T0229239

Heuristic Search

Heuristic Search
Theory and Applications

Stefan Edelkamp

Stefan Schrödl

AMSTERDAM • BOSTON • HEIDELBERG • LONDON
NEW YORK • OXFORD • PARIS • SAN DIEGO
SAN FRANCISCO • SINGAPORE • SYDNEY • TOKYO

Morgan Kaufmann is an imprint of Elsevier

Acquiring Editor: Rachel Roumeliotis
Development Editor: David Bevans
Project Manager: Sarah Binns
Designer: Joanne Blank

Morgan Kaufmann Publishers is an imprint of Elsevier.
225 Wyman Street, Waltham, MA 02451, USA

This book is printed on acid-free paper. ∞

Library of Congress Cataloging-in-Publication Data

Edelkamp, Stefan.
   Heuristic search: theory and applications / Stefan Edelkamp, Stefan Schrödl.
      p. cm.
   ISBN 978-0-12-372512-7 (hardback : acid-free paper)
1. Heuristic algorithms. I. Schrödl, Stefan. II. Title.
   QA76.9.A43E34 2011
   005.1'1–dc22

                                                            2011005844

British Library Cataloguing-in-Publication Data

A catalogue record for this book is available from the British Library.

For information on all Morgan Kaufmann publications,
visit our Web site at www.mkp.com or www.elsevierdirect.com

Printed in the United States of America
11 12 13 14 15   5 4 3 2 1

Contents

List of Algorithms xvii

Preface xxiii

PART I HEURISTIC SEARCH PRIMER

CHAPTER 1 **Introduction** **3**

  1.1 Notational and Mathematical Background 3

      1.1.1 Pseudo Code 3

      1.1.2 Computability Theory 4

      1.1.3 Complexity Theory 5

      1.1.4 Asymptotic Resource Consumption 7

      1.1.5 Symbolic Logic 8

  1.2 Search 9

  1.3 Success Stories 9

  1.4 State Space Problems 12

  1.5 Problem Graph Representations 14

  1.6 Heuristics 15

  1.7 Examples of Search Problems 19

      1.7.1 Sliding-Tile Puzzles 19

      1.7.2 RUBIK'S CUBE 22

      1.7.3 SOKOBAN 22

      1.7.4 ROUTE PLANNING 24

      1.7.5 TSP 25

      1.7.6 MULTIPLE SEQUENCE ALIGNMENT 26

  1.8 General State Space Descriptions 29

      1.8.1 Action Planning 29

      1.8.2 *Production Systems 32

      1.8.3 Markov Decision Processes 35

      1.8.4 Generic Search Model 36

  1.9 Summary 37

  1.10 Exercises 39

  1.11 Bibliographic Notes 45

CHAPTER 2 **Basic Search Algorithms** **47**

  2.1 Uninformed Graph Search Algorithms 48

      2.1.1 Depth-First Search 50

      2.1.2 Breadth-First Search 51

      2.1.3 Dijkstra's Algorithm 53

2.1.4 Negatively Weighted Graphs 57

2.1.5 Relaxed Node Selection 58

2.1.6 *Algorithm of Bellman-Ford 60

2.1.7 Dynamic Programming 62

2.2 Informed Optimal Search 68

2.2.1 A* 69

2.2.2 On the Optimal Efficiency of A* 74

2.3 *General Weights 75

2.3.1 Cost Algebras 76

2.3.2 Multiobjective Search 79

2.4 Summary 80

2.5 Exercises 82

2.6 Bibliographic Notes 86

CHAPTER 3   ***Dictionary Data Structures** **89**

3.1 Priority Queues 89

3.1.1 Bucket Data Structures 90

3.1.2 Heap Data Structures 97

3.2 Hash Tables 110

3.2.1 Hash Dictionaries 111

3.2.2 Hash Functions 112

3.2.3 Hashing Algorithms 121

3.2.4 Memory-Saving Dictionaries 130

3.2.5 Approximate Dictionaries 134

3.3 Subset Dictionaries 138

3.3.1 Arrays and Lists 139

3.3.2 Tries 139

3.3.3 Hashing 139

3.3.4 Unlimited Branching Trees 141

3.4 String Dictionaries 142

3.4.1 Suffix Trees 143

3.4.2 Generalized Suffix Trees 146

3.5 Summary 151

3.6 Exercises 154

3.7 Bibliographic Notes 157

CHAPTER 4   **Automatically Created Heuristics** **161**

4.1 Abstraction Transformations 162

4.2 Valtorta's Theorem 164

4.3 *Hierarchical A* 165

4.4 Pattern Databases 167

4.4.1 FIFTEEN-PUZZLE 168
4.4.2 RUBIK'S CUBE 169
4.4.3 Directed Search Graphs 170
4.4.4 Korf's Conjecture 170
4.4.5 Multiple Pattern Databases 172
4.4.6 Disjoint Pattern Databases 173
4.5 *Customized Pattern Databases 177
4.5.1 Pattern Selection 178
4.5.2 Symmetry and Dual Pattern Databases 179
4.5.3 Bounded Pattern Databases 180
4.5.4 On-Demand Pattern Databases 183
4.5.5 Compressed Pattern Databases 183
4.5.6 Compact Pattern Databases 185
4.6 Summary 185
4.7 Exercises 187
4.8 Bibliographic Notes 190

PART II HEURISTIC SEARCH UNDER MEMORY CONSTRAINTS

CHAPTER 5 Linear-Space Search **195**
5.1 *Logarithmic Space Algorithms 195
5.1.1 Divide-and-Conquer BFS 196
5.1.2 Divide-and-Conquer Shortest Paths Search 196
5.2 Exploring the Search Tree 197
5.3 Branch-and-Bound 198
5.4 Iterative-Deepening Search 201
5.5 Iterative-Deepening A* 204
5.6 Prediction of IDA* Search 206
5.6.1 Asymptotic Branching Factors 206
5.6.2 IDA* Search Tree Prediction 212
5.6.3 *Convergence Criteria 217
5.7 *Refined Threshold Determination 218
5.8 *Recursive Best-First Search 219
5.9 Summary 220
5.10 Exercises 222
5.11 Bibliographic Notes 223

CHAPTER 6 Memory-Restricted Search **227**
6.1 Linear Variants Using Additional Memory 228
6.1.1 Transposition Tables 228
6.1.2 Fringe Search 231

       6.1.3 *Iterative Threshold Search 233
       6.1.4 MA*, SMA, and SMAG 235
   6.2 Nonadmissible Search 240
       6.2.1 Enforced Hill-Climbing 240
       6.2.2 Weighted A* 243
       6.2.3 Overconsistent A* 244
       6.2.4 Anytime Repairing A* 246
       6.2.5 k-Best-First Search 250
       6.2.6 Beam Search 251
       6.2.7 Partial A* and Partial IDA* 251
   6.3 Reduction of the Closed List 254
       6.3.1 Dynamic Programming in Implicit Graphs 255
       6.3.2 Divide-and-Conquer Solution Reconstruction 255
       6.3.3 Frontier Search 257
       6.3.4 *Sparse Memory Graph Search 259
       6.3.5 Breadth-First Heuristic Search 261
       6.3.6 Locality 264
   6.4 Reduction of the Open List 266
       6.4.1 Beam-Stack Search 266
       6.4.2 Partial Expansion A* 270
       6.4.3 Two-Bit Breadth-First Search 271
   6.5 Summary 273
   6.6 Exercises 275
   6.7 Bibliographic Notes 279

CHAPTER 7 **Symbolic Search** **283**
   7.1 Boolean Encodings for Set of States 284
   7.2 Binary Decision Diagrams 286
   7.3 Computing the Image for a State Set 290
   7.4 Symbolic Blind Search 291
       7.4.1 Symbolic Breadth-First Tree Search 291
       7.4.2 Symbolic Breadth-First Search 293
       7.4.3 Symbolic Pattern Databases 294
       7.4.4 Cost-Optimal Symbolic Breadth-First Search 296
       7.4.5 Symbolic Shortest Path Search 298
   7.5 Limits and Possibilities of BDDs 299
       7.5.1 Exponential Lower Bound 299
       7.5.2 Polynomial Upper Bound 300
   7.6 Symbolic Heuristic Search 302
       7.6.1 Symbolic A* 302
       7.6.2 Bucket Implementation 305

7.6.3 Symbolic Best-First Search 307
7.6.4 Symbolic Breadth-First Branch-and-Bound 308
7.7 *Refinements 309
7.7.1 Improving the BDD Size 309
7.7.2 Partitioning 310
7.8 Symbolic Algorithms for Explicit Graphs 311
7.9 Summary 311
7.10 Exercises 313
7.11 Bibliographic Notes 317

CHAPTER 8 **External Search** **319**
8.1 Virtual Memory Management 320
8.2 Fault Tolerance 321
8.3 Model of Computation 321
8.4 Basic Primitives 323
8.5 External Explicit Graph Search 324
8.5.1 *External Priority Queues 324
8.5.2 External Explicit Graph Depth-First Search 325
8.5.3 External Explicit Graph Breadth-First Search 326
8.6 External Implicit Graph Search 328
8.6.1 Delayed Duplicate Detection for BFS 328
8.6.2 *External Breadth-First Branch-and-Bound 330
8.6.3 *External Enforced Hill-Climbing 332
8.6.4 External A* 334
8.6.5 *Lower Bound for Delayed Duplicate Detection 340
8.7 *Refinements 342
8.7.1 Hash-Based Duplicate Detection 342
8.7.2 Structured Duplicate Detection 343
8.7.3 Pipelining 344
8.7.4 External Iterative-Deepening A* Search 345
8.7.5 External Explicit-State Pattern Databases 346
8.7.6 External Symbolic Pattern Databases 348
8.7.7 External Relay Search 348
8.8 *External Value Iteration 349
8.8.1 Forward Phase: State Space Generation 349
8.8.2 Backward Phase: Update of Values 349
8.9 *Flash Memory 353
8.9.1 Hashing 354
8.9.2 Mapping 354
8.9.3 Compressing 356
8.9.4 Flushing 358

8.10 Summary 358
8.11 Exercises 361
8.12 Bibliographic Notes 364

PART III HEURISTIC SEARCH UNDER TIME CONSTRAINTS

CHAPTER 9 **Distributed Search** **369**
   9.1 Parallel Processing 370
      9.1.1 Motivation for Practical Parallel Search 374
      9.1.2 Space Partitioning 374
      9.1.3 Depth Slicing 375
      9.1.4 Lock-Free Hashing 378
   9.2 Parallel Depth-First Search 379
      9.2.1 *Parallel Branch-and-Bound 379
      9.2.2 Stack Splitting 380
      9.2.3 Parallel IDA* 382
      9.2.4 Asynchronous IDA* 382
   9.3 Parallel Best-First Search Algorithms 385
      9.3.1 Parallel Global A* 385
      9.3.2 Parallel Local A* 387
   9.4 Parallel External Search 388
      9.4.1 Parallel External Breadth-First Search 388
      9.4.2 Parallel Structured Duplicate Detection 391
      9.4.3 Parallel External A* 392
      9.4.4 Parallel Pattern Database Search 398
   9.5 Parallel Search on the GPU 400
      9.5.1 GPU Basics 401
      9.5.2 GPU-Based Breadth-First Search 401
      9.5.3 Bitvector GPU Search 407
   9.6 Bidirectional Search 408
      9.6.1 Bidirectional Front-to-End Search 409
      9.6.2 *Bidirectional Front-to-Front Search 410
      9.6.3 Perimeter Search 412
      9.6.4 Bidirectional Symbolic Breadth-First Search 416
      9.6.5 *Island Search 416
      9.6.6 *Multiple-Goal Heuristic Search 418
   9.7 Summary 419
   9.8 Exercises 422
   9.9 Bibliographic Notes 425

CHAPTER 10   State Space Pruning **429**
    10.1 Admissible State Space Pruning 430
        10.1.1 Substring Pruning 430
        10.1.2 Pruning Dead-Ends 440
        10.1.3 Penalty Tables 445
        10.1.4 Symmetry Reduction 447
    10.2 Nonadmissible State Space Pruning 449
        10.2.1 Macro Problem Solving 449
        10.2.2 Relevance Cuts 452
        10.2.3 Partial Order Reduction 453
    10.3 Summary 458
    10.4 Exercises 460
    10.5 Bibliographic Notes 463

CHAPTER 11   Real-Time Search **465**
    11.1 LRTA* 466
    11.2 LRTA* with Lookahead One 473
    11.3 Analysis of the Execution Cost of LRTA* 474
        11.3.1 Upper Bound on the Execution Cost of LRTA* 476
        11.3.2 Lower Bound on the Execution Cost of LRTA* 477
    11.4 Features of LRTA* 479
        11.4.1 Heuristic Knowledge 479
        11.4.2 Fine-Grained Control 479
        11.4.3 Improvement of Execution Cost 480
    11.5 Variants of LRTA* 482
        11.5.1 Variants with Local Search Spaces of Varying Sizes 482
        11.5.2 Variants with Minimal Lookahead 482
        11.5.3 Variants with Faster Value Updates 484
        11.5.4 Variants That Detect Convergence 488
        11.5.5 Variants That Speed Up Convergence 488
        11.5.6 Nonconverging Variants 491
        11.5.7 Variants for Nondeterministic and Probabilistic State Spaces 494
    11.6 How to Use Real-Time Search 496
        11.6.1 Case Study: Off line Search 496
        11.6.2 Case Study: Goal-Directed Navigation in Unknown Terrain 497
        11.6.3 Case Study: Coverage 500
        11.6.4 Case Study: Localization 501
    11.7 Summary 507
    11.8 Exercises 509
    11.9 Bibliographic Notes 514

PART IV HEURISTIC SEARCH VARIANTS

CHAPTER 12 Adversary Search **519**
    12.1 Two-Player Games 520
        12.1.1 Game Tree Search 524
        12.1.2 $\alpha\beta$-Pruning 525
        12.1.3 Transposition Tables 530
        12.1.4 *Searching with Restricted Windows 530
        12.1.5 Accumulated Evaluations 534
        12.1.6 *Partition Search 535
        12.1.7 *Other Improvement Techniques 537
        12.1.8 Learning Evaluation Functions 538
        12.1.9 Retrograde Analysis 543
        12.1.10 *Symbolic Retrograde Analysis 544
    12.2 *Multiplayer Games 547
    12.3 General Game Playing 550
    12.4 AND/OR Graph Search 552
        12.4.1 AO* 554
        12.4.2 *IDAO* 554
        12.4.3 *LAO* 557
    12.5 Summary 559
    12.6 Exercises 563
    12.7 Bibliographic Notes 567

CHAPTER 13 Constraint Search **571**
    13.1 Constraint Satisfaction 572
    13.2 Consistency 575
        13.2.1 Arc Consistency 575
        13.2.2 Bounds Consistency 577
        13.2.3 *Path Consistency 578
        13.2.4 Specialized Consistency 579
    13.3 Search Strategies 580
        13.3.1 Backtracking 581
        13.3.2 Backjumping 583
        13.3.3 Dynamic Backtracking 584
        13.3.4 Backmarking 585
        13.3.5 Search Strategies 587
    13.4 NP-Hard Problem Solving 591
        13.4.1 Boolean Satisfiability 592
        13.4.2 Number Partition 596

13.4.3 *Bin Packing 598
13.4.4 *Rectangle Packing 601
13.4.5 *Vertex Cover, Independent Set, Clique 604
13.4.6 *Graph Partition 606
13.5 Temporal Constraint Networks 609
13.5.1 Simple Temporal Network 609
13.5.2 *PERT Scheduling 611
13.6 *Path Constraints 612
13.6.1 Formula Progression 614
13.6.2 Automata Translation 615
13.7 *Soft and Preference Constraints 617
13.8 *Constraint Optimization 618
13.9 Summary 619
13.10 Exercises 623
13.11 Bibliographic Notes 629

CHAPTER 14 **Selective Search** **633**
14.1 From State Space Search to Minimization 634
14.2 Hill-Climbing Search 635
14.3 Simulated Annealing 637
14.4 Tabu Search 638
14.5 Evolutionary Algorithms 639
14.5.1 Randomized Local Search and $(1 + 1)$ EA 639
14.5.2 Simple GA 641
14.5.3 Insights to Genetic Algorithm Search 643
14.6 Approximate Search 645
14.6.1 Approximating TSP 646
14.6.2 Approximating MAX-k-SAT 646
14.7 Randomized Search 647
14.8 Ant Algorithms 652
14.8.1 Simple Ant System 652
14.8.2 Algorithm Flood 654
14.8.3 Vertex Ant Walk 654
14.9 *Lagrange Multipliers 657
14.9.1 Saddle-Point Conditions 658
14.9.2 Partitioned Problems 661
14.10 *No-Free-Lunch 662
14.11 Summary 662
14.12 Exercises 664
14.13 Bibliographic Notes 668

PART V HEURISTIC SEARCH APPLICATIONS

CHAPTER 15 **Action Planning** **673**

    15.1 Optimal Planning 675

        15.1.1 *Graphplan* 675

        15.1.2 *Satplan* 677

        15.1.3 Dynamic Programming 678

        15.1.4 Planning Pattern Databases 680

    15.2 Suboptimal Planning 685

        15.2.1 Causal Graphs 685

        15.2.2 Metric Planning 687

        15.2.3 Temporal Planning 691

        15.2.4 Derived Predicates 695

        15.2.5 Timed Initial Literals 696

        15.2.6 State Trajectory Constraints 696

        15.2.7 Preference Constraints 697

    15.3 Bibliographic Notes 697

CHAPTER 16 **Automated System Verification** **701**

    16.1 Model Checking 702

        16.1.1 Temporal Logics 702

        16.1.2 The Role of Heuristics 703

    16.2 Communication Protocols 705

        16.2.1 Formula-Based Heuristic 705

        16.2.2 Activeness Heuristic 707

        16.2.3 Trail-Directed Heuristics 709

        16.2.4 Liveness Model Checking 710

        16.2.5 Planning Heuristics 710

    16.3 Program Model Checking 713

    16.4 Analyzing Petri Nets 717

    16.5 Exploring Real-Time Systems 721

        16.5.1 Timed Automata 721

        16.5.2 Linearly Priced Timed Automata 722

        16.5.3 Traversal Politics 723

    16.6 Analyzing Graph Transition Systems 723

    16.7 Anomalies in Knowledge Bases 726

    16.8 Diagnosis 727

        16.8.1 General Diagnostic Engine 728

        16.8.2 Symbolic Propagation 729

16.9 Automated Theorem Proving 730
    16.9.1 Heuristics 732
    16.9.2 Functional A* Search 733
16.10 Bibliographic Notes 734

CHAPTER 17   **Vehicle Navigation** **737**
  17.1 Components of Route Guidance Systems 737
    17.1.1 Generation and Preprocessing of Digital Maps 737
    17.1.2 Positioning Systems 739
    17.1.3 Map Matching 741
    17.1.4 Geocoding and Reverse Geocoding 744
    17.1.5 User Interface 744
  17.2 Routing Algorithms 744
    17.2.1 Heuristics for Route Planning 745
    17.2.2 Time-Dependent Routing 746
    17.2.3 Stochastic Time-Dependent Routing 747
  17.3 Cutting Corners 749
    17.3.1 Geometric Container Pruning 749
    17.3.2 Localizing A* 752
  17.4 Bibliographic Notes 756

CHAPTER 18   **Computational Biology** **759**
  18.1 BIOLOGICAL PATHWAY 759
  18.2 MULTIPLE SEQUENCE ALIGNMENT 760
    18.2.1 Bounds 763
    18.2.2 Iterative-Deepening Dynamic Programming 763
    18.2.3 Main Loop 764
    18.2.4 Sparse Representation of Solution Paths 767
    18.2.5 Use of Improved Heuristics 769
  18.3 Bibliographic Notes 771

CHAPTER 19   **Robotics** **773**
  19.1 Search Spaces 773
  19.2 Search under Incomplete Knowledge 777
  19.3 Fundamental Robot-Navigation Problems 778
  19.4 Search Objective 780
  19.5 Search Approaches 781
    19.5.1 Optimal Off line Search 782
    19.5.2 Greedy On line Search 784

19.6 Greedy Localization 786

19.7 Greedy Mapping 787

19.8 Search with the Freespace Assumption 789

19.9 Bibliographic Notes 791

Bibliography 793

Index 825

List of Algorithms

1.1   Computing the approximation of the relaxed planning heuristic 34
2.1   Skeleton of search algorithms in implicitly given graphs 49
2.2   Tracing back the solution path using predecessor links 50
2.3   Improve procedure with duplicate detection and predecessor links 50
2.4   Choosing path to v through minimum of $f(v)$ and $f(u) + w(u,v)$ 54
2.5   An update routine that copes with negative edge weights 57
2.6   Relaxing the node expansion order in Algorithm A 59
2.7   Edge relaxation for implicit version of Bellman and Ford's algorithm.................... 61
2.8   Bellman-Ford algorithm in an implicit graph... 62
2.9   Floyd-Warshall algorithm... 63
2.10 Pairwise sequence alignment with dynamic programming in column order 64
2.11 Policy iteration 67
2.12 Value iteration 68
2.13 A* 70
3.1   Initializing a 1-LEVEL BUCKET 91
3.2   Inserting an element into a 1-LEVEL BUCKET 91
3.3   Deleting the minimum element in a 1-LEVEL BUCKET 91
3.4   Updating the key in a 1-LEVEL BUCKET 92
3.5   Creating a RADIX HEAP 94
3.6   Inserting an element into a RADIX HEAP 94
3.7   Inserting an element into a RADIX HEAP 94
3.8   Delete the minimum from a RADIX HEAP 95
3.9   Finding the successor in a VAN EMDE BOAS PRIORITY QUEUE 96
3.10 Inserting an element in a VAN EMDE BOAS PRIORITY QUEUE 97
3.11 Deleting an element from a VAN EMDE BOAS PRIORITY QUEUE............................ 97
3.12 Inserting an element into a HEAP 99
3.13 Decreasing the key of an element in a HEAP... 99
3.14 Extracting the minimum element from a HEAP 100
3.15 Rearrange HEAP 100
3.16 Rearrange PAIRING HEAP 101
3.17 Implementation of different subroutines for WEAK HEAPS............................... 103
3.18 Restoration of WEAK HEAPS 103
3.19 Extracting the minimum element from a WEAK HEAP 104
3.20 Inserting an element into a WEAK HEAP 104
3.21 Decreasing the key of an element in a WEAK HEAP 105
3.22 Consolidation with bitvectors and heuristic factor in a FIBONACCI HEAP 106
3.23 Reducing number of markings in a RELAXED WEAK QUEUE 110
3.24 Algorithm of Rabin and Karp 114
3.25 Rank operation for permutations 119
3.26 Unrank operation for permutations... 120

3.27 Recursion-free unranking and signature computation 120
3.28 Recursion-free ranking operation for permutations 122
3.29 Searching a chained hash table 122
3.30 Inserting an element into a chained hash table... 122
3.31 Deleting an element from a chained hash table 123
3.32 Searching an element in an open hash table 124
3.33 Inserting an element into an open hash table 125
3.34 Deleting an element from an open hash table... 125
3.35 Inserting an element for ordered hashing 125
3.36 Lookup for a key in a cuckoo hash table 128
3.37 Inserting a key into a cuckoo hash table 130
3.38 Searching a TRIE for a partial match 140
3.39 Searching a hash table for a partial match 140
3.40 Inserting a set in an UNLIMITED BRANCHING TREE 142
3.41 Searching for subsets in an UNLIMITED BRANCHING TREE 142
3.42 Algorithm to construct a SUFFIX TREE in linear time 145
3.43 Insertion of one suffix in a GENERALIZED SUFFIX TREE 149
3.44 Deleting a string in a GENERALIZED SUFFIX TREE 150
 4.1 Construction of pattern database using a backward search 168
 4.2 Pattern database construction in directed and weighted problem graphs................... 171
 5.1 Computing the BFS level with logarithmic space 196
 5.2 Searching the shortest paths with logarithmic space 197
 5.3 Depth-first branch-and-bound algorithm... 199
 5.4 Depth-first branch-and-bound subroutine 200
 5.5 Depth-first iterative-deepening algorithm.. 202
 5.6 DFS subroutine for DFID search 202
 5.7 Driver loop for IDA* 204
 5.8 The IDA* algorithm (no duplicate detection) 205
 5.9 The RBFS algorithm, implemented recursively 220
 6.1 IDA* driver with transposition table 230
 6.2 IDA* with transposition table and cost revision... 230
 6.3 Fringe search algorithm 232
 6.4 Algorithm ITS 234
 6.5 Pruning nodes in ITS.. 235
 6.6 Procedure SMAG 237
 6.7 Update procedure in SMAG for newly generated nodes 238
 6.8 Deleting unpromising nodes in SMAG 239
 6.9 Backing up heuristic values in SMAG 239
6.10 Recursive deletion of unused *Closed* nodes 239
6.11 Enforced hill-climbing 241
6.12 BFS searching for a better state v 241
6.13 A* search with i-values 245
6.14 A* with an arbitrary overconsistent initialization 246
6.15 Subroutine for anytime repairing A* 248
6.16 Main function of anytime repairing A* 248

6.17   Algorithm *k*-best-first search 250
6.18   Algorithm *k*-beam search 252
6.19   A* search with (single) bit-state hashing 253
6.20   Partial IDA* search with (single) bit-state hashing...................................... 254
6.21   Dynamic programming search algorithm 256
6.22   Edge relaxation step in dynamic programming.. 256
6.23   Solution reconstruction in sparse-memory graph search 260
6.24   Improve procedure for SMGS 261
6.25   Pruning the list of expanded nodes in SMGS 261
6.26   Breadth-first heuristic search 263
6.27   Update of a problem graph edge in Algorithm 6.26 264
6.28   The beam-stack search algorithm 269
6.29   Algorithm PEA* 271
6.30   Update procedure in PEA* for newly generated nodes 272
6.31   Breadth-first search with two bits 272
6.32   Extended IDA*.. 276
6.33   Traversing the search space with one bit per state....................................... 279
 7.1   BDD arithmetics via fixpoint computation 290
 7.2   Symbolic breadth-first tree search implemented with BDDs 292
 7.3   Symbolic BFS 293
 7.4   Symbolic pattern database construction.. 295
 7.5   Cost-optimal symbolic BFS algorithm 297
 7.6   Dijkstra's algorithm implemented with BDDs.. 299
 7.7   A* implemented with BDDs 303
 7.8   Symbolic A* in a bucket implementation.. 306
 7.9   Greedy best-first search implemented with BDDs... 307
7.10   Symbolic breadth-first branch-and-bound with buckets.................................. 308
7.11   Relational product algorithm to compute the image of a state set 314
7.12   Dijkstra's algorithm on buckets 316
7.13   Shortest path A* algorithm on buckets.. 316
 8.1   External BFS by Munagala and Ranade 327
 8.2   Delayed duplicate detection algorithm for BFS 329
 8.3   File subtraction for external duplicate elimination 330
 8.4   External breadth-first branch-and-bound.. 331
 8.5   Main routine for external enforced hill-climbing... 333
 8.6   External BFS searching for a better state *v* 333
 8.7   External A* for consistent and integral heuristics 338
 8.8   External value iteration algorithm.. 350
 8.9   External value iteration—backward update... 352
 9.1   Algorithm to compute $a_1 + \cdots + a_n$ in parallel..................................... 372
 9.2   Algorithm to compute all prefix sums in parallel.. 373
 9.3   Transposition-driven scheduling 376
 9.4   The depth-slicing parallelization method 377
 9.5   Searching and inserting an element in a lock-free hash table 379
 9.6   Parallel branch-and-bound with global synchronization 380

9.7 Parallel DFS with stack splitting 381
9.8 Parallel IDA* with global synchronization 383
9.9 Distributing IDA* with respect to different search thresholds 383
9.10 Parallel external breadth-first search 390
9.11 Parallel external A* for consistent and integral heuristics 396
9.12 Large-scale breadth-first search on the GPU.................................... 403
9.13 Expanding a layer on the GPU 404
9.14 Detecting duplicates via sorting on the GPU 404
9.15 Bidirectional search with BHPA.. 410
9.16 Bidirectional BFS implemented with BDDs..................................... 417
10.1 Computation of failure function 437
10.2 Incremental learning of duplicates in A* 439
10.3 Bottom-up propagation in the search decomposition tree.......................... 443
10.4 The decomposition and bottom-up propagation algorithm................................ 444
10.5 An algorithm for checking ample sets 455
11.1 LRTA* 471
11.2 Value-update step of LRTA*.. 472
11.3 LRTA* with lookahead one... 474
11.4 Min-LRTA* 482
11.5 RTAA*.. 485
11.6 Variant of LRTA* (1) 489
11.7 FALCONS... 490
11.8 Variant of LRTA* (2) 513
11.9 Variant of LRTA* (3) 514
12.1 The negmax game tree labeling procedure....................................... 525
12.2 Minimax game tree search.. 525
12.3 $\alpha\beta$ negmax game tree pruning.. 527
12.4 Minimax game tree search with $\alpha\beta$-pruning.................................... 528
12.5 Negmax game tree search with $\alpha\beta$-pruning and transposition table...................... 531
12.6 Principal-variation search in negmax formulation................................ 532
12.7 MTD algorithm framework.. 533
12.8 The minimax game tree search procedure for accumulated node evaluations 535
12.9 Partition search 536
12.10 One iteration in the UCT algorithm 539
12.11 Temporal difference learning 541
12.12 Q-learning 543
12.13 Calculating the set of reachable positions...................................... 546
12.14 Classification 547
12.15 The $\alpha\beta$-branch-and-bound algorithm for multiplayer games 550
12.16 The AO* search algorithm for AND/OR trees 555
12.17 The AO* search algorithm for stochastic shortest path 556
12.18 The IDAO* search algorithm.. 556
12.19 The IDAO*-DFS search subroutine 557
12.20 The LAO* algorithm... 558

13.1 Simple consistency algorithm 575
13.2 Arc consistency with AC-3 576
13.3 Arc consistency with AC-8 577
13.4 Algorithm for path consistency... 580
13.5 Backtracking search algorithm 582
13.6 Pure backtracking search algorithm 582
13.7 Backjumping search algorithm 584
13.8 Simple consistency for backjumping.. 585
13.9 Backmarking search algorithm 587
13.10 One iteration in limited discrepancy search.. 589
13.11 One iteration in improved limited discrepancy search 590
13.12 Depth-bounded discrepancy search 592
13.13 Algorithm of Davis-Putnam and Logmann-Loveland...................................... 594
13.14 Computing strong and weak backdoors 596
13.15 Recursive computation of feasible sets for bin completion 600
13.16 Minimal network computation in simple temporal network 611
13.17 Computing the critical path with PERT scheduling 612
13.18 Formula progression algorithm... 614
13.19 LTL path constraint solver 615
13.20 BDD construction algorithm for linear and bound arithmetic constraint................... 628
14.1 Hill-climbing 635
14.2 Simulated annealing.. 637
14.3 Tabu search 638
14.4 Randomized tabu search 639
14.5 Randomized local search 640
14.6 Randomized $(1 + 1)$ EA 641
14.7 Simple GA on solution strings 643
14.8 Deterministic approximation algorithm for MAX-k-SAT................................. 647
14.9 Monien-Speckenmeyer algorithm 648
14.10 Algorithm of Paturi, Pudlák, and Zane... 648
14.11 Hamming sphere algorithm... 649
14.12 Algorithm random walk 651
14.13 The ant system algorithm for solving TSP... 653
14.14 Flood algorithm 655
14.15 Vertex ant walk.. 655
14.16 Saddle-point iteration method for finding a CLM 660
14.17 Lagrangian method for finding a CLM.. 662
15.1 Max-atom heuristic 679
15.2 Approximation of a plan with causal graph... 688
15.3 Plan graph construction for numerical relaxed planning heuristic.......................... 691
15.4 Extraction of a numerical relaxed plan... 692
15.5 Fixpoint for applying a set of rules to a planning state 696
16.1 The unification algorithm for first-order logic 731
16.2 Resolution refutation procedure 731

16.3 Functional implementation of the A* algorithm 734
17.1 Creating shortest path containers 750
17.2 Bounding-box graph search algorithm 751
17.3 Access operations on HEAP OF HEAPS 753
17.4 Maintenance of active heap 754
18.1 Iterative-deepening dynamic programming 765
18.2 Edge expansion in IDDP 765
18.3 Edge relaxation step for IDDP 766
18.4 Recursive deletion of edges that are no longer part of any solution path 766
18.5 Divide-and-conquer solution reconstruction in reverse order 767
18.6 Sparsification of *Closed* list under restricted memory 768

Preface

This book is intended to serve as a comprehensive introduction to artificial intelligence (AI) heuristic state space search. It includes many developments that are not yet covered by any textbook, including pattern databases, symbolic search, search with efficient use of external memory, and parallel processing units. Thus, the book is suitable for readers who do not yet have a background in search and are looking for a good introduction to the field, as well as for readers who do have some background in search and are interested in reading up on the latest developments in the field. It serves as a unique reference to the large body of research and provides many pointers to the literature.

The book is intended to strike a balance between search algorithms and their theoretical analysis on one hand, and their efficient implementation and application to important real-world problems on the other hand. It is intended to cover the field comprehensively, from well-known basic results to recent proposals that push the state of the art.

The book supplements broad textbooks on AI and, more importantly, serves as a primary textbook for more advanced AI classes on search. It discusses search applications in a variety of subfields of AI, including puzzle solving, game playing, constraint satisfaction, action planning, and robotics. However, the book is also suitable for self-study and provides a valuable source of information for graduate students, researchers, and practitioners in a variety of decision sciences (including AI and operations research), as well as application programmers who need to use search algorithms to solve their problems.

The book is relatively self-contained. In particular, we do not require the readers to have any prior knowledge of AI. Instead, we assume the reader to have basic knowledge of algorithms, data structures, and calculus. It uses examples to introduce the search algorithms and motivate their properties. The text often contains proofs of the correctness and other properties of search algorithms to give it formal rigor and introduces the readers to important proof techniques. (This aspect of the book is especially important for graduate students and researchers.)

The presented material also teaches how to implement search algorithms. It includes pseudo code to avoid the typical problems that practitioners (or students) have with converting ideas into running programs if textbooks describe algorithms only verbally or do not explicitly discuss implementation details. The book discusses how to implement the data structures needed to run the search algorithms, from very simple but somewhat slow implementations to highly sophisticated and extremely fast implementations. Moreover, the book includes exercises that can be used either as homework exercises in classes or as self-tests.

This text gives the readers a feeling for when to use which search algorithm. For example, it discusses the time and space complexities of search algorithms and which properties make some of them well suited for a given search problem and others less suited for the same search problem. Finally, it provides case studies that show how search algorithms can be applied to a large variety of problems from different application areas. Thus, it contains cookbook solutions for a variety of important real-world problems, demonstrates the impact that search techniques already have in practice, and gives the reader a feeling for the amount of work that is needed to adapt search algorithms to specific applications. (This aspect of the book is especially important for practitioners.)

The book is divided into five main parts: *Heuristic Search Primer* (I), *Heuristic Search Under Memory Constraints* (II), *Heuristic Search Under Time Constraints* (III), *Heuristic Search Variants* (IV), and *Heuristic Search Applications* (V). Part I introduces basic problems, algorithms, and heuristics. Parts II and III address refined solutions in the context of existing resource limitations in time and space. Part II considers memory-limited, symbolic, and disk-based search, and Part III addresses parallel search, various pruning techniques, and move-committing search strategies. Part IV attacks related search methods that apply more general notions of search heuristics, including game evaluations, constraint satisfaction, as well as local search approaches. Part V is dedicated to different real-world application areas and shows how the concepts of the first four parts have been turned into rather complex search engines. We address application areas traditionally closer to AI, such as action planning and robotics, and other areas not originating in AI, such as vehicle navigation, computational biology, and automated system verification. You will notice some sections preceded by an asterisk; the asterisks in front of chapter and section headings indicate advanced material that can be skipped in a first reading of the book.

Heuristic Search Primer

Introduction

In this book, we study the theory and the applications of heuristic search algorithms. The general model is the guided exploration in a space of states.

After providing some mathematical and notational background and motivating the impact of search algorithms by reflecting several success stories, we introduce different *state space* formalisms. Next we provide examples of *single-agent puzzles* such as the $(n^2 - 1)$-PUZZLE and extensions to it, the RUBIK'S CUBE, as well as SOKOBAN problems. Furthermore, the practically important application areas of ROUTE PLANNING and MULTIPLE SEQUENCE ALIGNMENT are introduced. The former is fundamental to vehicle navigation and the latter is fundamental to computational biology. In the TSP we consider the computation of round trips. For each of the domains, we introduce *heuristic evaluation functions* as a means to accelerate the search. We motivate them graphically and formalize them. We define properties of heuristics, such as *consistency* and *admissibility*, and how they are related. Moreover, we define the general descriptive schemes of *production systems*, *Markov decision process problems*, and *action planning*. For the case of a *production system*, we will see that general state space problem solving is in fact *undecidable*. For the case of action planning, we will see how to derive some problem-independent heuristics.

1.1 NOTATIONAL AND MATHEMATICAL BACKGROUND

Algorithms are specifications of action sequences, similar to recipes for cooking. The description should be concrete enough to cook a tasteful meal. On the other hand, some abstraction is necessary to keep the presentation readable; we don't teach the cook how to dice onions. In presenting algorithms in computer science, the situation is similar. The presentation should be concrete enough to allow analysis and reimplementation, but abstract enough to be ported on different programming languages and machines.

1.1.1 Pseudo Code

A program representation in a fictitious, partly abstract programming language is called *pseudo code*. However, its intention is to give a high-level description of an algorithm to a human, not to a machine. Therefore, irrelevant details (e.g., memory management code) are usually omitted, and sometimes natural language is used when convenient.

Most programs consist of assignments ($\leftarrow$), selection (e.g., branching based on *if* conditions), and iteration (e.g., *while* loops). Subroutine calls are important to structure the program and to implement recursion, and are shown in italics. In the pseudo code implementations, we use the following constructs.

> **if** ($\langle condition \rangle$) $\langle body \rangle$ **else** $\langle alternative \rangle$
> Branching of the program based on the case selected in the Boolean predicate *condition*.
> **and, or, not**
> Logical operation on Boolean conditions.
> **while** ($\langle condition \rangle$) $\langle body \rangle$
> Loop to be checked prior to the execution of its body.
> **do** $\langle body \rangle$ **while** ($\langle condition \rangle$)
> Loop to be checked after the execution of its body.
> **for each** $\langle element \rangle$ **in** $\langle Set \rangle$
> Variable *element* iterates on the (often ordered) set *Set*.
> **return**
> Backtrack to calling procedure with result.

Conditional and loop constructs introduce *compound statements*; that is, the parts of the statements constitute lists of statements (*blocks*) themselves. To clarify the hierarchical structure of the program, sometimes explicit *begin* and *end* statements are given. Different from this convention, in this book, in the interest of succinctness we chose to rely solely on *indentation*. For example, in the following fragment, note the end of the block that is executed in case the condition evaluates to *false*:

> **if** ($\langle condition \rangle$)
> $\langle$if-true-statement 1$\rangle$
> $\langle$if-true-statement 2$\rangle$
>   . . .
> **else**
> $\langle$if-false-statement 1$\rangle$
> $\langle$if-false-statement 2$\rangle$
>   . . .
> $\langle$after-if-statement 1$\rangle$
> . . .

For easier understanding, each line in the pseudo code is annotated with some short comments, separated from the program code by a double semicolon.

1.1.2 Computability Theory

Computability theory is the branch of theoretical computer science that studies which problems are computationally solvable using different computation models. Computability theory differs from the related discipline of computational complexity theory (see next section) in asking whether a problem can be solved at all, given any finite but arbitrarily large amount of resources.

A common model of computation is based on an abstract machine, the *Turing machine* (see Fig. 1.1). The computational model is very simple and assumes a computer M in the form of a 7-tuple $M = (Q, \Sigma, \Gamma, \delta, B, F, q_0)$, with state set Q, input alphabet Σ, tape alphabet Γ, transition function $\delta : Q \times \Gamma \rightarrow Q \times \Gamma \times \{L, R, N\}$, blank symbol B, final state set F, and head position q_0.

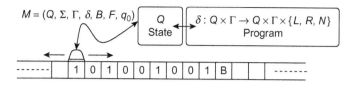

FIGURE 1.1

A Turing machine.

The machine takes some input word $(w_1, \ldots, w_n)$ over the alphabet Σ and assumes that it is already located on the tape at position $1, \ldots, n$. The initial head position is 1. The process of computation terminates, if some final state in F is reached. The state transition function δ sets the new state in Q, which can be interpreted as performing on step in the program that is run on the Turing machine. Then a character is written on the tape at the current head position. Depending on the value in $\{L, R, N\}$ the head is moved to the left (L), to the right (R), or remains unchanged (N), respectively. The output of the computation is the content of the tape after termination. The machine solves a *decision problem* when for an input string, it produces a binary output signifying "yes" or "no." A problem is *decidable* if a Turing machine exists that always gives an answer in finite time.

Since the time of Turing, many other formalisms for describing effective computability have been proposed, including recursive functions, the lambda calculus, register machines, Post systems, combinatorial logic, and Markov algorithms. The computational equivalence of all these systems corroborates the validity of the *Church-Turing thesis*: Every function that would naturally be regarded as computable can be computed by a Turing machine.

A *recursively enumerable* set S is a set such that a Turing machine exists that successively outputs all of its members. An equivalent condition is that we can specify an algorithm that always terminates and answers "yes" if the input is in S; if the input is not in S, computation might not halt at all. Therefore, recursively enumerable sets are also called *semi-decidable*.

A function $f(x)$ is *computable* if the set of all input–output pairs is recursively enumerable. Decision problems are often considered because an arbitrary problem can always be reduced to a decision problem, by enumerating possible pairs of domain and range elements and asking, "Is this the correct output?"

1.1.3 Complexity Theory

Complexity theory is part of the theory of computation dealing with the resources required during computation to solve a given problem, predominantly time (how many steps it takes to solve a problem) and space (how much memory it takes). Complexity theory differs from computability theory, which deals with whether a problem can be solved at all, regardless of the resources required.

The class of algorithms that need space $s(n)$, for some function $s(n)$, is denoted by the class DSPACE($s(n)$); and those that use time $t(n)$ is denoted by DTIME($t(n)$). The problem class P consists of all problems that can be solved in polynomial time; that is, it is the union of complexity classes DTIME($t(n)$), for all polynomials $t(n)$.

A *nondeterministic* Turing machine is a (nonrealizable) generalization of the standard deterministic Turing machine of which the transition rules can allow more than one successor configuration, and all these alternatives can be explored in parallel (another way of thinking of this is by means of an *oracle* suggesting the correct branches). The corresponding complexity classes for nondeterministic Turing machines are called NSPACE($s(n)$) and NTIME($s(n)$). The complexity class NP (for nondeterministic polynomial) is the union of classes NTIME($t(n)$), for all polynomials $t(n)$. Note that a deterministic Turing machine might not be able to *compute* the solution for a problem in NP in polynomial time, however, it can *verify* it efficiently if it is given enough information (a.k.a. *certificate*) about the solution (besides the answer "yes" or "no").

Both P and NP are contained in the class PSPACE, which is the union of DSPACE($s(n)$) for any polynomial function $s(n)$; PSPACE doesn't impose any restriction on the required time.

A problem S is *hard* for a class C if *all* other problems $S' \in C$ are *polynomially reducible* to C; this means that there is a polynomial algorithm to transform the input x' of S' to an input x to S, such that the answer for S applied to x is "yes" if and only if the answer for S' applied to x' is "yes." A problem S is *complete* for a class C if it is a member of C and it is hard for C.

One of the big challenges in computer science is to prove that P $\neq$ NP. To refute this conjecture, it would suffice to devise a deterministic polynomial algorithm for some NP-complete problem. However, most people believe that this is not possible. Figure 1.2 graphically depicts the relations between the mentioned complexity classes.

Although the model of a Turing machine seems quite restrictive, other, more realistic models, such as random access machines, can be simulated with polynomial overhead. Therefore, for merely deciding if an algorithm is efficient or not (i.e., it inherits at most a polynomial time or at least an exponential time algorithm), complexity classes based on Turing machines are sufficiently expressive. Only when considering hierarchical and parallel algorithms will we encounter situations where this model is no longer adequate.

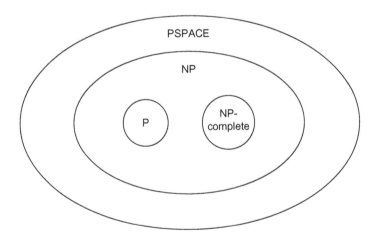

FIGURE 1.2

Assumed inclusion relation of some complexity classes.

1.1.4 **Asymptotic Resource Consumption**

In the previous section, we had a quite crude view on complexity classes, distinguishing merely between polynomial and more than polynomial complexity. While the actual degree of the polynomial can be preeminently important for practical applications (a "polynomial" algorithm might still not be practically feasible), exponential complexity cannot be deemed efficient because multiple resources are needed to increase the input size.

Suppose the two functions $f_1(n) = 100,000 + n$ and $f_2(n) = 8n^2$ describe the time or space used by two different algorithms for an input of size n. How do we determine which algorithm to use? Although f_2 is certainly better for small n, for large inputs its complexity will increase much more quickly. The constant factors depend only on the particular machine used, the programming language, and such, whereas the order of growth will be transferable.

The *big-oh notation* aims at capturing this asymptotic behavior. If we can find a bound c for the ratio $f_1(n)/f_2(n)$, we write $f_1(n) = O(f_2(n))$. More precisely, the expression $f_1(n) = O(f_2(n))$ is defined that there exist two constants n_0 and c such that for all $n \geq n_0$ we have $f_1(n) \leq c \cdot f_2(n)$. With the previous example we could say that $f_1 \in O(n)$ and $f_2 = O(n^2)$.

The *little-oh notation* constitutes an even stricter condition: If the ratio approaches zero in the limit, we write $f_1(n) \in o(f_2(n))$. The formal condition is that there exists an n_0 such that for all $n \geq n_0$, we have $f_1(n) \leq c \cdot f_2(n)$, for each $c > 0$. Analogously, we can define lower bounds: $f_1(n) = \omega(f_2(n))$ and $f_1(n) = \Omega(f_2(n))$, by changing the $\leq$ in the definition by $\geq$, and $<$ by $>$. Finally, we have $f_1(n) = \Theta(f_2(n))$ if both $f_1 = O(f_2(n))$ and $f_1(n) = \Omega(g(n))$ hold.

Some common complexity classes are constant complexity ($O(1)$), logarithmic complexity ($O(\lg n)$), linear complexity ($O(n)$), polynomial complexity ($O(n^k)$, for some fixed value of k and exponential complexity (e.g., $O(2^n)$).

For refined analysis we briefly review the basics on *amortized complexity*. The main idea is to pay more for cheaper operations and use the savings to cover the more expensive ones. Amortized complexity analysis distinguishes between t_l, the real cost for operation l; Φ_l, the potential after execution operation l; and a_l, the amortized costs for operation l. We have $a_l = t_l + \Phi_l - \Phi_{l-1}$ and $\Phi_0 = 0$,

$$\sum_{l=1}^{m} a_l = \sum_{l=1}^{m} t_l + \Phi_l - \Phi_{l-1} = \sum_{l=1}^{m} t_l - \Phi_0 + \Phi_m$$

and

$$\sum_{l=1}^{m} t_l = \sum_{l=1}^{m} a_l + \Phi_0 - \Phi_m \leq \sum_{l=1}^{m} a_l,$$

so that the sum of the real costs can be bounded by the sum of the amortized costs.

To ease the representation of the exponential algorithms, we abstract from polynomial factors. For two polynomials p and q and any constant $\epsilon > 0$, we have that $O(p(n)2^{q(n)}) = O((2+\epsilon)^{q(n)})$. Therefore, we introduce the following notation:

$$f(n) \doteq g(n) \Leftrightarrow f \text{ and } g \text{ differ by polynomial factors only}$$

$$\Leftrightarrow \exists q(n) \text{ with } g(n)/q(n) \leq f(n) \leq g(n)q(n).$$

1.1.5 Symbolic Logic

Formal logic is a powerful and universal representation formalism in computer science, and also in this book we cannot completely get around it. *Propositional logic* is defined over a domain of discourse of allowed predicate symbols, *P*. An *atom* is an occurrence of a predicate. A *literal* is either an atom *p* or the negation of an atom, ¬*p*. A *propositional formula* is recursively defined as an atom or a compound formula, obtained from connecting simpler formulas using the connectives ∧ (and), ∨ (or), ¬ (not), →
(if-then), ⇔ (equivalent), and ⊕ (exclusive-or).

While the syntax governs the construction of well-formed formulas, the semantics determine their meaning. An *interpretation* maps each atom to either *true* or *false* (sometimes these values are given as 0 and 1). Atoms can be associated with propositional statements such as "the sun is shining." In *compositional* logic, the truth of a compound formula is completely determined by its components and its connectors. The following truth table specifies the relations. For example, if *p* is true in an interpretation *I*, and *q* is false, then $p \wedge q$ is false in *I*.

p	q	$\neg p$	$p \wedge q$	$p \vee q$	$p \rightarrow q$	$p \Leftrightarrow q$	$p \oplus q$
0	0	0	0	0	1	1	0
0	1	0	0	1	1	0	1
1	0	1	0	1	0	0	1
1	1	1	1	1	1	1	0

A propositional formula *F* is *satisfiable* or *consistent* if it is true in some interpretation *I*; in this case, *I* is called a *model* of *F*. It is a *tautology* (or *valid*) if it is true in every interpretation (e.g., $p \vee \neg p$). A formula *G* is *implied* by *F* if *G* is true in all models of *F*.

Propositional formulas can always be equivalently rewritten either in *disjunctive normal form* (i.e., as a disjunction of conjunctions over atoms) or in *conjunctive normal form* (i.e., as a conjunction of disjunctions over atoms).

First-order predicate logic is a generalization of propositional logic that permits the formulation of quantified statements such as "there is at least one X such that ..." or "for any X, it is the case that...."
The domain of discourse now also contains *variables*, *constants*, and *functions*. Each predicate or function symbol is assigned an *arity*, the number of arguments. A *term* is defined inductively as a variable and a constant, or has the form $f(t_1, \ldots, t_k)$, where f is a function of arity k, and the t_i are terms. An *atom* is a well-formed formula of the form $p(t_1, \ldots, t_k)$, where p is a predicate of arity k and the t_i are terms.

First-order predicate logic expressions can contain the *quantifiers* ∀ (read "for all") and ∃ (read "exists"). Compound formulas can be constructed as in propositional logic from atoms and connectors; in addition, if *F* is a well-formed formula, then $\exists x F$ and $\forall x F$ are as well, if *x* is a variable symbol. The *scope* of these quantifiers is *F*. If a variable *x* occurs in the scope of a quantifier, it is *bound*, otherwise it is *free*. In first-order logic, *sentences* are built up from terms and atoms, where a term is a constant symbol, a variable symbol, or a function of *n* terms. For example, *x* and $f(x_1, \ldots, x_n)$ are terms, where each x_i is a term. Hence, a *sentence* is an atom, or, if *P* is a sentence and *x* is a variable, then $(\forall x)P$ and $(\exists x)P$ are sentences. A *well-formed formula* is a sentence containing no *free* variables. For example, $(\forall x)P(x,y)$ has *x* bound as a universally quantified variable, but *y* is free.

An *interpretation I* for predicate logic comprises the set of all possible objects in the domain, called the *universe U*. It evaluates constants, free variables, and terms with some of these objects. For a bound variable, the formula $\exists x F$ is true if there is some object $o \in U$ such that *F* is true if all occurrences of *x* in *F* are interpreted as *o*. The formula ∀*xF* is true under *I* if *F* is for each possible substitution of an object in *U* for *x*.

A *deductive system* consists of a set of axioms (valid formulas) and *inference rules* that transform valid formulas into other ones. A classic example of an inference is *modus ponens*: If *F* is true, and $F \rightarrow G$ is true, then also *G* is true. Other inference rules are *universal elimination*: If $(\forall x)P(x)$ is true, then $P(c)$ is true, where *c* is constant in the domain of *x*; *existential introduction*: If $P(c)$ is true, then $(\exists x)P(x)$ is inferred; or *existential elimination*: From $(\exists x)P(x)$ infer $P(c)$, with *c* brand new. A deductive system is *correct* if all derivable formulas are valid; on the other hand, it is *complete* if each valid formula can be derived.

Gödel proved that first-order predicate logic is not *decidable*; that is, no algorithm exists that, given a formula as input, always terminates and states whether it is valid or not. However, first-order predicate logic is recursively enumerable: algorithms can be guaranteed to terminate in case the input is valid indeed.

1.2 SEARCH

We all search. The first one searches for clothes in the wardrobe, the second one for an appropriate television channel. Forgetful people have to search a little more. A soccer player searches for an opportunity to score a goal. The main restlessness of human beings is to search for the purpose of life.

The term *search* in research relates the process of finding solutions to yet unsolved problems. In computer science research, the word *search* is used almost as generally as in the human context: Every algorithm searches for the completion of a given task.

The process of problem solving can often be modeled as a search in a state space starting from some given initial state with rules describing how to transform one state into another. They have to be applied over and over again to eventually satisfy some goal condition. In the common case, we aim at the best one of such paths, often in terms of path length or path cost.

Search has been an important part of artificial intelligence (AI) since its very beginning, as the core technique for problem solving. Many important applications of search algorithms have emerged since then, including ones in action and route planning, robotics, software and hardware verification, theorem proving, and computational biology.

In many areas of computer science, *heuristics* are viewed as practical rules of thumb. In AI search, however, heuristics are well-defined mappings of states to numbers. There are different types of search heuristics. This book mainly focuses on one particular class, which provides an estimate of the remaining distance or cost to the goal. We start from this definition. There are other classes of search heuristics that we will touch, but with less emphasis. For example, in game tree or in local search, heuristics are estimates of the value of a particular (game) state and not giving an estimate of the distance or cost to the goal state. Instead, such search heuristics provide an evaluation for how *good* a state is. Other examples are variable and value ordering heuristics for constraint search that are not estimates of the distance to a goal.

1.3 SUCCESS STORIES

Refined search algorithms impress with recent successes. In the area of single-player games, they have led to the first optimal solutions for challenging instances of SOKOBAN, the RUBIK'S CUBE, the

$(n^2 - 1)$-PUZZLE, and the TOWERS-OF-HANOI problem, all with a state space of about or more than a *quintillion* (a billion times a billion) of states. Even when processing a million states per second, naively looking at all states corresponds to about 300,000 years. Despite the reductions obtained, time and space remain crucial computational resources. In extreme cases, weeks of computation time, gigabytes of main memory, and terabytes of hard disk space have been invested to solve these search challenges.

In RUBIK'S CUBE, with a state space of 43,252,003,274,489,856,000 states, first random problems have been solved optimally by a general-purpose strategy, which used 110 megabytes of main memory for guiding the search. For the hardest instance the solver generated 1,021,814,815,051 states to find an optimum of 18 moves in 17 days. The exact bound for the worst possible instance to be solved is 20 moves. The computation for the lower bound on a large number of computers took just a few weeks, but it would take a desktop PC about 35 CPU years to perform this calculation.

With recent search enhancements, the average solution time for optimally solving the FIFTEEN-PUZZLE with over 10^{13} states is only milliseconds. The state space of the FIFTEEN-PUZZLE has been completely generated in 3 weeks using 1.4 terabytes of hard disk space.

The TOWERS-OF-HANOI problem (with 4 pegs and 30 disks) spawns a space of 1,152,921,504,606, 846,976 states. It was solved by integrating a number of advanced search techniques in about 400 gigabytes of disk space and 17 days.

In SOKOBAN, more than 50 of a set of 90 benchmark instances have been solved push-optimally by looking at less than 160 million states in total. Since standard search algorithms solved none of the instances, enhancements were crucial.

Search refinements have also helped to beat the best human CHESS player in tournament matches, to show that CHECKERS is a draw, and to identify the game-theoretical values in CONNECT 4 variants. CHESS has an expected search space of about 10^{44}, CHECKERS of about 10^{20}, and CONNECT 4 of 4,531,985,219,092 states (counted with binary decision diagrams in a few hours and validated with brute-force explicit-state search in about a month, by running 16,384 jobs).

The *Deep Blue* system, beating the human CHESS world champion in 1997, considered about 160 million states per second on a massive parallel system with 30 processors and 480 single-chip search engines, applying some search enhancements on the hardware. The *Deep Fritz* system won against the human world champion in 2006 on a PC, evaluating about 10 million states per second.

CHECKERS has been shown to be a draw (assuming optimal play). Endgame databases of up to 10 pieces were built, for any combination of kings and checkers. The database size amounts to 39 trillion positions. The search algorithm has been split into a front-end proof tree manager and a back-end prover. The total number of states in the proof for a particular opening was about 10^{13}, searched in about 1 month on an average of seven processors, with a longest line of 67 moves (*plies*).

The standard problem for CONNECT 4 is victory for the first player, however, the 9×6 version is won for the second player (assuming optimal play). The latter result used a database constructed in about 40,000 hours. The search itself considered about $2 \cdot 10^{13}$ positions and took about 2,000 hours.

Search algorithms also solved multiplayer games. For mere play, BRIDGE programs outplay world-class human players and, together with betting, computer BRIDGE players match expert performance. Pruning techniques and randomized simulation have been used to evaluate about 18,000 cards per second. In an invitational field consisting of 34 of the world's best card players, the best-playing BRIDGE program finished twelfth.

Search also applies to games of chance. Probabilistic versions of the $(n^2 - 1)$-PUZZLE have been solved storing 1,357,171,197 annotated edges on 45 gigabytes of disk space. The algorithm (designed for solving general MDPs) terminated after two weeks and 72 iterations using less than 1.4 gigabytes RAM. For BACKGAMMON with about 10^{19} states, over 1.5 million training games were played to *learn* how to play well. Statistical, so-called *roll-outs* guide the search process.

As illustrated in recent competitions, *general game playing* programs play many games at acceptable levels. Given the rules of a game, *UCT*-based search algorithms can infer a strategy for playing it, without any human intervention. Additionally, perfect players can be constructed using BDDs.

Many industrial online and offline route planning systems use search to answer shortest- and quickest-route queries in fractions of the time taken by standard single-source shortest paths search algorithms. A time and memory saving exploration is especially important for smaller computational devices like smart phones and PDAs. A recent trend for such handheld devices is to process GPS data.

Nowadays domain-independent state space action planning systems solve BLOCKSWORLD problems with 50 blocks and more, and produce close to step-optimal plans in LOGISTICS with hundreds of steps. For planning with numbers, potentially infinite search spaces have to be explored. As application domains, nowadays planners control the ground traffic on airports, control the flow of oil derivatives through a pipeline network, find deadlocks in communication protocols, resupply a number of lines in a faulty electricity network, collect image data with a number of satellites, and set up applications for mobile terminals. With the appropriate selection of search techniques, optimal plans can be obtained.

Search algorithms effectively guide industrial and autonomous robots in known and unknown environments. As an example, the time for path planning on Sony's humanoid robot with 38 degrees of freedom (in a discretized environment with 80,000 configurations) was mostly below 100 milliseconds on the robot's embedded CPUs. Parallel search algorithms also helped solve the collision-free path planning problem of industrial robot arms for assembling large work pieces.

Search algorithms have assisted finding bugs in software. Different model checkers have been enhanced by directing the search toward system errors. Search heuristics also accelerate symbolic model checkers for analyzing hardware, on-the-fly verifiers for analyzing compiled software units, and industrial tools for exploring real-time domains and finding resource-optimal schedules. Given a large and dynamic changing state vector of several kilobytes, external memory and parallel exploration scale best. A sample exploration consumed 3 terabytes hard disk space, while using 3.6 gigabytes RAM. It took 8 days with four dual CPUs connected via NFS-shared hard disks to locate the error, and 20 days with a single CPU.

Search is currently the best known method for solving sequence alignment problems in computational biology optimally. Alignments for benchmarks of five benchmark sequences (length 300–550) have to be computed by using parallel and disk-based search algorithms. The graphs for the most challenging problems contain about 10^{13} nodes. One sample run took 10 days to find an optimal alignment.

Encouraging results for search in *automated theorem proving* with first- and higher-order logic proofs could not be obtained without search guidance. In some cases, heuristics have helped to avoid being trapped on large and infinite plateaus.

In summary, there is lot of progress in making search algorithms more efficient and in applying them to additional real-world domains. Moreover, it is not hard to predict that the success of search algorithms will likely continue in the future.

1.4 STATE SPACE PROBLEMS

A multitude of algorithmic problems in a variety of application domains, many of which will be introduced in this and the following chapters, can be formalized as a *state space problem*. A state space problem $P = (S, A, s, T)$ consists of a set of states S, an initial state $s \in S$, a set of goal states $T \subseteq S$, and a finite set of actions $A = \{a_1, \dots, a_n\}$ where each $a_i : S \rightarrow S$ transforms a state into another state.

Consider a circular railway track with a siding, as in Figure 1.3. The goal is to exchange the location of the two cars, and to have the engine back on the siding. A railroad switch is used to enable the trains to be guided from the circular track to the siding. To frame this RAILROAD SWITCHING problem as a state space problem, note that the exact position of the engines and the car is irrelevant, as long as their relative position to each other is the same. Therefore, it is sufficient to consider only *discrete* configurations where the engine or the cars are on the siding, above or below the tunnel. Actions are all switching movements of the engine that result in a change of configuration. In the literature, different notions are often used depending on the application. Thus, states are also called *configurations* or *positions*; *moves*, *operators*, or *transitions* are synonyms for actions.

Looking at a state space problem in this way, it is immediately conducive to visualize it by drawing it. This leads to a graph-theoretical formalization, where we associate states with *nodes* and actions with *edges* between nodes. For the example problem, the state space is shown as a graph in Figure 1.4.

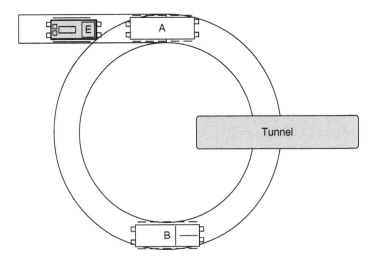

FIGURE 1.3

RAILROAD SWITCHING problem. An engine (E) at the siding can push or pull two cars (A and B) on the track. The railway passes through a tunnel that only the engine, but not the rail cars, can pass.

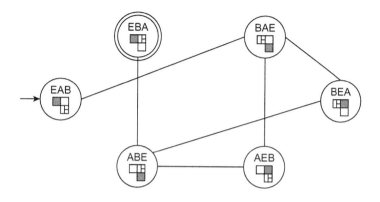

FIGURE 1.4

Discretized state space of the RAILROAD SWITCHING problem. Possible states are labeled by the locations of the engine (E) and the cars (A and B), either in the form of a string or of a pictogram; EAB is the start state, EBA is the goal state.

Definition 1.1. *(State Space Problem Graph) A problem graph $G = (V, E, s, T)$ for the state space problem $P = (S, A, s, T)$ is defined by $V = S$ as the set of nodes, $s \in S$ as the initial node, T as the set of goal nodes, and $E \subseteq V \times V$ as the set of edges that connect nodes to nodes with $(u, v) \in E$ if and only if there exists an $a \in A$ with $a(u) = v$.*

Note that each edge corresponds to a unique action, but often an action is specified in such a way that it can induce multiple edges. Each edge of the graph can be labeled by a respective action. In chess, for example, an action could be "move the king one square to the left," and could be applied in many different positions with as many different outcomes. For the RAILROAD SWITCHING problem, we could label the transitions by the sequence of executed actions of the engine; for example, *(exit-right, couple-A, push-A, uncouple-A, cycle-left, couple-B, pull-B, exit-left, uncouple-B, exit-right, cycle-left)* for the transition from state EAB to BAE. It is often possible to devise much smaller label sets.

Actions can be strung together into a sequence by applying an action to the result of another one. The objective of solving a state space problem is finding a *solution*.

Definition 1.2. *(Solution) A solution $\pi = (a_1, \ldots, a_k)$ is an ordered sequence of actions $a_i \in A$, $i \in \{1, \ldots, k\}$ that transforms the initial state s into one of the goal states $t \in T$; that is, there exists a sequence of states $u_i \in S$, $i \in \{0, \ldots, k\}$, with $u_0 = s$, $u_k = t$, and u_i is the outcome of applying a_i to u_{i-1}, $i \in \{1, \ldots, k\}$.*

A solution for our example problem would be defined by the path (EAB, BAE, AEB, ABE, EBA). Note that several different solutions are possible, such as (EAB, BAE, BEA, ABE, EBA), but also as (EAB, BAE, BEA, ABE, AEB, BAE, AEB, ABE, EBA). Typically, we are not only interested in finding any solution path, but a *shortest* one—one with the minimum number of edges.

Frequently, we are not only interested in the *solution length* of a problem (i.e., the number of actions in the sequence), but more generally in its *cost* (again, depending on the application, authors use synonyms such as *distance* or *weight*). For the RAILROAD SWITCHING example problem, costs could be given by travel time, distance, number of couplings/uncouplings, or power consumption. Each edge is assigned a weight. Unless stated otherwise, a key assumption we will make is that weights are *additive*; that is, the cost of a path is the sum of the weights of its constituting edges. This is a natural concept when counting steps or computing overall costs on paths from the initial state to the goal. Generalizations to this concept are possible and discussed later. The setting motivates the following definition.

Definition 1.3. *(Weighted State Space Problem) A weighted state space problem is a tuple* $P = (S, A, s, T, w)$, *where w is a cost function* $w : A \rightarrow \mathbb{R}$. *The cost of a path consisting of actions* $a_1, \ldots, a_n$ *is defined as* $\sum_{i=1}^{n} w(a_i)$. *In a weighted search space, we call a solution optimal if it has minimum cost among all feasible solutions.*

For a weighted state space problem, there is a corresponding weighted problem graph $G = (V, E, s, T, w)$, *where w is extended to* $E \rightarrow \mathbb{R}$ *in the straightforward way. The graph is* uniform(ly weighted), *if* $w(u, v)$ *is constant for all* $(u, v) \in E$. *The weight or cost of a path* $\pi = (v_0, \ldots, v_k)$ *is defined as* $w(\pi) = \sum_{i=1}^{k} w(v_{i-1}, v_i)$.

Unweighted (or unit cost) problem graphs, such as the RAILROAD SWITCHING *problem, arise as a special case with* $w(u, v) = 1$ *for all edges* (u, v).

Definition 1.4. *(Solution Path) Let* $\pi = v_0, \ldots, v_k$ *be a path in G. If* $v_0 = s$ *and* $v_k \in T$ *for the designated start state s and the set of goal nodes T, then* π *is called a solution path. In addition, it is optimal if its weight is minimal among all paths between s and* v_k; *in this case, its cost is denoted as* $\delta(s, v)$. *The optimal solution cost can be abbreviated as* $\delta(s, T) = \min\{t \in T \mid \delta(s, t)\}$.

For example, the RAILROAD SWITCHING problem has $\delta(s, T) = 4$. Solution paths to *uniformly weighted problem graphs with* $w(u, v) = k$ *for all edges* (u, v) are solved by considering the unit cost problem and multiplying the optimal solution cost with k.

1.5 PROBLEM GRAPH REPRESENTATIONS

Graph search is a fundamental problem in computer science. Most algorithmic formulations refer to *explicit graphs*, where a complete description of the graph is specified.

A graph $G = (V, E)$ is usually represented in two possible ways (see Fig. 1.5). An *adjacency matrix* refers to a two-dimensional Boolean array M. The entry $M_{i,j}$, $1 \leq i, j \leq n$, is *true* (or 1) if and only if an edge contains a node with index i as a source and a node with index j as the target; otherwise, it is *false* (or 0). The required size of this graph representation is $O(|V|^2)$. For *sparse graphs* (graphs with

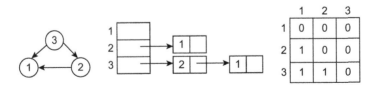

FIGURE 1.5

An unweighted but directed problem graph (left) together with its adjacency list (middle), and its adjacency matrix representation (right).

relatively few edges) an *adjacency list* is more appropriate. It is implemented as an array L of pointers to node lists. For each node u in V, entry L_u will contain a pointer to a list of all nodes v with $(u,v) \in E$. The space requirement of this representation is $O(|V| + |E|)$, which is optimal.

Adding weight information to these explicit graph data structures is simple. In case of the adjacency matrix, the distance values are substituting the Boolean values so that entries $M_{i,j}$ denote corresponding edge weights; the entries for nonexisting edges are set to ∞. In the adjacency list representation, with each node list element v in list L_u we associate the weight $w(u,v)$.

Solving state space problems, however, is sometimes better characterized as a search in an *implicit graph*. The difference is that not all edges have to be *explicitly* stored, but are generated by a set of rules (e.g., in games). This setting of an implicit generation of the search space is also called *on-the-fly*, *incremental*, or *lazy* state space generation in some domains.

Definition 1.5. *(Implicit State Space Graph) In an* implicit state space graph, *we have an initial node* $s \in V$, *a set of goal nodes determined by a predicate* Goal: $V \to \mathbb{B} = \{false, true\}$, *and a node expansion procedure* Expand: $V \to 2^V$.

Most graph search algorithms work by iteratively lengthening candidate paths $(u_0, \ldots, u_n = u)$ by one edge at a time, until a solution path is found. The basic operation is called *node expansion* (a.k.a. *node exploration*), which means generation of all neighbors of a node u. The resulting nodes are called *successors* (a.k.a. *children*) of u, and u is called a *parent* or *predecessor* (if u_{n-1} additionally is a neighbor it might not be generated if expand is clever, but it can still be a successor). All nodes $u_0, \ldots, u_{n-1}$ are called *ancestors* of u; conversely, u is a *descendant* of each node $u_0, \ldots, u_{n-1}$. In other words, the terms *ancestor* and *descendant* refer to paths of possibly more than one edge. These terms relate to the exploration order in a given search, whereas the *neighbors* of a node are all nodes adjacent in the search graph. To abbreviate notation and to distinguish the node expansion procedure from the successor set itself, we will write *Succ* for the latter.

An important aspect to characterize state space problems is the *branching factor*.

Definition 1.6. *(Branching Factor) The* branching factor *of a state is the number of successors it has. If* Succ(u) *abbreviates the successor set of a state* $u \in S$ *then the branching factor is* $|$Succ$(u)|$; *that is, the cardinality of* Succ(u).

In a problem graph, the branching factor corresponds to the *out-degree* of a node; that is, its number of neighbors reachable by some edge. For the initial state EAB in the RAILROAD SWITCHING example, we have only one successor, whereas for state BAE we have a branching factor of 3.

For a problem graph, we can define an average, minimum, and maximum branching factor. The average branching factor b largely determines the search effort, since the number of possible paths of length l grows roughly as b^l.

1.6 HEURISTICS

Heuristics are meant to be estimates of the remaining distance from a node to the goal. This information can be exploited by search algorithms to assess whether one state is *more promising* than the rest. We will illustrate that the computational search effort can be considerably reduced if between two candidate paths, the algorithm prefers to expand the one with the lower estimate. A detailed introduction to search algorithms is deferred to the next section.

A search *heuristic* provides information to orient the search into the direction of the search goal. We refer to the graph $G = (V, E, s, T, w)$ of a weighted state space problem.

Definition 1.7. *(Heuristic)* A heuristic h is *a* node evaluation function, *mapping V to $\mathbb{R}_{\geq 0}$.*

If $h(t) = 0$ for all t in T and if for all other nodes $u \in V$ we have $h(u) \neq 0$, the goal check for u simplifies to the comparison of $h(u)$ with 0.

Before plunging into the discussion of concrete examples of heuristics in different domains, let us briefly give an intuitive description of how heuristic knowledge can help to guide algorithms; the notions will be made precise in Chapter 2.

Let $g(u)$ be the path cost to a node u and $h(u)$ be its estimate. The value $g(u)$ varies with the path on which u is encountered. The equation

$$f(u) = g(u) + h(u)$$

is very important in understanding the behavior of heuristic search algorithms. In words, the f-value is the estimate of the total path cost from the start node to the target destination, which reaches u on the same path.

As general state spaces are difficult to visualize, we restrict ourselves to an extremely simplified model: the states are linearly connected along the horizontal axis, like pearls on a string (see Fig. 1.6). In each step, we can look at one state connected to a previously explored state.

If we have no heuristic information at all, we have to conduct a blind (uninformed) search. Since we do not know if the target lies on the left or the right side, a good strategy is to expand nodes alternatively on the left and on the right, until the target is encountered. Thus, in each step we expand a node of which the distance g from s is minimal.

When a heuristic h is given, an extension of this strategy always prefers to expand the most promising node, the one of which the estimated total distance to the target, $f = g + h$, is minimal. Then, at least all nodes with f-value less than the optimal solution cost f^* will be expanded; however, since h increases the estimate, some nodes can be pruned from consideration. This is illustrated in Figure 1.7, where h amounts to half the true goal distance. In a *perfect heuristic*, the two are identical. In our example (see Fig. 1.8), this reduces the number of expanded nodes to one-half, which is optimal.

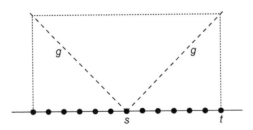

FIGURE 1.6

A state space without heuristic knowledge. s is the start state and t is the target state; the search depth g is illustrated with dots along the horizontal axis, and the search cost is illustrated along the vertical axis.

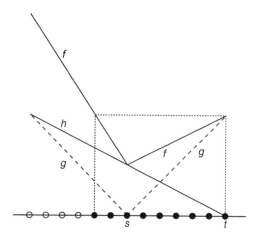

FIGURE 1.7

A state space with some heuristic knowledge. The amplitudes of heuristic h and search depth g accumulate to the amplitude of f.

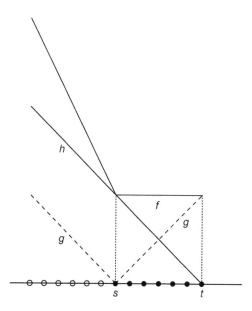

FIGURE 1.8

A state space with perfect heuristic knowledge. All states between s and t have the same f-value.

Finally, Figure 1.9 depicts the case of a heuristic that is misleading. The path going away from the goal looks better than the path to the goal. In this case, the heuristic search traversal will expand more nodes than blind exploration.

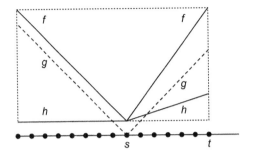

FIGURE 1.9

A state space with misleading heuristic knowledge, indicating that by a smaller f-value the search will more likely search the part of the search space that contains no goal.

Heuristics are particularly useful if we can make sure that they sometimes may underestimate, but never overestimate, the true goal distance.

Definition 1.8. *(Admissible Heuristic) An estimate h is an* admissible heuristic *if it is a lower bound for the optimal solution costs; that is, $h(u) \leq \delta(u,T)$ for all $u \in V$.*

Other useful properties of heuristics are *consistency* and *monotonicity*.

Definition 1.9. *(Consistent, Monotonic Heuristic) Let $G = (V,E,s,T,w)$ be a weighted state space problem graph.*

- *A goal estimate h is a* consistent heuristic *if $h(u) \leq h(v) + w(u,v)$ for all edges $e = (u,v) \in E$.*
- *Let $(u_0,\ldots,u_k)$ be any path, $g(u_i)$ be the path cost of $(u_0,\ldots,u_i)$, and define $f(u_i) = g(u_i) + h(u_i)$. A goal estimate h is a* monotone heuristic *if $f(u_j) \geq f(u_i)$ for all $j > i$, $0 \leq i,j \leq k$; that is, the estimate of the total path cost is nondecreasing from a node to its successors.*

The next theorem shows that these properties are actually equivalent.

Theorem 1.1. *(Equivalence of Consistent and Monotone Heuristics) A heuristic is consistent if and only if it is monotone.*

Proof. For two subsequent states u_{i-1} and u_i on a path $(u_0,\ldots,u_k)$ we have

$$
\begin{aligned}
f(u_i) &= g(u_i) + h(u_i) & \text{(by the definition of } f) \\
&= g(u_{i-1}) + w(u_{i-1},u_i) + h(u_i) & \text{(by the definition of path cost)} \\
&\geq g(u_{i-1}) + h(u_{i-1}) & \text{(by the definition of consistency)} \\
&= f(u_{i-1}) & \text{(by the definition of } f)
\end{aligned}
$$

Moreover, we obtain the following implication. ∎

Theorem 1.2. *(Consistency and Admissibility) Consistent estimates are admissible.*

Proof. If h is consistent we have $h(u) - h(v) \leq w(u,v)$ for all $(u,v) \in E$. Let $p = (v_0, \ldots, v_k)$ be any path from $u = v_0$ to $t = v_k$. Then we have

$$w(p) = \sum_{i=0}^{k-1} w(v_i, v_{i+1}) \geq \sum_{i=0}^{k-1} (h(v_i) - h(v_{i+1})) = h(u) - h(t) = h(u).$$

This is also true in the important case of p being an optimal path from u to $t \in T$. Therefore, $h(u) \leq \delta(u,T)$. ∎

In addition, the following conditions hold (see Exercises):

- The maximum of two admissible heuristics is an admissible heuristic.
- The maximum of two consistent heuristics is a consistent heuristic.
- Admissible heuristics are not necessarily consistent (although most practically used ones are).

1.7 EXAMPLES OF SEARCH PROBLEMS

In this section, we introduce some standard search problems we will refer to throughout the book. Some of them are puzzles that have been used extensively in the literature for benchmarking algorithms; some are real-world applications.

1.7.1 Sliding-Tile Puzzles

Our first example, illustrated in Figure 1.10, is a class of single-player sliding-tile toy games called the EIGHT-PUZZLE, the FIFTEEN-PUZZLE, the TWENTY-FOUR-PUZZLE, and, generally, the $(n^2 - 1)$-PUZZLE. It consists of $(n^2 - 1)$ numbered tiles, squarely arranged, that can be slid into a single empty position, called the *blank*. The task is to rearrange the tiles such that a certain goal state is reached.

FIGURE 1.10

Classic goal states for the EIGHT-PUZZLE (left), FIFTEEN-PUZZLE (middle), and TWENTY-FOUR-PUZZLE (right).

The state space for these problems grows exponentially in n. The total number of reachable states[1] is $(n^2)!/2$.

For modeling the puzzle as a state space problem, each state can be represented as a permutation vector, each of the components of which corresponds to one location, indicated by which of the tiles (including the blank) it occupies. For the EIGHT-PUZZLE instance of Figure 1.10 the vector representation is $(1,2,3,8,0,4,7,6,5)$. Alternatively, we can devise a vector of the *locations* of each tile $(5,1,2,3,8,5,7,6,4)$ in the example. The last location in the vector representation can be omitted.

The first vector representation naturally corresponds to a physical $(n \times n)$ board layout. The initial state is provided by the user; for the goal state we assume a vector representation with value i at index $i+1$, $1 \leq i \leq n^2 - 1$. The *tile movement* actions modify the vector as follows. If the blank is at index j, $1 \leq j \leq n^2$, it is swapped with the tile either in direction *up* (index $j-n$), *down* (index $j+n$), *left* (index $j-1$), or *right* (index $j+1$) *unless* the blank is already at the top-most (or, respectively, bottom-most, left-most, or right-most) fringe of the board. Here we see an instance where a labeled action representation comes in handy: We let Σ be $\{U,D,L,R\}$ with U, D, L, and R denoting a respective *up*, *down*, *left*, or *right* movement (of the blank). Although strictly speaking, up movements from a different blank position are different actions, in each state at most one action with a given label is applicable.

The GENERAL SLIDING-TILE PUZZLE (a.k.a. KLOTZKI) is an extension of the $(n^2 - 1)$-PUZZLE where the pieces can have different shapes. It consists of a collection of possibly labeled pieces to be slid on adjacent positions on a given board in either of the four directions *up*, *down*, *left*, and *right*. Each piece is composed of a set of tiles. Pieces of the same shape and labeling are indistinguishable. Figure 1.11 visualizes typical GENERAL SLIDING-TILE PUZZLE instances. The goal is to move the 2×2 block toward the arrow head. A compact representation is the list of tiles according to fixed reference coordinates and some traversal of the board. For the DONKEY PUZZLE example, and a natural reference spot and traversal of the board, we obtain the list *2x1*, *blank*, *blank*, *2x1*, *2x2*, *2x1*, *2x1*, *1x2*, *1x1*, *1x1*, *1x1*, and *1x1*. Let s, the total number of pieces, be partitioned into sets of f_i pieces of the same type for $\{1,\ldots,k\}$; then the number of configurations is bounded by $s!/(f_1! \cdots f_k!)$. The exact number can be determined utilizing a turn out of which the next piece to be placed is drawn. If a piece fits into the current configuration the next one is drawn, otherwise an alternative piece is chosen. With this approach we can compute the total state count for the puzzles: DAD'S PUZZLE, 18,504; DONKEY

---

[1] The original version of this puzzle was invented by Sam Lloyd in the 1870s, and was made with 15 wooden blocks in a tray. He offered a reward of $1,000 to anyone who could prove they'd solved it from the state where the 14 and 15 were switched. All sorts of people claimed they had solved the puzzle, but when they were asked to demonstrate how they'd done it (without actually picking the blocks off the tray and replacing them), none of them could do it. Apparently, one clergyman spent a whole freezing winter night standing under a lamp post trying to remember what he'd done to get it right.

Actually, there exists no solution for this; the concept that made Sam Lloyd rich is called *parity*. Assume writing the tile numbers of a state in a linear order, by concatenating, consecutively, all the rows. An *inversion* is defined as a pair of tiles x and y in that order such that x occurs before y in that order, but $x > y$. Note that a horizontal move does not affect the order of the tiles. In a vertical move, the current tile always skips over the three intermediate tiles following in the order, and these are the only inversions affected by that move. If one of these intermediate tiles contributes an inversion with the moved tile, it no longer does so after the move, and vice versa. Hence, depending on the magnitudes of the intermediate tiles, in any case the number of inversions changes by either one or three. Now, for a given puzzle configuration, let N denote the sum of the total number of inversions, plus the row number of the blank. Then ($N \bmod 2$) is invariant under any legal move. In other words, after a legal move an odd N remains odd, whereas an even N remains even. Consequently, from a given configuration, only half of all possible states are reachable.

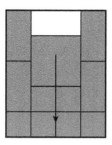 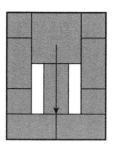 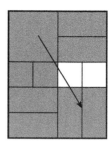

FIGURE 1.11

Instances of the GENERAL SLIDING-TILE PUZZLE: DONKEY PUZZLE (left), CENTURY PUZZLE (middle), and DAD'S PUZZLE (right).

PUZZLE, 65,880; and CENTURY PUZZLE, 109,260. A successor can be generated in time linear to the number of tiles (see Exercises).

One of the simplest heuristics for sliding-tile puzzles is to count the number of tiles that are not at their respective goal location. This *misplaced-tile heuristic* is consistent, since it changes by at most one between neighboring states.

The $(n^2 - 1)$-PUZZLE has another lower bound estimate, called the *Manhattan distance heuristic*. For each two states $u = ((x_1, y_1), (x_2, y_2), \ldots, (x_{n^2-1}, y_{n^2-1}))$ and $v = ((x'_1, y'_1), (x'_2, y'_2), \ldots, (x'_{n^2-1}, y'_{n^2-1}))$, with coordinates $x_i, y_i \in \{0, \ldots, n-1\}$ it is defined as $\sum_{i=1}^{n^2-1} (|x_i - x'_i| + |y_i - y'_i|)$; in words, it is the sum of moves required to bring each tile to its target position independently. This yields the heuristic estimate $h(u) = \sum_{i=1}^{n^2-1} (|x_i - \lfloor i/n \rfloor| + |y_i - (i \bmod n)|)$.

The Manhattan distance and the misplaced-tile heuristic for the $(n^2 - 1)$-PUZZLE are both consistent, since the difference in heuristic values is at most 1; that is, $|h(v) - h(u)| \leq 1$, for all u, v. This means $h(v) - h(u) \leq 1$ and $h(u) - h(v) \leq 1$. Together with $w(u, v) = 1$, the latter inequality implies $h(v) - h(u) + w(u, v) \geq 0$.

An example is given in Figure 1.12. Tiles 5, 6, 7, and 8 are not in final position. The number of misplaced tiles is 4, and the Manhattan distance is 7.

An improvement for the Manhattan distance is the *linear conflict heuristic*. It concerns pairs of tiles that both are in the correct row (column), but in the wrong order in column (row) direction. In this case, two extra moves not accommodated in the Manhattan distance will be needed to get one tile out of the way of the other one. In the example, tiles 6 and 7 are in a linear conflict and call for an offset 2 to the Manhattan distance. Implementing the full linear conflict heuristic requires checking the permutation orders for all pairs of tiles in the same row/column.

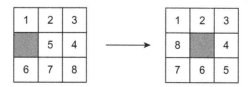

FIGURE 1.12

Example for heuristic estimates in the EIGHT-PUZZLE.

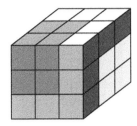

FIGURE 1.13

A scrambled RUBIK'S CUBE; colors are in grayscale.

1.7.2 RUBIK'S CUBE

RUBIK'S CUBE (see Fig. 1.13), invented in the late 1970s by Erno Rubik, is another known challenge for a single-agent search. Each face can be rotated by 90, 180, or 270 degrees and the goal is to rearrange the subcubes, called *cubies*, of a scrambled cube such that all faces are uniformly colored. The 26 visible cubies can be classified into 8 corner cubies (three colors), 12 edge cubies (two colors), and 6 middle cubies (one color). There are $8! \cdot 3^8 \cdot 12! \cdot 2^{12}/12 \approx 43 \cdot 10^{18}$ possible cube configurations. Since there are six faces—left (L), right (R), up (U), down (D), front (F), and back (B)—this gives an initial branching factor of $6 \cdot 3 = 18$. The move actions are abbreviated as $L, L^2, L^-, R, R^2, R^-, U,$ $U^2, U^-, D, D^2, D^-, F, F^2, F^-, B, B^2,$ and B^-. (Other notations consist of using $'$ or -1 for denoting inverted operators, instead of $-$.)

We never rotate the same face twice in a row, however, since the same result can be obtained with a single twist of that face. This reduces the branching factor to $5 \cdot 3 = 15$ after the first move. Twists of opposite faces are independent of each other and hence commute. For example, twisting the left face followed by the right face gives the same result as twisting the right face followed by the left face. Thus, if two opposite faces are rotated consecutively, we assume them to be ordered without loss of generality. For each pair of opposite faces, we arbitrarily label one a *first* face and the other a *second* face. After a first face is twisted, there are three possible twists of each of the remaining five faces, resulting in a branching factor of 15. After a second face is twisted, however, we can only twist four remaining faces, excluding the face just twisted and its corresponding first face, for a branching factor of 12.

Humans solve the problem by a general strategy that generally consists of *macro actions*, fixed move sequences that correctly position individual or groups of cubes without violating previously positioned ones. Typically, these strategies require 50 to 100 moves, which is far from optimal.

We generalize the Manhattan distance to RUBIK'S CUBE as follows. For all cubies, we cumulate the minimum number of moves to a correct position and orientation. However, since each move involves eight cubies, the result has to be divided by 8. A better heuristic computes the Manhattan distance for the edge and corner cubies separately, takes the maximum of the two, and divides it by 4.

1.7.3 SOKOBAN

SOKOBAN was invented in the early 1980s by a computer games company in Japan. There exists a set of benchmark problems (see Fig. 1.14), ordered roughly easiest to hardest in difficulty for a human to solve. The start position consists of *n balls* (a.k.a. *stones*, *boxes*) scattered over a maze. A *man*,

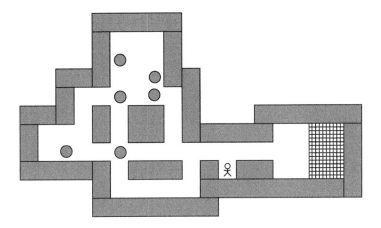

FIGURE 1.14

First level in SOKOBAN benchmark suite. Walls define the maze to be traversed by the man; balls have to be pushed to the goal area located to the right of the maze.

controlled by the puzzle solver, traverses the board and pushes balls onto an adjacent empty square. The aim is to move the balls onto n designated goal fields.

One important aspect of SOKOBAN is that it contains traps. Many state space problems like the RAILROAD SWITCHING problem are *reversible*; that is, for each action $a \in A$ there exists an action $a^{-1} \in A$, so that $a(a^{-1}(u)) = u$ and $a^{-1}(a(u)) = u$. Each state that is reachable from the start state can itself reach the start state. Hence, if the goal is reachable, then it is reachable from every state. *Directed state space problems*, however, can include *dead-ends*.

Definition 1.10. *(Dead-End) A state space problem has a* dead-end $u \in S$ *if u is reachable and $P_u = (S,A,u,T)$ is unsolvable.*

Examples for *dead-ends* in SOKOBAN are four balls placed next to each other in the form of a square, so that the man cannot move any of them; or balls that lie at the boundary of the maze (excluding goal squares). We see that many dead-ends can be identified in the form of *local patterns*. The instance in Figure 1.14, however, is solvable.

For a fixed number of balls, the problem's complexity is polynomial. In general, we distinguish three problems: DECIDE is just the task to solve the puzzle (if possible), PUSHES additionally asks to minimize the number of ball pushes, whereas MOVES request an optimal number of man movements. All these problems are provably hard (PSPACE complete).

We see that complexity theory states results on a scaling set of problems, but does not give an intuitive understanding on the hardness for a single problem at hand. Hence, Figure 1.15 compares some search space properties of solitaire games. The *effective branching factor* is the average number of children of a state, after applying pruning methods. For SOKOBAN, the numbers are for typical puzzles from the humanmade test sets; common SOKOBAN board sizes are 20×20.

One good lower bound estimate for SOKOBAN (PUSHES variant) is found using a *minimal matching* approach. We are interested in a matching of balls to goal fields, such that the sum of all ball paths

Characteristic	TWENTY-FOUR-PUZZLE	RUBIK'S CUBE	SOKOBAN
Branching Factor	2–4	12–18	0–50
– effective –	2.13	13.34	10
Solution Length	80–112	14–18	97–674
– typical –	100	16	260
Search Space Size	10^{25}	10^{18}	10^{18}
Graph	Undirected	Undirected	Directed

FIGURE 1.15

Search space properties of some puzzles (numbers are approximate).

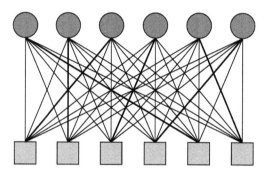

FIGURE 1.16

Matching balls (top row) to goal fields (bottom row) in SOKOBAN. Bold edges illustrate a match; a matched edge connects a ball to its particular goal field.

is minimal. The one part of the bipartite graph (see Fig. 1.16) is composed of nodes for the balls, the other half consists of nodes for the goal fields, and the edge weight between every selected pair (*ball, goal*) of nodes is the shortest path cost for moving the *ball* to *goal* (assuming all other balls were removed from the problem). The standard algorithm to compute the best weighted matching runs in time cubic in the number of balls. More efficient algorithms reduce the problem to the *maximum flow* problem by inserting additional start and sink nodes connected to the ball nodes and to the goal fields, respectively.

In the case of a group of goal fields that is only reachable via a single door, the minimal matching heuristic can be simplified as shortest path calculations through this *articulation* (an articulation of a connected graph is a node that if removed will disconnect the graph). The heuristic is consistent, since moving one ball reduces the individual shortest path to each goal by at most one, and any matching will include only one of the updated shortest path distance values.

1.7.4 ROUTE PLANNING

A practically important application domain for search algorithms is ROUTE PLANNING. The (explicit) search graph consists of a road network, where intersections represent nodes and edges represent drivable connections. The graph is relatively sparse, since the degree of nodes is bounded (intersections with five or more participating roads are very rare). The task consists of finding a path between a start location s and a target location t that minimizes distance, expected travel time, or a related measure. A common approach to estimate travel time is to classify roads into a number of road classes (e.g., freeway, highway, arterial road, major road, local connecting road, residential street), and to associate an average speed with each one. The problem can become challenging in practice due to the large size of maps that have to be stored on external memory, and on tight time constraints (e.g., of navigation systems or online web search). In ROUTE PLANNING, nodes have associated coordinates in some coordinate space (e.g., the Euclidean). We assume a layout function $L : V \rightarrow \mathbb{R}^2$. A lower bound for the road distance between two nodes u and v with locations $L(u) = (x_u, y_u)$ and $L(v) = (x_v, y_v)$ can be obtained as $h(u) = ||L(v) - L(u)||_2 = \sqrt{(x_u - x_v)^2 + (y_u - y_v)^2}$, where $|| \cdot ||_2$ denotes the *Euclidean distance* metric. It is admissible, since the shortest way to the goal is at least as long as the beeline. The heuristic $h(u) = ||L(t) - L(u)||_2$ is consistent, since $h(u) = ||L(t) - L(u)||_2 \leq ||L(t) - L(v)||_2 + ||L(v) - L(u)||_2 = ||L(t) - L(v)||_2 + ||L(u) - L(v)||_2 = h(v) + w(u, v)$ by the *triangle inequality* of the Euclidean plane.

Due to its commercial relevance, we will cover ROUTE PLANNING in Chapter 17.

1.7.5 TSP

One other representative for a state space problem is the TSP (*traveling salesman problem*). Given a distance matrix between n cities, a tour with minimum length has to be found, such that each city is visited exactly once, and the tour returns to the first city. We may choose cities to be enumerated with $\{1, 2, \ldots, n\}$ and distances $d(i, j) \in \mathbb{R}^+$ and $d(i, i) = 0$ for $1 \leq i, j \leq n$. Feasible solutions are permutations τ of $(1, 2, \ldots, n)$ and the objective function is $P(\tau) = \sum_{i=1}^{n} d(\tau(i), \tau((i+1) \bmod n + 1))$ and an optimal solution is a solution τ with minimal $P(\tau)$. The state space has $(n - 1)! / 2$ solutions, which is about 4.7×10^{157} for $n = 101$. This problem has been shown to be NP complete in the general case; entire books have been dedicated to it. Figure 1.17 (left) shows an example of the TSP problem, and Figure 1.17 (right) a corresponding solution.

Various algorithms have been devised that *quickly* yield *good* solutions with *high* probability. Modern methods can find solutions for extremely large problems (millions of cities) within a reasonable time with a high probability just 2 to 3% away from the optimal solution.

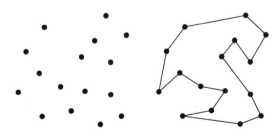

FIGURE 1.17

METRIC TSP problem instance (left) and its solution (right); edge costs are straight-line distances.

In the special case of the METRIC TSP problem, the additional requirement of the *triangle inequality* is imposed. This inequality states that for all vertices u, v, and w, the distance function d satisfies $d(u,w) \leq d(u,v) + d(v,w)$. In other words, the cheapest or shortest way of going from one city to another is the direct route between two cities. In particular, if every city corresponds to a point in Euclidean space, and distance between cities corresponds to Euclidean distance, then the triangle inequality is satisfied. In contrast to the general TSP, METRIC TSP can be 1.5-approximated, meaning that the approximate solution is at most 50% larger than the optimal one.

When formalizing TSP as a search problem, we can identify states with incomplete tours, starting with any arbitrary node. Each expansion adds one more city to the partial path. A state denoting a completed, closed tour is a goal state.

A *spanning tree* of a graph is a subgraph without cycles connecting all nodes of the graph. A MINIMUM SPANNING TREE (MST) is a spanning tree such that the sum of all its edge weights is minimum among all spanning trees of the graph. For n nodes, it can be computed as follows. First, choose the edge with minimum weight and mark it. Then, repeatedly find the cheapest unmarked edge in the graph that does not close a cycle. Continue until all vertices are connected. The marked edges form the desired MST.

A heuristic that estimates the total length of a TSP cycle, given a partial path, exploits that the yet unexplored cities have to be at least connected to the ends of the existing part (to both the first and the last city). So if we compute a MST for these two plus all unexplored cities, we obtain a lower bound for a connecting tree. This must be an admissible heuristic, since a connecting tree that additionally fulfills the linearity condition cannot be shorter. A partial solution and the MST used for the heuristic are shown in Figure 1.18.

1.7.6 MULTIPLE SEQUENCE ALIGNMENT

The MULTIPLE SEQUENCE ALIGNMENT problem, in computational biology, consists of aligning several sequences (strings; e.g., related genes from different organisms) to reveal similarities and differences across the group. Either *DNA* can be directly compared, and the underlying alphabet Σ consists of the set {C,G,A,T} for the four standard *nucleotide bases* cytosine, guanine, adenine and thymine; or we can compare *proteins*, in which case Σ comprises the 20 *amino acids*.

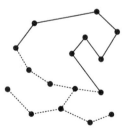

FIGURE 1.18

TSP partial solution (solid line) and MST for heuristic (dotted line).

Roughly speaking, we try to write the sequences one above the other such that the columns with matching letters are maximized; thereby, gaps (denoted here by an additional letter _) may be inserted into either of them to shift the remaining characters into better corresponding positions. Different letters in the same column can be interpreted as being caused by point mutations during the course of evolution that substituted one amino acid by another one; gaps can be seen as insertions or deletions (since the direction of change is often not known, they are also collectively referred to as *indels*). Presumably, the alignment with the fewest mismatches reflects the biologically most plausible explanation.

The state space consists of all possible alignments of prefixes of the input sequences $m_1, \ldots, m_k$. If the prefix lengths serve as vector components we can encode the problem as a set of vertices $x = (x_1, \ldots, x_k)$, $x_i \in \{0, \ldots, |m_i|\}$ with associated cost vector v_x. A state x' is a (potential) successor of x if $x'_i - x_i \in \{0, 1\}$ for all i. The underlying problem graph structure is directed and acyclic and follows a k-dimensional *lattice* or *hypercube*.

There is a host of applications of sequence alignment within *computational biology*; for example, for determining the evolutionary relationship between species, for detecting functionally active sites that tend to be preserved best across homologous sequences, and for predicting three-dimensional protein structures.

Formally, we associate a cost with an alignment and try to find the (mathematically) *optimal* alignment, the one with the minimum cost. When designing a cost function, computational efficiency and biological meaning have to be taken into account. The most widely used definition is the *sum-of-pairs* cost function. First, we are given a symmetric $(|\Sigma| + 1)^2$ matrix containing penalties (scores) for substituting a letter with another one (or a gap). In the simplest case, this could be one for a mismatch and zero for a match, but more biologically relevant scores have been developed. A *substitution matrix* corresponds to a model of molecular evolution and estimates the exchange probabilities of amino acids for different amounts of evolutionary divergence. Based on such a substitution matrix, the sum-of-pairs cost of an alignment is defined as the sum of penalties between all letter pairs in corresponding column positions. An example of the calculation of the sum-of-pairs cost is depicted in Figure 1.19. The value $6 = (3 + 3)$ is based on entry (A/_) in the substitution matrix, and the second value 7 is based on entry (B,_) plus 1 for a still-opened gap.

```
A  B  C  _  B
_  B  C  D  _
_  _  _  D  B
```

	A	B	C	D	_
A	0	2	4	2	3
B		1	3	3	3
C			2	2	3
D				1	3
_					0

FIGURE 1.19

Fictitious alignment problem with sum-of-pair cost: $6 + 7 + 8 + 7 + 7 = 35$; alignment (left), substitution matrix (right).

A number of improvements can be integrated into the sum-of-pairs cost, like associating weights with sequences, and using different substitution matrices for sequences of varying evolutionary distance. A major issue in MULTIPLE SEQUENCE ALIGNMENT algorithms is their ability to handle gaps. Gap penalties can be made dependent on the neighbor letters. Moreover, it has been found that assigning a fixed score for each indel sometimes does not produce the biologically most plausible alignment. Since the insertion of a sequence of x letters is more likely than x separate insertions of a single letter, gap cost functions have been introduced that depend on the length of a gap. A useful approximation is *affine gap costs*, which distinguish between opening and extension of a gap and charge $a + b * x$ for a gap of length x, for appropriate a and b. Another frequently used modification is to waive the penalties for gaps at the beginning or end of a sequence. A real alignment problem is shown in Figure 1.20.

The sequence alignment problem is a generalization of the problem of computing the *edit distance*, which aims at changing a string into another by using the three main edit operations of modifying, inserting, or deleting a letter. Each edit operation is charged, and the minimum-cost operations sequence is sought. For instance, a *spell checker* could determine the lexicon word of which the edit distance from a (possibly misspelled) word typed by the user is minimal. The same task arises in *version control systems*.

Lower bounds on the cost of aligning k sequences are often based on optimal alignments of subsets of $m < k$ sequences. In general, for a vertex v in k-space, we are looking for a lower bound for a path from v to the target corner t. Consider first the case $m = 2$. The cost of such a path is, by definition, the sum of its edge costs, where each edge cost in turn is the sum of all pairwise (replacement or gap) penalties. Each MULTIPLE SEQUENCE ALIGNMENT induces a pairwise alignment for sequences i and j, by simply copying rows i and j and ignoring columns with a "_" in both rows.

By exchanging the summation order, the sum-of-pairs cost is the sum of all pairwise alignment costs of the respective paths projected on a face, each of which cannot be smaller than the optimal pairwise path cost. Thus, we can construct an admissible heuristic h_{pair} by computing, for each pairwise alignment and for each cell in a pairwise problem, the cheapest path cost to the goal node.

The optimal solutions to all pairwise alignment problems needed for the lower-bound h values are usually computed prior to the main search in a preprocessing step. Since this time we are interested in the lowest cost of a path from v to t, it runs in a backward direction, proceeding from the bottom-right

```
1thx     _aeqpvlvyfwaswcgpcqlmsplinlaantysdrlkvvkleidpnpttvkky...
1grx     __mqtvi__fgrsgcpysvrakdlaeklsnerdd_fqyqyvdiraegitkedl...
1erv     agdklvvvdfsatwcgpckmikpffhslsekysn_viflevdvddcqdvasec...
2trcP    _kvttivvniyedgvrgcdalnssleclaaeypm_vkfckira_sntgagdrf...


1thx     ...k_____vegvpalrlvkgeqildstegvis__kdkllsf_ldthln_____
1grx     ...qqkagkpvetvp__qifvdqqhiggytdfaawvken_____1da_____
1erv     ...e_____vksmptfqffkkgqkvgefsgan___kek_____leatine__1v____
2trcP    ...s_____sdvlptllvykggelisnfisvaeqfaedffaadvesflneygllper_
```

FIGURE 1.20

Alignment of problem 2trx of BALiBase, computed with a biologically relevant substitution matrix.

corner to the top-left corner in the alingment matrix, expanding all possible parents of a vertex in each step.

1.8 GENERAL STATE SPACE DESCRIPTIONS

In this section, we introduce some general formalisms to describe state space problems: *action planning*, *production systems*, and *generic search models* including *nondeterministic search* and *Markov decision processes*.

1.8.1 Action Planning

Action planning refers to a world description in logic. A number of atomic propositions *AP* describe what can be true or false in each state of the world. By applying operations in a state, we arrive at another state where different propositions might be true or false. For example, in a BLOCKSWORLD a robot might try to reach a target state by actions that stack and unstack blocks, or put them on the table. Usually, only a few atoms are affected by an action, and most of them remain the same. Therefore, a concise representation is the following STRIPS formalism.

Definition 1.11. *(Propositional Planning Problem) A propositional planning problem (in STRIPS notation) is a finite-state space problem $P = (S, A, s, T)$, where $S \subseteq 2^{AP}$ is the set of states, $s \in S$ is the initial state, $T \subseteq S$ is the set of goal states, and A is the set of actions that transform states into states. We often have that T is described by a simple list of propositions* Goal $\subseteq AP$. *Actions $a \in A$ have propositional preconditions* pre(a), *and propositional effects* (add(a), del(a)), *where* pre$(a) \subseteq AP$ *is the precondition list of a,* add$(a) \subseteq AP$ *is its add list, and* del$(a) \subseteq AP$ *is the delete list. Given a state u with* pre$(a) \subseteq u$, *then its successor $v = a(u)$ is defined as $v = (u \setminus \text{del}(a)) \cup \text{add}(a)$.*

Effects are seen as updates to the current states. To avoid conflicts, delete effects are eliminated from the state *before* add effects are included.

Even though we have defined STRIPS on sets of propositions it is not difficult to transfer the description into logic. Boolean variables for propositions are called *facts*. The goal condition is shorthand for $\bigwedge_{p \in Goal}(p = true)$ and preconditions are interpreted as $\bigwedge_{p \in pre(a)}(p = true)$. The application of the add and delete lists are short for setting p to *false* for all $p \in del(a)$ followed by setting p to *true* for all $p \in add(a)$. STRIPS planning assumes a *closed world*. Everything that is not stated true is assumed to be false. Therefore, the notation of the initial state s is shorthand for the assignment to *true* of the propositions included in s, and to *false* of the ones that are not.

It is often not difficult to encode a state space problem in STRIPS. For modeling the $(n^2 - 1)$-PUZZLE we introduce atomic propositions $at(t, p)$, denoting the truth of the tile t to be located at position p, and $blank(p)$, denoting that the blank is located at position p. An action would be $slide(t, p, p')$, which has $at(t, p)$ and $blank(p')$ as preconditions, $at(t, p')$ and $blank(p)$ as add effects, as well as $at(t, p)$ and $blank(p')$ as delete effects.

To encode finite-domain state space problems with numbers, we observe that a variable with k possible value assignment can be encoded with $O(\lg k)$ (logarithmic encoding)—or $O(k)$ (unary encoding)—atomic propositions. Of course, this is only feasible if k is small.

In BLOCKSWORLD (see Fig. 1.21) there are labeled blocks that can be moved using a robot arm that can grasp one block at a time. Additionally, there is a table large enough to hold all blocks. The

FIGURE 1.21

BLOCKSWORLD configuration with seven blocks; grayscales label different blocks.

four operations are *stack* (put block onto one tower), *unstack* (remove block from one tower), *pickup* (remove block from table), and *putdown* (put block onto table). Let us consider a BLOCKSWORLD problem with l blocks $b_1,\ldots,b_l$ placed on a table t as an example. State variables for each block are *on* that can take values from $\{\perp,t,b_1,\ldots,b_l\}$, a Boolean variable *clear* for each block, and an additional variable *holding* that can take values from $\{\perp,b_1,\ldots,b_l\}$. Actions are *stack, unstack, putdown, pickup*; for example, $stack(a,b)$ has preconditions $holding = a$ and $clear(b) = true$ and the four update operations $on(a) \leftarrow b$, $holding \leftarrow \perp$, $clear(b) \leftarrow false$, and $clear(a) \leftarrow true$. In a unary encoding, for each block a and b we devise the fluents $on(a,b)$, $clear(a)$, and $holding(a)$. The corresponding STRIPS action for $stack(a,b)$ has the two preconditions $holding(a)$ and $clear(b)$, the two add effects $on(a,b)$ and $clear(a)$, as well as the two delete effects $holding(a)$ and $clear(b)$.

Planning domains can either be *parametric* or *grounded* (fully instantiated). Parametric descriptions feature predicates and actions based on a bounded number of domain objects. A (*Lisp*-like) formal representation for both parametric or grounded planning problems is referred to as the *problem domain description language* (PDDL). A PDDL example for a more complex LOGISTICS domain illustrated in Figure 1.22 is provided in Figure 1.24. The task is to transport packages within cities using trucks, and between cities using airplanes. Locations within a city are connected and trucks can move between any two such locations. In each city there is exactly one truck, and each city has one airport. The airports are connected for airplanes to operate. One particular problem instance is shown in Figure 1.23.

STRIPS-type planning is known to be PSPACE complete. Including types, numbers, and durations to the problem description in the developments of PDDL leads to specification formalisms that are *undecidable*. Nonetheless, there are enumeration algorithms and acceleration techniques that are practical for a large set of benchmarks. In recent years, the performance of state-of-the-art systems has improved drastically, and with that, more realistic examples came within reach. We have devoted an entire application chapter to address these developments (See Chapter 15, "Action Planning").

Next, we present the *relaxed planning heuristic* h^+ for planning in STRIPS notation with each action a, having precondition list $pre(a)$, add list $add(a)$, and delete list $del(a)$.

The *relaxation* a^+ of an action a is a with the delete list omitted. The *relaxation of a planning problem* is the one in which all actions are substituted by their relaxed counterparts. Any solution that solves the original plan also solves the relaxed one. Value h^+ is defined as the length of the shortest plan that solves the relaxed problem. This heuristic is consistent: The relaxed plan starting at v with

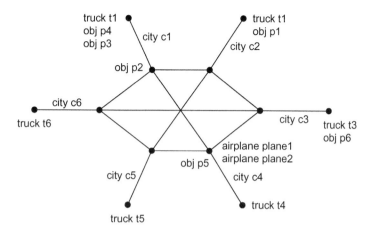

truck t1
obj p4
obj p3
city c1

truck t1
obj p1
city c2

obj p2

city c6
truck t6

city c3
truck t3
obj p6

obj p5
city c5

airplane plane1
airplane plane2
city c4

truck t4

truck t5

FIGURE 1.22

A map of a LOGISTICS problem with six cities of two locations each. Trucks operate within the cities, and airplanes connect the cities. Both mobiles transport objects when loaded. The planning task is to move the objects from their initial locations to their respective target locations (not shown in the figure).

cost $h^+(v)$ can be extended to a plan from u by adding the action that leads from u to v. Therefore, we have $h^+(u) \leq h^+(v) + 1$.

Solving relaxed plans is still computationally hard. It can, however, efficiently be approximated by the number of actions in a parallel plan that solves the relaxed problem. The polynomial time algorithm builds a relaxed problem graph followed by a greedy plan generation process. A pseudo-code implementation is provided in Algorithm 1.1. The variables l and i denote the layer for the forward and the backward phases, respectively.

An illustration for its work is given in Figure 1.25. The graph consists of five (encircled) layers for propositions, the last one containing the only goal. Layers are connected by actions. Propositions are identified with nodes and actions are identified with rectangles. Dotted lines denote the application of *noop*, an additional action that incurs no change. Propositions and actions in the relaxed plan are shaded.

The first phase constructs the layered graph of propositional facts, performing a fixpoint computation on $A^+ = \{a^+ \mid a \in A\}$ starting with the initial state. In layer i all facts are considered that are reachable by applying an action with satisfied precondition facts in any layer j with $1 \leq j < i$. In layer 0 we have all facts present in the initial state. Since we have a finite number of grounded propositions the process eventually reaches a *fixpoint*. The next loop marks the goal facts.

The second phase is the *greedy plan extraction phase*. It performs a backward search to match facts to enabling actions. The goal facts build the first unmarked facts. As long as there are unmarked facts in layer i, select an action that makes this fact true and mark all add effects, and queue all preconditions as unmarked new goals. If there is no unmarked fact left in layer i, continue with layer $i - 1$ until the only unmarked facts are the initial ones in layer 0. The heuristic is constructive; that is, it not only returns the estimated distance but also a corresponding sequence of actions.

The heuristic is neither admissible nor consistent, but it is effective in practice, especially for structurally simpler benchmark problems (problem graphs with no or recognized dead-end and small plateaus).

```
(define (problem strips-log-x-1)
  (:domain logistics-strips)
  (:objects p6 p5 p4 p3 p2 p1 c6 c5 c4 c3 c2 c1
            t6 t5 t4 t3 t2 t1 plane2 plane1
            c6-1 c5-1 c4-1 c3-1 c2-1 c1-1
            c6-2 c5-2 c4-2 c3-2 c2-2 c1-2)
  (:init (obj p6) (obj p5) (obj p4) (obj p3) (obj p2) (obj p1)
         (city c6) (city c5) (city c4) (city c3) (city c2) (city c1)
         (truck t6) (truck t5) (truck t4)
         (truck t3) (truck t2) (truck t1)
         (airplane plane2) (airplane plane1)
         (location c6-1) (location c5-1)
         (location c4-1) (location c3-1)
         (location c2-1) (location c1-1)
         (airport c6-2) (location c6-2) (airport c5-2) (location c5-2)
         (airport c4-2) (location c4-2) (airport c3-2) (location c3-2)
         (airport c2-2) (location c2-2) (airport c1-2) (location c1-2)
         (in-city c6-2 c6) (in-city c6-1 c6) (in-city c5-2 c5)
         (in-city c5-1 c5) (in-city c4-2 c4) (in-city c4-1 c4)
         (in-city c3-2 c3) (in-city c3-1 c3) (in-city c2-2 c2)
         (in-city c2-1 c2) (in-city c1-2 c1) (in-city c1-1 c1)
         (at plane2 c4-2) (at plane1 c4-2)
         (at t6 c6-1) (at t5 c5-1) (at t4 c4-1)
         (at t3 c3-1) (at t2 c2-1) (at t1 c1-1)
         (at p6 c3-1) (at p5 c4-2) (at p4 c1-1)
         (at p3 c1-1) (at p2 c1-2) (at p1 c2-1))
  (:goal (and (at p6 c1-2) (at p5 c6-2) (at p4 c3-2)
              (at p3 c6-1) (at p2 c6-2) (at p1 c2-1))))
```

FIGURE 1.23

An (untyped) STRIPS problem description in PDDL.

1.8.2 *Production Systems

Another classic AI representation for a search problem is a *production system*.

Definition 1.12. *(Production System) A production system is a state space problem $P = (S, A, s, T)$, of which the states are strings over the alphabet Σ, and the actions are given in form of grammar inference rules $\alpha \rightarrow \beta$, with α, β being strings over Σ.*

The following theorem shows that any *Turing machine* computation can be casted as a special kind of a production system.

Theorem 1.3. *(Undecidability for Production Systems) The problem to solve a general production system for arbitrary start and goal state is* undecidable.

Proof. The proof is done via reduction to the *halting problem for Turing machines*. Given a *Turing machine* $M = (Q, \Sigma, \Gamma, \Delta, B, q_0, F)$ with input alphabet $\Sigma = \{a_0, \ldots, a_n\}$, tape alphabet $\Gamma = \Sigma \cup \{B\}$,

```
(define (domain logistics-strips)
  (:requirements :strips)
  (:predicates (OBJ ?obj) (TRUCK ?t) (LOCATION ?loc) (AIRPLANE ?a)
               (CITY ?c) (AIRPORT ?airport)
               (at ?obj ?loc) (in ?obj1 ?obj2) (in-city ?obj ?c))
(:action LOAD-TRUCK :parameters (?obj ?t ?loc)
  :precondition (and (OBJ ?obj) (TRUCK ?t) (LOCATION ?loc)
                     (at ?t ?loc) (at ?obj ?loc))
  :effect (and (not (at ?obj ?loc)) (in ?obj ?t)))
(:action LOAD-AIRPLANE :parameters  (?obj ?a ?loc)
  :precondition (and (OBJ ?obj) (AIRPLANE ?a) (LOCATION ?loc)
                     (at ?obj ?loc) (at ?a ?loc))
  :effect (and (not (at ?obj ?loc)) (in ?obj ?a)))
(:action UNLOAD-TRUCK :parameters (?obj ?t ?loc)
  :precondition  (and (OBJ ?obj) (TRUCK ?t) (LOCATION ?loc)
                      (at ?t ?loc) (in ?obj ?t))
  :effect (and (not (in ?obj ?t)) (at ?obj ?loc)))
(:action UNLOAD-AIRPLANE :parameters (?obj ?a ?loc)
  :precondition (and (OBJ ?obj) (AIRPLANE ?a) (LOCATION ?loc)
                     (in ?obj ?a) (at ?a ?loc))
  :effect (and (not (in ?obj ?a)) (at ?obj ?loc)))
(:action DRIVE-TRUCK :parameters (?t ?from ?to ?c)
  :precondition (and (TRUCK ?t) (LOCATION ?from) (LOCATION ?to) (CITY ?c)
                     (at ?t ?from) (in-city ?from ?c) (in-city ?to ?c))
  :effect (and (not (at ?t ?from)) (at ?t ?to)))
(:action FLY-AIRPLANE :parameters (?a ?from ?to)
  :precondition (and (AIRPLANE ?a) (AIRPORT ?from) (AIRPORT ?to)
                     (at ?a ?from))
  :effect (and (not (at ?a ?from)) (at ?a ?to))))
```

FIGURE 1.24

An (untyped) STRIPS domain description in PDDL.

$Q = \{q_0, \ldots, q_m\}$, initial state q_0, transition function $\Delta : Q \times \Gamma \to Q \times \Gamma \times \{L, R, N\}$, and goal state set $F = \{q_e\}$, we construct a state space problem as follows.

States are configurations of the Turing machine M; that is, words of $\{B\}^+ \times \Gamma^* \times Q \times \Gamma^* \times \{B\}^+$. (With "$*$" we denote *Kleene's hull*: For a single letter σ, the term σ^* refers to the set $\{\epsilon, \sigma, \sigma^2, \sigma^3, \ldots\}$, where $\epsilon \in \Sigma^*$ is the empty word. For all $\alpha, \beta \in \Sigma^*$ we have $\alpha\beta \in \Sigma^*$.)

The initial state is state $B^* q_0 B^*$ and the goal state is $B^* q_e B^*$. Depending on the value of d we assign each $aq \to bq'd$ to words $wcqaw' \to s$, $s \in \{wcq'bw', wcbq'w', wq'cbw'\}$ with $w \in \{B\}^+ \times \Gamma^*$ and $w' \in \Gamma^* \times \{B\}^+$. For $d = N$ we have $wcqaw' \to wq'bw'$; for $d = R$ we have $wcqaw' \to wvq'bw'$; and for $d = L$ we have $wqcaw' \to wq'cbw'$. Last, but not least, the rules $wq_e BBw' \to wq_e Bw'$ and $wBBq_e w' \to wBq_e w'$ shorten the empty tape. Hence, we have deduced that M halts on an empty input tape starting from q_0 in finitely many steps in terminal state q_e if and only if the initial state $B^* q_0 B^*$ can be transformed into goal state $B^* q_e B^*$ in finitely many steps. ∎

Procedure Relaxed-Plan
Input: Relaxed planning problem with current state u and condition $Goal \subseteq 2^{AP}$
Output: Value of the relaxed planning heuristic for u

$P_0 \leftarrow u;\ l \leftarrow 0$	;; Set initial layer and iteration counter
while $(Goal \nsubseteq P_l)$	;; Forward search phase
$\quad P_{l+1} \leftarrow P_l \cup \bigcup_{pre(a) \subseteq P_l} add(a)$	;; Build next layer
$\quad$ **if** $(P_{l+1} = P_l)$ **return** ∞	;; Fixpoint reached
$\quad l \leftarrow l+1$	;; Increase counter
for each i **in** $\{0,\dots,l-1\}$	;; Backward traversal
$\quad T_{l-i} \leftarrow \{t \in Goal \mid layer(t) = l-i\}$	;; Initialize goal queues
for each i **in** $\{0,\dots,l-1\}$	;; Backward search phase
$\quad$ **for each** t **in** T_{l-i}	;; Consider each open goal in layer $l-i$
$\quad\quad$ **if** $(a$ **in** A **with** t **in** $add(a)$ **and** $layer(a) = l-i-1)$	;; Match found
$\quad\quad RelaxedPlan \leftarrow RelaxedPlan \cup \{a\}$	;; Include action to relaxed plan
$\quad\quad$ **for each** p **in** $pre(a)$	;; Select preconditions
$\quad\quad\quad T_{layer(p)} \leftarrow T_{layer(p)} \cup \{p\}$	;; Append to queues
return $\|RelaxedPlan\|$	;; Size of action set is heuristic estimate

Algorithm 1.1

Computing the approximation of the relaxed planning heuristic.

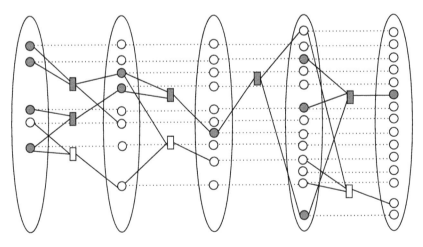

FIGURE 1.25

Working of the approximation of the relaxed planning heuristic. Nodes are propositions and rectangles are actions connected in the form of a layered graph constructed in the forward plan graph generation phase. The propositions in the initial state are shown on the left; the goal layer is depicted on the right. Shaded operators illustrate the relaxed plans and have been selected in the greedy backward extraction phase.

However, individual state space problems, including the ones with finite-state spaces, are decidable, so that most combinatorial problems like instances to the $(n^2 - 1)$-PUZZLE are solvable by general node expanding algorithms.

A convenient though less expressive formalism than general production systems is *PSVN*, or *vector notation for productions systems*. It is defined by a triple (s, A, L), where s is a seed state, A is the set of actions, and L is the finite set of labels. States are represented by fixed-length vectors of labels from L. For example, the states of the THREE-PUZZLE (the $(n^2 - 1)$-PUZZLE for $n = 2$) can be described as a 4-tuple, of which the components are chosen out of $L = \{0, 1, 2, 3\}$ to indicate which tile is located at the top-left, top-right, bottom-left, and bottom-right squares, respectively. Actions are defined by a *left-hand side* (LHS), representing the precondition, and a *right-hand side* (RHS), defining the resulting state. Each side has the same length as the state vector. The semantics are defined in a way resembling Prolog unification rules; each position can hold a constant, a named variable, or an unnamed variable, denoted "_". A constant in LHS represents an exact match for a state at that position. A named variable in LHS represents a binding of the label in the state to which LHS is being applied, and basically leaves a label unchanged. Every variable of RHS must be bound in LHS and every constant label must belong to the set of declared labels. The state space is the transitive closure of applying any sequence of actions to s.

For example, consider the following action definition $a = (A, A, 1, \_, B, C) \rightarrow (2, \_, \_, \_, C, B)$. The action applies to states of which the first two labels are identical and the third label is 1. The fifth and sixth labels are bound to B and C, respectively. Applying a to state $u = (4, 4, 1, 7, 5, 6)$ results in $a(u) = (2, 4, 1, 7, 6, 5)$. In the THREE-PUZZLE, the action $(0, A, \_, \_) \rightarrow (A, 0, \_, \_)$ moves the blank from the top-left to the top-right square.

1.8.3 Markov Decision Processes

Markov decision process problems (MDPs) assume a finite number of states and actions. At each time the agent *observes* a state and *executes* an action, which incurs intermediate *costs* to be minimized (or, in the inverse scenario, *rewards* to be maximized). The cost and the successor state depend only on the current state and the chosen action. Successor generation may be probabilistic, based on the uncertainty we have on the environment in which the search takes place. For example, an action might sometimes fail to result in the desired target state, instead staying in the current state with a small probability.

We should point out that in this book we assume that we always have perfect knowledge of what state we are in. This assumption is dropped in the concept of a *partially observable Markov decision process problem* (POMDP). Here, instead, we are given some observations based on which we can estimate the probability of being in a certain state.

Definition 1.13. *(MDP) A Markov decision process problem is a tuple (S, A, w, p), where S is the underlying state space, A is the set of actions, $w : S \times A \rightarrow \mathbb{R}$ is the cost or immediate reward function, and $p(v \mid u, a)$ is the probability that action a in state u will lead to state v. In some MDPs, additional costs c incur when arriving at a goal state. The goal is to minimize the (expected) accumulated costs or, equivalently, to maximize the (expected) accumulated rewards.*

As Markov decision processes are defined on sequences of actions they are an extension of *Markov chains*.

Definition 1.14. *(Policy) A solution to an MDP is provided in terms of a* policy π, *which maps each state to an action to take in this state.*

In some cases the policy may be realized by means of a lookup table, whereas in others it may involve extensive computation. Applying action a in u incurs costs $w(u,a)$. The goal is to minimize the expected costs $f^{\pi}(u)$ for a state u over the set of all possible policies π, where the *value function* $f^{\pi}(u)$ at u is often called *expected return*, starting from u. The optimal value function is denoted by f^{*}.

1.8.4 Generic Search Model

A generalized model of a state space search problem consists of a discrete and finite-state space S, an initial state s, and a nonempty set of terminal states T. Furthermore, a set of actions $A(u) \subseteq A$ applicable in each nonterminal state u, an action cost function $w : (S \setminus T) \times A \to \mathbf{X}$ for nonterminal states, and a terminal cost function $c : T \to \mathbf{X}$ are assumed. In the general case, $\mathbf{X}$ is a real-valued cost function, but in many practical cases $\mathbf{X}$ is a small set of integers.

In deterministic models, the successors of a node u are $Succ(u) = \{v \in S \mid \exists a \in A(u)$ and $a(u) = v\}$. For the nondeterministic search model, we have $Succ(u,a) = \{v \in S \mid a \in A(u)$ and $a(u)=v\}$. Successor outcomes are either added or maximized. For MDPs with probabilities $p(v \mid u,a)$ we have that $\sum_{v \in Succ(u,a)} p(v \mid u,a) = 1$.

A simple example of an MDP is a probabilistic version of the $(n^2 - 1)$-PUZZLE with noisy actions that achieve their intended effects with probability $p = 0.9$ and have no effect with probability $1 - p$.

The solutions to the models can be expressed in terms of *Bellman equations*, which induce options to compute *optimal policies*. For the deterministic case we have

$$f(u) = \begin{cases} 0 & \text{if } u \in T \\ \min_{v \in Succ(u)}\{w(u,v)+f(v)\} & \text{otherwise} \end{cases}.$$

For the nondeterministic case we have either (additive model)

$$f(u) = \begin{cases} 0 & \text{if } u \in T \\ \displaystyle\min_{a \in A(u)} \left\{ w(u,a) + \sum_{v \in Succ(u,a)} f(v) \right\} & \text{otherwise} \end{cases}$$

or (max model)

$$f(u) = \begin{cases} 0 & \text{if } u \in T \\ \displaystyle\min_{a \in A(u)} \left\{ w(u,a) + \max_{v \in Succ(u,a)} f(v) \right\} & \text{otherwise} \end{cases}.$$

For the MDP case we have

$$f(u) = \begin{cases} c(u) & \text{if } u \in T \\ \displaystyle\min_{a \in A(u)} \left\{ w(u,a) + \sum_{v \in Succ(u,a)} p(v \mid u,a) \cdot f(v) \right\} & \text{otherwise} \end{cases}.$$

In a unified perspective, the functions f^* are solutions to the set of Bellman equations, and, hence, optimal value functions. Policies $\pi : S \to A$ for the nondeterministic and probabilistic cases are extensions of plans that map states to actions. In practice, they are used in the form of controllers to simulate the solution process. Policies are *greedy* if they match any given value function, and policies π^* that are greedy with respect to the optimal value function are called *optimal*.

For the deterministic setting, the outcome of applying an action is unique, such that π can be reduced to a sequence of states. In this case the optimal value function f^* exactly estimates the total distance from each state to a goal state; that is,

$$f^* = \min_{\pi=(u_0,\dots,u_k)} \left\{ \sum_{i=1}^{k} w(u_{i-1},a) \mid s = u_0, u_k \in T \right\},$$

and the *optimal plan* π^* is the one that minimizes its total cost; that is,

$$\pi^* = \arg\min_{\pi=(u_0,\dots,u_k)} \left\{ \sum_{i=1}^{k} w(u_{i-1},a) \mid s = u_0, u_k \in T \right\}.$$

In some implementations, the update is performed on the *Q-value* $q(a,u)$, an intermediate term in the preceding equations, which also depends on the model. It is defined for deterministic models as

$$q(a,u) = w(a) + f(a(u)),$$

for nondeterministic (additive and max) models as

$$q(a,u) = w(u,a) + \sum_{v \in Succ(u,a)} f(v),$$

$$q(a,u) = w(u,a) + \max_{v \in Succ(u,a)} f(v),$$

and for MDPs as

$$q(a,u) = w(u,a) + \sum_{v \in S} p(v \mid u,a) \cdot f(v).$$

1.9 SUMMARY

In this chapter, we introduced the kinds of problems that we study in most chapters of this book, namely graph search problems where we are given a weighted directed graph (where edges are directed and have a cost), a start node, and a set of goal nodes, and the objective is to find a shortest path in the graph from the start node to any goal node. We introduced the terminology used in artificial intelligence for such graph search problems. The nodes, for example, are called states and the edges are called actions. We then discussed ways of categorizing graphs, for example, their branching factor (the number of outgoing edges averaged over all nodes). We also discussed two ways of representing graphs, namely explicitly (by enumerating all nodes and edges) and implicitly (by giving a procedure of which the input is a node and the output is a list of outgoing edges together with the nodes that they point to). Implicit graph representations can be problem-specific or general, for example, using STRIPS or production systems. Implicit representations can be much more compact than explicit representations, which allow implicit representations to represent large graph search problems by exploiting their structure. However, a shortest path can be found in time polynomial in the size of an explicit representation, but often not in time polynomial in the size of an implicit representation.

We then discussed several problems that can be formulated as graph search problems, some of which are used as typical test domains for graph search algorithms and some of which are important in practice, including for transportation systems and biology. In many of these domains, the shortest path is important since it allows one to move from the start node to a goal node. In some domains (e.g., in the TSP), however, only the goal node reached by the shortest path is important since it encodes how to move. To be efficient, graph search algorithms need to exploit some knowledge of the graphs they search. This knowledge can be provided by the domain expert in the form of encoding the heuristic function manually, or, as illustrated later in this book, obtained automatically from the problem structure.

Table 1.1 gives an overview on the state space problems in this chapter and their characteristics (implicit/explicit graph, reversible/irreversible actions, range of weight function, complexity). These search problems dominate the content of the book but are not the only ones that we discuss; we also discuss different two-player games.

One powerful piece of knowledge for solving state space problems is a heuristic. A heuristic assigns a heuristic value to every node, where a heuristic value is an estimate of the goal distance of the node (the length of a shortest path from the node to any goal node). Good heuristics are close to the goal distances and fast to calculate. They can be found easily for most graph search problems. Two important properties are their admissibility (does not overestimate the goal distances) and consistency (satisfies the triangle inequality), where consistency implies admissibility. In Chapter 2, we introduce a graph search algorithm that is able to exploit a given heuristic.

Table 1.2 depicts the properties of the heuristics that have been introduced. Additionally, we show the order of runtime for computing the heuristic estimate for a state (measured in the size of the state vector).

Table 1.1 State spaces and their characteristics.

Problem	Implicit	Reversible	Weight	Complexity
$(n^2 - 1)$-PUZZLE	✓	✓	unit	NP-hard
RUBIK'S CUBE	✓	✓	unit	fixed
SOKOBAN	✓	–	unit	PSPACE-hard
TSP	✓	✓	$\mathbb{R}_{>0}$	NP-hard
MSA	✓	–	$\mathbb{R}_{\geq 0}$	NP-hard
ROUTE PLANNING	–	–	unit	fixed
STRIPS	✓	–	unit	PSPACE-hard
Production System	✓	–	unit	undecidable

Table 1.2 State spaces and their heuristics.

Problem	Name	Admissible	Consistent	Complexity
(n^2-1)-PUZZLE	Manh. Distance	✓	✓	linear
RUBIK'S CUBE	Manh. Distance	✓	✓	linear
SOKOBAN	Min. Matching	✓	✓	cubic
TSP	MST	✓	✓	superlinear
MSA	Sum-of-Pairs	✓	✓	quadratic
ROUTE PLANNING	Eucl. Distance	✓	✓	constant
STRIPS	Relax	–	–	polynomial

Some heuristics (e.g., the relaxed planning or the Euclidean distance) do not shrink the problem graph but introduce new edges. In other heuristics (e.g., the Manhattan distance or minimal matching), sets of nodes are contracted to *super-nodes*, and adjacent edges are merged (the principle will be reconsidered in Chapter 4). One problem in deriving well-informed heuristics based on problem projections is to devise problem simplifications, so that the individual estimates based on solving the subproblems can be added admissibly.

1.10 EXERCISES

1.1   Write a Turing machine program in pseudo code for the following problems:
1. Addition of two numbers in unary representation.
2. Increment of a number in binary representation.
3. Decrement of a number in binary representation.
4. Addition of two numbers in binary representation (use parts (b) and (c)).

1.2   1. Determine constants c and n_0, to show $(n+1)^2 = O(n^2)$.
2. If the limit of $f(n)/g(n)$ for large n is bounded by a constant c we have that $f(n) = O(g(n))$. Use this result to show $(n+1)^2 = O(n^2)$.
3. The *Rule of L'Hôpital* states that if the limit of $f'(n)/g'(n)$ for large n is bounded then it is equal to the limit of $f(n)/g(n)$ for large n. Use this rule to prove $(n+1)^2 = O(n^2)$.

1.3   Prove the *big-oh*
1. addition rule: $O(f) + O(g) = O(\max\{f,g\})$
2. multiplication rule: $O(f) \cdot O(g) = O(f \cdot g)$, for given functions f and g.
Explain the practical use of the rules.

1.4   1. Let a, b, c be real values with $1 < b, 1 \le a, c$. Show $\lg_b(an+c) = \Theta(\lg_2 n)$.
2. Let $p(n)$ be a polynomial of constant degree k. Show $O(\lg p(n)) = O(\lg n)$.
3. Show $(\lg n)^3 = O(\sqrt[3]{n})$ and, more generally, $(\lg n)^k = O(n^\epsilon)$ for all $k, \epsilon > 0$.

1.5   Show that according to the definition of $\doteq$
1. $n2^n \doteq 2^n$
2. $n^2 2^n + (n+1)^4 3^n \doteq 3^n$

1.6 Show that a problem L is in NP if and only if there exist a polynomially decidable predicate P and a polynomial p such that L can be expressed as the set of all words w for which there exists a w' with $|w'| \leq p(|w'|)$ and $P(w, w')$ is true.

1.7 Show that the bit-flipping efforts for a binary counter according to the following table are amortized constant.

Step	Operation	Φ_i	t_i	$a_i = t_i + \Phi_{i+1} - \Phi_i$
	0	0		
0	↓		1	2
	1	1		
1	↓		2	2
	10	1		
2	↓		1	2
	11	2		
3	↓		3	$3 + (1 - 2) = 2$
	100	1		
4	↓		1	2
	101	2		
5	↓		2	2
	110	2		
6	↓		1	2
	111	3		
7	↓		4	$4 + (1 - 3) = 2$
	1000	1		
8	↓		1	2
	1001	2		

1.8 The pseudo code we consider uses different loop and case statements. Show that
1. *for* $(i \in \{1, \ldots, n\})$ $\langle B \rangle$
2. *do* $\langle B \rangle$ *while* $(\langle A \rangle)$
3. *if* $(\langle A \rangle)$ $\langle B \rangle$ *else* $\langle C \rangle$
are all *syntactic sugar* and can be expressed with a classic *while* loop.

1.9 The *Fibonacci numbers* are recursively defined as follows:

$$F(0) = 0$$
$$F(1) = 1$$
$$F(n) = F(n-1) + F(n-2), \text{ for } n \geq 2.$$

Show by induction that
1. for $n \geq 6$ we have $F(n) \geq 2^{n/2}$
2. for $n \geq 0$ we have $F(0) + \cdots + F(n) = F(n+2) - 1$
3. for $n \geq 1$ we have $F^2(n) = F(n-1)F(n+1) + (-1)^{n+1}$

1.10   The *Ackermann function* is defined as follows:

$$a(0,y) = y + 1$$
$$a(x+1,0) = a(x,1)$$
$$a(x+1,y+1) = a(x,a(x+1,y)).$$

Use induction to show
1. $a(1,y) = y + 2$
2. $a(2,y) = 2y + 3$

1.11   Use a *truth table* to show
1. $((A \rightarrow (\neg B \rightarrow C)) \wedge (A \rightarrow \neg B)) \wedge \neg(A \rightarrow C)$
2. $(A \wedge (B \vee C)) \Leftrightarrow ((A \wedge B) \vee (A \wedge C))$

1.12   Given four pieces of chain (initial state shown in Fig. 1.26, left), the CHEAP NECKLACE problem is characterized as follows. It costs 20 cents to open and 30 cents to close a link. Join all links into a single necklace (goal state in Figure 1.26, right) at the lowest cost.

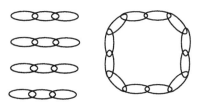

FIGURE 1.26

The CHEAP NECKLACE problem: initial state (left) and goal state (right).

1. What are the states? What are the actions? What is the start state? What are the goal states? What are the weights? What are the costs for an optimal solution?
2. How many states are there? What is the average branching factor?
3. Is the graph directed or undirected? Does the graph contain dead-ends?

1.13   For the GENERAL SLIDING-TILE PUZZLE:
1. Compute the number of reachable system states for the instances of Figure 1.27. In the HARLEQUIN PUZZLE (left) the two corner pieces have to be assembled to a 2×3 block. In the MAN AND BOTTLE PUZZLE (right), the man at the left side has to move to the right next to the bottle.
2. Give a suitable generalization of the Manhattan distance heuristic.
3. Show that the test for successor generation can be performed in total time linear to the number of tiles (counting blanks as *empty* tiles).

1.14   Consider the example level in SOKOBAN shown in Figure 1.14.
1. Determine an optimal solution for PUSHES and for MOVES.
2. Show that, in general, optimal solutions for both problems differ.

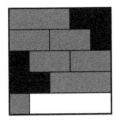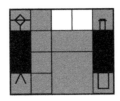

FIGURE 1.27

Further instances of the GENERAL SLIDING-TILE PUZZLE.

1.15   Consider the minimal MULTIPLE SEQUENCE ALIGNMENT problem between ACGTACGACGT and ATGTCGTACACGT. Take as a cost function the one that assigns cost 1 to a mismatch and cost 2 to a gap. Find the minimal alignment of the two sequences.

1.16   For BLOCKSWORLD:
1. Model the problem of Figure 1.21 in STRIPS using the predicates *on*, *clear*, and *holding*.
2. Show that finding a solution that is at most twice as long as the optimal one can be computed in polynomial time.

1.17   Another scalable sliding-tile puzzle FROGS AND TOADS invented by Gardner additionally allows tile jumps (see Fig. 1.28). The goal is to exchange the sets of black and white tiles in the minimum number of moves.
1. Give a state space characterization of the puzzle.
2. Determine the number of reachable configurations in a formula depending on n.
3. Devise a heuristic for the puzzle.

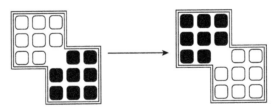

FIGURE 1.28

An instance of Gardner's game. A tile can either slide or jump if the target location is empty.

1.18   The goal of ATOMIX (see Fig. 1.29) is to assemble a given molecule from atoms. The player can select an atom at a time and *push* it toward one of the four directions left, right, up, and down; it will keep moving until it hits an obstacle or another atom. The game is won when the atoms form the same constellation (the *molecule*) as depicted beside the board. Note that the interconnection of the atoms matters.

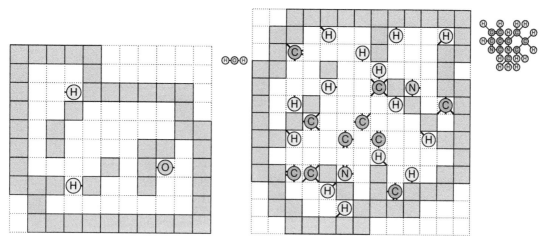

FIGURE 1.29

Two levels of ATOMIX. The molecule to be assembled is shown to the top-right of each problem instance. The problem to the left can be solved with 13 moves. Atom 1: DL; Atom 3: LDRURDLDR; Atom 2: D; Atom 1: R. The instance to its right illustrates a more complex problem; it takes at least 66 moves to solve.

1. Formalize ATOMIX as a state space problem.
2. Extend Figure 1.15 with the characteristics of ATOMIX.
3. Obtain an easily computable heuristic that allows an atom to slide through other atoms or share a place with another atom.
4. Find a solution for Figure 1.29.

1.19 An *n*-WUSEL (see Fig. 1.30) consists of *n* connected blocks. In motion, a group of blocks is simultaneously moved. The possible directions are *left*, *right*, *up*, *down*, *forward*, and *backward*. A move group is connected. An example for a sequence of moves is given in Figure 1.31.

Cubes connected to the ground can only be moved upward. At least one block has to stay on the ground. All other blocks have to be arranged such that the WUSEL is in balance. The WUSEL tumbles if the projection of the *center of mass* is outside the *convex hull* of the blocks on the floor (the convex hull includes all points on lines between any two points).

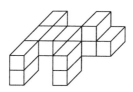

FIGURE 1.30

A particular WUSEL of 15 blocks (3 blocks are not visible).

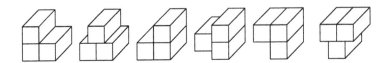

FIGURE 1.31

A valid move sequence for a particular 3-WUSEL with intermediate configurations to illustrate the transition.

1. Give a (coarse) estimate for the number of n-WUSELs.
2. Choose an appropriate representation that allows fast connectivity checks.
3. Find out how to efficiently perform stability checks for the WUSEL.
4. Devise an efficient function for a successor generation.
5. Devise a heuristic estimate for the WUSEL wrt. a target location for the center of mass.

1.20   For the ROUTE PLANNING problem devise a consistent heuristic for finding:
1. The shortest-fastest route.
2. The fastest-shortest route.
3. A weighted combination of the two.

1.21   Test your structural knowledge on heuristics.
1. Prove that the maximum of several consistent heuristics is a consistent heuristic.
2. Show that the sum of two consistent estimates is not necessarily admissible.
3. Give an example of an admissible heuristic that is not consistent.

1.22   Devise a PSVN characterization of the state and state change for the RUBIK'S CUBE.

1.23   Prove that a PSVN action is reversible, if and only if there is no i such that the label at i of the left side is _, the label at i of the right side is different to _, and every variable bound on the left side is *present* on the right side; that is, if it is used to assign a label on the right side, or if there is a j so that the label at j on the left side is some variable A, and on the right side, it is either _ or A.

1.24   The *cross-product state space* $P = (S, A, s, T)$ of the state space problems $P_1, \ldots, P_n$ is defined as $S = S_1 \times \cdots \times S_n$, $s = (s_1, \ldots, s_n)$, $T = \{(u_1, \ldots, u_n) | \forall i \in \{1, \ldots, n\} : u_i \in T_i\}$, and $A = \{((u_1, \ldots, u_n), (v_1, \ldots, v_n)) \, | \, \exists i \in \{1, \ldots, n\} : \exists a \in A_i : a(u_i) = v_i \text{ and } \forall i \neq j : u_j = v_j\}$. Let heuristic h_i be the minimal solution length from the current local state S_i to reach a goal in T_i for problem P_i. Show that h_i is consistent.

1.25   Devise an MDP model for a variant of the the $(n^2 - 1)$-PUZZLE domain, where each intended move fails with a probability of 10%.

1.26   An instance of the pen-and-paper game RACETRACK is defined by a racetrack divided into grid cells together with cars initially standing behind a starting line. The goal is to cross an additional finish line. The task is to find the control for driving a car from an initial state into a set of goal states, minimizing the number of time steps and without hitting the racetrack's boarder. Each applied action achieves its intended effect with probability 0.7. Provide an MDP model for RACETRACK with states consisting of coordinates (x, y) and velocity vectors (Δ_x, Δ_y).

1.11 **BIBLIOGRAPHIC NOTES**

Milestones in single-agent games refer to publications of Korf (1985a), Korf and Schultze (2005) (FIFTEEN-PUZZLE), Korf and Felner (2002), Korf and Taylor (1996) (TWENTY-FOUR-PUZZLE), Edelkamp et al. (2008b) (THIRTY-FIVE-PUZZLE), Korf and Felner (2007) (TOWERS-OF-HANOI), Junghanns (1999) (SOKOBAN) and Korf (1997), Kunkle and Cooperman (2008) (RUBIK'S CUBE). Reid has shown in 1995 that the one position (corners correct, edges placed but flipped) requires at least 20 moves; the according lower bound has been proven in 2010 by Rokicki, Kociemba, Davidson, and Dethridge.[2] The presentation of multiplayer game efficiencies refers to the work of Campbell et al. (2002) (CHESS), Schaeffer et al. (2005, 2007) (CHECKERS), Tesauro (1995) (BACKGAMMON), Allen (2010), Allis (1998), Tromp (2008) (CONNECT 4), and Ginsberg (1999) and Smith et al. (1998) (BRIDGE). The number 4,531,985,219,092 computed by Edelkamp and Kissmann (2008b) for CON-NECT 4 has been validated by John Tromp in 2010. Large-scale search in probabilistic environments has been studied by Edelkamp et al. (2007).

The set of remarkable results in planning have been published in the context of the international planning competitions. Parallel optimal planning has been addressed by Blum and Furst (1995) and Kautz and Selman (1996), while sequential optimal planning has been considered by Helmert et al. (2007), among others. UCT for general game playing goes back to Kocsis and Szepesvári (2006).

Multiple sequence alignment problems have been solved with AI search methods by Edelkamp and Kissmann (2007), and Korf and Zhang (2000), Schrödl (2005), and Zhou and Hansen (2002b). Recent entries to verification via AI search are given by Edelkamp et al. (2004b) (explicit-state model checking), Bloem et al. (2000) (hardware verification), Groce and Visser (2002) (program model checking), Jabbar (2008) (external model checking), Wijs (1999) (quantitative model checking), and Kupferschmid et al. (2007) (real-time model checking). Vehicle navigation results refer to work by Bast et al. (2007), Wagner and Willhalm (2003) (maps), Edelkamp et al. (2003) and Schrödl et al. (2004) (GPS). From the broad range of applying search in robotics we highlighted results of Gutmann et al. (2005) and Henrich et al. (1998).

The motivating example is taken from Wickelgren (1995). Ratner and Warmuth (1990) have shown that optimally solving the $(n^2 - 1)$-PUZZLE is NP-hard. First optimal solutions to the EIGHT-PUZZLE have been provided by Schofield (1967), for the FIFTEEN-PUZZLE by Korf (1985a), and for the TWENTY-FOUR-PUZZLE by Korf and Taylor (1996), with an improvement by Korf and Felner (2002). The GENERAL SLIDING-TILE PUZZLE problems are either commercially available or taken from Berlekamp et al. (1982). Many suboptimal solutions to RUBIK'S CUBE have been published but random instances have been solved optimally by Korf (1997) for the first time.

TSP is a touchstone for many general heuristics devised for combinatorial optimization: genetic algorithms, simulated annealing, Tabu search, neural nets, ant system, some of which will be discussed later in this book. For METRIC TSP, Christofides (1976) gives a constant-factor approximation algorithm that always finds a tour of length at most 1.5 times the shortest one.

SOKOBAN is one of the remaining single-player games in which the human solution quality is competitive to automatic solving strategies. Culberson (1998a) has proven that SOKOBAN is PSPACE-hard. In his PhD thesis, Junghanns (1999) has discussed an implementation that could solve 56 of the 90

---

[2] *http://www.cube20.org.*

problems push-optimally. Computing the *minimal matching* is reduced to *network flow*. An initially empty matching is iteratively enlarged by computing single-source shortest paths. Dijkstra's original algorithm has to be modified to handle edges with negative weights.

The results on branching factors, solution lengths, and search space sizes of block sliding games are contained in the work of Edelkamp and Korf (1998) and Junghanns (1999). Block sliding complexities have been studied by Demaine et al. (2000). ATOMIX has been studied by Hüffner et al. (2001). Holzer and Schwoon (2001) have proven that it is PSPACE complete. The WUSEL problem has appeared as a challenge in a computer science competition for high school students in Germany.

Gusfield (1997) and Waterman (1995) have given introductions to computational molecular biology and MULTIPLE SEQUENCE ALIGNMENT. Dayhoff et al. (1978) have proposed a model of molecular evolution where they estimate the exchange probabilities of amino acids for different amounts of evolutionary divergence; this gives rise to the so-called PAM matrices, where PAM250 is generally the most widely used. Jones et al. (1992) have refined the statistics based on a larger body of experimental data. The preprocessed heuristic is due to Ikeda and Imai (1994).

STRIPS-type planning has been invented by Fikes and Nilsson (1971). Bylander (1994) has proven that propositional planning is PSPACE complete. He has also shown that finding optimal solutions for the relaxed planning problem is NP-hard. Hoffmann and Nebel (2001) have studied the polynomial time approximation based on greedily extracting a relaxed plan in a layered planning graph. The heuristic has been incorporated in many actual planning systems and has been extended to numerical planning domains (Hoffmann, 2003) and to temporal domains (Edelkamp, 2003c). Decidability and undecidability results for planning with numbers were given by Helmert (2002). PSVN has been discussed by Hernádvögyi and Holte (1999). MDP instances are found in Barto et al. (1995), in Hansen and Zilberstein (2001), as well as in Bonet and Geffner (2006).

Basic Search Algorithms

2

Exploring state space problems often corresponds to a search for a shortest path in an underlying problem graph. *Explicit* graph search algorithms assume the entire graph structure to be accessible either in adjacency matrix or list representation. In case of *implicit* graph search, nodes are iteratively generated and expanded without access to the unexplored part of the graph. Of course, for problem spaces of acceptable size, implicit search can be implemented using an explicit graph representation, if that helps to improve the runtime behavior of the algorithm.

Throughout the book, we will be concerned mostly with the SINGLE-SOURCE SHORTEST PATH problem; that is, the problem of finding a solution path such that the sum of the weights of its constituent edges is minimized. However, we also mention extensions to compute the ALL PAIRS SHORTEST PATHS problem, in which we have to find such paths for every two vertices. Obviously, the latter case is only feasible for a finite, not too large number of nodes, and since the solution involves *storing* a number of distances, it is quadratic to the number of nodes in the problem graph. The most important algorithms for solving shortest path problems are:

- *Breadth-first search* and *depth-first search* refer to different search orders; for depth-first search, instances can be found where their naive implementation does not find an optimal solution, or does not terminate.
- *Dijkstra's algorithm* solves the SINGLE-SOURCE SHORTEST PATH problem if all edge weights are greater than or equal to zero. Without worsening the runtime complexity, this algorithm can in fact compute the shortest paths from a given start point *s* to all other nodes.
- The *Bellman-Ford algorithm* also solves the SINGLE-SOURCE SHORTEST PATHS problem, but in contrast to Dijkstra's algorithm, edge weights may be negative.
- The *Floyd-Warshall algorithm* solves the ALL PAIRS SHORTEST PATHS problem.
- The *A* algorithm* solves the SINGLE-SOURCE SHORTEST PATH problem for nonnegative edge costs.

The difference of A* from all preceding algorithms is that it performs a *heuristic search*. A *heuristic* can improve search efficiency by providing an estimate of the remaining, yet unexplored distance to a goal. Neither depth-first search, nor breadth-first, nor Dijkstra's algorithm take advantage of such an estimate, and are therefore also called *uninformed* search algorithms.

In this chapter, we prove correctness of the approaches and discuss the optimal efficiency of A* (with regard to other search algorithms). We show that the A* algorithm is a variant of the implicit variant of Dijkstra's SINGLE-SOURCE SHORTEST PATH algorithm that traverses a reweighted problem graph, transformed according to the heuristic. With nonoptimal A* variants we seek for a trade-off between solution optimality and runtime efficiency. We then propose the application of heuristic search to problem graphs with a general or algebraic notion of costs. We solve the optimality problem within those cost structures by devising and analyzing cost-algebraic variants of Dijkstra's algorithm and A*. Generalizing cost structures for action execution accumulates in a multiobjective search, where edge costs become vectors.

2.1 UNINFORMED GRAPH SEARCH ALGORITHMS

In *implicit graph search,* no graph representation is available at the beginning; only while the search progresses, a partial picture of it evolves from those nodes that are actually explored. In each iteration, a node is *expanded* by generating all adjacent nodes that are reachable via edges of the implicit graph (the possible edges can be described for example by a set of transition rules). This means applying all allowed actions to the state. Nodes that have been generated earlier in the search can be kept track of; however, we have no access to nodes that have not been generated so far. All nodes have to be reached at least once on a path from the initial node through successor generation. Consequently, we can divide the set of *reached nodes* into the set of *expanded nodes* and the set of *generated nodes* that are not yet expanded. In AI literature the former set is often referred to as the *Open list* or the *search frontier,* and the latter set as the *Closed list.* The denotation as a *list* refers to the legacy of the first implementation, namely as a simple linked list. However, we will see later that realizing them using the right data structures is crucial for the search algorithm's characteristics and performance.

The set of all explicitly generated paths rooted at the start node and of which the leaves are the *Open* nodes constitutes the *search tree* of the underlying problem graph. Note that while the *problem graph* is defined solely by the problem domain description, the search tree characterizes the part explored by a search algorithm at some snapshot during its execution time. Figure 2.1 gives a visualization of a problem graph and a corresponding search tree.

In tree-structured problem spaces, each node can only be reached on a single path. However, it is easy to see that for finite acyclic *graphs,* the search tree can be exponentially larger than the original

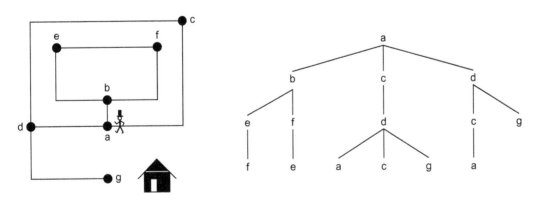

FIGURE 2.1

The problem graph (left) and its search tree (right). As a trivial improvement (to any search algorithm) we do not generate ancestors; for example the node *a* from *a-c-d* and from *a-d-c* has been pruned.

Procedure Implicit-Graph-Search
Input: Implicit problem graph with start node s, weight function w,
    successor generation function *Expand*, and predicate *Goal*
Output: Path from s to a goal node $t \in T$, or $\emptyset$ if no such path exists

$Closed \leftarrow \emptyset$	;; Initialize structures
$Open \leftarrow \{s\}$	;; Insert s into empty search frontier
while $(Open \neq \emptyset)$	;; As long as there are frontier nodes
Remove some u from $Open$	;; Select node in algorithm-specific way
Insert u into $Closed$	;; Update list of expanded nodes
if $(Goal(u))$ **return** $Path(u)$	;; Reconstruct solution using Alg. 2.2
$Succ(u) \leftarrow Expand(u)$	;; Generate successor set
for each v **in** $Succ(u)$	;; For all successors v of u
$Improve(u,v)$	;; Call Alg. 2.3, update structures
return $\emptyset$	;; No solution exists

Algorithm 2.1

Skeleton of search algorithms in implicitly given graphs.

---

search space. This is due to the fact that a node can be reached multiple times, at different stages of the search via different paths. We call such a node a *duplicate*; for example, in Figure 2.1 all shown leaves at depth 3 are duplicates. Moreover, if the graph contains cycles, the search tree can be infinite, even if the graph itself is finite.

In Algorithm 2.1 we sketch a framework for a general node expansion search algorithm.

Definition 2.1. *(Closed/Open Lists) The set of already expanded nodes is called* Closed *and the set of generated but yet unexpanded nodes is called* Open. *The latter is also denoted as the search frontier.*

As long as no solution path has been established, a frontier node u in *Open* is selected and its successors are generated. The successors are then dealt with in the subroutine *Improve*, which updates *Open* and *Closed* accordingly (in the simplest case, it just inserts the child node into *Open*). At this point, we deliberately leave the details of how to *Select* and *Improve* a node unspecified; their subsequent refinement leads to different search algorithms.

Open and *Closed* were introduced as data structures for sets, offering the opportunities to insert and delete nodes. Particularly, an important role of *Closed* is duplicate detection. Therefore, it is often implemented as a hash table with fast lookup operations.

Duplicate identification is *total*, if in each iteration of the algorithm, each node in *Open* and *Closed* has one unique representation and generation path. In this chapter, we are concerned with algorithms with total duplicate detection. However, imperfect detection of already expanded nodes is quite frequent in state space search out of necessity, because very large state spaces are difficult to store with respect to given memory limitations. We will see many different solutions to this crucial problem in upcoming chapters.

Generation paths do not have to be fully represented for each individual node in the search tree. Rather, they can be conveniently stored by equipping each node u with a *predecessor link parent(u)*, which is a pointer to the parent in the search tree (or $\emptyset$ for the root s). More formally, $parent(v) = u$

Procedure Path
Input: Node u, start node s, with start node s, weight function w,
        parent pointers set by search algorithm
Output: Path from s to u

$Path \leftarrow (u)$	;; Path with single element
while ($parent(u) \neq s$)	;; Loop through predecessors
$Path \leftarrow (u, Path)$	;; Extend path by u
$u \leftarrow parent(u)$	;; Continue with predecessor
return $(s, Path)$	;; Beginning of path reached

Algorithm 2.2
Tracing back the solution path using predecessor links.

Procedure Improve
Input: Nodes u and v, v successor of u
Side effects: Update parent of v, *Open*, and *Closed*

if (v **not in** *Closed* $\cup$ *Open*)	;; v not yet reached
Insert v into Open	;; Update search frontier
$parent(v) \leftarrow u$	;; Set predecessor pointer

Algorithm 2.3
Improve procedure with duplicate detection and predecessor links.

---

if $v \in Succ(u)$. By tracing the links back in bottom-up direction until we arrive at the root s, we can reconstruct a solution path $Path(u)$ of length k as $(s = parent^k(u),\dots,parent(parent(u)),parent(u),u)$ (see Alg. 2.2).

Algorithm 2.3 sketches an implementation of *Improve* with duplicate detection and predecessor link updates.[1] Note that this first, very crude implementation does not attempt to find a shortest path; it merely decides if a path exists at all from the start node to a goal node.

To illustrate the behavior of the search algorithms, we take a simple example of searching a goal node at $(5, 1)$ from node $(3, 3)$ in the GRIDWORLD of Figure 2.2. Note that the potential set of paths of length i in a grid grows exponentially in i; for $i = 0$ we have at most $1 = 4^0$, for $i = 1$ we have at most $4 = 4^1$, and for $i = k$ we have at most 4^k paths.

2.1.1 Depth-First Search

For *depth-first search* (DFS), the *Open* list is implemented as a *stack* (a.k.a. a LIFO, or *last-in first-out queue*), so that *Insert* is in fact a *push* operation and *Select* corresponds to a *pop* operation. Operation

---

[1] In this chapter we explicitly state the calls to the underlying data structure, which are considered in detail Chapter 3. In later chapters of the book we prefer sets for *Open* and *Closed*.

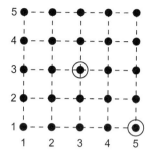

FIGURE 2.2

The GRIDWORLD search space.

Table 2.1 Steps in DFS (with duplicate detection) for the example in Figure 2.1.

Step	Selection	Open	Closed	Remarks
1	{}	{a}	{}	
2	a	{b,c,d}	{a}	
3	b	{e,f,c,d}	{a,b}	
4	e	{f,c,d}	{a,b,e}	f is duplicate
5	f	{c,d}	{a,b,e,f}	e is duplicate
6	c	{d}	{a,b,e,f,c}	d is duplicate
7	d	{g}	{a,b,e,f,c,d}	c is duplicate
8	g	{}	{a,b,e,f,c,d,g}	Goal reached

push places an element and operation *pop* extracts an element at the top of this data structure. Successors are simply pushed onto the stack. Thus, each step greedily generates a successor of the last visited node, unless it has none, in which case it backtracks to the parent and explores another not yet explored sibling.

It is easy to see that in finite search spaces DFS is *complete* (i.e., will find a solution path if there is some), since each node is expanded exactly once. It is, however, not optimal. Depending on which successor is expanded first, any path is possible. Take, for example, the solution ((3,3), (3,2), (2,2), (2,3), (2,4), (2,5), (3,5), (3,4), (4,4), (4,3), (5,3), (5,4), (5,5)) in the GRIDWORLD example. The path length, defined as the number of state transitions, is 12 and hence larger than the minimum.

Table 2.1 and Figure 2.3 show the expansion steps and the search tree explored by DFS when run on the example of Figure 2.1. Without loss of generality, we assume that children are expanded in alphabetical order.

Without duplicate elimination, DFS can get trapped in cycles of the problem graph and loop forever without finding a solution at all.

2.1.2 Breadth-First Search

For *breadth-first search (BFS)*, the set *Open* is realized as a *first-in first-out queue (FIFO)*. The *Insert* operation is called *Enqueue*, and adds an element to the end of the list; the *Dequeue* operation selects

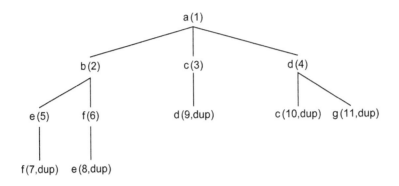

FIGURE 2.3

DFS search tree for the example in Figure 2.1. The numbers in brackets denote the order of node generation.

Table 2.2 Steps in BFS (with duplicate detection) for the example in Figure 2.1.

Step	Selection	Open	Closed	Remarks
1	{}	{a}	{}	
2	a	{b,c,d}	{a}	
3	b	{c,d,e,f}	{a,b}	
4	c	{d,e,f}	{a,b,c}	d is duplicate
5	d	{e,f,g}	{a,b,c,d}	c is duplicate
6	e	{f,g}	{a,b,c,d,e}	f is duplicate
7	f	{g}	{a,b,c,d,e,f}	e is duplicate
8	g	{}	{a,b,c,d,e,f,g}	Goal reached

and removes its first element. As a result, the neighbors of the source node are generated layer by layer (one edge apart, two edges apart, and so on).

As for DFS, *Closed* is implemented as a hash table, avoiding nodes to be expanded more than once. Since BFS also expands one new node at a time, it is complete in finite graphs. It is optimal in uniformly weighted graphs (i.e., the first solution path found is the shortest possible one), since the nodes are generated in level order with respect to the tree expansion of the problem graph.

One BFS search order in the GRIDWORLD example is ((3,3), (3,2), (2,3), (4,3), (3,4), (2,2), (4,4), (4,2), (2,4), (3,5), (5,3), (1,3), (3,1), ..., (5,5)). The returned solution path ((3,3), (4,3), (4,4), (4,5), (5,5)) is optimal.

Table 2.2 and Figure 2.4 list steps of the BFS algorithm in the example in Figure 2.1.

A possible drawback for BFS in large problem graphs is its large memory consumption. Unlike DFS, which can find goals in large search depth, it stores all nodes with depth smaller than the shortest possible solution length.

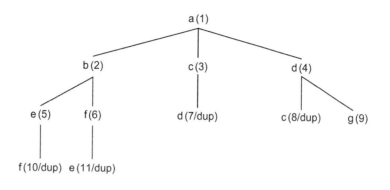

FIGURE 2.4

BFS search tree for the example in Figure 2.1. The numbers in brackets denote the order of node generation.

2.1.3 Dijkstra's Algorithm

So far we have looked at uniformly weighted graphs only; that is, each edge counts the same. Now let us consider the generalization that edges are weighted with a *weight function* (a.k.a. *cost function*) w. In weighted graphs, BFS loses its optimality. Take, for example, weights on the DFS solution path p of 1/12, and weights of 1 for edges not on p. This path is of total weight 1, and the BFS solution path is of weight $1 + 3/12 > 1$.

To compute the shortest (cheapest) path in graphs with nonnegative weights, Dijkstra proposed a greedy search strategy based on the *principle of optimality*. It states that *an optimal path has the property that whatever the initial conditions and control variables (choices) over some initial period, the control (or decision variables) chosen over the remaining period must be optimal for the remaining problem, with the node resulting from the early decisions taken to be the initial condition.* Applying the principle developed by Richard Bellman to shortest path search results in

$$\delta(s,v) = \min_{v \in Succ(u)} \{\delta(s,u) + w(u,v)\}.$$

In words, the minimum distance from s to v is equal to the minimum of the sum of the distance from s to a predecessor u of v, plus the edge weight between u and v. This equation implies that any subpath of an optimal path is itself optimal (otherwise it could be replaced to yield a shorter path).

The search algorithm maintains a tentative value of the *shortest distance*. More precisely, an upper bound $f(u)$ on $\delta(s,u)$ for each node u; initially set to ∞, $f(u)$ is successively decreased until it matches $\delta(s,u)$. From this point on, it remains constant throughout the rest of the algorithm.

A suitable data structure for maintaining *Open* is a *priority queue*, which associates each element with its f-value, and provides operations *Insert* and *DeleteMin* (accessing the element with the minimum f-value and simultaneously removing it from the priority queue). Additionally, the *DecreaseKey* operation can be thought of as deleting an arbitrary element and reinserting it with a lower associated f-value; executing these two steps together can be performed more efficiently in some implementations. Note that the signature of *Insert* requires now an additional parameter: the *value* used to store the node in the priority queue.

Procedure Improve
Input: Nodes u and v, v successor of u
Side effects: Update parent of v, $f(v)$, *Open*, and *Closed*

if (v **in** *Open*)   ;; Node already generated but not expanded
  if ($f(u) + w(u,v) < f(v)$)   ;; New path is shorter
    parent(v) $\leftarrow u$;; Set predecessor pointer
    Update $f(v) \leftarrow f(u) + w(u,v)$;; *DecreaseKey*, might reorganize *Open*
else   ;; Node not yet reached
  if (v **not in** *Closed*)   ;; Not yet expanded
    parent(v) $\leftarrow u$;; Set predecessor pointer
    Initialize $f(v) \leftarrow f(u) + w(u,v)$;; First estimate
    Insert v into *Open* with $f(v)$;; Update search frontier

Algorithm 2.4

Choosing path to v through minimum of $f(v)$ and $f(u) + w(u,v)$.

FIGURE 2.5

An example for a node relaxation.

The algorithm initially inserts s into the priority queue with $f(s)$ set to zero. Then, in each iteration an *Open* node u with minimum f-value is selected, and all its children v reachable by outgoing edges are generated. The subroutine *Improve* of Algorithm 2.1 now updates the stored estimate $f(v)$ for v if the newly found path via u is shorter than the best previous one. Basically, if for a path you can take a detour via another path to shorten the path, then it should be taken. *Improve* inserts v into *Open*, in turn. The pseudo code is listed in Algorithm 2.4. This update step is also called a *node relaxation*. An example is given in Figure 2.5.

For illustration, we generalize our running example by assuming edge weights, as given in Figure 2.6. The execution of the algorithm is given in Table 2.3 and Figure 2.7.

The correctness argument of the algorithm is based on the fact that for a node u with minimum f-value in *Open*, f is *exact*; that is, $f(u) = \delta(s,u)$.

Lemma 2.1. *(Optimal Node Selection) Let $G = (V,E,w)$ be a positively weighted graph and f be the approximation of $\delta(s,u)$ in Dijkstra's algorithm. At the time u is selected in the algorithm, we have $f(u) = \delta(s,u)$.*

Proof. Assume the contrary and let u be the first selected node from *Open* with $f(u) \neq \delta(s,u)$; that is, $f(u) > \delta(s,u)$. Furthermore, let $(s,\ldots,x,y,\ldots,u)$ be a shortest path for u with y being the first node on the path that is not expanded (see Fig. 2.8).

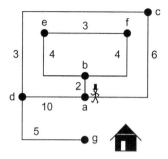

FIGURE 2.6

Extended example in Figure 2.1 with edge weights.

Table 2.3 Steps in Dijkstra's algorithm for the example in Figure 2.6. *s* in brackets denote the *f*-value.

Step	Selection	Open	Closed	Remarks
1	{}	{a(0)}	{}	
2	a	{b(2),c(6),d(10)}	{a}	
3	b	{e(6),f(6),c(6),d(10)}	{a,b}	Ties broken arbitrarily
4	e	{f(6),c(6),d(10)}	{a,b,e}	f is duplicate
5	f	{c(6),d(10)}	{a,b,e,f}	e is duplicate
6	c	{d(9)}	{a,b,e,f}	d reopened, parent changes to c
7	d	{g(14)}	{a,b,e,f,c,d}	a is duplicate
8	g	{}	{a,b,e,f,c,d,g}	Goal reached

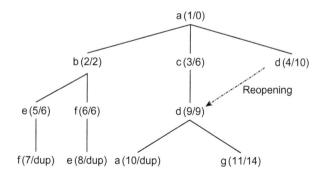

FIGURE 2.7

SINGLE-SOURCE SHORTEST PATHS search tree for the example in Figure 2.6. The numbers in brackets denote the order of node generation/*f*-value.

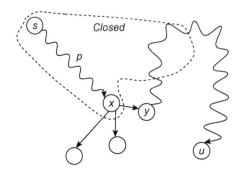

FIGURE 2.8

Selecting u from *Open* in Dijkstra's algorithm.

Then $f(x) = \delta(s,x)$, since $x \in Closed$ given the minimality of u. Furthermore, the edge (x,y) has been relaxed. Hence,

$$f(y) \le f(x) + w(x,y) = \delta(s,x) + w(x,y) = \delta(s,y) \le \delta(s,u) < f(u)$$

(in the second-last step, the positivity of weights is used). This inequality is a contradiction to the selection of u from the priority queue, instead of y. ∎

It is important to observe that Lemma 2.1 suits Dijkstra's exploration scheme to implicit enumeration, because at the first encountering of a goal node t we already have $f(t) = \delta(s,t)$.

Theorem 2.1. *(Correctness Dijkstra's Algorithm) In weighted graphs with nonnegative weight function the algorithm of Dijkstra's algorithm is optimal; that is, at the first node $t \in T$ that is selected for expansion, we have $f(t) = \delta(s,T)$.*

Proof. With nonnegative edge weights, for each pair (u,v) with $v \in Succ(u)$ we always have $f(u) \le f(v)$. Therefore, the values f for selected nodes are monotonically increasing. This proves that at the first selected node $t \in T$ we have $f(t) = \delta(s,t) = \delta(s,T)$. ∎

In infinite graphs we have to guarantee that a goal node will eventually be reached.

Theorem 2.2. *(Dijkstra's Algorithm on Infinite Graphs) If the weight function w of a problem graph $G = (V,E,w)$ is strictly positive and if the weight of every infinite path is infinite, then Dijkstra's algorithm terminates with an optimal solution.*

Proof. The premises induce that if the cost of a path is finite, the path itself is finite. Therefore, there are only finitely many paths of cost smaller than $\delta(s,T)$. We further observe that no path of cost $\ge \delta(s,T)$ can be a prefix of an optimal solution path. Therefore, Dijkstra's algorithm examines the problem graph only on a finite subset of all infinite paths. A goal node $t \in T$ with $\delta(s,t) = \delta(s,T)$ will eventually be reached, so that Dijkstra's algorithm terminates. The solution will be optimal by the correctness argument of Theorem 2.1. ∎

Note that for all nodes u in *Closed*, an optimal path from s to u has been found. Thus, a slight modification of Dijkstra's algorithm that only stops when *Open* runs empty can not only find the shortest path between a single source s and a single target t, but also to all other nodes (provided, of course, that the number of nodes is finite).

2.1.4 Negatively Weighted Graphs

Unfortunately, the correctness and optimality argument in Lemma 2.1 is no longer true for graphs with negative edge weights. As a simple example, consider the graph consisting of three nodes s, u, v having edges (s, u) with $w(s, u) = 5$, (s, v) with $w(s, v) = 4$, and edge (v, u) with $w(v, u) = -2$, for which the algorithm of Dijkstra computes $\delta(s, u) = 5$ instead of the correct value, $\delta(s, u) = 3$.

An even worse observation is that negatively weighted graphs may contain negatively weighted cycles, so that the shortest path may be infinitely long and of value $-\infty$. This has led to the *Bellman-Ford algorithm* to be described later. However, we can still handle graphs with negative weights using a modified Dijkstra algorithm if we impose a slightly less restrictive condition on the graph, namely that $\delta(u, T) = \min\{\delta(u, t)| \ t \in T\} \geq 0$ for all u. That is, the distance from each node to the goal is nonnegative. Figuratively speaking, we can have negative edges when far from the goal, but they get "eaten up" when coming closer. The condition implies that no negatively weighted cycles exist.

In the sequel, we will denote the extended version of Dijkstra's algorithm as algorithm A. As can be gleaned from the comparison between Algorithm 2.5 and Algorithm 2.4, with negative edges it can be necessary to reopen not only *Open* nodes, but also *Closed* ones.

Procedure Improve
Input: Nodes u and v, v successor of u
Side effects: Update parent of v, $f(v)$, *Open*, and *Closed*

if (v **in** *Open*)	;; Node already generated but not expanded
if ($f(u) + w(u, v) < f(v)$)	;; New path is shorter
parent(v) $\leftarrow u$	;; Set predecessor pointer
Update $f(v) \leftarrow f(u) + w(u, v)$	;; *DecreaseKey* operation
else if (v **in** *Closed*)	;; Node v already expanded
if ($f(u) + w(u, v) < f(v)$)	;; New path cheaper
parent(v) $\leftarrow u$	;; Set predecessor pointer
Update $f(v) \leftarrow f(u) + w(u, v)$	;; Update estimate
Remove v from *Closed*	;; Reopening of v
Insert v into *Open* with $f(v)$	;; Changing lists
else	;; Node not visited before
parent(v) $\leftarrow u$	;; Set predecessor pointer
Initialize $f(v) \leftarrow f(u) + w(u, v)$	
Insert v into *Open* with $f(v)$	;; Update search frontier

Algorithm 2.5

An update routine that copes with negative edge weights.

Lemma 2.2. *(Invariance for Algorithm A) Let* $G = (V, E, w)$ *be a weighted graph,* $p = (s = v_0, \ldots, v_n = t)$ *be a least-cost path from the start node s to a goal node* $t \in T$, *and f be the approximation in the algorithm A. At each selection of a node u from* Open, *we have the following invariance:*

(I) *Unless* v_n *is in* Closed *with* $f(v_n) = \delta(s, v_n)$, *there is a node* v_i *in* Open *such that* $f(v_i) = \delta(s, v_i)$, *and no* $j > i$ *exists such that* v_j *is in* Closed *with* $f(v_j) = \delta(s, v_j)$.

Proof. Without loss of generality let i be maximal among the nodes satisfying (I). We distinguish the following cases:

1. Node u is not on p or $f(u) > \delta(s, u)$. Then node $v_i \neq u$ remains in *Open*. Since no v in *Open* $\cap$ p $\cap$ $Succ(u)$ with $f(v) = \delta(s, v) \leq f(u) + w(u, v)$ is changed and no other node is added to *Closed*, (I) is preserved.
2. Node u is on p and $f(u) = \delta(s, u)$. If $u = v_n$, there is nothing to show.

    First assume $u = v_i$. Then *Improve* will be called for $v = v_{i+1} \in Succ(u)$; for all other nodes in $Succ(u) \setminus \{v_{i+1}\}$, the argument of case 1 holds. According to (I), if v is in *Closed*, then $f(v) > \delta(s, v)$, and it will be reinserted into *Open* with $f(v) = \delta(s, u) + w(u, v) = \delta(s, v)$. If v is neither in *Open* nor *Closed*, it is inserted into *Open* with this merit. Otherwise, the *DecreaseKey* operation will set it to $\delta(s, v)$. In either case, v guarantees the invariance (I).

    Now suppose $u \neq v_i$. By the maximality assumption of i we have $u = v_k$ with $k < i$. If $v = v_i$, no *DecreaseKey* operation can change it because v_i already has optimal merit $f(v) = \delta(s, u) + w(u, v) = \delta(s, v)$. Otherwise, v_i remains in *Open* with an unchanged f-value and no other node besides u is inserted into *Closed*; thus, v_i still preserves (I). ∎

Theorem 2.3. *(Correctness of Algorithm A) Let* $G = (V, E, w)$ *be a weighted graph so that for all u in V we have* $\delta(u, T) \geq 0$. *Algorithm A is optimal; that is, at the first extraction of a node t in T we have* $f(t) = \delta(s, T)$.

Proof. Assume that the algorithm does terminate at node $t' \in T$ with $f(t') > \delta(s, T)$. According to (I) there is a node u with $f(u) = \delta(s, u)$ in *Open*, which lies on an optimal solution path p_t to t. We have

$$f(t') > \delta(s, T) = \delta(s, u) + \delta(u, T) \geq \delta(s, u) = f(u),$$

in contradiction to the fact that t' is selected from *Open*. ∎

In infinite graphs we can essentially apply the proof of Theorem 2.2.

Theorem 2.4. *(A in Infinite Graphs) If the weight of every infinite path is infinite, then algorithm A terminates with an optimal solution.*

Proof. Since $\delta(u, T) \geq 0$ for all u, no path of cost $\geq \delta(s, T)$ can be a prefix of an optimal solution path. ∎

2.1.5 Relaxed Node Selection

Dijkstra's algorithm is bound to always expand an *Open* node with minimum f-value. However, as we will see in later chapters, sometimes it can be more efficient to choose nodes based on other criteria. For example, in route finding in large maps we might want to explore neighboring streets in subregions together to optimize disk access.

Procedure Node-Selection A
Input: Implicit problem graph with start node s, weight function w, heuristic h,
　　　successor generation function *Expand*, and predicate *Goal*
Output: Cost-optimal path to a goal node $t \in T$, or $\emptyset$ if no such path exists

$Closed \leftarrow \emptyset; Open \leftarrow \{s\}$ 　　　　　　　　　　;; Initialize structures
$f(s) \leftarrow h(s)$ 　　　　　　　　　　　　　　　;; Initialize estimate
$U \leftarrow \infty; bestPath \leftarrow \emptyset$ 　　　　　　　;; Initialize solution path values
while $(Open \neq \emptyset)$ 　　　　　　　　;; As long as there are frontier nodes
　Remove some u from $Open$ 　　;; Select *arbitrary* node from search frontier
　Insert u into $Closed$ 　　　　　　;; Update list of expanded nodes
　if $(f(u) > U)$ **continue** 　　　;; Prune expansions if costs are too high
　if $(Goal(u)$ **and** $f(u) < U)$ 　　　;; Improved solution established
　　$U \leftarrow f(u); bestPath \leftarrow Path(u)$ 　　　;; Update solution path
　else
　　$Succ(u) \leftarrow Expand(u)$ 　　　　;; Generate successor set
　　for each v **in** $Succ(u)$ 　　　　;; For all successor nodes
　　　$Improve(u,v)$ 　　　　　　;; Update data structures
return $bestPath$ 　　　　　　　　;; Return optimal solution

Algorithm 2.6

Relaxing the node expansion order in Algorithm A.

In Algorithm 2.6 we give a pseudo-code implementation for a relaxed node selection scheme that gives us precisely this freedom. In contrast to Algorithm A and Dijkstra's algorithm, reaching the first goal node will no longer guarantee optimality of the established solution path. Hence, the algorithm has to continue until the *Open* list runs empty. A global current best solution path length U is maintained and updated; the algorithm improves the solution quality over time.

If we want the algorithm to be optimal we have to impose the same restriction on negatively weighted graphs as in the case of Algorithm A.

Theorem 2.5. *(Optimality Node-Selection A, Conditioned) If we have $\delta(u,T) \geq 0$ for all nodes $u \in V$, then node selection A terminates with an optimal solution.*

Proof. Upon termination, each node inserted into *Open* must have been selected at least once. Suppose that invariance (I) is preserved in each loop; that is, that there is always a node v in the *Open* list on an optimal path with $f(v) = \delta(s,v)$. Thus, the algorithm cannot terminate without eventually selecting the goal node on this path, and since by definition it is not more expensive than any found solution path and *best* maintains the currently shortest path, an optimal solution will be returned. It remains to show that the invariance (I) holds in each iteration. If the extracted node u is not equal to v there is nothing to show. Otherwise, $f(u) = \delta(s,u)$. The bound U denotes the currently best solution length. If $f(u) \leq U$, no pruning takes place. On the other hand, $f(u) > U$ leads to a contradiction since $U \geq \delta(s,u) + \delta(u,T) \geq \delta(s,u) = f(u)$ (the latter inequality is justified by $\delta(u,T) \geq 0$). ∎

If we do allow $\delta(u,T)$ to become negative, we can at least achieve the following optimality result.

Theorem 2.6. *(Optimality Node-Selection A, Unconditioned) For $f(u) + \delta(u, T) > U$-as the pruning condition in the node selection A algorithm, it is optimal.*

Proof. By analogy to the previous theorem, it remains to show that (I) holds in each iteration. If the extracted node u is not equal to v there is nothing to show. Otherwise, $f(u) = \delta(s, u)$. The bound U denotes the currently best solution length. If $f(u) + \delta(u, T) \leq U$, no pruning takes place. On the other hand, $f(u) + \delta(u, T) > U$ leads to a contradiction since $\delta(s, T) = \delta(s, u) + \delta(u, T) = f(u) + \delta(u, T) > U$, which is impossible given that U denotes the cost of some solution path; that is, $U \geq \delta(s, T)$.   ∎

Unfortunately, we do not know the value of $\delta(s, T)$, so the only thing that we can do is to approximate it; in other words, to devise a bound for it.

2.1.6 *Algorithm of Bellman-Ford

Bellman and Ford's algorithm is the standard alternative to Dijkstra's algorithm when searching graphs with negative edge weights. It can handle any such finite graphs (not just those with nonnegative goal distances), and will detect if negative cycles exist.

The basic idea of the algorithm is simple: relax all edges in each of $n - 1$ passes (n is the number of nodes in the problem graph), where node relaxation of edge (u, v) is one update of the form $f(v) \leftarrow \min\{f(v), f(u) + w(u, v)\}$. It satisfies the invariant that in pass i, all cheapest paths have been found that use at most $i - 1$ edges. In a final pass, each edge is checked once again. If any edge can be further relaxed at this point, a negative cycle must exist; the algorithm reports this and terminates. The price we pay for the possibility of negative edges is a time complexity of $O(|E||V|)$, worse than Dijkstra's algorithm by a factor of $|V|$.

Most of the time, the Bellman-Ford algorithm is described in terms of explicit graphs, and is used to compute shortest paths from a source to all other nodes. In the following, however, we develop an implicit version of the algorithm of Bellman and Ford that makes it comparable to the previously introduced algorithms. One advantage is that we can exploit the fact it is necessary to perform this relaxation in iteration i only if the f-value of u has changed in iteration $(i - 1)$.

Note that the Bellman-Ford algorithm can be made to look almost identical to Dijkstra's algorithm by utilizing a queue instead of a priority queue: For all nodes u extracted from one end of the queue, relax every successor v of u, and insert v into the tail of the queue. The reasoning is as follows. For graphs with negative edge weights it is not possible to have perfect choice on the extracted element that is known to be contained in the *Open* list by invariance (I) (see page 58). As we have seen, considering already expanded nodes is necessary. Suppose that u is the extracted node. Before u is selected for next time the optimal node v_i with $f(v_i) = \delta(s, v_i)$ has to be selected at least once, such that the solution path $p = (v_1, \ldots, v_n)$ that is associated with v_i is extended by at least one edge. To implement this objective for convenience we redisplay the *Improve* procedure that has been devised so far for the situation where the *Open* list is a queue. Algorithm 2.7 shows the pseudo code.

The implicit version of Bellman and Ford is listed in Algorithm 2.8. In the original algorithm, detection of negative cycles is accomplished by checking for optimal paths longer than the total number of nodes, after *all* edges have been relaxed $n - 1$ times. In our implicit algorithm, this can be done more efficiently. We can maintain the length of the path, and as soon as any one gets longer than n, we can exit with a failure notice. Also, more stringent checking for duplicates in a path can be implemented.

We omitted the termination condition at a goal node, but it can be implemented analogously as in the *node selection A* algorithm. That is, it is equivalent whether we keep track of the current best

---

Procedure Improve
Input: Nodes u and v, v successor of u, number of problem graph nodes n
Side effects: Update parent of v, $f(v)$, *Open*, and *Closed*

if (v in *Open*)	;; Node already generated but not expanded
if ($f(u) + w(u,v) < f(v)$)	;; New path is cheaper
if (*length*(*Path*(v)) $\geq n - 1$)	;; Path contains some node twice
exit	;; Negative cycle detected
parent(v) $\leftarrow u$	;; Set predecessor pointer
Update $f(v) \leftarrow f(u) + w(u,v)$	;; Improved estimate
else if (v in *Closed*)	;; Node v already expanded
if ($f(u) + w(u,v) < f(v)$)	;; New path cheaper
if (*length*(*Path*(v)) $\geq n - 1$)	;; Path contains some node twice
exit	;; Negative cycle detected
parent(v) $\leftarrow u$	;; Set predecessor pointer
Remove v from *Closed*	
Update $f(v) \leftarrow f(u) + w(u,v)$	;; Reopening of v
Enqueue v into *Open*	;; Changing lists
else	;; Node not seen before
parent(v) $\leftarrow u$	;; Set predecessor pointer
Initialize $f(v) \leftarrow f(u) + w(u,v)$	;; First estimate
Enqueue v into *Open*	;; Add to search frontier

Algorithm 2.7

Edge relaxation for implicit version of Bellman and Ford's algorithm.

---

solution during the search or (as in the original formulation) scan all solutions after completion of the algorithm.

Theorem 2.7. *(Optimality of Implicit Bellman-Ford) Implicit Bellman-Ford is correct and computes optimal cost solution paths.*

Proof. Since the algorithm only changes the ordering of nodes that are selected, the arguments for the correctness and optimality of the implicit version of Bellman and Ford's and the node selection A algorithm are the same. ∎

Theorem 2.8. *(Complexity of Implicit Bellman-Ford) Implicit Bellman-Ford applies no more than $O(ne)$ node generations.*

Proof. Let $Open_i$ be the set *Open* (i.e., the content of the queue) when u is removed for the ith time from *Open*. Then, by applying the Invariant (I) (Lemma 2.2) we have that $Open_i$ contains at least one element, say u_i, with optimal cost. Since *Open* is organized as a queue, u_i is deleted from *Open* before u is deleted for the $(i + 1)$-th time. Since u_i is on the optimal path and will never be added again, we have the number of iterations i is smaller than the number of nodes in the expanded problem graph. This proves that each edge is selected at most n times, so that at most ne nodes are generated. ∎

Procedure Implicit Bellman-Ford
Input: Problem graph with start node s, weight function w,
       successor generation function *Expand*, and predicate *Goal*
Output: Cheapest path cost from s to $t \in T$ stored in $f(s)$

Open $\leftarrow \{s\}$	;; Initialize search frontier
$f(s) \leftarrow h(s)$	;; Initialize estimate
while (*Open* $\neq \emptyset$)	;; As long as there are frontier nodes
Dequeue u from *Open*	;; Select node in breadth-first manner
Insert u into *Closed*	;; Update list of expanded nodes
Succ(u) $\leftarrow$ *Expand(u)*	;; Generate successor set
for each v in *Succ(u)*	;; Consider all successors
Improve(u,v)	;; Node relaxation according to Alg. 2.7

Algorithm 2.8

Bellman-Ford algorithm in an implicit graph.

2.1.7 Dynamic Programming

The *divide-and-conquer* strategy in algorithm design suggests to solve a problem recursively by splitting it into smaller subproblems, solving each of them separately, and then combining the partial results into an overall solution. *Dynamic programming* was invented as a similarly general paradigm. It addresses the problem that a recursive evaluation can give rise to solving overlapping subproblems repeatedly, invoked for different main goals. It suggests to store subresults in a table so that they can be reused. Such a tabulation is most efficient if an additional *node order* is given that defines the possible subgoal relationships.

All Pair Shortest Paths

For example, consider the problem of finding the shortest distance for each pair of nodes in $1, \ldots, n$. We could run either SINGLE-SOURCE SHORTEST PATHS algorithms discussed so far—BFS or Dijkstra's algorithm—repeatedly, starting from each node i in turn, but this would traverse the whole graph several times. A better solution is to apply the ALL PAIRS SHORTEST PATHS *Floyd-Warshall* algorithm. Here, all distances are recorded in an n-by-n matrix D, where element $D_{i,j}$ indicates the shortest path costs from i to j. A sequence of matrices $D^0, D^1, \ldots, D^k$ is computed, where D^0 contains only the edge weights (it is the adjacency matrix), and D^k contains the shortest distances between nodes with the constraint that intermediate nodes have no index larger than k.

According to the *principle of optimality* it holds that

$$D_{i,j}^k = \min\left\{ D_{i,j}^{(k-1)}, D_{i,k}^{(k-1)} + D_{k,j}^{(k-1)} \right\}.$$

In particular, if no path between i and j passes through k, then $D_{i,j}^k = D_{i,j}^{(k-1)}$. Algorithm 2.9 solves the ALL PAIRS SHORTEST PATHS problem in $O(n^3)$ time and $O(n^2)$ space.

Multiple Sequence Alignment

Dynamic programming is a very effective means in many domains. Here, we will give a MULTIPLE SEQUENCE ALIGNMENT example (see Sec. 1.7.6). Let w define the cost of substituting one character

---

Procedure Floyd-Warshall
Input: n-by-n adjacency matrix A
Output: Matrix D containing shortest path distances between all pairs of nodes

$D \leftarrow M$;; Initialize distance matrix
for each k **in** $\{1,\ldots,n\}$;; Loop over intermediate node
  for each i **in** $\{1,\ldots,n\}$;; Loop over start node
    for each j **in** $\{1,\ldots,n\}$;; Loop over end node
      $D_{i,j}^{(k)} \leftarrow \min\{D_{i,j}^{(k-1)}, D_{i,k}^{(k-1)} + D_{k,j}^{(k-1)}\}$
return D

Algorithm 2.9

Floyd-Warshall algorithm.

---

with another, and denote the distance between two strings $m_1 = m_1' x_1$ and $m_2 = m_2' y_2$ as δ. Then, according to the principle of optimality, the following recurrence relation holds:

$$\delta(m_1, m_2) = \begin{cases} \delta(m_1, m_2') + w('\_', x_2) & \text{if } |m_1| = 0 \\ \delta(m_1', m_2) + w(x_1, '\_') & \text{if } |m_2| = 0 \\ \min\{\delta(m_1, m_2') + w('\_', x_2), & \text{(insertion of } x_2\text{)} \\ \quad\quad \delta(m_1', m_2) + w(x_1, '\_'), & \text{(insertion of } x_1\text{)} \quad\quad \textbf{otherwise} \\ \quad\quad \delta(m_1', m_2') + w(x_1, x_2)\} & \text{(match of } x_1 \text{ and } x_2\text{)} \end{cases}$$

A pairwise alignment can be conveniently depicted as a path between two opposite corners in a two-dimensional grid: one sequence is placed on the horizontal axis from left to right, the other one on the vertical axis from top to bottom. If there is no gap in either string, the path moves diagonally down and right; a gap in the vertical (horizontal) string is represented as a horizontal (vertical) move right (down), since a letter is consumed in only one of the strings. The alignment graph is directed and acyclic, where a (nonborder) vertex has incoming edges from the left, top, and top-left adjacent vertices, and outgoing edges to the right, bottom, and bottom-right vertices.

The algorithm progressively builds up alignments of prefixes of m and m' in a bottom-up fashion. The costs of partial alignments are stored in a matrix D, where $D_{i,j}$ contains the distance between $m[1..i]$ and $m'[1..j]$. The exact order of the scan can vary (e.g., rowwise or columnwise), as long as it is compatible with a *topological order* of the graph; a topological order of a directed, acyclic graph is a sorting of the nodes $u_0, u_1, \ldots$, such that if u_i is reachable from u_j, then it must hold that $j \geq i$. In particular, u_0 has no incoming edges, and if the number of nodes is some finite n, then u_n has no outgoing edges. In general, many different topological orderings can be constructed for a given graph.

For instance, in the alignment of two sequences, a cell value depends on the values of the cells to the left, top, and diagonally top-left, and these have to be explored before it. Algorithm 2.10 shows the case of columnwise traversal. Another particular such ordering is that of *antidiagonals*, which are diagonals running from top-right to bottom-left. The antidiagonal number of a node is simply the sum of its coordinates.

As an example, the completed matrix for the edit distance between the strings sport and sort is shown in Figure 2.9. After all matrix entries have been computed, the solution path has to be

Procedure Align-Pairs
Input: Substitution costs w, Strings m, and m'
Output: Matrix D containing shortest distances between all pairs of string prefixes

for each i in $\{0,\dots,|m|\}$ $D_{i,0} \leftarrow w('\_',m_i)$	;; Initialize first column
for each $i \leftarrow \{1,\dots,|m'|\}$ $D_{0,i} = w('\_',m'_i)$	;; Initialize first row
for each i in $\{1,\dots,|m|\}$	;; For all columns
for each j in $\{1,\dots,|m'|\}$	;; For all rows
$D_{i,j} \leftarrow \min\{D_{i,j-1} + w('\_',m'_j),$	;; Insertion into m'
$D_{i-1,j} + w(m_i,'\_'),$	;; Insertion into m
$D_{i-1,j-1} + w(m_i,m'_j)\}$	;; Letter match

return D

Algorithm 2.10

Pairwise sequence alignment with dynamic programming in column order.

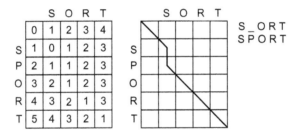

FIGURE 2.9

Edit distance matrix for strings "sport" and "sort" (left); solution path (right).

reconstructed to obtain the actual alignment. This can be done iteratively in a backward direction starting from the bottom-right corner up to the top-left corner, and selecting in every step a parent node that allows a transition with the given cost. Alternatively, we could store in each cell an additional pointer to the relevant predecessor.

It is straightforward to generalize pairwise sequence alignment to the case of aligning k sequences simultaneously, by considering higher-dimensional lattices. For example, an alignment of three sequences can be visualized as a path in a cube. Figure 2.10 illustrates an example for the alignment

```
A B C _ B
_ B C D _
_ _ _ D B
```

If the sequence length is at most n, the generalization of Algorithm 2.10 requires $O(n^k)$ time and space to store the dynamic programming table. In Section 6.3.2, we will present a refined algorithm

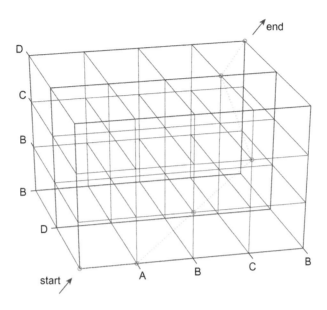

FIGURE 2.10

Alignment of the three sequences ABCB, BCD, and DB.

that reduces the space complexity by one order of magnitude.[2] An example of how successor costs are calculated, with the cost matrix of Figure 2.10 and a gap opening penalty of 4, is shown in Figure 2.11.

Markov Decision Process Problems

A common way of calculating an optimal policy is by means of dynamic programming using either *policy iteration* or *value iteration.*

Both policy iteration and value iteration are based on the Bellman optimality equation,

$$f^*(u) = \min_{a \in A} \left\{ w(u,a) + \sum_{v \in S} p(v \mid u,a) \cdot f^*(v) \right\}.$$

In some cases, we apply a *discount* δ to handle infinite paths. Roughly speaking, we can define the value of a state as the total reward/cost an agent can expect to accumulate when traversing the graph according to its policy, starting from that state. The discount factor defines how much more we should value immediate costs/rewards, compared to costs/rewards that are only attainable after two or more

---

[2]As a technical side note, we remark that to deal with the biologically more realistic *affine gap costs*, we can no longer identify nodes in the search graph with lattice vertices; this is because the cost associated with an edge depends on the preceding edge in the path. Similarly, as in route planning with turn restrictions, in this case, it is more suitable to store lattice edges in the priority queue, and let the transition costs for $u \to v, v \to w$ be the sum-of-pairs substitution costs for using one character from each sequence or a gap, plus the incurred gap penalties for $v \to w$ followed by $u \to v$. Note that the state space in this representation grows by a factor of 2^k.

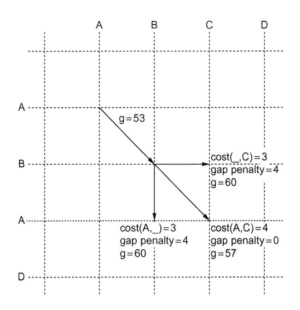

FIGURE 2.11

Example of computing path costs with affine gap function; the substitution matrix of Figure 2.10 and a gap opening penalty of 4 is used.

steps. Formally, the corresponding equation according to the principle of optimality is

$$f^*(u) = \min_{a \in A} \left\{ w(u,a) + \delta \cdot \sum_{v \in S} p(v \mid u,a) \cdot f^*(v) \right\}.$$

Policy iteration successively improves a policy π by setting

$$\pi(u) \leftarrow \arg\min_{a \in A} \left\{ w(u,a) + \sum_{v \in S} p(v \mid u,a) \cdot f^\pi(v) \right\}$$

for each state u, where the *evaluation* of π, $f^\pi(u)$, can be computed as a system of $|S|$ linear equations:

$$f^\pi(u) \leftarrow w(u,\pi(u)) + \sum_{v \in S} p(v \mid u, \pi(u)) \cdot f^\pi(v).$$

A pseudo-code implementation for policy iteration is shown in Algorithm 2.11.

    Value iteration improves the estimated *cost-to-go* function f by successively performing the following operation for each state u:

$$f(u) \leftarrow \min_{a \in A} \left\{ w(u,a) + \sum_{v \in S} p(v \mid u,a) \cdot f(v) \right\}.$$

Procedure Policy-Iteration
Input: Markov decision process problem, some initial policy π
Output: Optimal policy

do	;; Loop until convergence
$\quad f^\pi = Evaluate(\pi)$	;; Evaluate policy
$\quad changed \leftarrow false$	;; Loop control
$\quad$ **for each** $u \in S$	;; For all expanded states
$\quad\quad bestVal \leftarrow \infty$	;; Dynamically updated bound
$\quad\quad A \leftarrow -1$	;; For updating operator
$\quad\quad$ **for each** $a \in A$	;; For all operators
$\quad\quad\quad V \leftarrow w(u,a)$	;; Cost/reward
$\quad\quad\quad$ **for each** $v \in S$	;; For all successor states
$\quad\quad\quad\quad V \leftarrow V + \delta \cdot p(v \mid u,a) \cdot f^\pi(v)$	;; Compute cost
$\quad\quad\quad$ **if** $(V < bestVal)$	;; Improvement achieved
$\quad\quad\quad\quad bestVal \leftarrow V; bestAct \leftarrow a$	;; Backup best results
$\quad\quad$ **if** $(\pi(u) \neq bestAct)$	;; Policy changed
$\quad\quad\quad changed \leftarrow true; \pi(u) \leftarrow bestAct$	;; Protocol change
while $(changed)$	;; Loop until flag unset

Algorithm 2.11

Policy iteration.

The algorithm exits if an error bound on the policy evaluation falls below a user-supplied threshold ϵ, or a maximum number of iterations have been executed. If the optimal cost f^* is known for each state, the optimal policy can be easily extracted by choosing an operation according to a single application of the Bellman equation. Value iteration is shown in pseudo code in Algorithm 2.12. The procedure takes a heuristic h for initializing the value function as an additional parameter.

The error bound on the value function is also called the *residual*, and can, for example, be computed in form $\max_{u \in S} |f_t(u) - f_{t-1}(u)|$. A residual of zero denotes that the process has converged. An advantage of policy iteration is that it converges to the exact optimum, whereas value iteration usually only reaches an approximation. On the other hand, the latter technique is usually more efficient on large state spaces.

For implicit search graphs the algorithms proceed in two phases. In the first phase, the whole state space is generated from the initial state s. In this process, an entry in a hash table (or vector) is allocated to store the f-value for each state u; this value is initialized to the cost of u if $u \in T$, or to a given (not necessarily admissible) heuristic estimate (or zero if no estimate is available) if u is nonterminal. In the second phase, iterative scans of the state space are performed updating the values of nonterminal states u as

$$f(u) = \min_{a \in A(u)} q(u,a), \tag{2.1}$$

where $q(u,a)$, which depends on the search model (see Sec. 1.8.4).

Procedure Value-Iteration
Input: Markov decision process problem, tolerance $\epsilon > 0$, heuristic h, and
       maximum iteration number t_{max}
Output: ϵ-Optimal policy π

$t \leftarrow 0$	;; Iteration count
for each $u \in S$	;; For all states
$f_0(u) \leftarrow h(u)$	;; Set default value function
while (Residual on $f_t > \epsilon$ **and** $t < t_{max}$)	;; Convergence criterion
$t \leftarrow t + 1$	;; Next iteration number
for each $u \in S$	;; For all expanded states
$bestVal \leftarrow \infty$	;; For monitoring updates
for each $a \in A$	;; For all actions
$V \leftarrow w(u,a)$	;; Compute cost/reward
for each $v \in S$	;; For all successor states
$V \leftarrow V + \delta \cdot p(v \mid u,a) \cdot f_{t-1}(v)$	;; Compute value
if $(V < bestVal)$ $\pi(u) \leftarrow a$; $bestVal \leftarrow V$	;; Update values
$f_t(u) \leftarrow M$	;; Set value
return $Policy(f_t)$	;; Using arg-min

Algorithm 2.12

Value iteration.

Value iteration converges to the solution optimal value function provided that its values are finite for all $u \in S$. In the case of MDPs, which may have cyclic solutions, the number of iterations is not bounded and value iteration typically only converges in the limit. For this reason, for MDPs, value iteration is often terminated after a predefined bound of t_{max} iterations are performed, or when the residual falls below a given $\epsilon > 0$.

Monte Carlo policy evaluation estimates f^{π}, the value of a state under a given policy. Given a set of iterations, value f^{π} is approximated by following π. To estimate f^{π}, we count the *visits* to a fixed state u. Value f^{π} is computed by averaging the returns in a set of iterations. Monte Carlo policy evaluation converges to f^{π} as the number of visits goes to infinity. The main argument is that by the law of large numbers the sequence of averages will converge to their expectation.

For convenience of terminology, in the sequel we will continue referring to nodes when dealing with the search algorithm.

2.2 INFORMED OPTIMAL SEARCH

We now introduce *heuristic search algorithms*; that is, algorithms that take advantage of an estimate of the remaining goal distance to prioritize node expansion. Domain-dependent knowledge captured in this way can greatly prune the search tree that has to be explored to find an optimal solution. Therefore, these algorithms are also subsumed under the category *informed search*.

FIGURE 2.12

Approximating the cost of a solution path.

2.2.1 **A***

The most prominent heuristic search algorithm is A*. It updates estimates $f(u)$ (a.k.a. *merits*) defined as

$$f(u) = g(u) + h(u),$$

where $g(u)$ is the weight of the (current optimal) path from s to u, and $h(u)$ is an estimate (lower bound) of the remaining costs from u to a goal, called the *heuristic function*. Hence, the combined value $f(u)$ is an approximation for the cost of the entire solution path (see Fig. 2.12). For the sake of completeness, the entire algorithm is shown in Algorithm 2.13.

For illustration, we again generalize our previous example by assuming that we can obtain heuristic estimates from an unknown source, as shown in Figure 2.13. The execution of the A* algorithm is given in Table 2.4 and Figure 2.14, respectively. We see that compared to Dijkstra's algorithm, nodes b, e, and f can be pruned from expansion since their f-value is larger than the cheapest solution path.

The attentive reader might have noticed our slightly sloppy notation in Algorithm 2.13: We use the term $g(u)$ in the *Improve* procedure, however, we don't initialize these values. This is because in light of an efficient implementation, it is necessary to store either the g-value or the f-value of a node, but not both. If only the f-value is stored, we can derive the f-value of node v with parent u as $f(v) \leftarrow f(u) + w(u, v) - h(u) + h(v)$.

By following this reasoning, it turns out that algorithm A* can be elegantly cast as Dijkstra's algorithm in a reweighted graph, where we incorporate the heuristic into the weight function as $\hat{w}(u, v) = w(u, v) - h(u) + h(v)$. An example of this *reweighting* transformation of the implicit search graph is shown in Figure 2.15. One motivation for this transformation is to inherit correctness proofs, especially for graphs. Furthermore, it bridges the world of traditional graphs with an AI search. As a by-product, the influence heuristics have is clarified. Let us formalize this idea.

Lemma 2.3. *Let G be a weighted problem graph and $h : V \to \mathbb{R}$. Define the modified weight $\hat{w}(u, v)$ as $w(u, v) - h(u) + h(v)$. Let $\delta(s, t)$ be the length of the shortest path from s to t in the original graph and $\hat{\delta}(s, t)$ be the corresponding value in the reweighted graph.*

1. *For a path p, we have $w(p) = \delta(s, t)$, if and only if $\hat{w}(p) = \hat{\delta}(s, t)$.*
2. *Moreover, G has no negatively weighted cycles with respect to w if and only if it has none with respect to $\hat{w}$.*

Proof. For proving the first assertion, let $p = (v_0, \ldots, v_k)$ be *any* path from start node $s = v_0$ to a goal node $t = v_k$. We have

$$\hat{w}(p) = \sum_{i=1}^{k} (w(v_{i-1}, v_i) - h(v_{i-1}) + h(v_i))$$
$$= w(p) - h(v_0).$$

Procedure A*
Input: Implicit problem graph with start node s, weight function w, heuristic h,
     successor generation function *Expand*, and predicate *Goal*
Output: Cost-optimal path from s to $t \in T$, or $\emptyset$ if no such path exists

Closed $\leftarrow \emptyset$	;; Initialize structures
Open $\leftarrow \{s\}$	;; Insert s into search frontier
$f(s) \leftarrow h(s)$	;; Initialize estimate
while (*Open* $\neq \emptyset$)	;; As long as there are frontier nodes
Remove u from *Open* with minimum $f(u)$	;; Select node for expansion
Insert u into *Closed*	;; Update list of expanded nodes
if (*Goal*(u)) **return** *Path*(u)	;; Goal found, return solution
else *Succ*(u) $\leftarrow$ *Expand*(u)	;; Expansion yields successor set
for each v **in** *Succ*(u)	;; For all successors v of u
Improve(u,v)	;; Call relaxation subroutine
return $\emptyset$	;; No solution exists

Procedure Improve
Input: Nodes u and v, v successor of u
Side effects: Update parent of v, $f(v)$, *Open*, and *Closed*

if v **in** *Open*	;; Node already generated but not expanded
if $(g(u) + w(u,v) < g(v))$	;; New path is cheaper
parent(v) $\leftarrow u$	;; Set predecessor pointer
$f(v) \leftarrow g(u) + w(u,v) + h(v)$	;; *DecreaseKey* operation
else if v **in** *Closed*	;; Node v already expanded
if $(g(u) + w(u,v) < g(v))$	;; New path cheaper
parent(v) $\leftarrow u$	;; Set predecessor pointer
$f(v) \leftarrow g(u) + w(u,v) + h(v)$	;; Update estimate
Remove v from *Closed*	;; Reopening of v
Insert v into *Open* with $f(v)$	;; Reopening of node
else	;; Node not seen before
parent(v) $\leftarrow u$	;; Set predecessor pointer
Initialize $f(v) \leftarrow g(u) + w(u,v) + h(v)$	;; First estimate
Insert v into *Open* with $f(v)$	;; Add v to search frontier

Algorithm 2.13

A*.

Assume that there is a path p' with $\hat{w}(p') < \hat{w}(p)$ and $w(p') \geq w(p)$. Then, $w(p') - h(v_0) < w(p) - h(v_0)$ and thus $w(p') < w(p)$, a contradiction. The other direction is dealt with analogously.

For the second assertion let $c = (v_0, \dots, v_l = v_0)$ be any cycle in G. Then we have $\hat{w}(c) = w(c) + h(v_l) - h(v_0) = w(c)$. ∎

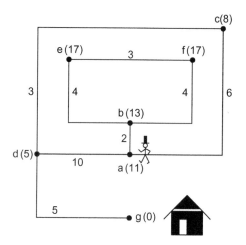

FIGURE 2.13

Extended example of Figure 2.6 with heuristic estimates (in parentheses).

Table 2.4 Steps in A* for the example of Figure 2.13. The numbers in brackets denote the g-value and f-value.

Step	Selection	Open	Closed	Remarks
1	{}	{a(0,11)}	{}	
2	a	{c(6,14),b(2,15),d(10,15)}	{a}	
3	c	{d(9,14),b(2,15)}	{a,c}	update d, change parent to c
4	d	{g(14,14),b(2,15)}	{a,c,d}	a is duplicate
5	g	{b(2,15)}	{a,c,d,g}	goal reached

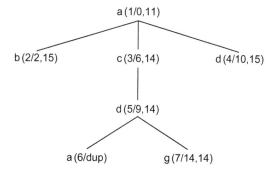

FIGURE 2.14

A* search tree for the example of Figure 2.13. The numbers in parentheses denote the order of node generation / h-value, f-value.

FIGURE 2.15

The process of reweighting edges.

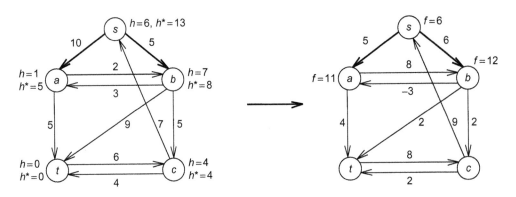

FIGURE 2.16

A problem graph before (left) and after (right) reweighting.

As an example, consider the two graphs in Figure 2.16. To the left the original problem graph with heuristic estimates attached to each node is shown. Each node u is additionally labeled by the value $h^*(u) = \delta(u,t)$. In the reweighted graph to the right the computed f-values after expanding node s are shown. The inconsistency on the original graph on edge (b,a) generates a negative weight in the reweighted graph.

The usual approach to deal with inconsistent but admissible heuristics in the context of A* is called *pathmax*. It takes the maximum of the accumulated weights on the path to a node to enforce a monotone growth in the cost function. More formally for a node u with child v the pathmax equation sets $f(v)$ to $\max\{f(v), f(u)\}$ or, equivalently, $h(v)$ to $\max\{h(v), h(u) - w(u,v)\}$, such that h does not overestimate the distance from the parent to the goal.

The approach is wrong if we apply its reasoning to a graph search as A*. In the example in Figure 2.16, after expanding nodes s and a we have $Open = \{(b,12),(t,15)\}$ and $Closed = \{(s,6),(a,11)\}$. Now a is reached once more via b by means $(b,12)$, it is moved to $Closed$, and $(a,12)$ is compared to the closed list. We have that 12 is the pathmax on path (s,b,a). Wrongly we keep $(a,11)$ and all information contained in $(a,12)$ is lost forever.

The equation $h(u) \leq h(v) + w(u,v)$ is equivalent to $\hat{w}(u,v) = h(v) - h(u) + w(u,v) \geq 0$. A consistent heuristic yields a first A* variant of Dijkstra's algorithm.

Theorem 2.9. *(A* for Consistent Heuristics) Let h be consistent. If we set $f(s) = h(s)$ for the initial node s and update $f(v)$ with $f(u) + \hat{w}(u,v)$ instead of $f(u) + w(u,v)$, at each time a node $t \in T$ is selected, we have $f(t) = \delta(s,t)$.*

Proof. Since h is consistent, we have $\hat{w}(u,v) = w(u,v) - h(u) + h(v) \geq 0$. Therefore, the preconditions of Theorem 2.1 are fulfilled for weight function $\hat{w}$, so that $f(u) = \hat{\delta}(s,u) + h(s)$, if u is selected from *Open*. According to Lemma 2.3, shortest paths remain invariant through reweighting. Hence, if $t \in T$ is selected from *Open* we have

$$f(t) = \hat{\delta}(s,t) + h(s) = \hat{w}(p_t) + h(s) = w(p_t) = \delta(s,t).$$

Since $\hat{w} \geq 0$, we have $f(v) \geq f(u)$ for all successors v of u. The f-values increase monotonically so that at the first extraction of $t \in T$ we have $\delta(s,t) = \delta(s,T)$. ∎

In case of negative values for $w(u,v) - h(u) + h(v)$, shorter paths to already expanded nodes may be found later in the search process. These nodes are *reopened*.

In the special case of unit edge cost and *trivial heuristic* (i.e., $h(u) = 0$ for all u), A* proceeds similarly to the breadth-first search algorithm. However, the two algorithms can have different stopping conditions. BFS stops as soon as it *generates* the goal. A* will not stop–it will insert the goal in the priority queue and it will finish level $d - 1$ before it terminates (assuming the goal is at distance d from the start node). Therefore, the difference between the two algorithms can be as large as the number of nodes at level $d - 1$, which is usually a significant fraction (e.g., half) of the total number of nodes expanded. The reason BFS can do this and A* cannot is because the stopping condition for BFS is correct only when all the edge weights in the problem graph are the same. A* is general-purpose–it has to finish level $d - 1$ because there might be an edge leading to the goal of which the edge has value 0, leading to a better solution. There is an easy solution to this. If node u is adjacent to a goal node then define $h(u) = \min\{w(u,t) \mid t \in T\}$. The new weight of an optimal edge is 0 so that it is searched first.

Lemma 2.4. *Let G be a weighted problem graph, h be a heuristic, and $\hat{w}(u,v) = w(u,v) - h(u) + h(v)$. If h is admissible, then $\hat{\delta}(u,T) \geq 0$.*

Proof. Since $h(t) = 0$ and since the shortest path costs remain invariant under reweighting of G by Lemma 2.3, we have

$$\hat{\delta}(u,T) = \min\{\hat{\delta}(u,t) \mid t \in T\}$$
$$= \min\{\delta(u,t) - h(u) + h(t) \mid t \in T\}$$
$$= \min\{\delta(u,t) - h(u) \mid t \in T\}$$
$$= \min\{\delta(u,t) \mid t \in T\} - h(u)$$
$$= \delta(u,T) - h(u) \geq 0.$$
  ∎

Theorem 2.10. *(A* for Admissible Heuristics) For weighted graphs $G = (V,E,w)$ and admissible heuristics h, algorithm A* is complete and optimal.*

Proof. Immediate consequence of Lemma 2.4 together with applying Theorem 2.3. ∎

A first remark concerning notation: According to the original formulation of the algorithm, the * in A^*, f^*, h^*, and so on was used to denote optimality. As we will see, many algorithms developed later were named conforming to this standard. Do not be surprised if you see many stars!

With respect to the search objective $f = g + h$, Figure 2.17 illustrates the effect of applying DFS, BFS, A*, and *greedy best-first search*, the A* derivate with $f = h$.

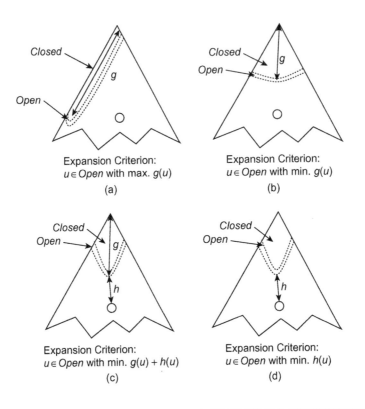

FIGURE 2.17

Different search strategies: (a) DFS, (b) BFS, (c) A*, and (d) greedy best-first search.

2.2.2 On the Optimal Efficiency of A*

It is often said that A* does not only yield an optimal solution, but that it expands the minimal number of nodes (up to tie breaking). In other words, A* has *optimal efficiency* for any given heuristic function, or no other algorithm can be shown to expand fewer nodes than A*. The result, however, is only partially true. It does hold for *consistent* heuristics, but not necessarily for *admissible* heuristics. We first give a proof for the first case and a counterexample for the second one.

Consistent Heuristics

We remember that we can view a search with a consistent heuristic as a search in a reweighted problem graph with nonnegative costs.

Theorem 2.11. *(Efficiency Lower Bound) Let G be a problem graph with nonnegative weight function, with initial node s and final node set T, and let $f^* = \delta(s, T)$ be the optimal solution cost. Any optimal algorithm has to visit all nodes $u \in V$ with $\delta(s, u) < f^*$.*

Proof. We assume the contrary; that is, that an algorithm A finds an optimal solution p_t with $w(p_t) = f^*$ and leaves some u with $\delta(s, u) < f^*$ unvisited. We will show that there might be another solution path q with $w(q) < f^*$ that is not found. Let q_u be the path with $w(q_u) = \delta(s, u)$, let t be a supplementary

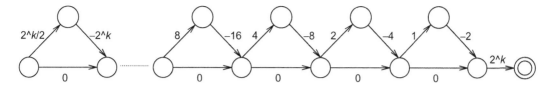

FIGURE 2.18

A problem graph with an exponential number of reopenings.

special node in T and V, and let (u,t) be a new edge with $w(u,t) = 0$. Since u is not expanded, for A we do not know if (u,t) exists. Let $q = (q_u,t)$. Then $w(q) = w(q_u) + w(u,t) = w(q_u) = \delta(s,u) < f^*$. ∎

If the values $\delta(s,u)$ are pairwise different, then there is no tie, and the number of nodes that A expands will have to be larger than or equal to the number of nodes that A* expands.

Nonconsistent Heuristics

If we have admissibility but not consistency, A* will reopen nodes. Even worse, as we will indicate later, A* might reopen nodes *exponentially* many times, even if the heuristic is admissible. This leads to an exponential time consumption in the size of the graph. Fortunately, this strange behavior does not appear frequently in practice, as in most cases we deal with unit costs, limiting the number of possible improvements for a particular node to the depth of the search.

Based on the process of reweighting edges, we can better reflect what happens when we reopen nodes. If we consider nonconsistent heuristics, the reweighted problem graph may contain negative edges. If we consider $w(u,v) + h(v) - h(u)$ as the new edge costs, Figure 2.18 gives an example for a problem graph that leads to exponentially many reopenings. The second last node is reopened for every path with weight $\{1,2,\ldots,2^k - 1\}$.

It is not difficult to restore a heuristic function with nonnegative edge costs. For the top-level nodes in the triangles we have $2^k + 2^{k/2}$, ..., 24, 12, 6, and 3, and for the bottom level node we have 2^k, $2^{k/2},\ldots,16, 8$, 4, 2, 1, and 0. The weights for the in- and outgoing edges at the top-level nodes are zero, and the bottom-level edges are weighted $2^{k/2}, \ldots, 8, 4, 2, 1$, and 2^k.

Recourse to basic graph theory shows that there are algorithms that can do better. First of all, we notice that the problem graph structure is directed and acyclic so that a linear-time algorithm *relaxes* the nodes in topological order. General problem graphs with negative weights are dealt with by the algorithm of Bellman and Ford (see Alg. 2.8), which has a polynomial complexity. But even if we call the entire algorithm of Bellman and Ford for every expanded node, we have an accumulated complexity of $O(n^2 \cdot e)$, which is large but not exponential as with A* and reopening. As a consequence, the efficiency of A* is not optimal. Nonetheless, in the domains that are used in problem solving practice, reopenings are rare, so that A*'s strategy is still a good choice. One reason is that for bounded weights, the worst-case number of reopenings is polynomial.

2.3 *GENERAL WEIGHTS

Next we consider generalizing the state space search by considering an abstract notion of costs. We will consider optimality with respect to a certain cost or weight associated to edges. We abstract costs by an algebraic formalism and adapt the heuristic search algorithms accordingly. We first define the cost algebra we are working on. Then we turn to a cost-algebraic search in graphs, in particular for solving the optimality problem. Cost-algebraic versions of Dijkstra's algorithm and A* with consistent and admissible estimates are discussed. Lastly we discuss extensions to a multiobjective search.

2.3.1 Cost Algebras

Cost-algebraic search methods generalize edge weights in a rather straightforward way to more general cost structures. Our formalism for cost is called *cost algebra*. We recall some required definitions of algebraic concepts.

Let A be a set and $\times : A \times A \to A$ be a binary action. A *monoid* is a tuple $\langle A, \times, 1 \rangle$ if $1 \in A$ and for all $a, b, c \in A$,

$$
\begin{array}{lll}
- & a \times b \in A & \text{(closeness)} \\
- & a \times (b \times c) = (a \times b) \times c & \text{(associativity)} \\
- & a \times 1 = 1 \times a = a & \text{(identity)}
\end{array}
$$

Intuitively, set A will represent the domain of the costs and $\times$ is the operation representing the cumulation of costs.

Let A be a set. A relation $\preceq \in A \times A$ is a *total order* whenever for all $a, b, c \in A$,

$$
\begin{array}{lll}
- & a \preceq a & \text{(reflexivity)} \\
- & a \preceq b \wedge b \preceq a \Rightarrow a = b & \text{(antisymmetry)} \\
- & a \preceq b \wedge b \preceq c \Rightarrow a \preceq c & \text{(transitivity)} \\
- & a \preceq b \vee b \preceq a & \text{(total)}
\end{array}
$$

We write $a \prec b$ if $a \preceq b$ and $a \neq b$. We say that a set A is *isotone* if $a \preceq b$ implies both $a \times c \preceq b \times c$ and $c \times a \preceq c \times b$ for all $a, b, c \in A$.

Definition 2.2. *(Cost Algebra)* A cost algebra *is a 5-tuple* $\langle A, \times, \preceq, 0, 1 \rangle$, *such that* $\langle A, \times, 1 \rangle$ *is a monoid,* $\preceq$ *is a total order,* $0 = \sqcap A$ *and* $1 = \sqcup A$, *and* A *is isotone.*

The least *and* greatest *operations are defined as follows:* $\sqcup A = c$ *such that* $c \preceq a$ *for all* $a \in A$, *and* $\sqcap A = c$ *such that* $a \preceq c$ *for all* $a \in A$.

Intuitively, A is the domain set of cost values, $\times$ is the operation used to cummulate values and $\sqcup$ is the operation used to select the best (the least) among values. Consider, for example, the following cost algebras:

- $\langle R^+ \cup \{+\infty\}, +, \leq, +\infty, 0 \rangle$ (optimization)
- $\langle R^+ \cup \{+\infty\}, \min, \geq, 0, +\infty \rangle$ (max/min)

The only nontrivial property to be checked is isotonicity.

$\langle R^+ \cup \{+\infty\}, +, \leq, +\infty, 0 \rangle$: Here we have to show that $a \leq b$ implies both $a + c \leq b + c$ and $c + a \leq c + b$ for all $a, b, c \in R^+ \cup \{\infty\}$, which is certainly true.

$\langle R^+ \cup \{+\infty\}, \min, \geq, 0, +\infty \rangle$: $a \geq b$ implies $\min\{a, c\} \geq \min\{b, c\}$ and $\min\{c, a\} \geq \min\{c, b\}$, $a, b, c \in R^+ \cup \{\infty\}$.

Not all algebras are isotone; for example, take $A \subseteq \mathbb{R} \times \mathbb{R}$ with $(a,c) \times (b,d) = (\min\{a,b\}, c+d)$ and $(a,c) \preceq (b,d)$ if $a > b$ or $c < d$ if $a = b$. We have $(4,2) \times (3,1) = (3,3) \succ (3,2) = (3,1) \times (3,1)$ but $(4,2) \prec (3,1)$. However, we may easily verify that the related cost structure implied by $(a,c) \times (b,d) = (a+b, \min\{c,d\})$ is isotone.

More specific cost structures no longer cover all the example domains. For example, the slightly more restricted property of *strict isotonicity*, where we have that $a \prec b$ implies both $a \times c \prec b \times c$ and $c \times a \prec c \times b$ for all $a,b,c \in A$, $c \neq \mathbf{0}$, is not sufficient. For the *max/min* cost structure we have $\min\{3,3\} = \min\{3,5\}$, but $3 < 5$.

Definition 2.3. *(Multiple-Edge Graph) A multiple-edge graph G is a tuple (V, E, in, out, w), where V is a set of nodes, E is a set of edges, $in, out : E \to V$ are a source and target functions, and $w : E \to A$ is a weight function.*

The definition generalizes ordinary graphs as it includes a function that produces the source of an edge, and a target function that produces the destination of an edge, so that different edges can have the same source and target. An example is provided in Figure 2.19.

Why haven't we insisted on multiple-edge graphs right away? This is because with the simple cost notion we used in Chapter 1 we can remove multiple edges by keeping only the cheapest ones between the edges for each pair of nodes. The removed edges are superfluous because we are interested in shortest paths. In contrast, we need multiple edges to evidence the need of isotonicity in algebraic costs.

Therefore, the definition of *in* and *out* includes graphs with multiple edges on node pairs. Multiple-edge problem graphs have a distinguished start node s, which we denote with u_0^G, or just $s = u_0$ if G is clear from the context. For an alternating sequence of nodes and edges $u_0, a_0, u_1, \ldots$, such that for each $i \geq 0$ we have $u_i \in V$, $a_i \in E$, $in(a_i) = u_i$, and $out(a_i) = u_{i+1}$, or, shortly $u_i \xrightarrow{a_i} u_{i+1}$.

An initial path is a path starting at s. Finite paths are required to end at nodes. The length of a finite path p is denoted by $|p|$. The concatenation of two paths p, q is denoted by pq, where we require p to be finite and end at the initial node of q. The cost of a path is given by the cumulative cost of its edges.

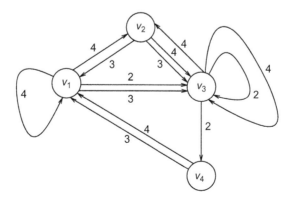

FIGURE 2.19

A multiple-edge graph.

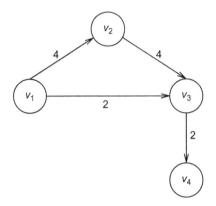

FIGURE 2.20

The problem of prefix-optimality.

On general cost structures, not all subpaths of an optimal path are necessarily optimal. A path $p = (s = u_0 \overset{a_0}{\to} \ldots \overset{a_{k-1}}{\to} u_k)$ is *prefix-optimal* if all prefixes of this path $p = (s = u_0 \overset{a_0}{\to} \ldots \overset{a_{i-1}}{\to} u_i)$ with $i < k$ form an optimal path. As an example consider the (max/min) cost structure of the problem graph in Fig. 2.20. Path (v_1, v_3, v_4) and path (v_1, v_2, v_3, v_4) are optimal with cost 2, but only (v_1, v_2, v_3, v_4) is prefix-optimal.

Reachability and optimality problems can be solved with traditional search algorithms. For the reachability problem, for instance, we can use, among others, depth-first search. For the optimality problem, on the other hand, only Dijkstra's algorithm or A* are appropriate. They are traditionally defined over a simple instance of our cost algebra, namely the optimization cost algebra $\langle \mathbb{R}^+ \cup \{+\infty\}, +, \le, +\infty, 0 \rangle$. Thus, we need to generalize the results that ensure the *optimality* of the search algorithms; that is, the fact that they correctly solve the optimality problem.

The design of cost-algebraic algorithms depends on a different notion for the *principle of optimality*, which intuitively means that the optimality problem can be decomposed.

Definition 2.4. *(Principle of Optimality) The* principle of optimality *requires* $\delta(s,v) = \sqcup \{\delta(s,u) \times w(a) \mid u \overset{a}{\to} v\}$, *where s is the start node in a given problem graph G.*

Lemma 2.5. *Any cost algebra* $\langle A, \times, \le, 0, 1 \rangle$ *satisfies the principle of optimality.*

Proof. We have

$$\sqcup \{\delta(s,u) \times w(a) \mid u \overset{a}{\to} v\} = \sqcup \{\sqcup \{w(p) \mid p = (s, \ldots, u)\} \times w(a) \mid u \overset{a}{\to} v\}$$

$$= \sqcup \{w(p) \times w(a) \mid p = s \to \cdots \to u \overset{a}{\to} v\}$$

$$= \sqcup \{w(p') \mid p' = s \to \cdots \to v\} = \delta(s, v).$$

The first step is by definition and the second step by the distributivity of $\times$. The third step is by isotonicity, since $c \times b \le a \times b$ for all a implies $\sqcup \{b \mid b \in B\} \times c = \sqcup \{b \times c \mid b \in B\}$, and the last step is by definition. ∎

Next we adapt the notions of admissibility and consistency of heuristic functions.

Definition 2.5. *(Cost-Algebraic Heuristics) A heuristic function h with $h(t) = \mathbf{1}$ for each goal node $t \in T$ is*

- admissible, *if for all $u \in V$ we have $h(u) \preceq \delta(u, T)$;*
- consistent, *if for each $u, v \in V$, $a \in E$ with $u \overset{a}{\to} v$ we have $h(u) \preceq w(a) \times h(v)$.*

We can generalize the fact that consistency implies admissibility.

Lemma 2.6. *(Consistency Implies Admissibility) If h is consistent, then it is admissible.*

Proof. We have $\delta(u, T) = w(p)$ for some solution path $p = (u = u_0 \overset{a_0}{\to} u_1 \overset{a_1}{\to} \ldots u_{k-1} \overset{a_{k-1}}{\to} u_k = t)$, $t \in T$, and $h(u) \preceq w(a_0) \times h(v) \preceq w(a_0) \times w(a_1) \times \ldots \times w(a_{k-1}) \times h(u_k) = \delta(u, T)$. ∎

We can extend the approach to more than one optimization criterion; for example, for the prioritized Cartesian product of two cost algebras $C_1 = \langle A_1, \sqcup_1, \times_1, \preceq_1, \mathbf{0}_1, \mathbf{1}_1 \rangle$ and $C_2 = \langle A_2, \sqcup_2, \times_2, \preceq_2, \mathbf{0}_2, \mathbf{1}_2 \rangle$, which is defined by $C_1 \times C_2$ is a tuple $\langle A_1 \times A_2, \sqcup, \times, \preceq, (\mathbf{0}_1, \mathbf{0}_2), (\mathbf{1}_1, \mathbf{1}_2) \rangle$, where $(a_1, a_2) \times (b_1, b_2) = (a_1 \times b_1, a_2 \times b_2)$, $(a_1, a_2) \preceq (b_1, b_2)$ if and only if $a_1 \prec b_1 \vee (a_1 = b_1 \wedge a_2 \preceq b_2)$, and $a \sqcup b = a$ if and only if $a \preceq b$. Cartesian products that prioritize one criteria among the others have the problem to deliver nonisotone algebras in general (see Exercises).

Lemma 2.7. *(Cartesian Product Cost Algebra) If C_1, C_2 are cost algebras and C_1 is strictly isotone then $C_1 \times C_2$ is a cost algebra.*

Proof. The only nontrivial part is isotonicity. If we have $(a_1, a_2) \preceq (b_1, b_2)$ then there are two cases. First, $a_1 \prec a_2$, in which case (by strict isotonicity) we have $a_1 \times c_1 \prec b_1 \times c_1$ and $c_1 \times a_1 \prec c_1 \times b_1$, which clearly implies $(a_1, a_2) \times (c_1, c_2) \preceq (b_1, b_2) \times (c_1, c_2)$ and $(c_1, c_2) \times (a_1, a_2) \preceq (c_1, c_2) \times (b_1, b_2)$.

The second case is $a_1 = b_1$ and $a_1 \preceq b_2$. This trivially implies $a_1 \times c_1 = b_1 \times c_1$ and $a_1 \times c_1 = b_1 \times c_1$ and, by isotonicity, $a_2 \times c_2 \preceq b_2 \times c_2$ and $c_2 \times a_2 \preceq c_2 \times b_2$. Clearly, we have $(a_1, a_2) \times (c_1, c_2) \preceq (b_1, b_2) \times (c_1, c_2)$ and $(c_1, c_2) \times (a_1, a_2) \preceq (c_1, c_2) \times (b_1, b_2)$. ∎

Similarly, we can show that if C_1 and C_2 are strictly isotone then $C_1 \times C_2$ is strictly isotone (see Exercises).

2.3.2 Multiobjective Search

Many realistic optimization problems, particularly those in design, require the simultaneous optimization of more than one objective function. As an example for bridge construction, a good design is characterized by low total mass and high stiffness. A good aircraft design requires simultaneous optimization of fuel efficiency, payload, and weight. A good sunroof design in a car minimizes the noise the driver hears and maximizes the ventilation. With cost algebras we could preserve the work on certain cross-products of criteria. In the multiobjective case we have now arrived at vectors and partial orders.

A *multiobjective search* is an extension to traditional search algorithms, where edge costs are vectors. It generalizes a cost-algebraic search and is applicable in various domains where one has several conflicting objectives with solutions that are optimal for the one but not the others. More formally, multiobjective search can be stated as follows. We are given a weighted problem graph G with n nodes, e edges, and cost function $w : E \to \mathbb{R}^k$. We additionally have a start node s and a set of goal nodes T. The goal is to find the set of nondominated solution paths in G from s to T, where *dominance* is

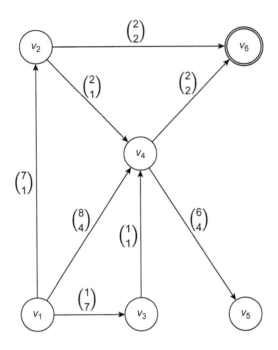

FIGURE 2.21

Example graph for multiobjective search.

given in the form of the following partial order relation $\preceq$: For all $v \in R^k$ we have $v \preceq v'$ if $v_i \leq v'_i$ for all $i \in \{1,\ldots,k\}$. A vector $v \in A$ is *dominated* in set $A \subseteq R^k$ if there is a $v' \neq v$ in A with $v' \preceq v$. The aim is to find solutions that are nondominated such that there exists no other feasible solution that will yield an improvement in one objective without causing a degradation in at least one other objective. Figure 2.21 provides a graph with six nodes and cost vector pairs associated with each edge.

In difference to the cost-algebraic search, relation $\preceq$ is not a total order. Hence, it is not always possible to rank two elements in R with respect to $\preceq$. For example, take $\binom{3}{4}$ and $\binom{4}{3}$. Heuristics $h : V \to R^k$ estimate the accumulated cost vectors of paths to set T. Heuristic h is admissible if for all nondominated solution paths, $p = (s = u_0, u_1, \ldots, u_k = t)$, $t \in T$, and for all prefix paths $p_i = (s = u_0, u_1, \ldots, u_i)$ we have $w(p_i) + h(u_i) \preceq w(p) = w(p_t)$.

Since most approaches illustrated earlier do not easily translate into a multiobjective search, solving them remains being a challenge.

2.4 SUMMARY

In this chapter, we discussed several search algorithms and their properties. Some search algorithms find a path from the given start state to any of the given goal states; others find paths from the given start state to all other states; and even others find paths from all states to all other states. Desirable properties of search algorithms include their correctness (they find a path if and only if one exists), optimality (they find a shortest path), a small runtime, and small memory consumption. In some cases, the correctness or optimality of a search algorithm is only guaranteed on special kinds of graphs, such as unit or nonnegative cost graphs, or where the goal distances of all states are nonnegative. We are often forced to make trade-offs between the different properties, for example, find suboptimal paths because the runtime or memory consumption would otherwise be too large.

We discussed that most search algorithms perform dynamic programming as an underlying technique. Dynamic programming is a general problem-solving technique that assembles the solutions of complex problems from solutions to simpler problems, which are calculated once and reused several times. Dynamic programming works over the entire state space as a whole, in contrast to heuristic search algorithms, which focus on finding only the optimal path for a single current state and prune everything else for efficiency.

On the other hand, most heuristic search algorithms apply dynamic programming updates and traverse the state space in the same way. They build a tree from the given start state to the goal state, maintaining an estimate of the start distances of all states in the search tree. The interior nodes are in the *Closed* list and the leaf nodes are in the *Open* list. They repeatedly pick a leaf of the search tree and expand it; that is, generate its successors in the state space and then add them as its children in the search tree. (They differ in which leaves they pick.) They can find a path from the start state to any of the given goal states if they stop when they are about to expand a goal state and return the only path from the root of the search tree to this goal state. They can find paths from the start state to all other states if they stop only when they have expanded all leaf nodes of the search tree. We distinguished uninformed and informed search algorithms. Uninformed search algorithms exploit no knowledge in addition to the graphs they search. We discussed depth-first search, breadth-first search, Dijkstra's algorithm, the Bellman-Ford algorithm, and the Floyd-Warshall algorithm in this context.

Informed (or synonymously, heuristic) search algorithms exploit estimates of the goal distances of the nodes (heuristic values) to be more efficient than uninformed search algorithms. We discussed A* in this context. We discussed the properties of A* in detail since we discuss many variants of it in later chapters. A* with consistent heuristics has many desirable properties:

- A* can find a shortest path even though it expands every state at most once. It does not need to reexpand states that it has expanded already.
- A* is at least as efficient as every other search algorithm in the sense that every search algorithm (that has the same heuristic values available as A*) needs to expand at least the states that A* expands (modulo tie-breaking; that is, possibly except for some states of which the f-values are equal to the length of the shortest path).
- A* with any given heuristic values cannot expand more states than A* with heuristic values that are dominated by the given heuristic values (again modulo tie-breaking).

Many of these properties followed from the properties of Dijkstra's algorithm, since A* for a given search problem and heuristic values behave identically to Dijkstra's algorithm on a search problem that can be derived from the given search problem by changing the edge costs to incorporate the heuristic values.

Table 2.5 summarizes the uninformed and informed search algorithms, namely how to implement their *Open* and *Closed* lists, whether they can exploit heuristic values, which values their edge costs can take on, whether they find shortest paths, and whether or not they can reexpand states that they

Table 2.5 Overview of implicit graph search algorithms.

Algorithm	Open	Closed	Heur	Weight	Optimal	Reopen
DFS (2.1/2.3)	stack	set	–	unit	–	–
BFS (2.1/2.3)	queue	set	–	unit	✓	–
Dijkstra (2.1/2.4)	pq	set	–	$R_{\geq 0}$	✓	–
Bellm.-Ford (2.7/2.8)	queue	set	–	R	✓	✓
A (2.1/2.5)	pq	set	–	R	✓	✓
Node-Sel. A (2.1/2.6)	set	set	–	R	✓	✓
Floyd-Warshall (2.9)	row	matrix	–	R	✓	–
A*, cons. (2.1/2.4)	pq	set	✓	$R_{\geq 0}$	✓	–
A*, admis. (2.1/2.5)	pq	set	✓	$R_{\geq 0}$	✓	✓
Policy-Iteration (2.11)	set	set	–	prob.	✓	✓
Value-Iteration (2.12)	set	set	✓	prob.	ϵ	✓

have expanded already. (The figures that describe their pseudo code are given in parentheses.) Most search algorithms build either on depth-first search or on breadth-first search, where depth-first search trades off runtime and optimality for a small memory consumption and breadth-first search does the opposite. Many discussed algorithms relate to breadth-first search: Dijkstra's algorithm is a specialized version of A* in case no heuristic values are available. It is also a specialized and optimized version of the Bellman-Ford algorithm in case all edge costs are nonnegative. Breadth-first search, in turn, is a specialized and optimized version of Dijkstra's algorithm in case all edge costs are uniform. Finally, we discussed algebraic extension to the operator costs and generalizations for search problems of which the edge costs are vectors of numbers (e.g., the cost and time required for executing an action), explaining why dynamic programming often cannot solve them as efficiently as graphs of which the edge costs are numbers because they often need to maintain many paths from the start state to states in the search tree.

2.5 EXERCISES

2.1 The MISSIONARY AND CANNIBALS (or HOBBITS AND ORCS) problem is defined as follows (see Fig. 2.22). At one side of a river there are three missionaries and three cannibals. They have a boat that can transport at most two persons. The goal for all persons is to cross the river. At no time should the number of cannibals exceed the number of missionaries for obvious reasons.

1. Draw the problem graph and provide its adjacency list representation.

2. Solve the problem via DFS and BFS by annotating the graph with numbers.

3. Consider a heuristic function that counts the number of people on the other side of the river. Do you observe an inconsistency?

4. Consider a compressed problem graph with actions that correspond to two successive river crossings. Use the same heuristic function as before. Is it consistent?

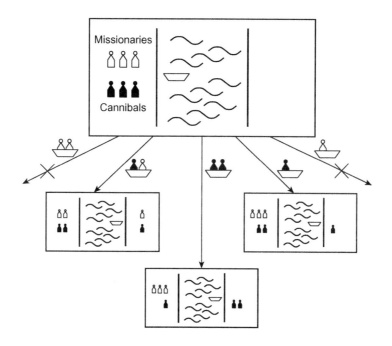

FIGURE 2.22

The MISSIONARY AND CANNIBALS problem.

2.2 Solve the following two additional famous RIVER CROSSING problems optimally.
1. A man, a fox, a goose, and some corn are together on one side of the river. The boat can carry the man and one other subject. The goal is to move them on the other side. Neither the goose and the corn, nor the fox and the goose can be left alone.
2. Four couples have to cross a river that has one island. The boat carries only two persons and because partners are jealous, no person can be left alone with another single of a different sex.

2.3 The KNIGHT'S TOUR problem asks for a square disjoint on a $(n \times n)$-size chess board; that is, for a path that covers the entire board and visits each square only once.
1. Show that there is no KNIGHT'S TOUR on a 4×4 board.
2. A KNIGHT'S TOUR on the 5×5 board is as follows:

1	18	13	22	7
12	23	8	19	14
17	2	21	6	9
24	11	4	15	20
3	16	25	10	5

Compute a KNIGHT'S TOUR starting top-left and ending two squares right of the bottom-left corner for boards sized 6×6, 7×7, 8×8, and 9×9.

3. A KNIGHT'S TOUR on a square board of size 6×6 with a square of size 1×1 omitted in the bottom-right corner, which starts top-right, and ends two squares right of the bottom-left corner looks as follows:

32	3	14	9	26	1
13	24	33	2	15	10
4	31	12	25	8	27
23	20	29	34	11	16
30	5	18	21	28	7
19	22	35	6	17	

Construct similar tours for the boards 7×7 with a subsquare of size 2×2 omitted, 8×8 with a subsquare of size 3×3 omitted, and 9×9 with a subsquare of size 4×4 omitted.

4. Use the previous results to devise a KNIGHT'S TOUR strategy for covering any $n \times n$ board, $n > 6$, starting top-right. You will have to reflect some of the subtour patterns along the axes and diagonals.

2.4 Consider the MULTIPLE SEQUENCE ALIGNMENT problem between ACGTACGACGT and ATGTCG-TACACGT. Take the same cost function as in Exercise 1.16.

1. Fill the dynamic programming table. How best to traverse it?

2. Display the extracted solution path, after the table has been filled.

2.5 Consider the graph in Figure 2.23. Denote the order of expanded nodes (and their f-values) as generated by DFS and BFS, as well as by A* and a greedy best-first search with the Euclidean distance estimate. To resolve ties, nodes should be inserted into the according data structures with respect to their alphabetic order.

2.6 Let graph $G = (V, E, w)$ be a weighted graph, and T be a set of goal nodes. Suppose that for each node $u \in V$ reachable from the source we have $\delta(u, T) = \min\{\delta(u, t) \mid t \in T\} \geq 0$. Show that the graph contains no negative cycle that is reachable from the source.

2.7 Consider the algorithm of Bellman and Ford (on a connected graph).

1. Show that the number of reopenings of a node can be bounded by the length (number of edges) L of an optimal solution path, so that the complexity of the algorithm is $O(L \cdot |E|)$.

2. Assign an order $v_1, \ldots, v_n$ to the nodes of the input graph and partition E in E_f and E_b, where $E_f = \{(v_i, v_j) \in E : i < j\}$ and $E_b = \{(v_i, v_j) \in E : i > j\}$. $G_f = (V, E_f)$ is acyclic with topological order $v_1, \ldots, v_n$ and $G_b = (V, E_b)$ is acyclic with topological order $v_n, \ldots, v_1$. Now relax all edges in E_f leaving v_i for all v_i in $\{v_1, \ldots, v_n\}$ and all edges in E_b leaving v_i for all v_i in $\{v_n, \ldots, v_1\}$. Show that $n/2$ passes suffice.

3. Another refinement is that if $(V_j, E_j), j \in \{1, \ldots, l\}$ are the *strongly connected components* of G. (Recall that a and b are in the same strongly connected components if a can reach b and b can reach a.) Show that the algorithm now runs in time $O(|E| + \sum_j |V_j||E_j|)$.

2.8 KNAPSACK has the following inputs: weights $w_1, \ldots, w_n$, utilities $u_1, \ldots, u_n$, and weight limit W. Putting an item i into the knapsack increases the weight of the knapsack by w_i and gives an additional utility of u_i. The optimization problem is to maximize the utility in the set of all possible

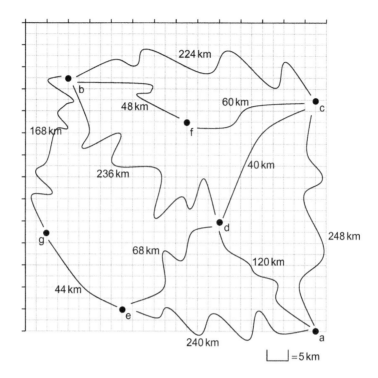

FIGURE 2.23

A map.

packings, while respecting the weight limit. The corresponding decision problem additionally takes a bound U for the utility as the input.

1. Show that KNAPSACK can be solved in time $O(nW)$ by dynamic programming.
2. Extend the algorithm to compute the optimal packing.

2.9 The product C of two matrices A and B having respective sizes $n \times m$ and $m \times l$ is defined by $c_{ij} = \sum_{i=1}^{m} a_{ik} \cdot b_{kj}$, for $1 \le i \le n$ and $1 \le j \le l$. Devise a dynamic programming algorithm to compute the matrix product of $A_1, \ldots, A_6$ (of sizes 6×2, 2×6, 6×3, 3×2, 2×7, and 7×8) with a minimal number of multiplications.

1. Determine the number of multiplications needed to compute $(((A_1A_2)A_3)A_4)A_5)A_6)$ and $(((A_1A_2)A_3)(A_4(A_5A_6)))$.
2. Find an arrangement of brackets with the least number of multiplications.
3. How many options are there to place brackets?

2.10 Prove the correctness of cost-algebraic search variants.

1. Show that the cost-algebraic version of Dijkstra's algorithm solves the optimality problem on multiple-edge graphs.
2. Show that cost-algebraic A* for consistent estimates solves the optimality problem on multiple-edge graphs.

3. Prove the invariance condition for a cost-algebraic heuristic search.
4. Infer that cost-algebraic A* with reopening solves the optimality problem for admissible estimates on multiple-edge graphs.

2.11   Prove that if C_1 and C_2 are both strictly isotone, then $C_1 \times C_2$ is strictly isotone.

2.12   Find and discuss differences and similarities of the algorithms value iteration (2.8) and Bellman-Ford (2.12).

2.13   Solve the following WUMPUS WORLD problem via *value iteration* and *policy iteration*: a 4×3 GRIDWORLD with a hole at $(2,2)$, and two goals at $(4,3)$ and $(4,2)$. The agent starts at $(1,1)$; the rewards are: 1, for arriving at $(4,3)$, and -1, for arriving at $(4,2)$. Transition probabilities for the four possible move directions are as follows. With probability 0.8 the move is successful; with probability of 0.1 (each) the move direction misplaced at right angles. If a wall is encountered, the agent stays at its position. As discount value δ take 24/25. For both cases restrict the number of iterations to 50.
1. Display the stochastic transition system, with states and transition probabilities.
2. Provide the reward cost table.

2.14   Show that the ϵ-greedy policies with respect to π_q are an improvement over every policy with $\pi(u,a) > 0$.

2.6 BIBLIOGRAPHIC NOTES

Shortest path search is a classic topic in the field of combinatorial optimization. The algorithm of Dijkstra (1959) to find shortest paths in graphs with nonnegative edge weights is one of the most important algorithms in computer science. Sound introductions to shortest path search are given by Tarjan (1983) and Mehlhorn (1984). The linear-time shortest path algorithm for acyclic graphs can be found in Lawler (1976).

Using lower bound to prune search goes back to the late 1950s, where branch-and-bound search was proposed. The first use of distance goal estimates to guide state space search is probably due to Doran and Michie (1966) in a program called *GraphTraverser*. Original A* search as proposed by Hart, Nilsson, and Raphael (1968) refers to Dijkstra's algorithm, but in most AI textbooks the link to standard graph theory has vanished. The reweighting transformation is found in Cormen, Leiserson, and Rivest (1990) in the context of the ALL PAIRS SHORTEST PATHS problem of Johnson (1977). It makes it abundantly clear that heuristics do not change the branching factor of a space, but affect the relative depth of the goal, an issue stressed while predicting the search efforts of IDA*. The general problem of finding the shortest path in a graph containing cycles of negative length is NP-hard (Garey and Johnson, 1979).

Bellman (1958) and Ford and Fulkerson (1962) discovered the algorithm for shortest path search in negative graphs independently. A nondeterministic version is discussed by Ahuja, Magnanti, and Orlin (1989). Gabow and Tarjan (1989) showed that if C is the weight of the largest edge the algorithm of Bellman and Ford can been improved to $O(\sqrt{n}e\lg(nC))$. To alleviate the problem of exponentially many node expansions in A*, Martelli (1977) suggested a variation of the Bellman-Ford algorithm, where the relaxation is performed for the entire set of expanded nodes each time a new node is considered. His algorithm has been slightly improved by Bagchi and Mahanti (1983). The heuristic search version of the Bellman-Ford algorithm were entitled *C*, *ProbA*, and *ProbC* (Bagchi and Mahanti, 1985). Mero (1984) has analyzed heuristic search with a modifiable estimate in an algorithm B' that extends the B algorithm of Martelli (1977). A taxonomy of shortest path search has been given by Deo and Pang (1984) and a general framework that includes heuristic search has been presented by Pijls and Kolen (1992). Sturtevant, Zhang, Holte, and Schaeffer (2008) have analyzed inconsistent heuristics for A* search, and propose a new algorithm that introduces a delay list for a better trade-off.

The technique of dynamic programming has been introduced by Bellman (1958). One of the most important applications of this principle in computer science is probably the parsing of context-free languages (Hopcroft and Ullman, 1979; Younger, 1967). Computing edit-distances with dynamic programming is a result that goes back to mathematicians like Ulam and Knuth. In computational biology, the work of Needleman and Wunsch (1981) is considered as the first publication that applies dynamic programming to compute the similarity of two strings. A neat application also used for compiling this textbook is the optimal line break algorithm of Knuth and Plass (1981). A good introduction to the subject of dynamic programming is found in the textbook of Cormen et al. (1990). The lattice edge representation for multiple sequence alignment has been adopted in the program MSA by Gupta, Kececioglu, and Schaffer (1996).

The term *best-first search* appears in AI literature in two different meanings. Pearl (1985) uses this term to define a general search algorithm that includes A* as a special case. Others use it to describe an algorithm that always expands the node estimated closest to the goal. Russell and Norvig (2003) coined the term *greedy best-first search* to avoid confusion. In our notation an algorithm is *optimal* if it computes a shortest solution path. We chose an optimal instead of an admissible algorithm as done by Pearl (1985). Optimality in our notation does not mean *optimal efficiency*. The optimality efficiency argument on the number of node expansions in A* with consistent heuristics has been given by Dechter and Pearl (1983). Common misconceptions of heuristic search have been highlighted by Holte (2009).

The cost formalism extends the one of Sobrinho (2002) with an additional set, to where the heuristic function is mapped. The problem of Cartesian products and power constructions as defined for semirings by Bistarelli, Montanari, and Rossi (1997) is that they provide partial orders. Observations on multiobjective A* have been provided by Mandow and de-la Cruz (2010a,b). Multiobjective IDA* has been considered by Coego, Mandow, and de-la Cruz (2009). Speed-up techniques for a Dijkstra-like search have been studied by Berger, Grimmer, and Müller-Hannemann (2010). Advances in multiobjective search also include work on minimum spanning trees by Galand, Perny, and Spanjaard (2010) as well as KNAPSACK problems by Delort and Spanjaard (2010).

*Dictionary Data Structures

The exploration efficiency of algorithms like A* is often measured with respect to the number of expanded/generated problem graph nodes, but the actual runtimes depend crucially on how the *Open* and *Closed* lists are implemented. In this chapter we look closer at efficient data structures to represent these sets.

For the *Open* list, different options for implementing a priority queue data structure are considered. We distinguish between integer and general edge costs, and introduce bucket and advanced heap implementations.

For efficient duplicate detection and removal we also look at hash dictionaries. We devise a variety of hash functions that can be computed efficiently and that minimize the number of collisions by approximating uniformly distributed addresses, even if the set of chosen keys is not (which is almost always the case). Next we explore memory-saving dictionaries, the space requirements of which come close to the information-theoretic lower bound and provide a treatment of approximate dictionaries.

Subset dictionaries address the problem of finding partial state vectors in a set. Searching the set is referred to as the SUBSET QUERY or the CONTAINMENT QUERY problem. The two problems are equivalent to the PARTIAL MATCH retrieval problem for retrieving a partially specified input query word from a file of k-letter words with k being fixed. A simple example is the search for a word in a crossword puzzle. In a state space search, subset dictionaries are important to store partial state vectors like dead-end patterns in SOKOBAN that generalize pruning rules (see Ch. 10).

In state space search, *string dictionaries* are helpful to exclude a set of forbidden action sequences, like UD or RL in the $(n^2 - 1)$-PUZZLE, from being generated. Such sets of excluded words are formed by concatenating move labels on paths that can be learned and generalized (see Ch. 10). Therefore, string dictionaries provide an option to detect and eliminate duplicates without hashing and can help to reduce the efforts for storing all visited states. Besides the efficient insertion (and deletion) of strings, the task to determine if a query string is the substring of a stored string is most important and has to be executed very efficiently. The main application for string dictionaries are web search engines. The most flexible data structure for efficiently solving this DYNAMIC DICTIONARY MATCHING problem is the GENERALIZED SUFFIX TREE.

3.1 PRIORITY QUEUES

When applying the A* algorithm to explore a problem graph, we rank all generated but not expanded nodes u in list *Open* by their priority $f(u) = g(u) + h(u)$. As basic operations we need to find the element of the minimal f-value: to insert a node together with its f-value and to update the structure if a node becomes a better f-value due to a shorter path. An abstract data structure for the three operations *Insert, DeleteMin,* and *DecreaseKey* is a *priority queue.*

In Dijkstra's original implementation, the *Open* list is a plain array of nodes together with a bitvector indicating if elements are currently open or not. The minimum is found through a complete scan, yielding quadratic execution time in the number of nodes. More refined data structures have been developed since, which are suitable for different classes of weight functions. We will discuss integer and general weights; for integer cost we look at bucket structures and for general weights we consider refined heap implementations.

3.1.1 Bucket Data Structures

In many applications, edge weights can only be positive integers (sometimes for fractional values it is also possible and beneficial to achieve this by rescaling). As a general assumption we state that the difference between the largest key and the smallest key is less than or equal to a constant C.

Buckets

A simple implementation for the priority queues is a 1-LEVEL BUCKET. This priority queue implementation consists of an array of $C+1$ buckets, each of which is the first link in a linked list of elements. With the array we associate the three numbers *minValue, minPos,* and n: *minValue* denotes the smallest f value in the queue, *minPos* fixes the index of the bucket with the smallest key, and n is the number of stored elements. The ith bucket $b[i]$ contains all elements v with $f(v) = (minValue + (i - minPos)) \bmod (C+1)$, $0 \leq i \leq C$. Figure 3.1 illustrates an example for the set of keys $\{16, 16, 18, 20, 23, 25\}$. The implementations for the four main priority queue operations *Initialize, Insert, DeleteMin,* and *DecreaseKey* are shown in Algorithms 3.1 through 3.4.

With doubly linked lists (each element has a predecessor and successor pointer) we achieve constant runtimes for the *Insert* and *DecreaseKey* operations, while the *DeleteMin* operation consumes $O(C)$ time in the worst-case for searching a nonempty bucket. For *DecreaseKey* we generally assume that a pointer to the element to be deleted is available. Consequently, Dijkstra's algorithm and A* run in $O(e + nC)$ time, where e is the number of edges (generated) and n is the number of nodes (expanded).

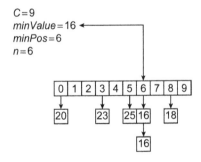

FIGURE 3.1

Example for a 1-LEVEL BUCKET data structure.

Procedure Initialize
Input: 1-LEVEL BUCKET array $b[0..C]$ (implicit constant C)
Side Effect: Updated 1-LEVEL BUCKET $b[0..C]$

$n \leftarrow 0$	;; No element in so far
$minValue \leftarrow \infty$	;; Default value for current minimum

Algorithm 3.1

Initializing a 1-LEVEL BUCKET.

Procedure Insert
Input: 1-LEVEL BUCKET $b[0..C]$, element x with key k
Side Effect: Updated 1-LEVEL BUCKET $b[0..C]$

$n \leftarrow n + 1$	;; Increase number of elements
if $(k < minValue)$	;; Element with smallest key
$\quad minPos \leftarrow k \ mod \ (C + 1)$	;; Update location of minimum
$\quad minValue \leftarrow k$	;; Update current minimum
Insert x in $b[k \ mod \ (C + 1)]$	;; Insert into list

Algorithm 3.2

Inserting an element into a 1-LEVEL BUCKET.

Procedure DeleteMin
Input: 1-LEVEL BUCKET $b[0..C]$
Output: Element x with key $minPos$
Side Effect: Updated 1-LEVEL BUCKET $b[0..C]$

Remove x in $b[minPos]$ from doubly ended list	;; Eliminate element
$n \leftarrow n - 1$	;; Decrease number of elements
if $(n > 0)$	;; Structure nonempty
$\quad$ **while** $(b[minPos] = \emptyset)$	;; Bridge possible gaps
$\quad\quad minPos \leftarrow (minPos + 1) \ mod \ (C + 1)$	;; Update location of pointer
$\quad minValue \leftarrow Key(x), x \in b[minPos]$	;; Update current minimum
else $minValue \leftarrow \infty$	;; Structure empty
return x	;; Feedback result

Algorithm 3.3

Deleting the minimum element in a 1-LEVEL BUCKET.

Given that the f-value can often be bounded by a constant f_{max} in a practical state space search, authors usually omit the modulo operation $mod \ (C + 1)$, which reduces the space for array b to $O(C)$, and take a plain array addressed by f instead. If f_{max} is not known in advance a doubling strategy can be applied.

Procedure DecreaseKey
Input: 1-LEVEL BUCKET $b[0..C]$, element x, key k
Side Effect: Updated 1-LEVEL BUCKET $b[0..C]$ with x moved

Remove x from doubly ended list   ;; Eliminate element
$n \leftarrow n - 1$;; Decrease number of elements
Insert x with key k in b ;; Reinsert element

Algorithm 3.4

Updating the key in a 1-LEVEL BUCKET.

Multilayered Buckets

In state space search, we often have edge weights that are of moderate size, say realized by a 32-bit integer for which a bucket array b of size 2^{32} is too large, whereas 2^{16} can be afforded.

The space complexity and the worst-case time complexity $O(C)$ for *DeleteMin* can be reduced to an *amortized* complexity of $O(\sqrt{C})$ operations by using a 2-LEVEL BUCKET data structure with one top and one bottom level, both of length $\lceil \sqrt{C+1} \rceil + 1$.

In this structure we have two pointers for the minimum position, *minPosTop* and *minPosBottom*, and a number *nbot* of bottom elements. Although each bucket in the bottom array holds a list of elements with the same key as before, the top layer points to lower-level arrays. If after a *DeleteMin* operation that yields a minimum key k no insertion is performed with a key less than k (as it is the case for a consistent heuristic in A*), it is sufficient to maintain only one bottom bucket (at *minPosTop*), and collect elements in higher buckets in the top level; the lower-level buckets can be created only when the current bucket at *minPosTop* becomes empty and *minPosTop* moves on to a higher one. One advantage is that in the case of maximum distance between keys, *DeleteMin* has to inspect only the $\lceil \sqrt{C+1} \rceil + 1$ buckets of the top level; moreover, it saves space if only a small fraction of the available range C is actually filled.

As an example, take $C = 80$, *minPosTop* $= 2$, *minPosBottom* $= 1$, and the set of element keys $\{7, 7, 11, 13, 26, 35, 48, 57, 63, 85, 86\}$. The intervals and elements in the top buckets are $b[2] : [6, 15] = \{7, 7, 11, 13\}$, $b[3] : [16, 25] = \emptyset$, $b[4] : [26, 35] = \{26, 35\}$, $b[5] : [36, 45] = \emptyset$, $b[6] : [46, 55] = \{48\}$, $b[7] : [56, 65] = \{57, 63\}$, $b[8] : [66, 75] = \emptyset$, $b[9] : [76, 85] = \{85\}$, $b[0] : [86, 95] = \{86\}$, and $b[1] : [96, 105] = \emptyset$. Bucket $b[2]$ is expanded with nonempty bottom buckets 1, 5, and 7 containing the elements 7, 11, and 13, respectively. Figure 3.2 illustrates the example.

Since *DeleteMin* reuses the bottom bucket in case it becomes empty, in some cases it is fast and in other cases it is slow. In our case of the 2-LEVEL BUCKET, let Φ_l be the number of elements in the top-level bucket, for the lth operation, then *DeleteMin* uses $O(\sqrt{C} + m_l)$ time in the worst-case, where m_l is the number of elements that move from top to bottom. The term $O(\sqrt{C})$ is the worst-case distance passed by in the top bucket, and m_l are efforts for the reassignment, which costs are equivalent to the number of elements that move from top to bottom. Having to wait until all moved elements in the bottom layer are dealt with, the worst-case work is amortized over a longer time period. By amortization we have $O(\sqrt{C} + m_l + (\Phi_l - \Phi_{l-1})) = O(\sqrt{C})$ operations. Both operations *Insert* and *DecreaseKey* run in real and amortized constant time.

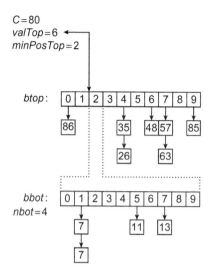

FIGURE 3.2

Example for 2-LEVEL BUCKET data structure.

Radix Heaps

For achieving an even better amortized runtime, namely $O(\lg C)$, a so-called RADIX HEAP maintains a list of $\lceil \lg(C+1) \rceil + 1$ buckets of sizes 1, 1, 2, 4, 8, 16, and so on (see Fig. 3.3). The main difference to layered buckets is to use buckets of exponentially increasing sizes instead of a hierarchy. Therefore, only $O(\lg C)$ buckets are needed.

For the implementation we maintain buckets $b[0..B]$ and bounds $u[0..B+1]$ with $B = \lceil \lg(C+1) \rceil + 1$ and $u[B+1] = \infty$. Furthermore, the bucket number $\phi(k)$ denotes the index of the actual bucket for key k. The invariants of the algorithms are (1) all keys in $b[i]$ are in $[u[i], u[i+1]]$; (2) $u[1] = u[0] + 1$; and (3) for all $i \in \{1, \ldots, B-1\}$ we have $0 \le u[i+1] - u[i] \le 2^{i-1}$.

The operations are as follows. *Initialize* generates an empty RADIX HEAP according to the invariants (2) and (3). The pseudo code is shown in Algorithm 3.5.

To insert an element with key k, in a linear scan a bucket i is searched, starting from the largest one ($i = B$). Then the new element with key k is inserted into the bucket $b[i]$ with $i = \min\{j \mid k \le u[j]\}$. The pseudo-code implementation is depicted in Algorithm 3.6.

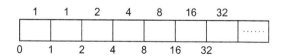

FIGURE 3.3

Example for a RADIX HEAP. The bottom row numbers denote current values of the bounds u and the top row numbers denote the size of the interval defined by two successive u-values.

Procedure Initialize
Input: Array $b[0..B]$ of lists and array $u[0..B]$ of bounds
Side Efect: Initialized RADIX HEAP with arrays b and u

for each i **in** $\{0,...,B\}$ $b[i] \leftarrow \emptyset$	;; Initialize buckets
$u[0] \leftarrow 0; u[1] \leftarrow 1$	;; Initialize bounds
for each i **in** $\{2,...,B\}$ $u[i] \leftarrow u[i-1] + 2^{i-2}$	;; Initialize bounds

Algorithm 3.5

Creating a RADIX HEAP.

Procedure Insert
Input: RADIX HEAP with array $b[0..B+1]$ of lists and array $u[0..B+1]$, key k
Side Effect: Updated RADIX HEAP

$i \leftarrow B$	;; Initialize index
while $(u[i] > k)$ $i \leftarrow i-1$	;; Decrease index
Insert k in $b[i]$	;; Insert element in list

Algorithm 3.6

Inserting an element into a RADIX HEAP.

Procedure DecreaseKey
Input: RADIX HEAP with array $b[0..B+1]$ of lists and array $u[0..B+1]$,
 index i in which old key k is stored, new key k'
Side Effect: Updated RADIX HEAP

while $(u[i] > k')$ $i \leftarrow i-1$	;; Decrease index
Insert k' in $b[i]$	;; Insert element in list

Algorithm 3.7

Inserting an element into a RADIX HEAP.

For *DecreaseKey*, bucket i for an element with key k is searched linearly. The difference is that the search starts from the actual bucket i for key k as stored in $\phi(k)$. The implementation is shown in Algorithm 3.7.

For *DeleteMin* we first search for the first nonempty bucket $i = min\{j \mid b[j] \neq \emptyset\}$ and identify the element with minimum key k therein. If the smallest bucket contains an element it is returned. For the other case $u[0]$ is set to k and the bucket bounds are adjusted according to the invariances; that is, $u[1]$ is set to $k+1$ and for $j > 2$ bound $u[j]$ is set to $min\{u[j-2] + 2^{j-2}, u[i+1]\}$. Lastly, the elements of $b[i]$ are distributed to buckets $b[0], b[1], ..., b[i-1]$ and the minimum element is extracted from the nonempty smallest bucket. The implementation is shown in Algorithm 3.8.

Procedure DecreaseMin
Input: RADIX HEAP with array $b[0..B+1]$ of lists and array $u[0..B+1]$
Output: Minimum element
Side Effect: Updated RADIX HEAP

$i \leftarrow 0$	;; Start with first bucket
$r \leftarrow Select(b[i])$	;; Select (any) minimum key
$b[i] \leftarrow b[i] \setminus \{r\}$	;; Eliminate minimum key
while $(b[i] = \emptyset)$ $i \leftarrow i+1$	;; Search for first nonempty bucket
if $(i > 0)$	;; First bucket empty
$k \leftarrow \min b[i]$	;; Select smallest key
$u[0] \leftarrow k, u[1] \leftarrow k+1$	;; Update bounds
for each j **in** $\{2,\ldots,i\}$	;; Loop on array indices
$u[j] \leftarrow \min\{u[j-1]+2^{j-2}, u[i+1]\}$	;; Update bounds
$j \leftarrow 0$	;; Initialize index
for each k **in** $b[i]$	;; Keys to distribute
while $(k > u[j+1])$ $j \leftarrow j+1$	;; Increase index
$b[j] \leftarrow b[j] \cup \{k\}$	;; Distribute
return r	;; Output minimum element

Algorithm 3.8

Delete the minimum from a RADIX HEAP.

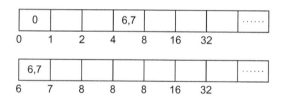

FIGURE 3.4

Example for *DeleteMin* operation in a RADIX HEAP.

As a short example for *DeleteMin* consider the following configuration (written as $[u[i]] : b[i]$) of a RADIX HEAP $[0] : \{0\}, [1] : \emptyset, [2] : \emptyset [4] : \{6,7\}, [8] : \emptyset, [16] : \emptyset$ (see Fig. 3.4). Extracting key 0 from bucket 1 yields $[6] : \{6,7\}, [7] : \emptyset, [8] : \emptyset, [8] : \emptyset, [8] : \emptyset, [16] : \emptyset$. Now, key 6 and 7 are distributed. If $b[i] \neq \emptyset$ then the interval size is at most 2^{i-1}. In $b[i]$ we have $i-1$ buckets available. Since all keys in $b[i]$ are in $[k, \min\{k + 2^{i-1} - 1, u[i+1] - 1\}]$ all elements fit into $b[0],\ldots,b[i-1]$.

The amortized analysis of the costs of maintaining a RADIX HEAP uses the potential $\Phi_l = \sum_{x \in R} \phi_l(x)$ for operation l. We have that *Initialize* runs in $O(B)$, and *Insert* runs in $O(B)$. *DecreaseKey* has an amortized time complexity in $O(\phi_l(x) - \phi_{l-1}(x)) + 1 + (\Phi_l - \Phi_{l-1}) = O((\phi_l(x) - \phi_{l-1}(x)) - (\phi_l(x) - \phi_{l-1}(x)) + 1) = O(1)$, and *DeleteMin* runs in time $O(B + (\sum_{x \in b[i]} \phi_l(x) - \sum_{x \in b[i]} \phi_{l-1}(x)) + (\Phi_l - \Phi_{l-1})) = O(1)$ amortized. In total we have a running time of $O(m \lg C + l)$ for m *Insert* and l *DecreaseKey* and *ExtractMin* operations.

Utilizing this representation, A* runs in time $O(e + n \lg C)$ time. For current computers, the value of $\lg C$ for encompassing the entire integer range is small (32 or 64), so that A* on integers using a RADIX HEAP runs in linear time in practice.

Van Emde Boas Priority Queues

A VAN EMDE BOAS PRIORITY QUEUE is efficient when $n > \lg N$ for a universe $U = \{0, \ldots, N-1\}$ of keys. In this implementation, all priority queue operations reduce to successor computation, which takes $O(\lg \lg N)$ time. The space requirements are $O(N \lg \lg N)$.

We start by considering a data structure T_N on the elements $\{0, \ldots, N-1\}$ defining only three operations: *Insert(x)*, *Delete(x)*, and *Succ(x)*, where the two first ones have an obvious semantics and the last one returns the smallest item in T_N that is larger than or equal to x. All priority queue operations use the recursive operation *Succ(x)* that finds the smallest y in the structure T_N with $y > x$. For the priority queue data structure, *DeleteMin* is simply implemented as *Delete(Succ(0))*, assuming positive key values, and *DecreaseKey* is a combination of a *Delete* and an *Insert* operation.

Using an ordinary bitvector, *Insert* and *Delete* are constant-time operations, but *Succ* is inefficient. Using balanced trees, all operations run in time $O(\lg N)$. A better solution is to implement a recursive representation with $\sqrt{N}$ distinct versions of $T_{\sqrt{N}}$. The latter trees are called *bottom*, and an element $i = a \cdot \sqrt{N} + b$ is represented by the entry b in *bottom(a)*. The conversion from i to a and b in bit-vector representation is simple, since a and b refer to the most and least significant half of the bits. Moreover, we have another version $T_{\sqrt{N}}$ called *top* that contains a only if a is nonempty.

Algorithm 3.9 depicts a pseudo-code implementation of *Succ*. The recursion for the runtime is $T(N) = T(\sqrt{N}) + O(1)$. If we set $N \sim 2^k$ then $T(2^k) = T(2^{k/2}) + O(1)$ so that $T(2^k) = O(\lg k)$ and $T(N) = O(\lg \lg N)$. The subsequent implementations for *Insert* and *Delete* are shown in Algorithms 3.10 and 3.11. Inserting element x in T_N locates a possible place by first seeking the successor *Succ(x)* of x. This leads to a running time of $O(\lg \lg N)$. *Deletion* used the doubly linked structure and the successor relation. It also runs in $O(\lg \lg N)$ time.

A VAN EMDE BOAS PRIORITY QUEUE *k-structure* is recursively defined. Consider the example $k = 4$ (implying $N = 16$) with the set of five elements $S = \{2, 3, 7, 10, 13\}$. Set *top* is a 2-structure

---

Procedure Succ
Input: VAN EMDE BOAS PRIORITY QUEUE structure T_N, $i = a\sqrt{N} + b$
Output: $\min\{k \in T_N | k \geq i\}$
Side Effect: Updated VAN EMDE BOAS PRIORITY QUEUE structure T_N

if (*maxValue(bottom(a))* $\geq b$)	;; Maximum in bottom exceeds b
$\quad j \leftarrow a\sqrt{N} + Succ(bottom(a), b)$	;; Search in bottom list
else	;; Maximum in bottom structure smaller than b
$\quad z \leftarrow Succ(top, a+1)$	;; Compute temporary
$\quad j \leftarrow c\sqrt{z} + minValue(bottom(z))$	;; Search in next-to-bottom
return j	;; Return obtained value

Algorithm 3.9

Finding the successor in a VAN EMDE BOAS PRIORITY QUEUE.

Procedure Insert
Input: VAN EMDE BOAS PRIORITY QUEUE structure T_N, $i = a\sqrt{N} + b$
Side Effect: Updated VAN EMDE BOAS PRIORITY QUEUE structure T_N

if $(Size(bottom(a)) = 0)$;; Bottom structure empty
    $Insert(top, a)$;; Recursive call
$Insert(bottom, b)$;; Insert element to bottom structure

Algorithm 3.10

Inserting an element in a VAN EMDE BOAS PRIORITY QUEUE.

Procedure Delete
Input: VAN EMDE BOAS PRIORITY QUEUE structure T_N, $i = a\sqrt{N} + b$
Side Effect: Updated VAN EMDE BOAS PRIORITY QUEUE structure T_N

$Delete(bottom, b)$;; Remove element from bottom structure
if $(Size(bottom(a)) = 0)$;; Bottom structure now empty
    $Delete(top, a)$;; Recursive call

Algorithm 3.11

Deleting an element from a VAN EMDE BOAS PRIORITY QUEUE.

---

on $\{0, 1, 2, 3\}$ based on the set of possible prefixes in the binary encoding of the values in S. Set *bottom* is a vector of 2-structures (based on the suffixes of the binary state encodings in S) with $bottom(0) = \{2, 3\}$, $bottom(1) = \{3\}$, $bottom(2) = \{2\}$, and $bottom(3) = \{1\}$, since $(2)_2 = 00|10$, $(3)_2 = 00|11$, $(7)_2 = 01|11$, $(10)_2 = 10|10$, and $(13)_2 = 11|01$. Representing *top* as a 2-structure implies $k = 2$ and $N = 4$, such that the representation of $\{0, 1, 2, 3\}$ with $(0)_2 = 0|0$, $(1)_2 = 0|1$, $(2)_2 = 1|0$, and $(3)_2 = 1|1$ leads to a sub-*top* structure on $\{0, 1\}$ and two sub-*bottom* structures $bottom(0) = \{0, 1\}$ and $bottom(1) = \{0, 1\}$.

To realize the structures in practice, a mixed representation of the element set is appropriate. On one hand, a doubly connected linked list contains the elements sorted according to the values they have in the universe. On the other hand, a bitvector b is devised, with bit i denoting if an element with value b_i is contained in the list. The two structures are connected via links that point from each nonzero element to an item in the doubly connected list. The mixed representation (bitvector and doubly ended leaf list) for the earlier 4-structure (without unrolling the references to the single *top* and four *bottom* structures) is shown Figure 3.5.

3.1.2 Heap Data Structures

Let us now assume that we can have arbitrary (e.g., floating-point) keys. Each operation in a priority queue then divides into compare-exchange steps. For this case, the most common implementation of a priority queue (besides a plain list) is a BINARY SEARCH TREE or a HEAP.

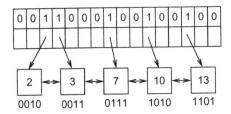

FIGURE 3.5

An example of a 4-structure for the VAN EMDE BOAS PRIORITY QUEUE.

Binary Search Trees

A BINARY SEARCH TREE is a binary tree implementation of a priority queue in which each internal node x stores an element. The keys in the left subtree of x are smaller than (or equal) to the one of x, and keys in the right subtree of x are larger than the one of x. Operations on a binary search tree take time proportional to the height of the tree. If the tree is a linear chain of nodes, linear comparisons might be induced in the worst-case. If the tree is balanced, a logarithmic number of operations for insertion and deletion suffice. Because balancing can be involved, in the following we discuss more flexible and faster data structures for implementing a priority queue.

Heaps

A HEAP is a complete binary tree; that is, all levels are completely filled except possibly the lowest one, which is filled from the left. This means that the depth of the tree (and every path length from the root to a leaf) is $\Theta(\lg n)$. Each internal node v satisfies the *heap property*: The key of v is smaller than or equal to the key of either of its two children.

Complete binary trees can be embedded in an array A as follows. The elements are stored levelwise from left to right in ascending cells of the array; $A[1]$ is the root; the left and right child of $A[i]$ are $A[2i]$ and $A[2i+1]$, respectively; and its parent is $A[\lfloor i/2 \rfloor]$. On most current microprocessors, the operation of multiplication by two can be realized as a single shift instruction. An example of a HEAP (including its array embedding) is provided in Figure 3.6.

To insert an element into a HEAP, we first tentatively place it in the next available leaf. As this might violate the heap property, we restore the heap property by swapping the element with its parent, if the parent's key is larger; then we check for the grandparent key, and so on, until the heap property is valid or the element reaches the root. Thus, *Insert* needs at most $O(\lg n)$ time. In the array embedding we start with the last unused index $n+1$ in array A and place key k into $A[n+1]$. Then, we climb up the ancestors until a correct HEAP is constructed. An implementation is provided in Algorithm 3.12.

DecreaseKey starts at the node x that has changed its value. This reference has to be maintained with the elements that are stored. Algorithm 3.13 shows a possible implementation.

To extract the minimum key is particularly easy: It is always stored at the root. However, we have to delete it and guarantee the heap property afterward. First, we tentatively fill the gap at the root with the last element on the bottom level of the tree. Then we restore the heap property using two comparisons per node while going down. This operation is referred to as *SiftDown*. That is, at a node we determine the minimum of the current key and that of the children; if the node is actually the minimum of the three, we are done, otherwise it is exchanged with the minimum, and the balancing

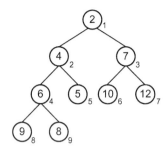

FIGURE 3.6

Example of a HEAP. Array indices are attached to the nodes.

Procedure Insert
Input: Key k, HEAP of size n embeded in Array A
Side Effect: Updated HEAP of size $n + 1$

$A[n + 1] \leftarrow k$; $x \leftarrow n + 1$;; Place element at empty place at end of array
while $(x \neq 1)$ **and** $(A[parent(x)] > A[x])$;; Unless finished or root visited
   Swap$(parent(x), x)$;; Exchange keys
   $x \leftarrow parent(x)$;; Climb up structure
$n \leftarrow n + 1$;; Increase size

Algorithm 3.12

Inserting an element into a HEAP.

Procedure DecreaseKey
Input: HEAP, index x of element that has improved to value k
Side Effect: Updated HEAP

$A[x] \leftarrow k$;; Update key value
while $(x \neq 1)$ **and** $(A[parent(x)] > A[x])$;; Unless finished or root visited
   Swap$(parent(x), x)$;; Exchange keys
   $x \leftarrow parent(x)$;; Climb up structure

Algorithm 3.13

Decreasing the key of an element in a HEAP.

---

continues at its previous position. Hence, the running time for *DeleteMin* is again $O(\lg n)$ in the worst-case. The implementation is displayed in Algorithm 3.14. Different *SiftDown* procedures are known: (1) top-down (as in Alg. 3.15); (2) bottom-up (first following the special path of smaller children to the leaf, then sifting up the root element as in *Insert*); or (3) with binary search (on the special path).

Procedure DeleteMin
Input: HEAP of size n
Output: Minimum element
Side Effect: Updated HEAP of size $n - 1$

$Swap(A[1],A[n])$	;; Swap last element to root position
$SiftDown(1)$	;; Restore heap property
$n \leftarrow n - 1$	;; Decrease size
return $A[n + 1]$	;; Return minimum element

Algorithm 3.14

Extracting the minimum element from a HEAP.

Procedure SiftDown
Input: HEAP of size n, index i
Output: Restored HEAP

$j \leftarrow 2i$	;; First child
while $(j \leq n)$	;; Leaf not reached
if $(j + 1 \leq n)$ **and** $(A[j + 1] \leq A[j])$	;; Compare both children
$j \leftarrow j + 1$	;; Select second child
if $(A[j] \leq A[i])$	;; Heap property violated
$Swap(i,j)$	;; Exchange elements at i and j
$i \leftarrow j$	;; Follow path
$j \leftarrow 2i$	;; First child
else return	;; Rearranging heap

Algorithm 3.15

Rearrange HEAP.

An implementation of the priority queue using a HEAP leads to an $O((e + n) \lg n)$ algorithm for A*, where n (resp. e) is the number of generated problem graph nodes (resp. edges). The data structure is fast in practice if n is small, say a few million elements (an accurate number depends on the efficiency of the implementation).

PAIRING HEAPS

A PAIRING HEAP is a heap-ordered (not necessarily binary) self-adjusting tree. The basic operation on a PAIRING HEAP is *pairing*, which combines two PAIRING HEAPS by attaching the root with the larger key to the other root as its left-most child. More precisely, for two PAIRING HEAPS with respective root values k_1 and k_2, pairing inserts the first as the left-most subtree of the second if $k_1 > k_2$, and otherwise inserts the second into the first as its left-most subtree. Pairing takes constant time and the minimum is found at the root.

In a multiway tree representation realizing the priority queue operations is simple. Insertion pairs the new node with the root of the heap. *DecreaseKey* splits the node and its subtree from the heap (if the node is not the root), decreases the key, and then pairs it with the root of the heap. Delete splits the node to be deleted and its subtree, performs a *DeleteMin* on the subtree, and pairs the resulting tree with the root of the heap. *DeleteMin* removes and returns the root, and then, in pairs, pairs the remaining trees. Then, the remaining trees from right to left are incrementally paired (see Alg. 3.16).

Since the multiple-child representation is difficult to maintain, the child-sibling binary tree representation for PAIRING HEAPS is often used, in which siblings are connected as follows. The left link of a node accesses its first child, and the right link of a node accesses its next sibling, so that the value of a node is less than or equal to all the values of nodes in its left subtree. It has been shown that in this representation *Insert* takes $O(1)$ and *DeleteMin* takes $O(\lg n)$ amortized, and *DecreaseKey* takes at least $\Omega(\lg \lg n)$ and at most $O(2^{\sqrt{\lg \lg n}})$ steps.

WEAK HEAPS

A WEAK HEAP is obtained by relaxing the HEAP requirements. It satisfies three conditions: the key of a node is smaller than or equal to all elements to its right, the root has no left child, and leaves are found on the last two levels only.

The array representation uses extra bits $Reverse[i] \in \{0,1\}$, $i \in \{0,\ldots,n-1\}$. The location of the left child is located at $2i + Reverse[i]$ and the right child is found at $2i + 1 - Reverse[i]$. By flipping $Reverse[i]$ the locations of the left child and the right child are exchanged. As an example take $A = [1,4,6,2,7,5,3,8,15,11,10,13,14,9,12]$ and $Reverse = [0,1,1,1,1,1,1,0,1,1,1,1,1,1,1]$ as an array representation of a WEAK HEAP. Its binary tree equivalent is shown in Figure 3.7.

Procedure DeleteMin
Input: PAIRING HEAP, h pointer to root
Output: Restored PAIRING HEAP

$h \leftarrow first(h)$; $parent(h) \leftarrow 0$;	;; Eliminate root node
$h_1 \leftarrow h$; $h_2 \leftarrow right(h)$	;; Pass 1
while(h_2)	;; Left to right
$\quad h \leftarrow right(right(h_1))$	;; Successive pairs of root nodes
$\quad pairing(h_1, h_2)$;	;; Link nodes
$\quad$ **if** (h)	;; First node exists
$\quad\quad$ **if**($right(h)$)	;; Second node exists
$\quad\quad\quad h_2 \leftarrow right(h)$; $h_1 \leftarrow h$;	;; Update pointers
$\quad\quad$ **else**	;; Second node does not exist
$\quad\quad\quad h_2 \leftarrow 0$;	;; Update pointers
$\quad$ **else**	;; First node does not exist
$\quad\quad h \leftarrow h_1$; $h_2 \leftarrow 0$	;; Update pointers
$h_1 \leftarrow parent(h)$; $h_2 \leftarrow h$;	;; Pass 2
while(h_1)	;; Right to left
$\quad pair(h_1, h_2)$;	;; Always the two right-most nodes
$\quad h \leftarrow h_1$; $h_2 \leftarrow h_1$; $h_1 \leftarrow parent(h_1)$;	;; Update pointers
return h;	;; Pointer to the very first node

Algorithm 3.16

Rearrange PAIRING HEAP.

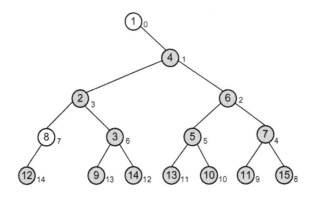

FIGURE 3.7

Example of a WEAK HEAP. Reflected nodes are shown in gray.

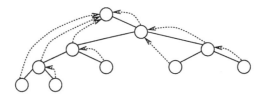

FIGURE 3.8

Grandparent relationship in a WEAK HEAP indicated using dashed arrows.

The function *Grandparent* is defined as $Grandparent(i) = Grandparent(parent(i))$ in case i is a left child, and $parent(i)$ if i is a right one. In a WEAK HEAP, $Grandparent(i)$ refers to the index of the deepest element known to be smaller than or equal to the one at i. An illustration is given in Figure 3.8.

Let node v be the root of a balanced tree T and let node u with the left subtree of T and v with the right subtree of T each form a WEAK HEAP. *Merging* u and v yields a new WEAK HEAP. If $A[u] \leq A[v]$ then the tree with root u and right child v is a WEAK HEAP. If, however, $A[v] < A[u]$ we swap $A[v]$ with $A[u]$ and reflect the subtrees in T (see Fig. 3.9, right). Algorithm 3.17 provides the pseudo-code implementation for *Merge* and *Grandparent*.

To restore the WEAK HEAP all subtrees corresponding to grandchildren of the root are combined. Algorithm 3.18 shows the implementation of this *Merge-Forest* procedure. The element at position m serves as a root node. We traverse the grandchildren of the root in which the second largest element is located. Then, in a bottom-up traversal, the WEAK HEAP property is restored by a series of *Merge* operations.

For *DeleteMin* we restore the WEAK HEAP property after exchanging the root element with the last one in the underlying array. Algorithm 3.19 gives an implementation.

To construct a WEAK HEAP from scratch all nodes at index i for decreasing i are merged to their grandparents, resulting in the minimal number of $n-1$ comparisons.

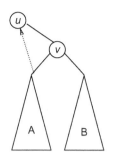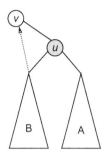

FIGURE 3.9

Merging operation in a WEAK HEAP.

Procedure Grandparent
Input: Index j
Output: Index for the grandparent for j

while $(Even(j))$ $j \leftarrow j/2$;; Left child
return $\lfloor j/2 \rfloor$;; Right child

Procedure Merge
Input: Indices i and j, i is (virtual) grandparent of j
Output: Combined sub–WEAK HEAPS rooted at i and j

if $(A[i] > A[j])$;; Wrong order
    $Swap(i,j)$; $Reverse[j] \leftarrow \neg Reverse[j]$;; Swap elements and flip bit

Algorithm 3.17

Implementation of different subroutines for WEAK HEAPS.

Procedure Merge-Forest
Input: Index m
Side Effect: Restored WEAK HEAP in a bottom-up merging phase

$x \leftarrow 1$;; Start at second index
while $(2x + Reverse[x] < m)$ $x \leftarrow 2x + Reverse[x]$;; Go left
while $(x > 0)$ $Merge(m,x)$; $x \leftarrow \lfloor x/2 \rfloor$;; Climb up

Algorithm 3.18

Restoration of WEAK HEAPS.

For *Insert* given a key k, we start with the last unused index x in array A and place k into $A[x]$. Then we climb up the grandparents until the WEAK HEAP property is satisfied (see Alg. 3.20). On the average, the path length of grandparents from a leaf node to a root is approximately half of the depth of the tree.

Procedure DeleteMin
Input: WEAK HEAP of size n
Output: Minimum element
Side Effect: Updated WEAK HEAP of size $n - 1$

$Swap(A[0], A[n - 1])$;; Swap last element to root position
$Merge\text{-}Forest(0)$;; Restore WEAK HEAP property
$n \leftarrow n - 1$;; Decrease size
return $A[n]$;; Return minimum element

Algorithm 3.19

Extracting the minimum element from a WEAK HEAP.

Procedure Insert
Input: Key k, WEAK HEAP of size n
Side Effect: Updated WEAK HEAP of size $n + 1$

$A[n] \leftarrow k; x \leftarrow n$;; Place element at empty place at end of array
$Reverse[x] \leftarrow 0$;; Initialize bit
while $(x \neq 0)$ **and** $(A[Grandparent(x)] > A[x])$;; Unless finished or root node found
    $Swap(Grandparent(x), x)$;; Exchange keys
    $Reverse[x] \leftarrow \neg Reverse[x]$;; Rotate subtree rooted at x
    $x \leftarrow Grandparent(x)$;; Climb up structure
$n \leftarrow n + 1$;; Increase size

Algorithm 3.20

Inserting an element into a WEAK HEAP.

For the *DecreaseKey* operation we start at the node x that has changed its value. Algorithm 3.21 shows an implementation.

FIBONACCI HEAPS

A FIBONACCI HEAP is an involved data structure with a detailed presentation that exceeds the scope of this book. In the following, therefore, we only motivate FIBONACCI HEAPS.

Intuitively, FIBONACCI HEAPS are relaxed versions of BINOMIAL QUEUES, which themselves are extensions to BINOMIAL TREES. A BINOMIAL TREE B_n is a tree of height n with 2^n nodes in total and $\binom{n}{i}$ nodes in depth i. The structure of B_n is found by unifying 2-structure B_{n-1}, where one is added as an additional successor to the second.

BINOMIAL QUEUES are unions of heap-ordered BINOMIAL TREES. An example is shown in Figure 3.10. Tree B_i is represented in queue Q if the ith bit in the binary representation of n is set. The partition of a BINOMIAL QUEUE structure Q into trees B_i is unique as there is only one binary representation of a given number. Since the minimum is always located at the root of one B_i, operation *Min* takes $O(\lg n)$ time. BINOMIAL QUEUES Q_1 and Q_2 of sizes n_1 and n_2 are *meld* by simulating binary addition of n_1 and n_2. This corresponds to a parallel scan of the root lists of Q_1 and Q_2. If

---

Procedure DecreaseKey
Input: WEAK HEAP, index x of element that has improved to k
Side Effect: Updated WEAK HEAP

$A[x] \leftarrow k$;; Update key value
while $(x \neq 0)$ **and** $(A[Grandparent(x)] > A[x])$;; Unless finished or root node found
   $Swap(Grandparent(x), x)$;; Exchange keys
   $Reverse[x] \leftarrow \neg Reverse[x]$;; Rotate subtree rooted at x
   $x \leftarrow Grandparent(x)$;; Climb up structure

Algorithm 3.21

Decreasing the key of an element in a WEAK HEAP.

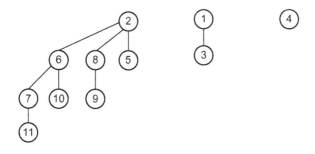

FIGURE 3.10

Example of a BINOMIAL QUEUE.

$n \sim n_1 + n_2$ then meld can be performed in time $O(\lg n)$. Having to meld the queues $Q_1 = (B_2, B_1, B_0)$ and $Q_2 = (B_0)$ leads to a queue $Q_3 = (B_3)$.

BINOMIAL QUEUES are themselves priority queues. Operations *Insert* and *DeleteMin* both use procedure *meld* as a subroutine. The former creates a tree B_0 with one element, and the latter extracts tree B_i containing the minimal element and splits it into its subtrees $B_0, \ldots, B_{i-1}$. In both cases the resulting trees are merged with the remaining queue to perform the update. *DecreaseKey* for element v updates the BINOMIAL TREE B_i in which v is located by propagating the element change bottom-up. All operations run in $O(\lg n)$.

A FIBONACCI HEAP is a collection of heap-ordered BINOMIAL TREES, maintained in the form of a circular doubly linked unordered list of root nodes. In difference to BINOMIAL QUEUES, more than one BINOMIAL TREE of rank i may be represented in one FIBONACCI HEAP. Consolidation traverses the linear list and merges trees of the same rank (each rank is unique). For this purpose, an additional array is devised that supports finding the trees of the same rank in the root list. The minimum element in a FIBONACCI HEAP is accessible in $O(1)$ time through a pointer in the root list. *Insert* performs a meld operation with a singleton tree.

For the critical operation *consolidate* (see Algorithm 3.22) a node is marked if it loses a child. Before it is marked twice, a *cut* is performed, which separates the node from its parent. The subtree of the node is inserted in the root list (where the node becomes unmarked again). The cut may *cascade* as it is propagated to the parent node. An example for a cascading cut is shown in Figure 3.11. Nodes

---

Procedure Consolidate
Input: FIBONACCI HEAP, of size n, bitvector o, p
Side Effect: Simplified FIBONACCI HEAP of size $n + 1$

$\Delta \leftarrow 1 + 1.45 \lg n$	;; Heuristic degree
if ($|o| \le \Delta$) **return**	;; loop, if only a few trees
$r \leftarrow head$	;; Start at head pointer of list
do	;; Construct temporary array A and bitvectors
$d \leftarrow degree(r)$	;; Binomial tree size
$set(o,d)$	;; Set occupancy bit
if($A[d]$)	;; List not empty
$set(p,d)$	;; Set bit in pairs bitvector
$link(r) \leftarrow A[d]$; $A[d] \leftarrow r$; $r \leftarrow right(r)$	;; Progress to next element
while($r \ne head$)	;; Circular list completely processed
while($|p|$)	;; Bits in pairs bitvector exist
$d \leftarrow Select(p)$	;; Choose any bit
$x \leftarrow A[d]$; $y \leftarrow link(x)$; $link(x) \leftarrow 0$	;; Remove x
$z \leftarrow link(y)$; $link(y) \leftarrow 0$; $A[d] \leftarrow z$	;; Remove y
if ($z = 0$)	;; List empty
$clear(o,d)$; $clear(p,d)$	;; Delete bit in bitvectors
else if($link(z) = 0$) $clear(p,d)$	;; Delete bit in pair bitvector
$set(o,d+1)$	;; Delete bit in occupancy bitvector
if ($A[d+1]$) $set(p,d+1)$	;; Set bit in pairs bitvector next degree
if ($x \le y$)	;; Key comparison
$Swap(x,y)$	;; Exchange links
$Cut(x,y)$	;; Cut x and join y with x
$link(y) \leftarrow A[d+1]$ $A[d+1] \leftarrow y$	;; Insert y
if ($head = x$) $head \leftarrow y$	;; New head of root list

Algorithm 3.22

Consolidation with bitvectors and heuristic factor in a FIBONACCI HEAP.

---

with the keys 3, 6, and 8 are already marked. Now we decrease the key 9 to 1, so that 3, 6, and 8 will lose their second child.

DecreaseKey performs the update on the element in the heap-ordered tree. It removes the updated node from the child list of its parent and inserts it into the root list while updating the minimum. *DeleteMin* extracts the minimum and includes all subtrees into the root list and consolidates it.

A heuristic parameter can be set to call consolidation less frequently. Moreover, a bitvector can improve the performance of consolidation, as it avoids additional links and faster access to the trees of the same rank to be merged. In an eager variant Fibonacci heaps maintain the consolidation heap store at any time.

RELAXED WEAK QUEUES

RELAXED WEAK QUEUES are worst-case efficient priority queues, by means that all running times of FIBONACCI HEAPS are worst-case instead of amortized.

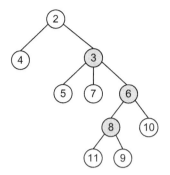

FIGURE 3.11

Cascading cut in heap-ordered tree.

WEAK QUEUES contribute to the observation that PERFECT WEAK HEAPS inherit a one-to-one correspondence to BINOMIAL QUEUES by only taking edges that are defined by the *Grandparent* relation. Note that in PERFECT WEAK HEAPS the right subtree of the root is a complete binary tree. A WEAK QUEUE stores n elements and is a collection of disjoint (nonembedded) PERFECT WEAK HEAPS based on the binary representation of $n = \sum_{i=0}^{\lfloor \lg n \rfloor} c_i 2^i$. In its basic form, a WEAK QUEUE contains a PERFECT WEAK HEAP H_i of size 2_i if and only if $c_i = 1$.

RELAXED WEAK QUEUES relax the requirement of having exactly one WEAK HEAP of a given rank in the WEAK QUEUE and allow some inconsistent elements that violate the WEAK HEAP property. A structure (of logarithmic size) called the *heap store* maintains PERFECT WEAK HEAPS of the same rank similar to FIBONACCI HEAPS. At most two heaps per rank suffice to efficiently realize injection and ejection of the heaps. To keep the worst-case complexity bounds, merging WEAK HEAPS of the same rank is delayed by maintaining the following structural property on the sequence of numbers of PERFECT WEAK HEAPS of the same rank.

The *rank sequence* $(r_{-1}, r_0, \ldots, r_k) \in \{0, 1, 2\}^{k+1}$ is *regular* if any digit 2 is preceded by a digit 0, possibly having some digits 1 in between. A subsequence of the form $(01^l 2)$ is called a *block*. That is, every digit 2 must be part of a block, but there can be digits, 0s and 1s, that are not part of a block. For example, the rank sequence (1011202012) contains three blocks. For injecting a WEAK HEAP, we join the first two WEAK HEAPS that are of the same size, if there are any. They are found by scanning the rank sequence. For $O(1)$ access, a stack of pending joins, the so-called *join schedule* implements the rank sequence of pending joins. Then we insert the new WEAK HEAP, which will preserve the regularity of the rank sequence. For ejection, the smallest WEAK HEAP is eliminated from the heap sequence and, if this PERFECT WEAK HEAP forms a pair with some other PERFECT WEAK HEAP, the top of the join schedule is also popped.

To keep the complexity for *DecreaseKey* constant, resolving WEAK HEAP order violations is also delayed. The primary purpose of a *node store* is to keep track and reduce the number of *potential violation nodes* at which the key may be smaller than the key of its grandparent. A node that is a potential violation node is *marked*. A marked node is *tough* if it is the left child of its parent and also the parent is marked. A chain of consecutive tough nodes followed by a single nontough marked node is called a *run*. All tough nodes of a run are called its *members*; the single nontough marked node of that run is called its *leader*. A marked node that is neither a member nor a leader of a run is called a *singleton*. To summarize, we can divide the set of all nodes into four disjoint node type categories: unmarked nodes, run members, run leaders, and singletons.

A pair *(type, height)* with *type* being either unmarked, member, leader, or singleton and *height* being a value in $\{0, 1, \ldots, \lfloor \lg n \rfloor - 1\}$ denotes the *state* of a node. Transformations induce a constant number of state transitions. A simple example of such a transformation is a *join*, where the height of the new root must be increased by one. Other operations are cleaning, parent, sibling, and pair transformations (see Fig. 3.12). A *cleaning transformation* rotates a marked left child to a marked right one, provided its neighbor and parent are unmarked. A *parent transformation* reduces the number of marked nodes or pushes the marking one level up. A *sibling transformation* reduces the markings by eliminating two markings in one level, while generating a new marking one level up. A *pair transformation* has a similar effect, but also operates on disconnected trees.

All transformations run in constant time. The node store consists of different list items containing the type of the node marking, which can either be a *fellow*, a *chairman*, a *leader*, or a *member* of a run, where fellows and chairmen refine the concept of singletons. A fellow is a marked node, with an unmarked parent, if it is a left child. If more than one fellow has a certain height, one of them is elected a chairman. The list of chairmen is required for performing a singleton transformation. Nodes that are left children of a marked parent are members, while the parent of such runs is entitled the leader. The list of leaders is needed for performing a run transformation.

The four primitive transformations are combined to a *λ-reduction*, which invokes either a *singleton* or *run transformation* (see Alg. 3.23). A singleton transformation reduces the number of markings in a given level by one, not producing a marking in the level above; or it reduces the number of markings in a level by two, producing a marking in the level above. A similar observation applies to a run transformation, so that in both transformations the number of markings is reduced by at least one in a constant amount of work and comparisons. A λ-reduction is invoked once for each *DecreaseKey* operation. It invokes either a singleton or a run transformation and is enforced, once the number of marked nodes exceeds $\lfloor \lg n \rfloor - 1$.

Table 3.1 measures the time in μ-seconds (for each operation) for inserting n integers (randomly assigned to values from n to $2n - 1$). Next, their values are decreased by 10 and then the minimum element is deleted n times. (The lack of results in one row is due to the fact that FIBONACCI HEAPS ran out of space.)

Table 3.1 Performance of priority queue data structures on n integers.

	$n = 25'000'000$			$n = 50'000'000$		
	Insert	**Dec.Key**	**Del.Min**	**Insert**	**Dec.Key**	**Del.Min**
RELAXED WEAK QUEUES	0.048	0.223	4.38	0.049	0.223	5.09
PAIRING HEAPS	0.010	0.020	6.71	0.009	0.020	8.01
FIBONACCI HEAPS	0.062	0.116	6.98	—	—	—
HEAPS	0.090	0.064	5.22	0.082	0.065	6.37

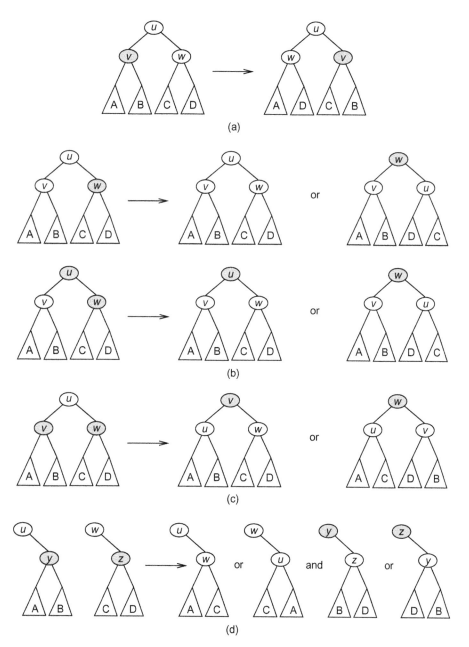

FIGURE 3.12

Primitives used in a λ-reduction: (a) cleaning transformation, (b) parent transformation, (c) sibling transformation, and (d) pair transformation.

Procedure λ-Reduction
In/Output: RELAXED WEAK QUEUE

if (*chairmen* ≠ ∅)	;; Fellow pair on some level
f ← *first(chairmen)*; *firstparent* ← *parent(f)*	;; 1st item and its parent
if (*left(firstparent)* = *f* **and** *marked(right(firstparent))* **or**	;; 2 childs . . .
left(firstparent) ≠ *f* **and** *marked(left(firstparent))*)	;; . . . marked
siblingtrans(firstparent); **return**	;; Case (c) suffices
s ← *second(chairmen)*; *secondparent* ← *parent(s)*	;; 2nd item
if (*left(secondparent)* = *s* **and** *marked(right(secondparent))* **or**	;; 2 childs . . .
left(secondparent) ≠ *s* **and** *marked(left(secondparent))*)	;; . . . are marked
siblingtrans(secondparent); **return**	;; Case (c) suffices
if (*left(firstparent)* = *first*) *cleaningtrans(firstparent)*	;; Toggle children marking
if (*left(secondparent)* = *second*) *cleaningtrans(secondparent)*	;; Case (a) applies
if (*marked(firstparent)* **or** *root(firstparent)*)	;; Parent also marked
parenttrans(firstparent); **return**	;; Case (b) applies
if (*marked(secondparent)* **or** *root(secondparent)*)	;; Parent also marked
parenttrans(secondparent); **return**	;; Case (b) applies
pairtrans(firstparent, secondparent)	;; Case (d) applies
else if (*leaders* ≠ ∅)	;; Leader exists on some level
leader ← *first(leaders)* ; *leaderparent* ← *parent(leader)*	;; Select leader and parent
if (*leader* = *right(leaderparent)*)	;; Leader is right child
parenttrans(leaderparent)	;; Transform into left child
if (¬*marked(leaderparent)* ∧ *marked(leader)*)	;; Parent also marked
if (*marked(left(leaderparent))*) *siblingtrans(leaderparent)*; **return**	;; Case (c)
parenttrans(leaderparent)	;; Case (b) applies first time
if (*marked(right(leaderparent))*) *parenttrans(leader)*	;; Case (b) applies again
else	;; Leader is left child
sibling ← *right(leaderparent)*	;; Temporary variable
if (*marked(sibling)*) *siblingtrans(leaderparent)*; **return**	;; Case (c) suffices
cleaningtrans(leaderparent)	;; Toggle marking of leader's children
if (*marked(right(sibling))*) *siblingtrans(sibling)*; **return**	;; Case (c) suffices
cleaningtrans(sibling)	;; Toggle marking of sibling's children
parenttrans(sibling)	;; Case (b) applies
if (*marked(left(leaderparent))*) *siblingtrans(leaderparent)*	;; Case (c) suffices

Algorithm 3.23

Reducing number of markings in a RELAXED WEAK QUEUE.

3.2 **HASH TABLES**

Duplicate detection is essential for state space search to avoid redundant expansions. As no access to all states is given in advance, a dynamically growing dictionary to represent sets of states has to be provided. For the *Closed* list, we memorize nodes that have been expanded and for each generated state we check whether it is already stored. We also have to search for duplicates in the *Open* list, so another dictionary is needed to assist lookups in the priority queue. The DICTIONARY problem consists of providing a data structure with the operations *Insert*, *Lookup*, and *Delete*. In search applications, deletion is not always necessary. The slightly easier *membership* problem neglects any associated information. However, many implementations of membership data structures can be easily generalized to dictionary data structures by adding a pointer. Instead of maintaining two dictionaries for *Open* and *Closed* individually, more frequently, the *Open* and *Closed* lists are maintained together in a combined dictionary.

There are two major techniques for implementing dictionaries: (balanced) search trees and hashing. The former class of algorithms can achieve all operations in $O(\lg n)$ worst-case time and $O(n)$ storage space, where n is the number of stored elements. Generally, for hashing constant time for lookup operations is required, so we concentrate on hash dictionaries. We first introduce different hash functions and algorithms. *Incremental hashing* will be helpful to enhance the efficiency of computing hash addresses. In *perfect hashing* we consider bijective mapping of states to addresses. In *universal hashing*, we consider a class of hash functions that will be useful for more general perfect hashing strategies. Because memory is a big concern in state space search we will also address memory-saving dictionary data structures. At the end of this section, we show how to save additional space by being imprecise (saying *in the dictionary* when it is not).

3.2.1 Hash Dictionaries

Hashing serves as a method to store and retrieve states $u \in S$ efficiently. A *dictionary* over a universe $S = \{0, \ldots, N-1\}$ of possible keys is a partial function from a subset $R \subseteq S$ (the *stored keys*) to some set I (the associated information). In state space hashing, every state $x \in S$ is assigned to a key $k(x)$, which is a part of the representation that uniquely identifies S. Note that every state representation can be interpreted as a binary integer number. Then not all integers in the universe will correspond to valid states. For simplicity, in the following we will identify states with their keys.

The keys are mapped into a linear array $T[0..m-1]$, called the *hash table*. The mapping $h : S \to \{0, \ldots, m-1\}$ is called the *hash function* (see Fig. 3.13). The lack of injectiveness yields *address collisions*; that is, different states that are mapped to the same table location. Roughly speaking, hashing is all about computing keys and detecting collisions. The overall time complexity for hashing depends on the time to compute the hash function, the collision strategy, and the ratio between the number of stored keys and the hash table size, but usually not on the size of the keys.

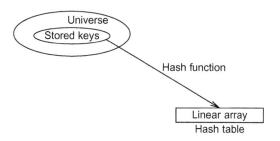

FIGURE 3.13

Basic principle of hashing.

The choice of a good hash function is the central problem for hashing. In the worst-case, all keys are mapped to the same address; for example, for all $x \in S$ we have $h(x) = const$, with $0 \leq const < m$. In the best case, we have no collisions and the access time to an element is constant. A special case is that of a fixed stored set R, and a hash table of at least m entries; then a suitable hash function is $h(x_i) = i$ with $x_i \in R$ and $0 \leq i < m$.

These two extreme cases are more of theoretical interest. In practice, we can avoid the worst-case by a proper design of the hash function.

3.2.2 Hash Functions

A *good* hash function is one that can be computed efficiently and minimizes the number of address collisions. The returned addresses for given keys should be uniformly distributed, even if the set of chosen keys in S is not, which is almost always the case.

Given a hash table of size m and the sequence $k_1, \ldots, k_n$ of keys to be inserted, for each pair (k_i, k_j) of keys, $i, j \in \{1, \ldots, n\}$, we define a random variable

$$X_{ij} = \begin{cases} 1 & \text{if } h(k_i) = h(k_j) \\ 0 & \text{otherwise} \end{cases}.$$

Then $X = \sum_{i<j} X_{ij}$ is the sum of collisions. Assuming a random hash function with uniform distribution, the expected value of X is

$$E(X) = E\left(\sum_{i<j} X_{ij}\right) = \sum_{i<j} E(X_{ij}) = \sum_{i<j} \frac{1}{m} = \binom{n}{2} \cdot \frac{1}{m}.$$

Using a hash table of size $m = 10^7$, for 1 million elements, we expect about $\binom{10^6}{2} \cdot \frac{1}{m} \approx 4,999$ address collisions.

Remainder Method

If we can extend S to $\mathbb{Z}$, then $\mathbb{Z}/m\mathbb{Z}$ is the *quotient space* with equivalence classes $[0], \ldots, [m-1]$ induced by the relation

$$z \sim w \text{ if and only if } z \bmod m = w \bmod m.$$

Therefore, a mapping $h : S \to \{0, 1, \ldots, m-1\}$ with $h(x) = x \bmod m$ distributes S on T. For the uniformity, the choice of m is important; for example, if m is even then $h(x)$ is even if and only if x is.

The choice $m = r^w$, for some $w \in \mathbb{N}$, is also not appropriate, since for $x = \sum_{i=0}^{l} a_i r^i$ we have

$$x \bmod m = \left(\sum_{i=w}^{l} a_i r^i + \sum_{i=0}^{w-1} a_i r^i\right) \bmod m = \left(\sum_{i=0}^{w-1} a_i r^i\right) \bmod m$$

This means that the distribution takes only the last w digits into account.

A good choice for m is a prime that does not divide a number $r^i \pm j$ for small j, because $m \mid r^i \pm j$ is equivalent to $r^i \bmod m = \mp j$ so that (case $+$)

$$x \bmod m = j \cdot \sum_{i=0}^{l} a_i \bmod m;$$

that is, keys with same sum of digits are mapped to the same address.

Multiplicative Hashing

In this approach the product of the key and an irrational number ϕ is computed and the fractional part is preserved, resulting in a mapping into $[0, 1) \subset \mathbb{R}$. This can be used for a hash function that maps the key x to $\{0, \ldots, m-1\}$ as follows:

$$h(x) = \lfloor m(x\phi - \lfloor x\phi \rfloor) \rfloor.$$

One of the best choices for ϕ for *multiplicative hashing* is $(\sqrt{5} - 1)/2 \approx 0.6180339887$, the *golden ratio*. As an example take $k = 123{,}456$ and $m = 10{,}000$; then $h(k) = \lfloor 10{,}000 \cdot (123456 \cdot \phi) \rfloor = 41$.

Rabin and Karp Hashing

For incremental hashing based on the idea of Rabin and Karp, states are interpreted as strings over a fixed alphabet. In case no natural string representation exists it is possible to interpret the binary representation of a state as a string over the alphabet $\{0, 1\}$. To increase the effectiveness of the method the string of bits may be divided into blocks. For example, a state vector consisting of bytes yields 256 different *characters*.

The idea of Rabin and Karp originates in matching a pattern string $M[1..m] \in \Sigma^m$ to a text $T[1..n] \in \Sigma^n$. For a certain hash function h, pattern M is mapped to the number $h(M)$, assuming that $h(M)$ fits into a single memory cell and can be processed in constant time. For $1 \le j \le n - m + 1$ the algorithm checks if $h(M) = h(T[j..j+m-1])$. Due to possible collisions, this check is a necessary but not a sufficient condition for a valid match of M and $T[j..j+m-1]$. To validate that the match is indeed valid in case $h(M) = h(T[j..j+m-1])$, a character-by-character comparison has to be performed.

To compute $h(T[j+1..j+m])$ in constant time, the value is calculated incrementally—the algorithm takes the known value $h(T[j..j+m-1])$ into account to determine $h(T[j+1..j+m])$ with a few CPU operations. The hash function has to be chosen carefully to be suited to the incremental computation; for example, linear hash functions based on a radix number representation such as $h(M) = \sum_{i=1}^{m} M[i] r^i \bmod q$ are suitable, where q is a prime and the radix r is equal to $|\Sigma|$.

Algorithmically, the approach works as follows. Let q be a sufficiently large prime and $q > m$. We assume that numbers of size $q \cdot |\Sigma|$ fit into a memory cell, so that all operations can be performed with single precision arithmetic. To ease notation, we identify characters in Σ with their order. The algorithm of Rabin and Karp as presented in Algorithm 3.24 performs the matching process.

The algorithm is correct due to the following observation.

Procedure Rabin-Karp
Input: String T, pattern M, alphabet Σ
Output: Occurrence of M in T

$p \leftarrow t \leftarrow 0; u \leftarrow |\Sigma|^{m-1}$ *mod q*	;; Initialization
for each i **in** $\{1,\ldots,m\}$	;; Traverse pattern positions
$\quad p \leftarrow (|\Sigma| \cdot p + M[i])$ *mod q*	;; Precompute hash function of pattern
for each i **in** $\{1,\ldots,m\}$	;; Traverse text prefix
$\quad t \leftarrow (|\Sigma| \cdot p + T[i])$ *mod q*	;; Precompute hash function for text prefix
for each j **in** $\{1,\ldots,n-m+1\}$	;; Main comparison loop
$\quad$ **if** $(p = t)$	;; Hash function matches
$\quad\quad$ **if** $(check\ (M,T[j..j+m-1]))$	;; Exact string comparison required
$\quad\quad\quad$ **return** j	;; Pattern found at position j
$\quad$ **if** $(j \leq n-m)$	;; Text fully processed
$\quad\quad t \leftarrow ((t - T[j] \cdot u) \cdot |\Sigma| + T[j+m])$ *mod q*	;; Shift using Horner's rule

Algorithm 3.24

Algorithm of Rabin and Karp.

Theorem 3.1. *(Correctness Rabin-Karp) Let the steps of Algorithm 3.24 be numbered wrt. the loop counter j. At the start of the jth iteration we have*

$$t_j = \left(\sum_{i=j}^{m+j-1} T[i]|\Sigma|^{m-i+j-1} \right) \bmod q.$$

Proof. Certainly, $t_1 = \left(\sum_{i=1}^{m} T[i]|\Sigma|^{m-i} \right) \bmod q$ and inductively we have

$$t_j = \left((t_{j-1} - T[j-1] \cdot u) \cdot |\Sigma| + T[j+m-1] \right) \bmod q$$

$$= \left(\left(\left(\sum_{i=j-1}^{m+j-2} T[i]|\Sigma|^{m-i+j-2} \right) - T[j-1] \cdot u \right) \cdot |\Sigma| + T[j+m-1] \right) \bmod q$$

$$= \left(\sum_{i=j}^{m+j-1} T[i]|\Sigma|^{m-i+j-1} \right) \bmod q. \qquad \blacksquare$$

As an example take $\Sigma = \{0,\ldots,9\}$ and $q = 13$. Furthermore, let $M = 31415$ and $T = 2359023141526739921$. The application of the mapping h is illustrated in Figure 3.14.

We see h produces collisions. The incremental computation works as follows.

$$h(14,152) \equiv (h(31,415) - 3 \cdot 10,000) \cdot 10 + 2 \ (mod \ 13)$$

$$\equiv (7 - 3 \cdot 3) \cdot 10 + 2 \ (mod \ 13) \equiv 8 \ (mod \ 13).$$

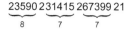

FIGURE 3.14

Example of Rabin-Karp hashing for string matching.

The computation of all hash addresses has a resulting running time of $O(n+m)$, which is also the best-case overall running time. In the worst-case, the matching is still of order $\Omega(nm)$, as the example problem of searching $M = 0^m$ in $T = 0^n$ shows.

Incremental Hashing

For a state space search, we have often the case that a state transition changes only a part of the representation. In this case, the computation of the hash function can be executed incrementally. We refer to this approach as *incremental state space hashing*. The alphabet Σ denotes the set of characters in the string to be hashed. In the state space search, the set Σ will be used for denoting the domain(s) of the state variables.

Take, for example, the FIFTEEN-PUZZLE. With $\Sigma = \{0, \ldots, 15\}$, a natural vector representation for state u is $(t_0, \ldots, t_{15}) \in \Sigma^{16}$, where $t_i = l$ means that the tile labeled with l is located at position i, and $l = 0$ is the blank. Because successor generation is fast and Manhattan distance heuristic can be computed incrementally in constant time (using a table addressed by the tile's label $l \in \Sigma \setminus \{0\}$, the tile's move direction $d \in \{U, D, L, R\}$, and the position $p \in \Sigma$ of the tile that is being moved), the computational burden is on computing the hash function.

One hash value of a FIFTEEN-PUZZLE state u is $h(u) = (\sum_{i=0}^{15} t_i \cdot 16^i) \bmod q$. Let state u' with representation $(t'_0, \ldots, t'_{15})$ be a successor of u. We know that there is only one transposition in the vectors t and t'. Let j be the position of the blank in u and k be the position of the blank in u'. We have $t'_j = t_k, t'_k = 0$, and for all $1 \leq i \leq 16$, with $i \neq j, i \neq k$, it holds that $t'_i = t_i$. Therefore,

$$h(u') = \left(\left(\sum_{i=0}^{15} t_i \cdot 16^i\right) - t_j \cdot 16^j + t'_j \cdot 16^j - t_k \cdot 16^k + t'_k \cdot 16^k\right) \bmod q$$

$$= \left(\left(\left(\sum_{i=0}^{15} t_i \cdot 16^i\right) \bmod q\right) - 0 \cdot 16^j + t'_j \cdot 16^j - t_k \cdot 16^k + 0 \cdot 16^k \bmod q\right) \bmod q$$

$$= (h(u) + (t'_j \cdot 16^j) \bmod q - (t_k \cdot 16^k) \bmod q) \bmod q.$$

To save time, we may precompute $(k \cdot 16^l) \bmod q$ for each k and l in $\{0, \ldots, 15\}$. If we were to store $(k \cdot 16^j) \bmod q - (k \cdot 16^l) \bmod q$ for each value of j, k, and l, we would save another addition. As $h(u) \in \{0, \ldots, q-1\}$ and $(k \cdot 16^j) \bmod q - (k \cdot 16^k) \bmod q \in \{0, \ldots, q-1\}$, we may further substitute the last *mod* by faster arithmetic operations.

As a particular case, we look at an instance of the FIFTEEN-PUZZLE, where the tile 12 is to be moved downward from its position 11 to position 15. We have $h(u') = (h(u) - 12 \cdot (16^{11}) \bmod q + 12 \cdot (16^{15}) \bmod q) \bmod q$.

Next we generalize our observations. The savings are larger, when the state vector grows. For the $(n^2 - 1)$-PUZZLE nonincremental hashing results in $\Omega(n^2)$ time, whereas in incremental hashing the efforts remain constant. Moreover, incremental hashing is available for many search problems that obey a static vector representation. Hence, we assume that state u is a vector $(u_1, \ldots, u_k)$ with u_i in finite domain Σ_i, $i \in \{1, \ldots, k\}$.

Theorem 3.2. (*Efficiency of Incremental Hashing*) *Let $I(a)$ be the set of indices in the state vector that change when applying a, and $I_{max} = \max_{a \in A} |I(a)|$. The hash value of v for successor u of v via a given the hash value for u is available in time:*

1. $O(|I(a)|)$; *using an $O(k)$-size table.*
2. $O(1)$; *using an $O(\binom{k}{I_{max}}) \cdot (\Sigma_{max})^{I_{max}})$-size table. where $\Sigma_{max} = \max_{1 \leq i \leq k}\{|\Sigma_i|\}$.*

Proof. We define $h(u) = \sum_{i=1}^{k} u_i M_i \mod q$ as the hash function, with $M_1 = 1$ and $M_i = |\Sigma_1| \cdot \ldots \cdot |\Sigma_{i-1}|$ for $1 < i \leq k$. For case 1 we store $M_i \mod q$ for all $1 \leq i \leq k$ in a precomputed table, so that $|I(a)|$ lookups are needed. For case 2 we compute $\sum_{j \in I(a)} -u_j M_j + v_j M_j \mod q$ for all possible actions $a = (u, v)$. The number of possible actions is bounded by $\binom{k}{I_{max}} \cdot (\Sigma_{max})^{I_{max}}$, since at most $\binom{k}{I_{max}}$ indices may change to at most $(\Sigma_{max})^{I_{max}}$ different values. ∎

Note that the number of possible actions is much smaller in practice. The effectiveness of incremental hashing relies on two factors: on the *state vector's locality* (i.e., how many state variables are affected by a state transition) and on the *node expansion efficiency* (i.e., the running time of all other operations to generate one successor). In the RUBIK'S CUBE, exploiting locality is limited. If we represent position and orientation of each subcube as a number in the state vector, then for each twist, 8 of the 20 entries will be changed. In contrast, for SOKOBAN the node expansion efficiency is small; as during move execution, the set of pushable balls has to be determined in linear time to the board layout, and the (incremental) computation of the minimum matching heuristic requires at least quadratic time in the number of balls.

For incremental hashing the resulting technique is very efficient. However, it can also have drawbacks, so take care. For example, as with ordinary hashing, the suggested schema induces collisions, which have to be resolved.

Universal Hash Functions

Universal hashing requires a set of hash functions to have on average a good distribution for any subset of stored keys. It is the basis for FKS and cuckoo hashing and has a lot of nice properties. Universal hashing is often used in a state space search, when restarting a randomized incomplete algorithm with a different hash function.

Let $\{0, \ldots, m-1\}$ be the set of hash addresses and $S \subseteq N$ be the set of possible keys. A set of hash function H is universal, if for all $x, y \in S$,

$$\frac{|\{h \in H \mid h(x) = h(y)\}|}{|H|} \leq 1/m.$$

The intuition in the design of universal hash functions is to include a suitable random number generator inside the hash computation. For example, the *Lehmer generator* refers to linear congruences.

It is one of the most common methods for generating random numbers. With respect to a triple of constants a, b, and c a sequence of pseudo-random numbers x_i is generated according to the recursion

$$x_0 \leftarrow b$$

$$x_{i+1} \leftarrow (ax_i + c) \bmod m \quad i \geq 0.$$

Universal hash functions lead to a good distribution of values on the average. If h is drawn randomly from H and S is the set of keys to be inserted in the hash table, the expected cost of each *Lookup*, *Insert*, and *Delete* operation is bounded by $(1 + |S|/m)$. We give an example of a class of universal hash functions. Let $S \subseteq \mathbb{N}$, p be prime with $p \geq |S|$. For $1 \leq a \leq p - 1, 0 \leq b \leq p - 1$, define

$$h_{a,b} = ((ax + b) \bmod p) \bmod m.$$

Then

$$H = \{h_{a,b} \mid 1 \leq a \leq p - 1, 0 \leq b \leq p - 1\}$$

is a set of universal hash functions. As an example, take $m = 3$ and $p = 5$. Then we have 20 functions in H:

$$
\begin{array}{cccc}
x+0 & 2x+0 & 3x+0 & 4x+0 \\
x+1 & 2x+1 & 3x+1 & 4x+1 \\
x+2 & 2x+2 & 3x+2 & 4x+2 \\
x+3 & 2x+3 & 3x+3 & 4x+3 \\
x+4 & 2x+4 & 3x+4 & 4x+4 \\
\end{array}
$$

all taken *mod 5 mod 3*. Hashing 1 and 4 yields the following address collisions:

$$(1 \cdot 1 + 0) \bmod 5 \bmod 3 = 1 = (1 \cdot 4 + 0) \bmod 5 \bmod 3$$
$$(1 \cdot 1 + 4) \bmod 5 \bmod 3 = 0 = (1 \cdot 4 + 4) \bmod 5 \bmod 3$$
$$(4 \cdot 1 + 0) \bmod 5 \bmod 3 = 1 = (4 \cdot 4 + 0) \bmod 5 \bmod 3$$
$$(4 \cdot 1 + 4) \bmod 5 \bmod 3 = 0 = (4 \cdot 4 + 4) \bmod 5 \bmod 3$$

To prove that H is universal, let us look at the probability that two keys $x \neq y$ are mapped to locations r and s by the inner part of the hash function,

$$P([(ax + b) = r(\bmod p)] \text{ and } [(ay + b) = s(\bmod p)]).$$

This means that $a(x - y) = r - s(\bmod p)$, which has exactly one solution $(\bmod p)$ since $Z_p^* = (\mathbb{Z}/p\mathbb{Z} \setminus \{[0]\}, \cdot)$ is a field (we needed $p \geq |S|$ to ensure that $x \neq y \bmod p$). Value r cannot be equal to s, since this would imply $a = 0$, contrary to the definition of the hash function. Therefore, we now assume $r \neq s$. Then there is a 1 in $(p - 1)$ chance that a has the right value. Given this value of a, we need $b = r - ax(\bmod p)$, and there is a $1/p$ chance that b gets this value. Consequently, the overall probability that the inner function maps x to r and y to s is $1/p(p-1)$.

Now, the probability that x and y collide is equal to this $1/p(p-1)$, times the number of pairs $r \neq s \in \{0, \ldots, p-1\}$ such that $r = s \pmod m$. We have p choices for r, and subsequently at most $\lceil p/m \rceil - 1$ choices for s (the -1 is for disallowing $s = r$). Using $\lceil v/w \rceil \leq v/w + 1 - 1/w$ for integers v and w, the product is at most $p(p-1)/m$.

Putting this all together, we obtain for the probability of a collision between x and y,

$$P((ax+b \bmod p) \bmod m = (ay+b \bmod p) \bmod m) \leq \frac{p(p-1)}{m} \cdot \frac{1}{p(p-1)} = \frac{1}{m}.$$

Perfect Hash Functions

Can we find a hash function h such that (besides the efforts to compute the hash function) all lookups require constant time? The answer is yes—this leads to *perfect hashing*. An injective mapping of R with $|R| = n \leq m$ to $\{1, \ldots, m\}$ is called a *perfect hash function*; it allows an access without collisions. If $n = m$ we have a *minimal perfect hash function*. The design of perfect hashing yields an optimal worst-case performance of $O(1)$ accesses. Since perfect hashing uniquely determines an address, a state S can often be reconstructed given $h(S)$.

If we invest enough space, perfect (and incremental) hash functions are not difficult to obtain. In the example of the EIGHT-PUZZLE for a state u in vector representation $(t_0, \ldots, t_8)$ we may choose $(\ldots((t_0 \cdot 9 + t_1) \cdot 9 + t_2) \ldots) \cdot 9 + t_8$ for $9^9 = 387{,}420{,}489$ different hash addresses (equivalent to about 46 megabytes space). Unfortunately, this approach leaves most hash addresses vacant. A better hash function is to compute the rank of the permutation in some given ordering, resulting in 9! states or about 44 kilobytes.

Lexicographic Ordering

The *lexicographic rank* of permutation π (of size N) is defined as $rank(\pi) = d_0 \cdot (N-1)! + d_1 \cdot (N-2)! + \cdots + d_{N-2} \cdot 1! + d_{N-1} \cdot 0!$, where the coefficients d_i are called the *inverted index* or *factorial base*.

By looking at a permutation tree it is easy to see that such a hash function exists. Leaves in the tree are all permutations and at each node in level i, the ith vector value is selected, reducing the range of available values in level $i+1$. This leads to an $O(N^2)$ algorithm. A linear algorithm for this maps a permutation to its factorial base $\sum_{i=0}^{k-1} d_i \cdot i!$ with d_i being equal to t_i minus the number of elements $t_j, j < i$ that are smaller than t_i; that is; $d_i = t_i - c_i$ with the number of *inversions* c_i being set to $|\{0 \leq l < t_i \mid l \in \{t_0, \ldots, t_{i-1}\}|$. For example, the lexicographic rank of permutation $(1,0,3,2)$ is equal to $(1-0) \cdot 3! + (0-0) \cdot 2! + (3-2) \cdot 1! + (2-2) \cdot 0! = 7$, corresponding to $c = (0,0,2,2)$ and $d = (1,0,1,0)$. The values c_i are computed in linear time using a table lookup in a 2^{k-1}-size table T. In the table T we store the number of ones in the binary representation of a value, $T(x) = \sum_{i=0}^{m} b_i$ with $(x)_2 = (b_m, \ldots, b_0)$. For computing the hash value, while processing vector position t_i we mark bit t_i in bitvector x (initially set to 0). Thus, x denotes the tiles we have seen so far and we can take $T(x_0, \ldots, x_{i-1})$ as the value for c_i. Since this approach consumes exponential space, time-space trade-offs have been discussed.

For the design of a minimum perfect hash function of the sliding-tile puzzles we observe that in a lexicographic ordering every two successive permutations have an alternating signature (parity of the number of inversions) and differ by exactly one transposition. For minimal perfect hashing a $(n^2 - 1)$-PUZZLE state to $\{0, \ldots, n^2!/2 - 1\}$ we consequently compute the lexicographic rank and divide it by 2. For unranking, we now have to determine which one of the two uncompressed permutations of the

---

Procedure Rank
Input: Depth N, permutation π, inverse permutation π^{-1}
Output: Rank of π
Side Effect: (π and π^{-1} are modified)

if ($N = 1$) **return** 0	;; End of recursion
$l \leftarrow \pi_{N-1}$	;; Memorize location
$Swap(\pi_{N-1}, \pi_{\pi_{N-1}^{-1}})$	;; Update in π
$Swap(\pi_l^{-1}, \pi_{N-1}^{-1})$	;; Update in π^{-1}
return $l \cdot (N-1)! + Rank(N-1, \pi, \pi^{-1})$	;; Recursive call

Algorithm 3.25

Rank operation for permutations.

---

puzzle is reachable. This amounts to finding the signature of the permutation, which allows us to separate solvable from insolvable states. It is computed as $sign(\pi) = (\sum_{i=0}^{N-1} d_i) \, mod \, 2$. For example, with $N = 4$ we have $sign(17) = (2 + 2 + 1) \, mod \, 2 = 1$.

There is one subtle problem with the blank. Simply taking the minimum perfect hash value for the alternation group in S_{n^2} does not suffice, since swapping a tile with the blank does not necessarily toggle the solvability status (e.g., it may be a move). To resolve this problem, we partition state space along the position of the blank. Let $B_0, \ldots, B_{n^2}$ denote the sets of blank-projected states. Then each B_i contains $(n^2 - 1)!/2$ elements. Given index i and the rank inside B_i, it is simple to reconstruct the state.

Myrvold Ruskey Ordering

We next turn to alternative permutation indices proposed by Myrvold and Ruskey. The basic motivation is the generation of a random permutation according to swapping π_i with π_r, where r is a random number uniformly chosen in $0, \ldots, i$, and i decreases from $N-1$ down to 1.

One (recursive) algorithm *Rank* is shown in Algorithm 3.25. The permutation π and its inverse π^{-1} are initialized according to the permutation, for which a rank has to be determined.

The inverse π^{-1} of π can be computed by setting $\pi_{\pi_i}^{-1} = i$, for all $i \in \{0, \ldots, k-1\}$. Take as an example permutation $\pi = \pi^{-1} = (1, 0, 3, 2)$. Then its rank is $2 \cdot 3! + Rank(102)$. This unrolls to $2 \cdot 3! + 2 \cdot 2! + 0 \cdot 1! + 0 \cdot 0! = 16$. It is also possible to compile a rank back into a permutation in linear time. The inverse procedure *Unrank*, initialized with the identity permutation, is shown in Algorithm 3.26. The depth value N is initialized with the size of the permutation, and the rank r is the value computed with Algorithm 3.25. (As a side effect, if the algorithm is terminated at the Nth step, the positions $N - l, \ldots, N - 1$ hold a random l-permutation of the numbers $\{0, \ldots, N - 1\}$.)

Algorithm 3.27 shows another (in this case nonrecursive) unrank algorithm proposed by Myrvold and Ruskey. It also detects the *parity* of the number of inversions (the *signature* of the permutation) efficiently and fits to the ranking function in Algorithm 3.28. All permutations of size $N = 4$ together with their signature and ranked according to the two approaches are listed in Table 3.2.

Theorem 3.3. *(Myrvold-Ruskey Permutation Signature) Given the Myrvold-Ruskey rank (as computed by Alg. 3.28), the signature of a permutation can be computed in $O(N)$ time within Algorithm 3.27.*

Procedure Unrank
Input: Value N, rank r, permutation π
Side Effect: Updated global permutation

if $(N = 0)$ **return**	;; End of recursion
$l \leftarrow \lfloor r/(k-1)! \rfloor$	;; Determine swapping location
$Swap(\pi_{N-1}, \pi_l)$	;; Perform the exchange
$Unrank(N-1, r-l \cdot (N-1)!, \pi)$	;; Recursive call

Algorithm 3.26

Unrank operation for permutations.

Procedure Unrank
Input: Value r, size N
Output: Permutation π and its signature

$\pi \leftarrow id$	;; Initialize permutation with identity
$parity \leftarrow false$	;; Initialize sign of permutation
while $(N > 0)$	;; Loop on size of permutation
$\quad i \leftarrow N-1 ; j \leftarrow r \bmod N$	;; Temporary variables
$\quad$ **if** $(i \neq j)$	;; Only in case there is change
$\quad\quad parity \leftarrow \neg parity$	;; Toggle signature
$\quad\quad swap(\pi_i, \pi_j)$	;; Exchange values
$\quad\quad r \leftarrow r \text{ div } N$	;; Compute reduced number
$\quad n \leftarrow n-1$	;; Reduce size
return $(parity, \pi)$	;; Permutation found

Algorithm 3.27

Recursion-free unranking and signature computation.

Proof. In the *unrank* function we always have $N-1$ element exchanges. For swapping two elements u and v at respective positions i and j with $i = j$ we count $2 \cdot (j-i-1)+1$ transpositions: $uxx \ldots xxv \rightarrow xux \ldots xxv \rightarrow \cdots \rightarrow xx \ldots xxuv \rightarrow xx \ldots xxvu \rightarrow \cdots \rightarrow vxx \ldots xxu$. As $2 \cdot (j-i-1)+1 \ mod \ 2 = 1$, each transposition either increases or decreases the parity of the number of inversion, so that the parity for each iteration toggles. The only exception is if $i = j$, where no change occurs. Hence, the sign of the permutation can be determined by executing the Myrvold-Ruskey algorithm in $O(N)$ time. ∎

Theorem 3.4. *(Compression of Alternation Group) Let* $\pi(i)$ *denote the value returned by the Myrvold and Ruskey's* Unrank *function (Alg. 3.28) for index* i. *Then* $\pi(i)$ *matches* $\pi(i+N!/2)$ *except for transposing* π_0 *and* π_1.

Proof. The last call for $swap(n-1, r \bmod n)$ in Algorithm 3.27 is $swap(1, r \bmod 2)$, which resolves to either $swap(1,1)$ or $swap(1,0)$. Only the latter one induces a change. If $r_1, \ldots, r_{N-1}$ denote the

Table 3.2 Myrvold and Ruskey's perfect permutation hash functions.

Index	Unrank (Alg. 3.26)	Signature	Unrank (Alg. 3.27)	Signature
0	(2,1,3,0)	0	(1,2,3,0)	0
1	(2,3,1,0)	1	(3,2,0,1)	0
2	(3,2,1,0)	0	(1,3,0,2)	0
3	(1,3,2,0)	1	(1,2,0,3)	1
4	(1,3,2,0)	1	(2,3,1,0)	0
5	(3,1,2,0)	0	(2,0,3,1)	0
6	(3,2,0,1)	1	(3,0,1,2)	0
7	(2,3,0,1)	0	(2,0,1,3)	1
8	(2,0,3,1)	1	(1,3,2,0)	1
9	(0,2,3,1)	0	(3,0,2,1)	1
10	(3,0,2,1)	0	(1,0,3,2)	1
11	(0,3,2,1)	1	(1,0,2,3)	0
12	(1,3,0,2)	0	(2,1,3,0)	1
13	(3,1,0,2)	1	(2,3,0,1)	1
14	(3,0,1,2)	0	(3,1,0,2)	1
15	(0,3,1,2)	1	(2,1,0,3)	0
16	(1,0,3,2)	1	(3,2,1,0)	1
17	(0,1,3,2)	0	(0,2,3,1)	1
18	(1,2,0,3)	1	(0,3,1,2)	1
19	(2,1,0,3)	0	(0,2,1,3)	0
20	(2,0,1,3)	1	(3,1,2,0)	0
21	(0,2,1,3)	0	(0,3,2,1)	0
22	(1,0,2,3)	0	(0,1,3,2)	0
23	(0,1,2,3)	1	(0,1,2,3)	1

indices of $r \bmod n$ in the iterations $1, \ldots, N-1$ of Myrvold and Ruskey's *Unrank* function, then $r_{N-1} = \lfloor \ldots \lfloor r/(N-1) \rfloor \ldots /2 \rfloor$, which is 1 for $r \geq n!/2$ and 0 for $r < n!/2$. ∎

3.2.3 Hashing Algorithms

There are two standard options for dealing with colliding items: *chaining* or *open addressing*. In *hashing with chaining*, keys x are kept in linked overflow lists. The dictionary operations *Lookup*, *Insert*, and *Delete* amount to computing $h(x)$ and then performing pure list manipulations in $T[h(x)]$. Their pseudo-code implementation is provided in Algorithms 3.29 through 3.31. They assume a *null* pointer $\perp$ and a link *Next* to the successor in the chained list. Operations *Insert* and *Delete* suggest a call to *Lookup* prior to their invocation to determine whether or not the element is contained in the hash table. An example for hashing the characters in *heuristic search* in a table of 10 elements with respect to their lexicographical order modulo 10 is depicted in Figure 3.15.

Procedure Rank
Input: Depth N, permutation π, inverse permutation π^{-1}
Output: Rank of π
Side Effect: (π and π^{-1} are modified)

for each i **in** $\{1,\ldots,N-1\}$	;; Traverse the vector
$\quad l \leftarrow \pi_{N-i}$	;; Temporary variable
$\quad swap(\pi_{N-i}, \pi_{\pi_{N-i}^{-1}})$	;; Update π
$\quad swap(\pi_l^{-1}, \pi_{N-i}^{-1})$	;; Update π^{-1}
$\quad rank_i \leftarrow l$	;; Store intermediate result
return $\prod_{i=1}^{N-1}(rank_{N-i+1} + i)$	;; Compute result

Algorithm 3.28

Recursion-free ranking operation for permutations.

Procedure Lookup
Input: Chained hash table T, key x
Output: Pointer to element or $\bot$ if not in T

$p \leftarrow T[h(x)]$	;; Table entry
while $(p \neq \bot)$ **and** $(p \neq x)$	;; Until found or empty
$\quad p \leftarrow Next(p)$	;; Go to next element in chained list
if $(p \neq \bot)$ **return** p	;; Feedback result, element found
else return $\bot$	;; Feedback result, element not found

Algorithm 3.29

Searching a chained hash table.

Procedure Insert
Input: Chained hash table T, key x
Output: Updated hash table T

$p \leftarrow T[h(x)]$	;; Table entry
if $(p = \bot)$ $T[h(x)] \leftarrow x$; **return**	;; Free location, set table entry and exit
while $(Next(p) \neq \bot)$ **and** $(p \neq x)$	;; Until found or empty
$\quad p \leftarrow Next(p)$	;; Go to next element in chained list
if $(p \neq x)$ $Next(p) \leftarrow \bot$	;; Insert if not already contained

Algorithm 3.30

Inserting an element into a chained hash table.

Procedure Delete
Input: Chained hash table T, key x
Output: Updated hash table T

$p \leftarrow T[h(x)]$;; Table entry
$T[h(x)] \leftarrow RecDelete(p,x)$;; Delete and feedback modified list

Procedure RecDelete
Input: Table entry p, key x
Output: Pointer to modified chain

if $(p = \perp)$ **return** $\perp$;; End of list detected
if $(p = x)$ **return** $Next(p)$;; Element found
$Next(p) \leftarrow RecDelete(Next(p),x)$;; Recursive call

Algorithm 3.31

Deleting an element from a chained hash table.

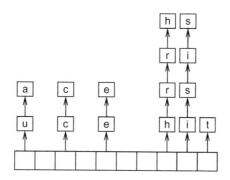

FIGURE 3.15

Hashing the characters of the term *heuristic search* with chaining.

Hashing with *open addressing* integrates the colliding elements at free locations in the hash table; that is, if $T[h(x)]$ is occupied, it searches for an alternative location for x. Searching a key x starts at $h(x)$ and continues in the probing sequence until either x or an empty table entry is found. When deleting an element, some keys may have to be moved back to fill the hole in the lookup sequence.

The *linear probing* strategy considers $(h(x) - j) \bmod m$ for $0 \le j < m$. In general, we have the sequence

$$(h(x) - s(j,x)) \bmod m \quad 0 \le j < m$$

Procedure Lookup
Input: Open hash table T of size q, key x, probing function s
Output: Pointer to element, or $\perp$ if x not in T

$i \leftarrow h(x)$	;; Compute initial location
$j \leftarrow 1$	;; Index in probing sequence
while ($Tag[i] \neq Empty$) **and** ($x \neq T[i]$)	;; Traverse sequence
$\quad i \leftarrow (h(k) - s(j,x)) \bmod q$	;; Next location
$\quad j \leftarrow j+1$	;; Next index
if ($x = T[i]$) **and** ($Tag[i] = Occupied$)	;; Element found
$\quad$ **return** $T[i]$	;; Feedback element
else return $\perp$	;; Element not found

Algorithm 3.32

Searching an element in an open hash table.

---

for probing function $s(j,x)$. There is a broad spectrum of suitable probing sequences, for example,

$$s(j,x) = j \qquad \text{(linear probing)}$$

$$s(j,x) = (-1)^j \cdot \left\lceil \frac{j}{2} \right\rceil^2 \quad \text{(quadratic probing)}$$

$$s(j,x) = j \cdot h'(x) \qquad \text{(double hashing)}$$

$$s(j,x) = r_x \qquad \text{(ideal hashing),}$$

where r_x is a random number depending on x, and h' is a second function, which determines the step size of the probing sequence in *double hashing*.

To exploit the whole table, $(h(x) - s(0,x)) \bmod m$, $(h(x) - s(1,x)) \bmod m$, $\ldots$, $(h(x) - s(m - 2,x)) \bmod m$, and $(h(x) - s(m - 1,x)) \bmod m$ should be a permutation of $\{0,\ldots,m - 1\}$.

An implementation of the procedure *Lookup* for a generic probing function s is provided in Algorithm 3.32. The implementation assumes an additional array *Tag* that associates one of the values *Empty*, *Occupied*, and *Deleted* with each element. Deletions (see Alg. 3.33) are handled by setting the *Deleted* tag for the cell of the deleted key. Lookups skip over deleted cells, and insertions (see Alg. 3.34) overwrite them.

When the hash table is nearly full, unsuccessful searches lead to long probe sequences. An optimization is *ordered hashing*, which maintains all probe sequences sorted. Thus, we can abort a *Lookup* operation as soon as we reach a larger key in the probe sequence. The according algorithm for inserting a key x is depicted in Algorithm 3.35. It consists of a search phase and an insertion phase. First, the probe sequence is followed up to a table slot that is either empty or contains an element that is larger than x. The insertion phase restores the sorting condition to make the algorithm work properly. If x replaces an element $T[i]$, the latter has to be reinserted into its respective probe sequence, in turn. This leads to a sequence of updates that end when an empty bin is found. It can be shown that the average number of probes to insert a key into the hash table is the same as in ordinary hashing.

Procedure Delete
Input: Open hash table T, key x
Output: Updated hash table T

$p \leftarrow Lookup(x)$;; Find location of key
if $(p \neq \perp)$;; State is contained in table
  $Tag[p] \leftarrow Deleted$;; Update flag

Algorithm 3.33

Inserting an element into an open hash table.

Procedure Insert
Input: Open hash table T of size q, key x
Side Effect: Updated hash table T

$j \leftarrow 1$;; Next index in probing sequence
$i \leftarrow h(x)$;; Compute initial location
while $(Tag[i] = Occupied)$;; Traverse sequence
  $i \leftarrow (h(k) - s(j,x)) \bmod q$;; Next location
  $j \leftarrow j+1$;; Next index
$T[i] \leftarrow x$;; Insert element
$Tag[i] \leftarrow Occupied$;; Update flag

Algorithm 3.34

Deleting an element from an open hash table.

Procedure Insert
Input: Key x, hash table T
Side Effect: Updated table T

$i \leftarrow h(x)$;; Compute hash function
while $(Tag[i] = Occupied)$ **and** $(T[i] \geq x)$;; Search phase
  if $(T[i] = x)$ **return**   ;; Key already present
  $i \leftarrow (i + h'(x)) \bmod m$;; Next probe location
while $(Tag[i] = Occupied)$;; Insertion phase
  if $(T[i] < x)$ $Swap(T[i],x)$;; x is at correct place in its probe chain
  $i \leftarrow (i + h'(x)) \bmod m$;; Net probe location
$T[i] \leftarrow x$;; Free space at end of chain found
$Tag[i] \leftarrow Occupied$;; Update flag

Algorithm 3.35

Inserting an element for ordered hashing.

For a hash table of size m that stores n keys, the quotient $\alpha = n/m$ is called the *load factor*. The load factor crucially determines the efficiency of hash table operations. The analysis assumes uniformness of h; that is, $P(h(x) = j) = 1/m$ for all $x \in S$ and $0 \leq j \leq m - 1$. Under this precondition, the expected number of memory probes for insertion and unsuccessful lookup is

$$\text{linear probing} \approx \frac{1}{2}\left(1 + \frac{1}{(1-\alpha)^2}\right)$$

$$\text{quadratic probing} \approx 1 - \frac{\alpha}{2} + \ln\left(\frac{1}{1-\alpha}\right)$$

$$\text{double hashing} \approx \frac{1}{1-\alpha}$$

$$\text{chained hashing} \approx 1 + \alpha$$

$$\text{ideal hashing} \approx \frac{1}{\alpha}\ln\left(\frac{1}{1-\alpha}\right)$$

Thus, for any $\alpha \leq 0.5$, in terms of number of probes we obtain the following rank order: ideal hashing, chained hashing, double hashing, quadratic probing, and linear probing. The order of the last four methods is true for any α.

Although chaining scores quite favorably in terms of memory probes, the comparison is not totally fair, since it dynamically allocates memory and uses extra linear space to store the pointers.

FKS Hashing Scheme

With a hash function h of a class H of universal hash functions, we can easily obtain constant lookup time if we don't mind spending a quadratic amount of memory. Say we allocate a hash table of size $m = n(n - 1)$. Since there are $\binom{n}{2}$ pairs in R, each with a chance $1/m$ of colliding with each other, the probability of a collision in the hash table is bounded by $\binom{n}{2}/m \leq 1/2$. In other words, the chance of drawing a *perfect hash function* for the set of stored keys is $1/2$. While for each given hash function there is a worst set of stored keys that maps all of them into the same bin, the crucial element of the algorithm is a *randomized rehashing*: If the chosen h actually leads to a collision, just try again with another hash function drawn with uniform probability from H.

Perfect hashing has important advances in storing and retrieving information in the visited list and, equally important, for fast lookup of pattern databases (see Ch. 4). The apparent question for practical search is whether memory consumption for perfect hashing can be reduced. The so-called *FKS hashing scheme* (named after the initials of the inventors Fredman, Komlós, and Szemerédi) ended a long dispute in research about whether it is also possible to achieve constant access time with a *linear storage size* of $O(n)$. The algorithm uses a two-level approach: First, hash into a table of size n, which will produce some collisions, and then, for each resulting bin, rehash it as just described, squaring the size of the hash bucket to get zero collisions.

Denote the subset of elements mapped to bin i as R_i, with $|R_i| = n_i$. We will use the property that

$$E\left[\sum_{i=0}^{n-1}\binom{n_i}{2}\right] < \frac{n(n-1)}{m}. \tag{3.1}$$

This can be seen by noting that $\sum_{i=0}^{n-1} \binom{n_i}{2}$ is the total number of ordered pairs that land in the same bin of the table; we have

$$E\left[\sum_{i=0}^{n-1} \binom{n_i}{2}\right] = \sum_{x \in S} \sum_{y \in S, y \neq x} P(x \text{ and } y \text{ are in the same bucket})$$

$$< n(n-1) \cdot \frac{1}{m} \text{ (by the definition of universal hash functions)}.$$

Using the Markov inequality $P(X \geq a) \leq E[X]/a$ with $a = t \cdot E[X]$ shows $P(X \geq t \cdot E[X]) \leq 1/t$. Consequently,

$$P\left(\sum_{i=0}^{n-1} \binom{n_i}{2} < \frac{2n(n-1)}{m}\right) \geq 1/2.$$

Choosing $m = 2(n-1)$, this implies that for at least half of the functions $h \in H$ we have

$$\sum_{i=0}^{n-1} \binom{n_i}{2} < n. \tag{3.2}$$

At the second level, we use the same property with the choice of the size of the hash table for R_i, $m_i = \max\{1, 2n_i(n_i - 1)\}$. Then, for at least half of the functions $h \in H_{m_i}$ we obtain

$$\sum_{j=0}^{|m_i|-1} \binom{n_{ij}}{2} < 1,$$

where n_{ij} is the number of elements in the second-level bin j of R_i; in other words, $n_{ij} \leq 1$ for all j.

So, the total space used is $O(n)$ for the first table (assuming it takes a constant amount of space to store each hash function), plus

$$O\left(\sum_{i=0}^{n-1} 2n_i(n_i - 1)\right) = O\left(4 \cdot \sum_{i=0}^{n-1} \frac{n_i(n_i - 1)}{2}\right) = O\left(\sum_{i=0}^{n-1} \binom{n_i}{2}\right) = O(n)$$

for the other tables. For the last equality we used Equation 3.2.

Dynamic Perfect Hashing

Unfortunately, the FKS hashing scheme is only applicable to the static case, where the hash table is created once with a fixed set of keys, and no insertions and deletions are allowed afterward.

Later the algorithm was generalized to allow for update operations. Deletion of an element is handled simply by tagging it, and subsequently ignoring tagged keys, overwriting them later.

A standard doubling strategy is used to cope with a growing or shrinking number of stored elements. Every time that a predetermined maximum number of update operations has occurred, the structure is recreated from scratch in the same way as in the static case, but slightly larger than necessary to accommodate future insertions. More precisely, it is planned for a maximum capacity of $m = (1 + c) \cdot n$, where n is the number of currently stored keys. The top-level hash function contains

$s(m)$ bins, which is defined as an $O(n)$ function. Each second-level bin is allocated for a capacity m_i of twice as many elements in it; that is, if n_i keys fall into bin i, its size is chosen as $2m_i(m_i - 1)$, with $m_i = 2n_i$. The resulting new structure will be used subsequently for at most $c \cdot n$ update operations.

Before this maximum update count is reached, an *insert* operation first tries to insert an element according to the given structure and hash functions; this is possible if Equation 3.2 is still valid, the bin i the element is mapped to has some spare capacity left (i.e., $n_i < m_i$), and the position within bin i assigned by the second-level hash function is empty. If only the last condition doesn't hold, bin i is reorganized by randomly drawing a new second-level hash function. If $n_i \geq m_i$, the bin's capacity is doubled (from m_i to $2m_i$) prior to reorganization. If, on the other hand, Equation 3.2 is violated, a new top-level hash function has to be selected, and hence the whole structure must be recreated.

It can be shown that this scheme uses $O(n)$ storage; *Lookup* and *Delete* are executed in constant worst-case time, whereas *Insert* runs in constant amortized expected time.

Cuckoo Hashing

The FKS hashing is involved and it is unclear whether the approach can be made incremental. For the first-level hash function this is possible, but for the selection of a universal hash function for each bucket we lack an appropriate answer.

Therefore, we propose an alternative conflict strategy. *Cuckoo hashing* implements the dictionary with two hash tables, T_1 and T_2, and two different hash functions, h_1 and h_2. Each key, k, is contained either in $T_1[h_1(k)]$ or in $T_2[h_2(k)]$. Algorithm 3.36 provides a pseudo-code implementation for searching a key. If an item produces a collision in the first table the detected synonym is deleted and inserted into the other table. Figure 3.16 gives an example—arrows point to the alternative bucket in the other hash table. If D is hashed into the first hash table where it preempts C, then C needs to go into the second hash table where it preempts B, and B needs to go into the first hash table where it found an empty location. During the insertion process the arrows have to be inverted. That is, B that has been moved to the first table points to C in the second table, and C that has been moved to the second table now points to the inserted element D in the first table.

There is a small probability that the *cuckoo process* may not terminate at all and loop forever; Figure 3.17 gives an example. If D is hashed into the first hash table where it preempts C, then C needs to go into the second hash table where it preempts A, A needs to go into the first hash table where it preempts E, E needs to go into the second hash table where it preempts B, B needs to go into the first hash table where it preempts D, D needs to go into the second hash table where it preempts G, G needs to go into the first hash table where it preempts F, F needs to go into the second hash table where it

---

Procedure Lookup
Input: Key k, hash tables T_1 and T_2
Output: Truth value, if k is stored in the dictionary

return $(T_1[h_1(k)] = k)$ **or** $(T_2[h_2(k)]) = k)$;; Constant-time lookup

Algorithm 3.36

Lookup for a key in a cuckoo hash table.

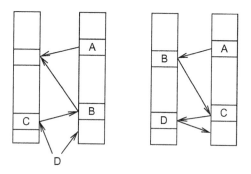

FIGURE 3.16

A successful insertion of an element via cuckoo hashing.

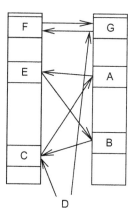

FIGURE 3.17

An infinite cuckoo process; rehashing is needed.

preempts D, D needs to go into the first hash table where it preempts B, and so on. The analysis shows that such a situation is rather unlikely, so that we can pick fresh hash functions and rehash the entire structure after a fixed number t of failures. Algorithm 3.37 provides an implementation for the insert procedure.

Although reorganization costs linear time it contributes a small amount to the expected runtime. The analysis reveals that if t is fixed appropriately ($3\lceil\lg_{1+\epsilon} r\rceil$ for r being the individual hash table sizes and $n > (1+\epsilon)r$) the probability of rehash is $O(1/n^2)$. Therefore, rehashing n elements causes no recursive rehash with probability $O(1-1/n)$. As the expected time for inserting one element is constant, the total expected time to reinsert all n elements is $O(n)$. This is also the total expected time for rehashing.

In summary, cuckoo hashing has worst-case constant access time and amortized worst-case insertion time. It is simple to implement and efficient in practice.

Procedure Insert
Input: Key k, hash tables T_1 and T_2
Side Effect: Updated tables T_1 and T_2

if ($Lookup(k)$) **return**	;; Lookup if element is already in dictionary
for each i **in** $\{1,\ldots,t\}$	;; Loop until predefined max number is exceeded
$Swap(k, T_1[h_1(k)])$	;; Exchange key with table element
if ($k = \emptyset$) **return**	;; Empty place for key found
$Swap(k, T_2[h_2(k)])$	;; Exchange key with table element
if ($k = \emptyset$) **return**	;; Empty place for key found
$Rehash$	;; No empty place found, reorganize entire dictionary
$Insert(k)$	;; Recursive call to put element in reorganized structure

Algorithm 3.37

Inserting a key into a cuckoo hash table.

3.2.4 Memory-Saving Dictionaries

The information-theoretic lower bound on the number of bits required to store an arbitrary subset of size n of a universe of size N is $B = \lg \binom{N}{n}$, since we have to be able to represent all possible combinations of selecting n values out of the N. Using Stirling's approximation and defining $r = N/n$, we obtain

$$B \approx n \lg \frac{N}{n} = n \lg r$$

with an error less than $n \lg e$, where e is Euler's constant. Alternatively, using

$$\lg \binom{N}{n} = \lg \frac{N \cdot (N-1) \cdot \cdots \cdot (N-n+1)}{n!} = \sum_{j=N-n+1}^{N} \lg j - \sum_{j=1}^{n} \lg j,$$

we can approximate the logarithm by two corresponding integrals. If we properly bias the integral limits we can be sure to compute a lower bound

$$\lg \binom{N}{n} \geq \int_{N-n+1}^{N} \lg(x) dx - \int_{2}^{n+1} \lg(x) dx.$$

For the case of *dynamic dictionaries* (where insertions and deletions are fully supported), we want to be able to maintain subsets of varying size, say, of zero up to a maximum of n elements. This results in a minimum number of

$$\left\lceil \lg \left(\sum_{i=0}^{n} \binom{N}{i} \right) \right\rceil$$

bits. For $n \leq (N-2)/3$ (which is usually the case for nontrivial search problems) we have

$$\binom{N}{n} \leq \sum_{i=0}^{n} \binom{N}{i} \leq 2 \cdot \binom{N}{n}.$$

The correctness follows from the property of binomial coefficients $\binom{n}{i}/\binom{n}{i+1} \leq 1/2$ for $i \leq (n-2)/3$. We are only interested in the logarithms, so we conclude

$$\lg\binom{N}{n} \leq \lg\left(\sum_{i=0}^{n} \binom{N}{i}\right) \leq \lg\left(2\binom{N}{n}\right) = \lg\binom{N}{n} + 1.$$

Obviously in this restricted range it is sufficient to concentrate on the last binomial coefficient. The error in our estimate is at most one bit. At the end, as we look at the logarithms, the dynamic case is not much different from the static case.

If N is large compared to n, listing all elements, for example, in a hash table comes close to the information-theoretic minimum number of bits B. In the other border case, for small r it is optimal to list the *answers*, for example, in the form of a bitvector of size N. The more difficult part is to find appropriate representations for intermediate sizes.

Suffix Lists

Given B bits of memory, for space-efficient state storage we want to maintain a dynamically evolving visited list closed under inserts and membership queries. For the ease of presentation, the entries of *Closed* are integers from $\{0,\ldots,n\}$. Using hashing with open addressing, the maximal size of *Closed* nodes m is limited to $O(n/\lg n)$, since $\lg n$ bits are required to encode a state. A gain is only to be expected if we can exploit redundancies in the state vector set. In the following we describe a simple but very space-efficient approach with small update and query times.

Let $bin(u)$ be the binary representation of an element $u \in \{1,\ldots,n\}$ from the set *Closed*. We split $bin(u)$ in p high bits and $s = \lceil \lg n \rceil - p$ low bits. Furthermore, $u_{s+p-1},\ldots,u_s$ denotes the prefix of $bin(u)$ and $u_{s-1},\ldots,u_0$ stands for the suffix of $bin(u)$.

A SUFFIX LIST data structure consists of a linear array P of size 2^p bits and of a two-dimensional array L of size $m(s+1)$ bits. The basic idea of a SUFFIX LIST is to store a common prefix of several entries as a single bit in P, whereas the distinctive suffixes form a group within L. P is stored as a bit array. L can hold several groups with each group consisting of a multiple of $s+1$ bits. The first bit of each $s+1$-bit row in L serves as a *group bit*. The first s-bit suffix entry of a group has group bit one, and the other elements of the group have group bit zero. We place the elements of a group together in lexicographical order (see Fig. 3.18).

First, we compute $k = \sum_{i=0}^{p-1} u_{s+i} \cdot 2^i$, which gives us the search position in the prefix array P. Then we simply count the number of ones in P starting from position $P[0]$ until we reach $P[k]$. Let z be this number. Finally, we search through L until we have found the zth suffix of L with group bit one. If we have to perform a membership query we simply search in this group. Note that searching a single entry may require scanning large areas of main memory.

To insert entry u we first search the corresponding group as described earlier. In case u opens a new group within L this involves setting group bits in P and L. The suffix of u is inserted in its group while maintaining the elements of the group sorted. Note that an insert may need to shift many rows in L to

Closed nodes	In sorted order
1011001	0011 011
0011011	0011 101
1011010	0101 000
0011101	0101 001
1011011	0101 111
0101000	1011 001
1011110	1011 010
0101001	1011 011
0101111	1011 110

Prefix-list

0000	0
	0
	0
0011	1
	0
0101	1
	0
	0
	0
	0
	0
1011	1
	0
	0
	0
1111	0

Suffix-list

1	011
0	101
1	000
0	001
0	111
1	001
0	010
0	011
0	110

FIGURE 3.18

Example for a SUFFIX LIST with $p = 4$ and $s = 3$.

create space at the desired position. The maximum number m of elements that can be stored in B bits is limited as follows: We need 2^p bits for P and $s + 1 = \lceil \lg n \rceil - p + 1$ bits for each entry of L. Hence, we choose p so that r is maximal subject to

$$m \leq \frac{B - 2^p}{\lceil \lg n \rceil - p + 1}.$$

For $p = \Theta(\lg B - \lg \lg (n/B))$ the space requirement for both P and the suffixes in L is small enough to guarantee $m = \Theta \left(\frac{B}{\lg(n/B)} \right)$.

We now show how to speed up the operations. When searching or inserting an element u we have to compute z to find the correct group in L. Instead of scanning potentially large parts of P and L for each single query we maintain checkpoints, *one-counters*, to store the number of ones seen so far. Checkpoints are to lie close enough to support rapid search but must not consume more than a small fraction of the main memory. For $2^p \leq m$ we have $z \leq m$ for both arrays, so $\lceil \lg m \rceil$ bits are sufficient for each one-counter.

Keeping one-counters after every $c_1 \cdot \lfloor \lg m \rfloor$ entries limits the total space requirement. Binary search on the one-counters of P now reduces the scan area to compute the correct value of z to $c_1 \cdot \lfloor \lg m \rfloor$ bits.

Searching in L is slightly more difficult because groups could extend over 2^s entries, thus potentially spanning several one-counters with equal values. Nevertheless, finding the beginning and the end of large groups is possible within the stated bounds. As we keep the elements within a group sorted, another binary search on the actual entries is sufficient to locate the position in L.

We now turn to insertions where two problems remain: adding a new element to a group may need shifting large amounts of data. Also, after each insert the checkpoints must be updated. A simple solution uses a second buffer data structure BU that is less space efficient but supports rapid inserts and lookups. When the number of elements in BU exceeds a certain threshold, BU is merged with the old SUFFIX LIST to obtain a new up-to-date space-efficient representation. Choosing an appropriate size of BU, amortized analysis shows improved computational bounds for inserts while achieving asymptotically the same order of phases for the graph search algorithm.

Note that membership queries must be extended to BU as well. We implement BU as an array for hashing with open addressing. BU stores at most $c_2 \cdot m/\lceil \lg n \rceil$ elements of size $p + s = \lceil \lg n \rceil$, for some small constant c_2. As long as there is 10% space left in BU, we continue to insert elements into BU, otherwise BU is sorted and the suffixes are moved from BU into the proper groups of L. The reason not to exploit the full hash table size is again to bound the expected search and insert time within BU to a constant number of tests. Altogether, we can prove the following theorem.

Theorem 3.5. *(Time Complexity* SUFFIX LIST*) Searching and inserting n items into a* SUFFIX LIST *under space restriction amounts to a runtime of $O(n \lg n)$.*

Proof. For a membership query we perform binary searches on numbers of $\lceil \lg m \rceil$ bits or s bits, respectively. So, to search an element we need $O(\lg^2 m + s^2) = O(\lg^2 n)$ bit operations since $r \le n$ and $s \le \lg n$.

Each of the $O(m/\lg n)$ buffer entries consists of $O(\lg n)$ bits, hence sorting the buffer can be done with

$$O\left(\lg n \cdot \frac{m}{\lg n} \cdot \lg \frac{m}{\lg n} \right) = O(m \lg n)$$

bit operations. Starting with the biggest occurring keys merging can be performed in $O(1)$ memory scans. This also includes updating all one-counters. In spite of the additional data structures we still have

$$r = \Theta\left(\frac{B}{\lg(n/B)} \right).$$

Thus, the total bit complexity for n inserts and membership queries is given by

$$O(\#\textit{buffer-runs} \cdot (\#\textit{sorting-ops} + \#\textit{merging-ops}) +$$
$$\#\textit{elements} \cdot \#\textit{buffer-search-ops} + \#\textit{elements} \cdot \#\textit{membership-query-ops}) =$$
$$O(n/m \cdot \lg n \cdot (m \cdot \lg n + B) + n \cdot \lg^2 n + n \cdot \lg^2 n) =$$
$$O(n/m \cdot \lg n \cdot (m \cdot \lg n + r \cdot \lg(n/B)) + n \cdot \lg^2 n) = O(n \cdot \lg^2 n).$$

Assuming a machine word length of $\lg n$, any modification or comparison of entries with $O(\lg n)$ bits appearing in a SUFFIX LIST can be done using $O(1)$ machine operations. Hence, the total complexity reduces to $O(n \lg n)$ operations. ∎

The constants can be improved using the following observation: In the case $n = (1 + \epsilon) \cdot B$, for a small $\epsilon > 0$ nearly half of the entries in P will always be zero, namely those that are lexicographically bigger than the suffix of n itself. Cutting the P array at this position leaves more room for L, which in turn enables us to keep more elements.

Table 3.3 compares a SUFFIX LIST data structure with hashing and open addressing. The constants for the SUFFIX LIST are chosen so that $2 \cdot c_1 + c_2 \le 1/10$, which means that if m elements can be treated, we set aside $m/10$ bits to speed up internal computations. For hashing with open addressing we also leave 10% of memory free to keep the internal computation time moderate. When using a SUFFIX LIST instead of hashing, note that only the ratio between n and B is important.

Table 3.3 Fractions of n that can be accommodated in a SUFFIX LIST and in hashing with open addressing. *Note:* n is the size of the search space to be memorized, and B is the number of bits available for storing the data. The columns denote the maximal portion of the state space that can be stored according to the information theoretical bound, the SUFFIX LIST structure, and ordinary hashing according to two practical values of n.

n/B	Upper Bound	Suffix Lists	Hashing $n = 2^{20}$	$n = 2^{30}$
1.05	33.2%	22.7%	4.3%	2.9%
1.10	32.4%	21.2%	4.1%	2.8%
1.25	24.3%	17.7%	3.6%	2.4%
1.50	17.4%	13.4%	3.0%	2.0%
2.00	11.0%	9.1%	2.3%	1.5%
3.00	6.1%	5.3%	1.5%	1.0%
4.00	4.1%	3.7%	1.1%	0.7%
8.00	1.7%	1.5%	0.5%	0.4%
16.00	0.7%	0.7%	0.3%	0.2%

Hence, the SUFFIX LIST data structures can close the memory gap in search algorithms between the best possible and trivial approaches like hashing with open addressing.

3.2.5 Approximate Dictionaries

If we relax the requirements to a membership data structure, allowing it to store a slightly different key set than intended, new possibilities for space reduction arise.

The idea of erroneous dictionaries was first exploited by Bloom. A BLOOM FILTER is a bitvector v of length m, together with k independent hash functions $h_1(x),\ldots,h_k(x)$. Initially, v is set to zero. To *insert* a key x, compute $h_i(x)$, for all $i = 1,\ldots,k$, and set each $v[h_i(x)]$ to one. To *lookup* a key, check the status of $v[h_1(x)]$; if it is zero, x is not stored, otherwise continue with $v[h_2(x)], v[h_3(x)], \ldots$. If all these bits are set, report that x is in the filter. However, since they might have been turned on by different keys, the filter can make *false positive* errors. Deletions are not supported by this data structure, but they can be incorporated by replacing the bits by *counters* that are incremented in insertions rather than just set to one.

Bit-State Hashing

For large problem spaces, it can be most efficient to apply a depth-first search strategy in combination with duplicate detection via a membership data structure. Bit-state hashing is a BLOOM FILTER storage technique without storing the complete state vectors. If the problem contains up to 2^{30} states and more (which implies a memory consumption of 1 GB times state vector size in bytes), it resorts to approximate hashing. Obviously, the algorithm is no longer guaranteed to find a shortest solution (or any solution at all, for that matter). As an illustration of the bit-state hashing idea, Figures 3.19 through 3.21 depict the range of possible hash structures: usual hashing with chaining, single-bit hashing, and double-bit hashing.

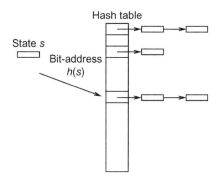

FIGURE 3.19

Ordinary hashing with chaining.

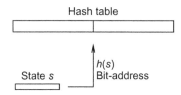

FIGURE 3.20

Single bit-state hashing.

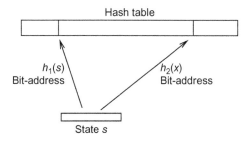

FIGURE 3.21

Double bit-state hashing.

Let n be the number of reachable states and m be the maximal number of bits available. As a coarse approximation for single bit-state hashing with $n < m$, the average probability P_1 of a false positive error during the course of the search is bounded by

$$P_1 \leq \frac{1}{n} \sum_{i=0}^{n-1} \frac{i}{m} \leq n/2m,$$

since the ith element collides with one of the $i-1$ already inserted elements with a probability of at most $(i-1)/m$, $1 \leq i \leq n$. For multibit hashing using h (independent) hash functions with the assumption $hn < m$, the average probability of collision P_h is reduced to $P_h \leq \frac{1}{n}\sum_{i=0}^{n-1}(h \cdot \frac{i}{m})^h$, since i elements occupy at most hi/m addresses, $0 \leq i \leq n-1$. In the special case of double bit-state hashing, this simplifies to

$$P_2 \leq \frac{1}{n}\left(\frac{2}{m}\right)^2 \sum_{i=0}^{n-1} i^2 = 2(n-1)(2n-1)/3m^2 \leq 4n^2/3m^2.$$

An attempt to remedy the incompleteness of partial search is to reinvoke the algorithm several times with different hash functions to improve the coverage of the search tree. This technique, called *sequential hashing*, successively examines various beams in the search tree (up to a certain threshold depth). In considerably large problems, sequential hashing succeeds in finding solutions (but often returns long paths). As a rough estimate on the error probability we take the following. If in sequential hashing exploration of which the first hash function covers c/n of the search space, the probability that a state x is not generated in d independent runs is $(1 - c/n)^d$, such that x is reached with probability $1 - (1 - c/n)^d$.

Hash Compaction

To increase the coverage of the search space, further lossy compression techniques have been considered in practice to best exploit the limited amount of memory. Like bit-state hashing, the *hash compaction* method aims at reducing the memory requirements for the state table. However, it stores a compressed state descriptor in a conventional hash table instead of setting bits corresponding to hash values of the state descriptor in a bitvector. The compression function c maps a state to a b-bit number in $\{0, \ldots, 2^b - 1\}$. Since different states can have the same compression, false positive errors can arise. Note, however, that if the probe sequence and the compression are calculated independently from the state, the same compressed state can occur at different locations in the table.

In the analysis, we assume that breadth-first search with ordered hashing using open addressing is applied. Let the goal state s_d be located at depth d, and $s_0, s_1, \ldots, s_d$ be a shortest path to it.

It can be shown that the probability p_k of a false positive error, given that the table already contains k elements, is approximately equal to

$$p_k = 1 - \frac{2}{2^b}(H_{m+1} - H_{m-k}) + \frac{2m + k(m-k)}{m2^b(m-k+1)}, \tag{3.3}$$

where $H_n = \sum_{i=1}^{n} \frac{1}{i} = \ln n + \gamma + \frac{1}{2n} - \frac{1}{12n^2} + O(\frac{1}{n^4})$ denotes a *harmonic number*.

Let k_i be the number of states stored in the hash table after the algorithm has completely explored the nodes in level i. Then there were at most $k_i - 1$ states in the hash table when we tried to insert s_i. Hence, the probability P_{miss} that *no* state on the solution path was omitted is bounded by

$$P_{miss} \geq \prod_{i=0}^{d} p_{k_i - 1}.$$

If the algorithm is run up to a maximum depth d, it can record the k_i values online and report this lower bound on the omission probability after termination.

To obtain an *a priori estimate*, knowledge of the depth of the search space and the distribution of the k_i is required. For a coarse approximation, we assume that the table fills up completely ($m = n$) and that half the states in the solution path experience an empty table during insertion, and the other half experiences the table with only one empty slot. This models (crudely) the typically bell-shaped state distribution over the levels $0, \ldots, d$. Assuming further that the individual values in Equation 3.3 are close enough to one to approximate the product by a sum, we obtain the approximation

$$P_{miss} = \frac{1}{2^b}(\ln n - 1.2).$$

Assuming, more conservatively, only one empty slot for all states on the solution path would increase this estimate by a factor of two.

Collapse Compression

A related memory-saving strategy is *collapse compression*. It stores complex state vectors in an efficient way. The main idea is to store different parts of the state space in separate descriptors and represent the actual state as an index to relevant states. Collapse compression is based on the observation that although the number of distinct search states can become very large, the number of distinct parts of the state vector are usually smaller. In contrast, to jointly store the leading part of the state vector, as in SUFFIX LISTS, different parts of the state can be shared (across all the visited states that are stored). This is especially important when only small parts of the state vector change and avoids storing the complete vector every time a new state is visited.

Essentially, different components are stored in separate hash tables. Each entry in one of the tables is given a unique number. A whole state vector is then identified by a vector of numbers that refer to corresponding components in the hash tables. This greatly reduces the storage needs for storing the set of already explored states. An illustration of this technique is provided in Figure 3.22. Besides the memory capacity for the state components, collapse compression additionally needs an overall hash table to represent the combined state. The collapsed state vector consists of (hash) IDs for the individual components. Therefore, there is a gain only if the individual state components that are collapsed are themselves complex data structures. Collapse compression can be implemented lossless or lossy.

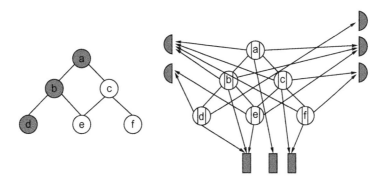

FIGURE 3.22

Effect of collapse compression. On the left there is the search tree. On the right, the states have been partitioned in three parts, which are stored individually and jointly addressed with indices. When moving from *a* to *b* only the part in the middle of the state vector changes and has to be newly stored.

3.3 SUBSET DICTIONARIES

The problem of finding an element in a set of elements such that this element is a subset (or a superset) of the query occurs in many search applications; for example, in the matching of a large number of production rules, in the identification of inconsistent subgoals in AI planning, and in finding string completions for constructing or solving crossword puzzles. Moreover, efficiently storing and searching partial information is central to many learning processes. The problem also occurs in search applications that allow the user to search for documents containing a given *set* of words, and therefore extends the setting in the previous section.

For a state space search the stored sets often correspond to partially specified state vectors (*patterns*). As an example, consider the solitaire game SOKOBAN (see Ch. 1), together with a selection of dead-end patterns. Since every given state is unsolvable, if the dead-end pattern is a subset of it, we want to quickly detect whether or not such a dead-end pattern is present in the data structure (see Ch. 10). We assume the patterns to sets of elements from a certain universe Γ (set of coordinates in SOKOBAN).

Definition 3.1. (*Subset and Containment Query Problem, Subset Dictionary*) *Let D be a set of n subsets over a universe Γ. The* SUBSET QUERY (CONTAINMENT QUERY) *problem asks for any query set $q \subseteq D$ if there is any $p \in D$ with $q \subseteq p$ ($p \subseteq q$).*

A subset dictionary is an abstract data structure providing insertion of sets to D while supporting subset and containment queries.

Since p is a subset of q if and only if its complement is a superset of the complement of q, the two query problems are equivalent.

For the SOKOBAN problem, we have that each board position is an element of Γ. Inserting a pattern amounts to inserting a subset of Γ to the subset dictionary. Subsequently, determining whether or not a state matches a stored pattern is a containment query to the dictionary.

From an implementation point of view we may think of subset dictionaries as hash tables that contain generalized information about sets of problem states. But before diving into implementation issues, we draw another equivalence, which turns out to be essential.

Definition 3.2. (PARTIAL MATCH) *Let $*$ denote a special* don't care *character that matches every character contained in an alphabet. Given a set D of n vectors over the alphabet Σ, the* PARTIAL MATCH *problem asks for a data structure, which for any query $q \in \Sigma \cup \{*\}$ detects if there is any entry p in D such that q matches p.*

The application for this problem is to solve approximate matching problems in information retrieval. A sample application is a crossword puzzle dictionary. A query like B*T**R in the CROSSWORD PUZZLE would be answered with words like BETTER, BITTER, BUTLER, or BUTTER.

Theorem 3.6. (*Equivalence* PARTIAL MATCH *and* SUBSET QUERY *Problems*) *The* PARTIAL MATCH *problem is equivalent to the* SUBSET QUERY *problem.*

Proof. As we can adjust any algorithm for solving the PARTIAL MATCH problem to handle binary symbols by using a binary representation, it is sufficient to consider the alphabet $\Sigma = \{0, 1\}$.

To reduce the PARTIAL MATCH to the SUBSET QUERY problem, we replace each $p \in D$ by a set of all pairs (i, p_i) for all $i = 1, \ldots, |\Gamma|$. Moreover, we replace each query q by a set of all pairs (i, q_i) provided that q is not the don't care symbol $*$. Solving this instance to the subset query problem also solves the PARTIAL MATCH problem.

To reduce the SUBSET QUERY to the PARTIAL MATCH problem, we replace each database set by its characteristic vector, and replace query set q by its characteristic vector, of which the zeros have been replaced with don't cares.   ∎

As the SUBSET QUERY is equivalent to the CONTAINMENT QUERY problem, the latter one can also be solved by algorithms for the PARTIAL MATCH. For the sake of simplicity, in the following data structures we restrict the alphabet for the PARTIAL MATCH problem to $\{0, 1\}$.

3.3.1 **Arrays and Lists**

These problems have two straightforward solutions. The first approach is to store all answers to all possible queries in a (perfect) hash table or array of size 2^m, with $m = |\Gamma|$. Query time is $O(m)$ to compute the hash address. For the CONTAINMENT QUERY each hash table entry contains a list of sets from the database corresponding to the query (state), which in turn is interpreted as a bitvector. Unfortunately, the memory requirements for this implementation are too large for most practical applications because we have to reserve a table entry for all queries (corresponding to the entire state space).

The list representation with each list item containing one database entry is the other extreme. The storage requirements with $O(n)$ are optimal but searching for a match now corresponds to time $O(nm)$, a term that is also too big for practical applications. In the following, we propose compromises in between storing plain arrays and lists.

3.3.2 **Tries**

One possible implementation that immediately comes to mind is a TRIE, which compares a query string to the set of stored entries. A TRIE is a lexicographic search tree structure, in which each node spawns at most $|\Sigma|$ children. The transitions are labeled by $a \in \Sigma$ and are mutually exclusive for two successors of a state. Leaf nodes correspond to stored strings. A TRIE is a natural and unique representation for a set of strings.

Since inserting and deleting strings in a TRIE is simple, in Algorithm 3.38 we consider the traversal of the tree for a search. For notational convenience, we consider the PARTIAL MATCH problem as introduced earlier. The recursive procedure *Lookup* is initially invoked with the root of the TRIE, the query $q = (q_1, \ldots, q_m)$ with $q_i \in \{0, 1, *\}$, $1 \leq i \leq m$, and the level 1. The expected sum of nodes examined has been estimated by $O(n^{\lg(2-s/m)})$, where s is the number of indices specified in a query.

3.3.3 **Hashing**

An alternative reduction of the space complexity for the array representation is to hash the query sets to a smaller table. The lists in the chained hash table again correspond to database sets. However, the lists have to be searched to filter the elements that match.

A refined implementation of the array approach appropriate for SOKOBAN is to construct containers L_i of all patterns that share a ball at position i. In the pattern lookup for position u we test whether or not $L_1 \cup \ldots \cup L_k$ is empty. Insertion and retrieval time correspond to the sizes $|L_i|$ and the individual storage structures for them (e.g., sorted lists, bitvectors, balanced trees).

Procedure Lookup
Input: TRIE node u, query q, level l
Output: Display all entries p with q matches p

if $(Leaf(u))$	;; Entry stored at leaf node
if $(Match(Entry(u),q))$	;; Match found
print $Entry(u)$	;; Return matching item
if $(q_l \neq *)$	;; Ordinary symbol at position l
if $(Succ(u,q_l) \neq \perp)$	;; Successor exists
$Lookup(Succ(u,q_l),q,l+1)$	;; One recursive call
else	;; Don't care symbol
if $(Succ(u,0) \neq \perp)$	;; 0-successor exists
$Lookup(Succ(u,0),q,l+1)$	;; First recursive call
if $(Succ(u,1) \neq \perp)$	;; 1-successor exists
$Lookup(Succ(u,1),q,l+1)$	;; Second recursive call

Algorithm 3.38

Searching a TRIE for a partial match.

Procedure Lookup
Input: Chained hash table T, hash function h, query q
Output: All entries p with q matches p

$L \leftarrow \emptyset$	;; Initialize list of matches
for each $j \in h(q)$	;; Determine all addresses for hash query
for each $p \in L_j$	;; Traverse list in bucket
if $(Match(p,q))$ $L \leftarrow L \cup p$	;; Report match
return L	;; Feedback all matches

Algorithm 3.39

Searching a hash table for a partial match.

Generalizing the idea for the PARTIAL MATCH problem leads to the following hashing approach. Let h be the hash function mapping Σ^m to the chained hash table. A record p is stored in the list L_j if and only if $j \in h(p)$.

For mapping queries q we have to hash all matching elements of Σ^m that are covered by q, and define $h(q)$ as the union of all p such that q matches p. The implementation of the *Lookup* procedure is shown in Algorithm 3.39.

The complexity of computing set $h(q)$ heavily depends on the chosen hash function h. For a *balanced hash function*, consider the partition of Σ^m induced by h; generating blocks $B_j = \{p \in \Sigma^m \mid h(p) = j\}$. A hash function is balanced if $|B_j|$ is equal to $|\Sigma^m|$ divided by the hash table size b for all j.

For large alphabets (as in the CROSSWORD PUZZLE problem) the hash table size b can be scaled to some value larger than 2^m and letters can be individually mapped. More precisely, we assume an auxiliary hash function h' that maps Σ to a small set of b bits. $h(\text{BETTER})$ is determined by the concatenation $h'(\text{B})h'(\text{E})h'(\text{T})h'(\text{T})h'(\text{E})h'(\text{R})$. A partial match query for queries q like B $*$ T $*$ $*$ R would be answered by inspecting all $2^{(m-s)b}$ table entries in $h(q)$, where s is the number of fixed bits.

For small alphabets (like the binary case) we have $2^m > b$. One suitable approach is to extract the first $l = \lceil \lg b \rceil$ bits of each record as a first hash table index. However, the worst-case behavior can be poor: If none of the bits occurs in the first m positions, then every list must be searched.

To obtain good hash functions also for the worst-case, they have to depend on every input character.

3.3.4 Unlimited Branching Trees

A compromise between the TRIE and hash table subset dictionary data structure is an ordered list of tries, called an UNLIMITED BRANCHING TREE. Insertion is similar to an ordinary TRIE insertion with the exception that we maintain a distinctive root for the first element in the sorted representation of the set.

Figure 3.23 displays the UNLIMITED BRANCHING TREE data structure during the insertion of $\{1,2,3,4\}$, $\{1,2,4\}$, and $\{3,4\}$. To the left of the figure, the first subset generates a new UNLIMITED BRANCHING TREE. In the middle of the figure, we see that insertion can result in branching. The insertion, which has been executed to the right of the figure, shows that a new TRIE is inserted into the root list. The corresponding pseudo code is provided in Algorithm 3.40. The algorithm traverses the root list to detect whether or not a matching root element is present. In case we do not establish a new root element the implementation of the ordinary insert routine for the corresponding TRIE (not shown) is called. In case there is no such element, a new one is constructed and added to the list.

The running time of the algorithm is $O(k + l)$, where k is the size of the current TRIE list and l the size of the sorted set, plus the time $O(l \lg l)$ to sort the elements. As with our example it is often the case that all elements are selected from the set $\{1, \ldots, n\}$ such that the running time is $O(n)$ altogether.

The data structure is designed to solve the SUBSET QUERY and the CONTAINMENT QUERY problem. In Algorithm 3.41 we show a possible implementation for the latter. First, all root elements matching the query are retrieved. Then the corresponding tries are searched individually for a possible match with the query. As both the query and the stored set are sorted, the match is available in linear time with respect to the query set. The number of root elements that have to be processed can grow considerably and is bounded by the size of the universe Γ.

The worst-case running time of the algorithm is $O(km)$, where k is the size of the current TRIE list and m is the size of the query set plus the time $O(m \lg m)$ to sort the elements. If all set elements have been selected from the set $\{1, \ldots, n\}$, the worst-case running time is bounded by $O(n^2)$.

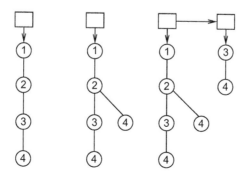

FIGURE 3.23

Evolution of an UNLIMITED BRANCHING TREE.

Procedure Insert
Input: UNLIMITED BRANCHING TREE $L = (T_1,\ldots,T_k)$, sorted set $p = \{p_1,\ldots,p_l\}$
Side Effect: Modified UNLIMITED BRANCHING TREE data structure

for each i **in** $\{1,\ldots,k\}$	;; Consider all tries
if $(p_1 = root(T_i))$	;; Matches root list
Trie-Insert(T_i,q) ; **return**	;; Insert into trie and quit
Generate a new trie T' for p	;; Temporary trie for inserted set
Insert T' into list L	;; Include new trie into sorted list

Algorithm 3.40

Inserting a set in an UNLIMITED BRANCHING TREE.

Procedure Lookup
Input: UNLIMITED BRANCHING TREE $L = (T_1,\ldots,T_k)$, query $q = \{q_1,\ldots,q_m\}$
Output: Flag indicating whether or not p is contained in L with $q \supseteq p$

$Q \leftarrow \emptyset$	;; Initialize queue
for each i **in** $\{1,\ldots,k\}$	;; Consider all tries
if $(root(T_i) \in q)$	;; Matches root list
$Q \leftarrow Q \cup \{T_i\}$	;; Insert trie to candidate set
for each T_i **in** Q	;; Process queue
if (*Trie-Lookup*(T_i,q)) **return** *true*	;; Search individual trie
return *false*	;; Search failed

Algorithm 3.41

Searching for subsets in an UNLIMITED BRANCHING TREE.

The matching efforts have been reduced using a data structure from rule-based production systems. The so-called *Rete algorithm* exploits the fact that the firing of rules, or playing moves as in our case, only changes a few parts of the state, and are of structural similarity, meaning that the same subpattern can occur in multiple rules. The Rete algorithm uses a rooted acyclic-directed graph, the Rete, where the nodes, with the exception of the root, represent patterns, and the edges represent dependencies (the relation $\subseteq$ defined earlier can be directly mapped).

3.4 STRING DICTIONARIES

String dictionaries offer substring and superstring queries, and are a specialization of subset dictionaries since substrings and superstrings are consecutive character vectors that do not include gaps. In the following, we study string dictionaries based on SUFFIX TREE.

A SUFFIX TREE is a compact trie representation of all suffixes of a given string. The substring information stored at each suffix node is simply given by the indices of the first and the last characters. In the following, the SUFFIX TREE data structure and its linear-time construction algorithm are explained in detail.

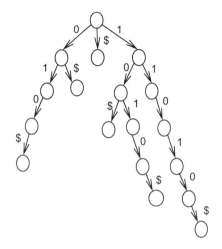

FIGURE 3.24

A SUFFIX TRIE for the string 11010$.

Inserting each suffix of string m in a TRIE yields a SUFFIX TRIE. To avoid conflicts at terminal nodes, we append a special character $ to m. For notational convenience, in the following this tag is commonly interpreted as an integral part of m. An example of a SUFFIX TRIE is shown in Figure 3.24. Each node in the SUFFIX TRIE corresponds to exactly one unique substring in m. Unfortunately, it can consist of $\Omega(|m|^2)$ nodes. Take, for example, the strings of the form 1^k0^k. They include $k^2 + 4k + 2$ different substrings (see Exercises).

3.4.1 Suffix Trees

A SUFFIX TREE (see Fig. 3.25) is a compact representation of a SUFFIX TRIE in which each node with only one successor is merged with its parent. (Such compressed structure of a TRIE is sometimes referred to as PATRICIA TRIE for *practical algorithms to retrieve information coded in alphanumeric*.) Each node in the SUFFIX TREE for m has more than one successor and $|m|$ leaves. As a consequence, it consumes at most $O(|m|)$ space.

For efficient SUFFIX TREE construction, we need some definitions. A *partial path* is a consecutive sequence of edges starting at the root. A *path* is a partial path that ends at a leaf. The *locus* of a string α is the node at the end of the path of α (if it exists). An extension of a string α is each string that has α as a prefix. The *extended locus* of α is the locus of the shortest extension of α. The *contracted locus* of a string α is the locus of the longest prefix of α. The term suf_i refers to the suffix of m starting at i, so that $suf_1 = m$. The string $head_i$ is the longest prefix of suf_i, which is also a prefix of suf_j for some $j < i$, and $tail_i$ is defined as $suf_i - head_i$; that is, $suf_i = head_i tail_i$. As an example take ababc, then $suf_3 = $ abc, $head_3 = $ ab, and $tail_3 = $ c. A naive approach starts with the empty tree T_0 and inserts suf_{i+1} to construct T_{i+1} from T_i for an increasing value of i.

To generate a SUFFIX TREE efficiently, *suffix links* are helpful, where a suffix link points from the locus of $a\alpha$, $a \in \Sigma$, $\alpha \in \Sigma^*$, to the locus of α. Suffix links are used as shortcuts during construction and search. We have that $head_i$ is the longest prefix of suf_i, which has an extended locus in T_{i-1}, since in T_i all suffixes $suf_j, j < i$ already have a locus.

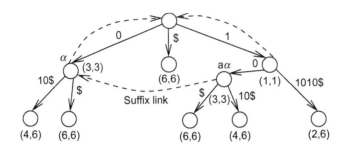

FIGURE 3.25

A SUFFIX TREE for the same string with suffix links.

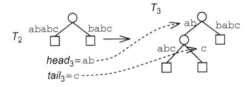

FIGURE 3.26

Inserting suf_i.

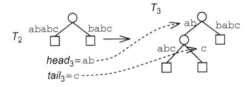

FIGURE 3.27

Insertion for the example string.

For inserting suf_i, tree T_{i+1} can be constructed from T_i as follows (see Fig. 3.26). First, we determine the extended locus $head_{i+1}$ in T_i, divide the last edge that leads to it in two new edges, and introduce a new node. Then, we create a new leaf for suf_{i+1}. For the given example string, Figure 3.27 depicts the modifications to transform T_2 into T_3.

The algorithm takes a linear number of steps. If the extended locus of $head_{i+1}$ in T_i is found, the extension of the tree can be accomplished in constant time. Algorithm 3.42 has two stages. First, it determines $head_{i+1}$ in T_i in amortized constant time. Then, it sets another suffix link.

We observe that if $head_i = a\gamma$ for character a and a (possibly empty) string γ, then γ is a prefix of $head_{i+1}$. Let $head_i = a\gamma$, then there is a $j < i$, such that $a\gamma$ is prefix of suf_i and suf_j according to the definition of $head_i$. Hence, γ is a prefix of suf_{i+1} and suf_{j+1}.

The loop invariants of the algorithm are (1) all internal nodes in T_{i-1} have a correct suffix link in T_i (I1), and (2) during the construction of T_i the contracted locus of $head_i$ in T_{i-1} is visited (I2). The

---

Procedure Construct-Suffix-Tree
Input: SUFFIX TREE T_i.
Output: SUFFIX TREE T_{i+1}.

Stage 1: Insertion of the locus of $head_{i+1}$.

1. Follow the suffix link of the contracted locus v' of $head_i$ to the node u.
2. If $\beta_i \neq \epsilon$, rescan β_i in T_i; that is, follow a path in T_i starting from u, so that the edge labels are β_i.
   i. If the locus w of $\alpha_i\beta_i$ in T_i does exists, scan γ_{i+1} starting from w; that is, follow a path in T_i starting from w, such that the edge labels coincide with suf_{i+1}, unless one falls off at edge (x,y).
   ii. If the locus w of $\alpha_i\beta_i$ in T_i does not exist let x be the contracted locus of $\alpha_i\beta_i$ and y be the extended locus of $\alpha_i\beta_i$. We have $head_{i+1} = \alpha_i\beta_i$.
3. At (x,y) create an internal node z for the locus of $head_{i+1}$ and a leaf for the locus of suf_{i+1}.

Stage 2: Insertion of the suffix link of the locus v of $head_i$.

1. Follow the suffix link from the contracted locus v' of $head_i$ to u.
2. If $\beta_i \neq \epsilon$, then *rescan* β_i in T_i until locus w of $\alpha_i\beta_i$. Set suffix link of the locus v of $head_i$ to w.

Algorithm 3.42

Algorithm to construct a SUFFIX TREE in linear time.

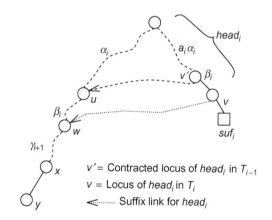

FIGURE 3.28

Partition of T_i.

invariants are certainly true if $i = 1$. If $i > 1$, then (I2) implies that construction T_{i+1} from T_i can start at the contracted locus of $head_i$ in T_{i-1}. If $head_i \neq \varepsilon$, then let α_i be the concatenation of the edge labels of the path to the contracted locus of $head_i$ without the first letter a_i. Moreover, $\beta_i = head_i - a_i\alpha_i$; that is, $head_i = a_i\alpha_i\beta_i$. If $head_i \neq \varepsilon$, then T_i can be visualized as shown in Figure 3.28.

Based on the lemma we have $head_{i+1} = \alpha_i \beta_i \gamma_{i+1}$. From the contracted locus v' of $head_i$ we already have a correct suffix link in T_i to a node u according to (I1). To build the locus of $head_{i+1}$ in T_i we start at u instead of the root of T_i in the naive approach. In an actual implementation both stages would have to be interleaved.

Lemma 3.1. *If the locus of $\alpha_i \beta_i$ in T_i does not exist, then $head_{i+1} = \alpha_i \beta_i$.*

Proof. Let v be the contracted locus and w be the extended locus of $\alpha_i \beta_i$. Let the labeling of the edges on the path to v be equal to γ and let the label of (v, w) be equal $\delta_1 \delta_2$ with $\delta_1, \delta_2 \neq \epsilon$ and $\gamma \delta_1 = \alpha_i \beta_i$. Then all suffixes with prefix $\alpha_i \beta_i$ are contained in the subtree of T with root node w, and all suffixes in T have a prefix $\alpha_i \beta_i \delta_2$. Therefore, $j < i + 1$ and suf_j has the prefix $\alpha_i \beta_i$. Hence, suf_j has the prefix $\alpha_i \beta_i \delta_2$. We have to show that $suf_j = \alpha_i \beta_i a \cdots$ and $suf_{i+1} = \alpha_i \beta_i b \cdots$ with $a \neq b$.

Let $suf_{j'}$ be a suffix with prefix $head_i = a_i \alpha_i \beta_i$. Then $suf_{j'+1}$ has prefix $\alpha_i \beta_i \delta_2$ and $suf_{j'}$ has prefix $a_i \alpha_i \beta_i \delta_2$. Since $head_i = a_i \alpha_i \beta_i$, the first letter a of δ_2 and the first letter b that follows $a_i \alpha_i \beta_i$ in suf_i are different. Therefore, the prefix of suf_{i+1} is $\alpha_i \beta_i b$ and the prefix of suf_j is $\alpha_i \beta_i a$, so that the longest common prefix is $\alpha_i \beta_i$. ∎

As an example take $W = b^5 abab^3 a^2 b^5 c$. The construction of T_{14} from T_{13} by inserting $suf_{14} = bbbbbc$ in T_{13} is shown in Figure 3.29.

Theorem 3.7. *(Time Complexity* SUFFIX TREE *Construction) Algorithm 3.42 takes $O(|m|)$ time to generate a* SUFFIX TREE *for m.*

Proof. In every step a suffix of m is scanned and rescanned. We first analyze rescanning. Since $\alpha_i \beta_i$ is a prefix of $head_{i+1}$, at an edge we only have to test how many characters we have to skip in β_i. Subsequently, we require constant time for each traversed edge so that the total number of steps during rescanning is proportional to the number of traversed edges. Let $res_i = \beta_{i-1} \gamma_i tail_i$. At each edge e, which is traversed while rescanning β_{i-1}, the string α_i is extended by δ of edge e; that is, δ is in res_i, but not in res_{i+1}. Since $|\delta| \geq 1$, we have $|res_{i+1}| \leq |res_i| - k_i$ with k_i as the number of rescanned edges in step i, and

$$\sum_{i=1}^{n} k_i \leq \sum_{i=1}^{n} |res_i| - |res_{i+1}| = |res_1| - |res_{n+1}| \leq n.$$

Next we analyze scanning. The number of scanned characters in step i equals $|\gamma_{i+1}|$, where $|\gamma_{i+1}| = |head_{i+1}| - |\alpha_i \beta_i| = |head_{i+1}| - (|head_i| - 1)$. Therefore, the total number of scanned characters is equal to

$$\sum_{i=0}^{n-1} |\gamma_{i+1}| = \sum_{i=0}^{n-1} |head_{i+1}| - |head_i| + 1 = n + |head_n| - |head_0| \in O(n).$$

∎

3.4.2 Generalized Suffix Trees

A GENERALIZED SUFFIX TREE is a string data structure appropriate for web search and for solving problems in computational biology. After introducing GENERALIZED SUFFIX TREES we first consider

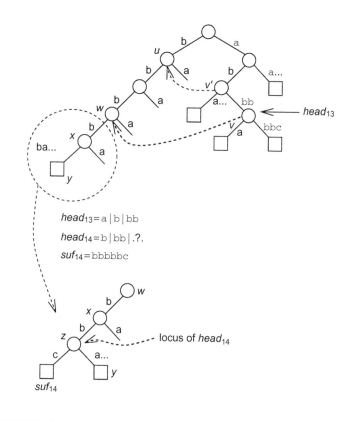

FIGURE 3.29

Construction of T_{14} from T_{13}.

the problem of updating the information to obtain optimal space performance even in a dynamic setting.

The efficient construction of a SUFFIX TREE can be extended naturally to more than one string by building the SUFFIX TREE of the string $m_1\$_1 \ldots m_n\$_n$. It is not difficult to show (see Exercises) that the SUFFIX TREE for $m_1\$_1 \ldots m_n\$_n$ is isomorphic to the compacted TRIE for all suffixes of $m_1\$_1$ up to all suffixes of $m_n\$_n$. Furthermore, the trees are identical except for the labels of the edges incident to leaves. This fact allows us to insert and search a string into an existing SUFFIX TREE.

A straightforward deletion of strings causes problems, since each edge stored at the subsequent nodes includes substring interval information of some previously inserted strings. Therefore, the update procedure also has to update substring references in the tree. The solution to this nontrivial problem is based on maintaining an additional INVERTED TRIE. Let M be the set of strings in the generalized SUFFIX TREE S and let T be the TRIE that contains all inverted strings. Then there is a bijection between the set of nodes in T and the set of leaf nodes in S: On one hand, each suffix of a string m_i corresponds to a leaf node; on the other hand, for each prefix of

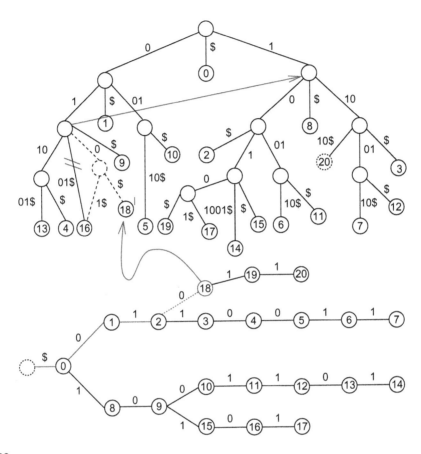

FIGURE 3.30

GENERALIZED SUFFIX TREE during insertion of 11010$.

m_i^{-1} there is a prefix in T. Figure 3.30 shows a snapshot of inserting string *11010$* in a GEN-ERALIZED SUFFIX TREE with an associated inverted trie. Nodes of the same index indicate the bijection.

Given the associated INVERTED TRIE, it is possible to delete a string from the largest suffix to the shortest. As a consequence, in each step the suffix links are correct. The problem that is often not dealt with in literature is that the deleted strings are indeed needed inside the generalized tree. The idea of the improvement is to extend the unique representation of the leaves given by T bottom to the internal nodes. Therefore, we invent *twins* that refer to the history of leaf generation. Figure 3.31 gives an example.

As with the algorithm for constructing an ordinary SUFFIX TREE, the insertion process can be divided into a sequence of update operations. In the pseudo-code implementation of Algorithm 3.43

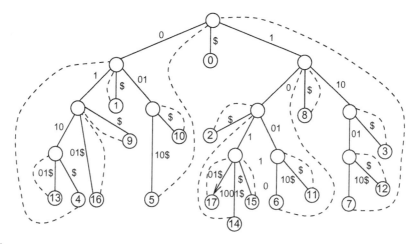

FIGURE 3.31

Twin structure in the GENERALIZED SUFFIX TREE.

Procedure Insert
Input: String m_j, pointer $head_{j-1}$, associated string uvw
      contracted locus cl, extended locus el, current offset at
Output: Pointer $head_j$ and associated decomposition uvw
Side Effect: Modifies cl, el, at

Decompose uvw into u, v and w	;; Partition string uvw
if $(v = \epsilon)$ $cl \leftarrow el \leftarrow root$ **else** $cl \leftarrow el \leftarrow link(uv)$	;; Shortcut via suffix link
if $(Rescan(w, at, cl, el))$	;; If rescanning ends at existing node
if $(link(head_{j-1}) = \perp)$ $link(head_{j-1}) \leftarrow el$	;; Set suffix link
if $(Scan(m_j, at, cl, el))$	;; If scanning ends on existing node
Insert m_j at cl	;; Insert suffix at existing node
$head_j \leftarrow cl$	;; Set next head to existing node
else	;; Scanning ends on an edge
Insert m_j between cl and el at distance at	;; Generates new node $inner$
$head_j \leftarrow inner$	;; Update new head
else	;; w does not fit, $z = \epsilon$, no scan
Insert m_j between cl and el at distance at	;; Generates new node $inner$
if $(link(head_{j-1}) = \perp)$ $link(head_{j-1}) \leftarrow inner$	;; Set suffix link of old head
$head \leftarrow inner$	;; Set next head to new node
Generate new string uvw from $head_j$	;; New head determines new prefix

Algorithm 3.43

Insertion of one suffix in a GENERALIZED SUFFIX TREE.

Procedure Delete
Input: String m, GENERALIZED SUFFIX TREE, associated INVERTED TRIE T
Output: Updated GENERALIZED SUFFIX TREE

$Stack \leftarrow Trie\text{-}Remove(T, m^{-1})$	;; Delete node and initialize stack
while $(Stack \neq \emptyset)$	;; As long as we can decrease
Pop q from $Stack$	;; Delete node from stack
$s \leftarrow parent(q); p \leftarrow parent(twin(q))$	;; Determine (twin) predecessor of q
if $(|Succ'(q)| > 0)$ **return**	;; At least two suffixes point to q
Find label j of edge $(twin(p), q)$	;; Label of outgoing edge
Remove child q from s; Remove child q from $twin(p)$	;; Delete leaf q
Let r be some twin child of $twin(s)$	;; Find twin successor of s
if $(s = p)$	;; Direct predecessors do not match
if $(|Succ'(s)| > 1)$	;; s has more than one successor
Change string reference at s to the one of r	;; Adjust representation
else	;; s has only one successor
Remove s	;; Delete inner node
else	;; Direct predecessors match
Remove child r from $twin(s)$	;; Extract twin child node
Add child r to $twin(p)$ with label j	;; Offer twin child to next node
Change string reference at $twin(r)$ to the one of r	;; Adjust representation
if $(Succ'(s) > 1)$	;; More than one successor
Let r' be some twin child of $twin(s)$	;; Find another twin successor
Change string reference at $twin(s)$ to the one of r'	;; Adjust representation
else	;; There is only one successor
Remove s	;; Delete internal node

Algorithm 3.44

Deleting a string in a GENERALIZED SUFFIX TREE.

---

we assume a procedure to insert a suffix at an existing locus, and a procedure to split an existing edge. Deletion, as shown in Algorithm 3.44, is based on a subroutine for removing a leaf that is called for each removed node while deleting the inverted string in the INVERTED TRIE T. If removing a leaf, we access and adjust the string representation of a twin. The correctness argument is based on the following result.

Lemma 3.2. *Let* Internal *and* Leaves *be the sets of all internal and leaf nodes in the* GENERALIZED SUFFIX TREE. *Let* Succ(p) *be the set of successor of p and* Succ$'(p)$ *be the set of twin successors of p. The following invariances are preserved:*

(Ia) *For all $p \in$ Internal there is a $q \in$ Leaves with $q \in$ Succ$'(p)$, which has the same string representative as p.*

(Ib) *For all $p \in$ Internal we have $|Succ'(p)| = |Succ(p)| - 1$; that is, the number of ordinary successors is always one larger to the number of twin successors.*

Proof. To prove the result we perform a case study:

Inserting a suffix at a given node A newly inserted leaf extends both sets *Succ* and *Succ′* for the existing node by one element. The string representation of the leaf and of the existing node is set to the inserted string m. Therefore, the invariances remain satisfied.

Inserting a suffix between two nodes In this case both newly generated nodes refer to m, so that we have (Ia). The internal node gets two successors and one twin successor (the new leaf node). Therefore, $2 = |Succ(p)| = |Succ′(p)| + 1$ and (Ib).

Removing a Leaf Let q be the node to be deleted, s be its predecessor, and p its twin predecessor. The algorithm considers two cases:

$s = p$ Since q in $Succ(s) \cap Succ′(s)$ invariance (Ib) is satisfied. If $|Succ(s)| > 1$, then there exists a leaf r in $Succ′(s)$. Leaf r changes the string representation such that s no longer refers to the string representation of q. Therefore, we have (Ia) for node s. If, however, $|Succ(s)| = 1$, then s is deleted for good, and nothing has to be shown.

$s \neq p$ This case is tricky. If $|Succ(s)| = 1$, then s is deleted. Moreover, $Succ′(p)$ is set to $Succ′(p) - \{q\} \cup \{r′\}$ such that $|Succ′(p)|$ remains unchanged. Otherwise, $|Succ(s)| = k > 1$. Using (Ib), then at the time when q was deleted we have $k + 1$ successors and k twin successors of s. Consequently, besides $r′$ there is another twin successor r of s. This node is used to determine the string representation for p; that is, $Succ′(p)$ is set to $Succ′(p) \setminus \{q\} \cup \{r\}$. We see that both invariances are maintained. ∎

Hence, we can prove the following result.

Theorem 3.8. *(Space Optimality* GENERALIZED SUFFIX TREE*) Let S be a* GENERALIZED SUFFIX TREE *after an arbitrary number of insert and delete operations and $d_{max} = \max_i d_i$ be the maximal number of all characters of strings in the dictionary M; that is, $d_i = \sum_{m \in M_i} |m|$, where i denotes the operation step. The space requirements of S are bounded by $O(d_{max})$.*

To find a substring of a given string m, we can determine the longest pattern prefix h of the string stored in the GENERALIZED SUFFIX TREE that matches m *starting* at position i, $i \in \{1, \ldots, |m|\}$. Similarly, we can determine the longest substring h of the strings stored in the GENERALIZED SUFFIX TREE that matches m *ending* at position i. In both cases we have to check if h is maximal; that is, if an accepting node that corresponds to a path for a full string m in the dictionary has been reached.

3.5 SUMMARY

The search algorithms discussed in the previous chapter need to keep track of the generated and expanded states. A*, for example, needs to be able to check whether a state is in the *Open* list, insert a state into the *Open* list, with a given f-value, decrease the f-value of a state in the *Open* list, extract the state with the smallest f-value from the *Open* list, check whether a state is in the *Closed* list, insert a state into the *Closed* list, and perhaps delete a state from the *Closed* list. These operations need to be fast since they are typically performed a large number of times during each search. In this chapter, therefore, we discussed algorithms and data structures for implementing them.

The *Open* list is basically a priority queue. The values of the priorities (e.g., the f-values for A*) determine how the operations on the *Open* list can be implemented. If the priorities are floating-point values, then the operations can be implemented with heaps, including advanced heap structures and data structures. A HEAP is a complete binary tree that stores a state at every node so that the priority of the state at a node is always higher than the priority of the states at the children of the node. A FIBONACCI HEAP, a WEAK HEAP, and a WEAK QUEUE relax this requirement in different ways. If the priorities are integers, then the operations can also be implemented with buckets of fixed or exponentially increasing sizes (RADIX HEAP) or hierarchical structures of buckets, including the VAN EMDE BOAS PRIORITY QUEUE. Buckets consist of randomly accessible storage locations in a consecutive address range that are labeled with consecutive ranges of priorities, where each storage location stores the set of states of which the priorities are in its range of priorities. Implementations that use buckets are usually faster than those that use heaps.

Table 3.4 gives an overview for the priority queue data structures introduced in this chapter. The complexities for integer-based methods are measured in the number of instructions. For generic weights we express complexities in the number of comparisons. The parameters are $C = $ max edge weight, $N = $ max key, $n = $ nodes stored, and $e = $ nodes visited. The star (*) denotes amortized costs.

The *Closed* list is a simple set. The operations on it can, therefore, be implemented with bitvectors, lists, search trees, or hash tables. Bitvectors assign a bit to every state in a set. The bit is set to one if the state is in the set. They are a good choice if the percentage of states in the set (out of all states) is large. Lists simply represent all states in the set, perhaps storing compressed versions of states by representing similar parts of several states only once (SUFFIX LIST). They are a good choice if the percentage of states in the set is small. The question then becomes how to test membership efficiently. To this end, lists are often represented as search trees or, more commonly since faster, hash tables rather than linked lists. Hash tables (hash dictionaries) consist of randomly accessible storage locations in a consecutive address range. Hashing maps each state to an address.

We discussed different hash functions. Perfect hashing (similar to bitvectors) maps every state to its own address. To insert a state into a hash table, we store the state at its address. To delete a state

---

Table 3.4 Priority queue data structures; top are bucket structures for integer keys, bottom are heap structures for general keys in a totally ordered set defined through a comparison function.

Data Structure	DecreaseKey	DeleteMin	Insert	Dijkstra/A*
1-LEVEL BUCKET (3.1–3.4)	$O(1)$	$O(C)$	$O(1)$	$O(e + Cn)$
2-LEVEL BUCKET	$O(1)$	$O(\sqrt{C})$	$O(1)$	$O(e + \sqrt{C}n)$
RADIX HEAP (3.5–3.8)	$O(1)^*$	$O(\lg C)^*$	$O(1)^*$	$O(e + n \cdot \lg C)$
EMDE BOAS (3.9–3.11)	$O(\lg \lg N)$	$O(\lg \lg N)$	$O(\lg \lg N)$	$O((e + n)\lg \lg N)$
BINARY SEARCH TREE	$O(\lg n)$	$O(\lg n)$	$O(\lg n)$	$O((e + n)\lg n)$
BINOMIAL QUEUE	$O(\lg n)$	$O(\lg n)$	$O(\lg n)$	$O((e + n)\lg n)$
HEAP (3.12–3.14)	$2\lg n$	$2\lg n$	$2\lg n$	$O((e + n)\lg n)$
WEAK HEAP (3.17–3.21)	$\lg n$	$\lg n$	$\lg n$	$O((e + n)\lg n)$
PAIRING HEAP (3.16)	$O(2^{\sqrt{\lg \lg n}})$	$O(\lg n)^*$	$O(1)$	$O(2^{\sqrt{\lg \lg n}}e + n \lg n)$
FIBONACCI HEAP (3.22)	$O(1)^*$	$O(\lg n)^*$	$O(1)$	$O(e + n\lg n)$
REL. WEAK QUEUE (3.23)	$O(1)$	$O(\lg n)$	$O(1)$	$O(e + n\lg n)$

from the hash table, we remove the state from its address. To check whether a state is in the hash table, we compare the state in question against the state stored at its address. If and only if there is a state stored at its address and it matches the state in question, then the state in question is in the hash table. Perfect hashing is memory intensive. Regular hashing can map two states to the same address, which is called an address collision. Address collisions can be handled either via chaining or open addressing. Chaining resolves the conflict by storing all states in the hash table that map to the same address in a linked list and stores a pointer to the linked list at this address. Open addressing resolves the conflict by storing a state at a different address in either the same or a different hash table when some other state is already stored at its address. We discussed different ways of determining this other address, including using more than one hash table.

We also discussed how to increase the size of the hash table, in case the number of successive address collisions is too large, until an empty address is found. Regular hashing is less memory intensive than perfect hashing but can still be memory intensive. Approximate hashing saves memory by storing an insufficient amount of information to implement the membership test exactly. For example, it might store only a compressed version of the state in one or more hash tables. In the extreme case, it might only set a single bit to one in one or more hash tables to indicate that some state is stored at an address. In case of several hash tables, the state is considered stored if and only if all hash tables report that it is stored. Approximate hashing can make the mistake to determine that a state is in the *Closed* list even though it is not, which means that a search might not expand a state since it thinks it has expanded the state already and thus might not be able to find a path even if one exists.

Table 3.5 gives an overview of the different hash methods and their time complexity. We indicate whether states are stored in a compressed or ordinary way, and whether or not the hashing method is lossy.

Moreover, we have seen two storage structures for partial information. The subset dictionary stores partial states in the form of sets, and the substring dictionary stores partial paths in the form of substrings. In the first case, different implementations have been discussed to solve one of the equivalent problems, SUBSET QUERY, CONTAINMENT QUERY, and PARTIAL MATCH; for the second case, we have concentrated on the SUFFIX TREE data structure and its extensions for solving the DYNAMIC DICTIONARY MATCHING problem.

Table 3.5 Hashing algorithms. With Y we denote $\max_y |\{x \mid h(x) = h(y)\}|$. With $p^+(\alpha)$ and $p^-(\alpha)$ we denote the time complexities for successful and unsuccessful search based on the current hash table load α. More accurate values depend on the conflict resolution strategy used.

	Insert	Lookup	Compressed	Lossy
Chaining (3.29–3.31)	$O(1)$	$O(Y)$	–	–
Open addressing (3.32–3.35)	$O(p^-(\alpha))$	$O(p^+(\alpha))$	–	–
SUFFIX LIST hashing	$O(\lg n)^*$	$O(\lg n)^*$	✓	–
FKS hashing	$O(1)^*$	$O(1)$	–	–
Cuckoo hashing (3.36–3.37)	$O(1)^*$	$O(1)$	–	–
Bit-state hashing	$O(1)$	$O(1)$	✓	✓
Hash compact	$O(1)$	$O(1)$	✓	✓

3.6 EXERCISES

3.1   Display the
1. 2-LEVEL BUCKET data structure ($C = 80$)
2. RADIX HEAP data structure

for the elements $\{28,7,69,3,24,7,72\}$.

3.2   A *union-find* data structure is a dictionary for maintaining partitions of a set. We may represent each interval by its right-most element, so that the partitioning $[1,x_1],\ldots,[x_k+1,n]$ is represented by the set $\{x_1,\ldots,x_k\}$. Consider the data type that represents a partition of $\{1,\ldots,n\}$ into intervals with the operations:
- *Find(x)* that returns the interval containing x.
- *Union(x)* that unifies an interval with the immediately following one.
- *Split(x)* that splits the interval T containing x into two intervals $I \cap [1,x]$ and $I \cap [x+1,n]$.
  1. How do the basic operations act on this set?
  2. Use a VAN EMDE BOAS PRIORITY QUEUE to implement this strategy.

3.3   In a randomly filled array with n entries the minimal and maximal elements have to be found. For the sake of simplicity, you may assume $n \geq 2$ to be a power of 2.
1. Describe a *divide-and-conquer* algorithm that uses $3n/2 - 2$ comparisons.
2. Use WEAK HEAPS to elegantly solve the problem with $3n/2 - 2$ comparisons.
3. Show as a lower bound $3n/2 - 2$ comparisons are required to solve the problem.
4. Show a similar bound to search the first- and second-smallest element.

3.4   1. Show that the path to index n in a HEAP is determined by the binary representation of n.
2. Let $f(n)$ be the number of HEAPS with n pairwise different keys and let s_i be the size of the subtree for root i, $1 \leq i \leq n$. Show that $f(n) = n! / \prod_{i=1}^{n} s_i$.

3.5   Merge two HEAPS with n_1 and n_2 elements efficiently.
1. Assume that n_1 und n_2 are very different; for example, n_1 is much larger than n_2.
2. Assume that n_1 and n_2 are *almost* the same, say $\lfloor n_1/2 \rfloor = \lfloor n_2/2 \rfloor$.

Provide the time complexities for both cases in big-oh notation.

3.6   *Double-ended queues* are priority queues that allow the insertion and the deletion of the minimum *and* maximum element.
1. Transform a HEAP/WEAK HEAP into its dual and estimate the number of required comparisons.
2. Show how to perform the transposition of elements in such a compare-exchange structure.

3.7   Transform a WEAK HEAP into a heap in-place with a small number of comparisons.
1. Study the base case of a WEAK HEAP of size 8.
2. Develop a recursive algorithm. For the ease of construction, you may assume $n = 2^k$.
3. Compare the number of comparisons with ordinary heap construction and top-down, bottom-up, and binary search sift-down.

3.8   In an initially empty BINOMIAL QUEUE perform the following operations:
   1. *Insert(45), Insert(33), Insert(28), Insert(21), Insert(17), Insert(14)*
   2. *Insert(9), Insert(6), Insert(5), Insert(1), DeleteMin*
   3. *DecreaseKey(33,11), Delete(21), DecreaseKey(28,3), DeleteMin*
   Display the data structure for all intermediate results.

3.9   Consider an initially empty hash table with 11 entries. Insert the keys 16, 21, 15, 10, 5, 19, and 8 according to the following hash algorithms and display the table after the last insertion. Use the two hash functions $h(x) = x \bmod 11$ and $h'(x) = 1 + (x \bmod 9)$.
   1. Linear probing using $s(j,k) = j$, quadratic probing using $s(j,k) = (-1)^j \lceil j/2 \rceil^2$.
   2. Double and ordered hashing, single and double bit-state hashing.

3.10 Let $u = (p_1, \ldots, p_m)$ be a state for an ATOMIX problem on a board of size $n \times n$. We define its hash value as $h(u) = \left(\sum_{i=1}^{m} p_i \cdot n^{2i} \right) \bmod q$. Let v be an immediate successor of u that differs from its predecessor u only in the position of atom i.
   1. Determine $h(v)$ based on $h(u)$ using incremental hashing.
   2. Use a precomputed table with $n^2 \cdot m$ entries to accelerate the computation.
   3. Avoid computationally expensive modulo operators by using addition/subtraction.

3.11 *Dynamic incremental hashing* considers hashing of state vectors of variable size.
   1. How does the hash function $h(u) = \sum_i u_i |\Sigma|^i \bmod q$ change if:
   - A value is added to/deleted at the end of the existing state vector of u?
   - A value is added to/deleted at the beginning of the existing state vector of u?
   For both cases devise a formula that can be computed in time $O(1)$.
   2. For the general case, where a value is changed somewhere in the state vector $u = (u_1, \ldots, u_n)$, compute the hash address in $O(\lg n)$ time.

3.12 In the SUFFIX LIST example of Figure 3.18, insert $(0101010)_2$ and delete $(0011101)_2$.

3.13 Compute the
   1. perfect hash value of the permutation (4 7 2 5 0 8 1 3 6)
   2. permutation (of size 15) for the rank 421, 123, 837, 658
   according to the lexicographic ordering and according to the one of Myrvold and Ruskey.

3.14 Devise two hash functions and a sequence of insertions that lead to an infinite cuckoo process.

3.15 Let $N = 2^k$. A NAVIGATION PILE is a complete binary tree with $2^{k+1} - 1$ nodes. The first $n \leq 2^k$ leaf elements store one element each and the remaining leaves are empty. Interior nodes (branches) contain links to the leaf nodes in the form of binary-encoded relative index information. For each branch the leaf is addressed that contains the smallest element of all elements stored in the leaf sequence.
   The representation of a NAVIGATION PILE are two sequences: $A[0..n-1]$ for the elements and $B[0..2^{k+1} - 1]$ for the navigation information, pointing to the elements in A. An example NAVIGATION PILE of size 14 and capacity 16 are shown in Figure 3.32. The parent/child relationship is shown with dotted arrows and the navigation information with solid arrows.

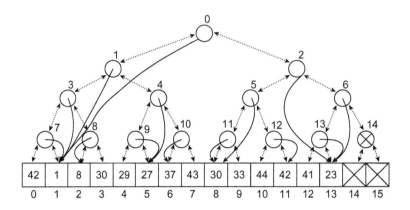

FIGURE 3.32

Example of a NAVIGATION PILE.

1. Show that all navigation information can be stored with $2^{k+1} = 2N$ bits.
2. Argue that the following operations can be supported in constant time: *depth, height, parent, first-leaf, last-leaf, first-child, second-child, root, is-root,* and *ancestor*.
3. Show that bottom-up construction of a NAVIGATION PILE requires $n - 1$ comparisons.
4. Show how to implement *Insert* with at most $\lg\lg n + O(1)$ comparisons and one element move (given that $O(\lg n)$ additional instructions are allowed).

3.16 Draw a SUFFIX TREE for 10100100110001100$ including the suffix links.

3.17 Consider a text t.
1. Show how to report all substrings in t in between two given strings with respect to their lexicographic ordering. For example, ACCGTA is in between ACA and ACCT.
2. Devise an efficient algorithm to find the longest substring that occurs at least twice in t.

3.18 There are $n^2/2$ substrings of string T of size n. Some of the substrings are identical.
1. Show that $1^k0^k$$ has $k^2 + 4k + 2$ different substrings.
2. Show how to print all different substrings in time proportional to their total length.

3.19 Let D be a set of k string of length $n_1, \ldots, n_k$.
1. Devise an efficient algorithm to determine for each string in D if it is a substring of another string in D.
2. Devise an algorithm that computes the longest common substring for all pairs of strings in D. The running time should be $O(kd)$, where d is the sum of the sizes of the strings in D.
3. Let $n_1 = \ldots = n_k = m$. Devise an algorithm that computes the longest common prefix for all pairs of strings in D. The running time should be $O(km + p)$, where p is the number of pairs, of which the common prefix is not empty.

3.20 Consider a (very long) text $T = t_1 \ldots t_n$ over the alphabet Σ to be searched for a maximal pattern $P = t_i t_{i+1} \ldots t_j$ such that the reflection $\tilde{P} = t_j \ldots t_{i+1} t_i$ is also a pattern in T. For example, in $T = 10000111100101111000001$ the pair $P = 000011110$ and $\tilde{P} = 011110000$ is maximal. Describe an efficient algorithm to solve the problem and provide its time and space complexities.

3.7 BIBLIOGRAPHIC NOTES

Dial (1969) has invented the 1-LEVEL BUCKET priority queue data structure. Its variants have been studied by Ahuja, Magnanti, and Orlin (1989). The 2-level architecture can be further refined to an arbitrary number k of levels, with k-arrays of the size $O(\sqrt[k]{C})$. Space and time can be improved to $O(\sqrt[4]{C})$, but the implementation becomes quite involved. Two-layered RADIX HEAP data structures improve the bound for *DeleteMin* to $O(\lg C / \lg \lg C)$ and a hybrid with a FIBONACCI HEAP yields an $O(\sqrt{\lg C})$ time algorithm. Alternative priority queue data structures based on keys have been studied by van Emde Boas, Kaas, and Zijlstra (1977). Dementiev, Kettner, Mehnert, and Sanders (2004) have provided cache-efficient implementations.

Fredman and Tarjan (1987) have given the amortized analysis for a FIBONACCI HEAP that apply *Insert* and *DecreaseKey* in amortized constant time and *DeleteMin* in amortized logarithmic time. Cherkassy, Goldberg, and Silverstein (1997b) compare different priority queue implementations and provide an efficient shortest path library (Cherkassy, Goldberg, and Ratzig, 1997a). Many priority queue implementations have been integrated in LEDA by Mehlhorn and Näher (1999).

The WEAK HEAP data structure has been introduced by Dutton (1993) and analyzed in detail by Edelkamp and Wegener (2000). Edelkamp and Stiegeler (2002) have implemented a sorting index based on WEAK-HEAPSORT with $O(n \lg n - 0.9n)$ comparisons in the worst-case and an in-place QUICK-SORT variant with $O(n \lg n + 0.2n)$ comparisons on average. The latter approach is based on replacing original HEAPSORT with WEAK-HEAPSORT in the hybrid of QUICK-HEAPSORT originally proposed by Cantone and Cinotti (2002).

Minimizing the number of moves has been considered by Munro and Raman (1996). The NAVIGATION PILE data structure has been introduced by Katajainen and Vitale (2003). It has been applied to sorting, yielding an algorithm with $n \lg n + 0.59n + O(1)$ comparisons, $2.5n + O(1)$ element moves, and $O(n \lg n)$ further instructions. Independently, Franceschini and Geffert (2003) devised a sorting algorithm with less than $17n + \epsilon n$ moves and $3n \lg n + 2 \lg \lg n$ comparisons. Other doubly ended priority queue structures are min-max HEAPS proposed by Atkinson, Sack, Santoro, and Strothotte (1986), DEAPS by Carlsson (1987), and INTERVAL HEAPS by van Leeuwen and Wood (1993).

Thorup (1999) has shown that for integer weights in undirected graphs a deterministic linear-time algorithm can be devised. It bypasses the requirement for extracting the minimum element. The data structure is substituted by a growing COMPONENT TREE. However, the algorithm is pretty involved and rather of theoretical interest, since its data structure, an ATOMIC HEAP, requires $n > 2^{12^{20}}$. Thorup (2000) has studied *RAM priority queues*. For a random access machine with arbitrary word size a priority queue is obtained supporting *Insert*, *Delete*, and *DeleteMin* operations in worst-case time $O(\lg \lg n)$. This improves $O(\sqrt{\lg C})$ for a hybrid RADIX HEAP.

RELAXED WEAK QUEUES (a.k.a. RUN-RELAXED WEAK QUEUES) by Elmasry, Jensen, and Katajainen (2005) are binary tree variants of run-relaxed heaps invented by Driscoll, Gabow, Shrairman, and Tarjan (1988), and implement a worst-case efficient priority queue (with constant-time efficiencies for INSERT and DECREASEKEY and logarithmic time for DELETE and DELETEMIN). Other structures achieving this performance are BRODAL HEAPS by Brodal (1996) and FAT HEAPS by Kaplan, Shafrir, and Tarjan (2002). By sacrificing worst for average case performance, RANK-RELAXED WEAK QUEUES achieve a better practical efficiency. Another promising competitor in this class are VIOLATION HEAPS proposed by Elmasry (2010). Policy-based benchmarking has been done by Bruun, Edelkamp, Katajainen, and Rasmussen (2010).

Theoretical advances for reducing the number of comparisons for deleting the minimum to $n \lg n + O(\lg \lg n)$ and $n \lg n + O(n)$ have been discussed by Elmasry, Jensen, and Katajainen (2008c) and Elmasry, Jensen, and Katajainen (2008b). PAIRING HEAPS have been suggested by Fredman, Sedgewick, Sleator, and Tarjan (1986). A refined implementation has been suggested by Stasko and Vitter (1987). A transformational approach and survey on efficient double-ended priority queues has been provided by Elmasry, Jensen, and Katajainen (2008a).

Hashing is fundamental to state space search and by the need of good distribution functions links to the generation of pseudo-random numbers. One generator has been proposed by Lehmer (1949) and its improvement has been suggested by Schrage (1979). The distribution and the selection of good random numbers have been analyzed by Park and Miller (1988).

Karp and Rabin (1987) have suggested incremental hashing for string search. A related incremental hashing for game playing has been introduced by Zobrist (1970). Its application to state space search and multiple pattern databases has been proposed by Mehler and Edelkamp (2005). For dynamic state vectors, incremental hashing has been extended by Mehler and Edelkamp (2006). Recursive hashing has been introduced by (Cohen, 1997) and most prominently implemented in the software model checker SPIN (Holzmann, 2004). Gains for incremental recursive hashing in SPIN are documented by Nguyen and Ruys (2008). In this context universal hashing has been shown to have advantages by Eckerle and Lais (1998). In experiments the authors have shown that the *ideal* circumstances for error prediction in sequential hashing are not found in practice and refine the model for coverage prediction to match the observation. Bit-state hashing has been adopted in protocol validator SPIN that parses the expressive concurrent Promela protocol specification language (Holzmann, 1998). Hash compaction has been contributed by Stern and Dill (1996), and collapse compression has been implemented by Holzmann (1997) and Lerda and Visser (2001).

The BLOOM FILTER has been invented by Bloom (1970) and been used in the web context by Marais and Bharat (1997) as a mechanism for identifying which pages have associated comments stored. Holzmann and Puri (1999) have suggested a finite-state machine description that shares similarities with binary decision diagrams. In work by Geldenhuys and Valmari (2003) the practical performance ratio has been shown to be close to the information theoretical bound for some protocols like the Dining Philosophers. As with the *suffix list* by Edelkamp and Meyer (2001) the construction aims at redundancies in the state vector. Similar ideas have been considered by Choueka, Fraenkel, Klein, and Segal (1986), but the data structure there is static and not theoretically analyzed. Another dynamic variant achieving asymptotically equivalent storage bounds is sketched in Brodnik and Munro (1999). Constants are only given for two static examples. Comparing with the numbers of Brodnik, a dynamic SUFFIX LIST can host up to five times more elements of the same value range. However, the data structure of Brodnik provides constant access time.

Ranking permutations in linear time is due to Myrvold and Ruskey (2001). Korf and Schultze (2005) have used lookup tables with a space requirement of $O(2^N \lg N)$ bits to compute lexicographic ranks, and Bonet (2008) has discussed different time-space trade-offs. Mares and Straka

(2007) proposed a linear-time algorithm for lexicographic rank, which relies on constant-time bitvector manipulations.

FKS hashing is due to Fredman, Komlós, and Szemerédi (1984). Dietzfelbinger, Karlin, Mehlhorn, auf der Heide, Rohnert, and Tarjan (1994) have devised the first dynamic version of it, yielding a worst-case constant-time hashing algorithm. Östlin and Pagh (2003) have shown that the space complexity for dynamical perfect hashing can be greatly reduced and Fotakis, Pagh, and Sanders (2003) have studied how to further reduce the space complexity to an information theoretical minimum. Practical perfect hashing has been analyzed by Botelho, Pagh, and Ziviani (2007) and an external memory perfect hash function variant has been given by Botelho and Ziviani (2007). The complexity is bounded by the need to sort all elements by their hash value in the partitioning step. Minimum perfect hash functions can be stored with less than four bits per item. With *cuckoo hashing*, Pagh and Rodler (2001) have devised a further practical and theoretical worst-case optimal hashing algorithm.

The SUFFIX TREE data structure is of widespread use in the context of web search (Stephen, 1994) and computational biology (Gusfield, 1997). The linear-time construction algorithm is due to McCreight (1976). DYNAMIC DICTIONARY MATCHING problems have been proposed and solved by Amir, Farach, Galil, Giancarlo, and Park (1994), and Amir, Farach, Idury, Poutré, and Schäffer (1995). The optimal space bound for arbitrary deletions has been proven by Edelkamp (1998b). Another class for string search based on bit manipulation has been contributed by Baeza-Yates and Gonnet (1992).

Probably the first nontrivial result for the PARTIAL MATCH problem has been obtained by Rivest (1976). He showed that the 2^m space of the exhaustive storage solution can be improved for $m \leq 2\lg N$. New algorithms for subset queries and partial matching have been provided by Charikar, Indyk, and Panigrahy (2002), studying two algorithms with different trade-offs. The *Rete* algorithm is due to Forgy (1982). The related TWO-DIMENSIONAL PATTERN STRING MATCHING problem has been studied intensively in literature, for example, by Fredriksson, Navarro, and Ukkonen (2005). Hoffmann and Koehler (1999) have suggested UNLIMITED BRANCHING TREES.

Automatically Created Heuristics

Where do heuristics come from? A common view is that heuristics are relaxations of constraints of the problem that solve a relaxed problem exactly. A prominent example for this is the straight-line distance estimate for routing problems. It can be interpreted as adding straight routes to the map. The notion of an *abstraction transformation* formalizes this concept, and makes it accessible to an automated generation of heuristics, as opposed to hand-crafted, domain-dependent solutions using human intuition. However, a negative result shows that such transformations cannot lead to a speed-up on their own; on the contrary, the power of abstractions lies in the reduction of multiple concrete states to a single abstract state.

Although earlier versions of heuristic search via abstraction generated heuristic estimates on-the-fly, *pattern databases* precompute and store the goal distances for the entire abstract search space in a lookup table. Successful approaches additionally combine the heuristics of multiple smaller pattern databases, either by maximizing or by cumulating the values, which is admissible under certain disjointness conditions. To save space, the computation of the database can be restricted using an upper bound on the length of an optimal solution path and by exploiting specialized data compression schemes.

Therefore, abstraction is the key to the automated design of heuristic estimates. Applying abstractions simplifies the problem, and the exact distances in the simplified version serve as heuristic estimates in the concrete state space. The combination of heuristics based on different abstractions often leads to better estimates. In some cases an abstraction hierarchy can be established. The selection of abstraction functions is usually supervised by the user, but first, progress in computing abstractions automatically are shown.

Abstraction is a method to reduce the exploration efforts for large and infinite state spaces. The abstract space is often smaller than the concrete one. If the abstract system has no solution, neither has the concrete one. However, abstractions may introduce so-called *spurious solution paths*, the inverse of which is not present in the concrete system. One option to deal with the problem of spurious solution paths is the design of an *abstract-and-refine loop*, in which the coarse abstraction is refined for one that is consistent with the solution path established, so that the search process can start again. In contrast, we exploit the duality of abstraction and heuristic search. Abstract state spaces are explored to create a database that stores the exact distances from abstract states to the set of abstract goal states. Instead of checking whether or not the abstract path is present in the concrete system, efficient heuristic state space search algorithms exploit the database as a guidance. Many abstractions remove state variables, others are based on *data abstraction*. They assume a state vector with state components of finite domain and map these domains to abstract variables with smaller domain.

4.1 ABSTRACTION TRANSFORMATIONS

In AI search, researchers have investigated *abstraction transformations* as a way to create admissible heuristics automatically.

Definition 4.1. *(Abstraction Transformation) An abstraction transformation* $\phi : S \to S'$ *maps states u in the concrete problem space to abstract states* $\phi(u)$ *and concrete actions a to abstract actions* $\phi(a)$.

If the distance between all states $u, v \in S$ in the concrete space is greater than or equal to the distance between $\phi(u)$ and $\phi(v)$, the distance in the abstract space can be used as an admissible heuristic for the concrete search space. It is possible to either compute the heuristic values on demand, as in hierarchical A* (see Sec. 4.3), or to precompute and store the goal distance for all abstract states when searching with *pattern databases* (see Sec. 4.4).

Intuitively, this agrees with a common explanation of the origin of heuristics, which views them as the cost of exact solutions to a *relaxed problem*. A relaxed problem is one where we drop constraints (e.g., on move execution). This can lead to inserting additional edges in the problem graph, or to a merging of nodes, or both.

For example, the Manhattan distance for sliding-tile puzzles can be regarded as acting in an abstract problem space that allows multiple tiles to occupy the same square. At first glance, by this relaxation there could be more states than in the original, but fortunately the problem can be decomposed into smaller problems.

Two frequently studied types of abstraction transformations are *embeddings* and *homomorphisms*.

Definition 4.2. *(Embedding and Homomorphism) An abstraction transformation* ϕ *is an embedding transformation if it* adds edges *to S such that the concrete and abstract state sets are the same; that is,* $\phi(u) = u$ *for all* $u \in S$. Homomorphism *requires that for all edges* (u, v) *in S, there must also be an edge* $(\phi(u), \phi(v))$ *in S'.*

By definition, embeddings are special cases of homomorphisms, since existing edges remain valid in the abstract state space. Homomorphisms group together concrete states to create a single abstract state. The definition is visualized in Figure 4.1.

Some rare abstractions are *solution preserving*, meaning a solution path in the abstract problem also introduces a solution path in the concrete problem. In this case, the abstraction does not introduce

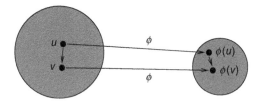

FIGURE 4.1

Concrete states and connecting edge mapped to abstract states and connecting edge via a state space homomorphism. Note that the concrete state space can be much larger than the abstraction, inducing a potentially large group of states mapped to the identical abstract state.

spurious paths. As a simple example for introducing a spurious path consider edges (u, y) and (x, v) in the concrete space. Then there is no path from x to y in the concrete space, but there is one after merging u and v.

For an example of a solution-preserving abstraction, we assume that v is the only successor of u and that the abstraction would merge them. The concrete edge from u to v is converted to a self-loop and thus introduces infinite paths in the abstract space. However, a solution path exists in the abstract problem if and only if a solution path exists in the concrete problem.

Some solution-preserving reductions are not homomorphic. For example, consider that two paths (x, u, y) and (x, v, y) in the concrete state space are reduced to (x, u, y) and (x, v) in the abstract state spaces. In other words, diamond subgraphs are broken according to move transpositions.

Another issue is whether the costs of abstract paths are lower or equal. In our case, we generally assume that the cost of the actions in abstract space are the same as in concrete space. In most cases, we refer to unit cost problem graphs. The usefulness of heuristics derived from abstraction transformations is due to the following result.

Theorem 4.1. *(Admissibility and Consistency of Abstraction Heuristics) Let S be a state space and $S' = \phi(S)$ be any homomorphic abstraction transformation of S. Let heuristic function $h_\phi(u)$ for state u and goal t be defined as the length of the shortest path from $\phi(u)$ to $\phi(t)$ in S'. Then h_ϕ is an admissible, consistent heuristic function.*

Proof. If $p = (u = u_1, \ldots, u_k = t)$ is a shortest solution in S, $\phi(u_1), \ldots, \phi(t)$ is a solution S', which obviously cannot be shorter than the optimal solution in S'.

Now recall that a heuristic h is consistent, if for all u and u' in S, $h(u) \leq \delta(u, u') + h(u')$. Because $\delta_\phi(u, t)$ is the length of the shortest path between $\phi(u)$ and $\phi(t)$, we have $\delta_\phi(u, t) \leq \delta_\phi(u, u') + \delta_\phi(u', t)$ for all u and u'. Substituting h_ϕ results in $h_\phi(u) \leq \delta_\phi(u, u') + h_\phi(u')$ for all u and u'. Because ϕ is an abstraction, $\delta_\phi(u, u') \leq \delta(u, u')$ and, therefore, $h_\phi(u) \leq \delta(u, u') + h_\phi(u')$ for all u and u'. ∎

The type of abstraction usually depends on the state representation. For example, in logical formalisms, such as STRIPS, techniques that omit a predicate from a state space description induce homomorphisms. These predicates are removed from the initial state and goal and from the precondition (and effect) lists of the actions.

The STAR *abstraction* is another general method of grouping states together by neighborhood. Starting with a state u with the maximum number of neighbors, an abstract state is constructed of which the range consists of all the states reachable from u within a fixed number of edges.

Another kind of abstraction transformations are *domain abstractions*, which are applicable to state spaces described in PSVN notation, which was introduced in Section 1.8.2. A domain abstraction is a mapping of labels $\phi : L \to L'$. It induces a state space abstraction by relabeling all constants in both concrete states and actions; the abstract space consists of all states reachable from $\phi(s)$ by applying sequences of abstract actions. It can be easily shown that a domain abstraction induces a state space homomorphism.

For instance (see Fig. 4.2), consider the EIGHT-PUZZLE with vector representation, where tiles 1, 2, and 7 are replaced by the don't care symbol x. We have $\phi_1(v) = v'$ with $v'_i = v_i$ if $v_i \in \{0, 3, 4, 5, 6, 8\}$, and $v_i = x$, otherwise. In addition to mapping tiles 1, 2, and 7 to x, in another domain abstraction ϕ_2 we might additionally map tiles 3 and 4 to y, and tiles 6 and 8 to z. The generalization allows refinements to the *granularity* of the relaxation, defined as a vector indicating how many constants in the concrete

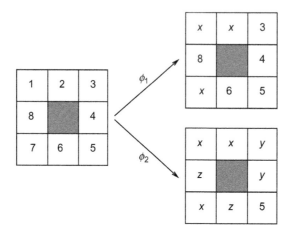

FIGURE 4.2

Two abstractions of the EIGHT-PUZZLE; top abstraction maps all involved tiles to one don't care symbol x; in the bottom abstraction, two tile labels x and y have been introduced.

domain are mapped to each constant in the abstract domain. In the example, the granularity of ϕ_2 is $(3,2,2,1,1)$ because three constants are mapped to x, two are mapped to each of y and z, and constants 5 and 0 (the blank) remain unique.

In the sliding-tile puzzles, a granularity $(g_1,\ldots,g_k)$ implies that the size of the abstract state space is $n^2!/(c \cdot g_1! \cdots g_k!)$, with the choice of $c \in \{1,2\}$ depending on whether or not half of all states are reachable due to parity (see Sec. 1.7). In general, however, we cannot directly derive the size from the granularity of the abstraction: ϕ might not be *surjective*; for some abstract states u' there might not exist a concrete state u such that $\phi(u) = u'$. In this case, the abstract space can even comprise more states than the original one, thereby rendering the method counterproductive. In general, unfortunately, it is not efficiently decidable if an abstract space is surjective.

4.2 VALTORTA'S THEOREM

Without a heuristic, we can only search *blindly* in the original space; the use of a heuristic focuses this search, and saves us some computational effort. However, this is only beneficial if the cost of the auxiliary search required to compute h doesn't exceed these savings. Valtorta found an important theoretical limit of usefulness.

Theorem 4.2. *(Valtorta's Theorem) Let u be any state necessarily expanded, when the problem (s,t) is solved in S with BFS; $\phi : S \to S'$ be any abstraction mapping; and the heuristic estimate $h(u)$ be computed by blindly searching from $\phi(u)$ to $\phi(t)$. If the problem is solved by the A^* algorithm using h, then either u itself will be expanded, or $\phi(u)$ will be expanded.*

Proof. When A* terminates, u will either be *closed*, *open*, or *unvisited*.

- If u is *closed*, it has already been expanded.
- If u is *open*, then $h_\phi(u)$ must have been computed during search. $h_\phi(u)$ is computed by searching in S' starting at $\phi(u)$; if $\phi(u) \neq \phi(t)$, the first step in this auxiliary search is to expand $\phi(u)$; otherwise, if $\phi(u) = \phi(t)$ then $h_\phi(u) = 0$, and u itself is necessarily expanded.
- If u is *unvisited*, on every path from s to u there must be a state that was added to *Open* during search but never expanded.

  Let v be any such state on the shortest path from s to u. Because v was opened, $h_\phi(v)$ must have been computed. We will now show that in computing $h_\phi(v)$, $\phi(u)$ is necessarily expanded.

  From the fact that u is necessarily expanded by blind search, we have $\delta(s,u) < \delta(s,t)$. Because v is on the shortest path, we have $\delta(s,v) + \delta(v,u) = \delta(s,u) < \delta(s,t)$. From the fact that v was never expanded by A*, we have $\delta(s,v) + h_\phi(v) \geq \delta(s,t)$. Combining the two inequalities, we get $\delta(v,u) < h_\phi(v) = \delta_\phi(v,t)$. Since ϕ is an abstraction mapping, we have $\delta_\phi(v,u) \leq \delta(v,u)$, which gives $\delta_\phi(v,u) < \delta_\phi(v,t)$. Therefore, $\phi(u)$ is necessarily expanded. ∎

As a side remark note that Valtorta's theorem is sensitive to whether the goal counts as expanded or not. Many textbooks including this one assume that A* stops immediately before expanding the goal.

Since $\phi(u) = u$ in an embedding, we immediately obtain the following consequence of Valtorta's theorem.

Corollary 4.1. *For an embedding ϕ, A*—using h computed by blind search in the abstract problem space—necessarily expands every state that is expanded by blind search in the original space.*

Of course, this assumes that the heuristic is computed once for a single problem instance; if it were stored and reused over multiple instances, its calculation could be amortized.

Contrary to the case of embeddings, this negative result of Valtorta's theorem does not apply in this way to abstractions based on homomorphisms; they can reduce the search effort, since the abstract space is often smaller than the original one.

As an example, consider the problem of finding a path between the corners $(1,1)$ and $(N,1)$ on a regular $N \times N$ GRIDWORLD, with the abstraction transformation ignoring the second coordinate (see Fig. 4.3 for $N = 10$; the reader may point out the expanded nodes explicitly and compare with nodes expanded by informed search). Uninformed search will expand $\Omega(N^2)$ nodes. On the other hand, an online heuristic requires $O(N)$ steps. If A* applies this heuristic to the original space, and resolves ties between nodes with equal f-value by preferring the one with a larger g-value, then the problem demands $O(N)$ expansions.

4.3 *HIERARCHICAL A*

Hierarchical A makes use of an arbitrary number of abstraction transformation layers $\phi_1, \phi_2, \ldots$. Whenever a heuristic value for a node u in the base level problem is requested, the abstract problem to find a shortest path between $\phi_1(u)$ and $\phi_1(t)$ is solved on demand, before returning to the original

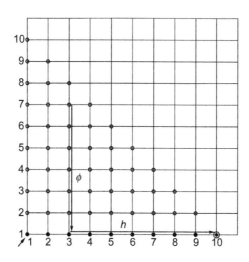

FIGURE 4.3

Two-dimensional GRIDWORLD problem with initial state (1, 1) and goal state (10, 1) illustrating the validity of Valtorta's theorem; the abstraction projects a state to its x-axis, such that the h-value is the size of the line from the projected point to the goal.

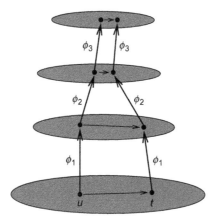

FIGURE 4.4

Layered abstraction in hierarchical A* with regard to the current state u and goal state t (in the original state space) according to three abstractions.

problem. In turn, the search at level 2 utilizes a heuristic computed on a third level as the shortest path between $\phi_2(\phi_1(u))$ and $\phi_2(\phi_1(t))$, and so on (see Fig. 4.4).

This naive scheme would repeatedly solve the same instances at the higher levels requested by different states at the base level. An immediate remedy for this futile overhead is to cache the heuristic values of all the nodes in a shortest path computed at an abstract level.

The resulting heuristic will no longer be monotone: Nodes that lay on the solution path of a previous search can have high h-values, whereas their neighbors off this path still have their original heuristic value. Generally, a nonmonotone heuristic leads to the need for reopening nodes; they can be closed even if the shortest path to them has not yet been found. However, this is not a concern in this case: A node u can only be prematurely closed if every shortest path passes through some node v for which the shortest path is known. If no such v is part of a shortest path from s to t, neither is u, and the premature closing is irrelevant. On the other hand, all nodes on the shortest path from v to t have already cached the exact estimate, and hence will only be expanded once.

An optimization technique, known as *optimal path caching*, records not only the value of $h^*(u) = \delta(u, T)$, but also the exact solution path found. Then, whenever a state u with known value $h^*(u)$ is encountered during the search, we can directly insert a goal into the *Open* list, instead of explicitly expanding u.

In controlling the granularity of abstractions, there is a trade-off to be made. A coarse abstraction leads to a smaller problem space that can be searched more efficiently; however, since a larger number of concrete states are assigned the same estimate, the heuristic becomes less discriminating and hence less informative.

4.4 PATTERN DATABASES

In the previous setting, heuristic values are computed on demand. With caching, a growing number of them will be stored over time. An alternative approach is to completely evaluate the abstract search space prior to the base level search. For a fixed goal state t and any abstraction space $S' = \phi(S)$, a *pattern database* is a lookup table indexed by $u' \in S'$ containing the shortest path length from u' to $\phi(t)$ in S' for $t \in T$. The size of a pattern database is the number of states in S'.

It is easy to create a pattern database by conducting a breadth-first search in a backward direction, starting at $\phi(t)$. This assumes that for each action a we can devise an inverse action a^{-1} such that $v = a(u)$ iff $u = a^{-1}(v)$. If the set of backward actions $A^{-1} = \{a^{-1} \mid a \in A\}$ is equal to A, the problem is reversible (leading to an undirected problem graph). For backward pattern database construction, the uniqueness of the actions' inverse is sufficient. The set of all states generated by applying inverse actions to a state u is denoted as $Pred(u)$. It is generated by the inverse successor generating function $Expand^{-1}(u)$. Pattern databases can cope with weighted state spaces. Moreover, by additionally associating the shortest path predecessor with each state it is possible to maintain the shortest abstract path that leads to the abstract goal. To construct a pattern database for weighted graphs, the shortest path exploration in abstract space uses inverse actions and Dijkstra's algorithm.

Algorithm 4.1 shows a possible implementation for pattern database construction. It is not difficult to see that the construction is in fact a variant of Dijktra's algorithm (as introduced in Ch. 2) executed backward in abstract space (with successor set generation $Expand^{-1}$ instead of $Expand$ for abstract states $\phi(u)$ instead of u). Even though in many cases pattern databases are constructed for a single goal state t it extends nicely the search for multiple goal states T. Therefore, in Algorithm 4.1 *Open* is initialized with T.

For the sake of readability in the pseudo codes we often use the *set notation* for the accesses to the *Open* and *Closed* lists. In an actual implementation, the data structures of Chaper 3 have to be used. This pattern database construction procedure is sometimes termed *retrograde analysis*.

Procedure Backward-Pattern-Database-Construction
Input: Abstract problem graph with abstract start node $\phi(s)$,
      abstract goal nodes $\phi(t)$, $t \in T$, weight function w, and
      abstract inverse successor generation function $Expand^{-1}$
Output: Pattern database

$Closed \leftarrow \emptyset$;; Initialize expanded node set
$Open \leftarrow \{\phi(t), t \in T\}$;; Insert abstract initial state into search frontier
while $(Open \neq \emptyset)$;; As long as there are horizon nodes
    Remove $\phi(u)$ from $Open$ with minimum $f(u)$;; Select most promising node
    Insert $\phi(u)$ into $Closed$;; Update list of expanded nodes
    $Pred(\phi(u)) \leftarrow Expand^{-1}(\phi(u))$;; Expansion memorizes predecessors
    for each $\phi(v)$ **in** $Pred(\phi(u))$;; For all abstract successors $\phi(v)$ of $\phi(u)$
        $Improve(\phi(u), \phi(v))$;; Set backward distances
return $Closed$;; List, together with distances, is pattern database

Algorithm 4.1

Construction of pattern database using a backward search.

Since pattern databases represent the set *Closed* of expanded nodes in abstract space, a straightforward implementation for storing and retrieving the computed distance information are hash tables. As introduced in Chapter 3, many different options are available such as hash tables with chaining, open addressing, suffix lists, and others. For search domains with a regular structure (like the $(n^2 - 1)$-PUZZLE), the database can be time- and space-efficiently implemented as a *perfect hash table*. In this case the hash address uniquely identifies the state that is searched, and the hash entries themselves consist of the shortest path distance value only. The state itself has not been stored. A simple and fast (though not memory-efficient) implementation of such a perfect hash table is a multidimensional array that is addressed by the state components. More space-efficient indexes for permutation games have been introduced in Chapter 3. They can be adapted to partial state/pattern addresses.

The pattern database technique was first applied to define heuristics for sliding-tile puzzles. The space required for pattern database construction can be bounded by the length of the abstract goal distance encoding times the size of the perfect hash table.

4.4.1 FIFTEEN-PUZZLE

For this case, problem abstraction consists of ignoring a selected subset of tiles on the board. Their labels are replaced by a special "don't care" symbol; the remaining set of tiles is referred to as the *pattern*. Sample fringe and corner patterns are illustrated in Figure 4.5.

In experiments it has been shown that taking the maximum of the Manhattan distance and the fringe (corner) pattern database reduces the number of expanded nodes by two orders of magnitude of the algorithm using only the Manhattan distance. Using both databases together even leads to an improvement according to three orders of magnitude. Table 4.1 shows further exploration results for the FIFTEEN-PUZZLE in reducing the number of search nodes and increasing mean heuristic value.

FIGURE 4.5

Fringe and corner target pattern for the FIFTEEN-PUZZLE.

Table 4.1 Effect of pattern databases in the FIFTEEN-PUZZLE.		
Heuristic	**Nodes**	**Mean Heuristic Value**
Manhattan Distance	401,189,630	36.942
Linear Conflict Heuristic	40,224,625	38.788
5-Tile Pattern Database	5,722,922	41.562
6-Tile Pattern Database	3,788,680	42.924

4.4.2 RUBIK'S CUBE

A state in RUBIK'S CUBE (see Sec. 1.7.2) is uniquely specified by the position and orientation of the 8 edge cubies and the 12 corner cubies. For the implementation, this can be represented as an array of 20 elements, one for each cubie. The values encode the position and orientation as one of 24 different values—$8 \cdot 3$ for the corners and $2 \cdot 12$ for the edges.

Uninformed search is impractical on large RUBIK'S CUBE problems, since the number of generated nodes grows rapidly. In Depth 10 we expect 244,686,773,808 nodes, and in Depth 18 we have more than $2.46 \cdot 10^{20}$ nodes.

If we consider the eight corner cubies as a pattern, the position and orientation of the last cubie is determined by the remaining seven, so there are exactly $8! \cdot 3^7 = 88,179,840$ possible combinations. Using backward breadth-first search starting from the goal state, we can enumerate these states and build a pattern database. Perfect hashing can be used, allocating four bits to encode the heuristic value for each abstract state. The mean heuristic value is about 8.764. In addition, we may consider the edge cubies separately. Since taking all edge cubies into consideration would lead to a memory-exceeding pattern database, the set of edge cubies is divided, leading to two pattern databases of size $12!/6! \cdot 2^6 = 42,577,922$. The mean heuristic value for the maximum of all three pattern database heuristics is about 8.878.

Using the previous databases, Korf solved 10 random instances to the RUBIK'S CUBE move optimally. The solvable instances were generated by making 100 random moves each starting from the goal state. His results are shown in Table 4.2. The optimal solution for the hardest possible instance has 20 moves (see Ch. 1).

Table 4.2 Solutions to 10 random
Rubik's Cube instances.

Problem	Depth	Nodes Generated
1	16	3,720,885,493
2	17	11,485,155,726
3	17	64,937,508,623
4	18	126,005,368,381
5	18	262,228,269,081
6	18	344,770,394,346
7	18	502,417,601,953
8	18	562,494,969,937
9	18	626,785,460,346
10	18	1,021,814,815,051

4.4.3 Directed Search Graphs

A precondition for the above construction is that actions are *inversible*; that is, the set of legal reachable states that can be transformed into a target state must be efficiently computable. This is true for regular problems like the $(n^2 - 1)$-Puzzle and Rubik's Cube. However, applying inversible actions is not always possible. For example, in PSVN the action $(A, A, \_) \rightarrow (1, 2, \_)$ is not inversible, since in a backward direction, it is not clear which label to set at the first and second position (although we know it must be the same one). In other words, we no longer have an inverse abstract successor generation function to construct set *Pred*.

Fortunately, there is some hope. If inverse actions are not available, we can reverse the state space graph generated in a forward chaining search. With each node v we attach the list of *all* predecessor nodes u (assuming $v \in Succ(u)$) from which v is generated. In case a goal is encountered, the traversal is not terminated, but the abstract goal states are collected in a (priority) queue. Next, backward traversal is invoked on the inverse of the (possibly weighted) state space graph, starting with the queued set of abstract goal states. The established shortest path distances to the abstract goal state are associated with each state in the hash table. Algorithm 4.2 shows a possible implementation. Essentially, a forward search to explore the whole state space is executed, memorizing the successors of all states, so that we can then construct their predecessors. Then we perform *Backward-Pattern-Database-Construction* without the need to apply inverse node expansion.

4.4.4 Korf's Conjecture

In the following we are interested in the performance of pattern databases. We will argue that for the effectiveness of an (admissible) heuristic function, the expected value is a very good predictor. This average can be approximated by random sampling, or for pattern databases determined as the average of the database values. This value is *exact* for the distribution of heuristic values in the abstract state space but, as abstractions are nonuniform in general, only approximate for the concrete state space.

Procedure Forward-Pattern-Database-Construction
Input: Abstract problem graph with start node $\phi(s)$, weight function w (inducing f),
     abstract successor generation function, and abstract goal predicate
Output: Pattern database

Closed $\leftarrow \emptyset$	;; Initialize structure for expanded node set
Open $\leftarrow \{\phi(s)\}$	;; Insert abstract initial state into search frontier
while (*Open* $\neq \emptyset$)	;; As long as there are horizon nodes
Remove some $\phi(u)$ from *Open*	;; Select node based on any criteria
Insert $\phi(u)$ into *Closed*	;; Update list of expanded nodes
if (*Goal*($\phi(u)$)) $Q \leftarrow Q \cup \{\phi(u)\}$	;; If abstract goal is found, store it
Succ($\phi(u)$) $\leftarrow$ *Expand*($\phi(u)$)	;; Expansion memorizes predecessors
for each $\phi(v)$ **in** *Succ*($\phi(u)$)	;; For all abstract successors $\phi(v)$ of $\phi(u)$
if ($v \notin$ *Open* $\cup$ *Closed*)	;; Successor is reached for the first time
Pred($\phi(v)$) $\leftarrow \emptyset$	;; Initialize set
else	;; Successor already stored
Pred($\phi(v)$) $\leftarrow$ *Pred*($\phi(v)$) $\cup \{\phi(u)\}$	;; Update set
Improve($\phi(u),\phi(v)$)	;; Set forward distances
Closed $\leftarrow \emptyset$	;; Initialize structure for backward search
Open $\leftarrow Q$	;; Insert abstract goals into search frontier
while (*Open* $\neq \emptyset$)	;; As long as there are horizon nodes
$\phi(u) \leftarrow$ arg min$_f$ *Open*	;; Select most promising node
Open $\leftarrow$ *Open* $\setminus \{\phi(u)\}$	;; Update search horizon
Closed $\leftarrow$ *Closed* $\cup \{\phi(u)\}$	;; Update list of expanded nodes
for each $\phi(v)$ **in** *Pred*($\phi(u)$)	;; Predecessors stored in first search
Improve($\phi(u),\phi(v)$)	;; Set backward distances
return *Closed*	;; List, together with backward distances, is pattern database

Algorithm 4.2

Pattern database construction in directed and weighted problem graphs.

In general, the larger the values of an admissible heuristic, the better the corresponding database should be judged. This is due to the fact that the heuristic values directly influence the search efficiency in the original search space. As a consequence, we compute the mean heuristic value for each database. More formally, the average estimate of a pattern database *PDB* with *entries* in the range $[0..\max_h]$ is

$$\overline{h} = \sum_{h=0}^{\max_h} h \cdot |\{u \in PDB \mid entry(u) = h\}|/|PDB|.$$

A fundamental question about memory-based heuristics concerns the relationship between the size of the pattern database and the number of nodes expanded when the heuristic is used to guide the search. One problem of relating the performance of a search algorithm to the accuracy of the heuristic is it is hard to measure. Determining the exact distance to the goal is computationally infeasible for large problems.

If the heuristic value of every state is equal to its expected value $\overline{h}$, then a search to depth d is equivalent to searching to depth $d - \overline{h}$ without a heuristic, since the f-value for every state would be its depth plus $\overline{h}$. However, this estimate turns out to be much too low in practice. The reason for the discrepancy is that the states encountered are not random samples. States with large heuristic values are pruned and states with small heuristic values spawn more children.

On the other hand, we can predict the expected value of a pattern database heuristic during the search. The minimal depth of a search tree covering a search space of n nodes with constant branching factor of b will be around $d = \lg_b n$. This is because with d moves, we can generate about b^d nodes. Since we are ignoring possible duplicates, this estimate is generally too low.

We assume d to be the average optimal solution length for a random instance and that our pattern database is generated by caching heuristic values for all states up to distance d from the goal. If the abstract search tree is also branching with factor b, a lower bound on the expected value of a pattern database heuristic is $\lg_b m$, where m is the number of stored states in the database (being equal to the size of the abstract state space). The derivation of $\lg_b m$ is similar to the one of $\lg_b n$ for the concrete state space.

The hope is that the combination of an overly optimistic estimate with a too-pessimistic estimate results in a more realistic measure. Let t be the number of nodes generated in an A* search (without duplicate detection). Since d is the depth to which A* must search, we can estimate $d \approx \lg_b n$. Moreover, as argued earlier, we have $\overline{h} \approx \lg_b m$ and $t \approx b^{d-\overline{h}}$. Substituting the values for d and $\overline{h}$ yields

$$t \approx b^{d-\overline{h}} \approx b^{\lg_b n - \lg_b m} = n/m.$$

Since the treatment is insightful but informal, this estimate has been denoted as *Korf's conjecture*; it states that the number of generated nodes in an A* search without duplicate detection using a pattern database may be approximated by $O(n/m)$, the size of the problem space divided by the available memory. Using experimental data from the RUBIK'S CUBE problem shows that the prediction is very good. We have $n \approx 4.3252 \cdot 10^{19}$, $m = 88,179,940 + 2 \cdot 42,577,920 = 173,335,680$, $n/m = 149,527,409,904$, and $t = 352,656,042,894$, which is off only by a factor of 1.4.

4.4.5 Multiple Pattern Databases

The most successful applications of pattern databases all use *multiple* ones.

This raises the question on improved main memory consumption: Is it best to use one large database, or rather split the available space up into several smaller ones? Let m be the number of patterns that we can store in the available memory, and p be the number of pattern databases. In many experiments on the performance of p pattern databases of size m/p (e.g., in the domain of the sliding-tile puzzle and in RUBIK'S CUBE) it has been observed that small values of p are suboptimal. The general observation is that the use of maximized smaller pattern databases reduces the number of nodes. For example, heuristic search in the EIGHT-PUZZLE with 20 pattern databases of size 252 performs less state expansions (318) than 1 pattern database of size 5,040 (yielding 2,160 state expansions).

The observation remains true if maximization is performed on a series of different partitions into databases. The first heuristic of the TWENTY-FOUR-PUZZLE partitions the tiles into four groups of 6 tiles each. When partitioning the 24 tiles into eight different pattern databases with four groups of 5 tiles and one group of 4 tiles this results $8 \cdot (4 \cdot 25!/20! + 25!/21!) = 206,448,000$ patterns.

Compared to the first heuristic that generates $4 \cdot 25!/19! = 510,048,000$ patterns, this is roughly one-third. However, the second heuristic performs better, with a ratio of nodes generated in between 1.62 to 2.53.

Of course, the number of pattern databases cannot be scaled to an arbitrary amount. With very few states the distances in abstract state space are very imprecise. Moreover, since node generation in sliding-tile puzzles is very fast, the gains of a smaller node count are counterbalanced by the larger efforts in addressing the multiple databases and computing the maximum.

The explanation of this phenomenon, that many smaller pattern databases may perform better than one larger one, is based on two observations:

- The use of smaller pattern databases instead of one large pattern database usually reduces the number of patterns with high h-value; maximizing the values of the smaller pattern databases can make the number of patterns with low h-values significantly smaller than the number of low-valued patterns in the larger pattern database.
- Eliminating low h-values is more important for improving search performance than for retaining large h-values.

The first assertion is intuitively clear. A smaller pattern database means a smaller pattern space with fewer patterns with high h-values. Maximization of the smaller pattern databases reduces the number of patterns with very small h-values.

The second assertion refers to the number of nodes expanded. If pattern databases differ only in their maximum value, this only affects the nodes with a large h-value, corresponding to a number of nodes that is typically small. If the two pattern databases, on the contrary, differ in the fraction of nodes with a small h-value, this has a large effect on the number of nodes expanded, since the number of nodes that participate in those values is typically large.

As multiple pattern database lookups can be time consuming, we gain efficiency by computing bounds on the heuristic estimate prior to the search, and avoiding database lookups if the bounds are exceeded.

4.4.6 Disjoint Pattern Databases

Disjoint pattern databases are important to derive admissible estimates. It is immediate that the *maximum* of two heuristics is admissible. On the other hand, we would like to *add* the heuristic estimates of two pattern databases to arrive at an even better estimate. Unfortunately, adding heuristics does not necessarily preserves admissibility. Additivity can be applied if the cost of a subproblem is composed from costs of objects from a corresponding pattern only. For the $(n^2 - 1)$-PUZZLE, every operator moves only one tile, but RUBIK'S CUBE is a counterexample.

Consider the example of a small graph with four nodes s, u, v, and t arranged along one path (see Fig. 4.6), where s is the start and t is the goal node. The first abstraction merges nodes s and u, and the second abstraction merges u with v. Because self-loops do not contribute to optimal solutions they have been omitted from the abstract graph. As the incoming edge to t remains in both abstractions, being in state v gives the cumulated abstract distance value 2, which is larger than the concrete distance 1.

The reason why we could only take the maximum of the fringe and corner heuristics for the EIGHT-PUZZLE is that we want to avoid counting some action twice. The minimum number of moves stored

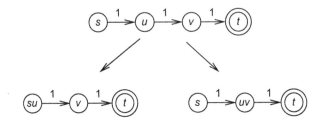

FIGURE 4.6

Two nonadditive abstractions of a graph (top) obtained by merging nodes s with u (left) and u with v (right).

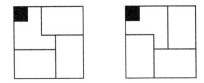

FIGURE 4.7

Disjoint pattern databases for a 24-PUZZLE; tiles (in the goal) selected for the pattern are shown together.

in the database does not involve only the tiles' movements that are part of the actual pattern. Since the nonpattern moves can be part of the abstract solution path for the other pattern, adding the two values might result in a nonadmissible heuristic.

A solution for the problem is not to record the total solution path length, but to count moves of the tiles in the pattern for computing the heuristic estimate only. Since at each point in time only one tile is moved, this makes it possible to *add* the heuristic values rather than maximizing them. As an extreme case, we can think of the Manhattan distance as the sum of $n^2 - 1$ patterns consisting of one tile each. Since each move changes only the shifted tile, addition is admissible. Generally, we can resort to this partitioning technique if we make sure that the subgoal solutions are independent.

Different disjoint pattern databases' heuristics can additionally be combined using the maximization of their outcome. For example, when solving random instances of the TWENTY-FOUR-PUZZLE, we might compute the maximum of two additive groups of four disjoint pattern databases each. As shown in Figure 4.7 each tile group (indicated by the enclosed areas) consists of six tiles for generating databases with $25!/19! = 127,512,000$ patterns (the location of the blank is indicated using a black square).

If, for all states, the same partitioning is applied, we speak of *statically partitioned* disjoint pattern databases. There is an alternative way of *dynamically* choosing among several possible partitions the one with the maximum heuristic value. For example, a straightforward generalization of the Manhattan distance for sliding-tile puzzles is to precompute the shortest solution for every pair of tiles, rather than considering each tile individually. Then, we can construct an admissible heuristic by choosing half of these pairs such that each tile is covered exactly once. With an odd number of tiles, one of them will be left out, and simply contributes with its Manhattan distance.

To compute the most accurate heuristic for a given state, we have to solve a *maximum weighted bipartite matching* problem in a graph where each vertex in both sets corresponds to a tile, and each edge between the two sets is labeled with the pairwise solution cost of the corresponding pair of tiles. An algorithm is known that accomplishes this task in $O(k^3)$ time, where k is the number of tiles. However, it has also been shown that the corresponding matching problem for *triples* of tiles is NP-complete. Thus, in general, dynamic partitioning might not be efficiently computable, and we would have to resort to approximate the largest heuristic value.

If we partition the state variables into disjoint subsets (patterns), such that no action affects variables in more than one subset, then a lower bound for the optimal solution of an instance is the sum of the optimal costs of solving optimally each pattern corresponding to the variable values of the instance.

Definition 4.3. *(Disjoint State Space Abstractions) Let actions be* trivial *(a no-op) if they induce a self-cycle in the abstract state space graph. Two state space abstractions ϕ_1 and ϕ_2 are disjoint, if for all nontrivial actions a' in the abstraction generated by ϕ_1 and for all nontrivial actions a'' in the abstraction generated by ϕ_2, we have $\phi_1^{-1}(a') \cap \phi_2^{-1}(a'') = \emptyset$, where $\phi_i^{-1}(a') = \{a \in A \mid \phi_i(a) = a'\}$, $i \in \{1,2\}$. Trivial actions correspond to self-loops in the problem graph.*

If we have more than one pattern database, then for each state u in the concrete space and each abstraction $\phi_i, i \in \{1, \ldots, k\}$ we compute the values $h_i(u) = \delta_{\phi_i}(u, t)$. The heuristic estimate $h(u)$ is the accumulated cost of the costs in the different abstractions; that is, $h(u) = \sum_{i=0}^{k} h_i(u)$. To preserve *admissibility*, we require *disjointness*, where two pattern databases with regard to the abstractions ϕ' and ϕ'' are *disjoint*, if or all $u \in S$ we have $\delta_{\phi'}(u, T) + \delta_{\phi''}(u, T) \leq \delta(u, T)$.

Theorem 4.3. *(Additivity of Disjoint Pattern Databases) Two disjoint pattern databases are additive, by means that their distance estimates can be added while still providing a lower bound for the optimal solution path length.*

Proof. Let P_1 and P_2 be abstractions of $P = < S, A, s, T >$ according to ϕ_1 and ϕ_2, respectively, and let $\pi = (a_1, \ldots, a_k)$ be an optimal sequential plan for P. Then, the abstracted plan $\pi_1 = (\phi_1(a_1), \ldots, \phi_1(a_k))$ is a solution for the state space problem P_1, and $\pi_2 = (\phi_2(a_1), \ldots, \phi_2(a_k))$ is a solution for the state space problem P_2. We assume that all void actions in π_1 and π_2, if any, are removed. Let k_1 and k_2 be the resulting respective lengths of π_1 and π_2. Since the pattern databases are disjoint, for all $a' \in \pi_1$ and all $a'' \in \pi_2$ we have $\phi_1^{-1}(a') \cap \phi_2^{-1}(a'') = \emptyset$. Therefore, $\delta_{\phi_1}(u, T) + \delta_{\phi_2}(u, T) \leq k_1 + k_2 \leq \delta(u, T)$. ∎

Consider a slight modification of the example graph with four nodes s, u, v, and t, now arranged as shown in Figure 4.8. The first abstraction merges nodes s with u and v with t and the second abstraction merges s with v and u with t. Now each edge remains valid in only one abstraction, so that being in state v gives the cumulated abstract distance value 1, which is equal to the concrete distance 1.

In Figure 4.10 a plain pattern database (left) and a pair of disjoint pattern databases (right) are shown. All pattern databases (gray bars) refer to underlying partial state vectors (represented as thin rectangles). The first rectangle in both cases represents the state vector in original space with all parts of it being relevant (no shading). The second (and third) rectangle additionally indicates the selected part of don't care variables in the state vector (shaded in black) for each abstraction. The heights of the pattern database bars that are erected on top of the state vector indicate the sizes of the pattern databases (number of states stored), and the widths of the pattern database rulers correlate with the

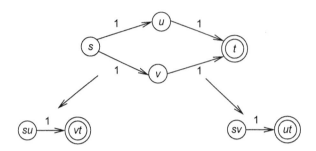

FIGURE 4.8

Disjoint abstractions of a small graph (top), obtained by merging nodes s with u and v with t (left) and s with v and u with t (right).

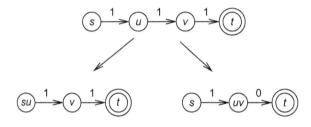

FIGURE 4.9

Admissible but nondisjoint abstraction of a small graph obtained by merging nodes s with u (left) and u with v (right), and adjusting the edge weights to avoid multiple-edge counting.

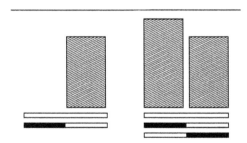

FIGURE 4.10

Single (left) and two disjoint databases (right); height of bars denote size of the pattern database, horizontal line on top of the bars denote the limit of main memory, and the rulers below the bar denote selected pattern parts in a state vector (black stands for don't care variable, and white denotes a pattern variable).

selected parts of the state vector. The maximum size of a pattern database is determined by the amount of main memory available and is illustrated by a line above the databases.

Finding disjoint state space abstractions in general is difficult. Therefore, in pattern database practice, an alternative approach for enforcing disjointness is used: If an action has a nonempty

Table 4.3 Effect of disjoint pattern databases in the FIFTEEN-PUZZLE.

Heuristic	Nodes	Mean Heuristic Value
Manhattan Distance	401,189,630	36.942
Disjoint 7- and 8-Tile Pattern Databases	576,575	45.632

intersection with one more than one chosen pattern, it is assigned to cost 0 in all but one database. Alternatively, we can assign 1 divided by the number of times the action is valid for an abstraction.

For the $(n^2 - 1)$-PUZZLE, at most one tile can move at a time. Hence, if we restrict the count to only pattern tile moves, we can add entries of pattern databases with a disjoint tile set. Table 4.3 shows the effect of disjoint pattern databases in reducing the number of search nodes and increasing the mean heuristic value.

Reconsider the example of the graph with four nodes s, u, v, and t arranged along a path with its two abstraction functions. The edge to t is assigned to cost 1 in the first abstraction and to cost 0 in the second abstraction such that, when being in state v, the cumulated abstract distance value is now 1, which is equal to the concrete distance 1. The resulting mapping is shown in Figure 4.9.

In general, we cannot expect that each action contributes costs to only one pattern database. For this case, concrete actions can be counted multiple times in different abstractions. This implies that the inferred heuristic is no longer admissible. To see this, suppose that this action immediately reaches the goal with cost 1. In contrast, the cumulated cost for being nonvoid in two abstractions is 2.

Another option is to *count* an action in only one abstraction. In a modified breadth-first pattern database construction algorithm this is achieved as follows. In each BFS level we compute the *transitive hull* of zero-cost actions: each zero-cost action is applied until no zero-cost action is applicable. In other words, the impact of an action is added to the overall cost, only if it does not appear for the construction of another pattern database.

A general theory of additive state space abstraction has been defined on top of a directed abstract graph by assigning two weights per edge, one for the primary cost w_P and residual cost w_R. Having two costs per abstract edge instead of just one is inspired by counting distinguished moves differently than don't care moves. In that example, our primary cost is the cost associated with the distinguished moves, and our residual cost is the cost associated with the don't care moves.

It is not difficult to see that if for all edges (u, v) and state space abstractions ϕ_i in the original space the edge $(\phi_i(u), \phi_i(v))$ is contained in the abstract space, and if for all paths π in the original space we have $w_p(\pi) \geq w_p(\phi_i(\pi)) + w_r(\phi_i(\pi))$, the resulting heuristic is consistent. Moreover, if for all paths π we have $w_p(\pi) \geq \sum w_p(\phi_i(\pi))$, the resulting additive heuristic is also consistent.

4.5 *CUSTOMIZED PATTERN DATABASES

So far we looked at manual selection of pattern variables. On the one hand, this implies that pattern-database design is not domain independent. On the other hand, finding good patterns for the design of one pattern database is involved, as there is an exponential number of possible choices. This problem of pattern selection becomes worse when general abstractions and multiple pattern databases are considered. Last, but not least, the quality of pattern databases is far from being obvious.

4.5.1 Pattern Selection

To automate the pattern selection process is a challenge. For domain-independent choices of the patterns, we have to control the size of the abstract state space that corresponds to this choice. State spaces for fixed-size state vectors can be interpreted as products of state space abstractions for individual state variables. An upper bound of the abstract state space is to multiply the preimages of the remaining variables.

Upper bounds on the size of the abstract spaces can be used to distribute the pattern variables. Since the number of state variables can be considerably large, we simplify the problem of finding a suitable partition of the state vector into patterns to a form of BIN PACKING. Consequently, the aim for automated pattern selection is to distribute the state variables to abstract state space bins in such a way that a minimal number of bins is used. A state variable is added to an already existing bin, until the (expected) abstract state space size exceeds main memory.

In constrast to ordinary BIN PACKING that adds object sizes, the PATTERN PACKING variant is suited to automated pattern selection. For PATTERN PACKING the domain sizes to estimate the abstract state space growth multiply. More formally, adding a variable to a pattern corresponds to a multiplication of its domain size to the (already computed) abstract state size (unless it exceeds the RAM limit). As an example, the abstract state space for the variables v_1 and v_2 is bounded from above by $|dom(v_1)| \cdot |dom(v_2)|$, where $dom(v_i)$ denotes the set of possible assignments to v_i. Adding v_3 yields an upper bound for the abstract state space size of $|dom(v_1)| \cdot |dom(v_2)| \cdot |dom(v_3)|$.

Figure 4.11 illustrates an example, plotting the sizes of the pattern databases against the set of chosen abstractions. BIN PACKING is NP-complete, but efficient approximations (like first- or best-fit strategies) have been used successfully in practice.

As argued earlier, a linear gain in the mean heuristic value $\bar{h}$ corresponds to an exponential gain in the search. For the pattern selection problem we conclude that the higher the average distance stored, the better the corresponding pattern database. For computing the strength of multiple pattern databases we compute the mean heuristic value for each of the databases individually and add (or maximize) the outcome.

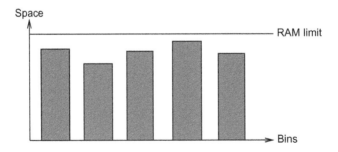

FIGURE 4.11

Bin packing for automated pattern selection; bars illustrate the contents of each pattern of databases, and the horizontal line indicates the limit of main memory.

In the following we show that there is a unique way of combining several pattern database heuristics into one.

Definition 4.4. *(Canonical Pattern Database Heuristic) Let C be a collection of abstractions* $\phi_1,\ldots,\phi_k$ *and let X be a collection of all disjoint subsets Y of C maximal with respect to set inclusion. Let h_i be the pattern database for ϕ_i. The* canonical pattern database heuristic h^C *is defined as*

$$h^C = \max_{Y \in X} \sum_{\phi_i \in Y} h_i.$$

Theorem 4.4. *(Consistency and Quality of Canonical Pattern Database Heuristic) The canonical pattern database heuristic is consistent and is larger than or equal to any admissible combination of maximums and sums.*

Proof. Intuitively, the proof is based on the fact that for this case the maximum over all sums is equal to the sum over the maxima, such that no maximum remains nested inside. We illustrate this for two pattern databases. Suppose we are given four abstractions $\phi_1,\ldots,\phi_4$ with ϕ_i and ϕ_j being disjoint for $i \in \{1,2\}$ and $j \in \{3,4\}$. Let $h' = \max\{h_1,h_2\} + \max\{h_3,h_4\}$ and $h'' = \max\{h_1 + h_3, h_1 + h_4, h_2 + h_3, h_2 + h_4\}$. We show $h' \leq h''$ and $h'' \leq h'$. Since for all u the value $h''(u)$ is the maximum over all sums $h_i(u) + h_j(u)$, $i \in \{1,2\}$ and $j \in \{3,4\}$, it cannot be less than the particular pair $h_{i'}(u) + h_{j'}(u)$ that is selected in h'. Conversely, the maximum in $h''(u)$ is attained by $h_{i''}(u) + h_{j''}(u)$ for some $i'' \in \{1,2\}$ and $j'' \in \{3,4\}$. As the pattern database heuristics are derived from different terms, this implies that $i' = i''$ and $j' = j''$. ∎

A heuristic h *dominates* a heuristic h' if and only if $h(u) \geq h'(u)$ for all $u \in S$. It is simple to see that h^C dominates all h_i, $i \in \{1,\ldots,k\}$ (see Exercises).

4.5.2 Symmetry and Dual Pattern Databases

Many solitaire games like the $(n^2 - 1)$-PUZZLE can be mapped onto themselves by using symmetry operations, for example, along some board axes. Such automorphisms can be used to improve the memory consumption of pattern databases in the sense that one database is reused for all symmetric state space abstractions. For example, the $(n^2 - 1)$-PUZZLE is symmetric according to the mappings that correspond to a rotation of the board by 0, 90, 180, and 270 degrees and symmetric according to the mappings that correspond to the vertical and horizontal axes.

What is needed are symmetries that preserve shortest path information with respect to the abstract goal. Hence, *symmetry pattern database lookups* exploit physical symmetries of the problem that do exist for the goal state(s). For example, because of the length-preserving symmetry along the main diagonal in the $(n^2 - 1)$-PUZZLE, the pattern database built for the tiles 2, 3, 6, and 7 can also be used to estimate the number of moves required for patterns 8, 9, 12, and 13 as shown in Figure 4.12. More formally, for a given $(n^2 - 1)$-PUZZLE with a state $u = (u_0,\ldots,u_{n^2-1})$ and a symmetry $\psi : \{0,\ldots,n^2 - 1\} \rightarrow \{0,\ldots,n^2 - 1\}$, the symmetry lookup is executed on state u' with $u'_i = \psi(u_{\psi(i)})$, where $i \in \{0,\ldots,n^2 - 1\}$ and $\psi = (0,4,8,12,1,5,9,13,2,6,10,14,3,7,11,15)$.

Another example is the well-known TOWERS-OF-HANOI problem. It consists of three pegs of different-size discs, which are sorted in decreasing order of size on one of the pegs. A solution has to move all discs from their initial peg to a goal peg, subject to the constraint that a smaller disk is

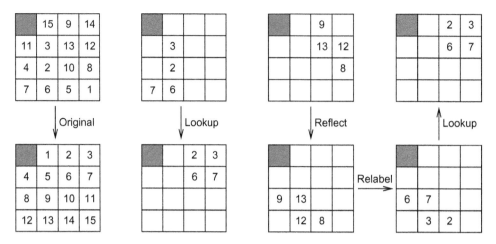

FIGURE 4.12

Ordinary (left) and symmetry (right) pattern database lookup tiles are reflected along the main diagonal, relabeled, and queried in the original pattern database for retrieving the exact goal distance.

above a larger one. A pattern database symmetry is found by exploiting that the two nongoal pegs are indistinguishable. Note that the three-peg problem is not a challenging combinatorial problem any more because the lower and upper bounds of $2^n - 1$ moves match by simple arguments on a recursive solution (to build an n tower from peg A to C move the top $n - 1$ tower to B, then the largest disk from A to C, and finally the $n - 1$ tower from B to C). The four-peg TOWERS-OF-HANOI problem, however, is a search challenge.

A related aspect to symmetry is *duality. Dual pattern database lookups* require a bijection between objects and locations of the domain in the sense that each object is located in one location and each location occupies only one object. There are three main assumptions: Every state is a permutation, the actions are location-based, and the actions are inversible. An example is provided in Figure 4.13. The dual question is generated by first selecting the goal positions for the tiles that are in the pattern locations (inversion) and then substituting the tiles with their indexes. The dual lookup itself can reuse the database.

Experimental results show that the average heuristic value increases when using symmetry or duality or both. Symmetry pattern database lookups are used for the same search direction as for the original pattern database lookup, whereas dual lookups result in estimates for backward search.

4.5.3 Bounded Pattern Databases

Most pattern database heuristics assume that a memory-based heuristic is computed for the entire state space, and the cost of computing it is amortized over many problem instances. But in some cases, it may be useful to compute pattern database heuristics for a single problem instance. If we know an upper bound U for the minimum cost solution f^* in original space S, one option to reduce the memory needs is to limit the exploration in abstract space to a superset of the ones that are relevant for being queried in the concrete state space search. Assume that A* search with cost function f is applied in the backward

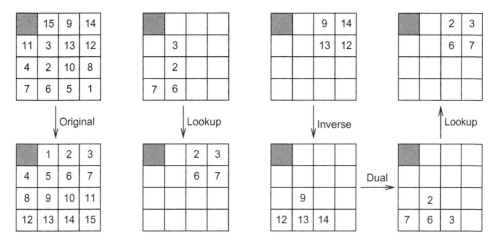

FIGURE 4.13

Ordinary and dual pattern database lookups initial and goal states (far left); ordinary lookup in the pattern database for the tiles 2, 3, 6, and 7 (left, the pattern itself is shown on the top, its respective goal is shown on the bottom). For a dual lookup we generate a dual question (right, top to bottom) followed by a lookup in the pattern database for the tiles 2, 3, 6, and 7 (far right, bottom to top).

traversal of the abstract space to guide the search toward the abstract start state $\phi(s)$. When terminating at $\phi(s)$ not all relevant abstract goal distances have been computed. Pattern database construction has to continue according to a different termination criterion. The following simple observation limits the exploration in the focused traversal of abstract space. In other words, goal distances of some particular abstract states can be safely ignored, based on the following result.

Theorem 4.5. *(Bounded Computation of Pattern Database) Let U be an upper bound on f^*, the cost of the optimal solution to the original problem, let ϕ be the state space abstraction function, and let f be the cost function in the backward traversal of the abstract space. A pattern database entry for u only needs to be computed if $f(\phi(u)) < U$.*

Proof. Since the f-value in an abstract state for a state $\phi(u)$ provides a lower bound on the cost of an optimal solution in abstract space, which in turn is a lower bound on the cost of the optimal solution to the original problem, it follows that for any projected state $\phi(v)$ of which the f-value exceeds U, it cannot lead to any better solution with cost lower than U and thus can be safely ignored in the computation. ∎

The situation is shown to the left in Figure 4.14, where we see the concrete state space on top of the abstract one. The relevant part that could be queried by the top-level search is shaded. It is contained in the cover $C = \{\phi(u) \mid f(\phi(u)) < U\}$.

Consequently, A* for pattern database creation terminates when condition $f(\phi(u)) < U$ is not satisfied. The following result shows that the technique is particularly useful in computing a set of disjoint pattern database heuristics.

Theorem 4.6. *(Bounded Construction of Disjoint Pattern Databases) Let Δ be the difference between an upper bound U and a lower bound $L = \sum_i h_i(\phi_i(s))$ on the cost of an optimal solution to the original*

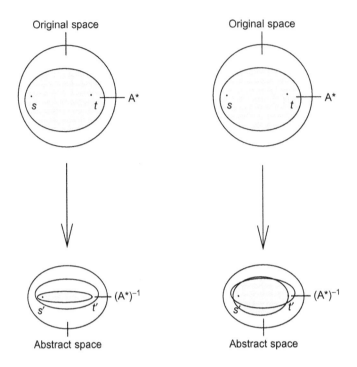

FIGURE 4.14

Successful one-pass A* pattern database construction (left), and demand for extension of secondary A* search in abstract state space (right). Nodes searched by A* in the original graph and states needed for the database lookup are shaded gray, and nodes searched by A* in the inverse abstract state space graph, $(A^*)^{-1}$ for short, are indicated with an ellipse.

problem, where h is a consistent heuristic and $\phi_i(s)$ is the initial state for the abstract problem. A state $\phi_i(u)$ for the construction of a disjoint pattern database heuristic needs to be processed only if $f_i(\phi_i(u)) < h_i(\phi_i(s)) + \Delta$.

Proof. In disjoint pattern database heuristics, the cost of optimal solution to each abstract problem can be added to obtain an admissible heuristic to the original problem. Therefore, it can be shown that a pattern database heuristic needs only to be computed for $\phi_i(u)$ if $\sum_i f_i(\phi_i(u)) < U$. Subsequently, for every abstraction ϕ_j we have $f_j(\phi_j(u)) < U - \sum_{i\neq j} f_i(\phi_i(u))$. Since all heuristics are consistent, we have $f_i(\phi_i(u)) \geq h_i(\phi_i(s))$. It follows that

$$f_j(\phi_j(u)) < U - \sum_{i\neq j} f_i(\phi_i(u)) \leq U - \sum_{i\neq j} h_i(\phi_i(s)).$$

Because $\sum_{i\neq j} h_i(\phi_i(s)) = \left(\sum_i h_i(\phi_i(s))\right) - h_j(\phi_j(s))$, we get

$$f_j(\phi_j(u)) < U + h_j(\phi_j(s)) - \sum_i h_i(\phi_i(s)) = U - L + h_j(\phi_j(s)) = \Delta + h_j(\phi_j(s)).$$

■

4.5.4 On-Demand Pattern Databases

Another option for reducing the space occupied by the pattern databases is not to apply heuristic backward search in the abstract space. For the sake of simplicity, we assume a problem graph, in which the initial and goal state are unique. In the abstract space the pattern database is constructed backward from the goal using a heuristic that estimates the distance to the abstract initial state. When the initial pattern is reached, pattern construction is suspended. The set of expanded nodes in abstract space can be used for lookups in forward search, as they contain optimal distance values to the goal (assuming a consistent heuristic and maintaining the g-value).

Consider the situation as shown in Figure 4.14. The left part of the figure displays the concrete state space and the mapping of the initial state s and goal state t to their corresponding abstract counterparts. We see that A* executed in the concrete state space and abstract A* executed in the abstract state space do not fully traverse their state spaces. As said, the search in abstract state space is suspended once the goal has been found, and the information computed corresponds to a partially constructed pattern database.

In the best case, all states queried in the concrete search will be mapped to states that have been generated in the abstract state space. To the right in Figure 4.14 we see, however, that the abstract states generated for queries in the original A* (indicated by another ellipse, labeled with A*) can be located outside the states set already generated in an abstract A* search. In this case, heuristic values for the concrete state space have to be computed *on demand*. The suspended exploration in abstract state space is resumed until the state that has been queried is contained in the enlarged set. Hence, the pattern database grows dynamically (until memory is exhausted).

There is a subtle issue that influences the runtime of the approach. To allow the secondary search to be guided toward the new abstract query states (that failed the lookup procedure), the entire search frontier of the suspended abstract A* search has to be reorganized. Let $h_{t'}$ be the heuristic for the first and $h_{t''}$ be the estimator for the subsequent abstract goal, then the priorities in the search frontier have to be changed from $g(u) + h_{t'}(u)$ to $g(u) + h_{t''}(u)$.

4.5.5 Compressed Pattern Databases

Generally, the larger patterns become, the more powerful the heuristic will be in reducing the search efforts. Unfortunately, due to its size we might reach the physical memory limits of the computer very soon. Therefore, it can be beneficial to consider hash compression techniques to push the limits further.

Compressed pattern databases partition the abstract search space into clusters or groups of nodes. They contribute to the fact that it is possible to generate abstract search spaces beyond the limit of main memory. These spaces are generated but not stored completely, either by omitting the visited set from the search (see Ch. 6), or by maintaining the state space externally on the hard disk (see Ch. 8).

The compression mapping folds the hash table representation of the pattern databases. A group of entries is projected to one representative location and if hash conflicts are detected, the entry stored will be the minimum of all patterns that map to the same address to preserve admissibility. Unfortunately, this induces that the heuristic can drop by more than the edge costs, giving rise to possible inconsistencies.

Theorem 4.7. *(Nearby Pattern Database Compression) Assume that for two abstract states $\phi(u)$ and $\phi(v)$ we have $\delta_\phi(u,v) \le c$. Then $h_\phi(u) - h_\phi(v) \le c$.*

Proof. By applying the triangular inequality for shortest paths $\delta_\phi(u,v) + \delta_\phi(v,T) \geq \delta_\phi(u,T)$ we obtain

$$h_\phi(u) - h_\phi(v) = \delta_\phi(u,T) - \delta_\phi(v,T) \leq \delta_\phi(u,v) \leq c.$$

∎

As a consequence, if nearby patterns are compressed, the loss of information is bounded. Finding domain-dependent problem projections that preserve the locality in the abstract search graph is a challenge. Hence, one compression technique is based on connected subgraphs that appear in the search space and that are contracted using the projection function. The most prominent examples are *cliques*, sets of nodes that are fully connected via edges. In this case the entries in the pattern database for these nodes will differ from one another by at most 1. Of course, cliques in pattern space are domain dependent and do not exist in every problem graph. Furthermore, when cliques exist, their usage for compressing the pattern database depends heavily on the index function used. Nonetheless, at least for permutation-type domains, the hope is that cliques will appear quite often.

Suppose that k nodes of the pattern space form a clique. If we can identify a general subgraph structure for k adjacent entries, we can compress the pattern database by contracting it. Instead of storing k entries, we map all nodes in the subgraph to one entry. An *admissible compression* stores the *minimum* of the k nodes.

This compression can be generalized and included into pattern database construction as follows. Suppose that we can generate but not fully store an abstract state space. At each abstract state generated, we further map it to a smaller range, and address a pattern database hash table of this compressed index range. As several abstract states now share the same address in the compressed pattern database, we store the smallest distance value. An example is provided in Table 4.4.

Viewed differently, such compression is a hash abstraction in the form of an equivalence relation. It clusters nodes with the same hash value, updating costs and using the minimum. There is a tight connection of pattern database compression to other hash compression techniques like bit-state hashing (see Ch. 3).

For the compression, the state space that is traversed is larger than the one that is stored. The search frontier for exploring the entire abstract space has to be maintained space-efficiently, for example, on disk (see Ch. 8).

Table 4.4 Compressing a pattern database: original pattern database (left), compressed database (right).

Address	Value		Compressed Address (stored)	Original Address (not stored)	Value (stored)
1	4				
2	5		1	{1,2}	4
3	6		2	{3,4}	6
4	7		3	{5,6}	3
5	5		4	{7,8}	1
6	3				
7	2				
8	1				

Traversing the larger abstract state space does pay off. We show that the values in compressed pattern databases are in general significantly better than the ones generated in corresponding uncompressed databases bound by the available memory.

Theorem 4.8. *(Performance of Pattern Database Compression) For permutation problems with n variables and a pattern of p variables, let h_ψ^k denote the database heuristic when abstracting k and let h_ϕ^k denote the database heuristic when removing k of the p variables. Then the sizes of the pattern databases match and for all states u we have $h_\psi^k(u) \geq h_\phi^k(u)$.*

Proof. Both abstract search spaces contain $n!/(n-p+k)!$ states. Whereas ϕ simply ignores the k variables, ψ takes the minimum value for all possible combinations of the k variables. ∎

4.5.6 Compact Pattern Databases

An alternative for reducing the space requirement for a pattern database is to exploit the representation of a state as a string and a *trie* implementation for the pattern database. For each pattern, a path in a trie is generated, with the heuristic value at the leaves. This representation is sensible to orderings of characters in the string that describe the pattern, and might be optimized for better space consumption. Leaves of common heuristic values can be merged and isomorphic subtrees can be eliminated. In contrast to the pattern database compression, compaction is *lossless*, since the accuracy of the pattern database is not affected.

Lastly, there are various compression techniques known from literature (e.g., run-length, Huffman, and Lempel-Ziv) that can be applied to pattern databases to reduce their memory consumption. The core problem with these techniques is that a pattern database (or parts of it) have to be uncompressed to perform a lookup.

4.6 SUMMARY

A* and its variants are more focused if they use heuristic estimates of the goal distances and then find shortest paths potentially much faster than when using the uninformed zero heuristics. In this chapter, we therefore discussed different ways of obtaining such informed heuristics, which is often done by hand but can be automated to some degree.

Abstractions, which simplify search problems, are the key to the design of informed heuristics. The exact goal distances of the abstract search problem can be used as consistent heuristics for the original search problem. Computing the goal distances of the abstract search problem on demand does not reduce the number of expanded states, and the goal distances just need to be memorized. The goal distances of several abstractions can be combined to yield more informed heuristics for the original search problem. Abstractions can also be used hierarchically by abstracting the abstract search problem further. Most consistent heuristics designed by humans for some search problem turn out to be the exact goal distances for an abstract version of the same search problem, which was obtained either by adding actions (embeddings) or grouping states into abstract states. Embeddings, for example, can be obtained by dropping preconditions of operators, whereas groupings can be obtained by clustering close-by states, dropping predicates from the STRIPS representations of states, or replacing predicates with don't care symbols independent of their parameters (resulting in so-called patterns). This insight allows us to derive consistent heuristics automatically by solving abstract versions of search problems.

We discussed a negative speed-up result for embeddings: Assume that one version of A* solves a search problem using the zero heuristics. Assume further that a different version of A* solves the same search problem using more informed heuristics that, if needed, are obtained by determining the goal distances for an embedding of the search problem with A* using the zero heuristics. Then, we showed that the second scheme expands at least all states that the first scheme expands and thus cannot find shortest paths faster than the first scheme. This result does not apply to groupings but implies that embeddings are helpful only if the resulting heuristics are used to solve more than one search problem or if they are used to solve a single search problem with search methods different from the standard version of A*.

We discussed two ways of obtaining heuristics by grouping states into abstract states. First, Hierarchical A* calculates the heuristics on demand. Hierarchical A* solves a search problem using informed heuristics that, if needed, are obtained by determining the goal distances for a grouping of the search problem with A* that can either use the zero heuristics or heuristics that, if needed, are obtained by determining the goal distances for a further grouping of the search problem. The heuristics, once calculated, are memorized together with the paths found so that they can be reused. Second, pattern databases store in a lookup table a priori calculated heuristics for abstract states of a grouping that typically correspond to the smallest goal distances in the original state space of any state that belongs to the abstract states.

Pattern databases result in the most powerful heuristics currently known for many search problems. We discussed Korf's conjecture that the number of states generated by A* (without duplicate detection) using a pattern database is approximately proportional to the ratio of the number of states in the state space and the size of the pattern database. Instead of using one large pattern database, we can often obtain more informed consistent heuristics by using several smaller pattern databases and taking the maximum or, if each operator application is counted in at most one of the pattern databases (resulting in so-called disjoint pattern databases), the sum of their heuristics. Sometimes we can also obtain more informed consistent heuristics from a plain pattern database by exploiting symmetry and duality, a special form of symmetry. We can design good pattern databases by hand or automatically compute the heuristics stored in the pattern database for all abstract states or only a superset of the relevant ones (if we know an upper bound on the length of the shortest path), compute these heuristics a priori or on demand, store these heuristics in a compressed or uncompressed form, and choose statically or dynamically which pattern databases to combine to guarantee that the pattern databases are disjoint.

Table 4.5 summarizes different ways of constructing pattern databases, where k is the number of (not necessarily disjoint) patterns and l is the number of disjoint patterns. Then we list the search methods used in the forward and backward search directions separately. A dash denotes that an (additional) search in the given direction is not needed, and an asterisk denotes that any search method can be used. *User* lists the information provided by the designer of the pattern database. *Lookup* lists the number of heuristics retrieved from the pattern database to calculate the heuristic of one state. *Admissible* lists the condition under which the resulting heuristics are admissible. A checkmark denotes that they are guaranteed to be admissible in any case, otherwise it is shown how the heuristics of several pattern databases need to be combined to guarantee admissibility.

Table 4.5 Overview pattern databases: ϕ is a state space abstraction, ψ a state space partition; *maxMem* denotes the use of automated pattern selection with regard to pattern database size threshold, and U denotes an upper bound on the length of the shortest path for the search problem in the original state space. Notation $\sqrt{} \Rightarrow \sqrt{}$ is ad hoc for saying that if the pattern database heuristic is admissible then the dual is admissible as well.

Pattern Database	Forward	Backward	User	Lookup	Admissible
Ordinary	-	BFS	ϕ	1	$\sqrt{}$
Directed	Any	BFS	ϕ	1	$\sqrt{}$
Weighted	Any	Dijkstra	ϕ	1	$\sqrt{}$
Multiple	$k \times$Any	$k \times^*$	ϕ_i, maxMem	k	max
Disjoint	$l \times$Any	$l \times^*$	ϕ_i, maxMem	l	add
Multiple Disjoint	$kl \times$Any	$kl \times^*$	ϕ_i, maxMem	kl	add/max
Bounded	-	BFS	ϕ, U	1	$\sqrt{}$
On-Demand	-	A*	ϕ	1	$\sqrt{}$
Symmetry	-	-	ϕ, Symmetry	s	$\sqrt{}$
Dual	-	-	ϕ, Duality	2	$\sqrt{} \Rightarrow \sqrt{}$
Compressed	-	BFS	ϕ, ψ	1	$\sqrt{}$

4.7 EXERCISES

4.1 Consider the FIFTEEN-PUZZLE with all labels of the tiles removed. Display the abstract state space and annotate the distances to the goal.

4.2 The THIRTY-FIVE-PUZZLE is the $n = 6$ variant of the $(n^2 - 1)$-PUZZLE.
   1. Determine the sizes of the abstract state spaces for a growing number of tiles in the pattern.
   2. Assuming a perfect hash table with one byte per entry, estimate the amount of memory needed for a disjoint set of 6-tile and a disjoint set of 7-tile pattern databases.

4.3 Provide a sufficient condition for the inversion of an operator in PSVN.

4.4 The ARROW PUZZLE asks for changing the order of the arrows in an arrangement, while flipping two adjacent arrows at a time.
   1. Transform the initial state $\uparrow\uparrow\uparrow\downarrow\downarrow\downarrow$ into $\uparrow\downarrow\uparrow\downarrow\uparrow\downarrow$.
   2. Devise an abstraction by solving any 4-ARROW PUZZLE subproblem. How many subproblems do you obtain?
   3. Illustrate that the solution length reduces linearly, but the state space reduces exponentially.

4.5 Consider the three-disk TOWERS-OF-HANOI PUZZLE with the disks *small*, *middle*, and *big* and three pegs.

1. Depict the entire state space (level 0). How many states does it have?
2. Depict the entire state space for the problem where only the middle and smallest disk are provided (level 1). How many states does it have?
3. Depict the entire state space for the problem where only the smallest disk is provided (level 2). How many states does it have?
4. Show levels 0, 1, and 2 of the abstraction hierarchy formed for the initial state.

4.6 In a BLOCKSWORLD problem involving n blocks b_i it is possible to define n patterns and relaxations as follows. The variables $pos(b_i)$ encode the position of block b_i. The value $pos(b_i)$ is 0 if b_i is located on the table and j if it is located on another block $b_j, j \neq i$.
1. Show that such patterns are disjoint; that is, no action affects more than one variable.
2. For all blocks that are on the table to build an n-tower show that an according pattern database heuristic results in the value n.
3. For an n-tower, where only the two bottom-most blocks are to be exchanged, show that the preceding pattern database heuristic results in the value 1.

4.7 For the FIFTEEN-PUZZLE instance $(14, 13, 15, 7, 11, 12, 9, 5, 6, 0, 2, 1, 4, 8)$ compute the disjoint pattern database value with respect to the goal state and
1. one tile in each pattern. What is the name of the heuristic?
2. two tiles in each pattern; that is, group the tiles $(1,2), (1,3), \ldots, (14,15)$.

4.8 Consider the disjoint 6-tile pattern databases in Figure 4.7.
1. Validate that the maximal depth of the regular 6-pattern databases is 35 and explain why the construction of only one of the three pattern databases is sufficient.
2. The irregular 6-tile pattern database encloses the blank, which limits the last two moves of the tiles (e.g., the last tile that can move is either tile 1 or tile 5 for the standard layout of the puzzle). How far does this technique increase the initial maximal depth of 32? Does this affect the consistency of the database? Why or why not?

4.9 Explain how to construct a pattern database if the abstract state space contains more than one abstract goal state.

4.10 Show that
1. $\max\{h_1, h_2\}$ induced by ϕ_1 and ϕ_2 dominates h_1 and h_2.
2. $h_1 + h_2$ induced by disjoint ϕ_1 and ϕ_2 dominates h_1 and h_2.
3. h' for ϕ' generated by unifying ϕ_1, ϕ_2 dominates both $\max\{h_1, h_2\}$ and $h_1 + h_2$.
4. h^C dominates all h_i, induced by $\phi_i, i \in \{1, \ldots, k\}$.

4.11 Explain why in SOKOBAN we have used the *minimum* weighted matching, but in the sliding-tile puzzle we have used the *maximum* weighted matching to combine the subproblems.

4.12 For the 2×2 version of the $(n^2 - 1)$-PUZZLE:
1. Display the concrete and the abstract state spaces generated by mapping all labels to 1.
2. Show that introducing two blanks leads to *spurious* states that have no concretization.
3. Give a general characterization that no *spurious* state is generated.

4.13 Consider the 4×4 GRIDWORLD with initial state at the bottom-left and the goal state at the top-right corner. Additionally, insert edges along the diagonal, and connect (i,i) with $(i+1,i+1)$ for all available values of i by undirected edges. Let h_r denote the row distance of a node to the goal and h_c the column distance.

1. Perform BFS on the problem.
2. Show that using either h_r or h_c alone reduces the amount of search by a factor of two.
3. Show that maximizing the two heuristics leads to a search that proceeds directly down the optimal solution path along the diagonal edges.

4.14 Consider a FIFTEEN-PUZZLE instance $(5, 10, 14, 7, 8, 3, 6, 1, 15, 0, 12, 9, 2, 11, 4, 13)$.

1. Determine the abstract goal distances for the two pattern tile selections $(1,2,4,5,6,8,9,10)$ and $(3,7,11,12,13,14,15)$ by counting *each move* in abstract space. Maximize the values to compute an admissible heuristic estimate.
2. Determine the abstract goal distances for the two pattern tile selections $(1,2,3,4,5,6,7)$ and $(8,9,10,11,12,13,14,15)$ counting each *pattern tile move* in abstract space. Add the values to compute an admissible heuristic.

4.15 Given a weighted graph, the SEQUENTIAL ORDERING problem asks for a minimal-cost Hamiltonian path from the start node to the goal vertex, which also observes precedence constraints. An instance to the problem can be defined by a cost matrix, where the entry is the cost of the edge, or it is -1 to represent that the first node must precede the second node in the solution path. A state corresponds to a partial completion of the trip. It records the current last vertex in this partial tour as well as the nodes that have not been reached yet.

1. Provide a representation of a state space in the form of a lattice with the start state at the top and the goal state at the bottom. Your lattice should have as many layers as there are nodes in the graph. Draw an example problem with three nodes.
2. Construct an abstract state space lattice with the same number of levels but with a lesser number of states. The abstract lattice should be obtained by clustering states on the same level. In your chosen example you should merge nodes 1 and 3 in level 1, and nodes 1 and 2 in levels 2 and 3. Show the outcome of the abstraction.
3. Describe the modifications to the cost matrix and prove that the abstraction is a lower bound.

4.16 Explain why maximizing of two heuristics can fail to produce better search results than one of the individual exploration. Hint: Use the odd/even parity of the f-value in the $(n^2 - 1)$-PUZZLE.

4.17 For the EIGHT-PUZZLE use the domain abstractions ϕ_1, which maps the vector of tiles $(1,2,3,4,5,6,7,8,0)$ to the vector $(x,x,3,4,5,6,x,8,0)$, and ϕ_2, which maps $(1,2,3,4,5,6,7,8,0)$ to $(x,x,y,y,5,z,x,z,0)$.

1. Determine the sizes of the abstract space generated by ϕ_1 and ϕ_2.
2. Why can it be better to map values to more than one don't care symbol?

4.18 The granularity of a domain abstraction is a vector indicating how many constants in the original domain are mapped to each constant in the abstract domain. For example, the granularity of ϕ_2 in Exercise 4.17 is $(3,2,2,1,1)$ because three constants are mapped to x, two are mapped to y, two are mapped to z, and constants 5 and 0 remain unique.

1. Determine the granularity of ϕ_1.
2. Determine the expected sizes of the abstract spaces for the EIGHT-PUZZLE based on the granularity $(3,3,2,1)$ by first determining n, the number of different domain abstractions with this granularity, and m, the pattern space size for each of the abstractions.
3. Provide an EIGHT-PUZZLE example that shows that different granularities can produce pattern state space of the same size.

4.19 Graph abstractions ensure that if there is an initial goal path in the concrete cost-algebraic graph, there is one in the abstract system, and that the cost of the optimal initial goal path in the concrete system is smaller (w.r.t. $\preceq$) than the cost of the one in the abstract system.

1. Illustrate the merging of nodes v_1, v_2 in a (multiple-edge) graph with edges $v_1 \xrightarrow{e_1} v_3$, $v_2 \xrightarrow{e_2} v_3$, $v_3 \xrightarrow{e_1} v_1$, and $v_3 \xrightarrow{e_2} v_2$.
2. Show that merging nodes to super-nodes leads to a graph abstraction.
3. Show how merging of edges reduces the search effort.
4. Show that self-loops can be eliminated because they do not contribute to a better solution.

4.20 RUBIK'S CUBE (see Ch. 1) is one of the best examples to apply symmetries. The cube has 48 symmetries including reflections. Show that these symmetries can be generated by four basic symmetries.

4.21 Let us now look at conjugation for the RUBIK'S CUBE, a fundamental concept in group theory. For example, the operation $g = RUR^{-1}RU^2R^{-1}R^{-1}L^{-1}U^{-1}LU^{-1}L^{-1}U^2L$ twists two specific corners on a face. For any element h in the cube group, $h^{-1}gh$ will twist some pair of corners. Repeating the conjugate operation n times yields $h^{-1}(g)^n h$.

1. Show that conjugacy, as defined for the RUBIK'S CUBE, is an equivalence relation.
2. Enumerate the conjugacy classes of S_4.
3. Consider the RUBIK'S CUBE and apply the commutator $RUR^{-1}U^{-1}$ and the conjugated commutator $F(RUR^{-1}U^{-1})F^{-1}$. Display your result!
4. Now raise conjugation to a power, $F(RUR^{-1}U^{-1})^2F^{-1}$, $F(RUR^{-1}U^{-1})^3F^{-1}$, and so on.

4.22 If you turn the faces of a solved cube and do not use the moves R, R^{-1}, L, L^{-1}, F, F^{-1}, B, and B^{-1}, you will only generate a subset of all possible cubes. This subset is denoted by $G_1 = (U, D, R2, L2, F2, B2)$. In this subset, the orientations of the corners and edges cannot be changed and the four edges in the UD-slice (between the U-face and D-face) stay isolated.

1. Show that mapping a concrete cube position to one in G_1 is a state space abstraction.
2. How many states are contained in G_1?
3. Determine the goal distances in G_1 using backward BFS.
4. Devise a *two-phase* algorithm that first searches for the shortest path for any state to one in G_1 and that then searches for the shortest path within G_1. Is this strategy optimal (i.e., does it yield optimal solutions)?

4.8 BIBLIOGRAPHIC NOTES

Using abstraction transformations to guide the search goes back to Minski who defined abstractions as the unification of a simplified problem and refinement in the early 1960s. The ABSTRIPS solver technology is due to Sacerdoti (1997). The history on automated creation of admissible heuristics ranges from early work of Gaschnig (1979b), Pearl (1985), and Preditis (1993), to Guida and Somalvico (1979). Gaschnig has proposed that the cost of solutions can be computed by exact solution in auxiliary space. He observed that search with abstract information can be more time consuming than breadth-first search. Valtorta (1984) has proven this conjecture and published a seminal paper, which has been reconsidered by Holte, Perez, Zimmer, and Donald (1996). An update on Valtorta's result is due to Hansson, Mayer, and Valtorta (1992). Hierarchical A* has been revisited by Holte, Grajkowski, and Tanner (2005). The authors have also invented hierarchical IDA*. *Absolver* by Mostow and Prieditis (1989) was the first system to break the barrier imposed by the theorems. They implemented the idea of searching through the space of abstractions and speed-up transformations. In later research, one of the authors suggests to store all heuristic values before base-level search in a hash table.

Pattern databases have been introduced by Culberson and Schaeffer (1998) in the context of the Fifteen-Puzzle. The name refers to (don't care) pattens as abstractions. This suggests to revise the name to *abstraction databases* since any abstraction (based on patterns or not) can be used. Despite such attempts, for example by Qian (2006), in AI research the term pattern database has settled. They have shown to be very effective in solving random instances of the Rubik's Cube by Korf (1997) and the Twenty-Four-Puzzle by Korf and Felner (2002) optimally. Holte and Hernádvölgyi (1999) have given a time-space trade for pattern database search (Korf, Reid, and Edelkamp, 2001). Additive pattern databases have been proposed by Felner, Korf, and Hanan (2004a) and general theory on additive state space abstraction has been given by Yang, Culberson, Holte, Zahavi, and Felner (2008). Edelkamp (2002) has shown how to construct pattern databases symbolically. Hernádvölgyi (2000) has applied pattern databases to significantly shorten the length of *macro actions*.

Multiple pattern databases have been studied by Furcy, Felner, Holte, Meshulam, and Newton (2004) in the context of puzzle solving. The authors also discuss limits and possibilities of different pattern partitions. Breyer and Korf (2010a) have shown that independent additive heuristics reduce search multiplicatively. Zhou and Hansen (2004b) have analyzed a compact space-efficient representation of pattern databases. *Multivalued pattern databases* are variants of multiple goal pattern databases that improve the performance of single-valued pattern databases in practice, and have been suggested by Linares López (2008), and *vectorial pattern databases*, as proposed by Linares López (2010), induce nonconsistent heuristic functions by recognizing admissible heuristic values.

Machine learning methods for multiple pattern database search, including their selection and compression, are discussed by Samadi, Felner, and Schaeffer (2008a) and by Samadi, Siabani, Holte, and Felner (2008b). Symmetric pattern databases have already been considered by Culberson and Schaeffer (1998). Lookups based on the duality of positions and state vector elements have been studied by Felner, Zahavi, Schaeffer, and Holte (2005). In Zahavi, Felner, Holte, and Schaeffer (2008b) general notions of duality are discussed, but are limited to location-based permutations. On-demand or instance-dependent pattern databases have been introduced by Felner and Alder (2005), and compressed databases are due to Felner, Meshulam, Holte, and Korf (2004b). Bitvector pattern databases based on two-bit BFS are proposed by Breyer and Korf (2010b). A method for learning good compression has been suggested by Samadi et al. (2008b). For large range of planning domains, Ball and Holte (2008) have shown that BDD sometimes achieve very large compression ratios. A first theoretical study on BDD growth in state space search has been provided by Edelkamp and Kissmann (2008c). Counterintuitively, inconsistencies (e.g., due to random selection of pattern databases) positively reduce search efforts, see work by (Zahavi, Felner, Schaeffer, and Sturtevant, 2007). Applying machine learning for bootstrapping has been proposed by Jabbari, Zilles, and Holte (2010).

The interrelation of abstraction and heuristics has been emphasized by Larsen, Burns, Ruml, and Holte (2010). Neccessary and sufficient conditions for avoiding spurious states have been studied by Zilles and Holte (2010), and abstraction-based heuristics with *true distance heuristics* have been considered by Felner and Sturtevant (2009) as a way to obtain admissible heuristics for explicit state spaces. In a variant, called *portal heuristic*, the domain is partitioned into regions and portals between regions are identified. True distances between all pairs of portals are stored and used to obtain admissible heuristics for A* search.

The application of pattern databases are manifold. The multiple sequence alignment problem as introduced in Chapter 1 calls for sets of n sequences to be optimally aligned with respect to some similarity measurement. The heuristic estimates as applied in Korf and Zhang (2000); McNaughton, Lu, Schaeffer, and Szafron (2002); and Zhou and Hansen (2004b) is to find and add the lookup values of alignments of disjoint subsets for $k < n$ sequences. Pattern databases together with A* have been applied by Klein and Manning (2003) to find the best parsing of a sentence. The estimate correlates to the cost of completing a partial parse and is derived by simplifying the grammar. Finding a least-cost path in quality-of-service routing problems (see Ch. 2) has been considered by Li, Harms, and Holte (2007) with different estimate functions for each of the resources. Each estimate is derived by considering only the constraint on the considered resource. The approach relates to finding the shortest path subject to multiple constraints by Li, Harms, and Holte (2005).

The SEQUENTIAL ORDERING problem has been analyzed by Hernádvölgyi (2003) using pattern databases. Another application area for pattern databases is *interactive entertainment*. For cooperative plan finding in computer games many agents search for individual paths but are allowed to help each other to succeed. Silver (2005) has shown how to incorporate memory-based heuristics. In *constraint optimization*, bucket elimination as proposed by Kask and Dechter (1999) shares similarities with pattern databases, providing an optimistic bound on the solution cost.

Knoblock (1994) has found that techniques that drop a predicate entirely from a state space in domain-independent *action planning* are homomorphisms. Haslum, Bonet, and Geffner (2005) have discussed the automated selection of pattern databases in the context of optimal planning. The paper extends the work of Edelkamp (2001a), who has applied pattern database search to AI planning (see Ch. 15).

Abstraction is a fundamental concept in the area of *model checking* (Clarke, Grumberg, and Long, 1994). Cleaveland, Iyer, and Yankelevich (1995) have presented an alternative setting. The concept of path preservation is called *simulation* and has been explained by Milner (1995). Merino, del Mar Gallardo, Martinez, and Pimentel (2004) have presented a tool to perform data abstraction for the verification of communication protocols. *Predicate abstraction* is a related abstraction method that is important to control the branching in software programs and has been introduced by S. Graf and H. Saidi (1997). It is the basis of the counterexample-guided abstract-and-refinement paradigm, invented by Clarke, Grumberg, Jha, Lu, and Veith (2001), and integrated in state-of-the-art tools, for example, by Ball, Majumdar, Millstein, and Rajamani (2001). The first applications of pattern databases in verification are due to Qian and Nymeyer (2004) and Edelkamp and Lluch-Lafuente (2004).

Heuristic Search Under Memory Constraints

Linear-Space Search

5

A* always terminates with an optimal solution and can be applied to solve general state space problems. However, its memory requirements increase rapidly over time. Suppose that 100 bytes are required for storing a state and all its associated information, and that the algorithm generates 100,000 new states every second. This amounts to a space consumption of about 10 megabytes per second. Consequently, main memory of, say, 1 gigabyte is exhausted in less than two minutes. In this chapter, we present search techniques with main memory requirements that scale linear with the search depth. The trade-off is a (sometimes drastic) increase in time.

As a boundary case, we show that it is possible to solve a search problem with logarithmic space. However, the time overhead makes such algorithms only theoretically interesting.

The standard algorithms for linear-space search are *depth-first iterative-deepening* (DFID) and *iterative-deepening A** (IDA*), which, respectively, simulate a BFS and an A* exploration by performing a series of depth- or cost-bounded (depth-first) searches. The two algorithms analyze the *search tree* that can be much larger than the underlying problem graph. There are techniques to reduce the overhead of repeat evaluations, which are covered later in the book.

This chapter also predicts the running time of DFID and IDA* for the restricted class of so-called *regular search spaces*. We show how to compute the size of a brute-force search tree, and its asymptotic branching factor, and use this result to predict the number of nodes expanded by IDA* using a consistent heuristic. We formalize the problem as the solution of a set of simultaneous equations. We present both analytic and numerical techniques for computing the exact number of nodes at a given depth, and for determining the asymptotic branching factor. We show how to determine the exact brute-force search tree size even for a large depth and give sufficient criteria for the convergence of this process. We address refinements to IDA* search, such as *refined threshold determination* that controls the threshold increases more liberally, and *recursive best-first search*, which uses slightly more memory to back up information.

The exponentially growing search tree has been also addressed with *depth-first branch-and-bound* (DFBnB). The approach computes lower *and* upper bounds for the solution quality to prune the search (tree). DFBnB is often used when *algorithmic lower bounds* are complemented by *constructive upper bounds* that correspond to the costs of obtained solutions.

5.1 *LOGARITHMIC SPACE ALGORITHMS

First of all, we might ask for the limit of space reduction. We assume that the algorithms are not allowed to modify the input, for example, by storing partial search results in nodes. This corresponds to the situation where large amounts of data are kept on read-only (optical storage) media.

Given a graph with n nodes we devise two $O(\lg n)$ space algorithms for the SINGLE-SOURCE SHORTEST PATHS problem, one for unit cost graphs and one for graphs with bounded-edge costs.

5.1.1 Divide-and-Conquer BFS

Given an unweighted graph with n nodes we are interested in an algorithm that computes the *level* (the smallest length of a path) for all nodes. To cope with very limited space, we apply a *divide-and-conquer algorithm* that solves the problem recursively. The top-level procedure *DAC-BFS* calls *Exists-Path* (see Alg. 5.1), which reports whether or not there is a path from a to b with l edges, by calling itself twice. If $l = 1$ and there is an edge from a to b, the procedure immediately returns true. Otherwise, for each intermediate node index j, $1 \leq j \leq n$, it recursively calls *Exists-Path*$(a, j, \lceil l/2 \rceil)$ and *Exists-Path*$(j, b, \lfloor l/2 \rfloor)$. The recursion stack has to store at most $O(\lg n)$ frames, each of which contains $O(1)$ integers. Hence, the space complexity is $O(\lg n)$.

However, this space efficiency has to be paid with a high time complexity. Let $T(n, l)$ be the time needed to determine if there is a path of l edges, where n is the total number of nodes. T obeys the recurrence relation $T(n, 1) = 1$ and $T(n, l) = 2n \cdot T(n, l/2)$, resulting in $T(n, n) = (2n)^{\lg n} = n^{1+\lg n}$ time for one test. Varying b and iterating on l in the range of $\{1, \ldots, n\}$ gives an overall performance of at most $O(n^{3+\lg n})$ steps.

5.1.2 Divide-and-Conquer Shortest Paths Search

We can generalize the idea to the SINGLE-SOURCE SHORTEST PATHS problem (see Alg. 5.2) assuming integer weights bounded by a constant C. For this case, we check the weights

---

Procedure DAC-BFS
Input: Explicit problem graph G with n nodes and start node s
Output: Level of every node

for each i **in** $\{1, \ldots, n\}$;; For all nodes i
   for each l **in** $\{1, \ldots, n\}$;; For all distances l
      if (*Exists-Path*(s, i, l))   ;; If path of length l exists
         print (s, i, l); **break**   ;; Output level and terminate

Procedure Exists-Path
Input: Nodes a and b, expected distance l between a and b
Output: Boolean, denoting if path of this length does exist

if $(l = 1)$;; If path has come down to one edge
   return $((a, b) \in E)$;; Feedback if edge between a and b exists
for each j **in** $\{1, \ldots, n-1\}$;; For all intermediate values
   if (*Exists-Path*$(a, j, \lceil l/2 \rceil)$ **and** *Exists-Path*$(j, b, \lfloor l/2 \rfloor)$)   ;; Recursive check
      return *true*   ;; If both calls are successful, a path exists
return *false*   ;; No path possible

Algorithm 5.1

Computing the BFS level with logarithmic space.

Procedure DAC-SSSP
Input: Explicit problem graph G with n nodes and start node s
Output: Weighted distance of every node

for each i in $\{1,\ldots,n\}$;; For all nodes
   for each w in $\{1,\ldots,C \cdot n - 1\}$;; For all intermediate weights
      if (*Exists-Path*(s,i,w))   ;; Path of weight w exists
         print (s,i,w); **break**   ;; Output distance and terminate

Procedure Exists-Path
Input: Nodes a and b, expected weight w of path between a and b
Output: Boolean, denoting if path of this length does exist

if $(w(a,b) = w)$ **return** *true*   ;; If weight on edge fits report path found
for each j in $\{1,\ldots,n\}$;; For each intermediate node
   for each s in $\{\max\{1, \lfloor w/2 \rfloor - \lceil C/2 \rceil\},\ldots,$;; From minimum weight ...
      $\min\{w-1, \lfloor w/2 \rfloor + \lceil C/2 \rceil\}\}$;; ... to maximum weight
      if (*Exists-Path*(a,j,s) **and** *Exists-Path*$(j,b,w-s)$)   ;; Divide and conquer
         return *true*   ;; Path with cost w found
return false   ;; No path found

Algorithm 5.2

Searching the shortest paths with logarithmic space.

$\lfloor w/2 \rfloor - \lceil C/2 \rceil$ for path $a \to j$, $\lfloor w/2 \rfloor + \lceil C/2 \rceil$ for path $j \to b$,
$\lfloor w/2 \rfloor - \lceil C/2 \rceil + 1$ for path $a \to j$, $\lfloor w/2 \rfloor + \lceil C/2 \rceil - 1$ for path $j \to b$,
$\cdots$ $\cdots$
$\lfloor w/2 \rfloor + \lceil C/2 \rceil$ for path $a \to j$, $\lfloor w/2 \rfloor - \lceil C/2 \rceil$ for path $j \to b$.

If there is a path with total weight w then it can be decomposed into one of these partitions, assuming that the bounds are contained in the interval $[1..w-1]$. The worst-case reduction on weights is $Cn \to Cn/2 + C/2 \to Cn/4 + 3C/4 \to \cdots \to C \to C-1 \to C-2 \to C-3 \to \cdots \to 1$.

    Therefore, the recursion depth is bounded by $\lg(Cn) + C$, which results in a space requirement of $O(\lg n)$ integers. As in the BFS case the running time is exponential (scale-up factor C for partitioning the weights).

5.2 EXPLORING THE SEARCH TREE

Search algorithms that do not eliminate duplicates necessarily view the set of search tree nodes as individual elements in search space. Probably the best way to explain how they work is to express the algorithms as a search in a space of paths. Search trees are easier to analyze than problem graphs because for each node there is a unique path to it.

In other words, we investigate a state space in the form of a search tree (formally a tree expansion of the graph rooted at the start node s), so that elements in the search space are paths. We mimic the tree searching algorithms and internalize their view.

Recall that to certify optimality of the A* search algorithm, we have imposed the admissibility condition on the weight function that

$$\delta(u, T) = \min\{\delta(u, t) \mid t \in T\} \geq 0$$

for all $u \in S$. In the context of search trees, this assumption translates as follows. The *search tree problem space* is characterized by a set of states $\mathbf{S}$, where each state is a path starting at s. The subset of paths that end with a goal node is denoted by $\mathbf{T} \subseteq \mathbf{S}$. For the *extended weight function* $w : \mathbf{S} \to \mathbb{R}$, admissibility implies that

$$\min\{w(q) \mid (p, q) \in \mathbf{T}\} \geq 0$$

for all paths $p \in \mathbf{S}$.

Definition 5.1. *(Ordered Search Tree Algorithm) Let $w_{max}(p_v)$ be the maximum weight of any prefix of a given path $p_v \in \mathbf{S}$; that is,*

$$w_{max}(p_v) = \max_{p_m \in \mathbf{S}}\{w(p_m) \mid \exists q : p_v = (p_m, q)\}.$$

An ordered search tree algorithm expands paths with regard to increasing values of w_{max}.

Lemma 5.1. *If w is admissible, then for all solution paths $p_t \in \mathbf{T}$, we have $w_{max}(p_t) = w(p_t)$.*

Proof. If $\min\{w(q) \mid p_t = (p_u, q) \in \mathbf{T}\} \geq 0$ for all p_u in $\mathbf{S}$, then for all $p_t = (p_u, q) \in \mathbf{T}$ with p_u in $\mathbf{S}$ we have $w(q) \geq 0$, especially for path p_u with $w_{max}(p_t) = w(p_u)$. This implies $w(p_t) - w_{max}(p_t) = w(p_t) - w(p_u) = w(q) \geq 0$. On the other side, $w(p_t) \leq w_{max}(p_t)$ and, therefore, $w(p_t) = w_{max}(p_t)$. ∎

The following theorem states conditions on the optimality of any algorithm that operates on the search tree.

Theorem 5.1. *(Optimality of Search Tree Algorithms) Let G be a problem graph with admissible weight function w. For all ordered search tree algorithms operating on G it holds that when selecting $p_t \in \mathbf{T}$ we have $w(p_t) = \delta(s, T)$.*

Proof. Assume $w(p_t) > \delta(s, T)$; that is, there is a solution path $p_t' \in \mathbf{T}$ with $w(p_t') = \delta(s, T) < w(p_t)$ that is not already selected. When terminating this implies that there is an encountered unexpanded path $p_u \in \mathbf{S}$ with $p_t' = (p_u, q) \in \mathbf{T}$. By Lemma 5.1 we have $w_{max}(p_u) \leq w_{max}(p_t') = \delta(s, T) < w(p_t) = w_{max}(p_t)$ in contradiction to the ordering of the search tree algorithm and the choice of p_t. ∎

5.3 BRANCH-AND-BOUND

Branch-and-bound (BnB) is a general programming paradigm used, for example, in operations research to solve hard combinatorial optimization problems. *Branching* is the process of spawning subproblems, and *bounding* refers to ignoring partial solutions that cannot be better than the current

---

Procedure DFBnB-Driver
Input: Implicit problem graph with start node s, weight function w, heuristic h,
    successor generation function *Expand* and goal predicate *Goal*
Output: Shortest path to a goal node $t \in T$, or $\emptyset$ if no such path exists

Initialize upper bound U ;; e.g., ∞
$bestPath \leftarrow \emptyset$;; Initialize solution path
$DFBnB(s, 0, U)$;; Call Alg. 5.4
return $bestPath$;; Output optimal solution path

Algorithm 5.3

Depth-first branch-and-bound algorithm.

best solution. To this end, lower and upper bounds L and U are maintained. Since global control values on the solution quality improve over time, branch-and-bound is effective in solving *optimization problems*, in which a cost-optimal assignment to the problem variables has to be found.

For applying branch-and-bound search to general state space problems, we concentrate on DFS extended with upper and lower bounds. In this context, branching corresponds to the generation of successors, so that DFS can be casted as generating a *branch-and-bound search tree*. We have already seen that one way of obtaining a lower bound L for the problem state u is to apply an admissible heuristic h, or $L(u) = g(u) + h(u)$ for short. An initial upper bound can be obtained by constructing any solution, such as one established by a greedy approach.

As with standard DFS, the first solution obtained might not be optimal. With DFBnB, however, the solution quality improves over time together with the global value U until eventually the lower bound $L(u)$ at some node u is equal to U. In this case an optimal solution has been found, and the search terminates.

The implementation of DFBnB is shown in Algorithm 5.3. At the beginning of the search, the procedure is invoked with the start node and with the upper bound U set to some reasonable estimate (it could have been obtained using some heuristics; the lower it is, the more can be pruned from the search tree, but in case no upper bound is known, it is safe to set it to ∞). A global variable *bestPath* keeps track of the actual solution path.

The recursive search routine is depicted in Algorithm 5.4. Sorting the set of successors according to increasing L-values is an optional refinement to the algorithm that often aids in accelerating the search for finding an early solution.

Theorem 5.2. *(Optimality Depth-First Branch-and-Bound) Algorithm depth-first branch-and-bound is optimal for admissible weight functions.*

Proof. If no pruning was taking place, every possible solution would be generated so that the optimal solution would eventually be found. Sorting of children according to the L-values has no influence on the algorithm's completeness. Condition $L(v_j) < U$ confirms that the node's lower bound is smaller than the global upper bound. Otherwise, the search tree is pruned, since admissible weight functions exploring the subtree cannot lead to better solutions than the one stored with U. ∎

Procedure DFBnB
Input: Node u, path cost g, upper bound U
Side effects: Update of threshold U, solution path *bestPath*

if $(Goal(u))$	;; Goal found
if $(g < U)$	;; Improvement to currently shortest path
bestPath ← *Path*(u)	;; Record solution path
$U \leftarrow g$	;; Update global maximum
else	;; Nongoal node
Succ(u) ← *Expand*(u)	;; Generate successor set
Let $\{v_0,\ldots,v_n\}$ be *Succ*(u), sorted according to h	;; Optimize search order
for each j **in** $\{1,\ldots,n\}$	;; Successor iteration
if $(g + h(v_j) < U)$	;; Apply upper bound pruning
DFBnB$(v, g + w(u,v), U)$	;; Recursive call

Algorithm 5.4

Depth-first branch-and-bound subroutine.

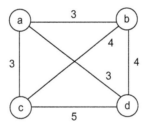

FIGURE 5.1

TSP with four cities to be visited on roundtrip.

An important advantage of *branch-and-bound* algorithms is that we can control the quality of the solution to be expected, even if it is not yet found. The cost of an optimal solution is only up to $U - L$ smaller than the cost of the best computed one.

A prototypical example for DFBnB search is the TSP, as introduced in Chapter 1. As one choice for branching, the search tree may be generated by assigning edges to a partial tour. A suboptimal solution might be found quickly.

Consider the TSP of Figure 5.1 together with the MINIMUM SPANNING TREE heuristic. The corresponding branch-and-bound search tree is shown in Figure 5.2. We have chosen an asymmetric interpretation and a branching rule that extends a partial tour by an edge if possible. If in case of a tie the left child is preferred, we see that the optimal solution was not found on the first trial, so the first value for U is 15. After a while the optimal tour of cost 14 is found. The example is too small for the lower bound to prune the search tree based on condition $L > U$.

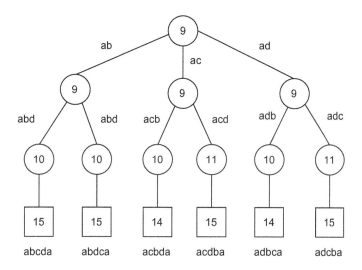

FIGURE 5.2

Branch-and-bound-tree for TSP of Figure 5.1.

Analogously to a depth-first scheme, we can also modify BFS to create an algorithm for *breadth-first branch-and-bound*. The search expands nodes in breadth-first order and uses bounds to prune the search space.

5.4 ITERATIVE-DEEPENING SEARCH

We have seen that the first solution found by DFBnB doesn't have to be optimal. Moreover, if the heuristic bounds are weak, the search can turn into exhaustive enumeration. *Depth-first iterative-deepening* (DFID) tries to control these aspects. The search mimics a breadth-first search with a series of depth-first searches that operate with a successively increasing search horizon. It combines optimality of BFS with the low space complexity of DFS. A successively increasing global threshold U for the solution cost is maintained, up to which a recursive DFS algorithm has to expand nodes.

The main driver loop (see Alg. 5.5) maintains U and U', the bound for the next iteration. It repeatedly calls the DFID subroutine of Algorithm 5.6, which searches for an optimal goal path p_t in the thresholded search tree. It updates the global variable U' to the minimal weight of all generated, except unexpanded nodes in the current iteration, and yields the new threshold U for the next iteration. Note that if the graph contains no goal and is infinite, then the algorithm will run forever; however, if it is finite, then the f-values also are bounded, and so when U reaches this value, U' will not be updated, it will be ∞ after the last search iteration. In contrast to A*, DFID can track the solution path on the stack, which allows predecessor links to be omitted (see Ch. 2).

Consider the example of Figure 5.3, a weighted version of a sample graph introduced in Chapter 1. Table 5.1 traces the execution of DFID on this graph. The contents of the search frontier in the form

Procedure DFID-Driver
Input: Implicit problem graph with start node s, weight function w,
      successor generation function *Expand*, and goal predicate *Goal*
Output: Path from s to $t \in T$, or $\emptyset$ if no such path exists

$U' \leftarrow 0$	;; Initialize global threshold
$bestPath \leftarrow \emptyset$	;; Initialize solution paths
while ($bestPath = \emptyset$ **and** $U' \neq \infty$)	;; Goal not found, unexplored nodes left
$\quad U \leftarrow U'$	;; Reset threshold
$\quad U' \leftarrow \infty$	;; Initialize new global threshold
$\quad bestPath \leftarrow DFID(s,0,U)$	;; Invoke Alg. 5.6 at s
return $bestPath$	;; Terminate with solution path

Algorithm 5.5

Depth-first iterative-deepening algorithm.

Procedure DFID
Input: Node u, path length g, upper bound U
Output: Solution path, or $\emptyset$ if no goal found
Side effects: Update of threshold U'

if ($Goal(u)$)	;; Goal found
$\quad$**return** (u)	;; Output solution path
$Succ(u) \leftarrow Expand(u)$	;; Generate successor set
for each v **in** $Succ(u)$	;; For all successors
$\quad$**if** ($g + w(u,v) \leq U$)	;; Node within thresholded tree
$\quad\quad p \leftarrow DFID(v, g + w(u,v), U)$	;; Recursive call
$\quad\quad$**if** ($p \neq \emptyset$) **return** (u,p)	;; Solution found
$\quad\quad$**else if** ($g + w(u,v) < U'$) $U' \leftarrow g + w(u,v)$	;; Set new threshold

Algorithm 5.6

DFS subroutine for DFID search.

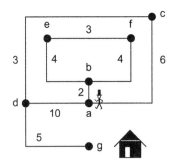

FIGURE 5.3

Example of weighted graph with initial node a and goal node g.

Table 5.1 Steps in DFID (with predecessor elimination) for the example of Figure 5.3.

Step	Iteration	Selection	Pending Calls	U	U′	Remarks
1	1	{}	{(a,0)}	0	∞	
2	1	a	{}	0	2	g(b), g(c), and g(d) > U
3	2	{}	{(a,0)}	2	∞	New iteration starts
4	2	a	{(b,2)}	2	6	g(c) and g(d) > U
5	2	b	{}	2	6	g(e) and g(f) > U
6	3	{}	{(a,0)}	6	∞	New iteration starts
7	3	a	{(b,2),(c,6)}	6	10	g(d) > U
8	3	b	{(e,6),(f,6),(c,6)}	6	10	
9	3	e	{(f,6),(c,6)}	6	10	g(f) > U
10	3	f	{(c,6)}	6	10	g(e) > U
11	3	c	{}	6	9	g(d)
12	4	{}	{(a,0)}	9	∞	New iteration starts
13	4	a	{(b,2),(c,6)}	9	10	g(d) > U
14	4	b	{(c,6),(e,6),(f,6)}	9	10	
15	4	c	{(e,6),(f,6),(d,9)}	9	10	
16	4	e	{(f,6),(d,9),(f,9)}	9	10	
17	4	f	{(d,9),(f,9),(e,9)}	9	10	
18	4	d	{(f,9),(e,9)}	9	10	g(g) and g(c) > U
19	4	f	{(e,9)}	9	10	g(b) > U
20	4	e	{(d,9)}	9	10	g(b) > U
⋮	⋮	⋮	⋮	⋮	⋮	⋮
44	7	{}	{(a,0)}	14	∞	New iteration starts
45	7	a	{(b,2),(c,6),d(10)}	14	∞	
46	7	b	{(c,6),(d,10),(e,6),(f,6)}	14	∞	
47	7	c	{(d,10),(e,6),(f,6))}	14	∞	
48	7	d	{(e,6),(f,6),(e,9),(c,13)}	14	15	g(g) > U
49	7	e	{(f,6),(d,9),(c,13),(f,9)}	14	15	
50	7	f	{(d,9),(c,13),(f,9),(e,9)}	14	15	
51	7	d	{(c,13),(f,9),(e,9),(g,14)}	14	15	
52	7	c	{(f,9),(e,9),(g,14)}	14	15	g(a) > U
53	7	f	{(e,9),(g,14),(b,13)}	14	15	
54	7	e	{(g,14),(b,13),(b,13)}	14	15	
55	7	g	{(b,13),b(13)}	14	15	Goal reached

of pending calls to the subroutine are provided. For the sake of conciseness, we assume that the predecessor of a node u is not generated again (as a successor of u) and that the update of value U' takes part before the recursive call.

Theorem 5.3. *(Optimality Depth-First Iterative Deepening) Algorithm DFID for unit cost graphs with admissible weight function is optimal.*

Proof. We have to show that by assuming uniform weights for the edges DFID is ordered. We use induction over the number of *while* iterations k. Let E_k be the set of newly encountered paths in iteration k and R_k be the set of all generated but not expanded paths. Furthermore, let U_k be the threshold of iteration k. After the first iteration, for all $p \in E_1$ we have $w_{max}(p) = 0$. Furthermore, for all $q \in R_1$ we have $w_{max}(q) = 1$. Let $w_{max}(p) = U_k = k - 1$ for all $p \in E_k$. This implies $w_{max}(q) > U_k$ for all q in R_k. Hence, $U_{k+1} = \min_{q \in R_k}\{w_{max}(q)\} = k$. For all $p \in E_{k+1}$ we have $w_{max}(p) = U_{k+1} = k$. Therefore, for all $p \in E_{k+1}$ the condition $U_k < w_{max}(p) = U_{k+1}$ is satisfied. Hence, DFID is ordered. ∎

5.5 ITERATIVE-DEEPENING A*

Iterative deepening A* (IDA*) extends the idea of DFID to heuristic search by including the estimate h. IDA* is the most often used alternative in cases when memory requirements are not allowed to run A* directly. As with DFID, the algorithm is most efficient if the implicit problem graph is a tree. In this case, no duplicate detection is required and the algorithm consumes space linear in the solution length.

Algorithms 5.7 and 5.8 provide a recursive implementation of IDA* in pseudo code: The value $w(u, v)$ is the weight of the edge (u, v), and $h(u)$ and $f(u)$ are the heuristic estimate and combined cost for node u, respectively. During one depth-first search stage, only nodes that have an f-value no larger than U (the current threshold) are expanded. At the same time, the algorithm maintains an upper bound U' on the threshold for the next iteration. This threshold is determined as the smallest f-value of a generated node that is larger than the current threshold, U. This minimum increase in the bound ensures that at least one new node is explored in the next iteration. Moreover, it guarantees that we can stop at the first solution encountered. This solution must indeed be optimal due, since no solution was found in the last iteration with an f-value smaller than or equal to U, and U' is the minimum cost of any path not explored before.

Procedure IDA*-Driver
Input: Implicit problem graph with start node s, weight function w, heuristic h,
　　　　successor generation function *Expand*, and goal predicate *Goal*
Output: Path from s to $t \in T$, or $\emptyset$ if no such path exists

$U' \leftarrow h(s)$	;; Initialize global threshold
bestPath $\leftarrow \emptyset$	;; Initialize solution path
while (*bestPath* $= \emptyset$ **and** $U' \neq \infty$)	;; Goal not found, unexplored nodes left
$U \leftarrow U'$	;; Reset global threshold
$U' \leftarrow \infty$	;; Initialize new global threshold
bestPath $\leftarrow$ IDA*$(s, 0, U)$	;; Invoke Alg. 5.8 at s
return *bestPath*	;; Terminate with solution path

Algorithm 5.7

Driver loop for IDA*.

Procedure IDA*
Input: Node u, path length g, upper bound U
Output: Shortest path to a goal node $t \in T$, or $\emptyset$ if no such path exists
Side effects: Update of threshold U'

if $(Goal(u))$ **return** $Path(u)$	;; Terminate search
$Succ(u) \leftarrow Expand(u)$	;; Generate successor set
for each v **in** $Succ(u)$	;; For all successors
if $(g + w(u,v) + h(v) > U)$	;; Cost exceeds old bound
if $(g + w(u,v) + h(v) < U')$	;; Cost smaller than new bound
$U' \leftarrow g + w(u,v) + h(v)$	;; Update new bound
else	;; f-value below current threshold
$p \leftarrow$ IDA*$(v, g + w(u,v), U)$	;; Recursive call
if $(p \neq \emptyset)$ **return** (u,p)	;; Solution found
return $\emptyset$	;; No solution exists

Algorithm 5.8

The IDA* algorithm (no duplicate detection).

Table 5.2 Steps in IDA* (with predecessor elimination) for the example of Figure 5.3. The numbers in brackets denote f-values.

Step	Iteration	Selection	Pending Calls	U	U'	Remarks
1	1	{}	{(a,11)}	11	∞	h(a)
2	1	a	{}	11	14	f(b), f(d), and f(c) larger than U
3	2	{}	{(a,11)}	14	∞	New iteration starts
4	2	a	{(c,14)}	14	15	f(b), f(d) > U
5	2	c	{(d,14)}	14	15	
6	2	d	{(g,14)}	14	15	f(a) > U
7	2	g	{}	14	15	Goal found

Table 5.2 traces the execution of DFID on our example graph. Note that the heuristic drastically reduces the search effort from 55 steps in DFID to only 7 in IDA*.

The more diverse the f-values are, the larger the overhead induced through repeated evaluations. Therefore, in practice, iterative deepening is limited to graphs with a small number of distinct integral weights. Still, it performs well in a number of applications. An implementation of it using the Manhattan distance heuristic solved random instances of the FIFTEEN-PUZZLE for the first time. Successor nodes that equal a node's predecessor are not regenerated. This reduces the length of the shortest cycle in the resulting problem graph to 12, such that at least for shallow searches the space is "almost" a tree.

Theorem 5.4. *(Optimality Iterative-Deepening A*) Algorithm IDA* for graphs with admissible weight function is optimal.*

Proof. We show that IDA* is ordered. We use induction over the number of *while* iterations k. Let E_k be the set of newly encountered paths in iteration k and R_k be the set of all generated but not expanded paths. Furthermore, let U_k be the threshold of iteration k.

After the first iteration, for all $p \in E_1$ we have $w_{max}(p) = U_1$. Moreover, for all $q \in R_1$ we have $w_{max}(q) > U_1$. Let $w_{max}(p) = U_k$ for all $p \in E_k$. This implies $w_{max}(q) > U_k$ for all q in R_k. Hence, $U_{k+1} = \min_{q \in R_k}\{w_{max}(q)\}$. For all $p \in E_{k+1}$ we have $w_{max}(p) = U_{k+1}$, since assuming the contrary contradicts the monotonicity of w_{max}, since only paths p with $w(p) \leq U_{k+1}$ are newly expanded. Therefore, for all $p \in E_{k+1}$ the condition $U_k < w_{max}(p) = U_{k+1}$ is satisfied. Hence, IDA* is ordered. ∎

Unfortunately, if the search space is a graph, then the number of paths can be exponentially larger than the number of nodes; a node can be expanded multiple times, from different parents. Therefore, duplicate elimination is essential. Moreover, in the worst case, IDA* expands only one new node in each iteration. Consider a linear-space search represented by the path $p = (v_1, \ldots, v_k)$. If n_{A^*} denotes the number of expanded nodes in A*, IDA* will expand $\Omega((n_{A^*})^2)$ many nodes. Such worst cases are not restricted to lists. If all nodes in a search tree have different priorities (which is common if the weight function is rational) IDA* also degrades to $\Omega((n_{A^*})^2)$ many node expansions.

5.6 PREDICTION OF IDA* SEARCH

In the following we will focus on tree-shaped problem spaces. The reason is that while many search spaces are in fact graphs, IDA* potentially explores every path to a given node, and searches the search tree as explained in Section 5.5; complete duplicate detection cannot be guaranteed due to the size of the search space.

The size of a brute-force search tree can be characterized by the *solution depth d*, and by its *branching factor b*. Recall that the branching factor of a node is the number of children it has. In most trees, however, different nodes have different numbers of children. In that case, we define the *asymptotic branching factor* as the number of nodes at a given depth, divided by the number of nodes at the next shallower depth, in the limit as the depth goes to infinity.

5.6.1 Asymptotic Branching Factors

Consider RUBIK'S CUBE with the two pruning rules described in Section 1.7.2. Recall that we divided the faces of the cube into two classes; a twist of a first face can be followed by a twist of any second face, but a twist of a second face cannot be followed immediately by a twist of the opposite first face. We call nodes where the last move was a twist of a first face *type-1 nodes*, and those where it was a twist of a second face *type-2 nodes*. The branching factors of these two types are 12 and 15, respectively, which also gives us bounds on the asymptotic branching factor.

To determine the asymptotic branching factor exactly, we need the proportion of type-1 and type-2 nodes. Define the *equilibrium fraction* of type-1 nodes as the number of type-1 nodes at a given depth, divided by the total number of nodes at that depth, in the limit of large depth. The fraction of type-2 nodes is one minus the fraction of type-1 nodes. The equilibrium fraction is not $1/2$: Each type-1 node generates $2 \cdot 3 = 6$ type-1 nodes and $3 \cdot 3 = 9$ type-2 nodes as children, the difference being that you can't twist the same first face again. Each type-2 node generates $2 \cdot 3 = 6$ type-1 nodes and $2 \cdot 3 = 6$ type-2 nodes, since you can't twist the opposite first face next, or the same second face again. Thus, the number of type-1 nodes at a given depth is six times the number of type-1 nodes at the previous depth, plus six times the number of type-2 nodes at the previous depth. The number of type-2 nodes at a given depth is nine times the number of type-1 nodes at the previous depth, plus six times the number of type-2 nodes at the previous depth.

Let f_1 be the fraction of type-1 nodes, and $f_2 = 1 - f_1$ the fraction of type-2 nodes at a given depth. If n is the total number of nodes at that depth, then there will be nf_1 type-1 nodes and nf_2 type-2 nodes at that depth. In the limit of large depth, the fraction of type-1 nodes will converge to the equilibrium fraction, and remain constant. Thus, at large depth,

$$f_1 = \frac{6nf_1 + 6nf_2}{6nf_1 + 6nf_2 + 9nf_1 + 6nf_2} = \frac{6f_1 + 6f_2}{15f_1 + 12f_2} = \frac{6}{3f_1 + 12} = \frac{2}{f_1 + 4}.$$

Cross multiplying gives us the quadratic equation $f_1^2 + 4f_1 = 2$, which has a positive root at $f_1 = \sqrt{6} - 2 \approx 0.44949$. This gives us an asymptotic branching factor of $15 \cdot f_1 + 12 \cdot (1 - f_1) = 3\sqrt{6} + 6 \approx 13.34847$.

In general, this analysis produces a system of simultaneous equations. For another example, consider the FIVE-PUZZLE, the 2×3 version of the well-known sliding-tile puzzles shown in Figure 5.4 (left). In this problem, the branching factor of a node depends on the blank position. The position types are labeled s and c, representing side and corner positions, respectively (see Fig. 5.4, middle). We don't generate the parent of a node as one of its children, to avoid duplicate nodes representing the same state. This requires keeping track of both the current and previous blank positions. Let cs denote a node where the blank is currently in a side position, and the last blank position was a corner position. Define ss, sc, and cc nodes analogously. Since cs and ss nodes have two children each, and sc and cc nodes have only one child each, we have to know the equilibrium fractions of these different types of nodes to determine the asymptotic branching factor. Figure 5.4 (right) shows the different types of states, with arrows indicating the type of children they generate. For example, the double arrow from ss to sc indicates that each ss node generates two sc nodes at the next level.

Let $N(t, d)$ be the number of nodes of type t at depth d in the search tree. Then we can write the following recurrence relations directly from the graph in Figure 5.4. For example, the last equation comes from the fact that there are two arrows from ss to sc, and one arrow from cs to sc.

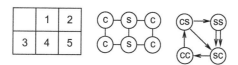

FIGURE 5.4

The FIVE-PUZZLE (left); position types for corner and side positions of the blank, unpruned search (middle) and search with predecessor pruning (right).

$$N(cc, d+1) = N(sc, d)$$

$$N(cs, d+1) = N(cc, d)$$

$$N(ss, d+1) = N(cs, d)$$

$$N(sc, d+1) = 2N(ss, d) + N(cs, d).$$

The initial conditions are that the first move either generates an ss node and two sc nodes, or a cs node and a cc node, depending on whether the blank starts in a side or corner position, respectively.

A simple way to compute the branching factor is to numerically compute the values of successive terms of these recurrences, until the relative frequencies of different state types converge. Let f_{cc}, f_{cs}, f_{ss}, and f_{sc} be the number of nodes of each type at a given depth, divided by the total number of nodes at that depth. After a hundred iterations, we get the equilibrium fractions $f_{cc} = 0.274854, f_{cs} = 0.203113, f_{ss} = 0.150097$, and $f_{sc} = 0.371936$. Since cs and ss states generate two children each, and the others generate one child each, the asymptotic branching factor is $f_{cc} + 2 \cdot f_{cs} + 2f_{ss} + f_{sc} = 1.35321$. Alternatively, we can simply compute the ratio between the total nodes at two successive depths to get the branching factor. The running time of this algorithm is the product of the number of different types of states (e.g., four in this case) and the search depth. In contrast, searching the actual tree to depth 100 would generate over 10^{13} states.

To compute the exact branching factor, we assume that the fractions eventually converge to constant values. This generates a set of equations, one from each recurrence. Let b represent the asymptotic branching factor. This allows us to rewrite the recurrences as the following set of equations. The last one constrains the fractions to sum to one.

$$bf_{cc} = f_{sc}$$

$$bf_{cs} = f_{cc}$$

$$bf_{ss} = f_{cs}$$

$$bf_{sc} = 2f_{ss} + f_{cs}$$

$$1 = f_{cc} + f_{cs} + f_{ss} + f_{sc}.$$

Repeated substitution to eliminate variables reduces this system of five equations in five unknowns to the single equation, $b^4 + b - 2 = 0$, with a solution of $b \approx 1.35321$. In general, the degree of the polynomial will be the number of different types of states. The FIFTEEN-PUZZLE without predecessor elimination has three types of states: c-nodes with node branching factor 2, side or s-nodes with node branching factor 3, and middle or m-nodes with node branching factor 4. Figure 5.5 shows the type of transition graph for the EIGHT-PUZZLE, FIFTEEN-PUZZLE, and TWENTY-FOUR-PUZZLE.

For the TWENTY-FOUR-PUZZLE, however, the search tree of two side or two middle states may differ. For this case we need six classes with a blank at position 1, 2, 3, 7, 8, and 13 according to the tile labeling in Figure 1.10. In the general case the number of different node branching classes in the $(n^2 - 1)$-PUZZLE (without predecessor elimination) is

$$\sum_{i=0}^{\lceil n/2 \rceil} i = \binom{\lceil n/2 \rceil}{2} = \lceil n/2 \rceil (\lceil n/2 \rceil - 1)/2.$$

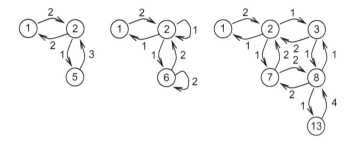

FIGURE 5.5

The state-type transition graph for the EIGHT-PUZZLE (left), FIFTEEN-PUZZLE (middle), and TWENTY-FOUR-PUZZLE (right); node labels correspond to the tile label in the goal state of the puzzle; weights denote the number of successors generated along the edge.

This still compares well to a partition according to the n^2 equivalent classes in the first factorization (savings of a factor of about eight) and, of course, to the $(n^2)!/2$ states in the overall search space (exponential savings).

Let F be the vector of node frequencies and P the transposed matrix of the matrix representation of the state-type graph G. Then the underlying mathematical issue turns out to be an *eigenvalue problem*. Transforming $bF = PF$ leads to $0 = (P - bI)F$ for the identity matrix I. The solutions for b are the roots of the characteristic equation $\det(P - bI) = 0$ where det is the determinant of the matrix. Since $\det(P - bI) = \det(P^T - bI)$, the transposition of the equivalence graph matrix preserves the value of b. For the case of the FIFTEEN-PUZZLE with corner, side, and middle nodes, we have

$$\det \begin{pmatrix} 0-b & 2 & 0 \\ 1 & 1-b & 1 \\ 0 & 2 & 2-b \end{pmatrix} = 0,$$

which simplifies to $(1-b)(b-2)b + 4b - 4 = 0$. The solutions to this equation are 1, $1 + \sqrt{5} = 3.236067978$, and $1 - \sqrt{5} = -1.236067978$. The value $1 + \sqrt{5}$ matches experimental data for the asymptotic branching factor.

The equation $N^{(d)} = PN^{(d-1)}$ can be unrolled to $N^{(d)} = P^d N^{(0)}$. We briefly sketch how to compute P^d for large values of d. Matrix P is *diagonalizable* if there exists an inversible matrix C and a diagonal matrix Q with $P = CQC^{-1}$. This simplifies the calculation of P^d, since we have $P^d = CQ^dC^{-1}$ (the remaining terms $C^{-1}C$ cancel). By the diagonal shape of Q, the value of Q^d is obtained by simply taking the matrix elements $q_{i,i}$ to the power of d. These elements are the eigenvalues of P.

For the FIFTEEN-PUZZLE the basis-transformation matrix C and its inverse C^{-1} are

$$C = \begin{pmatrix} 1 & -1 & 1 \\ 1 - \sqrt{5} & -1 & 1 + \sqrt{5} \\ 3/2 - 1/2\sqrt{5} & 1 & 3/2 + 1/2\sqrt{5} \end{pmatrix}$$

and

$$C^{-1} = \begin{pmatrix} 1/50 \left(5+3\sqrt{5}\right)\sqrt{5} & -1/50 \left(5+\sqrt{5}\right)\sqrt{5} & 1/5 \\ -2/5 & -1/5 & 2/5 \\ 1/50 \left(-5+3\sqrt{5}\right)\sqrt{5} & -1/50 \left(-5+\sqrt{5}\right)\sqrt{5} & 1/5 \end{pmatrix}.$$

The vector of node counts is

$$N^{(d)} = \begin{pmatrix} 1/50 \left(1-\sqrt{5}\right)^d \left(5+3\sqrt{5}\right)\sqrt{5}+2/5 \\ +1/50 \left(1+\sqrt{5}\right)^d \left(-5+3\sqrt{5}\right)\sqrt{5} \\[6pt] 1/50 \left(1-\sqrt{5}\right)\left(1-\sqrt{5}\right)^d \left(5+3\sqrt{5}\right)\sqrt{5}+2/5 \\ +1/50 \left(1+\sqrt{5}\right)\left(1+\sqrt{5}\right)^d \left(-5+3\sqrt{5}\right)\sqrt{5} \\[6pt] 1/50 \left(3/2-1/2\sqrt{5}\right)\left(1-\sqrt{5}\right)^d \left(5+3\sqrt{5}\right)\sqrt{5}-2/5 \\ +1/50 \left(3/2+1/2\sqrt{5}\right)\left(1+\sqrt{5}\right)^d \left(-5+3\sqrt{5}\right)\sqrt{5} \end{pmatrix}$$

such that the exact total number of nodes in depth d is

$$1/50 \left(7/2-3/2\sqrt{5}\right)\left(1-\sqrt{5}\right)^d \left(5+3\sqrt{5}\right)\sqrt{5}+2/5$$
$$+1/50 \left(7/2+3/2\sqrt{5}\right)\left(1+\sqrt{5}\right)^d \left(-5+3\sqrt{5}\right)\sqrt{5}.$$

The number of corner nodes $(1,0,2,2,10,26,90,\ldots)$, the number of side nodes $(0,2,2,10,26,90,$ $282,\ldots)$, and the number of middle nodes $(0,0,6,22,70,230,\ldots)$ grow as expected. The largest eigenvalue $1+\sqrt{5}$ dominates the growth of the search tree in the limit for large values of d.

When incorporating pruning to the search, symmetry of the underlying graph structure may be affected. We consider the EIGHT-PUZZLE. The adjacency matrix for predecessor elimination now consists of four classes: cs, sc, mc, and cm, where the class ij indicates that the predecessor of a j-node in the search tree is an i-node, and m stands for the center position.

$$\begin{pmatrix} 0 & 1 & 0 & 0 \\ 1 & 0 & 0 & 1 \\ 2 & 0 & 0 & 0 \\ 0 & 0 & 3 & 0 \end{pmatrix}.$$

In this case we cannot infer diagonalizability according to the set of real numbers. Fortunately, we know that the branching factor is a positive real value since the iteration process is real. Therefore, we may perform all calculations to predict the search tree growth with complex numbers, for which the characteristic polynomial factorizes. The branching factor and the search tree growth can be calculated analytically and the iteration process eventually converges.

In the example, the set of (complex) eigenvalues is $i\sqrt{2}$, $-i\sqrt{2}$, $\sqrt{3}$, and $-\sqrt{3}$. Therefore, the asymptotic branching factor is $\sqrt{3}$. The vector $N^{(d)}$ is equal to

$$
\begin{pmatrix}
1/5\left(i\sqrt{2}\right)^d + 1/5\left(-i\sqrt{2}\right)^d + 3/10\left(\sqrt{3}\right)^d + 3/10\left(-\sqrt{3}\right)^d \\
-1/10\,i\sqrt{2}\left(i\sqrt{2}\right)^d + 1/10\,i\sqrt{2}\left(-i\sqrt{2}\right)^d + 1/10\sqrt{3}\left(\sqrt{3}\right)^d - 1/10\sqrt{3}\left(-\sqrt{3}\right)^d \\
3/20\,i\sqrt{2}\left(i\sqrt{2}\right)^d - 3/20\,i\sqrt{2}\left(-i\sqrt{2}\right)^d + 1/10\sqrt{3}\left(\sqrt{3}\right)^d - 1/10\sqrt{3}\left(-\sqrt{3}\right)^d \\
-1/10\left(i\sqrt{2}\right)^d - 1/10\left(-i\sqrt{2}\right)^d + 1/10\left(\sqrt{3}\right)^d + 1/10\left(-\sqrt{3}\right)^d
\end{pmatrix}.
$$

Finally, the total number of nodes in depth d is

$$
n^{(d)} = 1/5\left(1/2 + 1/4\,i\sqrt{2}\right)\left(i\sqrt{2}\right)^d + 1/5\left(1/2 - 1/4\,i\sqrt{2}\right)\left(-i\sqrt{2}\right)^d
$$
$$
+ 1/10\left(4 + 2\sqrt{3}\right)\left(\sqrt{3}\right)^d + 1/10\left(4 - 2\sqrt{3}\right)\left(-\sqrt{3}\right)^d.
$$

For small values of d the value $n^{(d)}$ equals 1, 2, 4, 8, 10, 20, 34, 68, 94, 188, and so on.

Table 5.3 gives the even- and odd-depth branching factors of the $(n^2 - 1)$-PUZZLE up to 10×10. As n goes to infinity, all the values converge to 3, the branching factor of an infinite sliding-tile puzzle, since most positions have four neighbors, one of which was the previous blank position.

In some problem spaces, every node has the same branching factor. In other spaces, every node may have a different branching factor, requiring exhaustive search to compute the average branching factor. The technique described earlier determines the size of a brute-force search tree in intermediate cases, where there are a small number of different types of states, the generation of which follows a regular pattern.

Table 5.3 The asymptotic branching factor for the $(n^2 - 1)$-PUZZLE with predecessor elimination. The last column is the geometric mean (the square root of their product); the best estimate of the overall branching factor.

n	$n^2 - 1$	Even Depth	Odd Depth	Mean
3	8	1.5	2	$\sqrt{3}$
4	15	2.1304	2.1304	2.1304
5	24	2.30278	2.43426	2.36761
6	35	2.51964	2.51964	2.51964
7	48	2.59927	2.64649	2.62277
8	63	2.69590	2.69590	2.69590
9	80	2.73922	2.76008	2.74963
10	99	2.79026	2.79026	2.79026

5.6.2 IDA* Search Tree Prediction

We measure the time complexity of IDA* by the number of node expansions. If a node can be expanded and its children evaluated in constant time, the asymptotic time complexity of IDA* is simply the number of node expansions. Otherwise, it is the product of the number of node expansions and the time to expand a node. Given a consistent heuristic function, both A* and IDA* must expand all nodes of which the total cost, $f(u) = g(u) + h(u)$, is less than c, the cost of an optimal solution. Some nodes with the optimal solution cost may be expanded as well, until a goal node is chosen for expansion, and the algorithms terminate. In other words, $f(u) < c$ is a sufficient condition for A* or IDA* to expand node u, and $f(u) \leq c$ is a necessary condition. For a worst-case analysis, we adopt the weaker necessary condition.

An easy way to understand the node expansion condition is that any search algorithm that guarantees optimal solutions must continue to expand every possible solution path, as long as it is smaller than the cost of an optimal solution. On the final iteration of IDA*, the cost threshold will equal c, the cost of an optimal solution. In the worst case, IDA* will expand all nodes u of which the cost $f(u) = g(u) + h(u) \leq c$. We will see later that this final iteration determines the overall asymptotic time complexity of IDA*.

We characterize a heuristic function by the distribution of heuristic values over the nodes in the problem space. In other words, we need to know the number of states with heuristic value 0, how many states have heuristic value 1, the number with heuristic value 2, and so forth. Equivalently, we can specify this distribution by a set of parameters $D(h)$, which is the fraction of total states of the problem of which the heuristic value is less than or equal to h. We refer to this set of values as the *overall distribution* of the heuristic. $D(h)$ can also be defined as the probability that a state chosen randomly and uniformly from all states in the problem space has a heuristic value less than or equal to h. Heuristic h can range from zero to infinity, but for all values of h greater than or equal to the maximum value of the heuristic, $D(h) = 1$. Table 5.4 shows the overall distribution for the Manhattan distance heuristic on the FIVE-PUZZLE.

The overall distribution is easily obtained for any heuristic. For heuristics implemented in the form of a *pattern database*, the distribution can be determined exactly by scanning the table. Alternatively, for a heuristic computed by a function, such as Manhattan distance on large sliding-tile puzzles, we can randomly sample the problem space to estimate the overall distribution to any desired degree of accuracy. For heuristics that are the maximum of several different heuristics, we can approximate the distribution of the combined heuristic from the distributions of the individual heuristics by assuming that the individual heuristic values are independent.

The distribution of a heuristic function is not a measure of its accuracy, and says little about the correlation of heuristic values with actual costs. The only connection between the accuracy of a heuristic and its distribution is that given two admissible heuristics, the one with higher values will be more accurate than the one with lower values on average.

Although the overall distribution is the easiest to understand, the complexity of IDA* depends on a potentially different distribution. The *equilibrium distribution* $P(h)$ is defined as the probability that a node chosen randomly and uniformly among all nodes at a given depth of the brute-force search tree has a heuristic value less than or equal to h, in the limit of large depth.

If all states of the problem occur with equal frequency at large depths in the search tree, then the equilibrium distribution is the same as the overall distribution. For example, this is the case with the RUBIK'S CUBE search tree. In general, however, the equilibrium distribution may not equal the overall distribution. In the FIVE-PUZZLE, for example, the overall distribution assumes

Table 5.4 Heuristic distributions for the Manhattan distance on the FIVE-PUZZLE. The first column gives the heuristic value. The second column gives the number of states of the FIVE-PUZZLE with each heuristic value. The third column gives the total number of states with a given or smaller heuristic value, which is simply the cumulative sum of the values from the second column. The fourth column gives the overall heuristic distribution $D(h)$. These values are computed by dividing the value in the third column by 360, the total number of states in the problem space. The remaining columns are explained in the text.

h	States	Sum	$D(h)$	Corner	Side	Csum	Ssum	$P(h)$
0	1	1	0.002778	1	0	1	0	0.002695
1	2	3	0.008333	1	1	2	1	0.008333
2	3	6	0.016667	1	2	3	3	0.016915
3	6	12	0.033333	5	1	8	4	0.033333
4	30	42	0.116667	25	5	33	9	0.115424
5	58	100	0.277778	38	20	71	29	0.276701
6	61	161	0.447222	38	23	109	52	0.446808
7	58	219	0.608333	41	17	150	69	0.607340
8	60	279	0.775000	44	16	194	85	0.773012
9	48	327	0.908333	31	17	225	102	0.906594
10	24	351	0.975000	11	13	236	115	0.974503
11	8	359	0.997222	4	4	240	119	0.997057
12	1	360	1.000000	0	1	240	120	1.000000

that all states, and, hence, all blank positions, are equally likely. At deep levels in the tree, the blank is in a side position in more than one-third of the nodes, and in a corner position in less than two-thirds of the nodes. In the limit of large depth, the equilibrium frequency of side positions is $f_s = f_{cs} + f_{ss} = 0.203113 + 0.150097 = 0.35321$. Similarly, the frequency of corner positions is $f_c = f_{cc} + f_{sc} = 0.274854 + 0.371936 = 0.64679 = 1 - f_s$. Thus, to compute the equilibrium distribution, we have to take these equilibrium fractions into account. The fifth and sixth columns of Table 5.4, labeled *corner* and *side*, give the number of states with the blank in a corner or side position, respectively, for each heuristic value. The seventh and eighth columns give the cumulative numbers of corner and side states with heuristic values less than or equal to each particular heuristic value. The last column gives the equilibrium distribution $P(h)$. The probability $P(h)$ that the heuristic value of a node is less than or equal to h is the probability that it is a corner node, 0.64679, times the probability that its heuristic value is less than or equal to h, given that it is a corner node, plus the probability that it is a side node, 0.35321, times the probability that its heuristic value is less than or equal to h, given that it is a side node. For example, $P(2) = 0.64679 \cdot (3/240) + 0.35321 \cdot (3/120) = 0.016915$. This differs from the overall distribution $D(2) = 0.016667$.

The equilibrium heuristic distribution is not a property of a problem, but of a problem space. For example, including the parent of a node as one of its children can affect the equilibrium distribution by changing the equilibrium fractions of different types of states. When the equilibrium distribution differs from the overall distribution, it can still be estimated from a pattern database, or by random sampling of the problem space, combined with the equilibrium fractions of different types of states, as illustrated earlier.

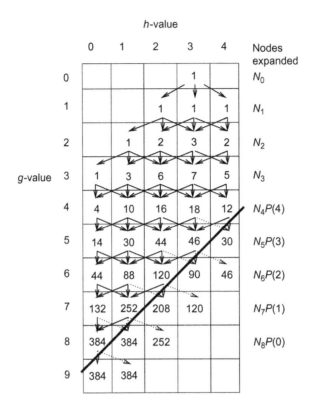

FIGURE 5.6

Sample tree for analysis of IDA*. The vertical axis represents the depth of a node, which is also its g-value, and the horizontal axis represents the heuristic value of a node. Each box represents a set of nodes at the same depth with the same heuristic value, labeled with the number of such nodes. The arrows represent the relationship between parent and child node sets. The thick diagonal line separates the fertile node sets from the sterile node sets.

To provide some intuition behind our main result, Figure 5.6 shows a schematic representation of a search tree generated by an iteration of IDA* on an abstract problem instance, where all edges have unit cost. The numbers were generated by assuming that each node generates one child each with a heuristic value one less, equal to, and one greater than the heuristic value of the parent. For example, there are six nodes at depth 3 with heuristic value 2, one with a parent that has a heuristic value 1, two with parents that have a heuristic value 2, and three with parents that have a heuristic value 3. In this example, the maximum value of the heuristic is 4, and the heuristic value of the initial state is 3.

One assumption of our analysis is that the heuristic is consistent. Because of this, and since all edges have unit cost ($w(u,v) = 1$ for all u,v) in this example, the heuristic value of a child must be at least the heuristic value of its parent, minus one. We assume a cutoff threshold of eight moves for this iteration of IDA*. Solid arrows represent sets of *fertile* nodes that will be expanded, and dotted arrows represent sets of *sterile* nodes that will not be expanded because their total cost, $f(u) = g(u) + h(u)$, exceeds the cutoff threshold.

The values at the far right of Figure 5.6 show the number of nodes expanded at each depth, which is the number of fertile nodes at that depth. N_i is the number of nodes in the brute-force search tree at depth i, and $P(h)$ is the equilibrium heuristic distribution. The number of nodes generated is the branching factor times the number expanded.

Consider the graph from top to bottom. There is a root node at depth 0, which generates N_1 children. These nodes collectively generate N_2 child nodes at depth 2. Since the cutoff threshold is eight moves, in the worst case, all nodes n of which the total cost $f(u) = g(u) + h(u) \leq 8$ will be expanded. Since 4 is the maximum heuristic value, all nodes down to depth $8 - 4 = 4$ will be expanded. Thus, for $d \leq 4$, the number of nodes expanded at depth d will be N_d, the same as in a brute-force search. Since 4 is the maximum heuristic value, $P(4) = 1$, and, hence, $N_4 P(4) = N_4$.

The nodes expanded at depth 5 are the fertile nodes, or those for which $f(u) = g(u) + h(u) = 5 + h(u) \leq 8$, or $h(u) \leq 3$. At sufficiently large depths, the distribution of heuristic values converges to the equilibrium distribution. Assuming that the heuristic distribution at depth 5 approximates the equilibrium distribution, the fraction of nodes at depth 5 with $h(u) \leq 3$ is approximately $P(3)$. Since all nodes at depth 4 are expanded, the total number of nodes at depth 5 is N_5, and the number of fertile nodes is $N_5 P(3)$.

There exist nodes at depth 6 with heuristic values from 0 to 4, but their distribution differs from the equilibrium distribution. In particular, nodes with heuristic values 3 and 4 are underrepresented relative to the equilibrium distribution, because these nodes are generated by parents with heuristic values from 2 to 4. At depth 5, however, the nodes with heuristic value 4 are sterile, producing no offspring at depth 6, hence reducing the number of nodes at depth 6 with heuristic values 3 and 4. The number of nodes at depth 6 with $h(u) \leq 2$ is completely unaffected by any pruning however, since their parents are nodes at depth 5 with $h(u) \leq 3$, all of which are fertile. In other words, the number of nodes at depth 6 with $h(u) \leq 2$, which are the fertile nodes, is exactly the same as in the brute-force search tree, or $N_6 P(2)$.

Due to consistency of the heuristic function, all possible parents of fertile nodes are themselves fertile. Thus, the number of nodes to the left of the diagonal line in Figure 5.6 is exactly the same as in the brute-force search tree. In other words, heuristic pruning of the tree has no effect on the number of fertile nodes, although it does effect the sterile nodes. If the heuristic was inconsistent, then the distribution of fertile nodes would change at every level where pruning occurred, making the analysis far more complex.

When all edges have unit cost, the number of fertile nodes at depth i is $N_i P(d - i)$, where N_i is the number of nodes in the brute-force search tree at depth i, d is the cutoff depth, and P is the equilibrium heuristic distribution. The total number of nodes expanded by an iteration of IDA* to depth d is

$$\sum_{i=0}^{d} N_i P(d - i).$$

Let us now generalize this result to nonunit edge costs. First, we assume that there is a minimum edge cost; we can, without loss of generality, express all costs as multiples of this minimum cost, thereby normalizing it to one. Moreover, for ease of exposition these transformed actions and heuristics are assumed to be integers; this restriction can easily be lifted.

We replace the depth of a node by $g(u)$, the sum of the edge costs from the root to the node. Let N_i be the number of nodes u in the brute-force search tree with $g(u) = i$. We assume that the heuristic is consistent, meaning that for any two nodes u and v, $h(u) \leq \delta(u,v) + h(v)$, where $\delta(u,v)$ is the cost of an optimal path from u to v.

Theorem 5.5. *(Node Prediction Formula) For larger values of c the expected number $E(N,c,P)$ of nodes expanded by IDA* up to cost c, given a problem-space tree with N_i nodes of cost i, with a heuristic characterized by the equilibrium distribution P, is*

$$E(N,c,P) = \sum_{i=0}^{c} N_i P(c - i).$$

Proof. Consider the nodes u for which $g(u) = i$, which is the set of nodes of cost i in *the brute-force search tree*. There are N_i such nodes. The nodes of cost i that will be expanded by IDA* in an iteration with cost threshold c are those for which $f(u) = g(u) + h(u) = i + h(u) \leq c$, or $h(u) \leq c - i$. By definition of P, in the limit of large i, the number of such nodes in the brute-force search tree is $N_i P(c - i)$. It remains to show that all these nodes in the brute-force search tree are also in the tree generated by IDA*.

Consider an ancestor node v of such a node u. Then there is only one path between them in the tree, and $g(u) = i = g(v) + w(v,u)$, where $w(v,u)$ is the cost of the path from node v to node u. Since $f(v) = g(v) + h(v)$, and $g(v) = i - w(v,u)$, $f(v) = i - \delta(v,u) + h(v)$. Since the heuristic is consistent, $h(v) \leq \delta(v,u) + h(u)$, where $\delta(v,u) \leq w(v,u)$ is the cost of an optimal path from v to u in the problem graph, and hence, $h(v) \leq w(v,u) + h(u)$. Thus, $f(v) \leq i - w(v,u) + w(v,u) + h(u)$, or $f(v) \leq i + h(u)$. Since $h(u) \leq c - i, f(v) \leq i + c - i$, or $f(v) \leq c$. This implies that node m is fertile and will be expanded during the search. Therefore, since all ancestors of node u are fertile and will be expanded, node u must eventually be generated itself. In other words, all nodes u in the brute-force search tree for which $f(u) = g(u) + h(u) \leq c$ are also in the tree generated by IDA*. Since there can't be any nodes in the IDA* tree that are not in the brute-force search tree, the number of such nodes at level i in the IDA* tree is $N_i \cdot P(c - i)$, which implies the claim. ∎

The effect of earlier iterations (small values of c) on the time complexity of IDA* depends on the rate of growth of node expansions in successive iterations. The *heuristic branching factor* is the ratio of the number of nodes expanded in a search-to-cost threshold c, divided by the nodes expanded in a search-to-cost $c - 1$, or $E(N,c,P)/E(N,c-1,P)$, where the normalized minimum edge cost is 1. Assume that the size of the brute-force search tree grows exponentially as $N_i = b^i$, where b is the brute-force branching factor. In that case, the heuristic branching factor $E(N,c,P)/E(N,c-1,P)$ is

$$\frac{\sum_{i=0}^{c} b^i P(c - i)}{\sum_{i=0}^{c-1} b^i P(c - 1 - i)} = \frac{b^0 P(c) + b^1 P(c - 1) + b^2 P(c - 2) + \cdots + b^c P(0)}{b^0 P(c - 1) + b^1 P(c - 2) + \cdots + b^{c-1} P(0)}.$$

The first term of the numerator, $b^0 P(c)$, is less than or equal to one, and can be dropped without significantly affecting the ratio. Factoring b out of the remaining numerator gives

$$\frac{b(b^0 P(c - 1) + b^1 P(c - 2) + \cdots + b^{c-1} P(0))}{b^0 P(c - 1) + b^1 P(c - 2) + \cdots + b^{c-1} P(0)} = b.$$

Thus, if the brute-force tree grows exponentially with branching factor b, then the running time of successive iterations of IDA* also grows by a factor of b. In other words, the heuristic branching factor is the same as the brute-force branching factor. In that case, it is easy to show that the overall time complexity of IDA* is $b/(b-1)$ times the complexity of the last iteration (see Exercises).

Our analysis shows that on an exponential tree, the effect of a heuristic is to reduce search complexity from $O(b^c)$ to $O(b^{c-k})$, for some constant k, which depends only on the heuristic function; contrary to previous analyses, however, the branching factor remains basically the same.

5.6.3 *Convergence Criteria

We have not yet looked closely at the convergence conditions of the process for computing the asymptotic branching factor.

The matrix for calculating the population of nodes implies $N^{(d)} = PN^{(d-1)}$, with $N^{(d)}$ being the vector of node sizes of different types. The asymptotic branching factor b is the limit of $||N^{(d)}||_1/||N^{(d-1)}||_1$, where $||x||_1 = \sum_i |x|$. We observe that in most cases $||N^{(d)}||_1/||N^{(d-1)}||_1 = N_i^{(d)}/N_i^{(d-1)}$ for every $i \in \{1,\ldots,k\}$, where k is the number of state types. Evaluating $N_i^{(d)}/N_i^{(d-1)}$ for increasing depth d is exactly what is considered in the *algorithm of van Mises* for approximating the largest eigenvalue (in absolute terms) of P. The algorithm is also referred to as the *power iteration* method.

As a precondition, the algorithm requires that P be diagonalizable. This implies that we have n different eigenvalues $\lambda_1,\ldots,\lambda_n$ and each eigenvalue λ_i with multiplicity of α_i has α_i linear-independent eigenvectors. Without loss of generality, we assume that the eigenvalues are given in decreasing order $|\lambda_1| \geq |\lambda_2| \geq \cdots \geq |\lambda_k|$. The algorithm further requires that the start vector $N^{(0)}$ has a representation in the basis of eigenvectors in which no coefficient according to λ_1 is trivial.

We distinguish the following two cases: $|\lambda_1| > |\lambda_2| \geq \cdots \geq |\lambda_k|$ and $|\lambda_1| = |\lambda_2| > \cdots \geq |\lambda_k|$. In the first case we obtain that (independent of the choice of $j \in \{1,\ldots,k\}$) the value of $\lim_{d\to\infty} N_j^{(d)}/N_j^{(d-1)}$ equals $|\lambda_1|$. Similarly, in the second case, $\lim_{d\to\infty} N_j^{(d)}/N_j^{(d-2)}$ is in fact λ_1^2. The cases $|\lambda_1| = \cdots = |\lambda_l| > \cdots \geq |\lambda_k|$ for $l > 2$ are dealt with analogously. The outcome of the algorithm and therefore the limit in the number of nodes in layers with difference l is $|\lambda_1|^l$, so that once more the geometric mean turns out to be $|\lambda_1|$.

We indicate the proof of the first case only. Diagonalizability implies a basis of eigenvectors $b_1,\ldots,b_k$. Due to $|\lambda_1| > |\lambda_2| \geq \cdots \geq |\lambda_n|$ the quotient of $|\lambda_i/\lambda_1|^d$ converges to zero for large values of d. If the initial vector $N^{(0)}$ with respect to the eigenbasis is given as $x_1 b_1 + x_2 b_2 + \cdots + x_k b_k$, applying P^d yields $x_1 P^d b_1 + x_2 P^d b_2 + \cdots + x_k P^d b_k$ by linearity of P, which further reduces to $x_1 b_1 \lambda_1^d + \lambda_2^d x_2 b_2 + \cdots + \lambda_n^d x_k b_k$ by the definition of eigenvalues and eigenvectors. The term $x_1 b_1 \lambda_1^d$ will dominate the sum for increasing values of d. Factorizing λ_1^d in the numerator and λ_1^{d-1} in the denominator of the quotient of $N_j^{(d)}/N_j^{(d-1)}$ results in an equation of the form $x_1 b_1 \lambda_1 + R$, where $\lim_{d\to\infty} R$ is bounded by a constant, since except for the leading term $x_1 b_1 \lambda_1$, both the numerator and the denominator in R only involve expressions of the form $O(|\lambda_i/\lambda_1|^d)$. Therefore, to find the asymptotic branching factor analytically, it suffices to determine the set of eigenvalues of P and take the largest one. This corresponds to the results of the asymptotic branching factors in the (n^2-1)-Puzzle.

For the Fifteen-Puzzle for increasing depth d the value $N_1^{(d)}/N_1^{(d-1)}$ equals 1, 3, 13/5, 45/13, 47/15, 461/141, 1485/461, 4813/1485, 15565/4813, 50381/15565, 163021/50381, 527565/163021

$= 3.236178161$, and so on, a sequence approximating $1 + \sqrt{5} = 3.236067978$. Moreover, the ratio of $n^{(d)}$ and $(1 + \sqrt{5})^d$ quickly converges to $1/50 \left(7/2 + 3/2\sqrt{5} \right) \left(-5 + 3\sqrt{5} \right) \sqrt{5} = 0.5236067984$.

5.7 *REFINED THRESHOLD DETERMINATION

A drawback of IDA* is its overhead in computation time introduced by the repeated node evaluations in different iterations. If the search space is a uniformly weighted tree, this is not a concern: Each iteration explores b times more nodes than the last one, where b is the effective branching factor. If the solution is located at level k, then it holds for the number n_{A*} of expansion in A* that

$$1 + \sum_{i=0}^{i=k-1} b^i = 2 + \frac{b(b^{k-1} - 1)}{b - 1} \leq n_{A*} \leq 1 + \frac{b(b^k - 1)}{b - 1} = \sum_{i=0}^{i=k} b^i,$$

depending on the random location of the solution in the last layer.

On the other hand, IDA* performs between $2 + \frac{b(b^{k-1}-1)}{b-1}$ and $1 + \frac{b(b^k-1)}{b-1}$ expansions in the last iteration like A*, and additional

$$\sum_{i=0}^{k} \frac{b(b^i - 1)}{b - 1} = \frac{b}{b - 1} \sum_{i=0}^{k} (b^i - 1) = \frac{b^2(b^k - 1) - k(b - 1)}{(b - 1)^2}$$

expansions in all previous iterations. Thus, ignoring lower-order terms the overhead for $k > 2$ in the range number of iterations is

$$\frac{2b}{b - 1} \leq \frac{n_{IDA*}}{n_{A*}} \leq \frac{2b^2}{b - 1}.$$

In other words, since the number of leaves in a tree is about $(b - 1)$ times larger than the number of interior nodes, the overhead of bounded searches to nonleaf levels is acceptable. However, the performance of IDA* can be much worse for general search spaces. In the worst case, if all merits are distinct, in each iteration only one new node is explored, such that it expands $1 + 2 + \cdots + n = O(n^2)$ nodes. Similar degradation occurs, for example, if the graph is a chain. To speed up IDA* for general graphs, it has been proposed to not always use the smallest possible threshold increase for the next iteration, but to augment it by larger amounts. One thing we have to keep in mind in this case is that we cannot terminate the search at the first encountered solution, since there might still be cheaper solutions in the yet unexplored part of the search iteration. This necessarily introduces *overshooting* behavior; that is, the expansion of nodes with merit larger than the optimal solution.

The idea is to dynamically adjust the increment such that the overhead can be bounded similarly to the case of the uniform tree. One way to do so is to choose a threshold sequence $\theta_1, \theta_2, \ldots$ such that the number of expansions n_i in stage i satisfies

$$n_i = r n_{i-1}$$

for some fixed ratio r. If we choose r too small, the number of reexpansions and hence the computation time will grow rapidly; if we choose it too big, then the threshold of the last iteration can exceed the optimal solution cost significantly, and we will explore many irrelevant edges. Suppose that $n_0 r^p \leq n_{A^*} < n_0 r^{p+1}$ for some value p. Then IDA* will perform $p+1$ iterations. In the worst case, the overshoot will be maximal if A* finds the optimal solution just above the previous threshold, $n_{A^*} = n_0 r^p + 1$. The total number of expansions is $n_0 \sum_{i=0}^{p+1} r^i = n_0 \frac{r(r^{p+1}-1)}{r-1}$, and the ratio v becomes approximately $\frac{r^2}{r-1}$. By setting the derivative of this expression to zero, we find that the optimal value for r is 2; that is, the number of expansions should double from one search stage to the next. If we achieve doubling, we will expand at most four times as many nodes as A*.

The cumulative distribution of expansions is problem dependent; however, the function type is often specific to the class of problems to be solved, whereas its parameters depend on the individual problem instance. We record the runtime information of the sequence of expansion numbers and thresholds from the previous search stages, and then use curve fitting for estimating the number of expansions at higher thresholds. For example, if the distribution of nodes with f-value smaller or equal to threshold c can be adequately modeled according to an exponential formula

$$n_c = A \cdot B^c,$$

(for adequately chosen parameters A and B) then to attempt to double the number of expansions we choose the next threshold according to

$$\theta_{i+1} = \theta_i + 1/\lg B.$$

This way of dynamically adjusting the threshold such that the estimated number of nodes expanded in the next stage grows by a constant ratio is called RIDA*, for *runtime regression* IDA*.

5.8 *RECURSIVE BEST-FIRST SEARCH

Algorithms RBFS (*recursive best-first search*) and IE (*iterative expansion*) were developed independently, but are very similar. Therefore, we will only describe RBFS.

RBFS improves on IDA* by expanding nodes in best-first order, and backing up heuristic values to make the node selection more informed. RBFS expands nodes in best-first order even when the cost function is nonmonotone. Whereas iterative deepening uses a global cost threshold, RBFS uses a local cost threshold for each recursive call. RBFS stores the nodes on the current search path and all their siblings; the set of these nodes is called the *search skeleton*. Thus, RBFS uses slightly more memory than IDA*, namely $O(db)$ instead of $O(d)$, where b is the branching factor of the search tree. The basic observation is that with an admissible heuristic, the backed-up heuristics can only increase. Therefore, when exploring the children of a node, the descendants of the child with lowest f-value should be explored first, until the merits of all nodes in the search frontier exceed the f-value of the second best child. To this end, each node remembers its backup merit, initially set to its f-value. The algorithm is most easily described as a recursive procedure, which takes a node and a bound as arguments (see Alg. 5.9). At the root, it is called with the start node and ∞.

It has been proposed to augment RBFS such that it can exploit additionally available memory to reduce the number of expansions. The resulting algorithm is called *memory-aware recursive best-first search* (MRBFS). Whereas the basic RBFS algorithm stores the search skeleton on the stack, in MRBFS the generated nodes have to be allocated permanently; they are not automatically dropped with the end of a recursive procedure call. Only when the overall main memory limit is reached, previously generated nodes other than those on the skeleton are dropped. Three pruning strategies were

---

Procedure RBFS
Input: Node u, upper bound U
Output: Smallest f-value of a fringe node larger than U

if $(f(u) > U)$ **return** $f(u)$	;; Threshold exceeded
if $(Goal(u))$ **exit with** $Path(u)$	;; Abort search with success
$Succ(u) \leftarrow Expand(u)$	;; Generate successor set
if $(Succ(u) = \emptyset)$	;; No successors
return ∞	;; No bound
else if $(|Succ(u)| = 1)$	;; One successor
return $RBFS(v_0, U)$	;; Pass call through to child
else	;; More than one successor
$Succ(u) \leftarrow Expand(u)$	;; Generate successor set
for each $v \in Succ(u)$	;; For all successors
$backup(v) = \max\{f(u) + w(u,v), backup(u)\}$	;; Initialize update value
Let $\{v_0,\ldots,v_n\}$ be $Succ(u)$, sorted according to $backup$	;; Prior sorting
while $(backup(v_0) < U)$	;; Below threshold
$backup(v_0) \leftarrow RBFS(v_0, \min\{U, f(v_1)\})$	;; Recursive call for first successor
Let $\{v_0,\ldots,v_n\}$ be $Succ(u)$, resorted according to $backup$	;; Posterior sorting
return $backup(v_0)$	;; Feedback f-value

Algorithm 5.9

The RBFS algorithm, implemented recursively.

---

suggested: pruning all nodes except the skeleton, pruning the worst subtree rooted from the skeleton, or pruning individual nodes with the highest backup value. In experiments, the last strategy was proven to be the most efficient. It is implemented using a separate priority queue for deletions. When entering a recursive call, the node is removed from the queue since it is part of the skeleton and cannot be deleted; conversely, it is inserted upon termination.

5.9 SUMMARY

We showed that divide-and-conquer methods can find optimal solutions with a memory consumption that is only logarithmic in the number of states, which is so small that they cannot even store the shortest path in memory. However, these search methods are impractical due to their large runtime. Depth-first search has a memory consumption that is linear in its depth cutoff since it stores only the path from the root node of the search tree to the state that it currently expands. This allows depth-first search to search large state spaces with a reasonable runtime. We discussed depth-first branch-and-bound, a version of depth-first search that reduces the runtime of depth-first search by maintaining an upper bound on the cost of a solution (usually the cost of the best solution found so far), which allows it to prune any branch of the search tree of which the admissible cost estimate is larger than the current upper bound. Unfortunately, depth-first search needs to search up to the depth cutoff, which can waste computational resources if the depth cutoff is too large, and cannot stop once it finds a path from the start state to any goal state (since the path might not be optimal). Breadth-first search and A* do not have these problems but fill up the available memory on the order of minutes and are thus not able to solve large search problems.

Researchers have addressed this issue by trading off their memory consumption and runtime, which increases their runtime substantially. They have developed a version of breadth-first search, called depth-first iterative-deepening (DFID), and A*, called iterative-deepening A* (IDA*), of which the memory consumption is linear in the length of a shortest path from the start state to any goal state. The idea behind these search methods is to use a series of depth-first searches with increasing depth cutoffs to implement breadth-first search and A*, in the sense that they expand states for the first time in the same order as breadth-first search and A* and thus inherit their optimality and completeness properties. The depth cutoff is set to the smallest depth or f-value of all generated but not expanded states during the preceding depth-first search. Thus, every depth-first search expands at least one state for the first time.

We also discussed a version of IDA* that increases the depth cutoff more aggressively, in an attempt to double the number of states expanded for the first time from one depth-first search to the next one. Of course, DFID and IDA* expand some states repeatedly, both from one depth-first search to the next one and within the same depth-first search. The first disadvantage implies that the runtime of the search methods is small only if every depth-first search expands many states (rather than only one) for the first time. The second disadvantage implies that these search methods work best if the state space is a tree but, in case the state space is not a tree, can be mitigated by not generating those children of a state s in the search tree that are already on the path from the root of the search tree to state s (a pruning method discussed earlier in the context of depth-first search). Note, however, that the information available for pruning is limited since the memory limitation prohibits, for example, to store a closed list.

We predicted the runtime of IDA* in case the state space is a tree. We showed how to compute the number of nodes at a given depth and its asymptotic branching factor, both analytically and numerically, and used this result to predict the number of nodes expanded by IDA* with consistent heuristics. IDA* basically stores only the path from the root node of the search tree to the state that it currently expands. We also discussed recursive best-first search (RBFS), a more sophisticated version of A* of which the memory consumption is also linear in the length of a shortest path from the start state to any goal state (provided that the branching factor is bounded). RBFS stores the same path as IDA* plus all siblings of states on the path and manipulates their f-values during the search, which no longer consists of a series of depth-first searches but still expands states for the first time in the same order as A*, a property that holds even for inadmissible heuristics.

Table 5.5 gives an overview on the algorithms introduced in this chapter. We refer to the algorithm's pseudo code, the algorithm it simulates, and its space complexity. In case of DFID, IDA*, and DFBnB,

Table 5.5 Linear-space algorithms; d is the search depth, b is the maximum branching factor.

Algorithm	Simulates	Complexity	Optimal	Ordered
DAC-BFS (5.1)	BFS	logarithmic in $|S|$	✓	—
DAC-SSSP (5.2)	Dijkstra	logarithmic in $|S|$	✓	—
DFID (5.6, 5.5)	BFS	$O(d)$	✓	✓
IDA* (5.7, 5.8)	A*	$O(d)$	✓	✓
RBFS (5.9)	A*	$O(db)$	✓	✓
DFBnB (5.3, 5.4)	BnB	$O(d)$	✓	—

the complexity $O(d)$ assumes that at most one successor of a node is stored to perform a backtrack. If all successors were stored, the complexity would rise to $O(db)$ as with RBFS.

5.10 EXERCISES

5.1 Apply DAC-BFS to the (3×3) GRIDWORLD. The start node is located at the top-left and the goal node is located at the bottom-right corner.
1. Protocol all calls to *Exists-Path*.
2. Report all output due to **print**.

5.2 We have seen that DFID simulates BFS, and IDA* simulates A*. Devise an algorithm that simulates Dikstra's algorithm. Which assumptions on the weight function are to be imposed?

5.3 Consider the random TSP with 10 cities in Figure 5.7. Solve the problem with depth-first branch-and-bound using:
1. No lower bound.
2. The cost of the MINIMUM SPANNING TREE as a lower bound.

Denote the value of α each time it improves.

6,838	5,758	113	7,515	1,051	5,627	3,010	7,419	6,212	4,086
7,543	5,089	1,183	5,137	5,566	6,966	4,978	495	311	1,367
524	8,505	8,394	2,102	4,851	9,067	2,754	1,653	6,561	7,096
1,406	4,165	3,403	5,562	4,834	1,353	920	444	4,803	7,962
4,479	9,983	8,751	3,894	8,670	8,259	6,248	7,757	5,629	3,306
5,262	7,116	2,825	3,181	3,134	5,343	8,022	1,233	7,536	9,760
2,160	4,005	729	7,644	7,475	1,693	5,514	4,139	2,088	6,521
6,815	4,586	9,653	6,306	7,174	8,451	3,448	6,473	2,434	8,193
2,956	4,162	4,166	4,997	7,793	2,310	1,391	9,799	7,926	4,905
965	120	2,380	5,639	6,204	4,385	2,475	5,725	7,265	3,214

FIGURE 5.7

A distance matrix for a TSP.

5.4 A MÁZE is an $(m \times n)$-size GRIDWORLD with walls. Generate a random maze for small values of $n = 100$ and $m = 200$ and a probability of a wall of 30%. Write a program that finds a path from the start to the goal or reports insolvability using:
1. Breadth-first and depth-first search.
2. Depth-first iterative-deepening search.
3. Iterative-deepening A* search with Manhattan distance heuristic.

Compare the number of expanded and generated nodes.

5.5 Solve instance $(17, 1, 20, 9, 16, 2, 22, 19, 14, 5, 15, 21, 0, 3, 24, 23, 18, 13, 12, 7, 10, 8, 6, 4, 11)$ of the TWENTY-FOUR-PUZZLE with IDA*, Manhattan distance heuristic, and predecessor elimination step-optimally and report the number of generated states in each iteration. You will need efficient successor generation.

5.6 To see why the even and odd branching factors in the $(n^2 - 1)$-PUZZLE are different, color the positions of a puzzle in a checkerboard pattern. If the sets of different-colored squares are equivalent, as in the FIVE-PUZZLE and FIFTEEN-PUZZLE, there is one branching factor. If the sets of different-colored squares are different, however, as in the EIGHT-PUZZLE, there will be different even and odd branching factors.
   1. Check the assertion for the 2×7 and 4×6 board (with predecessor elimination).
   2. Prove the assertion.

5.7 Compute the successor generation matrix P for the EIGHT-PUZZLE, FIFTEEN-PUZZLE, and TWENTY-FOUR-PUZZLE without predecessor elimination. Take Figure 5.5 as the state-type transition graph.

5.8 Determine the exact node count vectors $N^{(d)}$ of the brute-force search tree in the EIGHT-PUZZLE and TWENTY-FOUR-PUZZLE without predecessor elimination by recursively applying the system of recursive equations, starting with a blank in the (top-left) corner.

5.9 Compute the eigenvalues of $(P - bI)$ and the exact node count vectors $N^{(d)}$ in the EIGHT-PUZZLE and TWENTY-FOUR-PUZZLE without predecessor elimination. Provide the base-transformation matrices. For the EIGHT-PUZZLE this can be done by hand; for the TWENTY-FOUR-PUZZLE symbolic mathematical tools are needed.

5.10 Test the theoretical analysis experimentally by predicting the performance of IDA* on the FIFTEEN-PUZZLE using the Manhattan distance heuristic. Use a random sample of a million solvable instances to approximate the heuristic. For N_i, use the exact numbers of nodes at depth i that are computed from the recurrence relations. Determine the
   1. Average heuristic value and maximum number of moves.
   2. Average solution length and the relative error of the prediction.

5.11 Show that if the brute-force tree grows exponentially with branching factor b, the overall time complexity of IDA* is $b/(b - 1)$ times the complexity of the last iteration.

5.12 Explain where and why consistency of the heuristic is essential in proving Theorem 5.5. What can happen with the successors with regard to the sample tree analysis if we have
   1. An admissible but not a consistent estimate?
   2. Not even an admissible estimate?

5.13 Provide an example of a state space graph for which RBFS gives a better search result as IDA*.

5.11 BIBLIOGRAPHIC NOTES

The principle of minimal-space breadth-first and single-source shortest path search is similar to the simulation of nondeterministic Turing machines as proposed by Savitch (1970). For the same restricted memory setting similar problems of node reachability (i.e., determine whether there is any path between two nodes) and graph connectivity have been efficiently solved using random-walk strategies

(Feige, 1996, 1997). Reingold (2005) has developed a deterministic, log-space algorithm that solves the problem of start-to-goal node connectivity in undirected graphs. The result implies a way to construct in log-space a fixed sequence of directions that guides a deterministic walk through all the vertices of any connected graph.

The origins of iterative-deepening search trace back to the late 1960s, when programmers sought a reliable mechanism to control the time consumption of the newly emerging tournament chess programs, so that the search process can halt with the best available answer at hand. IDA* has been invented by Korf (1985a) in the context of solving the FIFTEEN-PUZZLE. In this work Korf provides a list of 100 random problem instances that have been solved with IDA* search. Algorithms that reduce the number of regenerations by increasing the threshold more liberally include IDA*_CR by Russell (1992), DFS* by Rao, Kumar, and Korf (1991), and MIDA* by Wah (1991). The first solution found by these algorithms is often the best possible. Extensions like branch-and-bound are needed to guarantee optimal solutions. Recent results on the predicting IDA* search have been provided by Breyer and Korf (2008).

The analysis of the average branching factor for regular search spaces has been given by Edelkamp and Korf (1998). Search tree prediction for IDA* search, as presented here, has been studied by Korf and Reid (1998). The two aspects have some overlap; a joint exposition has been given by Korf, Reid, and Edelkamp (2001). Exact node counts and sufficient convergence criteria have been given by Edelkamp (2001b). A more complex prediction formula based on including successor values surface in the form of conditional distributions has been provided by Zahavi, Felner, Burch, and Holte (2008a). It extends the analysis discussed in this chapter of the book to the case of inconsistent heuristics, and shows different ways to create more accurate analysis (by considering dependences of different lengths and even making predictions for particular states). Since inconsistency is common in settings such as automated planning and has been proven to be beneficial in others, some work has been already done in predicting the performance of inconsistent heuristic functions by Zahavi, Felner, Schaeffer, and Sturtevant (2007) and by Zhang, Sturtevant, Holte, Schaeffer, and Felner (2009).

Search tree prediction formulas have been used by Holte and Hernádvölgyi (1999) and by Haslum, Botea, Helmert, Bonet, and Koenig (2007) to select expressive pattern databases for the search. Furcy, Felner, Holte, Meshulam, and Newton (2004) exploit the prediction formula to argue why a larger collection of smaller databases often performs better than a smaller collection of large databases. The average solution length for the FIFTEEN-PUZZLE has been computed by Korf and Felner (2002).

Most previous theoretical analyses of heuristic search focused on A*; for example, see the PhD thesis of Gaschnig (1979a), the book of Pearl (1985), and the work of Pohl (1977b). Based on different assumptions, the authors assumed that the effect of a heuristic function is to reduce search complexity from $O(b^c)$ to $O(a^c)$, where $a < b$, reducing the effective branching factor. All used an abstract problem-space tree where every node has b children, every edge has unit cost, and there is a single goal node at depth d. The heuristic is characterized by its error in estimating the actual solution cost. This model predicts that a heuristic with constant absolute error results in linear-time complexity, and constant relative error results in exponential time complexity. There are several limitations of this model. The first is that it assumes only one path from the start to the goal state, whereas most problem spaces contain multiple paths to each state. The second limitation is that to determine the accuracy of the heuristic on even a single state, we have to determine the optimal solution cost from that state, which is expensive to compute. Doing this for a significant number of states is impractical for large problems. Finally, the results are only asymptotic, and don't predict actual numbers of node generations.

An attempt for a probabilistic analysis of the A* algorithm has been given by Huyn, Dechter, and Pearl (1980). However, as in similar analyses (e.g., by Sen and Bagchi, 1988, and Davis, 1990), the approach only refers to a tree search with A*. The behavior of A* in acyclic graphs that arise in many search problems have been theoretically analyzed by Zhang, Sen, and Bagchi (1999). The authors consider graph structures that arise, for example, in the exploration of JOB SEQUENCING problems and the TSP. To assign a probability distribution on the heuristic estimates, the average analysis is done with respect to three models: linear, less-than-linear, and logarithmic. For the linear model (and some further assumptions), the expected number of distinct nodes is exponential, and for the logarithmic model (and some further assumptions), the number of distinct nodes remains polynomial. A* search using accurate heuristics has been predicted by Dinh, Russell, and Su (2007).

Branch-and-bound has been formulated first by Land and Doig (1960). A simple implementation has been provided by Dakin (1965). Depth-first branch-and-bound in the form of a linear-space search algorithm has been suggested by Korf (1993).

Memory-Restricted Search

6

In the previous chapter, we saw instances of search graphs, which were so large that they inherently call for algorithms capable of running under limited memory resources. So far, we have restricted the presentation to algorithms that consume memory that scales at most linear to the search depth. By the virtue of lower memory requirements, IDA* can solve problems that A* cannot. On the other hand, it cannot avoid revisiting nodes. Thus, there are many problems that neither A* nor IDA* can solve, because A* runs out of memory and IDA* takes too long. There have been several solutions being proposed to use the entire amount of main memory more effectively to store more information on potential duplicates. One problem of introducing memory for duplicate removal is a possible interaction with depth-bounded search. We observe an anomaly that goals are not found even if they have smaller costs than the imposed threshold.

We can coarsely classify the attempts by denoting whether or not they sacrifice completeness or optimality, and if they prune the *Closed* list, the *Open* list, or both. A broad class of algorithms that we focus on first uses all the memory that is available to temporarily store states in a cache. This reduces the number of reexpansions. We start with fixed-size hash tables in depth-bounded and iterative-deepening search. Next we consider memory-restricted state-caching algorithms that dynamically extend the search frontier. They have to decide which state to retain in memory and which one to delete.

If we are willing to sacrifice optimality or completeness, then there are algorithms that can obtain good solutions faster. This class includes exploration approaches that strengthen the influence of search heuristics in best-first searches and search algorithms that have limited coverage and look only at some parts of the search space. Approaches that are not optimal but are complete are useful mainly for overcoming inadmissibilities in the heuristic evaluation function and ones that sacrifice completeness.

Another class of algorithms reduces the set of expanded nodes, as full information might not be needed to avoid redundant work. Such a reduction is effective for problems that induce a small search frontier. In most cases, a regular structure of the search space (e.g., an undirected or acyclic graph structure) is assumed. As states on solution paths might no longer be present, after a goal has been found, the according paths have to be *reconstructed*.

The last class of algorithms applies a reduction to the set of search frontier nodes. The general assumption is that search frontier is large compared to the set of visited nodes. In some cases, the storage of all successors is avoided. Another important observation is that the breadth-first search frontier is smaller than the best-first search frontier, leading to cost-bounded BFS. We present algorithms closer to A* than to IDA*, which are not guaranteed to always find the optimal solution within the given memory limit, but significantly improve the memory requirements.

6.1 LINEAR VARIANTS USING ADDITIONAL MEMORY

A variety of algorithms have been proposed that are guaranteed to find optimal solutions, and that can exploit additionally available memory to reduce the number of expansions and hence the running time.

To emphasize the problems that can arise when introducing space for duplicate detection, let us introduce a *Closed* list in DFS. Unfortunately, bounding the depth to some value d (e.g., to improve some previously encountered goal) does not necessarily imply that every state reachable at a search depth less than d will eventually be visited. To see this, consider depth-bounded DFS as applied in the search tree of Figure 6.1.

The anomaly can be avoided by either reopening expanded nodes if reached on a smaller g-value or by applying an iterative-deepening strategy, which has searched for a low-cost solution before larger thresholds are applied. Table 6.1 shows the execution of such depth-first iterative-deepening exploration together with full duplicate detection for the example of Figure 2.1 (see also Figure 5.3 in Ch. 5).

6.1.1 Transposition Tables

The storage technique of *transposition tables* is inherited from the domain of two-player games; the name stems from duplicate game positions that can be reached by performing the same moves in a different order. Especially for single-agent searches, the name *transposition table* is unfortunate as transposition tables are full-flexible dictionaries that detect duplicates, even if not generated by move transpositions.

At least for problems with fast successor generators (like the $(n^2 - 1)$-PUZZLE) the construction and maintenance of the generated search space can be a time-consuming task compared to depth-first search approaches like IDA*. Transposition tables implemented as hash dictionaries (see Ch. 3),

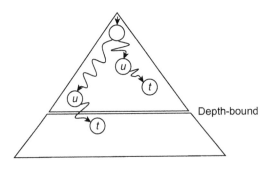

FIGURE 6.1

Anomaly in depth-bounded DFS. First it visits node u (bottom-left copy) and stores it. The goal node t in the subtree of u cannot be reached due to the depth-bound. When the search reaches u for the second time along a shallower path (top-right copy) it stops exploring the successor, since u has been already stored. Hence, the goal is not found, even though it is located in depth smaller than the bound.

Table 6.1 Expansion steps in DFID (with duplicate detection) in the example of Figure 5.3.

Step	Iteration	Selection	Open	Closed	U	U′	Remarks
1	1	{}	{a}	{}	0	∞	
2	1	a	{}	{a}	0	2	g(b)
3	2	{}	{a}	{}	2	∞	New iteration starts
4	2	a	{b}	{a}	2	6	g(c) and g(d) > U
5	2	b	{}	{a,b}	2	6	
6	3	{}	{a}	{}	6	∞	New iteration starts
7	3	a	{b,c}	{a}	6	10	g(d) > U
8	3	b	{e,f,c}	{a,b}	6	10	
9	3	e	{f,c}	{a,b,e}	6	10	Duplicate
10	3	f	{c}	{a,b,e,f}	6	10	Duplicate
11	3	c	{}	{a,b,e,f,c}	6	9	g(d)
12	4	{}	{a}	{}	9	∞	New iteration starts
13	4	a	{b,c}	{a}	9	10	g(d) > U
14	4	b	{e,f,c}	{a,b}	9	10	
15	4	e	{f,c}	{a,b,e}	9	10	Duplicate
16	4	f	{c}	{a,b,e,f}	9	10	Duplicate
17	4	c	{d}	{a,b,e,f,c}	9	10	d Duplicate
18	4	d	{}	{a,b,e,f,c}	9	10	
19	5	{}	{a}	{}	10	∞	New iteration starts
20	5	a	{b,c,d}	{a}	10	∞	
21	5	b	{e,f,c,d}	{a,b}	10	∞	
22	5	e	{f,c,d}	{a,b,e}	10	∞	Duplicate
23	5	f	{c,d}	{a,b,e,f}	10	∞	Duplicate
24	5	c	{d}	{a,b,e,f,c}	10	∞	
25	5	d	{}	{a,b,e,f,c,d}	10	14	g(g)
26	6	{}	{a}	{}	14	∞	New iteration starts
27	6	a	{b,c,d}	{a}	14	∞	g(d) > U
28	6	b	{e,f,c,d}	{a,b}	14	∞	
29	6	e	{f,c,d}	{a,b,e}	14	∞	Duplicate
30	6	f	{c,d}	{a,b,e,f}	14	∞	Duplicate
31	6	c	{d}	{a,b,e,f,c}	14	∞	
32	6	d	{g}	{a,b,e,f,c,d}	14	∞	
33	6	g	{}	{a,b,e,f,c,d}	14	∞	Goal reached

preserve a high performance. They store visited states u together with a cost value $H(u)$ that is updated during the search.

We present the use of transposition tables here as a variant of IDA* (compare Alg. 5.8 on page 205). We assume the implementation of a top-level driver routine (see Alg. 6.1), which matches the one of IDA* except that *Closed* is additionally initialized to the empty set. Furthermore, we see that Algorithm 6.2 returns the threshold U' for the next iteration. *Closed* stores previously explored nodes

---

Procedure IDA*-TT-Driver
Input: Implicit problem graph with start node s, weight function w,
      successor generation function *Expand*, and predicate *Goal*
Output: Path from s to $t \in T$, or $\emptyset$ if no such path exists

$U \leftarrow h(s)$	;; Initialize global thresholds
while $(U \neq \infty)$	;; Goal not found, unexplored nodes left
$\quad U \leftarrow$ IDA*-TT(s, U)	;; Invoke Alg. 6.2 at s

Algorithm 6.1

IDA* driver with transposition table.

Procedure IDA*-TT
Input: Node u, upper bound U
Output: Shortest path to a goal node, or bound for next iteration

if $(Goal(u))$ **exit with** $Path(u)$	;; Terminate search
$Succ(u) \leftarrow Expand(u)$	;; Generate successor set
for each v in $Succ(u)$	;; For all successors
$\quad U' \leftarrow \infty$	;; New bound
$\quad$ **if** $(v$ in *Closed*$)$	;; Node v in transposition table
$\quad\quad b(v) \leftarrow w(u,v) + H(v)$	;; Use revised costs
$\quad$ **else**	;; Node v not in transposition table
$\quad\quad b(v) \leftarrow w(u,v) + h(v)$	;; Compute heuristic estimate
$\quad$ **if** $(b(v) > U)$	;; Cost exceeds old bound
$\quad\quad t \leftarrow b(v)$	;; Used computed value
$\quad$ **else**	;; Cost within old bound
$\quad\quad t \leftarrow w(u,v) +$ IDA*-TT$(v, U - w(u,v))$	;; Recursive call
$\quad U' \leftarrow \min\{U', t\}$	;; Update new bound
Insert u into *Closed* with $H(u) \leftarrow U'$	;; Save node and bound in transposition table
return U'	;; No solution exists

Algorithm 6.2

IDA* with transposition table and cost revision.

---

u, together with a threshold $H(u)$, such that the path costs from the root via u to a descendant of u is $g(u) + H(u)$. Each newly generated node v is first tested against *Closed*; if this is the case, then the stored value H is a tighter bound than $h(v)$.

The application of the algorithm to the example problem is shown in Table 6.2. We see that the (remaining) upper bound decreases. The approach applies one step less than the original IDA*, since node d is not considered twice.

Of course, if we store *all* expanded nodes in the transposition table, we would end up with the same memory requirement as A*, contrary to the original intent of IDA*. One solution to this problem is

Table 6.2 Steps in IDA* (with transposition table) for the example of Figure 5.3.

Step	Iteration	Selection	Open	Closed	U	U′	Remarks
1	1	{}	{a}	{}	11	∞	h(a)
2	1	a	{}	{a}	11	14	b(b), b(c), and b(d) exceed U
3	2	{}	{a}	{(a,14)}	14	∞	New iteration starts
4	2	a	{c}	{(a,14)}	14	∞	b(b) and b(d) exceed U
5	2	c	{d}	{(a,14)}	8	∞	b(a) exceeds U
6	2	d	{g}	{(a,14)}	5	∞	b(a) exceeds U
7	2	g	{}	{(a,14)}	0		Goal found

to embed a replacement strategy into the algorithm. One candidate would be to organize the table in the form of a *first-in first-out* queue. In the worst case, this will not provide any acceleration. By an adversary strategy argument, it may always happen that nodes just deleted are being requested.

Stochastic node caching can effectively reduce the number of revisits. While transposition tables always cache as many expanded nodes as possible, it stochastically caches expanded nodes. Whenever a node is expanded, we decide whether to keep the node in memory by flipping a (possibly biased) coin. This selective caching allows storing, with high probability, only nodes that are visited most frequently. The algorithm takes an additional parameter p, which is the probability of a node being cached every time it is expanded. It follows that the overall probability of a node being stored after it is expanded t times is $1 - (1 - p)^t$; the more frequent the same node is expanded, the higher the probability of it being cached becomes.

6.1.2 Fringe Search

Fringe search also reduces the number of revisits in IDA*. Regarded as a variant of A*, the key idea in *fringe search* is that *Open* does not need to be fully sorted, avoiding access to complex data structures. The essential property that guarantees optimal solutions is the same as in IDA*: A state with an f-value exceeding the largest f-value expanded so far must not be expanded, unless there is no state in *Open* with a smaller f-value.

Fringe search iterates over the frontier of the search tree. The data structure are two plain lists: $Open_t$ for the current iteration and $Open_{t+1}$ for the next iteration; $Open_0$ is initialized with the initial node s and $Open_1$ is initialized to the empty set.

Unless the goal is found the algorithm simulates IDA*. The first node u in $Open_t$ (head) is examined. If $f(u) > U$ then u is removed from *Open* and inserted into $Open_{t+1}$ (at the end). Node u is only generated but not expanded in this iteration, so we save it for the next iteration. If $f(u) \leq U$ then we generate its successors and insert them into $Open_t$ (at the front), after which u is discarded. When a goal has not been found and the iteration completes, the search threshold is increased. Moreover, $Open_{t+1}$ becomes $Open_t$, and $Open_{t+2}$ is set to empty. It is not difficult to see that fringe search expands nodes in the exact same order as IDA*.

Compared to A*, *fringe search* may visit nodes that are irrelevant for the current iteration, and A* must insert nodes into a priority queue structure (imposing some overhead). To the contrary, A*'s ordering means that it is more likely to find a goal sooner.

Algorithm 6.3 displays the pseudo code. The implementation is a little tricky, as it embeds $Open_t$ and $Open_{t+1}$ in one list structure. All nodes before the currently expanded nodes belong to the next search frontier in $Open_{t+1}$, whereas all nodes after the currently expanded nodes belong to the current search frontier $Open_t$. Nodes u that are simply passed by executing the *continue* statement in case $f(v) > U$ move from one list to the other. All other expanded nodes are deleted since they do not belong to the next search frontier. Successors are generated and checked whether or not they are duplicates of already expanded or generated nodes. If one matches a state, then the one with the best g-value (matches the f-value as the h-values are the same) will survive. If not refuted, the new state is inserted directly after the expanded nodes as still to be processed. The order of insertion is chosen such that the expansion order matches the depth-first strategy.

An illustration comparing fringe search (right) with IDA* (left) is given in Figure 6.2. The heuristic estimate is the distance to a leaf (height of the node). Both algorithms start with an initial threshold

---

Procedure Fringe Search
Input: Implicit problem graph with start node s, weight function w, heuristic h,
      successor generating function *Expand*, and predicate *Goal*
Output: Shortest path to a goal node if such path exists

Insert s into *Open*	;; Initialize search frontier
Insert pair $(0, \perp)$ for s into *Closed*	;; Initialize visited list
$U \leftarrow h(s)$	;; Initialize bound
while $(Open \neq \emptyset)$	;; Unless problem unsolvable
$U' \leftarrow \infty$	;; Next search threshold
for each u **in** *Open*	;; Traverse search frontier
Lookup $(g, parent)$ for u in *Closed*	;; Search stored entry
$f \leftarrow g + h(u)$	;; Compute path cost, call estimate
if $(f > U)$	;; Threshold exceeded
$U' \leftarrow \min\{f, U'\}$ **continue**	;; Next threshold
if $(Goal(u))$ **return** $Path(u)$	;; Terminal node, construct solution
$Succ(u) \leftarrow Expand(u)$	;; Generate successors
for each $v \in Succ(u)$	;; Traverse successors
$g(v) \leftarrow g + w(u, v)$	;; Compute g-value
if $(v$ in *Closed*$)$	;; Successor already visited
Lookup $(g', parent)$ for v in *Closed*	;; Search stored entry
if $(g(v) \geq g')$ **continue**	;; No improvement at successor
if $(v \in Open)$	;; Successor already present
Delete v from *Open*	;; Eliminate this successor from search frontier
Insert v into *Open* after u	;; Simulating depth-first search
Insert (g', u) into *Closed*	;; Update depth value for expanded node
Delete u from *Open*	;; Remove expanded node
$U \leftarrow U'$	;; Set new bound

Algorithm 6.3

Fringe search algorithm.

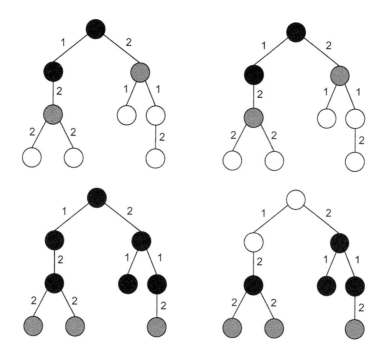

FIGURE 6.2

Comparing IDA* (left) with fringe search (right) for the first two iterations; black nodes denote expanded, gray nodes are generated nodes, and the two hollow nodes at the root of the search tree for fringe search denote the potential for savings.

of $h(s) = 3$. Before the algorithm proves the problem to be unsolvable with a cost threshold of 3, two nodes are expanded and two nodes are generated. An expanded node has its children generated. A generated node is one where no search is performed because the f-value exceeds the threshold. In the next iteration, the threshold is increased to 4.

6.1.3 *Iterative Threshold Search

The memory-restricted *iterative threshold search algorithm* (ITS) also closely resembles that of IDA*. Similar to fringe search its exploration order is depth-first and not best-first. In contrast to fringe search, which assumes enough memory to be available and which does not need a complex data structure to support its search, ITS requires some tree data structure to retract nodes when running out of memory.

Compared to the previous approaches, ITS provides a strategy to replace elements in memory by their cost value. One particular feature is that it maintains information not only for nodes, but also for edges. The value $f(u,v)$ stores a lower-bound estimate of a solution path using edge (u,v). Node v does not have to be generated—it suffices to know the operator leading to it without actually applying it. When a node u is created for the first time, all estimates $f(u,v)$ are initialized to the usual bound $f(u) = g(u) + h(u)$ (to deal with the special case that u has no successors, a dummy node d is assumed with $f(u,d) = \infty$; for brevity, this is not shown in the pseudo code). An edge (u,v), where v has not been created, is called a *tip edge*; a *tip node* is a node of which all outgoing edges are tip edges.

An implementation of the approach is shown in Algorithms 6.4 and 6.5. The similarity of the algorithm to IDA* is slightly obscured by the fact that it is formulated in an iterative rather than recursive way; however, this alleviates its exposition. Note that IDA* uses a *node ordering* that is implicitly defined by the arbitrary but fixed sequence in which successors are generated. It is the same order that we refer to in the following when speaking, for example, of a *left-most* or *right-most* tip node.

As before, an upper threshold U bounds the depth-first search stage. The search tree is expanded until a solution is found, or all tip nodes exceed the threshold. Then the threshold is increased by the smallest possible increment to include a new edge, and a new iteration starts. If ITS is given no more memory than (plain) IDA*, every node generated by ITS is also generated by IDA*. However, when additional memory is available, ITS reduces the number of node expansions by storing part of the search tree and backing up heuristic values as more informed bounds.

The inner search loop always selects the left-most tip branch of which the f-value is at most U. The tail of the edge is expanded; that is, its g-value and f-value are computed, and its successor structures are initialized with this value. Finally, it is inserted into the search tree.

Procedure ITS
Input: Implicit problem graph with start node s, weight function w, heuristic h,
      successor generating function *Expand*, and predicate *Goal*
Output: Shortest path to a goal node, or $\emptyset$ if no such path exists

$g(s) \leftarrow 0$	;; Initialize initial costs
$Succ(s) \leftarrow Expand(s)$	;; Expand node
for each u **in** $Succ(s)$	;; Consider all successors of root node
$f(s,u) \leftarrow g(s) + h(s)$	;; Initialize estimate
$Open \leftarrow \{s\}$	;; Initialize search tree structure
$U \leftarrow 0$	;; Initialize cost threshold
while $(U \neq \infty)$	;; Unless termination criterion satisfied
Select left-most u, v with $f(u,v) < U$, u in $Open$, v not in $Open$;; Tip edge
or break	;; No such nodes exist
if $(Goal(u))$ **return** $Path(u)$	;; Terminate search with success
$MemoryControl(Open, U, maxMem)$	;; Call Alg. 6.5 to allocate space
$g(v) \leftarrow g(u) + w(u,v)$	;; Initialize outgoing edges
$Succ(v) \leftarrow Expand(v)$	;; Expand node
for each $w \in Succ(v)$	;; Consider all successors of node
$f(v,w) \leftarrow g(v) + h(v)$	;; Initialize estimate
Insert v into $Open$	;; Update search frontier
$U \leftarrow \min\{f(u,v) \mid u \in Open, v \notin Open\}$	;; Minimum f-value of all tip nodes
return $\emptyset$	;; No solution found

Algorithm 6.4

Algorithm ITS.

Procedure MemoryControl
Input: *Open*, upper bound U, memory threshold *maxMem*
Side effects: Delete unpromising nodes from memory, back up their heuristic values

if ($|Open| \geq$ *maxMem* **and** $|\{u \in Open \mid v \notin Open$ **for each** $v \in Succ(u)\}| \geq 2$)
                                                                          ;; Memory limit
                                                                          ;; . . . reached, at least
                                                                          ;; . . . two tip nodes exist

    Select left-most u in *Open* such that
      $f(u,v) > U$, v **not in** *Open* **for each** $v \in Succ(u)$;; Left-most tip node
  or   ;; No such node exists
    Select right-most u in *Open* such that
      v **not in** *Open* **for each** $v \in Succ(u)$;; Right-most tip node
    $f(parent(u),u) \leftarrow \min\{f(u,v) \mid v \in Succ(u)\}$;; Back up f-value along edge
    Remove u from *Open*   ;; Delete node in search tree structure

Algorithm 6.5

Pruning nodes in ITS.

Global memory consumption is limited by a threshold *maxMem*. If this limit is reached, the algorithm first tries to select a node for deletion of which all the successor edges exceed the upper bound. From several such nodes, the left-most one with this condition is chosen. Otherwise, the right-most tip node is chosen. Before dropping the node, the minimum f-value over its successors is backed up to its parent to improve the latter one's estimate and hence reduce the number of necessary reexpansions. Thus, even though the actual nodes are deleted, the heuristic information gained from their expansion is saved.

An example of a tree-structured problem graph for applying IDA* (top) and ITS (bottom) is provided in Figure 6.3. The tree is searched with the trivial heuristic ($h \equiv 0$). The initial node is the root and a single goal node is located at the bottom of the tree. After three iterations (left) all nodes in the top half of the search tree have been traversed by the algorithm. Since the edges to the left of the solution path have not led to a goal they are assigned to cost ∞. As a result, ITS avoids revisits of the nodes in the subtrees below. In contrast, IDA* will reexplore these nodes several times. In particular, in the last iteration (right), IDA* revisits several nodes of the top part.

6.1.4 MA*, SMA, and SMAG

The original algorithm MA* underwent several improvements, during the course of which the name changed to SMA* and later to SMAG. We will restrict ourselves to describing the latter.

Contrary to A*, SMAG (see Alg. 6.6) generates one successor at a time. Compared to ITS, its cache decisions are based on problem graph nodes rather than on problem graph edges. Memory restoration is based on maintaining reference count(er)s. If a counter becomes 0, the node no longer needs to be stored. The algorithm assumes a fixed upper bound on the number of allocated edges in $Open \cup Closed$. When this limit is reached, space is reassigned by dynamically deleting one previously expanded node at a time, and if necessary, moving its parent back to *Open* such that it can be regenerated. A least-promising node (i.e., one with the maximum f-value) is replaced. If there are several

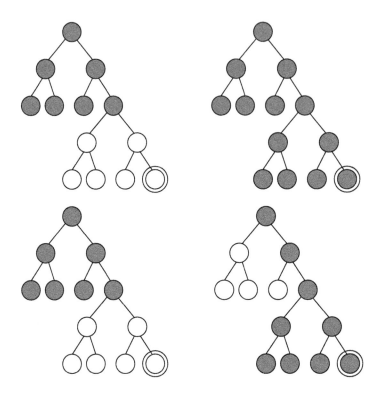

FIGURE 6.3

Two selected iterations of IDA* (top) and ITS (bottom) within a search tree; nodes generated in one iteration are shaded, goal state is encircled.

nodes with the same maximum f-value, then the shallowest one is taken. Nodes with the minimum f-value are selected for expansion; correspondingly, the tie-breaking rule prefers the deepest one in the search tree.

The update procedure *Improve* is shown in Algorithm 6.7. Here, reference counts and depth values are adapted. If the reference count (at some parent place) decreases to zero, a (possible recursive) node delete procedure for unused nodes is invoked. The working of the function is close to the one of a garbage collector for dynamic memory regions in some programming languages like Java. In the assignment to $ref(parent(v))$ nothing will happen if v is equal to the initial node s.

Thus, the *Open* list contains *partially expanded nodes*. It would be infeasible to keep track of all nodes storing pointers to all successors; instead we assume that each node keeps track of an iterator index *next* indicating the smallest unexamined child. The information about forgotten nodes is preserved by backing up the minimum f-value of descendants in a completely expanded subtree (see Alg. 6.9). Because $f(u)$ is an estimate of the least-cost solution path through u, and the solution path is restricted to pass one of u's successors, we can obtain a better estimate from

$$\max\{f(u), \min\{f(v) \mid v \in Succ(u)\}\}.$$

Procedure SMAG
Input: Implicit problem graph with start node s, weight function w, heuristic h,
      successor generating function *Expand*, and predicate *Goal*
Output: Shortest path to a goal node, or $\emptyset$ if no such path exists

$Closed \leftarrow \emptyset$	;; Initialize structures
$f(s) \leftarrow h(s); g(s) \leftarrow 0$	;; Initialize merit and cost values
$depth(s) \leftarrow 0$	;; Initialize depth value
$next(s) \leftarrow 0; ref(s) \leftarrow 0$	;; Initialize link structures
$Open \leftarrow \{s\}$	;; Insert s into search frontier
while $(Open \neq \emptyset)$	;; As long as there are frontier nodes
Let M be the nodes in $Open$ with minimum $f(u)$	;; Minimum elements
Select u from M with minimum $depth(u)$	;; Minimum depth element
Remove u from $Open$	;; Deepest node with best f-value
if $(Goal(u))$ **return** $Path(u)$	;; If goal is found, return solution
$v \leftarrow next(u)$-th successor of u	;; Generate one successor at a time
$next(u) \leftarrow next(u) + 1$	;; Increment u's successor iterator
$next(v) \leftarrow 0$	;; Initialize v's successor iterator
$Improve(u,v)$	;; Call Alg. 6.7
if $(next(u) > last(u))$	;; All successors have been examined
$Backup(u)$	;; Backup value (Alg. 6.9)
if $(Succ(u) \subseteq Open \cup Closed)$	;; All successors are stored in memory
if $(ref(u) = 0)$	;; Reference count is zero
$DeleteRec(u)$	;; Recursive deletion, Alg. 6.10
else	;; Reference count not zero
Insert u into $Closed$	;; Update list of expanded nodes
else	;; Unexamined successors left
Insert u into $Open$	;; Keep partially expanded node
return $\emptyset$	;; No solution found

Algorithm 6.6

Procedure SMAG.

If all successors of u have been dropped, we will not know which way to go from u, but we still have an idea of how worthwhile it is to go anywhere from u. The backed-up values provide a more informed estimate.

When regenerating *forgotten* nodes, to reduce the number of repeated expansions we would also like to use the most informed estimate. Unfortunately, the estimates of individual paths are lost. One considerable improvement is the so-called *path-max heuristic* (as introduced in Sec. 2.2.1): If the heuristic is at least admissible, since a child's goal distance can only be smaller than the parent's by the edge cost, it is valid to apply the bound $\max\{f(v), f(u)\}$, where $v \in Succ(u)$.

One complication of the algorithm is the need to prune a node from the $Closed$ list if it does not occur on the best path to any fringe node. Since these nodes are essentially useless, they can cause *memory leaks*. The problem can be solved by introducing a reference counter for each node that keeps

Procedure Improve
Input: Nodes u and v, v successor of u
Side effects: Update parent of v, *Open*, and *Closed*

if (v **not in** (*Open* $\cup$ *Closed*))	;; Newly generated
MemoryControl	;; If necessary, create space by pruning (Alg. 6.8)
$g(v) \leftarrow g(u) + w(u,v)$	;; Initialize path cost
$f(v) \leftarrow \max\{g(v) + h(v), f(u)\}$	;; Apply path-max heuristic
$depth(v) \leftarrow depth(u) + 1$	;; Set depth value
$ref(v) \leftarrow 0$	;; Set reference count
$parent(v) \leftarrow u$	;; Set parent link
$ref(u) \leftarrow ref(u) + 1$	;; Increment reference count of parent
Insert v into *Open*	;; Update search frontier
else if ($g(u) + w(u,v) < g(v)$)	;; Shorter path found
if (v **in** *Closed*)	;; Node already visited
Remove v from *Closed*	;; Update list of expanded nodes
$g(v) \leftarrow g(u) + w(u,v)$	;; Update path costs
$f(v) \leftarrow \max\{g(v) + h(v), f(u)\}$	;; Apply path-max heuristic
$depth(v) \leftarrow depth(u) + 1$	;; Increase depth value
$ref(v) \leftarrow 0$	;; Set reference count
$ref(u) \leftarrow ref(u) + 1$	;; Increment reference count of new parent
$ref(parent(v)) \leftarrow ref(parent(v)) - 1$	;; Update counter of old parent
if ($ref(parent(v)) = 0$)	;; Previous parent doesn't lie on a solution path
DeleteRec($parent(v)$)	;; Call Alg. 6.10
$parent(v) \leftarrow u$	;; Update predecessor link
if (v **not in** *Open*) Insert v into *Open*	;; Reinsert

Algorithm 6.7

Update procedure in SMAG for newly generated nodes.

track of the number of successor nodes of which the parent pointer refers to them. When this count goes to zero, the node can be deleted; moreover, this might give rise to a chain of ancestor deletions as sketched in Algorithm 6.10.

Since the algorithm requires the selection of both the minimum and the maximum f-value, the implementation needs a refined data structure. For example, we could use two heaps or a balanced tree. To select a node according to its depth, a tree of trees could also be employed.

As an example of state generation in SMAG, we take a search tree with six nodes as shown in Figure 6.4. Let the memory limit be assigned to store at most three nodes. Initially, node a is stored in memory with a cost of 20, then nodes b and c are generated next with a costs of 30 and 25, respectively. Now a node has to be deleted to continue exploration. We take node c because it has the highest cost. Node a is annotated with a cost of 30, which is the lowest cost for a deleted child. Successor node d of node b is generated with a cost of 45. Since node d is not a solution it is deleted and node b is annotated with 45. The next child of b, node e, is then generated. Since node e is not a solution either, node e is deleted and node b is regenerated, because node b is the node with the next best cost. After node b is regenerated, node c is deleted, so that goal node f with zero cost is found.

Procedure MemoryControl
Input: Nodes u and v, memory limit *maxMem*
Side effects: Delete unpromising nodes from memory

if $(|Closed| + |Open| \geq maxMem)$	;; Memory limit reached
Let M be the nodes in *Open* with maximum $f(u)$	;; Minimum elements
Select u from M with maximum $depth(u)$	;; Minimum depth element
Remove u from *Open*	;; Deepest node with max f-value
$next(parent(u)) \leftarrow \min\{next(parent(u)), index(u)\}$	;; Add u to $parent(u)$'s list
$ref(parent(u)) \leftarrow ref(parent(u)) - 1$	;; Update counter of old parent
if ($parent(u)$ **not in** *Open*)	;; Parent not in search frontier
Insert $parent(u)$ into *Open*	;; Reinsert
if ($parent(u)$ **in** *Closed*)	;; Parent already expanded
Remove $parent(u)$ from *Closed*	;; Update list of expanded nodes

Algorithm 6.8

Deleting unpromising nodes in SMAG.

Procedure Backup
Input: Node u
Side effects: Update heuristic estimates for u's ancestors

$U \leftarrow \min\{f(v) \mid v \in Succ(u)\}$	;; Best successor merit
if $(U > f(u))$	;; Worse than current merit
$f(u) \leftarrow U$	;; Reorder frontier according to new f-value
if ($parent(u) \neq \emptyset$ **and**	;; All successors
$Succ(parent(u)) \subseteq Open \cup Closed$)	;; Contained in memory
$Backup(parent(u))$	;; Recursive call

Algorithm 6.9

Backing up heuristic values in SMAG.

Procedure DeleteRec
Input: Node u
Side effects: Delete nodes with zero reference count

if ($parent(u) \neq \emptyset$)	;; If parent exists
$ref(parent(u)) \leftarrow ref(parent(u)) - 1$	;; Update reference count
if ($ref(parent(u)) = 0$)	;; If parent no longer exists
$DeleteRec(parent(u))$	;; Recursive call
$Delete(u)$	;; Physical change

Algorithm 6.10

Recursive deletion of unused *Closed* nodes.

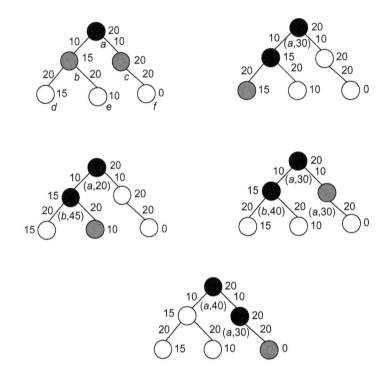

FIGURE 6.4

Example of SMAG (stages left-to-right, top-to-bottom). Annotations for the nodes include its unique label and the *h*-cost associated with it, and annotations for the edges provide its weight. Additionally, backup *f*-values are provided. Black nodes illustrate expanded, gray nodes are generated nodes in the cache with a capacity of three elements, and hollow nodes are deleted from the memory.

6.2 NONADMISSIBLE SEARCH

In Section 2.2.1 we have seen that the use of an admissible heuristic guarantees that algorithm A* will find an optimal solution. However, as problem graphs are so huge, waiting for the algorithm to terminate becomes unacceptable, if regarding the limitation of main memory the algorithm can be carried out at all. Therefore, variants of heuristic search algorithms were developed that do not insist on the optimal solution, but a good solution in feasible time and space. Some strategies even sacrifice completeness and may fail to find a solution of a solvable problem instance. These algorithms usually come with strategies that decrease the likelihood of such errors. Moreover, they are able to obtain optimal solutions to problems where IDA* and A* fail.

6.2.1 Enforced Hill-Climbing

Hill-climbing is a greedy search engine that selects the best successor node under evaluation function *h*, and commits the search to it. Then the successor serves as the actual node, and the search continues.

Procedure Enforced-Hill-Climbing
Input: Implicitly given graph with start node s,
　　　successor generating function *Expand*
Output: Path to node $t \in T$

$u \leftarrow s; h \leftarrow h(s)$	;; Initialize search
while $(h \neq 0)$	;; As far as goal node not found
$(u', h') \leftarrow EHC\text{-}BFS(u, h)$	;; Search for improvement
if $(h' = \infty)$ **return** $\emptyset$	;; No better evaluation found
$u \leftarrow u'$	;; Update u for next iteration
$h \leftarrow h'$	;; Update h
return $Path(u)$	;; Return solution path

Algorithm 6.11

Enforced hill-climbing.

Procedure EHC-BFS
Input: Node u with evaluation $h(u)$
Output: Node v with evaluation $h(v) < h(u)$ or failure

$Enqueue(Q, u)$	;; Add initial node to queue
while $(Q \neq \emptyset)$	;; As far as queue not empty
$v \leftarrow Dequeue(Q)$	;; Take first node from queue
if $(h(v) < h(u))$ **return** $(v, h(v))$	;; Abort search
$Succ(v) \leftarrow Expand(v)$	;; Generate successor set
for each w **in** $Succ(w)$	;; For all successors
$Enqueue(Q, w)$	;; Add result to end of queue
return $(\cdot, \infty)$	;; No improvement found

Algorithm 6.12

BFS searching for a better state v.

Of course, hill-climbing does not necessarily find optimal solutions. Moreover, it can be trapped in state space problem graphs with dead-ends. On the other hand, the method proves to be extremely efficient for some problems, especially the easiest ones.

A more stable version is *enforced hill-climbing*. It picks a successor node, only if it has a strictly better evaluation than the current node. Since this node might not be in the immediate neighborhood of the current node, *enforced hill-climbing* searches for that node in a breadth-first manner. We have depicted the pseudo code for the driver in Algorithm 6.11. The BFS procedure is shown in Algorithm 6.12. We assume a proper heuristic with $h(t) = 0$, if and only if t is a goal. An example is provided in Figure 6.5.

Theorem 6.1. *(Completeness Enforced Hill-Climbing) If the state space graph contains no dead-ends then Algorithm 6.12 will find a solution.*

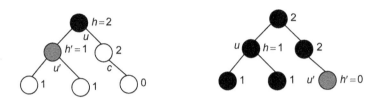

FIGURE 6.5

Example of enforced hill-climbing (two iterations). Black nodes are expanded within the BFS, gray nodes are exit states. The first BFS iteration (left), starting at the root, with an h-value 2, generates a successor of a smaller h-value 1 immediately. The second BFS iteration (right) searches for a node with an h-value smaller than 1. It generates the goal, so that the algorithm terminates.

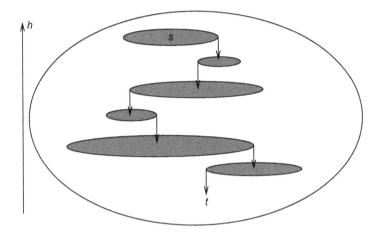

FIGURE 6.6

Search plateaus generated with enforced hill-climbing. The start node s is located in the first (top) layer and the goal node t is found in the last (bottom) layer.

Proof. There is only one case that the algorithm does not find a solution; that is, for some intermediate node v, no better evaluated node v can be found. Since BFS is a complete search method, it will find a node on a solution path with better evaluation. In fact, if it were not terminated in the case of $h(v) < h(u)$, but in the case of $h(v) = 0$, it would find a full solution path. ∎

If we have an unweighted problem graph, then it contains no dead-ends. Moreover, any complete algorithm can be used instead of BFS. However, there is no performance guarantee on the solution path obtained. An illustration of the search plateaus generated by the enforced hill-climbing algorithm is provided in Figure 6.6. The plateaus do not have to be disjoint, as intermediate nodes in one layer can exceed the h-value for which the BFS search was invoked.

Besides being incomplete in directed graphs the algorithm has other drawbacks. There is evidence that when the heuristic estimation is not very accurate, enforced hill-climbing easily suffers from stagnation or is led astray.

6.2.2 **Weighted A***

We often have that the heuristic h drastically underestimates the true distance, so that we can obtain a more realistic estimate by scaling up its influence with regard to some parameter. Although this compromises optimality, it can lead to a significant speedup; this is an appropriate choice when searching under time or space constraints.

If we parameterize $f_l(u) = l \cdot h(u) + (1-l) \cdot g(u)$ with $l \in [0,1]$, we obtain a continuous range of best-first search variants A_l, also denoted as *weighted A**. For $l = 0$, we simulate a breadth-first traversal of the problem space; for $l = 1$, we have *greedy best-first search*. Algorithm $A_{0.5}$ selects nodes in the same order as original A*.

If we choose l appropriately, the monotonicity of f is preserved.

Lemma 6.1. *For $l \leq 0.5$ and a consistent estimate h, f_l is monotone.*

Proof. Since h is consistent we have f monotone; that is, $f(v) \geq f(u)$ for all pairs (u, v) on a solution path. Consequently,

$$
\begin{aligned}
f_l(v) &= l \cdot h(v) + (1-l) \cdot g(v) \\
&= l \cdot h(v) + (1-l) \cdot (g(u) + w(u,v)) \\
&\geq l \cdot (h(u) - w(u,v)) + (1-l) \cdot (g(u) + w(u,v)) \\
&= l \cdot h(u) + (1-l) \cdot g(u) + (1 - 2l) \cdot w(u,v) \\
&\geq l \cdot h(u) + (1-l) \cdot g(u) = f_l(u),
\end{aligned}
$$

since $(1-l) \cdot w(u,v) - l \cdot w(u,v) = w(u,v)(1 - 2l) \geq 0$. ∎

Let us now relax the restrictions on l to obtain more efficient, though nonadmissible, algorithms. The quality of the solution can still be bounded in the following sense.

Definition 6.1. *(ϵ-Optimality) A search algorithm is ϵ-optimal if it terminates with a solution of maximum cost $(1 + \epsilon) \cdot \delta(s, T)$, with ϵ denoting an arbitrary small positive constant.*

Lemma 6.2. *A* where $f(u) = g(u) + (1 + \epsilon) \cdot h(u)$ for an admissible estimate h is ϵ-optimal.*

Proof. For nodes u in *Open* that satisfy invariant (I) (Lemma 2.2) we have $f(u) = \delta(s, u) + h(u)$ and $g(u) = \delta(s, u)$ due to the reweighting process. Therefore,

$$
\begin{aligned}
f(u) &\leq \delta(s, u) + \delta(u, T) + \epsilon \cdot \delta(u, T) \\
&\leq \delta(s, T) + \epsilon \cdot \delta(u, T) \\
&\leq \delta(s, T) + \epsilon \cdot \delta(s, T) \\
&\leq (1 + \epsilon) \cdot \delta(s, T).
\end{aligned}
$$

Thus, if a node $t \in T$ is selected we have $f(t) \leq (1 + \epsilon) \cdot \delta(s, T)$. ∎

ϵ-Optimality allows for more liberal selection of nodes for expansion.

Lemma 6.3. *Let* Focal $= \{u \mid f(u) \le (1+\epsilon) \cdot \min_{u' \in Open} f(u')\}$. *Then any selection of a node in* Focal *yields an ϵ-optimal algorithm.*

Proof. Let u be the node in invariant (I) (Lemma 2.2) with $f(u) = \delta(s,u) + h(u) \le \delta(s,u) + \delta(u,T) = \delta(s,T)$ and let v be the node with the minimal f-value in *Open*. Then $f(v) \le f(u)$, and for a goal t we have $f(t) \le f(v) \cdot (1+\epsilon) \le f(u) \cdot (1+\epsilon) \le \delta(s,T) \cdot (1+\epsilon)$. ∎

6.2.3 Overconsistent A*

We can reformulate A* search to reuse the search results of its previous executions. To do this, we define the notion of an *inconsistent node* and then formulate A* search as the repeated expansion of inconsistent nodes. This formulation can reuse the results of previous executions simply by identifying all the nodes that are inconsistent.

We will first introduce a new variable, called i. Intuitively, these i-values will be estimates of start distances, just like g-values. However, although $g(u)$ is always the cost of the best path found so far from s to u, $i(u)$ will always be equal to the cost of the best path from s to u found at the time of the last expansion of u. If u has never been expanded then $i(u)$ is set to ∞. Thus, every i-value is initially set to ∞ and then it is always reset to the g-value of the node when the node is expanded. The pseudo code of A* that maintains these i-values is given in Algorithm 6.13.

Since we set $i(u)$ to $g(u)$ at the beginning of the expansion of u and we assume nonnegative edge costs, $i(u)$ remains equal to $g(u)$ while u is being expanded. Therefore, setting $g(v)$ to $g(u) + w(u,v)$ is equivalent to setting $g(v)$ to $i(u) + w(u,v)$. As a result, one benefit of introducing i-values is the following invariant that A* always maintains: For every node $v \in S$,

$$g(v) = \begin{cases} 0 & \text{if } v = t \\ \min_{z \in Pred(z)} \{i(z) + w(z,v)\} & \text{otherwise.} \end{cases} \tag{6.1}$$

More importantly, however, it turns out that *Open* contains exactly all the nodes u visited by the search for which $i(u) \ne g(u)$. This is the case initially, when all nodes except for s have both i- and g-values infinite and *Open* only contains s, which has $i(s) = \infty$ and $g(s) = 0$. Afterward, every time a node is being selected for expansion it is removed from *Open* and its i-value is set to its g-value on the very next line. Finally, whenever the g-value of any node is modified it has been decreased and is thus strictly less than the corresponding i-value. After each modification of the g-value, the node is made sure to be in *Open*.

Let us call a node u with $i(u) \ne g(u)$ *inconsistent* and a node with $i(u) = g(u)$ *consistent*. Thus, *Open* always contains exactly those nodes that are inconsistent. Consequently, since all the nodes for expansion are chosen from *Open*, A* search expands only inconsistent nodes.

An intuitive explanation of the operation of A* in terms of inconsistent node expansions is as follows. Since at the time of expansion a node is made consistent by setting its i-value equal to its g-value, a node becomes inconsistent as soon as its g-value is decreased and remains inconsistent until the next time the node is expanded. That is, suppose that a consistent node u is the best predecessor for some node v: $g(v) = \min_{z \in Pred(v)} \{i(z) + w(z,v)\} = i(u) + w(u,v) = g(u) + w(u,v)$. Then, if $g(u)$ decreases we get $g(v) > g(u) + w(u,v)$ and therefore $g(v) > \min_{z \in Pred(v)} \{g(w) + w(w,v)\}$. In other words, the decrease in $g(s)$ introduces an inconsistency between the g-value of u and the g-values of its successors. Whenever u is expanded, on the other hand, this inconsistency is corrected by reevaluating

---

Procedure A* with Inconsistent Nodes
Input: Implicit problem graph with start node s, weight function w,
    successor generation function *Expand*, and predicate *Goal*
Output: Path from s to a goal node $t \in T$

$g(s) \leftarrow 0$, $i(s) \leftarrow \infty$, *Open* $\leftarrow \{s\}$	;; Initialize search
while (*Open* $\neq \emptyset$)	;; Goal state not reached
Remove u with the smallest $f(u)$ from *Open*	;; Extract node to be expanded
if (*Goal*(u)) **return** *Path*(u)	;; Reconstruct solution using Alg. 2.2
$i(u) \leftarrow g(u)$	;; Set inconsistency value of expanded node
Succ(u) $\leftarrow$ *Expand*(u)	;; Generate successor set
for each v in *Succ*(u)	;; For all successors v of u
if (v was never initialized)	;; Successor new
$i(v) \leftarrow g(v) \leftarrow \infty$	;; Initialize inconsistency value
if ($g(v) > g(u) + w(u,v)$)	;; Better path found
$g(v) \leftarrow g(u) + w(u,v)$	;; Improve g-value
Insert/Update v in *Open* with $f(v) = g(v) + h(v)$	;; Update structure

Algorithm 6.13

A* search with i-values.

---

the g-values of the successors of u. This in turn makes the successors of u inconsistent. In this way the inconsistency is propagated to the children of u via a series of expansions. Eventually the children no longer rely on u, none of their g-values are lowered, and none of them are inserted into the *Open* list.

The operation of this new formulation of A* search is identical to the original version of A* search. The variable i just makes it easy for us to identify all the nodes that are inconsistent: These are all the nodes u with $i(u) \neq g(s)$. In fact, in this version of the subroutine, the g-values only decrease, and since the i-values are initially infinite, all inconsistent nodes have $i(u) > g(u)$. We will call such nodes *overconsistent*, and nodes u with $i(u) < g(u)$ are called *underconsistent*.

In the versions of A* just presented, all nodes had their g-values and i-values initialized at the outset. We set the i-values of all nodes to infinity, we set the g-values of all nodes except for s to infinity, and we set $g(s)$ to 0. We now remove this initialization step and the only restriction we make is that no node is underconsistent and all g-values satisfy equation 6.1 except for $g(s)$, which is equal to zero. This arbitrary overconsistent initialization will allow us to reuse previous search results when running multiple searches.

The pseudo code under this initialization is shown in Algorithm 6.14. The only change necessary for the arbitrary overconsistent initialization is the terminating condition of the while loop. For the sake of simplicity we assume a single goal node $t \in T$. The loop now terminates as soon as $f(s)$ becomes less than or equal to the key of the node to be expanded next; that is, the smallest key in *Open* (we assume that the min operator on an empty set returns ∞). The reason for this addition is that under the new initialization t may never be expanded if it was already correctly initialized. For instance, if all nodes are initialized in such a way that all of them are consistent, then *Open* is initially empty, and the search terminates without a single expansion. This is correct, because when all nodes are consistent

---

Procedure Overconsistent A*
Input: Problem graph with start node s and goal node t,
      each initialized node u must have $i(u) \geq g(u)$ and $g(u)$ set wrt. Eq. 6.1,
      Open must contain exactly all nodes u of which $i(u) \neq g(u)$
Output: Solution path from s to t

while $(f(t) > \min_{u \in Open} \{f(u)\})$	;; Termination criterion
Remove u with the smallest $f(u)$ from *Open*	;; Extract node to be expanded
$i(u) \leftarrow g(u)$	;; Set inconsistency value
$Succ(u) \leftarrow Expand(u)$	;; Generate successor set
for each v **in** $Succ(u)$	;; For all successors v of u
if (v was never initialized)	;; Node is new
$i(v) \leftarrow g(v) \leftarrow \infty$	;; Set inconsistency value of new node
if $(g(v) > g(u) + w(u,v))$	;; Better path found
$g(v) \leftarrow g(u) + w(u,v)$	;; Improve g-value
Insert/Update v in *Open* with $f(v) = g(v) + h(v)$	;; Update structure
return *Path(t)*	;; Reconstruct solution

Algorithm 6.14

A* with an arbitrary overconsistent initialization.

---

and $g(s) = 0$, then for every node $u \neq s$, $g(u) = \min_{v \in Pred(u)} \{i(v) + w(v,u)\} = \min_{v \in Pred(u)} \{g(v) + w(v,u)\}$, which means that the g-values are equal to the corresponding start distances and no search is necessary—the solution path from s to t is an optimal solution.

Just like the original A* search, for consistent heuristics, at the time the test of the while loop is being executed, for any node u with $h(u) < \infty$ and $f(u) \leq f(v)$ for all v in *Open*, it holds that the extracted solution path from u to t is optimal.

Given this property and the terminating condition of the algorithm, it is clear that after the algorithm terminates the returned solution is optimal. In addition, this property leads to the fact that no node is expanded more than once if heuristics are consistent: Once a node is expanded its g-value is optimal and can therefore never decrease afterward. Consequently, the node is never inserted into *Open* again. These properties are all similar to the ones A* search maintains. Different from A* search, however, the *Improve* function does not expand all the necessary nodes relevant to the computation of the shortest path. It does not expand the nodes of which the i-values were already equal to the corresponding start distances. This property can result in substantial computational savings when using it for repeated search. A node u is expanded at most once during the execution of the *Improve* function and only if $i(u)$ was not equal to the start distance of u before invocation.

6.2.4 Anytime Repairing A*

In many domains A* search with inflated heuristics (i.e., A* search with f-values equal to g plus ϵ h-values for $\epsilon \geq 1$) can drastically reduce the number of nodes it has to examine before it produces a solution. While the path the search returns can be suboptimal, the search also provides a bound on the suboptimality, namely, the ϵ by which the heuristic is inflated. Thus, setting ϵ to 1 results in standard A* with an uninflated heuristic and the resulting path is guaranteed to be optimal. For $\epsilon > 1$ the length of the found path is no larger than ϵ times the length of the optimal path, while the search can often be much faster than its version with uninflated heuristics.

To construct an anytime algorithm with suboptimality bounds, we could run a succession of these A* searches with decreasing inflation factors. This naive approach results in a series of solutions, each one with a suboptimality factor equal to the corresponding inflation factor. This approach has control over the suboptimality bound, but wastes a lot of computation since each search iteration duplicates most of the efforts of the previous searches. In the following we explain the ARA* (anytime repairing A*) algorithm, which is an *efficient* anytime heuristic search that also runs A* with inflated heuristics in succession but reuses search efforts from previous executions in such a way that the suboptimality bounds are still satisfied. As a result, a substantial speedup is achieved by not recomputing the node values that have been correctly computed in the previous iterations.

Anytime repairing A* works by executing A* multiple times starting with a large ϵ and decreasing ϵ prior to each execution until $\epsilon = 1$. As a result, after each search a solution is guaranteed to be within a factor ϵ of optimal. ARA* uses the overconsistent A* subroutine to reuse the results of the previous searches and therefore can be drastically more efficient.

The only complication is that the heuristics inflated with ϵ may no longer be consistent. It turns out that the same function applies equally well when heuristics are inconsistent. Moreover, in general, when consistent heuristics are inflated the nodes in A* search may be reexpanded multiple times. However, if we restrict the expansions to no more than one per node, then A* search is still complete and possesses ϵ-suboptimality: the cost of the found solution is no worse than ϵ times the cost of an optimal solution.

The same holds true for the subroutine as well. We therefore restrict the expansions in the function (see Alg. 6.15) using the set *Closed*: Initially, *Closed* is empty; afterward, every node that is being expanded is added to it, and no node that is already in *Closed* is inserted into *Open* to be considered for expansion. Although this restricts the expansions to no more than one per node, *Open* may no longer contain all inconsistent nodes. In fact, *Open* contains only the inconsistent nodes that have not yet been expanded. We need, however, to keep track of *all* inconsistent nodes since they will be the starting points for the inconsistency propagation in the future search iterations. We do this by maintaining the set *Incons* of all the inconsistent nodes that are not in *Open* in Algorithm 6.15. Thus, the union of *Incons* and *Open* is exactly the set of all inconsistent nodes, and can be used to reset *Open* before each call to the subroutine.

The main function of ARA* (see Alg. 6.16) performs a series of search iterations. It does initialization, including setting ϵ to a large value ϵ_0, and then repeatedly calls the subroutine with a series of decreasing values of ϵ. Before each call to the subroutine, however, a new *Open* list is constructed by moving to it the contents of the set *Incons*. Consequently, *Open* contains all inconsistent nodes before each call to the subroutine. Since the *Open* list has to be sorted by the current f-values of nodes, it is reordered. After each call to the function ARA* publishes a solution that is suboptimal by at most a factor of ϵ. More generally, for any node s with an f-value smaller than or equal to the minimum f-value in *Open*, we have computed a solution path from s to u that is within a factor of ϵ of optimal.

Each execution of the subroutine terminates when $f(t)$ is no larger than the minimum key in *Open*. This means that the extracted solution path is within a factor ϵ of optimal. Since before each iteration ϵ is decreased, ARA* gradually decreases the suboptimality bound and finds new solutions to satisfy the bound.

Procedure ARA*
Input: Problem graph with start node s and goal node t
Output: Solution path from s to t

$Closed \leftarrow Incons \leftarrow \emptyset$	;; Initialize structures
while $(f(t) > \min_{u \in Open}\{f(u)\})$	;; Termination criterion
Remove u with the smallest $f(u)$ from $Open$	;; Extract node to be expanded
Insert u into $Closed$	;; Extend visited set
$i(u) \leftarrow g(u)$	;; Set i value
$Succ(u) \leftarrow Expand(u)$	;; Generate successor set
for each v **in** $Succ(u)$	;; For all successors v of u
if (v was never initialized)	;; Node is new
$i(v) \leftarrow g(v) \leftarrow \infty$	;; Set i-value of new node
if $(g(v) > g(u) + w(u,v))$	;; Better path found
$g(v) \leftarrow g(u) + w(u,v)$	;; Improve g-value
if ($v \notin Closed$)	;; Node not visited
Insert/Update v in $Open$ with $f(v) = g(v) + \epsilon\, h(v)$	;; Update structure
else	;; Node is already in closed
Insert v into $Incons$	;; Move to temporary list

Algorithm 6.15

Subroutine for anytime repairing A*.

Procedure Anytime Repairing A*
Input: Problem graph with start node s and t and consistent heuristics
Output: A series of solutions

$g(t) \leftarrow i(t) \leftarrow \infty$; $i(s) = \infty$	;; Initialize search
$g(s) \leftarrow 0$; $Open \leftarrow \emptyset$; $\epsilon \leftarrow \epsilon_0$	;; Initialize suboptimality bound
insert s into $Open$ with $f(s) = g(s) + \epsilon\, h(s)$	;; Initialize structures
$ARA^*(s,t)$	;; Call search subroutine
print ϵ-suboptimal solution	;; Report current best solution
while $(\epsilon > 1)$	;; Optimum certified at $\epsilon = 1$
decrease ϵ	;; Call search subroutine
move nodes from $Incons$ into $Open$	;; Reinitialize search
for each $u \in Open$	;; Prepare restart
update the priorities according to $f(u) = g(u) + \epsilon\, h(u)$	;; Weighted A*
$ARA^*(s,t)$	;; Call search subroutine
print ϵ-suboptimal solution	;; Report current best solution

Algorithm 6.16

Main function of anytime repairing A*.

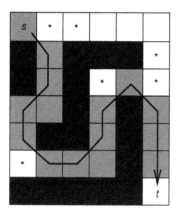 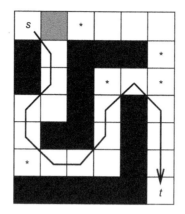 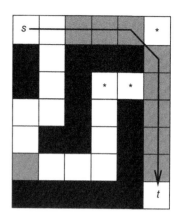

FIGURE 6.7

Example for ARA*: initial search ($\epsilon = 2.5$) (left), second search ($\epsilon = 1.5$) (middle), and third search ($\epsilon = 1.0$) (right).

Figure 6.7 shows the operation of ARA* in a simple maze example. Nodes that are inconsistent at the end of an iteration are shown with an asterisk. Although the first call ($\epsilon = 2.5$) is identical to the weighted A* call with the same ϵ, the second call ($\epsilon = 1.5$) expands only one cell. This is in contrast to large number cells expanded by A* search with the same ϵ. For both searches the suboptimality factor, ϵ, decreases from 2.5 to 1.5. Finally, the third call with ϵ set to 1 expands only nine cells.

ARA* gains efficiency due to the following two properties. First, each search iteration is guaranteed not to expand nodes more than once. Second, it does not expand nodes of which the i-values before a subroutine call function have already been correctly computed by some previous search iteration.

Each solution ARA* publishes comes with a suboptimality equal to ϵ. In addition, an often tighter suboptimality bound can be computed as the ratio between $g(t)$, which gives an upper bound on the cost of an optimal solution, and the minimum unweighted f-value of an inconsistent node, which gives a lower bound on the cost of an optimal solution. This is a valid suboptimality bound as long as the ratio is larger than or equal to one. Otherwise, $g(t)$ is already equal to the cost of an optimal solution. Thus, the actual suboptimality bound, ϵ', for each solution ARA* publishes can be computed as the minimum between ϵ and this new bound:

$$\epsilon' = \min\left\{\epsilon, \max\left\{1, \frac{g(t)}{\min_{u \in Open \, \cup \, Incons}\{g(u) + h(u)\}}\right\}\right\}. \tag{6.2}$$

The anytime behavior of ARA* strongly relies on the properties of the heuristics they use. In particular, it relies on the assumption that a sufficiently large inflation factor ϵ substantially expedites the search process. Although in many domains this assumption is true, this is not guaranteed. In fact, it is possible to construct pathological examples where the best-first nature of searching with a large ϵ can result in much longer processing times. In general, the key to obtaining anytime behavior in ARA* is finding heuristics for which the difference between the heuristic values and the true distances these heuristics estimate is a function with only shallow local minima. Note that this is not the same as just the magnitude of the differences between the heuristic values and the true distances. Instead, the difference will have shallow local minima if the heuristic function has a shape similar to the shape of the true distance function. For example, in the case of robot navigation a local minimum can be a U-shaped obstacle placed on the straight line connecting a robot to its goal (assuming the heuristic function is Euclidean distance). The size of the obstacle determines how many nodes weighted A*, and consequently ARA*, will have to visit before getting out of the minimum. The conclusion is that with ARA*, the task of developing an anytime planner for various hard search domains becomes the problem of designing a heuristic function that results in shallow local minima. In many cases (although certainly not always) the design of such a heuristic function can be a much simpler task than the task of designing a whole new anytime search algorithm for solving the problem at hand.

6.2.5 k-Best-First Search

A very different nonoptimal search strategy modifies the selection condition in the priority-queue data structure by considering larger sets of nodes without destroying its internal f-order. The algorithm k-best-first search is a generalization of best-first search in that each cycle expands the best k-nodes from *Open* instead of the first best node only. Successors are not examined until the rest of the previous k-best nodes are expanded. A pseudo-code implementation is provided in Algorithm 6.17.

In light of this algorithm, best-first search can be regarded as 1-best-first search, and breadth-first search as ∞-best first search, since in each expansion cycle, all nodes in *Open* are expanded.

Procedure k-Best-First-Search
Input: Implicit problem graph with start node s, weight function w, heuristic h,
        successor-generating function *Expand*, predicate *Goal*, and memory limit k
Output: Shortest path from s to goal node, or $\emptyset$ if no such path exists

```
Closed ← Ø                                              ;; Initialize structures
Open ← {s}                                              ;; Insert s into search frontier
f(s) ← h(s)                                             ;; Initialize estimate
while (Open ≠ Ø)                                        ;; As long as there are frontier nodes
    k' ← min{k,|Open|}                                 ;; No more nodes than there are in frontier
    Remove elements u₁,...,u_k' from Open with smallest f(u_i)    ;; Select k nodes
    Insert u₁,...,u_k' into Closed                     ;; Update list of expanded nodes
    for i in {1,...,k'}                                 ;; Expand all selected nodes
        Succ(u_i) ← Expand(u_i)                        ;; Generate successor set
        for each v in Succ(u_i)                         ;; For all successors v of u_i
            if (Goal(v)) return Path(v)                 ;; Goal found, return solution
            Improve(u_i,v)                              ;; Call relaxation subroutine
return Ø                                                ;; No solution exists
```

Algorithm 6.17

Algorithm k-best-first search.

The rationale of the algorithm is that if the level of impreciseness in a nonadmissible heuristic function increases, k-best-first search avoids running in the wrong direction and temporarily abandoning overestimated, optimal solution paths. It has been shown to outperform best-first search in a number of domains.

On the other hand, it will not be advantageous in conjunction with admissible, monotonic heuristics, since in this case all nodes that have a cost less than the optimal solution must be expanded anyway. However, when suboptimal solutions are affordable, k-best-first search can be a simple yet sufficiently powerful choice. From this point of view, k-best-first search is a natural competitor not for A*, but for weighted A* with $l > 0.5$.

6.2.6 Beam Search

A variation of k-best-first search is *k-beam search* (see Algorithm 6.18). The former keeps all nodes in the *Open* list, and the latter discards all but the best k nodes before each expansion step. The parameter k is also known as the *beam width* and can scale close to the limits of main memory. Different from k-best-first search, beam search makes local decisions and does not move to another part of the search tree.

Restricted to blind breadth-first search exploration, only the most promising nodes at each level of the problem graph are selected for further branching with the other nodes pruned off permanently. This pruning rule is inadmissible; that is, it does not preserve the optimality of the search algorithm. The main motivation to sacrifice optimality and to restrict the beam width is the limit of main memory. By varying the beam width, it is possible to change the search behavior; with width 1 it corresponds to a greedy search behavior, with no limits on width to a complete search using A*. By bounding the width, the complexity of the search becomes linear in the depth of the search instead of exponential. More precisely, the time and memory complexity of beam search is $O(kd)$, where d is the depth of the search tree. *Iterative broadening* (a.k.a. *iterative weakening*) performs a sequence of beam searches in which a weaker pruning rule is used in each iteration. This strategy is iterated until a solution of sufficient quality has been obtained, and is illustrated in Figure 6.8 (left).

6.2.7 Partial A* and Partial IDA*

During the study of partial hash functions such as *bit-state hashing*, *double bit-state hashing*, and *hash compact* (see Ch. 3), we have seen that the sizes of the hash tables can be decreased considerably. This is paid for by giving up search optimality, since some states can no longer be disambiguated. As we have seen, partial hashing is a compromise to the space requirements that full state storage algorithms have and can be casted as a nonadmissible simplification to traditional heuristic search algorithms. In the extreme case, partial search algorithms are not even complete, since they can miss an existing goal state due to wrong pruning. The probability can be reduced either by enlarging the number of bits in the remaining vector or by reinvoking the algorithm with different hash functions (see Fig. 6.8, right).

*Partial A** applies bit-state hashing for A*'s *Closed* list. The hash table degenerates to a bit array without any collision strategy (we write *Closed*[i] to highlight the difference). Note that partial A* is applied without reopening, even if the estimate is not admissible, since the resulting algorithm cannot guarantee optimal solutions anyway. The effect of partial state storage is illustrated in Figure 6.9. If only parts of states are stored, more states fit into main memory.

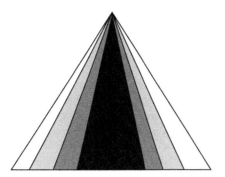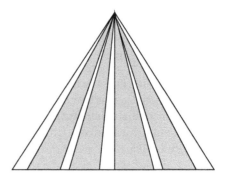

FIGURE 6.8

Improving coverage: iterative broadening (left), enlarging the beam width and restarts (right); for example, with regard to different hash functions.

Procedure *k*-Beam-Search
Input: Implicit problem graph with start node s, weight function w, heuristic h,
        successor-generating function *Expand*, predicate *Goal*, and memory limit k
Output: Shortest path from s to goal node, or $\emptyset$ if no such path exists

```
Closed ← ∅                                              ;; Initialize structures
Open ← {s}                                              ;; Insert s into search frontier
f(s) ← h(s)                                             ;; Initialize estimate
while (Open ≠ ∅)                                        ;; As long as there are frontier nodes
    k' ← min{k,|Open|}                                 ;; Not more nodes than in search frontier
    Remove elements u₁,...,uₖ' from Open with smallest f(uᵢ)      ;; Select k nodes
    for i in {1,...,k'}                                 ;; Expand all selected nodes
        Succ(uᵢ) ← Expand(uᵢ)                          ;; Generate successor set
        for each v in Succ(uᵢ)                         ;; For all successors v of uᵢ
            if (Goal(v)) return Path(v)                ;; Goal found, return solution
            Insert v as successor of uᵢ into Open      ;; Call relaxation subroutine
return ∅                                                ;; No solution exists
```

Algorithm 6.18

Algorithm *k*-beam search.

To analyze the consequences of applying nonreversible compression methods, we concentrate on bit-state hashing. Our focus on this technique is also motivated by the fact that bit-state hashing compresses states drastically down to one or a few bits emphasizing the advantages of depth-first search algorithms. Algorithm 6.19 depicts the A* search algorithm with (single) bit-state hashing.

Given M bits of memory, single bit-state hashing is able to store M states. This saves memory of factor $\Omega(\lg|S|)$, since the space requirements for an explicit state are at least $\lg|S|$ bits. For large state spaces and less efficient state encodings the gains in state space coverage for bit-state hashing are considerable.

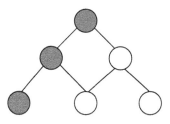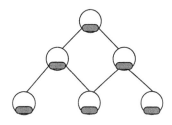

FIGURE 6.9

Effect of partial state storage (right) on the coverage of the state space with regard to full state storage (left); shaded areas illustrate main memory capacity.

Procedure Partial-A*
Input: Implicit problem graph with start node s, weight function w, heuristic h,
       successor-generating function *Expand*, predicate *Goal*, hash table size M
Output: Shortest path to goal node, or $\emptyset$ if no such path exists

for each i in $\{1,\ldots,M\}$ *Closed* $[i] \leftarrow$ *false*	;; Initialize bit-state list
Open $\leftarrow \{s\}$	;; Initialize search frontier
$f(s) \leftarrow h(s)$	;; Set initial cost value
while $(Open \neq \emptyset)$	;; Loop until goal found or not reachable
Remove u from *Open* with minimum $f(u)$	;; Select node for expansion
Closed $[hash(u)] \leftarrow$ *true*	;; Mark element visited
if $(Goal(u))$	;; Check for termination
return *Path*(u)	;; Return solution
Succ$(u) \leftarrow$ *Expand*(u)	;; Generate successor set
for each v in *Succ*(u)	;; For all successors of u
if $(v$ in *Open*$)$	;; Successor in search frontier
$f(v) \leftarrow \min\{f(v), g(u) + w(u,v) + h(v)\}$	;; Update cost
if $(v$ **not in** *Open* **and** *Closed* $[hash(v)] =$ *false*$)$	;; Successor new
$f(v) \leftarrow g(u) + w(u,v) + h(v)$	;; Compute cost
Insert v into *Open*	;; Update search frontier
return $\emptyset$	;; No solution exists

Algorithm 6.19

A* search with (single) bit-state hashing.

First of all, states in the search frontier can hardly be compressed. Second, it is often necessary to keep track of the path that leads to each state. An additional observation is that many heuristic functions and algorithms must access the length (or cost) of the optimal path through which the state was reached.

There are two solutions to these problems: either information is recomputed by traversing the path that leads to the state, or it is stored together with the state. The first so-called *state reconstruction*

Procedure Partial-IDA*
Input: Node u, path cost g, upper bound U, hash table size M, hash function *hash*
Output: Shortest path to a goal node $t \in T$, or $\emptyset$ if no such path exists
Side effects: Update threshold U'

if $(Goal(u))$ **exit with** $Path(u)$	;; Terminate search
$Succ(u) \leftarrow Expand(u)$	;; Generate successor set
for each v **in** $Succ(u)$	;; For all successors
if not $(Closed\,[hash(v)])$	;; State not in hash table
$Closed\,[hash(v)] \leftarrow true$	;; Insert fingerprint
$f(v) \leftarrow g + w(u,v) + h(v)$	;; Compute heuristic estimate
if $(f(v) > U)$	;; Cost exceeds old bound
if $(f(v) < U')$	;; Cost smaller than new bound
$U' \leftarrow f(v)$	;; Update new bound
else	;; f-value below current threshold
$Partial\text{-}IDA^*(v, g + w(u,v))$	;; Recursive call
return $\emptyset$	;; No solution exists

Algorithm 6.20

Partial IDA* search with (single) bit-state hashing.

---

method increases time complexity, and the second one increases the memory requirements. Still, state reconstruction needs to store a predecessor link, which on a W-bit processor typically requires W bits.

It is not trivial to analyze the amount of information needed to store the set *Open*, especially considering that problem graphs are not regular. However, experimental results show that the search frontier frequently grows exponentially with the search depth, such that compressing the set of closed states does not help much. Hence, applying bit-state hashing for search algorithms such as BFS is not as effective as it is in DFS.

Nonadmissible bit-state hashing can also be used in combination with linear IDA* search. The implementation of *Partial IDA** is shown in Algorithm 6.20. Bit-state hashing can be combined with transposition table updates propagating f-values or h-values back to the root, but as the pruning technique is incomplete and annotating any information at a partially stored state is memory intensive, it is simpler to initialize the hash table in each iteration.

Refreshing large bitvector tables is fast in practice, but for shallow searches with a small number of expanded nodes this scheme can be improved by invoking ordinary IDA* with transposition table updates for smaller thresholds and by applying bitvector exploration in large depths only.

6.3 REDUCTION OF THE CLOSED LIST

When searching tree-structured state spaces, the *Closed* list is usually much smaller than the *Open* list, since the number of generated nodes is exponentially growing with search depth. However, in some problem domains its size might actually dominate the overall memory requirements. For example, in the GRIDWORLD problem, the *Closed* list is roughly described as an area of quadratic size, and the *Open* list of linear size. We will see that search algorithms can be modified such that, when running out of space during the search, much or all of the *Closed* list can be temporarily discarded and only later be partially reconstructed to obtain the solution path.

6.3.1 Dynamic Programming in Implicit Graphs

The main precondition of most dynamic programming algorithms is that the search graph has to be acyclic. This ensures a topological order $\preceq$ on the nodes such that $u \preceq v$ whenever u is an ancestor of v.

For example, this is the case for the rectangular *lattice* of the MULTIPLE SEQUENCE ALIGNMENT problem. Typically, the algorithm is described as explicitly filling out the cells of a fixed-size, preallocated matrix. However, we can equivalently transfer the representation to implicitly defined graphs in a straightforward way by modifying Dijkstra's algorithm to use the *level* of a node as the heap key instead of its g-value. This might save us space, in case we can prune the computation to only a part of the grid. A topological sorting can be partitioned into levels $level_i$ by forming disjoint, exhaustive, and contiguous subsequences of the node ordering. Alignments can be computed by proceeding in rows, columns, antidiagonals, and many more possible partitions.

When dynamic programming traverses a k-dimensional lattice in antidiagonals, the *Open* list consists of at most k levels (e.g., for $k = 2$, the parents to the left and top of a cell u at *level* are at $level - 1$, and the diagonal parent to the top-left at $level - 2$); thus, it is of order $O(kN^{k-1})$, one dimension smaller than the search space $O(N^k)$.

The only reason to store the *Closed* list is for tracing back the solution path once the target has been reached. A means to reduce the number of nodes that have to be stored for path reconstruction is to associate, similar as in Section 6.1.4, a *reference count* with each node that maintains the number of children on the optimal path it lies. The pseudo code is shown in Algorithm 6.21, and the corresponding node relaxation step in Algorithm 6.22, where procedure *DeleteRec* is the same as in Algorithm 6.10.

In general, reference counting has been experimentally shown to be able to drastically reduce the size of the stored *Closed* list.

6.3.2 Divide-and-Conquer Solution Reconstruction

Hirschberg first noticed that when we are only interested in determining the cost of an optimal alignment, it is not necessary to store the whole matrix; instead, when proceeding by rows, for example, it suffices to keep track of only k of them at a time, deleting each row as soon as the next one is completed. This reduces the space requirement by one dimension, from $O(N^k)$ to $O(kN^{k-1})$; a considerable improvement for long sequences. Unfortunately, this method doesn't provide us with the actual solution path. To recover it after termination of the search, recomputation of the lost cell values is needed. The solution is to apply the algorithm twice to half the grid each, once in a forward direction and once in a backward direction, meeting at some intermediate relay layer. By adding the corresponding forward and backward distances, the cell lying on an optimal path can be recovered. This cell essentially splits the problem into two smaller subproblems, one starting at the top-left corner and the other at the bottom-right corner they can be recursively solved using the same method. Since in two dimensions, solving a problem of half the dimension is roughly four times easier, the overall computation time is

---

Procedure Dynamic-Programming
Input: Implicit problem graph with start node s, weight function w,
      successor-generating function *Expand*, predicate *Goal*, function *level(u)*
Output: Shortest path to a goal node $t \in T$, or $\emptyset$ if no such path exists

Closed $\leftarrow \emptyset$	;; Initialize structures
$g(s) \leftarrow 0$	;; Initialize path costs
Open $\leftarrow \{s\}$	;; Insert s into search frontier
while (*Open* $\neq \emptyset$)	;; As long as there are frontier nodes
Remove u from *Open* with minimum *level(u)*	;; Levelwise expansion
if (*Goal(u)*) **return** *Path(u)*	;; If goal is found, return solution
Succ(u) $\leftarrow$ *Expand(u)*	;; Generate successor set
for each v in *Succ(u)*	;; For all successors
Improve(u,v)	;; Update search structures, g-value, and f-value (Alg. 6.22)
if (*ref(u)* $= 0$)	;; No goal found in subtree
DeleteRec(u)	;; Call Alg. 6.10
return $\emptyset$	;; No solution found

Algorithm 6.21

Dynamic programming search algorithm.

Procedure Improve
Input: Nodes u and v, v successor of u
Side effects: Update parent of v, $g(v)$, *Open*, and *Closed*

if (v **not in** (*Open* $\cup$ *Closed*) **or** $g(u) + w(u,v) < g(v)$)	;; New or shorter
$g(v) \leftarrow g(u) + w(u,v)$	;; Update shortest found path
ref(u) $\leftarrow$ *ref(u)* $+ 1$	;; Increment new parent's reference count
if (*parent(v)* $\neq \emptyset$)	;; Previous parent exists
ref(parent(v)) $\leftarrow$ *ref(parent(v))* $- 1$	;; Decrement reference count of old parent
if (*ref(parent(v))* $= 0$)	;; Node v was the last child left
DeleteRec(parent(v))	;; No longer useful (Alg. 6.10)
parent(v) $\leftarrow u$	;; Reset parent
if (v **not in** *Open*)	;; Node is not generated
Insert v into *Open*	;; Update search frontier
if (v **in** *Closed*)	;; Node already visited
Remove v from *Closed*	;; Update list of expanded nodes

Algorithm 6.22

Edge relaxation step in dynamic programming.

---

at most double of that when storing the full *Closed* list; the overhead reduces even more in higher dimensions. Further refinements of Hirschberg's algorithm exploit additionally available memory to store more than one node on an optimal path, thereby reducing the number of recomputations.

6.3.3 **Frontier Search**

Frontier search is motivated by the attempt of generalizing the space reduction for the *Closed* list achieved by Hirschberg's algorithm to a general best-first search. It mainly applies to problem graphs that are undirected or acyclic but has been extended to more general graph classes. It is especially effective if the ratio of *Closed* to *Open* list sizes is large. Figure 6.10 illustrates a frontier search in an undirected GRIDWORLD. All generated nodes as well as tags for the used incoming operators prevent reentering the set of expanded nodes, which initially consists of the start state.

In directed acyclic graphs a frontier search is even more apparent. Figure 6.11 schematically depicts a snapshot during a two-dimensional alignment problem, where all nodes with an f-value no larger than the current f_{min} have been expanded. Since the accuracy of the heuristic decreases with the distance to the goal, the typical onion-shaped distribution results, with the bulk being located closer to the start node, and tapering out toward higher levels.

However, in contrast to the Hirschberg algorithm, A* still stores all the explored nodes in the *Closed* list. As a remedy, we obtain two new algorithms.

Divide-and-conquer bidirectional search performs a bidirectional breadth-first search with *Closed* lists omitted. When the two search frontiers meet, an optimal path has been found, as well as a node on it in the intersection of the search frontiers. At this point, the algorithm is recursively called for the two subproblems: one from the start node to the middle node, and the other from the middle node to the target.

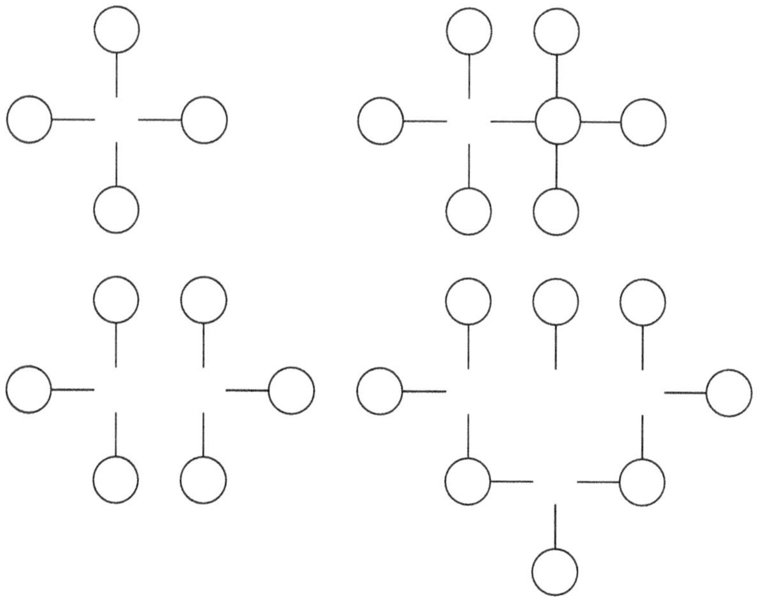

FIGURE 6.10

Snapshots during a frontier search in the GRIDWORLD. Situation after expanding the first node (top left), after expanding another node memorizing the incoming edges (top right), after deleting the node that has been expanded (bottom left), and after two more expansions (bottom right).

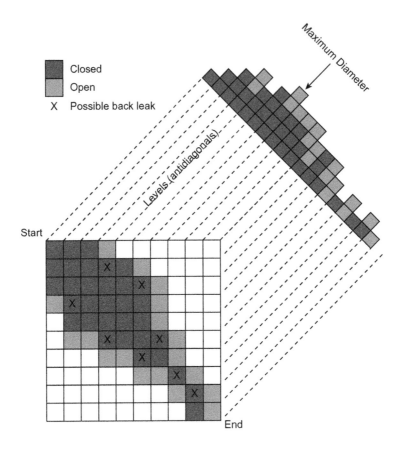

FIGURE 6.11

Snapshot of search in pairwise alignment (schematically).

Divide-and-conquer forward frontier search searches only in a forward direction, without the *Closed* list. In the first phase, a goal t with optimal cost f^* is searched. In the second phase the search is reinvoked with a relay layer at about $f^*/2$. When a node on a relay layer is encountered, all its children store it as their parent. Subsequently, every node past the relay layer saves its respective ancestor on the relay layer that lies on its shortest path from the start node. When the search terminates, the stored node in the relay layer is an intermediate node roughly halfway on an optimal solution path. This intermediate state i from s to t is detected; in the last phase the algorithm is recursively called for the two subproblems from s to i, and from i to t. Figure 6.12 depicts the recursion step (left) and the problem in directed graphs of falling back behind the current search frontier (right), if the width of the search frontier is too small. For this case, several duplicates are generated.

Apart from keeping track of the solution path, A* uses the stored *Closed* list to prevent the search from *leaking back*, in the following sense. A consistent heuristic ensures that (as in the case of Dijkstra's algorithm) at the time a node is expanded, its g-value is optimal, and hence it is never

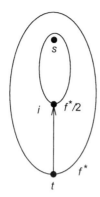 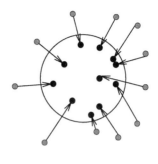

FIGURE 6.12

Divide-and-conquer forward frontier search (left) and the problem of *back leaks* (right); *s* is the start, *t* the goal, and *i* an intermediate state that is located in a relay layer in or close to $\lfloor \delta(s,t)/2 \rfloor$.

expanded again. However, if we try to delete the *Closed* nodes, then there can be topologically smaller nodes in *Open* with a higher *f*-value; when those are expanded at a later stage, they can lead to the regeneration of the node at a nonoptimal *g*-value, since the first instantiation is no longer available for duplicate checking. In Figure 6.11, nodes that might be subject to spurious reexpansion are marked "X." The problem of the search frontier "leaking back" into previously expanded *Closed* nodes is the main obstacle for *Closed* list reduction in a best-first search.

One suggested workaround is to save, with each state, a list of move operators describing *forbidden* moves leading to *Closed* nodes. However, this implies that the node representation cannot be constant, but grows exponentially with the problem dimension. Another way out is to insert all possible parents of an expanded node into *Open* specially marked as not yet reached. However, this inflates the *Open* list and is incompatible with many other pruning schemes.

6.3.4 *Sparse Memory Graph Search

The reduction of frontier search has inspired most of the upcoming algorithms. A promising attempt at memory reduction is *sparse memory graph search* (*SMGS*). It is based on a compressed representation of the *Closed* list that allows the removal of many, but not all, nodes. Compared to frontier search it describes an alternative scheme of dealing with back leaks.

Let *Pred*(*v*) denote the set of predecessors for node *v*; that is, $Pred(v) = \{u \mid (u,v) \in E\}$. The *kernel* *K*(*Closed*) of the set of visited nodes *Closed* is defined as the set of nodes for which all predecessors are already contained in *Closed*:

$$K(Closed) = \{u \in Closed \mid \forall v \in Pred(u) : p \in Closed\}.$$

The rest of the *Closed* nodes are called the *boundary B*(*Closed*):

$$B(Closed) = Closed \setminus K(Closed) = \{v \in Closed \mid \exists u \in Pred(v), u \notin Closed\}.$$

The *Closed* nodes form a *volume* in the search space enclosing the start node; nodes outside this volume cannot reach any node inside it without passing through the boundary. Thus, storing the boundary is sufficient to avoid back leaks.

A *sparse solution path* is an ordered list $(s = v_0, \ldots, v_d = t)$ with $d \geq 1$ and $\sum_{i=1}^{d-1} \delta(v_i, v_{i+1}) = \delta(s, t)$; that is, it consists of a sequence of ancestor nodes on an optimal path where v_i doesn't necessarily have to be a direct parent of v_{i+1}. All *Closed* nodes except boundary nodes and *relay* nodes can be deleted, such as nodes that are used to reconstruct the corresponding solution path from the sparse representation. SMGS tries to make maximum use of available memory by lazily deleting nodes only if necessary because the algorithm's memory consumption approaches the computer's limit.

The algorithm SMGS assumes that the in-degree $|Pred(v)|$ of each node v can be computed. Moreover, the heuristic h must be consistent, $w(u, v) + h(u) - h(v) \geq 0$ for edge u, v, so that no reopening can take place. SMGS is very similar to the standard algorithm, except for the reconstruction of the solution path, which is shown in Algorithm 6.23. Starting from a goal node, we follow the ancestor pointers as usual. However, if we encounter a gap, the problem is dealt with a recursive call of the search procedure. Two successive nodes on the sparse path are taken as start and goal node. Note that these decomposed problems are by far smaller and easier to solve than the original one.

Algorithm 6.24 illustrates the edge relaxation step for SMGS. Each generated and stored node u keeps track of the number of unexpanded predecessors in a variable $ref(u)$. It is initialized with the in-degree of the node minus one, accounting for its parent. During expansion the ref-value is appropriately decremented; kernel nodes can then be easily recognized by $ref(u) = 0$.

The pruning procedure (see Alg. 6.25) prunes nodes in two steps. Before deleting kernel nodes, it updates the ancestral pointer of its boundary successors to the next higher boundary node. Further pruning of the resulting relay nodes is prevented by setting its ref-value to infinity.

Figure 6.13 gives a small example for the algorithm in the context of the MULTIPLE SEQUENCE ALIGNMENT problem. The input consists of the two strings TGACTGC and ACGAGAT, assuming that a match incurs no cost, a mismatch introduces cost 1, and a gap corresponds to cost 2.

Procedure Path
Input: Goal node u
Output: Complete solution path from s to u

$Path \leftarrow (u)$	;; Initialize path
while $(ancestor(u) \neq \emptyset)$	;; Root not yet reached
if $(ancestor(u)$ **in** $Pred(u))$	;; Ordinary edge
$Path \leftarrow (ancestor(u), Path)$	;; Add ancestor to path
else	;; Contracted edge
$subPath \leftarrow SMGS(ancestor(u), u)$	;; Recursive call to fill in gap
$Path \leftarrow (subPath, Path)$	;; Add partial path
$u \leftarrow ancestor(u)$	;; Continue loop
return $Path$	;; Path complete

Algorithm 6.23

Solution reconstruction in sparse-memory graph search.

Procedure Improve
Input: Nodes u and v, v successor of u; memory limit *maxMem*
Side effects: Update parent of v, *Open*, and *Closed*;
                  if memory limit reached, delete Closed nodes

if (v **in** *Open*)	;; Node already in search frontier
$ref(v) \leftarrow ref(v) - 1$	;; Decrease predecessor counter
if $(g(u) + w(u,v) + h(v) < f(v))$	;; New path shorter
$f(v) \leftarrow g(u) + w(u,v) + h(v)$	;; *DecreaseKey* operation
$ancestor(v) \leftarrow u$	;; Update predecessor
else if (v **in** *Closed*)	;; Node already expanded
$ref(v) \leftarrow ref(v) - 1$	;; Decrease predecessor counter
else	;; New node
$ref(v) \leftarrow |Pred(v)| - 1$	;; Compute in-degree
$ancestor(v) \leftarrow u$	;; Set ancestor
Insert v into *Open* with $f(v)$	;; Add new node to search frontier
if ($|Open \cup Closed| > maxMem$)	;; Memory capacity exceeded
PruneClosed	;; Release memory (Alg. 6.25)

Algorithm 6.24

Improve procedure for SMGS.

Procedure PruneClosed
Side effects: Delete *Closed* nodes with zero reference counts

for each (u **in** *Open* $\cup$ *Closed*)	;; For all generated nodes
if ($ancestor(u)$ **in** $Pred(u)$)	;; Ancestor is predecessor
$v \leftarrow ancestor(u)$	;; Set temporary variable
while (v **in** *Closed* **and** $ref(v) = 0$)	;; Node v visited and completed
$v \leftarrow ancestor(v)$	;; Go to ancestor
if ($v \neq ancestor(u)$)	;; If temporary is not initial ancestor
$ancestor(u) \leftarrow v$	;; Set ancestor
$ref(v) \leftarrow \infty$	;; Do not remove relay nodes
for each ($u \in$ *Closed*)	;; For all visited nodes u
if ($ref(u) = 0$)	;; If predecessor value is zero
Remove u from *Closed*	;; Free memory

Algorithm 6.25

Pruning the list of expanded nodes in SMGS.

6.3.5 Breadth-First Heuristic Search

The term *breadth-first heuristic search* is short for the sparse-memory algorithm breadth-first branch-and-bound search with layered duplicate detection. It is based on the observation that the storage of nodes serves two purposes. First, duplicate detection allows recognition of states that are reached

	A	C	G	A	G	A	T
	0	2	4	6			
T	2	1	3	4	6		
G	4	3	2	4	4	6	
A	6	4	4	3	5	4	6
C		6	4	5	4	6	5
T							
G							
C							

	A	C	G	A	G	A	T
	0			6			
T				4	6		
G				4	6		
A	6	4			5	4	6
C		6	4	5	4	6	5
T							
G							
C							

FIGURE 6.13

Example for pruning MULTIPLE SEQUENCE ALIGNMENT with SMGS; exploration process before the reduction of the *Closed* list (left), compressed representation after the reduction (right) (nodes in *Closed* are highlighted).

along a different path. Second, it allows reconstruction of the solution path after finding the goal using the links to the predecessors. IDA* can be seen as a method that gives up duplicate detection, and breadth-first heuristic search gives up solution reconstruction.

Breadth-first search divides the problem graph into layers of increasing depth. If the graph is unit cost, then all nodes in one layer have the same g-value. Moreover, as shown for frontier search at least for regular graphs, we can omit the *Closed* list and reconstruct the solution path based on an existing relay layer kept in main memory.

Subsequently, *breadth-first heuristic search* combines breadth-first search with an upper-bound pruning scheme (that allows the pruning of frontier nodes according to the combined cost function $f = g + h$) together with frontier search to eliminate already expanded nodes. The assumption is that the sizes of the search frontiers for breadth-first and best-first search differ and that using divide-and-conquer solution reconstruction is more memory efficient for breadth-first search.

Instead of maintaining *used operator* edges together with each problem graph node, the algorithms maintain a set of layers of parent nodes. In undirected graphs two parent layers are sufficient, as the successor of a node that is a duplicate has to appear either in the actual layer or in the layer of previous nodes. More formally, assume that the levels $Open_0, \ldots, Open_{i-1}$ have already been computed correctly. We consider a successor v of a node $u \in Open_{i-1}$: The distance from s to v is at least $i - 2$ because otherwise the distance of u would be less than $i - 1$. Thus, $v \in Open_{i-2} \cup Open_{i-1} \cup Open_i$. Therefore, we can correctly subtract $Open_{i-1}$ and $Open_{i-2}$ from the set of all successors of $Open_{i-1}$ to build the duplicate-free search frontier $Open_i$ for the next layer.

Suppose that an upper bound U on the optimal solution cost f^* is known. Then node expansion can immediately discard successor nodes of which the f-values are larger than U. The pseudo-code implementation using two backup BFS layers for storing states assumes an undirected graph and is shown in Algorithms 6.26 and 6.27. The lists *Open* and *Closed* are partitioned along the nodes' depth values. The relay layer r is initially set to $\lfloor U/2 \rfloor$. During the processing of layer l the elements are moved from $Open_l$ to $Closed_l$ and new elements are inserted into $Open_{l+1}$. After a level is completed l increases. The *Closed* list for layer l and the *Open* list for layer $(l + 1)$ are initialized to the empty set. In case a solution is found the algorithm is invoked recursively to enable divide-and-conquer solution reconstruction from s to m and from m to the established goal u, where m is the node in relay layer r that realizes minimum costs with regard to u. Node m is found using the link $ancestor(u)$, which in case a previous layer is deleted, is updated as follows. For all nodes u below the relay layer we set

---

Procedure BFHS
Input: Implicit problem graph with start node s, weight function w, heuristic h,
      successor generating function *Expand*, predicate *Goal*, threshold U
Output: Shortest path to a goal node $t \in T$, or $\emptyset$ if no such path exists

$ancestor(s) \leftarrow \emptyset$	;; Initialize link for solution reconstruction
$Open_0 \leftarrow \{s\}$; $Open_1 \leftarrow Closed_0 \leftarrow \emptyset$	;; Initialize structures
$l \leftarrow 0$; $r \leftarrow \lfloor U/2 \rfloor$	;; Initialize BFS level and relay layer
while $(Open_l \cup Open_{l+1} \neq \emptyset)$	;; Horizon not empty
while $(Open_l \neq \emptyset)$	;; Current level not empty
Remove u from $Open_l$ with minimum $f(u)$	;; Extract best frontier node
Insert u into $Closed$	;; Update list of expanded nodes
if $(Goal(u))$	;; Terminal node reached
$m \leftarrow ancestor(u)$	;; Node in relay layer
if $(u$ in $Succ(s))$	;; Node m is direct successor of s
$P_1 \leftarrow (s,m)$	;; Simple path
else $P_1 \leftarrow BFHS(s,m,g(m))$	;; Recursive call
if $(u$ in $Succ(s))$	;; Node u is direct successor of m
$P_2 \leftarrow (m,u)$	;; Simple path
else $P_2 \leftarrow BFHS(m,u,g(u)-g(m))$	;; Recursive call
return $P_1 P_2$	;; Concatenate two paths
$Succ(u) \leftarrow Expand(u)$	;; Generate successor set
for each v in $Succ(u)$	;; Traverse successor set
$Improve(u,v)$	;; Change lists and prune wrt. U
if $(l \neq r)$	;; Relay layer not met
$PruneLayer(l)$	;; Remove layer, updating ancestor links
$l \leftarrow l+1$; $Open_{l+1} \leftarrow Closed_l \leftarrow \emptyset$	;; Prepare next layer
return $\emptyset$	;; No solution found

Algorithm 6.26

Breadth-first heuristic search.

$ancestor(u)$ to s. For all nodes above the relay layer we set $ancestor(u)$ to $ancestor(ancestor(u))$ unless we encounter a node in the relay layer. (The implementation of *DeleteLayer* is left as an exercise.)

If all nodes were stored in the main memory, breadth-first heuristic search would usually traverse more nodes than A*. However, like sparse memory graph search, the main impact of *breadth-first heuristic search* lies in its combination with divide-and-conquer solution reconstruction. We have already encountered the main obstacle for this technique in heuristic search algorithms—the problem of back leaks; to avoid node regeneration, a boundary between the frontier and the interior of the explicitly generated search graph has to be maintained, which dominates the algorithm's space requirements. The crucial observation is that this boundary can be expected to be much smaller for breadth-first search than for best-first search; an illustration is given in Figure 6.14. Essentially, a fixed number of layers suffices to isolate the earlier layers. In addition, the implementation is easier.

As said, BFHS assumes an upper bound U on the optimal solution cost f^* as an input. There are different strategies to find U. One option is to use approximate algorithms like hill-climbing or

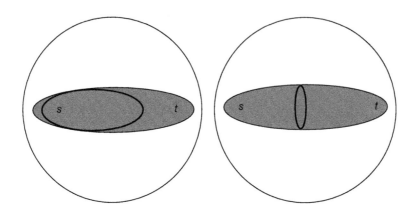

FIGURE 6.14

Effect of breadth-first heuristic search: area expanded by A* shaded gray, best-first search frontier (left), and breadth-first search frontier (right) illustrated as ellipses in boldface.

Procedure Improve
Input: Nodes u and v, v successor of u, layer l
Side effects: Update ancestor link of v, change in $Open_{l+1}$

> **if** $(g(u) + w(u,v) + h(v) \leq U)$;; Search threshold condition
>   **if** $(v$ **not in** $Closed_{l-1} \cup Closed_l)$;; Frontier pruning condition
> $ancestor(v) \leftarrow u$;; Initialize predecessor link
>   Insert v into $Open_{l+1}$ with $f(v)$;; Update next search frontier

Algorithm 6.27

Update of a problem graph edge in Algorithm 6.26.

---

weighted A* search. Alternatively, we can use an iterative-deepening approach as in IDA*, starting with $U \leftarrow h(s)$ and continuously increasing the bound. Since the underlying search strategy is BFS, the algorithm has been called *breadth-first iterative deepening*.

6.3.6 Locality

How many layers are sufficient for full duplicate detection in general is dependent on a property of the search graph called *locality*.

Definition 6.2. *(Locality) For a weighted problem graph G the* locality *is defined as*

$$\text{locality}_G = \max\{\delta(s,u) - \delta(s,v) + w(u,v) \mid u \in S, v \in \text{Succ}(u)\}.$$

For undirected and unweighted graphs we have $w \equiv 1$. Moreover, $\delta(s,u)$ and $\delta(s,v)$ differ by at most 1, so that the locality turns out to be 2. The locality determines the *thickness* of the search frontier needed to prevent duplicates in the search. Note that the layer that is currently expanded is included in the computation of the locality but the layer that is currently generated is not.

While the locality is dependent on the graph, the *duplicate detection scope* also depends on the search algorithm applied. We call a search graph a g-ordered best-first search graph if each node is maintained in buckets matching its g-value. For breadth-first search, the search tree is generated with increasing path lengths, whereas for weighted graphs the search tree is generated with increasing path cost (this corresponds to Dijkstra's exploration strategy in 1-LEVEL BUCKET data structure).

Theorem 6.2. *(Locality Determines Boundary) The number of buckets of a g-ordered best-first search graph that need to be retained to prevent a duplicate search effort is equal to the locality of the search graph.*

Proof. Let us consider two nodes u and v, with $v \in Succ(u)$. Assume that u has been expanded for the first time, generating the successor v, which has already appeared in the layers $0,\ldots,\delta(s,u) - locality_G$, implying $\delta(s,v) \leq \delta(s,u) - locality_G$. We have

$$locality_G \geq \delta(s,u) - \delta(s,v) + w(u,v) \geq \delta(s,u) - \delta(s,u) - locality_G + w(u,v)$$
$$= locality_G + w(u,v).$$

This is a contradiction to $w(u,v) > 0$.   ∎

To determine the number of shortest path layers prior to the search, it is important to establish sufficient criteria for the locality of a search graph. However, the condition $\delta(s,u) - \delta(s,v) + w(u,v)$ maximized over all nodes u and $v \in Succ(u)$ is not a property that can be easily checked before the search. So the question is, can we find a sufficient condition or upper bound for it? The following theorem proves the existence of such a bound.

Theorem 6.3. *(Upper Bound on Locality) The locality of a problem graph can be bounded by the minimal distance to get back from a successor node v to u, maximized over all u, plus $w(u,v)$.*

Proof. For any nodes s,u,v in a graph, the triangular property of shortest paths $\delta(s,u) \leq \delta(s,v) + \delta(v,u)$ is satisfied, in particular for $v \in Succ(u)$. Therefore, $\delta(v,u) \geq \delta(s,u) - \delta(s,v)$ and $\max\{\delta(v,u) \mid u \in S, v \in Succ(u)\} \geq \max\{\delta(s,u) - \delta(s,v) \mid u \in S, v \in Succ(u)\}$. In positively weighted graphs, we have $\delta(v,u) \geq 0$, such that $\max\{\delta(v,u) \mid u \in S, v \in Succ(u)\} + w(u,v)$ is larger than the locality.   ∎

Theorem 6.4. *(Upper Bounds in Weighted Graphs) For undirected graphs with maximum edge weight C we have $locality_G \leq 2C$.*

Proof. For undirected graphs with with maximum edge cost C we have

$$locality_G \leq \max_{u \in V, v \in Succ(u)} \{\delta(v,u)\} + C = \max_{u \in V, v \in Succ(u)} \{\delta(u,v)\} + C$$
$$= \max_{u \in V, v \in Succ(u)} \{w(u,v)\} + C = 2C.$$

∎

6.4 REDUCTION OF THE OPEN LIST

In this section we analyze different strategies that reduce the number of nodes in the search frontier. First we look at different traversal policies that can be combined with a branch-and-bound algorithm.

Even if the number of stored layers k is less than the locality of the graph, the number of times a node can be reopened in breadth-first heuristic search is only linear in the depth of the search. This contrasts the exponential number of possible reopenings for linear-space depth-first search strategies.

6.4.1 Beam-Stack Search

We have seen that beam search accelerates a search by not maintaining in each layer just one node, but a fixed number, *maxMem*. No layer of the search graph is allowed to grow larger than the beam width so that the least-promising nodes are pruned from a layer when the memory is full. Unfortunately, this *inadmissible pruning* scheme means that the algorithm is not guaranteed to terminate with an optimal solution.

Beam-stack search is a generalization of beam search that essentially turns it into an admissible algorithm. It first finds the same solution like beam search, but then continues to backtrack to pruned nodes to improve the solution over time. It can also be seen as a modification of branch-and-bound search, and includes depth-first branch-and-bound search and breadth-first branch-and-bound search as special cases. In the first case the beam width is 1, and in the second case, the beam width is greater than or equal to the size of the largest layer.

The first step toward beam-stack search is *divide-and-conquer beam search*. It limits the layer width of breadth-first heuristic search to the amount of memory available. For undirected search spaces, divide-and-conquer beam search stores three layers for duplicate detection and one relay layer for solution reconstruction. The difference from traditional beam search is that it uses divide-and-conquer solution reconstruction to reduce memory. Divide-and-conquer beam search has been shown to outperform, for example, weighted A* in planning problems. Unfortunately, as with beam search, it is neither complete nor optimal. An illustration of this strategy is provided in Figure 6.15. To the left we see the four layers (including the relay layer) of currently stored breadth-first heuristic search. To the right we see that divide-and-conquer beam search explores a smaller corridor, leading to less nodes to be stored in main memory.

The beam-stack search algorithm utilizes a specialized data structure called the *beam stack*, a generalization of an ordinary stack used in DFS. In addition to the nodes, each layer also contains one record of the breadth-first search graph. To allow backtracking, the beam stack exploits the fact that the nodes can be sorted by their cost function f. We assume that the costs are unique, and that ties are broken by refining the cost function to some secondary order comparison criteria. On the stack in each layer a half-open interval $[f_{min}, f_{max})$ is stored, such that all nodes u are pruned with $f(p_u) < f_{min}$ and all nodes are eliminated with an $f(p_u) \geq f_{max}$. All layers are initialized to $[0, U)$ with U being the current upper bound.

An illustration of beam-stack search is provided in Figure 6.16. The algorithm is invoked with a beam width of 2 and an initial upper bound of ∞. The problem graph is shown at the top of the figure. Nodes currently under consideration are shaded. Light shading corresponds to the fact that a node cannot be stored based on the memory restriction. To the bottom of the graphs, the current value for U and the contents of the beam stack are provided. We have highlighted four iterations. The first

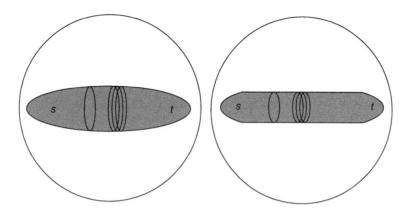

FIGURE 6.15

Comparing breadth-first heuristic search (left) and divide-and-conquer beam search (right); area expanded by A* shaded gray, breadth-first search frontier and relay layer shown as ellipses.

iteration expands the start node and generates two of three successors for the next search depth. As all weights are integers, the next possible value 3 is stored as the upper bound for the first layer. When expanding the second layer, again one node does not satisfy the width. In the next iteration we arrive at the goal on two possible paths, suggesting a minimal solution of 8. The value overwrites the initial upper bound and is propagated bottom-up such that 8 is the next upper bound to start with. As we have searched all paths corresponding to a solution value smaller than 3, the lower bound is set to 3. The last step shows the situation for searching the graph with the solution interval [3, 8]. It illustrates that beam-stack search eventually finds the optimal solution of value 6, which in turn is assigned to U and reported at the root node.

Divide-and-conquer beam-stack search combines divide-and-conquer solution reconstruction with the beam stack search. If the memory becomes full, the nodes with the highest f-values are deleted from the *Open* list. In *divide-and-conquer beam-stack search* there are two complications to be resolved. First, divide-and-conquer solution reconstruction has to be combined with backtracking. Since there are only a bounded number of layers in memory, the layer to which the algorithm backtracks may not be in memory, so that it has to be recovered. Fortunately, the beam-stack search contains the interval of f-values to recover a missing layer. The algorithm goes back to the start node and generates successor nodes at each layer according to the corresponding beam-stack item, until all nodes in the layer preceding the missing layer have been expanded. The other problem is the decision on solution reconstruction or continuation of the search. If the algorithm starts reconstructing the solution path using large amounts of memory, then the search information computed so far is affected. For these cases a delayed solution reconstruction approach is useful. Solution construction starts only if the search algorithm backtracks, since this will delete search layers anyway.

Algorithm 6.28 shows a recursive pseudo-code implementation of the search algorithm. Initially, the entire interval $[0, U]$ is pushed onto the beam stack. As long as no solution is found, which means that there are unexplored intervals on the beam stack, a recursive search procedure *beam-stack-search* works on one interval from the initial node. If a solution is found, then the upper-bound value is

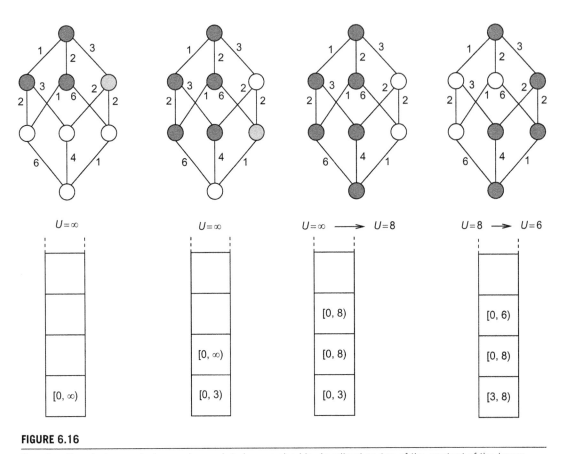

FIGURE 6.16

Four iterations in beam-stack search; graph to be searched is visualized on top of the content of the beam stack; the graph's top node is the initial state, the node at the bottom level is the goal.

updated. Subsequently, the refined upper-bound value truncates and eliminates the intervals on the beam stack. A goal has been found if the upper-bound is exceeded, otherwise the interval can be shortened by the explored part.

To arrive at linear space performance of $O(d \cdot maxMem)$ elements, procedure *PruneLayer* restricts the number of nodes stored. When beam-stack search prunes nodes in a layer, it changes the f_{max} of the previous layer's stack item to the lowest costs of the nodes that have been pruned. This ensures that the search algorithm will not generate any successor with a larger f-cost before backtracking to this layer. Backtracking is invoked if all successors of nodes in the current layer have a w-value greater than U. On every backtrack, beam-stack search forces the search beam to admit a different set of successors by shifting the interval $(f_{min}, f_{max}]$; that is, the new f_{min}-value is initialized with f_{max} and f_{max} is initialized with U.

Theorem 6.5. *(Optimality of Beam-Stack Search) Beam-stack search is guaranteed to find an optimal solution.*

Procedure Beam-Stack-Search
Input: Level l of beam stack, main memory bound *maxMem*
Side effects: Improvement to global variables U, *bestPath*

$f_{min,l} \leftarrow 0$; $f_{max,l} \leftarrow U$;; Initialize top of beam stack
while $(f_{max,l} < U)$;; Promising nodes left
   while $(Open_l \neq \emptyset)$;; Unexplored nodes in level l
     Select u from $Open_l$ with minimum $f(u)$;; Select node to expand
     if $(Goal(u))$;; Goal encountered
        $U \leftarrow f(u)$; $bestPath \leftarrow Path(u)$;; Update bounds and solution path
     $Succ(u) \leftarrow Expand(u)$;; Generate successor set
     $Open_{l+1} \leftarrow Open_{l+1} \cup Succ(u)$;; Level completed, start next level
     $PruneLayer(l+1, maxMem)$;; Remove nodes no longer needed
   $Beam\text{-}Stack\text{-}Search(l+1)$;; Call recursive search
   $f_{min,l} \leftarrow f_{max,l}$; $f_{max,l} \leftarrow U$;; Update top of beam stack

Procedure PruneLayer
Input: Level l of beam stack, main memory bound k
Side effects: Update $Open_l$, $f_{max,l-1}$

if $(|Open_l| > k)$;; Layer too large
   $\{u_{i_1}, \ldots, u_{i_k}\} \leftarrow Sort(Open_l)$;; Sort open list according to increasing f-values
   $f_{max,l-1} \leftarrow f(u_{i_{k+1}})$;; Update parent beam-stack level
   $Open_l \leftarrow \{u_{i_1}, \ldots, u_{i_k}\}$;; Prune successors with larger f-value

Algorithm 6.28

The beam-stack search algorithm.

Proof. We first show that beam-stack search always terminates. If $\Delta > 0$ is the least operator cost then the maximum length of a path and the maximum depth of the beam stack is at most $\lceil U/\Delta \rceil$. If b is the maximal number of applicable operators (a.k.a. the maximal out-degree of the problem graph), the number of backtracks in beam stack search is bounded by $O(b^{\lceil U/\Delta \rceil})$.

Moreover, beam-stack search systematically enumerates all successors of a level by shifting the interval (f_{min}, f_{max}) of path costs. Therefore, no path will be ignored forever, unless the beam stack contains a node u with $f(p_u) > U$ or a node to which a lower-cost path has already been found. Thus, an optimal path must be found eventually. ∎

As beam-stack search is a generalization to the two other branch-and-bound algorithms mentioned earlier, with this proof we have also shown their optimality.

An illustration of divide-and-conquer beam-stack search is provided in Figure 6.17 (right). Different from ordinary beam-stack search (left), intermediate layers are eliminated from main memory. If a solution has been found, it has to be reconstructed. The beam width is induced by the resources of main memory.

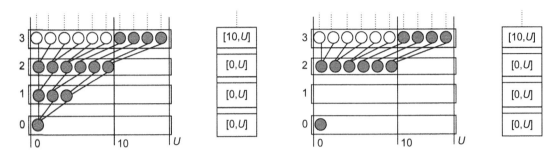

FIGURE 6.17

Snapshots for ordinary (left) and divide-and-conquer beam-stack search (right). The search tree is generated from the bottom to the top to match the beam-stack intervals. The active nodes that are contained in the beam are shaded. Each BFS layer is sorted by the f-value.

6.4.2 Partial Expansion A*

The main observation that led to the development of *Partial Expansion A** (PEA*) is that classic A* search expands a node by always generating *all* of its successors. However, many of these nodes have an f-value larger than the optimal solution and hence will never be selected. They just clutter the *Open* list and waste space.

In PEA* (see Alg. 6.29 and 6.30), each node stores an additional value F, which is the minimum f-value of all of its yet nongenerated children. In each iteration, only a node in $Succ_\leq$ with the minimum F-value is expanded, and only those children with $f = F$ can be inserted into *Open*. After expansion, a node is moved to the *Closed* list, only if it has no more nongenerated successors left; otherwise, its F-value is updated to reflect the possible increase in f-value due to the shrinking of set $Succ_>$.

This algorithm has the advantage of only generating nodes with an f-value smaller than the optimal cost, which cannot be avoided altogether. In experimental results in the domain of MULTIPLE SEQUENCE ALIGNMENT, it has been shown to be able to reduce the space memory requirement by about a factor of a hundred. However, the overhead in computation time can be considerable, since for minimum determination all possible edges have to be considered, while only a few of them will actually be retained. As a remedy, it was proposed to relax the condition by generating all children with $f \leq F + c$ at once, for some small constant c.

Figure 6.18 illustrates an example for PEA*. We see the first four expansion steps. In the first expansion the f-value of the root is initialized to 1. Only one child node is stored at this expansion, because the f-value of it equals the f-value of the root. The root's f-value is revised to 2, and it is reinserted into *Open*. In the second expansion there are no successors with the same f-value as the expanded node, so nothing is stored during this expansion. The expanded node is reinserted into *Open* after revising its f-value 3. In the third expansion the root is expanded again and the second successor is stored. The root's f-value is revised to 4, and again inserted into *Open*.

Note the similarity of the underlying idea to that of algorithm RBFS (see Sec. 5.8, p. 219), which also prunes the search tree below a node if the f-values start to exceed that of a sibling.

Procedure PEA*
Input: Implicit problem graph with start node s, weight function w, heuristic h,
      successor-generating function *Expand*, predicate *Goal*, constant C
Output: Shortest path to a goal node $t \in T$, or $\emptyset$ if no such path exists

$Closed \leftarrow \emptyset$	;; Initialize visited list structure
$g(s) \leftarrow 0$	;; Initialize path costs
$F(s) \leftarrow h(s)$	;; Initialize merit
$Open \leftarrow \{s\}$	;; Insert s into search frontier
while ($Open \neq \emptyset$)	;; As long as there are frontier nodes
Select node u from $Open$ with minimum $F(u)$	;; Select node for expansion
if ($Goal(u)$) **return** $Path(u)$	;; If goal is found, return solution
$Succ(u) \leftarrow Expand(u)$	;; Generate successor set
$Succ_{\leq}(u) \leftarrow \{v \mid v \in Succ(u), f(v) \leq F(u)+c\}$	;; Minimal successors
$Succ_{>}(u) \leftarrow \{v \mid v \in Succ(u), f(v) > F(u)+c\}$	;; Nonminimal successors
for each v in $Succ_{\leq}(u)$	;; For all successors v of u
$Improve(u,v)$	;; Update search structures, g-, f-, and F-value
if ($Succ_{>}(u) = \emptyset$)	;; All successors generated
Insert u into $Closed$	;; Update list of expanded nodes
else	;; Still nongenerated successors left
$F(u) \leftarrow \min\{f(v) \mid v \in Succ_{>}\}$	;; Update F-value
Insert u into $Open$ with $F(u)$	;; Reopen with new value
return $\emptyset$	;; No solution exists

Algorithm 6.29

Algorithm PEA*.

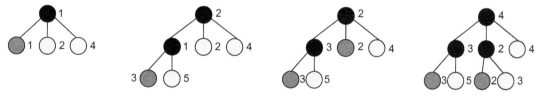

FIGURE 6.18

First four iterations of PEA* for an example graph; black nodes represent stored nodes and gray nodes represent omitted states. The numbers denote the f-values of the nodes, which are revised after expansion.

6.4.3 Two-Bit Breadth-First Search

Two-bit breadth-first search integrates a tight compression method into the BFS algorithm. The approach designed for solving the large search problems requires a reversible minimum perfect hash functions to be available. It applies a space-efficient representation for a bitvector state space representation in breadth-first search with two bits per state.

Procedure Improve
Input: Nodes u and v, v successor of u
Side effects: Update parent of v, *Open*, and *Closed*

if (v **not in** ($Open \cup Closed$) **or** $g(u) + w(u,v) < g(v)$)	;; New or shorter
$\quad f(v) \leftarrow g(u) + w(u,v) + h(v)$	;; Update shortest found path
$\quad F(v) \leftarrow f(v)$	;; Initialize F-value to usual merit
$\quad$ **if** (v **not in** *Open*)	;; Node is not contained in search frontier
$\quad\quad$ Insert v into *Open*	;; Update search frontier
$\quad$ **if** (v **in** *Closed*)	;; Node is already expanded
$\quad\quad$ Remove v from *Closed*	;; Update list of expanded nodes

Algorithm 6.30

Update procedure in PEA* for newly generated nodes.

Procedure Two-Bit-Breadth-First-Search
Input: Implicit problem graph with start node s and successor generator *Expand*,
$\quad$ bitvector *Open*, and reversible perfect hash function (with *Rank* and *Unrank*)

for each i **in** $\{0,\ldots,|S|-1\}$	;; Scan array
$\quad Open[i] \leftarrow 3$	;; Initialize array
$Open[Rank(s)] \leftarrow level \leftarrow 0$	;; Insert initial state
loop	;; Until no more new states are encountered
$\quad level \leftarrow level + 1$	;; Increase BFS layer
$\quad$ **for each** i **in** $\{1,\ldots,|S|-1\}$	;; Scan array
$\quad\quad$ **if** ($Open[i] = (level - 1) \bmod 3$)	;; State on search frontier
$\quad\quad\quad Succ \leftarrow Expand(Unrank(i))$	;; Reconstruct state and generate children
$\quad\quad\quad$ **for each** v **in** $Succ$	;; Consider all successors
$\quad\quad\quad\quad$ **if**($Open[Rank(v)] = 3$)	;; Only unvisited states are considered
$\quad\quad\quad\quad\quad Open[Rank(v)] \leftarrow level \bmod 3$	;; Set depth value

Algorithm 6.31

Breadth-first search with two bits.

Algorithm 6.31 shows how to generate the state spaces according to such a bitvector. The running time is (roughly) determined by the size of the search space times the maximum BFS layer (times the efforts to generate the children).

The algorithm uses two bits encoding the numbers from 0 to 3, with 3 denoting an unvisited state, and 0, 1, and 2 denoting the mod-3 value of the current depth. The main effect is to distinguish newly generated states and already visited states from the current layer that is scanned. If a bit is set to be expanded the array index is unranked and the successors are produced. The successor state bits are computed using a rank function and then marked with the mod-3 value of their depth.

In the advent of a *move-alternation property* that lets us distinguish states in one BFS level from the previous ones we can perform bitvector BFS using only one bit per state. For the example of such property changes with each depth, consider the $(n^2 - 1)$-PUZZLE with an even number of columns. The position of the blank can be used to derive the parity of the BFS layer (the blank position in puzzles with an odd number of columns at an even BFS level is even and for each odd BFS level it is odd).

Two-bit breadth-first search suggests the use of bitvectors to compress pattern databases to $\lg 3 \approx 1.6$ bits per abstract state (value 3 for an unvisited state is obsolete). If we stored the mod-3 value of the BFS level in a hash table, we can determine its absolute value by backward construction incrementally as one shortest path predecessor with a mod-3 value of BFS-level k contained in level $k - 1$ mod 3.

6.5 SUMMARY

We have seen a sizable number of attempts to tame the explosion of the state space working at the limit of main memory. Exploiting various hybrids of A* and IDA* exploration has given rise to different trade-offs between the time of regenerating a node and the space for storing it to detect duplicates. The presented techniques provide a portfolio for tackling a challenging state space exploration problem at the edge of main memory, provided that no better guidance is known.

There are three sources of inefficiency of IDA* that have been addressed. First, in a graph where we have multiple paths to a node, IDA* repeats work due to the large number of duplicates. Second, each IDA* iteration repeats all the work of the previous iteration. This is necessary because IDA* uses essentially no storage. IDA* uses a left-to-right traversal of the search frontier. If thresholds are increased too rapidly, then IDA* may expand more nodes than necessary. In contrast, A* maintains the frontier in sorted order, expanding nodes in a best-first manner, which incurs some cost for handling the data structures.

The repeated states problems have been solved using a transposition table as a cache of visited states. The table is usually implemented as a large hash dictionary to minimize the lookup costs. A transposition table entry essentially stores and updated h-values. It serves two purposes and its information can be split in the minimal g-value for this state and the backed-up f-value obtained from searching this state. The g-values are used to eliminate provably nonoptimal paths from the search. The f-values are used to show that additional search at the node for the current iteration threshold is unnecessary. For larger state vectors a better coverage of the search space has been achieved by applying inadmissible compaction methods like bit-state hashing.

If heuristics are rather weak, their influence can be scaled in weighted heuristic search variants like weighted A* using node priorities $f(u) = g(u) + \lambda \cdot h(u)$. In some cases, the loss of solution quality can be bounded to obtain ϵ-optimal solutions. Another completeness preserving strategy, appropriate especially for inconsistent heuristics, is k-best-first search, which selects the k-best nodes from the priority queue. Its aggressive variant, k-beam search, removing all other nodes from the queue, is often faster but incomplete.

ITS aims to span the gap between A* and IDA* by using whatever memory is available to reduce the duplicated node generations that make IDA* inefficient. SMA* chooses for expansion the deepest, least f-cost node. ITS exploration order, by contrast, is left-to-right depth-first. New nodes are inserted into a data structure representing the search tree, and the node chosen for expansion is the deepest, left-most node of which the f-value does not exceed the current cost bound. ITS requires the whole tree structure to retract nodes if it runs out of memory. Fringe search also explores successors from left to right but with a simpler data structure.

The advantage of *state-caching algorithms* is that they explore the middle ground between time and space of IDA* and A* searches. The disadvantages of many state-caching algorithms is that their successes in practice are rather small. State-caching distinguishes between the *virtual search tree* that has been traversed so far and the part of it that resides in main memory. The main challenge is to dynamically change the set of stored nodes according to the (possibly asymmetrically) growing search tree, without losing efficiency gains for node expansion. We observe a trade-off between the depth of the search and its width, or, more generally speaking, between *exploration* and *exploitation* of the search space.

Another set of memory-restricted algorithms, including frontier search, breadth-first heuristic search, sparse-memory graph search, and beam-stack search, eliminate already expanded nodes from the memory while preventing the algorithms to take a back-edge to fall behind the search frontier. The largest of such back-edges defines the locality and is, therefore, dictated by the structure of the problem graph. In undirected graphs, only three BFS layers need to be stored in the RAM, while in acyclic graphs, only one layer is needed.

Some of the algorithms, like breadth-first heuristic search, sparse-memory graph search, and beam-stack search, additionally stress the fact that for a limited duplicate detection, scope, breadth-first search together with an upper bound on the solution cost saves more memory. The problem of reconstructing the solution path is considered using divide-and-conquer based on information stored in relay layers.

For reducing the search frontier, we have looked at partial expansion algorithms, which expand nodes but but only store one successor. Such algorithms show a benefit in case the search frontier grows exponentially.

Table 6.3 Overview of memory-restricted search algorithms.

Name	Reduces	Space	Weights	Optimal
IDA*-TT (6.2)	None	*maxMem* Nodes	$\mathbb{N}$	✓
Stochastic Node Caching	–	*maxMem* Nodes	$\mathbb{N}$	✓
Fringe Search (6.3)	None	*maxMem* Nodes	$\mathbb{N}$	✓
Weighted A*	Both	*maxMem* Nodes	$\mathbb{R}$	–
ARA* (6.15, 6.16)	Both	*maxMem* Nodes	$\mathbb{R}$	–
k-best (6.17)	Both	*maxMem* Nodes	$\mathbb{R}$	–
k-beam (6.18)	Both	*kd* Nodes	$\mathbb{R}$	–
Partial A* (6.19)	Closed	*M* Bits	$\mathbb{R}$	–
Partial IDA* (6.20)	Closed	*M* Bits	$\mathbb{N}$	–
ITS (6.4,6.5)	Open	*maxMem* Nodes	$\mathbb{N}$	✓
(S)MA*/SMAG (6.6-6.10)	Open	*maxMem* Nodes	$\mathbb{N}$	✓
DP/Frontier Search (6.21,6.22)	Closed	*maxMem* Nodes	$\mathbb{N}$	✓
SMGS (6.23-6.25)	Closed	*maxMem* Nodes	$\mathbb{R}$	✓
BFHS (6.26,6.27)	Closed	*maxMem* Nodes	unif.	✓
Beam-Stack Search (6.28)	Both	*maxMem* Nodes	unif.	✓
PEA* (6.29,6.30)	Open	*maxMem* Nodes	$\mathbb{R}$	✓
Two-Bit BFS (6.31)	Both	$2|S|$ Bits	unif.	✓

Moreover, we have shown that provided a perfect and reversible hash function, two bits are sufficient to conduct a complete breadth-first exploration of the search space.

Table 6.3 summarizes the presented approaches to memory-restricted search. We give information on the algorithm's implementation and whether to save space it mainly reduces the *Open* or the *Closed* list. We also give information if the space limit is on the number of states or bits or if it is logarithmic in the state space size. We provide information on possible edge weights in the problem graph. For constant-depth solution reconstruction implementations, undirected graphs are assumed. Most of the algorithms can be extended to weighted and directed problem graphs. However, including these extensions can be involved. Last but not least, the table shows whether or not the algorithm is optimal when assuming admissible heuristic estimates.

For an exploration at the edge of the main memory, it is obvious that due to time overhead for swapping of memory pages, saving memory eventually saves time.

6.6 EXERCISES

6.1 Consider depth-first search (with duplicate detection) that continues the exploration when a goal has been found and that bounds the search to the depth of that state minus 1. Initially, there is a depth bound that is set to a certain upper-bound value by the user.

    1. Show that the strategy can also be trapped by the anomaly described in the text.

    2. Given an example of an unweighted problem graph with not more than six nodes, where does the anomaly arise? How large is your depth bound?

    3. Fix the problem to make the algorithm admissible.

6.2 Figure 6.19 provides an example for the effect of SNC. On the left it shows that IDA* with a transposition table caches nodes a, b, d in the order of expansion. In contrast, SNC is likely to store node e that is visited more often. As e is detected as a duplicate state, the entire subtree below e (not shown) is not repeatedly explored.

    1. Generate a random 100 maze and plot the probability of caching nodes $p = 0$, $p = 0.2$, $p = 0.4$, $p = 0.6$, $p = 0.8$, and $p = 1$ with respect to the number of times the same node is expanded.

    2. To which algorithm does SNC reduce for $p = 0$ and $p = 1$?

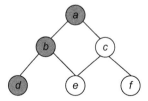 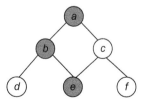

FIGURE 6.19

Comparing IDA*-TT-DFS (left) with IDA*-SNC-DFS (right).

6.3 In *Extended IDA** (see Alg. 6.32) states are expanded in A*-like fashion with the exception that the maximum cost value in the priority queue is not exceeded. The first stage collects at most m states in running memory-bounded IDA*. The queue additionally allows access to the element of maximal cost. In the second stage of the algorithm the collected frontier nodes in D are selected and expanded. Successor nodes v of u are reinserted into D if they are *safe* (i.e., if D is not full and the f-value of v is smaller than the maximal f-value in the priority queue). This is done until D eventually becomes empty. The very last expanded node in the second phase then gives the bound for the next IDA* exploration. Show that

1. All x in D have not been expanded.
2. For each x in D we have $f(x) \geq U'$ and $f(x) \leq f(u)$ of all generated but not expanded nodes u.
3. For all expanded nodes u we have $U' > f(u)$, and if $f(u) < U'$ then u has been expanded.
4. The algorithm terminates with an optimal solution.

Procedure Extended IDA*
Input: Problem graph G, start node s, stack S priority queue D
Output: Shortest path to a goal node $t \in T$ if it exists

$Push(S, s, h(s)); U' \leftarrow U \leftarrow h(s)$	;; Initialize stack and thresholds
while $(U' \neq \infty)$	;; New threshold not trivial
$\quad U \leftarrow U'; U' \leftarrow \infty$	;; Update thresholds
$\quad$ **while** $(S \neq \emptyset)$	;; Loop until stack becomes empty
$\quad\quad (u, f(u)) \leftarrow Pop(S)$	;; Extract top node
$\quad\quad$ **if** $(Goal(u))$ **return** $Path((u))$	;; Check for termination
$\quad\quad Succ(u) \leftarrow Expand(u)$	;; Expand node
$\quad\quad$ **for each** v **in** $Succ(u)$	;; For all successors
$\quad\quad\quad$ **if** $(f(u) + w(u,v) - h(u) + h(v) \leq U)$	;; Small cost values
$\quad\quad\quad\quad Push(S, v, f(u) + w(u,v) - h(u) + h(v))$	;; Continue IDA*
$\quad\quad\quad$ **else**	;; Large cost values
$\quad\quad\quad\quad$ insert v with $f(u) + w(u,v) - h(u) + h(v)$ into D	;; Collect frontier nodes
$\quad$ **while** $(D \neq \emptyset)$	;; Process queue structure
$\quad\quad u \leftarrow \arg\min_f D$	;; Select minimum
$\quad\quad$ **if** $(Goal(u))$ **return** $Path((u))$	;; Check for termination
$\quad\quad Succ(u) \leftarrow Expand(u)$	;; Expand node
$\quad\quad$ **for each** v **in** $Succ(u)$	;; Consider successors
$\quad\quad\quad$ **if** $(f(u) + w(u,v) - h(u) + h(v) \leq \max_f D)$	;; If costs not too large
$\quad\quad\quad\quad$ insert v with $f(u) + w(u,v) - h(u) + h(v)$ into D	;; Include to queue
$\quad\quad U' \leftarrow f(u)$	;; Set new threshold

Algorithm 6.32

Extended IDA*.

6.4 In enforced hill-climbing search give plausible definitions for
1. A harmless, a recognized, and an unrecognized dead-end.
2. A local minima and a (maximal) exit distance.

6.5 Use enforced hill-climbing to solve the FIFTEEN-PUZZLE together with the Manhattan distance estimate. Test your implementation to generate a solution for the instance $(15,2,12,11,14,13,9,5,1,3,8,7,0,10,6,4)$.

6.6 Let us investigate the notion of node inconsistency:
1. Suppose that every node in the state space is consistent. Show that a solution path from s to t is then an optimal one in the graph.
2. Suppose that no node in the state space is underconsistent. Can you say anything about the relationship between the cost of a solution path from s to t and $g(t)$? If yes, then prove the relationship.
3. Suppose that every underconsistent node s in the state space has $v(s) + h(s) > g(t)$. Can you then say anything about the relationship between the cost of a solution path from s to t and $g(t)$? If yes, then prove the relationship.

6.7 Anytime A* continues to expand nodes after the first solution is found according to the same priority function, prune away from *Open* the nodes with unweighted f-values $(g(u) + h(u)$, where $h(u)$ is uninflated) larger than the cost of the best solution found so far, $g(t)$.

Analyze the amount of work (in terms of nodes expanded) that anytime algorithms have to do to generate their first solutions. Assume that all algorithms have the same tie-breaking criteria when choosing between two nodes with the same priorities for expansion.
1. Given the same consistent heuristics, is it possible for ARA* to do more work than (uninflated) A* before generating a first solution? Prove the answer.
2. Given the same consistent heuristics and the same initial ϵ, is it possible for ARA* to do more work than anytime A* before generating a first solution? Prove the answer.
3. Given the same consistent heuristics and the same initial ϵ, is it possible for anytime A* to have more nodes in *Open* than for ARA* at the time each algorithm generates a first solution? What about the other way around? Prove your answers.

6.8 Compare k-best-first search with weighted A* and beam search on a randomly generated graph of 15 nodes with a consistent heuristic and a nonadmissible heuristic. To generate the graph, throw a biased coin with probability of 20% for drawing an edge between a pair of vertices.

6.9 Figure 6.20 shows a typical tree in SMAG, where the left subtree has been pruned to make room for the more promising right subtree. The f-costs that are propagated bottom-up are shown with their original f-costs. Nodes are generated in the order of their number. The pruned region is shown.
1. In which order are the nodes pruned?
2. Explain how node 9 will receive a value of 5, although it was known to have a value of 6.

6.10 Run frontier breadth-first search in the GRIDWORLD.
1. Compute the exact number of nodes in level i.
2. Determine the accumulated number of nodes in the levels $1,\ldots,i$.
3. Quantify the ratio of *Open* and *Closed* list sizes for a given level.
4. Determine the ratio of *Open* and *Closed* list sizes in the limit for a large BFS level.

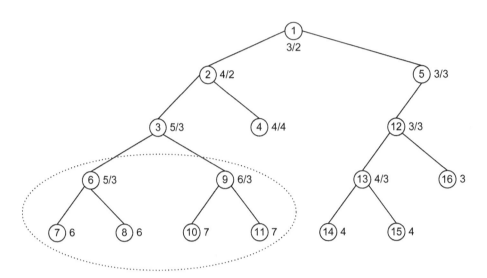

FIGURE 6.20

Example graph for memory-restricted search in SMAG.

6.11 Construct a small example, where the sizes of the breadth-first search frontier and the best-first search frontier are considerably different.

6.12 Complete the table in Figure 6.13 for pruning the MULTIPLE SEQUENCE ALIGNMENT problem with SMGS.
  1. Compute the optimal alignment costs.
  2. Invoke one additional memory reduction phase.
  3. Reconstruct the solution path.

6.13 Implement procedure *PruneLayer* for breadth-first heuristic search in pseudo code.

6.14 One problem of beam-stack search are large plateaus of nodes that have the same f-value and that exceed the memory capacity. Discuss beam-stack variants that
  1. Solve the problem by refining the comparison operation.
  2. Explore such plateaus completely using disk.
  3. Enforce a monotone cost function by considering a lexicographic ordering on states.

6.15 A simplification of the two-bit breadth-first search algorithm allows us to generate the entire state space using only one bit. Algorithm 6.33 participates from the implicit ordering imposed by the minimum perfect hash function for the $(n^2 - 1)$-PUZZLE (see Ch. 3). As the algorithm does not distinguish between *Open* and *Closed* nodes, the algorithm may expand a node multiple times. If the successor's position is smaller than the actual one, it will be expanded in the next run, otherwise in the same one.
  1. Show that the number of scans in the algorithm *one-bit-reachability* is bounded by the maximum BFS layer.
  2. Can you avoid multiple node expansions?

Procedure One-Bit-Reachability
Input: Implicit problem graph with start node s,
        successor-generating function *Expand*, bitvector *Open*, and
        reversible perfect hash function (with *Rank* and *Unrank*)

  for each i in $\{0 \ldots N!/2 - 1\}$;; Initialize array
      $Open[i] \leftarrow false$;; Set each bit to not visited
  $Open[Rank(s) \bmod N!/2] \leftarrow true$;; Insert initial state
  loop   ;; Endless loop for full state space coverage
    for each i in $\{0 \ldots N!/2 - 1\}$;; Perform a scan
      if $(Open[i] = true)$;; State seen before
        $(valid, \pi) \leftarrow Unrank(i)$;; Inverse of perfect hash function
        if $(\neg valid)$ $Swap(\pi_0, \pi_1)$;; Uncompress puzzle state
        $Succ \leftarrow Expand(\pi)$;; Generate children
        for each v in $Succ$;; Consider them one by one
          $Open[Rank(v) \bmod N!/2] \leftarrow true$;; Mark successor

Algorithm 6.33

Traversing the search space with one bit per state.

6.7 BIBLIOGRAPHIC NOTES

Memory-restricted search has been studied from different angles for the last three decades. We only refer to some milestones. There are many others like *m-depth search* by Ibaraki (1978) and *speculative search* by Gooley and Wah (1990). The anomaly of depth-bounded DFS has been described in Edelkamp, Leue, and Lluch-Lafuente (2004c). Admissible DFS has been implemented in the model checker SPIN by Holzmann (2004).

One of the first memory-restricted algorithms is the recursive best-first-search algorithm MREC that has been proposed by Sen and Bagchi (1989). The algorithm is a generalization of IDA* that uses additional memory. It grows an explicit search graph until the main memory limit is reached. The memory usage is static and supports no caching strategy. If the pool size is set to 0, then MREC behaves identical to IDA*. Like IDA*, MREC starts all iterations at the root node, so that the underlying problem graph is repeatedly searched. This avoids a priority queue representation of the list of generated nodes.

Transposition tables have been suggested for IDA* exploration by Reinefeld and Marsland (1994) in the context on improved puzzle solving. The term is inherited from two-player game search, where move transpositions are detected by hashing. Avoiding multiple searches from identical nodes, transposition tables speed up the search of the game/search tree considerably. Stochastic node caching is due to Miura and Ishida (1998) and has been successfully applied to multiple sequence alignment problems. Different to our exposition, SNC is presented in the context of the MREC algorithm.

MA* has been introduced by Chakrabarti, Ghose, Acharya, and DeSarkar (1989). Russell (1992) has simplified the exposition and improved it by incorporating the path-max heuristic (SMA*). Kaindl and Khorsand (1994) have generalized it to graph search (SMAG). Zhou and Hansen (2003b) have improved its efficiency when reopening nodes. Iterative threshold search (ITS) has been proposed by Ghosh, Mahanti, and Nau (1994). IDA* with bit-state hashing has first been proposed in the context of protocol validation by Edelkamp, Leue, and Lluch-Lafuente (2004b). It has been brought to AI by Hüffner, Edelkamp, Fernau, and Niedermeier (2001) to optimally solve Atomix instances.

As discussed in the text, earlier approaches in memory-restricted search had only limited success in exploring the middle-ground between A* and IDA*. As one reason, the overhead for implementing the caching policies often did not pay off. Recent algorithms appear more careful in testing applicability. Often acyclic or undirected search spaces are assumed. Algorithm RIDA* has been presented by Wah and Shang (1994). Zhou and Hansen (2003a) have presented the approach to prune the *Closed* list in A* and Yoshizumi, Miura, and Ishida (2000) introduced Partial Expansion A*. The algorithm of Hirschberg (1975) has influenced Korf (1999) in the development of the divide-and-conquer strategy *frontier search* for multiple sequence alignment problems. The approach has been improved by Korf and Zhang (2000) into a forward search algorithm. Divide-and-conquer beam search has been presented by Zhou and Hansen (2004a) and its extension to beam-stack search by Zhou and Hansen (2005b).

The time complexity of SMAG has also been established for the algorithm DBIDA*, developed by Eckerle and Schuierer (1995). It dynamically balances the search tree. The algorithm, its bidirectional variant, and a lower-bound example have been studied by Eckerle (1998),. The question of how to add diversity into the search has been posed in the context of a memory-restricted k-breadth-first search algorithm by Linares López and Borrajo (2010).

The discussion of inadmissable heuristics in weighted A* is kept rather short. Pearl (1985) already dedicated one entire chapter to that subject. In Chapter 2 we saw that the number of reopenings can be exponential. We followed the approach of inadmissible nodes by Likhachev (2005). On top of work by Zahavi, Felner, Schaeffer, and Sturtevant (2007) and by Zhang, Sturtevant, Holte, Schaeffer, and Felner (2009), Thayer and Ruml have studied both an inadmissible heuristic to quickly find a solution and an admissible one to guarantee optimality.

Enforced hill-climbing has been proposed by Hoffmann and Nebel (2001) in the context of action planning. It has been adapted to both propositional and numerical planning by Hoffmann (2003). In case of failure in a directed problem graph the planner chooses best-first search (with $f = g + 5h$ as a default) as complete back-end. In the book by Hoos and Stützle (2004) (on the very first page) the pseudo code of the *iterative improvement* algorithm is presented. The algorithm shares many similarities with *enforced hill-climbing* and was known before enforced hill-climbing was introduced.

Adjusting the weights in A* has been studied in detail by Pohl (1977a). The presentation of ϵ-optimal approximation for A* with node selection based on search efforts refers to results presented by Pearl (1985). The algorithm k-best-first search is introduced by Felner (2001) and empirically evaluated in the incremental random trees with dead-ends, in sliding-tile puzzles, and in number partition problems. Although beam search is often associated with a breadth-first strategy, Rich and Knight (1991) have suggested applying it to best-first search. A more general definition has been given by Bisani (1987), where any search algorithm that uses pruning rules to discard nonpromising alternatives is called beam search. One example for the adaption to the depth-first branch-and-bound search algorithm is provided by Zhang (1998). He used iterative weakening, as introduced by Provost (1993), to regain completeness. A closely related technique is iterative broadening by Ginsberg and Harvey (1992). Beam search has been applied to accelerate bug-hunting in model checking by Wijs (1999).

The idea of anytime search was proposed in the AI community a while ago (Dean and Boddy, 1988), and much work has been done on the development of anytime planning algorithms since then (e.g., Ambite and Knoblock, 1997; Hawes, 2002; Pai and Reissell, 1998; Prendinger and Ishizuka,

1998; Zilberstein and Russell, 1993). A* and its variants, such as weighted A*, can easily run out of memory in cases when the heuristics guide the search in a wrong direction and the state space is large. Consequently, these properties extend to the anytime algorithms that are based on weighted A* such as ARA* by Likhachev (2005). Specific memory-bounded anytime heuristic searches, for example, have been developed by Furcy (2004), Kumar (1992), Zhang (1998). The term *potential search* has been coined by Stern, Puzis, and Felner (2010b) to describe an approach to greedy anytime heurstic search. A framework on anytime heuristic search has been provided by Thayer and Ruml (2010).

An anytime search algorithm is suitable for solving complex planning problems under the conditions where time is critical. An *incremental search* is suitable for planning in domains that require frequent replanning (e.g., dynamic environments). Search methods for dynamic graph updates have been suggested in the algorithms literature; for example, by Ausiello, Italiano, Marchetti-Spaccamela, and Nanni (1991); Even and Shiloach (1981); Even and Gazit (1985); Edelkamp (1998a); Feuerstein and Marchetti-Spaccamela (1993); Franciosa, Frigioni, and Giaccio (2001); Frigioni, Marchetti-Spaccamela, and Nanni (1996); Goto and Sangiovanni-Vincentelli (1978); Italiano (1988); Klein and Subramanian (1993); Lin and Chang (1990); Ramalingam and Reps (1996); Rohnert (1985); and Spira and Pan (1975). They are all uninformed; that is, they do not use heuristics to focus their search, but differ in their assumptions; for example, whether they solve single-source or all-pairs shortest path problems, which performance measure they use, when they update the shortest paths, which kinds of graph topology and edge costs they apply to, and how the graph topology and edge costs are allowed to change over time (see Frigioni, Marchetti-Spaccamela, and Nanni, 1998). If arbitrary sequences of edge insertions, deletions, or weight changes are allowed, then the dynamic shortest path problems are called fully dynamic shortest path problems by Frigioni, Marchetti-Spaccamela, and Nanni (2000). The lifelong planning A* algorithm (closely related to an uninformed algorithm by Ramalingam and Reps, 1996) is an incremental search method that solves fully dynamic shortest path problems but, different from the incremental search methods cited earlier, uses heuristics to focus its search and thus combines two different techniques to reduce its search effort. As shown by Likhachev and Koenig (2005) it can also be configured to return solutions for any bound of suboptimality. Thus it may also be suitable to the domains where optimal planning is infeasible.

Breadth-first heuristic search, breadth-first iterative deepening, and divide-and-conquer beam search have been introduced by Zhou and Hansen (2004a). These advanced algorithms are based on early findings of memory-bounded A* search by Zhou and Hansen (2002a). Beam-stack search was introduced as a generalization to depth-first and breadth-first branch-and-bound search by Zhou and Hansen (2005b). It showed good performance in finding an optimal solution to STRIPS-type planning problems.

The space-efficient representation in breadth-first search with two frontier bits has been applied to state space search by Kunkle and Cooperman (2008), with an idea that goes back to Cooperman and Finkelstein (1992). For large instances to the PANCAKE problem, two-bit breadth-first search has been applied by Korf (2008). Breyer and Korf (2010b) have built compressed pattern databases based on the observation of Cooperman and Finkelstein (1992) that, after BFS construction, three bits of information suffice for the relative depth of each state. One-bit breadth-first search variants have been discussed by Edelkamp, Sulewski, and Yücel (2010b).

Symbolic Search

7

In previous chapters we have seen that there is a strong interest in improving the scalability of search algorithms. The central challenge in scaling up search is the *state/space explosion problem*, which denotes that the size of the state space grows exponentially in the number of state variables (problem components). In recent years, *symbolic* search techniques, originally developed for verification domains, have shown a large impact on improving AI search. The term *symbolic search* originates in the research area and has been chosen to contrast *explicit-state search*.

Symbolic search executes a functional exploration of the problem graph. Symbolic state space search algorithms use Boolean functions to represent sets of states. According to the space requirements of ordinary search algorithms, they save space mainly by sharing parts of the state vector. Sharing is realized by exploiting a functional representation of the state set. The term *functional* often has different meanings in computer science (nondestructive, emphasis on functions as first-order objects). In contrast, here, we refer to the representation of the sets in form of characteristic functions. For example, the set of all states in the $(n^2 - 1)$-PUZZLE with the blank located on the second or fourth position with regard to the state vector $(t_0, \ldots, t_{n^2-1})$ is represented by the *characteristic function* $(t_1 = 0) \vee (t_3 = 0)$. The characteristic function of a state set can be much smaller than the number of states it represents. The main advantage of symbolic search is that it operates on the functional representation of both state and actions. This has a drastic impact on the design of available search algorithms, as known explicit-state algorithms have to be adapted to the exploration of sets of states.

In this chapter we will first see how to represent states and action as (characteristic) functions, and then briefly address the problem of obtaining an efficient state encoding. The functional representations of states and actions then allow us to compute the functional representation of a set of successors, or the *image*, in a specialized operation. As a by-product, the functional representation of the set of predecessors, or the *preimage*, can also be effectively determined.

We refer to the functional (or implicit) representation of state and action sets in a data structure as their *symbolic representation*. We select BINARY DECISION DIAGRAMS (BDDs) as the appropriate data structure for characteristic functions. BDDs are directed, acyclic, and labeled graphs. Roughly speaking, these graphs are restricted deterministic finite automata, accepting the state vectors (encoded in binary) that are contained in the underlying set. In a scan of a state vector starting at the start node of the BDD at each intermediate BDD node, a state variable is processed, following a fixed variable ordering. The scan either terminates at a nonaccepting leaf labeled *false* (or 0), which means that a state is not contained in the set, or at an accepting leaf labeled *true* (or 1), which means that the state is contained in the set. Compared to a host of ambiguous representations of Boolean formulas, the BDD representation is unique. As in usual implementations of BDD libraries, different BDDs share their structures. Such libraries have efficient operations of combining BDDs and subsequently support the computation of images. Moreover, BDD packages often support arithmetic operations on variables of finite domains with BDDs. To avoid notational conflicts in this chapter, we denote vertices of the problem graph as *states* and vertices of the BDDs as *nodes*.

Symbolic uninformed search algorithms (e.g., *symbolic breadth-first search* and *symbolic shortest path search*), as well as symbolic heuristic search algorithms (e.g., *symbolic A**, *symbolic best-first search*, as well as *symbolic-branch-and-bound search*) are introduced. For the case of symbolic A* search, a complexity analysis shows that, assuming consistent heuristics, the algorithm requires a number of images that is at most quadratic in the optimal solution length.

We also consider symbolic search to cover general cost functions. As state vectors are of finite domain, such cost functions require arithmetics for BDDs.

Subsequent to the presentation of the algorithms, we consider different implementation refinements to the search. Next we turn to symbolic algorithms that take the entire graph as an input in the form of a BDD.

7.1 BOOLEAN ENCODINGS FOR SET OF STATES

Symbolic search avoids (or at least lessens) the costs associated with the exponential memory requirement for the state set involved as problem sizes get bigger. Representing fixed-length state vectors (of finite domain) in binary is uncomplicated. For example, the FIFTEEN-PUZZLE can be easily encoded in 64 bits, with 4 bits encoding the label of each tile. A more concise description is the binary code for the ordinal number of the permutation associated with the puzzle state yielding $\lceil \lg 16!/2 \rceil = 44$ bits (see Ch. 3). For SOKOBAN we have different options; either we encode the position of the balls individually, or we encode their layout on the board. Similarly, for propositional planning, we can encode the valid propositions in a state by using the binary representation of their index, or we take the bitvector of all facts being true and false. More generally, a state vector can be represented by encoding the domains of the vector, or—assuming a perfect hash function of a state vector—using the binary representation of the hash address.

Given a fixed-length binary state vector for a search problem, *characteristic functions* represent state sets. A characteristic function evaluates to true for the binary representation of a given state vector if and only if the state is a member of that set. As the mapping is one-to-one, the characteristic function can be identified with the state set.

Let us consider the following SLIDING-TOKEN PUZZLE as a running example. We are given a horizontal bar, partitioned into four locations (see Fig. 7.1) with one sliding token moving between adjacent locations. In the initial state, the token is found on the left-most position $0 = (00)_2$. In the goal state, the token has reached position $3 = (11)_2$. Since we only have four options, two variables x_0 and x_1 are sufficient to uniquely describe the position of the token and, therefore, each individual state. They refer to the bits for the states. The characteristic function of all states is provided in Table 7.1.

The characteristic function for combining two or more states is the disjunction of characteristic functions of the individual states. For example, the combined representation for the two positions $0 = (00)_2$ and $1 = (01)_2$ is $\neg x_0$. We observe that the representation for these two states is smaller than for the single ones. A symbolic representation for several states, however, is not always smaller than an explicit one. Consider the two states $0 = (00)_2$ and $3 = (11)_2$. Their combined representation is $\neg x_0 \neg x_1 \vee x_0 x_1$. Given the offset for representing the term, in this case the explicit representation is actually the better one, but in general, the gain for sharing the encoding is big.

FIGURE 7.1

The SLIDING-TOKEN PUZZLE and its binary encoding.

Table 7.1 Encoding of states in the SLIDING-TOKEN PUZZLE.

State ID	State Role	Binary Code	Boolean Formula
0	Initial	00	$\neg x_0 \neg x_1$
1	–	01	$\neg x_0 x_1$
2	–	10	$x_0 \neg x_1$
3	Goal	00	$x_0 x_1$

Table 7.2 Comparison of concepts in explicit-state and symbolic search.

Explicit Concept	Notation	Symbolic Concept	Notation
State	u	Characteristic Function	$\phi_{\{u\}}(x)$
State Set	S	Characteristic Function	$\phi_S(x)$
Search Frontier	*Open*	Characteristic Function	*Open*(x)
Expanded State	*Closed*	Characteristic Function	*Closed*(x)
Initial State	s	Characteristic Function	$\phi_{\{s\}}(x)$
Successor State Set	*Succ*	Characteristic Function	*Succ*(x)
Goal (State Set)	T	Characteristic Function	$\phi_T(x)$
Action	a	Individual Transition Relation	$Trans_a(x,x')$
Action Set	A	Full Transition Relation	$Trans(x,x')$
Action Costs	$w(a)$	Weighted Transition Relation	$Trans(w,x,x')$
Heuristic Function	h	Heuristic Relation	$Heur(value,x)$

Actions are also formalized as relations; that is, as sets of state pairs, or alternatively, as the characteristic function of such sets. The *transition relation* has twice as many variables as the encoding of the state. The transition relation *Trans* is defined in a way such that if x is the binary encoding of a given position and if x' is the binary encoding of a successor state, *Trans*(x,x') will evaluate to true. To construct *Trans*, we observe that it is the disjunction of all individual state transitions. In our case we have the six actions $(00) \rightarrow (01)$, $(01) \rightarrow (00)$, $(01) \rightarrow (10)$, $(10) \rightarrow (01)$, $(10) \rightarrow (11)$, and $(11) \rightarrow (10)$, such that

$$Trans(x,x') = (\neg x_0 \neg x_1 \neg x'_0 x'_1) \vee (\neg x_0 x_1 \neg x'_0 \neg x'_1) \vee (\neg x_0 x_1 x'_0 \neg x'_1) \vee$$
$$(x_0 \neg x_1 \neg x'_0 x'_1) \vee (x_0 \neg x_1 x'_0 x'_1) \vee (x_0 x_1 x'_0 \neg x'_1).$$

Table 7.2 relates the concepts needed for explicit-state heuristic search to their symbolic counterparts. As a feature, all algorithms in this chapter work for initial state *sets*, reporting a path from one member to the goal. For the sake of coherence, we nonetheless stick to singletons. Weighted transition relations $Trans(w,x,x')$ include action cost values encoded in binary. Heuristic relations $Heur(value,x)$ partition the state space according to the heuristic estimates encoded in *value*.

7.2 BINARY DECISION DIAGRAMS

BINARY DECISION DIAGRAMS (BDDs) are fundamental to various areas such as model checking and the synthesis of hardware circuits. In AI search, they are used to space-efficiently represent huge sets of states.

In the introduction, we informally characterized BDDs as deterministic finite automata. For a more formal treatment, a binary decision diagram G_f is a data structure for representing Boolean functions f (acting on variables $x_1,\ldots,x_n$). Assignments to the variables are mapped to either *true* or *false*.

Definition 7.1. *(BDD) A binary decision diagram (BDD) is a directed node- and edge-labeled acyclic graph with a single root node and two sinks labeled 1 and 0. The nodes are labeled by variables x_i, $i \in \{1,\ldots,n\}$, and the edge labels are either 1 or 0.*

For evaluating the represented function for a given input, a path is traced from the root node to one of the sinks, quite similar to the way DECISION TREES are used. What distinguishes BDDs from DECISION TREES is the use of two reduction rules, detecting unnecessary variable tests and isomorphisms in subgraphs, leading to a unique representation that is polynomial in the length of the bit strings for many interesting functions.

Definition 7.2. *(Reduced and Ordered BDD) A* reduced and ordered BDD *is a BDD where on each path a fixed ordering of variables is preserved (ordered BDD) and where nodes with identical successors are omitted and isomorphic sub-BDDs are merged (reduced BDD).*

Figure 7.2 illustrates the application of these two rules. An unreduced and a reduced BDD for the goal state of the example problem is shown in Figure 7.3.

Throughout this chapter we write BDDs, although we always mean reduced and ordered BDDs. The reason that the reduced representation is unique is that each node in a BDD represents an essential subfunction. The uniqueness of BDD representation of a Boolean function implies that the satisfiability test is available in $O(1)$ time. (If the BDD merely consists of a 0-sink, then it is unsatisfiable, otherwise it is satisfiable.) This is a clear benefit to a general satisfiability test of Boolean formulas, which by the virtue of *Cook's theorem* is an NP-hard problem. Some other operations on BDDs are:

SAT-Count Input: BDD G_f. Output: $|f^{-1}(1)| = |\{a \in \{0,1\}^n \mid f(a) = 1\}|$. Running time: $O(|G_f|)$.
    Description: The algorithm considers a topological ordering of the nodes in the BDD. It

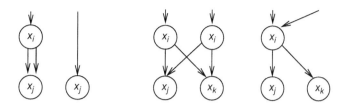

FIGURE 7.2

BDD reduction: common edge (left) and common successor sets (right).

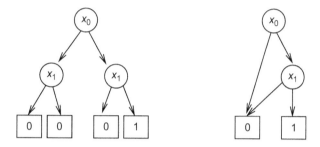

FIGURE 7.3

Unreduced (left) and reduced (right) BDD, where the left edge denotes the 0-successor, and the right edge denotes 1-successor.

propagates the number of possible assignments at each internal node bottom-up. Application: For state space search, the operation determines the number of explicit states that are represented by a BDD. In AI literature, this operation is also referred to as *model counting*.

Synthesis Input: BDDs G_f and G_g, operator $\otimes \in \{\wedge, \Leftrightarrow, \oplus, \Rightarrow, \vee, \ldots\}$. Output: BDD for $f \otimes g$. Running time: $O(|G_f||G_g|)$. Description: The implementation traverses both input graphs in parallel and generates the result by merging matching subtrees bottom-up. The synchronization between the two parallel depth-first searches is the variable ordering. If the index in the first BDD is larger than in the other, it has to wait. As the traversal is depth-first, the bottom-up construction is organized *postorder*. For returning a reduced BDD the application of both reduction rules is included in the parallel traversal. Application: For state space search, synthesis is the main operation to construct unions and intersections of state sets.

Negation Input: BDD G_f. Output: BDD for $\neg f$. Running time: $O(1)$. Description: The algorithm simply exchanges the labels of the sinks. Analogous to the satisfiability test it assumes the sinks are accessible in constant time. Application: In state space search, negation is needed to remove a state set, as set subtraction is realized via a combination of a conjunction and a negation.

Substitution-by-Constant Input: BDD G_f, variable x_i, and constant $c \in \{0, 1\}$. Output: BDD $f|_{x_i=c}$. Running time: $O(|G_f|)$. Description: The algorithm sets all $(1-c)$ successors of x_i to the zero sink (followed by BDD reduction). Application: In state space search, variants for substitution-by-constant are needed to reconstruct the solution path.

Quantification Input: BDD G_f, variable x_i. Output: BDD $\exists x_i : f = f|_{x_i=0} \vee f|_{x_i=1}$ (or $\forall x_i : f = f|_{x_i=0} \wedge f|_{x_i=1}$). Running time: $O(|G_f|^2)$. Description: The algorithm applies the synthesis algorithm for $f|_{x_i=0}, f|_{x_i=1}$, and $\vee$ (or $\wedge$). Application: In state space search, quantification is used when projecting a state set to a subset of variables.

Relational Product Input: BDDs G_f and G_g, variable x_i. Output: BDD $\exists x_i : f \wedge g = (f \wedge g)|_{x_i=0} \vee (f \wedge g)|_{x_i=1}$ (or $\forall x_i : f \Rightarrow g = (f \Rightarrow g)|_{x_i=0} \wedge (f \rightarrow g)|_{x_i=1}$). Running time: $O((|G_f||G_g|)^2)$. Description: The basic algorithm applies the synthesis algorithm for $(f \wedge g)|_{x_i=0}, (f \wedge g)|_{x_i=1}$ and $\vee$ (or $(f \Rightarrow g)|_{x_i=0}$ and $(f \rightarrow g)|_{x_i=1}$, and $\wedge$). Algorithm 7.11 (see Exercises) shows how to integrate quantification with the additional operator $\wedge$ (or $\rightarrow$). Application: In state space search, the relational is used when computing the images and preimages of a state set.

Substitution-by-Variable Input: BDD G_f, variable x_i and x_i' (f does not depend on x_i'). Output: BDD $f[x_i' \leftrightarrow x_i] = f|_{x_i=x_i'}$. Running time: $O(|G_f|^2)$. Description: The function $f|_{x_i=x_i'}$ can be written as $f|_{x_i=x_i'} = \exists x_i : f \wedge x_i = x_i'$, so that a substitution by variable is a relational product. (If x_i' follows x_i in the variable ordering the algorithm simply relabels all x_i nodes with x_i' in $O(|G_f|^2)$ time.) Application: In state space search, substitution-by-variable is needed to change the variable labels.

The variable ordering has a huge influence on the *size* (the space complexity in terms of the number of nodes to be stored) of a BDD. For example, the function $f = x_1 x_2 \vee x_3 x_4 \vee \cdots \vee x_{2n-1} x_{2n}$ has linear size ($2n + 2$ nodes) if the ordering matches the permutation $(1, 2, 3, 4, \ldots, 2n - 1, 2n)$, and exponential size ($2^{n+1}$ nodes) if the ordering matches the permutation $(1, 3, \ldots, 2n - 1, 2, 4, \ldots, 2n)$. Unfortunately, the problem of finding the best ordering (the one that minimized the size of the BDD) for a given function f is NP-hard. The worst case are functions that have exponential size for all orderings (see Exercises) and, therefore, do not suggest the use of BDDs.

For transition relations, the variable ordering is also important. The *standard variable ordering* simply appends the variables according to the binary representation of a state; for example, (x_0, x_1, x_0', x_1'). The *interleaved variable ordering* alternates x and x' variables; for example, (x_0, x_0', x_1, x_1').

The BDD for the transition relation $Trans(x, x') = (\neg x_0 \neg x_1 \neg x_0' x_1') \vee (\neg x_0 x_1 \neg x_0' \neg x_1') \vee (\neg x_0 x_1 x_0' \neg x_1') \vee (x_0 \neg x_1 \neg x_0' x_1') \vee (x_0 \neg x_1 x_0' x_1') \vee (x_0 x_1 x_0' \neg x_1')$ for a noninterleaved variable ordering is shown in Figure 7.4. (Drawing the BDD for the interleaved ordering is left as an exercise.)

There are many different possibilities to come up with an encoding of states for a problem and a suitable ordering among the state variables. The more obvious ones often waste a lot of space. So it is worthwhile to spend efforts in finding a good ordering. Many applications select orderings based upon an approximate analysis of available input information. One approach is a *conflict analysis*, which determines how strong a state variable assignment depends on another. Variables that are dependent of each other appear as close as possible in the variable encoding.

Alternatively, advanced variable ordering techniques have been developed, such as the *sifting* algorithm. It is roughly characterized as follows. Because a BDD has to respect the variable ordering on each path, it is possible to partition it according to levels of nodes with the same variable index. Let $L(x_i)$ be the level of nodes with variable index i, $i \in \{1, \ldots, n\}$. The sifting algorithm repeatedly seaks a better position in the variable ordering for a variable (or an entire group of variables) by moving it up (or down) in the current order, and evaluating the result by measuring the resulting BDD size. In fact, variables x_i are selected, for which the levels $L(x_i)$ in the BDDs are at their widest; that is, for which $|L(x_i)|$ is maximal. Interestingly, the reordering technique can be invoked *dynamically* during the course of computations.

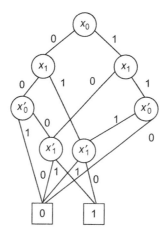

FIGURE 7.4

The BDD for the transition relation *Trans* in the SLIDING-TOKEN PUZZLE; for the sake of clarity arrowheads are omitted.

Performing arithmetics is essential for many BDD-based algorithms. In the following we illustrate how to perform addition with finite-domain variables using BDDs (multiplication is dealt with analogously). Since most BDD packages support finite-domain variables, we abstract from the binary representation. Because it is not difficult to shift a domain from [min, max] to [0, max − min], without loss of generality, in the following we assume all variable domains start with value 0 and end with value max.

First, the BDD $Inc(a,b)$ that encodes the binary relation $a + 1 = b$ can be constructed by enumerating all possible assignments of the form $(i, i+1)$, $0 \leq i < \mathrm{max}$,

$$Inc(a,b) = ((a=0) \wedge (b=1)) \vee ((a=1) \wedge (b=2)) \vee \cdots \vee ((a=\mathrm{max}-1) \wedge (b=\mathrm{max})),$$

assuming that the binary relation $Equal(a,b)$, written as $a = b$, is provided by the underlying BDD package.

BDD $Add(a,b,c)$ represents the ternary relation $a + b = c$. For the construction, we might enumerate all possible assignments to the variables a, b, and c. For large domains, however, the following recursive computation should be preferred:

$$Add(a,b,c) = ((b=0) \wedge (a=c)) \vee \exists\, b',c'\ (Inc(b',b) \wedge Inc(c',c) \wedge Add(a,b',c')).$$

Hence, *Add* is the result of a *fixpoint* computation. Starting with the base case $(b=0) \wedge (a=c)$, which unifies all cases in which the according relation is true, the closure of *Add* is computed by applying the second part of the equation until the BDD representation no longer changes. The pseudo code is shown in Algorithm 7.1. To allow multiple quantification, in each iteration the sets of variables (for the parameters b and c) are swapped (denoted by $[b \leftrightarrow b', c \leftrightarrow c']$). The BDDs *From* and *New* denote the same set, but are kept as separate concepts: one is used for termination detecting and the other for initiating the next iteration.

Procedure Construct-Add
Input: BDD for relation *Inc*
Output: BDD for relation *Add*

$Reach(a,b,c) \leftarrow From(a,b,c) \leftarrow (a = c \wedge b = 0)$;; Initialize construction
repeat   ;; Until convergence
$\quad To(a,b',c') \leftarrow From(a,b,c)[b \leftrightarrow b', c \leftrightarrow c']$;; Change variable labels in BDD
$\quad To(a,b,c) \leftarrow \exists b',c'(Inc(b',b) \wedge Inc(c',c) \wedge To(a,b',c'))$;; Apply equation
$\quad From(a,b,c) \leftarrow New(a,b,c) \leftarrow To(a,b,c) \wedge \neg Reach(a,b,c)$;; Prepare next iteration
$\quad Reach(a,b,c) \leftarrow Reach(a,b,c) \vee New(a,b,c)$;; Update relation
until $(New(a,b,c) = \emptyset)$;; Fixpoint reached
return $Reach(a,b,c)$;; Fixpoint is the relation *Add*

Algorithm 7.1

BDD arithmetics via fixpoint computation.

7.3 COMPUTING THE IMAGE FOR A STATE SET

What have we achieved so far? We are able to reformulate the initial and final states in a state space problem as BDDs. As an end in itself, this does not help much. We are interested in a sequence of actions that transforms an initial state into one that satisfies the goal.

By conjoining the transition relation with a formula describing a set of states, and quantifying the predecessor variables, we compute the representation of all states that can be reached in one step from some state in the input set. This is the *relational product* operator. Hence, what we are really interested in is the image of a state set S with respect to a transition relation *Trans*, which is equal to applying the operation

$$Image_S(x') = \exists x\ (Trans(x,x') \wedge \phi_S(x)),$$

where ϕ_S denotes the characteristic function of set S. The result is a characteristic function of all states reachable from the states in S in one step. For the running example, the image of the state set $\{0,2\}$ represented by $\phi_S = \neg x_1$ is given by

$$Image_S(x') = \exists x_0 \exists x_1\ \neg x_1 \wedge ((\neg x_0 \neg x_1 \neg x_0' x_1') \vee (\neg x_0 x_1 \neg x_0' \neg x_1') \vee$$
$$(\neg x_0 x_1 x_0' \neg x_1') \vee (x_0 \neg x_1 \neg x_0' x_1') \vee (x_0 \neg x_1 x_0' x_1') \vee (x_0 x_1 x_0' \neg x_1'))$$
$$= \exists x_0 \exists x_1\ (\neg x_0 \neg x_1 \neg x_0' x_1') \vee \exists x_0 \exists x_1\ (x_0 \neg x_1 \neg x_0' x_1') \vee$$
$$\exists x_0 \exists x_1\ (x_0 \neg x_1 x_0' x_1') = \neg x_0' x_1' \vee \neg x_0' x_1' \vee x_0' x_1' = x_1'$$

and represents the state set $\{1,3\}$.

More generally, the relational product of a vector of Boolean variables x and two Boolean functions f and g combines quantification and conjunction in one step and is defined as $\exists x(f(x) \wedge g(x))$. Since existential quantification of a Boolean variable x_i in the Boolean function f is equal to $f|_{x_i=0} \vee f|_{x_i=1}$, the quantification of the entire vector x results in a sequence of subproblem disjunctions. Although computing the relational product (for the entire vector) is NP-hard in general, specialized algorithms have been developed leading to an efficient determination of the image for many practical applications.

7.4 SYMBOLIC BLIND SEARCH

First, we turn to undirected search algorithms that originate in symbolic model checking.

7.4.1 Symbolic Breadth-First Tree Search

In a symbolic variant of BFS we determine the set of states S_i reachable from the initial state s in i steps. The search is initialized with $S_0 = \{s\}$. The following image equation determines ϕ_{S_i} given both $\phi_{S_{i-1}}$ and the transition relation $Trans$:

$$\phi_{S_i}(x') = \exists x \, (\phi_{S_{i-1}}(x) \wedge Trans(x,x')).$$

Informally, a state x' belongs to S_i if it has a predecessor x in the set S_{i-1} and there exists an operator that transforms x into x'. Note that on the right side of the equation ϕ depends on x, compared to x' on the left side. Thus, it is necessary to substitute x' with x in ϕ_{S_i} for the next iteration. There is no need to reorder or reduce, because the substitution can be done by a textual replacement of the node labels in the BDD.

To terminate the search we test whether or not a state is represented in the intersection of the set S_i and the set of goal states T. Since we enumerated the sets $S_0, \ldots, S_{i-1}$, the first iteration index i with $S_i \cap T \neq \emptyset$ denotes the optimal solution length.

Let $Open$ be the representation of the search frontier and let $Succ$ be the BDD for the set of successors. Then the algorithm *symbolic breadth-first tree search* can be realized as the pseudo code Algorithm 7.2 suggests. (For the sake of simplicity, in this and upcoming algorithms we generally assume that the start state is not a goal.) It leads to three iterations for the example problem (see Fig. 7.5). We start with the initial state represented by a BDD of two inner nodes for the function $\neg x_0 \wedge \neg x_1$. After the first iteration we obtain a BDD representing the function $x_0 \wedge \neg x_1$. The next iteration leads to a BDD of one internal node for $\neg x_1$, and the last iteration results in a BDD for x_1 that contains the goal state. The corresponding content of the $Open$ list is made explicit in Table 7.3.

Theorem 7.1. (*Optimality and Complexity of Symbolic Breadth-First Tree Search*) *The solution returned by* symbolic breadth-first tree search *has the minimum number of steps while applying the same number of images.*

Proof. The algorithm generates every reachable state in the search tree with repeated image operations in a breadth-first manner, such that the first goal state encountered has optimal depth. ∎

By keeping track of the intermediate BDDs, a legal sequence of states linking the initial state to a goal state can be extracted, which in turn can be used to find a corresponding sequence of actions. The goal state is on the optimal path. A state in an optimal path that comes before the detected goal

---

Procedure Symbolic-Breadth-First-Tree-Search
Input: State space problem with transition relation *Trans*
Output: Optimal solution path

$Open(x) \leftarrow \phi_{\{s\}}(x)$;; Initialize search frontier
do   ;; Repeat-until loop
    $Succ(x') \leftarrow \exists x \ (Open(x) \wedge Trans(x,x'))$;; Determine successor set
    $Open(x) \leftarrow Succ(x')[x' \leftrightarrow x]$;; Iterate with new search frontier
  while $(Open(x) \wedge \phi_T(x) = false)$;; Until goal is found
  return $Construct(Open(x) \wedge \phi_T(x))$;; Reconstruct solution

Algorithm 7.2

Symbolic breadth-first tree search implemented with BDDs.

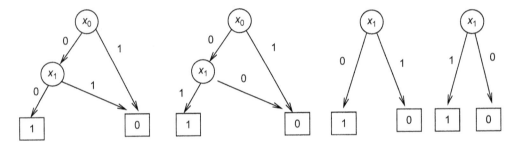

FIGURE 7.5

Four iterations in symbolic breadth-first tree search.

Table 7.3 State sets in the four iterations of symbolic breadth-first tree search.

Step	State Set	Binary Codes	Boolean Formula
0	$\{0\}$	$\{00\}$	$\neg x_0 \neg x_1$
1	$\{1\}$	$\{01\}$	$\neg x_0 x_1$
2	$\{0,2\}$	$\{00,10\}$	$\neg x_1$
3	$\{1,3\}$	$\{01,11\}$	x_1

state must be contained in the previous BFS level. We, therefore, intersect the predecessors of the goal state with that level. All states that are in the intersection are reachable in an optimal number of steps and reach the goal with an optimal number of steps, so any of these states can be chosen to continue solution reconstruction until the initial state is found.

If all previous BFS levels remain in main memory, sequential solution reconstruction is sufficient. If levels are eliminated (as in frontier search; see Ch. 6), a solution reconstruction from BFS levels flushed to disk is recommended.

7.4.2 **Symbolic Breadth-First Search**

The introduction of a list *Closed* containing all states ever expanded is the common approach in the explicit-state exploration to avoid duplicates. In symbolic breadth-first search (see Alg. 7.3) this technique is realized through the refinement *Succ* $\land$ $\neg Closed$ for the successor state set *Succ*. The operation is called *forward* or *frontier set simplification*. One additional advantage is that the algorithm terminates in case no solution exists.

The BDDs for exploring the SLIDING-TOKEN PUZZLE are shown in Figure 7.6 with formula representations listed in Table 7.4. For bigger examples, memory savings by applying the functional state set representation in the BDD are expected to grow. Figure 7.7 shows a typical behavior.

Theorem 7.2. *(Optimality and Complexity of Symbolic BFS) The solution returned by symbolic BFS has the minimum number of steps. The number of images is equal to the solution length. It stops if a problem obeys no solution.*

Proof. The algorithm expands each possible node in the problem graph with repeated image operations at most once, such that the first goal state encountered has optimal depth. If no goal is returned the entire reachable search space has been explored. ∎

Procedure Symbolic-Breadth-First-Search
Input: State space problem with transition relation *Trans*
Output: Optimal solution path

$Closed(x) \leftarrow Open(x) \leftarrow \phi_{\{s\}}(x)$	;; Initialize search sets
do	;; Repeat-until loop
if $(Open(x) = false)$ **return** "Exploration completed"	;; Full graph has been seen
$Succ(x) \leftarrow \exists x(Open(x) \land Trans(x,x'))[x' \leftrightarrow x]$	;; Image computation
$Open(x) \leftarrow Succ(x) \land \neg Closed(x)$	;; Delete set of expanded states
$Closed(x) \leftarrow Closed(x) \lor Succ(x)$	;; Update visited list
while $(Open(x) \land \phi_T(x) = false)$	;; Until goal found
return $Construct(Open(x) \land \phi_T(x))$	;; Generate solution

Algorithm 7.3

Symbolic BFS.

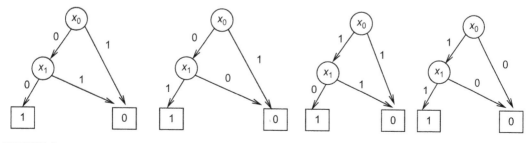

FIGURE 7.6

Four steps in symbolic BFS.

Table 7.4 State sets in the four iterations of symbolic BFS.

Step	State Set	Binary Codes	Boolean Formula
0	{0}	{00}	$\neg x_0 \neg x_1$
1	{1}	{01}	$\neg x_0 x_1$
2	{2}	{10}	$x_0 \neg x_1$
3	{3}	{11}	$x_0 x_1$

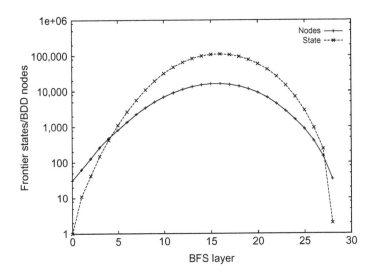

FIGURE 7.7

State and BDD growth in symbolic BFS.

In Chapter 6, we saw that for some problem classes like undirected or acyclic graphs, duplicate elimination can be limited from all to a reduced number of BFS levels. In undirected search spaces, it is also possible to apply frontier search (see Ch. 6). In the $(n^2 - 1)$-PUZZLE for each BFS level, all permutations (vectors) have the same *parity* (minimum transpositions needed to transform the state vector into the identity modulo 2, either even or odd). This implies that states in odd depths cannot reappear in an even depth and vice versa. As a consequence, only BFS level $i - 2$ has to be subtracted from BFS level i to remove all duplicates from the search.

7.4.3 Symbolic Pattern Databases

We have seen that the main limitation for applying pattern databases in search practice is the restricted amount of (main) memory and that the objective in symbolic search is to represent large sets of states with BDD nodes.

Symbolic pattern databases are pattern databases that have been constructed symbolically for later use either in symbolic or explicit heuristic search. It is based on the advantage of the fact that *Trans* has been defined as a relation. In backward breadth-first search we start with the goal set $B_0 = T$ and iterate until we encounter the start state. We then successively compute the *preimage* according to the formula

$$\phi_{B_i}(x) = \exists x' \, (\phi_{B_{i-1}}(x') \wedge Trans(x,x')).$$

Each state set is efficiently represented by a corresponding characteristic function. Different to the posterior compression of the state set, the construction itself works on the compressed representation, allowing much larger databases to be constructed.

For symbolic pattern database construction, backward symbolic BFS is used. For an abstraction function ψ the symbolic pattern database *Heur(value,x)* is initialized with the projected goal set $\psi(T)$ and, as long as there are newly encountered states, we take the current list of frontier nodes and generate the predecessor list with respect to the abstracted transition relation $Trans_\psi$. Then we attach the current BFS level to the new states, merge them with the set of already reached state states, and iterate. In Algorithm 7.4 *Closed* is the set of visited states for backward search, *Open* is the current abstract search frontier, and *Pred* is the set of abstract predecessor states.

Note that in addition to the capability to represent large sets of states in the exploration, symbolic pattern databases have one further advantage to explicit ones: fast initialization. In the definition of most problems the goal is not given as a collection of states but as a formula to be satisfied. In explicit-pattern database construction all goal states have to be generated and inserted into the backward exploration queue, but for the symbolic construction, initialization is immediate by building the BDD for the goal formula.

If we consider the example of the THIRTY-FIVE-PUZZLE with x tiles in the pattern, the abstract state space consists of $36!/(36-x)!$ states. A perfect hash table for the THIRTY-FIVE-PUZZLE has space requirements of 43.14 megabytes ($x = 5$), 1.3 gigabytes ($x = 6$), and 39.1 gigabytes ($x = 7$). The memory required for storing symbolic pattern databases is plotted in Figure 7.8, suggesting a moderate

---

Procedure Construct-Symbolic-Pattern-Database
Input: Abstract state space problem wrt, ψ and transition relation $Trans_\psi$
Output: Symbolic pattern database $H_\psi(value,x')$

$Closed(x') \leftarrow Open(x') \leftarrow \psi(T)(x')$;; Initialize search
$i \leftarrow 0$;; Initialize BFS layer
while $(Open(x') \neq false)$;; Abstract state space fully traversed?
    $Pred(x') \leftarrow \exists x' \, (Open(x') \wedge Trans_\psi(x,x'))[x \leftrightarrow x']$;; Determine predecessor set
    $Open(x') \leftarrow Pred(x') \wedge \neg Closed(x')$;; Frontier set simplification
    $H_\psi(value,x') \leftarrow H_\psi(value,x') \vee (value = i \wedge Open(x'))$;; Add to database
    $Closed(x') \leftarrow Closed(x') \vee Open(x')$;; Increase set of explored states
    $i \leftarrow i+1$;; Increase BFS layer
return $H_\psi(value,x')$;; Exploration complete

Algorithm 7.4

Symbolic pattern database construction.

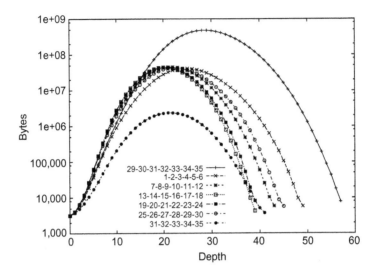

FIGURE 7.8

Memory profile for symbolic THIRTY-FIVE-PUZZLE pattern databases (on a logarithmic scale); six 6-tile pattern databases (one database has 5 tiles) and one seven-tile pattern databases are selected; tiles involved in each abstraction are used to label the curves.

but noticeable reduction with regard to the corresponding explicit construction; that is, the seven-tile pattern database requires 6.6 gigabytes of RAM. In other domains, it has been observed that the savings of symbolic pattern databases scale to several orders of magnitude.

Another key performance of symbolic pattern databases is a fast construction time. Given that pattern construction is an exploration in abstract state spaces, in some cases the search performance corresponds to billions of states being generated in a second.

7.4.4 Cost-Optimal Symbolic Breadth-First Search

Symbolic BFS finds the optimal solution in the number of solution steps. BDDs are also capable of space-efficiently optimizing a cost function f over the problem space. In this section, we do not make any specific assumption about f (e.g., being monotone or being composed of g or h), except that f operates on variables of finite domains. The problem has become prominent in the area of (oversubscribed) action planning, where a cost function encodes and accumulates the desire for the satisfaction of soft constraints on planning goals, which has to be maximized. As an example, consider that in addition to an ordinary goal description, we prefer certain blocks in BLOCKSWORLD to be placed on the table. For the sake of simplicity, we restrict ourselves to minimization problems. This implies that we want to find the path to a goal node in T that has the smallest f-value.

To compute a BDD $F(value, x)$ for the cost function $f(x)$ over a set of finite-domain state variables $x = (x_1, \ldots, x_k)$ with $x_i \in [\min_{x_i}, \max_{x_i}]$, we first compute the minimum and maximum values that f can take. This defines the range $[\min_f, \max_f]$ that has to be encoded in binary. For example, if f is a linear function $\sum_{i=1}^{k} a_i x_i$ with $a_i \geq 0$, $i \in \{1, \ldots, k\}$ then $\min_f = \sum_{i=1}^{k} a_i \min_{x_i}$ and $\max_f = \sum_{i=1}^{k} a_i \max_{x_i}$.

To construct $F(value, x)$ we build sub-BDD $Partial(value, x)$, with $value$ representing $a_i x_i$, $i \in \{1, \ldots, k\}$, and combine the intermediate results to the relation $F(value, x)$ using the relation Add. As the a_i are finite the relation $Partial(value, x)$ can be computed by using $value = x_i + \cdots + x_i$ (a_i times) or by adapting the ternary relation $Mult$. This shows that all operations to construct F can be realized using finite-domain arithmetics on BDDs. Actually, there is a direct option for constructing the BDD of a linear function directly from the coefficients in $O(\sum_{i=0}^{n} |a_i|)$ time and space.

Algorithm 7.5 displays the pseudo code for symbolic BFS incrementally improving an upper bound U on the solution cost. The algorithm applies symbolic BFS until the entire search space has been traversed and stores the current best solution. As before, state sets are represented in the form of BDDs. Additionally, the search frontier is reduced to those states that have a cost value of at most U. In case an intersection with the goal is found, the breadth-first exploration is suspended to construct a solution with the smallest f-value for states in the intersection. The cost gives a new upper bound U denoting the quality of the current best solution minus 1. After the minimal cost solution has been found, the breadth-first exploration is resumed.

Procedure Cost-Optimal-Symbolic-BFS
Input: State space problem with transition relation $Trans$ and cost relation F
Output: Cost-optimal solution path

$U \leftarrow \max_f$	;; Initialize bound U
$Closed(x) \leftarrow Open(x) \leftarrow \phi_{\{s\}}(x)$	;; Initialize search sets
$Intersect(x) \leftarrow \phi_{\{s\}}(x) \wedge \phi_T(x)$	;; Intersection of search frontiers
loop	;; Endless loop
$\quad Bound(value, x) \leftarrow F(value, x) \wedge \bigvee_{i=\min_f}^{U} (value = i)$	;; Omit states from frontier
$\quad$ **loop**	;; Until improvement has been made
$\quad\quad$ **if** $(Open(x) = false)$ **return** sol	;; Full state space seen
$\quad\quad Succ(x) \leftarrow \exists x \, (Trans(x, x') \wedge Open(x))[x \leftrightarrow x']$	;; Determine successor set
$\quad\quad Open(x) \leftarrow Succ(x) \wedge \neg Closed(x)$	;; Subtract state seen before
$\quad\quad Closed(x) \leftarrow Closed(x) \vee Succ(x)$	;; Update set of reachable states
$\quad\quad Intersect(x) \leftarrow Open(x) \wedge \phi_T(x)$	;; Search frontiers meet
$\quad\quad Eval(value, x) \leftarrow Intersect(x) \wedge Bound(value, x)$	;; Evaluate full solution cost
$\quad\quad$ **if** $(Eval(value, x) \neq false)$	;; Solution found
$\quad\quad\quad$ **for each** $i \in \{\min_f, \ldots, U\}$	;; Find best solution
$\quad\quad\quad\quad$ **if** $(F(value, x) \wedge (value = i) \wedge Eval(value, x) \neq false)$	;; (in discretization)
$\quad\quad\quad\quad\quad U \leftarrow i - 1$	;; Lower the bound
$\quad\quad\quad\quad\quad sol \leftarrow Construct(Eval(value, x))$	;; Generate the solution
$\quad\quad\quad\quad\quad$ **break**	;; Do not look for worse solutions

Algorithm 7.5

Cost-optimal symbolic BFS algorithm.

Theorem 7.3. *(Optimality and Complexity of Cost-Optimal Symbolic BFS) The solution constructed by* cost-optimal symbolic BFS *has minimum cost. The number of images is bounded by the maximum BFS level.*

Proof. The algorithm applies duplicate detection and traverses the entire state space. It generates each possible state exactly once. Eventually, the state with the minimal f-value will be found. Only those goal states are abandoned from the cost evaluation that have an f-value larger than or equal to the current best solution. The exploration terminates if all BFS levels have been generated. Thus, the number of images matches the maximum BFS-level. ∎

7.4.5 Symbolic Shortest Path Search

Before turning to the symbolic algorithms for directed search, we take a closer look at the bucket implementation of Dijkstra's SINGLE-SOURCE SHORTEST PATH algorithm for solving search problems with action costs.

Finite action costs are a natural search concept. In many applications, costs can only be positive integers (sometimes for fractional values it is also possible and beneficial to achieve this by rescaling). Since BDDs allow sets of states to be represented efficiently, the priority queue of a search problem with integer-valued cost function can be partitioned to a list of buckets. We assume that the highest action cost and f-value are bounded by some constant.

The priority queue of a search problem with an integer-valued cost function can be implemented as a set of pairs, of which the first component is the f-value and the second component is the x-value. In a functional representation pairs correspond to satisfying paths in a BDD $Open(f,x)$. The variables for the encoding of f can be assigned smaller indices than the variables encoding x, since, aside from the potential to generate smaller BDDs, this allows an intuitive understanding of the BDDs and its association with the priority queue. Figure 7.11 (left) illustrates the representation of the priority queue in the form of BDDs.

The symbolic version of Dijkstra's algorithm can be implemented as shown in Algorithm 7.6. For the sake of simplicity, the algorithm has no *Closed* list, so that it can contain identical states with different f-values. (As with symbolic breadth-first tree search, duplicate elimination is not difficult to add, but may induce additional complexity to the BDD.)

The working of the algorithm is as follows. The BDD *Open* is set to the representation of the start state with f-value 0. Unless we establish a goal state, in each iteration we extract *all* states with minimum f-value f_{min}. The easiest option to find the next value of f_{min} is to test all internal values f starting from the last value of f_{min} for intersection with *Open*. A more efficient option is to exploit the BDD structure in case the f-variables are encoded on top of the BDD.

Given f_{min}, next we determine the successor set and update the priority queue. The BDD *Min* of all states in the priority queue with value f_{min} is extracted, resulting in the BDD *Rest* of the remaining set of states. If no goal state is found, the variables in *Min* (the transition relation $Trans(w,x',x)$ is applied to) determine the BDD for the set of successor states. To calculate $f = f_{min} + w$ and to attach new f-values to this set, we store the old f-value f_{min}. Finally, the BDD *Open* for the next iteration is obtained by the disjunction of the successor set with the remaining queue.

Theorem 7.4. *(Optimality of Symbolic Shortest Path Search) For action weights $w \in \{1, \ldots, C\}$, the solution computed by the symbolic shortest path search algorithm is optimal.*

Procedure Symbolic-Shortest-Path-Search
Input: State space problem with weighted transition relation *Trans*
Output: Optimal solution path

$Open(f,x) \leftarrow (f=0) \wedge \phi_{\{s\}}(x)$;; Initialize search frontier
loop   ;; Endless loop
  $f_{min} \leftarrow \min\{f \mid \exists f'.f = f' \wedge Open(f',x) \neq false\}$;; Find minimum
  $Min(x) \leftarrow \exists f(Open(f,x) \wedge f = f_{min})$;; Extract minimum bucket
  if $(Min(x) \wedge \phi_T(x) \neq false)$;; If goal has been found
    return $Construct(Min(x) \wedge \phi_T(x))$;; Generate solution
  $Rest(f,x) \leftarrow Open(f,x) \wedge \neg Min(x)$;; Delete set of states from queue
  $Succ(f,x) \leftarrow \exists x,f',w$;; Cost-assigned image
    $(Min(x) \wedge Trans(w,x,x') \wedge Add(f',w,f) \wedge f' = f_{min})[x \leftrightarrow x']$;; ... of *Min* bucket
  $Open(f,x) \leftarrow Rest(f,x) \vee Succ(f,x)$;; Include successor set to frontier
                                                                                           ;; Until goal has been found

Algorithm 7.6

Dijkstra's algorithm implemented with BDDs.

Proof. The algorithm mimics the SINGLE-SOURCE SHORTEST PATH algorithm of Dijkstra on a 1-LEVEL BUCKET structure (see Ch. 3). Eventually, the state with the minimum f-value is found. As f is monotonically increasing, the first goal reached has optimal cost. ∎

Theorem 7.5. *(Complexity of Symbolic Shortest Path Search) For positive transition weights $w \in \{1,\ldots,C\}$, the number of iterations (BDD images) in the symbolic shortest path search algorithm is $O(f^*)$, where f^* is the optimal solution cost.*

Proof. The number of iterations (BDD images) is dependent on the number of buckets that are considered during the exploration. Since the edge weight is a positive integer, we have at most $O(f^*)$ iterations, where f^* is the optimal solution cost. ∎

7.5 LIMITS AND POSSIBILITIES OF BDDS

To uncover the causes for good and bad BDD performance we aim at lower and upper bounds for BDD growth in various domains.

7.5.1 Exponential Lower Bound

We first consider permutation games on $(0,\ldots,N-1)$, such as the (n^2-1)-PUZZLE, where $N = n^2$. The characteristic function f_N of all permutations on $(0,\ldots,N-1)$ has $N\lceil \lg N \rceil$ binary state variables and evaluates to *true*, if every block of $\lceil \lg N \rceil$ variables corresponds to the binary representation of an integer and every satisfying path of N integers is a permutation.

It is known that the BDD for f_N needs more than $\lfloor \sqrt{2^N} \rfloor$ BDD nodes for any variable ordering. This suggests that permutation games are hard for BDD exploration.

```
(define (domain gripper)
   (:predicates (room ?r) (ball ?b) (gripper ?g)
                (at-robby ?r) (at ?b ?r) (free ?g) (carry ?o ?g))
   (:action move
      :parameters  (?from ?to)
      :precondition (and  (room ?from) (room ?to) (at-robby ?from))
      :effect (and  (at-robby ?to) (not (at-robby ?from))))
   (:action pick
      :parameters (?obj ?room ?gripper)
      :precondition  (and  (ball ?obj) (room ?room) (gripper ?gripper)
     (at ?obj ?room) (at-robby ?room) (free ?gripper))
      :effect (and (carry ?obj ?gripper)
                   (not (at ?obj ?room)) (not (free ?gripper))))
   (:action drop
      :parameters  (?obj  ?room ?gripper)
      :precondition  (and  (ball ?obj) (room ?room) (gripper ?gripper)
     (carry ?obj ?gripper) (at-robby ?room))
      :effect (and (at ?obj ?room) (free ?gripper)
                   (not (carry ?obj ?gripper)))))
```

FIGURE 7.9

The STRIPS planning domain description for GRIPPER.

7.5.2 Polynomial Upper Bound

In other state spaces, we obtain an exponential gain using BDDs. Let us consider a simple planning domain, called GRIPPER. The domain description is provided in Figure 7.9. There is one robot to transport $2k = n$ balls from one room A to another room B. The robot has two grippers to pick up and put down a ball.

It is not difficult to observe that the state space grows exponentially. Since we have $2^n = \sum_{i=0}^n \binom{n}{i} \le n\binom{n}{k}$, the number of all states with k balls in one room is $\binom{n}{k} \ge 2^n/n$. The precise number of all reachable states is $S_n = 2^{n+1} + n2^{n+1} + n(n-1)2^{n-1}$, where $S_n^0 = 2^{n+1}$ corresponds to the number of all states with no ball in a gripper.

The basic observation is that all states with an even number of balls in each room (apart from the two states with all balls in the same room and the robot in the other one) are part of an optimal plan. For larger values of n, therefore, heuristic search planners even with a constant error of only 1 are doomed to fail.

The robot's cycle for delivering two balls from one room to the other in any optimal plan has length six (picking up the two balls, moving from one room to the other, putting down the two balls, and moving back), such that every sixth BFS layer contains the states on an optimal plan with no ball in a gripper. Yet there are still exponentially many of these states, namely, $S_n^0 - 2$.

Theorem 7.6. (*Exponential Representation Gap for* GRIPPER) *There is a binary state encoding and an associated variable ordering, in which the BDD size for the characteristic function of the states on any optimal path in the breadth-first exploration of* GRIPPER *is polynomial in n.*

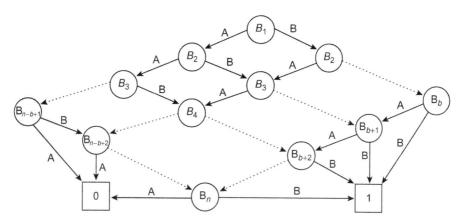

FIGURE 7.10

BDD structure for representing at least b balls in room B in the GRIPPER domain. Nodes for variables are labeled by the balls in question: The zero edge labeled with A denotes that the ball is located in room A, and the one edge labeled with B denotes that the ball is located in room B.

Proof. To encode states in GRIPPER, $1 + 2 \cdot \lceil \lg(n+1) \rceil + 2n$ bits are required: one for the location of the robot, $\lceil \lg(n+1) \rceil$ for each of the grippers to denote which ball it currently carries, and 2 for the location of each ball. According to BFS, we divide the set of states on an optimal path into levels l, $0 \leq l \leq 6k - 1$. If both grippers are empty and the robot is in the right room, all possible states with $b = 2d$ balls in the right room have to be represented, which is available using $O(bn)$ BDD nodes. See Figure 7.10 for a BDD representing at least b balls in room B. The BDD for representing exactly b balls in room B is a slight extension and includes an additional tail of $O(n)$ nodes (see Exercises). The number of choices with one or two balls in the gripper that are addressed in the $2 \lceil \lg(n+1) \rceil$ variables is bounded by $n + n^2 = O(n^2)$, such that intermediate levels may lead to at most a quadratic growth. Hence, each layer restricted to the states on the optimal plan contains less than $O(n^2 \cdot dn) = O(dn^3) = O(n^4)$ BDD nodes in total. Accumulating the numbers along the path, of which the size is linear in n, we arrive at less than $O(n^5)$ BDD nodes needed for the entire exploration. ∎

We next look at the SOKOBAN domain, where we observe another exponential gap between explicit-state and symbolic representation.

As we have $\binom{n}{k} \leq \left(\frac{n}{k}\right)^k$, the number of all reachable states is clearly exponential.

Theorem 7.7. *(Exponential Representation Gap for* SOKOBAN*) If all $\binom{n}{k} \cdot (n-k)$ configurations with k balls in a maze of n cells in* SOKOBAN *are reachable, there is a binary state encoding and an associated variable ordering, in which the BDD size for the characteristic function of all reachable states in* SOKOBAN *is polynomial in n.*

Proof. To encode states in SOKOBAN, $2n$ bits are required; that is, 2 bits for each cell (stone/player/none). If we were to omit the player, we would observe a similar pattern to the one in Figure 7.10, where the left branch would denote an empty cell and the right branch a stone, leaving a BDD of $O(nk)$ nodes. Integrating the player results in a second BDD of size $O(nk)$ with links from the first to the second. Therefore, the complexity for representing all reachable SOKOBAN positions requires a polynomial number of BDD nodes. ∎

7.6 SYMBOLIC HEURISTIC SEARCH

We have seen that in *heuristic search*, with every state in the search space we associate a lower-bound estimate h on the optimal solutions cost. Further, at least for consistent heuristics by reweighting the edges, the algorithm of A* reduces to Dijkstra's algorithm. The rank of a node is the combined value $f = g + h$ of the generating path length g and the estimate h.

7.6.1 Symbolic A*

A* can be cast as a variant of Dijkstra's algorithm with (consistent) heuristics. Subsequently, in the symbolic version of A* the relational product algorithm determines all successors of the set of states with minimum f-value in one image operation. It remains to determine their f-values. For the dequeued state u we have $f(u) = g(u) + h(u)$. Since we can access the f-value, but usually not the g-value, the new f-value of a successor v has to be calculated in the following way:

$$f(v) = g(v) + h(v) = g(u) + w(u,v) + h(v) = f(u) + w(u,v) - h(u) + h(v).$$

The estimator *Heur* can be seen as a relation of tuples $(value, x)$, which is *true* if and only if the heuristic value of the states represented by x is equal to a number represented by *value*. We assume that the heuristic relation *Heur* can be represented as a BDD for the entire problem space (see Fig. 7.11, right).

There are different options to determine *Heur*. One approach tries to implement the function directly from its specification (see Exercises for an implementation of the Manhattan distance heuristic in the $(n^2 - 1)$-PUZZLE). Another option simulates explicit-pattern databases (as introduced in Ch. 4) that *Heur* is the outcome of a symbolic backward BFS or Dijkstra exploration in abstract space. The implementation of symbolic A* is shown in Algorithm 7.7. Since all successor states are reinserted in the queue we expand the search tree in best-first manner.

The BDD arithmetics for computing the relation $Formula(h, h', w, f', f)$ based on the old and new heuristic values (h and h', respectively) and the old and new costs (f' and f, respectively) are involved:

$$Formula(h, h', w, f', f) = \exists\, t_1, t_2 \; Add(t_1, h, f') \;\wedge\; Add(t_1, w, t_2) \;\wedge\; Add(h', t_2, f).$$

Optimality and completeness of symbolic A* are inherited from the fact that given an admissible heuristic, explicit-state A* will find an optimal solution.

By pushing variables inside the calculation of *Succ* can be simplified to

$$\exists w, x' (Min(x) \wedge Trans(w, x, x') \wedge \exists h(Heur(h, x) \wedge \exists h'(Heur(h', x') \wedge Formula(h, h', w, f_{\min}, f)))).$$

Let us consider our SLIDING-TOKEN PUZZLE example once again. The BDD for the estimate h is depicted in Figure 7.12, where the estimate is set to 1 for states 0 and 1, and set to 0 for states 3 and 4.

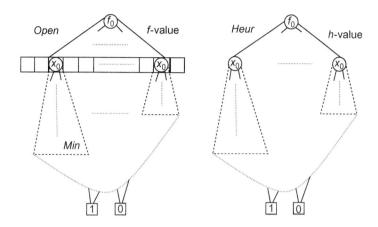

FIGURE 7.11

Schematic view on BDD representations of the priority queue (left) and the estimate relation (right). Variables encoding the f-value (left) and h-value (right) in finite domain are queried at the top layers of the BDDs and naturally partition the state sets queried in the bottom layers of the BDD. On the left, an alternative bucket representation of the priority queue in the form of an array of BDDs for the states is indicated. The state sets with the minimum value can be found by locating the first nonempty bucket (*Min*) corresponding to the left-most branch to a state variable node in the BDD.

Procedure Symbolic-A*
Input: State space problem with weighted transition *Trans* and estimate relation *Heur*
Output: Optimal solution path

$Open(f,x) \leftarrow Heur(f,x) \wedge \phi_{\{s\}}(x)$	;; Initialize and evaluate search frontier
loop	;; Endless loop
$\quad f_{min} \leftarrow \min\{f \mid \exists f'. f = f' \wedge Open(f',x) \neq false\}$	;; Compute minimum priority
$\quad Min(x) \leftarrow \exists f(Open(f,x) \wedge f = f_{min})$	;; Determine according to state set
$\quad$ **if** $(Min(x) \wedge \phi_T(x) \neq false)$	;; If goal has been found
$\quad\quad$ **return** $Construct(Min(x) \wedge \phi_T(x))$	;; Generate solution
$\quad Rest(f,x) \leftarrow Open(x) \wedge \neg Min(x)$	;; Extract set from queue
$\quad Succ(f,x) \leftarrow \exists w,x,h,h',f' Min(x) \wedge Trans(w,x,x') \wedge$	;; Image with estimates
$\quad\quad Heur(h,x) \wedge Heur(h',x') \wedge Formula(h,h',w,f',f) \wedge f' = f_{min}[x \leftrightarrow x']$	
$\quad Open(f,x) \leftarrow Rest(f,x) \vee Succ(f,x)$	;; Insert result in priority queue

Algorithm 7.7

A* implemented with BDDs.

The minimum f-value is 1. Assuming that f^* will be bounded by 4 we need only *two* variables, f_0 and f_1, to encode f (by adding 1 to the binary encoded value).

After the initialization step, the priority queue *Open* is filled with the initial state represented by the term $\neg x_0 \neg x_1$. The h-value is 1 and so is the initial f-value (represented by $(00)_2$). There is only one successor to the initial state, namely $\neg x_0 x_1$, which has an h-value of 1 and, therefore, an f-value of $2 \equiv (01)_2$. Applying *Trans* to the resulting BDD-we obtain the combined characteristic function of the states with index 0 and 2. Their h-values differ by 1. Therefore, the term $x_0 \neg x_1$ is assigned to an f-value of $2 \equiv (01)_2$ and $\neg x_0 \neg x_1$ is assigned to $3 \equiv (10)_2$ (the status of the priority queue is depicted in Fig. 7.13, left). In the next iteration we extract $x_0 \neg x_1$ with value 2 and find the successor set, which in this case consists of $1 = (01)_2$ and $3 = (11)_2$. By combining the characteristic function x_1 with the estimate h we split the BDD of x_1 into two parts, since $x_0 x_1$ relates to an h-value 0, whereas $\neg x_0 x_1$ relates to 1 (the resulting priority queue is shown in Fig. 7.13, right). Since *Min* now has a nonempty intersection with the characteristic function of the goal, we have found a solution. The represented state sets and their binary encoding are shown in Table 7.5. The minimum f-value is 3, as expected.

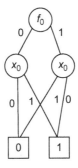

FIGURE 7.12

The BDD for the heuristic function for the SLIDING-TOKEN PUZZLE. The variables on top represent the heuristic estimate value, which is 1 for the two states to the left of the bar, and 0 for the two states to the right of the bar. To distinguish between these two state sets, variable x_1 does not need to be queried at all.

Table 7.5 State sets for the four iterations of symbolic A* (states that belong to the state set *Min* shown in bold).

Step	*Open* Set	Binary Codes	Boolean Formula
0	$\{(\mathbf{1},\mathbf{0})\}$	$\{(\mathbf{00},\mathbf{00})\}$	$\neg f_0 \neg f_1 \neg x_0 \neg x_1$
1	$\{(\mathbf{2},\mathbf{1})\}$	$\{(\mathbf{01},\mathbf{01})\}$	$\neg f_0 f_1 \neg x_0 x_1$
2	$\{(3,0),(\mathbf{2},\mathbf{2})\}$	$\{(10,00),(\mathbf{01},\mathbf{10})\}$	$(f_0 \neg f_1 \neg x_0 \neg x_1) \vee$ $(\neg f_0 f_1 x_0 \neg x_1)$
3	$\{(\mathbf{3},\mathbf{0}),(4,1),(\mathbf{3},\mathbf{3})\}$	$\{(\mathbf{10},\mathbf{00}),(11,01),(\mathbf{10},\mathbf{11})\}$	$(f_0 \neg f_1 \neg x_0 \neg x_1) \vee$ $(f_0 f_1 \neg x_0 x_1) \vee$ $(f_0 \neg f_1 x_0 x_1)$

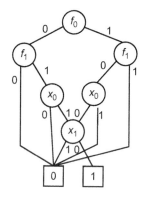 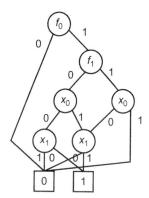

FIGURE 7.13

The priority queue *Open* after two (left) and after three (right) exploration steps in symbolic A* search for the SLIDING-TOKEN PUZZLE example. Variables encoding the f-value are encoded by f_0 and f_1. Variables encoding the state are x_0 and x_1. After two steps the BDD for function $(f_0 \neg f_1 \neg x_0 \neg x_1) \vee (\neg f_0 f_1 x_0 \neg x_1)$ is shown and after three steps the BDD for function $(f_0 \neg f_1 \neg x_0 \neg x_1) \vee (f_0 f_1 \neg x_0 x_1) \vee (f_0 \neg f_1 x_0 x_1)$ is shown (the represented sets are explicified in Table 7.5).

To exemplify the effectiveness of the approach, we consider the SOKOBAN problem. To compute the step-optimal solution for the problem of Figure 1.14 symbolic A* has been invoked with a heuristic that counts the number of balls not on a goal position. Symbolic BFS finds the optimal solution with a peak BDD of 250,000 nodes (representing 61 million states) in 230 iterations, and symbolic A* leads to 419 iterations and to a peak BDD of 68,000 nodes (representing 4.3 million states).

7.6.2 Bucket Implementation

Symbolic A* applies to unweighted graphs or graphs with integer action costs. Its functional implementation can be applied even to infinite state spaces by using more expressive representation formalisms than BDDs (like automata for state sets induced by linear constraints over the integers).

For small values of C and a maximal h-value $\max_h$, it is possible to avoid arithmetic computations with BDDs. We assume unit action costs and that the heuristic relation is partitioned into $Heur[0](x), \ldots, Heur[\max_h](x)$, with

$$Heur(value, x) = \bigvee_{i=0}^{\max_h} (value = i) \wedge Heur[i](x).$$

We use a two-dimensional bucket layout for the BDDs as shown in Figure 7.14. The advantages are two-fold. First, the state sets to be expanded next are generally smaller, and the hope is that the BDD representation is as well. Second, given the bucket by which a state set is addressed, each state set already has both the g-value and the h-value attached to it, and the arithmetic computations that were needed to compute the f-values for the set of successors are no longer needed. The refined pseudo-code implementation for symbolic A* is shown in Algorithm 7.8.

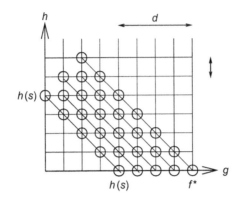

FIGURE 7.14

The number of iterations in symbolic A*.

Procedure Symbolic-A*

Input: State space problem with transition relation *Trans* and estimate relation *Heur*

Output: Optimal solution path

$Open[0, h(s)](x) \leftarrow \phi_{\{s\}}(x)$	;; Initialize frontier bucket
$f_{min} \leftarrow h(s)$	;; Initial minimum
while $(f_{min} \neq \infty)$	;; Search frontier not empty
$\quad g \leftarrow \min\{i \mid Open[i, f_{min} - i](x) \neq false\}$	;; Determine minimum depth
$\quad$ **while** $(g \leq f_{min})$	;; As far as merit not exceeded
$\quad\quad Min(x) \leftarrow Open[g, f_{min} - g](x)$	;; Determine according to state set
$\quad\quad$ **if** $(Min(x) \wedge \phi_T(x) \neq false)$	;; Goal found
$\quad\quad\quad$ **return** $Construct(Min(x) \wedge \phi_T(x))$	;; Generate solution
$\quad\quad Succ(x) \leftarrow \exists x\, Min(x) \wedge Trans(x, x')[x \leftrightarrow x']$	;; Compute image
$\quad\quad$ **for each** $h \in \{0, \dots, \max_h\}$	;; Traverse all possible h values
$\quad\quad\quad Open[g+1, h](x) \leftarrow Open[g+1, h](x) \vee Succ(x) \wedge Heur[h](x)$	;; Distribute
$\quad\quad g \leftarrow g+1$	;; Increase depth
$\quad f_{min} \leftarrow \min\{i+j > f_{min} \mid Open[i, j](x) \neq false\} \cup \{\infty\}$	;; Minimum f-value

Algorithm 7.8

Symbolic A* in a bucket implementation.

Theorem 7.8. *(Optimality of Symbolic A*) Given a unit cost problem graph and a consistent heuristic, the solution cost computed by symbolic A* is optimal.*

Proof. The algorithm mimics the execution of the reweighted version of Dijkstra's algorithm on a 1-LEVEL BUCKET structure. Eventually, the state of the minimum f-value will be encountered. Since the reweighted action costs are nonnegative, f is monotonic increasing. Hence, the first encountered goal state has optimal cost. ∎

For an optimal heuristic, one that estimates the shortest path distance exactly, we have at most $h(s) = f^*$ iterations in symbolic A*. On the other hand, if the heuristic is equivalent to the zero function (breadth-first search), we need f^* iterations, too.

Theorem 7.9. *(Complexity Symbolic A*) Given a unit cost problem graph and a consistent heuristic the worst-case number of iterations (BDD operations) in symbolic A* is $O((f^*)^2)$, with f^* being the optimal solution length.*

Proof. There are at most $f^* + 1$ different h-values and at most $f^* + 1$ different g-values that are encountered during the search process. Consequently, for each period between two successive increases of the minimum f-value, we have at most f^* iterations. Consider Figure 7.14, in which the g-values are plotted with respect to the h-value, such that nodes with the same g-value and h-value appear on the diagonals $f = g + h$. Each bucket is expanded at most once. All iterations (marked by a circle) are located on or below the (f^*)-diagonal, so that $O((f^*)^2)$ is an upper bound on the number of iterations. ∎

For heuristics that are not consistent, we cannot terminate at the first goal that we encounter (see Exercises). One solution is to constrain the g-value to be less than the current best solution cost value f.

7.6.3 Symbolic Best-First Search

A variant of the symbolic execution of A*, called *symbolic greedy best-first search*, is obtained by ordering the priority queue *Open* only according to the h-values. In this case the calculation of the successor relation simplifies to $\exists x' \ (Min(x') \wedge Trans(x',x) \wedge Heur(f,x))$ as shown in the pseudo code of Algorithm 7.9. The old f-values are ignored.

Unfortunately, even for admissible heuristics the algorithm is not optimal. The hope is that in huge problem spaces the estimate is good enough to lead the solver into a promising goal direction. Therefore, especially inadmissible heuristics can support this aim.

Procedure Symbolic-Greedy-Best-First-Search
Input: State space problem with transition *Trans* and estimate relation *Heur*
Output: Optimal solution path

$Open(x) \leftarrow Heur(f,x) \wedge \phi_{\{s\}}(x)$;; Insert and evaluate initial state
do   ;; Repeat-until loop
  $f_{min} \leftarrow \min\{f \mid f \wedge Open(f,x) \neq false\}$;; Determine minimum priority
  $Min(x) \leftarrow \exists f \ Open(f,x) \wedge f = f_{min}$;; Compute corresponding state set
  $Rest(f,x) \leftarrow Open(f,x) \wedge \neg Min(x)$;; Extract state set
  $Succ(f,x) \leftarrow \exists x' Min(x) \wedge Trans(x,x') \wedge Heur(f,x')[x \leftrightarrow x']$;; Compute image
  $Open(f,x) \leftarrow Rest(f,x) \vee Succ(f,x)$;; Determine new frontier list
while $(Open(f,x) \wedge \phi_T(x) \equiv false)$;; Until goal found
return $Construct(Open(f,x) \wedge \phi_T(x))$;; Generate solution

Algorithm 7.9

Greedy best-first search implemented with BDDs.

On solution paths the heuristic values eventually decrease. Hence, *symbolic greedy best-first search* profits from the fact that the most promising states are in the front of the priority queue and are explored first. This compares to symbolic A* in which the f-value on the solution paths eventually increases.

In between A* and *greedy best-first search*, there are different best-first algorithms. For example, scaling the heuristic estimate similar to the weighted A* algorithm is as follows. If $Heur(f,x)$ denotes the heuristic relation a weight factor λ can be introduced by constructing $Heur(\lambda \cdot h,x)$.

7.6.4 Symbolic Breadth-First Branch-and-Bound

Even for symbolic search, memory consumption remains a critical resource for a successful exploration. This motivates a breadth-first instead of a best-first traversal of the search space (as illustrated in the context of breadth-first heuristic search in Ch. 6).

Symbolic breadth-first branch-and-bound generates the search tree in breadth-first instead of best-first order. The core search routine is invoked with a bound U on the optimal solution length, which can be provided by the user or automatically inferred by nonoptimal search algorithms like beam search. Using the bound U, buckets are neglected from the search if their $(g+h)$-value is larger than U.

Algorithm 7.10 shows an implementation of this strategy for symbolic search. The algorithm traverses the matrix of buckets (g,h) with increasing depth g, where each breadth-first level is pruned by the bound U.

In the exposition of the strategy again we assume a unit cost problem graph in the input and the implementation of a construction algorithm for extracting the solution path (e.g., using a divide-and-conquer approach by keeping an additional relay layer in main memory). For the sake of clarity, we have also omitted symbolic duplicate elimination.

If the graph has been fully explored without generating any solution, we know that there is no solution of length $\leq U$. Hence, breadth-first branch-and-bound returns the optimal solution, if the value U is chosen minimally in providing a solution. As a consequence, *breadth-first iterative-deepening A** operating with an increasing threshold U is optimal.

Procedure Symbolic-Breadth-First-Branch-and-Bound
Input: State space problem with transition *Trans* and estimate relation *Heur*, bound U
Output: Solution path

$Open[0,h(s)](x) \leftarrow \phi_{\{s\}}(x)$;; Initialize frontier bucket
for each $g \in \{0,\ldots,U\}$;; Traverse state set breadth-first
    for each $h \in \{0,\ldots,U-g\}$;; Prune h-values that are out of bounds
        $Min(x) \leftarrow Open[g,h](x)$;; Select state set
        if $(Min(x) \wedge \phi_T(x) \neq false)$;; Goal found
           return $Construct(Min(x) \wedge \phi_T(x))$;; Generate solution
        $Succ(x) \leftarrow \exists x\ Min(x) \wedge Trans(x,x')[x \leftrightarrow x']$;; Compute image
        for each $h' \in \{0,\ldots,U-g-1\}$;; Distribute according to possible h-values
           $Open[g+1,h'](x) \leftarrow Open[g+1,h'](x) \vee \exists h(Succ(x) \wedge Heur[f](x) \wedge f = h')$

Algorithm 7.10

Symbolic breadth-first branch-and-bound with buckets.

If the bound to solution length U provided to the algorithm is minimal, we can also expect time and memory savings with regard to symbolic A* search, since states that exceed the given bound are neither generated nor stored. If the bound, however, is not optimal, the iterative-deepening algorithm may explore more states than symbolic A*, but retain the advantage in memory.

Theorem 7.10. *(Complexity of Symbolic Breadth-First Branch-and-Bound) Provided with the optimal cost threshold $U = f^*$, symbolic breadth-first branch-and-bound (without duplicate elimination) computes the optimal solution in at most $O((f^*)^2)$ image operations.*

Proof. If $U = f^*$, the buckets considered with a $(g + h)$-value smaller than or equal to f^* are the same as in symbolic A*, this algorithm also considers the buckets on the diagonals with rising g-value. Subsequently, we obtain the same number of images. ∎

In search practice, the algorithm shows some memory advantages. In an instance of the FIFTEEN-PUZZLE for which explicit-state A* consumes 1.17 gigabytes of main memory, and *breadth-first heuristic search* consumes 732 megabytes, symbolic A* consumes 820 megabytes, and symbolic heuristic (branch-and-bound) search consumes 387 megabytes.

As said, finding the optimal cost threshold can be involved and the iterative computation is more time consuming than applying A* search. Moreover, symbolic A* may also be implemented with a *delayed expansion* strategy. Consider the case of the $(n^2 - 1)$-PUZZLE with Manhattan Distance heuristic, where each bucket is expanded twice for each f-value. In the first pass, only the successors on the active diagonal are generated, leaving out the generation of the successors on the $(f + 2)$-diagonal. In the second pass, the remaining successors on the $(f + 2)$-diagonal are generated. We can avoid computing the estimate twice, since all successor states that do not belong to the bucket $(g + 1, h - 1)$ belong to the bucket $(g + 1, h + 1)$. In the second pass we can therefore generate all successors and subtract bucket $(g + 1, h - 1)$ from the result. The complexity of this strategy decreases from exploring $E = \{(u, v) \mid v \in Succ(u) \ \wedge \ f(u) \leq f^*\}$ edges to exploring $E' = \{(u, v) \mid v \in Succ(u) \ \wedge \ f(v) \leq f^*\}$. Hence, expanding each state twice compensates for a large number of generated nodes above the f^*-diagonal that are not stored in the first pass.

7.7 *REFINEMENTS

Besides *forward set simplification* there are several improvement tricks that can be played to improve the performance of the BDD exploration.

7.7.1 Improving the BDD Size

Any set smaller than the successor set *Succ* and larger than the successor set *Succ* with simplified set *Closed* of all states reached already will be a valid choice for the frontier *Open* in the next iteration.

In the Shannon-expansion of a Boolean function f with respect to another function g, defined by $f = (g \wedge f_g) \vee (\neg g \wedge f_{\neg g})$, this determines f_g and $f_{\neg g}$ at the position $(x_1, \ldots, x_n)$ with $g(x_1, \ldots, x_n) = 1$ and $\neg g(x_1, \ldots, x_n) = 1$. However, if $g(x_1, \ldots, x_n) = 0$ or $\neg g(x_1, \ldots, x_n) = 0$ we have some flexibility. Therefore, we may choose a set that minimizes the BDD representation instead of minimizing the set of represented states. This is the idea of the *restrict operator* $\Downarrow$, which itself is a refinement to the *constrain operator* $\downarrow$. Since both operators are dependent of the ordering, we assume the ordering π to be the trivial permutation. We define the distance $|a - b|$ of two Boolean vectors a and b of length n by the sum of $|a_i - b_i| 2^{n-i}$ for $i \in \{1, \ldots, n\}$. The *constrain operator* $f \downarrow g$ of two Boolean functions f and

g evaluated at a vector a is then determined as $f(a)$ if $g(a) = 1$, and as $f(b)$ if $g(a) = 0$, $g(b) = 1$, and $|a - b|$ is minimum. The *restrict operator* $f \Downarrow g$ now incorporates the fact that for the function $h = \exists x_i\, g$ we have $g \wedge f_g = g \wedge f_h$. Without going into more details we denote that such optimizing operators are available in several BDD packages.

7.7.2 Partitioning

The image *Succ* of the state set *Open* with respect to the transition relation *Trans* has been computed as $Succ(x') = \exists x\, (Trans(x,x') \wedge Open(x))$. In this image, $Trans(x',x)$ is assumed to be monolithic; that is, represented as one big relation. For several domains, constructing such a transition relation prior to the search consumes huge amounts of the available computational resources. Fortunately, it is not required to build *Trans* explicitly. Hence, we can keep it partitioned, keeping in mind that $Trans = \bigvee_{a \in A} Trans_a$ for each individual transition relation $Trans_a$ and each action $a \in A$.

The image now reads as

$$Succ(x') = \exists x \left(\bigvee_{a \in A} Trans_a(x,x') \wedge Open(x) \right) = \bigvee_{a \in A} \left(\exists x\, (Trans_a(x,x') \wedge Open(x)) \right).$$

Therefore, the monolithic construction of *Trans* can be bypassed. The execution sequence of the disjunction has an effect on the overall running time. The recommended implementation organizes this partitioned image in the form of a balanced tree.

For heuristic functions that can be computed incrementally in a small integer range, there is the choice to group state pairs (u,v) that have a common heuristic difference d. This leads to a limited set of relations $Heur(u,v,d)$. One example is the Manhattan distance heuristic with $h(u) - h(v) \in \{-1,1\}$ for all successors v of u. For this case, we split the possible transition $Heur(x,x',d)$ into two parts $Heur_1(x,x',-1)$ and $Heur_2(x,x',+1)$. The successors of a frontier bucket *Open* with coordinates g and h can now be inserted either into bucket $[g+1,h-1]$ or into $[g+1,h+1]$.

Such incremental computations are exploited in images via *branching partitions*. The abstracted transition expressions are partitioned according to which variables they modify. Take, for example, the set of transitions $(0,0) \to (1,0)$, $(0,1) \to (1,1)$, and $(1,0) \to (0,0)$ that modify variable x_0, as well as $(0,0) \to (0,1)$ and $(1,1) \to (1,0)$ that modify variable x_1. Figure 7.15 depicts the transition system with solid arrows for one and dashed arrows for the other branching partition.

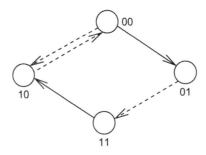

FIGURE 7.15

A transition system for branching partitions.

7.8 SYMBOLIC ALGORITHMS FOR EXPLICIT GRAPHS

Symbolic search approaches are also under theoretical and empirical investigation for classic graph algorithms, like TOPOLOGICAL SORTING, STRONGLY CONNECTED COMPONENT, SINGLE-SOURCE SHORTEST PATH, ALL-PAIRS SHORTEST PATH, and MAXIMUM FLOW. The difference from the earlier implicit setting is that the graph is now supposed to be an input of the algorithms. In other words, we are given a graph $G = (V, E, w)$ with source $s \in V$ represented in the form of a Boolean function or BDD $Graph : V \times V \times \{0, \ldots, C\} \rightarrow \{0, 1\}$, such that $Graph(u, v, w) = 1$ if and only if $(u, v) \in E$ and $0 \leq w(u, v) \leq C$ for all u and v.

For the encoding of the $|V|$ nodes, a bit string of length $k = \lceil \lg |V| \rceil$ is used, so that edges are represented by a relation with $2k$ variables. To perform an equality check $x = y$ in linear time an interleaved ordering $(x_{k-1}, y_{k-1}, \ldots, x_0, y_0)$ is preferred to a sequential ordering $(x_{k-1}, \ldots, x_0, y_{k-1}, \ldots, y_0)$.

Since the maximum accumulated weight on a path can be nC, the fixed size of the encoding of the weight function should be of size $O(\lg nC)$. It is well known that the BDD size for a Boolean function on l variables is bounded by $O(2^{l - \lg l}) = O(2^l / l)$ nodes, since given the reduced structure, the deepest levels *have* to converge to the two sinks. Using a binary encoding for V and weights in nd we have that the worst-case size of the BDD $Graph$ is of order $O(2^{2\lg n + \lg(nC)}/(2\lg n + \lg(nC))) = O(n^2 nC/\lg(nC)) = O((nC)^3/\lg(nC))$, and the hope is that many structured graphs have a sublinear BDD with size $o(nC)$. Since we cannot expect a gain for general graphs in the worst case, symbolic versions for explicit-graph algorithms are designed for sublinear runtime on special graphs and acceptable average-case behavior.

The symbolic SINGLE-SOURCE SHORTEST PATH algorithm maintains distance function $f : V \rightarrow \mathbb{N} \cup \{\infty\}$ in the form of a BDD $Dist$ such that $Dist(v, d) = 1$ if and only if $f(v) = d$. As we have discussed before, *Dijkstra's algorithm* considers nodes in the set *Closed* that already have a shortest path, selects nodes $u \in Open = V \setminus Closed$ with minimum $f(u)$, and adds u to *Closed*. Then it updates f for neighbors v of u according to $f(v) = \min\{f(v), f(u) + w(u, v)\}$. With BDD operations and n being the number of nodes in the graph, one iteration can be performed with $O(\lg(nC))$ BDD operations. Having at most $O(n)$ iterations, we have at most $O(n \lg(nC))$ BDD operations in total.

For the *Bellman-Ford algorithm* we *relax* every node $(u, v) \in E$ with $f(u) + w(u, v) < f(v)$ followed by an update of $f(v)$. This can be achieved using a BDD representation for *Relax* on the variables for u, v, and d that evaluates to true if $f(u) + w(u, v) = d < f(v)$. In other words, the relation *Relax* is defined by

$$\exists d_1, d_2 (f(u, d_1) \wedge Graph(u, v, d_2) \wedge d = d_1 + d_2) \wedge \neg (\exists d_1 (f(v, d_1) \wedge (d_1 \leq d)).$$

In total, we have $O(ne \lg(nC))$ BDD operations. The observation is that Dijkstra's algorithm leads to many fast operations, since the symbolic sets are fairly structured, whereas the algorithm of Bellman and Ford relaxes edges in parallel, which leads to fewer operations, but each operation is considerably slow. Experiments on random graphs show that even though Dijkstra needs space almost linear in the size of the BDD representation of the input graph, Bellman-Ford is usually faster.

7.9 SUMMARY

Symbolic search algorithms use a functional representation to express large but finite sets of states based on a finite-domain state encoding. We have chosen binary decision diagrams (BDDs) for the space-efficient unique representation of these functions. Other representations for Boolean functions (e.g., ALGEBRAIC DECISION DIAGRAMS (ADDs), AND INVERTER GRAPHS, and DECOMPOSABLE NEGATIONAL NORMAL FORMS (DNNFs)) do not change the exploration algorithms. Other symbolic data structures (e.g., *Presburger automata* and *difference bound matrices*) can cover infinite state sets, but follow similar algorithmic principles.

The advantages of symbolic search with BDDs for representing state sets include

- The exploitation of similarities within the state vector (due to path sharing in the graph structure of the BDD).
- The observation that a polynomially sized BDD may contain exponentially many paths.
- The uniqueness of the representation (which avoids any form of duplicate detection within the represented set).
- The functional[1] exploration of the state space (which avoids an intermediate uncompressed representation during the exploration).

During the exploration, a minimized binary variable encoding (e.g., $x_0 x_1 = (11)_2$ for $x = 3$) outperforms a unary encoding of predicates (e.g., $x_0 x_1 x_2 = (111)_1$ for $x = 3$). Using an appropriate relevance measure on the dependency of variables, good orderings can be obtained that lead to smaller BDDs. As an immediate consequence, precondition and effect variables should be interleaved. Permutation games are likely to be hard for BDDs, whereas games that are based on selecting indistinguishable objects appear to be easier.

Symbolic search relies on a transition relation that takes twice the number of state variables. The relation features both forward and backward search and can be extended to include action costs. If possible, the transition relation should be kept partitioned to keep the most expensive image operation tractable for larger problems. As enumerating all problem graph edges is out of reach for an implicit graph search, we have introduced partitions by individual actions (disjunctive partitioning), by abstract distance values (pattern database partitioning), by hash differences (branching partitioning), and by discrete action costs (cost value partitioning). Using a discretization into $f = (g, h)$ buckets, BDD arithmetics can be avoided.

Duplicate detection with respect to previous exploration sets is not necessarily an advantage, as it may complicate the BDD representation, but as a trade-off, we can detect a nonsolvable search problem due to a complete exploration. Even though it is difficult to formalize by the series of subproblem disjunctions, the number of represented states seems to have some influence on the hardness of computing the image of a state set. The number of previous levels that need to be maintained in the RAM to preserve full duplicate detection has been introduced in previous chapters (e.g., Ch. 6).

We have emphasized the similarities to other implicit graph search algorithms, and propose symbolic search variants for breadth-first search, Dijkstra search, and A*. The two *blind* search algorithms were used to construct pattern databases in suitable abstract spaces. The advantages with respect to explicit-state pattern databases have been made visible in time and space.

Symbolic heuristic and branch-and-bound search is an apparent integration of compaction (using BDDs) and pruning (using pruning by the f-cost). In difference to symbolic A*, symbolic versions

---

[1] Functionality already has a specific meaning like being nondestructive, with emphasis on functions as (first-order) objects. In contrast, here we refer to the representation of the sets in form of functions.

Table 7.6 Overview of symbolic search algorithms.

Name	Partition	DDD	Arith.	Guided	Optimal
Symbolic-BFTS (7.2)	✓	–	–	–	length
Symbolic-BFS (7.3)	✓	✓	–	–	length
Symbolic-SSSP (7.6)	✓	–	✓	–	weight
Symbolic-A* (7.7–7.8)	✓	–	✓/–	✓	weight
Symbolic-GBFS (7.9)	✓	–	–	✓	–
Symbolic-BFBnB (7.10)	✓	–	–	✓	weight
Cost-Opt. Symbolic-BFS (7.5)	✓	✓	✓	–	cost

of branch-and-bound take the solution bound as an additional input parameter. For problems with exponentially increasing state set sizes, iterative deepening applies.

Table 7.6 summarizes the presented approaches. We indicate if disjunctive transition function splitting can be used to compute the image. We also denote whether or not the provided implementations use a visited list for duplicate detection (DDD). The table also shows whether BDD arithmetic is used, if the search is guided by a heuristic relation, and if the result is optimal.

Additionally, we have seen an alternative application for symbolic search methods. We have discussed a symbolic algorithm for solving the SINGLE-SOURCE SHORTEST PATH problem in explicit but symbolically represented graphs.

7.10 EXERCISES

7.1 Extend the arithmetics on finite domains with BDDs to perform multiplication.
    1. Write a recursive Boolean formula for *Mult* based on the *add* relation.
    2. Provide the pseudo code for computing *Mult*.

7.2 Display the structure of the BDD for function $f = x_1 x_2 \vee x_3 x_4 \vee \cdots \vee x_{2n-1} x_{2n}$ with respect to the identity permutation ordering and the ordering $(1, 3, \ldots, 2n - 1, 2, 4, \ldots, 2n)$.

7.3 Show that the BDD for the hidden weighted bit function $HWB(x) = x_{|x|}$, where $|x|$ denotes the number of 1s in the assignment to x, has exponential size for all variable orderings and, therefore, does not suggest the use of BDDs.

7.4 In Algorithm 7.11 we have depicted the nontrivial pseudo-code implementation of the relational product algorithm that consists of an interleaved execution of conjunctions, deletion of variables, and disjunction of the subtrees due to the existential quantification. The procedure uses two hash tables: a *transposition table TT* to detect if nodes have already been constructed beforehand, and a *unique table UT* to apply the reduction rule of isomorphic subtrees.

1. The pseudo code extends the ordinary $\wedge$-synthesis operation in the additional call *if (x-index(m)) return Synthesis($s_0, s_1, \vee$)*. Illustrate this algorithm for conjoining two BDDs for the Boolean functions $f(x) = x_1 x_2$ and $g(x) = x_1 \vee x_3$ according to the variable order (x_1, x_2, x_3).
2. Illustrate the working of the algorithm in computing the relational product on $\exists x_2 (f \wedge g)$.

7.5 How many Boolean functions $\boldsymbol{B}^n \to \boldsymbol{B}$ do we have? Show that the number of (reduced-ordered) BDD representations is exactly the same.

7.6 Supply pseudo-code implementations for the main BDD operations.
1. *Substitution by constant* with integrated reduction rule application.
2. *SAT-count* backing up countervalues at internal nodes.

7.7 Give a 64-bit binary encoding for the FIFTEEN-PUZZLE.
1. Depict the characteristic function for the goal state in this encoding.
2. Explain how to compute the Manhattan distance function as a BDD in this encoding. You may start with sub-BDDs for each tile and combine the results using a relational product on temporary variables to connect them to build the overall sum.

Procedure RelationalProduct
Input: Two BDDs for $Trans(x, x')$ and $S(x)$
Output: BDD $G_{\exists x (Trans(x,x') \wedge S(x))}$

if ($Search(TT, root(G_{Trans}), root(G_S))$)	;; Node visited twice
return $Search(TT, root(G_{Trans}), root(G_S))$	;; Return found node
if ($sink_0(G_{Trans})$ **or** $sink_0(G_S)$) **return** $sink_0$	;; Return 0-sink
if ($sink_1(G_{Trans})$) **return** $sink_1$	;; Return 1-sink
if ($index(root(G_{Trans})) < index(root(G_S))$)	;; Variable index in G_{Trans} smaller
$s_0 \leftarrow RelationalProduct(left(G_{Trans}), G_S)$	;; Use 0-edge in G_{Trans}
$s_1 \leftarrow RelationalProduct(right(G_{Trans}), G_S)$	;; Use 1-edge in G_{Trans}
else if ($index(root(G_{Trans})) > index(root(G_S))$)	;; Variable index in G_S smaller
$s_0 \leftarrow RelationalProduct(G_{Trans}, left(G_S))$	;; Use 0-edge in G_S
$s_1 \leftarrow RelationalProduct(G_{Trans}, right(G_S))$	;; Use 1-edge in G_S
else	;; Indices in G_{Trans} and G_S are equal
$s_0 \leftarrow RelationalProduct(left(G_{Trans}), left(G_S))$	;; Use 0-edge in G_{Trans} and G_S
$s_1 \leftarrow RelationalProduct(right(G_{Trans}), right(G_S))$	;; Use 1-edge in G_{Trans} and G_S
$m \leftarrow \min\{index(top(G_{Trans})), index(top(G_S))\}$	;; Minimum index of G_{Trans} and G_S
if ($s_0 = s_1$) **return** s_0	;; Reduction rule 1
if ($Search(UT, s_0, s_1, m)$) **return** $Search(UT, s_0, s_1, m)$	;; Reduction rule 2
if (x-$index(m)$) **return** $Synthesis(s_0, s_1, \vee)$	;; If quantified, compute disjunction
return $new(s_0, s_1, m)$	;; Otherwise generate node and include it in TT and UT

Algorithm 7.11

Relational product algorithm to compute the image of a state set.

7.8   Provide two different encoding schemes for the level-1 SOKOBAN instance (see Ch. 1):
1. One that encodes each ball in binary based on the index of the maze layout.
2. One that encodes each ball using one bit.
3. Try to improve your encoding, for example, by omitting squares that can be excluded in finding a solution.
4. How many variables do you need?
5. Which one is the better encoding and how would you encode the man?

7.9   Provide an encoding for states and actions for STRIPS-type planning problems (see Ch. 1). Show how to combine the operator encodings to a monolithic transition relation. You may use one bit for each grounded proposition to obtain a state descriptor with $|AP|$ bits. Take care of propositions that are not mentioned in the initial or goal state.

7.10   Display the transition relation *Trans* for the SLIDING-TOKEN PUZZLE for an interleaved ordering.

7.11   Perform a partitioned BFS exploration based on the set of transitions $(0,0) \rightarrow (1,0)$, $(0,1) \rightarrow (1,1)$, and $(1,0) \rightarrow (0,0)$ that modify variable x_0, as well as $(0,0) \rightarrow (0,1)$ and $(1,1) \rightarrow (1,0)$ that modify variable x_1. The starting node is $(0,0)$.

7.12   Give a consistent and nonredundant rule set for the academic knowledge database verification example.
1. Display the BDDs for all instantiated rules.
2. Compute the BDD labels that are reached in a forward chaining algorithm.

7.13   Draw the BDD for representing exactly b balls in room B in the GRIPPER domain.

7.14   Prove that the expressions that are generated in a labeling approach in a knowledge-based system can require exponential size, with the exponent being in the depth of the rule set.

7.15   For admissible heuristics there might be successors that address a bucket below the f_{min} diagonal in symbolic A*. Moreover, for explicit search we have seen that always considering the smallest bucket as in A* may lead to an exponential number of reopenings.

   Show that for admissible estimates there exists an implementation of symbolic A* for which the number of images can be bounded by $O((f^*)^4)$.

7.16   The bucket-based implementation of Dijkstra's algorithm is as follows. In one iteration we first choose the bucket with the minimum f-value together with the BDD *Min* of all states in the priority queue having this value. Next, the partitioned transition relation $Trans_a$ with $c(a) = i$ is applied to determine the BDD for the subset of all successor states that can be reached with cost i. To attach new f-values to this set, we simply insert the result into bucket $f + i$. The pseudo code is shown in Algorithm 7.12.
1. Give a slightly more compact implementation for the priority queue using a 1-LEVEL BUCKET priority queue (see Ch. 3).
2. Integrate duplicate elimination to the algorithm.

7.17   In the extension of symbolic A* to discrete weights shown in Algorithm 7.13, we determine all successors of the set of states with the minimum f-value, current cost total g, and action cost i. It remains to determine their h-values by a lookup in a (multiple)-pattern database.

Procedure Symbolic-Shortest-Path-Search
Input: Discrete cost state space planning problem $P = (S,A,s,T)$ in symbolic form
  with $\phi_{\{s\}}(x)$, $\phi_T(x)$, and $Trans_a(x,x')$
Output: Optimal solution path

$Open[0](x) \leftarrow \phi_{\{s\}}(x)$
for each $f = 0,\ldots,f_{max}$;; Scan buckets
  $Min(x) \leftarrow Open[f](x)$;; Extract minimum state set
  if $(Min(x) \wedge \phi_T(x) \neq false)$;; If goal has been found
    return $Construct(Min(x) \wedge \phi_T(x))$;; Generate solution
    for all $i = 1,\ldots,C$;; Consider all action costs
      $Succ_i(x) \leftarrow \bigvee_{a \in A, w(a)=i}(\exists x'(Min(x) \wedge Trans_a(x,x'))[x \leftrightarrow x']$;; Image
      $Open[f+i](x) \leftarrow Open[f+i](x) \vee Succ_i(x)$;; Insert result in search frontier
return "Exploration completed"   ;; Full graph has been seen

Algorithm 7.12

Dijkstra's algorithm on buckets.

Procedure Symbolic-A*
Input: Discrete cost state space planning problem $P = (S,A,s,T)$ in symbolic form
  with $\phi_{\{s\}}(x)$, $\phi_T(x)$ and $Trans_a(x,x')$, shortest path locality L
Output: Optimal solution path

for all $h = 0,\ldots,h_{max}$
  $Open[0,h](x) \leftarrow Evaluate(s,h)$
for all $f = 0,\ldots,f_{max}$
  for all $g = 0,\ldots,f$
    $h \leftarrow f - g$
    for all $l = 1,\ldots,L$ with $g - l \geq 0$
      $Open[g,h](x) \leftarrow Open[g,h](x) \setminus Open[g-l,h](x)$
    $Min(x) \leftarrow Open[g,h](x)$
    if $(Min(x) \wedge \phi_T(x) \neq false)$
      return $Construct(Min(x) \wedge \phi_T(x))$
    for all $i = 1,\ldots,C$
      $Succ_i(x) \leftarrow \exists x \bigvee_{a \in A, w(a)=i}(Min(x) \wedge Trans_a(x,x'))[x \leftrightarrow x']$
      for each $h \in \{0,\ldots,h_{max}\}$
        $Open[g+i,h](x) \leftarrow Open[g+i,h](x) \vee Evaluate(Succ_i,h)$
return $false$

Algorithm 7.13

Shortest path A* algorithm on buckets.

1. Annotate the pseudo code with comments.
2. Perform the lookup and the combination of multiple-pattern databases $PDB_1,\dots,PDB_k$ entries on-the-fly (either by taking the sum or the max). Provide pseudo code.
3. Prove that for transition weights $w \in \{1,\dots,C\}$, and the algorithm finds the optimal solution with at most $O(C \cdot (f^*)^2)$ images, where f^* is the optimal solution cost.

7.18   Adapt the symbolic branch-and-bound algorithm to a cost-optimal search with a monotonic-increasing objective function $f = g + h$ represented as a BDD.

7.19   BDDs can serve alternative data structures for solving the SUBSET QUERY or CONTAINMENT QUERY problem (see Ch. 3). The characteristic function of each encountered pattern is taken into disjunct with the Boolean representation of the subset dictionary. In the example of SOKOBAN, if variable b_i denotes the existence of a ball at position i, we build the following Boolean function:

$$PatternStore \leftarrow \bigvee_{p \in D} \bigwedge_{i \in p} b_i.$$

1. Denote how to add a pattern into the pattern store and derive its time complexity for insertion.
2. Denote how to search a position for a contained pattern in the pattern store and derive the time complexity of the operation.

7.11 BIBLIOGRAPHIC NOTES

BDDs together with efficient operations on them have been made prominent by Bryant (1992), but binary decision diagrams go back to Lee (1959) and Akers (1978). Minato, Ishiura, and Yajima (1990) have shown how to store several BDDs in a joint structure. One of the best libraries is CUDD, maintained by Fabio Somenzi. Improved implementation issues are found in Yang et al. (1998). The authors have shown that the number of subproblem disjunctions is a good platform-independent measure of the work to be performed in computing the image. Lower bounds and some generalized BDD structures have been studied by Sieling (1994). A survey on theory and applications of BDDs has been given by Wegener (2000).

The use of BDDs for model checking, known as *symbolic model checking*, has been introduced by McMillan (1993). Implementations for symbolic model checkers based on BDDs include nuSMV by Cimatti, Giunchiglia, Giunchiglia, and Traverso (1997) and μcke by Biere (1997). Alternatives for symbolic exploration with BDDs are *bounded model checkers* introduced by Biere, Cimatti, Clarke, and Zhu (1999) that base on thresholded SAT solving as in the *Satplan* system by Kautz and Selman (1996). The rise of heuristic search procedures for explicit and symbolic model checking tools (e.g., by Edelkamp, Leue, and Lluch-Lafuente, 2004b, and by Qian and Nymeyer, 2004) indicate that synergies between the disciplines are many-fold.

Symbolic A* (alias BDDA*) has been invented by Edelkamp and Reffel (1998) in the context of solving the $(n^2 - 1)$-PUZZLE and SOKOBAN. The work estimated the maximum number of iterations.

The algorithm has been ported to hardware verification problems (Reffel and Edelkamp, 1999) and has been integrated in the presented planning context by Edelkamp and Helmert (2001). ADDA* developed by Hansen, Zhou, and Feng (2002) is an alternative implementation of symbolic A* with ADDs. Jensen, Bryant, and Veloso (2002) have refined the partitioning in symbolic A*. The authors also have exploited on a matrix representation of g-values and h-values. An extensive treatment, including applications in nondeterministic and adversarial domains, has been provided by Jensen (2003). Symbolic branch-and-bound search has been proposed by Jensen, Hansen, Richards, and Zhou (2006).

In an experimental study, Qian and Nymeyer (2003) indicated that for BDD exploration with heuristics with smaller range and inducing a simpler BDD structure, sometimes to speedup the overall search process better than more complex heuristics (having more involved BDDs). However, this has not been shown to be a general trend.

Different symbolic approaches are under theoretical and empirical investigation for classic graph algorithms. The used upper bound $O(2^n/n)$ for the BDD size on n variables is due to the work of Breitbart, Hunt, and Rosenkrantz (1995). In fact, Breitbart, Hunt, and Rosenkrantz (1992) already have determined this lower bound and a matching upper bound function. The presented study for TOPOLOGICAL SORTING has been proposed by Woelfel (2006). MAXIMUM FLOW has been studied by Hachtel and Somenzi (1992), with an improvement given by Sawatzki (2004b). A treatment for shortest paths based on a symbolical representation of the entire state space is also subject to current research; for example, the ALL-PAIRS SHORTEST PATH problem has been considered by Sawatzki (2004a).

External Search

8

Often search spaces are so large that even in compressed form they fail to fit into the main memory. During the execution of a search algorithm, only a part of the graph can be processed in the main memory at a time; the remainder is stored on a disk.

It has been observed that the law of Intel cofounder Gordon Moore moves toward external devices. His prediction, popularly known as *Moore's Law*, states that the number of transistors on a chip doubles about every two years. The costs for large amounts of disk space have decreased considerably. But hard disk operations are about 10^5 to 10^6 times slower than main memory accesses and technological progress yields annual rates of about 40% increase in processor speeds, while disk transfers improve only by about 10%. This growing disparity has led to a growing attention to the design of *I/O-efficient algorithms* in recent years.

Most modern operating systems hide secondary memory accesses from the programmer, but offer one consistent address space of *virtual memory* that can be larger than internal memory. When the program is executed, virtual addresses are translated into physical addresses. Only those portions of the program currently needed for the execution are copied into main memory. Caching and prefetching heuristics have been developed to reduce the number of page faults (the referenced page does not reside in the cache and has to be loaded from a higher memory level). By their nature, however, these methods cannot always take full advantage of the locality inherent in algorithms. Algorithms that explicitly manage the *memory hierarchy* can lead to substantial speedups, since they are more informed to predict and adjust future memory access.

We first give an introduction to the more general topic of I/O-efficient algorithms. We introduce the most widely used computation model, which counts inputs/outputs (I/Os) in terms of block transfers of fixed-size records to and from secondary memory. As external memory algorithms often run for weeks and months, a fault-tolerant hardware architecture is needed and discussed in the text. We describe some basic external memory algorithms like *scanning* and *sorting*, and introduce data structures relevant to graph search.

Then we turn to the subject of external memory graph search. In this part we are mostly concerned with breadth-first and SINGLE-SOURCE SHORTEST PATH search algorithms that deal with graphs stored on disk, but we also provide insights on external (memory) depth-first search. The complexity for the general case is improved by exploiting properties of certain graph classes.

For state space search, we adapt external breadth-first search to implicit graphs. As the use of early duplicate pruning in a hash table is limited, in external memory search the pruning concept has been coined to the term *delayed duplicate detection* for *frontier search*. The fact that no external access to the adjacency list is needed reduces the I/O complexity to the minimum possible.

External breadth-first branch-and-bound conducts a cost-bounded traversal of the state space for more general cost functions. Another impact of external breadth-first search is that it serves as a subroutine in *external enforced hill-climbing*. Next, we show how external breadth-first search can be extended to feature A*. As *external A** operates on sets of states, it shares similarities with the symbolic implementation of A*, introduced in Chapter 7.

We discuss different sorts of implementation refinements; for example, we improve the I/O complexity for regular graphs and create external pattern databases to compute better search heuristics. Lastly, we turn to the external memory algorithm for nondeterministic and probabilistic search spaces. With *external value iteration* we provide a general solution for solving Markov decision process problems on disk.

8.1 VIRTUAL MEMORY MANAGEMENT

Modern operating systems provide a general-purpose mechanism for processing data larger than available main memory called *virtual memory*. Transparent to the program, *swapping* moves parts of the data back and forth from disk as needed. Usually, the virtual address space is divided into units called *pages*; the corresponding equal-size units in physical memory are called *page frames*. A *page table* maps the virtual addresses on the page frames and keeps track of their status (loaded/absent). When a *page fault* occurs (i.e., a program tries to use an unmapped page), the CPU is interrupted; the operating system picks a rarely picked page frame and writes its contents back to the disk. It then fetches the referenced page into the page frame just freed, changes the map, and restarts the trapped instruction. In modern computers memory management is implemented on hardware with a page size commonly fixed at 4,096 bytes.

Various *paging strategies* have been explored that aim at minimizing page faults. Belady has shown that an optimal offline page exchange strategy deletes the page that will not be used for a long time. Unfortunately, the system, unlike possibly the application program itself, cannot know this in advance. Several different online algorithms for the paging problem have been proposed, such as *last-in-first-out* (LIFO), *first-in-first-out* (FIFO), *least-recently-used* (LRU), and *least-frequently-used* (LFU). Despite that Sleator and Tarjan proved that LRU is the best general online algorithm for the problem, we reduce the number of page faults by designing data structures that exhibit *memory locality*, such that successive operations tend to access nearby memory cells.

Sometimes it is even desirable to have explicit control of secondary memory manipulations. For example, fetching data structures larger than the system page size may require multiple disk operations. A file buffer can be regarded as a kind of *software paging* that mimics swapping on a coarser level of granularity. Generally, an application can outperform the operating system's memory management because it is well informed to predict future memory access.

Particularly for search algorithms, system paging often becomes the major bottleneck. This problem has been experienced when applying A* to the domain of route planning. Moreover, A* does not respect memory locality at all; it explores nodes in the strict order of f-values, regardless of their neighborhood, and hence jumps back and forth in a spatially unrelated way.

8.2 FAULT TOLERANCE

External algorithms often run for a long time and have to be robust with respect to the reliability of existing hardware. Unrecoverable error rates on hard disks happen at a level of about 1 in 10^{14} bits. If such an error occurs in critical system areas, the entire file system is corrupted. In conventional usage, such errors happen every 10 years. However, in extensive usage with file I/O in the order of terabytes per second, such a worst-case scenario may happen every week. As one solution to the problem, a *redundant array of inexpensive disks* (RAID)[1] is appropriate. Some of its levels are: 0 (striping: efficiency improvement for the exploration due to multiple disk access without introducing redundancy); 1 (mirroring: reliability improvement for the search due to option of recovering data); and 5 (performance and parity: reliability and efficiency improvement for the search, automatically recovers from one-bit disk failures).

Another problem with long-term experiments are environmental faults that lead to switched-down power supply. Even if data is stored on disk, it is not certain that all data remains accessible in case of a failure. As hard disks may have individual reading and writing buffers, disk access is probably not under full control by the application program or the operating system. Therefore, it can happen that a file is deleted when the file reading buffer is still unprocessed. One solution to this problem is *uninteruptable power supplies* (UPSs) that assist in writing volatile data to disk. In many cases like external breadth-first search it continues the search from some certified flush like the last layer fully expanded.

8.3 MODEL OF COMPUTATION

Recent developments of hardware significantly deviate from the von Neumann architecture; for example, the next generation of processors has multicore processors and several processor cache levels (see Fig. 8.1). Consequences like *cache anomalies* are well known; for example, recursive programs like QUICKSORT perform unexpectedly well in practice when compared to other theoretically stronger sorting algorithms.

The commonly used model for comparing the performances of external algorithms consists of a single processor, small internal memory that can hold up to M data items, and unlimited secondary memory. The size of the input problem (in terms of the number of records) is abbreviated by N. Moreover, the *block size B* governs the bandwidth of memory transfers. It is often convenient to refer to these parameters in terms of blocks, so we define $m = M/B$ and $n = N/B$. It is usually assumed that at the beginning of the algorithm, the input data is stored in contiguous blocks on external memory, and the same must hold for the output. Only the number of block read and writes are counted, and computations in internal memory do not incur any cost (see Fig. 8.2). An extension of the model considers D disks that can be accessed simultaneously. When using disks in parallel, the technique of *disk striping* can be employed to essentially increase the block size by a factor of D. Successive blocks are

---

[1]Nowadays this acronym also is used for *redundant array of independent disks*.

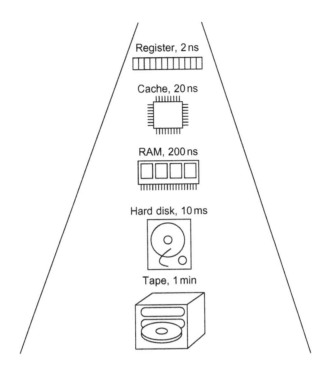

FIGURE 8.1

The memory hierarchy.

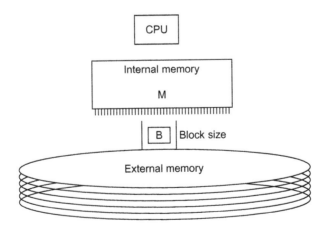

FIGURE 8.2

The external memory model.

distributed across different disks. Formally, this means that if we enumerate the records from zero, the ith block of the jth disk contains record number $(iDB + jB)$ through $(iDB + (j+1)B - 1)$. Usually, it is assumed that $M < N$ and $DB < M/2$.

We distinguish two general approaches of external memory algorithms: either we can devise algorithms to solve specific computational problems while explicitly controlling secondary memory access, or we can develop general-purpose *external memory data structures*, such as stacks, queues, search trees, priority queues, and so on, and then use them in algorithms that are similar to their internal memory counterparts.

8.4 BASIC PRIMITIVES

It is often convenient to express the complexity of external memory algorithms using two frequently occurring primitive operations. These primitives, together with their complexities, are summarized in Table 8.1. The simplest operation is *external scanning*, which means reading a stream of records stored consecutively on secondary memory. In this case, it is trivial to exploit disk and block parallelism. The number of I/Os is $N/DB = n/D$.

Sorting is a fundamental problem that arises in almost all areas of computer science. For the heuristic search exploration, sorting is essential to arrange similar states together, for example, to find duplicates. For this purpose, sorting is useful to eliminate I/O accesses. The proposed *external sorting* algorithms fall into two categories: those based on the *merging paradigm*, and those based on the *distribution paradigm*.

EXTERNAL MERGESORT converts the input into a number of elementary sorted sequences of length M using internal memory sorting. Subsequently, a merging step is applied repeatedly until only one run remains. A set of k sequences $S_1, \ldots, S_k$ can be merged into one run with $O(N/B)$ I/O operations by reading each sequence in a blockwise manner. In internal memory, k cursors p_k are maintained for each of the sequences; moreover, it contains one buffer block for each run, and one output buffer. Among the elements pointed to by the p_k, the one with the smallest key, say p_i, is selected; the element is copied to the output buffer, and p_i is incremented. Whenever the output buffer reaches the block size B, it is written to disk and emptied; similarly, whenever a cached block for an input sequence has been fully read, it is replaced with the next block of the run in external memory. When using one internal buffer block per sequence and one output buffer, each merging phase uses $O(N/B)$ operations. The best result is achieved when k is chosen as big as possible, $k = M/B$. Then sorting can be accomplished in $O\left(\lg_{M/B} \frac{N}{B}\right)$ phases, resulting in the overall optimal complexity.

On the other hand, EXTERNAL QUICKSORT partitions the input data into disjoint sets S_i, $1 \leq i \leq k$, such that the key of each element in S_i is smaller than that of any element in S_j, if $i < j$. To produce this

Table 8.1 Primitives of external memory algorithms.

Operation	Complexity	Optimality Achieved By
scan(N)	$(N/DB) = (n/D)$	Trivial sequential access
sort(N)	$\Theta\left(\frac{N}{DB} \lg_{M/B} \frac{N}{B}\right) = \Theta\left(\frac{n}{D} \lg_m n\right)$	merge or distribution sort

partition, a set of *splitters* $-\infty = s_0 < s_1 < \cdots < s_k < s_{k+1} = \infty$ is chosen, and S_i is defined to be the subset of elements $x \in S$ with $s_i < x \leq s_{i+1}$. The splitting can be done I/O-efficiently by streaming the input data through an input buffer, and using an output buffer. Then each subset S_i is recursively processed, unless its size allows sorting in internal memory. The final output is produced by concatenating all the elementary sorted subsequences. Optimality can be achieved by a good choice of splitters, such that $|S_i| = O(N/k)$. It has been proposed to calculate the splitters in linear time based on the classic internal memory *selection algorithm* to find the k-smallest element. We note that although we will be concerned only with the case of a single disk ($D = 1$), it is possible to make optimal use of multiple disks with $\Theta\left(\frac{N}{DB} \lg_{M/B} \frac{N}{B}\right) = \Theta\left(\frac{n}{D} \lg_m n\right)$ I/Os. Simple disk striping, however, does not lead to optimal external sorting. It has to be ensured that each read operation brings in $\Omega(D)$ blocks, and each write operation must store $\Omega(D)$ blocks on disk. For EXTERNAL QUICKSORT, the buckets have to be hashed to the disks almost uniformly. This can be achieved using a randomized scheme.

8.5 EXTERNAL EXPLICIT GRAPH SEARCH

External explicit graphs are problem graphs that are stored on disk. Examples are large maps for route planning systems. Under *external explicit graph search*, we understand search algorithms that operate in explicitly specified directed or undirected graphs that are too large to fit in main memory. We distinguish between assigning BFS or DFS numbers to nodes, assigning BFS levels to nodes, or computing the BFS or DFS tree edges. However, for BFS in undirected graphs it can be shown that all these formulations are reducible to each other in $O(\text{sort}(|V| + |E|))$ I/Os, where V and E are the sets of nodes and edges of the input graph (see Exercises).

The input graph consists of two arrays, one that contains all edges sorted by the start node, and one array of size $|V|$ that stores, for each vertex, its out-degree and offset into the first array.

8.5.1 *External Priority Queues

External priority queues for general weights are involved. An I/O-efficient algorithm for the SINGLE-SOURCE SHORTEST PATHS problem simulates Dijkstra's algorithm by replacing the priority queue with the TOURNAMENT TREE data structure. It is a priority queue data structure that was developed with the application to graph search algorithms in mind; it is similar to an external heap, but it holds additional information. The tree stores pairs (x, y), where $x \in \{1, \dots, N\}$ identifies the element, and y is called the *key*. The TOURNAMENT TREE is a complete binary tree, except for possibly some right-most leaves missing. It has N/M leaves. There is a fixed mapping of elements to the leaves, namely, IDs in the range from $(i - 1)M + 1$ through the iM map to the ith leaf. Each element occurs exactly once in the tree. Each node has an associated list of $M/2$ to M elements, which are the smallest ones among all descendants. Additionally, it has an associated buffer of size M. Using an amortization argument, it can be shown that a sequence of k *Update*, *Delete*, or *DeleteMin* operations on a tournament tree containing N elements requires at most $O\left(\frac{k}{B} \lg \frac{N}{B}\right)$ accesses to external memory.

The BUFFERED REPOSITORY TREE is a variant of the TOURNAMENT TREE that provides two operations: *Insert*(x, y) inserts element x under key y, where several elements can have the same key. *ExtractAll*(y) returns and removes all elements that have key y. As in a TOURNAMENT TREE, keys come from a key set $\{1, \dots, N\}$, and the leaves in the static height-balanced binary tree are associated with the key ranges in the same fixed way. Each internal node stores elements in a buffer of size B, which is recursively distributed to its two children when it becomes full. Thus, an *Insert* operation needs $O\left(\frac{1}{B}\lg|V|\right)$ I/O amortized operations. An *ExtractAll* operation requires $O\left(\lg|V|+\frac{x}{B}\right)$ accesses to secondary memory, where the first term corresponds to reading all buffers on the path from the root to the correct leaf, and the second term reflects reading the x reported elements from the leaf. Moreover, a BUFFERED REPOSITORY TREE T is used to remember nodes that were encountered earlier. When v is extracted, each incoming edge (u, v) is inserted into T under key u. If at some later point u is extracted, then *ExtractAll(u)* on T yields a list of edges that should not be traversed because they would lead to duplicates. The algorithm takes $O(|V|+|E|/B)$ I/Os to access adjacency lists. The $O(|E|)$ operations on the priority queues take at most $O(|V|)$ times, leading to a cost of $O(|V|+sort(|E|))$. Additionally, there are $O(|E|)$ *Insert* and $O(|V|)$ *ExtractAll* operations on T, which add up to $O((|V|+|E|/B)\cdot\lg|V|)$ I/Os; this term also dominates the overall complexity of the algorithm.

More efficient algorithms can be developed by exploiting properties of particular classes of graphs. In the case of *directed acyclic graphs* (DAGs) like those induced in MULTIPLE SEQUENCE ALIGNMENT problems, we can solve the shortest path problem following a topological ordering, in which for each edge (u, v) the index of u is smaller than that of v. The start node has index 0. Nodes are processed in this order. Due to the fixed ordering, we can access all adjacency lists in $O(scan(|E|))$ time. Since this procedure involves $O(|V|+|E|)$ priority queue operations, the overall complexity is $O(sort(|V|+|E|))$.

It has been shown that the SINGLE-SOURCE SHORTEST PATHS problem can be solved with $O(sort(|V|))$ I/Os for many subclasses of *sparse graphs*; for example, for *planar graphs* that can be drawn in a plane in the natural way without having edges cross between nodes. Such graphs naturally decompose the plane into faces. For example, route planning graphs without bridges and tunnels are planar. As most special cases are local, virtual intersections may be inserted to exploit planarity.

We next consider external DFS and BFS exploration for more general graph classes.

8.5.2 **External Explicit Graph Depth-First Search**

External DFS relies on an external stack data structure. The search stack is often small compared to the overall search but in the worst-case scenario it can become large. For an external stack, the buffer is just an internal memory array of $2B$ elements that at any time contains the $k < 2B$ elements most recently inserted. We assume that the stack content is bounded by at most N elements. A *pop* operation incurs no I/O, except for the case when the buffer has run empty, where $O(1)$ I/O to retrieve a block of B elements is sufficient. A *push* operation incurs no I/O, except for the case the buffer has run full, where $O(1)$ I/O is needed to retrieve a block of B elements. Insertion and deletion take $1/B$ I/Os in the amortized sense.

The I/O complexity for external DFS for explicit (possibly directed) graphs is $O(|V|+|V|/M \cdot scan(|E|))$. There are $|V|/M$ phases where the internal buffer for the visited state set becomes full, in which case it is flushed. Duplicates are eliminated not via sorting (as in the case of external BFS) but by removing marked states from the external adjacency list representation by a file scan. This is possible as the adjacency is explicitly represented on disk and done by generating a simplified copy of the graph and writing it to disk. Successors in the unexplored adjacency lists that are visited are marked not to be generated again, such that all states in the internal visited list can be eliminated. As with external BFS in explicit graphs, $O(|V|)$ I/Os are due to the unstructured access to the external adjacency list. Computing strongly connected components in explicit graphs also takes $O(|V| + |V|/M \cdot scan(|E|))$ I/Os.

Dropping the term of $O(|V|)$ I/O as with external BFS, however, is a challenge. For implicit graphs, no access to an external adjacency list is possible, so that we cannot access the search graph that has not been seen so far. Therefore, the major problem for external DFS exploration in implicit graphs is that adjacencies defining the successor relation cannot be filtered out as done for explicit graphs.

8.5.3 External Explicit Graph Breadth-First Search

Recall the standard internal memory BFS algorithm, visiting each reachable node of the input problem graph G one by one utilizing a FIFO queue. After a node is extracted, its adjacency list (the sets of successors in G) is examined, and those that haven't been visited so far are inserted into the queue in turn. Naively running the standard internal BFS algorithm in the same way in external memory will result in $\Theta(|V|)$ I/Os for unstructured accesses to the adjacency lists, and $\Theta(|E|)$ I/Os to check if successor nodes have already been visited. The latter task is considerably easier for *undirected graphs*, since duplicates are constrained to be located in adjacent levels.

The algorithm of Munagala and Ranade improves I/O complexity for the case of undirected graphs, in which duplicates are constrained to be located in adjacent levels.

The algorithm builds $Open(i)$ from $Open(i-1)$ as follows: Let $A(i) = Succ(Open(i-1))$ be the multiset of successors of nodes in $Open(i-1)$; $A(i)$ is created by concatenating all adjacency lists of nodes in $Open(i-1)$. Then the algorithm removes duplicates by external sorting followed by an external scan. Since the resulting list $A'(i)$ is still sorted, filtering out the nodes already contained in the sorted lists $Open(i-1)$ or $Open(i-2)$ is possible by parallel scanning. This completes the generation of $Open(i)$. Set U maintains all unvisited nodes necessary to be looked at when the graph is not completely connected. Algorithm 8.1 provides the implementation of the algorithm of Munagala and Ranade in pseudo code. The algorithm can record the nodes' BFS level in additional $O(|V|)$ time using an external array.

Theorem 8.1. (*Efficiency Explicit Graph External BFS*) *On an undirected explicit problem graph, the algorithm of Munagala and Ranade requires at most $O(|V| + sort(|E|))$ I/Os to compute the BFS level for each state.*

Proof. For the correctness argument, we assume that the state levels $Open(0), \ldots, Open(i-1)$ have already been assigned to the correct BFS level. Now we consider a successor v of a node $u \in Open(i-1)$: The distance from s to v is at least $i-2$ because otherwise the distance of u would be less than $i-1$. Thus, $v \in Open(i-2) \cup Open(i-1) \cup Open(i)$. Therefore, we can correctly assign $A'(i) \setminus (Open(i-1) \cup Open(i-2))$ to $Open(i)$.

For the complexity argument we assume that after preprocessing, the graph is stored in adjacency-list representation. Hence, successor generation takes $O(|Open(i-1)| + |Succ(Open(i-1))|/B)$ I/Os. Duplicate elimination within the successor set takes $O(sort(A(i)))$ I/Os. Parallel scanning can be done using $O(sort(|Succ(Open(i-1))|) + scan(|Open(i-1)| + |Open(i-2)|))$ I/Os. Since $\sum_i |Succ(Open(i))| = O(|E|)$ and $\sum_i |Open(i)| = O(|V|)$, the execution of external BFS requires $O(|V| + sort(|E|))$ time, where $O(|V|)$ is due to the external representation of the graph and the initial reconfiguration time to enable efficient successor generation. ∎

Procedure External-Explicit-BFS
Input: Explicit external problem graph with start node s
Output: BFS layers $Open(i)$, $i \in \{0,1,\ldots,k\}$

$Open(-1) \leftarrow Open(-2) \leftarrow \emptyset; \; U \leftarrow V$	;; Initialize frontier and unvisited list
$i \leftarrow 0$	;; Initialize iteration counter
while $(Open(i-1) \neq \emptyset \; \vee \; U \neq \emptyset)$	;; Loop while states are available
if $(Open(i-1) = \emptyset)$	;; Graph component empty
$Open(i) \leftarrow \{x\}, where \; x \in U$	;; Insert unvisited
else	;; Component not empty
$A(i) \leftarrow Succ(Open(i-1))$	;; Determine successor list
$A'(i) \leftarrow RemoveDuplicates(A(i))$	;; Simplify list
$Open(i) \leftarrow A'(i) \setminus (Open(i-1) \cup Open(i-2))$	;; Subtract levels
for each $v \in Open(i)$	;; Remaining nodes
$U \leftarrow U \setminus \{v\}$	;; Mark visited
$i \leftarrow i+1$	;; Increase counter

Algorithm 8.1

External BFS by Munagala and Ranade.

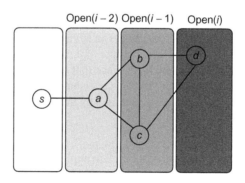

FIGURE 8.3

Example for the algorithm of Munagala and Ranade.

An example is provided in Figure 8.3. When generating $Succ(Open(i-1))$ we unify $Succ(b) = \{a,c,d\}$ with $Succ(c) = \{a,b,d\}$. Removing the duplicates in $Succ(b) \cup Succ(c)$ yields set $\{a,b,c,d\}$. Removing $Open(i-1)$ reduces the set to $\{a,d\}$; omitting $Open(i-2)$ results in the final node set $\{d\}$.

The bottleneck of the algorithm are the $O(|V|)$ unstructured accesses to adjacency lists. The following refinement of Mehlhorn and Meyer consists of a preprocessing and a BFS phase, arriving at a complexity of $O(\sqrt{|V| \cdot scan(|V| + |E|)} + sort(|V| + |E|))$ I/Os.

The preprocessing phase partitions the graph into K disjoint subgraphs $\{G_i \mid 1 \leq i \leq K\}$ with small internal shortest path distances; the adjacency lists are accordingly partitioned into consecutively stored sets $\{F_i \mid 1 \leq i \leq K\}$ as well. The partitions are created by choosing *seed nodes* independently with uniform probability μ. Then K BFS are run in parallel, starting from the seed nodes, until all nodes of the graph have been assigned to a subgraph. In each round, the active adjacency lists of nodes lying on the boundary of their partition are scanned; the requested destination nodes are labeled with the partition identifier, and are sorted (ties between partitions are arbitrarily broken). Then, a parallel scan of the sorted requests and the graph representation can extract the unvisited part of the graph, as well as label the new boundary nodes and generate the active adjacency lists for the next round. The expected I/O bound for the graph partitioning is $O((|V| + |E|)/\mu DB + sort(|V| + |E|))$; the expected shortest path distance between any two nodes within a subgraph is $O\left(\frac{1}{\mu}\right)$. The main idea of the second phase is to replace the nodewise access to adjacency lists by a scanning operation on a file H that contains all F_i in sorted order such that the current BFS level has at least one node in S_i. All subgraph adjacency lists in F_i are merged with H completely, not node by node. Since the shortest path within a partition is of order $O\left(\frac{1}{\mu}\right)$, each F_i stays in H accordingly for at most $O\left(\frac{1}{\mu}\right)$ levels. The second phase uses $O(\mu|V| + (|V| + |E|)/\mu DB + sort(|V| + |E|))$ I/Os in total; choosing $\mu = \min\{1, \sqrt{(|V| + |E|)/\mu DB}\}$, we arrive at a complexity of $O(\sqrt{|V| \cdot scan(|V| + |E|)} + sort(|V| + |E|))$ I/Os. An alternative to the randomized strategy of generating the partition described here is a deterministic variant using a *Euler tour* around a minimum spanning tree. Thus, the bound also holds in the worst case.

8.6 EXTERNAL IMPLICIT GRAPH SEARCH

An *implicit graph* is a graph that is not residing on disk but generated by successively applying a set of actions to nodes selected from the search frontier. The advantage in implicit search is that the graph is generated by a set of rules, and hence no disk accesses for the adjacency lists are required.

Considering the I/O complexities, bounds like those that include $|V|$ are rather misleading, since we are often trying to avoid generating all nodes. Hence, value $|V|$ is needed only to derive worst-case bounds. In almost all cases, $|V|$ can safely be substituted by the number of expanded nodes.

8.6.1 Delayed Duplicate Detection for BFS

A variant of Munagala and Ranade's algorithm for BFS in implicit graphs has been coined with the term *delayed duplicate detection* for *frontier search*. Let s be the initial node, and *Succ* be the implicit successor generation function. The algorithm maintains BFS layers on disk. Layer $Open(i - 1)$ is scanned and the set of successors are put into a buffer of a size close to the main memory capacity. If the buffer becomes full, internal sorting followed by a duplicate elimination phase generates a sorted duplicate-free node sequence in the buffer that is flushed to disk. The outcome of this phase are k presorted files. Note that delayed internal duplicate elimination can be improved by using hash tables for the blocks before being flushed to disk. Since the node set in the hash table has to be stored anyway, the savings by early duplicate detection are often small.

In the next step, *external merging* is applied to unify the files into $Open(i)$ by a simultaneous scan. The size of the output files is chosen such that a single pass suffices. Duplicates are eliminated. Since the files were presorted, the complexity is given by the scanning time of all files. We also have to eliminate $Open(i - 1)$ and $Open(i - 2)$ from $Open(i)$ to avoid recomputations; that is, nodes extracted from the external queue are not immediately deleted, but kept until the layer has been completely generated and sorted, at which point duplicates can be eliminated using a parallel scan. The process is repeated until $Open(i - 1)$ becomes empty, or the goal has been found.

Procedure External-BFS
Input: Problem graph with start node s
Output: Optimal solution path

$Open(-1) \leftarrow \emptyset, Open(0) \leftarrow \{s\}$	;; Initialize frontier lists
$i \leftarrow 1$	;; Initialize counter
while $(Open(i-1) \neq \emptyset)$	;; Loop until done
$\quad A(i) \leftarrow Succ(Open(i-1))$	;; Determine successor list
$\quad$ **if** $(Goal(Open(i)))$	;; Terminal state in set
$\quad\quad$ **return** $Construct(Open(i))$	;; Generate solution path
$\quad A'(i) \leftarrow RemoveDuplicates(A(i))$	;; Simplify list
$\quad Open(i) \leftarrow A'(i) \setminus (Open(i-1) \cup Open(i-2))$	;; Remove previous levels
$\quad i \leftarrow i+1$	;; Increase counter

Algorithm 8.2

Delayed duplicate detection algorithm for BFS.

The corresponding pseudo code is shown in Algorithm 8.2. Note that the explicit partition of the set of successors into blocks is implicit. Termination is not shown, but imposes no additional implementation problem.

Theorem 8.2. *(Efficiency Implicit External BFS) On an undirected implicit problem graph, external BFS with delayed duplicate elimination requires at most $O(\text{scan}(|V|) + \text{sort}(|E|))$ I/Os.*

Proof. The proof for implicit problem graphs is essentially the same for explicit problem graphs with the exception that the access to the external device for generating the successors of a state resulting in at most $O(|V|)$ I/Os is not needed.

As with the algorithm of Munagala and Ranade, delayed duplicate detection applies $O(\text{sort}(|Succ(Open(i-1))|) + \text{scan}(|Open(i-1)| + |Open(i-2)|))$ I/Os. As no explicit access to the adjacency list is needed, by $\sum_i |Succ(Open(i))| = O(|E|)$ and $\sum_i |Open(i)| = O(|V|)$, the total execution time is $O(\text{sort}(|E|) + \text{scan}(|V|))$ I/Os. ∎

In search problems with a bounded branching factor we have $|E| = O(|V|)$, and thus the complexity for implicit external BFS reduces to $O(\text{sort}(|V|))$ I/Os. If we keep each $Open(i)$ in a separate file for sparse problem graphs (e.g., simple chains), file opening and closing would accumulate to $O(|V|)$ I/Os. The solution for this case is to store the nodes in $Open(i)$, $Open(i+1)$, and so forth, consecutively in internal memory. Therefore, I/O is needed, only if a level has at most B nodes.

The algorithm shares similarities with the internal frontier search algorithm (see Ch. 6) that was used for solving the MULTIPLE SEQUENCE ALIGNMENT problem. In fact, the implementation has been applied to external memory search with considerable success. The BFS algorithm extends to graphs with bounded locality. For this case and to ease the description of upcoming algorithms, we assume to be given a general file subtraction procedure as implemented in Algorithm 8.3.

In an internal, not memory-restricted setting, a plan is constructed by backtracking from the goal node to the start node. This is facilitated by saving with every node a pointer to its predecessor. For

---

Procedure Subtract
Input: State set *Open(i)* and sets *Open(j)* for $j < i$, locality l
Output: Refined state set *Open(i)*

for *loc* ← 1 **to** *l*   ;; Locality determines boundary
    Open'(i) ← *Open'(i)*\ *Open(i − loc)*   ;; Subtraction of previous levels

Algorithm 8.3

File subtraction for external duplicate elimination.

memory-limited frontier search, a divide-and-conquer solution reconstruction is needed for which certain relay layers have to be stored in the main memory. In external search divide-and-conquer solution reconstruction and relay layers are not needed, since the exploration fully resides on disk.

There is one subtle problem: predecessors of the pointers are not available on disk. This is resolved as follows. Plans are reconstructed by saving the predecessor together with every state, by scanning with decreasing depth the stored files, and by looking for matching predecessors. Any reached node that is a predecessor of the current node is its predecessor on an optimal solution path. This results in a I/O complexity that is at most linear to scanning time $O(scan(|V|))$.

Even if conceptually simpler, there is no need to store the *Open* list in different files Open(*i*), $i \in \{0, 1, \ldots, k\}$. We may store successive layers appended in one file.

8.6.2 *External Breadth-First Branch-and-Bound

In weighted graphs, external BFS with delayed duplicate detection does not guarantee an optimal solution. A natural extension of BFS is to continue the search when a goal is found and keep on searching until a *better* goal is found or the search space is exhausted. In searching with nonadmissible heuristics we hardly can prune states with an evaluation larger than the current one. Essentially, we are forced to look at all states. However, if $f = g + h$ with monotone heuristic function h we can prune the exploration.

For the domains where cost $f = g + h$ is monotonically increasing, *external breadth-first branch-and-bound* (external BFBnB) with delayed duplicate detection does not prune away any node that is on the optimal solution path and ultimately finds the optimal solution. In Algorithm 8.4, the algorithm is presented in pseudo code. The sets *Open* denote the BFS layers and the sets A, A', A'' are temporary variables to construct the search frontier for the next iteration. States with $f(v) > U$ are pruned and states with $f(v) < U$ lead to a bound that is updated.

Theorem 8.3. *(Cost-Optimality External BFBnB with Delayed Duplicate Detection) For a state space with $f = g + h$, where g denotes the depth and h is a consistent estimate, external BFBnB with delayed duplicate detection terminates with the optimal solution.*

Proof. In BFBnB with cost function $f = g + h$, where g is the depth of the search and h a consistent search heuristic, every duplicate node with a smaller depth has been explored with a smaller f-value. This is simple to see as the h-values of the query node and the duplicate node match, and BFS generates a duplicate node with a smaller g-value first. Moreover, u is safely pruned if $f(u)$ exceeds the current threshold, as an extension of the path to u to a solution will have a larger f-value. Since external BFBnB

Procedure External-Breadth-First-Heuristic-Search
Input: Weighted problem graph with start node s
Output: Optimal solution cost U

$U \leftarrow \infty$	;; Initialize upper bound
$f(s) \leftarrow h(s)$	;; Evaluate initial node
$Open(-1) \leftarrow \emptyset$; $Open(0) \leftarrow \{s\}$	;; Initialize frontier layers
$j \leftarrow 0$	;; Initialize BFS iteration counter
while $(Open(j-1) \neq \emptyset)$	;; Termination criterion
$\quad A(j) \leftarrow Succ(Open(j-1))$	;; Generate successors
$\quad$ **for each** $v \in A(j), v \in Succ(u)$	;; For each successor
$\qquad f(v) \leftarrow f(u) + w(u,v) + h(v) - h(u)$	;; Set cost
$\qquad$ **if** $(Goal(v)$ **and** $f(v) < U)$ $U \leftarrow f(v)$	;; Update bound
$\quad A'(j) \leftarrow A(j) \setminus \{u \in A(j) \mid f(u) > U\}$	;; Prune nodes
$\quad A''(j) \leftarrow RemoveDuplicates(A'(j))$	;; Remove duplicates in layer
$\quad A''(j) \leftarrow Subtract(A''(j))$	;; Subtract previous layers
$\quad Open(j) \leftarrow A''(j)$	;; Set next layer
$\quad j \leftarrow j+1$	;; Increase iteration counter
return U	;; Optimal solution cost

Algorithm 8.4

External breadth-first branch-and-bound.

---

with delayed duplicate detection expands all nodes u with $f(u) < f^*$ the algorithm terminates with the optimal solution. ∎

Furthermore, we can easily show that if there exists more than one goal node in the state space with a different solution cost, then external BFBnB with delayed duplicate detection will explore less nodes than a complete external BFS with delayed duplicate detection.

Theorem 8.4. *(Gain of External BFBnB wrt. External BFS) If n_{BFBnB} is the number of nodes expanded by external BFBnB with delayed duplicate detection for $U \geq f^*$, and n_{BFS} the number of nodes expanded by a complete run of external BFS with delayed duplicate detection, then $n_{BFBnB} \leq n_{BFS}$.*

Proof. External BFBnB does not change the order in which nodes are looked at during a complete external BFS. There can be two cases. In the first case, there exists just one goal node t, which is also the last node in a BFS tree. For this case, clearly $n_{BFBnB} = n_{BFS}$. If there exists more than one goal node in the search tree, let $t_1, t_2 \in T$ be the two goal nodes with $f(t_1) > f(t_2) = f^*$ and $depth(t_1) < depth(t_2)$. Since t_1 will be expanded first, $f(t_1)$ will be used as the pruning value for all the next iterations. In this case, there does not exist any node u in the search tree between t_1 and t_2 with $f(u) > f(t_2)$, $n_{BFBnB} = n_{BFS}$, otherwise $n_{BFBnB} \leq n_{BFS}$. ∎

Table 8.2 gives an impression of cost-optimal search in a selected optimization problem, reporting the number of nodes in each layer obtained after refinement with respect to the previous layers. An entry in the goal cost column corresponds to the best goal cost found in that layer.

Table 8.2 Results of cost-optimal search on a selected search domain.

BFS Layer	Nodes	Space (GB)	Goal Cost
0	1	0.000000536	105
1	2	0.00000107	–
2	10	0.00000536	–
3	61	0.0000327	–
4	252	0.000137	–
5	945	0.000508	104
6	3,153	0.00169	–
7	9,509	0.00585	–
8	26,209	0.0146	103
9	66,705	0.0361	–
10	158,311	0.0859	–
11	353,182	0.190	101
12	745,960	0.401	–
13	1,500,173	0.805	–
14	2,886,261	1.550	97
15	5,331,550	2.863	–
16	9,481,864	5.091	–
17	16,266,810	8.735	96
18	26,958,236	14.476	–
19	43,199,526	23.197	–
20	66,984,109	35.968	95
21	100,553,730	53.994	–
22	146,495,022	78.663	–
23	205,973,535	110.601	93
⋮	⋮	⋮	⋮

For unit cost search graphs the external branch-and-bound algorithm simplifies to *external breadth-first heuristic search* (see Ch. 6).

8.6.3 *External Enforced Hill-Climbing

In Chapter 6 we have introduced enforced hill-climbing (a.k.a. iterative improvement) as a more conservative form of hill-climbing search. Starting from a start state, a (breadth-first) search for a successor with a better heuristic value is started. As soon as such a successor is found, the hash tables are cleared and a fresh search is started. The process continues until the goal is reached. Since the algorithm performs a complete search on every state with a strictly better heuristic value, it is guaranteed to find a solution in directed graphs without dead-ends.

Having external BFS in hand, an external algorithm for enforced hill-climbing can be constructed by utilizing the heuristic estimates. In Algorithm 8.5 we show the algorithm in pseudo-code format.

Procedure External-Enforced Hill-Climbing
Input: Problem graph with start node s, successor set generation function *Succ*
Output: Path to goal node

$u \leftarrow s$	;; Initialize search
while $(h \neq 0)$	;; As far as goal node not found
$\quad (u',h') \leftarrow$ *External-EHC-BFS*(u,h)	;; Search for improvement
$\quad$ **if** $(h' = \infty)$ **return** $\emptyset$	;; No better evaluation found
$\quad u \leftarrow u'$	;; Update u for next iteration
$\quad h \leftarrow h'$	;; Update h
return *Construct*(u)	;; Return solution path

Algorithm 8.5

Main routine for external enforced hill-climbing.

Procedure External-EHC-BFS
Input: Node u with evaluation $h(u)$
Output: Node v with evaluation $h(v) < h(u)$ or failure

$Open(0,h) \leftarrow u$	;; Add initial node to queue
$i \leftarrow 1$	;; Initialize BFS layer
while $(Open(i-1,h) \neq \emptyset)$	;; As far as queue not empty
$\quad A(i) \leftarrow Succ(Open(i-1,h))$	;; Compute successors
$\quad$ **for each** v in $A(i)$	;; Traverse successors
$\quad\quad$ **if** $h(v) < h(u)$	;; Improvement found
$\quad\quad\quad$ **return** (v,h')	;; New seed state together with new heuristic
$\quad A'(i) \leftarrow RemoveDuplicates(A(i))$	;; Eliminate duplicates in current layer
$\quad A'(i) \leftarrow Subtract(A'(i))$	;; Duplicates in previous layers
$\quad Open(i,h) \leftarrow A'(i)$	;; Update next frontier
$\quad i \leftarrow i+1$	;; Increase BFS layer
return (i,∞)	;; Failure

Algorithm 8.6

External BFS searching for a better state v.

The externalization is embedded in the subprocedure Algorithm 8.6 that performs external BFS for a state that has an improved heuristic estimate. Figure 8.5 shows parts of an exploration for solving a action planning instance. It provides a histogram (logarithmic scale) on the number of nodes in BFS layers for external enforced hill-climbing in a selected planning problem.

Theorem 8.5. *(Complexity External Enforced Hill-Climbing) Let $h(s)$ be the heuristic estimate of the initial state. External enforced hill-climbing with delayed duplicate elimination in a problem graph with bounded locality requires at most $O(h(s) \cdot (\mathrm{scan}(|V|) + \mathrm{sort}(|E|)))$ I/Os.*

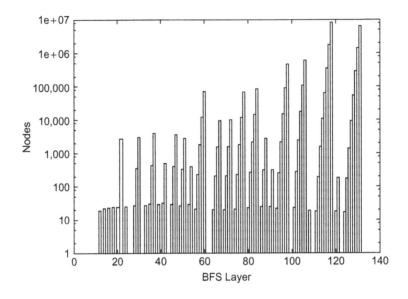

FIGURE 8.4

Typical memory profile of external enforced hill-climbing.

Proof. The I/O complexity is bounded by the number of calls to BFS times the I/O complexity of each run, by $O(h(s) \cdot (scan(|V|) + sort(|E|)))$ I/Os. ∎

Enforced hill-climbing has one important drawback: its results are not optimal. Moreover, in directed search spaces with unrecognized dead-ends it can be trapped, without finding a solution to a solvable problem.

8.6.4 External A*

In the following we study how to extend external breadth-first exploration in implicit graphs to an A*-like search. If the heuristic is consistent, then on each search path, the evaluation function f is nondecreasing. No successor will have a smaller f-value than the current one. Therefore, the A* algorithm, which traverses the node set in f-order, expands each node at most once. Take, for example, a sliding-tile puzzle. As the Manhattan distance heuristic is consistent, for every two successive nodes u and v the difference of the according estimate evaluations $h(v) - h(u)$ is either -1 or 1. By the increase in the g-value, the f-values remain either unchanged, or $f(v) = f(u) + 2$.

As earlier, *external A** maintains the search frontier on disk, possibly partitioned into main memory–size sequences. In fact, the disk files correspond to an external representation of a bucket implementation of a priority queue data structure (see Ch. 3). In the course of the algorithm, each bucket addressed with index i contains all nodes u in the set *Open* that have priority $f(u) = i$. An external representation of this data structure will memorize each bucket in a different file.

We introduce a refinement of the data structure that distinguishes between nodes with different g-values, and designates bucket $Open(i,j)$ to all nodes u with path length $g(u) = i$ and heuristic estimate $h(u) = j$. Similar to external BFS, we do not change the identifier *Open* to separate generated from expanded nodes. In external A* (see Alg. 8.7), bucket $Open(i,j)$ refers to nodes that are in the current search frontier or belong to the set of expanded nodes. During the exploration process, only nodes from one currently *active bucket Open(i,j)*, where $i+j=f_{min}$, are expanded, up to its exhaustion. Buckets are selected in lexicographic order for (i,j); then, the buckets $Open(i',j')$ with $i' < i$ and $i'+j' = f_{min}$ are *closed*, whereas the buckets $Open(i',j')$ with $i'+j' > f_{min}$ or with $i' > i$ and $i'+j' = f_{min}$ are *open*. Depending on the actual node expansion progress, nodes in the active bucket are either *open* or *closed*.

To estimate the maximum number of buckets once more we consider Figure 7.14 as introduced in the analysis of the number of iteration in Symbolic A* (see Ch. 7), in which the g-values are plotted with respect to the h-values, such that nodes with the same $f = g+h$ value are located on the same diagonal. For nodes that are expanded in $Open(g,h)$ the successors fall into $Open(g+1,h-1)$, $Open(g+1,h)$, or $Open(g+1,h+1)$. The number of naughts for each diagonal is an upper bound on the number of buckets that are needed. In Chapter 7, we have already seen that the number is bounded by $O((f^*)^2)$.

By the restriction for f-values in the (n^2-1)-PUZZLE only about half the number of buckets have to be allocated. Note that f^* is not known in advance, so that we have to construct and maintain the files on-the-fly.

Figure 8.5 shows the memory profile of external A* on a THIRTY-FIVE-PUZZLE instance (with 14 tiles permuted). The exploration started in bucket $(50,0)$ and terminated while expanding bucket

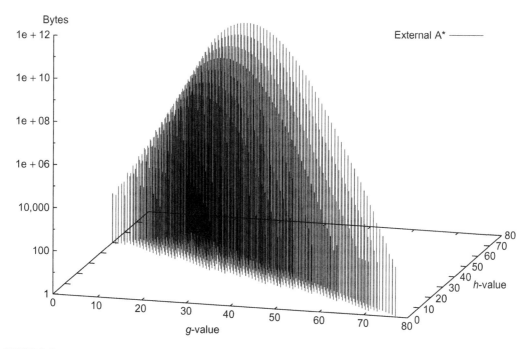

FIGURE 8.5

Memory profile external A* (on a logarithmic scale).

(77,1). Similar to external BFS but in difference to ordinary A*, external A* terminates while generating the goal, since all states in the search frontier with a smaller g-value have already been expanded. For this experiment three disjoint 3-tile and three disjoint 5-tile pattern databases were loaded, which, together with the buckets for reading and flushing, consumed about 4.9 gigabytes of RAM. The total disk space taken was 1,298,389,180,652 bytes, or 1.2 terabytes, with a state vector of $188 = 32 + 2 \times (6 \times 12 + 6 \times 1) = 188$ bytes: 32 bytes for the state vector plus information for incremental heuristic evaluation; 1 byte for each value stored, multiplied by six sets of at most 12 pattern databases plus 1 value each for their sum. Factor 2 is due to symmetry lookups. The exploration took about two weeks.

The following result restricts duplicate detection to buckets of the same h-value.

Lemma 8.1. *In external A* for all i,i',j,j' with $j \neq j'$ we have* Open$(i,j) \cap$ Open$(i',j') = \emptyset$.

Proof. As in the algorithm of Munagala and Ranade, we can exploit the observation that in an undirected problem graph, duplicates of a node with BFS level i can at most occur in levels i, $i-1$, and $i-2$. In addition, since h is a total function, we have $h(u) = h(v)$ if $u = v$. ∎

For ease of describing the algorithm, we consider each bucket for the *Open* list as a different file. Very sparse graphs can lead to bad I/O performance, because they may lead to buckets that contain by far less than B elements and dominate the I/O complexity. For the following, we generally assume large graphs for which $(f^* + 1)^2 = O(scan(|V|))$ and $(f^*)^2 = O(sort(|E|))$.

Algorithm 8.7 depicts the pseudo code of the external A* algorithm for consistent estimates and unit cost and undirected graphs. The algorithm maintains the two values g_{min} and f_{min} to address the currently considered buckets. The buckets of f_{min} are traversed for increasing g_{min} up to f_{min}. According to their different h-values, successors are arranged into three different frontier lists: $A(f_{min})$, $A(f_{min} + 1)$, and $A(f_{min} + 2)$; hence, at each instance only four buckets have to be accessed by I/O operations. For each of them, we keep a separate buffer of size $M/4$; this will reduce the internal memory requirements to M. If a buffer becomes full then it is flushed to disk. As in BFS it is practical to presort buffers in one bucket immediately by an efficient internal algorithm to ease merging, but we could equivalently sort the unsorted buffers for one bucket externally.

There can be two cases that can give rise to duplicates within an active bucket (see Fig. 8.6, black bucket): two different nodes of the *same* predecessor bucket generating a common successor, and two nodes belonging to *different* predecessor buckets generating a duplicate. These two cases can be dealt with by merging all the presorted buffers corresponding to the same bucket, resulting in one sorted file. This file can then be scanned to remove the duplicate nodes from it. In fact, both the merging and duplicates removal can be done simultaneously.

Another special case of the duplicate nodes exists when the nodes that have already been evaluated in the upper layers are generated again (see Fig. 8.6). These duplicate nodes have to be removed by a file subtraction process for the next active bucket $Open(g_{min} + 1, h_{max} - 1)$ by removing any node that has appeared in $Open(g_{min}, h_{max} - 1)$ and $Open(g_{min} - 1, h_{max} - 1)$ (buckets shaded in light gray). This file subtraction can be done by a mere parallel scan of the presorted files and by using a temporary file in which the intermediate result is stored. It suffices to remove duplicates only in the bucket that is expanded next, $Open(g_{min} + 1, h_{max} - 1)$. The other buckets might not have been fully generated, and hence we can save the redundant scanning of the files for every iteration of the innermost *while* loop.

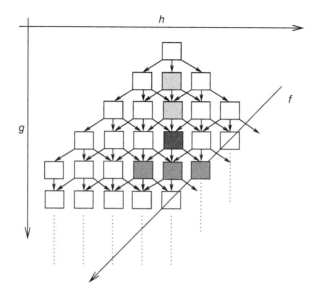

FIGURE 8.6

External A* with consistent heuristic in a unit cost undirected graph. The bucket (g,h) in dark gray is expanded, its successors fall into $(g+1,h-1)$, $(g+1,h)$, and $(g+1,h+1)$. It suffices to eliminate duplicate in (g,h) (by sorting and scanning) and by subtracting $(g-2,h)$ and $(g-1,h)$ (parallel scan through the sorted files). Arrow indicates traversal ordering.

When merging the presorted sets A' with the previously existing *Open* buckets (both residing on disk), duplicates are eliminated, leaving the sets $Open(g_{min}+1,h_{max}-1)$, $Open(g_{min}+1,h_{max})$, and $Open(g_{min}+1,h_{max}+1)$ duplicate free. Then the next active bucket $Open(g_{min}+1,h_{max}-1)$ is refined not to contain any node in $Open(g_{min}-1,h_{max}-1)$ or $Open(g_{min},h_{max}-1)$. This can be achieved through a parallel scan of the presorted files and by using a temporary file in which the intermediate result is stored, before $Open(g_{min}+1, h_{max}-1)$ is updated. It suffices to perform file subtraction lazily only for the bucket that is expanded next.

Theorem 8.6. *(Optimality of External A*) In a unit cost graph external A* is complete and optimal.*

Proof. Since *external A** simulates A* and only changes the order of expanded nodes that have the same f-value, completeness and optimality are inherited from the properties shown for A*. ∎

Theorem 8.7. *(I/O Performance of External A* in Undirected Graphs) The complexity for external A* in an implicit unweighted and undirected graph with a consistent estimate is bounded by $O(\text{sort}(|E|) + \text{scan}(|V|))$ I/Os.*

Proof. By simulating internal A*, delayed duplicate elimination ensures that each edge in the problem graph is looked at at most once. Similar to the analysis for external implicit BFS $O(sort(|Succ(Open(g_{min}+1,h_{max}-1))|)$, I/Os are needed to eliminate duplicates in the successor lists. Since each node is expanded at most once, this adds $O(sort(|E|))$ I/Os to the overall runtime.

Procedure External A*
Input: Problem graph with start node s
Output: Optimal solution path

$Open(0,h(s)) \leftarrow \{s\}$;; Initialize frontier bucket
$f_{min} \leftarrow h(s)$;; Initialize merit
while $(f_{min} \neq \infty)$;; Termination criterion for full exploration
 $g_{min} \leftarrow \min\{i \mid Open(i,f_{min}-i) \neq \emptyset\}$;; Determine minimal depth
 while $(g_{min} \leq f_{min})$;; As far as merit not exceeded
  $h_{max} \leftarrow f_{min} - g_{min}$;; Determine corresponding h-value
  $A(f_{min}),A(f_{min}+1),A(f_{min}+2) \leftarrow Succ(Open(g_{min},h_{max}))$;; Successors
  $Open(g_{min}+1,h_{max}+1) \leftarrow A(f_{min}+2)$;; New bucket
  $Open(g_{min}+1,h_{max}) \leftarrow A(f_{min}+1) \cup Open(g_{min}+1,h_{max})$;; Merge
  $Open(g_{min}+1,h_{max}-1) \leftarrow A(f_{min}) \cup Open(g_{min}+1,h_{max}-1)$;; Merge
  if $(Goal(Open(g_{min}+1,h_{max}-1)))$;; Terminal state in set
   return $Construct(Open(g_{min}+1,h_{max}-1))$;; Generate solution path
  $Open(g_{min}+1,h_{max}-1) \leftarrow$;; Simplify list
   $RemoveDuplicates(Open(g_{min}+1,h_{max}-1))$;; Sort/scan
  $Open(g_{min}+1,h_{max}-1) \leftarrow Open(g_{min}+1,h_{max}-1)\backslash$;; Omit duplicates from
   $(Open(g_{min},h_{max}-1) \cup Open(g_{min}-1,h_{max}-1))$;; ... previous levels
  $g_{min} \leftarrow g_{min}+1$;; Increase depth
 $f_{min} \leftarrow \min\{i+j > f_{min} \mid Open(i,j) \neq \emptyset\} \cup \{\infty\}$;; Find minimal f-value

Algorithm 8.7

External A* for consistent and integral heuristics.

Filtering, evaluating nodes, and merging lists is available in scanning time of all buckets in consideration. During the exploration, each bucket *Open* will be referred to at most six times, once for expansion, at most three times as a successor bucket, and at most two times for duplicate elimination as a predecessor of the same h-value as the currently active bucket. Therefore, evaluating, merging, and file subtraction add $O(scan(|V|) + scan(|E|))$ I/Os to the overall runtime. Hence, the total execution time is $O(sort(|E|) + scan(|V|))$ I/Os. ■

If we additionally have $|E| = O(|V|)$, the complexity reduces to $O(sort(|V|))$ I/Os. We next generalize the result to directed graphs with bounded locality.

Theorem 8.8. *(I/O Performance of External A* in Graphs with Bounded Locality) The complexity for external A* in an implicit unweighted problem graph with bounded locality and consistent estimate is bounded by $O(\mathrm{sort}(|E|) + \mathrm{scan}(|V|))$ I/Os.*

Proof. Consistency implies that we do not have successors with an f-value that is smaller than the current minimum. If we subtract a bucket $Open(j,h)$ from $Open(i,h)$ with $i < j$ and $i - j$ being smaller than the locality l, then we arrive at full duplicate detection. Consequently, during the exploration each problem graph node and edge is considered at most once. The efforts due to removing nodes in each bucket individually accumulate to at most $O(sort(|E|))$ I/Os, and subtraction adds $O(locality_G \cdot scan(|V|)) = O(scan(|V|))$ I/Os to the overall complexity. ■

Internal costs have been neglected in this analysis. Since each node is considered only once for expansion, the internal costs are $|V|$ times the time t_{exp} for successor generation, plus the efforts for internal duplicate elimination and sorting. By setting the weight of all edges (u,v) to $h(u) - h(v) + 1$ for a consistent heuristic h, A* can be cast as a variant of Dijkstra's algorithm that requires internal costs of $O(C \cdot |V|)$, $C = \max\{w(u,v) \mid v \text{ successor of } u\}$ on a bucket-based priority queue. Due to consistency we have $C \leq 2$, so that, given $|E| = O(|V|)$, internal costs are bounded by $O(|V| \cdot (t_{exp} + \lg |V|))$, where $O(|V| \lg |V|))$ refers to the total internal sorting efforts.

To reconstruct a solution path, we store predecessor information with each node on disk (thus doubling the state vector size), and apply backward chaining, starting with the target node. However, this is not strictly necessary: For a node in depth g, we intersect the set of possible predecessors with the buckets of depth $g - 1$. Any node that is in the intersection is reachable on an optimal solution path, so that we can iterate the construction process. The time complexity is bounded by the scanning time of all buckets in consideration, namely by $O(scan(|V|))$ I/Os.

Up to this point, we have made the assumption of unit cost graphs; in the rest of this section, we generalize the algorithm to small integer weights in $\{1, \ldots, C\}$. Due to consistency of the heuristic, it holds for every node u and every successor v of u that $h(v) \geq h(u) - w(u,v)$. Moreover, since the graph is undirected, we equally have $h(u) \geq h(v) - w(u,v)$, or $h(v) \leq h(u) + w(u,v)$; hence, $|h(u) - h(v)| \leq w(u,v)$. This means that the successors of the nodes in the active bucket are no longer spread across three, but over $3 + 5 + \cdots + 2C + 1 = C \cdot (C+2)$ buckets. In Figure 8.7, the region of successors is shaded in dark gray, and the region of predecessors is shaded in light gray.

For duplicate reduction, it is sufficient to subtract the $2C$ buckets $Open(i-1,j), \ldots, Open(i-2C,j)$ from the active bucket $Open(i,j)$ prior to the expansion of its nodes (indicated by the shaded rectangle in Fig. 8.7). We assume $O(C^2)$ I/Os for accessing the files is negligible.

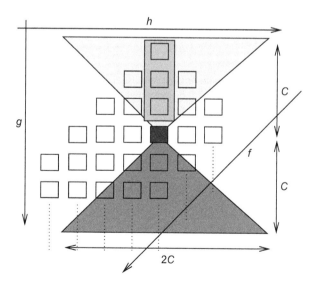

FIGURE 8.7

External A* with consistent estimate in a nonunit cost undirected graph.

Theorem 8.9. *(I/O Performance of External A* in Nonunit Cost Graphs) The I/O complexity for external A* in an implicit undirected unit cost graph, where the weights are in $\{1,\ldots,C\}$, with a consistent estimate, is bounded by $O(\text{sort}(|E|) + C \cdot \text{scan}(|V|))$.*

Proof. It can be shown by induction over $f = i + j$ that no duplicates exist in smaller buckets. The claim is trivially true for $f \le 2C$. In the induction step, assume to the contrary that for some node $v \in Open(i,j)$, $Open(i',j)$ contains a duplicate v' with $i' < i - 2C$; let $u \in Open(i - w(u,v), j_u)$ be the predecessor of v. Then, by the undirected graph structure, there must be a duplicate $u' \in Open(i' + w(u,v), j_u)$. But since $f(u') = i' + w(u,v) + j_u \le i' + C + j_u < i - C + j_u \le i - w(u,v) + j_u = f(u)$, this is a contradiction to the induction hypothesis.

The derivation of the I/O complexity is similar to the unit cost case; the difference is that each bucket is referred to at most $2C + 1$ times for bucket subtraction and expansion. Therefore, each edge in the problem graph is considered at most once. ∎

If we do not impose a bound C on the maximum integer weight, or if we allow directed graphs, the runtime increases to $O(\text{sort}(|E|) + f^* \cdot \text{scan}(|V|))$ I/Os. For larger edge weights and f^*-values, buckets become sparse and should be handled more carefully.

Let us consider how to externally solve FIFTEEN-PUZZLE problem instances that cannot be solved internally with A* and the Manhattan distance estimate. Internal sorting is implemented by applying QUICKSORT. The external merge is performed by maintaining the file pointers for every flushed buffer and merging them into a single sorted file. Since we have a simultaneous file pointers capacity bound imposed by the operating system, a two-phase merging applies. Duplicate removal and bucket subtraction are performed on single passes through the bucket file. As said, the successor's f-value differs from the parent node by exactly 2.

In Table 8.3 we show the diagonal pattern of nodes that is developed during the exploration for a simple problem instance. Table 8.4 illustrates the impact of duplicate removal (*dr*) and bucket subtraction (*sub*) for problem instances of increasing complexity. In some cases, the experiment is terminated because of the limited hard disk capacity.

One interesting feature of our approach from a practical point of view is the ability to pause and resume the program execution in large problem instances. This is desirable, for example, in the case when the limits of secondary storage are reached, because we can resume the execution with more disk space.

8.6.5 *Lower Bound for Delayed Duplicate Detection

Is the complexity for external A* I/O-optimal?

Recall the definition of big-oh notation in Chapter 1: We say $f(n) = O(g(n))$ if there are two constants n_0 and c, such that for all $n \ge n_0$ we have $f(n) \le c \cdot g(n)$. To devise lower bounds for external computation, the following variant of the big-oh notation is appropriate: We say $f(N) \in O(g(N,M,B))$ if there is a constant c, such that for all M and B there is a value N_0, such that for all $N \ge N_0$ we have $f(N) \le c \cdot g(N,M,B)$. The classes Θ and Ω are defined analogously. The intuition for universally

Table 8.3 Nodes inserted in the buckets. Rows denote depth of search (g-value) and columns denote estimated goal distance (h-value).

g\h	1	2	3	4	5	6	7	8	9	10	11
0	–	–	–	1	–	–	–	–	–	–	–
1	–	–	–	–	2	–	–	–	–	–	–
2	–	–	–	4	–	2	–	–	–	–	–
3	–	–	–	–	10	–	4	–	–	–	–
4	–	–	–	7	–	17	–	10	–	–	–
5	–	–	–	–	20	–	34	–	24	–	–
6	–	–	–	6	–	38	–	74	–	44	–
7	–	–	–	–	19	–	71	–	156	–	76
8	–	–	–	8	–	40	–	185	–	195	–
9	–	–	–	–	21	–	97	–	203	–	–
10	–	–	–	3	–	62	–	92	–	–	–
11	–	–	–	–	21	–	46	–	–	–	–
12	–	–	–	5	–	31	–	–	–	–	–
13	–	–	2	–	10	–	–	–	–	–	–
14	–	2	–	5	–	–	–	–	–	–	–
15	2	–	5	–	–	–	–	–	–	–	–

Table 8.4 Impact of duplicate removal and bucket subtraction on the number of generated nodes.

Instance	N	N_{dr}	N_{dr+sub}
1	530,401	2,800	1,654
2	71,751,166	611,116	493,990
3	<out of disk space>	7,532,113	5,180,710
4	<out of disk space>	<out of disk space>	297,583,236
5	<out of disk space>	<out of disk space>	2,269,240,000
6	<out of disk space>	<out of disk space>	2,956,384,330

quantifying M and B is that the adversary first chooses the machine, and then we, as the *good guys*, evaluate the bound.

External sorting in this model has the aforementioned complexity of $\Omega\left(N \lg \frac{N}{B} / B \lg \frac{M}{B}\right)$ I/Os. As internal *set inequality*, *set inclusion*, and *set disjointness* require at least $N \lg N - O(N)$ comparisons, the lower bounds on the number of I/Os for these problems are also $\Omega(sort(N))$.

For the internal duplicate elimination problem the known lower bound on the number of comparisons needed is $N \lg N - \sum_{i=1}^{k} N_i \lg N_i - O(N)$, where N_i is the multiplicity of record i. The main argument is that after the duplicate removal, the total order of the remaining records is known. This result can be lifted to external search and leads to an I/O complexity of at most

$$\Omega\left(\max\left\{\frac{N\lg\frac{N}{B} - \sum_{i=1}^{k} N_i\lg N_i}{B\lg\frac{M}{B}}, N/B\right\}\right)$$

for external delayed duplicate detection. For the sliding-tile puzzle with two preceding buckets and a branching factor $b \leq 4$ we have $N_i \leq 8$. For general consistent estimates in unit cost graphs we have $N_i \leq 3c$, with c being an upper bound on the maximal branching factor.

Theorem 8.10. *(I/O Performance Optimality for External A*) If $|E| = \Theta(|V|)$, delayed duplicate bucket elimination in an implicit unweighted and undirected graph A* search with consistent estimates that need at least $\Omega(\text{sort}(|V|))$ I/O operations.*

Proof. Since each node gives rise to at most c successors and there are at most three preceding buckets in A* search with consistent estimates in a unit cost graph, given that previous buckets are mutually duplicate free, we have at most $3c$ nodes that are the same. Therefore, all sets N_i are bounded by $3c$. Since k is bounded by N we have that $\sum_{i=1}^{k} N_i\lg N_i$ is bounded by $k \cdot 3c\lg 3c = O(N)$. Therefore, the lower bound for duplicate elimination for N nodes is $\Omega(\text{sort}(N) + \text{scan}(N))$. ∎

A related lower bound also applicable to the multiple disk model establishes that solving the duplicate elimination problem with N elements having P different values needs at least $\Omega(\frac{N}{P}\text{sort}(P))$ I/Os, since the depth of any decision tree for the duplicate elimination problem is at least $N\lg(P/2)$. For a search with consistent estimates and a bounded branching factor, we assume to have $P = \Theta(N) = \Theta(|E|) = \Theta(|V|)$, so that the I/O complexity reduces to $O(\text{sort}(|V|))$.

8.7 *REFINEMENTS

As an additional feature, external sorting can be avoided to some extent, by a single or a selection of hash functions that splits larger files into smaller pieces until they fit into main memory. As with the h-value in the preceding case a node and its duplicate will have the same hash address.

8.7.1 Hash-Based Duplicate Detection

Hash-based duplicate detection is designed to avoid the complexity of sorting. It is based on either one or two orthogonal hash functions. The primary hash function distributes the nodes to different files. Once a file of successors has been generated, duplicates are eliminated. The assumption is that all nodes with the same primary hash address fit into the main memory. The secondary hash function (if available) maps all duplicates to the same hash address. This approach can be illustrated by sorting a card deck of 52 cards. If we have only 13 internal memory places the best strategy is to hash cards to different files based on their suit in one scan. Next, we individually read each of the files to the main memory to sort the cards or search for duplicates.

The idea goes back to BUCKET SORT. In its first phase, real numbers $a \in [0,1)$ are thrown into n different buckets $b_i = [i/n, (i+1)/n)$. All the lists that are contained in one bucket can be sorted independently by some other internal sorting algorithm. The sorted lists for b_i are concatenated to a fully sorted list. In the worst case, each element is thrown into the same bucket, such that BUCKET SORT does not improve the sorting. However, in the average case, the (internal) algorithm is much better. Let X_i be a random variable that denotes how many elements fall into *bucket i*; that is, X_i denotes the length of bucket list b_i. For every bucket we might assume that the probability that an element falls into bucket b_i for $j \in \{1,\dots,n\}$ is $1/n$. Therefore, X_i follows a binomial distribution with parameters n and $p = 1/n$. The mean is $E[X_i] = np = 1$ and the variance is $V[X_i] = np(1-p) = 1 - 1/n$.

By iterating BUCKET SORT, it is not difficult to come up with an external version of RADIX SORT that scans the files more than once according to a radix representation of the key values. We briefly illustrate how it works. Say that we have some numbers in the range of 0 and 99, say 48, 26, 28, 87, 14, 86, 50, 23, 34, 69; and 17 in decimal (10-ary) representation. We devise 10 buckets $b_0, \dots b_9$, representing the numbers $0, \dots, 9$. We have two distribution and collection phases. In the first phase we distribute according to the right-most decimal, yielding $b_0 = [50]$, $b_1 = []$, $b_2 = []$, $b_3 = [23]$, $b_4 = [14, 34]$, $b_5 = []$, $b_6 = [26, 86]$, $b_7 = [87, 17]$, $b_8 = [48, 28]$, and $b_9 = [69]$. We collect the data by scanning 50, 23, 14, 34, 26, 86, 87, 17, 48, 28, 69, and distribute this set according to the left-most decimal, yielding $b_0 = []$, $b_1 = [14, 17]$, $b_2 = [26, 28]$, $b_3 = [34]$, $b_4 = [48]$, $b_5 = [50]$, $b_6 = [69]$, $b_7 = []$, $b_8 = [86, 87]$, and $b_9 = []$ for a final scan that produces the sorted outcome.

For the FIFTEEN-PUZZLE problem in ordinary vector representation with a number for each board position, we have 16 phases for radix sort using 16 buckets.

If we have N data elements with a radix representation of length l with base b then the internal time complexity of RADIX SORT is $O(l(N + b))$, and the internal space complexity $O(N + b)$. Since all operations can be buffered, the external time complexity reduces to $O(l(\text{scan}(|V|) + b))$ I/Os. Since we may assume that the number b of buckets needed is small, we have an improvement to EXTERNAL MERGESORT, if $l \cdot \text{scan}(N) < \text{sort}(N)$.

8.7.2 Structured Duplicate Detection

Structured duplicate detection incorporates a hash function that maps nodes into an *abstract* problem graph; this reduces the successor scope of nodes that have to be kept in main memory. Such hash projections are state space homomorphisms (as introduced in Ch. 4), such that for each pair of consecutive abstract nodes the pair of original nodes are also connected. A bucket now corresponds to the set of original states, which all map to the same abstract state. In difference to delayed duplicate detection, structured duplicate detection detects duplicates *early*, as soon as they are generated. Before expanding a bucket, not only the bucket itself, but all buckets that are potentially affected by successor generation have to be loaded and, consequently, fit into main memory.

This gives rise to a different definition of locality, which determines a handle for the duplicate detection scope. In difference to the *locality for delayed duplicate detection* the *locality for structured duplicate detection* is defined as the maximum node branching factor $b_{\max} = \max_{v \in \phi(S)} |Succ(v)|$ in the abstract state space $\phi(S)$.

If there are different abstractions to choose from, a suggestion is to take those that have the smallest ratio of maximum node branching factor $b_{\max}$ and abstract state space size $|\phi(S)|$. The idea is that smaller abstract state space sizes should be preferred but usually lead to larger branching factors.

In the example of the FIFTEEN-PUZZLE (see Fig. 8.8), the projection is based on nodes that have the same blank position. This state space abstraction also preserves the additional property that the

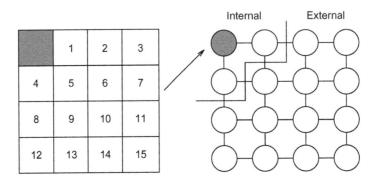

FIGURE 8.8

Example for structured duplicate detection.

successor set and the expansion sets are disjoint, yielding no self-loops in the abstract problem graph. The duplicate scope defines the successor buckets that have to be read into main memory.

The method is crucially dependent on the availability and selection of suitable abstraction functions ϕ that adapt to the internal memory constraints. In contrast, delayed duplicate detection does not rely on any partitioning beside the heuristic function and it does not require the duplicate scope to fit in the main memory.

Structured duplicate detection is compatible with ordinary and hash-based duplicate detection; in case the files that have to be loaded into the main memory no longer fit, we have to delay. However, the structured partitioning may have truncated the file sizes for duplicate detection to a manageable number. Each heuristic or hash function defines a partitioning of the search space but not all partitions provide a good locality with respect to the successor or predecessor states. State space abstractions are specialized hash functions in which we can study the successor relationship.

8.7.3 Pipelining

Many external memory algorithms arrange the data flow in a directed acyclic graph, with nodes representing physical sources. Every node writes or reads *streams* of elements.

Pipelining is a technique inherited from the database community, and improves algorithms that read data from and write data to buffered files. Pipelining allows algorithms to feed the output as a data stream directly to the algorithm that consumes the output, rather than writing it to the disk first.

Streaming nodes is equivalent to scan operations in nonpipelined external memory algorithms. The difference is that nonpipelined conventional scanning needs a linear number of I/Os, whereas streaming often does not incur any I/O, unless a node needs to access external memory data structures.

The nonpipelined and pipelined version of external breadth-first search are compared in Figure 8.9. In the pipelined version the whole algorithm is implemented in one scanner module that reads the nodes in $Open(i-1)$ and $Open(i-2)$ and scans through the stream in just one pass, and outputs the nodes in the current level $Open(i)$ and the multiset $Succ(Open(i))$, which is passed directly to the sorter. The output of the sorter is scanned once to delete duplicates and its output is used as $Open(i+1)$ in the next iteration.

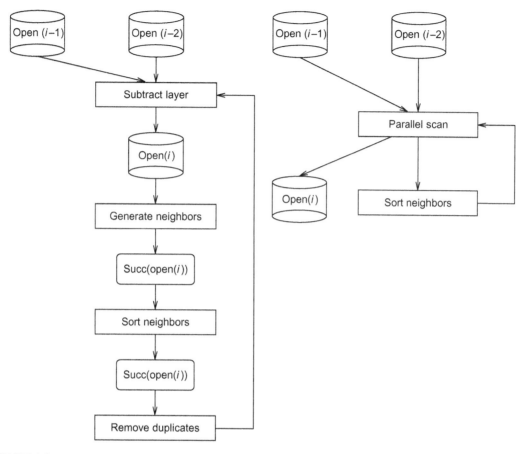

FIGURE 8.9

Pipelining in external BFS.

Pipelining can save constant factors in the I/O complexity of an algorithm. There is a trade-off, since it usually increases internal computational costs.

8.7.4 External Iterative-Deepening A* Search

While external A* requires a constant amount of memory for the internal read and write buffers, IDA* requires very little memory that scales linear with the search depth. External A* removes all duplicates from the search, but to succeed it requires access to disk, which tends to be slow. Moreover, in search practice disk space is limited, too. Therefore, one option is to combine the advantages of IDA* and external A*.

As a first observation, pruning strategies for IDA* search (e.g., omitting predecessors from the successor lists) can help save external space and access time. The reason is that when detecting duplicates late, larger amounts of disk space may be required for generating them.

Table 8.5 Combining IDA* with external A* for a
TWENTY-FOUR-PUZZLE instance.

Split at f-Value	Solution Length	Nodes Generated
68 (IDA*)	82	94,769,462
70 (Hybrid)	82	133,633,811
72 (Hybrid)	82	127,777,529
74 (Hybrid)	82	69,571,621
76 (Hybrid)	82	63,733,384
78 (Hybrid)	82	108,334,552
80 (Hybrid)	82	96,612,234
82 (Hybrid)	82	229,965,025
84 (External A*)	82	171,814,208

The integration of IDA* in external A* is simple. Starting with external A*, the buckets up to a predefined f-value f_{sp} (the *split value*) are generated. Then with increasing depth all buckets on the f_{sp} diagonal are read, and all states contained in the buckets are fed into IDA* as initial states, which is initialized to an anticipated solution length $U = f_{sp}$. As a side effect of all such runs being pairwise independent they can be easily distributed (e.g., on different processor cores).

Table 8.5 shows the results of solving a TWENTY-FOUR-PUZZLE instance according to different f-value splits to document the potential of such hybrid algorithms. In another instance (with an optimal step plan of 100 moves) a split value of 94 generated 367,243,074,706 nodes using 4.9 gigabytes on disk. A split value of 98 resulted in 451,034,974,741 generated nodes and 169 gigabytes on disk. We see that there is potential savings based on the different ordering of moves. By its breadth-first ordering, external A* necessarily expands the entire f^*-diagonal, whereas by its depth-first ordering IDA* does not need to look at all states in the f^*-diagonal. It can stop at the first goal found.

8.7.5 External Explicit-State Pattern Databases

External pattern databases correspond to complete explorations of abstract state spaces. Most frequently they correspond to external BFS with delayed duplicate detection. The construction of external pattern databases is especially suited to *frontier search*, as no solution path has to be reconstructed.

During construction each BFS layer i has been assigned to an individual file B_i. All states in B_i have the same goal distance, and all states that map to a state in i share the heuristic estimate i. For determining the h-value for some given state u in algorithms like external A* we first have to scan the files to find u.

As this is a cost-intensive operation, whenever possible, pattern database lookup should be delayed, so that the heuristic estimates for a larger set of states can be retrieved in one scan. For example, external A* distributes the set of successor states of each bucket according to their heuristic estimates. Hence, it can be adapted to delayed lookup, intersecting the set of successor states with (the state set represented by) the abstract states in the file of a given h-value.

To keep the pattern database partitioned, we have to assume that the number of files that can be opened simultaneously does not exceed $\Delta = \max\{h(v) - h(u)) + 1 \mid u, v \in Succ(u)\}$. We observe that Δ matches the *locality* of an abstract state space graph.

Theorem 8.11. *(Complexity External Pattern Databases Search) In an unweighted problem graph $G = (V, E)$ with pattern database abstraction $\phi(G) = (\phi(V), \phi(E))$ external A* with bounded concrete and abstract locality requires $O(sort(|E|) + scan(|V|) + sort(|\phi(E)|) + f^* \cdot scan(|\phi(V)|))$ I/Os.*

Proof. Constructing the pattern database externally yields $O(sort(|\phi(E)|) + scan(|\phi(V)|))$ I/Os, whereas external A* without external pattern database lookups requires $O(sort(|E|) + scan(|V|))$ I/Os. If we sort the successors with respect to the sorting criteria that has been used to generate the abstract state space we can evaluate the entire successor set in one scan of the entire external pattern database. As we look at most $O((f^*)^2)$ buckets in external A*, this gives a trivial bound of $O((f^*)^2 \cdot scan(|\phi(V)|))$ I/Os. In case of graphs with bounded locality at most a constant number of pattern database files are addressed for each successor set, such that each file is considered as a candidate for a lookup at most $O(f^*)$ times. Moreover, each successor set is additionally scanned at most a constant number of times. Hence, the additional work for pattern database lookup is $O(f^* \cdot scan(|\phi(V)|))$ I/Os. In total, we arrive at $O(sort(|E|) + scan(|V|) + sort(|\phi(E)|) + f^* scan(|\phi(V)|))$ I/Os. ∎

Note that external breadth-first heuristic search with optimal bound $U = f^*$ directly leads to $O(sort(|E|) + scan(|V|) + sort(|\phi(E)|) + f^* \cdot scan(|\phi(V)|))$ I/Os, but iteratively searching for f^* is involved.

Can we avoid the additional sorting requests on the successor set? One solution is to already sort the successor sets in original space according to the order in abstract space. To allow full duplicate elimination, synonyms have to be disambiguated. A hash function h will be called *order preserving*, if for all u in original space $h(u) \leq h(u')$ implies $h(\phi(u)) \leq h(\phi(u'))$. For a pattern database heuristics it not difficult to obtain an order-preserving hash function. In concrete space with state comparison function $\leq_c$ we can include any hash function h_ϕ that has been used to order the states in abstract space as a prefix to $\leq_c$. We extend state u to $u_h = (h_\phi(\phi(u)), u)$ and define $h(u_h) \leq h(u'_h)$ if either $h_\phi(\phi(u)) < h_\phi(\phi(u'))$ or $h_\phi(\phi(u)) < h_\phi(\phi(u'))$ and $u \leq_c u'$.

When using maximization over multiple-pattern databases, a hash function that is order preserving with respect to more than one abstraction is more difficult to obtain. However, successive projection and resorting always works. As the successor sets for resorting have no duplicates, external sorting can be attributed to the set V not to E. For this case, the number of pattern databases k leads to the overall complexity of $O(sort(|E|) + k \cdot sort(|V|) + \sum_{i=1}^{k}(sort(|\phi_i(E)|) + f^* \cdot scan(|\phi_i(V)|)))$ I/Os.

If a heuristic estimate is needed as soon as a node is generated, an appropriate choice for creating external memory pattern databases is a backward BFS with structured duplicate detection, as structured duplication already provides locality with respect to a state space abstraction function. Afterwards, the construction patterns are arranged according to pattern blocks, one for each abstract state. When a concrete heuristic search algorithm expands nodes, it must check whether the patterns from the pattern-lookup scope are in the main memory, and if not, it reads them from disk. Pattern blocks that do not belong to the current pattern-lookup scope are removed. When the part of internal memory is full, the search algorithm must decide which pattern block to remove from internal memory, for example, by adopting the least-recently used strategy.

8.7.6 **External Symbolic Pattern Databases**

Symbolic pattern databases can also be constructed externally. Each BFS level (in the form of a BDD) can be flushed to disk, so that the memory for representing this level can be reused. Again the heuristic is partitioned into files and pattern database lookup in algorithms like external A* is delayed.

As the BDD representation of a state set is unique, during symbolic pattern database construction no effort for eliminating duplicates in one BFS level is required. Before expanding a state set, however, we have to apply duplicate detection with regard to previous BFS levels. If this is too expensive in some critical level, we may afford some states to be represented more than once, but have to ensure termination.

For the construction of larger pattern databases, the intermediate result of the symbolic successor sets (the image) can also become too large to be completed in the main memory. As a solution, we can compute all subimages individually (one for each individual action), flush them, and externally compute their disjunction (e.g., in the form of a binary tree) in a separate program.

8.7.7 **External Relay Search**

Even if all refinements are played, the external exploration might still be too heavy to complete on disk. Besides starting from scratch with some approximate search, *relay search* can be directly applied to the best search bucket(s) found on an completed *f*-diagonal. All other buckets are eliminated from the search. As a result a lower and upper bound on the problem instances are produced.

Figure 8.10 illustrates the memory profile for a *relay solution* that solves fully random instances of the THIRTY-FIVE-PUZZLE with symbolic pattern databases. We observe three exploration peaks, where the search consumed too much resources and it was restarted with the currently best solution

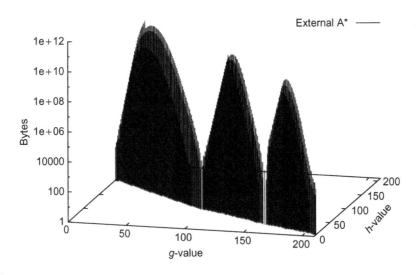

FIGURE 8.10

Memory profile of relay solution for the THIRTY-FIVE-PUZZLE.

buckets. Starting with an initial estimate 152 as a lower bound the obtained range for the optimal solution was [166, 214]. The large-scale exploration consumed $2, 566, 708, 604, 768 + 535, 388, 038, 560 + 58, 618, 421, 920$ bytes (≈ 2.9 terabytes).

8.8 *EXTERNAL VALUE ITERATION

We now discuss an approach for extending the search model to cover uncertainty. More precisely, we extend the value iteration procedure (introduced in Ch. 2) to work on large state spaces that cannot fit into the RAM. The algorithm is called *external value iteration*. Instead of working on states, we work on edges for reasons that shall become clear soon. In our case, an edge is a 4-tuple

$$(u, v, a, f(v)),$$

where u is called the predecessor state, v the stored state, a the action that transforms u into v, and $f(v)$ is the current assignment of the value function to v. Clearly, v must belong to $Succ(a, u)$. In deterministic problems, v is determined by u and a and so it can be completely dropped, but for the nondeterministic problems, it is a necessity.

Similarly to the internal version of value iteration, the external version works in two phases. A forward phase, where the state space is generated, and a backward phase, where the heuristic values are repeatedly updated until an ϵ-optimal policy is computed, or t_{max} iterations are performed.

We will explain the algorithm in a running example using the graph in Figure 8.11. The states are numbered from 1 to 10, the initial state is 1, and the terminal states are 8 and 10. The numbers next to the states are the initial heuristic values.

8.8.1 Forward Phase: State Space Generation

Typically, a state space is generated by a depth-first or a breadth-first exploration that uses a hash table to avoid reexpansion of states. We choose an external breadth-first exploration to handle large state spaces. Since in an external setting a hash table is not affordable, we rely on delayed duplication detection. It consists of two phases, first removing duplicates within the newly generated layer, and then removing duplicates with respect to previously generated layers. Note that an edge $(u, v, a, f(v))$ is a duplicate if and only if its predecessor u, its state v, and the action a match an existing edge. Thus, in undirected graphs, there are two different edges for each undirected edge. In our case, sorting-based delayed duplicate detection is best suited as the sorted order and is further exploited during the backward phase.

Algorithm 8.8 shows external value iteration in pseudo code. For each depth value d the algorithm maintains the BFS layers $Layer(d)$ on disk. The first phase ends up by concatenating all layers into one *Open* list that contains all edges reachable from s. For bounded locality, the complexity of this phase is $O(scan(|E|) + sort(|E|))$ I/Os.

8.8.2 Backward Phase: Update of Values

This is the most critical part of the approach and deserves more attention. To perform the update on the value of state v, we have to bring together the value of its successor states. Because they both

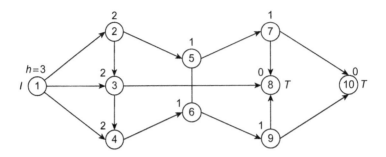

FIGURE 8.11

An example graph with initial ($f = h$)-values.

Procedure External-Value-Iteration
Input: Problem graph with start node s and heuristic h,
       tolerance $\epsilon > 0$, max. iterations t_{max}
Output: ϵ-optimal value function (on disk) if $t_{max} = \infty$

$Layer(0) \leftarrow \{(\emptyset, s, \perp, h(s))\}$	;; Initial state has no predecessor state and action
$d \leftarrow 0$	;; Initialize depth value
while $(Layer(d) \neq \emptyset)$	;; Unless state space fully traversed
$d \leftarrow d + 1$	;; Maintain depth of BFS layer
$Layer(d) \leftarrow \{(u, v, a, h(v)) \,\|$	
$u \in Layer(d-1), a \in A(u), v \in Succ(a, u)\}$	;; Next bucket
Sort $Layer(d)$ with respect to edges (u, v)	;; Prepare delayed duplicate detection
Remove duplicate edges in $Layer(d)$	;; Duplicate elimination within bucket...
Subtract duplicate edges from $Layer(d)$	;; ... and wrt. previous ones
$Open_0 \leftarrow Layer(0) \cup Layer(1) \cup \ldots \cup Layer(d-1)$	;; Merge BFS layers
Sort $Open_0$ with respect to states v	;; Sorting with respect to second component
$t \leftarrow 0; Residual \leftarrow +\infty$	;; Initialize iteration and approximation quality
while $t < t_{max} \wedge Residual > \epsilon$	;; Termination criterion
$Residual \leftarrow Backward\text{-}Update(Open_t)$	;; Call subroutine
$t \leftarrow t + 1$	;; Increase iteration

Algorithm 8.8

External value iteration algorithm.

---

are contained in one file, and there is no arrangement that can bring all successor states close to their predecessor states, we make a copy of the entire graph (file) and deal with the current state and its successor differently. To establish the adjacencies, the second copy, called *Temp*, is sorted with respect to the node u. Remember that *Open* is sorted with respect to the node v.

A parallel scan of files *Open* and *Temp* gives us access to all the successors and values needed to perform the update on the value of v. This scenario is shown in Figure 8.12 for the graph in the example. The contents of *Temp* and $Open_t$, for $t = 0$, are shown along with the heuristic values computed so far for each edge (u, v). The arrows show the flow of information (alternation between dotted and dashed arrows is just for clarity). The results of the updates are written to the file $Open_{t+1}$ containing the new

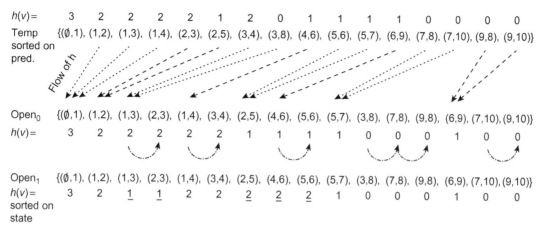

FIGURE 8.12

Backward phase in external value iteration. The files $Open_0$ and $Temp$ are stored on disk. A parallel scan of both files is done from left to right. The file $Open_1$ is the result of the first update; values that changed in the first update are shown with bold underline typeface.

values for each state after $t+1$ iterations. Once $Open_{t+1}$ is computed, the file $Open_t$ can be removed since it is no longer needed.

Algorithm 8.9 shows the backward update algorithm for the case of MDP models; the other models are similar. It first copies the $Open_t$ list in $Temp$ using buffered I/O operations, and sorts the new $Temp$ list according to the predecessor states u. The algorithm then iterates on all edges from $Open_t$ and searches for the successors in $Temp$. Since $Open_t$ is sorted with respect to states v, *the algorithm never goes back and forth in any of the* $Open_t$ *or* $Temp$ *files.* Note that all reads and writes are buffered and thus can be carried out very efficiently by always doing I/O operations in blocks.

We now discuss the different cases that might arise when an edge $(u,v,a,f(v))$ is read from $Open_t$. States from Figure 8.11 that comply with each case are referred to in parentheses. The flow of the values in h for the example is shown in Figure 8.12.

- *Case I:* v is terminal (states 8 and 10). Since no update is necessary, the edge can be written to $Open_{t+1}$.
- *Case II:* v is the same as the last updated state (state 3). Write the edge to $Open_{t+1}$ with this last value. (Case shown in Figure 8.12 with curved arrows.)
- *Case III:* v has no successors. That means that v is a terminal state and so is handled by case I.
- *Case IV:* v has one or more successors (remaining states). For each action $a \in A(v)$, compute the value $q(a,v)$ by summing the products of the probabilities and the stored values. Such value is kept in the array $q(a)$.

For edges (x,y,a',f') read from $Temp$, we have:

- *Case A:* y is the initial state, implying $x = \emptyset$. Skip this edge since there is nothing to do. By taking $\emptyset$ as the smallest element, the sorting of $Temp$ brings all such edges to the front of the file. (Case not shown for sake of brevity.)

• *Case B: x = v*, the predecessor of this edge, matches the current state from *Open$_t$*. This calls for an update in the $q(a)$-value.

The array $q : A \rightarrow \mathbb{R}$ is initialized to the edge weight $w(a,v)$, for each $a \in A(v)$. Once all the successors are processed, the new value for v is the minimum of the values stored in the q-array for all applicable actions.

An important point to note here is that the last edge read from *Temp* isn't used. The operation *Push-back* puts back this edge into *Temp*. This operation incurs in no physical I/O since the *Temp* file is buffered. Finally, to handle case II, a copy of the last updated node and its value are stored in variables v_{last} and h_{last}, respectively.

Theorem 8.12. *(I/O Complexity External Value Iteration) Assuming bounded locality the algorithm external value iteration performs at most $O(\text{scan}(|E|) + t_{max} \cdot \text{sort}(|E|))$ I/Os.*

Proof. For bounded locality, the forward phase requires $O(\text{scan}(|E|) + \text{sort}(|E|))$ I/Os. Moreover, the backward phase performs at most t_{max} iterations. Each such iteration consists of one sorting and two scanning operations for a total of $O(t_{max} \cdot \text{sort}(|E|))$ I/Os. ∎

Procedure Backward-Update
Input: Edge state space *Open$_t$* (stored on disk)
Output: Edge state space *Open$_{t+1}$* (stored in disk)
Side Effect: Files *Temp* and *Open$_{t+1}$* written

$Residual \leftarrow 0$	;; Initialize approximation quality
$Temp \leftarrow Open_t$	;; Copy file
Sort *Temp* with respect to states u	;; Sorting with respect to first component
for each $(u,v,a,f) \in Open_t$	;; Scan entire search space
if $v \in T$	;; Special case (I), goal found
Write (u,v,a,f) to *Open$_{t+1}$*	;; Copy value to next iteration
else if $v = v_{last}$	;; Case (II), successor has not changed
Write (u,v,a,f_{last}) to *Open$_{t+1}$*	;; Copy value to next iteration
else	;; Predecessor match
Read (x,y,a',f') from *Temp*	;; Case (IV) is $x = v$; case (III) is $x \neq v$
for each $a \in A(v)$ $q(a) \leftarrow w(a,v)$	;; Compute initial q-value
while $x = v$	;; Predecessor match
$q(a') \leftarrow q(a') + P_{a'}(y|x)f'$	;; Update q-value
Read (x,y,a',f') from *Temp*	;; Read next
Push back (x,y,a',f') in *Temp*	;; Last value needed to detect change
$f_{last} \leftarrow \min_{a\in A(v)} q(a)$	;; Update value function
$v_{last} \leftarrow v$	;; Copy to temporary
Write (u,v,a,f_{last}) to *Open$_{t+1}$*	;; Flush information
$Residual \leftarrow \max\{|f_{last} - f|, Residual\}$	;; Update approximation quality
return *Residual*	;; Generate output

Algorithm 8.9

External value iteration—backward update.

As an example domain we consider the sliding-tile puzzle, performing two experiments: one with deterministic moves, and the other with noisy actions that achieve their intended effects with probability $p = 0.9$ and no effect with probability $1 - p$. The rectangular 3×4 sliding-tile puzzle cannot be solved with internal value iteration because the state space did not fit in RAM. External value iteration generated a total of 1,357,171,197 edges taking 45 gigabytes of disk space. The backward update has finished successfully in 72 iterations using 1.4 gigabytes RAM. The value function for initial state converged to 28.8889 with a residual smaller than $\epsilon = 10^{-4}$.

8.9 *FLASH MEMORY

Mechanical hard disks have provided us with reliable service over these years. Their dominance at least on mobile devices is about to change with the advent of solid state disk (SSD). An SSD is electrically, mechanically, and software compatible with a conventional (magnetic) hard disk drive. The difference is that the storage medium is not magnetic (like a hard disk) or optical (like a CD), but a solid state semiconductor (NAND flash) such as a battery-backed RAM or other electrically erasable RAM-like chip. In the last few years, NAND flash memories outpaced RAM in terms of bit density, and the market with SSDs continues to grow. This provides faster access time than a disk because the data can be randomly accessed and does not rely on a read/write interface head synchronizing with a rotating disk. Typical values for data transfer bandwidth and access time for both magnetic and solid state disks is shown in Figure 8.13. (These values are, of course, subject to hardware changes, where SSDs seem to advance faster than HDDs.)

The speed of random reads for an SSD built with NAND flash memory lies roughly at the geometric mean of the speeds of RAM and a magnetic hard disk drive (HDD). The only factor limiting SSDs from being massively spread is the cost of the device if expressed per stored bit. The cost per stored bit is still significantly higher for SSDs than for magnetic disks.

We observe that random read operations on SSDs are substantially faster than on mechanical disks, while other parameters are similar. Therefore, it appears natural to ask whether it is necessary to employ *delayed duplicate detection* (DDD) known from the current I/O-efficient graph search algorithms, or if is possible to build an efficient SSD algorithm using standard *immediate duplicate detection* (IDD), hashing in particular.

Note that the external memory model is no longer a good match, since it does not cover the different access times for random read and write operations. For SSDs, therefore, it is suitable to extend

Characteristic	Hard Disk	Solid State Disk
Read Bandwidth	65 MB/s	72 MB/s
Write Bandwidth	60 MB/s	70 MB/s
Random Read Access Time	11 ms	0.1 ms
Random Write Access Time	11 ms	5 ms

FIGURE 8.13

Characteristics of solid state and hard disk drives.

the external memory model just introduced. One option is to work with different buffer sizes for read and write. Another option that we have chosen is to include a penalty factor p for random write operations.

There are different options to exploit SSDs in state space search. First, we study direct access to the SSD without exploiting RAM. This implies both random read and random write operations. The implementation serves as a reference, and can be scaled to any implicit graph search with a visited state space that fits on the SSD. As an improvement, a bit-state table in RAM can then be used to avoid unsuccessful lookups.

Next, we compress the state in internal memory to include the address on secondary memory. For this case, states are written sequentially to the external memory in the order of generation. For resolving hash synonyms, state lookups in the form of random reads are needed. Even though linear probing shows performance deficiencies for internal hashing, for blockwise strategies, it is the apparent candidates. Alternative hashing strategies can further reduce the number of random reads.

The third approach flushes the internal hash table to the external device once it becomes full. In this case, full state vectors are stored internally. For large amounts of external memory and small vector sizes, large state spaces can be looked at. Usually the exploration process is suspended while flushing the internal hash table. We observe different trade-offs for the amount of randomness for reading and writing, which mainly depend on increasing the locality of the access.

8.9.1 Hashing

The general setting (see Fig. 8.14) is a background hash table H_b kept on the SSD, which can hold $m = 2^b$ entries. We additionally assume a foreground hash table H_f with $m' = 2^f$ entries. The ratio between foreground and background is, therefore, $r = 2^k = 2^{b-f}$. Collisions especially on the background hash table can yield additional burden. As chaining requires overhead for storing and following links, we are left with open addressing and adequate probing strategies.

As indicated earlier, SSDs prefer sequential writes and sequential reads, but can cope with an acceptable number of random reads. As linear probing finds elements through sequential scanning, it is I/O efficient. For load factor α, a successful search requires about $1/2\,(1 + 1/(1 - \alpha))$ accesses on the average, but an unsuccessful search requires about $LP_\alpha = 1/2\left(1 + 1/(1 - \alpha)^2\right)$ accesses on the average. For a hash table that is filled up to $\alpha = 50\%$ we have less than three states to look at on the average, which easily fit into the I/O buffer. Given that random access is slower than sequential access, this implies that unless the hash table becomes filled, linear probing with one I/O per lookup per node is an appropriate option for SSD-based hashing.

8.9.2 Mapping

The simplest method to apply SSDs in graph search is to store each node at its background hash address in a file, and if occupied, to apply a conflict resolution strategy on disk. By their large seek times, this option is clearly infeasible for HDDs, but it does apply to some extent to SSDs. Nonetheless, besides extensive use of random writes that operate blockwise and are, thus, expected to be slow, one problem of the approach is the initialization time, incurred by erasing all existing data stored in the background hash table.

Hence, we apply a refinement to speed up search. With one additional bitvector array kept in RAM, we denote whether or not a state is already stored on disk. This limits initialization time to reset all

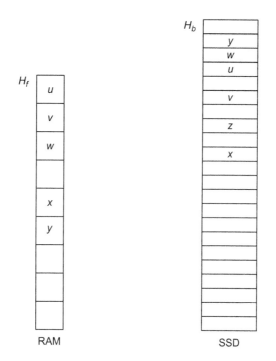

FIGURE 8.14

Foreground and background hash table, such as RAM and SSD.

bits in main memory, which is much faster. Moreover, this saves lookup time in case of hashing a new state with an unused table entry. Figure 8.15 (left) illustrates the approach. The bitvector *occupied* memorizes, if the address on the SSD is in use.

The extra amount of RAM additionally limits the size of the search spaces to be processed. In search practice with a full state vector of several hundred bytes to be stored in the background hash table, however, investing one bit per state in RAM does no harm, given that the ratio between main and external memory remains moderate. The only limit for the exploration is imposed by the number of states that can be stored on the solid state disk, which we assume to be sufficiently large.

For analyzing the approach, let n be the number of nodes and e be the number of edges in the state space graph that are looked at. Without occupied vector, this requires e lookup and n insert operations. Let B be the size of a block (amount of data retrieved, or written with one I/O operation) and $|s|$ be the fixed length of the state vector. As long as $LP_\alpha \cdot |s| \leq B$, at most two blocks are read for each lookup (when linear probing arrives at the end of the table, an additional seek to the start of the file is needed). For $LP_\alpha \cdot |s| > B$ no additional random read access is necessary. After the lookup, an insert operation results in one random write. This results in a flash I/O complexity of $O(e + pn)$, where p is the penalty factor for random write operations. Using the occupied vector, the number of read operations reduces from e to n, assuming that no collisions take place.

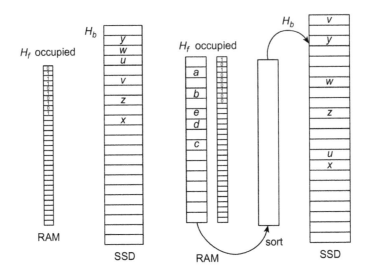

FIGURE 8.15

External hashing without and with merging.

As the main bottleneck of the approach is random writing to the background hash table, as another refinement we can additionally employ a foreground hash table as a write buffer. Due to numerous insert operations, the foreground hash table will become filled, and then has to be flushed to the background, which incurs writes and subsequent reads. One option that we call *merging* is to sort the internal hash table with regard to the external hash function before flushing. If the hash functions are correlated, the sequence is already presorted, by means that the number of inversions $inv(H_f) = |\{(i,j) \mid h_f(s_i) < h_f(s_j) \land h_b(s_i) > h_b(s_j)\}|$ is small. If $inv(H_f)$ is small we use an algorithm like *adaptive sort* that exploits presorting. While flushing we now have a sequential write (due to the linear probing strategy), such that the total worst-case I/O time for flushing is bounded by the number of flushes times the efforts for sequential writes. Figure 8.15 (right) illustrates the approach. Since we are able to exploit sequential data processing, updating the background hash table corresponds to a scan (see Fig. 8.16). Blocks are read into the RAM and merged with the internal information and then flushed back to SSD.

8.9.3 Compressing

Here we store all state vectors in a file on the external storage device, and substitute the state vector by its relative file pointer position. For an external hash table of size m this requires $\lceil \lg m \rceil$ bits per entry and $m \lceil \lg m \rceil$ bits in total. Figure 8.17 illustrates the approach with arrows denoting the position on external memory. An additional bitvector is no longer needed.

This strategy also results in e lookups and n insert operations. Since the ordering of states on the SSD does not necessarily correlate with the order in main memory, the lookup of states due to linear probing induces multiple random reads. Hence, the amount of individual blocks that have to be read is

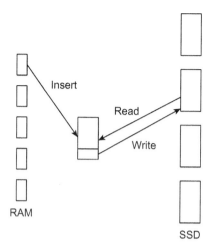

FIGURE 8.16

Updating tables in hashing with linear probing while merging.

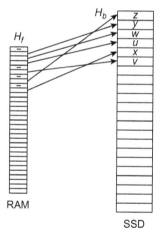

FIGURE 8.17

State compressing strategy.

bounded by $LP_\alpha \cdot e$. In contrast, all insert operations are performed sequentially, utilizing a cache of B bytes in memory. Subsequently, this approach performs $O(LP_\alpha \cdot e)$ random reads to the SSD. As long as $LP_\alpha < 2$ this approach performs less random read operations than mapping. By using another internal hashing strategy, for example, cuckoo hashing (see Ch. 3), we can reduce the maximum number of lookups to 2. As sequential writing of n states of s bytes requires $n|s|/B$ I/Os, the total flash-memory I/O complexity is $O(LP_\alpha \cdot e + n|s|/B)$.

8.9.4 Flushing

The previous approaches either require significant time to write data according to h_b or request significant sizes of foreground memory. There are further trade-offs that we will consider next.

One first solution, called *padding*, appends the entire foreground hash table as it is to the existing data on the background table. Hence, the background hash function can be roughly characterized as $h_b(s) = i \cdot m' + h_f(s)$, where i denotes the current number of flushes, and s the state to be hashed.

Writing is sequential, and conflict resolution strategy is inherited from the internal memory. For several flushing readings, a state for answering membership queries becomes involved, as the search for one state incurs up to r many table lookups. Conflict resolution may lead to an even worse performance. For a moderate number of states that exceed RAM resources only by a very small factor, however, the average performance is expected to be good. As far as all states can reside in main memory no access to the background hash table is needed.

We can safely assume that load factor α is small enough, so that the extra amount of work due to linear probing is transparent by using block accesses. Again, e lookups and n insert operations are performed. Let e_i be the number of successors generated in phase i, $i \in \{0, \dots, r-1\}$. For phase 0 no access to the background table is needed. For phase i, $i > 0$, at most $O(i \cdot e_i)$ blocks have to be read. Together with the sequential write of n elements (in r rounds) this results in a flash-memory complexity of $O(n|s|/B + rp + \sum_{0 \le i < r} i \cdot e_i)$ I/Os. An illustration is provided in Figure 8.18 (left). The entire foreground hash table has been flushed once, and the maximum number of flushes is set to 3.

The obvious alternative is to *slice* the background hash table, such that $h_b(s)$ becomes $h_f(s) \cdot r$ plus the number of flushes. An illustration is provided in Figure 8.18 (right); this is the situation after one flush, and again, at most three flushes are assumed.

The disadvantage of processing the entire external hash table during flushing is compensated by the fact that the probing sequences in the hash tables can now be searched concurrently. For the lookup we use a bit vector (of size equal to the number of flushes) that monitors if an individual probing sequence has terminated with an empty bucket. If all probing sequences fail, the query itself has failed.

8.10 SUMMARY

By the rapid increase in size and sequential access time and the rapid decrease in prices, in this chapter we have studied external (memory) search algorithms that explore the problem graph by utilizing hard disks.

Graph search algorithms, such as BFS, depth-first search, and A*, use duplicate detection to recognize when the same node is reached via alternative paths in a graph. This traditionally involves storing already explored nodes in random access memory (RAM) and checking newly generated nodes against the stored nodes. However, the limited size of RAM creates a memory bottleneck that severely limits the range of problems that can be solved with this approach. All clever techniques that have been developed for searching with limited RAM eventually are limited in terms of scalability, and many practical graph search problems are too large to be solved using any of these techniques. Relying on virtual memory slows down the exploration due to an excessive number of page faults. We have shown that the scalability of graph search algorithms can be dramatically improved by using external memory, such as a disk, to store generated nodes for use in duplicate detection. However, this requires very

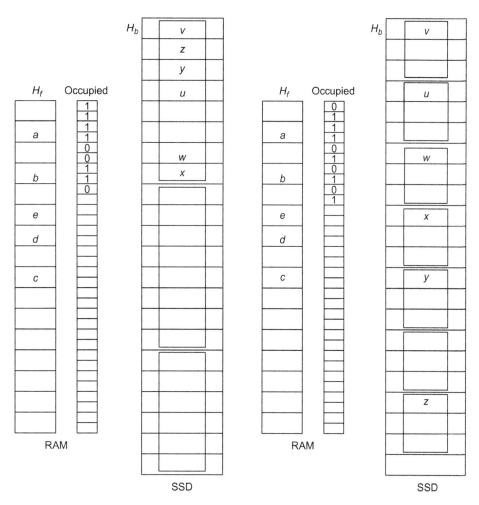

FIGURE 8.18

Padding and slicing strategies.

different search strategies to overcome the six orders-of-magnitude difference in random access speed between RAM and disk.

Disk access is supervised by the exploration algorithms rather than by the underlying operating system. Thus, the algorithm design is mainly concerned about access locality. Efficient designs provide alternative implementations to an internal hash table and allow a *delayed* detection of duplicates. If disk space becomes sparse, *early merging* delayed duplicate detections is invoked on demand. In *hash-based duplicate detection* coarse hash codes are effective for accelerating external sorting. If according to the hash value, the neighboring sets fit into main memory, so-called *structured duplicate detection* ensures that all duplicates are caught in the RAM.

The partitioning of the state space into buckets has much in common with the symbolic (blind and heuristic) search algorithm in Chapter 7. As the exploration is explicit-state, duplicates within one bucket have to be found by external sorting followed by an external scan operation.

External BFS was discovered for explicit graph search, but is much more effective in implicit graph search because no access to the adjacency list is required. Some algorithmic techniques such as preprocessing the explicit graph become obsolete, while others like pipelining become more attractive. Using one file as a queue, external BFS is I/O optimal in undirected graphs (either sparse or not). When looking at directed graphs, once again, the locality of the problem graphs becomes the important measurement to determine the duplicate detection scope. Besides the sorting it influences the I/O complexity the most.

Given the optimal solution bound, external A* and external breadth-first heuristic search both operate with a growing g-value and thus explore the same state sets. Although external A* has some difficulties in obtaining optimal efficiency in very sparse graphs (e.g., a chain of states) inducing extremely long solutions (file buffers are needed for every active bucket), external breadth-first heuristic search will have difficulties when searching with an unknown solution depth (for a rising threshold new states hardly squeeze in existing files).

We have extended external memory search from deterministic to the general search model that includes nondeterministic and probabilistic search spaces, like MDPs. Different to the deterministic setting, the external value iteration algorithm generates the entire set of reachable states, requires many passes over the problem graph, and operates on the problem graph edges instead of the problem graph nodes.

Table 8.6 gives an overview of the external algorithms presented in this chapter. To ease the denotation of the complexities, we assume constant locality as implied be undirected graph structures and use $|G|$ to abbreviate $|V| + |E|$. Nonetheless, most algorithms extend to integer edge weights and directed

Table 8.6 Overview of external search algorithms. Complexities assume constant locality; MR is the algorithm of Munagala and Ranade; MM is the algorithm of Mehlhorn and Meyer.

Name	I/O Complexity	Weight	Graph	Optimal
MR (8.1)	$O(|V| + sort(|E|))$	uniform	undirected	✓
MM	$O(\sqrt{|V|scan(|G|)} + sort(|G|))$	uniform	undirected	✓
Ext.-SSSP	$O(sort(|G|))$	$\mathbb{R}$	regular	✓
Ext.-BFS (8.2)	$O(scan(|V|) + sort(|E|))$	uniform	undirected	✓
Ext.-A* (8.7)	$O(scan(|V|) + sort(|E|))$	uniform	undirected	✓
Ext.-PDB-A*	$O(sort(|E|) + scan(|V|) +$ $sort(|\phi(E)|) + f^*scan(|\phi(V)|))$	uniform	undirected	✓
Ext.-BFBnB (8.4)	$O(scan(|V|) + sort(|E|))$	$\mathbb{R}$	undirected	✓
Ext.-BFHS (8.4)	$O(scan(|V|) + sort(|E|))$	uniform	undirected	✓
Ext.-EHC (8.5,8.6)	$O(h(s) \cdot (scan(|V|) + sort(|E|)))$	$\mathbb{N}$	undirected	-
Ext.-SDD	$O(|G|)$	uniform	structured	✓
Ext.-VI (8.8,8.9)	$O(scan(|E|) + t_{max} \cdot sort(|E|)))$	general	structured	✓

graphs. In directed graphs, a larger set of buckets has to be traversed to subtract duplicates from earlier search levels. In weighted graphs, nonadjacent buckets have to be addressed. Explicit graph search is only efficient for regular graph subclasses. For external BFS and external A* with delayed duplicate detection we have a matching lower bound.

Structured duplicate detection is assigned to an I/O complexity of $O(|G|)$, which is apparent if the projection function is the identity. In theory, such worst-case performance can occur in any abstraction that forces singleton nodes to be retrieved from disk. In terms of *cache-oblivious algorithms*, it is worth mentioning that the localized exploration that uses RAM and hard disks also optimizes the CPU cache performance.

With the advent of solid state disk technology, immediate duplicate detection becomes tractable, offering more flexibility for the choice of the exploration strategy. Monitoring CPU performances suggests that I/O waits are present, but not thrashing. With SSDs' random access time decreasing, SSDs will likely become fast enough to rise the CPU usage to full speed making the SSD fully transparent to the user. Compression, likely the best performing strategy, requires substantial main memory, which according to current ratios of space between RAM and SSDs is still no bottleneck.

8.11 EXERCISES

8.1   For an *external stack*, the buffer is an internal memory array of $2B$ elements that at any time contains the $k < 2B$ elements most recently inserted. We assume that the stack content is bounded by at most N elements.

   1. Implement a remove operation with no I/O, except for the case when the buffer has run empty. In this case a single I/O to retrieve a block of B elements is allowed.
   2. Implement an insert operation with no I/O, except for the case when the buffer has run full. In this case a single I/O to write a block of B elements is allowed.
   3. Show that insertion and deletion take $1/B$ I/Os in the amortized sense.
   4. Why does a stack not use a buffer of size B, but $2B$ instead?
   5. Implement an external queue using two stacks to achieve $1/B$ I/Os amortized for insertion and deletion.

8.2   An external linked list preserves locality: Elements that are near each other in the list must tend to be stored in the same block.

   1. Show that a simple approach of putting B consecutive elements in each block yields a list scan of N elements in $O(N/B)$ I/Os.
   2. Show that such a simple implementation requires $\Omega(N/B)$ I/Os for insertion and deletion.

8.3   A refined implementation of an external linked list maintains the following invariant: There are more than $2B/3$ elements in every pair of consecutive blocks.

   1. Show that the number of I/Os for a sequential scan grows by at most a factor of three.
   2. If either neighbor of the block for an insertion is full, we split the block into two blocks of at most $B/2$ elements. Show that the invariant is maintained.
   3. If one of the neighbors of the block for a deletion has $2B/3$ elements or less, we merge the two blocks. Show that the invariant is maintained.

   4. Show that splitting and merging can be done in $O(1)$ I/Os.
   5. Show that this approach ensures a constant number of I/Os to update a linked list.
   6. Show that this approach gives $O(1 + N/B)$ I/Os for N consecutive inserts.
   7. Show that after an insertion at least $B/6$ deletions are needed to violate the invariance.
   8. Increase the space utilization from $1/3$ to $1/\epsilon$.

8.4   Suppose we are given three large arrays A, B, and C of size n that exceed main memory. Moreover C is a permutation $\{C[1],\ldots,C[n]\} = \{1,\ldots,n\}$. The task is to assign $A[i]$ to $B[C[i]]$ for
   $i \in \{1,\ldots,n\}$.
   1. Show that the naive approach of sequentially processing the input implies $O(n)$ I/Os.
   2. Devise a strategy that has an I/O complexity of $O(sort(n))$.

8.5   Let the *BFS number* be the order of node visits in a BFS traversal and the *BFS tree* be the tree
   associated with a BFS search. (For each node v the parent of v in the BFS tree is the node with
   $bfsnum = \min_{v,w} bfsnum(w)$.) Show that for undirected graphs the following transformation can
   be done using $O(sort(|V| + |E|))$ I/Os:
   1. BFS numbers in BFS tree.
   2. BFS tree in BFS level.
   3. BFS level in BFS numbers.

8.6   As a simple external implementation of a balanced binary search tree incurs $O(\lg N)$ I/Os,
   B-trees have been proposed as a generalization to trees of degree $\Theta(B)$. For external usage,
   a B-tree node guides searches to one of the $\Theta(B)$ subtrees. The balance invariant requires that
   (1) for every node at level i smaller than the height of the tree h the number of leaves below
   are at least $(B/8)^i$ and (2) for every node at level $i \leq h$ the number of leaves below is at most
   $4(B/8)^i$. Show that the balance invariant implies the following assertions:
   1. Any node has at most $B/2$ children.
   2. The height of the B-tree is at most $1 + \lceil \lg_{B/8} N \rceil$.
   3. Any nonroot node has as at least $B/32$ children.
   4. Infer that the worst case for searching a B-tree is $1 + \lceil \lg_{B/8} N \rceil$ I/Os.
   5. Show a lower bound of $\Theta(\lg_B N)$ on the height of the B-tree.
   6. Explain how to perform insertions and deletions in $O(\lg_B N)$ I/Os.

8.7   Explain the working of the algorithm of Munagala and Ranade with respect to the graph in
   Figure 8.19 starting at node 1. What are the generated nodes in $Succ(Open(i))$ for $i > 0$? For
   each iteration remove the duplicates in this set and display the nodes that are remaining. For
   each iteration remove the lists $Open(i-1)$ and $Open(i-2)$.

8.8   Derive an external implementation of the implicit version of the Bellman-Ford algorithm
   (see Ch. 2) that uses $O(k \cdot (sort(|E|) + scan(|V|)))$ I/Os, where k is the length of the cost-
   optimal solution path. You may restrict to undirected unit cost problem graphs. Use a derivate of
   Munagala and Ranade's external BFS implementation and restrict duplicate elimination to
   allow reopening. Show that each edge and each node is considered at most k times to arrive
   at the stated complexity.

8.9   Show that the number of buckets $Open(i,j)$ that are considered by external A* in a unit cost
   problem graph with a consistent heuristic is bounded by $(f^* + 1)^2/3$.

Open(*i* − 2)   Open(*i* − 1)   Open(*i*)

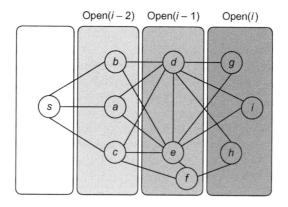

FIGURE 8.19

Extended example for the algorithm of Munagala and Ranade.

8.10 Give a pseudo-code implementation for external BFS exploration for cost-optimizing search, incrementally improving an upper bound U on the solution cost. The state sets that are used should be represented in the form of files. The search frontier denoting the current BFS layer is tested for an intersection with the goal, and this intersection is further reduced according to the already established bound.

8.11 Show that external A* with one pattern database heuristic can be executed in $O(sort(|E|) + scan(|V|) + sort(|\phi(E)|) + (f^* - h(s)) \cdot scan(|\phi(V)|))$ I/Os. (The only change is the factor $f^* - h(s)$ compared to f^* in the text.)

8.12 The PANCAKE problem is defined as follows. Given an n-stack of pancakes of different sizes, how many flips of the first k pancakes are needed to get them into ascending order? The problem is illustrated in Figure 8.20. It is known that $(5n + 5)/3$ flips alway suffice, and that $15n/14$ is a lower bound. In the BURNED PANCAKE problem the pancakes are burned on one side and the additional requirement is to bring all burned sides down. It is known that $(2n - 2)$ flips always suffice and that $3n/2$ is a lower bound.

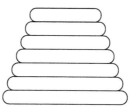

FIGURE 8.20

The PANCAKE problem.

1. Show that by iteratively putting the next largest element in its proper place we can obtain a solution with $2n - 3$ flips, and when the initial permutation has none of the desired adjacencies, at least n flips are needed.
2. An unproven conjecture for the BURNED PANCAKE problem is that the worst-case scenario is the original stack with all burned sides up. Validate it for $n = 1, 2, 3, 4$.
3. Derive a heuristic for the PANCAKE problem that is defined on the number of times the order changes from smaller to larger pancakes and vice versa.
4. Solve the problem with external BFS up to $n = 16$ for the ordinary and up to $n = 11$ for the BURNED PANCAKE problem. How far can you scale with external A* search?

8.12 BIBLIOGRAPHIC NOTES

The single disk model for external memory algorithms has been invented by Aggarwal and Vitter (1988). A detailed introduction has been given by Sanders, Meyer, and Sibeyn (2002). The buffer tree data structure is due to Arge (1996). A number of other variants for external priority queues have been suggested in the literature (Kumar and Schwabe, 1996; Fadel et al., 1997; Brengel et al., 1999). The tournament tree and its application to graph search has been proposed by Kumar and Schwabe (1996), and the buffered repository tree and its use in external graph search has been studied in Buchsbaum, Goldwasser, Venkatasubramanian, and Westbrook (2000).

There is no major difference in the application algorithm of Munagala and Ranade (1999) for explicit and implicit graphs. However, the precomputation and access efforts are by far larger for the explicit graphs. The extension to the algorithm proposed by Mehlhorn and Meyer (2002) has been the first attempt to break the $O(|V|)$ I/O barrier for explicit graphs. The I/O lower bound for delayed duplicate detection refers to Aggarwal and Vitter (1987), who have given such a lower bound for external sorting. Arge, Knudsen, and Larsen (1993) has extended this work to the issue of duplicate detection.

The term *delayed duplicate detection* has been coined by Korf (2003a) in the context of complete BFS explorations of rectangular $(n \times m)$-PUZZLES. As said in the text, the approach shares similarities with internal *frontier search* by Korf, Zhang, Thayer, and Hohwald (2005). In the published exposition of Korf (2003a), the elimination of nodes with respect to previous lists is mentioned. External sorting based on hash functions (hash-based delayed duplicate detection) has been proposed in the context of complete BFS of the FIFTEEN-PUZZLE by Korf and Schultze (2005). For permutation games like PANCAKE and BURNED PANCAKE, already considered by Gates and Papadimitriou (1976), featuring fast rank and unrank operations, Korf (2008) has shown how to perform BFS with two bits only. The treatment discusses an I/O-efficient implementation of how to partially flush the bit-state table to disk, in case RAM still becomes exhausted. The assumption of having a perfect and inversible hash function available may be difficult to obtain in nonregular domains. An effective heuristic for the PANCAKE problem based on relative ordering has been suggested by Helmert and Röger (2010).

External A* has been suggested by Edelkamp, Jabbar, and Schrödl (2004a) where the results as given in the text are found. Zhou and Hansen (2004c) have incorporated *structured duplicate detection* to external memory graph search. A refinement by Zhou and Hansen (2007a), called *edge partitioning*, trades less RAM requirements for multiple scans in structured duplicate detection. Korf (2004a) has successfully extended delayed duplicate detection to best-first search and also considered omission of the visited list as proposed in *frontier search*. In his proposal, it turned out that any two of the three options are compatible yielding the following set of algorithms: *breadth-first frontier search with delayed duplicate detection*, *best-first frontier search*, and *best-first search with external nonreduced closed list*. In the last case, a buffered traversal in a bucket-based priority queue is simulated. External A* satisfies all three requirements.

External pattern databases have been used by Zhou and Hansen (2005a) together with structured duplicate detection. Edelkamp (2005) has explored abstract STRIPS and MULTIPLE SEQUENCE ALIGNMENT problems with external explicit and symbolic pattern databases. The construction process is based on external BFS. In weighted abstract problem graphs, an external version of Dijkstra's algorithm is needed in the form of a derivate to external A*.

External BFBnB relates to the memory-restricted breadth-first heuristic search algorithm of Zhou and Hansen (2004a). Implementations for external model checking algorithms have been proposed by Kristensen and Mailund (2003), who suggested a sweep-line technique for scanning the search space according to a given partial order, and by Jabbar and Edelkamp (2005), who have implemented a model checking algorithm on top of external A*. Jabbar and Edelkamp (2006) have provided a distributed implementation of the algorithm of Jabbar and Edelkamp (2005) for model checking safety properties, and Edelkamp and Jabbar (2006c) have extend the approach to general LTL properties. External iterative broadening has been suggested in the context of model checking real-time domains by Edelkamp and Jabbar (2006b), and the internal technique has been introduced by Ginsberg and Harvey (1992). I/O-efficient probabilistic search with external value iteration refers to the work of Edelkamp, Jabbar, and Bonet (2007).

Some search algorithms by Edelkamp, Sanders, and Simecek (2008c) and Edelkamp and Sulewski (2008) have included perfect hash functions for what has been coined semi-external search. After generating the state space externally, a space-efficient perfect hash function (Botelho and Ziviani, 2007) with a small number of bits per state is constructed and features immediate duplicate detection for disk-based search.

As observed by Ajwani, Malinger, Meyer, and Toledo (2008), flash-memory devices, like solid-state disk, have slightly different characteristics than traditional hard disks: random read operations on SSDs are substantially faster than on mechanical disks, while other parameters are similar. Edelkamp, Sulewski, Barnat, Brim, and Simecek (2011) have re-invented immediate duplicate detection based on flash memory. Libraries for improved secondary memory maintenance are LEDA-SM (Crauser, 2001) developed at MPI and TPIE developed at Duke University. Another library for large data sets is STXXL by Dementiev et al. (2005).

Heuristic Search Under Time Constraints

Distributed Search

Modern computers exploit parallelism on the hardware level. *Parallel* or *distributed* algorithms are designed to solve algorithmic problems by using many processing devices (processes, processors, processor cores, nodes, units) simultaneously. The reason that parallel algorithms are required is that it is technically easier to build a system of several communicating slower processors than a single one that is multiple times faster.

Multicore and many-core processing units are widely available and often allow fast access to the shared memory area, avoiding slow transfer of data across data links in the cluster. Moreover, the limit of memory addresses has almost disappeared on 64-bit systems. The design of the parallel algorithm thus mainly follows the principle that time is the primary bottleneck. Today's microprocessors are using several parallel processing techniques like instruction-level parallelism, pipelined instruction fetching, among others.

Efficient parallel solutions often require the invention of original and novel algorithms, radically different from those used to solve the same problems sequentially. The *speedup* compared to a one-processor solution depends on the specific properties of the problem at hand. The aspects of general algorithmic problems most frequently encountered in designing parallel algorithms are compatibility with machine architecture, choice of suitable shared data structures, and compromise between processing and communication overhead. An efficient solution can be obtained only if the organization between the different tasks can be optimized and distributed in a way that the working power is effectively used. *Parallel algorithms* commonly refer to a *synchronous* scenario, where communication is either performed in regular clock intervals, or even in a fixed architecture of computing elements performing the same processing or communication tasks (*single-instruction multiple-data* architectures) in contrast to the more common case of *multiple-instructions multiple-data* computers. On the other hand, the term *distributed algorithm* is preferably used for an *asynchronous* setting with looser coupling of the processing elements. The use of terminology, however, is not consistent. In AI literature, the term *parallel search* is preferred even for a distributed scenario. The exploration (generating the successors, computing the heuristic estimates, etc.) is distributed among different processes, be it workstation clusters or multicore processor environments. In this book we talk about *distributed search* when more than one search process is invoked, which can be due to partitioning the workload among processes, as in parallel search, or due to starting from different ends of the search space, as addressed in *bidirectional search*. The most important problem in distributed search is to minimize the communication (overhead) between the search processes.

After introducing parallel processing, we turn to *parallel state space search* algorithms, starting with *parallel depth-first search* heading toward *parallel heuristic search*. Early parallel formulations of A* assume that the graph is a tree, so that there is no need to keep a *Closed* list to avoid duplicates. If the graph is not a tree, most frequently hash functions distribute the workload. We identify differences in shared memory algorithm designs (e.g., multicore processors) and algorithms for distributed memory architectures (e.g., workstation clusters). One distributed data structure that is introduced features the capabilities of both heaps and binary search trees. Newer parallel implementations of A* include frontier search and large amounts of disk space. Effective data structures for concurrent access especially for the search frontier are essential. In external algorithms, parallelism is often necessary for maximizing input/output (I/O) bandwidth. In *parallel external search* we consider how to integrate external and distributed search. As a large-scale example for parallel external breadth-first search, we present a complete exploration in the FIFTEEN-PUZZLE.

It is not hard to predict that, due to economic pressure, parallel computing on an increased number of cores both in central processing units (CPUs) and in graphics processing units (GPUs) will be essential to solve challenging problems in the future: The world's fastest computers have thousands of CPUs and GPUs, whereas a combination of powerful multicore CPUs and many-core GPUs is standard technology for the consumer market. As they require different designs for parallel search algorithms, we will thus especially look at GPU-based search.

Bidirectional search algorithms are distributed in the sense that two search frontiers are searched concurrently. They solve the ONE-PAIR SHORTEST-PATH problem. Multiple goals are typically merged to a single *super-goal*. Subsequently, bidirectional algorithms search from two sides of the search space. Bidirectional breadth-first search comes at a low price. For heuristic bidirectional search, however, this is no longer true. The original hope was that the search frontiers meet in the middle. However, contrary to this intuition, advantages of bidirectional heuristic search could not be validated experimentally for a long time, due to several misconceptions. We describe the development of various approaches, turn to their analysis of drawbacks, and explain refined algorithms that could finally demonstrate the usefulness of the bidirectional idea. When splitting the search space, *multiple-goal heuristic search* can be very effective. We illustrate the essentials for computing optimal solutions to the 4-peg TOWERS-OF-HANOI problem.

While reading this chapter, keep in mind that practical parallel algorithms are an involved topic to cover in sufficient breadth and depth, because existing hardware and models change rapidly over the years.

9.1 PARALLEL PROCESSING

In this section we start with the theoretical concept of a parallel random access machine (PRAM) and give examples for the summation of n numbers in parallel that fit well into this setting. One problem with the PRAM model in practice is that it does not match well with current (nor generalize well to different) parallel computer environments. For example, multicore systems are shared memory architectures that differ in many aspects from vector machines and computer clusters. Hence, in the following we motivate practical parallel search with an early approach that showed successes in the exploration of state spaces, namely computing worst-possible inputs for the FIFTEEN-PUZZLE for the first time. To allow for parallel duplicate detection, state space partitioning in the form of appropriate hash functions is a natural concept, in which communication overhead can be reduced. An alternative solution for the problem of load balancing closes the section.

As an illustrative example for a parallel algorithm, consider the problem of adding eight numbers $a_1, \ldots, a_8$. One option is to compute $a_1 + (a_2 + (a_3 + (a_4 + (a_5 + (a_6 + (a_7 + a_8))))))$ in a sequence. Obviously seven additions are necessary. Alternatively, we may add the numbers as $(((a_1 + a_2) + (a_3 + a_4)) + ((a_5 + a_6) + (a_7 + a_8)))$. The corresponding trees are shown in Figure 9.1. The second sequence can be computed more efficiently in parallel if more than one process is available. If we have four processes only three parallel steps are necessary. In general, we have reduced the (parallel) running time from $O(n)$ to $O(\lg n)$ by using $n/2$ processes. The procedure for the single process i is depicted in Algorithm 9.1. Each processor executes the loop $O(\lg n)$ times. The variables h, x, and y are local for each process. The algorithm is correct if the process works in *lock-step* mode, meaning that they execute the same steps at the same time. An example for the computation is provided in Figure 9.2.

One prominent computational model to analyze parallel algorithms is the *parallel random access machine* (PRAM). A PRAM has p processes, each equipped with some local memory. Additionally, all processes can access shared memory in which each process can directly access all memory cells. This is a coarse approximation of the most commonly used computer architectures. It concentrates on

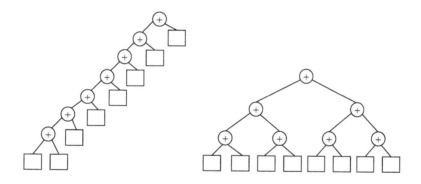

FIGURE 9.1

Computing the sum of eight numbers linearly (left) or in parallel (right).

Procedure Sum
Input: Numbers $a_1, \ldots, a_n$, $n = 2^k$
Output: Sum of $a_1, \ldots, a_n$

for each $h \in \{1, \ldots, k\}$;; Iteration
   for each $i \in \{1, \ldots, n/2^h\}$ **in parallel**   ;; Select parts
      $a_i \leftarrow a_{2i-1} + a_{2i}$;; Compute sum, write back
   return a_1 ;; Special case, process 1 has result

Algorithm 9.1

Algorithm to compute $a_1 + \cdots + a_n$ in parallel.

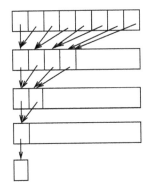

FIGURE 9.2

Recursion schema for procedure *Sum* on eight numbers.

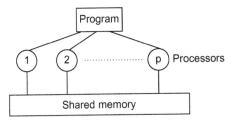

FIGURE 9.3

The PRAM model.

the partitioning of parts of computation and guarantees that data are present at the right point in time. The PRAM is programmed with a simple program that is parameterized with the process ID. A step in the execution consists of three parts: reading, calculating, and writing. A schematic view on a PRAM is shown in Figure 9.3.

To measure the performance of PRAM algorithms with respect to a problem of size n, the number of processes is denoted with $p(n)$ and the parallel running time with $t_p(n)$, such that the total work is $w_p(n) = p(n) \cdot t_p(n)$. In a good parallelization the work of the parallel algorithm matches the time complexity $t(n)$ of the sequential one. Since this is rarely the case, the term $t(n)/w_p(n)$ denotes the *efficiency* of the parallel algorithm. Sometimes a parallel algorithm is called *efficient* if for some constants k, k' we have $t_p(n) = O(\lg^k t(n))$ and $w_p(n) = O(t(n) \lg^{k'} n)$, by means that the time is reduced to a logarithmic term and the work is only a logarithmic factor from the minimum possible. The *speedup* is defined as $O(t(n)/t_p(n))$, and is called *linear in the number of processes*, if $p = O(t(n)/t_p(n))$. In rare cases, due to additional benefits of the parallelization, *super-linear* speedups can be obtained.

For our example problem of computing the sum of n numbers procedure *Sum* is efficient, as $t(n) = O(n)$ and $t_p(n) = O(\lg n)$. However, the work for the $p(n) = O(n)$ processors is $w_p(n) = O(n \lg n)$, which is not optimal. A *work-optimal algorithm* for adding n numbers has two steps. In step 1 only $n/\lg n$ processors are used and $\lg n$ numbers are assigned to each processor. Each processor then adds $\lg n$ numbers sequentially in $O(\lg n)$ time. In step 2 there are $n/\lg n$ numbers left and we execute our original algorithm on these $n/\lg n$ numbers. Now we have $t_p(n) = O(\lg n)$ and $w_p(n) = O(n)$.

Using parallel computation it is possible to compute not only the final result $s_n = a_1 + \cdots + a_n$ but also all *prefix sums* (or *partial sums*) of the elements, namely all values $s_j = a_1 + \cdots + a_j$, $1 \le j \le n$. The idea is to add all pairs of elements in parallel to produce $n/2^1$ sums, then add all pairs of those sums in parallel to produce $n/2^2$ sums, then add all pairs of those sums in parallel to produce $n/2^3$ sums, and so on. An implementation for such *parallel scan* computing of all prefix sums is provided in Algorithm 9.2, and an example of the application of the algorithm is given in Figure 9.4. Algorithm 9.2 is efficient, as $t_p(n) = O(\lg n)$, but the work is $O(n\lg n)$. Fortunately, this can be reduced to $w_p(n) = O(n)$ (see Exercises).

Procedure Prefix-Sum
Input: Numbers $a_1, \ldots, a_n$, $n = 2^k$
Output: Prefix-sum $a_1, \ldots, a_n$

for each $j \in \{0, \ldots, k-1\}$;; Main loop
  for each $i \in \{2^j, \ldots, n-1\}$ **in parallel**   ;; Distributed computation
    $a_{i+1} \leftarrow a_{i+1} + a_{i-2^j+1}$;; Compute sum, write back

Algorithm 9.2

Algorithm to compute all prefix sums in parallel.

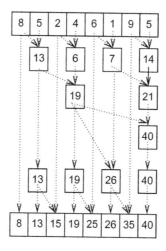

FIGURE 9.4

Computing the prefix sums of eight numbers in parallel (input array shown at the top, output array shown on the bottom level, arrows indicate the flow of computation: if arrows meet, an addition is performed).

The prefix sum algorithm has been applied as a subroutine in many parallel algorithms. For example, it helps to efficiently compress a sparse array or linked list or to simulate a finite-state machine (see Exercises).

Other basic building blocks for parallel algorithms are list ranking (compute distances of each element to the end of the list), matrix multiplication, and Euler tours (compute edge-disjoint cycles traversing all nodes). Fundamental PRAM algorithms include parallel merging and parallel sorting, parallel expression evaluation, and parallel string matching. Similar to the NP-completeness theory there is a theory on P-complete problems, which are sequentially simple but not parallel efficient. One representative problem in that class is the CIRCUIT VALUE PROBLEM: Given a circuit, the inputs to the circuit, and one gate in the circuit, calculate the output of that gate.

9.1.1 Motivation for Practical Parallel Search

For an early practical example of parallel state space search, we reconsider computing the most difficult problem instances for the FIFTEEN-PUZZLE in two stages. First, a candidate set is determined, which contains all positions that require more than k moves (and some positions requiring less than k moves) using some upper-bound function. Then, for each candidate, iterative-deepening search using the Manhattan distance heuristic is applied to show that it can be excluded from the candidate set, or that it requires more than k moves.

The candidate set is generated by applying an upper-bound function U to all positions u in the FIFTEEN-PUZZLE. Whenever $U(u) > k$, u becomes a candidate. The requirements on U are that it is fast to compute, so that it can be evaluated for all 10^{13} positions, and that it is a good upper-bound, so that the candidate set does not contain too many simple candidates. A first pattern database stores the optimal goal distances for all permutations of a subset of tiles. In the second step, the remaining tiles are moved to their goal location without moving the tiles fixed in the first step. A second pattern database contains the optimal goal distances for all permutations of the remaining tiles on the remaining board.

The obvious approach of actually solving each candidate requires too much time. For reducing the candidate set consistency constraints are applied. As an example, let u be a candidate and v its successor. If $\min\{U(v) \mid v \in Succ(u)\} < U(u) - 1$, a shorter path for u can be found. Both steps of the algorithm are computationally expensive.

After applying consistency constraints, the following candidate set for $k = 79$ can be computed in parallel: $U = 80$, number of candidates $33,208$; $U = 81$, number of candidates $1,339$; and $U = 82$, number of candidates 44. The remaining $1,383$ candidates with 81 or more moves can be solved in parallel. A bounded-depth macro move generator avoids repeating positions in shallow levels of the search tree (reducing the number of nodes in the very large search trees by roughly a factor of 4). The computation shows that all $1,383$ candidates require less than 81 moves. Moreover, six positions require exactly 80 moves, for example, $(15, 14, 13, 12, 10, 11, 8, 9, 2, 6, 5, 1, 3, 7, 4, 0)$. Therefore, this parallel computation proves that the hardest FIFTEEN-PUZZLE positions require 80 moves to be solved.

The lesson to be learned is that for practical parallel search, traditional PRAM techniques are not sufficient to solve hard problems; refined engineering is needed.

9.1.2 Space Partitioning

Another outcome of this case study is that parallel duplicate detection is a challenge. It can lead to large communication overhead and, in some cases, considerable waiting times. What is needed is a projection of the search space onto the processing elements that maps successors of nodes to the same or a nearby process.

An important step is the choice of a suitable *partition function* to evenly distribute the search space over the processes. One option is a *hash-based distribution* with a hash function defined on the state vector. A hash-based distribution is effective if with high probability the successors of a state expanded at a particular process also map to the process. This results in low communication overhead.

The *independence ratio* measures how many nodes on average can be generated and processed locally. If it is equal to 1 all successors must be communicated. The larger the ratio, the better the distributed algorithm. Given 100 processors and a randomized distribution of successors, the ratio is 1.01, close to the worst case. A *state space partitioning* function should achieve two objectives: a roughly equal distribution of work on all processing units and a large independence ratio.

For large states *full state hashing* can become computationally expensive. As one solution to the problem, *incremental hashing* exploits the hash value difference between a state and its successors (see Ch. 3). Another approach is *partial state hashing*, truncates the state vector before computing the hash function and restricts to those parts that are changed least frequently.

Transposition-driven scheduling is a solution that integrates asynchronous search with distributed hash tables for duplicate detection. The address returned by the hash function refers to both the process number and the local hash table. Rather than waiting for a result if a successor of an expanded node does not reside in the same process, the generated node is migrated to the destination process P_i. The latter one searches the node in the local table $Closed_i$ and stores the node in its work queue $Open_i$. To reduce communication, several nodes with the same source and destination process are bundled into packages.

Figure 9.5 illustrates the main differences to *distributed response strategies*, where the result of the table lookup is communicated through the network. In contrast, transposition-driven scheduling includes the successor v of node u into the local work queue. This eases asynchronous behavior, since process P_2 no longer has to wait for the response of process P_1.

All processes are synchronized after all nodes for a given search threshold have been exhausted. The algorithm achieves the goal of preventing duplicate searches with local transposition tables. It has the advantage that all communication is asynchronous (nonblocking). No separate load balancing strategy is required; it is implicitly determined by the hash function.

Transposition-driven scheduling applies to general state space search. In the pseudo code of Algorithm 9.3 we show how a node is expanded and how its successors are sent to the neighbor based on the partitioning of the search space.

9.1.3 Depth Slicing

One drawback of *static load balancing* via fixed partition functions is that the partitioning may yield different search efforts in different levels of the search tree, so that processes far from the root will encounter frequent idling. Subsequent efforts for *load balancing* can raise considerable especially for small- and medium-size problems.

A dynamic partitioning method suitable for shared memory environments is *depth-slicing*. The rationale behind it is that if a hash-based partition function is used, there is a high probability that the successor states will not be handled by the node that generated them, resulting in a high network overhead. Roughly speaking, depth-slicing horizontally slices the depth-first search tree and assigns

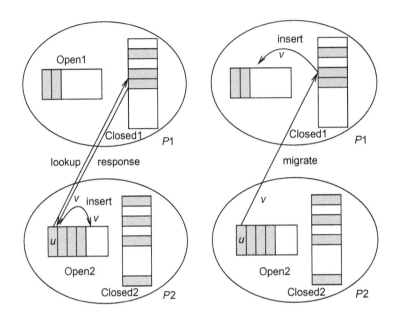

FIGURE 9.5

Distributed response strategy (left); transposition-driven scheduling (right).

Procedure Transposition-Driven Scheduling
Input: Problem graph partitioned wrt. distribution function ψ, number of processes N
Output: Solution if exists, or $\emptyset$

$Open_{\psi(s)} \leftarrow \{s\}$	;; Initialize search
for each $i \in \{1,\dots,N\}$ **in parallel**	;; Distributed computation
while $(Open_i \neq \emptyset$ **and not** $GoalFound)$	;; Still work to do
Select and eliminate node in $Open_i$	;; Choose a node for expansion
if $(Goal(u))$	;; Terminal state found
return $Announce(GoalFound)$	;; Distributed solution path extraction
$Succ(u) \leftarrow Expand(u)$	;; Generate successor set
for each $v \in Succ(u)$	;; Traverse successor set
$Send(v, P_{\psi(v)})$	;; Communicate children to responsible process
return $\emptyset$	;; No goal found

Algorithm 9.3

Transposition-driven scheduling.

---

each slice to a different node. For the sake of simplicity, let us assume a unit cost state space, where we have access to the local depth d of every generated node. Each process decides to communicate a successor if $d(u)$ exceeds a bound L. When a node is transmitted, the target processing unit will generate the search space with a newly initialized stack. The local depth will be initialized to zero. If the depth exceeds L again, it will be transmitted. The effect of this procedure will be a set of horizontal splits of the search tree (see Fig. 9.6). In every L level, states are transmitted from one process to the other. This induces that at about every $d \bmod L$ steps, a state will be transferred. As a result, the independence ratio is close to L. If no *hand-off* is available, the process continues with its exploration. Since all processes are busy by then, the load is balanced.

Because only one stack on each process is available, the remaining question for the implementation (shown in Alg. 9.4) is when to select a node from the incoming queue, and when to select a node from the local stack. If incoming nodes are preferred, then the search may continue breadth-first instead of depth-first. On the other hand, if a node on the local stack is preferred, then a process would not leave

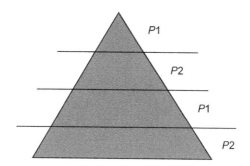

FIGURE 9.6

Slicing the search tree with respect to depth.

Procedure Depth-Slicing
Input: Problem graph with start node s, communication channels *In* and *Out*,
number of processes N
Output: Path from s to goal node

$Open_1 \leftarrow \{s\}$	;; Master takes start node
for each $i \in \{1,\ldots,N\}$ **in parallel**	;; Distributed computation
while not (*GoalFound*)	;; Termination check
Select u with maximal g-value in $Open_i \cup In$	;; Select node
Delete u from $Open_i$	;; Remove u from search frontier
$Succ(u) \leftarrow Expand(u)$	;; Select start node
for each v in $Succ(u)$	;; Consider all successors
if (*Goal(v)*) **return** *Announce(GoalFound)*	;; To output solution path
if ($g(u) \bmod L = 0$ **and** *avail(Out)*)	;; Hand-off depth, open channel
Insert u into *Out*	;; Forward borderline node to channel
else	;; Continue locally
Insert u into $Open_i$	;; Call subroutine on process

Algorithm 9.4

The depth-slicing parallelization method.

Procedure Lock-free Hashing
Input: Node u, bound on probing Θ, hash table size q
Output: Boolean, denoting if state is already stored

$j \leftarrow 1$	;; Set probing counter
while $(j < \Theta)$	;; Probing counter sufficiently small
$\quad i \leftarrow h(u) - s(j,u) \bmod q$	;; Follow probing sequence
$\quad$ **if** $(bucket[i] = \emptyset)$	;; Bucket is free
$\quad\quad$ **if** $(CAS(bucket[i], \emptyset, (h(u), \perp)))$	;; Swap out element and block
$\quad\quad\quad data[i] \leftarrow u$	;; Insert state
$\quad\quad\quad bucket[i] \leftarrow (h(u), \top)$	;; Release bucket
$\quad\quad\quad$ **return** *false*	;; Return failure
$\quad$ **if** $((h(u), \cdot) = bucket[i])$	;; Element found
$\quad\quad$ **while** $((\cdot, \perp) = bucket[i])$	;; Until lock released
$\quad\quad\quad$ **wait**	;; Wait for access
$\quad\quad$ **if** $(data[i] = u)$	;; State found
$\quad\quad\quad$ **return** *true*	;; Return success
$\quad j \leftarrow j + 1$	;; Increase counter

Algorithm 9.5

Searching and inserting an element in a lock-free hash table.

---

its part of the tree. The solution is to maintain all nodes in a g-value-ordered list in which the local and communicated successors are inserted. For each expansion, the node with the maximum g-value is preferred. In the code, subindex i refers to the *client* process P_i that executes the code. The process P_1 often takes a special role in initializing, finalizing, and coordinating the work among the processes, and is called the *master*.

Similar to horizontal depth-slicing a vertical partitioning of the search tree can be based on the heuristic values. The motivation for load balancing is that the expected distance to the goal (used here) is a similar measure compared to the distance to the start state (used in the previous method). The core advantage is that it is not only suited to depth-first but any general state expanding strategy.

9.1.4 Lock-Free Hashing

Lock-free algorithms guarantee systemwide progress in a concurrent environment of several running processing threads. The key is that modern CPUs implement an atomic *compare-and-swap* operation (CAS), so that always some thread can continue its work. For duplicate detection in state space search with a multicore CPU we require a *lock-free hash table*.

In this setting, however, we can only provide statistical progress guarantees and avoid explicit locks by CAS, which leads to a simpler implementation at no (visible) penalty in performance.

Strictly speaking, a lock-free hash algorithm in state space search locks *in-place*—it needs no additional variables for implementing the locking mechanism. CAS ensures atomic memory modification while preserving data consistency. This can be done by reading the value from memory, performing the desired computation on it, and writing the result back.

The problem with lock-free hashing is that it relies on low-level CAS operations with an upper limit on the data size that can be stored (one memory cell). To store state vectors that usually exceed the size of a memory cell, we need two arrays: the *bucket* and the *data* array.

Buckets store memorized hashes and the write status bit of the data in the data array. If h is the memorized hash, the possible values of the buckets are thus: $(\cdot, \top)$ for being empty, $(h, \bot)$ for being blocked for writing, and $(h, \top)$ for releasing the lock. In the *bucket* the locking mechanism is realized by CAS. The specialized value $(\bot)$ is a bitvector that indicates that the cell is used for writing. In the other cells the hash values are labeled unblocked. In a second background hash table *data* the states themselves are stored. A pseudo-code implementation is provided in Algorithm 9.5.

9.2 PARALLEL DEPTH-FIRST SEARCH

In this section we consider parallel depth-first search both in a *synchronous* and in an *asynchronous* setting, a notation that refers to the exchange of exploration information (nodes to expand, duplicates to eliminate) among different (depth-first) search processes. We also consider parallel IDA*–inspired search and algorithmic refinements like stack splitting and parallel window search.

Parallel depth-first search is often used synonymously to parallel branch-and-bound. For iterative-deepening search we distinguish between a synchronous and an asynchronous distribution. In the first case, work is distributed only within one iteration, and in the second case a process seeks work also within the next iteration. Therefore, asynchronous versions of IDA* are not optimal for the first solution found.

9.2.1 *Parallel Branch-and-Bound

Recall that a branch-and-bound algorithm consists of a branching rule that defines how to generate successors, a bounding rule that defines how to compute a bound, and an elimination rule that recognizes and eliminates subproblems, which cannot result in an optimal solution. In sequential depth-first branch-and-bound, a heuristic function governs the order in which the subproblems are branched from, and in case of being admissible it also defines the elimination rule. Different selections or bounding lead to different search trees.

The main difference between parallel implementations of branch-and-bound lies in the way information about the search process is shared. It consists of the states already generated, the lower bounds of the optimal solutions, and the upper bounds established. If the underlying state space is a graph, duplicate elimination is essential. Other parameters are the way that information is used in the individual processes, and the way it is divided.

In the following we present a simple generic high-level asynchronous branch-and-bound algorithm. Every process stores the cost of the best solutions and broadcasts every improvement to the other processes, which in turn use the information on the global best solution cost for pruning.

Algorithm 9.6 shows a prototypical implementation. Like in the corresponding sequential version (see Alg. 5.3), U denotes a global upper bound, and *sol* the best solution found so far. Subroutine *Bounded-DFS* is called for individual searches on process P_i. The procedure works in the same way as Algorithm 5.4. It updates U and *sol*; the only difference is that the search is aborted if resources are exceeded. That is, the additional input variable k indicates that based on existing resources in time and

---

Procedure Parallel-Branch-and-Bound
Input: Problem graph with start node s, number of processes N, number of nodes k
Output: Path from s to goal node, or $\emptyset$ if no solution is found

$Open_1 \leftarrow Bounded\text{-}Search(s,k)$	;; Initialize search
$U \leftarrow \infty$; $sol \leftarrow \emptyset$	;; Initialize global variable
while $(Open_1 \neq \emptyset)$	;; Termination criterion
for each $i \in \{2,\dots,N\}$ **in parallel**	;; Distributed computation
$u \leftarrow Select(Open_1)$	;; Select next start node
Delete u from $Open_1$	;; Removal from search frontier
$Bounded\text{-}DFS(P_i,u,k)$	;; Call subroutine on process i and ...
	;; ...Broadcast improvements on U
if $(sol \neq \emptyset)$ **return** sol	;; Output solution path
else return $\emptyset$	;; No goal found

Algorithm 9.6

Parallel branch-and-bound with global synchronization.

---

space the work on each process is limited to a set of k-generated nodes. For the sake of simplicity we assume that the value is uniform for each participating process. In practice, this value can vary a lot, depending on the distribution of computational resources. We further assume that the sizes for the set of states for the master and the subprocesses are the same. In practice, the initial search tree and the subtree sizes have to be adjusted individually.

If within the given resource bound the search cannot be completed, value k can be increased to start a new run. Alternatively, the master's search frontier can be extended. Up to the communication of bounds and according solutions, the implementation of bounded DFS is equal to the sequential one. A real implementation depends on how information is exchanged: via files in a shared memory architecture, or via network communication in a cluster.

9.2.2 Stack Splitting

The parallel depth-first variant that we consider next is a task attraction scheme that shares subtrees among the processes on demand. This scheme works for depth-first search (see Alg. 9.7) but here we concentrate on iterative-deepening search.

In the denotation derived earlier we consider a synchronous search approach that performs *stack splits* to explicit transfer nodes, where a *stack split* divides a larger stack of pending nodes to be expanded into pieces that can be distributed among available idle processes. In parallel stack-splitting search, each process works on its own local stack of frontier nodes. When the local stack is empty, a process issues a work request to another process. The donor then splits its stack and sends a part of its own work to the requester. Figure 9.7 illustrates the approach for two stacks P and Q, where the stack of requester Q is initially empty and the stack of donor P is split.

Initially, all work is given to the master. The other processes start with an empty stack, immediately asking for work. If the master has generated enough nodes, it splits its stack, donating subtrees to the requesting process.

Procedure Stack-Splitting
Input: Problem graph with start node s, number of processes N, number of nodes k
Output: Path from s to goal node

$Push(S_1, s)$	;; Initialize search
$idle \leftarrow \{2,\ldots,N\}$	;; Master maintains set of idle processes
while not $(GoalFound)$	;; Termination criterion
for each $i \in \{2,\ldots,N\}$ **in parallel**	;; Distribute the computation
if $(|S_i| = 0)$	;; Client runs out of work
$idle \leftarrow idle \cup \{i\}$	;; Update list
else	;; Client has work
if $(|S_i| > k)$ **and** $(idle \neq \emptyset)$	;; Too much work, distribute
$j \leftarrow Select(idle)$	;; Select partner process
$idle \leftarrow idle \setminus \{j\}$	;; Remove from idle list
$StackSplit(P_i, P_j)$	;; Divide work
$u \leftarrow Pop(S_i)$	;; Select node for expansion
if $(Goal(u))$ **return** $Announce(GoalFound)$	;; Terminate search
$Succ(u) \leftarrow Expand(u)$	;; Extract top node
for each v **in** $Succ(u)$	;; For all successors
$Push(S_i, v)$	;; Continue with successor

Algorithm 9.7

Parallel DFS with stack splitting.

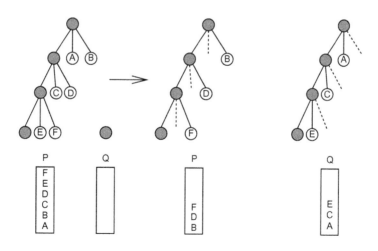

FIGURE 9.7

Stack splitting in parallel DFS (to the left the search tree before the partitioning and to the right the search tree after the split is shown). Nodes on the stack for backtrack are successors to the nodes that are currently searched in the search.

There are several possible splitting strategies. If the search space is irregular, then picking half the states above the cutoff depth as in Figure 9.7 is appropriate. However, if strong heuristics are available, picking a few nodes closer to the threshold is recommended.

9.2.3 Parallel IDA*

For parallel heuristic search, sequential IDA* is an appropriate candidate to distribute, since it shares many algorithmic features with depth-first branch-and-bound. In contrast to A*, it can run with no or limited duplicate detection.

For a selected set of sliding-tile problems, parallel IDA* with stack splitting achieves almost linear speedups. These favorable results, however, apply only for systems with small communication diameters, like a hypercube, or a butterfly architecture. The identified bottleneck for massively parallel systems is that it takes a long time to equally distribute the initial workload, and that recursive stack splitting generates work packets with rather unpredictable processing times per packet. Moreover, the stack-splitting method requires implementation of explicit stack handling routines, which can be involved. A possible implementation for parallel IDA* with global synchronization is indicated in Algorithm 9.8.

In *parallel window search*, each process is given a different IDA* search threshold. In other words, we give different processes different estimates of the depth of the goal. In this way, parallelization cuts off many iterations of wrong guesses. All processes traverse the same search tree, but with different cost thresholds simultaneously. If a process completes an iteration without finding a solution it is given a new threshold. Some processes may consider the search tree with a threshold that is larger than others.

The advantage of parallel window search is that the redundant search inherent in IDA* is not performed serially. Another advantage of parallel window search is if the problem graph contains a larger density of goal nodes. Some processes may find an early solution in the search tree given a larger threshold while the others are still working on the smaller thresholds. A pseudo-code implementation is provided in Algorithm 9.9. Since sequential IDA* stops searching after using the right search bound, parallel window search can result in a large number of wasted node expansions.

The two ideas of parallel window search and node ordering have been combined to eliminate the weaknesses of each approach while retaining their strengths. In ordinary IDA* search, children are expanded in a depth-first manner from left to right, bounded in depth by the cost threshold. In parallel window search, the search algorithm expands the tree a few levels and sorts the search frontier by increasing h-value. This frontier set is updated for each iteration. Nodes with smaller h-values are preferred. The resulting merge finds near-optimal solutions quickly, improves the solution until it is optimal, and then finally guarantees optimality, depending on the amount of time available.

An example on how search tree nodes are spread among different processes is provided in Figure 9.8. We see that the process with threshold 5 can find a suboptimal solution earlier than one that searches with optimal threshold 4.

9.2.4 Asynchronous IDA*

A generic scheme for highly parallel iterative-deepening search on asynchronous systems is *asynchronous IDA**. The algorithm is based on a data partitioning, where different parts of the search space

Procedure Parallel-IDA*

Input: Problem graph with start node s, number of processes N,
number of nodes k, old threshold U, new threshold $U' \neq \infty$

Output: Path from s to goal node

$Push(S_1, \{s, h(s)\})$	;; Initialize search
$idle \leftarrow \{2, \dots, N\}$	;; Master maintains set of idle process
while not $(GoalFound)$	;; Termination criterion
for each $i \in \{2, \dots, N\}$ **in parallel**	;; Distribute the computation
if $(|S_i| = 0)$	;; Client has run out of work
$idle \leftarrow idle \cup \{i\}$	;; Update list
else	;; Client has work
if $(|S_i| > k)$ **and** $(idle \neq \emptyset)$	;; Too much work, distribute
$j \leftarrow Select(idle)$	;; Select partner process
$idle \leftarrow idle \setminus \{j\}$	;; Remove from idle list
$StackSplit(P_i, P_j)$	;; Divide work
$u \leftarrow Pop(S_i)$	;; Select node for expansion
if $(Goal(u))$ **return** $Announce(GoalFound)$	;; Terminate search
$Succ(u) \leftarrow Expand(u)$	;; Extract top node
for each v **in** $Succ(u)$	;; For all successors
if $(f(u) + w(u,v) - h(u) + h(v) > U)$	;; Cost exceeds bound
if $(f(u) + w(u,v) - h(u) + h(v) < U')$	;; Below new bound
$U' \leftarrow f(u) + w(u,v) - h(u) + h(v)$	;; Update new bound
else	;; f-value below current threshold
$Push(S_i, \{v, f(u) + w(u,v) - h(u) + h(v)\})$	;; Continue with v

Algorithm 9.8

Parallel IDA* with global synchronization.

Procedure Parallel-Window-Search

Input: Problem graph with start node s, number of processes N, global solution sol

Output: Path from s to goal node

$U \leftarrow \infty$; $sol \leftarrow \emptyset$	;; Initialize global variable
$k \leftarrow h(s) - 1$	;; Initialize iteration counter
for each $i \in \{1, \dots, N\}$ **in parallel**	;; Distribute the computation
while $(k < U)$	;; Termination criterion, threshold lower than best solution found
$k \leftarrow k + 1$	;; Next unprocessed search threshold
$IDA^*\text{-}DFS(s, k)$	;; Invoke IDA* at s, improve global solution sol, cost U
return sol	;; Goal found

Algorithm 9.9

Distributing IDA* with respect to different search thresholds.

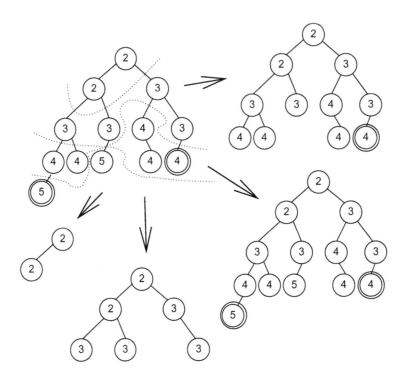

FIGURE 9.8

Distribution of IDA* search tree in parallel window search (nodes are annotated with according f-values; the dotted lines indicate cuts in the search tree due to different thresholds; the different IDA* iterations executed in parallel are shown in clockwise order).

are processed asynchronously by sequential routines running in parallel on the distributed processing elements. The algorithm consists of three phases:

- *Data Partitioning:* All processes redundantly expand the first few tree levels until a sufficient amount of nodes is generated.
- *Distribution:* Each process selects some nodes from the frontier nodes of the first phase for further expansion. One way of obtaining a widespread distribution of nodes is to assign nodes $i, p + i, \ldots,$ $k \cdot p + i$ to process i. The nodes are expanded to produce a larger set of, say, some thousand fine-grained work packets for the subsequent asynchronous search phase.
- *Asynchronous Search:* The processes generate and explore different subtrees in an iterative-deepening manner until one or all solutions are found. Since the number of expanded nodes in each work package usually varies and is not known in advance, dynamic load balancing is needed.

None of these three phases requires a hard synchronization. Processors are allowed to proceed with the next phase as soon as they finished the previous one. Only in the third phase, some mechanism is needed to keep all processes working on about the same search iteration. However, this synchronization is a weak one. If a process runs out of work, it requests unsolved work packages from a designated neighborhood (the original algorithm was run on a *transputer* system, where processors are connected in a two-dimensional grid structure). If such a package is found, its ownership is transferred to the previously idle processor. Otherwise, it is allowed to proceed with the next iteration. Load balancing ensures that all processors finish their iterations at about the same time.

9.3 PARALLEL BEST-FIRST SEARCH ALGORITHMS

At first glance, best-first search is more difficult to parallelize than IDA*. The challenge lies in the distributed management of the *Open* and *Closed* lists. It is no longer guaranteed that the first goal is optimal. It can happen that the optimal solution is computed by some other process such that a global termination criterion has to be established. One nonadmissible solution is to accept a goal node that has been found by one process only if no other process has a better f-valued node to expand.

From the host of different suggestions we exemplarily selected one global approach that takes shared memory and flexible data structures to rotate locks down a tree. For local A* search that is based on a hash partitioning of the search space, different load balancing and pruning strategies are discussed.

9.3.1 Parallel Global A*

A simple parallelization of A*, called *parallel global A**, follows an asynchronous concurrent scheme. It lets all available processes work in parallel on one node at a time, accessing data structures *Open* and *Closed* that are stored in global, shared memory. As opposed to that, *parallel local A* (PLA*)* uses data structures local to each process; they are discussed in the next section.

The advantage of parallel global A* is that it provides small search overheads, because especially in a multiprocessor environment with shared memory, global information is available for all processors. However, it also introduces difficulties. Since the two lists *Open* and *Closed* are accessed asynchronously, we have to choose data structures that ensure consistency for efficient parallel search.

If several processes wish to extract a node from *Open* and modify the data structure, consistency can only be guaranteed by granting mutually exclusive access rights or *locks*. In addition, if the *Closed* structure is realized by storing pointers to nodes in *Open*, it too would have to be partially locked. These locks reserialize parts of the algorithm and can limit the speedup.

*Treaps

One proposal is to use a *priority search tree* data structure, called a *treap*, to represent *Open* and *Closed* jointly. This saves the effort of having to manage two separate data structures.

Treaps exhibit the properties of *binary search trees* and *heaps* (see Ch. 3) at the same time. Let X be a set of n items, associated both with a *key* and a *priority*. Keys and priorities come from two ordered universes that need not be the same. A treap for X is a binary tree with node set X that is arranged such that the priorities satisfy the heap property and, as in an ordinary search tree, the keys are sorted in an *in-order traversal*. More precisely, the following invariants hold for nodes u and v:

- If v is a left child of u, then $key(v) < key(u)$.
- If v is a right child of u, then $key(v) > key(u)$.
- If v is a child of u, then $priority(v) > priority(u)$.

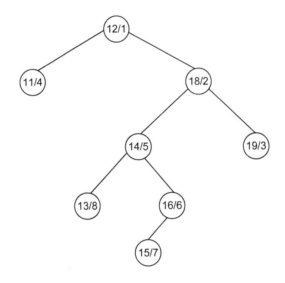

FIGURE 9.9

An example treap; keys (shown in the first component) form a search tree, and priorities (shown in the second component) form a heap.

It is easy to see that for any set X a treap exists and that by the heap property of the priorities the item with the smallest priority is located at the root. To construct a treap for X from scratch (assuming that the *key* is unique), we first select the element $x \in X$ with the smallest priority. Then, we partition X into $X' = \{y \in X \mid key(y) < key(x)\}$ and $X'' = \{y \in X \mid key(y) > key(x)\}$ and construct the treaps for the sets X' and X'' recursively, until we reach a singleton set that corresponds to a leaf. Figure 9.9 shows a treap for the set of $(priority, key)$-pairs $\{(11,4), (12,1), (13,8), (14,5), (15,7), (16,6), (18,2), (19,3)\}$.

The access operations on a treap T are as follows. *Lookup(key)* finds the item x in T with matching *key* using the binary tree search. *Insert(x)* adds the item x to T. Let y be an item already in T with matching *key*. If the priority of y is smaller than the one of x then x is not inserted; otherwise, y is removed and x is inserted. *DeleteMin* selects and removes the item x with the smallest priority and *Delete(x)* removes the item x from T.

Insertion makes use of the *subtree rotation* operation, an operation known from other (balanced) binary search tree implementations (see Fig. 9.10). First, using the key of x we search the position with respect to the in- and heap-ordering among the nodes. The search stops when an item y is found with a priority larger than the one of x, or an item z is encountered with the matching *key* component. In the first case, the item x is inserted between y and the parent of y. In the second case, x must not be inserted in the treap since the priority of x is known to be larger than the one of z. In the modified tree all nodes are in heap-order. To reestablish the in-order, the *splay operation* is needed that splits the subtree rooted at x into two parts: one with the nodes that have a key smaller than x and one with the nodes that have a key larger than x. All nodes y that turn out to have the same *key* component during the *splay* operation are deleted. The splay operation is implemented using a sequence of rotations.

The operations *Delete* and *DeleteMin* are similar in structure. Both rotate x down until it becomes a leaf, where it can be deleted for good. The time complexity for each of the operations is proportional

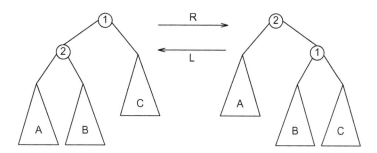

FIGURE 9.10

Rotation operations to restructure a treap.

to the depth of the treap, which can be linear in the worst case but remains logarithmic for random priorities.

Locking

Using a treap the need for exclusive locks can be alleviated to some extent. Each operation on the treap manipulates the data structure in the same *top-down* direction. Moreover, it can be decomposed into successive elementary operations. The *tree partial locking protocol* uses the paradigm of *user view serialization*. Every process holds exclusive access to a sliding window of nodes in the tree. It can move this window down a path in the tree, which allows other processes to access different, nonoverlapping windows at the same time.

Parallel A* using a treap with partial locking has been tested for the FIFTEEN-PUZZLE on different architectures, with a speedup for eight processors in between 2 and 5.

9.3.2 Parallel Local A*

In *parallel local A**, each process is allocated a different portion of the search space represented in its own local data structures. In this case, the inconsistencies of multiple lists introduce a number of inefficiencies. Processes run out of work and become idle. Since processes perform local rather than global best-first search, many processes may expand nonessential nodes, additionally causing a memory overhead. In a state space search graph duplicates arise in different processes, so that load balancing is needed to minimize nonessential work and *pruning strategies* to avoid duplicate work.

Different solutions for load balancing have been proposed. Earlier approaches use either quantitative balancing strategies like *round-and-robin* and *neighborhood averaging*, or qualitative strategies like *random communication*, *AC*, and *LM*. In *round-and-robin*, a process that runs out of work requests work from its busy neighbors in a circular fashion. In *neighborhood averaging*, the number of active nodes among the neighboring processors are averaged. In *random communication*, each processor donates the newly generated children generated in each iteration to a random neighbor. In the AC and LM strategies, each processor periodically reports the nondecreasing list of costs of nodes in *Open* to its neighbors, and computes its relative load to decide which nodes to transfer. One compromise between quantitative and qualitative load balancing is *quality equalizing*, in which processors utilize load information of neighboring processes to balance the load via nearest-neighbor work transfers. In summary, most load balancing schemes transfer work from a *donor processor* to an *acceptor processor*.

There are two essentially different strategies for pruning: *global* and *local hashing*. For global hashing, for example, multiplicative hash functions (Ch. 3) apply. By using the hash function also to balance the load, all duplicates will be hashed to the same process and can be eliminated. As a drawback, transmissions for duplicate pruning are global and increase message latency. In local hashing a search space partition scheme is needed. This ensures that any set of duplicate nodes arises only within a particular process group. Finding suitable local hash functions is a domain-dependent task and is sensible to the parallel architecture. Design principles that have been exploited are *graph leveling*, *clustering*, and *folding*. State space graph leveling applies to many combinatorial optimization problems, and every search node has a unique level. In clustering, the effect on the throughput requirements of duplicate pruning is analyzed, while folding is meant to achieve static load balance across parallel hardware substructures. Speedups obtained for global hashing are better than without hashing, but often smaller than for local hashing. In both cases, quality equalizing improves the speedup substantially.

The number of generated nodes in parallel A* search can grow quickly, so that strategies for searching with restricted or fixed amount of memory may become necessary. In this case, we apply memory-restricted search algorithms (see Ch. 6) extended to the situation, where main memory, even if shared among different processors, becomes rare. Partial expansion is one of the best choices to improve the performance of A* processes that run in parallel.

9.4 PARALLEL EXTERNAL SEARCH

Good parallel and I/O-efficient designs have much in common. Moreover, large-scale parallel analyses often exceed main memory capacities. Hence, combined parallel and external search executes an external memory exploration (see Ch. 8) in distributed environments like multiprocessor machines and workstation clusters. One main advantage is that duplicate detection can often be parallelized from avoiding concurrent writes.

In similarity to the parallel memory model of a PRAM the distributed memory model by Vitter and Shriver is a PDISK model. Each processor has its own local hard disk and the processes communicate with each other via the network and access a global hard disk (see Fig. 9.11).

As with the PRAM model, complexity analyses do not always map to practical performance, since either the disk transfer or the internal calculations can become the computational bottleneck.

In this section we first consider parallel external BFS with delayed, hash-based duplicate detection in the example of completely exploring the FIFTEEN-PUZZLE. Next, we consider parallelizing structured duplicate detection with a partitioning based on abstract state spaces, and parallel external A* with a partitioning based on g-values and h-values. We close the section with the parallel and disk-based computation of heuristic values based on selected patterns and corresponding distributed (possibly additive) databases.

9.4.1 Parallel External Breadth-First Search

In *parallel external breadth-first search* with delayed duplicate detection, the state space is partitioned into different files using a global hash function to distribute and locate states. For example, in state

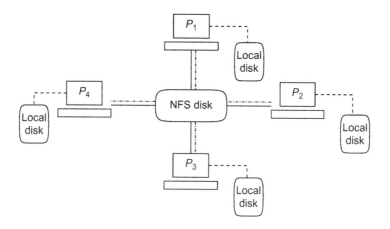

FIGURE 9.11

Distributed memory model with four processors.

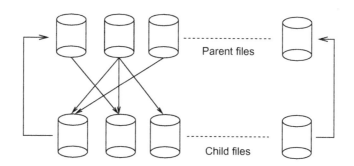

FIGURE 9.12

Externally stored state space with parent and child files.

spaces like the FIFTEEN-PUZZLE that are regular permutation games, each node can be perfectly hashed to a unique index, and some prefix of the state vector can be used for partitioning. Recall that if state spaces are undirected, frontier search (see Sec. 6.3.3, p. 257) can distinguish neighboring nodes that have already been explored from those that have not, and, in turn, omit the *Closed* list.

Figure 9.12 depicts the layered exploration on the external partition of the state space with a hash function that partitions both the current *parent* layer and the *child* layer for the successors into files. If a layer is done, child files are renamed into parent files to iterate the exploration.

It turned out that even on a single processor, multiple threads maximize the performance of the disks. The reason is that a single-threaded implementation will block until the read from or write to disk has been completed.

Hash-based delayed duplicate detection on the state vector prefix works well to generate a suitable partition for the FIFTEEN-PUZZLE. Within one iteration, most file accesses can be performed independently. The two processes will be in conflict only if we simultaneously expand two parent files that have a child file in common.

To realize parallel processing a work queue is maintained, which contains parent files waiting to be expanded and child files waiting to be merged. At the start of each iteration, the queue is initialized to contain all parent files. Once all parents of a child file are expanded, the child file is inserted into the queue for *early* merging.

Each process works as follows. It first locks the work queue. The algorithm checks whether the first parent file conflicts with any other file expansion. If so, it scans the queue for a parent file with no conflicts. It swaps the position of that file with the one at the head of the queue, grabs the nonconflicting file, unlocks the queue, and expands the file. For each file it generates, it checks if all of its parents have been expanded. If so, it puts the child file at the head of the queue for expansion, and then returns to the queue for more work. If there is no more work in the queue, any idle process waits for the current iteration to complete. At the end of each iteration the work queue is reinitialized to contain all parent files for the next iteration. Algorithm 9.10 shows a pseudo-code implementation. Figure 9.13 illustrates the distribution of a bucket among three processors.

A complete search for the FIFTEEN-PUZZLE with its 16!/2 states has been executed using a maximum of 1.4 terabytes of disk storage. Three parallel threads on two processors completed the search in about four weeks. The results are shown in Table 9.1 and validate that the diameter of the FIFTEEN-PUZZLE is 80.

Procedure Parallel-External-BFS
Input: Undirected problem graph with start node s,
number of processes N, hash partition ψ
Output: Partitioned BFS layers $Open_j(i)$, $i \in \{0, 1, \ldots, k\}$, $j \in \{1, \ldots, N\}$

$g \leftarrow 0$	;; Master initializes layer
$Open_1(g) \leftarrow \{s\}$	;; Master initializes search
while $(\cup_{i=1}^{N} Open_i(g) = \emptyset)$	;; Search not terminated
for each $j \in \{1, \ldots, N\}$ **in parallel**	;; Distribute computation
if $(Goal(Open_j(g))$	;; Terminal state in set
return $Announce(GoalFound)$	;; Generate solution path
$A_j \leftarrow Succ(Open_j(g))$	;; Generated successors
$RemoveDuplicates(A_j)$	;; Sorting/scanning current elements
for each $j \in \{1, \ldots, N\}$ **in parallel**	;; Distribute computation
$A'_j \leftarrow \{v \in \cup_{i=1}^{N} A_i \mid \psi(v) = j\}$	;; Acquire nodes to sort
$RemoveDuplicates(A'_j)$	;; Sorting/scanning
$Open_j(g+1) \leftarrow A'_j \setminus (Open_j(g) \cup Open_j(g-1))$	;; Frontier subtraction
$g \leftarrow g + 1$	;; Increase depth
return $Open_j(i)$, $i \in \{0, 1, \ldots, k\}$, $j \in \{1, \ldots, N\}$	

Algorithm 9.10

Parallel external breadth-first search.

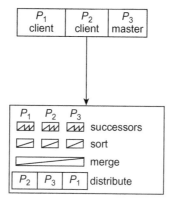

FIGURE 9.13

Distribution of buckets in parallel external BFS. The top bucket is the one for the actual level that is expanded, the bottom one is the one for the next level in which successors are generated. One dedicated processor, called master, additionally merges the data and otherwise works as a client. Successors are generated in parallel and duplicated detection is delayed. The sawtooth curves illustrate the partial sorting of the states in the files with regard to the comparison function as a result of sorting in the main memory.

9.4.2 Parallel Structured Duplicate Detection

Structured duplicate detection (Ch. 6) performs early duplicate detection in the RAM. Each abstract state represents a file containing every concrete state mapping to it. Since all adjacent abstract states were loaded into main memory, duplicate detection for concrete successor states remains in the RAM.

We assume breadth-first heuristic search as the underlying search algorithm (see Ch. 6), which generates the search space with increasing depth, but prunes it with respect to the f-value, provided that the optimal solution length is known. If not, external A* or iterative-deepening breadth-first heuristic search applies.

Structured duplicate detection extends nicely to a parallel implementation. In *parallel structured duplicate detection* abstract states together with their abstract neighbors are assigned to a process. We assume that the parallelization takes care of synchronization after one breadth-first search iteration has been completed, because a concurrent expansion in different depths likely affects the algorithm's optimality.

If in one BFS level two abstract nodes together with their successor do not overlap, their expansion can be executed fully independently on different processors. More formally, let $\phi(u_1)$ and $\phi(u_2)$ be the two abstract nodes; then the scopes of $\phi(u_1)$ and $\phi(u_2)$ are disjoint if $Succ(\phi(u_1)) \cap Succ(\phi(u_2)) = \emptyset$. This parallelization maintains locks only for the abstract space. No locks for individual states are needed.

The approach applies to both shared and distributed memory architectures. In the shared implementation each processor has a private memory pool. As soon as this is exhausted it asks the master process (that has spawned it as a child process) for more memory that might have been released using a completed exploration by some other process.

Table 9.1 Number of states in the FIFTEEN-PUZZLE with respect to their BFS level.

d	$|S_d|$	d	$|S_d|$	d	$|S_d|$	d	$|S_d|$
1	2	21	3,098,270	41	83,099,401,368	61	232,306,415,924
2	4	22	5,802,411	42	115,516,106,664	62	161,303,043,901
3	10	23	10,783,780	43	156,935,291,234	63	105,730,020,222
4	24	24	19,826,318	44	208,207,973,510	64	65,450,375,310
5	54	25	36,142,146	45	269,527,755,972	65	37,942,606,582
6	107	26	65,135,623	46	340,163,141,928	66	20,696,691,144
7	212	27	116,238,056	47	418,170,132,006	67	10,460,286,822
8	446	28	204,900,019	48	500,252,508,256	68	4,961,671,731
9	946	29	357,071,928	49	581,813,416,256	69	2,144,789,574
10	1,948	30	613,926,161	50	657,076,739,307	70	868,923,831
11	3,938	31	1,042,022,040	51	719,872,287,190	71	311,901,840
12	7,808	32	1,742,855,397	52	763,865,196,269	72	104,859,366
13	15,544	33	2,873,077,198	53	784,195,801,886	73	29,592,634
14	30,821	34	4,660,800,459	54	777,302,007,562	74	7,766,947
15	60,842	35	7,439,530,828	55	742,946,121,222	75	1,508,596
16	119,000	36	11,668,443,776	56	683,025,093,505	76	272,198
17	231,844	37	17,976,412,262	57	603,043,436,904	77	26,638
18	447,342	38	27,171,347,953	58	509,897,148,964	78	3,406
19	859,744	39	40,271,406,380	59	412,039,723,036	79	70
20	1,637,383	40	58,469,060,820	60	317,373,604,363	80	17

For a proper (conflict-free) distribution of work for undirected search spaces, numbers $I(\phi(u))$ were assigned to each abstract node $\phi(u)$, denoting the accumulated influence that currently is imposed to this node by running processes. If $I(\phi(u)) = 0$ the abstract node $\phi(u)$ can be picked for expansion from every processor that is currently idle. Function I is updated as follows. In a first step, for all $\phi(v) \neq \phi(u)$ with $\phi(u) \in Succ(\phi(v))$ value $\phi(v)$ is incremented by one: All abstract nodes that include $\phi(u)$ in their scope cannot be expanded, since $\phi(u)$ is chosen for expansion. In a second step, for all $\phi(v) \neq \phi(u)$ with $\phi(v) \in Succ(\phi(u))$ and all $\phi(w) \neq \phi(v)$ with $\phi(w) \in Succ(\phi(v))$ value $\phi(v)$ is incremented by one: All abstract nodes that include any $\phi(v)$ as a successor of $\phi(u)$ cannot be expanded, since they are also assigned to the processor.

Figure 9.14 illustrates the working of parallel structural duplicate detection for the FIFTEEN-PUZZLE with the currently expanded abstract nodes shaded. The left-most part of the figure shows the abstract problem graph together with four processes working independently at expanding abstract states. The numbers $I(\phi(u))$ are associated with each abstract node $\phi(u)$. The middle part of the figure depicts the situation after one process has finished, and the right part shows the situation after the process has been assigned to a new abstract state.

9.4.3 Parallel External A*

The distributed version of external A*, called *parallel external A*$*$, is based on the observation that the internal work in each individual bucket of external A* can be parallelized among different processes.

More precisely, each two states in a bucket $Open(g,h)$ can be expanded in different processes at the same time. An illustration is given in Figure 9.15, indicating a uniform partition available for each $Open(g,h)$-bucket. We discuss disk-based message queues to distribute the load among different processes.

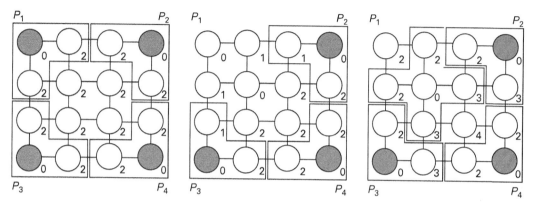

FIGURE 9.14

Example for parallel structured duplicate detection with four processes: before P_1 releases its work (left), after P_1 has released its work (middle), and after P_1 has allocated new work (right).

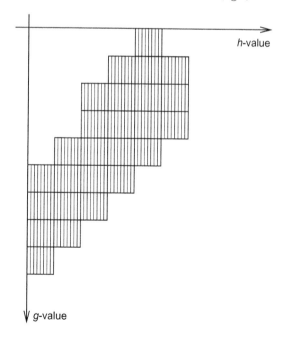

FIGURE 9.15

Partition of buckets in parallel and external A* (schematic view, buckets are sliced into parts according to the independent expansion of state sets of different processors).

Disk-Based Queues

To organize the communication between the processes a work queue is maintained on disk. The work queue contains the requests for exploring parts of a (g,h)-bucket together with the part of the file that has to be considered. (Since processes may have different computational power and processes can dynamically join and leave the exploration, the size of the state space partition does not necessarily have to match the number of processes. By utilizing a queue, we also may expect a process to access a bucket multiple times. However, for the ease of a first understanding, it is simpler to assume that the jobs are distributed uniformly among the processes.) For improving the efficiency, we assume a distributed environment with one master and several client processes. In the implementation, the *master* is in fact an ordinary process defined as the one that finalized the work for a bucket. This applies to both the cases when each client has its own hard disk or if they work together on one hard disk (e.g., residing on the master). We do not expect all processes to run on one machine, but allow clients to log on the master machine, suitable for workstation clusters. Message passing between the master and client processes is purely done on files, so that all processes are fully autonomous. Even if client processes are killed, their work can be redone by any other idle process that is available.

One file, which we call the *expand-queue*, contains all current requests for exploring a node set that is contained in a file (see Fig. 9.16). The filename consists of the current g-values and h-values.

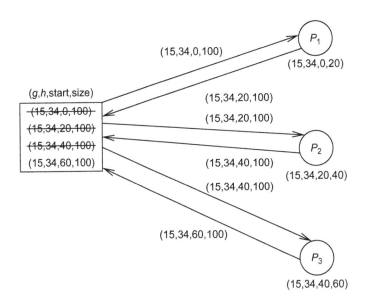

FIGURE 9.16

A parallel work queue (left) for heuristic search with set states to be expanded contained in a bucket of common $g = 15$ and $h = 34$. Snapshot taken after the successful request of work of three processors (right); each processor has taken a share, modified the remaing total amount of work in the queue, and released the lock for the access in the queue.

In case of larger files, file pointers for processing parts of a file are provided to allow for better load balancing. There are different strategies to split a file into equidistance parts, depending on the number and performance of logged-on clients. Since we want to keep the exploration process distributed, we select the file pointer windows into equidistant parts of a fixed number of C bytes for the nodes to be expanded. For improved I/O, the number C is supposed to divide the system's block size B. As concurrent read operations are allowed for most operating systems, multiple processes reading the same file impose no concurrency conflicts.

The expand-queue is generated by the master process and is initialized with the first block to be expanded. Additionally, we maintain the total number of requests, the size of the queue, and the current number of satisfied requests. Any logged-on client reads a request and increases the count once it finishes. During the expansion process, in a subdirectory indexed by the client's name it generates different files that are indexed by the g-values and h-values of the successor nodes.

The other queue is the *refine-queue*, which is also generated by the master process once all processes are done. It is organized in a similar fashion as the expand queue and allows clients to request work. The refine-queue contains filenames that have been generated above, namely the name of the client (that does not have to match with the one of the current process), the block number, and the g-values and h-values. For a suitable processing the master process will move the files from subdirectories indexed by the slave's name to ones that are indexed by the block number. Because this is a sequential operation executed by the master thread, changing the file locations is fast in practice.

To avoid redundant work, each process eliminates the requests from the queue. Moreover, after finishing the job, it writes an acknowledgment to an associated file, so that each process can access the current status of the exploration and determine if a bucket has been completely explored or sorted.

All communication between different processes can be realized via shared files so that a message passing unit is not required. However, a mechanism for mutual exclusion is necessary. A rather simple but efficient method to avoid concurrent writes accesses is the following. Whenever a process has to write on a shared file, it issues an operating system command to rename the file. If the command fails, it implies that the file is currently being used by another process.

Sorting and Merging

For each bucket under consideration, we establish four stages in Algorithm 9.11. These stages are visualized in Figure 9.17 (top to bottom). Zig-zag curves illustrate the order of the nodes in the files with regard to the comparison function used. As the states are presorted in internal memory, every peak corresponds to a flushed buffer. The sorting criteria are defined first by the node's hash key and then by the low-level comparison based on the (compressed) state vector.

In the *exploration stage* (generating the first row in the figure), each process p flushes the successors with a particular g-value and h-value to its own file (g, h, p). Each process has its own hash table and eliminates some duplicates already in main memory. The hash table is based on chaining, with chains sorted along the node comparison function. However, if the output buffer exceeds memory capacity it writes the entire hash table to disk. By the use of the sorting criteria as given earlier, this can be done using a mere scan of the hash table.

Procedure Parallel-External-A*
Input: Undirected problem graph with start node s, goal predicate *Goal*,
       number of processes N, hash partition ψ
Output: Optimal solution path

$$g \leftarrow 0; h \leftarrow h(s) \qquad\qquad\qquad\qquad\qquad\qquad\qquad \text{;; Initial bucket}$$
$$Open_1(g,h) \leftarrow \{s\} \qquad\qquad\qquad\qquad\qquad \text{;; Master initializes search}$$

while not (*goalFound*)   ;; Search not terminated
   for each $j \in \{1,\dots,N\}$ **in parallel**   ;; Distribute computation
     if ($Goal(Open_j(g,h))$)   ;; Terminal state in set
       return *Announce*(*GoalFound*)   ;; Generate solution path
     $A_j(h-1), A_j(h), A_j(h+1) \leftarrow Succ(Open_j(g,h))$;; Generated successors
     $Open_j(g+1,h+1) \leftarrow A_j(h+1)$;; Prepare next level
     $Open_j(g+1,h) \leftarrow A_j(h) \cup Open_j(g+1,h)$;; Prepare next level
     $RemoveDuplicates(A_j(h-1))$;; Sorting/scanning
   for each $j \in \{1,\dots,N\}$ **in parallel**   ;; Distribute computation
     $A'_j(h-1) \leftarrow \{u \in \cup_{i=1}^{N} A_i(h-1) \mid \psi(u) = j\}$;; Allocate work
     $Open_j(g+1,h-1) \leftarrow A'_j(h-1) \cup Open_j(g+1,h-1)$;; Prepare next level
     $RemoveDuplicates(Open_j(g+1,h-1))$;; Sorting/scanning
     $Open_j(g+1,h-1) \leftarrow Open_j(g+1,h-1) \backslash$;; Eliminate duplicates
        $(Open_j(g,h-1) \cup Open_j(g-1,h-1))$
   $f \leftarrow \min\{k+l \mid \cup_{i=1}^{N} Open_i(k,l) \neq \emptyset\}$;; Update f-value
   $g \leftarrow \min\{l \mid \cup_{i=1}^{N} Open_i(l, f-l) \neq \emptyset\}; h \leftarrow f-g$;; Next nonempty bucket

Algorithm 9.11

Parallel external A* for consistent and integral heuristics.

In the *first sorting stage* (generating the second row in the figure), each process sorts its own file. In the distributed setting we exploit the advantage that the files can be sorted in parallel, reducing internal processing time. Moreover, the number of file pointers needed is restricted by the number of flushed buffers, and illustrated by the number of peaks in the figure. Based on this restriction, we only need a merge of different sorted buffers.

In the *distribution stage* (generating the third row in the figure), all nodes in the presorted files are distributed according to the hash value's range. As all input files are presorted this is a mere scan. No all-including file is generated, keeping the individual file sizes small. This stage can be a bottleneck to the parallel execution, as processes have to wait until the distribution stage is completed. However, if we expect the files to reside on different hard drives, traffic for file copying can be parallelized.

In the *second sorting stage* (generating the last row in the figure), processes resort the files (with buffers presorted wrt. the hash value's range) to find further duplicates. The number of peaks in each individual file is limited by the number of input files (= number of processes), and the number of output files is determined by the selected partitioning of the hash index range. Using the hash index as the sorting key we establish that the concatenation of files is sorted.

Figure 9.18 shows the distribution of states into buckets with three processors.

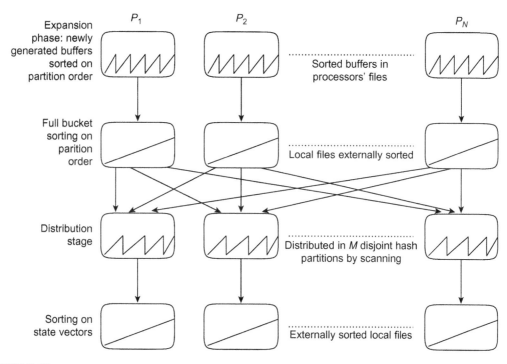

FIGURE 9.17

Sorting expanded stages during parallel bucket expansions in parallel external A*. Zig-zag lines indicate partial sortedness of the data due to internal sorting (top row) or distribution (third row); straight lines indicate fully sorted files with respect to partition order or state vector order.

Complexity

The lower bound for the I/O complexity for delayed duplicate elimination in an implicit undirected unit-cost graph A* search with consistent estimates is $\Omega(sort(|E|))$, where E is the set of explored edges in the search graph. Fewer I/Os can only be expected if structural properties can be exploited. But by assuming a sufficient number of file pointers, the external memory sorting complexity reduces to $\Omega(scan(|E|))$ I/Os, since a constant number of merging iterations suffice to sort the file.

Strictly speaking, the total number of I/Os cannot be reduced by parallel search. More disks, however, reduce the number of I/Os; that is, $scan(|E|) = O(|E|/DB)$. If the number of disks D equals the number of processes N then we can have a speedup of N either with local or global hard disk access. Using this we can achieve in fact a linear number of I/Os for delayed duplicate elimination and sorting.

An important observation is that the more processes we invest, the finer the partitioning of the state space, and the smaller the individual file sizes will be. Therefore, a side effect of having more processes at hand is an improvement in I/O performance.

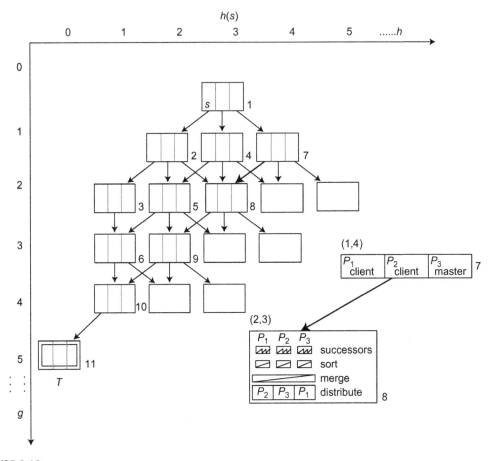

FIGURE 9.18

Distribution of parallel external A* using three processors. Subscript numbers indicate traversal ordering along the f-values. Successors are generated along the arrows and are distributed according to the change in heuristic value. The expansion of bucket $(1, 4)$ and its successor generation into bucket $(2, 3)$ is magnified to the right.

9.4.4 Parallel Pattern Database Search

Disjoint pattern databases can be constructed embarrassingly parallel. The subsequent search, however, faces the problem of high memory consumption due to many large pattern databases, since loading pattern databases on demand significantly slows down the performance.

One solution is to distribute the lookup to multiple processes. For external A* this works as follows. As buckets are fully expanded, the order in a bucket does not matter, so we can distribute the work for expansion, evaluation, and duplicate elimination. For the THIRTY-FIVE-PUZZLE we choose one master to distribute generated states to 35 client processes P_i, each one responsible for one tile i for $i \in \{1, \dots, 35\}$. All client processes operate individually and communicate via shared files.

During the expansion of a bucket (see Fig. 9.19), the master writes a file T_i for each client process $P_i, i \in \{1,\ldots,35\}$. Once it has finished the expansion of a bucket, the master P_m announces that each P_i should start evaluating T_i. Additionally, the client is informed on the current g-value and h-value. After that, the master P_m is suspended, and waits for all P_i's to complete their task. To relieve the master from load, no sorting takes place during distribution. Next, the client processes start evaluating T_i, putting their results into $E_i(h-1)$ or $E_i(h+1)$, depending on the observed difference in the h-values. All files E_i are additionally sorted to eliminate duplicates, internally (when a buffer is flushed) and externally (for each generated buffer). Because only three buckets are opened at a time (one for reading and two for writing) the associated internal buffers can be large.

After the evaluation phase is completed, each process P_i is suspended. When all clients are done, the master P_m is resumed and merges the $E_i(h-1)$ and $E_i(h+1)$ files into $E_m(h-1)$ and $E_m(h+1)$. The merging preserves the order in the files $E_i(h-1)$ and $E_i(h+1)$, so that the files $E_m(h-1)$ and $E_m(h+1)$ are already sorted with all duplicates within the bucket eliminated. The subtraction of the bucket $(g-1,h-1)$ from $E_m(h-1)$ and $(g-1,h+1)$ from $E_m(h+1)$ now eliminates duplicates from the search using a parallel scan of both files.

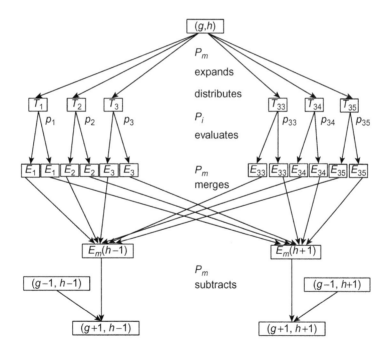

FIGURE 9.19

Distributed pattern database usage in the example of the THIRTY-FIVE-PUZZLE. The distribution of successor states of 1 bucket into 35 buckets according to the tile that moves is followed by the distributed heuristic evaluation with regard to the pattern databases including the tile chosen. Next, the merging into the bucket $h-1$ (or $h+1$) is shown. Finally, the result in bucket $(g+1,h-1)$ (or $(g+1,h+1)$) is generated and duplicates are eliminated, subtracting states residing in $(g-1,h-1)$ (or $(g-1,h+1)$).

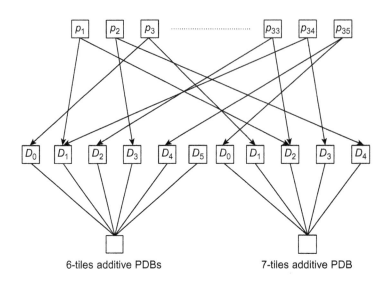

FIGURE 9.20

Selection of pattern databases for distributed evaluation; for example, processor p_1 responsible for tile t_1 has to have a local copy of a part of the 6-tiles pattern database (D_1) and a local copy of a part of the 7-tiles pattern database (D_2) to evaluate a state.

Besides the potential for speeding up the evaluation, the chosen distribution mainly saves space. On one hand, the master process does not need any additional memory for loading pattern databases. It can invest all its available memory for internal buffers required for the distribution, merging, and subtraction of nodes. On the other hand, during the entire lifetime of client process P_i, it has to maintain only the pattern database D_j that includes tile i in its pattern (see Fig. 9.20).

9.5 PARALLEL SEARCH ON THE GPU

In the last few years there has been a remarkable increase in the performance and capabilities of the graphics processing unit (GPU). Modern GPUs are not only powerful, but also parallel programmable processors featuring high arithmetic capabilities and memory bandwidths. High-level programming interfaces have been designed for using GPUs as ordinary computing devices. These efforts in *general-purpose GPU programming* (GPGPU) have positioned the GPU as a compelling alternative to traditional microprocessors in high-performance computing. The GPU's rapid increase in both pro-grammability and capability has inspired researchers to map computationally demanding, complex problems to it. However, it is a challenge to effectively use these massively parallel processors to achieve efficiency and performance goals. This imposes restrictions on the programs that should be executed on GPUs.

Since the memory transfer between the card and main board on the express bus is extremely fast, GPUs have become an apparent candidate to speed up large-scale computations. In this section we consider the time-efficient generation of state spaces on the GPU, with state sets made available via a transfer from/to main and secondary memory. We start with describing typical aspects of an existing GPU. Algorithmically, the focus is on GPU-accelerated BFS, delayed duplicate detection, and state compression. We then look into GPU-accelerated bitvector breadth-first search. As an application domain, we chose the exploration in sliding-tile puzzles.

9.5.1 GPU Basics

GPUs are programmed through *kernels* that are selected as threads to run on each core, which is executed as a set of *threads*. Each thread of the kernel executes the same code. Threads of a kernel are grouped in *blocks*. Each block is uniquely identified by its index and each thread is uniquely identified by the index within its block. The dimensions of the thread and the thread block are specified at the time of launching the kernel.

Programming GPUs is facilitated by APIs and support special declarations to explicitly place variables in some of the memories (e.g., shared, global, local), predefined keywords (variables) containing the block and thread IDs, synchronization statements for cooperation between threads, runtime API for memory management (allocation, deallocation), and statements to launch functions on GPU. This minimizes the dependence of the software from the given hardware.

The memory model loosely maps to the program thread-block-kernel hierarchy. Each thread has its own *on-chip registers*, which are fast, and *off-chip local memory*, which is quite slow. Per block there is also an on-chip *shared memory*. Threads within a block cooperate via this memory. If more than one block is executed in parallel then the shared memory is equally split between them. All blocks and threads within them have access to the off-chip *global memory* at the speed of RAM. Global memory is mainly used for communication between the host and the kernel. Threads within a block can communicate also via lightweight synchronization.

GPUs have many cores, but the computational model is different from the one on the CPU. A core is a *streaming processor* with some floating point and arithmetic logic units. Together with some special function units, streaming processors are grouped together to form streaming multiprocessors (see Fig. 9.21).

Programming a GPU requires a special compiler, which translates the code to native GPU instructions. The GPU architecture mimics a *single instruction multiply data* computer with the same instructions running on all processors. It supports different layers for accessing memory. GPUs forbid simultaneous writes to a memory cell but support concurrent reads.

On the GPU, memory is structured hierarchically, starting with the GPU's global memory called *video RAM*, or *VRAM*. Access to this memory is slow, but can be accelerated through *coalescing*, where adjacent accesses with less than word-width number bits are combined to full word-width access. Each streaming multiprocessor includes a small amount of memory called *SRAM*, which is shared between all streaming multiprocessors and can be accessed at the same speed as registers. Additional registers are also located in each streaming multiprocessor but not shared between streaming processors. Data have to be copied to the VRAM to be accessible by the threads.

9.5.2 GPU-Based Breadth-First Search

We assume a hierarchical GPU memory structure of SRAM (small, but fast and parallel access) and VRAM (large, but slow access). The general setting is displayed in Figure 9.22. In the following we illustrate how to perform GPU-based breadth-first search, generating the entire search space.

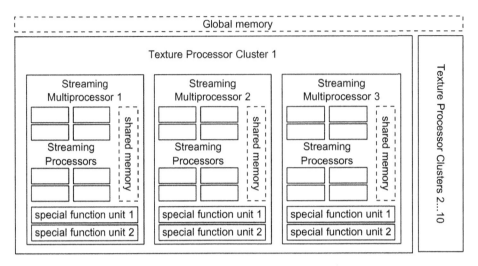

FIGURE 9.21

Sample GPU architecture.

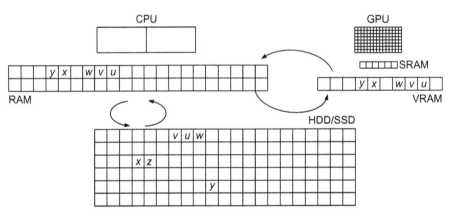

FIGURE 9.22

External memory search utilizing the GPU.

Algorithm 9.12 displays the main search algorithm running on the CPU. For each BFS level it divides into two computational parts that are executed on the GPU: applying actions to generate the set of successors, and detecting and eliminating duplicates in a delayed fashion via GPU-based sorting.

The two according kernel functions that are executed on the graphics card are displayed in Algorithms 9.13 and 9.14. For the sake of clarity we haven't shown the transfer from hard disk to

Procedure GPU-BFS
Input: State space problem with initial state s
Output: State space partitioned into BFS-levels

$g \leftarrow 0$; $Layer[g] \leftarrow \{s\}$;; Initialize search
while ($Layer[g] \neq \emptyset$)   ;; Until search levels off
    $Layer[g+1] \leftarrow SuccLayer \leftarrow LayerPart \leftarrow \emptyset$;; Initialize sets
    for each u **in** $Layer[g]$;; Process BFS level
        $LayerPart \leftarrow LayerPart \cup \{u\}$;; Add node to part
        if ($|LayerPart| = |VRAM|$)   ;; RAM temporary for VRAM
            $SuccLayer \leftarrow SuccLayer \cup GPU\text{-}ExpandLayer(LayerPart)$;; Call kernel
            $LayerPart \leftarrow \emptyset$;; Reinitialize structure
    $SuccLayer \leftarrow SuccLayer \cup GPU\text{-}ExpandLayer(LayerPart)$;; Call kernel function
    for each $v \in SuccLayer$;; Consider all successors
        $H[hash(v)] \leftarrow H[hash(v)] \cup \{v\}$;; Insert in bucket
        if $H[hash(v)]$ **full**   ;; Overflow in bucket
            $Sorted \leftarrow GPU\text{-}DetectDuplicates(H)$;; Call kernel function
            $CompactedLayer \leftarrow ScanAndRemoveDuplicates(Sorted)$;; Compaction
            $DuplicateFreeLayer \leftarrow Subtract(CompactedLayer, Layer[0..g])$;; Subtraction
            $Layer[g+1] \leftarrow Merge(Layer[g+1], DuplicateFreeLayer)$;; Combine result
            $H[0..m] \leftarrow \emptyset$;; Reset BFS-level
    $Sorted \leftarrow GPU\text{-}DetectDuplicates(H)$;; Call kernel function
    $CompactedLayer \leftarrow ScanAndRemoveDuplicates(Sorted)$;; Compaction
    $DuplicateFreeLayer \leftarrow Subtract(CompactedLayer, Layer[0..g])$;; Subtraction
    $Layer[g+1] \leftarrow Merge(Layer[g+1], DuplicateFreeLayer)$;; Combine result
    $g \leftarrow g+1$;; Next BFS-level
return $Layer[0..g-1]$;; Final result on disk

Algorithm 9.12

Large-scale breadth-first search on the GPU.

RAM and back for BFS-levels that do not fit in RAM, nor the copying from RAM to VRAM and from VRAM to the SRAM, as needed for GPU computation.

One example for the subtleties that arise is that for better compression in RAM and on disk, we keep the search frontier and the set of visited states distinct, since only the first one needs to be accessible in uncompressed form.

Delayed Duplicate Detection on the GPU

For delayed elimination of duplicates, we have to order a BFS level with regard to a comparison function that operates on states (sorting phase). The array is then scanned and duplicates are removed (compaction). Considering the strong set of assumptions of orthogonal, disjoint, and concise hash functions, ordinary hash-based delayed duplicate detection is often infeasible. Therefore, we propose a trade-off between sorting-based and hash-based delayed duplicate detection by sorting buckets that have been filled through applying a hash function. The objective is that hashing in RAM performs

Procedure GPU-Kernel ExpandLayer
Input: $Layer = \{u_1, \ldots, u_k\}$
Output: $SLayer = \{v_1, \ldots, v_l\}$

for each group g **do**	;; Select part
for each thread t **do in parallel**	;; Distributed computation
$u_i \leftarrow SelectState(Layer, g, t)$	;; Project VRAM to SRAM
$V_i \leftarrow Expand(effects, u_i)$	;; Generate successors
$SLayer \leftarrow SLayer \cup V_i$	;; Write successors
return $SLayer$	;; Feedback result to CPU

Algorithm 9.13

Expanding a layer on the GPU.

Procedure GPU-Kernel DetectDuplicates
Input: H (unsorted)
Output: H (partially sorted)

for each group g	;; Select part
$i \leftarrow SelectTable(H, g)$	;; Split table
$H'[i] \leftarrow Sort(H[i])$	;; Invoke BITONIC SORT
return H'	;; Feedback partially sorted result to CPU

Algorithm 9.14

Detecting duplicates via sorting on the GPU.

more costly distant data moves, while subsequent sorting addresses local changes, and can be executed on the GPU by choosing the bucket sizes appropriately. If the buckets fit into the SRAM, they can be processed in parallel.

Disk-based sorting refers to one of the major success stories for GPU computation. Various implementations have been proposed, including variants of BITONIC SORT and GPU-based QUICKSORT. Applying the algorithms to larger state vectors, however, fails as their movements within the VRAM slows down the computation significantly. Trying to sort an array of indexes also fails, since now the comparison operator exceeds the boundary of the SRAM. This leads to an alternative design of GPU sorting for state space search.

Hash-Based Partitioning

The first phase of sorting smaller blocks in BITONIC SORT is fast, but merging the presorted sequences for a total ordered slows down the performance. Therefore, we employ hash-based partitioning on the CPU to distribute the elements into buckets of adequate size (see Fig. 9.23). The state array to be sorted is scanned once. Using hash function h and a distribution of the VRAM into k blocks, the

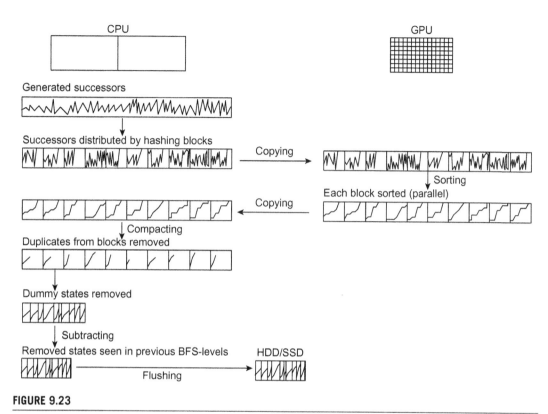

FIGURE 9.23

Schematic illustration of hash-based partitioning in GPU-based search. Unsorted successors are hashed into buckets of fixed length and sorted on the GPU. Partial sorted blocks together with hash value give a total order. Duplicates are eliminated on the CPU and the state set is compacted before merging with the external storage device.

state s is written to the bucket with index $h'(s) = h(s) \bmod k$. If the distribution of the hash function is appropriate and the maximal bucket sizes are not too small, a first overflow occurs when the entire hash table is occupied to more than a half. All remaining elements are set to a predefined illegal state vector that realizes the largest possible value in the ordering of states.

This hash-partitioned vector of states is copied to the graphics card and sorted by the first phase of BITONIC SORT. The crucial observation is that, due to the presorting, the array is not only partially sorted with regard to the comparison function operating on states s, but totally sorted with regard to the extended comparison function operating on the pairs $(h'(s), s)$. The sorted vector is copied back from VRAM to RAM, and the array is compacted by eliminating duplicates with another scan through the elements. Subtracting visited states is made possible through scanning all previous BFS-levels residing on disk. Finally, we flush the duplicate-free file for the current BFS-level to disk and iterate. To accelerate discrimination and to obey the imposed order on disk, the hash bucket value $h'(s)$ is added to the front of the state s.

If a BFS-level becomes too large to be sorted on the GPU, we split the search frontier into parts that fit in the VRAM. This yields some additional state vector files to be subtracted to obtain a duplicate-free BFS-level, but in practice, time performance is still dominated by expansion and sorting. For the case that subtraction becomes harder, we can exploit the hash partitioning, inserting previous states into files partitioned by the same hash value. States that have a matching hash value are mapped to the same file. Provided that the sorting order is defined first on the hash value then on the state vector itself, after the concatenation of files (even if sorted separately) we obtain a total order on the sets of states. This implies that we can restrict duplicate detection including subtraction to states that have matching hash values.

Instead of sorting the buckets after they have been filled, it is possible to use chaining right away, checking each individual successor for having a duplicate against the states stored in its bucket. Keeping the list of states sorted, as in ordered hashing, accelerates the search, but requires additional work for insertion and does not speed up the computation, if compared to parallel sorting the buckets on the GPU. A refinement checks the state to be inserted in a bucket with the top element to detect some duplicates quickly.

State Compression

With a 64-bit hash address collision even in very large state spaces are rare. Henceforth, given hash function h, we compress the state vector for u to $(h(u), i(u))$, where $i(u)$ is the index of the state vector residing in RAM that is needed for expansion. We sort the pairs on the GPU with respect to the lexicographic ordering of h. The shorter the state vector, the more elements fit into one group, and the better the expected speedup on the GPU.

To estimate the error probability assume a state space of $n = 2^{30}$ elements uniformly hashed to the $m = 2^{64}$ possible bitvectors of length 64. According to the *birthday problem*, the probability of having no duplicates is $m!/(m^n(m-n)!)$. One known upper bound is $e^{-n(n-1)/2m}$, which in our case leads to a less than 96.92% chance of having no collision at all. But how much less can this be? For better confidence on our algorithm, we need a lower bound. We have

$$m!/(m^n(m-n)!) = m \ldots (m-n+1)/m^n = m/m \ldots (m-n+1)/m$$
$$\geq ((m-n+1)/m)^n \geq (1-n/m)^n.$$

For our case this resolves to a confidence of at least 93.94% that no duplicate arises while hashing the entire state space to 64 bits (per state). Recall that missing a duplicate harms, only if the missed state is the only way to reach the goal. If this confidence is too low, we may rerun the experiment with another independent hash function, certifying that with more than a 99.6% chance, the entire state space has been traversed.

Array Compaction

The compaction operation for sorted state sets can be accelerated on a parallel machine using an additional vector *unique* as follows. The vector is initialized with 1s, denoting that we initially assume that states are unique. In a parallel scan, we then compare a state with its left neighbor and mark the ones that are not unique by setting its entry to 0. Next, we compute the prefix sum to compute the final indices for compaction.

Duplicates in previous levels can be eliminated in parallel as follows. First we map as many BFS-levels as possible into the GPU. Processor p_i scans the current BFS-level t and a selected previous layer $i \in \{0, \ldots, t-1\}$. As both arrays $Open(t)$ and $Open(i)$ are sorted, the time complexity for the parallel scan is acceptable, because the arrays have to be mapped from RAM to VRAM and back anyway. If a match is found, array *unique* is updated, setting the according bit in $Open_t$ to 0. The parallelization we obtain for level subtraction is due to processing different BFS levels, and for sorting and scanning due to partitioning the array. Because all processors read the array $Open_t$ we allow concurrent read. Additionally, we allow each processor to write into the array *unique*. Since previous layers are mutually disjoint, no processor will access the same position, so that the algorithm preserves exclusive writes.

Expansion on the GPU

The remaining bottleneck is the CPU performance in generating the successors, which can also be reduced by applying parallel computation. For this we port the expansion for states to the GPU, parallelizing the search.

For BFS, the order of expansions within one bucket does not matter, so that no communication between threads is required. Each processor simply takes its share and starts expanding. Having fixed the set of applicable actions for each state, generating the successors in parallel on the GPU is immediate by replicating each state to be expanded by the number of applicable actions. All generated states are copied back to RAM (or by directly applying the GPU sorting).

9.5.3 Bitvector GPU Search

In the advent of perfect and inversible hash functions (see Ch. 3), a bitvector exploration of the search space can be fortunate (see Ch. 6). The GPU-assisted exploration will rank and unrank states during the expansion process.

The entire (or partitioned) state space bitvector is kept in RAM, while copying an array of indices (ranks) to the GPU. One additional scan through the bitvector is needed to convert its bits into integer ranks, but on the GPU the work to unrank, generate the successors, and rank them is identical for all threads. If the number of successors is known in advance, with each rank we reserve space for its successors. In larger instances that exceed main memory capacities, we additionally maintain write buffers in RAM to avoid random access on disk. Once the buffer is full, it is flushed to disk. Then, in one streamed access, all corresponding bits are set.

Consider the $(n^2 - 1)$-PUZZLE in Figure 9.24. The partition $B_0, \ldots, B_{n^2-1}$ into buckets has the advantage that we can determine whether the state belongs to an odd or even BFS-level and to which bucket a successor belongs. With this move-alternation property we can perform the 1- instead of 2-bit BFS with speedup results shown in Table 9.2. To avoid unnecessary memory access, the rank given to expand could be overwritten with the rank of the first child.

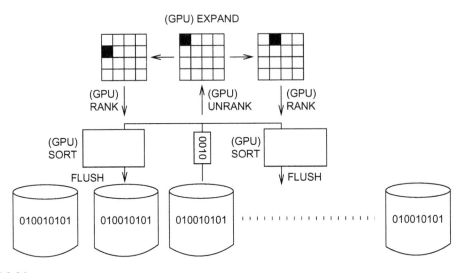

FIGURE 9.24

GPU exploration of a sliding-tile puzzle stored as a bitvector in RAM.

Table 9.2 Comparing CPU with GPU performances in one-bit and two-bit BFS in various sliding-tile puzzle (o.o.m. means out of memory, and o.o.t. denotes out of time).

Problem	2-Bit		1-Bit	
	Time GPU	Time CPU	Time GPU	Time CPU
(2×6)	70s	176s	163s	1517s
(3×4)	55s	142s	98s	823s
(4×3)	64s	142s	104s	773s
(6×2)	86s	160s	149s	1110s
(7×2)	o.o.m.	o.o.m.	13590s	o.o.t.

9.6 BIDIRECTIONAL SEARCH

Bidirectional search is a distributed search option executed from both ends of the search space, the initial and the goal node.

Bidirectional breadth-first search can accelerate the exploration by an exponential factor. Whether the bidirectional algorithm is more efficient than a unidirectional algorithm particularly depends on the structure of the search space. In heuristic search, the largest state sets are typically in the middle of the search space. In shallow depth, the set of explored states is small based on their limited reachability, and in large depth they are small due to the pruning power of the heuristic. Roughly speaking, when the search frontiers meet in the middle, then we have invested twice as much space as in unidirectional search for storing the *Open* lists. If the search frontiers meet earlier or later, there can be substantial savings.

After illustrating the application of bidirectional BFS in this section we introduce Pohl's path algorithm and a *wave-shaping* alternative to it, called *heuristic front-to-front search*. A nonoptimal approximation to *wave-shaping* and an improvement to Pohl's algorithms are provided. A practical relevant trade-off between heuristic and breadth-first search is *perimeter search*, a form of *target enlargement*. Due to its success in practice we have included bidirectional symbolic search to save memory, and island search to partition the search space in case a small cut of intermediate states is known. We close the section with investigating the multigoal heuristic search approach.

9.6.1 Bidirectional Front-to-End Search

The first approach to bidirectional search was the *bidirectional heuristic path algorithm* (*BHPA*). It applies front-to-end evaluations; that is, heuristic evaluation functions $h_d(u)$ that estimate the distance from u to s or to t, respectively, depending on the search direction $d \in \{0, 1\}$. Two A*-type searches are carried out quasi-simultaneously; that is, the search direction is changed from time to time. The *cardinality criterion* selects the *Open* list with the minimum number of elements. If the two search frontiers meet, a solution path is found. However, even if the two parts of the search paths are optimal, the concatenation doesn't need to be. Therefore, the termination condition of the algorithm is that the cost of the best solution found so far is no larger than the maximum of the two minimum f-values in either of the *Open* lists.

In the worst case, BHPA might have to perform the two A* searches completely, with the exception of at least one node expansion; if an optimal solution is found only in the last step, the termination condition is fulfilled immediately thereafter, and one expansion can be saved on the opposite frontier.

Disappointingly, experimental studies showed that the performance was actually close to the worst case. At that time, this was erroneously attributed to the assumption that the frontiers pass each other, which led to the algorithms described in the next section. However, in fact, the frontiers go through each other, and a large search subspace is explored twice.

This is avoided by the improved algorithm BS*, which exploits four optimizations:

Trimming: Nodes extracted from *Open* can be immediately discarded if their f-value is larger than the current best solution.

Screening: Successor nodes with an f-value larger than the current best solution need not be inserted into *Open*.

Nipping: Nodes extracted from $Open_d$ do not have to be expanded if they are already contained in $Closed^{1-d}$.

Pruning: In the same situation, descendants of these nodes in $Open^{1-d}$ can be removed.

Algorithm 9.15 gives the pseudo code for BS; BHPA is the algorithm with all the lines marked with BS* removed. Figure 9.25 illustrates the search strategies.

Although algorithm BS* saves a lot of time and memory, compared to BHPA, in experiments it still couldn't significantly outperform A* search. Usually the frontiers meet, and the optimal solution path is found early in the computation; most of the effort is in proving that this found path is indeed optimal.

Procedure BHPA / BS
Input: Graph G, start node s, goal node t
Output: Shortest path from s to t

$Open^0 \leftarrow \{s\}$; $Open^1 \leftarrow \{t\}$	;; Initialize search frontiers
$Closed^0 \leftarrow \{\}$; $Closed^1 \leftarrow \{\}$	;; Initialize visited list
$\alpha \leftarrow \infty$	;; Best solution cost found so far
while $(\alpha > \max\{\min\{f_0(x) \mid x \in Open^0\}, \min\{f_1(x) \mid x \in Open^1\}\})$	;; Termination
Fix search direction d	;; Perform forward or backward search
Select and delete u in $Open^d$	;; Delete minimum
Insert u into $Closed^d$	;; Update according to visited list
if $(f(u) \geq \alpha)$ **continue**	;; BS^*: Trimming
if $(u \in Closed^{1-d})$	;; Solution path found
$\alpha \leftarrow \min\{\alpha, g_d(u) + g_{1-d}(u)\}$	;; Update threshold
Delete descendants from u in $Open^{1-d}$	;; BS^*: Pruning
continue	;; BS^*: Nipping
$Succ^d(u) \leftarrow Expand^d(u)$	;; Generate successors
for all v in $Succ^d(u)$	;; Consider successors
if $(g_d(u) + w(u, v) + h_d(v) \geq \alpha)$ **continue**	;; BS^*: Screening
$Improve_d(u, v)$	;; Insert v into $Open^d$
	;; Remove v from $Closed^d$, if shorter path found

return α

Algorithm 9.15

Bidirectional search with BHPA.

9.6.2 *Bidirectional Front-to-Front Search

Over a long time, researchers believed that the experimental inefficiency of BHPA was due to the fact the search frontiers passed each other. Therefore, *wave-shaping* techniques were invented that would guide the two search frontiers toward each other. These algorithms use *front-to-front* evaluations that directly estimate the distance between the search frontiers.

The *bidirectional heuristic front-to-front algorithm* (BHFFA) computes the value $f(u, v) = g_0(u) + h(u, v) + g_1(v)$ for all pairs $(u, v) \in Open^0 \times Open^1$. Then it selects two nodes u_{min} and v_{min} for expansion in the two search frontiers that minimize the f-value, $f(u_{min}, v_{min}) = \min\{f(u, v) \mid (u, v) \in Open^0 \times Open^1\}$. Different than in front-to-end evaluation, the algorithm can admissibly terminate with the first solution path found. There are subtle problems with the front-to-front approach; the first version of BHFFA was wrong in the sense that it failed to find optimal solutions.

BHFFA was experimentally shown to improve on unidirectional search in terms of node expansions. However, the computational complexity is extremely high, and outweighs this advantage by far. In a straightforward implementation, each step requires $n_0 \cdot n_1$ heuristic evaluations, where n_i is the number of nodes in search frontier i. The total time complexity is $O(n^3)$, since there are at most n iterations for a total number of n expansions. When storing the result in $O(n_0 \cdot n_1)$ memory, the number of evaluations per expansion can be reduced to the number of successors of the expanded node, times the size of the opposite search frontier.

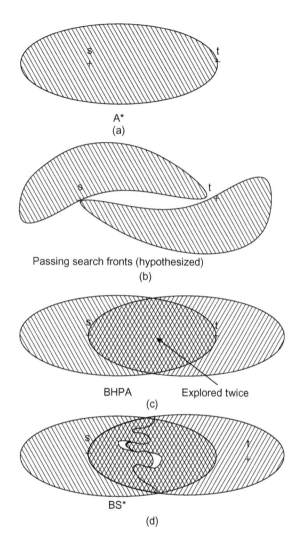

FIGURE 9.25

Exploration of search space (schematically): normal A* search (a), hypothesized passing of search fronts in bidirectional search (b), redundant evaluation in BHPA (c), and improvement by BS*(d).

To ease this overhead, Politowski and Pohl proposed another important derivate of BHFFA, called *d-node retargeting*. It guides the search frontier only toward one "central" node in the opposite search frontier, the *d*-node, where *d* is fixed as the furthest search node from the origin. Every *k* iterations, the search direction is switched, and a new *d*-node is computed on the opposite search frontier.

Unfortunately, *d*-node retargeting is also not admissible. Moreover, parameter *k* has to be chosen carefully. For a small parameter *k* we will get worse solutions when the two search frontiers meet; for a larger value of *k*, we imitate unidirectional search.

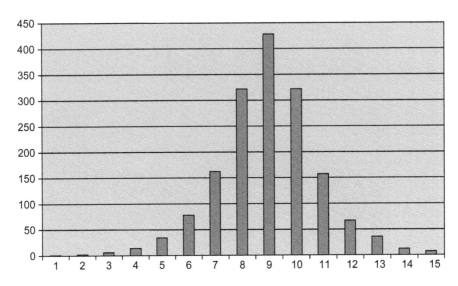

FIGURE 9.26

Distribution on the number of generated nodes in A* with respect to a given search depth.

Problems with maintaining two concurrently growing search trees can be avoided. A combination of forward and backward search is to look at one search tree that consists of pairs of forward and backward states. In each node either the forward or the backward state is expanded.

The most challenging question, however, is why bidirectional heurstic search algorithms often perform rather poorly in practice, whereas in blind search the savings of bidirectional state space traversals are obvious. One of the answers is found when looking at the number of nodes that A* explores with respect to a given search depth. We choose a simple FIFTEEN-PUZZLE problem example together with Manhattan distance heuristic and A*. Figure 9.26 shows the number of generated nodes with respect to a growing search depth. In difference to breadth-first search the number of expanded nodes drop significantly at both ends. The reason is that the heuristic estimate for the nodes closer to the goal is better. According to the IDA* search tree prediction, in depth i we expect about $N_i P(c - i)$ nodes for large f-cost threshold values c. If we assume P to be approximately normal distributed and N_i to be approximately equal to b^i with brute-force branching factor b, we often observe that the reduction in P for smaller values of x is larger than the growth of N_i, so that $N_i P(c - i)$ decreases exponentially also at the end.

The mean for the distribution is of course not exactly equal to half of the solution depth, but quite often it is not far off from this value. For our example with data values v_i, $i \in \{1, \ldots, 15\}$ we compute $\sum_{i=1}^{15} v_i = 1,647$ and $\sum_{i=1}^{15} i \cdot v_i = 14,761$, so that we have a mean of 8.962.

9.6.3 Perimeter Search

Perimeter search tries to reap the benefits of front-to-front evaluations, while avoiding the computational efforts involved in retargeting the heuristics toward a continuously changing search frontier. The search direction only changes once. It conducts a depth-bounded breadth-first search starting from the goal node; the nodes on the final search frontier, called the *perimeter*, are stored. Then a forward search, starting from s, employs front-to-front evaluation with respect to these nodes. Algorithm PS* does this in a A*-like fashion, and algorithms IDPS* and BIDA* carry out IDA*. The difference between the latter two is that BIDA* removes nodes from the perimeter that cannot influence the heuristic evaluation. For retrieving the solution path, either the optimal solution path is stored with each node or all nodes together with pointers to their parents are stored as well. Moreover, whereas IDPS* evaluates the distance to each perimeter node, BIDA* is a little bit more elegant, since it introduced a condition to avoid the consideration of a number of perimeter nodes in the presence of consistent heuristic functions.

During the search we compute the heuristic value of each node outside the parameter as the minimal value of the heuristic estimate to each perimeter node, plus the diameter of the perimeter. The main advantages of perimeter search is that the minimum heuristic value together with the diameter is generally more accurate than a single heuristic, and the search can terminate once a state in the perimeter has been found. The disadvantages are that the memory requirements for storing the perimeter and, more crucially, that the multiple heuristic computations are considerable. For the former concern, it has been proven already that very small perimeters can significantly enhance the heuristic estimation. Later we will see that in the context of pattern databases the latter concern can be bypassed.

The forward search evaluation function is $H(u) = \min_{p \in P}\{h(u,p) + \delta(p,t)\}$. This implies $H(u) = \delta(u,t)$ for all $u \in P$.

Theorem 9.1. *(Admissibility of H) Heuristic $H(u)$ is admissible if h is admissible.*

Proof. We have to show that $H(u) \leq \delta(u,t)$ for all $u \in V \setminus P$. Since $h(u,v) \leq \delta(u,v)$ we have

$$\delta(u,t) = \min_{v \in P}\{\delta(u,v) + \delta(v,t)\} \geq \min_{v \in P}\{h(u,v) + \delta(v,t)\} = H(u).$$ ∎

Theorem 9.2. *(Consistency of H) Heuristic $H(u)$ is consistent if h is consistent.*

Proof. We have to show that $H(u) \leq H(v) + w(u,v)$:

$$H(v) + w(u,v) = \min_{w \in P}\{h(v,w) + \delta(w,t)\} + w(u,v)$$

$$= \min_{w \in P}\{h(v,w) + w(u,v) + \delta(w,t)\}$$

$$\geq \min_{w \in P}\{h(u,w) + \delta(w,t)\} = H(u).$$ ∎

For the correctness of perimeter search, it is helpful to consider the *perimeter reduction* G_p of G, in which the entire perimeter is reduced to a single super node t^* and all incoming edges to the perimeter starting at u are reassigned to $w(u,t^*) = w(u,v) + \delta(v,t)$.

Theorem 9.3. *(Perimeter Reduction) For all nongoal nodes u in the perimeter reduced graph G_P of G, we have $\delta_G(s,t) = \delta_{G_P}(s,t^*)$.*

Proof. Let $p = (u_0, \ldots, u_k)$ be a solution path from s to t in G, then we have for a prefix $p' = (u_0, \ldots, u_l)$ that (p', t^*) is a solution path in G_P. We have $g(p) = w(u_0, u_1) + \cdots + w(u_{l-1}, u_l) + w(u_l, u_{l+1}) + \cdots + w(u_{k-1}, u_k)$. The condition $w(u_l, u_{l+1}) + \cdots + w(u_{k-1}, u_k) \leq \delta(u_l, u_t)$ implies that $g(p) \leq g(p', t^*)$. Moreover, for an optimal solution path we have $\delta_G(s,t) = \delta_G(s, u_{l-1}) + w(u_{l-1}, u_l) + \delta(u_l, t^*) = \delta_{G_P}(s, t^*)$. ∎

*Improvements of Perimeter Search

The following update procedure has been suggested to save time in computing $\min_{p\in P}\{h(u,p)+\delta(p,t)\}$. However, it requires $O(|P|)$ storage at each node to store the estimated distance to the target through each perimeter node; therefore, for large problems it can be used only in conjunction with the iterative-deepening procedure (IDPS*).

The improvement is based on the observation that with a consistent heuristic, it holds for each v and u that $|h(v) - h(u)| \leq w(u,v)$, where $w(u,v)$ is the weight of the edge between u and v. Thus, the estimate from v to a perimeter node can at most change by $w(u,v)$, where u is the parent of v. Therefore, the heuristic value does not need to be recomputed if its value cannot change enough to affect the minimum.

The heuristic is used once fully for the start node at the beginning of the search for each perimeter node, and these estimates are stored, along with the index of the minimum. Next, when a node v is generated from u, the heuristic value of the current minimum is recomputed. The edge weight $w(u,v)$ is then subtracted from the rest of the stored heuristic values; if any of these falls below the current minimum, it is recomputed using h, too.

In the FIFTEEN-PUZZLE domain, BIDA* expands only a fraction of the nodes A* expands. This reduction has to be balanced with the increased computation time needed for the heuristic evaluation. It turns out that when varying the perimeter diameter, the overall running time exhibits a minimum at depth 16; at this point, it amounts to 27.4% of A*'s running time and 0.9% of its expansions.

When analyzing the improvements, it becomes clear that the benefit of the bidirectional approach lies primarily in a dynamically improved heuristic estimate. For example, in the FIFTEEN-PUZZLE, using a perimeter of only 1 (which contains two nodes) saves already about half of the node generations of IDA*. The perimeter search discovers an improvement of the Manhattan distance heuristic under the name *last move heuristic*. In most cases the heuristic is increased by two units. The last move consists of bringing the blank into its goal position; therefore, before that, one of its neighbor tiles must be in the blank's goal position, which is not accommodated in the Manhattan distance.

Perhaps surprisingly, however, in other domains, it is hard to achieve any real improvements with perimeter search. This is, for example, the case in mazes under the same Manhattan distance. The reason is that the same perimeter achieves the same absolute improvement of the heuristic; however, since the solution length is longer by orders of magnitude, the relative impact is too insignificant. To obtain the same savings in expansions, a much larger perimeter would have to be computed, which would make perimeter search very expensive in terms of computation and memory.

*Front-to-Front Variants of Perimeter Search

To avoid the increased computational effort of front-to-front evaluations, it has been suggested to use the same scheme as in perimeter search, changing the direction only once and using the stored nodes of the first search in the second one, in conjunction with front-to-front evaluation. For the two search stages, different A*-like or IDA*-like algorithms can be instantiated (called BAA and BAI, respectively). If a *Closed* node of the backward stage is encountered, a solution path has been found, and it need not be expanded further (it can be nipped). The search terminates if the best solution found so far is no larger than the minimum f-value (in A*), respectively the next higher threshold (in IDA*).

In addition, bidirectional search allows for dynamic improvements of the heuristic, which are not possible in unidirectional search. One such method is called the *Add-method*. Let *MinDiff* be the minimum error of the heuristic on the perimeter around t, i.e., $MinDiff = \min\{g_1^*(u) - h_0(u)|u \in P\}$.

Lemma 9.1. *(Nonincreasing Error of Heuristic) If h_0 is consistent, then the error in the heuristic $Diff_0 = g_1^*(u) - h_0(u)$ cannot increase on an optimal solution path.*

Proof. Let u and v be two successor nodes on an optimal path to t. Then

$$Diff_0(v) = g_1^*(v) - h_0(v) \leq g_1^*(v) + w(u,v) - h_0(u) = g_1^*(u) - h_0(u) = Diff_0(u). \qquad \blacksquare$$

Using this lemma, the heuristic remains optimistic if we add the minimum error to it.

Theorem 9.4. *(Quality Bound for Add-Method) $H_0(u) = h_0(u) + MinDiff \leq h_0^*(u)$.*

Proof. The optimal path from u to t must go through some perimeter node p:

$$H_0(u) = h_0(u) + MinDiff \leq h_0(u) + Diff_0(p) \leq h_0(u) + Diff_0(u) = h_0^*(u). \qquad \blacksquare$$

Now unidirectional A* search wouldn't be affected at all by adding a constant to all heuristic values. However, recall that in BAI and BAA the current best solution is compared to the minimum estimate in *Open*; therefore, the addition can lead to earlier termination. For further optimization, to maximize *MinDiff*, the perimeter generation search can always select the node with the maximum error in the heuristic; this variant is called *Add-BDA*.

The second method, called the *Max-method*, uses the estimate $h_0'(u) = f_{\min,1} - h_1(u)$, where $f_{\min,1}$ is the minimum f-value of the perimeter, $f_{\min,1} = \min\{g_1^*(u) + h_1(u) | u \in P\}$.

Theorem 9.5. *(Admissibility Max-Method) $h_0'(u) \leq h_0^*(u)$.*

Proof. The optimal path from u to t must go through some perimeter node p:

$$h_0'(u) = f_{\min,1} - h_1(u) \leq h_1(p) - h_1(u) + g_1^*(p) \leq \delta(u,p) + g_1^*(p) = h_0^*(u). \qquad \blacksquare$$

This dynamic evaluation is not necessarily always better than the static function, but since both are admissible, we can combine them as $H_0(u) = \max\{h_0(u), f_{\min,1} - h_1(u)\}$.

In experimental studies, it was shown that *Max-BAI* with a transposition table can outperform IDA* (and all other bidirectional search algorithms) for the FIFTEEN-PUZZLE, and that *Add-BDA* has outperformed A* (and all other bidirectional search algorithms) on maze problems.

Near-Optimal Perimeter Search

Choosing $f(u) = g(u) + \lambda h(u)$ with $\lambda > 1$ in A* leads to inadmissible heuristics and nonoptimal solutions. Increasing values of λ results in finding solutions faster at the expense of an increased solution length. For perimeter search it seems irrational to calculate all these heuristics and then compute weighted versions. In near-optimal perimeter search the heuristic function is defined as $h(u,t)$ and not as $h(u,P)$, plus the depth of the perimeter as in perimeter search. For near-optimal perimeter search only constant time is needed to process each generated or expanded node. The match of a new node against the perimeter nodes that are saved in a hash table can be performed in a constant time.

Theorem 9.6. *(Quality Bound on Perimeter Search) Let d be the depth of the perimeter P and let $H_P = \min_{p \in P}\{h(p,t)\}$ for an admissible heuristic h. Let $\delta(s,t)$ be the length of an optimal solution and W be the cost of the solution found by near-optimal perimeter search. Then we have*

$$\delta(s,t) \leq W \leq \delta(s,t) + d - H_P.$$

Proof. For the first inequality we note that the cost of any path that leads to the goal cannot be smaller than the optimal path cost. Since W is composed of the path cost $g(u)$ and the heuristic estimate $H_P = \min_{p \in P}\{h(p,t)\} \le h(u) \le h^*(u)$, the combined cost $g(u) + H_P$ cannot be larger than $\delta(s,t)$.

Since *near-optimal perimeter search* uses an admissible heuristic, $0 \le H_P \le d$ and $d - H_P \ge 0$. Let u be the first encountered node on the perimeter; then we have $W = g(u) + d$. Since the cost function of A* and *near-optimal perimeter search* fulfill $f(u) = g(u) + h(u) \le \delta(s,t)$, we have $g(u) + d \le \delta(s,t) + d - h(u)$. In the worst case we can take the minimum heuristic value of all nodes in the perimeter and get $W \le \delta(s,t) + d - H_P$. ∎

The value $d - H_P$ can be viewed as the maximum mistake of heuristic values among nodes in the perimeter.

9.6.4 Bidirectional Symbolic Breadth-First Search

As a by-product for symbolic search for the construction of symbolic pattern databases we have already seen the advantage of the transition relation *Trans* to perform backward search. Recall that for state sets S_i we successively determine the preimages of the goal set, by computing

$$\phi_{S_i}(x') = \exists x \, (\phi_{S_{i-1}}(x) \wedge Trans(x',x))$$

for an increasing index i. Because the search is symbolic, large goal sets do not impose a burden to the search process.

In bidirectional breadth-first search, forward and backward search are carried out concurrently. On one hand, we have the symbolic forward search frontier $\phi_{\{s\}}$, and on the other, the backward search frontier ϕ_G. When the two search frontiers meet after f forward and b backward iterations we have found an optimal solution of length $f + b$. With the two horizons $Open^0$ and $Open^1$ the algorithm is implemented in pseudo code in Algorithm 9.16.

In a unit cost graph, the number of iterations remains equal to the optimal solution length f^*. Solution reconstruction now proceeds from the established intersection to the respective starting states.

The selection of the direction of the search is often critical for a successful exploration. There are three simple criteria: BDD size, number of represented states, and smaller exploration time. Since the former two are not well suited to predict the computational efforts for the next iteration, the third criterion should be preferred.

9.6.5 *Island Search

Consider the road network of a city through which a river runs in a north-south direction (see Fig. 9.27). Suppose we are trying to find the shortest path from a western to an eastern destination; then the path is constrained to pass through one of the bridges over the river. The idea of island search is to improve search efficiency by breaking the path up into two components, before and after a bridge. Reaching a bridge can be regarded as a subgoal that has to be achieved first.

In terms of a general search graph $G = (V, E)$, we assume that we know of a (not too large) subset of nodes $I \subset V$, such that any solution path must contain one element; in other words, I represents a *cut* of G. This can allow us to improve search efficiency by means of a tighter heuristic estimate. Instead of using the goal distance $h(u)$ from a node u to the goal t everywhere, we obtain a better bound for nodes before the cut as $\min\{h(u|i)\}$ for $i \in I$, where $h(u|i)$ denotes the estimated length of a minimum path from u to t, constrained to pass through node i. For instance, in the route planning example, we

Procedure Symbolic-Bidirectional-BFS
Input: State space problem with transition relation *Trans*, goal set T, and start node s
Output: Optimal solution path

$Open^0(x) \leftarrow \phi_{\{s\}}; Open^1(x) \leftarrow \phi_T$	;; Initialize horizon lists
while $(Open^0(x) \wedge Open^1(x) \equiv false)$	;; Loop if search frontiers do not meet
Fix search direction d	;; Perform forward or backward search
if $(d = 0)$	;; Forward search
$Open^0(x') \leftarrow \exists x ((x = x') \wedge Open^0(x))$	;; Variable replacement
$Succ(x) \leftarrow \exists x' (Open^0(x') \wedge Trans(x',x))$	;; Forward image
$Open^0(x) \leftarrow Succ(x)$	;; Iteration with new search frontier
else	;; Backward search
$Pred(x') \leftarrow \exists x (Open^1(x) \wedge Trans(x',x))$	;; Backward image
$Open^1(x') \leftarrow Pred(x')$	;; Iteration with new search frontier
$Open^1(x) \leftarrow \exists x' ((x = x') \wedge Open^1(x'))$	;; Variable replacement
return $Construct(Open^0(x) \wedge Open^1(x))$	;; Generate solution

Algorithm 9.16

Bidirectional BFS implemented with BDDs.

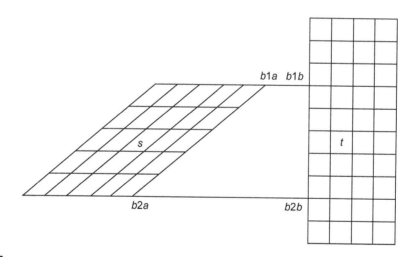

FIGURE 9.27

To route from s to t, either $b1a$ or $b2a$ (or equivalently, $b1b$ and $b2b$) must be traversed. Hence, the shortest path problem can be decomposed into finding the shortest paths from s to any of these bridges, and then from the bridges to t.

can replace the air distance from the current location to the goal destination by sum of the air distance from the current location to the bridge, plus the air distance from the bridge to the target destination, minimized over all bridges.

Island search can be incorporated both into A*-like and IDA*-like search algorithms. In the original paper, the A*-algorithm is described using two *Open* and *Closed* lists; however, this is not strictly necessary. It is sufficient if each node stores an additional flag indicating whether its generating path contains an ancestor in I. When a node is expanded, the successors inherit its flag, unless the node is in I, in which case it is switched on. Depending on its value, the h-value is estimated either conventionally or using the constraint form.

Island search differs from A* or IDA* essentially only in the improved heuristics; therefore, if the latter one is admissible, the algorithm is guaranteed to find an optimal path, if one exists.

Moreover, suppose that the triangle equality $h(x,y) \leq h(x,z) + h(z,y)$ holds for the heuristic estimate; this is obviously true for the air distance metric in our example. Then, the A* variant of island search is at least as efficient as A*; that is, it expands no more nodes.

The original algorithm has been generalized to more than two islands. In this scenario, there is a user-supplied lower-bound E on the minimum number of bridges that have to be passed on an optimal solution path. Each node stores a set of flags for the cuts passed by its ancestors; the goal distance is used as the heuristic only if this set has E elements.

The practical results of island search depend on how well the search graph can be partitioned. In general, this must be done prior to the search in a domain-specific way. It is important to obtain a small cut size: This limits the increased computation cost of the heuristic, and usually leads to larger improvements. For example, in a route planning application we could partition the road map into zones of urban areas, which are connected to each other by relatively few highways and major roads.

9.6.6 *Multiple-Goal Heuristic Search

Most of the search algorithms we have considered in previous chapters work with multiple goal states for which the condition *Goal* is tested. However, for bidirectional search so far we are limited to one-to-one shortest path search. Moreover, perimeter search has extended the goal set from one to many states and we would like to avoid a one-to-many heuristic frontier calculation.

The three-peg TOWERS-OF-HANOI problem illustrates the power of recursion. To move n disks from peg 1 to peg 2, first move $(n-1)$ disks from peg 1 to peg 3, then move disk n from peg 1 to peg 2, then move $(n-1)$ disks from peg 3 to peg 2. This leads to $2^n - 1$ moves. With three towers and n disks, the minimum number of moves is $2^n - 1$, so that the strategy is optimal.

An unproven conjecture on the four-peg TOWERS-OF-HANOI problem (see Fig. 9.28) states that an optimal solution begins by forming a substack of the k-smallest disks, then moving the rest, and then moving those k again, with k to be determined. If in the four-peg n-disk TOWERS-OF-HANOI problem we take two bits to encode the peg on which it is placed we arrive at a state vector of length $2n$ bits.

Based on the conjecture the minimum number of moves can be computed. The results are shown in Table 9.3. The numbers have been validated with parallel external heuristic search with up to 30 disks, which corresponds to a state space size of 4^{30} states. The parallel search explored over 7.1 million states and required about 1.28 terabytes disk space.

For the TOWERS-OF-HANOI problem the goal state and initial state are symmetrical. This allows the search depth in the four-peg problem to be cut to a half. The goal of the heuristic search was *any* middle state in which all but the largest disk are distributed over the two nongoal and noninitial pegs. If a middle state is found in depth l, then a complete solution in depth $2l + 1$ can always be constructed.

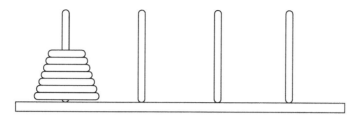

FIGURE 9.28

Four-peg TOWERS-OF-HANOI problem.

Table 9.3 Conjectured number of moves to solve the four-peg TOWERS-OF-HANOI problem.

n	1	2	3	4	5	6	7	8	9	10	11	12	13	14	15	16	17
$f(n)$	1	3	5	9	13	17	25	33	41	49	65	81	97	113	129	161	193
n	18	19	20	21	22	23	24	25	26	27	28	29	30				
$f(n)$	225	257	289	321	385	449	513	577	641	705	769	897	1,025				
n	31	32	33	34	35	36	37	38	39	40							
$f(n)$	1,153	1,281	1,409	1,537	1665	1,793	2,049	2,305	2,561	2,817							
n	41	42	43	44	45	46	47	48									
$f(n)$	3,073	3,329	3,585	3,841	4,097	4,609	5,121	5,633									

A depth 1,025 search for the 30-peg problem can thus be reduced to depth 512 to prove that no smaller solution exists.

The size of a single-goal pattern database is limited by the size of main memory, which by 1 GB is 2^{30} bytes. If we assume that the abstract solution length is below 256 steps, a pattern database is bound to 15 disks. To construct the pattern database with 15 pegs *all* states in which the 15 disks are distributed among two pegs are generated and assigned to a depth zero for initializing the backward heuristic search. Then the entire state space size of 4^{15} states is generated.

Multiple-goal pattern database search can overcome limitations of perimeter search. When constructing the database, we can seed backward database construction with all the states in the perimeter. During the overall search the minimum heuristic estimate is found by a simple table lookup. This technique requires that perimeter and abstract space computation are compatible.

9.7 SUMMARY

Scaling a problem often implies that expanding a state involves new actions and increases the internal computation time for generating the heuristic and for the heuristic evaluation of the successors. In extreme cases, internal time exceeds hard disk access time. We have divided this chapter on distributed search into two equally important parts: one on parallel search and one on multidirectional search. If we have more processors at hand, then any multidirectional search can be parallelized, even if some techniques may impose much communication overhead.

Parallel search algorithms are designed to solve algorithmic problems using a network of processes while distributing the workload among them. Processes communicate via files or message passing. An efficient solution is obtained, if different tasks can be distributed in a way that working power is effectively used. A speedup is expected if the load is distributed uniformly with low interprocess communication. Internal workload is divided among different processors either residing on the same or on different machines.

Synchronicity refers to what happens when a process completes its task; either one process waits for the other to complete their tasks, or it starts working on a new task immediately. In synchronous parallel search each node of the search space is assigned to one process, which performs a search on it. Subsequent work is distributed by this process to idle recipient ones. In this manner eventually all processes receive work and perform sequential search. Workload is distributed via sharing the work that is present on local stacks. Enforcing a synchronous execution usually increases the communication complexity. In asynchronous parallel search workload will not be balanced among different processes. The only shared information that is broadcast are current upper bounds and solution qualities. As a side effect, a different timing for the information exchange can lead to a nondeterministic behavior. On the other hand, the nondeterminism does not necessarily induce that the computed result is incorrect. The established solution cost is either the value of the best solution found, or the value of the best solution to the remaining subproblems. In such an asynchronous setting not all processes have complete search knowledge, such that information exchange is *delayed*.

We looked at different parallel implementations for depth-first-inspired search strategies, including parallel branch-and-bound and parallel iterative-deepening A* search. For the elimination of duplicates a (static or dynamic) function distributing states to the processes is crucial, inducing lookup requests or entire states to be communicated. A loosely coupled (asynchronous) computation is often faster than a tight (synchronous) one, but requires structural knowledge of the problem. Here the search tree is often generated to some search depth, and the search frontier distributed among the different processors, since one option for load balancing large stacks is split. Among the options for IDA* with parallel window search a rather simple parallelization has been presented. For parallelizing A* search, the search frontier has to be maintained in appropriate data structures. For shared memory architectures treaps trade access priority with the best-first ordering of keys induced by the f-value. For more loosely coupled, so-called local A* search approaches, load balancing together with controlling the extra efforts for expanding suboptimal states becomes a challenge.

With external parallel breadth-first and best-first search we then suggested an improved distributed duplicate detection scheme for multiple processors and multiple hard disks. We assumed a typical network scenario, where computers are interconnected through Ethernet or over TCP/IP. The computers have access to a shared hard disk through a network file system and a local hard disk can be present at each computer. The setting extends to multicore or multiple-processor systems. External designs often lead to new solutions for parallel computing. Additional to parallelizing delayed duplicate detection, we also studied parallel structured duplicate detection. To exploit larger joint RAM capacities in a computer network pattern-oriented, memory-based heuristics are evaluated in parallel. As an example, a client-server architecture for solving the $(n^2 - 1)$-PUZZLE has been discussed under the assumption that computing the heuristic takes more time than generating the successor set. With the distribution of disjoint pattern databases each client is responsible for (all) the pattern database(s) that have a specific

Table 9.4 Overview of parallel search algorithms together with synchronization option (sync) duplicate detection strategies (DD).

Name	DD	Sync	State Set	Iterative	Optimal
Parallel BnB (9.6)	–	–	Local	✓	✓
Parallel DFS (9.7)	–	✓	Local	–	–
Parallel IDA* (9.8)	–	✓	Local	✓	✓
Asynchronous IDA* (9.8)	–	–	Local	✓	✓
Parallel-Window-Search (9.9)	–	–	Local	✓	✓
TDS (9.3)	✓	✓	Local	✓	✓
Parallel Local A*	✓	✓	Local	–	✓
Parallel Global A*	✓	✓	Global	–	✓
Parallel-Ext.-BFS (9.10)	Delayed	–	Global	–	✓
Parallel-SDD	Early	–	Global	✓	✓
Parallel-Ext.-A* (9.11)	Delayed	–	Global	–	✓

tile in their pattern. It exploits the fact that pattern databases are selected based on the tile that moves. Individual RAM requirements are reduced, allowing larger pattern databases to be kept on one process.

Table 9.4 summarizes the parallel search algorithms that have been introduced. We provide information on how the algorithm performs duplicate detection, if it is synchronous or asynchronous, whether the node set is kept local or global if the approach is incremental (improves solution quality over time), and if it reports the optimal solution at termination time.

We have seen significant search improvements by integrating GPU computation. Speedups of more than one order of magnitude on a single, moderately advanced graphics card are possible, especially on more recent or multiple cards. We restricted our exposition to large-scale breadth-first search. Many other external memory algorithms that have been discussed in this book are also streamed and are suggested to be ported to the GPU.

As bidirectional algorithms we have introduced BS/BHPA and BHFFS, which use either front-to-end or front-to-front evaluations. Solutions quality is usually gradually improved. We have illustrated why the prospects on savings driven from bidirectional breadth-first search have not been fulfilled in search practices. As one solution, perimeter search avoids merging two opposite-directed search heuristics and uses complete search at one end of the search space to increase the effectiveness for a search from the other side, since all nodes of the perimeter have to be stored. Island Search is a multidirectional algorithm that exploits the structure of problem space to partitioning it into different pieces that are searched individually.

Table 9.5 summarizes the bi- and multidirectional search algorithms. We denote the state representation, the applied search approach in forward and backward search (if any), whether the algorithms improve the solution quality over time (anytime), and if it is optimal at the end.

Bidirectional search can already accelerate single-processor search, namely when the processor time-slices between the two search directions. It is also possible to implement bidirectional search on more than two processors, for example, by using the search methods discussed in the chapter to distribute the workload of the search in one (or both) directions.

Table 9.5 Overview of bidirectional search algorithms.

Name	Graph	Forward	Backward	Anytime	Optimal
Symb.-Bidir-BFS (9.16)	Symbolic	Blind	Blind	–	✓
BHPA/BS (9.15)	Explicit	Guided	Guided	✓	✓
BHFFS	Explicit	Guided	Guided	✓	✓
Island Search	Explicit	k Guided	–	–	✓
Perimeter Search	Explicit	Guided	Blind	–	✓
Multiple-Goal-A*	Explicit	Guided	Blind	–	✓

9.8 EXERCISES

9.1 Message passing interface libraries like MPI provide basic routines for message handling between different processes. Explain how critical sections of read and writes are to be avoided in MPI and compare the results with the alternative communication via (message) files as described in the text.

9.2 *Bounded DFS* depends on how information is exchanged. Produce pseudo code for two different information sharing approaches.

9.3 Consider the set of numbers $(a_1, \ldots, a_8) = (5, 3, 9, 4, 6, 2, 4, 1)$.
  1. Explain the working of the parallel computation for computing the sum of $a_1 \ldots a_8$ by displaying the array after each traversal of the loop of the procedure *Sum*.
  2. Explain the working of the parallel computation for computing the prefix sum $a_1 \ldots a_j$ by displaying the array after each traversal of the loop of the procedure *Prefix-Sum*.
  3. Show how procedure *Prefix-Sum* can be made work-optimal.
  4. Search an implementation for the GPU (e.g., in CUDA) on the Internet and explain it.

9.4 To simulate a finite-state automaton using prefix sum computations use state set $Q = \{1, 2, 3, 4\}$ and transition alphabet $\Sigma = \{a, b\}$ as an example. Let $q_0 = 1$ and let δ consist of the eight transitions $1 \xrightarrow{a} 2, 2 \xrightarrow{a} 3, 3 \xrightarrow{a} 4, 4 \xrightarrow{a} 1, 1 \xrightarrow{b} 3, 2 \xrightarrow{b} 1, 3 \xrightarrow{b} 2$, and $4 \xrightarrow{b} 4$ as shown in Figure 9.29. Let the input be string abbaabba.
  1. Compute the prefix sum over the associate function $\otimes$ that combines the sequential application of the transitions. For example, the combined transition function for string ab is $1 \rightarrow 1, 2 \rightarrow 2, 3 \rightarrow 4$, and $4 \rightarrow 3$, since $1 \rightarrow 2 \otimes 2 \rightarrow 1$ results in $1 \rightarrow 1$.
  2. Denote the state that is reached for each possible prefix by inserting the initial state q_0 in the transition function.

9.5 Use the solution of the previous exercise to compute the sum of two numbers x and y in binary in parallel logarithmic time.
  1. Devise a two-state finite-state automata for propagating the carry bit. A state in this automata represents the carry bit from the i-th state to the $(i+1)$th state. It depends on the sum of the two bits of x_i and y_i, so that the transition alphabet is $\Sigma = \{0, 1, 2\}$.

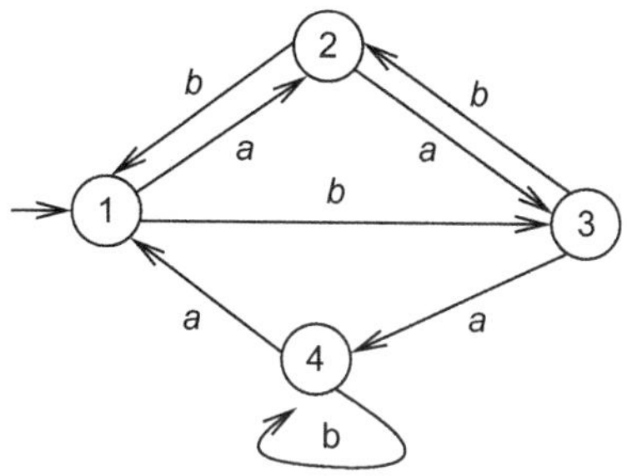

FIGURE 9.29

A state transition diagram of a finite-state machine.

2. Test your construction with the two numbers $u = (01010111)_2$ and $v = (00010011)_2$. Simulate the automata using the *Prefix Sum* algorithm in parallel logarithmic time.
3. Compute the result of the addition. For each bit position the carry bit has to be added to the input bits. If the solution is even then the result is 0, otherwise 1.

9.6   Show how to use prefix sums to eliminate duplicates in a sorted sequence. Use an additional array to mark the elements that are the same.

9.7   Insert $(17,0)$ in the treap depicted in Figure 9.9.
1. Where is the node containing $(17,0)$ finally located?
2. How many rotation steps do you need to satisfy the treap property? Distinguish between left and right rotations.
3. Display the treap after each rotation step.

9.8   Consider a treap in the form of a randomized search tree for a set S of n numbers, where the priorities are uniformly distributed random numbers.
1. Show that the average path in a randomized search tree has the length $O(\lg n)$.
2. Compute the average case time for insertion. (This is a tough one, since you have to consider all permutations of the numbers $\{1,\ldots,n\}$.)
3. Compute the average case time for deletion. Can you reuse the result of part (b)?

9.9   Sort large state sets (e.g., random strings) on the GPU.
- How can BITONIC SORT be of help?
- Can you beat CPU QUICKSORT?
- Discuss a strategy to parallelize QUICKSORT. What problems have to be resolved?

9.10   Transform the alignment of alternating black and white checkers depicted on the left side of Figure 9.30 into the arrangement shown on the right side of Figure 9.30. In this CHECKERS REARRANGEMENT problem you are allowed to move only two checkers of different, colors at a time, preserving their original order and the alignment. You may introduce gaps as needed.
1. Find a solution to the problem by hand. Work backward to reduce the set of options.
2. Use an evaluation function for backward search that computes the number of color transitions to apply a greedy heuristic search reasoning.

FIGURE 9.30

CHECKERS REARRANGEMENT problem.

9.11 Consider two jugs: one that contains seven units of water, and one that contains three units of water.
1. Find a solution sequence of fill and pouring operators that will result in one jar containing five units of water.
2. Work backward to obtain the solution more efficiently.

9.12 Draw a histogram on the number of expanded (or generated) nodes of A* in the FIFTEEN-PUZZLE with Manhattan distance with respect to a growing search depth for the instance (14 1 9 6 4 8 12 5 7 2 3 0 10 11 13 15). Compare your result with respect to bidirectional breadth-first search.

9.13 Take the distributed search model by Vitter/Shriver for a problem graph $G = (V, E)$ with locality L to be searched with N processors each having local disks. Show that parallel external BFS requires $O\left(\left(\frac{|E|}{NB} \lg_{M/B} \frac{|E|}{B}\right) + L \cdot |V|/NB\right)$ I/Os.

9.14 Show that for consistent heuristics parallel external A* terminates with the shortest path from an initial state to a target state, and does not expand any node that has a higher f-value than a state in T.

9.15 This exercise addresses the diameter of TOWERS-OF-HANOI problem, namely the largest distance of any node from the initial state.
1. For the three-peg TOWERS-OF-HANOI problem show that the minimum number of 2^{n-1} moves is the diameter of the problem by performing a complete BFS.
2. Show that for the four-peg TOWERS-OF-HANOI problem the depth is not always equal to the depth. While the condition is satisfied for smaller values n, for the 15-disk it is not. Run BFS on the 15-disk problem to validate that the optimal solution length is 129 and the diameter is 130. How many states are located in depth 130?

9.16 Compute all FIFTEEN-PUZZLE instances that lie on a perimeter of size 3 around the goal node.

9.17 Implement IDA* with perimeter search to solve some random instances of the FIFTEEN-PUZZLE problem.

9.18 Suppose the unit cost graph of Figure 9.27. Determine the intermediate f-values at b1b and b2b using
1. No additional heuristic.
2. A heuristic that counts the number of nonhorizontal lines between the actual node and the goal node (e.g., $h(s) = 4$).

Illustrate how *Island Search* continues given the information at the two nodes.

9.9 BIBLIOGRAPHIC NOTES

The textbook by Jájá (1992) covers the basic concepts of parallel computation. For the advanced readers the textbook by Zomaya (1996) may be appropriate. Applications of prefix sums have been studied by Eppstein and Galil (1988).

A number of parallel and distributed approaches to search have considerably improved the performance of the search process. Several parallelizations have been proposed for the branch-and-bound procedure with best-first traversal strategy.

Kumar, Ramesh, and Rao (1987) have given a survey on parallel best-first search. Kale and Saletore (1990) have considered parallel state space search for a first solution with consistent linear speedups. Minimal parallel window search is due to Powley and Korf (1991). Mahapatra and Dutt (1999) have analyzed parallel memory-restricted search and proposed an algorithm that iteratively extrapolates cost bounds. The application area is the traveling salesman problem. Exact extrapolations have been found via least-square curve fitting, and faster approximate extrapolations have been derived. A distributed termination criterion is due to Dijkstra and Scholten (1979).

The parallel search bench ZRAM, which solved the FIFTEEN-PUZZLE by showing that the hardest initial configuration requires 80 moves to be solved, has been developed by Bruengger, Marzetta, Fukuda, and Nievergelt (1999). The authors discovered two previously unknown positions, requiring exactly 80 moves to be solved. Large-scale parallel breadth-first search with hash-based delayed duplicate elimination has been implemented by Korf and Schultze (2005) to completely enumerate all states in the FIFTEEN-PUZZLE. Zhou and Hansen (2007b) have shown how to parallelize structured duplicate detection.

Different load balancing algorithms have been discussed by Dutt and Mahapatra (1994) while global and local hashing strategies for duplicate detections have been studied in Dutt and Mahapatra (1997). Adaptive parallel iterative-deepening A* by Cook and Varnell (1998) combines the benefits of many different approaches to parallel heuristic search. Results are generated from FIFTEEN-PUZZLE problems, robot arm motion problems, artificial search spaces, and planning problems, and indicate that the system is able to greatly reduce the search time for these applications. General and parallel branch-and-bound search has been discussed by Nau, Kumar, and Kanal (1984). A parallel implementation PRA* for the connection machine has been provided by Evett, Hendler, Mahanti, and Nau (1990). Transposition-driven scheduling has been introduced by Romein, Plaat, Bal, and Schaeffer (1999), and extended to two-player games by Kishimoto (1999). Recent implementation of A* and its derivatives on multicore machines include HDA* by Kishimoto, Fukunaga, and Botea (2009), and PBFS by Burns et al. (2009a,2009b). The former improves on transposition-driven scheduling and the latter improves on structured duplicate detection. Another refinement including edge partitioning suited to multicore search has been presented by Zhou, Schmidt, Hansen, Do, and Uckun (2010).

Lock-free (or *wait-free*) hash tables have been shown to be effective in state space search for reachability purposes by Laarman, van de Pol, and Weber (2010). The locking is realized without explicit lock variables using the atomic *compare-and-swap* operation. Sulewski, Edelkamp, and Kissmann (2011) have shown a domain-independent planner that exploits processing power available on the graphics card. To enhance precondition checks as well as assignments to effect variables on the GPU, a postfix notation of the expressions is used, and for duplicate detection, lock-free hash tables that yield optimal solutions are employed.

In the area of formal methods various authors have proposed ways of solving the problem of distributing the memory requirements over a cluster of workstations. Perhaps one of the first efforts is by Aggarwal, Alonso, and Courcoubetis (1988). Stern and Dill (1997) have employed a hash-based partitioning scheme to divide the whole state space into multiple computing nodes. The proposed approach was implemented on top of the Murφ verifier. Lerda and Sisto (1999) have experimented with a different partition function. The rationale behind their hash function is that a transition usually performs only few local changes in a system, so that with a high probability a successor might belong to the current node. Haverkort, Bell, and Bohnenkamp (1999) have introduced distributed search for stochastic Petri nets. Distributed verification in μ calculus has been reported by Bollig, Leucker, and Weber (2001) and for CTL* by Inggs and Barringer (2006). There are attempts by Behrmann, Hune, and Vaandrager (2000) to consider real-time settings and by Garavel, Mateescu, and Smarandache (2001) and Bollig et al. (2001) for SAT solving in a distributed environment. Edelkamp, Jabbar, and Sulewski (2008a) have parallized a C++ software model checker using state reconstruction and incremental hashing techniques. Distribution based on partitioning the Büchi automata has been contributed by Lluch-Lafuente (2003a). Another approach for distributed model checking based on BDDs has been reported by Grumberg, Heyman, and Schuster (2006).

Parallel external search with delayed duplication has been introduced by Jabbar and Edelkamp (2006) for model checking safety properties in SPIN. It shows that the approach is compatible with state vectors of varying length. The approach has been extended to LTL properties by Edelkamp and Jabbar (2006c). A wide body of important results on distributed verification for both safety and liveness is contributed by the Paradise Lab mostly implemented in the Divine environment (Barnat et al., 2006). A distributed cycle detection algorithm for LTL model checking based on parallel breadth-first search has been reported by Barnat, Brim, and Chaloupka (2003). An extension contributes an external memory variant of the same algorithm (Barnat, Brim, and Simecek, 2007). With depth-slicing Holzmann and Bosnacki (2007) have presented a method for N-core safety model checking. Their algorithm for liveness properties is limited to dual-core systems.

Owens et al. (2008) surveys the remarkable increase in the performance and capabilities of GPUs. They have outpaced CPUs in numerical algorithms as shown by Krueger and Westermann (2003) and by Harris, Sengupta, and Owens (2007). Applications include studying the folding behavior of proteins by Jaychandran, Vishal, and Pande (2006) and the simulation of biomolecular systems by Phillips et al. (2005). Since the memory transfer between the card and main board on the express bus is about one gigabyte per second, GPUs have become an apparent candidate to speed up large-scale computations like sorting numerical data on disk, as shown by Govindaraju, Gray, Kumar, and Manocha (2006) and by Cederman and Tsigas (2008). Its application for sorting-based delayed duplicate detection is apparent. By using perfect hash functions there is work by Edelkamp, Sulewski, and Yücel (2010b) on exploring single-agent search problems on the GPU and by Edelkamp, Sulewski, and Yücel (2010a) on solving two-player games. Explicit-state and probabilistic model checking problems have been ported to the GPU by Bosnacki, Edelkamp, and Sulewski (2009) and by Edelkamp and Sulewski (2010).

Priority search trees have been invented by McCreight (1985). The treap data structure has been proposed by Aragon and Seidel (1989), and the A* implementation based on them has been implemented by Cung and LeCun (1994).

One of the first references to bidirectional search is Pohl (1971). The effectiveness of method was surveyed later by Kaindl and Kainz (1997). The algorithm BIDA* was introduced by Manzini (1995). BHPA was invented by Pohl (1969). Kwa (1994) suggested BS* as an improvement to BHPA.

The front-to-front strategy has been proposed by DeChampeaux and Sint (1977). The first version of BHFFA was not able to grant optimality, a problem that was resolved by DeChampeaux in 1983. Politowski and Pohl (1984) suggested the use of *d-nodes* to focus the search. A time improvement has been contributed by Eckerle and Ottmann (1994). By the virtue of states pairs, of which either the first or the second state is expanded, there is an interesting transformation of bidirectional search to unidirectional frontier search (Felner, Moldenhauer, Sturtevant, and Schaeffer, 2010).

Perimeter search has been introduced by Dillenburg and Nelson (1994) and independently by Manzini (1995). A good exposition can be found in the PhD thesis of Dillenburg (1993). Improvements to perimeter search and near-optimal perimeter search are provided in the PhD thesis of Felner (2001). The proof that very small perimeters can significantly enhance the heuristic estimation is given in Linares López and Junghanns (2003).

Two approaches combine pattern database construction with perimeter search. Anderson, Schaeffer, and Holte (2007) have proposed *partial pattern databases* that consist of a set of abstract nodes and their distance to the goals less than some lower-bound threshold value. Felner and Ofek (2007) have used a perimeter to seed the pattern database, such that the perimeter acts as a goal node. Multiple-goal heuristic search for solving the four-peg TOWERS-OF-HANOI problem has been implemented by Korf and Felner (2007), a work that also suggests the use of perimeter pattern databases. Another multiple-goal task for focused web crawling has been addressed by Chakrabarti, van den Berg, and Dom (1999) and by Diligenty, Coetzee, Lawrence, Giles, and Gori (2000).

State Space Pruning

One of the most effective approaches to tackle large problem spaces is to *prune* (i.e., cut off branches from) the search tree. There are multiple reasons for pruning. Some branches might not lead to a goal state, others lead to inferior solutions; some result in positions already reached on different paths, and others are redundant; though these might lead to a solution, there are still alternatives that also lead to a solution.

All state space pruning techniques reduce the node (and subsequently the average) branching factor of the search tree such that less successor nodes have to be analyzed. Since a smaller part of the state space is generated, pruning saves both search time and space. However, there might be a trade-off between the two. Some techniques require rather complex data structures, such that the maintenance of pruning information may be involved.

Pruning itself is not necessarily bound to a specific search algorithm. Some pruning rules are erected on top of memory-restricted search algorithms like IDA*, for example, to enhance duplicate detection. Others support A* search, for example, to avoid being trapped in dead-ends. We will analyze implementation alternatives under an efficiencies aspect for storing and accessing pruning information.

Most approaches to pruning rely on observed regularities in the search space that have to be exploited to reduce the search efforts. Such regularities might be provided by a domain expert. In other cases, pruning knowledge can be constructed fully automatically. Often this information is inferred by searching some simpler spaces, like decomposed search spaces.

Static pruning techniques detect pruning knowledge prior to the main search routine. Other pruning rules may not be known to the search algorithm at its start, and have to be inferred during the execution of the program. This leads to layered search algorithms. In the top-level search, the search algorithms search for problem solutions, and in frequently invoked lower-level searches, pruning knowledge is refined.

We call a pruning rule *admissible* if at least one optimal solution will be reachable from the initial state and *solution preserving* if there exists at least one path from the initial state to the goal state in the reduced state space. *Admissible* pruning strategies and *admissible* estimates are fundamentally different concepts, but both refinements allow heuristic search algorithms like IDA* and A* to return optimal paths, and often are applied together to overcome the search bottleneck for large state spaces. Henceforth, we have divided the presentation in pruning algorithms that preserve optimality and those that do not.

- For *admissible state space pruning* we first address *substring pruning*, for which a set of forbidden operation sequences is omitted from the search. Subsequently, we turn to *dead-end* detection, for which we devise a decomposition approach. Finally, we address *symmetry reduction*, which reduces the state space by focusing on representatives.
- For *solution preserving state space pruning* we first address state spaces that are constructed by adding *macro actions* to the state space. In the macro problem solver a table is constructed that contains the macros to solve subproblems. When solving the state space problems the solver looks at the table entries to sequentially improve the current state to the goal one. We then look at *relevance cuts* that prevent a search algorithm from trying out every possible move in each state. *Partial order reduction* exploits commutativity of moves and reduces the state space with respect to a partially given goal.

10.1 ADMISSIBLE STATE SPACE PRUNING

As said, *admissible pruning* refers to a technique that reduces the branching factor of a state space problem while preserving the existence of optimal solutions, such that algorithms like A* and IDA* are capable of finding it.

10.1.1 Substring Pruning

Without mentioning them, most implementations of memory-restricted search algorithms perform already a basic form of pruning; when the successors of a node are generated, they prohibit using an inverse action to return to the node's parent. For example, in an infinitely large GRIDWORLD state space (see Fig. 10.1, left) with actions U, D, L, and R, the action sequence LR will always produce a duplicate node. Rejecting inverse action pairs, including RL, UD, and DU as well, reduces the number of children of a search node from four to three (see Fig. 10.1, middle).

In this section, we describe a method for pruning duplicate nodes that extends on this idea. The approach is suitable for heuristic search algorithms like IDA* that have imperfect duplicate detection

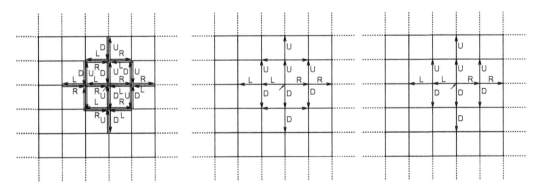

FIGURE 10.1

A GRIDWORLD search space: not pruned (left), pruned based on eliminating predecessors (middle), and pruned according to a small set of rules (right).

due to memory restrictions; it can be seen as an alternative to the use of transposition or hash tables.

We take advantage of the fact that the problem spaces of most combinatorial problems are described implicitly, and consider the state space problem in labeled representation, so that Σ is the set of different action labels. The aim of *substring pruning* is to prune paths from the search process that contain one of a set of *forbidden words* D over Σ^*. These words, called *duplicates*, are forbidden because it is known a priori that the same state can be reached through a different, possibly shorter, action sequence called a *shortcut*; only the latter path is allowed.

To distinguish between shortcuts and duplicates, we impose a lexicographical ordering $\leq_l$ on the set of actions in Σ. In the GRIDWORLD example, it is possible to further reduce the search according to the following rule: Go straight in the x-direction first, if at all, and then straight in the y-direction, if at all, making at most one turn. Rejecting the duplicates DR, DL, UR, and UL (with respective shortcuts RD, LD, RU, and LU) from the search space according to this rule leads to the state space of Figure 10.1 (right). As a result, each point (x, y) in the GRIDWORLD example is generated via a unique path. This reduces the complexity of the search tree to an optimal number of nodes (quadratic in the search depth), an exponential gain. The set of pruning rules we have examined depends on the fact that some paths always generate duplicates of nodes generated by other paths.

How can we find such string pairs (d, c), where d is a duplicate and c is a shortcut, and how can we guarantee admissible pruning, by means that no optimal solution is rejected?

First, we can initially conduct an exploratory (e.g., breadth-first) search up to a fixed-depth threshold. A hash table records all encountered states. Whenever a duplicate is indicated by the hash conflict, the lexicographically larger action sequence is recorded as a duplicate.

Another option that is applicable in undirected search spaces is to search for cycles, comparing a newly generated node in the search tree with all nodes in its generating path. The resulting cycle is split into one (or many) duplicate and shortcut (pairs). For example, the cycle in the $(n^2 - 1)$-PUZZLE RDLURDLURDLU with inverse DRULDRULDRUL is split as shown in Table 10.1. When splitting a full-length cycle, one part has to be inverted (all its actions have to be reversed). In case the length of one string is equal to the length of the other, we need some further criteria to draw a distinction between the two. One valid option is a lexicographic order on the set of actions Σ (and subsequently on the set of action strings Σ^*). For actions $\Sigma = \{U, R, D, L\}$, let $U \leq_l R \leq_l D \leq_l L$. The problem graph is undirected, so that we impose L to be inverse to R (written as $L^{-1} = R$), and U to be inverse to D.

Table 10.1 Splitting a cycle into duplicates and shortcuts.

First Part (Duplicate)	Second Part	Inverse (Shortcut)	First Part (Duplicate)	Second Part	Inverse (Shortcut)
RDLURDLURDL	ϵ				
RDLURDLURDL	U	D	DRULDRU	LURDL	RDLUR
RDLURDLURD	LU	DR	DRULDRUL	LURD	RDLU
RDLURDLUR	DLU	DRU	DRULDRULD	LUR	RDL
RDLURDLU	RDLU	DRUL	DRULDRULDR	LU	RD
RDLURDL	RDLUR	DRULD	DRULDRULDRU	L	R
RDLURD	RDLURD	DRULDR	DRULDRULDRUL	ϵ	ϵ

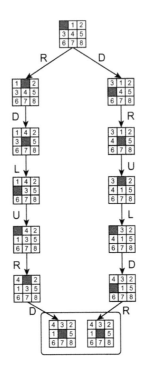

FIGURE 10.2

Example for a duplicate and a shortcut (string) for the EIGHT-PUZZLE.

For RDLURDLURDLU and duplicate DRULDR, we have RDLURD as its corresponding shortcut. The example is illustrated in Figure 10.2.

For generating cycles, a heuristic can be used that minimizes the distance back to the initial state, where the search was invoked. For such cycle-detecting searches, state-to-state estimates like the Hamming distance on the state vector are appropriate.

The setting for unit-cost state space graphs naturally extends to weighted search spaces with a weight function w on the set of action strings as follows.

Definition 10.1. *(Pruning Pair) Let G be a weighted problem graph with action label set Σ and weight function $w : \Sigma^* \to \mathbf{R}$. A pair $(d,c) \in \Sigma^* \times \Sigma^*$ is a pruning pair if:*

1. $w(d) > w(c)$, *or, if $w(d) = w(c)$, then $c \leq_l d$;*
2. *for all $u \in S$: d is applicable in u if and only if c is applicable in u; and*
3. *for all $u \in S$ we have that applying d on S yields the same result as applying c on S, if they are both applicable; that is, $d(u) = c(u)$.*

For sliding-tile puzzles, the applicability of an action sequence (condition 2) merely depends on the position of the blank. If in c the blank moves a larger distance in the x- or y-direction than in d, it cannot be a shortcut; namely, for some positions, d will be applicable, but not c. An illustration

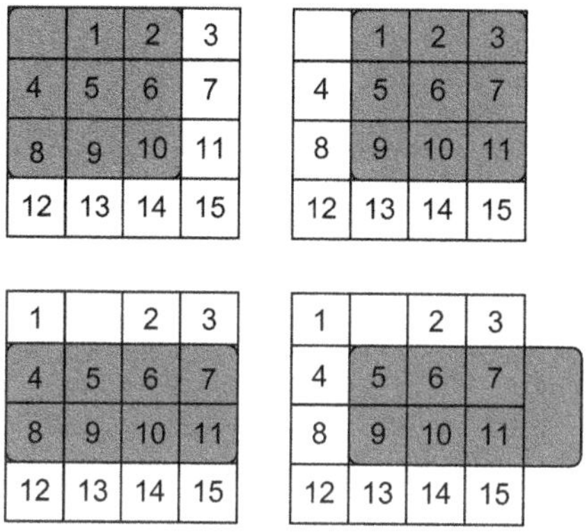

FIGURE 10.3

Moving blank area in the $(n^2 - 1)$-PUZZLE: duplicate (top) and shortcut (bottom). The area for action application validity is shaded gray.

is provided in Figure 10.3. If all three conditions for a pruning pair are valid the shortcut is no longer needed and the search refinement can rely only on the duplicates found, which in turn admissibly prune the search. It is easy to see that truncating a path that contains d preserves the existence of an optimal path to a goal state (see Exercises).

The conditions may have to be checked dynamically during the actual search process. If conditions 2 or 3 are violated, we have to test the validity of a proposed pair (d, c). Condition 2 is tested by executing the sequence $d^{-1}c$ at every encountered state, and condition 3 is tested via comparing the respective states before and after executing $d^{-1}c$.

Note that the state space does not have to include inversible actions to apply d^{-1} for testing conditions 2 and 3. Instead, we can use $|d^{-1}|$ *parent* pointers to climb up the search tree starting with the current state.

Pruning Automata

Assuming that we do not have to check conditions 2 or 3 for each encountered state, especially for depth-first, oriented search algorithms like IDA*, searching for a duplicate in the (suffix of the) current search tree path can slow down the exploration considerably, if the set of potential duplicates is large.

The problem of efficiently finding any of a set of strings in a text is known as the *bibliographic search problem*; it can be elegantly solved by constructing a *substring acceptor* in the form of a finite-state automaton, and feeding the text to it.

The automaton runs *synchronous* to the original exploration and prunes the search tree if the automaton reaches an accepting state. Each ordinary transition induces an automaton transition and vice versa. Substring pruning is important for search algorithms like IDA*, since constant-time pruning efforts fit well with enhanced DFS explorations. The reason is that the time to generate one successor for these algorithms is already reduced to a constant in many cases.

As an example, Figure 10.4 (left) shows the automaton for subset pruning with the string DU. The initial state is the most-left state and the accepting state is the most-right state in the automaton. Figure 10.4 (right) depicts the automaton for full predecessor elimination with accepting states omitted.

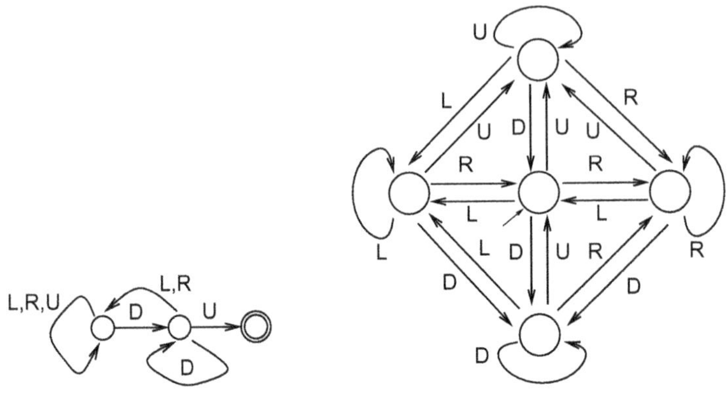

FIGURE 10.4

Automaton for string DU (left) and for full predecessor elimination (right).

Table 10.2 Reducing the branching factor by substring pruning.

Puzzle	Construction	Duplicate	States	Without	With
EIGHT-PUZZLE	BFS	35,858	137,533	1.732	1.39
FIFTEEN-PUZZLE	BFS	16,442	55,441	2.130	1.98
FIFTEEN-PUZZLE	CYC	58,897	246,768	2.130	1.96
TWENTY-FOUR-PUZZLE	BFS+CDBF	127,258	598,768	2.368	2.235
2^3 RUBIK'S CUBE	BFS	31,999	24,954	6.0	4.73
3^3 RUBIK'S CUBE	BFS	28,210	22,974	13.34	13.26

Table 10.2 shows the impact of substring pruning in the $(n^2 - 1)$-PUZZLE and in RUBIK'S CUBE (see Ch. 1). Note that the branching factor 13.34 for the RUBIK'S CUBE is already the result of substring pruning from the naïve space with a branching factor of 18, and the branching factors for the $(n^2 - 1)$-PUZZLE are already results of predecessor elimination (see Ch. 5). Different construction methods have been applied: BFS denotes that the search algorithm for generating duplicates operates breadth-first, with a hash conflict denoting the clash of two different search paths. An alternative method to find duplicates is cycle-detecting heuristic best-first search (CDBF). By unifying the generated sets of duplicates, both search methods can be applied in parallel (denoted as BFS+CDBF). We display the number of states in the pruning automaton and the number of duplicate strings that are used as forbidden words for substring matching.

As pruning strategies cut off branches in the search tree, they reduce the average node branching factor. We show this value with and without substring pruning (assuming that some basic pruning rules have been applied already).

Substring pruning automata can be included in the prediction of the search tree growth (see Ch. 5). This is illustrated in Figure 10.5 for substring pruning the grid by eliminating predecessors. In the

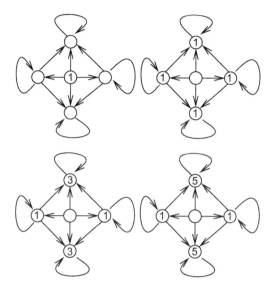

FIGURE 10.5

Search tree prediction with substring pruning automaton.

beginning (depth 0) there is only one state. In the next iteration (depth 1) we have 4 states, then 6 (depth 2), 8 (depth 3), 10 (depth 4), and so on.

To accept several strings $m_1,\ldots,m_n$, one solution is to construct a nondeterministic automaton that accepts them as substrings, representing the regular expression $\Sigma^* m_1 \Sigma^* | \Sigma^* m_2 \Sigma^* | \cdots | \Sigma^* m_n \Sigma^*$, and then convert the nondeterministic automaton into a deterministic one. Although this approach is possible, the conversion and minimization can be computationally hard.

Aho-Corasick Algorithm

The algorithm of *Aho and Corasick* constructs a deterministic finite-state machine for a number of search strings. It first generates a *trie* of the set of duplicate strings. Figure 10.6 shows a trie for the duplicates in the GRIDWORLD state space at depth 2. Every leaf corresponds to one forbidden action sequence and is considered to be accepting.

In the second step, the algorithm computes a *failure function* on the set of trie nodes. Based on the failure function, substring search will be available in linear time. Let u be a node in the trie and $string(u)$ the corresponding string. The failure node $failure(u)$ is defined as the location of the longest proper suffix of $string(u)$, which is also the prefix of a string in the trie (see Fig. 10.7, bold arrows).

The *failure* values are computed in a complete breadth-first traversal, where, inductively, the values in depth i rely on the values computed in depth $j < i$. Algorithm 10.1 shows the corresponding pseudo code. To highlight the different branching in a search tree and in a trie, we use $T(u,a)$ to denote a possible successor of u via a and write $\perp$ if this successor along a is not available.

First, all nodes in BFS level 1 are determined and inserted into the queue Q. For the example this includes the four nodes in depth 1. As long as Q is nonempty, the top element u is deleted and its successors v are processed. To compute $failure(v)$, the node in the sequence $failure(u)$, $failure^2(u)$,

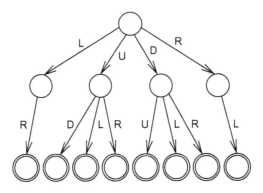

FIGURE 10.6

Trie of action sequences leading to duplicates in the GRIDWORLD domain.

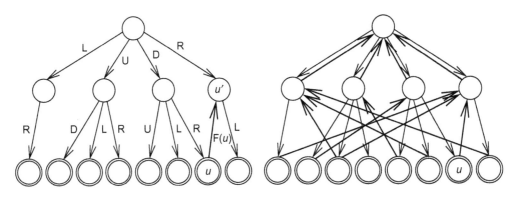

FIGURE 10.7

Partial (left) and complete (right) failure function on a set of strings.

$failure^3(u)$ is determined, which enables a transition with the chosen character a. As a rationale, if $string(failure(u))$ is the longest suffix of $string(u)$ in the trie, and $failure(u)$ has a child transition available labeled a, then $string(failure(u))a$ is the longest suffix of $string(u)$ that is contained in the trie.

In the example, to determine the failure value for node u in level 2 that was generated due to applying action R we go back via the link of its predecessor to the root node s and take the transition labeled R to u'. As a consequence, $failure(u) = u'$.

Each node is processed only once. Assuming the size of the alphabet to be bounded by a constant with an amortized analysis, we can show that computing the failure function takes time $O(d)$ in total, where d is the sum of string lengths in D, $d = \sum_{m \in D} |m|$.

Theorem 10.1. *(Time Complexity of Failure Computation) Let D be the set of duplicates and d be the total length of all strings in D. The construction of the failure function is O(d).*

Procedure Aho-Corasick-Failure
Input: Trie T with root s
Output: Failure function *failure*

failure$(s) \leftarrow s$	;; Initialize failure function
for each $a \in \Sigma$	;; For all action characters
$v \leftarrow T(s,a)$	;; Determine child
if $(v \neq \bot)$	;; If not void
Enqueue(Q,v)	;; Include in queue
failure$(v) \leftarrow s$	;; Failures in level 1 all link to root
while $(Q \neq \emptyset)$	;; As far as trie nodes are left
$u \leftarrow$ *Dequeue*(Q)	;; Take next one
for each $a \in \Sigma$	;; For all action characters
$v \leftarrow T(u,a)$	;; Determine child
if $(v \neq \bot)$	;; If not void
Enqueue(Q,v)	;; Include child in queue
$f \leftarrow$ *failure*(u)	;; Initialize failure node
while $(T(f,a) = \emptyset \wedge f \neq s)$	;; Determine failure node
$f \leftarrow$ *failure*(f)	;; Fix failure node
if $(T(f,a) = \emptyset)$ *failure*$(v) \leftarrow s$	;; Loop back
else *failure*$(v) \leftarrow T(f,a)$	;; Set failure function for child

Algorithm 10.1

Computation of failure function.

Proof. Let $|string(failure(u))|$ be the length of the longest proper suffix of $string(u)$, that is prefix of one string in D, where a string is proper if it is not empty. If u' and u are nodes on the path from the root node to a node i in T and u' is the predecessor of u we have $|string(failure(u))| \leq |string(failure(u'))| + 1$.

Choose any string m_i that corresponds to a path p_i in the trie for D. Then the total increase in the length for the failure function values of m_i is $\sum_{u \in p_i} |string(failure(u))| - |string(failure(u'))| \leq |m_i|$. On the other side, $|string(failure(u))|$ decreases on each failure transition by at least one and remains nonnegative throughout. Therefore, the total increase of the failure function strings for u on p_i is at most $|m_i|$. ∎

To construct the substring pruning automaton A from T, we also use breadth-first search, traversing the trie T together with its failure function. In other words, we have to compute $\Delta_A(u,a)$ for all automaton states u and all actions a in Σ. The skeleton of A is the trie T itself. The transitions $\Delta_A(u,a)$ for $u \in T$ and $a \in \Sigma$ that are not in the skeleton can be derived from the function *failure* as follows. At a given node u we execute a at $failure(u)$ using the already computed values of $\Delta_A(failure(u),a)$. In the example, we have included the transitions for node u in Figure 10.8. The time complexity to generate A is $O(d)$.

Searching existing substrings of a (path) string of length n is available in linear time by simply traversing automaton A. This leads to the following result.

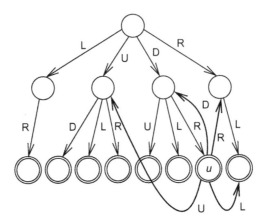

FIGURE 10.8

Partial automaton for substring pruning on a set of strings.

Theorem 10.2. *(Time Complexity Substring Matching) The earliest match of k strings of total length d in a text of length n can be determined in time $O(n+d)$.*

Automaton A can now be used for substring pruning as follows. With each node in the search process, we store a value $state(u)$, denoting the state in the automaton; since A has d states, this requires about $\lg_2 d$ memory bits per state. If u has successor v with an action that is labeled with a we have $state(v) = \Delta_A(a,s)$. This operation is available in constant time. Therefore, we can check in constant time if the generating path to u has one duplicate string as a suffix.

Incremental Duplicate Learning A

A challenge is to apply substring pruning dynamically, during the execution of a search algorithm. In fact, we have to solve a variant of the *dynamic dictionary matching problem*. Unfortunately, the algorithm of Aho and Corasick is not well suited to this problem.

In contrast to the static dictionary approach to prune the search space, generalized suffix trees (as introduced in Ch. 3) make it possible to insert and delete strings while maintaining a quick substring search. They can be adapted to a dictionary automaton as follows.

For incremental duplicate pruning with a set of strings, we need an efficient way to determine $\Delta(q,a)$ for a state q and action character a, avoiding the reconstruction of the path to the current state in the search tree.

Theorem 10.3. *(Generalized Suffix Trees as FSMs) Let string a be read from a_1 to a_{j-1}. There is a procedure Δ for which the returned value on input a_j is the longest suffix $a_i, \dots, a_j$ of $a_1, \dots, a_j$ that is also the substring of one string m stored in the generalized suffix tree. The amortized time complexity for Δ is constant.*

Proof. An automaton state q in the generalized suffix tree automaton is a pair $q = (i, l)$ consisting of the extended locus l and the current index i on the contracted edge incident to l. Recall that substrings referred to at l are denoted as intervals $[first, last]$ of the strings stored.

To find $q' = \Delta(q,a)$ starting at state (i,l) we search for a new extended locus l' and a new integer offset i', such that a corresponds to the transition stored at index position first $+ i$ of the substring stored at l. We use existing suffix links of the contracted loci and possible rescans if the character a does not match, until we have found a possible continuation for a. The extended locus of the edge and the reached substring index i' determines the pair (l', i') for the next state. In case of reaching a suffix tree node that corresponds to a full suffix we have encountered an accepting state q^*. The returned value in q^* is the substring corresponding to the path from the root to the new location. By amortization we establish the stated result. ∎

For a dynamic learning algorithm, we interleave duplicate detection with A*. As A* already has full duplicate detection based on states stored in the hash table, using substring pruning is optional. However, by following this case, it is not difficult to apply dynamic subset pruning to other memory-restricted search algorithms. For the sake of simplicity, we also assume that the strings m stored in the generalized suffix tree are *mutually substring free*; that is, no string is a substring of another one.

The resulting algorithm is denoted as *incremental duplicate learning A*** (IDLA*). Its pseudo code is shown in Algorithm 10.2. As usual, the update of the underlying data structures *Open* and *Closed*

Procedure IDLA*
Input: State space problem with start node s,
        dictionary automaton $D = (q_0, Q, F, \Sigma, \Delta)$
Output: Optimal solution path

Open ← {s}; *Closed* ← ∅; $q(s)$ ← q_0	;; Initialize structures
while (*Open* ≠ ∅)	;; If open empty, no solution
u ← **arg min**$_f$ *Open*	;; Find best node
Open ← *Open* \ {u}; *Closed* ← *Closed* ∪ {u}	;; Change lists
if (*Goal*(u)) **return** *Path*(u)	;; If goal reached, return solution path
Succ(v) ← *Expand*(u)	;; Generate successors
for each $v \in$ *Succ*(u), $u \xrightarrow{a} v, a \in \Sigma$	;; For all successors and enabling actions
$q(v)$ ← $\Delta(q(u), a)$	;; $q(v)$ is new automaton state
if ($q(v) \in F$) **continue**	;; Substring pruning automaton accepts, prune
if ($v \in$ *Closed*)	;; Duplicate state encountered
v' ← *Lookup*(*Closed*, v)	;; Find synonym
if (w(*Path*(v)) < w(*Path*(v')))	;; Path to v is shorter
m ← *Path*(v')	;; v' generates the duplicate string
else	;; Path to v' is shorter
m ← *Path*(v)	;; v generates the duplicate string
m ← m[*lcp*(*Path*(v), *Path*(v'))..|m|]	;; Remove longest common prefix
D ← $D \cup \{m\}$	;; Insert new duplicate
Improve(u, v)	;; Call update subroutine

Algorithm 10.2

Incremental learning of duplicates in A*.

are hidden in the call of *Improve*, which mainly implements the relaxation step $f(v) \leftarrow \{f(v), f(u) + w(u, v)\}$. The algorithm takes a state space problem and a (empty or preinitialized) dictionary automaton data structure D as input parameters. If according to the assumed regularity of the search space the detected tuples (d, c) are pruning pairs, we only have to store string d. If we are uncertain about the regularity at the accepting state of the dictionary automaton for d, we additionally store the proposed shortcut c and check whether or not it is actually applicable. Either way, inherited by the optimality of A*, the search algorithm outputs an optimal solution path.

The algorithm provides combined duplicate detection and usage. Before searching a node in the hash table, we search if we encounter an accepting state in D. Depending on the regularity of the search space, we might or might not check whether the proposed shortcut is valid. If D does not accept, then we use the hash table to find a synonym v' of the successor node v of u. If we do not find a match then we insert the new node in the ordinary search structures only.

If there is a counterpart v' of v in the hash table for *Closed* (computed using the generic *Lookup* procedure; see Ch. 3), we prune the longest common prefix (*lcp*) of both generating paths to construct the pair (d, c). This is useful to enhance the generality and pruning power of (d, c). The shorter the strings, the larger the potential for pruning. The correctness argument is simple: If (d, c) is a pruning pair, then every common prefix extension is also a pruning pair. As a result the reduced pair is inserted into the dictionary.

For a simple example we once more consider the GRIDWORLD. As a heuristic we choose the Manhattan distance estimate. Suppose that the algorithm is invoked with initial state $(3, 3)$ and goal state $(0, 0)$. Initially, we have *Open* $= \{((3, 3), 6)\}$, where the first entry denotes the state vector in the form of a GRIDWORLD location and the second entry denotes its heuristic estimate. Expanding the initial states yields the successor set $\{((4, 3), 8), ((3, 4), 8), ((3, 2), 6), ((2, 3), 6)\}$. Since no successor is hashed, all elements are inserted into *Open* and *Closed*. In the next step, $u = ((2, 3), 6)$ is inserted and one successor $v = ((3, 3), 8)$ turns out to have a counterpart $v' = ((3, 3), 6)$ in the hash table. This leads to the duplicate LR with corresponding shortcut ϵ, which is inserted into the dictionary automaton data structure. Next, $((3, 2), 6)$ is expanded. We establish another duplicate string DU with shortcut sequence ϵ. Additionally, we encounter the pruning pair (LD, DL), and so on.

10.1.2 Pruning Dead-Ends

In domains like the FIFTEEN-PUZZLE, every configuration that we can reach by executing an arbitrary move sequence remains solvable. This is not always the case, though. In several domains there are actions that can never be reversed (doors may shut if we go through). This directly leads to situations where a solution is out of reach.

A simple case of a dead-end in SOKOBAN can be obtained by pushing a ball into a corner, from where it cannot be moved. The goal of *dead-end pruning* is to recognize and avoid these branches as early as possible. There is, of course, an exception since a ball in a corner is a dead-end if and only if the corner position is not a goal field. In the following we exclude this subtle issue from our considerations.

This section presents an algorithm that allows us to generate, memorize, and generalize situations that are dead-ends. The strategy of storing unsolvable subpositions is very general, but to avoid introducing extensive notation, we take the SOKOBAN problem (see Ch. 1) as a welcome case study.

Two simple ways of identifying some special cases of dead-end positions in SOKOBAN can be described by the two procedures *IsolatedField* and *Stuck*. The former one checks for one or two connected, unoccupied fields that are surrounded by balls and not reachable by the man without pushes. If it is not possible to connect the squares only by pushing the surrounding balls "from the outside," the position one is a dead-end. The latter procedure, *Stuck*, checks if a ball is *free*; that is, if it has either no horizontal neighbor or no vertical neighbor. Initially, place all nonfree balls into a queue. Then, ignoring all free balls, iteratively try to remove the free balls from the queue until it becomes empty or nothing changes anymore. If in one iteration every ball stays inside the queue, some of which are not located on goal fields, the position is a dead-end. In the worst case, *Stuck* needs $O(n^2)$ operations for n balls, but in most cases it turns out to operate in linear time. The correctness is given by the fact that to free a ball with the men from a given position at least two of its neighbors have to be free.

Figure 10.9 illustrates the procedure and shows an example of a dead-end in SOKOBAN. Balls 1, 2, 5, or 6 cannot be moved, but balls 3, 4, 7, and 8 can be moved. It is obvious that without detecting the dead-end already on these balls, this position can be the root of a very large search tree. Initially all balls are put in a queue. If a ball is free it is removed, otherwise it is enqueued again. After a few iterations we reach a fixpoint. Balls 1, 2, 5, and 6 cannot be set free. Such a position is a valid end state only if the balls are correctly placed on goal fields.

We could perform these checks prior to every node expansion. Note, however, that they provide only sufficient but not necessary conditions for dead-ends. We can strengthen the pruning capabilities based on the following two observations:

- A dead-end position can be recursively defined as being either a position that can be immediately recognized as a dead-end, or a nongoal position in which every move that is available leads to a dead-end position. If all successors of a position are dead-ends, the position itself is a dead-end as well.
- Many domains allow a *generalization* of dead-end patterns; we can define a relation $\sqsubseteq$ and write $v \sqsubseteq u$ if v is a subproblem of u. If v is not solvable, then neither is u. For example, a (partial) dead-end SOKOBAN position remains a dead-end if we add balls to it. Thus, $\sqsubseteq$ turns out to be a simple pattern matching relation.

Decomposing a problem into parts has been successfully applied in divide-and-conquer algorithms, and storing solutions to already solved subproblems is called *memorizing*. The main difference to these

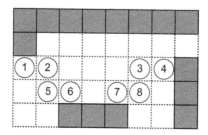

FIGURE 10.9

A discovered dead-end.

approaches is that we concentrate on *parts* of a position to be retrieved. For SOKOBAN, decomposing a position should separate unconnected positions and remove movable balls to concentrate on the intrinsic patterns that are responsible for a dead-end. For example, in Figure 10.9 the position can be decomposed by splitting the two ball groups. The idea of decomposing a position is a natural general-ization of the *isolated field* heuristic: A position with nongoal fields on which the man can never get is a likely dead-end. Take the graph G of all empty squares and partition G into connected components (using linear time). Examine each component separately. If every empty square can be reached by the man the position is likely to be alive. If one component is a dead-end, and indeed often they are, the entire position itself is a dead-end.

Our aim is to learn and generalize dead-end positions when they are encountered in the search; some authors also refer to this aspect as *bootstrapping*. Each dead-end subproblem found and inserted into the *subset dictionary* (see Ch. 3) can be used immediately to prune the search tree and therefore to get deeper into the search tree.

Depending on the given resources and heuristics, decomposition could be either invoked in every expansion step, every once in a while, or only in critical situations. The decomposition itself has to be carefully chosen to allow a fast dead-end detection and therefore a shallow search. A good trade-off has to be found: The characteristics responsible for the dead-end on one the hand should appear in only one component and, on the other hand, the problem parts should be far more easy to analyze than the original one. For SOKOBAN, we can consider the partial position that consists of all balls that cannot be safely removed by the procedure *Stuck*.

Before we turn to the implementation, we study the search tree for the SOKOBAN puzzle shown in Figure 10.10. It demonstrates how the preceding two observations, in conjunction with a simple dead-end detection, can use bottom-up propagation to generalize more complex patterns.

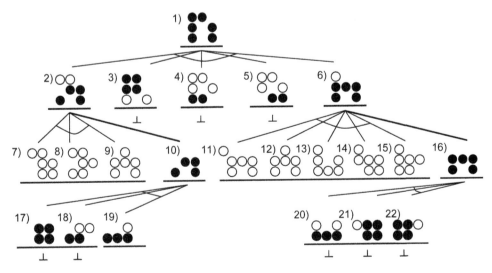

FIGURE 10.10

Example for learning a dead-end position in SOKOBAN.

The root position s is a dead-end, and although the *IsolatedField* procedure would immediately recognize this, we assume for the sake of the argument that only *Stuck* is used as the basic dead-end position detection. Initially, the subset dictionary is empty and the status of s is undefined. We expand u and generate its successor set $Succ(u)$. Three of the five elements in $Succ(u)$ are found to be a dead-end; the responsible balls are marked as filled circles. Marking can be realized through a Boolean array, with *true* denoting that the corresponding ball is relevant for the dead-end, and *false* otherwise. For usual transitions, a ball is a necessary constituent of a dead-end pattern if it is responsible for the unsolvability of *one* successor state; hence, unifying the *relevant* vectors is done by a Boolean or-operation. Generally, a state u is a dead-end if $relevant(u) \sqsubseteq u$ is a dead-end. Initially, *relevant* is the constantly false function for all states.

Since in this instance the status of two successors is not defined, overall solvability remains open. Therefore, the left-most and right-most nodes are both expanded (thin edges) and decomposed (bold edges). Decomposition is preferred, which is done by assigning a g-value of zero to the newborn child.

The expansion of the partial states is easier, and we find all of their successors dead-ended within one more step. As the root is a dead-end, we want to find a minimal responsible pattern by means of backpropagation. By unification, we see that all balls of the expanded nodes in the second-to-last level are relevant. Both positions are newly found dead-ended and inserted into the subset dictionary. Since we have now reached a decomposition node, it is sufficient to copy the relevant part to the parent; the failure of one component implies the failure of the complete state. All generated nodes in $Succ(u)$ are dead-ends, and we can further propagate our knowledge bottom-up by forming the disjunction of the successor's relevance information. Finally, the root is also inserted into the subset dictionary.

The corresponding pseudo code for this kind of bottom-up propagation is given in Algorithm 10.3. We assume that in addition to the vector of flags *relevant*, each node maintains a counter *succ* of the number of nondead-end children.

Procedure PropagateDeadEnd
Input: Partial state u to be propagated
Output: Updated information associated to search tree nodes

$PatternStore \leftarrow PatternStore \cup \{u\}$;; Update subset dictionary
if ($u = root$) **return**   ;; End of propagation
$p \leftarrow parent(u)$;; Predecessor of u
if (decomposed(u))   ;; Node u result of decomposition
    $relevant(p) \leftarrow relevant(u)$;; Copy relevance status
    $succ(p) \leftarrow 0$;; No successor
else   ;; Node u result of expansion
    $relevant(p) \leftarrow relevant(p) \cup relevant(u)$;; Combine relevance flags
    $succ(p) \leftarrow succ(p) - 1$;; Decrement number of nondead-end children
    if ($succ(p) = 0$) PropagateDeadEnd(p) ;; Recursive call

Algorithm 10.3

Bottom-up propagation in the search decomposition tree.

Procedure Abstraction-Decomposition-A*
Input: State space problem graph with start node s
Output: Shortest path to goal node

```
Open ← {s}; Closed ← Ø; PatternStore ← Ø;                    ;; Initialize structures
while (Open ≠ Ø)                                    ;; If horizon empty then no solution
    u ← arg min_f Open                             ;; Node u kept in H for reopening
    if (Goal(u))                                              ;; Goal is found
        if (decomposed(u)) solvable(u) ← true                 ;; In subsearch
        else return Path(u)                                   ;; In main search
    if (solvable(u) = unknown)                        ;; Status of u undefined
        if (DeadEnd(u)) or (u ∈ PatternStore)       ;; Stored or simple dead-ended
            solvable(u) ← false                         ;; Set u to unsolvable
    if (solvable(u) = false)                             ;; Node u is a dead-end
        PropagateDeadEnd(u)                            ;; Bottom-up propagation
        continue                         ;; Node u not expanded nor decomposed
    if (alive(u)) or (solvable(u))                            ;; Node u alive
        PropagateAlive(u)                 ;; Bottom-up propagation free positions
        continue                         ;; Node u not expanded nor decomposed
    Δ(u) ← Decompose(u)                                 ;; Invoke decomposition
    for each v ∈ Δ(u) decomposed(u) ← true             ;; Mark decomposed state
    Succ(u) ← expand(u)                              ;; Compute successor set
    for each v ∈ Δ(u) ∪ Succ(u)                       ;; Examine successor set
        Improve(u,v)                               ;; Update Open and Closed
```

Algorithm 10.4

The decomposition and bottom-up propagation algorithm.

The main procedure *Abstraction-Decomposition-A** (see Alg. 10.4) carries out the search for solvability (of possibly decomposed states) and for an optimal solution (in the main search tree) in an interleaved fashion; a flag *decomposed*(u) remembers which of the two modes is currently applied to state u. Moreover, *solvable*(u) keeps track of its status: *true, false*, or *unknown*.

Like in A*, until the priority queue gets empty, the node with the best f-value is selected. If it is a goal node and we are in the top search level, we have found the solution to the overall problem and can terminate; otherwise, the partial position is obviously solvable. For nongoal nodes, we try to establish their solvability by applying a simple dead-end check (e.g., using procedure *Stuck*), or by recognizing a previously stored pattern. Unsolvable partial positions are used to find larger dead-end patterns by backpropagation, as described earlier.

Since we are only interested in solvability of decomposed nodes, we do not have to search the subproblems all the way to the end. If we have enough information for a subproblem to be *alive*, we can back up this knowledge in the search tree in an analogous way. We might also allow a one-sided error without harming overall admissibility (i.e., let the *alive* procedure be overly optimistic).

The main difference to usual A* search is that for a node expansion of u, in addition to the set of successor nodes $Succ(u)$, decomposed positions $\Delta(u)$ are generated and then inserted into $Open$ with g set to zero to distinguish the new root from other search tree nodes. The ordinary successors are inserted, dropped, and reopened as usual in A*. Instead of using a lower-bound estimate h to solve the puzzle, in the learning process we can also try to actively focus the search to produce dead-ends.

Efficiently storing and searching dead-end (sub)positions is central to the whole learning process. We have called the abstract data structure providing insertion and lookup of substructures a *pattern store*. Possible implementations of such a dictionary data structure have been provided in Chapter 3.

10.1.3 Penalty Tables

In this section, an approach related to Abstraction-Decomposition-A* is described that tries to generalize, store, and reuse minimal dead-end patterns as well, but uses auxiliary, separate *pattern searches* instead of a dedicated decomposition/generalization procedure.

The approach can be conveniently described for the SOKOBAN domain. We refer to two different mazes: the *original maze* (i.e., the maze containing all the balls of the current position) and the *test maze*, which will be used for pattern searches. The pattern search algorithm's design is iterative and starts when a dead-end position has been found. Only the last ball moved is put into the test maze, and the algorithm tries to solve this simplified problem. If it succeeds, another A* test search is triggered, with some other ball of the original maze added; those balls are preferred that interfere with the path of the man or of a ball in the previous solution. If no solution is found, a dead-end is detected. An example is provided in Figure 10.11. Since this pattern need not yet to be minimal, successive iterations try to remove one ball at a time while preserving the dead-end property.

To fine-tune the trade-off between main and auxiliary search, a number of parameters control the algorithm, such as the maximum number of expansions max_n in each individual pattern search, the *maximal pattern size* max_b, and the *frequency* of pattern searches. One way to decide on the latter one

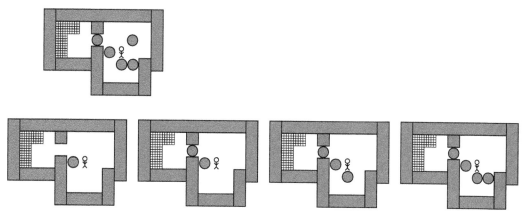

FIGURE 10.11

Example for pattern search: deadlock example (top), and sequence of test mazes (bottom).

is to trigger a pattern search for each position if the number of its descendants explored in the main search exceeds a certain threshold.

To improve search efficiency, we can make some further simplifications to the A* procedure: Since the pattern search is only concerned with solvability, as a heuristic it suffices to consider each ball's shortest distance to any goal field rather than computing a minimal matching, as usual. Moreover, balls on goal fields or balls that are reachable and free and can be immediately removed.

We can regard a dead-end subset dictionary as a table that associates each matching position with a heuristic value of ∞. This idea leads to the straightforward extension of dead-end detection to *penalty* tables, which maintain a corrective amount by which the simpler, procedural heuristic differs from the true goal distance. When a partial position has actually turned out to be solvable, the found solution distance might be larger than the standard heuristic indicates; in other words, the latter one is wrong. Multiple corrections from more than one applicable pattern can be added if the patterns do not overlap. Again, possible implementations for penalty tables are subset dictionaries as discussed in Chapter 3.

To apply *pattern search* in other domains, two properties are required: *reducibility* of the heuristic and *splittability* of the heuristic with regard to the state vector. These conditions are defined as follows. A state description S (viewed as a set of values) is called splittable, if for any two disjoint subsets S_1 and S_2 of S we have $\delta(S) = \delta(S_1) + \delta(S_2) + \delta(S \setminus (S_1 \cup S_2)) + C$; this means that the solution of S is at least as long as both subsolutions added. The third term accounts for additional steps that might be needed for conditions that are neither in S_1 nor in S_2, and C stands for subproblem interactions. A heuristic is reducible, if $h(S') \leq h(S)$ for $S' \subseteq S$. A heuristic is splittable, if for any two disjoint subsets S_1 and S_2 of S we have $h(S) = h(S_1) + h(S_2) + h(S \setminus (S_1 \cup S_2))$. The minimum matching heuristic introduced in Chapter 1 is not splittable but the sum of the distances to the closest goal results in a splittable heuristic.

If a heuristic is admissible, for $S' \subseteq S$ we additionally have a possible gap $\delta(S') - h(S') \geq 0$. We define the *penalty* with respect to S' as $pen(S') = \delta(S') - h(S')$.

Theorem 10.4. *(Additive Penalties) Let h be an admissible, reducible, and splittable heuristic; S be a state set; and $S_1, S_2 \subseteq S$ be disjoint subsets of S. Then we have $pen(S) \geq pen(S_1) + pen(S_2)$.*

Proof. Using admissibility of h and the definition of penalties, we deduce

$$
\begin{aligned}
pen(S) &= \delta(S) - h(S) \\
&= \delta(S_1) + \delta(S_2) + \delta(S \setminus (S_1 \cup S_2)) + C - (h(S_1) + h(S_2) + h(S \setminus (S_1 \cup S_2))) \\
&= \delta(S_1) - h(S_1) + \delta(S_2) - h(S_2) + \delta(S \setminus (S_1 \cup S_2)) - h(S \setminus (S_1 \cup S_2)) + C \\
&= pen(S_1) + pen(S_2) + pen(S \setminus (S_1 \cup S_2)) + C \\
&\geq pen(S_1) + pen(S_2).
\end{aligned}
$$
∎

As a corollary, the improved heuristic $h'(S) = h(S) + pen(S_1) + pen(S_2)$ is admissible since $h'(S) \leq h(S) + pen(S) = \delta(S)$. In other words, assuming *reducibility* and *splittability* for the domain and the heuristic, the penalties of nonoverlapping patterns can be added without affecting admissibility.

Pattern search was one of the most effective techniques for solving many SOKOBAN instances. It has also been used to improve the performance of search in the sliding-tile puzzle domains. In the FIFTEEN-PUZZLE the savings in the number of nodes are of about three to four orders of magnitude of difference compared to the Manhattan distance heuristic.

10.1.4 Symmetry Reduction

For multiple lookups in pattern databases (see Ch. 4), we already utilized the power of state space symmetries for reducing the search efforts. For every physical symmetry valid in the goal we apply it to the current state and get another estimate, which in turn can be larger than the original lookup and lead to stronger pruning. In this section, we expand on the observation and embed the observation in a more general context.

As a motivating example of the power of state space reduction through existing symmetries in the problem description, consider the ARROW PUZZLE problem, in which the task is to change the order of the arrows in the arrangement ↑↑↑↓↓↓ to ↑↓↑↓↑↓, where the set of allowed actions is restricted to reversing two adjacent arrows at a time. One important observation for a fast solution to the problem is that the order of arrow reversal does not matter. This exploits a form of action symmetry that is inherent in the problem. Moreover, two outermost arrows don't participate in an optimal solution and at least three reversals are needed. Therefore, any permutation of swapping the arrow index pairs (2,3), (3,4), and (4,5) leads to an optimal solution for the problem.

For state space reduction with respect to symmetries we expect to be provided by the domain expert, we use equivalence relations. Let $P = (S, a, s, T)$ be a state space problem as introduced in Chapter 1.

Definition 10.2. *(Equivalence Classes, Quotients, Congruences) A relation* $\sim \subseteq S \times S$ *is an* equivalence relation *if the following three conditions are satisfied:* $\sim$ *is reflexive (i.e., for all u in S we have* $u \sim v$*);* $\sim$ *is symmetric (i.e., for all u and v in S we have if* $u \sim v$ *then* $v \sim u$*); and* $\sim$ *is transitive (i.e., for all u, v, and w in S we have* $u \sim v$ *and* $v \sim w$ *implies* $u \sim w$*). Equivalence relations naturally yield equivalence classes* $[u] = \{v \in S \mid u \sim v\}$ *and a (disjoint) partition of the search space into equivalence classes* $S = [u_1] \cup \cdots \cup [u_k]$ *for some k. The state space* $(S/\sim) = \{[u] \mid u \in S\}$ *is called* quotient state space*. An equivalence relation* $\sim$ *of S is a* congruence relation *on P if for all* $u, u' \in S$ *with* $u \sim u'$ *and action* $a \in A$ *with* $a(u) = v$*, there is a* $v' \in S$ *with* $v \sim v'$ *and an action* $a' \in A$ *with* $a'(u') = v'$*. Any congruence relation induces a quotient state space problem* $(P/\sim) = (S/\sim), (A/\sim), [s], \{[t] \mid t \in T\})$*. In* $(P/\sim)$ *an action* $[a] \in (A/\sim)$ *is defined as follows. We have* $[a]([u]) = [v]$ *if and only if there is an action* $a \in A$ *mapping u to v so that* $u \in [u]$ *and* $v' \in [v']$*.*

Note that $(A/\sim)$ is sloppy in saying that the congruence relation $\sim$ partitions the action space A.

Definition 10.3. *(Symmetry) A bijection* $\phi : S \to S$ *is said to be a* symmetry *if* $\phi(s) = s$*,* $\phi(t) \in T$ *for all* $t \in T$ *and for any successor v to u there exists an action from* $\phi(u)$ *to* $\phi(v)$*. Any set Y of symmetries generates a subgroup* $g(Y)$ *called a* symmetry group*. The subgroup* $g(Y)$ *induces an equivalence relation* $\sim_Y$ *on states, defined as* $u \sim_Y v$ *if and only if* $\phi(u) = v$ *and* $\phi \in g(Y)$*. Such an equivalence relation is called a* symmetry relation *on P induced by Y.*

Any symmetry relation on P is a congruence on P. Moreover, u is reachable from s if and only if $[u]_Y$ is reachable from $[s]_Y$. This reduces the search for goal $t \in T$ to the reachability of state $[t]_Y$.

To explore a state space with respect to a state symmetry, we use a function *Canonicalize* each time a new successor node is generated, which determines a representative element for each equivalence class. Note that finding symmetries automatically is not easy, since it links to the computational problem of graph isomorphism, which is hard.

If a symmetry is known, then the implementation of symmetry detection is immediate, since both the *Open* set and *Closed* set can simply maintain the outcome of the *Canonicalize* action.

One particular technique for finding symmetries is as follows. In some search problems states correspond to (variable) valuations and goals are specified with partial valuations. Actions are often defined transparent to the assignments of values to the variables. For example, an important feature of (parametric) planning domains is that actions are generic to bindings of the parameters to the objects.

As a consequence, a symmetry in the form of a permutation of variables in the current and in the goal state has no consequence to the set of parametric actions.

Let V be the set of variables with $|V| = n$. There are $n!$ possible permutations of V, a number likely too large to be checked for symmetries. Taking into account type information on variable types reduces the number of all possible permutations of the variables to $\binom{n}{t_1, t_2, \ldots, t_k}$, where t_i is the number of variables with type i, $i \in \{1, \ldots, k\}$. Even for moderately sized domains, this number is likely still too large. To reduce the number of potential symmetries to a tractable size, we further restrict symmetries to *variable transpositions* $[v \leftrightarrow v']$ (i.e., a permutation of only two variables $v, v' \in V$), for which we have at most $n(n-1)/2 \in O(n^2)$ candidates. Using type information this number reduces to $\sum_{i=1}^{k} t_i(t_i - 1)/2$, which often is a practical value for symmetry detection.

We denote the set of (typed) variable transpositions by M. The outcome of a transposition of variables $(v, v') \in M$ applied to a state $u = (v_1, \ldots, v_n)$, written as $u[v \leftrightarrow v']$, is defined as $(v'_1, \ldots, v'_n)$, with $v'_i = v_i$ if $v_i \notin \{v, v'\}$, $v_i = v'$ if $v_i = v$, and $v_i = v$ if $v_i = v'$. It is simple to extend the definition to parametric actions.

In the example depicted in Figure 10.12, we have variables denoting the location of persons, so that we can write

$$(\text{at scott A})[\text{scott} \leftrightarrow \text{dan}] = (\text{at dan A}).$$

We observe that $u[v \leftrightarrow v'] = u[v' \leftrightarrow v]$ and $u[v \leftrightarrow v'][v \leftrightarrow v'] = u$.

Theorem 10.5. (*Time Complexity for Object Symmetry Detection*) *The worst-case complexity to determine the set of all variable transpositions for which a problem $P = (S, A, s, T)$ is symmetric is bounded by $O(|M| \cdot n)$ operations.*

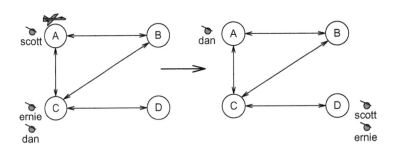

FIGURE 10.12

Example for symmetry in the transportation problem, where three passengers fly from their original location (left) to their respective destination (right).

Proof. A state space problem $P = (S, A, s, T)$ is symmetric with respect to the transposition $[v \leftrightarrow v']$, abbreviated as $P[v \leftrightarrow v']$, if $s[v \leftrightarrow v'] = s$ and $T[v \leftrightarrow v'] \in T$. The brute-force time complexity for computing $u[v \leftrightarrow v']$ is of order $O(n)$. However, by precomputing a lookup table containing the index of $u' = u[v \leftrightarrow v']$ for all $(v, v') \in M$, this complexity can be reduced to one lookup. ∎

For the example problem, the goal contains the three target locations of dan, ernie, and scott. In the initial state the problem contains no symmetry, since $s[\text{scott} \leftrightarrow \text{ernie}] \neq s$ and $T[\text{dan} \leftrightarrow \text{ernie}] \neq T$. In *forward-chaining search*, which explores the search space starting in a forward direction starting with the initial state s, symmetries that are present in s may vanish or reappear. Goals, however, do not change over time. Therefore, in an offline computation we can refine the set of symmetries M to $M' = \{(v, v') \in M \mid T[v \leftrightarrow v'] = T\}$. Usually, $|M'|$ is much smaller than $|M|$. For the example problem instance, the only variable symmetry left in M' is the transposition of scott and ernie. The remaining task is to compute the set $M''(u) = \{(v, v') \in M' \mid u[v \leftrightarrow v'] = u\}$ of symmetries that are present in the current state u. In the initial state s of the example problem, we have $M''(s) = \emptyset$, but once scott and ernie share the same location in a state u, this variable pair is included in $M''(u)$. With respect to Theorem 10.5 this additional restriction reduces the time complexity to detect all remaining variable symmetries to $O(|M'| \cdot n)$.

If a state space problem with current state $c \in S$ is symmetric with respect to the variable transposition $[v \leftrightarrow v']$ then applications of actions are neglected, significantly reducing the branching factor. The *pruning set* $A'(u)$ of a set of applicable actions $A(u)$ is the set of all actions that have a symmetric counterpart and that are of minimal index.

Theorem 10.6. *(Optimality of Symmetry Pruning) Reducing the action set $A(u)$ to $A'(u)$ for all states u during the exploration of state space problem $P = (S, A, s, T)$ preserves optimality.*

Proof. Suppose that for some expanded state u, reducing the action set $A(u)$ to $A'(u)$ during the exploration of planning problem $P = (S, A, s, T)$ does not preserve optimality. Furthermore, let u be the state with this property that is maximal in the search order. Then there is a solution $\pi = (a_1, \ldots, a_k)$ in $P_u = (S, A, u, T)$ with associated state sequence $(u_0 = u, \ldots, u_k \subseteq T)$. Obviously, $a_i \in a(u_{i-1})$, $i \in \{1, \ldots, k\}$. By the definition of the pruning set there exists $a'_1 = a_1[v \leftrightarrow v']$ of minimal index that is applicable in u_0.

Since $P_u = (S, A, u, T) = P_u[v \leftrightarrow v'] = (S, A, u[v \leftrightarrow v'] = u, T[v \leftrightarrow v'] = T)$, we have a solution $a_1[v \leftrightarrow v'], \ldots, a_k[v \leftrightarrow v']$ with state sequence $(u_0[v \leftrightarrow v'] = u_0, u_1[v \leftrightarrow v'], \ldots, u_k[v \leftrightarrow v'] = u_k)$ that reaches the goal T with the same cost. This contradicts the assumption that reducing the set $A(u)$ to $A'(u)$ does not preserve optimality. ∎

10.2 NONADMISSIBLE STATE SPACE PRUNING

In this section we consider different options for such reasoning that sacrifice solution optimality but yield large reductions to the search efficiency.

10.2.1 Macro Problem Solving

In some cases it is possible to group a sequence of operators to build a new one. This allows the problem solver to apply many primitive operators at once. For pruning the new combined operators substitute the original ones so that we reduce the set of applicable operators for a state. The pruning effect is that the strategy requires fewer overall decisions when ignoring choices within each sequence. Of course, if the substitution of operators is too generous, then the goal might not be found.

Here, we consider an approach for the formation of combined operators that may prune the optimal solutions, but preserve the existence of at least one solution path. A *macro operator* (*macro* for short) is a fixed sequence of elementary operators executed together. More formally, for a problem graph with node set V and edge set E a macro refers to an additional edge $e = (u, v)$ in $V \times V$ for which there are edges $e_1 = (u_1, v_1), \ldots, e_k = (u_k, v_k) \in E$ with $u = u_1$, $v = v_k$, and $v_i = u_{i+1}$ for all $1 \le i \le k - 1$. In other words, the path $(u_1, \ldots, u_k, v_k)$ between u and v is shortcut by introducing e.

Macros turn an unweighted problem graph into a weighted one. The weight of the macro is the accumulated weight of the original edges, $w(u, v) = \sum_{i=1}^{k} w(u_i, v_i)$. It is evident that inserting edges does not affect the reachability status of nodes. If there is no alternative in the choice of successors, $Succ(u_i) = \{v_i\}$, macros can simply substitute the original edges without loss of information. As an example, take maze areas of width one (tunnels) in SOKOBAN.

If there are more paths between a node, to preserve optimality of an underlying search algorithm, we have to take the shortest one, $w(u, v) = \delta(u, v)$. These macros are called *admissible*. The ALL-PAIRS SHORTEST PATHS algorithm of Floyd-Warshall (see Chapter 2) can be seen as one example of introducing admissible macros to the search space. At the end of the algorithm, all two nodes are connected (and assigned to the minimum path-cost value). The original edges are no longer needed to determine the shortest path value, such that omitting the original edges does not destroy the optimality of a search in the reduced graph.

Unfortunately, regarding the size of the search spaces we consider, computing ALL-PAIRS SHORTEST PATHS in the entire problem graph is infeasible. Therefore, different attempts have been suggested to approximate the information that is encoded in macros. If we are interested only in computing some solution, we can use *inadmissible* macros or delete problem graph edges after some but not all admissible macros have been introduced. The importance of macros in search practice is that they can be determined before the overall search starts. This process is called *macro learning*.

A way to use inadmissible macros is to insert them with a weight $w(u, v)$ smaller than the optimum $\delta(u, v)$ such that they will be used with higher priority. Another option is to restrict the search purely to the macros, neglecting all original edges. This is only possible if the goal remains reachable.

In the rest of this section, we give an example on how a macro problem solver can transform a search problem into an algorithmic scheme: The problem is decomposed into an ordered list of subgoals, and for each subgoal, a set of macros is defined that transform a state into the next subgoal.

We take the EIGHT-PUZZLE as an example. Again, actions are labeled by the direction in which the blank is moving. The entry in row r and column c in the *macro table* (see Table 10.3) holds the operator sequence to position the tile in position r into position c, such that after executing the macro at (r, c) the tiles in position 1 to $r - 1$ remain correctly placed.

Figure 10.13 shows the successive application of macro actions. For tile i, $1 \le i \le 6$, its current location c and its goal location r are determined, and the corresponding macro is applied.

Given a macro table, we can estimate the worst-case solution length needed by the macro solver by summing the string size maxima in the columns. For the EIGHT-PUZZLE we get a maximal length of $2 + 12 + 10 + 14 + 8 + 14 + 4 = 64$. As an estimate for the *average* solution length, we can add the

Table 10.3 Macro table for the EIGHT-PUZZLE.

	0	1	2	3	4	5	6
0							
1	DR						
2	D	LURD					
3	DL	URDL LURD	URDL				
4	L	RULD LURD	RULD	LURRD LULDR			
5	UL	DRUL DLUR ULDR	RDLU RULD	RULD RDLU URDL	RDLU		
6	U	DLUR ULDR	DRUULD	DLUU RDRU LLDR	DRUL	LURRD DLURU LLDR	
7	UR	LDRU ULDR	ULDDR ULURD	LDRUL URDRU LLDR	DLUR DRUL	DRULDL URRDLU	DLUR
8	R	ULDR	LDRR UULD	LURDR ULLDR	LDRRUL	DRUL LDRU RDLU	LDRU

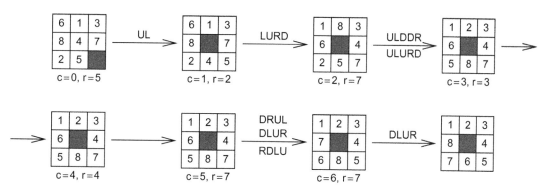

FIGURE 10.13

Macro solving the EIGHT-PUZZLE.

arithmetic means of the macro lengths in the columns, which yields

$$12/9 + 52/8 + 40/7 + 58/6 + 22/5 + 38/4 + 8/3 = 39.78.$$

To construct the macro table, it is most efficient to conduct a DFS or BFS search in a backward direction, starting from each goal state separately. For this purpose we need backward operators (which do not necessarily need to be valid operators themselves).

The row $r(m)$ of macro m is the position on which $p_{c(m)}$ is located, which has to be moved to $c(m)$ in the next macro application. The inverse of macro m will be denoted as m^{-1}.

For example, starting with the seventh subgoal, we will encounter a path $m^{-1} = $ LDRU, which alters goal position $p' = (0, 1, 2, 3, 4, 5, 6, 7, 8)$ into $p = (0, 1, 2, 3, 4, 5, 8, 6, 7)$. Its inverse is DLUR; therefore, $c(m) = 6$ and $r(m) = 7$, matching the last macro application in Figure 10.13.

10.2.2 Relevance Cuts

Humans can navigate through large state spaces due to an ability to use meta-level reasoning. One such meta-level strategy is to distinguish between relevant and irrelevant actions. They tend to divide a problem into several subgoals, and then to work on each subgoal in sequence. In contrast, standard search algorithms like IDA* always consider *all* possible moves available in each position. Therefore, it is easy to construct examples that are solvable by humans, but not by standard search algorithms. For example, in a mirror-symmetrical SOKOBAN position, it is immediately obvious that each half can be solved independently; however, IDA* will explore strategies that humans would never consider, switching back and forth between the two subproblems many times.

Relevance cuts attempt to restrict the way the search process chooses its next action, to prevent the program from trying all possible move sequences. Central to the approach is the notion of *influence*; moves that don't influence each other are called *distant* moves. A move can be cut off, if within the last m moves, more than k distant moves have been made (for appropriately chosen m and k); or, if it is distant to the last move, but not some move within the last m moves.

The definition of distant moves generally depends on the application domain; we sketch here one approach for SOKOBAN. First, we have to set up a measure for *influence*. We precompute a table for the *influence* of each square on each other one. The influence relation reflects the number of paths between the squares; the more alternatives exist, the less the influence. For example, in Figure 10.14 a and b influence each other less than c and d. Squares on the optimal path should have a stronger influence than others. Neighboring squares that are connected by a possible ball push are more influencing than if only the man can move between them. For example, in Figure 10.14 a influences c more than c influences a. In a tunnel, influence remains the same, regardless of the length of the tunnel. Note that the influence relation is not necessarily symmetric.

Given a relevance table, a move M_2 is regarded as *distant* from a previous move M_1, if its from-square influences M_1's from-square by less than some threshold, θ.

There are two possible ways that a move can be pruned. First, if within the last set of k moves more than l distant moves were made. This cut discourages arbitrary switches between nonrelated areas of the maze. Second a move that is distant with respect to the previous move, but not distant to a move in the past k moves. This will not allow switches back into an area previously worked on and abandoned just before. If we set $l = 1$, the first criterion entails the second. Through the restrictions

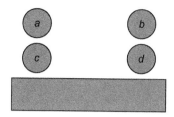

FIGURE 10.14

Influences of squares in SOKOBAN.

are imposed by relevance cuts, *optimality* of the solution can no longer be guaranteed. However, a number of previously unsolvable SOKOBAN instances could be handled based on this technique. To avoid pruning away optimal solutions, we can introduce randomness to the relevance cut decision. The probability determines if a cut is applied or not and reflects the confidence in the relevance cut.

Relevance cuts have been analyzed using the theoretical model of IDA* search (see Ch. 5). Unfortunately, in an empirical study the model turned out to be inadequate to handle the nonuniformity of the search space in SOKOBAN.

10.2.3 Partial Order Reduction

Partial order reduction methods exploit the commutativity of actions to reduce the size of the state space. The resulting state space is constructed in such a manner that it is equivalent to the original one. The algorithm for generating a reduced state space explores only some of the successors of a state. The set of enabled actions for node u is called the *enabled set*, denoted as *enabled*(u). The algorithm selects and follows only a subset of this set called the *ample set*, denoted as *ample*(u). A state u is said to be *fully expanded* when *ample*$(u) =$ *enabled*(u), otherwise it is said to be *partially expanded*.

Partial order reduction techniques are based on the observation that the order in which some actions are executed is not relevant. This leads to the concept of independence between actions.

Definition 10.4. *(Independent Actions) Two actions a_1 and a_2 are independent if for each state $u \in S$ the following two properties hold:*

1. Enabledness *is preserved: a_1 and a_2 do not disable each other.*
2. a_1 and a_2 are commutative: $a(a'(u)) = a'(a(u))$.

As a case study, we choose propositional STRIPS planning, where the planning goal is partially described by a set of propositions.

Definition 10.5. *(Independent STRIPS Planning Actions) Two STRIPS planning actions $a =$ $(pre(a), add(a), del(a))$ and $a' = (pre(a'), add(a'), del(a'))$ are independent if $del(a') \cap (add(a) \cup pre(a)) = \emptyset$ and $(add(a') \cup pre(a')) \cap del(a) = \emptyset$.*

Theorem 10.7. *(Commutativity of Independent Strips Actions) Two independent STRIPS actions are enabledness preserving and commutative.*

Proof. Let v be the state $(u \setminus del(a)) \cup add(a)$ and let w be the state $(u \setminus del(a')) \cup add(a')$. Since $(add(a') \cup del(a')) \cap pre(a) = \emptyset$, o is enabled in w, and since $(add(a) \cup del(a)) \cap pre(a') = \emptyset$, o' is enabled in v. Moreover,

$$a(a'(u)) = (((u \setminus del(a')) \cup add(a')) \setminus del(a)) \cup add(a)$$
$$= (((u \setminus del(a')) \setminus del(a)) \cup add(a')) \cup add(a)$$
$$= u \setminus (del(a') \cup del(a)) \cup (add(a') \cup add(a))$$
$$= u \setminus (del(a) \cup del(a')) \cup (add(a) \cup add(a'))$$
$$= (((u \setminus del(a)) \setminus del(a')) \cup add(a)) \cup add(a')$$
$$= (((u \setminus del(a)) \cup add(a)) \setminus del(a')) \cup add(a') = a'(a(u)).$$
∎

A further fundamental concept is the fact that some actions are *invisible* with respect to the goal. An action α is invisible with respect to the set of propositions in the goal T, if for each pair of states u, v, if $v = \alpha(u)$, we have $u \cap T = v \cap T$.

Figure 10.15 illustrates independence and invisibility of actions. Actions α, β, and γ are pairwise independent. Actions α and β are invisible with respect to the set of propositions $T = \{p\}$, but γ is not. The figure also illustrates why partial order reduction techniques are said to exploit *diamond properties* of a system.

The main goal of the *ample set* construction is to select a subset of the successors of a state such that the reduced state space is *stuttering equivalent* to the full state space with respect to a goal. The construction should offer a significant reduction without requiring a high computational overhead. Enough paths must be retained to give correct results. The following four conditions are necessary and sufficient for the proper construction of a partial order reduced state space for a given goal.

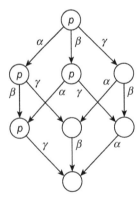

FIGURE 10.15

Illustration of independence and invisibility of actions.

C0: *ample(u)* is empty exactly when *enabled(u)* is empty.

C1: Along every path in the full state space that starts at u, an action that is dependent on an action in *ample(u)* does not occur without an action in *ample(u)* occurring first.

C2: If a state u is not fully expanded, then each action α in the ample set of u must be invisible with regard to the goal.

C3: If for each state of a cycle in the reduced state space an action α is enabled, then α must be in the ample set of some of the successors of some of the states of the cycle.

The general strategy to produce a reduced set of successors is to generate and test a limited number of ample sets for a given state, which is shown in Algorithm 10.5. Conditions **C0**, **C1**, and **C2** or their approximations can be implemented independently from the particular search algorithm used. Checking **C0** and **C2** is simple and does not depend on the search algorithm. Checking **C1** is more complicated. In fact, it has been shown to be at least as hard as establishing the goal for the full state space. It is, however, usually approximated by checking a stronger condition that can be checked independently of the search algorithm. We shall see that the complexity of checking the cycle condition **C3** depends on the search algorithm used.

Checking **C3** can be reduced to detecting cycles during the search. Cycles can be easily established in depth-first search: Every cycle contains a *backward edge*, one that links back to a state that is stored on the search stack. Consequently, avoiding ample sets containing backward edges except when the state is fully expanded ensures satisfaction of **C3** when using IDA*, since it performs a depth-first traversal. The resulting stack-based cycle condition **C3**$_{stack}$ can be stated as follows:

C3$_{stack}$: If a state u is not fully expanded, then at least one action in *ample(u)* does not lead to a state on the search stack.

Consider the example on the left of Figure 10.16. Condition **C3**$_{stack}$ does not characterize the set $\{\alpha_1\}$ as a valid candidate for the ample set. It accepts $\{\alpha_1, \alpha_2\}$ as a valid ample set, since at least one action (α_2) of the set leads to a state that is not on the search stack of the depth-first search.

The implementation of **C3**$_{stack}$ for DFS strategies marks each expanded state on the stack, so that stack containment can be checked in constant time.

Procedure CheckAmple
Input: State u, *ample(u)*
Output: Potentially reduced successor set $Succ(u)$

if (**C0**(*ample(u)*) **and** **C1**(*ample(u)*) **and** **C2**(*ample(u)*) **and** **C3**(*ample(u)*))
    $Succ(u) \leftarrow \{v \mid \exists \alpha \in ample(u) : \alpha(u) = v\}$;; Reduced set
else   ;; Conditions not satisfied
    $Succ(u) \leftarrow \{v \mid \exists \alpha \in enabled(u) : \alpha(u) = v\}$;; Unreduced set
return $Succ(u)$;; Return successors of u

Algorithm 10.5

An algorithm for checking ample sets.

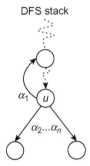

DFS stack

FIGURE 10.16

Reduction example for depth-first search.

Detecting cycles with general search algorithms that do not perform a depth-first traversal of the state space is more complex. For a cycle to exist, it is necessary to reach an already generated state. If during the search a state is found to be already generated, checking that this state is part of a cycle requires checking whether this state is reachable from itself. This increases the time complexity of the algorithm from linear to quadratic in the size of the state space. Therefore, the commonly adopted approach assumes that a cycle exists whenever an already generated state is found. Using this idea leads to weaker reductions. Fortunately for reversible state space the self-reachability check is trivial.

The cycle condition $C3_{stack}$ cannot be used without a search stack, since cycles cannot be efficiently detected. Therefore, we propose an alternative condition to enforce the cycle condition **C3**, which is sufficient to guarantee a correct reduction.

> **Condition $C3_{duplicate}$**: If a node u is not fully expanded, then at least one action in $ample(u)$ does not lead to an already generated node.

To prove the correctness of partial order reduction with condition $C3_{duplicate}$ for general node expanding algorithms, we use induction on the node expansion ordering, starting from a completed exploration and moving backward with respect to the traversal algorithm. For node u after termination of the search we ensure that each enabled action is executed either in the ample set of node u or in a node that appears later in the expansion process. Therefore, no action is omitted. Applying the result to all nodes u implies **C3**, which, in turn, ensures a correct reduction.

Partial order reduction does preserve the *completeness* of a search algorithm (no solution is lost) but not its optimality. In fact, the shortest path to a goal in the reduced state space may be longer than the shortest path to a goal in the full state space. Intuitively, the reason is that the concept of stuttering equivalence does not make assumptions about the length of equivalent blocks.

Suppose that actions α and β of the state space depicted in Figure 10.17 are independent and that α is invisible with respect to the set of propositions p. Suppose further that we want to search for a goal $\neg p$, where p is an atomic proposition. With these assumptions the reduced state space for the example is stuttering equivalent to the full one. The shortest path that violates the invariant in the reduced state

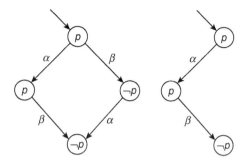

FIGURE 10.17

Example of a full state space (left) and a nonadmissible reduction (right).

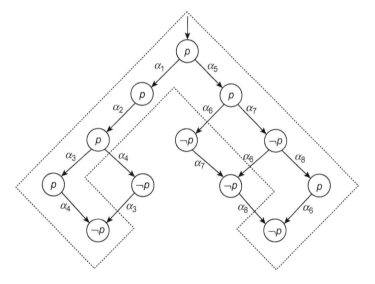

FIGURE 10.18

Another example of a full state space and a reduction (dashed region).

space consists of actions α and β, which has a length of 2. In the full one, the initial path with action β is the shortest path to a goal state, such that the corresponding solution path has a length of 1.

The problem can be partially avoided by postprocessing the solution. The intuitive idea is to ignore those actions that are independent from the action that directly led to the goal state, since they are not relevant. To get a valid solution path it is also necessary to require that the ignored actions *cannot enable* actions that occur after them in the original solution. The approach may be able to shorten the established solution path, but the resulting solution may not be optimal. Figure 10.18 depicts an example of a full state space and a possible reduction. As in the example in Figure 10.17, a goal state is one in which proposition p does not hold. Suppose that the following pairs of actions are independent—(α_3, α_4), (α_6, α_7), and (α_6, α_8)—and that only α_6 and α_4 are visible and negate the value of the proposition p. Then, the path formed by actions α_1, α_2, α_3, and α_4 can be established as the shortest path in the reduced state space denoted by the dashed region. Applying the approach can result in the solution path $\alpha_1\alpha_2\alpha_4$, which has a length of 3. This is possible since α_3 is invisible, independent from α_4 and cannot enable α_4. On the other hand, the optimal solution in the full state space is shorter: $\alpha_5\alpha_6$.

10.3 SUMMARY

In this chapter, we studied pruning to make searches more efficient. Pruning means to ignore parts of the search tree (and thus reduce the branching factor) to save runtime and memory. This can be tricky since we would like the search to find a shortest path from the start state to any goal state (admissible pruning) or at least some path from the start state to a goal state (solution preserving pruning) if one exists. Also, pruning itself requires runtime and memory, and thus we need to ensure that these costs are outweighed by the corresponding savings. Pruning often exploits regularities in the state space, knowledge of which can be supplied by an expert or learned automatically. The learning can happen either before the search (static pruning), often in similar but smaller state spaces than the ones to be searched, or during the search (dynamic pruning). If it is done during the search, it can be done as part of finding a path from the start state to a goal state or as part of a two-level architecture where the top-level search finds a path from the start state to a goal state and lower-level searches acquire additional pruning knowledge.

We discussed the following admissible pruning strategies:

- *Substring pruning* prunes action sequences (called duplicates) that result in the same state as at least one no-more-expensive nonpruned action sequence (called the shortcut). Thus, this pruning strategy is an alternative to avoiding the regeneration of already generated states for search algorithms that do not store all previously generated states in memory, such as IDA*, and thus cannot easily detect duplicate states. We discussed two static ways of finding duplicate action sequences, namely by a breadth-first search that finds action sequences that result in the same state when executed in the same state and by detecting action sequences that result in the same state in which they are executed (cycles). For example, URDL is a cycle in an empty GRIDWORLD, implying that UR is a duplicate action sequence of RU (the inverse of DL) and ULD is a duplicate action sequence of R (the inverse of L). We also discussed a dynamic way of finding duplicate action sequences, namely during an A* search. To be able to detect duplicate action sequences efficiently, we can encode them as finite-state machines, for example, using the Aho-Corasick algorithm. We used the EIGHT-PUZZLE to illustrate substring pruning.
- *Dead-end pruning* prunes states from which no goal state can be reached. A state can be labeled a dead-end if all successor states of it are dead-ends or by showing that one simplification (called decomposition) of it is a dead-end. We discussed a static way of finding dead-ends (called bootstrapping), namely using penalty tables. Penalty tables are a way of learning and storing more informed heuristics, and an infinite heuristic indicates a dead-end. We also discussed a dynamic

way of finding duplicate action sequences, namely during an A* search (resulting in abstraction decomposition A*). We used SOKOBAN to illustrate dead-end pruning.

- *Symmetry reduction* prunes action sequences that are similar (*symmetric*) to a same-cost, nonpruned action sequence. We discussed a dynamic way of symmetry reduction that exploits transpositions of state variables and uses some precompiled knowledge of symmetry between variables in the goal state.

We discussed the following nonadmissible pruning strategies:

- *Macro problem solving* prunes actions in favor of a few action sequences (called macros), which not only decreases the branching factor but also the search depth. We discussed a static way of macro learning for the EIGHT-PUZZLE where the macros bring one tile after the other into place without disturbing the tiles brought into place already.
- *Relevance cuts* prune actions in a state that are considered unimportant because they do not contribute to the subgoal currently pursued. Actions that do not influence each other are called distant actions. Relevance cuts can, for example, prune an action if more than a certain number of distant actions have been executed recently (because the action then does not contribute to the subgoal pursued by the recently executed actions) or if the action is distant to the last action but not a certain number of actions that have been executed recently (because the action then does not contribute to the subgoal pursued by the last action that already switched the subgoal pursued by the actions executed before). We used SOKOBAN to illustrate relevance cuts.
- Finally, *partial order reduction* prunes action sequences that result in the same state as at least one nonpruned action sequence. Different from substring pruning, the nonpruned action sequence can be more expensive than the pruned action sequence. The nonpruned actions are called ample actions. We discussed a way of determining the ample actions, utilizing properties of the actions, such as their independence and invisibility, so that action sequences from the start to the goal are not searched only if they are stuttering equivalent to an action sequence from the start to the goal that is searched. We discussed ways of postprocessing the found action sequence to make it shorter, even though neither the partial order–reduced sequence nor the postprocessed one can be guaranteed to be shortest.

Table 10.4 compares the state space pruning approaches. The strategies are classified along the criteria whether or not they are *admissible* (i.e., preserve optimal solutions in optimal solvers) or *incremental* (i.e., allow detection and processing of pruning information during the search). Pruning rules are hard criteria and can be seen as assigning a heuristic estimate ∞ to the search. Some rules extend to refinements to the admissible search heuristic, lower bound. The classification is not fixed; refer to the presentation in the text. Depending on weakening (strengthening) assumptions for the pruning scenario, admissible pruning techniques may become inadmissible (and vice versa). We also provide some time efficiencies for storing and applying the pruning, which, of course, depend on the implementation of the according data structure and neglect some subtleties provided in the text. For substring pruning we assume the Aho-Corasick automaton (IDA*) or suffix trees (IDLA*). For dead-end pruning and pattern search, a storage structure based on partial states is needed. Symmetries can either be provided by the domain experts or inferred by the system (action planning). For the sake of a concise notation, in action planning and SOKOBAN we assumed a unary Boolean encoding of the set of atoms (squares) to form the state vector.

Table 10.4 Overview state space pruning; $l(n)$ is the duplicate (solution path) length, S is the state vector of size k, P is the set of patterns, M is the set of symmetries (*amortized complexity).

Database	Admissible	Incremental	Storage	Retrieval
Substring Pruning (IDA*)	✓	–	$O(l)$	$O(1)^*$
Substring Pruning (IDLA*)	✓	✓	$O(l)$	$O(1)^*$
Pattern Search (naive)	✓	✓	$O(k)$	$O(k \cdot |P|)$
Symmetry (Planning)	✓	✓	$O(k)$	$O(k \cdot |M|)$
Macro Operators	–	–	$O(n)$	$O(n)$
Relevance Cuts	–	–	$O(k^2)$	$O(k)$
Partial Order Reduction	–	✓	$O(1)$	$O(n)$

10.4 EXERCISES

10.1 Assume that we have found a pruning pair (d,c) according to its definition. Show that pruning substrings d from search tree paths p is admissible.

10.2 Determine all duplicate/shortcut string pairs for the $(n^2 - 1)$-PUZZLE of accumulated length 12, by a hash lookup in depth 6 of a breadth-first search enumeration of the search space. Use the lexicographic ordering on the characters to differentiate between duplicate and shortcuts. Build the corresponding finite-state machine that accepts the duplicate strings.

10.3 Complex dead-end positions in SOKOBAN are frequent.
  1. Find a dead-end pattern u in SOKOBAN with more than eight balls.
  2. Show how *pattern search* determines the value ∞ for u.
  3. Display the tree structure for learning the dead-end position with root u.

10.4 In Dijkstra's DINING PHILOSOPHERS problem (see Fig. 10.19) n philosophers sit around a table to have lunch. There are n plates, one for each philosopher, and n forks located to the left and to the right of each plate. Since two forks are required to eat the spaghetti on the plates, not all philosophers can eat at a time. Moreover, no communication except taking and releasing the forks is allowed. The task is to devise a local strategy for each philosopher that lets all philosophers eventually eat. The simplest solution, to access the left fork followed by the right one, has an obvious problem. If all philosophers wait for the second fork to be released there is no possible progress: a dead-end has occurred.
  1. Give a state space characterization of the philosopher problem that pleases a rotational symmetry $\sim_r$. We have $(v_0, v_1, \ldots, v_{n-1}) \sim_r (w_0, w_1, \ldots, w_{n-1})$ if there exists a $k \in \{0, \ldots, n-1\}$ with

$$(v_{(1+k) \bmod n}, v_{(2+k) \bmod n}, \ldots, v_{(n-1+k) \bmod n}) = (w_0, w_1, \ldots, w_{n-1}).$$

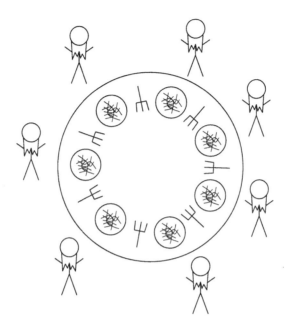

FIGURE 10.19

The DINING PHILOSOPHERS example.

    2. Show that $\sim_r$ is an equivalence relation.

    3. Show that $\sim_r$ is a congruence relation.

10.5 For computing symmetries in a logistic planning domain with 10 cities, 10 trucks, 5 airplanes, and 15 packages, determine

    1. The number of symmetries that respect the type information.

    2. The number of variable symmetries that respect variable types.

10.6 A *relevance analysis* precomputes a matrix D of influence numbers. The larger the influence number, the smaller the influence. One suggestion for calculating D is as follows. Each square on the path between start and goal squares adds 2 for each alternative route for the ball and 1 for each alternative route for a man. Every square that is part of an optimal path will only add half that amount. If the connection from the previous square on the path to the current square can be taken by a ball only 1 is added, else 2. If the previous square is in a tunnel, value 0 is added regardless of all other properties.

    1. Compute a relevance matrix D for the problem in Figure 10.20.

    2. Run a shortest path algorithm to find the largest influence between every two squares.

10.7 Provide macros for the (3-blocks) BLOCKSWORLD problem.

    1. Display the state space problem graph based on the actions *stack*, *pickup*, *putdown*, and *unstack*.

    2. Form all three-step macros, and establish a macro solution in which *a* is on top of *b* and *b* is on top of *c* starting from the configuration, where all blocks are on the table.

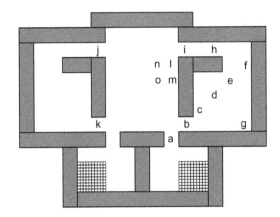

FIGURE 10.20

Relevance analysis for SOKOBAN.

10.8 Explain how to apply macros to solve RUBIK'S CUBE (see Ch. 1).
1. Define a state vector representation for RUBIK'S CUBE that allows you to build a macro table. How large is your table?
2. There are different solution strategies for incrementally solving the CUBE available on the Internet. Construct a macro table based on the 18 basic twist actions.
3. Construct a macro table automatically by writing a computer program searching for one (shortest) macro for each table entry.

10.9 Macro problem solving is only possible if the problem can be *serialized*; that is, if finding the overall goal can be decomposed into an incremental goal agenda.
1. Give a formal characterization of serialization based on a state vector representation $(v_1, \ldots, v_k)$ of the problem that is needed for macro problem solving.
2. Provide an example of a domain that is not serializable.

10.10 Show the necessity of condition **C3** in partial order reduction! Consider the original state space of Figure 10.21 (left). Proposition p is assumed to be contained in the goal description. Starting with S_1 we select $ample(S_1) = \alpha_1$, for S_2 we select $ample(S_2) = \alpha_2$, and for S_3 we select $ample(S_3) = \alpha_3$.
1. Explain that β is visible.
2. Show that the three ample sets satisfy **C0**, **C1**, and **C2**.
3. Illustrate that the reduced state graph in Figure 10.21 (right) does not contain any sequence, where p is changed from *true* to *false*.
4. Show that each state along the cycle has deferred β to a possible future state.

10.11 Prove the correctness of partial order reduction according to condition **C3**$_{duplicate}$ for depth-first, breadth-first, best-first, and A*-like search schemes. Show that for each node u the following is true: When the search of a general search algorithm terminates, each action $\alpha \in enabled(u)$ has been selected either in $ample(u)$ or in a node v such that v has been expanded after u.

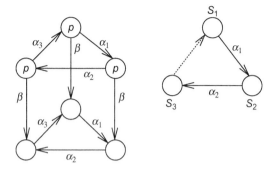

FIGURE 10.21

Original and reduced state space.

10.5 BIBLIOGRAPHIC NOTES

The pattern matching approach of Aho and Corasick (1975) is a generalization of the algorithm of Knuth, Morris, and Prat (1977). The latter has been extended to include character wild cards. Finite-state machine pruning based on Aho and Corasick's approach is best documented in Taylor's PhD thesis (1997). The usability of suffix trees in state space search is due to Edelkamp (1997).

Dead-end pruning in SOKOBAN has been first suggested by Junghanns and Schaeffer (1998). The presented algorithmic approach on abstraction and decomposition in A* is based on similar findings in Edelkamp (2003a). Pattern search has been introduced by Junghanns and Schaeffer (1998). The idea shares similarities with *Partition Search* by Ginsberg (1996), where the entries of a hash table are generalized to hold information about sets of problem states. Pattern searches are a conflict-driven top-down proof of correctness, whereas the *Method of Analogies* by Adelson-Velskiy, Arlazarov, and Donskoy (2003) is a bottom-up heuristic approximation.

State space reduction based on symmetry relations is frequently met in state space search literature. Symmetries are referred to in the context of pattern databases in Culberson and Schaeffer (1998). Action planning symmetries have been intensively studied by Fox and Long (1999), Rintanen (2003), and Edelkamp (2003c). In the area of model checking, symmetry reduction is also fundamental. A combination of symmetry reduction and directed search for the design of admissible symmetric estimates has been given by Lluch-Lafuente (2003b).

The *macro problem solver* by Korf (1985b) refers to his PhD thesis work. There is much work on the formation of macros in machine learning (Langley, 1996). STRIPS, nowadays used as an acronym for a basic specification language in action planning, actually refers to a planning system by Fikes and Nilsson (1971) that is based on macros. An application of so-called *partial order macros* to scale up action planners has been provided by Botea, Müller, and Schaeffer (2005).

Relevance cuts have been proposed and theoretically studied (Junghanns and Schaeffer, 2001) in the context of SOKOBAN. In two-player search, a number of meta-level reasonings such as null-move search (Goetsch and Campbell, 1990) and futility cut-offs (Schaeffer, 1986) are known.

Two main families of partial order techniques exist. The first one is based on net unfoldings as described by Bornot, Morin, Niebert, and Zennou (2002), and the second is based on the so-called diamond properties. We have focused on the latter, which are called partial order reduction techniques. Several partial order reduction approaches have been proposed, namely those based on *stubborn sets* by Valmari (1991), *persistent sets* by Godefroid (1991), and *ample sets* by Peled (1996). Although they differ in details, they are based on similar ideas. Due to its popularity, we mainly followed the ample sets approach. Nonetheless, most of the reasoning presented in this chapter can be adjusted to any of the other approaches. For an extended description of partial order reduction methods we refer to Peled (1998).

Real-Time Search

Sven Koenig

In this chapter, we describe real-time (heuristic) search and illustrate it with examples. Real-time search is sometimes used to describe search methods that only need a constant search time between action executions. However, we use a more restrictive definition of real-time search in this chapter, namely that of real-time search as a variant of agent-centered search. Interleaving or overlapping searches and action executions often has advantages for intelligent systems (agents) that interact directly with the world. *Agent-centered search* restricts the search to the part of the state space around the current state of the agent; for example, the current position of a mobile robot or the current board position of a game. The part of the state space around the current state of the agent is the part of the state space that is immediately relevant for the agent in its current situation (because it contains the states that the agent will soon be in) and sometimes might be the only part of the state space that the agent knows about. Agent-centered search usually does not search all the way from the start state to a goal state. Instead, it decides on the local search space, searches it, and determines which actions to execute within it. Then, it executes these actions (or only the first action) and repeats the process from its new state until it reaches a goal state.

The best-known example of agent-centered search is probably game playing, such as playing CHESS (as studied in Chapter 12). In this case, the states correspond to board positions and the current state corresponds to the current board position. Game-playing programs typically perform a minimax search with a limited lookahead (i.e., search horizon) around the current board position to determine which move to perform next. The reason for performing only a limited local search is that the state spaces of realistic games are too large to perform complete searches in a reasonable amount of time and with a reasonable amount of memory. The future moves of the opponent cannot be predicted with certainty, which makes the search tasks nondeterministic. This results in an information limitation that can only be overcome by enumerating all possible moves of the opponent, which results in large search spaces. Performing agent-centered search allows game-playing programs to choose a move in a reasonable amount of time while focusing on the part of the state space that is the most relevant to the next move decision.

Traditional search methods, such as A*, first determine minimal-cost paths and then follow them. Thus, they are *offline search* methods. Agent-centered search methods, on the other hand, interleave search and action execution and are thus *online search* methods. They can be characterized as revolving search methods with greedy action-selection steps that solve suboptimal search tasks. They are *suboptimal* since they are looking for any path (i.e., sequence of actions) from the start state to a goal state. The sequence of actions that agent-centered search methods execute is such a path. They are *revolving*, because they repeat the same process until they reach a goal state. Agent-centered search methods have the following two advantages:

Time constraints: Agent-centered search methods can execute actions in the presence of soft or hard time constraints since the sizes of their local search spaces are independent of the sizes of the state spaces and can thus remain small. The objective of the search in this case is to approximately minimize the execution cost subject to the constraint that the search cost (here: runtime) between action executions is bounded from above, for example, in situations where it is more important to act reasonably in a timely manner than to minimize the execution cost after a long delay. Examples include steering decisions when driving a car or movement decisions when crossing a busy street.

Sum of search and execution cost: Agent-centered search methods execute actions before their complete consequences are known and thus are likely to incur some overhead in terms of the execution cost, but this is often outweighed by a decrease in the search cost, both because they trade off the search and execution cost and because they allow agents to gather information early in nondeterministic state spaces, which reduces the amount of search they have to perform for unencountered situations. Thus, they often decrease the sum of the search and execution cost compared to search methods that first determine minimal-cost paths and then follow them, which can be important for search tasks that need to be solved only once.

Agent-centered search methods have to ensure that they do not cycle without making progress toward a goal state. This is a potential problem since they execute actions before their consequences are completely known. Agent-centered search methods have to ensure both that it remains possible to achieve the goal and that they eventually do so. The goal remains achievable if no actions exist of which the execution makes it impossible to reach a goal state, if the agent-centered search methods can avoid the execution of such actions in case they do exist, or if the agent-centered search methods have the ability to reset the agent into the start state. *Real-time search* methods are agent-centered search methods that store a value, called *h-value*, in memory for each state that they encounter during the search and update them as the search progresses, both to focus the search and avoid cycling, which accounts for a large chunk of their search time per search episode.

11.1 LRTA*

Learning real-time A* (LRTA*) is probably the most popular real-time search method, and we relate all real-time search methods in this chapter to it. The *h*-values of LRTA* approximate the goal distances of the states. They can be initialized using a heuristic function. They can be all zero if more informed *h*-values are not available. Figure 11.1 illustrates the behavior of LRTA* using a simplified goal-directed navigation task in known terrain without uncertainty about the start cell. The robot can move one cell to the north, east, south, or west (unless that cell is blocked). All action costs are one. The task of the robot is to navigate to the given goal cell and then stop. In this case, the states correspond to cells, and the current state corresponds to the current cell of the robot. We assume that there is no uncertainty in actuation and sensing. The *h*-values are initialized with the Manhattan distances. A robot under time pressure could reason as follows: Its current cell C1 is not a goal cell. Thus, it needs to move to one of the cells adjacent to its current cell to get to a goal cell. The *cost-to-go* of an action is its action cost plus the estimated goal distance of the successor state reached when executing the action, as given by

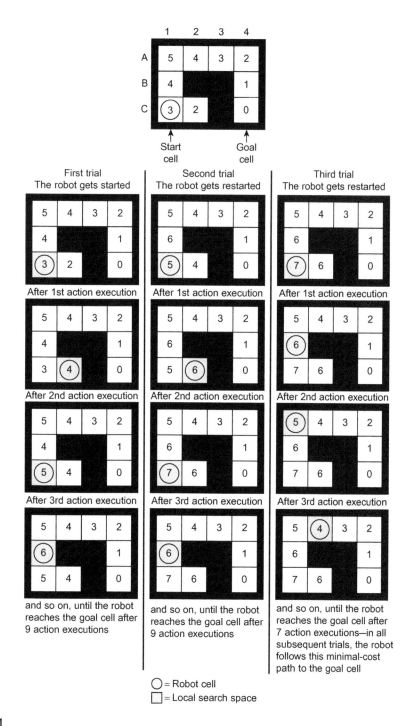

FIGURE 11.1

LRTA* in a simple GRIDWORLD, by Koenig (2001).

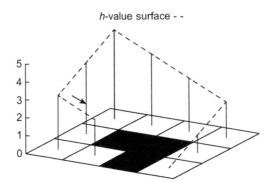

FIGURE 11.2

Initial *h*-value surface, by Koenig (2001).

the *h*-value of the successor state. If it moves to cell B1, then the action cost is one and the estimated goal distance from there is four as given by the *h*-value of cell B1. The cost-to-go of moving to cell B1 is thus five. Similarly, the cost-to-go of moving to cell C2 is three. Thus, it looks more promising to move to cell C2. Figure 11.2 visualizes the *h*-value surface formed by the initial *h*-values. However, a robot does not reach the goal cell if it always executes the move with the minimal cost-to-go and thus performs steepest descent on the initial *h*-value surface. It moves back and forth between cells C1 and C2 and thus cycles forever due to the local minimum of the *h*-value surface at cell C2.

We could avoid this problem by randomizing the action-selection process slightly, possibly together with resetting the robot into a start state (random restart) after the execution cost has become large. LRTA*, however, avoids this problem by increasing the *h*-values to fill the local minima in the *h*-value surface. Figure 11.3 shows how LRTA* performs a search around the current state of the robot to determine which action to execute next if it breaks ties among actions in the following order: north, east, south, and west. It operates as follows:

Local Search Space–Generation Step: LRTA* decides on the local search space. The *local search space* can be any set of nongoal states that contains the current state. We say that a local search space is *minimal* if and only if it contains only the current state. We say that it is *maximal* if and only if it contains all nongoal states. In Figure 11.1, for example, the local search spaces are minimal. In this case, LRTA* can construct a search tree around the current state. The local search space consists of all nonleaves of the search tree. Figure 11.3 shows the search tree for deciding which action to execute in the start cell C1.

Value-Update Step: LRTA* assigns each state in the local search space its correct goal distance under the assumption that the *h*-values of the states just outside of the local search space correspond to their correct goal distances. In other words, it assigns each state in the local search space the minimum of the execution cost for getting from it to a state just outside of the local search space, plus the estimated remaining execution cost for getting from there to a goal state, as given by the *h*-value of the state just outside of the local search space. The reason for this is that the local search space does not include any goal state. Thus, a minimal-cost path from a state in the local search space to a goal state has to contain a state just outside of the local search space. Thus, the smallest estimated cost of all paths from the state via a state just outside of the local search

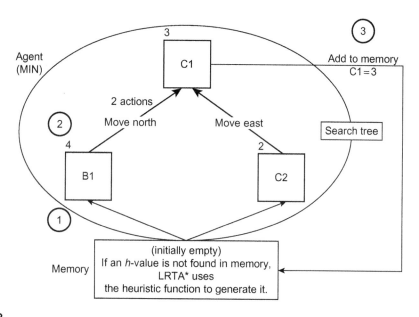

FIGURE 11.3

Illustration of LRTA*, by Koenig (2001).

space to a goal state is an estimate of the goal distance of the state. Since this lookahead value is a more accurate estimate of the goal distance of the state in the local search space, LRTA* stores it in memory, overwriting the existing h-value of the state.

In the example, the local search space is minimal and LRTA* can simply update the h-value of the state in the local search space according to the following rule provided that it ignores all actions that can leave the current state unchanged. LRTA* first assigns each leaf of the search tree the h-value of the corresponding state. The leaf that represents cell B1 is assigned an h-value of four, and the leaf that represents cell C2 is assigned an h-value of two. This step is marked ① in Figure 11.3. The new h-value of the root of the search tree, that represents cell C1, then is the minimum of the costs-to-go of the actions that can be executed in it, that is, the minimum of five and three. ②. This h-value is then stored in memory for cell C1 ③. Figure 11.4 shows the result of one value-update step for a different example where the local search space is nonminimal.

Action-Selection Step: LRTA* selects an action for execution that is the beginning of a path that promises to minimize the execution cost from the current state to a goal state (ties can be broken arbitrarily). In the example, LRTA* selects the action with the minimal cost-to-go. Since moving to cell B1 has cost-to-go five and moving to cell C2 has cost-to-go three, LRTA* decides to move to cell C2.

Action-Execution Step: LRTA* executes the selected action and updates the state of the robot, and repeats the process from the new state of the robot until the robot reaches a goal state. If its new state is outside of the local search space, then it needs to repeat the local search space–generation and value-update steps. Otherwise, it can repeat these steps or proceed directly to the action-selection step. Executing more actions before generating the next local search space typically results in a smaller search cost (because LRTA* needs to search less frequently);

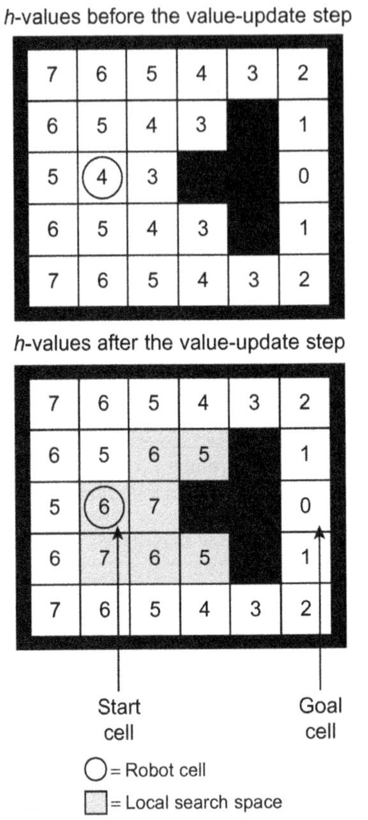

h-values before the value-update step

7	6	5	4	3	2
6	5	4	3		1
5	④	3			0
6	5	4	3		1
7	6	5	4	3	2

h-values after the value-update step

7	6	5	4	3	2
6	5	6	5		1
5	⑥	7			0
6	7	6	5		1
7	6	5	4	3	2

Start cell   Goal cell

O = Robot cell
☐ = Local search space

FIGURE 11.4

LRTA* with a larger local search space, by Koenig (2001).

executing fewer actions typically results in a smaller execution cost (because LRTA* selects actions based on more information).

The left column of Figure 11.1 shows the result of the first couple of steps of LRTA* for the example. The values in grey cells are the new *h*-values calculated by the value-update step because the corresponding cells are part of the local search space. The robot reaches the goal cell after nine action executions; that is, with execution cost nine. We assumed here that the terrain is known and the reason for using real-time search is time pressure. Another reason for using real-time search could be missing knowledge of the terrain and the resulting desire to restrict the local search spaces to the known parts of the terrain.

We now formalize LRTA*, using the following assumptions and notation for deterministic and nondeterministic search tasks, which will be used throughout this chapter: S denotes the finite *set of states* of the state space, $s \in S$ the *start state*, and $T \subseteq S$ the *set of goal states*. $A(u) \neq \emptyset$ denotes the finite, nonempty *set of* (potentially nondeterministic) *actions* that can be executed in state $u \in S$. $0 < w(u, a) < \infty$ denotes the *action cost* that results from the execution of action $a \in A(u)$ in state $u \in S$. We assume that all action costs are one unless stated otherwise. $w_{min} = \min_{u \in S, a \in A(u)} w(u,a)$ denotes the *minimal action cost* of any action. $Succ(u,a) \subseteq S$ denotes the *set of successor states* that can result from the execution of action $\in a \in A(u)$ in state $u \in S$. $a(u) \in Succ(u,a)$ denotes the state that results from an actual execution of action $a \in A(u)$ in state $u \in S$. In deterministic state spaces, $Succ(u,a)$ contains only one state, and we use $Succ(u,a)$ also to denote this state. Thus, $a(u) = Succ(u,a)$ in this case. An agent starts in the start state and has to move to a goal state. The agent always observes what its current state is and then has to select and execute its next action, which results in a state transition to one of the possible successor states. The search task is solved when the agent reaches a goal state. We denote the *number of states* by $n = |S|$ and the *number of state-action pairs* (loosely called actions) by $e = \sum_{u \in S} |A(u)|$; that is, an action that is applicable in more than one state counts more than once. Moreover, $\delta(u,T) \geq 0$ denotes the *goal distance* of state $u \in S$; that is, the minimal execution cost with which a goal state can be reached from state u. The *depth d* of the state space is its maximal goal distance, $d = \max_{u \in S} \delta(u,T)$. The expression $\arg\min_{x \in X} f(x)$ returns one of the elements $x \in X$ that minimize $f(x)$; that is, one of the elements from the set $\{x \in X | f(x) = \min_{x' \in X} f(x')\}$. We assume that all search tasks are deterministic unless stated otherwise, and discuss nondeterministic state spaces in Sections 11.5.7 and 11.6.4.

Algorithm 11.1 shows pseudo code for LRTA* in deterministic state spaces. It associates a nonnegative *h*-value $h(u)$ with each state $u \in S$. In practice, they are not initialized upfront but rather can be initialized as needed. LRTA* consists of a termination-checking step, a local search space–generation step, a value-update step, an action-selection step, and an action-execution step. LRTA* first checks whether it has already reached a goal state and thus can terminate successfully. If not, it generates the local search space $S_{lss} \subseteq S$. Although we require only that $u \in S_{lss}$ and $S_{lss} \cap T = \emptyset$, in practice LRTA* often uses forward search (that searches from the current state to the goal states) to select a continuous part of the state space around the current state u of the agent. LRTA* could determine the local search space, for example, with a breadth-first search around state u up to a given depth or with a (forward) A* search around state u until a given number of states have been expanded (or, in both cases, a goal state is about to be expanded). The states in the local search space correspond to the nonleaves of the corresponding search tree, and thus are all nongoal states. In Figure 11.1, a (forward) A* search that

---

Procedure LRTA*
Input: Search task with initial *h*-values
Side effect: Updated *h*-values

$u \leftarrow s$	;; Start in start state
while $(u \notin T)$	;; While goal not achieved
Generate S_{lss} with $u \in S_{lss}$ and $S_{lss} \cap T = \emptyset$	;; Generate local search space
Value-Update-Step(h, S_{lss})	;; Update *h*-values, see Algorithm 11.2
repeat	;; Repeat
$a \leftarrow \arg\min_{a \in A(u)} \{w(u,a) + h(Succ(u,a))\}$	;; Select action
$u \leftarrow a(u)$	;; Execute action
until $(u \notin S_{lss})$	;; Until local search space exited (optional)

Algorithm 11.1

LRTA*.

Procedure Value-Update-Step
Input: Search task with h-values and local search space
Side effect: Updated h-values

for each $u \in S_{lss}$;; For each state in local search space
   $temp(u) \leftarrow h(u)$;; Backup h-value
   $h(u) \leftarrow \infty$;; Initialize h-value
while $(|\{u \in S_{lss} | h(u) = \infty\}| \neq 0)$;; While infinite h-values exist
   $v \leftarrow \arg\min_{u \in S_{lss} | h(u) = \infty}$
     $\max\{temp(u), \min_{a \in A(u)}\{w(u,a) + h(Succ(u,a))\}\}$;; Determine state
   $h(v) \leftarrow \max\{temp(v), \min_{a \in A(v)}\{w(v,a) + h(Succ(v,a))\}\}$;; Update h-value
   if $(h(v) = \infty)$ **return**   ;; No improvement possible

Algorithm 11.2

Value-update step of LRTA*.

expands two states picks a local search space that consists of the expanded states C1 and C2. LRTA* then updates the h-values of all states in the local search space. Based on these h-values, LRTA* decides which action to execute next. Finally, it executes the selected action, updates its current state, and repeats the process.

Algorithm 11.2 shows how LRTA* updates the h-values in the local search space using a variant of Dijkstra's algorithm. It assigns each state its goal distance under the assumption that the h-values of all states in the local search space do not overestimate the correct goal distances and the h-values of all states outside of the local search space correspond to their correct goal distances. It does this by first assigning infinity to the h-values of all states in the local search space. It then determines a state in the local search space of which the h-value is still infinity and which minimizes the maximum of its previous h-value and the minimum over all actions in the state of the cost-to-go of the action. This value then becomes the h-value of this state, and the process repeats. The way the h-values are updated ensures that the states in the local search space are updated in the order of their increasing new h-values. This ensures that the h-value of each state in the local search space is updated at most once. The method terminates when either the h-value of each state in the local search space has been assigned a finite value or an h-value would be assigned the value infinity. In the latter case, the h-values of all remaining states in the local search space would be assigned the value infinity as well, which is already their current value.

Lemma 11.1. *For all times $t = 0,1,2,\ldots$ (until termination): Consider the $(t+1)$st value-update step of LRTA* (i.e., call to procedure Value-Update-Step in Algorithm 11.1). Let S_{lss}^t refer to its local search space. Let $h^t(u) \in [0,\infty]$ and $h^{t+1}(u) \in [0,\infty]$ refer to the h-values immediately before and after, respectively, the value-update step. Then, for all states $u \in S$, the value-update step terminates with*

$$h^{t+1}(u) = \begin{cases} h^t(u) & \text{if } s \notin S_{lss}^t \\ \max\{h^t(u), \min_{a \in A(u)}\{w(u,a) + h^{t+1}(Succ(u,a))\}\} & \text{otherwise} \end{cases}.$$

Proof by induction on the number of iterations within the value-update step (see Exercises). ∎

Lemma 11.2. *Admissible initial h-values (that is, initial h-values that are lower bounds on the corresponding goal distances) remain admissible after every value-update step of LRTA* and are monotonically nondecreasing. Similarly, consistent initial h-values (i.e., initial h-values that satisfy the triangle inequality) remain consistent after every value-update step of LRTA* and are monotonically nondecreasing.*

Proof by induction on the number of value-update steps, using Lemma 11.1 (see Exercises).   ∎

After the value-update step has updated the h-values, LRTA* greedily chooses the action $a \in A(u)$ in the current nongoal state u with the minimal cost-to-go $w(u,a) + h(Succ(u,a))$ for execution to minimize the estimated execution cost to a goal state. Ties can be broken arbitrarily, although we explain later that tie breaking can be important. Then, LRTA* has a choice. It can generate another local search space, update the h-values of all states that it contains, and select another action for execution. This version of LRTA* results when the repeat-until loop in Algorithm 11.1 is executed only once, which is why we refer to this version as *LRTA* without repeat-until loop*. If the new state is still part of the local search space (the one that was used to determine the action of which the execution resulted in the new state), LRTA* can also select another action for execution based on the current h-values. This version of LRTA* results when the repeat-until loop in Algorithm 11.1 is executed until the new state is no longer part of the local search space (as shown in the pseudo code), which is why we refer to this version as *LRTA* with repeat-until loop*. It searches less often and thus tends to have smaller search costs but larger execution costs. We analyze LRTA* without repeat-until loop, which is possible because LRTA* with repeat-until loop is a special case of LRTA* without repeat-until loop. After LRTA* has used the value-update step on some local search space, the h-values do not change if LRTA* uses the value-update step again on the same local search space or a subset thereof. Whenever LRTA* repeats the body of the repeat-until loop, the new current state is still part of the local search space S_{lss} and thus not a goal state. Consequently, LRTA* could now search a subset of S_{lss} that includes the new current state, for example, using a minimal local search space, which does not change the h-values and thus can be skipped.

11.2 LRTA* WITH LOOKAHEAD ONE

We now state a variant of LRTA* with minimal local search spaces, the way it is often stated in the literature. Algorithm 11.3 shows the pseudo code of *LRTA* with lookahead one*. Its action-selection step and value-update step can be explained as follows. The action-selection step greedily chooses the action $a \in A(u)$ in the current nongoal state u with the minimal cost-to-go $w(u,a) + h(Succ(u,a))$ for execution to minimize the estimated execution cost to a goal state. (The cost-to-go $w(u,a) + h(Succ(u,a))$ is basically the f-value of state $Succ(u,a)$ of an A* search from u toward the goal states.) The value-update step replaces the h-value of the current state with a more accurate estimate of the goal distance of the state based on the costs-to-go of the actions that can be executed in it, which is similar to temporal difference learning in reinforcement learning. If all h-values are admissible, then both $h(u)$ and the minimum of the costs-to-go of the actions that can be executed in state u are lower bounds on its goal distance, and the larger of these two values is the more accurate estimate. The value-update step then replaces the h-value of state u with this value. The value-update step of LRTA* is sometimes stated as $h(u) = w(u,a) + h(Succ(u,a))$. Our slightly more complex variant guarantees that the h-values are

---

Procedure LRTA*-with-Lookahead-One
Input: Search task with initial h-values
Side effect: Updated h-values

$u \leftarrow s$	;; Start in start state
while $(u \notin T)$	;; While goal not achieved
$\quad a \leftarrow \arg\min_{a \in A(u)}\{w(u,a) + h(Succ(u,a))\}$	;; Select action
$\quad h(u) \leftarrow \max\{h(u), w(u,a) + h(Succ(u,a))\}$	;; Update h-value
$\quad u \leftarrow a(u)$	;; Execute action

Algorithm 11.3

LRTA* with lookahead one.

---

nondecreasing. Since the h-values remain admissible and larger admissible h-values tend to guide the search better than smaller admissible h-values, there is no reason to decrease them. If the h-values are consistent then both value-update steps are equivalent. Thus, LRTA* approximates Bellman's optimal condition for minimal-cost paths in a way similar to Dijkstra's algorithm. However, the h-values of LRTA* with admissible initial h-values approach the goal distances from below and are monotonically nondecreasing, while the corresponding values of Dijkstra's algorithm approach the goal distances from above and are monotonically nonincreasing.

LRTA* with lookahead one and LRTA* with minimal local search spaces behave identically in state spaces where the execution of all actions in nongoal states necessarily results in a state change, that is, it cannot leave the current state unchanged. In general, actions that are not guaranteed to result in a state change can safely be deleted from state spaces because there always exists a path that does not include them (such as the minimal-cost path), if there exists a path at all. LRTA* with arbitrary local search spaces, including minimal and maximal local search spaces, never executes actions whose execution can leave the current state unchanged but LRTA* with lookahead one can execute them. To make them identical, one can change the action-selection step of LRTA* with lookahead one to "$a \leftarrow \arg\min_{a \in A(u)|Succ(u,a) \neq u}\{w(u,a) + h(Succ(u,a))\}$. However, this is seldom done in the literature.

In the following, we refer to LRTA* as shown in Algorithm 11.1 and not to LRTA* with lookahead one as shown in Algorithm 11.3 when we analyze the execution cost of LRTA*.

11.3 ANALYSIS OF THE EXECUTION COST OF LRTA*

A disadvantage of LRTA* is that it cannot solve all search tasks. This is so because it interleaves searches and action executions. All search methods can solve only search tasks for which the goal distance of the start state is finite. Interleaving searches and action executions limits the solvable search tasks because actions are executed before their complete consequences are known. Thus, even if the goal distance of the start state is finite, it is possible that LRTA* accidentally executes actions that lead to a state with infinite goal distance, such as actions that "blow up the world," at which point the search task becomes unsolvable for the agent. However, LRTA* is guaranteed to solve all search tasks in safely explorable state spaces. State spaces are *safely explorable* if and only if the goal distances of all states are finite; that is, the depth is finite. (For safely explorable state spaces where all action costs are one, it holds that $d \leq n - 1$.) To be precise: First, all states of the state space that cannot possibly be reached from the start state, or can be reached from the start state only by passing through a goal state, can be deleted. The goal distances of all remaining states have to be finite. Safely explorable state spaces guarantee that LRTA* is able to reach a goal state no matter which actions it has executed in the past. Strongly connected state spaces (where every state can be reached from every other state), for example, are safely explorable. In state spaces that are not safely explorable, LRTA* either stops in a goal state or reaches a state with goal distance infinity and then executes actions forever. We could modify LRTA* to use information from its local search spaces to detect that it can no longer reach a goal state (e.g., because the h-values have increased substantially) but this is complicated and seldom done in the literature. In the following, we assume that the state spaces are safely explorable.

LRTA* always reaches a goal state with a finite execution cost in all safely explorable state spaces, as can be shown by contradiction (the *cycle argument*). If LRTA* did not reach a goal state eventually, then it would cycle forever. Since the state space is safely explorable, there must be some way out of the cycle. We show that LRTA* eventually executes an action that takes it out of the cycle, which is a contradiction: If LRTA* did not reach a goal state eventually, it would execute actions forever. In this case, there is a time t after which LRTA* visits only those states again that it visits infinitely often; it cycles in part of the state space. The h-values of the states in the cycle increase beyond any bound, since LRTA* repeatedly increases the h-value of the state with the minimal h-value in the cycle by at least the minimal action cost w_{min} of any action. It gets into a state u with the minimal h-value in the cycle and all of its successor states then have h-values that are no smaller than its own h-value. Let h denote the h-values before the value-update step and h' denote the h-values after the value-update step. According to Lemma 11.1, the h-value of state u is then set to $h'(u) = \max\{h(u), \min_{a \in A(u)}\{w(u,a) + h'(Succ(u,a))\}\} \geq \min_{a \in A(u)}\{w(u,a) + h'(Succ(u,a))\} \geq \min_{a \in A(u)}\{w(u,a) + h(Succ(u,a))\} \geq \min_{a \in A(u)}\{w_{min} + h(u)\} = w_{min} + h(u)$. In particular, the h-values of the states in the cycle rise by arbitrarily large amounts above the h-values of all states that border the cycle. Such states exist since a goal state can be reached from every state in safely explorable state spaces. Then, however, LRTA* is forced to visit such a state after time t and leave the cycle, which is a contradiction.

The performance of LRTA* is measured by its execution cost until it reaches a goal state. The *complexity* of LRTA* is its worst-case execution cost over all possible topologies of state spaces of the same sizes, all possible start and goal states, and all tie-breaking rules among indistinguishable actions. We are interested in determining how the complexity scales as the state spaces get larger. We measure the sizes of state spaces as nonnegative integers and use measures x, such as $x = nd$, the product of the number of states and the depth. An *upper complexity bound* $O(x)$ has to hold for every x that is larger than some constant. Since we are mostly interested in the general trend (but not outliers) for the lower complexity bound, a *lower complexity bound* $\Omega(x)$ has to hold only for infinitely many different x. Furthermore, we vary only x. If x is a product, we do not vary both of its factors independently. This is sufficient for our purposes. A *tight complexity bound* $\Theta(x)$ *means both* $O(x)$ *and* $\Omega(x)$. To be able to express the complexity in terms of the number of states only, we often make the assumption that the state spaces are reasonable. *Reasonable state spaces* are safely explorable state spaces with $e \leq n^2$ (or, more generally, state spaces of which the number of actions does not grow faster than the number of states squared). For example, safely explorable state spaces where the execution of different actions in the same state results in different successor states are reasonable. For reasonable state spaces where all action costs are one, it holds that $d \leq n - 1$ and $e \leq n^2$. We also study Eulerian state spaces. A *Eulerian state space* is a state space where there are as many actions that leave a state as there are actions that enter it. For example, undirected state spaces are Eulerian. An *undirected state space* is a state space where every action in a state u of which the execution results in a particular successor state v has a unique corresponding action in state v of which the execution results in state u.

11.3.1 Upper Bound on the Execution Cost of LRTA*

In this section, we provide an upper bound on the complexity of LRTA* without repeat-until loop. Our analysis is centered around the invariant from Lemma 11.3. The time superscript t refers to the values of the variables immediately before the $(t+1)$st value-update step of LRTA*. For instance, u^0 denotes the start state s and a^{t+1} the action executed directly after the $(t+1)$st value-update step. Similarly, $h^t(u)$ denotes the h-values before the $(t+1)$st value-update step and $h^{t+1}(u)$ denotes the h-values after the $(t+1)$st value-update step. In the following, we prove an upper bound on the execution cost after which LRTA* is guaranteed to reach a goal state in safely explorable state spaces.

Lemma 11.3. *For all times $t = 0, 1, 2, \ldots$ (until termination) it holds that the execution cost of LRTA* with admissible initial h-values h^0 at time t is at most $\sum_{u \in S} \left[h^t(u) - h^0(u) \right] - (h^t(u^t) - h^0(u^0))$. (Sums have a higher precedence than other operators. For example, $\sum_i x + y = \sum_i [x] + y \neq \sum_i [x+y]$.)*

Proof by induction: The h-values are admissible at time t according to Lemma 11.2. Thus, they are bounded from above by the goal distances, which are finite since the state space is safely explorable. For $t = 0$, the execution cost and its upper bound are both zero, and the lemma thus holds. Now assume that the theorem holds at time t. The execution cost increases by $w(u^t, a^{t+1})$ and the upper bound increases by

$$\sum_{u \in S \setminus \{u^{t+1}\}} h^{t+1}(u) - \sum_{s \in S \setminus \{u^t\}} h^t(u)$$

$$= \sum_{u \in S \setminus \{u^t, u^{t+1}\}} [h^{t+1}(u) - h^t(u)] + h^{t+1}(u^t) - h^t(u^{t+1})$$

$$\overset{11.1}{=} \sum_{u \in S \setminus \{u^t, u^{t+1}\}} [h^{t+1}(u) - h^t(u)] + \max\{h^t(u^t), \min_{a \in A(u^t)} \{w(u^t, a) + h^{t+1}(Succ(u^t, a))\}\} - h^t(u^{t+1})$$

$$\geq \sum_{u \in S \setminus \{u^t, u^{t+1}\}} [h^{t+1}(u) - h^t(u)] + \min_{a \in A(u^t)} \{w(u^t, a) + h^{t+1}(Succ(u^t, a))\} - h^t(u^{t+1})$$

$$\geq \sum_{u \in S \setminus \{u^t, u^{t+1}\}} [h^{t+1}(u) - h^t(u)] + w(u^t, a^{t+1}) + h^{t+1}(u^{t+1}) - h^t(u^{t+1})$$

$$= \sum_{u \in S \setminus \{u^t\}} [h^{t+1}(u) - h^t(u)] + w(u^t, a^{t+1})$$

$$\overset{11.2}{\geq} w(u^t, a^{t+1}),$$

and the lemma thus continues to hold. ∎

Theorem 11.1 uses Lemma 11.3 to derive an upper bound on the execution cost.

Theorem 11.1. *(Completeness of LRTA*) LRTA* with admissible initial h-values h^0 reaches a goal state with an execution cost of at most $h^0(s) + \sum_{u \in S} [\delta(u, T) - h^0(u)]$.*

Proof. According to Lemma 11.3, the execution cost is at most

$$\sum_{u \in S}[h^t(u) - h^0(u)] - (h^t(u^t) - h^0(u^0)) \overset{11.2}{\leq} \sum_{u \in S}[\delta(u, T) - h^0(u)] + h^0(u^0)$$

$$= h^0(s) + \sum_{u \in S}[\delta(u, T) - h^0(u)]. \qquad \blacksquare$$

Since the goal distances are finite in safely explorable state spaces and the minimal action cost w_{min} of any action is strictly positive, Theorem 11.1 shows that LRTA* with admissible initial h-values reaches a goal state after a bounded number of action executions in safely explorable state spaces; that is, it is complete. More precisely: LRTA* reaches a goal state with an execution cost of at most $\sum_{u \in S}\delta(u, T)$, and thus after at most $\sum_{u \in S}\delta(u, T)/w_{min}$ action executions. Thus, it reaches a goal state with finite execution cost in safely explorable state spaces. One consequence of this result is that search tasks in state spaces where all states are clustered around the goal states are easier to solve with LRTA* than search tasks in state spaces that do not possess this property. Consider, for example, sliding-tile puzzles, which are sometimes considered to be hard search tasks because they have a small goal density. The EIGHT-PUZZLE has 181,440 states but only one goal state. However, the average goal distance of the EIGHT-PUZZLE (with the goal configuration where the tiles form a ring around the center) is only 21.5 and its maximal goal distance is only 30. This implies that LRTA* never moves far away from the goal state even if it makes a mistake and executes an action that does not decrease the goal distance. This makes the EIGHT-PUZZLE easy to search with LRTA* relative to other state spaces with the same number of states.

11.3.2 Lower Bound on the Execution Cost of LRTA*

LRTA* reaches a goal state with an execution cost of at most $\sum_{u \in S}\delta(u, T)$, and it holds that $\sum_{u \in S}\delta(u, T) \leq \sum_{i=0}^{n-1} i = n^2/2 - n/2$ in safely explorable state spaces where all action costs are one. Now assume that LRTA* with minimal local search spaces is zero-initialized, which implies that it is uninformed. In the following, we show that the upper complexity bound is then tight for infinitely many n. Figure 11.5 shows an example for which the execution cost of zero-initialized LRTA* with minimal local search spaces is $n^2/2 - n/2$ in the worst case until it reaches a goal state. The upper part of the figure shows the state space. All action costs are one. The states are annotated with their goal distances, their initial h-values, and their names. The lower part of the figure shows the behavior of LRTA*. On the right, the figure shows the state space with the h-values after the value-update step but before the action-execution step. The current state is shown in bold. On the left, the figure shows the searches that resulted in the h-values shown on the right. Again, the states are annotated with their h-values after the value-update step but before the action-execution step. The current state is on top. Ellipses show the local search spaces, and dashed lines show the actions that LRTA* is about to execute. For the example search task, after LRTA* has visited a state for the first time, it has to move through all previously visited states again before it is able to visit another state for the first time. Thus, the execution cost is quadratic in the number of states. If LRTA* breaks ties in favor of successor states with smaller indices, then its execution cost $f(n)$ until it reaches the goal state satisfies the recursive equations $f(1) = 0$ and $f(n) = f(n-1) + n - 1$. Thus, its execution cost is $f(n) = n^2/2 - n/2$ (for $n \geq 1$). The execution cost equals exactly the sum of the goal distances because LRTA* was

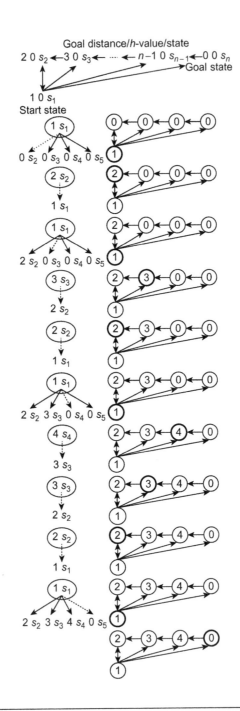

FIGURE 11.5

LRTA* in a state space with worst-case execution cost, by Koenig (2001).

zero-initialized and its final h-values are equal to the goal distances. For example, $n^2/2 - n/2 = 10$ for $n = 5$. In this case, LRTA* follows the path $s_1, s_2, s_1, s_3, s_2, s_1, s_4, s_3, s_2, s_1$, and s_5.

Overall, the previous section showed that the complexity of zero-initialized LRTA* with minimal local search spaces is $O(nd)$ over all state spaces where all actions costs are one, and the example in this section shows that it is $\Omega(nd)$. Thus, the complexity is $\Theta(nd)$ over all state spaces where all actions costs are one and $\Theta(n^2)$ over all safely explorable state spaces where all actions costs are one (see Exercises).

11.4 FEATURES OF LRTA*

In this section, we explain the three key features of LRTA*.

11.4.1 Heuristic Knowledge

LRTA* uses heuristic knowledge to guide its search. The larger its initial h-values, the smaller the upper bound on its execution cost provided by Theorem 11.1. For example, LRTA* is fully informed if and only if its initial h-values equal the goal distances of the states. In this case, Theorem 11.1 predicts that the execution cost is at most $h^0(s) = \delta(s, T)$ until LRTA* reaches a goal state. Thus, its execution cost is worst-case optimal and no other search method can do better in the worst case. In general, the execution cost is the smaller the more informed the initial h-values are although this correlation is not guaranteed to be perfect.

11.4.2 Fine-Grained Control

LRTA* allows for fine-grained control over how much search to perform between action executions by varying the sizes of its local search spaces. For example, LRTA* with repeat-until loop and maximal or, more generally, sufficiently large local search spaces performs a complete search without interleaving searches and action executions, which is slow but produces minimal-cost paths and thus minimizes the execution cost. On the other hand, LRTA* with minimal local search spaces performs almost no searches between action executions. There are several advantages to this fine-grained control.

In the presence of time constraints, LRTA* can be used as an anytime contract algorithm for determining which action to execute next, which allows it to adjust the amount of search performed between action executions to the search and execution speeds of robots or the time a player is willing to wait for a game-playing program to make a move. *Anytime contract algorithms* are search methods that can solve search tasks for any given bound on their search cost, so that their solution quality tends to increase with the available search cost.

The amount of search between action executions does not only influence the search cost but also the execution cost and thus also the sum of the search and execution cost. Typically, reducing the amount of search between action executions reduces the (overall) search cost but increases the execution cost (because LRTA* selects actions based on less information), although theoretically the search cost could also increase if the execution cost increases sufficiently (because LRTA* performs more searches). The amount of search between action executions that minimizes the sum of the search and execution cost depends on the search and execution speeds of the agent.

Fast-acting agents: A smaller amount of search between action executions tends to benefit agents of which the execution speed is sufficiently fast compared to their search speed since the resulting increase in execution cost is small compared to the resulting decrease in search cost, especially if heuristic knowledge focuses the search sufficiently well. For example, the sum of the search and execution cost approaches the search cost as the execution speed increases, and the search cost can often be reduced by reducing the amount of search between action executions. When LRTA* is used to solve search tasks offline, it only moves a marker within the computer (that represents the state of a fictitious agent), and thus action execution is fast. Small local search spaces are therefore optimal for solving sliding-tile puzzles with the Manhattan distance.

Slow-acting agents: A larger amount of search between action executions is needed for agents of which the search speed is sufficiently fast compared to their execution speed. For example, the sum of the search and execution cost approaches the execution cost as the search speed increases, and the execution cost can often be reduced by increasing the amount of search between action executions. Most robots are examples of slow-acting agents.

We will discuss later in this chapter that larger local search spaces sometimes allow agents to avoid executing actions from which they cannot recover in state spaces that are not safely explorable. On the other hand, larger local search spaces might not be practical in state spaces that are not known in advance and need to get learned during execution since there can be an advantage to restricting the search to the known part of the state space.

11.4.3 Improvement of Execution Cost

If the initial h-values are not completely informed and the local search spaces are small, then it is unlikely that the execution cost of LRTA* is minimal. In Figure 11.1, for example, the robot could reach the goal cell in seven action executions. However, LRTA* improves its execution cost, although not necessarily monotonically, as it solves search tasks with the same set of goal states (even with different start states) in the same state spaces until its execution cost is minimal; that is, until it has converged. Thus, LRTA* can always have a small sum of search and execution cost and still minimize the execution cost in the long run in case similar search tasks unexpectedly repeat, which is the reason for the "learning" in its name. Assume that LRTA* solves a series of search tasks in the same state space with the same set of goal states. The start states need not be identical. If the initial h-values of LRTA* are admissible for the first search task, then they are also admissible for the first search task after LRTA* has solved the search task and are statewise at least as informed as initially. Thus, they are also admissible for the second search task and LRTA* can continue to use the same h-values across search tasks. The start states of the search tasks can differ since the admissibility of h-values does not depend on them. This way, LRTA* can transfer acquired knowledge from one search task to the next one, thereby making its h-values more informed. Ultimately, more informed h-values result in an improved execution cost, although the improvement is not necessarily monotonic. (This also explains why LRTA* can be interrupted at any state and resume execution at a different state.) The following theorems formalize this knowledge transfer in the mistake-bounded error model. The *mistake-bounded error model* is one way of analyzing learning methods by bounding the number of mistakes that they make. Here, it counts as one mistake when LRTA* reaches a goal state with an execution cost that is larger than the goal distance of the start state and thus does not follow a minimal-cost path from the start state to a goal state.

Theorem 11.2. *(Convergence of LRTA*) Assume that LRTA* maintains h-values across a series of search tasks in the same safely explorable state space with the same set of goal states. Then, the number of search tasks for which LRTA* with admissible initial h-values reaches a goal state with an execution cost of more than $\delta(s,T)$ (where s is the start state of the current search task) is bounded from above.*

Proof. It is easy to see that the agent follows a minimal-cost path from the start state to a goal state if it follows a path from the start state to a goal state where the h-value of every state is equal to its goal distance. If the agent does not follow such a path, then it transitions at least once from a state u of which the h-value is not equal to its goal distance to a state v of which the h-value is equal to its goal distance, since it reaches a goal state and the h-value of the goal state is zero since the h-values remain admissible according to Lemma 11.2. Let a denote the action of which the execution in state u results in state v. Let h denote the h-values before the value-update step and h' denote the h-values after the value-update step. According to Lemma 11.1, the h-value of state u is set to $h'(u) = \max\{h(u), \min_{a \in A(u)}\{w(u,a) + h'(Succ(u,a))\}\} \geq \min_{a \in A(u)}\{w(u,a) + h'(Succ(u,a))\} = w(u,a) + h'(Succ(u,a)) \geq w(u,a) + h(Succ(u,a)) = w(u,a) + \delta(Succ(u,a),T) \geq \delta(u,T)$. Thus, $h'(u) = \delta(u,T)$ since the h-values cannot become inadmissible according to Lemma 11.2. After the h-value of state u is set to its goal distance, the h-value can no longer change since it could only increase according to Lemma 11.2 but would then make the h-values inadmissible, which is impossible according to the same lemma. Since the number of states is finite, it can happen only a bounded number of times that the h-value of a state is set to its goal distance. Thus, the number of times that the agent does not follow a minimal-cost path from the start state to a goal state is bounded. ∎

Assume that LRTA* solves the same search task repeatedly from the same start state, and that the action-selection step always breaks ties among the actions in the current state according to a fixed ordering of the actions. Then, the h-values no longer change after a finite number of searches, and LRTA* follows the same minimal-cost path from the start state to a goal state during all future searches. (If LRTA* breaks ties randomly, then it eventually discovers all minimal-cost paths from the start state to the goal states.) Figure 11.1 (all columns) illustrates this aspect of LRTA*. In the example, LRTA* with minimal local search spaces breaks ties among successor cells in the following order: north, east, south, and west. Eventually, the robot always follows a minimal-cost path to the goal cell. Figure 11.6 visualizes the h-value surface formed by the final h-values. The robot now reaches the goal cell on a

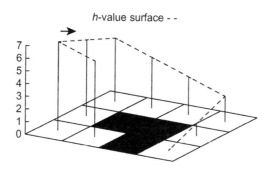

FIGURE 11.6

h-value surface after convergence, by Koenig (2001).

minimal-cost path if it always moves to the successor cell with the minimal h-value (and breaks ties in the given order) and thus performs steepest descent on the final h-value surface.

11.5 VARIANTS OF LRTA*

We now discuss several variants of LRTA*.

11.5.1 Variants with Local Search Spaces of Varying Sizes

LRTA* with small local search spaces executes a large number of actions to escape from depressions (that is, valleys) in the h-value surface (see Exercises). It can avoid this by varying the sizes of its local search spaces during a search, namely by increasing the sizes of its local search spaces in depressions. For example, LRTA* can use minimal local search spaces until it reaches the bottom of a depression. It can detect this situation because then the h-value of its current state is smaller than the costs-to-go of all actions that can be executed in it (before it executes the value-update step). In this case, it determines the local search space that contains all states that are part of the depression by starting with its current state and then repeatedly adding successor states of states in the local search space to the local search space so that, once a successor state is added, the h-value of each state in the local search space is less than the cost-to-go of all actions that can be executed in it and result in successor states outside of the local search space. The local search space is complete when no more states can be added. In Figure 11.1 (left), for example, LRTA* picks the minimal local search space that contains only state C1 when it is in state C1. It notices that it has reached the bottom of a depression and picks a local search space that consists of the states B1, C1, and C2 when it is in state C2. Its value-update step then sets the h-values of B1, C1, and C2 to 6, 7, and 8, respectively, which completely eliminates the depression.

11.5.2 Variants with Minimal Lookahead

LRTA* needs to predict the successor states of actions (i.e., the successor states resulting from their execution). We can decrease its lookahead further if we associate the values with state-action pairs rather than states. Algorithm 11.4 shows pseudo code for *Min-LRTA**, which associates a q-value $q(u,a)$ with each action $a \in A(u)$ that can be executed in state $u \in S$. The q-values are similar to

---

Procedure Min-LRTA*
Input: Search task with initial q-values
Side Effect: Updated q-values

$u \leftarrow s$;; Start in start state
while $(u \notin T)$;; While goal not achieved
    $a \leftarrow \arg\min_{a \in A(u)} q(u,a)$;; Select action
    $q(u,a) \leftarrow \max\{q(u,a), w(u,a) + \min_{a' \in A(Succ(u,a))} q(Succ(u,a),a')\}$;; Update q-value
    $u \leftarrow a(u)$;; Execute action

Algorithm 11.4

Min-LRTA*.

the signs used by SLRTA* and the state-action values of reinforcement-learning methods, such a Q-Learning, and correspond to the costs-to-go of the actions. The q-values are updated as the search progresses, both to focus the search and avoid cycling. Min-LRTA* has minimal lookahead (essentially lookahead zero) because it uses only the q-values local to the current state to determine which action to execute. Thus, it does not even project one action execution ahead. This means that it does not need to learn an action model of the state space, which makes it applicable to situations where the action model is not known in advance, and thus the agent cannot predict the successor states of actions before it has executed them at least once. The action-selection step of Min-LRTA* always greedily chooses an action with the minimal q-value in the current state. The value-update step of Min-LRTA* replaces $q(u,a)$ with a more accurate lookahead value. This can be explained as follows: The q-value $q(v,a')$ of any state-action pair is the cost-to-go of action a' in state v and thus a lower bound on the goal distance if one starts in state v, executes action a', and then behaves optimally. Thus, $\min_{a' \in A(v)} q(v,a')$ is a lower bound on the goal distance of state v, and $w(u,a) + \min_{a' \in A(Succ(u,a))} q(Succ(u,a),a')$ is a lower bound on the goal distance if one starts in state u, executes action a, and then behaves optimally. Min-LRTA* always reaches a goal state with a finite execution cost in all safely explorable state spaces, as can be shown with a cycle argument in a way similar to the proof of the same property of LRTA*.

Theorem 11.3. (*Execution Cost of Real-Time Search with Minimal Lookahead*) *The complexity of every real-time search method that cannot predict the successor states of actions before it has executed them at least once is* $\Omega(ed)$ *over all state spaces where all action costs are one. Furthermore, the complexity is* $\Omega(n^3)$ *over all reasonable state spaces where all action costs are one.*

Proof. Figure 11.7 shows a *complex state space*, which is a reasonable state space in which all states (but the start state) have several actions that lead back toward the start state. All action costs are one. Every real-time search method that cannot predict the successor states of actions before it has executed them at least once has to execute $\Omega(ed)$ or, alternatively, $\Omega(n^3)$ actions in the worst case to reach a goal state in complex state spaces. It has to execute each of the $\Theta(n^2)$ actions in nongoal states that lead away from the goal state at least once in the worst case. Over all of these cases, it has to execute $\Omega(n)$ actions on average to recover from the action, for a total of $\Omega(n^3)$ actions. In particular, it can execute at least $n^3/6 - n/6$ actions before it reaches the goal state (for $n \geq 1$). Thus, the complexity is $\Omega(ed)$ and $\Omega(n^3)$ since $e = n^2/2 + n/2 - 1$ (for $n \geq 1$) and $d = n - 1$ (for $n \geq 1$). ∎

Theorem 11.3 provides lower bounds on the number of actions that zero-initialized Min-LRTA* executes. It turns out that these lower bounds are tight for zero-initialized Min-LRTA* over all state

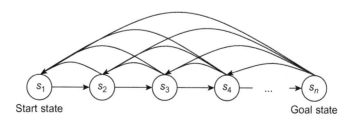

FIGURE 11.7

Complex state space, by Koenig and Simmons (1993).

spaces where all action costs are one and remain tight over all undirected state spaces and Eulerian state spaces where all action costs are one (see Exercises).

11.5.3 Variants with Faster Value Updates

Real-time adaptive A* (RTAA*) is a real-time search method that is similar to LRTA* but its value-update step is much faster. Assume that we have to perform several (forward) A* searches with consistent h-values in the same state space and with the same set of goal states but possibly different start states. Assume that v is a state that was expanded during such an A* search. The distance from the start state s to any goal state via state v is equal to the distance from the start state s to state v plus the goal distance $\delta(v,T)$ of state v. It clearly cannot be smaller than the goal distance $\delta(s,T)$ of the start state s. Thus, the goal distance $\delta(v,T)$ of state v is no smaller than the goal distance $\delta(s,T)$ of the start state s (i.e., the f-value $f(\bar{u})$ of the goal state $\bar{u}$ that was about to be expanded when the A* search terminates) minus the distance from the start state s to state v (i.e., the g-value $g(v)$ of state v when the A* search terminates):

$$g(v) + \delta(v,T) \geq \delta(s,T)$$
$$\delta(v,T) \geq \delta(s,T) - g(v)$$
$$\delta(v,T) \geq f(\bar{u}) - g(v).$$

Consequently, $f(\bar{u}) - g(v)$ provides a nonoverestimating estimate of the goal distance $\delta(v,T)$ of state v and can be calculated quickly. More informed consistent h-values can be obtained by calculating and assigning this difference to every state that was expanded during the A* search and thus is in the closed list when the A* search terminates. We now use this idea to develop RTAA*, which reduces to the case above if its local search spaces are maximal.

Algorithm 11.5 shows pseudo code for RTAA*, which follows the pseudo code of LRTA*. The h-values of RTAA* approximate the goal distances of the states. They can be initialized using a consistent heuristic function. We mentioned earlier that LRTA* could use (forward) A* searches to determine the local search spaces. RTAA* does exactly that. The (forward) A* search in the pseudo code is a regular A* search that uses the current h-values to search from the current state of the agent toward the goal states until a goal state is about to be expanded or *lookahead* > 0 states have been expanded. After the A* search, we require $\bar{u}$ to be the state that was about to be expanded when the A* search terminated. We denote this state consistently with $\bar{u}$. We require that $\bar{u} = false$ if the A* search terminated due to an empty open list, in which case it is impossible to reach a goal state with finite execution cost from the current state and RTAA* thus returns failure. Otherwise, $\bar{u}$ is either a goal state or the state that the A* search would have been expanded as the (*lookahead* $+ 1$)st state. We require the closed list *Closed* to contain the states expanded during the A* search and the g-value $g(v)$ to be defined for all generated states v, including all expanded states. We define the f-values $f(v) = g(v) + h(v)$ for these states v. The expanded states v form the local search space, and RTAA* updates their h-values by setting $h(v) = f(\bar{u}) - g(v) = g(\bar{u}) + h(\bar{u}) - g(v)$. The h-values of the other states remain unchanged. We give an example of the operation of RTAA* in Section 11.6.2. For example, consider Figure 11.16. The states in the closed list are shown in gray, and the arrows point to the states $\bar{u}$.

RTAA* always reaches a goal state with a finite execution cost in all safely explorable state spaces no matter how it chooses its values of *lookahead* and whether it uses the repeat-until loop or not, as can

---

Procedure RTAA*
Input: Search task with initial *h*-values
Side Effect: Updated *h*-values

$u \leftarrow s$;; Start in start state
while $(u \notin T)$;; While goal not achieved
   $(\bar{u}, Closed) \leftarrow A^*(u, lookahead)$;; A* search until *lookahead* states have been expanded
   if $(\bar{u} = false)$ **return** *false*   ;; Return if goal unachievable
   for each $v \in Closed$;; For each expanded state
     $h(v) \leftarrow g(\bar{u}) + h(\bar{u}) - g(v)$;; Update *h*-value
   repeat   ;; Repeat
     $a \leftarrow SelectAction(A(u))$;; Select action on minimal-cost path from u to $\bar{u}$
     $u \leftarrow a(u)$;; Execute action
   until $(u \notin Closed)$;; Until local search space exited (optional)

Algorithm 11.5

RTAA*.

---

be shown with a cycle argument in a way similar to the proof of the same property of LRTA*. We now prove several additional properties of RTAA* without repeat-until loop. We make use of the following known properties of A* searches with consistent *h*-values. First, they expand every state at most once. Second, the *g*-values of every expanded state v and state $\bar{u}$ are equal to the distance from the start state to state v and state $\bar{u}$, respectively, when the A* search terminates. Thus, we know minimal-cost paths from the start state to all expanded states and state $\bar{u}$. Third, the *f*-values of the series of expanded states over time are monotonically nondecreasing. Thus, $f(v) \leq f(\bar{u})$ for all expanded states v and $f(\bar{u}) \leq f(v)$ for all generated states v that remained unexpanded when the A* search terminates.

Lemma 11.4. *Consistent initial h-values remain consistent after every value-update step of RTAA* and are monotonically nondecreasing.*

Proof. We first show that the *h*-values are monotonically nondecreasing. Assume that the *h*-value of a state v is updated. Then, state v was expanded and it thus holds that $f(v) \leq f(\bar{u})$. Consequently, $h(v) = f(v) - g(v) \leq f(\bar{u}) - g(v) = g(\bar{u}) + h(\bar{u}) - g(v)$ and the value-update step cannot decrease the *h*-value of state v since it changes the *h*-value from $h(v)$ to $g(\bar{u}) + h(\bar{u}) - g(v)$. We now show that the *h*-values remain consistent by induction on the number of A* searches. The initial *h*-values are provided by the user and consistent. It thus holds that $h(v) = 0$ for all goal states v. This continues to hold since goal states are not expanded and their *h*-values thus not updated. (Even if RTAA* updated the *h*-value of state $\bar{u}$, it would leave the *h*-value of that state unchanged since $f(\bar{u}) - g(\bar{u}) = g(\bar{u}) + h(\bar{u}) - g(\bar{u}) = h(\bar{u})$. Thus, the *h*-values of the goal states would remain zero even in that case.) It also holds that $h(v) \leq w(v, a) + h(Succ(v, a))$ for all nongoal states v and actions a that can be executed in them, since the *h*-values are consistent. Let h denote the *h*-values before the value-update step and h' denote the *h*-values after the value-update step. We distinguish three cases for all nongoal states v and actions a that can be executed in them:

- First, both state v and state $Succ(v, a)$ were expanded, which implies that $h'(v) = g(\bar{u}) + h(\bar{u}) - g(v)$ and $h'(Succ(v, a)) = g(\bar{u}) + h(\bar{u}) - g(Succ(v, a))$. Also, $g(Succ(v, a)) \leq g(v) + w(v, a)$

since the A* search discovers a path from the current state via state v to state $Succ(v,a)$ of execution cost $g(v) + w(v,a)$. Thus, $h'(v) = g(\bar{u}) + h(\bar{u}) - g(v) \le g(\bar{u}) + h(\bar{u}) - g(Succ(v,a)) + w(v,a) = w(v,a) + h'(Succ(v,a))$.

- Second, state v was expanded but state $Succ(v,a)$ was not, which implies that $h'(v) = g(\bar{u}) + h(\bar{u}) - g(v)$ and $h'(Succ(v,a)) = h(Succ(v,a))$. Also, $g(Succ(v,a)) \le g(v) + w(v,a)$ for the same reason as in the first case, and $f(\bar{u}) \le f(Succ(v,a))$ since state $Succ(v,a)$ was generated but not expanded. Thus, $h'(v) = g(\bar{u}) + h(\bar{u}) - g(v) = f(\bar{u}) - g(v) \le f(Succ(v,a)) - g(v) = g(Succ(v,a)) + h(Succ(v,a)) - g(v) = g(Succ(v,a)) + h'(Succ(v,a)) - g(v) \le g(Succ(v,a)) + h'(Succ(v,a)) - g(Succ(v,a)) + w(v,a) = w(v,a) + h'(Succ(v,a))$.
- Third, state v was not expanded, which implies that $h'(v) = h(v)$. Also, $h(Succ(v,a)) \le h'(Succ(v,a))$ since the h-values of the same state are monotonically nondecreasing over time. Thus, $h'(v) = h(v) \le w(v,a) + h(Succ(v,a)) \le w(v,a) + h'(Succ(v,a))$.

Thus, $h'(v) \le w(v,a) + h'(Succ(v,a))$ in all three cases and the h-values thus remain consistent. ∎

Theorem 11.4. *(Convergence of RTAA*) Assume that RTAA* maintains h-values across a series of search tasks in the same safely explorable state space with the same set of goal states. Then, the number of search tasks for which RTAA* with consistent initial h-values reaches a goal state with an execution cost of more than $\delta(s,T)$ (where s is the start state of the current search task) is bounded from above.*

Proof. The proof is identical to the proof of Theorem 11.2, except for the part where we prove that the h-value of state v is set to its goal distance if the agent transitions from a state v of which the h-value is not equal to its goal distance to a state w of which the h-value is equal to its goal distance. When the agent executes some action $a \in A(v)$ in state v and transitions to state w, then state v is a parent of state w in the search tree produced during the last call of A* and it thus holds that (1) state v was expanded during the last call of A*, (2) either state w was also expanded during the last call of A* or $w = \bar{u}$, and (3) $g(w) = g(v) + w(v,a)$. Let h denote the h-values before the value-update step and h' denote the h-values after the value-update step. Then, $h'(v) = f(\bar{u}) - g(v)$ and $h'(w) = f(\bar{u}) - g(w) = \delta(w,T)$. The last equality holds because we assumed that the h-value of state w was equal to its goal distance and thus can no longer change since it could only increase according to Lemma 11.4 but would then make the h-values inadmissible and thus inconsistent, which is impossible according to the same lemma. Consequently, $h'(v) = f(\bar{u}) - g(v) = \delta(w,T) + g(w) - g(v) = \delta(w,T) + w(v,a) \ge \delta(v,T)$, proving that $h'(v) = \delta(v,T)$ since a larger h-value would make the h-values inadmissible and thus inconsistent, which is impossible according to Lemma 11.4. Thus, the h-value of state v is indeed set to its goal distance. ∎

RTAA* and a variant of LRTA* that uses the same (forward) A* searches to determine the local search spaces differ only in how they update the h-values after the (forward) A* search. We now prove that LRTA* with minimal local search spaces and RTAA* with minimal local search spaces behave identically if they break ties in the same way. They can behave differently for larger local search spaces, and we give an informal argument why the h-values of LRTA* tend to be more informed than the ones of RTAA* with the same local search spaces. On the other hand, it takes LRTA* more time to update the h-values and it is more difficult to implement, for the following reason: LRTA* performs one search to determine the local search space and a second search (using the variant of Dijkstra's algorithm from Algorithm 11.2) to determine how to update the h-values of the states in the local search space since it is unable to use the results of the first search for this purpose. Thus, there is a trade-off between the search cost and the execution cost.

Theorem 11.5. *(Equivalence of RTAA* and LRTA*) RTAA* and LRTA* with consistent initial h-values and minimal local search spaces behave identically if they break ties in the same way.*

Proof. We show the property by induction on the number of A* searches of RTAA*. The h-values of both search methods are initialized using the same heuristic function and are thus identical before the first A* search of RTAA*. Now consider any A* search of RTAA* and let $\bar{u}$ be the state that was about to be expanded when the A* search terminated. Let h denote the h-values of RTAA* before the value-update step and h' denote the h-values after the value-update step. Similarly, let $\bar{h}$ denote the h-values of LRTA* before the value-update step and $\bar{h}'$ denote the h-values after the value-update step. Assume that RTAA* and LRTA* are in the same state, break ties in the same way, and $h(v) = \bar{h}(v)$ for all states v. We show that $h'(v) = \bar{h}'(v)$ for all states v. Both search methods expand only the current state u of the agent and thus update only the h-value of this one state. It holds that $h'(u) = g(\bar{u}) + h(\bar{u}) - g(u) = g(\bar{u}) + h(\bar{u})$ and $\bar{h}'(u) = \max\{\bar{h}(u), \min_{a \in A(u)}\{w(u,a) + \bar{h}'(Succ(u,a))\}\} = \min_{a \in A(u)}\{w(u,a) + \bar{h}'(Succ(u,a))\} = \min_{a \in A(u)|Succ(u,a) \neq u}\{w(u,a) + \bar{h}'(Succ(u,a))\} = \min_{a \in A(u)|Succ(u,a) \neq u}\{g(Succ(u,a)) + \bar{h}(Succ(u,a))\} = g(\bar{u}) + \bar{h}(\bar{u}) = g(\bar{u}) + h(\bar{u})$, since the h-values of LRTA* remain consistent and are monotonically nondecreasing according to Lemma 11.2, which implies that $\bar{h}(u) \leq \bar{h}(Succ(u,a)) \leq \bar{h}'(Succ(u,a))$ for all $a \in A(u)$. Thus, both search methods set the h-value of the current state to the same value and, if they break ties identically, then move to state $\bar{u}$. Consequently, they behave identically. ∎

We now give an informal argument why the h-values of LRTA* with larger local search spaces *tend* to be more informed than the ones of RTAA* with the same local search spaces (if both real-time search methods execute the same number of actions after every search). This is not a proof but gives some insight into the behavior of the two search methods. Let h denote the h-values of RTAA* before the value-update step and h' denote the h-values after the value-update step. Similarly, let $\bar{h}$ denote the h-values of LRTA* before the value-update step and $\bar{h}'$ denote the h-values after the value-update step. Assume that both search methods with consistent initial h-values are in the same state, break ties in the same way, and $h(v) = \bar{h}(v)$ for all states v. We now prove that $h'(v) \leq \bar{h}'(v)$ for all states v. The A* searches of both search methods are identical if they break ties in the same way. Thus, they expand the same states and thus also update the h-values of the same states. We now show that the h-values h' cannot be consistent if $h'(v) > \bar{h}'(v)$ for at least one state v, contradicting Lemma 11.4. Assume that $h'(v) > \bar{h}'(v)$ for at least one state v. Pick a state v with the minimal $\bar{h}'(v)$ for which $h'(v) > \bar{h}'(v)$ and pick an action a with $a = \arg\min_{a \in A(v)}\{w(v,a) + \bar{h}'(Succ(v,a)\}$. State v must be a nongoal state and have been expanded since $h(v) = \bar{h}(v)$ but $h'(v) > \bar{h}'(v)$. Then, it holds that $\bar{h}'(v) \geq w(v,a) + \bar{h}'(Succ(v,a))$ according to Lemma 11.1. Since $\bar{h}'(v) \geq w(v,a) + \bar{h}'(Succ(v,a)) > \bar{h}'(Succ(v,a))$ and state v is a state with the minimal $\bar{h}'(v)$ for which $h'(v) > \bar{h}'(v)$, it must be the case that $h'(Succ(v,a)) \leq \bar{h}'(Succ(v,a))$. Put together, it holds that $h'(v) > \bar{h}'(v) \geq w(v,a) + \bar{h}'(Succ(v,a)) \geq w(v,a) + h'(Succ(v,a))$. This means that the h-values h' are inconsistent but they remain consistent according to Lemma 11.4, which is a contradiction. Consequently, it holds that $h'(v) \leq \bar{h}'(v)$ for all states v. However, this proof does not imply that the h-values of LRTA* always (weakly) dominate the ones of RTAA* since the search methods can move the agent to different states and then update the h-values of different states, but it suggests that the h-values of LRTA* with larger local search spaces tend to be more informed than the ones of RTAA* with the same local search spaces and thus that LRTA* tends to have a smaller execution cost than RTAA* with the same local search spaces (if both real-time search methods execute the same number of actions after every search).

11.5.4 **Variants That Detect Convergence**

We can modify LRTA* with admissible initial h-values to keep track of which h-values are already equal to the corresponding goal distances. For example, LRTA* could mark states so that a state is marked if and only if LRTA* knows that its h-value is equal to its goal distance, similar to the idea behind the proof of Theorem 11.2. Assume that LRTA* with minimal local search spaces maintains h-values and markings across a series of search tasks in the same safely explorable state space with the same set of goal states. Initially, only the goal states are marked. If several actions tie in the action-selection step and the execution of at least one of them results in a marked state (or if the execution of the only action results in a marked state), then LRTA* selects such an action for execution and marks its current state as well. The resulting variant of LRTA* then has the following properties: When a state is marked, its h-value is equal to its goal distance and then can no longer change. Once LRTA* reaches a marked state, it follows a minimal-cost path from there to a goal state and all states on that path are marked. If the start state of LRTA* is marked, then it follows a minimal-cost path to a goal state. If the start state of LRTA* is not marked, then it has marked one additional state by the time it reaches a goal state (see Exercises).

11.5.5 **Variants That Speed Up Convergence**

The convergence of LRTA* can be accelerated in different ways. For example, we can increase the sizes of its local search spaces. But we have several options even for LRTA* with minimal local search spaces:

- We can use LRTA* in abstractions of the state spaces (where clusters of states form meta-states), which effectively increases the sizes of its local search spaces.
- We can use more informed (but still admissible) initial h-values.
- We can weigh the h-values more heavily by using $\lambda \cdot h(Succ(u,a))$ instead of $h(Succ(u,a))$ in the action-selection and value-update steps, for a constant $\lambda > 1$, similar to weighted A*, which is what ϵ-*LRTA** does (see Exercises).
- We can change LRTA* to backtrack to the previous state (if possible) rather than execute the action selected by the action-selection step if the value-update step increased the h-value of the current state, with the idea that the action-selection step in the previous state might then select a different action than previously, which is what *SLA** does. (LRTA* could also use a learning quota and only backtrack after the sum of the increases of the h-values of a number of states are larger than the learning quota, which is what *SLA*T* does.)

There is also some speculation that the convergence of LRTA* can be accelerated in undirected state spaces if its action-selection step breaks ties toward successor states with minimal f-values rather than randomly or toward successor states with maximal f-values. Breaking ties toward successor states with minimal f-values is inspired by A*, which efficiently determines a minimal-cost path by always expanding a leaf of the search tree with the minimal f-value. If the g-values and h-values are perfectly informed (i.e., the g-value of each state is equal to its start distance and its h-value is equal to its goal distance), then the states with minimal f-values are exactly those on minimal-cost paths from the start state to a goal state. Thus, if LRTA* breaks ties toward successor states with minimal f-values, it breaks ties toward a minimal-cost path. If the g-values and h-values are not perfectly informed (the more common case), then LRTA* breaks ties toward what currently looks like a minimal-cost path.

To implement this tie-breaking criterion, LRTA* needs to maintain g-values. It can update the g-values in a way similar to how it updates the h-values, except that it uses the predecessor states instead of the successor states. Algorithm 11.6 shows pseudo code for the resulting variant of LRTA* with lookahead one: It executes actions with minimal cost-to-go and breaks ties toward actions of which the execution results in successor states with smaller f-values. *FAst Learning and CONverging Search (FALCONS)* implements this principle more consequently: It minimizes the f-value of the successor state and breaks ties toward actions with smaller costs-to-go. To understand why it breaks ties this way, consider g-values and h-values that are perfectly informed. In this case, all states on a minimal-cost path have the same (minimal) f-values and breaking ties toward actions with smaller costs-to-go ensures that FALCONS moves toward a goal state. Thus, while LRTA* focuses its h-value updates on what it believes to be a minimal-cost path from its current state to a goal state, FALCONS focuses its h-value updates on what it believes to be a minimal-cost path from the start state to a goal state. While LRTA* greedily tries to get quickly to a goal state, FALCONS greedily tries to get quickly to a minimal-cost path from the start state to a goal state and then follows the path, as shown in Figure 11.8. When it increases the g-value or h-value of a state on the path, then it might no longer consider the path to be a minimal-cost path from the start state to a goal state, and then again greedily tries to get quickly to a minimal-cost path from the start state to a goal state and then follows the path until it finally converges to a minimal-cost path from the start state to a goal state if it maintains its g-values and h-values across a series of search tasks in the same safely explorable state space with the same start state and set of goal states.

Algorithm 11.7 shows pseudo code for FALCONS. The initial g-values and h-values must be admissible (that is, they are lower bounds on the corresponding start and goal distances, respectively). We moved the termination-checking step after the value-update step because it makes sense to update the g-values in goal states. It turns out that care must be taken to ensure that FALCONS does not cycle

---

Procedure Variant-of-LRTA*-1
Input: Search task with initial g-values and h-values
Side Effect: Updated g-values and h-values

$u \leftarrow s$;; Start in start state
while (true)   ;; Repeat forever
   $a \leftarrow \arg\min_{a \in A(u)}\{w(u,a) + h(Succ(u,a))\}$;; Select action
       ;; Break ties in favor of an action a so that state $Succ(u,a)$ has a minimal
       ;; f-value, where $f(Succ(u,a)) = g(Succ(u,a)) + h(Succ(u,a))$
   if $(u \neq s)$;; If current state is not start state
     $g(u) \leftarrow \max\{g(u), \min_{v \in S, a' \in A(v) | Succ(v,a')=u}\{g(v) + w(v,a')\}\}$;; Update g-value
   if $(u \notin T)$;; If current state is not goal state
     $h(u) \leftarrow \max\{h(u), \min_{a' \in A(u)}\{w(u,a') + h(Succ(u,a'))\}\}$;; Update h-value
   else return   ;; Return if goal achieved
   $u \leftarrow a(u)$;; Execute action

Algorithm 11.6

Variant of LRTA* (1).

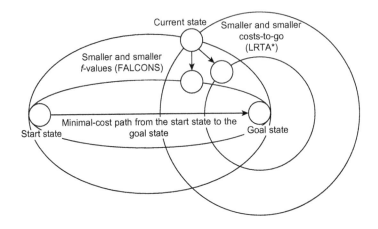

FIGURE 11.8

Illustration of FALCONS.

Procedure FALCONS
Input: Search task with initial g-values and h-values
Side Effect: Updated g-values and h-values

$u \leftarrow s$	;; Start in start state
while (true)	;; Repeat forever
$\quad a \leftarrow \arg\min_{a \in A(u)} \max\{g(Succ(u,a)) + h(Succ(u,a)), h(s)\}$	;; Select action
	;; Break ties in favor of an action a
	;; with the minimal cost-to-go $g(Succ(u,a)) + h(Succ(u,a))$
$\quad$ **if** $(u \neq s)$	;; If current state is not start state
$\quad\quad g(u) \leftarrow \max\{g(u),$	;; Update g-value
$\quad\quad\quad \min_{v \in S, a' \in A(v) \mid Succ(v,a')=u}\{g(v) + w(v,a')\},$	
$\quad\quad\quad \max_{a' \in A(u)}\{g(Succ(u,a')) - w(u,a')\}\}$	
$\quad$ **if** $(u \notin T)$	;; If current state is not goal state
$\quad\quad h(u) \leftarrow \max\{h(u),$	;; Update h-value
$\quad\quad\quad \min_{a' \in A(u)}\{w(u,a') + h(Succ(u,a'))\},$	
$\quad\quad\quad \max_{v \in S, a' \in A(v) \mid Succ(v,a')=u}\{h(v) - w(v,a')\}\}$	
$\quad$ **else return**	;; Return if goal achieved
$\quad u \leftarrow a(u)$	;; Execute action

Algorithm 11.7

FALCONS.

---

forever and converges to a minimal-cost path from the start state to a goal state if it maintains its
h-values across a series of search tasks in the same safely explorable state space with the same set
of goal states, which explains why the value-update step is so complicated. The value-update step for

the h-values, for example, basically simplifies to the one of LRTA* with lookahead one in case the h-values are consistent (see Exercises).

11.5.6 Nonconverging Variants

There are a large number of real-time search methods that basically operate like LRTA* but use h-values with different semantics and thus differ from LRTA* in their value-update steps, which allows them to reach a goal state but prevents them from converging if they maintain their h-values across a series of search tasks in the same safely explorable state space with the same set of goal states.

RTA*

A nonconverging variant of LRTA* is *real-time A* (RTA*)*. Its h-values correspond to approximations of the goal distances of the states, just like the h-values of LRTA*. RTA* with lookahead one uses the value-update step

$$h(u) \leftarrow \max\{h(u) \quad \min_{a' \in A(u) | Succ(u,a') \neq Succ(u,a)} \{w(u,a') + h(Succ(u,a'))\}\},$$

but is otherwise identical to LRTA* with lookahead one. (The minimum of an empty set is infinity.) Thus, RTA* basically updates the h-value of the current state based on the cost-to-go of the second-best action, whereas LRTA* updates the h-value of the current state based on the cost-to-go of the best action. Thus, the h-values of RTA* do not necessarily remain admissible but the h-values of LRTA* do. RTA* always reaches a goal state with a finite execution cost in all safely explorable state spaces, as can be shown with a cycle argument in a way similar to the proof of the same property of LRTA*. Although RTA* applies to all safely explorable state spaces, the motivation for its value-update step comes from state spaces that are trees, where the only reason for entering the current state again is to execute the currently second-best action. (If we execute an action that enters the current state again and then execute the currently best action again, then these two actions together have no effect and thus do not need to get executed.) Consider, for example, the state space shown in Figure 11.9. All action costs are one. LRTA* with lookahead one and RTA* with lookahead one move east in the start state. Then, however, LRTA* can move west and east before it is forced to move east, whereas RTA* is forced to move east right away. In general, RTA* tends to have a smaller execution cost than LRTA* but does not converge if it maintains its h-values across a series of search tasks in the same safely explorable state space with the same set of goal states.

Node Counting

Another nonconverging variant of LRTA* is *node counting*. Its h-values correspond to the number of times the states have been visited. It does not make sense to initialize them with a heuristic function.

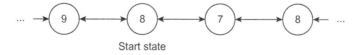

Start state

FIGURE 11.9

Example state space (1).

Rather, they are initialized with zero. Node counting then uses the value-update step

$$h(u) \leftarrow 1 + h(u)$$

(because the current state has been visited one additional time) but is otherwise identical to LRTA* with lookahead one from Algorithm 11.3 in state spaces where all action costs are one. Node counting always reaches a goal state with a finite number of action executions and thus a finite execution cost in all safely explorable state spaces, as can be shown with a cycle argument in a way similar to the proof of the same property of LRTA*.

We now analyze node counting in more detail and compare it to LRTA* in state spaces where all action costs are one. Theorem 11.1 implies that LRTA* always reaches a goal state with a finite execution cost in all safely explorable state spaces where all action costs are one. Furthermore, the complexity of zero-initialized LRTA* with minimal local search spaces is $\Theta(nd)$ over all state spaces where all action costs are one and $\Theta(n^2)$ over all safely explorable state spaces where all action costs are one. It turns out that these complexities remain tight over all undirected state spaces and over all Eulerian state spaces where all action costs are one (see Exercises). The complexity of zero-initialized node counting is at least exponential in n over all state spaces where all action costs are one. Figure 11.10 is a *reset state space*, which is a reasonable state space in which all states (but the start state) have an action that eventually resets one to the start state. All action costs are one. Node counting needs a number of action executions in the worst case to reach a goal state in reset state spaces that is at least exponential in n. In particular, if node counting breaks ties in favor of successor states with smaller indices, then it executes $2^{n/2+1/2} - 3$ actions before it reaches the goal state (for $n \geq 3$). Thus, the complexity of zero-initialized node counting is at least exponential in n over all state spaces where all action costs are one. It turns out that the complexity of zero-initialized node counting is also at least exponential in (the square root of) n even over all reasonable undirected state spaces where all action costs are one and over all reasonable Eulerian state spaces where all action costs are one, including (planar) undirected trees (see Exercises).

Thus, the complexity of zero-initialized LRTA* is smaller than the one of zero-initialized node counting in all of these cases. LRTA* has other advantages over node counting as well since it is able to use heuristic knowledge to guide its searches, can take action costs into account, allows for larger local search spaces, and converges if it maintains its h-values across a series of search tasks in the same safely explorable state space with the same set of goal states.

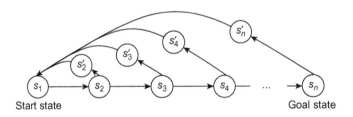

FIGURE 11.10

Reset state space.

Edge Counting

Another nonconverging variant of LRTA* is *edge counting*, which relates to node counting as Min-LRTA* relates to LRTA*. Its q-values correspond to the number of times the actions have been executed. It does not make sense to initialize them with a heuristic function. Rather, they are initialized with zero. Edge counting then uses the value-update step

$$q(u,a) \leftarrow 1 + q(u,a)$$

but is otherwise identical to Min-LRTA* in state spaces where all action costs are one. The action-selection step of edge counting always chooses the action for execution that has been executed the least number of times. This achieves the same result as random walks (namely, to execute all actions in a state equally often in the long run), but in a deterministic way. One particular tie-breaking rule, for example, is for edge counting to repeatedly execute all actions in a state in turn according to a fixed order, resulting in *edge ant walk*. In other words, edge counting executes the first action according to the given order when it visits some state for the first time, it executes the second action according to the given order when it visits the same state the next time, and so on. Edge counting always reaches a goal state with a finite number of action executions and thus a finite execution cost in all safely explorable state spaces, as can be shown with a cycle argument in a way similar to the proof of the same property of LRTA*.

The complexity of zero-initialized edge counting is at least exponential in n over all state spaces where all action costs are one (even over all reasonable state spaces where all action costs are one). Figure 11.11 is a variant of a reset state space, which is a reasonable state space in which all states (but the start state) have an action that resets one to the start state. All action costs are one. Edge counting needs a number of action executions in the worst case to reach a goal state in reset state spaces that is at least exponential in n. In particular, if edge counting breaks ties in favor of successor states with smaller indices, then it executes $3 \times 2^{n-2} - 2$ actions before it reaches the goal state (for $n \geq 2$).

Thus, the complexity of zero-initialized Min-LRTA* is smaller than the one of zero-initialized edge counting over all state spaces where all action costs are one. However, it turns out that the complexity of zero-initialized edge counting is $\Theta(ed)$ over all undirected state spaces where all action costs are one and over all Eulerian state spaces where all action costs are one (see Exercises). Furthermore, its complexity is $\Theta(n^3)$ over all reasonable undirected state spaces where all action costs are one and over all reasonable Eulerian state spaces where all action costs are one. Thus, the complexity of zero-initialized Min-LRTA* is equal to the one of zero-initialized edge counting in these state spaces.

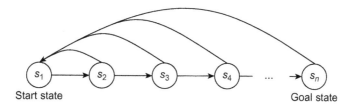

FIGURE 11.11

Variant of reset state space, by Koenig and Simmons (1996).

11.5.7 Variants for Nondeterministic and Probabilistic State Spaces

Search in nondeterministic and probabilistic state spaces is often more time consuming than search in deterministic state spaces since information limitations can only be overcome by enumerating all possible contingencies, which results in large search spaces. Consequently, it is even more important that agents take their search cost into account to solve search tasks efficiently. Real-time search in non-deterministic and probabilistic state spaces has an additional advantage compared to real-time search in deterministic state spaces, namely that it allows agents to gather information early. This information can be used to resolve some of the uncertainty and thus reduce the amount of search performed for unencountered situations. Without interleaving searches and action executions, an agent has to determine a complete conditional plan that solves the search task no matter which contingencies arise during its execution. Such a plan can be large. When interleaving searches and action executions, on the other hand, the agent does not need to plan for every possible contingency. It has to determine only the beginning of a complete plan. After the execution of this subplan, it can observe the resulting state and then repeat the process from the state that actually resulted from the execution of the subplan instead of all states that could have resulted from its execution, an advantage also exploited by game-playing programs.

Min-Max LRTA*

Min-max learning real-time A* (min-max LRTA*) uses minimax search to generalize LRTA* to nondeterministic state spaces. It views acting in nondeterministic state spaces as a two-player game in which it selects an action from the available actions in the current state. This action determines the possible successor states from which a fictitious agent, called nature, chooses one. Min-max LRTA* assumes that nature exhibits the most vicious behavior and always chooses the worst possible successor state.

Min-max LRTA* uses the maximal h-value of all successor states that can result from the execution of a given action in a given state everywhere in the pseudo code where LRTA* simply uses the h-value of the only successor state. Thus, the pseudo code of min-max LRTA* is identical to the pseudo code of LRTA* if every occurrence of $h(Succ(x,a))$ is replaced by $\max_{v \in Succ(x,a)} h(v)$ in Algorithms 11.1, 11.2, 11.3, and 11.8. For example, min-max LRTA* with lookahead one uses the action-selection step

$$a \leftarrow \arg \min_{a \in A(u)} \{w(u,a) + \max_{v \in Succ(u,a)} h(v)\}$$

and the value-update step

$$h(u) \leftarrow \max\{h(u), w(u,a) + \max_{v \in Succ(u,a)} h(v)\},$$

but is otherwise identical to LRTA* with lookahead one. Thus, min-max LRTA* is identical to LRTA* in deterministic state spaces. It turns out that min-max LRTA* has similar properties as LRTA* but the goal distance $\delta(u,T)$ of a state u now refers to its minimax goal distance; that is, the minimal execution cost with which a goal state can be reached from the state, even for the most vicious behavior of nature. For example, state spaces are now safely explorable if and only if the minimax goal distances of all states are finite and h-values are admissible if and only if they are lower bounds on the corresponding minimax goal distances. Then, Min-Max LRTA* with admissible initial h-values reaches a goal state with an execution cost of at most $\sum_{u \in S} \delta(u,T)$. Thus, it reaches a goal state with a finite execution cost in safely explorable state spaces.

The *h*-values of min-max LRTA* approximate the minimax goal distances of the states. (Informed) admissible *h*-values can be obtained as follows: We assume that nature decides in advance which successor state $g(u,a) \in Succ(u,a)$ to choose whenever action $a \in A(u)$ is executed in state $u \in S$; all possible states are fine. If nature really behaved this way, then the state space would effectively be deterministic. *h*-values that are admissible for this deterministic state space are admissible for the nondeterministic state space as well. This is so because additional successor states allow a vicious nature to cause more harm. How informed the obtained *h*-values are in the nondeterministic state space depends on how informed they are in the deterministic state space and how close the assumed behavior of nature is to its most vicious behavior.

Assume that min-max LRTA* maintains *h*-values across a series of search tasks in the same safely explorable state space with the same set of goal states. It turns out that the number of search tasks for which min-max LRTA* with admissible initial *h*-values reaches a goal state with an execution cost that is larger than $\delta(s,T)$ (where *s* is the start state of the current search task) is bounded from above. The action sequences that min-max LRTA* executes after convergence if it maintains its *h*-values across a series of search tasks in the same safely explorable state space with the same set of goal states depend on the behavior of nature and are not necessarily uniquely determined, but their execution costs are at most as large as the minimax goal distance of the start state. Thus, the execution cost of min-max LRTA* is either worst-case optimal or better than worst-case optimal. This is possible because nature might not be as vicious as a minimax search assumes. Min-max LRTA* might not be able to detect the existence of a successor state with a large minimax goal distance by introspection since it does not perform a complete minimax search but partially relies on observing the actual successor states of actions, and nature can wait an arbitrarily long time to reveal its existence or choose not to reveal it at all. This can prevent the *h*-values of the encountered states from converging after a bounded execution cost (or bounded number of search tasks) and is the reason why we analyzed the behavior of LRTA* using the mistake-bounded error model, although this problem cannot occur for LRTA* if its action-selection step always breaks ties among the actions in the current state according to a fixed ordering of the actions. It is important to realize that, since min-max LRTA* relies on observing the actual successor states of actions it can have computational advantages even over several search episodes compared to a complete minimax search. This is the case if some successor states do not occur in practice since min-max LRTA* plans only for states that it actually encounters during its searches.

Probabilistic LRTA*

Min-max LRTA* assumes that nature chooses the successor state that is worst for the agent. The *h*-value of a node in the minimax search tree where it is the turn of nature to move is thus calculated as the maximum of the *h*-values of its children, and min-max LRTA* attempts to minimize the worst-case execution cost. One advantage of using min-max LRTA* is that it does not depend on assumptions about the behavior of nature. If min-max LRTA* reaches a goal state for the most vicious behavior of nature, it also reaches a goal state if nature uses a different and therefore less vicious behavior. However, the assumption that nature chooses the successor state that is worst for the agent is often too pessimistic and can make search tasks wrongly appear to be unsolvable, for example, if a vicious nature could force the agent to cycle forever no matter which actions the agent executes. In such situations, min-max LRTA* can be changed to assume that nature chooses the successor state according to a probability distribution that depends only on the current state and the executed action, resulting in a totally observable *Markov decision process (MDP)* problem. In this case, the *h*-value of a node in the probabilistic search tree where it is the turn of nature to move is calculated as the average of the *h*-values of its children weighted with the probability of their occurrence as specified by the probability distribution. *Probabilistic LRTA**, this probabilistic variant of min-max LRTA*, then attempts to minimize the average execution cost rather than the worst-case execution cost. It uses the expected *h*-value of the successor states that can result from the execution of a given action in a given state everywhere in the pseudo code where LRTA* simply uses the *h*-value of the only successor state. Let $p(v|u,a)$ denote the probability with which the execution of action $a \in A(u)$ in state $u \in S$ results in successor state $v \in S$. Then, the pseudo code of probabilistic LRTA* is identical to the pseudo code of LRTA* if every occurrence of $h(Succ(x,a))$ is replaced by $\sum_{v \in Succ(x,a)} p(v \mid x,a)h(v)$ in Algorithms 11.3 and 11.8. For example, probabilistic LRTA* with lookahead one uses the action-selection step

$$a \leftarrow \arg\min_{a \in A(u)} \left\{ w(u,a) + \sum_{v \in Succ(u,a)} p(v \mid u,a)h(v) \right\}$$

and the value-update step

$$h(u) \leftarrow \max \left\{ h(u), w(u,a) + \sum_{v \in Succ(u,a)} p(v \mid u,a)h(v) \right\}$$

but is otherwise identical to LRTA* with lookahead one from Algorithm 11.3. However, the variant of Dijkstra's algorithm from Algorithm 11.2 cannot be used directly with the change since assigning each state in the local search space its new *h*-value requires the *h*-value of each state in the local search space to be updated multiple times. We can use value iteration, policy iteration, or other methods for solving MDPs for this purpose. Probabilistic LRTA* is identical to LRTA* in deterministic state spaces. It turns out that probabilistic LRTA* has similar properties as LRTA* but the goal distance of a state now refers to its expected goal distance. For example, state spaces are now safely explorable if and only if the expected goal distances of all states are finite, and *h*-values are admissible if and only if they are lower bounds on the corresponding expected goal distances.

11.6 HOW TO USE REAL-TIME SEARCH

We now discuss how to use real-time search using LRTA* as a basis. In addition to the case studies described in the following, real-time search methods have also been used in other nondeterministic state spaces from mobile robotics, including moving-target search, the task of catching moving prey.

11.6.1 Case Study: Offline Search

Many traditional state spaces from artificial intelligence are deterministic, including sliding-tile puzzles and blocks worlds. The successor states of actions can be predicted with certainty in deterministic state spaces. Real-time search methods can solve offline search tasks in these state spaces by moving a fictitious agent in the state space and thus provide alternatives to traditional search methods, such as A*. They have been applied successfully to traditional search tasks and STRIPS-type search tasks. For instance, real-time search methods easily determine suboptimal solutions for the TWENTY-FOUR PUZZLE, a sliding-tile puzzle with more than 10^{24} states, and blocks worlds with more than 10^{27} states.

For these search tasks, real-time search methods compete with other heuristic search methods such as greedy (best-first) search, which can determine suboptimal solutions faster than real-time search, or linear-space best-first search, which can consume less memory.

11.6.2 Case Study: Goal-Directed Navigation in A Priori Unknown Terrain

Goal-directed navigation in a priori unknown terrain requires a robot to move to a goal position in a priori unknown terrain. The robot knows the start and goal cell of the GRIDWORLD but not which cells are blocked. It can repeatedly move one cell to the north, east, south, or west (unless that cell is blocked). All action costs are one. On-board sensors tell the robot in every cell which of the four adjacent cells (to the north, east, south, or west) are blocked. The task of the robot is to move to the given goal cell, which we assume to be possible. We study this search task again in Chapter 19. The robot uses a navigation strategy from robotics: It maintains the blockage status of the cells that it knows so far. It always moves along a presumed unblocked path from its current cell toward the goal cell until it visits the goal cell. A *presumed unblocked path* is a sequence of adjacent cells that does not contain cells that the robot knows to be blocked. The robot moves on the presumed unblocked path toward the goal cell but immediately repeats the process if it observes a blocked cell on the planned path or reaches the end of the path. Thus, it has to search repeatedly.

The states of the state space correspond to the cells, and the actions correspond to moving from a cell to an adjacent cell. The action costs can increase between searches. Initially, they are all one. When the robot observes that a cell is blocked, then it removes all actions that enter or leave the cell, which corresponds to setting their action costs to infinity. LRTA* and RTAA* apply to this scenario since consistent (or admissible) h-values remain consistent (or admissible, respectively) if action costs increase.

Figure 11.12 shows a simple goal-directed navigation task in *a priori* unknown terrain that we use to illustrate the behavior of repeated (forward) A* (that repeatedly searches from the current cell of the robot to the goal cell), LRTA* with repeat-until loop, and RTAA* with repeat-until loop. Black cells are blocked. All cells are labeled with their initial h-values, which are the Manhattan distances. All search methods start a new search episode (i.e., run another search) when the action cost of an

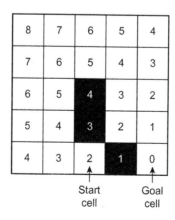

FIGURE 11.12

Goal-directed navigation task in a simple unknown GRIDWORLD, by Koenig and Likhachev (2006).

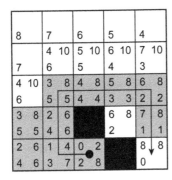

FIGURE 11.13

Repeated (forward) A* searches in the simple GRIDWORLD, by Koenig and Likhachev (2006).

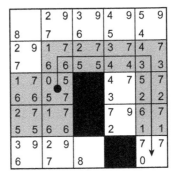

FIGURE 11.14

RTAA* with maximal local search spaces in the simple GRIDWORLD, by Koenig and Likhachev (2006).

action on their current path increases or, for LRTA* and RTAA*, when the new state is outside of their local search spaces, and break ties among cells with the same f-values in favor of cells with larger g-values and remaining ties in order from highest to lowest priority: east, south, west, and north. Figures 11.13, 11.14, 11.15, and 11.16 show the robot as a small black circle. The arrows show the found paths from the current cell of the robot to the goal cell, which is in the bottom-right corner. Cells that the robot has already observed to be blocked are black. All other cells have their h-value in the bottom-left corner. Generated cells have their g-value in the top-left corner and their f-value in the top-right corner. Expanded cells are gray and, for RTAA* and LRTA*, have their updated h-values in the bottom-right corner, which makes it easy to compare them to the h-values before the update in the bottom-left corner.

Repeated (forward) A*, RTAA* with maximal local search spaces (i.e., with *lookahead* $= \infty$), and LRTA* with the same local search spaces follow the same paths if they break ties in the same way. They differ only in the number of cell expansions until the robot reaches the goal cell, which is larger for repeated (forward) A* (23) than for RTAA* with maximal local search spaces (20) and larger for RTAA* with maximal local search spaces (20) than for LRTA* with maximal local search spaces (19). The first property is due to RTAA* and LRTA* updating the h-values while repeated (forward) A*

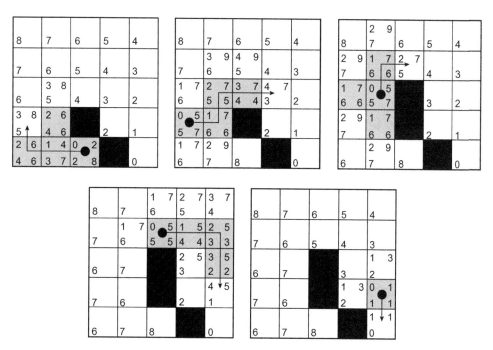

FIGURE 11.15

LRTA* with maximal local search spaces in the simple GRIDWORLD, by Koenig and Likhachev (2006).

FIGURE 11.16

RTAA* with *lookahead* = 4 in the simple GRIDWORLD, by Koenig and Likhachev (2006).

does not. Thus, repeated (forward) A* falls prey to the local minimum in the *h*-value surface and thus expands the three left-most cells in the bottom row a second time, whereas RTAA* and LRTA* avoid these cell expansions. The second property is due to some updated *h*-values of LRTA* being larger than the ones of RTAA*. However, most updated *h*-values are identical, although this is not guaranteed in general. We also compare RTAA* with *lookahead* = 4 to RTAA* with maximal local search spaces; that is, *lookahead* = ∞. Figures 11.14 and 11.16 show that smaller local search spaces increase the execution cost (from 10 to 12) but decrease the number of cell expansions (from 20 to 17) because smaller local search spaces imply that less information is used during each search episode. (The last search episode of RTAA* with *lookahead* = 4 expands only one cell since the goal cell is about to be expanded next.)

For goal-directed navigation in unknown terrain, smaller local search spaces tend to increase the execution cost of LRTA* and RTAA* but initially tend to decrease the number of cell expansions and the search cost. Increasing the execution cost tends to increase the number of search episodes. As the local search spaces become smaller, eventually the rate with which the number of search episodes increases tends to be larger than the rate with which the lookahead and the time per search episode decrease, so that the number of cell expansions and the search cost increase again. The number of cell expansions and the search cost tend to be larger for repeated (forward) A* than RTAA*, and larger for RTAA* than LRTA*. RTAA* with local search spaces that are neither minimal nor maximal tends to increase the *h*-values less per update than LRTA* with the same local search spaces. Consequently, its execution cost and number of cell expansions tend to be larger than the ones of LRTA* with the same local search spaces. However, it tends to update the *h*-values much faster than LRTA* with the same local search spaces, resulting in smaller search costs. Overall, the execution cost of RTAA* tends to be smaller than the one of LRTA* for given time limits per search episode because it tends to update the *h*-values much faster than LRTA*, which allows it to use larger local search spaces and overcompensate for its slightly less informed *h*-values.

11.6.3 Case Study: Coverage

Coverage requires a robot to visit each location in its terrain once or repeatedly. Consider a strongly connected state space without any goal states. Strongly connected state spaces guarantee that real-time search methods are always able to reach all states no matter which actions they have executed in the past. Then, LRTA* with lookahead one, RTA* with lookahead one, and node counting visit all states repeatedly, as can be shown with a cycle argument in a way similar to the proof that LRTA* always reaches a goal state with a finite execution cost. In fact, the worst-case cover time (where the cover time is measured as the execution cost until all states have been visited at least once) is the same as the worst-case execution cost until a goal state has been reached if an adversary can pick the goal state, for example, the state that was visited last when covering the state space. Thus, the earlier complexity results carry over to coverage.

The property of real-time search methods to visit all states of strongly connected state spaces repeatedly has been used to build *ant robots*—simple robots with limited sensing and computational capabilities. Ant robots have the advantage that they are easy to program and cheap to build. This makes it feasible to deploy groups of ant robots and take advantage of the resulting fault tolerance and parallelism. Ant robots cannot use conventional search methods due to their limited sensing and computational capabilities. To overcome these limitations, ant robots can use real-time search methods to leave markings in the state space that can be read by the other ant robots, similar to what real ants do when they use chemical (pheromone) traces to guide their navigation. For example, ant robots that all use LRTA* only have to sense the markings (in form of the *h*-values) of their adjacent states, and change the marking of their current state. They cover all states once or repeatedly even if they move asynchronously, do not communicate with each other except via the markings, do not have any kind of memory, do not know and cannot learn the topology of the state space, nor determine complete paths. The ant robots do not even need to be localized, which completely eliminates solving difficult and time-consuming localization tasks, and robustly cover all states even if they are moved without realizing that they have been moved (say, by people running into them), some ant robots fail, and some markings get destroyed.

Many of the real-time search methods discussed in this chapter could be used to implement ant robots. For example, the following properties are known if edge counting is used to implement ant robots, in addition to it executing all actions repeatedly. A *Eulerian cycle* is a sequence of action executions that executes each action in each state exactly once and returns to the start state. Consider edge ant walk, the variant of edge counting that repeatedly executes all actions in a state in turn according to a fixed order. In other words, edge counting executes the first action according to the given order when it visits some state for the first time, it executes the second action according to the given order when it visits the same state next time, and so on. It turns out that this variant of edge counting repeatedly executes a Eulerian cycle after at most $2ed'$ action executions in Eulerian state spaces without goal states, where the diameter d' of a state space is the maximal distance between any pair of its states. Furthermore, consider k ant robots that each execute one action in each time step so that they repeatedly execute all actions in a state in turn according to a fixed order. In other words, the first ant robot that executes an action in some state executes the first action according to the given order, the next ant robot that executes an action in the same state executes the second action according to the given order, and so on. It turns out that the numbers of times that any two actions have been executed differ by at most a factor of two after at most $2(k+1)ed'/k$ time steps in Eulerian state spaces without goal states.

Overall, it is probably easiest to use node counting to implement ant robots in GRIDWORLDS since each ant robot then marks cells and always increases the h-value of its current cell by the same amount. Figure 11.17 shows a simplified example. Each ant robot can repeatedly move one cell to the north, east, south, or west (unless that cell is blocked). We assume that there is no uncertainty in actuation and sensing. The ant robots move in a given sequential order (although this is not necessary in general). If a cell contains an ant robot, one of its corners is marked. Different corners represent different ant robots. Figure 11.17 (top) demonstrates how a single ant robot covers the GRIDWORLD, and Figure 11.17 (bottom) demonstrates how three ant robots cover it. Ant robots that leave more information in each cell (e.g., complete maps) tend to cover terrain even faster.

11.6.4 Case Study: Localization and Goal-Directed Navigation under Pose Uncertainty

Consider the goal-directed navigation task with pose uncertainty shown in Figure 11.18. The robot knows the GRIDWORLD, but is uncertain about its start pose, where a pose is a cell and orientation (north, east, south, or west). It can move one cell forward (unless that cell is blocked), turn left 90 degrees, or turn right 90 degrees. All action costs are one. On-board sensors tell the robot in every pose which of the four adjacent cells (front, left, behind, or right) are blocked. We assume that there is no uncertainty in actuation and sensing, and consider two navigation tasks. Localization requires the robot to gain certainty about its pose and then stop. We study this search task again in Chapter 19. Goal-directed navigation with pose uncertainty requires the robot to navigate to any of the given goal poses and then stop. Since there might be many poses that produce the same sensor reports as the goal poses, this navigation task includes localizing the robot sufficiently so that it knows that it is in a goal pose when it stops. We require that the GRIDWORLDS be strongly connected (every pose can be reached from every other pose) and not completely symmetrical (localization is possible). This modest

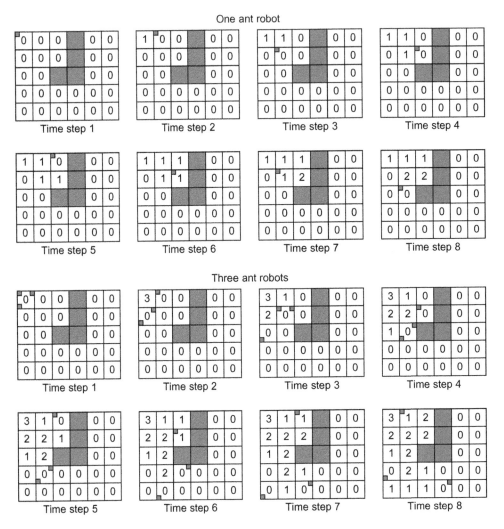

FIGURE 11.17

Ant robots using node counting in a simple GRIDWORLD, by Koenig, Szymanski and Liu (2001).

assumption makes all robot navigation tasks solvable, since the robot can always first localize itself and then, for goal-directed navigation tasks with pose uncertainty, move to a goal pose.

We now formally describe the navigation tasks, using the following notation: P is the finite set of possible robot poses. $A(p)$ is the finite set of possible actions that the robot can execute in pose $p \in P$: left, right, and possibly forward. $Succ(p,a)$ is the pose that results from the execution of action $a \in A(p)$ in pose $p \in P$. $o(p)$ is the observation that the robot makes in pose $p \in P$: whether or not there are blocked cells immediately adjacent to it in the four directions (front, left, behind, and right). The robot starts in pose $p_s \in P$ and then repeatedly makes an observation and executes an action until it decides to stop. It knows the GRIDWORLD, but is uncertain about its start pose. It could be in any pose

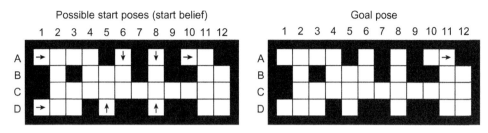

FIGURE 11.18

Goal-directed navigation task with pose uncertainty in a simple GRIDWORLD, by Koenig (2001).

in $P_s \subseteq P$. We require only that $o(p) = o(p')$ for all $p, p' \in P_s$, which automatically holds after the first observation, and $p_s \in P_s$, which automatically holds for $P_s = \{p \mid p \in P \wedge o(p) = o(p_s)\}$.

Since the robot does not know its start pose, the navigation tasks cannot be formulated as search tasks in small deterministic state spaces of which the states are the poses (pose space). Rather, the robot has to maintain a belief about its current pose. Analytical results about the execution cost of search methods are often about their worst-case execution cost (here, the execution cost for the worst possible start pose) rather than their average-case execution cost, especially if the robot cannot associate probabilities or other likelihood estimates with the poses. Then, all it can do is maintain a belief in the form of a set of possible poses, namely the poses that it could possibly be in. Thus, its beliefs are sets of poses and their number could be exponential in the number of poses. The beliefs of the robot depend on its observations, which the robot cannot predict with certainty since it is uncertain about its pose. For example, it cannot predict whether the cell in front of it will be blocked after it moves forward for the goal-directed navigation task with pose uncertainty from Figure 11.18. The navigation tasks are therefore search tasks in large nondeterministic state spaces of which the states are the beliefs of the robot (belief space). The robot will usually be uncertain about its current pose but can always determine its current belief for sure. For example, if the robot has no knowledge of its start pose for the goal-directed navigation task with pose uncertainty from Figure 11.18 but observes blocked cells all around it except in its front, then its start belief contains the following seven poses: A 1 →, A 6 ↓, A 8 ↓, A 10 →, D 1 →, D 5 ↑, and D 8 ↑.

We now formally describe the state spaces of the navigation tasks, using the following notation: B denotes the set of beliefs and b_s the start belief. $A(b)$ denotes the set of actions that can be executed when the belief is b. $O(b, a)$ denotes the set of possible observations that can be made after the execution of action a when the belief was b. $Succ(b, o, a)$ denotes the successor belief that results if observation o is made after the execution of action a when the belief was b. Then, for all $b \in B$, $a \in A(b)$, and $o \in O(b, a)$,

$$B = \{b \mid b \subseteq P \wedge o(p) = o(p') \text{ for all } p, p' \in b\}$$

$$b_s = P_s$$

$$A(b) = A(p) \text{ for any } p \in b$$

$$O(b, a) = \{o(Succ(p, a)) \mid p \in b\}$$

$$Succ(b, o, a) = \{Succ(p, a) \mid p \in b \wedge o(Succ(p, a)) = o\}.$$

To understand the definition of $A(b)$, notice that $A(p) = A(p')$ for all $p, p' \in b$ after the preceding observation since the observation determines the actions that can be executed.

For goal-directed navigation tasks with pose uncertainty, the robot has to navigate to any pose in $\emptyset \neq P_t \subseteq P$ and stop. In this case, we define the set of goal beliefs as $B_t = \{b | b \subseteq P_t \wedge o(p) = o(p')$ for all $p, p' \in b\}$. To understand this definition, notice that the robot knows that it is in a goal pose if and only if its belief is $b \subseteq P_t$. If the belief contains more than one pose, however, the robot does not know which goal pose it is in. If it is important that the robot knows which goal pose it is in, we use $B_t = \{b \mid b \subseteq P_t \wedge |b| = 1\}$. For localization tasks, we use $B_t = \{b \mid b \subseteq P \wedge |b| = 1\}$.

The belief space is then defined as follows. It is safely explorable since our assumptions imply that all navigation tasks are solvable:

$$S = B$$
$$s = b_s$$
$$T = B_t$$
$$A(u) = A(b) \quad \text{for } b = u$$
$$Succ(u, a) = \{Succ(b, o, a) | o \in O(b, a)\} \quad \text{for } b = u.$$

For goal-directed navigation tasks with pose uncertainty, we can use the admissible goal-distance heuristic, $h(u) = \max_{p \in u} \delta(p, P_t)$. (Thus, the robot determines for each pose in the belief state how many actions it would have to execute to reach a goal pose if it knew that it was currently in that pose. The maximum of these values then is an approximation of the minimax goal distance of the belief state.) For example, the goal-distance heuristic is 18 for the start belief state used earlier, namely the maximum of 18 for A 1 →, 12 for A 6 ↓, 10 for A 8 ↓, 1 for A 10 →, 17 for D 1 →, 12 for D 5 ↑, and 9 for D 8 ↑. The calculation of $\delta(p, P_t)$ involves no pose uncertainty and can be done efficiently without interleaving searches and action executions, by using traditional search methods in the pose space. This is possible because the pose space is deterministic and small. The h-values are admissible because the robot needs an execution cost of at least $\max_{p \in u} \delta(p, P_t)$ in the worst case to solve the goal-directed navigation task with pose uncertainty from pose $p' = \arg\max_{p \in u} \delta(p, P_t)$, even if it knows that it starts in that pose. The h-values are often only partially informed because they do not take into account that the robot might not know its pose and then might have to execute additional localization actions to overcome its pose uncertainty. For localization tasks, on the other hand, it is difficult to obtain more informed initial h-values than zero-initialized ones.

Figure 11.19 (excluding the dashed part) shows how min-max LRTA* with lookahead one performs a minimax search around the current belief state of the robot to determine which action to execute next. The local search space consists of all nonleaves of the minimax tree where it is the robot's turn to move (labeled "Agent" in the figure). Min-max LRTA* first assigns all leaves of the minimax tree the h-value determined by the heuristic function for the corresponding belief state ①. Min-max LRTA* then backs up these h-values toward the root of the minimax tree. The h-value of a node in the minimax tree where it is nature's turn to move (labeled "Nature" in the figure) is the maximum of the h-values of its children since nature chooses successor states that maximize the minimax goal distance ②. The h-value of a node in the minimax search tree where it is the robot's turn to move is the maximum of its previous h-value and the minimum over all actions in the node of the sum of the action cost plus the h-value of the corresponding child since min-max

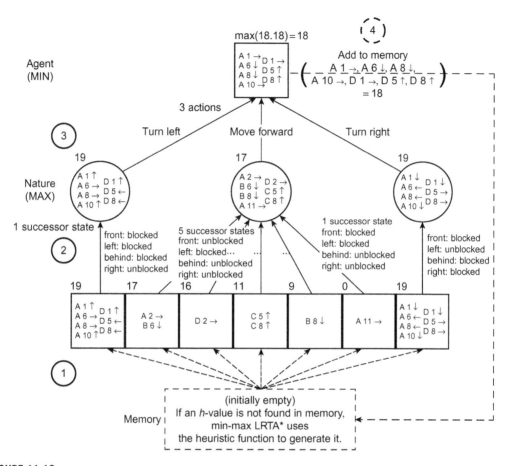

FIGURE 11.19

Illustration of min-max LRTA*, by Koenig (2001).

LRTA* chooses actions that minimize the minimax cost-to-go ③. Finally, min-max LRTA* selects the action in the root that minimizes the sum of the action cost plus the h-value of the corresponding child. Consequently, it decides to move forward. Min-max LRTA* then executes the selected action (possibly already searching for action sequences in response to the possible observations it can make next), makes an observation, updates the belief state of the robot based on this observation, and repeats the process from the new belief state of the robot until the navigation task is solved.

Min-max LRTA* has to ensure that it does not cycle forever. It can use one of the following two approaches to gain information between action executions and thus guarantee progress:

Direct Information Gain: If min-max LRTA* uses sufficiently large local search spaces, then it achieves a gain in information in the following sense. After executing the selected actions it is guaranteed that the robot has either solved the navigation task or at least reduced the number of poses it can be in. This way, it guarantees progress toward a solution. For example, moving forward reduces the number of possible poses from seven to at most two for the goal-directed navigation task with pose uncertainty from Figure 11.18. We study a search method with direct information gain, called greedy localization, in more detail in Chapter 19 since it performs agent-centered search but not real-time search.

Indirect Information Gain: Min-max LRTA* with direct information gain does not apply to all search tasks. Even if it applies, the local search spaces and thus the search cost that it needs to guarantee a direct information gain can be large. To operate with smaller local search spaces, it can use real-time search. It then operates as before, with the following two changes. First, when min-max LRTA* needs the h-value of a belief state just outside of the local search space (i.e., the h-value of a leaf of the minimax tree) in the value-update step, it now checks first whether it has already stored an h-value for this belief state in memory. If so, then it uses this h-value. If not, then it calculates the h-value using the heuristic function, as before. Second, after min-max LRTA* has calculated the h-value of a belief state in the local search space where it is the turn of the robot to move, it now stores it in memory, overwriting any existing h-value of the corresponding belief state. Figure 11.19 (including the dashed part) summarizes the steps of min-max LRTA* with indirect information gain before it decides to move forward. The increase of the potential $\sum_{u \in S \setminus \{u'\}} h^t(u)$, see the proof of Lemma 11.3, can be interpreted as an indirect information gain that guarantees that min-max LRTA* reaches a goal belief state in safely explorable state spaces. A disadvantage of min-max LRTA* with indirect information gain over min-max LRTA* with direct information gain is that the robot has to store potentially one h-value in memory for each belief state it has encountered during its searches. In practice, however, the memory requirements of real-time search methods often seem to be small, especially if the initial h-values are well informed and thus focus the searches well, which prevents them from encountering a large number of different belief states. Furthermore, real-time search methods only need to store the h-values of those belief states in memory that differ from the initial h-values. If the h-values are the same, then they can be automatically regenerated when they are not found in memory. For the example from Figure 11.19, for instance, it is unnecessary to store the calculated h-value 18 of the start belief state in memory.

An advantage of min-max LRTA* with indirect information gain over min-max LRTA* with direct information gain is that it is able to operate with smaller local search spaces, even local search spaces that contain only the current belief state. Another advantage is that it improves its worst-case execution cost, although not necessarily monotonically, until it converges if it maintains its h-values across a series of localization tasks in the same terrain or goal-directed navigation tasks with pose uncertainty with the same set of goal poses in the same terrain. The actual start poses or the beliefs of the robot about its start poses do not need to be identical.

So far, we have assumed that the robot can recover from the execution of each action. If this is not the case, then the robot has to guarantee that the execution of each action does not make it impossible to reach a goal belief state, which is often possible by increasing the local search spaces of real-time search methods. For example, if min-max LRTA* is applied to goal-directed navigation tasks with pose uncertainty in the presence of irreversible actions and always executes actions so that the resulting belief state is guaranteed to contain either only goal poses, only poses that are part of the current belief state of the robot, or only poses that are part of the start belief state, then either the goal-directed navigation task remains solvable in the worst case or it was not solvable in the worst case to begin with. We have also assumed that there is no actuator or sensor noise. Search tasks with actuator but no sensor noise can be modeled with MDPs, and search tasks with actuator and sensor noise can be modeled with partially observable MDPs (POMDPs). We have already shown that MDPs can be solved with probabilistic LRTA*. A POMDP can be expressed as an MDP of which the state space is the set of probability distributions over all states of the POMDP. Thus, the state space of the resulting MDP is continuous and needs to get discretized before we can use probabilistic LRTA* on it.

11.7 SUMMARY

In this chapter, we illustrated the concept of real-time search, described which kinds of search tasks it is suitable for, and discussed the design and the properties of some real-time search methods. We learned that real-time search methods have been applied to a variety of search tasks, including traditional off-line search, STRIPS-type planning, moving-target search, search of MDPs and POMDPs, reinforcement learning, and robot navigation (such as goal-directed navigation in unknown terrain, coverage and localization). We learned that real-time search methods have several advantages. First, different from the many existing ad hoc search and planning methods that interleave searches and action executions, they have a solid theoretical foundation and are state space independent. Second, they allow for fine-grained control over how much search to do between action executions. Third, they can use heuristic knowledge to guide their search, which can reduce the search cost without increasing the execution cost. Fourth, they can be interrupted at any state and resume execution at a different state. In other words, other control programs can take over control at arbitrary times if desired. Fifth, they amortize learning over several search episodes, which allows them to determine a solution with a suboptimal execution cost fast and then improve the execution cost as they solve similar search tasks, until the execution cost is satisficing or optimal. Thus, they still asymptotically minimize the execution cost in the long run in case similar search tasks unexpectedly repeat. Sixth, several agents can often solve search tasks cooperatively by performing an individual real-time search each but sharing the search information, thereby reducing the execution cost. For example, off-line search tasks can be solved on several processors in parallel by running a real-time search method on each processor and letting all real-time search methods share their h-values.

Although these properties can make real-time search methods the search methods of choice, we also learned that they are not appropriate for every search task. For example, real-time search methods execute actions before their consequences are completely known and thus cannot guarantee a small execution cost when they solve a search task for the first time. If a small execution cost is important, we might have to perform complete searches before starting to execute actions. Furthermore, real-time search methods trade off the search and execution costs but do not reason about the trade-off explicitly. In particular, it can sometimes be beneficial to update h-values of states that are far away from the current state, and repeated forward searches might not be able to determine these states efficiently. Time-bounded A*, for example, performs only one complete (forward) A* search and executes actions greedily until this search is complete. Finally, real-time search methods have to store an h-value in memory for each state encountered during their searches and thus can have large memory requirements if the initial h-values do not focus their searches well.

Table 11.1 Overview of real-time search methods.

Real-Time Search Method	Algorithm	State Space	Sizes of Local Search Spaces or Lookaheads	h-Values	Completeness	Convergence
LRTA*	11.1/11.2	deterministic	one to infinity	admissible	yes	yes
LRTA* with lookahead one	11.3	deterministic	one	admissible	yes	yes
Min-LRTA*	11.4	deterministic	zero	admissible	yes	yes
RTAA*	11.5	deterministic	one to infinity	consistent	yes	yes
FALCONS	11.7	deterministic	one	admissible	yes	yes
RTA*	—	deterministic	one (to infinity)	admissible	yes	no
Node counting	—	deterministic	one	zero	yes	no
Edge counting	—	deterministic	zero	zero	yes	no
Min-Max LRTA*	—	nondeterministic	one (to infinity)	admissible	yes	yes
Probabilistic LRTA*	—	probabilistic	one (to infinity)	admissible	yes	yes

Table 11.1 provides an overview of the real-time search methods introduced in this chapter, together with the kind of their state spaces, the sizes of their local search spaces, and whether they are complete and converge. We discussed LRTA* as a prototypical real-time search method and analyzed its properties, including its completeness, execution cost and convergence. We then discussed several variants of LRTA*, including variants with maximal local search spaces, minimal local search spaces, lookahead one (similar to minimal local search spaces) and lookahead zero (called minimal lookahead, where all information is local to the current state). We discussed variants of LRTA* that update their h-values faster than LRTA* (namely RTAA*), that detect convergence, that speed up convergence (including FALCONS) and that do not converge (including RTA*, node counting and edge counting). We also discussed variants of LRTA* for nondeterministic state spaces (min-max LRTA*) and probabilistic state spaces (probabilistic LRTA*).

11.8 EXERCISES

11.1 Consider the following algorithm for solving the $(n^2 - 1)$-Puzzle: If $n \leq 3$, then solve it by brute force. Otherwise, use a greedy method to put the first row and column into place, tile by tile, and then call the algorithm recursively to solve the remaining rows and columns. Show a greedy method that can put an additional tile in the first row or column into place without disturbing the tiles that it has already put into place, and that only needs a constant search time before the first action execution and between action executions. (It turns out that there exists a greedy method with this property so that the resulting algorithm solves the $(n^2 - 1)$-Puzzle with at most $5n^3 + O(n^2)$ action executions.)

11.2 List several similarities and differences of min-max LRTA* and the minimax search method used by game-playing programs.

11.3 Determine experimentally which value of *lookahead* minimizes the search cost (here: runtime) when using LRTA* to solve the Eight-Puzzle with the Manhattan distance on your computer if the local search spaces are generated by (forward) A* search until a goal state is about to be expanded or *lookahead* > 0 states have been expanded.

11.4 1. Simulate by hand LRTA* with lookahead one in the state space from Figure 11.20 where the initial h-values label the states. All action costs are one. Clearly, LRTA* with small local search spaces executes a large number of actions to escape from depressions in the h-value surface.

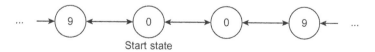

FIGURE 11.20

Example state space (2).

2. Show how LRTA* with local search spaces that vary during the search and RTA* with lookahead one avoid this behavior for the example.
3. Implement all three real-time search methods and experimentally compare them in more realistic state spaces of your choice.

11.5   We could add the additional value-update step $h(Succ(u,a)) \leftarrow \max(h(Succ(u,a)), h(u) - w(u,a))$ between the value-update step and the action-execution step of LRTA* with lookahead one, with the idea to update the h-value of a state not only based on the h-values of its successor states but also on the h-value of one of its predecessor states. Explain why this is only a good idea if the initial h-values are inconsistent.

11.6   Assume that LRTA* with minimal local search spaces maintains h-values and markings across a series of search tasks in the same safely explorable state space with the same set of goal states. Initially, only the goal states are marked. If several actions tie in the action-selection step and the execution of at least one of them results in a marked state (or if the execution of the only action results in a marked state), then LRTA* selects such an action for execution and marks its current state as well. Prove the following properties of the resulting variant of LRTA* with initial admissible h-values:
1. When a state is marked, its h-value is equal to its goal distance and then can no longer change.
2. Once LRTA* reaches a marked state, it follows a minimal-cost path from there to a goal state and all states on that path are marked.
3. If the start state of LRTA* is not marked, then it has marked one additional state by the time it reaches a goal state.

11.7   Assume that LRTA* with admissible initial h-values (very infrequently) gets teleported to a state close to its current state when it executes an action. How does this change its properties?
1. Are its h-values guaranteed to remain admissible?
2. Is it guaranteed to reach a goal state in safely explorable state spaces?
3. Is it guaranteed to converge to a minimal-cost path if it maintains its h-values across a series of search tasks in the same safely explorable state space with the same set of goal states?

11.8   Prove Lemmas 11.1 and 11.2.

11.9   Prove that the complexity of zero-initialized Min-LRTA* is $O(ed)$ over all state spaces where all action costs are one, in a way similar to the corresponding proof for LRTA*. As an intermediate step, prove results for Min-LRTA* similar to Lemma 11.3 and Theorem 11.1.

11.10   How do Lemma 11.3 and Theorem 11.1 change for LRTA* with lookahead one if some actions in nongoal states leave the current state unchanged in state spaces where all action costs are one?

11.11   Prove that the complexity of both zero-initialized Min-LRTA* and zero-initialized edge counting is $\Omega(ed)$ over all undirected state spaces where all action costs are one and over

This part of the state space is completely connected

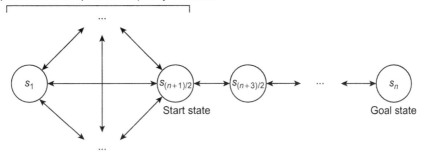

FIGURE 11.21

Lollipop state space, by Koenig and Simmons (1996).

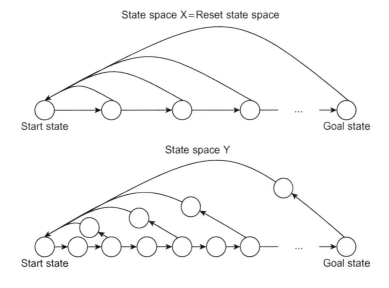

FIGURE 11.22

State space with intermediate states.

all Eulerian state spaces where all action costs are one, using the undirected *lollipop* state space from Figure 11.21.

11.12 Prove that the complexity of zero-initialized node counting is at least exponential in n even over all reasonable undirected state spaces where all action costs are one and over all reasonable Eulerian state spaces where all action costs are one.

11.13 Zero-initialized edge counting and zero-initialized node counting are related in state spaces where all action costs are one. Consider any state space X and a state space Y that is derived from state space X by replacing each of its directed edges with two directed edges that are connected with an intermediate state. Figure 11.22 gives an example. Then, node counting in state space Y, edge counting in state space Y, and edge counting in state space X behave identically (if ties are broken identically). This means that node counting in state space Y and edge counting in state space Y execute the same number of actions, which is twice the number of actions that edge counting executes in state space X (since they have to execute two actions for every action that edge counting executes in state space X). Is there a similar relationship between LRTA* and Min-LRTA*?

11.14   Section 11.6.2 mentions several experimental results in its last paragraph. Implement repeated (forward) A*, LRTA*, and RTAA* for goal-directed navigation in unknown terrain and confirm or disconfirm these results.

11.15   It turns out that goal-directed navigation tasks in unknown terrain can be solved with fewer cell expansions with repeated forward A* (that repeatedly searches from the current cell of the robot to the goal cell) than repeated backward A* (that repeatedly searches from the goal cell to the current cell of the robot), where cells are blocked randomly, the h-values of both variants of A* are initialized with the Manhattan distances, and all cell expansions are counted until the robot reaches the goal cell. The difference is substantial even though the branching factor is the same in both directions. Explain this phenomenon and then perform experiments to support your hypothesis in a GRIDWORLD where all action costs are one.

11.16   Implement a GRIDWORLD with five ant robots that all start in the same cell and use LRTA* with lookahead one to cover the GRIDWORLD repeatedly. All action costs are one. Test out different ideas for how to make the ant robots cover the GRIDWORLD faster or more uniformly.
1. Can you make the ant robots cover the GRIDWORLD faster or more uniformly by biasing them away from each other so that they spread out more quickly?
2. Can you make the ant robots cover the GRIDWORLD faster or more uniformly by letting them all use node counting instead of LRTA*?
3. Do the experimental cover times of LRTA* and node counting reflect the difference in their complexities?

11.17   Prove variants of Lemma 11.3, Theorem 11.1, and Theorem 11.2 for the variant of LRTA* from Algorithm 11.8 that does not constrain the order in which the h-values of the states are updated, which is sometimes called trial-based real-time dynamic programming. We can view it as repeating the value-update step with different local search spaces (at least one of which contains the current state) before it executes the action-selection step.

11.18   Describe how we can obtain (informed) admissible h-values for Probabilistic LRTA*, where the h-values approximate the expected goal distances of the states.

11.19   Consider one ant robot that performs an edge ant walk in the GRIDWORLD from Figure 11.1 with the start cell given in the figure. How many action executions does it need in the worst case to visit every state of this undirected state space at least once (that is, for the worst possible order of actions in each state). How many action executions does it need in the worst case before it repeatedly executes a Eulerian cycle?

11.20   Consider LRTA* with lookahead one that uses $\lambda \cdot h(Succ(u,a))$ instead of $h(Succ(u,a))$ in the action-selection and value-update steps, for a constant $\lambda > 1$. Assume that this variant of LRTA* maintains h-values across a series of search tasks in the same safely explorable state

---

Procedure Variant-of-LRTA*-2
Input: Search task with initial h-values
Side Effect: Updated h-values

$u \leftarrow s$;; Start in start state
while $(u \notin T)$;; While goal not achieved
 while desired   ;; Repeat zero or more times (as desired)
  $v \leftarrow SelectNongoalState(S)$;; Select any nongoal state
  $a \leftarrow \arg\min_{a \in A(v)}\{w(v,a) + h(Succ(v,a))\}$;; Select action
  $h(v) \leftarrow \max\{h(v), w(v,a) + h(Succ(v,a))\}$;; Update h-value
 $a \leftarrow \arg\min_{a \in A(u)}\{w(u,a) + h(Succ(u,a))\}$;; Select action
 $h(u) \leftarrow \max\{h(u), w(u,a) + h(Succ(u,a))\}$;; Update h-value
 $u \leftarrow a(u)$;; Execute action

Algorithm 11.8

Variant of LRTA* (2).

---

space with the same set of goal states. Prove or disprove that the number of search tasks for which this variant of LRTA* with admissible initial h-values reaches a goal state with an execution cost that is larger than $\lambda \cdot \delta(s, T)$ (where s is the start state of the current search task) is bounded from above.

11.21 The larger the sizes of the local search spaces of LRTA*, the smaller the execution cost of LRTA* tends to be. However, updating the h-values in larger local search spaces is time consuming. To run faster, LRTA* can update the h-values in its local search spaces only approximately, which is what RTAA* and the variant of LRTA* in Algorithm 11.8 do. There is also a variant of LRTA* that performs a branch-and-bound search, called minimin search, to set the h-value of the current state to the value calculated by our variant of Dijkstra's algorithm from Algorithm 11.2 but leaves the h-values of the other states in the local search space unchanged. In this general context, consider the variant of LRTA* from Algorithm 11.9. Initially, the non-negative h'-values are zero, and the s'-values are NULL. We use $h''(s,a)$ as a shorthand for $h'(succ(s,a))$ if $s'(succ(s,a)) = s$ and $h(succ(s,a))$ otherwise. (The minimum of an empty set is infinity.)
1. How does it relate to LRTA* with larger local search spaces?
2. How does it relate to RTA*?
3. Which properties does it have?
4. Can you improve on it?

11.22 Prove that edge counting always reaches a goal state with a finite number of action executions and thus finite execution cost in all safely explorable state spaces where all action costs are one.

11.23 Argue that Theorem 11.5 basically implies that the complexity results from Section 11.3 also apply to RTAA* with consistent initial h-values.

11.24 Simplify the value-update step of FALCONS in case its initial g-values and h-values are consistent.

Procedure Variant-of-LRTA*-3
Input: Search task with initial h-values
Side Effect: Updated h-values

$u \leftarrow s$	;; Start in start state
while $(u \notin T)$	;; While goal not achieved
$\quad a \leftarrow \arg\min_{a \in A(u)} \{w(u,a) + h''(u,a)\}$	;; Select action
$\quad h(u) \leftarrow \max\{h(u), w(u,a) + h''(u,a)\}$	;; Update h-value
$\quad s'(u) \leftarrow Succ(u,a)$	;; Select successor state
$\quad h'(u) \leftarrow \max\{h(u), \min_{a \in A(u) \mid Succ(u,a) \neq s'(u)} \{w(u,a) + h''(u,a)\}\}$	;; Update h-value
$\quad u \leftarrow a(u)$	;; Execute action

Algorithm 11.9

Variant of LRTA* (3).

11.25 The complexity of zero-initialized LRTA* with minimal local search spaces is $\Theta(nd)$ over all state spaces where all action costs are one and $\Theta(n^2)$ over all safely explorable state spaces where all action costs are one. Prove that these complexities remain tight over all undirected state spaces and Eulerian state spaces where all action costs are one. What are the corresponding complexities for RTAA*?

11.9 BIBLIOGRAPHIC NOTES

The term *agent-centered search* has been coined by Koenig (2001b); the term *real-time heuristic search* has been coined by Korf (1990); and the term *trial-based real-time dynamic programming* has been coined by Barto, Bradtke, and Singh (1995). Korf (1990) used real-time search originally for finding suboptimal solutions to large off-line search tasks, such as the NINETY-NINE-PUZZLE. Real-time search is related to pebble algorithms that agents can use to cover state spaces by marking otherwise indistinguishable states with colored pebbles (Blum, Raghavan, and Schieber, 1991). Real-time search is also related to plan-envelope methods that operate on MDPs and, like Probabilistic LRTA*, reduce the search cost by searching only small local search spaces (plan envelopes). If the local search space is left during execution, then they repeat the process from the new state, until they reach a goal state (Dean, Kaelbling, Kirman, and Nicholson, 1995). However, they search all the way from the start state to a goal state, using local search spaces that usually border at least one goal state and are likely not to be left during execution. Finally, real-time search is also similar to reinforcement learning (see work by Thrun, 1992 and Koenig and Simmons, 1996a) and to incremental search (see work by Koenig, 2004). Real-time search has been applied to traditional search tasks by Korf (1990, 1993); STRIPS-type planning tasks by Bonet, Loerincs, and Geffner (1997); moving-target search by Ishida (1997) and Koenig and Simmons (1995); coverage with ant robots by Wagner, Lindenbaum, and Bruckstein (1999), Koenig, Szymanski, and Liu (2001a), and Svennebring and Koenig (2004); localization by Koenig (2001a); MDPs by Barto, Bradtke, and Singh (1995); and POMDPs by Bonet and Geffner (2000).

LRTA* has been described by Korf (1990) (including minimin search) and analyzed by Koenig (2001a); SLA* has been described by Shue and Zamani (1993); SLA*T has been described by Shue, Li, and Zamani (2001); ϵ-LRTA* has been described by Ishida (1997); RTAA* has been described by Koenig and Likhachev (2006); RTA* has been described by Korf (1990); node counting has been described by Koenig and Szymanski (1999) and has been analyzed by Koenig, Szymanski, and Liu (2001a); Min-LRTA* has been described by Koenig and Simmons (1996a); SLRTA* has been described by Edelkamp and Eckerle (1997); edge counting has been described by Koenig and Simmons (1996b); edge ant walk has been described by Yanovski, Wagner, and Bruckstein (2003); FALCONS has been described by Furcy and Koenig (2000); and min-max LRTA* has been described by Koenig (2001a).

Variants of LRTA* have been studied by Russell and Wefald (1991); variants of min-max LRTA* have been studied by Bonet and Geffner (2000) and Hernández and Meseguer (2005 and 2007a,b); variants of node counting have been studied by Balch and Arkin (1993), Pirzadeh and Snyder (1990) and Thrun (1992); and variants of edge counting have been studied by Sutherland (1969). Improvements on these real-time search methods have been reported by Edelkamp and Eckerle (1997), Ishida (1997), Moore and Atkeson (1993), Pemberton and Korf (1992, 1994), Russell and Wefald (1991), Sutton (1991), Thorpe (1994), and Bulitko, Sturtevant, and Kazakevich (2005). Some of these improvements have been unified by Bulitko and Lee (2006).

Real-time search for cooperating agents other than ant robots has been studied by Ishida (1997), Knight (1993), and Felner, Shoshani, Altshuler, and Bruckstein (2006). A book-length overview on real-time search has been given by Ishida (1997) and covers many research results on real-time search by its author. Real-time search methods that do not satisfy our definition but only need a constant search time before the first action execution and between action executions, for example, have been described by Björnsson, Bultiko and Sturtevant (2009) for arbitrary state spaces (called time-bounded A*) and Parberry (1995) for sliding-tile puzzles.

Heuristic Search Variants

IV

Adversary Search

Adversaries introduce an element of uncertainty into the search process. One model for adversary search is *game playing*. It is a special case of a layered tree search that has been investigated in depth using specialized algorithms. Optimal strategies result in perfect play. In most settings, the players can take actions alternately and independently. We address the standard game playing algorithms *negmax* and *minimax* together with pruning options like $\alpha\beta$. Game tree searches are rather depth-bounded rather than cost-bounded, and values at the leaf nodes of the tree are computed through a static evaluation function. *Retrograde analysis* calculates entire databases of classified positions in a backward direction, starting from won and lost ones; these databases can be used in conjunction with specialized game playing programs as endgame lookup tables. Multiplayer and general game playing broaden this scope.

In nondeterministic or probabilistic environments, the adversary refers to the unpredictable behavior of nature. In contrast to the deterministic search models, the outcome of an executed action in a state is not unique. Each applicable action may spawn several successors. There are many reasons for such uncertainty: randomness that is in the real world, the lack of knowledge for modeling the real world precisely, the dynamic change in the environment that we cannot control, sensors and actuators that are imprecise, and so on.

Solutions to nondeterministic and probabilistic search tasks are no longer sequences of actions but mappings from state to actions. As opposed to linear solution sequences, adversary search requires state space traversal to return solution *policies* in the form of a tree or a graph. The policy is often implicitly represented in the form of a *value function* that assigns a value to each of the states. For the deterministic setting, the value function takes the role of the heuristic that is gradually improved to the goal distance. This links the solution process for adversary search problems to the ones presented for real-time search, where the value function for deterministic search models is improved over time.

To apply policies to the real world, we embed the solutions in the environment in the form of finite-state controllers. This means that solutions can be interpreted as being programs that react on inputs by issuing an action in the current internal state and changing this state based on the response of the environment.

In a probabilistic environment the standard formalism for a stochastic search problem is that of a Markov decision process. A simpler model of nondeterminism is an AND/OR graph, in which the solver controls the OR nodes, and the environment operates on the AND nodes. The main difference between the two is that outgoing edges when performing actions are labeled with probabilities.

We unify solving deterministic, nondeterministic, and probabilistic searches in one model. As with deterministic search, we usually search for policies that are optimal. In nondeterministic and probabilistic environments, the intended effect might be achieved or not; in this case, we maximize the *expected rewards* (or minimize the *expected costs*).

12.1 TWO-PLAYER GAMES

According to John McCarthy, CHESS is the *Drosophila* of AI, in an analogy with dominant use of that fruit fly to study inheritance. Since the early 1950s, CHESS (see Fig. 12.1) has advanced to one of the main successes in AI, resulting in the defeat of the human world champion in a tournament match, even if we may argue on how the computation-intense search resemblances to the intellectual approach used by human players.

Generally, a move in CHESS consists of transporting one of the pieces of the player to a different square, following the rules of movement for that piece. Up to one exception, a player can take a piece of the opponent by moving one of his own pieces to the square occupied by the opponent. The opponent's piece is removed from the board and remains out of play for the rest of the game. When the king is threatened and cannot make a move such that after the move the king is not threatened, then we have a mate position, which ends the game (see Fig. 12.1, right, for a mate in one move). When a player cannot make any legal move, but the king is not threatened, then the game is a draw. If the same position with the same player to move is repeated three times, he can also claim a draw.

The position to the right in Figure 12.1 illustrates a move in a recent human-machine game that has been overseen by the human world champion when playing against the program *Deep Fritz*. The

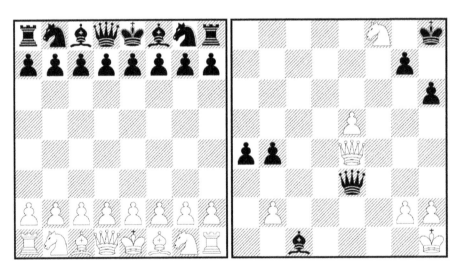

FIGURE 12.1

Initial and Mate-in-1 position in CHESS (white to move).

FIGURE 12.2

Intermediate states in TIC-TAC-TOE (left) and NIM (right).

personal computer won by 4:2. In contrast, *Deep Thought*, the first computer system that defeated a human world champion in a match, used a massively parallelized, hardware-oriented search scheme, evaluating and storing billions of nodes in a second with a fine-tuned evaluation function and a large, human-made opening book.

Besides competitive play, some combinatorial CHESS problems, like the 33,439,123,484,294 complete Knight's tours, have been solved using search.

TIC-TAC-TOE (see Fig. 12.2) is a game between two players, who alternate in setting their respective tokens O and X on a 3×3 board. The winner of the game has to complete either a row, a column, or a diagonal with his own tokens. Obviously, the size of the state space is bounded by $3^9 = 19,683$ states, since each field is either unmarked, or marked X or O. A complete enumeration shows that there is no winning strategy (for either side); the game is a draw (assuming optimal play).

NIM is a two-player game in which players remove one or more matches at a time from a single row. The player to take the last match wins. One classic NIM instance is shown in Figure 12.2 (right). By applying combinatorial game theory an optimal playing strategy can be obtained without much search (see Exercises).

Strong Go programs try to emphasize much of the human way of thinking rather than brute-force search methods for which computers are ideal, and from this point of view Go might have a chance to become the next fruit fly of AI, in the sense of McCarthy. Many techniques, like rule-based knowledge representation, pattern recognition, and machine learning, have been tried. The two players compete in acquiring territory by placing stones on a 19×19 board (see Fig. 12.3, left). Each player seeks to enclose territory with his stones and can capture opponent's ones. The object of the game is to enclose the largest territory. The game has been addressed by different strategies. One approach with exponential savings in some endgames uses a divide-and-conquer method in which some board situations are split into a sum of local games of tractable size. Another influencing search method exploits structure in samples of random play.

In CONNECT 4 (see Fig. 12.3, right), a player has to place tokens into one of the lowest unoccupied fields in each column. To win, four tokens of his color have to be lined up horizontally, vertically, or diagonally before the opponent does. This game has been proven to be a win for the first player in optimal play using a knowledge-based minimax-based search that introduces the third value *unknown* into the game search tree evaluation. The approach has a working memory requirement linear in the size of the search tree, whereas traditional $\alpha\beta$ pruning requires only memory linear to the depth of it.

The basic aim of the board game NINE-MEN-MORRIS (see Fig. 12.4) is to establish vertical or horizontal lines (a mill). Whenever a player completes a mill, that player immediately removes one opponent piece that does not form part of a mill from the board. If all the opponent's pieces form

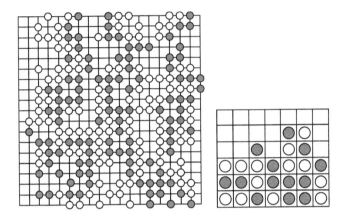

FIGURE 12.3

Intermediate positions in GO (left) and terminal one in CONNECT 4 (right).

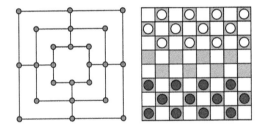

FIGURE 12.4

Initial positions in NINE-MEN-MORRIS and CHECKERS.

mills then an exception is made and the player is allowed to remove one. Initially, the players place a piece of their own color on any unoccupied point until all 18 pieces have been played. After that, play continues alternately but each turn consists of a player moving one piece along a line to an adjacent point. The game is lost for a player either by being reduced to two pieces or by being unable to move. NINE-MEN-MORRIS has been solved with parallel search and huge *endgame databases*. The outcome of a complete search is that the game is a draw.

In CHECKERS (see Fig. 12.4, right) the two players try to capture all the other players' pieces or render them immobile. A regular piece can move to a vacant square, diagonally forward. When such a regular piece reaches the last row, it becomes a king. A king can move to a vacant square diagonally forward or backward. A piece (piece or king) can only move to a vacant square. A move can also consist of one or more jumps, capturing an opponent piece if jumped. Nowadays, checker programs have perfect information for all CHECKERS positions involving 10 or fewer pieces on the board generated in large *retrograde analysis* using a network of workstations and various high-end computers. CHECKERS is a draw.

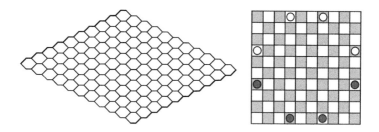

FIGURE 12.5

Initial positions in HEX and AMAZONS.

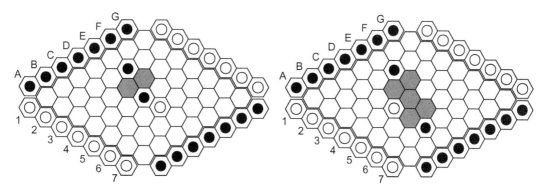

FIGURE 12.6

Virtual and virtual semiconnection in HEX.

HEX (see Fig. 12.5, left) is another PSPACE-complete board game. The players place balls in one of the cells with their color. Both players attempt to build a chain of his colored cells connecting his (opposing) borders. Since the game can never result in a draw, it is easy to prove that the game is won for the first player to move, since otherwise he can adopt the winning strategy of the second player to win the game. In HEX the current state-of-the-art programs use an unusual approach of electrical circuit theory to combine the influence of subpositions (virtual connections) to larger ones. A virtual semiconnection allows two groups of pieces to connect provided that one can move, and a full virtual connection allows groups to connect independent of the opponent's moves (see Fig. 12.6).

AMAZONS (see Fig. 12.5, right) is a board game, which has become popular in recent years, and has served as a platform for both game-theoretic study and AI games research. Players move queens on an $n \times n$ (usually 10×10) board. The pieces, called queens or amazons, move like CHESS queens. As part of each move an arrow is shot from the moved piece. The point where the arrow lands is reachable from the target position and is eliminated from the playing area, such that the arrows eventually block the movement of the queens. The last player to complete a move wins. AMAZONS is in PSPACE, since (unlike CHESS and GO) the number of moves in an AMAZONS game is polynomially bounded. Deciding the outcome of $n \times n$ AMAZONS is PSPACE-hard.

12.1.1 **Game Tree Search**

To select an optimal move in a two-person game, the computer constructs a *game tree*, in which each node represents a configuration (e.g., a board position). The root of the tree corresponds to the current position, and the children of a node represent configurations reachable in one move. Every other level (a.k.a. *ply*) corresponds to opponent moves. In terms of the formalism of Section 12.4, a game tree is a special case of an AND/OR graph, with alternating layers of AND and OR nodes. We are particularly concerned here with *zero-sum* games (the win of one player is the loss of the other), where both players have *perfect information* (unlike, for example, in a card game).

Usually, the tree is too large to be searched entirely, so the analysis is truncated at some fixed level and the resulting *terminal nodes* are evaluated by a heuristic procedure called a *static evaluation function*. The need for making a decision sooner than it takes to determine the optimal move and the bounded backup of horizon estimates is a characteristic that two-player search shares with real-time search.

The evaluation procedure assigns a numeric heuristic value to the position, where larger values represent positions more favorable to the player whose turn is to play. The static evaluator doesn't have to be correct, the only requirement is that it yields the correct values for terminal positions (e.g., checkmate or drawn configurations in CHESS), and the informal expectation that higher values correlate with better positions, on average. There is no notion of admissibility as in single-player games. A static evaluator can be implemented using basically any appropriate representation. One common, simple form is a weighted sum of game-specific features, such as material difference, figure mobility, attacked figures, and so on.

A major share of the secret of writing strong computer games lies in the "black magic" of crafting good evaluation functions. The challenge lies in striking the right balance between giving an indicative value without excessive computational cost. Indeed, easy games can be searched completely, so almost any heuristic will do; on the other hand, if we had an evaluation function at hand that is always correct, we wouldn't have to search in the first place. Usually, evaluation functions are developed by experts in laborious, meticulous trial-and-error experimentation. However, we will later also discuss approaches to let the computer "learn" the evaluation on its own.

It is a real challenge to find good evaluation functions for interesting games that can be computed efficiently. Often the static evaluation function is computed in two separate steps. First, a number of features are extracted, then these features are combined to an overall evaluation function. The features are described by human experts. The evaluation function is also often derived by hand, but it can also be learned or optimized by a program. Another problem is that all feature values have to be looked at and that the evaluation can become complex. We give a solution based on classification trees, a natural extension of decision trees, which are introduced first. Then we show how classification trees can be used effectively in $\alpha\beta$-search and how to find the evaluation functions with bootstrapping.

We will assume that the value of a position from the point of view of one player is the negative of its value from the point of view of the other. The *principal variation* is defined as the path from the root on which each player plays optimally; that is, chooses a move that maximizes his worst-case return (as measured by the static evaluator at the leaves of the tree). It may be found by labeling each interior node with the maximum of the negatives of the values of its children. Then the *principal variation* is defined as the path from the root to a leaf that follows from each node to its lowest-valued child; the value at the root is the value of the terminal position reached by this path (from the point of view of the first player). This labeling procedure is called the *negmax* algorithm, with its pseudo code shown in Algorithm 12.1.

Procedure Negmax
Input: Position u
Output: Value at root

if (*leaf(u)*) **return** *Eval(u)*	;; No successor, static evaluation
res ← −∞	;; Initialize value *res* for current frame
for each $v \in Succ(u)$	;; Traverse successor list
res ← max{*res*, −*Negmax(v)*}	;; Update value *res*
return *res*	;; Return final evaluation

Algorithm 12.1

The negmax game tree labeling procedure.

Procedure Minimax
Input: Position u
Output: Value at root

if (*leaf(u)*) **return** *Eval(u)*	;; No successor, static evaluation
if (*max-node(u)*) *val* ← −∞	;; Initialize return value for MAX node
else *val* ← +∞	;; Initialize return value for MIN node
for each $v \in Succ(u)$	;; Traverse successor list
if (*max-node(u)*) *val* ← max{*val*, *Minimax(v)*}	;; Recursive call at MAX node
else *val* ← min{*val*, *Minimax(v)*}	;; Recursive call at MIN node
return *res*	;; Return final evaluation

Algorithm 12.2

Minimax game tree search.

Minimax is an equivalent formulation of *negmax*, where the evaluation values for the two players do not necessarily have to be the negative of each other. The search tree consists of two different types of nodes: the *MIN nodes* for one player that tries to minimize the possible payoff, and the *MAX nodes* for the other player that tries to maximize it (see Alg. 12.2).

For all but some trivial games, the game tree cannot be fully evaluated. In practical applications, the number of levels that can be explored depends on a time limit for this move; in this respect, the interleaving of computation and action is reminiscent of the real-time search scenario (see Chapter 11). Since the actually required computation time is not known beforehand, most game playing programs apply an *iterative-deepening approach*; that is, they successively search to 2, 4, 6, ... plies until the available time is exhausted. As a side effect, we will see that the search to ply k can also provide valuable information to speed up the next deeper search to ply $k + 2$.

12.1.2 $\alpha\beta$-**Pruning**

We have seen how the *negmax* procedure performs depth-first search of the game tree and assigns a value to each node. The branch-and-bound method of $\alpha\beta$-*pruning* determines the root's *negmax* value while avoiding examination of a substantial portion of the tree. It requires two bounds that are used to restrict the search; taken together, these bounds are known as the $\alpha\beta$-*window*. The value α is meant to be the least value the player can achieve, while the opponent can surely keep it at no more than β. If the initial window is $(-\infty, \infty)$, the $\alpha\beta$-procedure will determine the correct root value. The procedure avoids many nodes in the tree by achieving *cut-offs*. There are two types to be distinguished: *shallow* and *deep cut-offs*.

We consider shallow cut-offs first. Consider the situation in Figure 12.7, where one child has value -8. Then the value of the root will be at least 8. Subsequently, the value of node d is determined as 5, and hence node c achieves at least -5. Therefore, the player at the root would always prefer moving to b, and the outcome of the other children of c is irrelevant.

In *deep* pruning, the bound used for the cut-off can stem not only from the parent, but from any ancestor node. Consider Figure 12.8. After evaluating the first child f of e, its value must be -5 or larger. But the first player can already achieve 8 at the root by moving to b, so he will never choose to move to e from d, and the remaining unexplored children of e can be pruned. The implementation of $\alpha\beta$-search is shown in Algorithm 12.3.

For any node u, β represents an upper bound that is used to restrict the node below u. A cut-off occurs when it is determined that u's negmax value is greater than or equal to β. In such a situation, the opponent can already choose a move that avoids u with a value no greater than β. From the opponent's standpoint, the alternate move is no worse than u, so continued search below p is not necessary. We say that u is *refuted*. It is obvious how to extend $\alpha\beta$-pruning to minimax search (see Alg. 12.4).

The so-called *fail-safe* version of $\alpha\beta$ initializes the variable *res* with $-\infty$, instead of with α. This modification allows the search for the case where the initial window is smaller than $(-\infty, \infty)$ to be generalized. If the search fails (i.e., the root value lies outside this interval), an estimate is returned that informs us if the true value lies below α, or above β.

Theorem 12.1. *(Correctness of Minimax Search with $\alpha\beta$-Pruning) Let u be an arbitrary position in a game and $\alpha < \beta$. Then the following three assertions are true.*

1. $MinimaxAlphaBeta(u, \alpha, \beta) \leq \alpha \Leftrightarrow Eval(u) \leq \alpha$.
2. $MinimaxAlphaBeta(u, \alpha, \beta) \geq \beta \Leftrightarrow Eval(u) \geq \beta$.
3. $\alpha < MinimaxAlphaBeta(u, \alpha, \beta) < \beta \Leftrightarrow \alpha < Eval(u) < \beta$.

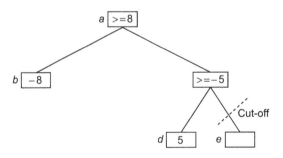

FIGURE 12.7

Shallow cut-off in $\alpha\beta$-pruning.

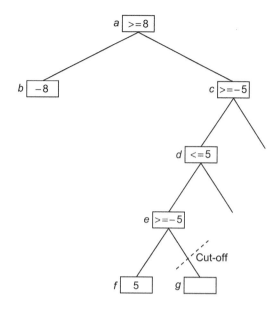

FIGURE 12.8

Deep cut-off in $\alpha\beta$-pruning.

Procedure NegmaxAlphaBeta
Input: Position u, bounds α, β
Output: Value at root

if (*leaf*(u)) **return** *Eval*(u)   ;; No successor, static evaluation
res $\leftarrow \alpha$;; Initialize value *res* for current frame
for each $v \in Succ(u)$;; Traverse successor list
    val $\leftarrow -$*NegmaxAlphaBeta*($v, -\beta, -res$)   ;; Initialize cut-off value
    if (*val* > *res*) *res* $\leftarrow$ *val*   ;; Update *res*
    if (*res* $\geq \beta$) **return** *res*   ;; Perform cut-off
return *res*   ;; Return final evaluation

Algorithm 12.3

$\alpha\beta$ negmax game tree pruning.

Proof. We only proof the second assertion—the others are inferred analogously. Let u be a MAX node. We have *MinimaxAlphaBeta*(u, α, β) $\geq \beta$ if and only if there exists a successor with *res* $\geq \beta$. Since for all further successors we have that the value *res* only increases and *res* for the chosen state is the maximum of all previous *res* values including α, we conclude that *res* for the chosen state is equal to *MinimaxAlphaBeta*(u, res', β) $\geq \beta$ for some value *res'* < *res*. By using induction we have that *Eval*(u) $\geq \beta$.

Procedure MinimaxAlphaBeta
Input: Position u, value α, value β
Output: Value at root

if (*leaf(u)*) **return** *Eval(p)*	;; No successor, return evaluation
if (*max-node(u)*)	;; MAX node
res ← α	;; Initialize result value
for each $v \in Succ(u)$	;; Traverse successor list
val ← *MinimaxAlphaBeta(v, res, β)*	;; Recursion for α
res ← max{*res, val*}	;; Take maximal value
if (*res* ≥ β)	;; Result exceeds threshold
return *res*	;; Propagate value
else	;; MIN node
res ← β	;; Initialize result value
for each $v \in Succ(u)$	;; Traverse successor list
val ← *MinimaxAlphaBeta(v, α, res)*	;; Recursion for β
res ← min{*res, val*}	;; Take minimal value
if (*res* ≤ α)	;; Result exceeds threshold
return *res*	;; Propagate value
return *res*	;; Propagate value

Algorithm 12.4

Minimax game tree search with $\alpha\beta$-pruning.

For the opposite direction we assume that $MinimaxAlphaBeta(u,\alpha,\beta) < \beta$, which means that for all successors the value *res* is smaller than β. Therefore, the value *val* for all successors is smaller than β and $Eval(u) < \beta$.

An example of minimax game tree search with $\alpha\beta$ pruning is shown in Fig. 12.9. In addition, the positive effect of pruning when additionally applying move ordering is illustrated. ∎

Performance of $\alpha\beta$-Pruning

To obtain a bound on the performance of $\alpha\beta$-pruning, we have to prove that for each game tree there is a *minimal (sub)tree* that has to be examined by any search algorithm, regardless of the values of the terminal nodes. This tree is called the *critical tree*, and its nodes are *critical nodes*. It is helpful to classify nodes into three types, called PV, CUT, and ALL. The following rules determine critical nodes.

- The root is a PV node.
- The first child of a PV node is a PV, the remaining children are CUT nodes.
- The first child of a CUT node is an ALL node.
- All children of an ALL node are CUT nodes.

If we do not implement deep cut-offs, only three rules for determining the minimal tree remain.

- The root is a PV node.
- The first child of a PV node is also a PV, the remaining children are CUT nodes.
- The first child of a CUT node is a PV node.

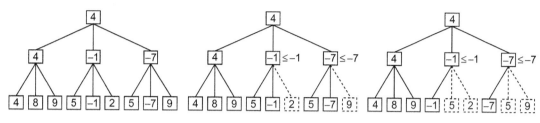

FIGURE 12.9

Minimax game search tree pruned by $\alpha\beta$ and additional move ordering.

The number of terminal leaves on the critical tree of a complete, uniform b-ary subtree of height d is

$$b^{\lceil d/2 \rceil} + b^{\lfloor d/2 \rfloor} - 1.$$

This can also be motivated as follows. To prove that the value of the root is *at least v*, $b^{\lceil d/2 \rceil}$ leaves must be inspected, since one move must be considered on each player level, and all moves on each opponent level (this subtree is also called the player's *strategy*). Conversely, to see that the value is *at most v*, $b^{\lfloor d/2 \rfloor} - 1$ leaf nodes have to be generated (the opponent's strategy). The principal variation lies in the intersection of the two.

If the tree is searched in best-first order (i.e., the best move is always chosen first for exploration), then $\alpha\beta$ will search *only* the critical tree. Thus, for the performance of this algorithm it is crucial to apply *move ordering* (i.e., sorting the moves heuristically according to their expected merit).

Note that the preceding term is approximately $2\sqrt{n}$, where $n = b^d$ is the number of leaves in the whole (unpruned) tree. Consequently, we can state that $\alpha\beta$-pruning has the potential to double the search depth.

Extending Pruning to the Static Evaluator

Depending on its complexity, the static evaluation can claim most of the computational effort in game tree search. One idea to cut down on unnecessary overhead is to extend $\alpha\beta$-pruning into the evaluation itself. It is no longer considered an atomic operation. For example, in a weighted sum type of the evaluator, one feature is computed at a time, and a partial estimate is available at each step. Suppose that, as is usually the case, all feature values and weights are positive. Then, as soon as the partial sum exceeds the $\alpha\beta$-search window, we can discard the position without taking the remaining features into consideration.

This type of pruning is particularly powerful if the heuristic is represented in the form of a tree. Each internal node in a *decision tree* contains a test condition (e.g., an attribute comparison with a threshold value) that determines which branch to descend next. Its leaves contain the actual outcome of the evaluation. Decision trees can be automatically induced from labeled training examples. One drawback is that if an attribute is close to a threshold value, the evaluation can abruptly jump based on an arbitrary change in the input feature. As a remedy, generalizations of decision trees have been developed and have been applied to game playing that make the decision boundary "soft" or "fuzzy."

12.1.3 Transposition Tables

As in single-agent search, *transposition tables* (see Sec. 6.1.1) are memory-intense dictionaries (see Ch. 3) of search information for valuable reuse. They are used to test if the value of a certain state has already been computed during a search in a different subtree. This can drastically reduce the size of the effective search game tree, since in two-player games it is very common to have different move sequences (or different orders of the same moves) lead to the same position.

The usual implementation of a transposition table is done by hashing. For fast hash function evaluations and large hash tables to be addressed a compact representation for the state is suggested.

We apply transposition table lookup to the *negmax* algorithm with $\alpha\beta$-pruning. Algorithm 12.5 provides a suitable implementation. To interpret the different stored flags, recall that in the $\alpha\beta$-pruning scheme not all values of α and β yield the *minimax* value at its root. There are three sets to be distinguished: *valid*, the value of the algorithm matches the one of *negmax* search; *lbound*, the value of the algorithm is a lower bound for the one of *negmax* search; and *ubound*, the value of the algorithm is an upper bound for the one of *negmax* search.

In addition, note that the same position can be encountered at different depths of the tree. This depth is also stored in the transposition table. Only if the stored search depth is larger or equal to the remaining search depth can the result replace the execution of the search.

Major nuances of the algorithm concern the strategy of when to overwrite an entry in the transposition table. In Algorithm 12.5, the scheme "always replace" is used, which simply overwrites anything that was already there. This may not be the best scheme, and in fact, there has been a lot of experimental work trying to optimize this scheme. An alternative scheme is "replace if same depth or deeper." This leaves a currently existing node alone unless the depth of the new one is greater than or equal to the depth of the one in the table.

As explained in the exposition of $\alpha\beta$-pruning (see Sec. 12.1.2), searching good moves first makes the search much more efficient. This gives rise to another important use of transposition tables, apart from eliminating duplicate work; along with a position's negmax value, it can also store the best move found. So if you find that there is a "best" move in your hash element, and you search it first, you will often improve your move ordering, and consequently reduce the effective branching factor. Particularly, if an iterative-deepening scheme is applied, the best moves from the previous, shallower search iteration tend to also be the best ones in the current iteration.

The *history heuristic* is another technique of using additional memory to improve move ordering. It is most efficient if all possible moves can be enumerated a priori; in CHESS, for instance, they can be stored in a 64×64 array encoding the start and end squares on the board. Regardless of the exact occurrence in the search tree, the history heuristic associates a statistic with each move about how effective it was in inducing cut-offs in the search. It has been proven that these statistics can be used for very efficient move ordering.

12.1.4 *Searching with Restricted Windows

Aspiration Search

Aspiration search is an inexact approximation of $\alpha\beta$ with higher cut-off rates. $\alpha\beta$-pruning uses an initial window $W = (-\infty, \infty)$ such that the game theoretical value is eventually found. If we initialize the window to some shorter range, we can increase the probability of pruning. For example, we can use a window $(v_0 - \epsilon, v_0 + \epsilon)$, where v_0 is a static estimate of the root value. If the bounds are chosen

Procedure NegmaxAlphaBeta-TT
Input: Position u, value α, value β, value d
Output: Value at root

if (*leaf*(u) **or** $d = 0$ **return** *Eval*(p)	;; No successor, return evaluation
if (*Search*(u) $\neq$ **nil**)	;; Transposition table contains entry for u
(*val*, *flag*, *depth*) $\leftarrow$ *Search*(u)	
if (*depth* $\geq d$)	;; Make sure that stored evaluation was at least as deep
if (*flag* = *valid*) **return** *val*	;; Stored value matches negmax value
if (*flag* = *lbound*) $\alpha \leftarrow \max\{\alpha, val\}$	;; Lower bound for negmax value
if (*flag* = *ubound*) $\beta \leftarrow \min\{\beta, val\}$	;; Upper bound for negmax value
if ($\alpha \geq \beta$) **return** *val*	;; Pruning
res $\leftarrow \alpha$	;; Initialize result value
for each $v \in Succ(u)$	;; Traverse successor list
val $\leftarrow$ $-$NegmaxAlphaBeta-TT($v, -\beta, -res, d - 1$)	;; Recursion for α
res $\leftarrow \max\{res, val\}$	;; Take maximal value
if (*res* $\geq \beta$)	;; Result exceeds threshold
Insert($u, (res, lbound, d)$)	;; Insert value in TT
return *res*	;; Propagate value
if (*res* $> \alpha$)	
Insert($u, (res, valid, d)$)	;; Insert computed value in TT
else	
Insert($u, (res, ubound, d)$)	;; Insert upper bound in TT
return *res*	;; Propagate value

Algorithm 12.5

Negmax game tree search with $\alpha\beta$-pruning and transposition table.

so large that for any position with a value at least that big we can be sure that it is won, then the exact outcome doesn't matter anymore. Alternatively, if the window was chosen too small, the fail-safe modification of $\alpha\beta$ will return an improved bound α' or β' for either α or β, and a re-search has to be conducted with an appropriately enlarged window (α', ∞) or $(-\infty, \beta')$. The hope is that the increased pruning outweighs the overhead of occasional repeated searches.

Null-Window Search

A special case of this algorithm is the so-called *null-window search*. Using the fact that the values of α and β are integral, the initial window is set to $(\alpha - 1, \alpha)$, so that no possible values lie between the bounds. This procedure will always fail, either low or high; it can essentially be used to decide whether the position is below or above a given threshold. Null-window search is mostly used as a subroutine for more advanced algorithms, as described in the following.

Principal-Variation Search

Principal-variation search (see Alg. 12.6) is based on the same rationale as aspiration search; that is, it is attempting to prune the search tree by reducing the evaluation window as much as possible. As

---

Procedure PVS
Input: Position u, bounds α, β
Output: Value at root

if ($leaf(u)$) **return** $Eval(u)$;; No successor, static evaluation
$v_0 \leftarrow first(Succ(u))$;; Try most promising successor first
$res \leftarrow -PVS(v_0, -\beta, -\alpha)$;; Initialize value res for current frame
for each $v \in Succ(u) \setminus \{v_0\}$;; Traverse successor list
    if ($res \geq \beta$) **return** res ;; CUT node
    if ($res > \alpha$) $\alpha \leftarrow res$;; Update bound
    $val \leftarrow -PVS(v, -\alpha - 1, -\alpha)$;; Null window search
    if ($val > res$)
        if ($val > \alpha$ **and** $val < \beta$)
            $res \leftarrow -PVS(v, -\beta, -val)$;; Re-search with enlarged window
    else
        $res \leftarrow val$;; Improved value
return res ;; Return final evaluation

Algorithm 12.6

Principal-variation search in negmax formulation.

---

soon as the value for one move has been obtained, it is assumed that this move is indeed the best one; a series of null-window searches is conducted to prove that its alternatives are inferior. If the null-window search fails high, then the search has to be repeated with the correct bounds.

Memory-Enhanced Test Framework

In contrast to principal-variation search, this class of algorithms relies *only* on a series of null-window searches to determine the negmax value of a position. The general outline of the framework is shown in Algorithm 12.7. It requires the programmer to implement two functions: *InitBound* calculates the test bound used in the first null-window search and *UpdateBound* does so for all successive iterations, depending on the outcome of the last search. The aim is to successively refine the interval (*lowerBound, upperBound*) in which the true negmax value lies, as fast as possible. To offset the cost of repeated evaluations, a transposition table is used.

One particular instantiation is called *MTD(f)*. It uses the following procedure to update the bound:

$$\textbf{if } (g = lower) \; test \; \leftarrow g + 1 \textbf{ else } \; test \; \leftarrow g.$$

That is, the new bound obtained from the last null-window search is used to split the interval.

It is clear that starting with an initial guess closer to the real negmax value should reduce the number of iterations and lead to faster convergence. One way to obtain such an estimate would be to use the static evaluation. Better yet, if, as usual, an iterative-deepening scheme is applied, the result of the previous shallower search can be exploited in *InitBound*.

Apart from MTD(f), other possible instantiations of the MTD framework include:

MTD(∞): *InitBound* returns ∞, *UpdateBound* sets *testBound* to g. While MTD(f) can be called realistic, this procedure is *optimistic* to the extent that it successively decreases an upper bound.

Procedure MTD
Input: Position u
Output: Value at root

$lower \leftarrow -\infty$
$upper \leftarrow \infty$
$test \leftarrow InitBound(u)$;; Set initial test value
repeat
    $g \leftarrow NegMaxAlphaBeta\text{-}TT(u,\ Bound-1, Bound)$;; Null-window search
    if $(g \leq test)$ $upper \leftarrow g$ **else** $lower \leftarrow g$;; Update bounds
    $test \leftarrow UpdateBound(u, g, lower, upper)$;; Determine next test bound
    until $upper = lower$;; Interval narrowed down to size zero
return g ;; Return final evaluation

Algorithm 12.7

MTD algorithm framework.

MTD($-\infty$): *InitBound* returns $-\infty$, *UpdateBound* sets *testBound* to $g+1$. This *pessimistic* algorithm successively increases a lower bound.
MTD(bi): *UpdateBound* sets *testBound* to the average of *lowerBound* and *upperBound* to *bisect* the range of possible outcomes.
MTD(step): Like in MTD(∞), an upper bound is successively lowered. However, by making larger steps at a time, the number of searches can be reduced. To this end, *UpdateBound* sets *testBound* to max($lower + 1, g - stepsize$).

Best-First Search

For over a decade prior to the introduction of the MTD framework, *best-first search* for two-player games had been shown to have theoretical advantages over the $\alpha\beta$-procedure. Like A*, the algorithm SSS* maintains an *Open* list of unexpanded nodes; as governed by a set of rules, in each step the node with the best evaluation is selected, and replaced by a number of other nodes, its children or its parent. In some cases, *Open* has to be purged of all ancestors of a node.

It was proven that in a statically ordered game tree, SSS* dominates $\alpha\beta$ in the sense of the number of evaluated leaf nodes that cannot be higher, and is often significantly lower. However, the algorithm never played a practically relevant role due to a number of perceived shortcomings:

- From the original formulation, the algorithm is hard to understand.
- It has large memory requirements.
- Purging of ancestor nodes is slow.

These problems could still not be completely overcome by subsequently developed improvements and variations, such as a recursive formulation, and an algorithm, which in analogy to SSS* successively increases a lower bound on the negmax value.

Now, with the advent of the MTD framework described in the previous section, a surprising breakthrough in game tree search research was achieved by clarifying the relation between the previously incomparable and disparate approaches of depth-first and best-first search. Specifically, with a sufficiently large transposition table, MTD(∞) and SSS* are equivalent to the extent that they expand the same nodes, in the same order. Since MTD only adds one loop around standard $\alpha\beta$-search, it is easy to see that the reason why SSS* can expand less leaf nodes is that searching with a null window allows for considerably more pruning. The memory requirements can be flexibly alleviated in dependence of available main memory by allocating less space for the transposition table (though it might be argued that this objection to SSS* is no longer valid for modern-day computers). No expensive priority queue operations are needed in the implementation, and the transposition table is usually realized as a hash table, resulting in constant-time access.

An experimental comparison of different depth-first and best-first algorithms on realistic game situations in CHECKERS and CHESS was conducted. All algorithms were given the same memory constraints. The results contradicted a number of previously held beliefs. MTD(f) turned out to consistently outperform other algorithms, both in terms of expansion numbers and execution times. SSS* yields only a modest improvement over $\alpha\beta$, and is sometimes outperformed both by depth-first and best-first algorithms. One reason is that the dominance proof of SSS* over $\alpha\beta$ assumes *static move ordering*; when, in an iterative-deepening scheme, a transposition table is used to explore the best moves from the previous iteration first, the latter algorithm can beat the former one. Contradicting earlier results with artificially generated trees, best-first search is generally not significantly better than depth-first search in practice, and can sometimes be even much worse. The reason is that additional, commonly applied search enhancements (some of which will be briefly discussed) are very effective in improving efficiency and reducing their advantage.

Another important lesson learned from the empirical algorithm comparison is that with search enhancements on realistic situations, the efficiency of all algorithms differed only by at most around 10%. Thus, we can say that the search enhancements used in high-performance game playing programs improve the search efficiency to an extent close to the critical tree, such that the question of which algorithm to use is no longer of prime importance.

12.1.5 Accumulated Evaluations

In some domains (e.g., some card games), the total evaluation at a leaf is in fact the sum of the evaluation at interior nodes. In this case, the $\alpha\beta$-routine for *minimax* search has to be implemented with care. The problem of usual $\alpha\beta$-pruning is that the accumulated value that will be compared in a transposition table lookup is influenced by the path. Algorithm 12.8 shows a possible implementation for this case.

Theorem 12.2. *(Correctness $\alpha\beta$ for Accumulated Estimates) Let u be any game position. Then we have*

$$AccMinimaxAlphaBeta'(u, \alpha - Eval(u), \beta - Eval(u)) + Eval(u) =$$
$$AccMinimaxAlphaBeta(u, \alpha, \beta).$$

Proof. The claim is proven by induction. Let $\alpha' = \alpha - Eval(u)$ and $\beta' = \alpha - Eval(u)$, then a call to $(AccMinimax)AlphaBeta'(u, \alpha', \beta')$ modifies α' as follows:

$$\alpha' = \max\{\alpha', Eval(v) + AlphaBeta'(\alpha' - Eval(v), \beta' - Eval(v))\}$$
$$= \max\{\alpha', Eval(v) + AlphaBeta'(\alpha - Eval(u) - Eval(v), \beta - Eval(u) - Eval(v))\}$$
$$= \max\{\alpha, AlphaBeta(v, \alpha, \beta)\} - Eval(v).$$

Procedure AccMinimaxAlphaBeta
Input: Position u, bounds α, β, leaf evaluation is sum of interior-node values
Output: Value at root

if ($leaf(u)$) **return** 0	;; No successor, return 0
for each $v \in Succ(u)$	;; Traverse successor list
if ($max\ node(u)$)	;; MAX node
$\alpha \leftarrow \max\{\alpha, Eval(v) + AccMinimaxAlphaBeta'(v, \alpha - Eval(v), \beta - Eval(v)\}$	
	;; Recursion for α
else	;; MIN node
$\beta \leftarrow \min\{\beta, Eval(v) + AccMinimaxAlphaBeta'(v, \alpha - Eval(v), \beta - Eval(v)\}$	
	;; Recursion for β
if $\alpha \geq \beta$ **break**	;; Pruning
if ($max\ node(u)$)	;; MAX node
return α	;; Propagate value
else	;; MIN node
return β	;; Propagate value

Algorithm 12.8

The minimax game tree search procedure for accumulated node evaluations.

Hence, $\alpha = \max\{\alpha, AlphaBeta(v, \alpha, \beta)\}$, and both update rules are equivalent. The proof for a MIN node is similar. ∎

12.1.6 *Partition Search

Partition search is a variation of $\alpha\beta$-search with a transposition table. The difference is that the transposition table not only contains single positions, but entire *sets* of positions that are equivalent.

The key observation motivating partition search is the fact that some *local* change in the state descriptor does not necessarily change the possible outcome. In CHESS, a checkmate situation can be independent of whether a pawn is on $a5$ or $a6$. For card games, changing two (possibly adjacent) cards in one hand can result in the same tree. First, we impose an ordering $\prec$ on the set of individual cards, then two cards c and c' are equivalent with respect to hands of cards C_1, and C_2, if $c, c' \in C_1$, and for all $d \in C_2$ we have $c \prec d$ if and only if $c' \prec d$.

The technique is contingent on having available an efficient representation for the relevant generalization sets. These formalisms are similar as in methods dealing with abstract search spaces (see Ch. 4). In particular, we need three generalization functions called P, C, and R, that map a position to a set. Let U be the set of all states, $S \subseteq U$ a set, and $u \in U$.

- $P: U \rightarrow 2^U$ maps positions to sets such that $u \in P(u)$; moreover, if u is a leaf, then $Eval(u) = Eval(u')$ for each $u' \in P(u)$ (i.e., P is any generalization function respecting the evaluation of terminal states).
- $R: U \times 2^U \rightarrow 2^U$ maps a position and a set to a set. It must hold that $u \in R(u, S)$, if some position in S is reachable from u; moreover, every $u' \in R(u, S)$ must have some successor in S (i.e., R is a generalization of u that contains only predecessors of states in S).

- $C : U \times 2^U \to 2^U$ also maps a position and a set to a set. It must hold that $u \in C(u, S)$, if *all* successors of u are elements of S; moreover, all successors of any $u' \in C(u, S)$ are constrained to lie in S (i.e., C is a generalization of u that contains only states of which the successors are constrained to a subset of S).

Note that if all states in a set S have a value of at least *val*, then this is also true for $R(p, S)$; analogously, an upper bound for the value of positions in S is also an upper bound for those in $C(p, S)$. Combining these two directions, if S_{all} denotes a superset of the successors of a position u with equal value, and S_{best} is a generalization of the best move with equal value, then all states in $R(u, S_{best}) \cap C(u, S_{all})$ will also have the same value as u. This is the basis for Algorithm 12.9.

In the game of BRIDGE, partition search has been empirically shown to yield a search reduction comparable to and on top of that of $\alpha\beta$-pruning.

Procedure PartitionSearch
Input: Position u, value α, value β, value d
Output: Value at root

if (*leaf*(u) **or** $d = 0$ **return** (*Eval*(p), $P(u)$)	;; No successor, return evaluation
$S_{res} \leftarrow U$; $S_{best} \leftarrow S_{all} \leftarrow \emptyset$	;; Initialize sets
if (*Search*(u) $\neq$ **nil**)	;; Transposition table contains entry for u
$\quad$ (S_{res}, *val*, *flag*, *depth*) $\leftarrow$ *Search*(u)	
$\quad$ **if** (*depth* $\geq d$)	;; Make sure stored evaluation was at least as deep
$\quad\quad$ **if** (*flag* = *valid*) **return** (*val*, S_{res})	;; Stored value matches negmax value
$\quad\quad$ **if** (*flag* = *lbound*) $\alpha \leftarrow$ max$\{\alpha, val\}$	;; Lower bound for negmax value
$\quad\quad$ **if** (*flag* = *ubound*) $\beta \leftarrow$ min$\{\beta, val\}$	;; Upper bound for negmax value
$\quad\quad$ **if** ($\alpha \geq \beta$) **return** (*val*, S_{res})	;; Pruning
res $\leftarrow \alpha$	;; Initialize result value
for each $v \in$ *Succ*(u)	;; Traverse successor list
$\quad$ (*val*, S_{new}) $\leftarrow$ $-$*PartitionSearch*(v, $-\beta$, $-res$, $d - 1$)	;; Recursion for α
$\quad$ **if** (*val* > *res*) (*res*, S_{best}) $\leftarrow$ (*val*, S_{new})	;; Update best move
$\quad$ $S_{all} \leftarrow S_{all} \cup S_{new}$	
$\quad$ **if** (*res* $\geq \beta$)	;; Result exceeds threshold
$\quad\quad$ $S_{res} = S_{res} \cap R(u, S_{best})$	;; Backup the generalization
$\quad\quad$ *Insert*(u, (S_{res}, *res*, *lbound*, d))	;; Insert value in TT
$\quad\quad$ **return** (S_{res}, *res*)	;; Propagate value
if (*res* > α)	
$\quad$ $S_{res} = S_{res} \cap R(u, S_{best}) \cap C(u, S_{all})$	;; Backup the generalization
$\quad$ *Insert*(u, (S_{res}, *res*, *valid*, d))	;; Insert computed value in TT
else	
$\quad$ $S_{res} = S_{res} \cap C(u, S_{best})$	;; Backup the generalization
$\quad$ *Insert*(u, (S_{res}, *res*, *ubound*, d))	;; Insert upper bound in TT
return (*res*, S_{res})	;; Propagate value

Algorithm 12.9

Partition search.

12.1.7 *Other Improvement Techniques

During the course of the development of modern game playing programs, several refinements and variations of the standard depth-first $\alpha\beta$-search scheme have emerged that greatly contributed to their practical success.

- A common drawback of searching the game tree up to a fixed depth is the *horizon effect*: If the last explored move was, for example, a capture, then the static evaluation might be arbitrarily bad, ignoring the possibility that the opponent can take another piece in exchange. The technique of *quiescence search*, therefore, extends evaluation beyond the fixed depth until a stable or *quiescent* position is reached. Apart from *null moves*, where a player essentially passes, only certain disruptive moves are taken into consideration that can significantly change the position's value, such as captures.
- *Singular extension* increases the search depth at forced moves. A MAX position p with depth d value v is defined to be singular if all of its siblings p' have a value at most $v - \delta$, for an appropriately chosen margin δ. Singular extensions are considered crucial in the strength of world-champion CHESS program *Deep Thought*.
- *Conspiracy search* can be seen as a generalization of both quiescence search and singular extensions. The basic rationale behind this approach is to dynamically let the search continue until a certain confidence in the root value has been established; this confidence is measured by the number of leaf nodes that would have to "conspire" to change their value to bring the strategy down. Thus, the higher the conspiracy number of a node, the more robust is its value to inaccuracies in the static evaluation function. The tree can be searched in a way that aims to increase the conspiracy number of the root node, and thus the confidence in its value, while expanding as few nodes as possible.

  The *ABC procedure* works similarly as $\alpha\beta$, except that the fixed-depth threshold is replaced by two separate *conspiracy-depth* thresholds, one for each player. The list of options is recursively passed on to the leaves, as an additional function argument. To account for dependencies between position values, the measure of conspiracy depth can be refined to the sum of an adjustment function applied to all groups of siblings. A typical function should exhibit "diminishing return" and approach a maximum value for large option sets. For the choice of the constant function, the algorithm reduces to ordinary $\alpha\beta$-search as a special case.
- *Forward pruning* refers to different cut-off techniques to break full-width search at the deepest level of the tree. If it is MAX's turn at one level above the leaves, and the static evaluation of the position is already better than β, the successor generation is pruned; the underlying assumption is that MAX's move will only improve the situation in his favor. Forward pruning might be unsafe because, for example, *zugzwang* positions are ignored.
- *Interior-node recognition* is another memorization technique in game playing that includes game theoretical information in the form of score values to cut-off whole subtrees for interior-node evaluation in $\alpha\beta$-search engines. Recognizers are only invoked, if transposition table lookups fail.
- *Monte Carlo search* (random game play) is an upcoming technique currently used with some success in 9×9 Go. Instead of relying on a heuristic to rank the moves that are available in a position (and then choosing the best one), their value is derived from a multitude of simulated, complete games starting from that position that the computer plays against itself.

  Before starting to play, the players form an ordered list of all available moves they are going to play. Then, in turn-taking manner they execute these moves regardless of the opponent's moves (unless it is not possible, in which case they simply skip to the subsequent one). The underlying assumption is made that the quality of the moves can be assessed independently of when they are played. Although this is certainly an oversimplification, it often holds in many games that a good move at one ply stays a good one two plys ahead.[1] The value of a move is the average score of the matches in which it occurred, and is updated after each game.

When generating the move list, first, all moves are sorted according to their value. Then, in a second pass, each element is swapped with another one in the list with a small probability. The probability of shifting n places down the list is $p(n) = e^{-n/T}$, where T is the so-called temperature parameter that slowly decreases toward zero between games. The intuition behind this annealing scheme is that in the beginning, larger variations are allowed to find the approximate "geographical region" of a good solution on a coarse scale. As T becomes smaller, permutations become less and less likely, allowing the solution to be refined, or, to use the spatial analogy, to find the lowest valley within the chosen region. In the end, the sequence is fixed, and the computer actually executes the first move in the list.

- The *UCT algorithm* is a value-based reinforcement learning algorithm. The action value function is approximated by a table, containing a subset of all state-action pairs. A distinct value is estimated for each state and action in the tree by Monte Carlo simulation. The policy used by UCT balances exploration with exploitation. UCT has two phases. In the beginning of each episode it selects actions according to knowledge contained within the search tree (see Algorithm 12.10). But once it leaves the scope of its search tree it has no knowledge and behaves randomly. Thus, each state in the tree estimates its value by Monte Carlo simulation. As more information propagates up the tree, the policy improves, and the Monte Carlo estimates are based on more accurate returns. Let $n(u,a)$ count the number of times that action a has been selected from state u (initialized to 1 on the first visit). Let $(s_1, a_1, s_2, a_2, ..., s_k)$ be a simulated path in which—if present—unused actions are chosen uniformly, and—if all applicable actions have been selected—preferred by the q-value. The updates are $n(u_t, a_t) = n(u_t, a_t) + 1$, and $q(u,a) = q(u_t, a_t) + (r_t - q(u_t, a_t))/n(u_t, a_t)$, where r_t is a constant to which $q(u,a)$ is also initialized. For two-player games, under some certain assumptions, UCT converges to the minimax value without using any prior knowledge on the evaluation function. UCT also applies to single-agent state space optimization problems with large branching factors (e.g., MORPION SOLITAIRE and SAME GAME, see Exercises).

- In some multiplayer games or games of incomplete information like BRIDGE we can use *Monte Carlo sampling* to model the opponents according to the information that is available. An exact evaluation of a set of samples for a given move option then gives a good decision procedure. The sampling approach is often implemented by a randomized algorithm that generates partial states efficiently. The drawback of sampling is that it cannot deal well with information-gathering moves.

12.1.8 Learning Evaluation Functions

As mentioned before, a crucial part of building good game playing programs lies in the design of the domain-specific evaluation heuristic. It takes a lot of time and effort for an expert to optimize this

---

[1] We could call this the zero-order algorithm. The first-order algorithm would record the value of the move dependent on the preceding move of the opponent, and so on. On the flip side, this also increases drastically the number of games that need to be played to reach an acceptable accuracy.

Procedure UCT-Iteration
Input: Search tree with root s, constant C
Output: Value at root

$u \leftarrow s$;; Start at root node
while (u is not a leaf)   ;; Determine leaf in UCT tree
   $Succ(u) \leftarrow Expand(u)$;; Generate successor set
   $umax \leftarrow 0$
   for each $v \in Succ(u)$;; For all successors
     if ($visits(v) = 0$)   ;; Preference to visit unexplored children
      $uct(v) \leftarrow \infty$;; Default value
     else   ;; All other children visited
      $umax \leftarrow \max\left\{umax, uct(v) + C \cdot \sqrt{\frac{\ln(visits(u))}{visits(v)}}\right\}$;; Apply UCT formula
   $u \leftarrow \left\{v \in Succ(u) \mid umax = uct(v) + C \cdot \sqrt{\frac{\ln(visits(u))}{visits(v)}}\right\}$;; Select best
if ($umax = \infty$ **and** $Succ(u) \neq \emptyset$)   ;; Leaf reached
   $u \leftarrow Extend\text{-}UCT(u)$;; Extend UCT tree by one node
$value \leftarrow Monte\ Carlo(u)$;; Sample game until it is over
$Update\text{-}Value(u, value)$;; Bottom-up evaluation, propagate counts and UCT values

Algorithm 12.10

One iteration in the UCT algorithm.

definition. Therefore, from the very beginning of computer game playing, researchers tried to automate some of this optimization, making it a testbed for early approaches to machine learning. For example, in the common case of an evaluation function being represented as a weighted sum of specialized feature values, the weight parameters could be adjusted to improve the program's quality of play based on its experience of previous matches. This scenario is closely related to that of determining an optimal policy for an MDP (see Sec. 1.8.3), so it will not come as a surprise that elements like the backup of estimated values play a role here, too. However, MDP policies are often formulated or implicitly assumed as a big table, with one entry for each state. For nontrivial games, this kind of *rote learning* is infeasible due to the huge number of possible states. Therefore, the static evaluator can be regarded as an approximation of the complete table, mapping states with similar features to similar values. In the domains of statistics and machine learning, a variety of frameworks for such approximators have been developed and can be applied, such as linear models, neural networks, decision trees, Bayes networks, and many more.

Suppose we have a parametric evaluation function $Eval_w(u)$ that depends on a vector of weights $w = w_1, \ldots, w_n$, and a couple of training examples $(u, Eval^*(u))$ supplied by a teacher consisting of pairs of positions and their "true" value. If we are trying to adjust the function so that it comes as close as possible to the teacher's evaluation, one way of doing this would be a *gradient descent* procedure. The weights should be modified in small steps, such as to reduce the *error E*, measured, for example, in terms of the squared differences $(Eval_w(u) - Eval^*(u))^2$ between the current output and the target value. The gradient $\nabla_w E$ of the error function is the vector of partial derivatives, and so the learning rule could be to change w by an amount,

$$\Delta w = \alpha(Eval^*(u) - Eval_w(u)) \cdot \nabla Eval_w(u),$$

with a small constant α called the learning rate.

Supervised learning requires a knowledgeable domain expert to provide a body of labeled training examples. This might make it a labor-intensive and error-prone procedure for training the static evaluator. As an alternative, it is possible to apply *unsupervised* learning procedures that improve the strategy while playing games against other opponents or even against themselves. These procedures are also called *reinforcement learning*, for they are not provided with a given position's true value—their only input is the observation of how good or bad the outcome is of a chosen action.

In game playing, the outcome is only known at the end of the game, after many moves of both parties. How do you find out which one(s) of them are really to blame for it, and to what degree? This general issue is known as the *temporal credit assignment problem*. A class of methods termed *temporal difference learning* is based on the idea that successive evaluations in a sequence of moves should be consistent.

For example, it is generally believed that the minimax value of a position u, which is nothing other than the backed-up static evaluation value of positions d moves ahead, is a more accurate predictor than the static evaluator applied to u. Thus, the minimax value could be directly used as a training signal for u. Since the evaluator can be improved in this way based on a game tree determined by itself, it is also a *bootstrap* procedure.

In a slightly more general setting, a discounted value function is applied: executing an action a in state u yields an *immediate reward* $w(u,a)$. The total value $f^\pi(u)$ under policy π is $w(u,a) + \delta f(v)$, where a is the action chosen by π in a, and v is the resulting state. For a sequence of states u_0, u_1, and so on, chosen by always following the actions a_0, a_1, and so on prescribed by π, the value is equal to the sum

$$w(u_0, a_0) + \delta \cdot w(u_1, a_1) + \delta^2 \cdot w(u_2, a_2) \ldots.$$

The optimal policy π^* maximizes the f^*-value.

An *action-value function* $Q^*(u,a)$ is defined to be the total (discounted) reward experienced when taking action a in state u. It is immediate that $f^*(u) = \max_a Q^*(u,a)$. Conversely, the optimal policy is $\pi^*(u) = \arg\max_a \{Q(u,a)\}$.

Temporal difference learning now starts with an initial estimate $Q(u,a)$ of $Q^*(u,a)$, and iteratively improves it until it is sufficiently close to the latter (see Alg. 12.11). To do so, it repeatedly generates episodes according to a policy π, and updates the Q-estimate based on the subsequent state and action.

In Figure 12.10 (left) we have displayed a simple directed graph with highlighted start and goal nodes. The optimal solution is shown to its right. The costs (immediate rewards) assigned to the edges are 1,000 in case it is the node with no successor, 0 in case it is the goal node, and 1 if it is an intermediate node.

Figure 12.11 displays the (ultimate) effect of applying temporal difference learning or Q-learning. In the left part of the figure the optimal value function is shown, and on the right part of the figure the optimal action-value function is shown (upward/downward cost values are annotated to the left/right of the bidirectional arrows).

Procedure Temporal Difference Learning
Input: Markov decision process problem, error bound ϵ
Output: Optimized policy π

$\pi \leftarrow InitialPolicy$	;; Initialize policy
while (Error bound on $Q > \epsilon$)	;; Convergence criterion
select some $u \in S$	;; Choose initial node
while $(u \notin T)$	;; Goal not reached
$a \leftarrow \pi(u),\ v \leftarrow a(u), a' \leftarrow \pi(v)$	;; Determine action and successor
$Q(u,a) \leftarrow Q(u,a) + \alpha \cdot \big(w(u,a) + \delta \cdot Q(v,a')\big)$	;; Update value
$u \leftarrow v$	;; Commit move
Update π	;; e.g., using arg min
return π	

Algorithm 12.11

Temporal difference learning.

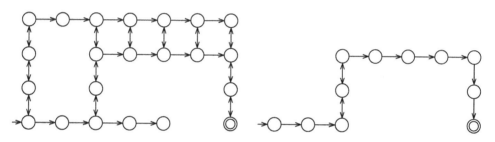

FIGURE 12.10

A graph to be searched (left) and its optimal solution (right).

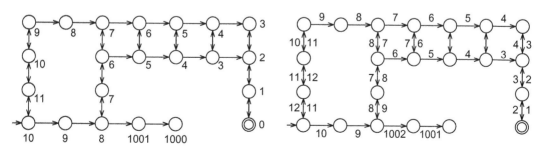

FIGURE 12.11

A graph with optimal value function (left) and with optimal action-value function (right).

The TD(λ) family of techniques has gained particular attention due to outstanding practical success. Here, the weight correction tries to correct the difference between successive estimates in a consecutive series of position $u_1, \ldots, u_t$; basically, we are dealing with the special case that the discount factor δ is 1, and all rewards are zero except for terminal (won or lost) positions. A hallmark of TD(λ) is that it tries to do so not only for the latest time step, but also for all preceding estimates. The influence of these previous observations is discounted exponentially, by a factor λ:

$$\Delta w_t = \alpha (Eval_w(u_{t+1}) - Eval_w(u_t)) \cdot \sum_{k=1}^{t} \lambda^{t-k} \nabla Eval_w(u_k).$$

As the two extreme cases, when $\lambda = 0$, no feedback occurs beyond the current time step, and the formula becomes formally the same as the supervised gradient descent, but the target value is replaced by the estimate at the next time step. When $\lambda = 1$, the error feeds back without decay arbitrarily far in time.

Discount functions other than exponential could be used, but this form makes it particularly attractive from a computational point of view. When going from one time step to the next, the sum factor can be calculated incrementally, without the need to remember all gradients separately:

$$e_{t+1} = \sum_{k=1}^{t+1} \lambda^{t+1-k} \nabla Eval_w(u_k)$$

$$= \nabla Eval_w(u_{t+1}) + \sum_{k=1}^{t} \lambda^{t+1-k} \nabla Eval_w(u_k)$$

$$= \nabla Eval_w(u_{t+1}) + \lambda \cdot e_t.$$

In Algorithm 12.11, the same policy being optimized is also used to select the next state to be updated. However, to ensure convergence, it has to hold that in an infinite sequence, all possible actions are selected infinitely often. One way to guarantee this is to let π be the greedy selection of the (currently) best action, except that it can select any action with a small probability ϵ. This issue is an instance of what is known as the *Exploration-Exploitation Dilemma* in Reinforcement Learning. We want to apply the best actions according to our model, but without sometimes making exploratory and most likely suboptimal moves, we will never obtain a good model.

One approach is to have a separate policy for exploration. This alley is taken by *Q-learning* (see Alg. 12.12). Note that

$$Q(u,a) \leftarrow \alpha \cdot \left(w(u,a) + \delta \cdot \max_{a'}\{Q(v,a') - Q(u,a)\} \right)$$

$$= (1 - \alpha)Q(u,a) + \alpha \cdot \left(w(u,a) + \delta \max_{a'}\{Q(v,a')\} \right).$$

Finally, it should be mentioned that besides learning the *parameters* of evaluation functions, approaches have been investigated to let machines derive useful *features* relevant for the evaluation of a game position. Some logic-based formalisms stand out where *inductive logic programming* attempts to

---

Procedure Q-Learning
Input: Markov decision process problem, error bound ϵ, exploration policy π
Output: Optimized estimates Q

$Q \leftarrow$ *InitialValueAction*   ;; Initialize Q-values
while (Error bound on $Q > \epsilon$)   ;; Convergence criterion
   select some $u \in S$;; Choose initial node
   while $(u \notin T)$;; Goal not reached
     $a \leftarrow \pi(u), v \leftarrow a(u)$;; Determine action and successor
     $Q(u,a) \leftarrow Q(u,a) + \alpha \left(w(u,a) + \delta \cdot \max_{a'} \{Q(v,a') - Q(u,a)\} \right)$;; Update Q-value
     $u \leftarrow v$;; Commit move

Algorithm 12.12

Q-learning.

---

find if-then classification rules based on training examples given as a set of elementary facts describing locations and relationships between pieces on the board. *Explanation-based learning* was applied to classes of endgames to generalize an entire minimax tree of a position such that it can be applied to other similar positions. To express minimax (or, more generally, AND/OR trees) as a logical expression, it was necessary to define a general explanation-based learning scheme that allows for *negative* preconditions (intuitively, we can classify a position as lost if *no* move exists such that the resulting position is *not* won for the opponent).

12.1.9 Retrograde Analysis

Some classes of CHESS endgames with very few pieces left on the board still require solution lengths that are beyond the capabilities of $\alpha\beta$-search for optimal play. However, the total number of all positions in this class might be small enough to store each position's value explicitly in a database. Therefore, many CHESS programs apply such special-case databases instead of forward search. In the last decade, many of such databases have been calculated, and some games of low to moderate complexity have even been solved completely. In this and the following sections, we will have a look at how such databases can be generated.

The term *retrograde analysis* refers to a method of calculation that finds the optimal play for all possible board positions in some restricted class of positions (e.g., in a specific CHESS endgame, or up to a limited depth). It can be seen as a special case of the concept of *dynamic programming* (see also Sec. 2.1.7). The characteristic of this method is that a backward calculation is performed, and all results are stored for reuse.

In the initialization stage, we start with all positions that are immediate wins or losses; all others are tentatively marked as draws, possibly to be changed later. From the terminal states, alternating *win backup* and *loss backup* phases successively calculate all won or lost positions in 1, 2, and further plies by executing reverse moves. The loss backup generates predecessors of states that are lost for the player in n plies; all of these are won for the opponent in $n + 1$ plies. *Win backup* requires more processing. It identifies all n-ply wins for the player, and generates their predecessor. For a position to be lost in $n+1$ plies for the opponent, *all* of its successors must be won for the player in at least n plies. The procedure iterates until no new positions can be labeled. The states that could not be labeled won or lost during the algorithm are either drawn or unreachable; in other words, illegal.

It would be highly inefficient to explicitly check each successor of a position in the win backup phase. Instead, we can use a counterfield to store the number of successors that have not yet been proven a win for the opponent. If it is found to be a predecessor of a won position, the counter is simply decremented. When it reaches zero, all successors have been proven wins for the opponent, and the position can be marked as a loss.

12.1.10 *Symbolic Retrograde Analysis

In this section, we describe an approach to how retrograde analysis can be performed *symbolically*, following the approaches of symbolic search described in Chapter 7. The sets of won and lost positions are represented as Boolean expressions; efficient realizations can be achieved through BDDs.

We exemplify the algorithmic considerations to compute the set of reachable states and the game theoretical values in this set for the game of TIC-TAC-TOE. We call the two players *white* and *black*.

To encode TIC-TAC-TOE, all positions are indexed as shown in Figure 12.12. We devise two predicates: $Occ(x,i)$ being 1 if position i is occupied, and $Black(x,i)$ evaluating to 1 if the position i, $1 \leq i \leq 9$ is marked by Player 2. This results in a total state encoding length of 18 bits. All final positions in which Player 1 has lost are defined by enumerating all rows, columns, and the two diagonals as follows.

$$WhiteLost(x) =$$

$$(Occ(x,1) \wedge Occ(x,2) \wedge Occ(x,3) \wedge Black(x,1) \wedge Black(x,2) \wedge Black(x,3)) \vee$$

$$(Occ(x,4) \wedge Occ(x,5) \wedge Occ(x,6) \wedge Black(x,4) \wedge Black(x,5) \wedge Black(x,6)) \vee$$

$$(Occ(x,7) \wedge Occ(x,8) \wedge Occ(x,9) \wedge Black(x,7) \wedge Black(x,8) \wedge Black(x,9)) \vee$$

$$(Occ(x,1) \wedge Occ(x,4) \wedge Occ(x,7) \wedge Black(x,1) \wedge Black(x,4) \wedge Black(x,7)) \vee$$

$$(Occ(x,2) \wedge Occ(x,5) \wedge Occ(x,8) \wedge Black(x,2) \wedge Black(x,5) \wedge Black(x,8)) \vee$$

$$(Occ(x,3) \wedge Occ(x,6) \wedge Occ(x,9) \wedge Black(x,3) \wedge Black(x,6) \wedge Black(x,9)) \vee$$

$$(Occ(x,1) \wedge Occ(x,5) \wedge Occ(x,9) \wedge Black(x,1) \wedge Black(x,5) \wedge Black(x,9)) \vee$$

$$(Occ(x,3) \wedge Occ(x,5) \wedge Occ(x,7) \wedge Black(x,3) \wedge Black(x,5) \wedge Black(x,7))$$

FIGURE 12.12

A state in TIC-TAC-TOE (left) and labeling of the board (right).

The predicate *BlackLost* is defined analogously. To specify the transition relation, we fix a *frame*, denoting that in the transition from state s to s', apart from the move in the actual grid cell i, nothing else will be changed.

$$FrameField(x,x',j) = (Occ(x,j) \wedge Occ(x',j)) \vee (\neg Occ(x,j) \wedge \neg Occ(x',j)) \wedge$$
$$(Black(x,j) \wedge Black(x',j)) \vee (\neg Black(x,j) \wedge \neg Black(x',j)).$$

These predicates are concatenated to express that with respect to board position i, the status of every other cell is preserved.

$$Frame(x,x',i) = \bigwedge_{1 \leq i \neq j \leq 9} FrameField(x,x',j).$$

Now we can express the relation of a black move. As a precondition, we have that one cell i is not occupied; the effects of the action are that in state s' cell i is occupied and black.

$$BlackMove(x,x') = \bigvee_{1 \leq i \leq 9} \neg Occ(x,i) \wedge Black(x',i) \wedge Occ(x',i) \wedge Frame(x,x',i).$$

The predicate *WhiteMove* is defined analogously.

To devise the encoding of all moves in the transition relation $Trans(x,x')$, we introduce one additional predicate *Move*, which it is true for all states with black to move.

$$Trans(x,x') = (\neg BlackMove(x) \wedge \neg WhiteLost(x) \wedge WhiteMove(x,x') \wedge Move(x')) \vee$$
$$(BlackMove(x) \wedge \neg BlackLost(x) \wedge BlackMove(x,x') \wedge \neg Move(x')).$$

There are two cases. If it is black's turn and if he has not already lost, execute all black moves; the next move is a white one. The other case is interpreted as follows. If white has to move, and if he has not already lost, execute all possible white moves and continue with a black one.

Reachability Analysis

In general, not all positions that are expressible in the domain language are actually reachable from the initial state (e.g., no TIC-TAC-TOE position can occur where both white and black have three marks in a row). To make symbolic retrograde analysis more efficient, we can restrict attention to reachable states. Therefore, to prepare for this, we describe *symbolic reachability analysis* first.

Essentially, it corresponds to a symbolic breadth-first search traversal, which successively takes the set *From* all positions in the current iteration and applies the transition relation to find the set of all *New* positions in the next iteration.

The algorithm terminates if no new position is available; that is, the expression for *New* is inconsistent. The union of all new positions is stored in the set *Reached*. The implementation is depicted in Algorithm 12.13.

Procedure Reachable
Input: State space problem with start state s, transition relation *Trans*
Side effect: Breadth-first search enumeration of state space

$Reach \leftarrow From \leftarrow s$	;; Initialize set representations
do	;; Loop
$To \leftarrow Replace(From, x', x)$	;; Rename variable set
$To \leftarrow \exists x\ (Trans(x, x') \wedge To(x))$	;; Perform one ply to state set
$From \leftarrow New \leftarrow To \wedge \neg Reach$	;; Update search frontier
$Reach \leftarrow Reach \vee New$	;; Update visited list
while $(New \neq false)$	;; Loop until there are no new states

Algorithm 12.13

Calculating the set of reachable positions.

Game-Theoretical Classification

As stated earlier, two-player games with perfect information are classified iteratively. Therefore, in contrast to reachability analysis, the direction of the search process is *backward*. Fortunately, backward search causes no problems, since the representation of all moves has already been defined as a relation.

Assuming optimal play and starting with all goal situations according to one player (here black's lost positions) all previous winning positions (here white's winning positions) are computed. A position is lost for black if all moves lead to an intermediate winning position in which white can force a move back to a lost position.

$$BlackLose(x) = BlackLost(x) \vee \forall x'\ (Trans(x, x') \Rightarrow (\exists x''\ Trans(x', x'') \wedge BlackLost(x''))).$$

This is also called a *strong preimage*. The choice of the actions $\wedge$ for existential quantification (weak preimage) and $\Rightarrow$ for universal quantification (strong preimage) are crucial.

The pseudo code for symbolic classification is shown in Algorithm 12.14. The algorithm *Classify* starts with the set of all final lost positions for black, and alternates between the set of positions that in which black (at move) will lose and positions in which white (at move) can win, assuming optimal play. In each iteration, each player moves once, corresponding to two quantifications in the analysis. The executed Boolean operations are exactly those established in the preceding recursive description. One important issue is to attach the player to move, since this information might not be available in the backward traversal. Furthermore, the computations can be restricted to the set of reachable states through conjunction. We summarize that given a suitable state encoding *Config*, for symbolic exploration and classification in a specific two-player game the programmer has to implement the procedures of the following interface.

1. *Start(Config)*: Definition of the initial state for reachability analysis.
2. *WhiteLost(Config)*: Final lost position for white.
3. *BlackLost(Config)*: Final lost position for black.
4. *WhiteMove(Config, Config)*: Transition relation for white moves.
5. *BlackMove(Config, Config)*: Transition relation for black moves.

Procedure Classify
Input: State space problem with start state s, transition relation *Trans*
Side effect: Backward breadth-first search enumeration of state space

WhiteWin ← *false*	;; Initialize set of winning position
BlackLose ← *From* ← *BlackLost(x)*	;; Initialize set of lost positions
do	;; Loop
To ← *Replace(From,x,x')*	;; Change variable set
To ← ∃x' (*Trans(x,x')* ∧ *To(x')*)	;; Perform on ply
To ← *To* ∧ ¬*Move(x)*	;; Update frontier
WhiteWin ← *WhiteWin* ∨ *To*	;; Update won position
To ← *Replace(WhiteWin,x,x')*	;; Change variable set
To ← ∀x' (*Trans(x,x')* ⇒ *To(x')*)	;; Perform on ply
To ← *To* ∧ *Move(x)*	;; Select player
From ← *New* ← *To* ∧ ¬*BlackLose*	;; Update frontier
BlackLose ← *BlackLose* ∨ *New*	;; Update lost position
while (*New* ≠ *false*)	;; As long as there are new states

Algorithm 12.14

Classification.

12.2 *MULTIPLAYER GAMES

Most of the work in computer game playing research has focused on *two-player* games. Games with three or more players have received much less attention. Nearly all *multiplayer games* involve negotiation or coalition-building to some degree, which makes it harder to define what an "optimal" strategy consists of.

The value of a game state is formalized by a vector of size p, where component i denotes the value for player i. In turn-taking games at the root, it is the first player's turn to move; at the first level of the game tree, it is the second player's turn, and so on, until the sequence repeats after p levels. These trees are called Max^n-trees.

The *negmax*-search formulation is based on the zero sum assumption, and on the fact that with only two players, the score of one of them trivially determines the other one. Therefore, in the following we will stick to the *minimax* formulation. The basic evaluation procedure can be readily transferred to the case of multiple players: at each node, the player i to move chooses the one that maximizes the ith component of the score vector.

However, computational difficulties arise when trying to adopt two-player pruning strategies, such as $\alpha\beta$-search. More precisely, *shallow pruning* works in the same way if bounds on the maximum and minimum score of a player and of the total score can be provided; *deep pruning*, however, is not applicable.

Let *minp* and *maxp* be the minimum and maximum score any player can achieve, and *minsum* and *maxsum* be the minimum and maximum sum of the scores of all players. For zero-sum games, these two are equal. Figure 12.13 illustrates shallow pruning in an example with three players, and

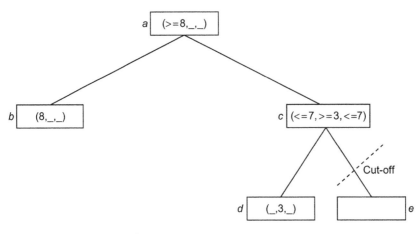

FIGURE 12.13

Shallow cut-off in Max^n for three players.

$maxsum = 10$. Player 1 can secure a value of 8 by moving from root a to b. Suppose subsequently node d is evaluated to a score of 3. Since Player 2 can score a 3 at c, both other players can achieve at most $10 - 3 = 7$ for their components in the remaining unexplored children of c. Therefore, no matter what their exact outcome is, Player 1 will not choose to move to c, and hence they can be pruned.

The following lemma states that shallow pruning requires that the maximum achievable score for any player must be at least half of the maximum total score.

Lemma 12.1. *Assume minp is zero. Then shallow pruning in a Max^n-tree requires $maxp \geq maxsum/2$.*

Proof. In Figure 12.13, denote the value for Player 1 at b as x, and that for Player 2 at d as y. A cut-off requires x being larger than the maximal achievable value at c, or $x \geq maxsum - y - (n-2) \cdot minp$, which is equivalent to $x + y \geq maxsum$ using $minp = 0$. The claim follows from $2 \cdot maxp \geq x + y$. ∎

The asymptotic branching factor for Max^n with shallow pruning is $(1 + \sqrt{4b-3})/2$ in the best case, where b is the branching factor without pruning. For a concrete game, the potential for pruning depends on the number of players and the values of $maxp$, $minsum$, and $maxsum$.

Let us now consider *deep* cut-offs. At first glance, following a similar argument as in the two-player case, the situation in Figure 12.14 should allow pruning all children of d but the first: Player 3 can achieve at least a value of 3, which leaves 7 for Player 1 at best, less than the 8 he can already achieve by moving from a to b. However, while the values of the other children of e cannot be the final outcome at the root, they can still influence the result. If the second child has the value $(6,0,4)$, it will be selected by Player 3; at c, Player 2 will then prefer its right child e with value $(9,1,0)$, which in turn yields the root value. In contrast, the branch would be irrelevant for the final outcome if Player 3 had selected the left child, f, instead.

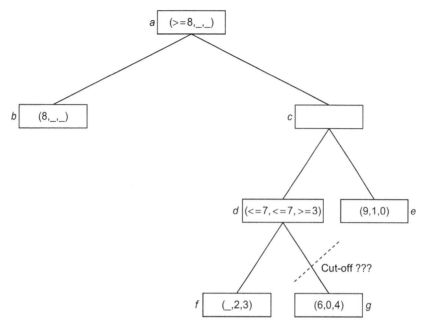

FIGURE 12.14

Deep cut-off in Max^n is not feasible.

In the shallow pruning discussed earlier, we obtained an upper bound for Player 2 by subtracting the minimum achievable score for Player 1 from *maxsum*. But often we can give tighter values, when lower and/or upper bounds for all players are available. This is the case for examples in card games, where the number of tricks or the total value of card values in tricks is counted. A lower bound comes from the tricks a player has already won, and an upper bound from the outstanding cards left on the table; that is, those that have not yet been scored by another player.

A recursive formulation of the resulting algorithm is shown in Algorithm 12.15. It assumed two heuristic functions $h_{low}(u,k)$ and $h_{up}(u,k)$ for lower and upper bounds on the score of player k in state u. The procedure performs shallow cut-offs based on a bound computed from the current best solution at the parent node.

As an alternative to Max^n, the tree evaluation can be reduced to the two-player case by making the *paranoid* assumption that all players form a coalition to conspire against the player at the root. This might result in nonoptimal play, however, reducing the search effort considerably. Player *Max* moves with a branching factor of b, while *Min* combines the rest of the players, and has therefore b^{p-1} choices. The reduced tree has depth $D = 2 \cdot d/p$, where d is the depth of the original tree. The best-case number of explored nodes is $b^{(p-1) \cdot D/2}$ for *Max*, and $b^{D/2}$ for *Min*, which together results in $O(b^{(p-1) \cdot D/2})$, or $O(b^{(p-1)/p})$ with respect to the original tree.

Procedure MultiPlayerAlphaBetaBnB
Input: Node u, Player i, bound U on i's score
Output: Best evaluation vector

$U' \leftarrow U - \sum_{k \neq i, k \neq i-1} h_{low}(u,k)$;; Compute improved bound
if $(h_{up}(u, i-1) \leq maxsum - U')$;; Shallow pruning
    return static value
$best \leftarrow (0, \dots, 0)$;; Initialize best score vector with minimum possible score
for each $v \in Succ(u)$;; For all children of u
    $current \leftarrow AlphaBetaBnB(v, i+1, maxsum - best[i])$;; Recursively call
    if $(current[i] > best[i])$;; Better solution found
        $best \leftarrow current$;; Update
        if $(best[i] \geq U'$ **or** $best[i] = h_{up}(u,i))$
            return $best$;; Shallow BnB cut-off
return $best$

Algorithm 12.15

The $\alpha\beta$-branch-and-bound algorithm for multiplayer games.

12.3 GENERAL GAME PLAYING

In *general game playing*, strategies are computed domain-independently without knowing which game is played. In other words, the AI designer does not know anything about the rules. The players attempt to maximize their individual outcome. To enforce finite games, the depth is often bounded by using a *step counter*.

The *game description language* (GDL) is designed for use in defining complete information games. It is a subset of first-order logic. GDL is a Datalog-inspired language for finite games with discrete outcomes for each player. Broadly speaking, every game specification describes the states of the game, the legal moves, and the conditions that constitute a victory for the players. This definition of games is similar to the traditional definition in *game theory* with a couple of exceptions. A game is a graph rather than a tree. This makes it possible to describe games more compactly, and it makes it easier for players to play games efficiently. Another important distinction between GDL and classic definitions from game theory is that states of the game are described succinctly, using logical propositions instead of explicit trees or graphs. An example game in GDL notation is provided in Figure 12.15.

As another example, take the game PEG, of which the initial state is shown in Figure 12.16. On the board 32 pegs are located at the depicted locations. The player can move one peg by jumping over an occupied field onto an empty one. This jump may only be performed in a horizontal or vertical direction. The peg then moves to the formerly empty field, leaving the field where it started its jump empty. The peg that was jumped over is deleted from the board leaving its field empty, too. The game ends when no more jumps are possible. As with each jump one peg is removed, this situation arises after 31 jumps at the most. The main goal is to remove all pegs except for one. This then should be located in the very middle (i.e., we aim at the inverse of the initial state). This situation with 26,856,243 states is classified to receive 100 points. We also give certain points for other final states: 99 points for one remaining peg that is not in the middle (only 4 states receive this value),

```
(init (cell 1 1 b))
...
(init (cell 3 3 b))
(init (control xplayer))
(<= terminal (line x))
(<= terminal (line o))
(<= terminal (not open))
(<= (goal xplayer 100) (line x))
(<= (goal xplayer 50) (not (line x)) (not (line o)) (not open))
(<= (goal xplayer 0) (line o))

(<= (row ?m ?x) (true (cell ?m 1 ?x)) (true (cell ?m 2 ?x)) (true (cell ?m 3 ?x)))
...
(<= (diagonal ?x) (true (cell 1 1 ?x)) (true (cell 2 2 ?x)) (true (cell 3 3 ?x)))
...
(<= (line ?x) (row ?m ?x))
...
(<= (line ?x) (diagonal ?x))
(<= open (true (cell ?m ?n b)))

(<= (next (cell ?m ?n x)) (does xplayer (mark ?m ?n)) (true (cell ?m ?n b)))
(<= (next (cell ?m ?n ?w)) (true (cell ?m ?n ?w)) (distinct ?w b))
(<= (next (cell ?m ?n b)) (does ?w (mark ?j ?k)) (true (cell ?m ?n b))
                          (or (distinct ?m ?j) (distinct ?n ?k)))
(<= (next (control oplayer)) (true (control xplayer)))
(<= (legal ?w (mark ?x ?y)) (true (cell ?x ?y b)) (true (control ?w)))
```

FIGURE 12.15

GDL description for TIC-TAC-TOE. Gains are associated with every terminating state.

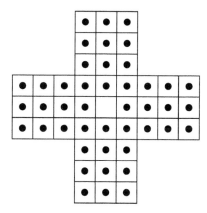

FIGURE 12.16

Initial state in PEG.

$90, \ldots, 10$ points for $2, \ldots, 10$ pegs remaining with respective 134,095,586; 79,376,060; 83,951,479; 25,734,167; 14,453,178; 6,315,974; 2,578,583; 1,111,851; and 431,138 states in the classification set. The remainder of 205,983 states have more than 10 pegs on the board.

Strategies for generalized game play include symbolic classification for solving, as well as variants of $\alpha\beta$ and Monte Carlo and UCT search for playing the games.

12.4 AND/OR GRAPH SEARCH

As before, we formalize a state space as a graph in which each node represents a problem state and each edge represents the application of an action. There are two conventional representations for AND/OR graphs, either with explicit AND and OR nodes, or as a *hypergraph*.

In the former representation, three different types of nodes exist. Apart from terminal (goal) nodes, interior nodes have an associate *type*, namely either *AND* or *OR*. Without loss of generality, we can assume that an AND node has only OR nodes as children, and vice versa; otherwise, we could transform it into one. As with regular search trees, edges can be assigned a weight, or cost. We will denote the cost of applying action a in state u (assuming it is applicable) as $w(u, a)$. AND/OR graphs are commonly used in artificial intelligence to model problem reduction schemes. To solve a nontrivial problem, we decompose it to a number of smaller subproblems. Successfully solving the partial problems will produce a final solution to the original problem according to the decomposition conditions.

A simple example for an AND/OR graph is the following (see Fig. 12.17, left). To play tennis, two conjunctive conditions have to be satisfied: good weather *and* an available court. A court is either public *or* private. In the former case, there is no further requirement. If the playground is private, we have to book it *and* to pay a deposit.

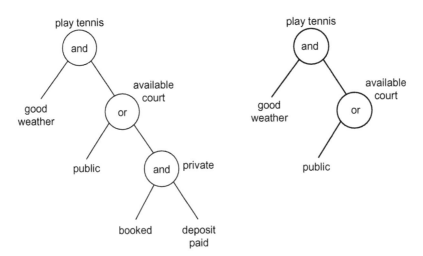

FIGURE 12.17

Play tennis example (left) and solution tree (right).

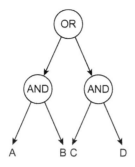 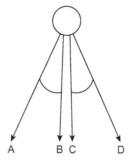

FIGURE 12.18

Conversion between AND/OR graphs (left) and hypergraphs (right).

Hypergraphs are an equivalent formalization to AND/OR graphs. Instead of arcs that connect pairs of nodes, a hypergraph has *hyperarcs* that connect a node to a set of k nodes. The two representations can be transformed into each other by absorbing respectively inserting AND nodes, as Figure 12.18 demonstrates.

Both AND/OR graphs and hypergraphs can be interpreted in different ways. In the *deterministic* interpretation, an OR node corresponds to the type of nodes in ordinary search trees, in that it is sufficient to solve a single successor. In contrast, *all* successor states of an AND node have to be solved in turn and are necessary parts of an overall solution. On the other hand, in the framework of the STOCHASTIC SHORTEST PATH problem, an action is regarded as a stochastic action that transforms a state into one of several possible successor states according to some probability distribution: $p(v \mid u, a)$ denotes the probability that applying action a to state u results in a transition to state v.

Because a hyperarc can have multiple successor states, AND/OR graph search generalizes the concept of a *solution* from a path to a tree (or, more generally, to a directed graph, if the same subgoal occurs in different branches). Starting from the initial state, it selects exactly one hyperarc for each state, each of its successors belong to the solution graph, in turn; each leaf is a goal node. The aim of the search algorithm is to find a solution tree (see Fig. 12.17, right) with minimal expected cost.

Recursively, a solution graph π satisfies the following properties. The root is part of the solution graph. Only one successor of an OR-node is contained in the solution graph. All of the successors of an AND node are part of π. The deepest directed paths must end with a goal node. The tennis example has two possible solution graphs.

In a solution graph, we can associate with each node the cost of solving the problem represented by that node. The cost of node u is defined by bottom-up recursion as follows. The cost $f(u)$ of a goal node is 0. At an internal node, an action a is applied. We have $f(u) = f(v) + w(u, a)$ if v is a successor of an OR node u, and

$$f(u) = w(u, a) + \sum_{v \in Succ(u,a)} f(v)$$

if u is an AND node. In the probabilistic interpretation, the latter formula becomes

$$f(u) = w(u, a) + \sum_{v \in Succ(u,a)} p(v \mid u, a) \cdot f(v).$$

In other words, the objective of a minimum-cost solution is generalized to a solution with *expected* minimum cost, averaging over all possible outcomes of an action.

12.4.1 **AO***

We now describe a heuristic search algorithm to determine the minimum-cost solution graph in an AND/OR tree. The algorithm starts with an initial node and then builds the AND/OR graph using the successor-generating subroutine *Expand*. At each time, it maintains a number of candidate *partial solutions*, which are defined in the same way as a solution, except that some tip nodes might not be terminal. To facilitate retrieval of the best partial solution, at each node the currently known best action is marked; it can then be extracted by following the marked edges top-down, starting at the root.

AO* as shown in Algorithm 12.16 works by repeatedly enlarging the best *partial solution* until a *complete solution* is found. The best partial solution is alleviated by associating with each iteration a nonterminal tip node from the currently best partial solution (which can be retrieved by following the marked paths from the root) that is selected for expansion. The f-value records a lower bound on the expected solution cost. For each successor, it is initialized with its h-value (or zero, for a goal state).

Eventually, the root becomes labeled as solved, in which case we obtain a minimum-cost solution graph by tracing down the marked edges. The performance of the algorithm depends on the informedness of the search heuristic.

Since the solution cost of a node depends on that of its successors, it has to be updated whenever the latter ones' estimate changes. Therefore, the algorithm interleaves *forward expansion* with a dynamic programming step that uses *backup induction*. The set Z of nodes possibly affected by the expansion of u consists of u and all its ancestors. More precisely, only those ancestors can change their value where u lies on a path of minimal cost. The nodes in Z are updated in an order so that all descendants of a node x are treated before x. In case of an OR node, we mark the edge that leads to the minimum heuristic estimate. In the case of an AND node, all edges are marked. Note that these updates can change the partial solution tree.

For sake of completeness, Algorithm 12.17 outlines the equivalent formalization of the AO* algorithm for a stochastic environment. This time, we provide the stochastic version, taking into account the probabilities $p(v \mid u,a)$. The deterministic algorithm can be derived by simply setting them to 1. For brevity, the labeling of *solved* nodes is omitted.

Both Algorithms 12.16 and 12.17 contain nondeterminism about which of the generally multiple terminal nodes of an optimal partial solution to choose for expansion. This choice will greatly affect the efficiency of the overall algorithm. Possible alternatives include the node with least cost, or with highest probability to be reached.

12.4.2 ***IDAO***

Like IDA* does with A* for regular search graphs, it is similarly possible to devise an iterative-deepening variant of AO* to cope with AND/OR graphs. The approach exploits the fact that the value function often maps to a small integer. It reassembles ideas for IDA* from the deterministic case. The main driver loop of the IDAO* algorithm (see Alg. 12.18) triggers searches with successively increasing upper thresholds U.

The main difference to IDA* is the DFS subroutine (see Alg. 12.19). When expanding an AND node, it recursively invokes the main procedure rather than the DFS function. As a result, for each successor to an AND node, the IDAO* algorithm performs a series of searches with increasing cost

---

Procedure AO*
Input: State space AND/OR graph problem with initial state (root) s
Output: Optimal solution graph π

$NTT \leftarrow \{s\}; f(s) \leftarrow 0$	;; Initialize nonterminal tip nodes and cost value
repeat until *solved*(s) **or** $(NTT = \emptyset)$	;; Unless proven or disproven
$\pi \leftarrow$ best partial solution	;; Expand best partial solution ...
$NTT \leftarrow$ nonterminal tip nodes of π	;; ... by following marked actions
$u \leftarrow Select(NTT)$	;; Select any horizon node
$NTT \leftarrow NTT \setminus \{u\}$	;; Node is no longer tip
$Succ(u) \leftarrow Expand(u)$	;; Generate successors
for each $v \in Succ(u) \setminus NTT$	;; Process successors
$NTT \leftarrow NTT \cup \{v\}$	;; New tip node
$f(v) \leftarrow h(v)$	;; Initialize costs with heuristic
if $(Goal(v))$ $solved(v) \leftarrow true$	;; Goal found
$Z \leftarrow \{u\}$	;; Start backup induction
while $Z \neq \emptyset$	;; Unless completed
$x \leftarrow Select(Z)$ **such that** $\pi_x \cap Z = \emptyset$	;; No descendant of x in Z
$Z \leftarrow Z \setminus \{x\}$	;; Eliminate x
if $(AND(x))$	;; AND node
$f(x) \leftarrow \sum_{y \in Succ(x)} f(y) + w(x,y)$	;; Compute cost
for each $y \in Succ(x) : mark(x,y) \leftarrow true$	;; Update π
$solved(x) \leftarrow \bigwedge_{y \in Succ(x)} solved(y)$	;; Update solvability status
else	;; OR node
$best \leftarrow \arg\min_{y \in Succ(x)} \{f(y) + w(x,y)\}$	;; Compute best successor
$solved(x) \leftarrow solved(best)$	;; Update solvability
$mark(x, best) \leftarrow true$	;; Update π
if $(f(x) > f(best) + w(x,y))$ **or** $solved(x)$	;; Update necessary
$f(x) \leftarrow f(best) + w(x,y)$	;; Update cost at x
$Z \leftarrow Z \cup \{z \mid z \in ancestor(x), mark(parent(z),z)\}$	;; Insert ancestors
if $(solved(s))$ **return** $\pi(s)$	;; Solution found
else return $\emptyset$	;; No solution found

Algorithm 12.16

The AO* search algorithm for AND/OR trees.

---

bound, starting from the heuristic estimate of the successor node and ending when a solution is found or the cost bound of the predecessor AND node is reached. This is because we prefer cheaper partial solutions, even if the overall cost (determined by the maximum over all children) does not increase. The cost value returned is always a lower bound on the optimal cost of the expanded node, and equal to the optimal cost if the node is solved.

IDAO* stops searching the successors of an AND node as soon as one is found to have a cost greater than the current bound, since this implies the cost of the AND node to also increase the bound. However, since the algorithm performs repeated depth-first searches with increasing bounds, the entire problem will eventually be solved.

Procedure AO*
Input: Probabilistic state space problem
Output: Shortest path subgraph π

$NTT \leftarrow \{s\}; f(s) \leftarrow 0$	;; Initialize nonterminal tip nodes and cost value
loop	
$\quad \pi \leftarrow$ best partial solution	;; Expand best partial solution ...
$\quad NTT \leftarrow$ nonterminal tip nodes of π	;; ... by following marked actions
$\quad$ **if** $(NTT = \emptyset)$	;; No nonterminal node
$\quad\quad$ **return** π	;; Return solution graph
$\quad u \leftarrow Select(NTT)$	;; Any nonterminal node
$\quad NTT \leftarrow NTT \setminus \{u\}$	;; Node is no longer tip
$\quad Succ(u) \leftarrow Expand(u)$	;; Generate successors
$\quad$ **for each** $v \in Succ(u)$	;; Traverse successor list
$\quad\quad f(v) \leftarrow h(v)$	;; Initialize costs with heuristic
$\quad\quad$ **if** $(Goal(v))$ $solved(v) \leftarrow true$	;; Goal found
$\quad Z \leftarrow \{u\}$	;; Start backup induction
$\quad$ **while** $Z \neq \emptyset$	;; Unless completed
$\quad\quad x \leftarrow Select(Z)$ **such that** $\pi_x \cap Z = \emptyset$	;; No descendant of x in Z
$\quad\quad Z \leftarrow Z \setminus \{x\}$	;; Eliminate x
$\quad\quad f(x) \leftarrow \min_{a \in A} \left\{ w(x,a) + \sum_y p(y \mid x,a) \cdot f(y) \right\}$	;; Update costs
$\quad\quad \pi(a) \leftarrow \operatorname{argmin}_{a \in A} \left\{ w(x,a) + \sum_y p(y \mid x,a) \cdot f(y) \right\}$	;; Best action

Algorithm 12.17

The AO* search algorithm for stochastic shortest path.

Procedure IDAO*
Input: State space AND/OR graph problem, start node s and cost bound b
Output: Optimal cost for solution subtre

$solved(s) \leftarrow false$
$U \leftarrow h(s)$
while $(U < b$ **and not** $solved(s))$
$\quad U \leftarrow$ IDAO*-DFS(s, U)
return U

Algorithm 12.18

The IDAO* search algorithm.

The algorithm shows how the f-value of a node can be made successively more accurate by backing up those of its children. When these improved bounds are stored in a transposition table that is always consulted prior to node expansion, the algorithm can be sped up considerably.

For brevity, we have not shown the reconstruction of the optimal solution. In contrast to AO*, this is performed in bottom-up fashion, starting at the leaves, and composing the solution from the partial

---

Procedure IDAO*-DFS
Input: Current node u and cost bound U
Output: New cost bound

if ($Goal(u)$)	;; Terminal node encountered
$solved(u) \leftarrow true$	;; Node is trivially solvable
return 0	;; Cost to reach node from itself
$Succ(u) \leftarrow Expand(u)$	;; Generate successors
if ($and\text{-}node(u)$)	;; AND node
for each $v \in Succ(u)$	;; Traverse successor list
$f(v) \leftarrow IDAO^*(v,U)$	;; Call to main routine
if ($f(v) > U$) **return** $f(v)$	;; Threshold exceeded
$solved(u) \leftarrow \bigwedge_{v \in Succ(u)} solved(v)$	;; All successors are solvable
$f(u) \leftarrow \max\{f(u), \max_{v \in Succ(u)} f(v)\}$	;; Cost values are stored
return $f(u)$	;; Cost values are maximized
else	;; OR node
for each $v \in Succ(u)$	;; Traverse successor list
if ($w(u,v) + h(v) \leq U$)	;; Cost below threshold
$f(v) \leftarrow IDAO^*\text{-}DFS(v,U - w(u,v))$	;; Call to subroutine
if ($solved(v)$) **return** $f(v)$	;; Successor is terminal
else $f(v) \leftarrow w(u,v) + h(v)$	;; Assign cost at horizon node
$f(u) \leftarrow \min\{f(u), \min_{v \in Succ(u)} w(u,v) + f(v)\}$	;; Cost values are stored
return $f(u)$	;; Feedback resulting costs

Algorithm 12.19

The IDAO*-DFS search subroutine.

---

solutions for the children at interior nodes. This could be implemented by augmenting the return value to comprise not only the cost of the solution, but the partial AND/OR tree as well.

12.4.3 *LAO*

Unlike dynamic programming, heuristic search can find an optimal solution graph starting from a given state s without evaluating the entire state space. In light of the similarities to Markov decision processes, the question arises whether AND/OR graph search can be extended to this scenario for improved efficiency.

The major issue in the transferability concerns the existence of *loops* in MDPs. That is, after executing an action, there might be a nonzero chance of staying in the same state. A plan might have to repeat an action until it succeeds. As a consequence, MDPs are said to have an *indefinite horizon*, since no worst-case upper bound on the solution length can be ascertained.

LAO* is a simple generalization of AO* that can find solutions with loops (see Alg. 12.20). The key observation is that the backup-induction step of AO* can be regarded as a special case of dynamic programming, and hence, can be substituted by either policy iteration or value iteration (see Ch. 2). Like AO*, LAO* has two main steps: a forward search step and a dynamic programming step. The forward search step is the same as in AO*, except that it allows a solution graph to contain loops.

Procedure LAO*
Input: State space AND/OR graph problem with cycles, heuristic estimate h
Output: Solution substructure π with loops

$NTT \leftarrow \{s\}; f(s) \leftarrow h(s)$	;; Initialize nonterminal tip nodes and cost value
loop	
$\pi \leftarrow$ best partial solution	;; Expand best partial solution ...
$NTT \leftarrow$ nonterminal tip nodes	;; ... by following marked actions
if $(NTT = \emptyset)$	;; No nonterminal node
return π	;; Return solution graph
$u \leftarrow Select(NTT)$	;; Any nonterminal node
$NTT \leftarrow NTT \setminus \{u\}$	;; Node is no longer tip
$Succ(u) \leftarrow Expand(u)$	;; Generate successors
for each $v \in Succ(u)$	;; Traverse successor list
$f(v) \leftarrow h(v)$	;; Compute estimate
$Z \leftarrow ancestor(u)$	;; Expanded node and ancestors
while $(Z \neq \emptyset)$	;; Backup induction
$x \leftarrow Select(Z \setminus \pi_x)$	;; No descendant of w in Z
$Z \leftarrow Z \setminus \{x\}$	;; Update Z
do either $Policy\text{-}Iteration(Z)$	;; Until convergence in Z
or $Value\text{-}Iteration(Z)$	;; One or more iterations
$mark(x) \leftarrow \arg\min_{a \in A} \left\{ w(x,a) + \sum_y p(y \mid x,a) \cdot f(y) \right\}$	;; Mark best action

Algorithm 12.20

The LAO* algorithm.

Forward search of a partial solution graph now terminates at a goal node, a nonterminal tip node, or a loop back to an already expanded node.

For admissible estimates and policy iteration, LAO* has the following properties.

Theorem 12.3. *(Optimality of LAO* for Policy Iteration) If h is admissible and policy iteration is used to perform dynamic programming in LAO*, then:*

1. *After each step for every state u we have* $f(u) \leq f^*(u)$.
2. *After termination, for every state u in the best solution graph* π, *we have* $f(u) = f^*(u)$.
3. *LAO* terminates after a finite number of iterations.*

Proof. The proof of the first assertion is by induction. Knowing that h is a lower bound, we have for every node u in the explicit graph an initial heuristic value $h(u) \leq f^*(u)$. The forward search step expands the best partial solution graph and does not change the cost of any node and so it is sufficient to consider the dynamic programming step. For building an invariance condition, we make the inductive assumption that before the step, for every state u we have $f(u) \leq f^*(u)$. If all tip nodes have optimal cost, then all the nontip nodes must converge to their optimal costs by the convergence for policy iteration. But by the induction hypothesis, all tip nodes have admissible costs. It follows that the nontip nodes must converge to costs that are as good or better than optimal when policy iteration is performed on them only.

To prove the second assertion, we observe that the search algorithm can only terminate if the solution graph is complete; that is, if it has no unexpanded nodes. For every state u in this solution graph it is contradictory to suppose $f(u) < f^*(u)$, since that implies a complete solution that is better than optimal. Together with Part 1 this yields $f(u) = f^*(u)$.

For proving the last assertion, it is clear that LAO* terminates after a finite number of iterations if the graph is finite, or equivalently the number of states in the MDP is finite. ∎

For admissible estimates and value iteration algorithm LAO* can be proven to have similar properties.

Theorem 12.4. *(Optimality of LAO* for Value Iteration) If h is admissible and value iteration is used to perform dynamic programming in LAO*, then:*

1. *After each step of LAO*, for every state u we have $f(u) \leq f^*(u)$.*
2. *For every state u of the best solution graph π, we have $f(u)$ converges to $f^*(u)$ in the limit.*

Proof. The proof of the first assertion is also by induction. Knowing that h is a lower bound, for every node u in the explicit graph we have $f(u) = h(u) \leq f^*(u)$. The hypothesis is that for every state u we have $f(u) \leq f^*(u)$. If value iteration is performed, by restating the Bellman optimality equation we have

$$f(u) = \min_{a \in A} \left\{ w(u,a) + \sum_{v \in S} p(v \mid u,a) \cdot f(v) \right\}$$

$$\leq \min_{a \in A} \left\{ w(u,a) + \sum_{v \in S} p(v \mid u,a) \cdot f^*(v) \right\} = f^*(u).$$

To prove the second assertion, we observe that the graph is finite, so that LAO* must eventually find a complete solution graph. In the limit, the nodes in their solution graph must converge to their exact costs by the convergence proof for value iteration. The solution graph must be optimal by the admissibility of the costs of all the nodes in the explicit graph. ∎

LAO* represents a solution as a mapping from states to actions in the form of a cyclic solution graph or, equivalently, a *finite-state controller*. The representation generalizes the graphical representations of a solution used by search algorithms like A* in the form of a simple path, and AO* in the form of an acyclic graph.

12.5 SUMMARY

In this chapter, we generalized deterministic shortest path problems in different ways. Deterministic shortest path problems assume that the successor state is completely determined by the current state and the action executed in it. However, action executions can sometimes result in more than one successor state from which one is chosen during execution either probabilistically or by an adversary, in which case the search problem is either a probabilistic or minimax (respectively) shortest path problem and either the expected or worst-case (respectively) goal distances of the states must be found. The optimal behavior can, in both cases, be specified by the action that we should execute every time we are in a given state (policy).

We generalized these search problems to search problems with three different kinds of nodes: The first kind of nodes are the goal nodes. The have a given value. The second kind of nodes are called OR or, synonymously, MIN nodes. They are nodes where the MIN player picks one of the available actions. Their values are the minimum over all outgoing edges (i.e., actions) of the sum of the cost of moving to the successor node (i.e., the cost of executing the action) and the value of the successor Node. The third kind of nodes depends on the search problem: For probabilistic shortest path problems, they are called AVE nodes. They are nodes where nature picks one of the outcomes of the chosen action. Their values are the average over all outgoing edges (i.e., outcomes) of the sum of the cost of moving to the successor node (typically zero) and the value of the successor node.

We argued that probabilistic shortest path problems can be specified using Markov decision process (MDP) models with goal states. For minimax shortest path problems, the third kind of nodes are MAX nodes. MAX nodes are nodes where an adversary (the MAX player) picks one of the outcomes of the chosen action. Their values are the maximum over all outgoing edges (i.e., outcomes) of the sum of the cost of moving to the successor node (typically zero) and the value of the successor node. We also discussed AND/OR search problems, which are typically solved for tree-shaped state spaces only. For AND/OR search problems, the third kind of nodes are AND nodes. AND nodes are nodes where the chosen action is decomposed into several actions that all need to be executed. Their values are the sum over all outgoing edges of the sum of the cost of moving to the successor node and the value of the successor node.

We discussed ways of determining the values of all nodes for these search problems. For tree-shaped state spaces (of which the root node is the start node and the leaves are the goal nodes) this can be done by expanding every node once, starting at the goal nodes. An example is the minimax search method for minimax shortest path problems. Minimax shortest path problems can be solved with a Dijkstra-like search method that expands every node once, starting at the goal nodes, even for state spaces with more general topologies as long as there are only positive-cost cycles. The reason is that the optimal policy is acyclic if the values of all nodes are finite. However, probabilistic shortest path problems typically cannot be solved by expanding every node only once because there might be no optimal policy that is acyclic even if the values of all nodes are finite. We discussed several dynamic programming methods that can be used to solve probabilistic shortest path problems, including policy iteration, value iteration, and Q-learning, where Q-learning is not told about the outcomes and costs of the actions but needs to learn them by executing actions (reinforcement-learning problem). We also generalized these three search methods to probabilistic shortest path problems without goal nodes, by using discounting to guarantee that the values of the nodes are finite.

We discussed that we can often utilize the knowledge of the start node to avoid having to determine the values of all nodes. In this case, we can use heuristic search methods that generalize A*. They start at the start node and use heuristics to focus the search toward the goal nodes. Examples are AO* (and its iterative-deepening version to save memory) for AND/OR search problems and LAO* for MDPs. Table 12.1 summarizes the algorithms for this class. It denotes whether the pseudo code assumes a nondeterministic or probabilistic environment and whether the AND/OR structure is assumed to be a tree or a general graph. Last, but not least, we mention if the algorithms operate on a single source or on multiple sources.

We then applied our insights to two-person zero-sum games with complete knowledge of the current state (e.g., board configuration in CHESS or CHECKERS), with a brief discussion of how to generalize the

Table 12.1 Overview of AND/OR search algorithms.

Algorithm	Environment	Structure	Source
AO* (12.16)	Nondeterministic	Tree	Single
AO* (12.17)	Probabilistic	Tree	Single
IDAO* (12.18,12.19)	Nondeterministic	Tree	Single
Q-Learning (12.12)	Nondeterministic	Graph	Single
LAO* (12.20)	Probabilistic	Graph	Single

approaches to multiperson zero-sum games with complete and incomplete information. In two-person zero-sum games with complete knowledge of the current state, we try to find the best move for a player (typically assumed to be the MAX player) under the assumption that the opponent (MIN player) plays optimally, which is reasonable if we find a strong move since the move remains strong if the opponent does not play optimally. Thus, game playing problems are basically minimax shortest path problems where all action costs are zero. The goal states are the terminal states. Their value is, say, infinity for a win of the MAX player (i.e., loss of the MIN player) and minus infinity for a loss of the MAX player (i.e., win of the MIN player).

These minimax shortest-path problems can be solved with the minimax search method. Around goal states, we can simply calculate the correct values of the states offline (retrograde analysis) and store them in endgame databases. However, the state spaces are typically much larger than the available memory, thus we cannot store the values of all states. Instead, we perform a search each time the MAX player has to move, generating only part of the state space around the current state (local search space). The perimeter states of the local search space then become the goal states. Their values correspond to how favorable the state appears to be for the MAX player based on a static evaluation heuristic that can either be hand-coded or learned from experience with machine learning methods, including reinforcement learning methods. Larger local search spaces tend to help the minimax search method to discover misleading static evaluations and thus result in better decisions (although this is not guaranteed). The minimax search method is typically implemented with depth-first search and thus operates on trees that contain many states multiple times. It then uses transposition tables to detect that the value of a state has already been computed and thus does not need to be computed again, which makes it more efficient.

We discussed different ways of making it even more efficient by not evaluating the values of states that are unimportant because they cannot be reached during optimal play. The alpha-beta search method, for example, maintains an alpha value (i.e., the best value that the MAX player is guaranteed to achieve, initialized with the value of a loss of the MAX player) and a beta value (i.e., the best value that the MIN player is guaranteed to achieve, initialized with the value of a loss of the MIN player) during its minimax search. The value of the root node of the tree is then guaranteed to be between the alpha and beta value, and we do not need to calculate the value of a state for which the alpha value is not strictly smaller than the beta value. The alpha-beta search method calculates the same values as the minimax search method and thus executes the same actions, given the same local search spaces. However, it calculates the values of many fewer states and can thus search much larger local search spaces (namely trees of up to twice the depth if actions in states are evaluated in order of decreasing strength for the person to play in the state) in the same time as the minimax search method and thus select better actions than the minimax search method.

We also discussed variants of the alpha-beta search method that initialize the alpha and beta values differently and are then able to calculate the value of the root node exactly only if it is between the initial alpha and beta values. These variants include aspiration search, principal-variation search, and search using the memory-enhanced test framework. We discussed various other enhancements of the alpha-beta search method, including search methods that generalize over similar states, that use static evaluations that are vectors of values, and that avoid horizon effects by enlarging the local search space until the static evaluations are stable.

There are also other search methods, including best-first search methods, but they are more complex than these versions of the alpha-beta search method (basically a depth-first search method) without being much more efficient for games like CHESS. Games with large branching factors (like GO), however, require fundamentally different approaches, for example, based on Monte Carlo search or problem decomposition. Games with probabilistic elements (e.g., BACKGAMMON and other games that require you to roll dice) or incomplete information (e.g., many card games) can be solved with variants of the minimax or alpha-beta methods. For card games, for example, sampling the hands of the opponents based on the available information and then playing as if we knew their hands seems to be a promising approach that transforms the problem to one of complete information and allows us to use variants of the alpha-beta method.

Table 12.2 displays the basic game playing programs of this chapter. We denote if the traversal direction is forward or backward search, on how many players are usually modeled, and a typical game playing application scenario. Analyzing games of chance like BACKGAMMON bridges the stochastic with game tree search. Moreover, we have attached the memory requirements, where d is the depth of the search tree and $|T|$ is its size.

Table 12.2 Overview of game playing search algorithms.

Algorithm	Forward	Players	Typical	Memory
Negmax (12.1)	✓	2	Board	$O(d)$
Minimax (12.2)	✓	2	Board	$O(d)$
NegmaxAlphaBeta (12.3)	✓	2	Board	$O(d)$
MiniMaxAlphaBeta (12.4)	✓	2	Board	$O(d)$
NegmaxAlphaBeta-TT (12.5)	✓	2	Board	$O(|T|)$
Principle-Variation Search (12.6)	✓	2	Board	$O(d)$
Memory-Test-Driver (12.7)	✓	2	Board	$O(|T|)$
AccumulateMinimaxAlphaBeta (12.8)	✓	2	Card	$O(d)$
PartitionSearch (12.9)	✓	2	Card	$O(|T|)$
Reachable (12.13)	✓	2	Board	$O(|T|)$
Classify (12.14)	–	2	Board	$O(|T|)$
AlphaBetaBnB (12.15)	✓	k	Card	$O(kd)$

12.6 **EXERCISES**

12.1   Consider the state space of the game as $Q = S \times \{0,1\}$. A game has an initial state and some predicate *goal* to determine whether the game has come to an end. We assume that every path from the initial state to a final one is finite. For the set of goal states $T = \{u \in Q \mid Goal(u)\}$, we define an evaluation function $Eval : T \rightarrow \{-1,0,1\}$, with -1 for a lost position, 1 for a winning position, and 0 for a drawing one. This function is extended to $Eval : Q \rightarrow \{-1,0,1\}$ asserting a game theoretical value to each state in the game. Let L_i be the set of lost positions for Player i, $i \in \{0,1\}$.

1. Define the sets L_1 and L_2 recursively assuming optimal play.
2. Let R be the set of all reachable states; with respect to the initial position and the rules of the game, define the set of draw games.

12.2   Represent the CONNECT 4 game efficiently and estimate the number of reachable states for board widths and heights in between 4 and 9.

12.3   In HEX, a goal pattern is a virtual connection between both sides of the board (see Fig. 12.19).

1. Show how to memorize goal patterns efficiently in an UNLIMITED BRANCHING TREE (see Ch. 3). Insert the patterns of Figure 12.19 into the empty dictionary.
2. As illustrated in Figure 12.19 there are many further patterns that can be obtained through translation, reflection, and rotation. Determine the number of symmetries and insert all symmetric patterns in the example into the UNLIMITED BRANCHING TREE.

12.4   In this partially completed TIC-TAC-TOE problem, both players were experts (neither one ever afforded the other an opportunity to force a win). What were the first and the last moves played?

```
X | O | O
---+---+---
  |   | X
---+---+---
  | X | O
```

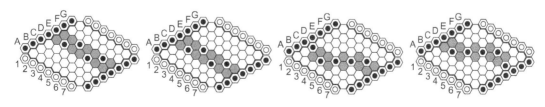

FIGURE 12.19

HEX goal patterns.

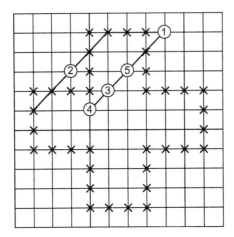

FIGURE 12.20

MORPION SOLITAIRE after drawing the first 5 lines.

12.5 The key to the theory NIM is the digital binary sum neglecting all carryovers; for example, the sum for $(011)_2$, $(100)_2$, and $(101)_2$ is $(010)_2$. The optimal strategy is finishing every move with sum 0.

  1. What is the optimal move for the configuration $(3,3,5)$?
  2. Show that there is always a move from a situation with a digital sum $\neq 0$ to one with a digital sum 0.
  3. Show that every possible move in a situation with digital sum 0 makes the sum different to 0.

12.6 The most common implementation of an incremental hash function in game playing is *Zobrist hashing*. Given a board with n squares and p different types of pieces (including the blank) an array Z of size $n \times 2p$ is filled with random numbers. The hash number is the XOR over the occupied squares of the entire board. For a typical game, it can be computed incrementally.

  If a piece is moved then an XOR of the current hash number with the Zobrist numbers for that piece corresponding to the two squares of the move is needed. For two-player games we often have to XOR in another random number for the side to move. Extend Zobrist hashing to capturing of pieces.

12.7 Provide the pseudo code for minimax-$\alpha\beta$ with transposition table pruning.

12.8 The 2004 CHESS world championship was almost won for Kramnik. However, Leko (playing black) won the Game 8 with very limited time, finding a brilliant move with regard to the board in Figure 12.21 (left), resulting in a win of black.

  Now Leko was in the lead. But the last game was again won by Kramnik for a final outcome of 7:7. At the end he found a checkmate in at most three moves on the board in Figure 12.21 (right).

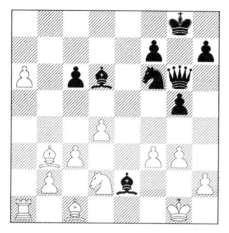 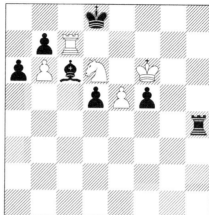

FIGURE 12.21

Black to move wins, and white to win in three moves.

1. Find the winning moves by hand.
2. Find them using any available chess program. Report the computer's analyses by explaining the evaluations in the search tree.

12.9 MORPION SOLITAIRE is a pen-and-pencil game played on an infinite grid with some set S of a marked intersection taken as the initial state. In each move $k - 1$ intersections are covered and a new one is produced by placing a (horizontal, vertical, or diagonal) line having $k - 1$ edges. Edges of two lines must not overlap. The usual setting is S being a Greek cross with $36 = 6 \cdot 4 + 6 \cdot 2$ marked intersections and k being 5 (see Figure 12.20). From a search perspective, MORPION SOLITAIRE is a longest path state space problem. The best human solution of 170 moves dates back to April 1976. In 2010 a new record with 172 moves was obtained with Monte Carlo search and a grid computer.
1. Explain that the graph to be searched can be reduced to a tree.
2. Show that the game of the usual setting with $k = 5$ is finite.
3. Find a good state encoding and compare various bitmap encodings with line stacks.
4. Implement a breadth-first tree searcher. How deep can you go?
5. Implement a random depth-first tree searcher. What is the largest depth you find?
6. Apply UCT to the problem to trade exploitation with exploration.

12.10 SAME GAME is a single-agent game played on an $n \times m$ grid covered with nm balls in k colors. In the ordinary case, we have $n = m = 15$ and $k = 5$. Balls can be removed if they form a connected group of at least l elements. The reward of the move is $(l - 2)^2$ points. If a group of balls is removed, others fall down. The goal of the game is to maximize reward. For total clearance, an additional reward of 1,000 points is given.

Speed-up Monte Carlo search.

1. Show that time $O(nm)$ suffices to determine all valid successors of a grid state. (Propagate first the connectivity and then the sizes of the ball groups.)
2. Derive the concept of *tabu colors* that shouldn't be touched for a long time to form larger groups of balls. What would be a good color to select?
3. Given an evaluation function that assigns successors to positive values, derive a random choice model (think of a *Roulette Wheel* for weighted random choices).
4. What are good evaluation functions? Try to trade execution time with quality.

12.11 SKAT is a popular three-player card game played on a 32 deck, where after bidding one player plays the other two. After bidding, computer SKAT can be played on a *double-dummy* strategy that traverses a two-player search tree strategy grouping the two opponents together. (To determine the strength of a hand, Monte Carlo simulation has to be put on top of the *double-dummy* solver.)

1. Find out how SKAT is played; that is, denote the value of each card and the rules of the game.
2. Find a 32-bit encoding for a hand, illustrate how to reverse the mapping, and determine a *card-to-index* procedure that allows you to efficiently determine if a card is better than another.
3. Explain how a card can be selected in $O(1)$ and on modern computers by computing the most significant bit.
4. Analyze the following game of seven cards (♣ is trump, player 1 to play first.):

> **Player 1:** ♣J ♣10 ♡8 ♡K ♡10 ♠7 ♠K
> **Player 2:** ♠J ♡J ♣8 ◇9 ◇Q ◇10 ◇A
> **Player 3:** ♣7 ♣Q ◇7 ♠8 ♠9 ♡7 ♡A

12.12 Apply symbolic retrograde analysis to TIC-TAC-TOE by using a symbolic model checking tool (e.g., SMV or μcke).

12.13 BLACKJACK is a card game, where a player tries to beat the dealer by obtaining a sum of card values that is higher than the dealer's. The limit is 21. The dealer stops hitting at 17. Explain how BLACKJACK can be solved with Q-learning. As the input, take the number of episodes for training, the number of games played per episode, the reinforcement values for a lost or won game, the step-size parameter, and the discount factor. Use epsilon-greedy for action selection. Higher epsilon values indicate higher exploration. Display the percentage of win games and the current learned Q-values.

12.14 In TETRIS the player is continually given pieces of varying shapes that must be positioned and rotated, then dropped on the pieces below. The shape of each subsequent piece is random. Since pieces begin to pile up, the player must try to stack them efficiently. If the player manages to complete a row, then that row disappears, freeing up more space. Describe a reinforcement strategy to learn to play TETRIS without directly programming its strategies. When given a random piece to add, it evaluates all the valid placements and chooses the action that results in the best one according to the evaluation function. Vary the value learning parameter and compare the efficiencies of Q-learning with temporal difference learning.

12.7 BIBLIOGRAPHIC NOTES

Good introductions to game theory have been given by Osborne and Rubinstein (1994) and by Owen (1982), and a general introduction to *two-person game theory* is found in the book by Rapoport (1966). Computer game playing goes back to the pioneer of computer science as a discipline (Turing et al., 1953) and the founding of information theory (Shannon, 1950). In 1950, Turing wrote the first computer chess program. The same year he proposed the *Turing test*, that in time, a computer could be programmed (e.g., playing CHESS) to acquire abilities rivaling human intelligence. If a human did not see the other human or computer during an imitation game such as chess, he or she would not know the difference between the human and the computer.

There is some variance in notation in literature in writing *Negmax/Negamax* and *MinMax/MiniMax*. The idea of Neg(a)max results from a simplification reported by Baudet (1978). Several enhancements to $\alpha\beta$ search including the *history heuristic* by Schaeffer (1989) have been proposed. Marsland and Reinefeld (1993) have treated principal-variation search. Plaat, Schaeffer, Pijls, and de Bruin (1996) have covered the MTD framework and its applications. SSS* has been proposed in Stockman (1997). Anantharaman, Campbell, and Hsu (1990) have described the concept of singular extensions. Classification tree and regression trees have been discussed by Breiman, Friedman, Olshen, and Stone (1984). Their application to $\alpha\beta$ evaluation functions has been discussed by Heinz and Hense (1993). It has been proven that evaluation functions can exhibit some pathologies; see, for example, work by Nau (1983). *Best-first minimax search*, proposed by Korf and Chickering (1994), has clearly enhanced the quality of an OTHELLO player. Generalization to $\alpha\beta$-search and SSS* have been discussed by Ibaraki (1986).

Conspiracy number search by McAllester (1988) and McAllester and Yuret (2002) search the game tree in a manner that several leaf evaluations have to change in order to change the root evaluation. *Proof-number search*, introduced by Allis, van der Meulen, and van den Herik (1994), proves or disproves the game-theoretical value. For this aim, it assigns a value to the root and shows that this value is equal to the minimax value. In every node, a proof number (and a disproof number) is stored that denotes the number of successors that have at least to be examined to prove (or disprove) the value. As proof-number search always considers the node with the largest influence on the root it is a best-first variant (with linear storage requirements). *Proof-set search* is a recent improvement to proof-number search, that trades node explorations for a higher memory consumption (Müller, 2002).

Samuel (1959) was the first researcher to implement a chess-playing program to apply learning in a game, and it was demonstrated on TV. His minimax algorithm included many heuristic extensions and cutoffs that we would call today $\alpha\beta$-pruning. He was also the first to use machine learning for improving the evaluation function, as a precursor of temporal-difference learning. The program played many thousand games against different versions of itself, and adjusted the weight parameters so as to approximate the minimax value of the position that resulted after two real plies in the match. $TD(\lambda)$ has been proposed by Sutton (1988). It is an extension of TD(0) on so-called *eligibility traces*. The most impressive application of $TD(\lambda)$ was Tesauro's *TDGammon* (1995) that is estimated to play close to the level of the best human players. *Monte Carlo* Go has been implemented by Bruegmann (1993) and has been played respectably on 9×9 Go. Most successful Go programs use UCT, as invented by Kocsis and Szepesvári (2006). UCT itself goes back to work by Auer, Cesa-Bianchi, and Fischer (2002). Known Go programs refer to initial work by Gelly and Silver (2007) and Coulom (2006).

Schrödl (1998) has introduced *negation as failure* to explanation-based learning and has used it to derive generalized logical descriptions of minimax trees for the chess endgame king-rook versus king-knight and could achieve up to 10-fold speedups.

A comprehensive reference for *combinatorial game theory* is contained in the book *Winning Ways* by Berlekamp, Conway, and Guy (1982), in which games are split into a sum of local games of tractable size. The divide-and-conquer decomposition search method by Müller (2001) propagates relative evaluations in the game tree and applies to all minimax search algorithms, such as $\alpha\beta$ and proof-number search. It has been shown to be very effective in Go endgames (Müller, 1995) with exponential savings in several positions. PSPACE hardness results for HEX (invented by the Danish mathematician Hein) and AMAZONS (invented by Walter Zamkauskas) have been given by Reisch (1981) and Furtak, Kiyomi, Uno, and Buro (2005).

Heinz (2000) has written a computer-chess primer introducing many of the standard and some advanced techniques. Early work on endgame databases has been surveyed by van den Herik and Herschberg (1986). Nowadays, Edward's table-bases and Thompson's databases are most important to the CHESS community. In CHECKERS, the distributed generation of a very large databases has eventually given the edge in favor to the computer. The story to beat the world champion has been revisited in a book by Schaeffer (1997). CONNECT 4 has been proven to be a win for the first player in optimal play by Allis (1998). The number of reachable positions has been counted by Edelkamp and Kissmann (2008b) with binary decision diagrams. NINE-MEN-MORRIS has been solved with huge databases by Gasser (1995), in which every position (after the initial setting) has been asserted to its game-theoretical value. The result has been validated by Edelkamp, Sulewski, and Yücel (2010a) using a GPU and a minimum perfect hash function to compress the state space to compute a *strong* solution, providing optimal play for each reachable state. Another parallel retrograde analysis (without GPU) has been applied by Romein and Bal (2003) to strongly solve AWARI on a bitvector.

Multiplayer games have been considered in Luckhardt and Irani (1986). Korf (1991) has introduced pruning in *Max^n* trees. The Soft-Max^n algorithm by Sturtevant and Bowling (2006) avoids the prediction of tie-breaking. It has been implemented with BDDs by Edelkamp and Kissmann (2008a). A branch-and-bound $\alpha\beta$-pruning strategy for multiplayer games has been proposed by Sturtevant and Korf (2000). UCT for multiplayer games has been studied by Sturtevant (2008). In MORPION SOLITAIRE Chris Rosin is the first to beat the 34-year-old record of 170 moves by C.-H. Bruneau.

Early BRIDGE players that use hierarchical planning have been proposed by Smith, Nau, and Throop (1998). A state-of-the-art BRIDGE playing program based on Monte Carlo sampling has been described by Ginsberg (1999), and the SKAT program has been contributed by Kupferschmid and Helmert (2006), and later extended with a bidding system by Keller and Kupferschmid (2008). Frank and Basin (1998) have shown that Monte Carlo sampling cannot determine optimal play.

In generalized game playing, as proposed by Love, Hinrichs, and Genesereth (2006), games are described using syntax from the knowledge interchangeable format (KIF). Early players have been contributed by Schiffel and Thielscher (2007) and Clune (2007). Recent players often use UCT (Finnsson and Björnsson, 2008). A two-player generalized game playing classification algorithm based on BDDs has been provided by Edelkamp and Kissmann (2008b), and improved in Kissmann and Edelkamp (2010b) with an instantiation module presented by Kissmann and Edelkamp (2010a).

Nilsson (1980) has introduced AO* search. A more recent implementation of AO* for adversarial planning has been provided by Bercher and Mattmüller (2008). LAO* has been proposed by Hansen and Zilberstein (1998) as an extended version of the AO* algorithm that is well-suited to MDP problems. Real-time dynamic programming as suggested by Barto, Bradtke, and Singh (1995) is based on the LRTA* search algorithm that has been introduced in Chapter 11. The difference to LAO* is trial-based exploration to explore the state space and to determine the order in which to update the state costs. On the other hand, LAO* finds a solution by systematically expanding a search graph in the manner of A* and AO*. In all these algorithms, dynamic value update and frontier extension are called in alternation. *Algebraic decision diagrams* (ADDs) are of common use for solving MDPs, as, for example, the publicly available library SPUDD (Hoey, St-Aubin, Hu, and Boutilier, 1999) shows. Feng and Hansen (2002) indicate how to incorporate guidance to MDP solving and devise a symbolic heuristic search implementation of LAO*. Applications of game playing in model checking includes work by Bakera, Edelkamp, Kissmann, and Renner (2008). Algorithm IDAO* with transposition tables has been provided by Haslum (2006) in the context of optimal temporal planning.

Learning DFS (LDFS) by Bonet and Geffner (2005) is a variant of IDA(O)* for AND/OR graphs and MDPs. While IDA* consists of a sequence of DFS iterations that backtrack upon encountering states with costs exceeding a given bound, LDFS consists of a sequence of DFS iterations that backtrack upon encountering states of which the values are not consistent with the values of its children. Upon encountering such inconsistent states, LDFS updates their values and backtracks, updating along the way ancestor states as well. In addition, when the DFS beneath a state does not find an inconsistent state, it is labeled as solved and not expanded again. *Bounded LDFS* by Bonet and Geffner (2005) is a slight variation of LDFS that accommodates an explicit bound parameter for focusing the search further on paths that are *critical*. For two-player games, bounded LDFS reduces to the memory-test driver algorithm MTD($-\infty$).

Bonet, Loerincs, and Geffner (1997) have shown applicability of real-time search in early development stages of their planner HSP (Bonet and Geffner, 2001). Bonet and Geffner (2000) have extended this approach to implement a general planning tool to solve partial observable MDPs. A state abstraction technique similar to the one presented here has been applied to Q-learning by Dietterich (2000), and state abstraction for prioritized-sweeping using a structured representation of the state space has been suggested by Dearden (2001).

Constraint Search

Constraint technology has evolved into one of the most effective search options, which is understandable because its declarative formulation makes it easy to use. The technology is open and extensible, because it differentiates among branching, propagation, and search. Constraint search has been integrated (e.g., in the form of a library) to many existing programming languages and is effective in many practical applications, especially in *time tabling*, *logistics*, and *scheduling* domains.

A search *constraint* is a restriction on the set of possible solutions to a search problem. For *goal constraints* (the standard setting in state space search), we specify goal states, and these incorporate constraints on the goal. In this case, constraints refer to the end of solution paths, denoting the restriction on the set of possible terminal states. For *path constraints*, constraints refer to the path as a whole. They are expressed in *temporal logic*, a common formalism for the specification of desired properties of software systems. Examples are conditions that have to be satisfied always, or achieved at least sometimes during the execution of a solution path.

In constraint modeling we have to decide about variables, their domains, and constraints. There are many different options to encode the same problem, and a good encoding may be essential for an efficient solution process.

Constraints can be of very different kinds; special cases are *binary* and *Boolean constraints*. The former ones include at most two constraint variables in each constraint to feature efficient propagation rules, and the latter ones refer to exactly two possible assignments (*true* and *false*) to the constraint variables and are known as *satisfiability problems*.

We further distinguish between *hard constraints* that have to be satisfied, and *soft constraints*, the satisfaction of which is preferred but not mandatory. The computational challenge with soft constraints is that they can be contradicting. In such cases, we say that the problem is *oversubscribed*. We consider soft constraints to be evaluated in a linear objective function with coefficients measuring their desirability.

Constraints express incomplete information such as properties and relations over unknown state variables. Search is needed to restrict the set of possible value assignments. The search process that assigns values to variables is called *labeling*. Any assignment corresponds to imposing a constraint on the chosen variable. Alternatively, general *branching rules* that introduce additional constraints may be used to split the search space.

The process to tighten and extend the constraint set is called *constraint propagation*. In constraint search, labeling and constraint propagation are interleaved. As the most important propagation techniques we exploit *arc consistency* and *path consistency*. Specialized consistency rules further enhance the propagation effectiveness. As an example, we explain insights to the inference based on the *all-different constraint* that requires all variable assignments to be mutually different.

Search heuristics determine an order on how to traverse the search tree. They can be used either to enhance pruning or to improve success rates, for example, by selecting the more promising nodes for a feasible solution. Different from the observation in previous chapters, for constraint search, diverse search paths turn out to be essential. Consequently, as one heuristic search option, we control the search by the number of *discrepancies* to the standard successor generation module.

Most of the text is devoted to strategies for solving *constraint satisfaction problems,* asking for satisfying assignments to a set of finite-domain variables. We also address the more general setting of solving *constraint optimization problems,* which asks for an optimal value assignment with respect to an additionally given *objective function.* For example, problems with soft constraints are modeled as a constraint optimization problem by introducing additional state variables that fine the violation of preference constraints. We will see how search heuristics in the form of lower bounds can be included into the constraint optimization, and how more general search heuristics apply.

In later parts of the chapter, we subject the search to solving some well-known NP-hard problems with specialized constraint solvers. We will consider instances of SAT, NUMBER PARTITION, BIN PACKING, and RECTANGLE PACKING, as well as graph problems like GRAPH PARTITION and VERTEX COVER. We present heuristic estimates and further search refinements to enhance the search for (optimal) solutions.

Temporal constraints are ones that restrict the set of possible time points; for example, to wake up between 7 A.M and 8 A.M. For this case variable domains are infinite. We introduce two algorithmic approaches that can deal with temporal constraints.

13.1 CONSTRAINT SATISFACTION

Constraint satisfaction is a technology for modeling and solving combinatorial problems. Its main parts are domain filtering and local consistency rules together with refined search techniques to traverse the resulting state space. Constraint satisfaction relies on a declarative problem description that consists of a set of variables together with their respective domains. Each domain itself is composed of a set of possible values. Constraints restrict the set of possible combinations of the variables.

Constraints are often expressed in the form of arithmetic (in)equalities over a set of unknown variables; for example, the unary integer constraints $X \geq 0$ and $X \leq 9$ denote that the value X consists of one digit. Combining a set of constraints can exploit information and yield a set of new constraints. Arithmetic linear constraints, such as $X + Y = 7$ and $X - Y = 5$, can be simplified to the constraints: $X = 6$ and $Y = 1$. In constraint solving practice, elementary calculus is often not sufficient to determine the set of feasible solutions. In fact, most constraint satisfaction domains we consider are NP-hard.

Definition 13.1. *(CSP, Constraint, Solution) A constraint satisfaction problem (CSP) consists of a finite set of variables $V_1, \ldots, V_n$ of finite domains $D_{V_1}, \ldots, D_{V_n}$, and a finite set of constraints, where a constraint is a(n arbitrary) relation over the set of variables. Constraints can be* extensional *in the form of a set of compatible tuples or* intentional *in the form of a formula. A* solution *to a CSP is a complete assignment of values to variables satisfying all the constraints.*

For the sake of simplicity this definition rules out continuous variables. Examples for extending this class are considered later in this chapter in the form of temporal constraints.

A binary constraint is a constraint involving only two variables. A *binary CSP* is a CSP with only binary constraints. Unary constraints can be compiled into binary ones, for example, by adding constraint variables with only assignment 0.

Any CSP is convertible to a binary CSP via its *dual encoding*, where the roles of variables and constraints are exchanged. The constraint variables are *encapsulated*, meaning one has assigned a domain that is a Cartesian product of the domains of individual variables. The valuation of original variables can to be extracted from the valuation of encapsulated variables. As an example, take the original (non-binary) CSP: $X + Y = Z$, $X < Y$, with $D_X = \{1, 2\}$, $D_Y = \{3, 4\}$, and $D_Z = \{5, 6\}$. The equivalent binary CSP consists of the two encapsulated variables $V = \{(X, Y, Z) \mid X + Y = Z\}$ and $W = \{(X, Y) \mid X < Z\}$ together with their domains $D_V = \{(1, 4, 5), (2, 3, 5), (2, 4, 6)\}$ and $D_W = \{(1, 3), (1, 4), (2, 3), (2, 4)\}$. The binary constraints between V and W require that the components that refer to the same original variables match; for example, the first component in V (namely X) is equal to the first component in W and the second component in V (namely Y) is equal to the second component in W.

One example is the EIGHT QUEENS problem (see Fig. 13.1). The task is to place eight queens on a chess board, but with at most one queen in the same row, column, or diagonal. If variable V_i denotes the column of the queen in row i, $i \in \{1, \ldots, 8\}$, we have that $D_{V_1} = \cdots = D_{V_8} = \{1, \ldots, 8\}$. An assignment to one variable will restrict the set of possible assignments to other ones. The constraints that induce no conflict are $V_i \neq V_j$ (vertical threat) and $|V_i - V_j| \neq |i - j|$ (diagonal threat) for all $1 \leq i \neq j \leq 8$. (Horizontal threats are already taken care of in the constraint model.)

Such a problem formulation calls for an efficient search algorithm to find a feasible variable assignment representing valid placements of the queens on the board. A naive strategy considers all 8^8 possible assignments, which can easily be reduced to 8!. A refined approach maintains a vector for a partial assignment in a vector, which grows with increasing depth and shrinks with each backtrack. To limit the branching during the search, we additionally maintain a global data structure to mark all places that are in conflict with the current assignment.

FIGURE 13.1

Solution to EIGHT QUEENS problem; no queen threatens another one.

		2	4					
	7		9			4		
5			8		2		7	
9	8						6	5
		2	9		5	4		
4	6						7	2
8		9		2		6		1
				5		3		
			1		8			

FIGURE 13.2

A SUDOKU; empty spaces have to be filled with numbers such that all rows, columns, and blocks are permutations of $1,\dots,9$.

```
??????? / ??? = ??8??
   ???
   - - -
   ????
   ???
   - - - -
    ????
```

FIGURE 13.3

The LONELY EIGHT problem; nonzero numbers have to be assigned to the wild cards such that the equation is true.

A SUDOKU (see Fig. 13.2) is a puzzle with rising popularity in the United States, but with a longer tradition in Asia and Europe. The rules are simple: fill all empty squares with numbers from $\{1,\dots,9\}$ such that in each column, in each row, and in each 3×3 block, all numbers from 1 to 9 are selected exactly once. If variable $V_{i,j}$ with $D_{V_{i,j}} = \{1,\dots,9\}$ denotes the number assigned to cell (i,j), where $i, j \in \{1,\dots,9\}$, as constraints we have

- $V_{i,j} \neq V_{i,j'}$ for all $i \in \{1,\dots,9\}$, $1 \leq j \neq j' \leq 9$ (vertical constraints)
- $V_{i,j} \neq V_{i'j}$ for all $j \in \{1,\dots,9\}$, $1 \leq i \neq i' \leq 9$ (horizontal constraints)
- $V_{i,j} \neq V_{i'j'}$ for all $(i,j) \neq (i',j')$, $\lfloor i/3 \rfloor = \lfloor i'/3 \rfloor$ and $\lfloor j/3 \rfloor = \lfloor j'/3 \rfloor$ (subsquare constraints)

As another typical CSP example, we consider a CRYPTARITHM (a.k.a *crypto-arithmetic* puzzle or *alphametic*), in which we have to assign numbers to each individual variable, so that the equation SEND + MORE = MONEY becomes true. The set of variables is $\{S,E,N,D,M,O,R,Y\}$. Each variable is an integer from 0 to 9, and leading characters and S and M cannot be assigned 0. The problem is to assign pairwise different values to the variables. It is not difficult to check that the (unique) solution to the problem is given by the assignments $[S, E, N, D, M, O, R, Y] = [9, 5, 6, 7, 1, 0, 8, 2]$ (vector notation).

Since we only consider problems with decimal digits, there are at most 10! different assignments of the digits to variables. So a CRYPTARITHM is a finite-state space problem, but generalizations to bases other than decimals are provably hard (NP-complete).

Another famous CSP problem is the LONELY EIGHT problem. The task is to determine all wild cards in the division that is shown in Figure 13.3. For a human using basic calculus and exclusions it is not difficult to obtain the only solution $10,020,316/124 = 80,809$. However, since no specialized constraints can be used, CSP solvers are often confronted with considerable work.

13.2 CONSISTENCY

Consistency is an inference mechanism to rule out certain variable assignments, which in turn enhances the search. The simplest consistency check tests a current assignment against the set of constraints. Such a simple consistency algorithm for a set of assigned variables and a set of constraints is provided in Algorithm 13.1. We use $Variables(c)$ to denote the set of variables that are mentioned in the constraint c, and $Satisfied(c, L)$ to denote if the constraint c is satisfied by the current label set L (assignment of values to variables).

In the following we introduce more powerful inference methods like *arc consistency* and *path consistency*, and discuss *specialized consistency* techniques like the *all-different constraint*.

13.2.1 Arc Consistency

Arc consistency is one of the most powerful propagation techniques for binary constraints. For every value of a variable in the constraint we search for a supporting value to be assigned to the other variable. If there is none, the value can safely be eliminated. Otherwise, the constraint is arc consistent.

Definition 13.2. *(Arc Consistency) The pair (X, Y) of constraint variables is* arc consistent *if for each value $x \in D_X$ there exists a value $y \in D_y$ such that the assignments $X = x$ and $Y = y$ satisfy all binary constraints between X and Y. A CSP is* arc consistent *if all variable pairs are arc consistent.*

Consider a simple CSP with the variables A and B subject to their respective domains $D_A = \{1, 2\}$ and $D_B = \{1, 2, 3\}$, as well as the binary constraint $A < B$. We see that value 1 can be safely removed from D_B based on constraint and the restriction we have on A.

Procedure Consistent
Input: Label set L, constraints C
Output: L satisfies C true/false

for each c **in** C ;; Consider all constraints
  if $(Variables(c) \subseteq L)$;; All variables are labeled
    if not $(Satisfied(c, L))$;; Check assignment
      return *false*   ;; No conflict
  return *true*   ;; Feedback success or failure

Algorithm 13.1

Simple consistency algorithm.

In general, constraints are used actively to remove inconsistencies from the problem. An inconsistency arises if we arrive at a value that cannot be contained in any solution. To abstract from different inference mechanisms we assume a procedure *Revise*, to be attached to each constraint, which governs the propagation of the domain restrictions.

AC-3 and AC-8

Algorithm AC-3 is one option to organize and perform constraint reasoning for arc consistency. The input of the algorithm are the set of variables V, the set of domains D, and the set of constraints C.

In the algorithm, a queue of constraints is frequently revised. Each time, when the domain of a variable changes, all constraints over this variable are enqueued. The pseudo code of the approach is shown in Algorithm 13.2. As a simple example, take the following CSP with the three variables $D_X = D_Y = D_Z = \{1,2,3,4,5,6\}$, subject to the binary constraints $X < Y$ and $Z < X - 2$. As $X < Y$, we have $D_X = \{1,2,3,4,5\}$, $D_Y = \{2,3,4,5,6\}$, and $D_Z = \{1,2,3,4,5,6\}$. Since $Z < X - 2$, we infer that $D_X = \{4,5\}$, $D_Y = \{2,3,4,5,6\}$, and $D_Z = \{1,2\}$. Now we take constraint $X < Y$ again to find the arc consistent set $D_X = \{4,5\}$, $D_Y = \{5,6\}$, and $D_Z = \{1,2\}$. Snapshots of the algorithms after selecting variable c are provided in Figure 13.4.

Procedure AC-3
Input: Set of variables V, set of domains D, set of constraints C
Output: Satisfiable *true/false*, restricted set of domains

$Q \leftarrow C$	;; Initialize queue
while $(Q \neq \emptyset)$	;; As far as constraints are available
$\quad c \leftarrow Select(Q)$	;; Choose one constraint
$\quad D' \leftarrow Revise(c,D)$	;; Restrict domains based on that choice
$\quad$ **if** (**exists** d **in** D' **with** $d = \emptyset$) **return** (*false,D'*)	;; Problem infeasible
$\quad Q \leftarrow (Q \cup \{c' \in C \mid \exists x \in Variables(c') : D'_x \neq D_x\}) \setminus \{c\}$	;; Update queue
$\quad D \leftarrow D'$	;; Update set of domains
return (*true,D*)	;; Return solution

Algorithm 13.2

Arc consistency with AC-3.

Q	D	c
$X < Y, Z < X - 2$	$D_X = D_Y = D_Z = \{1,2,3,4,5,6\}$	$X < Y$
$Z < X - 2$	$D_X = \{1,2,3,4,5\}, D_Y = \{2,3,4,5,6\},$	$Z < X - 2$
	$D_Z = \{1,2,3,4,5,6\}$	
$X < Y$	$D_X = \{4,5\}, D_Y = \{2,3,4,5,6\}, D_Z = \{1,2\}$	$X < Y$
	$D_X = \{4,5\}, D_Y = \{5,6\}, D_Z = \{1,2\}$	

FIGURE 13.4

Executing AC-3; Q is the queue of constraints, D_X the domain of variable X, and c the constraint selected.

An alternative to AC-3 is to use a queue of variables instead of a queue of constraints. The modified algorithm is referred to as AC-8. It assumes that a user will specify, for each constraint, when constraint revision should be executed. The pseudo code of the approach is shown in Algorithm 13.3 and a step-by-step example is given in Figure 13.5.

13.2.2 Bounds Consistency

Arc consistency works well in binary CSPs. However, if we are confronted with constraints that involve more than two variables (e.g., $X = Y + Z$), the application of arc consistency is limited. Unfortunately, *hyperarc consistency* techniques are involved, and similar to the complexity of SET COVERING and GRAPH COLORING-NP-hard for $n \geq 3$. The problem is that we must determine which values of the variables are legitimate and which is a nontrivial problem.

The trick is to use an approximation of the set of possible assignments in the form of an interval. A *domain range* $D = [a,b]$ denotes the set of integers $\{a, a+1, \ldots, b\}$ with $\min_D = a$ and $\max_D = b$.

Procedure AC-8
Input: Set of variables V, set of domains D, set of constraints C
Output: Satisfiable *true/false*, restricted set of domains

$Q \leftarrow V$	;; Initialize queue
while $(Q \neq \emptyset)$	;; As far as variables are available
$\quad v \leftarrow Select(Q)$	;; Choose one variable
$\quad Q \leftarrow Q \setminus \{v\}$	;; Eliminate variable from queue
$\quad$ **for each** c **in** C **with** v **in** *Variables*(c)	;; Determine respective constraint
$\quad\quad D' \leftarrow Revise(c, D)$	;; Restrict domains based on that choice
$\quad\quad$ **if** (**exists** d **in** D' **with** $d = \emptyset$) **return** (*false*, $\cdot$)	;; Problem infeasible
$\quad\quad Q \leftarrow Q \cup \{u \in Variables(c) \mid D'_u \neq D_u\}$	;; Update variable queue
$\quad\quad D \leftarrow D'$	;; Update set of domains
return (*true*, D)	;; Return solution

Algorithm 13.3

Arc consistency with AC-8.

Q	D	c
X, Y, Z	$D_X = D_Y = D_Z = \{1,2,3,4,5,6\}$	X
X, Y, Z	$D_X = \{4,5\}, D_Y = \{2,3,4,5,6\}, D_Z = \{1,2\}$	X
Y, Z	$D_X = \{4,5\}, D_Y = \{5,6\}, D_Z = \{1,2\}$	Y
Z	$D_X = \{4,5\}, D_Y = \{5,6\}, D_Z = \{1,2\}$	Z
	$D_X = \{4,5\}, D_Y = \{5,6\}, D_Z = \{1,2\}$	

FIGURE 13.5

Executing AC-8; Q is the queue of variables, D_X the domain of variable X, and v the variable selected.

For bounds consistency we only look at *arithmetic CSPs* that range over finite-domain variables for which all constraints are arithmetic expressions. A primitive constraint is *bounds consistent* if for each variable X that is in the constraint there is an assignment for all other variables (in their domain range) that is compatible with setting X to $\min_D$ and X to $\max_D$. An arithmetic CSP is bounds consistent if each primitive constraint is bounds consistent.

Consider the constraint $X = Y + Z$ and rewrite it as $X = Y + Z$, $Y = X - Z$, and $Z = X - Y$. Reasoning about minimum and maximum values on the right side, we establish the following six necessary conditions: $X \geq \min_D(Y) + \min_D(Z)$, $Y \geq \min_D(X) - \max_D(Z)$, $Z \geq \min_D(X) - \max_D(Y)$, $X \leq \max_D(Y) + \max_D(Z)$, $Y \leq \max_D(X) - \min_D(Z)$, and $Z \leq \max_D(X) - \min_D(Y)$. For example, the domains $D_X = [4..8]$, $D_Y = [0..3]$, and $D_Z = [2..2]$ are refined to $D_X = [4..5]$, $D_Y = [2..3]$, and $D_Z = [2..2]$ without missing any solution.

13.2.3 *Path Consistency

The good news about arc consistency is that it is fast in practice. The bad news is that arc consistency does not detect all inconsistencies. As a simple example consider the CSP shown in Figure 13.6 (left) with the three variables X, Y, Z with $D_X = D_Y = D_Z = \{1, 2\}$ subject to $X \neq Y$, $Y \neq Z$, and $X \neq Z$. The CSP is arc consistent but not solvable. Therefore, we introduce a stronger form of consistency.

Definition 13.3. *(Path Consistency) A path $(V_0, V_1, \ldots, V_m)$ is path consistent if, for all x in the domain of V_0, and for all y in the domain of V_m satisfying all binary constraints on V_0 and V_m, there exists an assignment to $V_1, \ldots, V_{m-1}$, s.t. all binary constraints between V_i and V_{i+1} for $i \in \{0, \ldots, m-1\}$ are satisfied.*
A CSP is path consistent, if every path is consistent.

This definition is long but not difficult to decipher. On top of binary constraints between two variables, path consistency certifies binary consistency between the variables on a path. It is not difficult to see that path consistency implies arc consistency. An example to show that path consistency is still incomplete is provided in Figure 13.6 (right).

For restricting the computational efforts, it is sufficient to explore paths of length two only (see Exercises). To come up with a path consistency algorithm, we consider the following example,

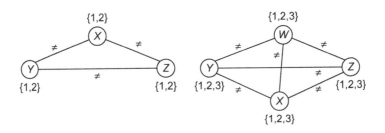

FIGURE 13.6

A graph for which path consistency but not arc consistency is complete (left), and a graph for which path consistency is incomplete (right).

consisting of the three variables A, B, C with $D_A = D_B = D_C = \{1, 2, 3\}$, subject to $B > 1, A < C, A = B$, and $B > C - 2$. Each constraint can be expressed in a (Boolean) matrix, denoting whether a variable combination is possible or not:

$$B > 1 \sim \begin{pmatrix} 000 \\ 010 \\ 001 \end{pmatrix}, A = B \sim \begin{pmatrix} 100 \\ 010 \\ 001 \end{pmatrix}, A < C \sim \begin{pmatrix} 011 \\ 001 \\ 000 \end{pmatrix}, B > C - 2 \sim \begin{pmatrix} 110 \\ 111 \\ 111 \end{pmatrix}.$$

Let $R_{i,j}$ be the matrix entry for the constraint between variable i and j; $R_{k,k}$ models the domain of k. Then consistency on the path (i, k, j) can be recursively determined by applying the equation

$$R_{i,j} \leftarrow R_{i,j} \wedge (R_{i,k} R_{k,k} R_{k,j}).$$

The concatenations correspond to Boolean matrix multiplications, such as the scalar product of the rows and columns in the matrix. The final conjunction is element-by-element.

For the example $R_{A,C} \leftarrow R_{A,C} \wedge R_{A,B} R_{B,B} R_{B,C}$, we establish the following equation:

$$\begin{pmatrix} 000 \\ 010 \\ 001 \end{pmatrix} \wedge \begin{pmatrix} 100 \\ 010 \\ 001 \end{pmatrix} \cdot \begin{pmatrix} 011 \\ 001 \\ 000 \end{pmatrix} \cdot \begin{pmatrix} 110 \\ 111 \\ 111 \end{pmatrix} = \begin{pmatrix} 000 \\ 001 \\ 000 \end{pmatrix}.$$

We observe that path consistency restricts the set of possible instantiations in the constraint.

For a path-consistent CSP, we have to repeat the earlier revisions of paths. The pseudo code is shown in Algorithm 13.4. It is a straightforward extension to the ALL-PAIRS SHORTEST PATHS algorithm of Floyd and Warshall (see Ch. 2). Mathematically spoken, it is the same algorithm applied to a different semiring, where minimization is substituted by conjunction and addition is substituted by multiplication.

13.2.4 Specialized Consistency

As path consistency is comparably slow with respect to arc consistency, it is not always the best solution for overall CSP solving. In some cases specialized constraints (together with effective propagation rules) are often more effective.

One important specialized constraint is the *all-different constraint* (AD) that we already came across in the SUDOKU and CRYPTARITHM domains at the beginning of this chapter.

Definition 13.4. *(All-Different Constraint) The* all-different constraint *covers a set of binary inequality constraints among all variables* $X_1 \neq X_2, X_1 \neq X_3, \ldots, X_{k-1} \neq X_k$:

$$AD(\{X_1, \ldots, X_k\}) = \{(d_1, \ldots, d_k) \mid \forall i : d_i \in D_i \wedge \forall i \neq j : d_i \neq d_j\}.$$

Propagating the all-different constraint, we achieve strong pruning. Its efficient implementation is based on matching *bipartite graphs*, where the set of nodes V is partitioned into two disjoint sets V' and V'': for each edge its source and target nodes are contained in a different set, and a *matching* is a node-disjoint selection of edges.

Procedure Path-Consistency
Input: Set of variables V, $n = |V|$, set of constraint matrices C
(one matrix between any pair of variables and for each variable)
Output: Path-consistent constraint matrices

$Y^n \leftarrow C$	;; Set of temporary matrix
repeat	;; Until fixpoint reached
$\quad Y^0 \leftarrow Y^n$	;; Initial matrix
$\quad$ **for each** k **in** $\{1,\ldots,n\}$	;; Loop on iteration number
$\quad\quad$ **for each** i **in** $\{1,\ldots,n\}$	;; Loop on start node
$\quad\quad\quad$ **for each** j **in** $\{1,\ldots,n\}$	;; Loop on end node
$\quad\quad\quad\quad Y^k_{i,j} \leftarrow Y^{k-1}_{i,j} \wedge (Y^{k-1}_{i,k} Y^{k-1}_{k,k} Y^{k-1}_{k,j})$	;; Perform update
until $(Y^n = Y^0)$	;; Fixpoint established
return Y^0	;; Return path-consistent constraint matrix

Algorithm 13.4

Algorithm for path consistency.

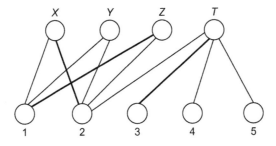

FIGURE 13.7

Example of the all-different constraint for the variables $\{X,Y,Z,T\}$ with $D_X = \{1,2\}$, and $D_Y = \{1,2\}$, $D_Z = \{1,2\}$, and $D_T = \{2,3,4,5\}$; matching edges (thick) show a selected assignment.

The assignment graph for the all-different constraint consists of two sets. On one hand, we have the variables, and, on the other hand, we have the values that are in the domain of at least one of the variables. Any assignment to the variables that satisfies the all-different constraint is a *maximum matching*. The running time for solving bipartite matching problems in graph $G = (V,E)$ is $O(\sqrt{|V|}|E|)$ (using *maximum flow* algorithms). An example for the propagation of the all-different constraint is provided in Figure 13.7.

13.3 SEARCH STRATEGIES

As with path consistency, even strong propagation techniques are often incomplete. Search is needed for resolving the set of remaining uncertainties for the current variable assignments.

The most important way to span a search tree is *labeling*, which assigns different values to variables. In a more general view, the search for solving constraint satisfaction problems resolves disjunctions. For example, an assignment not only assigns variables on one branch but also denotes that this value is no longer available on other branches of the search tree.

This observation leads to very different *branching rules* to generate a CSP search tree. They define the shape of the search tree. As an example, we can produce a binary search tree, by setting $X = x \vee X \neq x$ for one particular value x and branch on only these two constraints. Another important branching rule is *domain splitting*, which also generates a binary search tree. An example is to split the search tree according to the disjunction $X < 3 \vee X \geq 3$. The next option is disjunctions on the *variable ordering*, such as $X < Y \vee X \geq Y$.

Walking along this line, we see that each search tree node can be viewed as a set of constraints, indicating which knowledge on the set of variables is currently known for solving the problem. For example, assigning a value x to a variable X for generating a current search tree node u adds the constraint $X = x$ to the constraint set of the predecessor node *parent(u)*.

In the following we concentrate on labeling and on the selection of the variable to be labeled next. One often applied search heuristic is *first-fail*. It prefers the variable, the instantiation of which will lead to a failure with the highest probability. The intuition behind the strategy is to work on the simpler problems first. A consequent rule for this policy is to test variables with the smallest domain first. Alternatively, we may select most constrained variables first.

For *value selection*, the *succeed-first principle* has shown good performance. It prefers the values that might belong to the solution with the highest probability. Value selection criteria define the order of branches to be explored and are often problem-dependent.

13.3.1 Backtracking

The labeling process is combined with consistency techniques that prune the search space. For each search tree node we propagate constraints to make the problem *locally consistent*, which in turn reduces the options for labeling. The labeling procedure will backtrack upon failure, and continue with a search tree node that has not yet resolved completely.

The pseudo code for such a *backtracking* approach is shown in Algorithm 13.5. In the initial call of the recursive subprocedure *Backtrack*, the variable assignment set V is divided into the set of already labeled variables L and the set of yet unlabeled variables U. If all variables are successfully assigned the problem is solved and the assignment can be returned. As with the consistency algorithm an additional flag is attached to the return value to distinguish between success and failure.

There is a trade-off between the time spent for search and the time spent for propagation. The consistency call matches the parameters of the arc consistency algorithms AC-3 and AC-8. It is not difficult to include more powerful consistency methods like path consistency. On the other hand, more aggressive consistency mechanisms only check if the current assignment leads to no contradiction with the current set of constraints. Such a *pure backtracking* algorithm is shown in Algorithm 13.6. Other consistency techniques remove incompatible values only from connected but currently unlabeled variables. This technique is called *forward checking*. Forward checking is cheap. It does not increase the time complexity of pure backtracking, as the checks are only drawn earlier in the search process.

Procedure Backtrack
Input: Labeled/unlabeled variables L/U, domains D, and constraints C
Output: C satisfiable *true/false* and variable assignment

if $(U = \emptyset)$ **return** $(true, L)$	;; Feedback labeled variables
$x \leftarrow Select(U)$	;; Choose variable
for each v **in** D_x	;; Check domain of chosen variable
$\quad (b, D') \leftarrow AC\text{-}x(L, D, C \cup \{x = v\})$	;; Call subroutine, e.g., Alg. 13.2 or 13.3
$\quad$ **if** (b)	;; Subproblem consistent
$\qquad (b, R) \leftarrow Backtrack(U \setminus \{x\}, L \cup \{(x, v)\}, D', C \cup \{x = v\})$	;; Recursive call
$\qquad$ **if** (b) **return** $(true, R)$	;; Solution found
return $(false, \cdot)$	;; Problem inconsistent

Procedure Backtracking
Input: Variables V, domains D, constraints C
Output: Assignment for V if C satisfiable or *false*

$(b, L) \leftarrow Backtrack(\emptyset, V, D, C)$	;; Call of recursive procedure
if (b) **return** L **else return** *false*	;; Feedback success or failure

Algorithm 13.5

Backtracking search algorithm.

Procedure PureBacktrack
Input: Labeled/unlabeled variables L/U, constraints C
Output: C satisfiable *true/false* and variable assignment

if $(U = \emptyset)$ **return** $(true, L)$	;; Feedback labeled variables
$x \leftarrow Select(U)$	;; Choose variable
for each v **in** D_x	;; Check domain of chosen variable
$\quad b \leftarrow Consistent(L, C)$	;; Call subroutine, matches Alg. 13.1
$\quad$ **if** (b)	;; Subproblem consistent
$\qquad (b, R) \leftarrow PureBacktrack(U \setminus \{x\}, L \cup \{(x, v)\}, C)$	;; Recursive call
$\qquad$ **if** (b) **return** R	;; Solution returned
return $(false, \cdot)$	;; Problem inconsistent

Procedure PureBacktracking
Input: Variables V, constraints C
Output: Assignment for V if C satisfiable or *false*

$(b, L) \leftarrow PureBacktrack(\emptyset, V, C)$	;; Call of recursive procedure
if (b) **return** L **else return** *false*	;; Feedback success or failure

Algorithm 13.6

Pure backtracking search algorithm.

13.3.2 Backjumping

One weakness of the backtrack procedure is that it throws away the reason for the conflict. Suppose that we are given constraint variables A, B, C, D with $D_A = D_B = D_C = D_D = \{1,2,3,4\}$ and a constraint $A > D$. Backtracking starts with labeling $A = 1$, and then tries all the assignments for B and C before finding that A has to be larger than 1. A better option is to jump back to A at the first time D is labeled, since this is the source of the conflict.

We explain the working of the backjumping algorithm for the example with variables A, B, C, D, E, all of domain $\{1,2,3\}$, and constraints $A \neq C$, $A \neq D$, $A \neq E$, $B \neq D$, $E \neq B$, and $E \neq D$. The according constraint graph is shown in Figure 13.8. Some snapshots of the backjumping algorithm for this example are provided in Figure 13.9, where the variables are plotted against their possible value assignments following the order of labeling.

The pseudo code for the backjumping procedure is shown in Algorithm 13.7. The additional parameter for the algorithm is the previous level from which the procedure is invoked. The return value

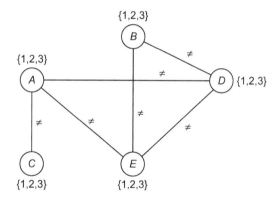

FIGURE 13.8

Constraint graph for a running example.

	1	2	3
A	✓		
B		✓	
C	×	✓	
D	×	×	✓
E	×	×	×

	1	2	3
A	✓		
B		✓	
C	×	✓	
D	×	×	×
E			

	1	2	3
A	✓		
B	✓	×	
C	×	✓	
D	×	✓	
E	×	×	✓

FIGURE 13.9

Conflict matrix evolution for backjumping in the example of Figure 13.8; matrix entries denote impossible assignment, and check denotes current assignment. Value assignment until first backtrack at E (left). After backtracking from E to the previous level, there is no possible variable assignment (middle). Backjumping to variable B, since this is the source of the conflict, eventually finds a satisfying assignment (right).

Procedure Backjump
Input: Labeled/unlabeled variables L/U, constraints C, previous level p
Output: Label set for satisfied C or jump level to conflicting variable

if $(U = \emptyset)$ **return** $(\lvert L \rvert + 1, L)$	;; Feedback labeled variables
$x \leftarrow Select(U)$	;; Select unlabeled variable
$m \leftarrow 0$	;; Initialize jump variable
for each v **in** D_x	;; Check domain of chosen variable
$\quad (b,j) \leftarrow Consistent(L,C,p+1)$	;; Compute closest conflict level, Alg. 13.8
$\quad$ **if** (b)	;; Test of consistency successful
$\quad\quad m \leftarrow p$	;; Standard backtrack
$\quad\quad (r,R) \leftarrow Backjump(U \setminus \{x\}, L \cup \{(x,v,p+1)\}, C, p+1)$	;; Recursive call
$\quad\quad$ **if** $(r \neq p+1)$ **return** (r,R)	;; Success or backjump
$\quad$ **else**	;; Conflict in level j
$\quad\quad m \leftarrow \max\{m,j\}$	;; Update jump variable
return $(m, \cdot)$	;; Jump to the conflicting variable

Procedure Backjumping
Input: Variables V, constraints C
Output: Assignment for V if C satisfiable or *false*

$(r,L) \leftarrow Backjump(\emptyset, V, C, 0)$	;; Call of subroutine
if $(r = \lvert V \rvert + 1)$ **return** L **else return** *false*	;; Feedback success or failure

Algorithm 13.7

Backjumping search algorithm.

---

includes the jump level instead of simply denoting success or failure. The values $\lvert L \rvert + 1 = \lvert V \rvert + 1$ are the otherwise impossible jump values chosen for success. The implementation is tricky. It invokes a variant of the (simple) consistency check, for which the closest conflicting level is computed, in addition to the test of satisfaction of the constraints. The pseudo code is shown in Algorithm 13.8. Its parameters are the currently label set L, the constraint set C, and the backjump level l. The implementation of Algorithm 13.8 is not much different from Algorithm 13.1 in the sense that it returns a Boolean value, denoting if the consistency check was successful and the level j on which the conflict has been detected. The update of j takes the current label set L into account, which now consists of triples with the third component being the level to which a variable is assigned. This value j then determines the return value in Algorithm 13.7 and the level m for the next backjump.

The reassignment of variable C that is in between B and D is actually not needed. This brings us to the next search strategy.

13.3.3 Dynamic Backtracking

A refinement to backjumping is *dynamic backtracking*. It handles the problem of losing the *in-between* assignments when jumping back. Dynamic backtracking remembers the source of the conflict, monitors the source of the conflict, and changes the order of variables.

Procedure Consistent
Input: Constraints C, level l
Output: Level to conflicting variable

$j \leftarrow l$	;; Level to be jumped
$b \leftarrow$ *false*	;; Flag denoting a conflict
for each c **in** C	;; Consider all constraints
if ($Variables(c) \subseteq L$)	;; All variables are labeled
if not ($Satisfied(c, L)$)	;; Check assignment
$b \leftarrow$ *true*	;; No conflict
$j \leftarrow \min\{j, \max\{k \mid v \in Variables(c) \wedge (x, v, l) \in L \wedge k < l\}\}$	;; Update
if (b) **then return** (*false*, j) **else return** (*true*, $\cdot$)	;; Feedback success or failure

Algorithm 13.8

Simple consistency for backjumping.

	1	2	3
A	√		
B		√	
C	A	√	
D	A	B	√
E	A	B	D

	1	2	3
A	√		
B		√	
C	A	√	
D	A	B	**AB**
E	A	B	

	1	2	3
A	√		
C	A	√	
B	√	A	
D	A	√	
E	A	B	√

FIGURE 13.10

Conflict matrix evolution for dynamic backtracking in the example of Figure 13.8; matrix entries denote source of conflict for chosen assignments, check denotes current assignment, bold variables are transposed.

Consider again the example of Figure 13.8. The iterations shown in Figure 13.10 illustrate how the sources of conflicts are maintained together with the assignments to the variables and how this information eventually allows the change of variable ordering. If we assign A to 1 and B to 2 we need no conflict information. When assigning C to 2 we store variable A at C as the source of a conflict of choosing 1. Setting D to 3 leads to the memorization of conflict with A (value 1) and B (value 2). Now E has no further assignment (left) so that we jump back to D but carry the conflict source AB from variable E to D (middle). This leads to another jump from D to C and a change of order of the variable B and C (right). A final assignment is A to 1, C to 2 (with conflict source A), B to 1 (with conflict source A), D to 2 (with conflict source A), and E to 3 (with conflict sources A and B). In difference to backjumping, vertex C is not reassigned.

13.3.4 Backmarking

Another problem for backtracking is redundant work for which unnecessary constraint checks are repeated. For example, consider A, B, C, D with $D_A = D_B = D_C = \{1, \ldots, 10\}$ with the constraints

$A + 8 < C$, $B = 5D$. Consider the search tree generated by labeling A, B, C, D (in this order). There is much redundant computation in different subtrees when labeling variable C (after setting $B = 1$, $B = 2, \ldots, B = 10$). The reason is that the change in B does not influence variable C at all. Therefore, we aim at removing redundant constraint checks.

The proposed solution is to remember previous (either good or no-good) assignments. This so-called *backmarking* algorithm removes redundant constraint checks by memorizing negative and positive tests. It maintains the values

- $Mark(x, v)$, for the farthest (instantiated) variable x in conflict with the current assignment v (conflict marking).
- $Back(x)$, for the farthest variable to which we backtracked since the last attempt to instantiate x (backtrack marking).

Constraint checks can be omitted for the case $Mark(x, v) < Back(x)$. An illustration is given in Figure 13.11. We detect that the assignment from X to 1 on the left branch on the tree is inconsistent with the assignment of Y to 1, but consistent with all other variables above X. The assignment from X to 1 on the right branch on the tree is still inconsistent with the assignment of Y to 1 and does not need to be checked again.

The pseudo-code implementation is provided in Algorithm 13.9 as an extension to the pure backtracking algorithm. We see that checking if the conflict marking is larger than or equal to the backtrack marking is performed before every consistency check. The algorithm also illustrates how the value *Back* is updated. The conflict marking is assumed to be stored together with each assignment. Note that as with backjumping (see Alg. 13.8), the consistency procedure is assumed to compute the conflict level together with each call.

The backmarking algorithm is illustrated for the EIGHT QUEENS problem of Figure 13.1 in Figure 13.12. The farthest conflict queen (the conflict marking) is denoted on the board, and the backtrack marking is written to the right of the board. The sixth queen cannot be allocated, despite the assignment to the fifth queen, such that all further assignments to the fifth queen are discarded. It is not difficult to observe that backmarking can be combined with backjumping.

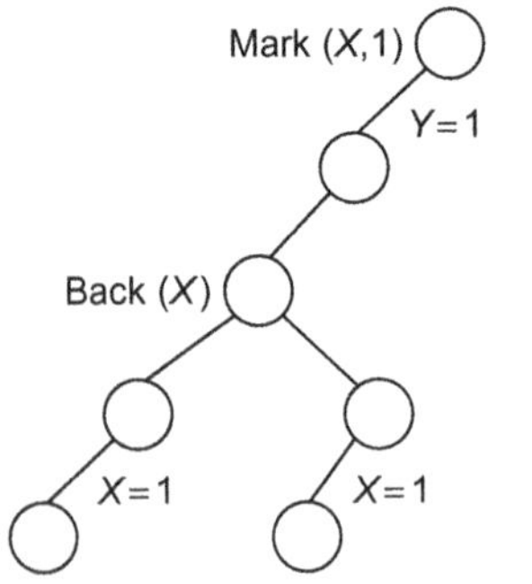

FIGURE 13.11

Fortunate case in backmarking.

Procedure Backmark
Input: Labeled/unlabeled variables L/U, constraints C, level l
Output: Label set for satisfied C

if $(U \neq \emptyset)$ return $(true, L)$;; Feedback labeled variables
$x \leftarrow Select(U)$;; Select unlabeled variable
for each v in D_x ;; Check domain of chosen variable
  if $(Mark(x,v) \geq Back(x))$;; Check marking
    if $(Consistent(L \cup \{(x,v)\}, C, l))$;; Check consistency
      $(b,R) \leftarrow BackMark(U \setminus \{x\}, \{(x,v,l)\} \cup L, C, l+1)$;; Recursive call
      if (b) return R ;; Return labeled set
$Back(X) \leftarrow l-1$;; Jump will be to the previous variable
for each Y in U ;; Broadcast the jump
  $Back(Y) \leftarrow \min\{l-1, Back(Y)\}$;; Update backtrack marking
return $(false, \cdot)$;; No assignment found

Procedure Backmarking
Input: Variables V, constraints C
Output: Assignment for V if C satisfiable or *false*

$(b,L) \leftarrow BackMark(\emptyset, V, C, 0)$;; Call of subroutine
if (b) return L else return *false* ;; Feedback success or failure

Algorithm 13.9

Backmarking search algorithm.

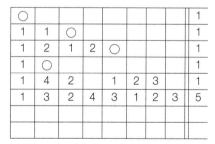

○								1
1	1	○						1
1	2	1	2	○				1
1	○							1
1	4	2		1	2	3		1
1	3	2	4	3	1	2	3	5

FIGURE 13.12

Example for backmarking in EIGHT QUEENS; queens are referred to as circles, numbers denote the farthest conflict queen, the ones far right denote the backtrack marking.

13.3.5 Search Strategies

In practical application of constraint satisfaction for real-life problems we frequently encounter that search spaces are so huge that they cannot be fully explored.

This immediately suggests heuristics to guide the search process into the direction of an assignment that satisfies the constraints and optimizes the objective function. In constraint satisfaction search heuristics are often encoded to recommend a value for an assignment in a labeling algorithm. This approach often leads to a fairly good solution on the early trials.

Backtracking mainly takes care of the bottom part of the search tree. It repairs later assignments rather than earliest ones. Consequently, backtracking search relies on the fact that search heuristics guide well in the top part of the search tree. As a drawback, backtracking is less reliable in the earlier parts of the search tree. This is due to the fact that, as the search process proceeds, more and more information is available and the number of violations to a search heuristic is small in practice.

Limited Discrepancy Search

Errors in the heuristic values have also been examined in the context of *limited discrepancy search* (*LDS*). It can be seen as a modification of depth-first search. On hard combinatorial problems like NUMBER PARTITION (see later) it outperforms traditional depth-first search.

Given a heuristic estimate, it would be most beneficial to order successors of a node according to their *h*-value, and then to choose the left one for expansion first. A *search discrepancy* means to stray from this heuristic preference at some node, and instead examine some other node that was not suggested by the heuristic estimate.

For ease of exposition, we assume binary search trees (i.e., two successors per node expansion). In fact, binary search trees are the only case that has been considered in literature and extensions to multi-ary trees are not obvious. A discrepancy corresponds to a right branch in an ordered tree. LDS performs a series of depth-first searches up to a maximum depth *d*. In the first iteration, it first looks at the path with no discrepancies, the left-most path, then at all paths that take one right branch, then with two right branches, and so forth. In Figure 13.13 paths with zero (first path), one (next three paths), two (next three paths), and three discrepancies (last path) in a binary tree are shown.

To measure the time complexity of LDS, we count the number of explored leaves.

Theorem 13.1. *(Complexity LDS) The number of leaves generated in limited discrepancy search in a complete binary tree of depth d is $(d+2)2^{d-1}$.*

Proof. The number of unique paths with *k* discrepancies is $\binom{d}{k}$. Therefore, for all $d+1$ iterations to completely search a tree of depth *d*, we have to evaluate the sum

$$S = (d+1)\binom{d}{0} + (d)\binom{d}{1} + \cdots + 2\binom{d}{d-1} + \binom{d}{d}.$$

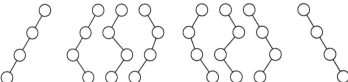

FIGURE 13.13

Paths with zero up to three discrepancies.

Writing the same terms in reverse order and adding the two equations together gives

$$2S = (d+2)\binom{d}{0} + (d+2)\binom{d}{1} + \cdots + (d+2)\binom{d}{d-1} + (d+2)\binom{d}{d},$$

so that $\left(\text{given } \binom{d}{d} = \binom{d}{0}\right)$,

$$S = \frac{d+2}{2}\left(\binom{d}{0} + \binom{d}{1} + \cdots + \binom{d}{d-1} + \binom{d}{d}\right) = (d+2)2^{d-1}.$$

■

The pseudo code for LDS is provided in Algorithm 13.10. Figure 13.14 visualizes the branches selected (bold lines) in different iterations of linear discrepancy search.

An obvious drawback of this basic scheme is that the ith iteration generates all paths with i discrepancies *or less*, hence it replicates the work of the previous iteration. In particular, to explore the right-most path in the last iteration, LDS regenerates the entire tree. LDS has been improved later using an upper bound on the maximum depth of the tree. In the ith iteration, it visits the leaf at the depth limit with exactly i discrepancies. The modified pseudo code for improved LDS is shown in Algorithm 13.11. An example is provided in Figure 13.15. This modification saves a factor of $(d+2)/2$.

Procedure Probe
Input: Node u with left/right successor *left(u)/right(u)*, discrepancy k
Output: Goal node if encountered, depth value

if $(Goal(u))$	;; Node u is a leaf
return $(true, 0)$	;; Return goal node or empty set
$(t, d_l) \leftarrow Probe(left(u), k)$	;; Try left
if (t) **return** $(true, 1 + d_l)$	;; If goal found, exit
if $(k > 0)$	;; Some discrepancy left
$(t, d_r) \leftarrow Probe(right(u), k - 1)$	;; Try right
if (t) **return** $(true, 1 + d_r)$	;; If goal found, exit
return $(false, \cdot)$	;; Return encountered depth

Procedure LDS
Input: Binary search with start node s, upper bond on discrepancy K
Output: Solution depth value or failure

for each k in $\{0, 1, 2, \ldots, K\}$	;; For all possible discrepancies
$(b, d) \leftarrow Probe(s, k)$	;; Call of subroutine
if (b) **return** d	;; Solution found
return *false*	;; No solution

Algorithm 13.10

One iteration in limited discrepancy search.

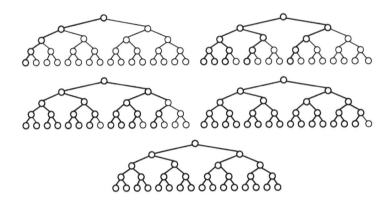

FIGURE 13.14

Limited discrepancy search in a binary tree changing the order of expansion; from left to right, paths are sorted by the number of discrepancies (right branches).

Function Probe
Input: Node u, depth d, discrepancy k
Output: Goal node if encountered, depth value

if $(Goal(u))$	;; Goal found or depth threshold encountered
if $(d = 0)$ **return** $(false, \cdot)$	;; Depth bound reached
return $(true, 0)$	;; Return goal node or empty set
if $(d > k)$	;; Depth exceeds discrepancy left
$(t, d_l) \leftarrow Probe(left(u), d - 1, k)$	;; Try left
if (t) **return** $(true, 1 + d_l)$	;; If goal found, exit
if $(k > 0)$	;; Some discrepancy left
$(t, d_r) \leftarrow Probe(right(u), d - 1, k - 1)$	;; Try right
if (t) **return** $(true, 1 + d_r)$	;; If goal found, exit
return $(false, \cdot)$	;; Return encountered depth

Procedure Improved-LDS
Input: Binary search with start node s, depth bound D, bound on discrepancy K
Output: Solution depth value or failure

for each k **in** $\{0, 1, 2, \ldots, K\}$	;; For all possible discrepancies
$(b, d) \leftarrow Probe(s, D, k)$	;; Call of subroutine
if (b) **return** d	;; Solution found
return $false$	;; No solution

Algorithm 13.11

One iteration in improved limited discrepancy search.

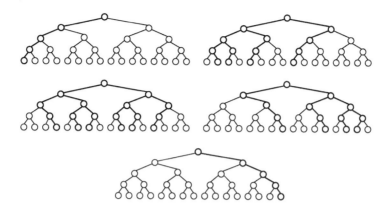

FIGURE 13.15

Improved limited discrepancy search: restricts number of discrepancies in iterations.

Theorem 13.2. *(Complexity-Improved LDS) The number of leaves generated in improved limited discrepancy search in a complete binary tree of depth d is 2^d.*

Proof. Since each iteration of improved LDS generates those paths with exactly k discrepancies, each leaf is generated exactly once for a total of 2^d leaf nodes.   ∎

A slightly different strategy, called *depth-bounded discrepancy search*, biases the search toward discrepancies high up in the search tree by means of an iteratively increasing depth bound. In the ith iteration, depth-bounded discrepancy explores those branches on which discrepancies occur at depth i or less. Algorithm 13.12 shows the pseudo code of depth-bounded discrepancy search. For the sake of simplicity, again we consider the traversal in binary search trees only.

Compared to improved LDS, depth-bounded LDS explores more discrepancies at the top of the search tree (see Fig. 13.16). While improved discrepancy search on a binary tree of depth d explores in its first iteration branches with at most one discrepancy, depth-bounded discrepancy search explores some branches with up to $\lg d$ discrepancies.

13.4 NP-HARD PROBLEM SOLVING

For an *NP-complete problem L* we require

NP-containment a *nondeterministic Turing machine M* that recognizes L in polynomial time, and

NP-hardness a *polynomial-time transformation f*, one for each problem L' in NP, such that $x \in L'$ if and only if $f(x) \in L$.

The running time of M is defined as the length of the shortest path to a final state. A *deterministic Turing machine* may simulate all possible computations of M in exponential time. Therefore, NP

Function Probe
Input: Node u, depth d, discrepancy k
Output: Goal node if encountered, depth value

if $(Goal(u))$ **return** $(true, 0)$	;; Return goal node
if $(d = 0)$ **return** $(false, \cdot)$	;; Depth bound reached
if $(k = 0)$	;; No discrepancy
$(t, d_l) \leftarrow Probe(left(u), d-1, 0)$	;; Go left
if (t) **return** $(true, 1 + d_l)$	;; If goal found, exit
if $(k = 1)$	;; One discrepancy
$(t, d_r) \leftarrow Probe(right(u), d-1, 0)$	;; Go right
if (t) **return** $(true, 1 + d_r)$	;; If goal found, exit
if $(k > 1)$	;; More than one discrepancy
$(t, d_l) \leftarrow Probe(left(u), d-1, k)$	;; Try left
if (t) **return** $(true, 1 + d_l)$	;; If goal found, exit
$(t, d_r) \leftarrow Probe(right(u), d-1, k-1)$	;; Try right
if (t) **return** $(true, 1 + d_r)$	;; If goal found, exit
return $(false, \cdot)$	;; Return encountered depth

Procedure Depth-Bounded Discrepancy Search
Input: Binary search with start node s, depth bound D, bound on discrepancy K
Output: Solution depth value or failure

for each k **in** $\{0, 1, 2, \ldots, K\}$	;; For all possible discrepancies
$(b, d) \leftarrow Probe(s, D, k)$	;; Call of subroutine
if (b) **return** d	;; Solution found
return $false$	;; No solution

Algorithm 13.12

Depth-bounded discrepancy search.

problems are state space problems with a state space of *configurations* of M, operators are transitions to successor configurations, the initial state is the start configuration of M, and the goal is defined by its final configuration(s).

NP-completeness makes scaling successful approaches difficult. Nonetheless, hard problems are frequent for search practice and for hundreds of thousands of problem instances that have been classified.

13.4.1 Boolean Satisfiability

Boolean CSPs are CSPs in which all variable domains are Boolean. Hence, the only two assignments that are allowed are *true* and *false*. If we are looking at variables of finite domains only, any CSP is convertible to a Boolean CSP, via an encoding of the variable domains. In such an encoding we impose an assignment of the form $X = x$ for each variable X and each value $x \in D_X$.

Let a literal be a positive or negated Boolean variable, and a clause be a disjunction of literals. We use the truth values *true/false* and their numerical equivalent 0/1 interchangeably.

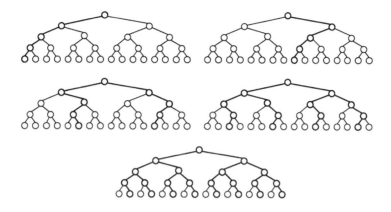

FIGURE 13.16

Depth-bounded discrepancy search: restricts discrepancies until given depth.

Definition 13.5. *(Satisfiability Problem) In* SATISFIABILITY *(SAT) we are given a formula f as a conjunction of* clauses *over the* literals $\{x_1,\ldots,x_n\} \cup \{\overline{x_1},\ldots,\overline{x_n}\}$. *The task is to search for an assignment* $a = (a_1,\ldots,a_n) \in \{0,1\}^n$ *for* $x_1,\ldots,x_n$, *so that* $f(a) =$ true.

By setting x_3 to *false* the example function $f(x_1,x_2,x_3) = (x_1 \vee x_2 \vee \overline{x_3}) \wedge (\overline{x_2} \vee \overline{x_3}) \wedge (\overline{x_1} \vee x_2 \vee \overline{x_3})$ is satisfiable.

Theorem 13.3. *(Complexity SAT) SAT is NP-complete.*

Proof. We only give the proof idea. The containment of SAT in NP is trivial since we can test a nondeterministically chosen assignment in linear time. To show that for all $L \in$ NP we have polynomial reduction to SAT, the computation of a nondeterministic Turing machine for L is simulated with (polynomially many) clauses. ∎

Definition 13.6. *(k-Satisfiability) In k-SAT the SAT instances consist of clauses of the form*

$$l_1 \vee l_2 \vee \cdots \vee l_k, \text{with } l_i \in \{x_1,\ldots,x_n\} \cup \{\overline{x_1},\ldots,\overline{x_n}\}.$$

Dealing with clauses of length smaller than k is immediate. For example, by adding the redundant literal $\overline{x_2}$ to the second clause, f is converted to 3-SAT notation. Even if k-SAT instances are simpler than general SAT problems, for $k \geq 3$ the k-SAT problem is still intractable.

Theorem 13.4. *(Complexity k-SAT) k-SAT is NP-hard for $k \geq 3$.*

Proof. The proof applies a simple *local replacement* strategy. For each clause C in the original formula, $|C| - 2$ extra variables are introduced for linking shorter clauses together. For example, satisfiability of $l_1 \vee l_2 \vee l_3 \vee l_4$ is equivalent to satisfiability of the 3-SAT formula $(l_1 \vee l_2 \vee y_1) \wedge (\overline{y_1} \vee l_3 \vee l_4)$. ∎

It is known that 2-SAT is in P. Since $a \vee b$ is equivalent to $\overline{a} \Rightarrow b$ and $\overline{b} \Rightarrow a$, respectively, we construct a graph G_f with nodes $\{x_1,\ldots,x_n\} \cup \{\overline{x_1},\ldots,\overline{x_n}\}$ and edges that correspond to the induced implications. It is not difficult to see that f is not satisfiable, if and only if G_f has a cycle that contains the same variable, once positive and once negative.

Procedure DPLL
Input: Clause set C of Boolean function f, partial assignment $a = (a_1, \ldots, a_k)$
Output: *true*, if C satisfiable; *false* if not

if $(\bigwedge_{c \in C} c\vert_a)$ **return** *true*	;; All clauses true in a
if not $(\bigvee_{c \in C} c\vert_a)$ **return** *false*	;; One clause false in a
if (**exists** c **in** C **with** $c\vert_a = l$)	;; Unit clause detected
return $DPLL(C, a \cup \{l \leftarrow true\})$	;; Unit clause preferred
if $(DPLL(C, a \cup \{l_{k+1} \leftarrow true\}))$	;; Try setting next literal
return *true*	;; Satisfied assignment found
return $DPLL(C, a \cup \{l_{k+1} \leftarrow false\})$	;; Backtrack, try failing next literal

Algorithm 13.13

Algorithm of Davis-Putnam and Logmann-Loveland.

David-Putnam Logmann-Loveland Algorithm

The most popular methods to solve Boolean satisfiability problems are refinements to the Davis-Putnam Logmann-Loveland algorithm (DPLL). DPLL (as shown in Alg. 13.13) is a depth-first variable labeling strategy with *unit (clause) propagation*. Unit propagation detects literals l in clauses c that have a forced assignment, since all other literals in the clause are *false*. For a given assignment a we write $c\vert_a = l$ for this case. The DPLL algorithm incrementally constructs an assignment and backtracks if this partial assignment already implies that the formula is not satisfiable. Refined implementations of the DPLL algorithm simplify the clauses parallel to the elimination of variables, that proved to be not satisfiable. Moreover, if a clause with only one literal is generated, the literal is preferred and its satisfaction can be propagated through the formula, which can lead to an early backtracking.

There are so many refinements to the basic algorithms that we can only discuss a few. First, we can preprocess the input to allow the algorithms to operate without branching as far as possible. Moreover, preprocessing can help to learn conflicts during the search.

DPLL is sensitive to the selection of the next variable. Many search heuristics have been applied that aim at a compromise between the *efficiency* to compute the heuristic and the *informedness* to guide the search process. As a thumb rule, it is preferable not to change the strategy too often during the search and to choose variables that appear often in the formula. For unit propagation we have to know how many literals are not false already. The update of these numbers can be time consuming. Instead, two literals in each clause are marked as *observed* literals. For each variable x, a list of clauses in which x is true and a list of clauses in which x is false are maintained. If x is assigned to a value, all clauses in its list are verified and another variable in each of these clauses is observed. The main advantage of the approach is that the lists of observables are not updated during backtracking.

Conflicts can be analyzed to determine when and to which depth to backtrack. Such a *backjump* is a nonchronological backtrack that forgets about the variable assignments that are not in the current conflict set, and has shown consistent performance gains.

As said, the running times of DPLL algorithms depend on the choice/ordering of branching variables in the top level of the search tree. A *restart* is a reinvocation of the algorithm after spending some fixed time without finding a solution. For each restart, a different set of branching variables can be chosen, leading to a completely different search tree. Often only a good choice of a few variable assignments are needed to show satisfiability or unsatisfiability. This is the reason why *rapid restarts* are often more effective than continuing the search.

An alternative for solving large satisfiability problems is GSAT, an algorithm that performs a randomized local search. The algorithm throws a coin and performs some variable flips to improve the number of satisfied clauses. If different variables are equally good one is chosen by random. Such and more advanced random strategies are considered in Chapter 14.

Phase Transition

One observation is that many randomly generated formulas are either trivially satisfiable or trivially nonsatisfiable. This reflects a fundamental problem to the complexity analysis of NP-hard problems. Even if the worst case may be hard, many instances can be very simple. As this observation is encountered in several other NP-hard problems, researchers have started to analyze the average case complexity with results much closer to practical problem solving. Another option is to separate problem instances into those that are hard and those that are trivial, and study problem parameters at which (randomly chosen) instances turn from simple to hard or from hard to simple. The change is also known as *phase transition*. In other words, these instances can be viewed as *witnesses* for the problem's (NP) hardness. Often it is the case that the phase transition is empirically studied. In some domains, however, theoretical results in the form of upper and lower bounds for the parameters are available.

For SATISFIABILITY, a phase transition effect has been analyzed by looking at the ratio of the number of clauses m and the number of variables n.

The generation of $m = \alpha n$ random formulas in 3-SAT is simple, for example, by a

- random choice of variables, followed by a
- random choice of their signs (positive or negated).

In such random 3-SAT samples, empirically the hard problems have been detected at $\alpha \approx 4.3$. Moreover, the complexity peak (measured in medium computational costs) appeared to be independent to the algorithms chosen. Problems with a ratio smaller than α are *underconstrained* and easy to satisfy, and problems with a ratio larger than 4.3 are *overconstrained* and easily shown to be nonsatisfiable.

A simple bound for unsatisfiability is derived as follows. A random clause with three (different) literals according to a fixed assignment a is satisfied with probability 7/8 (only one assignment fails the formula). Therefore, for a fixed assignment a, the entire formula is satisfied with probability $(7/8)^m$. Given that 2^n is the number of different assignments, this implies that the formula is satisfiable with probability $\leq 2^n(7/8)^m$ and unsatisfiable with probability $\geq 1 - 2^n(7/8)^m$. Subsequently, if $m \geq (n+1)/\lg_2(8/7) \approx 5.19n$, then the probability for unsatisfiability is larger than 50%. Similar observations have been made for many other problems.

Backbones and Backdoors

The *backbone* of an SAT problem is the set of literals that are true in every satisfying truth assignment. If a problem has a large backbone, then there are many options to choose an incorrect assignment to the critical variables. Search cost correlates with the backbone size. If the wrong value is assigned to such a critical backbone variable early during the search, the correction of this mistake is very costly. Backbone variables are hard to find.

Theorem 13.5. *(Hardness of Finding Backbones) If P $\neq$ NP, no algorithm can return a backbone literal of a (nonempty) SAT backbone in polynomial time for all formulas.*

Proof. Suppose there is such an algorithm. It returns a backbone literal, if the backbone is nonempty. We set this literal to true and simplify the formula. We then call the procedure and repeat. This procedure will find a satisfying assignment if one exists in polynomial time, contradicting the assumption that SAT is NP-hard. ∎

A *backdoor* into an SAT instance is a set of variables that eases solving the instance. It is *weak* if the set of variables defines a polynomially satisfiable formula, given a satisfiable instance. It is *strong* if it gives a polynomially tractable formula for a satisfiable or unsatisfiable problem. For example, there are strong *2-SAT* or *Horn* backdoors. In general, backdoors depend on the algorithm applied, but might be strengthened to the condition that unit propagation will directly solve the remaining problem.

It is not hard to see that that backbones and backdoors are not strongly correlated. There are problems, in which the backbone and backdoor variables are disjoint. However, statistical connections seem to exist. Hard combinatorial SAT problems appear to have large strong backdoors and backbones. Spoken otherwise, the sizes of strong backdoors and backbones are good predictors for the hardness of the problem.

A simple algorithm to calculate backdoors simply tests every combination of literals up to a fixed cardinality. Algorithm 13.14 has the advantage that for small problems, every weak and strong backdoor up to the given size is generated. However, this procedure can only be used for small problems.

13.4.2 Number Partition

The problem of dividing a set of numbers into two parts of equal sums is defined as follows.

Definition 13.7. *Let $a = (a_1, \ldots, a_n)$ be a set of numbers, and $N = \{1, \ldots, n\}$. In* NUMBER PARTITION *we search for an index set $I \subseteq N$, so that $\sum_{i \in I} a_i = \sum_{i \in N \setminus I} a_i$.*

Procedure Backdoor
Input: Formula f, maximal cardinality c_{max}
Output: A set of strong backdoors B_S and a set of weak backdoors B_W

$B_S \leftarrow B_W \leftarrow \emptyset$	;; Initialize backdoor sets
for each $X \subseteq \{x_1, \ldots, x_n\} \cup \{\overline{x_1}, \ldots, \overline{x_n}\}$, $|X| \leq c_{max}$	;; Subset literals
$\quad b \leftarrow true$	;; Initialize branching flag
$\quad$ **for each** $L \subseteq X$	;; Distinct set of literals
$\quad\quad b_L \leftarrow$ Unit-Propagate$(f|_L)$	;; Flag denotes unit propagation suffices
$\quad\quad$ **if** (b_L) $B_W \leftarrow B_W \cup L$	;; No branching required, weak backdoor
$\quad\quad b \leftarrow b \wedge b_L$	;; Update flag
$\quad$ **if** (b) $B_S \leftarrow B_S \cup L$	;; No branching required, strong backdoor
return B_S, B_W	;; Generate output

Algorithm 13.14

Computing strong and weak backdoors.

As an example take $a = (4,5,6,7,8)$. A possible index set is $I = \{1,2,3\}$ since $4+5+6 = 7+8$. The problem is solvable only if $\sum_{i \in N} a_i$ is even. The problem is NP-complete, so that we cannot expect a polynomial time algorithm for solving it.

Theorem 13.6. *(Complexity* NUMBER PARTITION*)* NUMBER PARTITION *is NP-hard.*

Proof. NUMBER PARTITION can be reduced from the following (specialized) *knapsack* problem: Given $a = (a_1, \ldots, a_n)$ and an integer A, decide whether there is a set $I \subseteq N$ for a $\sum_{i \in I} a_i = A$. (Knapsack itself can be shown to be NP-hard by a reduction from SAT.) Given $a = (a_1, \ldots, a_n, A)$ as an input for knapsack an instance of NUMBER PARTITION can be derived as $(a_1, \ldots, a_n, 1 - A + \sum_{i \in N} a_i, A + 1)$. If I is a solution to knapsack then $I \cup \{n+1\}$ is a solution of NUMBER PARTITION, since $\sum_{i \in I} a_i + \sum_{i \in N} a_i - A + 1 = \sum_{i \in N \setminus I} a_i + A + 1$. ∎

To improve the trivial 2^n algorithm for enumerating all possible partitions, we arbitrarily divide the original set of n elements into two of size $\lfloor n/2 \rfloor$ and $\lceil n/2 \rceil$. Then, all *subset sums* of these smaller sets are computed and sorted. Finally, the two lists are combined in a parallel scan to find value $\left(\sum_{i \in N} a_i \right)/2$.

For the example, we generate the lists $(4,6,8)$ and $(5,7)$. The sorted subset sums are $(0,4, 6,8,10,12,14,18)$ and $(0,5,7,12)$ with target value 15. The algorithm takes two pointers i and j; the first one starts at the beginning of the first list and is monotonic increasing, while the second one starts at the end of the second list and is monotonic decreasing. For $i = 1$ and $j = 4$ we have $0 + 12 = 12 < 15$. Increasing i yields $4 + 12 = 16 > 15$, which is slightly too large. Now we decrease j for $4 + 7 = 11 < 15$, and increase i twice in turn for $6 + 7 = 13 < 15$ and $8 + 7 = 15$, yielding the solution to the problem.

Generating all subset sums can be done in time $O(2^{n/2})$ by full enumeration of all subsets. They can be sorted in time $O(2^{n/2} \lg(2^{n/2})) = O(n \cdot 2^{n/2})$ using any efficient sorting algorithm (see Ch. 3). Scanning the two lists can be performed in linear time, for the overall time complexity of $O(n \cdot 2^{n/2})$. The running time can be improved to time $O(2^{n/2})$ by applying a refined sorting strategy (see Exercises).

Heuristics

We introduce two heuristics for this problem: *Greedy* and *Karmakar-Karp*. The first heuristic sorts the numbers in a in decreasing order, and successively places the largest number in the smaller subset. For the example we get the subset sums $(8,0)$, $(8,7)$, $(8,13)$, $(13,13)$, and $(13,17)$ for a final difference of 4. The algorithm takes $O(n \lg n)$ to sort and $O(n)$ to assign them for a total of $O(n \lg n)$.

The *Karmakar-Karp heuristic* also sorts the numbers in a in decreasing order. It successively takes the two largest numbers and computes their difference, which is reinserted into the sorted order of the remaining list of numbers. In the example, the sorted list is $(8,7,6,5,4)$ and 8 and 7 are taken. Their difference is 1, which is reinserted for the remaining list $(6,5,4,1)$. Now 6 and 5 are selected yielding $(4,1,1)$. The next step gives $(3,1)$ and the final difference 2.

To compute the actual partition, the algorithm builds a tree with one node for each original number. Each operation adds an edge between these nodes. The larger of the nodes *represents* the difference, so it remains active for subsequent computation. In the example, we have $(8,7) \rightarrow 1$, with 8 representing difference 1; $(6,5) \rightarrow 1$, with 6 representing difference value 1; $(4,1) \rightarrow 3$, with 4 representing the difference; and $(3,1) \rightarrow 2$ with 3 representing the difference. The edges inserted are $(8,7)$, $(6,5)$, $(4,8)$, and $(6,4)$. The resulting graph is a (spanning) tree on the set of nodes. This tree is to be two-colored to determine the actual partition. Using a simple DFS a two-coloring is available in $O(n)$ time. Therefore, due to the sorting requirement the total time for the Karmakar-Karp heuristic is $O(n\lg n)$ as in the previous case.

Complete Algorithms

The *complete greedy algorithm* (CGA) generates a binary search tree as follows. The left branch assigns the next number to one subset and the right one assigns it to the other one. If the difference of the two sides of the equation $\sum_{i \in I} a_i = \sum_{i \in N \setminus I} a_i$ at a leaf is zero, a solution has been established. The algorithm produces the greedy solution first and continuous to search for better solutions. At any node, where the difference between the current subset sums is greater than or equal to the sum of all remaining unassigned numbers, the remaining numbers are placed into the smaller subset. An optimization is that whenever the two subset sums are equal we only assign a number to one of the lists.

The *complete Karmakar-Karp algorithm* (CKKA) builds a binary tree from left to right, where at each node we replace the two largest of the remaining numbers. The left branch replaces them by their difference, the right branch replaces them by their sum. The difference is added to the list, as seen before, and the sum is added to the head of the list. Consequently, the first solution corresponds to the Karmakar-Karp heuristic, and the algorithm continues to find better partitions until a solution is found and verified. Similar pruning rules apply as in CGA. If the largest number at a node is greater than the subset sum of the others, it can be safely pruned.

If there is no solution, both algorithms have to traverse the entire tree, such that the algorithms perform equally bad in the worst case. However, CKKA produces better heuristic values and better partitions. Moreover, the pruning rule in CKKA is more effective. For example, in CKKA $(4,1,1)$ and $(11,4,1)$ are the successors of $(6,5,4,1)$, and the largest number is greater than the sum of the others, so that both branches are pruned. In CGA, the two children of the subtrees with difference 5 and difference 7 have to be expanded.

13.4.3 *Bin Packing

BIN PACKING (see Fig. 13.17) is a simplification to the KNAPSACK problem.

Definition 13.8. *(Bin Packing) Given n objects of size $a_1, \ldots, a_n$ the task in* BIN PACKING *is to distribute them among the bins of size b in such a way that a minimal number of bins is used. The corresponding decision problem is to find a mapping $f : \{1, \ldots, n\} \rightarrow \{1, \ldots, k\}$ for a given k such that for each j the sum of all objects a_i with $f(i) = j$ is not larger than b.*

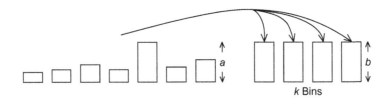

FIGURE 13.17

A BIN PACKING problem.

Here we see that optimization problems are identified with corresponding decision problems, thresholding the objective to be optimized to some fixed value.

Theorem 13.7. *(Complexity of Bin Packing) The decision problem for* BIN PACKING *is NP-hard.*

Proof. NP-hardness can be shown using a polynomial reduction from NUMBER PARTITION. Let $(a_1,\ldots,a_n)$ be the input of NUMBER PARTITION. The input for BIN PACKING is n objects of size $a_1,\ldots,a_n$ and $A = \lfloor(a_1 + \cdots + a_n)/2\rfloor$. If $\sum_{i=1}^{n} a_i$ is odd, then NUMBER PARTITION is not solvable. If $\sum_{i=1}^{n} a_i$ is even and the original problem is solvable, then the objects have a perfect fit into the two bins of size A. ∎

There are polynomial-time approximation algorithms for BIN PACKING like *first fit* (*best fit* and *worst fit*), which incrementally searches for the *first* (*best*, *worst*) placement of an object in the bins (the quality of the fit is measured in terms of the remaining space). First fit and best fit are known to have an asymptotic worst-case approximation ratio of 1.7, by means that they cannot generally produce solutions that are better than 1.7 times the optimum in the limit for large optimization values.

The modifications *first fit decreasing* and *best fit decreasing* presort the objects according to their size. The rationale is that starting with the larger objects first will be better than having them be placed at the end. Postponing the smaller ones, we can expect a better fit. Indeed using a decreasing order of object sizes together with either strategy *first fit* or *best fit* can be shown to guarantee solutions that are at most a factor of 11/9 off from the optimal one. Both algorithms run in $O(n\lg n)$ time.

Bin Completion

The algorithm for optimal BIN PACKING is based on depth-first branch-and-bound (see Ch. 5). The objects are first sorted in decreasing order. The algorithm then computes an approximate solution as initial upper bound, using the best solution among first fit, best fit, and worst fit decreasing. The algorithm next branches on the different bins in which an object can be placed.

The *bin completion strategy* is based on *feasible sets* of objects with a sum that fits with respect to the bin capacity. Rather than assigning objects one at a time to bins, it branches on the different feasible sets that can be used to complete each bin. Each node of the search tree, except the root node, represents a complete assignment of objects to a particular bin. The children of the root represent different ways of completing the bin containing the largest object. The nodes at the next level represent different feasible sets that include the largest remaining object. The depth of any branch of the tree is the number of bins in the corresponding solution.

The key property that makes bin completion more efficient is a *dominance condition* on the feasible completions of a bin. For example, let $A = \{20, 30, 40\}$ and $B = \{5, 10, 10, 15, 15, 25\}$ be two feasible sets. Now partition B into the subsets $\{5, 10\}$, $\{25\}$, and $\{10, 15, 15\}$. Since $5 + 10 \le 20$, $25 \le 30$, and $10 + 15 + 15 \le 40$, set A dominates set B.

To generate the nondominated feasible sets efficiently we use a recursive strategy illustrated in Algorithm 13.15. The algorithm generates feasible sets and immediately tests them for dominance, so it never stores multiple dominated sets. The inputs are sets of included, excluded, and remaining objects that are adjusted in the different recursive calls. In the initial call (not shown) the set of remaining elements is the set of all objects, while the other two sets are both empty. The cases are as follows. If all elements have been selected or rejected or we have a perfect fit, we continue with testing for

---

Procedure Feasible
Input: Sets I, E, and R of included, excluded, and remaining objects,
       residual capacity U
Output: None; calls test routine for undominated feasible subsets

if $(R = \emptyset)$ **or** $(U = 0)$	;; No remaining element or perfect fit
$Test(I, E, U)$	;; Apply subroutine, U residual capacity
else	;; Continue selection
$x \leftarrow argmax\ R$	;; Element x is largest in R
if $(x > U)$	;; Upper bound exceeded
$Feasible(I, E \cup \{x\}, R \setminus \{x\}, U)$	;; Drop element
if $(x = U)$	;; Upper bound met
$Feasible(I \cup \{x\}, E, R \setminus \{x\}, U - x)$	;; Include x
else	;; Check both
$Feasible(I \cup \{x\}, E, R \setminus \{x\}, U - x)$	;; Include x
$Feasible(I, E \cup \{x\}, R \setminus \{x\}, U)$	;; Exclude x

Algorithm 13.15

Recursive computation of feasible sets for bin completion.

dominance, otherwise we select the largest remaining object. If it is oversized with respect to remaining space we reject it. If it has a perfect fit we immediately include it (the best fit for the bin has been obtained) and continue with the rest; in the other cases we check for both inclusion and exclusion. Procedure *Test* checks dominance by comparing subset sums of included elements to excluded elements rather than comparing pairs of sets for dominance. The worst-case running time of procedure *Feasible* is exponential, since by reducing set R we obtain the recurrence relation $T(n) \leq 2 \cdot T(n-1)$.

Improvements

To improve the algorithm there are different options. The first idea is forced placements that reduce the branching. If only one more object can be added to a bin, which is easy to be checked by scanning through the set of remaining elements, then we only add the largest of such objects to it, and if only two more objects can be added, we generate all undominated two-element completions in linear time.

For pruning the search space, we consider the following strategy: Given a node with more than one child, when searching the subtree of any child but the first, we do not need to consider bin assignments that assign to the same bin all the objects used to complete the current bin in a previously explored child node. One implementation of this rule propagates a list of *no-good sets* along the tree. After generating the undominated completions for a given bin, we check each one to see if it contains any current no-good sets as a subset. If it does, we ignore that bin completion. The list of no-goods is pruned as follows. Whenever there is a no-good set, but the no-good set is not a subset of the bin completion, we remove that no-good set from the list that is passed down to the children of that bin completion. The reason is that by including at least one but not all the objects in the no-good set, we guarantee that it cannot be a subset of any bin completion below that node in the search tree.

13.4.4 *Rectangle Packing

RECTANGLE PACKING considers packing a set of rectangles into an enclosing rectangle. It is not difficult to devise a binary CSP for the problem. There is a variable for each rectangle, the legal values of which are the positions it could occupy without exceeding the boundaries of the enclosing rectangle. Additionally, we have a binary constraint between each pair of rectangles that they cannot overlap.

Definition 13.9. *(Rectangle Packing) In the decision variant of the* RECTANGLE PACKING *problem we are given a set of rectangles r_i of width w_i and height h_i, $i \in \{1,\ldots,n\}$ and an enclosing rectangle of width W and height H. The task is to find an assignment to all the left upper corner coordinates (x_i, y_i) of all rectangles r_i such that*

- *each rectangle is entirely contained in the enclosing rectangle; that is, for all $i \in \{1,\ldots,n\}$ we have $0 \le x_i$, $0 \le y_i$, $x_i + w_i \le W$, and $y_i + h_i \le H$.*
- *no two rectangles r_i and r_j with $1 \le i \ne j \le n$ overlap; that is,*

$$(x_i + w_i \le x_j \vee x_j + w_j \le x_i) \wedge (y_i + h_i \le y_j \vee y_j + h_j \le y_i).$$

The optimization variant of the rectangle problem asks the smallest enclosing rectangle for which an assignment to the variable is possible.

When placing unoriented rectangles, both orientations are to be considered.

RECTANGLE PACKING is important for VLSI and scheduling applications. Consider n jobs, where each job i requires a number of machines m_i and a specific processing time d_i, $i \in \{1,\ldots,n\}$. Finding a minimal-cost schedule is equivalent to RECTANGLE PACKING with $w_i = d_i$ and $h_i = m_i$ for $i \in \{1,\ldots,n\}$.

Theorem 13.8. *(Complexity Rectangle Packing) The decision problem for* RECTANGLE PACKING *is NP-hard.*

Proof. RECTANGLE PACKING can be polynomially reduced from NUMBER PARTITION as follows. Assume we have an instance of NUMBER PARTITION $a = (a_1,\ldots,a_n)$. Now we create an instance for RECTANGLE PACKING as follows. First we choose an enclosing rectangle with width W and height $H = \sum_{i=1}^{n} a_i/2$. If $\sum_{i=1}^{n} a_i$ is odd then there is no possible solution to NUMBER PARTITION. (W is chosen small enough to disallow changing orientation of the rectangle.) The rectangles to be placed have width $W/2$ and height a_i. Since the entire space of $\sum_{i=1}^{n} a_i$ cells has to be covered, any solution to the RECTANGLE PACKING problem immediately provides a solution to the NUMBER PARTITION. If we do not find a solution to the rectangle packing problem it is clear that there is no partitioning of a into two sets of equal sum. ∎

In the following we concentrate on rectangles of integer size. As an example, Figure 13.18 shows the smallest enclosing rectangle for 1×1 to 25×25. This suggests an alternative CSP encoding based on cells. Each cell c_{ij} with $1 \le i \le H$ and $1 \le j \le W$ corresponds to a finite-domain variable $C_{ij} \in \{0,\ldots,n\}$, which denotes if the cell c_{ij} is free (0) or the index of the rectangle that is placed on it. To check for overlapping rectangles, a two-dimensional array representing the actual layout of cells is used. When placing a new rectangle we only need to check if all cells on the boundary of the new rectangle are occupied.

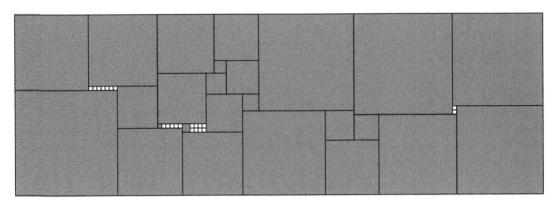

FIGURE 13.18

Packing of squares 1 × 1 to 25 × 25.

Wasted Space Computation

As rectangles are placed, the remaining empty space gets chopped up into smaller irregular regions. Many of these regions cannot accommodate any of the remaining rectangles and must remain empty. The challenge is to efficiently bound the amount in a partial solution.

A first option for computing wasted space is to perform horizontal and vertical slices of the empty space. Consider the example of Figure 13.19. Suppose that we have to pack one (1 × 1) and two (2 × 2) rectangles into the empty area. Looking on the vertical strips we find that there are five squares that can only accommodate the squares (1 × 1), such that $5 - 1 = 4$ squares have to remain empty. On the other hand, $11 - 4 = 7$ squares are not sufficient to accommodate the three rectangles of total size 9.

The key idea to improve the wasted space calculation is to consider the vertical and horizontal dimensions together rather than performing separate calculations in the two dimensions and taking the maximum. When packing oriented rectangles we have at least different choices for computing wasted space. One is to use our new lower bound that integrates both dimensions but using the minimum dimension of each rectangle to determine where it can fit. Another option is to use the new bound but use both the height and width of each empty rectangle.

For each empty cell, we store the width of the empty row and the height of the empty column it occupies. In an area of free cells, empty cells are grouped together if both values match. We refer to these values as the maximum width and height of the group of empty cells. A rectangle cannot occupy any of a group of empty cells if its width or height is greater than the maximum width or height of the group, respectively. This results in a BIN PACKING problem (see Fig. 13.20). There is one bin for each group of empty cells with the same maximum height and width. The capacity of each bin is the number of empty cells in the group. There is one element for each rectangle to be placed, the size of which is the area of the rectangle. There is a bipartite relation between the bins and the elements, specifying which elements can be placed in which bins, based on their heights and widths. These additional constraints simplify the BIN PACKING problem. For example, if any rectangle can only be placed in one bin, and the capacity of that bin is smaller than the area of the rectangle, then the problem is unsolvable. If any rectangle can only be placed in one bin, and the capacity of the bin is sufficient to accommodate it, then the rectangle is placed in the bin, eliminated from the problem, and the capacity of the bin is decreased

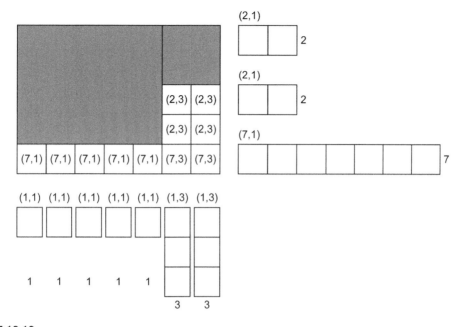

FIGURE 13.19

Partitioning of RECTANGLE PACKING into BIN PACKING problems.

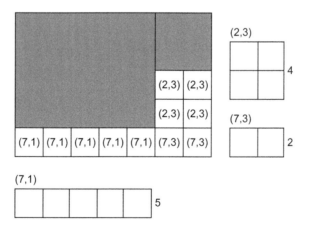

FIGURE 13.20

Refined partitioning of RECTANGLE PACKING into BIN PACKING problems.

by the area of the rectangle. If any bin can only contain a single rectangle, and its capacity is greater than or equal to the area of the rectangle, the rectangle is eliminated from the problem, and the capacity of the bin is reduced by the area of the rectangle. If any bin can only contain a single rectangle, and its capacity is less than the area of the rectangle, then the bin is eliminated from the problem, and the *remaining area* of the rectangle is reduced by the capacity of the bin.

Considering again the example of packing one (1×1) and two (2×2) rectangles, we immediately see that the first block can accommodate one (2×2) rectangle, but the second (2×2) rectangle has no fit.

Applying any of these simplifying rules may lead to further simplifications. When the remaining problem cannot be simplified further, we compute a lower bound on the wasted space. We identify a bin for which the total area of the rectangles it could contain is less than the capacity of the bin. The excess capacity is wasted space. The bin and the rectangles involved are eliminated from the problem. We then look for another bin with this property. Note that the order of bins can affect the total amount of wasted space computed.

Dominance Conditions

The largest rectangle is placed first in the top-left corner of the enclosing rectangle. Its next position will be one unit down. This leaves an empty strip one unit high above the rectangle. While this strip may be counted as wasted space, if the area of the enclosing rectangle is large relative to that of the rectangles to be packed, this partial solution may not be pruned based on wasted space. Partial solutions that leave empty strips to the left, of or above rectangle placements are often dominated by solutions that do not leave such strips, and hence can be pruned from considerations (see Fig. 13.21).

A simple *dominance condition* applies whenever there is a perfect rectangle of empty space of the same width immediately above a placed rectangle, with solid boundaries above, to the left, and to the right. The boundaries may consist of other rectangles or the boundary of the enclosing rectangle. Similarly, it also applies to a perfect rectangle of empty space of the same height immediately to the left of a placed rectangle.

13.4.5 *Vertex Cover, Independent Set, Clique

For the next set of NP-hard problems we are given an undirected graph $G = (V, E)$. The problems VERTEX COVER, CLIQUE, and INDEPENDENT SET are closely related.

Definition 13.10. *(Vertex Cover, Clique, Independent Set) In* VERTEX COVER *we are asked to find a node subset V' such that for all edges in E at least one of the end nodes is contained in V'. Given G and k,* CLIQUE *decides, whether or not there is a subset $V' \subseteq V$ such that for all $v, v' \in V$ we have $\{v, v'\} \in E$. Clique is the dual to the* INDEPENDENT SET *problem, which searches for a set of k nodes that contains no edge connecting any two of them.*

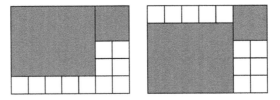

FIGURE 13.21

Right packing dominated by left packing.

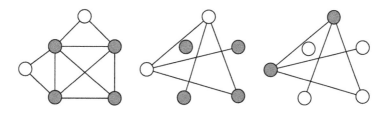

FIGURE 13.22

A clique (left), an independent set (middle), and a vertex cover (right); indicated by shaded nodes.

An illustration for the three problems is provided in Figure 13.22.

Theorem 13.9. *(Complexity Vertex, Cover, Clique, Independent Set)* VERTEX COVER, CLIQUE, *and* INDEPENDENT SET *are NP-hard.*

Proof. For CLIQUE and INDEPENDENT SET, we simply have to invert edges to convert the problem instances. To reduce INDEPENDENT SET to VERTEX COVER, we take an instance $G = (V, E)$ and k to INDEPENDENT SET and let the VERTEX COVER algorithm run on the same graph with bound $n - k$. An independent set with k nodes implies that all other $n - k$ nodes supervise all edges. Otherwise, if $n - k$ nodes cover the edge set, then all other k nodes build an independent set.

Therefore, we only have to show that one of the three graph problems is NP-hard. This can best be done using a reduction of 3-SAT to CLIQUE. Given a 3-SAT formula C consisting of the m clauses $c_1, \ldots, c_m$, the input for CLIQUE is defined as follows: V contains $3m$ nodes labeled by the pair (i, j). Nodes represent the variables in the clauses. Set E contains an edge between (i, j) and (i', j') if $i \neq i'$ and the literal corresponding to (i, j) is not negated at (i', j'). Value k is set to m. It is easy to see that we have a satisfying assignment for C if and only if the selected nodes form a clique of size k.   ■

Given these equivalences, from now on, we discuss only VERTEX COVER.

Enumeration

For search algorithms on graphs it is important to clarify terms. We distinguish between *nodes* in the search tree and *vertices* in the graph. A brute-force approach enumerates all 2^n different subsets and finds the smallest one that is a vertex cover. A search tree is built with internal nodes corresponding to partial assignments that branch on whether vertices are in V' or not, and the leaves corresponding to a complete assignment. Spanning a binary search tree of included and excluded vertices, the check of a vertex performed incrementally by traversing the tree, yields an $O(2^n)$ algorithm. For a partial assignment we have three sets: the set of included, the set of the excluded, and the set of free vertices.

A first improvement is to eliminate vertices u of degree one, while moving adjacent vertices v of u to the vertex cover. A more general observation is that if a node is not included in the vertex cover then all of its neighbors have to be included in the vertex cover. This will lead to forced assignments. The opposite idea is to eliminate all edges of a node that is selected, since they are already covered. During the search process this may lead to isolated free vertices that have to be included into the cover, or ones of degree one that are excluded with its neighbors included. Another improvement is to order the nodes in the search tree with respect to decreasing node degree. Nodes with many neighbors will be found high up in the search tree, while nodes with only a small number of neighbors are found to its bottom.

Lower Bounds

When looking at individual vertices in the *free graph* (the remaining graph that is induced by the not yet assigned nodes) there is not much to infer. But by looking at pairs of vertices we can devise a nontrivial heuristic as follows. For each pair of nodes (u,v) from the free graph we define the admissible pairwise cost 1, if $(u,v) \in E$, and 0 otherwise. This yields a bipartite graph. Since we look for edges with both endpoints that are not in the vertex cover, we are computing a *maximum matching* of the free graph, which can be computed in polynomial time.

13.4.6 *Graph Partition

The input of the GRAPH PARTITION problem (see Fig. 13.23) is a graph $G = (V,E)$.

Definition 13.11. *(Graph Partition Problem) In* GRAPH PARTITION *a graph G has to be divided into two equal-size sets of vertices $V', V'' \subseteq V$ with $V' \cup V'' = V$ and $V' \cap V'' = \emptyset$ such that the number of edges $|\{(v',v'') \in E \mid v' \in V' \wedge v'' \in V''\}|$ that go from one set to the other is minimized. The decision variant (a.k.a. minimum-cut problem) takes an additional parameter k, and asks whether or not $|\{(v',v'') \in E \mid v' \in V' \wedge v'' \in V''\}| \leq k$.*

The problem is very relevant in practice. Probably the most important application is parallel processing in a computer network. Given n tasks and p processors (here $p = 2$), there are many ways to assign n tasks to p processors, some of which have a low and some of which have a high communication overhead.

Theorem 13.10. *(Complexity* GRAPH PARTITION*)* GRAPH PARTITION *is NP-hard.*

Proof. We show that GRAPH PARTITION can be reduced from SIMPLE MAX CUT. This problem is known to be NP-hard by a polynomial reduction from 3-SAT (see Exercises) and defined as follows. Given a graph and an integer k the question is if there is a set N such that $|\{(v',v'') \in E \mid v' \in N \wedge v'' \in V \setminus N\}| \geq k$.

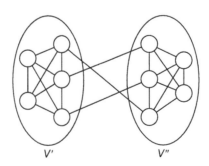

FIGURE 13.23

A graph partition.

For an input (V, E, k) of SIMPLE MAX CUT we construct an input (V^*, E^*, k^*) for GRAPH PARTITION as follows: $V^* = V \cup \{u_1, \ldots, u_n\}$, with $n = |N|$, $E^* = \{(v', v'') \in V^* \times V^* \mid (v', v'') \notin E\}$, and $k^* = n^2 - k$. Suppose there is a partition $N = V' \cup V''$ such that $|\{(v', v'') \in E \mid v' \in V' \wedge v'' \in V''\}| \geq k$. Since $k > 0$ we have $V' \neq \emptyset$ and $V'' \neq \emptyset$. Let $j = n - |V_1|$, $W' = V' \cup \{u_1, \ldots, u_j\}$, and $W'' = N \setminus V'$, then $N' = W' \cup W''$ is a partition of $G^* = (V^*, E^*)$ with $|W'| = |W''| = n$, $u_1 \in W'$, $u_n \in W''$, and

$$|\{(v', v'') \in E^* \mid v' \in W' \wedge v'' \in W''\}| = n^2 - |\{(v', v'') \notin E^* \mid v' \in W' \wedge v'' \in W''\}|$$

$$= n^2 - |\{(v', v'') \in E \mid v' \in V' \wedge v'' \in V''\}|$$

$$\leq n^2 - k = k^*.$$

Now suppose that there is a partition W' and W'' with $u_1 \in W'$, $u_n \in W''$, and $|W'| = |W''| = n$ such that $|\{(v', v'') \in E^* \mid v' \in W' \wedge v'' \in W''\}| \leq k^*$. Then $N = V' \cup V''$ where $V' = W' \cup N$ and $V'' = W'' \cup N$ is a partition of $G = (V, E)$ such that

$$|\{(v', v'') \in E \mid v' \in V' \wedge v'' \in V''\}| = |\{(v', v'') \notin E^* \mid v' \in W' \wedge v'' \in W''\}|$$

$$= n^2 - |\{(v', v'') \in E^* \mid v' \in W' \wedge v'' \in W''\}|$$

$$\geq n^2 - (n^2 - k) = k.$$

Therefore, G has a cut of size greater than or equal to k if and only if G^* has a partition into equal-size subsets with less than k^* edges. ∎

If no restriction to the size of the subsets is made, the problem can be solved in polynomial time (this is the famous max-cut or min-flow problem). However, other variants of GRAPH PARTITION are also NP-hard. The problem of dividing the vertices into an arbitrary number of sets with at most M vertices per set is NP-hard even when $M = 3$. If $M = 2$, it is not hard to see that the problem is equivalent to maximum matching.

In some variants of GRAPH PARTITION edge weights are introduced. An application for such extended domain is VLSI design, where the vertices are logical units on the chip, and the edges are wires connecting them. The goal is to place the units on the chip so as to minimize the numbers and lengths of the wires connecting them. In Gaussian elimination, graph partition can be used to reorder the rows and columns of the matrix to decrease the number of nonzero entries created during elimination.

Nodes in the search tree correspond to partial graph partitions of some of the vertices. At each such node, the left branch corresponds to an assignment of a vertex to V' and on the right branch we assign the same vertex to V''. It is obvious that the search tree is binary and has depth $n - 1$. We are only interested in leaves that partition the vertices into equal-size subsets. When pruning nodes with either $|V'| > n/2$ or $|V''| > n/2$ we have $\binom{n}{n/2}$ leaves remaining in the search tree.

Heuristics

Vertices not being assigned are called *free vertices*. Heuristic function proposes different completion strategies. Therefore, we distinguish between the assignment of vertices in V' (group A), the assignment

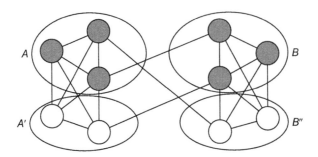

FIGURE 13.24

Sets for the computation of a heuristic in GRAPH PARTITION.

of vertices in V'' (group B), the proposed completion to V' (group A'), and the proposed completion to V'' (group B').

We can divide the edges in the graph into four types:

1. Edges within A and A' or within B and B' do not cross the partition and will not be counted by any heuristic.
2. Edges from A to B are already crossing the partition.
3. Edges from A' to B or from B' to A connect free to assigned vertices.
4. Edges from A' to B' connect free vertices (see Fig. 13.24).

The number of direct edges that connect a free vertex x to A (or B) is denoted by $d(x,A)$ (or $d(x,B)$). In the following we present two different heuristic functions for the GRAPH PARTITION problem.

For each free vertex let $h_1(x) = \min\{d(x,A), d(x,B)\}$. For a search node u we define $h_1(u)$ as the sum of $h_1(x)$ for all free vertices in u. We observe that up to the tie-breaking function $h_1(x)$ implicitly selects an appropriate set for each free variable x.

Let x and y be a pair of free vertices connected by an edge; then we define $h_2(x,y) = \min\{d(x,A) + d(y,A), d(x,B) + d(y,B), d(x,A) + d(y,B) + 1, d(x,B) + d(y,A) + 1\}$. It is a lower bound on the number of edges that must cross the partition. To compute $h_2(u)$ for a search node u we have to combine the values $h_2(x,y)$ for the free variables. This is done as follows. All pairwise distances are included into a *pair graph*, where an edge between x and y is weighted with $h_2(x,y)$. Once more, a *maximal matching* is used to avoid that the influence of a free variable is counted more than once. To improve the running time from cubic to quadratic, during the search process the maximal matching can be computed incrementally. Unfortunately, this heuristic turns out to be too complicated in practice. It is, however, effective to improve the heuristics by drawing inferences on the *free graph* that connects free vertices in A' and in B' (see Exercises).

Search Enhancements

The first option to enhance the search process that is similar to a strategy in BIN PACKING is to sort the vertices of the graph in decreasing order of degree and add new vertices to that order rather than taking a random order. The reason is that if we handle nodes with large branching factors at the top of the search tree then we have more flexibility for selecting sets in larger depth. This extension improves both IDA* and depth-first branch-and-bound.

Most of the nodes generated at the bottom of the search tree get pruned, and some of the heuristics are more complicated than others. Therefore, it is often effective first to check computationally simpler heuristics to detect failure, instead of selecting only the involved ones. For the GRAPH PARTITION problem this reduces the average time per node by more than 20% in practice.

13.5 TEMPORAL CONSTRAINT NETWORKS

A *temporal constraint network* consists of a set of variables $\{x_1, \ldots, x_n\}$ that denotes time points. It is a special case for *CSPs* with real-valued variables. Each constraint can be interpreted as a set of (closed) intervals $\{I_1, \ldots, I_k\} = \{[a_1, b_1], \ldots, [a_k, b_k]\}$.

A unary constraint $C(i)$ bounds the range of variables x_i to the disjunction of $(a_1 \leq x_i \leq b_1)$, $\ldots$, $(a_k \leq x_i \leq b_k)$, and a binary constraints $C(i, j)$ bounds the range of the difference $x_j - x_i$ to the disjunction of $(a_1 \leq x_j - x_i \leq b_1)$, $\ldots$, $(a_k \leq x_j - x_i \leq b_k)$. We implicitly assume that conditions are on pairwise different intervals.

A *binary constraint network* consists only of unary and binary constraints. It is interpreted as a *constraint graph* $G_c = (V, E)$, where V denotes the set of variables and E is defined by the constraints. Edges are annotated with the intervals that are in the corresponding constraints. A solution of a temporal CSP is an assignment to variables that satisfies all constraints.

A *minimal constraint network* is a constraint network where all intervals are minimal. It turns out that the decisions, if a network obeys a solution, and the task to determine possible assignment to x_i are NP-hard. Consequently, we have to work on *polynomial subclasses*. In the following we will see how to restrict the network to perform a consistency check and to compute the minimal network in $O(n^3)$ time.

The restriction we apply is to use at most one time interval for each pair of variables. This way, we disallow disjunctive conditions. Solving this *simple temporal network* subproblem also gives an algorithm for the overall problem via the application of branch-and-bound, where branching is obtained by selecting or neglecting one interval for a given edge. Let l be the number of edges in the constraint graph, and k be the maximal number of disjuncts at one edge. Having $O(n^3)$ time to solve one simple temporal network, we subsequently require $O(k^l n^3)$ time to obtain a solution for the disjunctive temporal constraint network (for each edge there are k options to choose from, so that k determines the branching factor in a search tree of depth l spanned by the constraints).

13.5.1 Simple Temporal Network

In a *simple (temporal) constraint network* all constraints are either of the form $x_i - x_j \leq c$ or $x_i \leq c$. The first form refers to a binary constraint and the second form corresponds to a unary constraint. Unary constraints can be eliminated by introducing an additional partner variable forced to be zero. Therefore, we arrive at a linear program with a simple structure. Referring to variables as time points, the set of constraints in a simple temporal network denote time intervals. As an *example* consider the following set of constraints: $x_4 - x_0 \leq -1$, $x_3 - x_1 \leq 2$, $x_0 - x_1 \leq 1$, $x_5 - x_2 \leq -8$, $x_1 - x_2 \leq 2$, $x_4 - x_3 \leq 3$, $x_0 - x_3 \leq -4$, $x_1 - x_4 \leq 7$, $x_2 - x_5 \leq 10$, and $x_1 - x_5 \leq 5$.

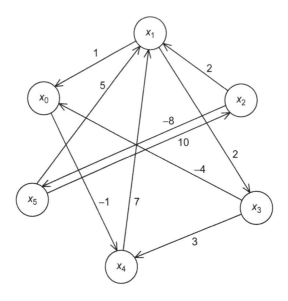

FIGURE 13.25

Example of a simple temporal constraint network graph.

In a weighted distance graph we associate weights to the edges of a graph, where each node represents a variable. The value $w(i, j)$ represents the inequality $x_j - x_i \leq w(i, j)$. The weighted distance graph for the example constraint set is shown in Figure 13.25. Consequently, for each path $i = i_0$ to $i_k = j$ via nodes $i_1, \ldots, i_{j-1}$ we have

$$x_j - x_i \leq \sum_{l=1}^{k} w(i_{l-1}, i_l).$$

Since there are several paths from i to j we have $x_j - x_i \leq \delta(x_i, x_j)$, where $\delta(x_i, x_j)$ is the minimum over $\sum_{l=1}^{k} w(i_{l-1}, i_l)$. Each negative cycle $C = i_1, \ldots, i_k = i_1$ corresponds to unsatisfiable inequality $x_{i_1} - x_{i_1} < 0$.

Theorem 13.11. *(Consistency Simple Temporal Network) A simple temporal constraint network is consistent if the distance graph contains no cycles.*

Proof. We start with a distance graph with no negative cycles. Henceforth, there exists a shortest path between every two connected nodes. For shortest path costs δ we have $\delta(x_0, x_j) \leq \delta(x_0, x_i) + w(i, j)$ or $\delta(x_0, x_j) - \delta(x_0, x_i) \leq w(i, j)$. Hence, the assignment $(\delta(x_0, x_1), \ldots, \delta(x_0, n))$ to the variables $x_i, \ldots, x_n$ is a solution to the temporal network. ∎

Moreover, we have that $(-\delta(x_1, x_0), \ldots, -\delta(x_n, x_0))$ is a solution and corresponds to the latest and earliest point in time. The *minimal temporal constraint network* is defined by constraints $[-\delta(x_j, x_i), \delta(x_i, x_j)]$. The set of possible assignments to x_i is defined by $[\delta(x_i, x_0), \delta(x_0, x_i)]$. The constraint network is inconsistent if we have $\delta(x_i, x_i) < 0$ for one index i.

Procedure Simple-Temporal-Network
Input: Weighted constraint graph
Output: Shortest path table δ

for each i **in** $\{1,\ldots,n\}$ $\delta(x_i,x_i) \leftarrow 0$;; Initialize diagonal
for each i, j **in** $\{1,\ldots,n\}$ $\delta(x_i,x_j) \leftarrow w(i,j)$;; Initialize weight matrix
for each k **in** $\{1,\ldots,n\}$;; Loop on middle node
  for each i **in** $\{1,\ldots,n\}$;; Loop on start node
    for each j **in** $\{1,\ldots,n\}$;; Loop on end node
      if $(\delta(x_i,x_j) \geq \delta(x_i,x_k) + \delta(x_k,x_j))$;; Better evaluation found
        $\delta(x_i,x_j) \leftarrow \delta(x_i,x_k) + \delta(x_k,x_j)$;; Update value

Algorithm 13.16

Minimal network computation in simple temporal network.

By the posterior calculations, the consistency problem is solved in $O(n^3)$ with a variant of the ALL-PAIRS SHORTEST PATH problem of Floyd and Warshall. Although the algorithm does not differ much from the presentation in Chapter 2, we have included the pseudo code of Algorithm 13.16.

13.5.2 *PERT Scheduling

The *project evaluation and review technique* (PERT) is a method to determine critical paths in project scheduling. We are given a set of operators O together with a precedence relationship among them. A simple example is provided in Figure 13.26. Let $e(o_i)$ be the earliest end time of o_i and $d(o_i)$ be the duration of o_i; then the earliest starting time is $t_i = e(o_i) - d(o_i)$.

The *critical path* is a sequence of operators, such that their total running time is greater than or equal to all other operator path costs. Any delay on the critical path enforces a delay within the project. The heart of the PERT scheduling problem is a network of operators, together with the precedence relationship $\preceq_d$, where $o_i \preceq_d o_j$ means that the end time of o_i is less than or equal to the start time of o_j.

Algorithmically, PERT scheduling can be seen as a shortest path algorithm for acyclic graphs. It is well known that an acyclic graph can be topologically sorted in linear time. This induces that a node is processed only if all its predecessors have been processed. Viewed from a different angle, PERT

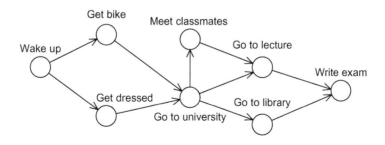

FIGURE 13.26

Example of a precedence network.

Procedure PERT
Input: Sequence of operators $o_1, \ldots, o_k$, precedence relationship $\preceq_d$
Output: Duration of optimal schedule

for each i in $\{1, \ldots, k\}$;; Loop on current operator
   $e(o_i) \leftarrow d(o_i)$;; Initialize earliest ending time
    for each j in $\{1, \ldots, i-1\}$;; Loop on previous operator
     if $(o_j \preceq_d o_i)$;; Test precedence relationship
       if $(e(o_i) < e(o_j) + d(o_i))$;; Larger evaluation demanded
         $e(o_i) \leftarrow e(o_j) + d(o_i)$;; Update value
   return $\max_{1 \leq i \leq k} e(o_i)$;; Critical path length

Algorithm 13.17

Computing the critical path with PERT scheduling.

---

scheduling can be interpreted as a specialized instance of a simple temporal constraint network, since we can model start and end times of each operator as time intervals using two constraint variables and the precedence relation as a binary constraint. The main advantage is that precedence scheduling problems can be solved roughly in quadratic time, whereas simple temporal network analysis requires cubic time. The pseudo code is shown in Algorithm 13.17.

Theorem 13.12. *(Optimality and Time Complexity PERT Scheduling) The schedule $\pi^* = ((o_1, t_1), \ldots, (o_k, t_k))$ defined by the PERT algorithm is optimal and can be computed in time $O(k + l)$, where l is the number of preferences induced by $\preceq_d$.*

Proof. The induction hypothesis is that after iteration i, the value of $e(o_i)$ is correct. For the base case, this is true, since $e(o_1) = d(o_1)$. For the step case, we assume the hypothesis to be true for $1 \leq j < i$. There are two cases.

1. There exists $j \in \{1, \ldots, i-1\}$ with $o_j \preceq_d o_i$. Hence, $e(o_i) \leftarrow \max_{j<i}\{e(o_j) + d(o_j) \mid o_j \preceq_d o_i\}$. The value of $e(o_i)$ is optimal, since o_i cannot start earlier as $\max_{j<i}\{e(o_j) \mid o_j \preceq_d o_i\}$ given that all $e(o_j)$ are the smallest possible.
2. There is no $j \in \{1, \ldots, i-1\}$ with $o_j \preceq_d o_i$. Therefore, $e(o_i) = d(o_i)$ as in the base case.

To summarize, the value $\max_{1 \leq i \leq k} e(o_i)$ is the duration of an optimal schedule.

To compute $t_1, \ldots, t_k$ we determine the earliest start times by setting set $t_i = e(o_i) - d(o_i)$, $i \in \{1, \ldots, n\}$. The time complexity of the algorithm is $O(k^2)$, which can be reduced to $O(k + l)$ using adjacency lists. ∎

13.6 *PATH CONSTRAINTS

Path constraints provide an important step toward the description of *temporally extended goals* and have also been used to prune the search in the form of additionally extended *control knowledge*. In

$$\pi \models \phi \equiv \pi \models (at\ end\ \phi) \quad \Leftrightarrow \quad u_n \models \phi$$

$$\pi \models (always\ \phi) \quad \Leftrightarrow \quad \forall 0 \le i \le n : u_i \models \phi$$

$$\pi \models (sometime\ \phi) \quad \Leftrightarrow \quad \exists 0 \le i \le n : u_i \models \phi$$

$$\pi \models (within\ t\ \phi) \quad \Leftrightarrow \quad \exists 0 \le i \le t : u_i \models \phi$$

$$\pi \models (at\text{-}most\text{-}once\ \phi) \quad \Leftrightarrow \quad \forall 0 \le i \le n : u_i \models \phi \Rightarrow$$
$$\exists i < j \le n : u_j \models \phi \wedge \forall j < l \le n : u_l \not\models \phi$$

$$\pi \models (sometime\text{-}after\ \phi\ \psi) \quad \Leftrightarrow \quad \forall 0 \le i \le n : u_i \models \phi \Rightarrow \exists i < j \le n : u_j \models \psi$$

$$\pi \models (sometime\text{-}before\ \phi\ \psi) \quad \Leftrightarrow \quad \forall 0 \le i \le n : u_i \models \psi \Rightarrow \exists 0 \le j < i : u_j \models \phi$$

$$\pi \models (always\text{-}during\ t\ t'\ \phi) \quad \Leftrightarrow \quad \forall t \le i \le t' : u_i \models \phi$$

$$\pi \models (always\text{-}after\ t\ \phi) \quad \Leftrightarrow \quad \forall t < i \le n : u_i \models \phi$$

FIGURE 13.27

Path constraints.

short, path constraints assert conditions that must be satisfied during the execution of the sequence of states visited during the execution of a solution path. Path constraints are often expressed through temporal *modal operators*. Basic modal operators are *always*, *sometime*, *at-most-once*, and *at end* (for goal constraints). The set is extended with *within*, which can be used to express deadlines. In addition, conditions like *sometime-before* and *sometime-after* indicate the option of operator nesting. For a solution path $\pi = (u_0, \ldots, u_n)$, such constraints are interpreted as illustrated in Figure 13.27, where $\models$ is chosen as the derivation symbol.

All these conditions can be combined with Boolean operators $\wedge, \vee, \neg$ to generate more complex expressions. In a more general setting, path constraints are expressed in linear temporal logic (LTL). LTL is a propositional logic over Boolean operators and includes arbitrary nesting of the temporal modalities.

LTL is defined on the notion of *infinite paths* in model M, which is a sequence of states $\pi = u_0, u_1, \ldots$. Moreover, let π^i for $i > 0$ denote the suffix of π starting at u_i.

Definition 13.12. *(Syntax and Semantics of LTL) LTL formulas have the form* always f, $\mathbf{A}f$ *for short, where f is a path formula. If p is an atomic proposition then p is a path formula. If f and g are path formulas then* $\neg f, f \vee g, f \wedge g, \mathbf{X}f, \mathbf{F}f, \mathbf{G}f, f\ \mathbf{U}\ g$ *are path formulas.*

For the next-time operator $\mathbf{X}$ *we have* $M, \pi \models \mathbf{X}f \Leftrightarrow M, \pi^1 \models f$. *For the* until operator $g\ \mathbf{U}\ f$ *we have* $M, \pi \models g\ \mathbf{U}\ f \Leftrightarrow \exists 0 \le k : M, \pi^k \models f \wedge \exists 0 \le j \le k : M, \pi^j \models g$. *For the* eventually operator *we have* $M, \pi \models \mathbf{F}\ f \Leftrightarrow \exists 0 \le k : M, \pi^k \models f$. *For the* globally operator *we have* $M, \pi \models \mathbf{G}\ f \Leftrightarrow \forall 0 \le k : M, \pi^k \models f$.

We give the following three examples (see Fig. 13.28).

1. The LTL formula $\mathbf{A}(\mathbf{G}\ p)$ means along every path, p will hold forever.
2. The LTL formula $\mathbf{A}(\mathbf{F}\ p)$ means along every path, there is some state in which p will hold.
3. The LTL formula $\mathbf{A}(\mathbf{FG}\ p)$ means along every path, there is some state from which p will hold forever.

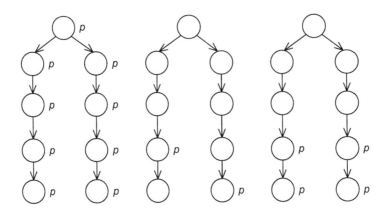

FIGURE 13.28

Three examples of an LTL formula.

For performing heuristic search on the extended plan conditions, we have to be able to evaluate the truth of the constraints on-the-fly for each encountered state. There have been two suggestions being made to associate the formula with the currently expanded state.

13.6.1 Formula Progression

One option to use LTL formulas for constraint search is *formula progression*. Depending on the structure of an LTL formula f a procedure *Progress* (see Alg. 13.18) propagates the satisfaction of f from a state to its successor.

Procedure *Progress*
Input: LTL formula f valid for node u
Output: LTL formula f valid for node v

case of	;; Switch on structure of formula
$f = \phi: f' \leftarrow (u \models f)$	;; Formula is an atomic
$f = f_1 \wedge f_2: f' \leftarrow Progress(f_1, u) \wedge Progress(f_2, u)$	;; Formula is a conjunction
$f = f_1 \vee f_2: f' \leftarrow Progress(f_1, u) \vee Progress(f_2, u)$	;; Formula is a disjunction
$f = \neg f_1: f' \leftarrow \neg Progress(f_1, u)$	;; Formula is a negation
$f = \mathbf{X} f_1: f' \leftarrow f_1$	;; Formula is of type *next-time*
$f = f_1 \mathbf{U} f_2: f' \leftarrow Progress(f_2, u) \vee (Progress(f_1, u) \wedge f)$	;; Formula is of type *until*
$f = \mathbf{F} f_1: f' \leftarrow Progress(f_1, u) \vee f$	;; Formula is of type *eventually*
$f = \mathbf{G} f_1: f' \leftarrow Progress(f_1, u) \wedge f$	;; Formula is of type *always*
return f'	;; Feedback result

Algorithm 13.18

Formula progression algorithm.

Procedure *LTL-Solve*
Input: Initial node *s* in a state space problem graph, LTL formula *f*
Output: Solution path

if (*Goal*(*u*)) **return** *Path*(*u*)   ;; Terminal state detected
f′ ← *Progress*(*f*, *u*)   ;; Progress formula at current state
if (*f*′ = *true*)   ;; Progression successful
    Succ(*u*) ← *Expand*(*u*)   ;; Determine successor set
    for each *v* **in** *Succ*(*u*)   ;; Traverse successor set
        LTL-Solve(*v*, *f*′)   ;; Recursive call

Algorithm 13.19

LTL path constraint solver.

As a running example we take BLOCKSWORLD. Suppose we want to propagate **G**(*on a b*) in a node for which we know that (*on a b*) is satisfied. We obtain a formula *true* ∧ **G**(*on a b*), which further simplifies to **G**(*on a b*). If (*on a b*) is not satisfied, we obtain *false* ∧ **G**(*on a b*), also *false*.

We briefly discuss a forward-chaining search algorithm that takes LTL control rules to prune the search tree. With each node in the search tree we associate a formula. When expanding a node *u* the associated formula f_u is progressed to the successor *v*. The pseudo code is shown in Algorithm 13.19. For the sake of simplicity we have chosen a depth-first search traversal, but the algorithm extends to any kind of search algorithm (see Exercises).

It is not difficult to see that if the algorithm *LTL-Solve* terminates at a node *u* with associated $f_u = false$, no successor will ever fulfill the imposed constraint (see Exercises).

Integrating a search heuristic to the LTL-Solver is not immediate. However, if we are able to determine a measurement on how far a temporal formula is from its satisfaction, we could order the states along this measurement to prefer the ones that are closer to it.

13.6.2 Automata Translation

LTL formulas are often translated into an equivalent automata that runs concurrently to the transitions taken in the overall search process and that accept when the constraint is satisfied. As LTL formulas have been designed to express properties of infinite paths the automaton models are *Büchi automata*. Syntactically, Büchi automata are the same as finite-state automata, but designed for the acceptance of infinite words. They generalize the finite case by having a slightly different acceptance condition. Let *ρ* be an infinite path and *inf*(*ρ*) be the set of states reached infinitely often in *ρ*; then a Büchi automaton accepts, if the intersection between *inf*(*ρ*) and the set of final states *F* is not empty. Because the paths are finite, we can view the Büchi automaton as an ordinary nondeterministic finite-state automaton, which accepts a word if it *terminates* in a final state. The labels of the automaton are conditions on the set of variables in a given state. For a more detailed treatment of searching with Büchi-Automata we refer the reader to Chapter 16.

Every LTL formula can be transformed into an equivalent *Büchi automaton*. (The contrary is not always possible, since Büchi automata are clearly more expressive than LTL expressions.) The application of automata in the search is that they run concurrent to the ordinary state exploration (each operator in the original state space induces a transition in the automaton). If the automaton accepts the LTL formula ϕ from which the automaton has been built, ϕ is fulfilled. As there are many elaborated tools for the nontrivial transformation of LTL expressions into automata representation, we do not dwell on how to derive the automaton construction automatically. Instead, we provide some examples.

For (*sometime* ϕ) with respect to some constraint ϕ, an automaton for the LTL formula $\mathbf{F}\phi$ is built. Let S be the original state space and $A_{\mathbf{F}\phi}$ be the constructed automaton for formula $A_{\mathbf{F}\phi}$ and $\otimes$ denote the interleaved (synchronous) cross-product between the state space and the automaton, then the combined state space is $S \otimes A_{\mathbf{F}\phi}$ with extended goal $T \otimes \{accepting(A_{\mathbf{F}\phi})\}$. The initial state s of the search problem is extended by the initial state of the automaton, which in this case is not accepting.

As an example consider the BLOCKSWORLD assertion that on every solution path *two blocks a and b should be put down on the table at least once*. This requirement corresponds to the LTL formula $\mathbf{F}ontable\_a \wedge \mathbf{F}ontable\_b$ with a Büchi automaton shown in Figure 13.29 (left, && corresponds to $\wedge$). The statement *in some state visited by the plan both blocks a and b are on the table* is expressed in LTL formula as $\mathbf{F}(ontable\_a \wedge ontable\_b)$ with a Büchi automata shown in Figure 13.29 (right).

For formulas like (*always* ϕ) we construct the cross-product $S \otimes A_{\mathbf{G}\phi}$. For nested expressions like (*sometime-before* $\phi\ \psi$) the temporal formula is more complicated, but the reasoning remains the same. We set

$$S \leftarrow S \otimes A_{(\neg\phi \wedge \neg\psi)\mathbf{U}((\neg\phi \wedge \psi) \vee (\mathbf{G}(\neg\phi \wedge \neg\psi)))}$$

and adapt the goal and the initial state accordingly.

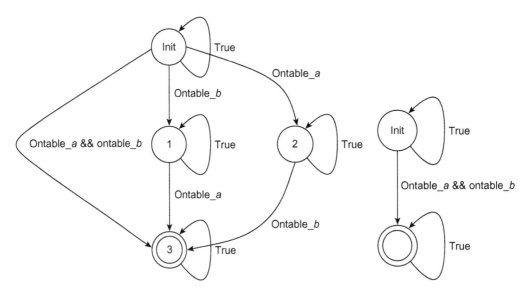

FIGURE 13.29

Büchi automata for the plan constraints $\mathbf{F}ontable\_a \wedge \mathbf{F}ontable\_b$ constraint (left) and for $\mathbf{F}(ontable\_a \wedge ontable\_b)$ (right).

For (*at-most-once* ϕ) we explore the combined state space $S \otimes A_{\mathbf{G}\phi \rightarrow (\phi \mathbf{U}(\mathbf{G}\neg\phi))}$ and for (*within t* ϕ) we first build the cross-product $S \otimes A_{\mathbf{F}\phi}$ as for *sometime*. Additionally, we enforce *accepting*($A_{\mathbf{F}\phi}$) to be fulfilled already in step t.

Constructing the Büchi automaton prior to the search can be a time-consuming task. However, the savings during the search are considerable, as for each state in the search space it only has to store and progress the state in the automaton instead of the formula description as a whole.

Concerning heuristics for the extended state spaces, it is not difficult to extend a distance heuristic for the original state space without the constraints with distance to an accepting state in the Büchi automaton. In other words, the minimum distance to an accepting state in the automaton is another admissible heuristic for finding a valid solution to the original problem. The state-to-accepting-state distances can be computed by invoking ALL-PAIRS SHORTEST PATHS in the automaton or by chaining backward from the goal (as in pattern databases).

13.7 *SOFT AND PREFERENCE CONSTRAINTS

Annotating goal conditions and temporal path constraints with *preferences* models *soft constraints*. A soft constraint is a condition on the trajectory generated by a solution that the user would prefer to see satisfied rather than not satisfied, but is prepared to accept not satisfying it because of the cost of satisfying it, or because of conflicts with other constraints or goals. In case a user has multiple soft constraints, there is a need to determine which of the various constraints should take priority if there is a conflict between them or if it should prove costly to satisfy them.

For example, in BLOCKSWORLD we might prefer block a to reside on the table if a goal is reached. In a more complex transportation task we might want that whenever a ship is ready at a port to load the containers it has to transport, and all such containers should be ready at that port. Moreover, at the end we would prefer all trucks to be clean and to be present at their source location. Additionally, we would like no truck to visit any destination more than once.

Such preference constraints are included into the *cost* or *objective function*. This function calls for searching cost-optimal plans.

Goal preferences refer to constraints that are added to the goal condition. For example, if we prefer block a to reside on the table during the plan execution, we may impose *preference p (on-table a)* with a indicator variable *isviolated$_p$* (denoting the violation of p) to be included in an objective function. Such indicators are interpreted as natural numbers that can be scaled and combined with other variable assignments in the objective function. More precisely, if we have a soft constraint of type *preference p ϕ_p*, we construct the indicator function $X_p(u) = (isviolated_p \wedge \neg\phi_p(u)) \vee (\neg isviolated_p \wedge \phi_p(u))$ and include *isviolated$_p$* as a variable into $f = \sum_p a_p \cdot isviolated_p$, which has to be minimized.

Preferences for plan constraints can, in principle, be dealt with automata theory. Instead of requiring to reach an accepting state we *prefer* to be there, by means that not arriving at an accepting state incurs costs to the evaluation of the objective function.

There is, however, a subtle problem. Because trajectory constraints may prune the search, a preference violation can also be due to a failed transition in the automata. For example, the constraints like $\mathbf{G}\phi$ prunes the search on each operator in which the only transition is not satisfied. The solution to this problem is to introduce extra transitions (one for each automata) that allow the enforced synchronization to be bypassed. Applying this transition is assigned to the corresponding costs and forces the automata to move into a dead(-end) state, from which there is no way back to any other automata state.

13.8 *CONSTRAINT OPTIMIZATION

The option for *constraint optimization* on top of constraint satisfaction is realized via a function that has to be minimized or maximized. Because we can negate the objective function, we can restrict constrained optimization to the minimization of an objective function subject to constraints on the possible values for the constraint variables. Constraints can be either equality constraints or inequality constraints.

The typical constrained optimization problem is to minimize some cost function $f(x)$ subject to constraints of the form $g(x) = 0$ or $h(x) \leq 0$. Function f is called the (scalar-valued) *objective function* and g and h are the vector-valued *constraint functions*. Strict convexity of the objective function is not sufficient to guarantee a unique minimum. In addition, each component of the constraint must be strictly convex to guarantee that the problem has a unique solution. In fact, solutions to the constrained problem are often not stationary points. Consequently, ad hoc techniques of searching for all stationary points that also satisfy the constraint do not work.

If we restrict the class of constraint and objective functions we can do much better. If we take linear constraints, depending on the domain of x this corresponds to either a linear program (LP) or integer linear program (ILP). While LP is polynomial time solvable, IP is NP-complete also for the case if the input variables x are either 0 or 1. Here we restrict integer programming concerning the satisfiability of a conjunction of linear constraints on integer variables. Constraint optimization problems on more general formalisms are considered in Chapter 14.

The efficiency of constraint processing is dependent on the representation of the constraint. A recent trend is to use BDDs (see Ch. 7) for bounded arithmetic constraints and linear expressions.

To compute a BDD $F(x)$ for a linear arithmetic function $f(x) = \sum_{i=1}^{n} a_i x_i$, we first compute the minimal and maximal value that f can take. This defines the range that has to be encoded in binary.

For the ease of presentation, we consider $x_i \in \{0, 1\}$. This restriction is sufficient to deal with goal preferences as introduced earlier.

Theorem 13.13. (*Time and Space Complexity Linear Arithmetic Constraint BDDs*) *The BDD for representing f has at most $O(n \sum_{i=1}^{n} a_i)$ nodes and can be constructed with matching time performance.*

Proof. For the construction, the BDD is interpreted as a serial processor that processes the integer variables $x_1, \ldots, x_n$ in this order. In the end the processor verifies whether or not $\sum_{i=1}^{n} a_i x_i > a_0$ or $-a_0 + \sum_{i=1}^{n} a_i x_i > 0$. If at any time the computation fails the BDD immediately evaluates to zero. Otherwise it continues. The processing starts with an initial value of $-a_0$ and then gradually adds $a_i x_i$ for increasing $i \in \{1, \ldots, n\}$. How many BDD nodes are needed in each level? The number can be bound by the range of the partial sum of all coefficients considered so far. This implies that the total number of nodes in the BDD is at most $n \cdot \sum_{i=0}^{n} a_i$ as stated. ∎

The approach extends to integer variables x_i, $1 \leq i \leq n$ with $0 \leq x_i \leq 2^b$ and to the conjunction/disjunction of several linear arithmetic formulas (see Exercises). This implies that integer programming on the satisfiability of a conjunction of m linear constraints can be solved in time

$O\left(nb\prod_{j=1}^{m}\sum_{i=1}^{n}a_{i,j}\right)$. The algorithm is polynomial in n and b but exponential in m, the number of constraints. If n can be fixed then a pseudo-polynomial algorithm exists.

13.9 SUMMARY

A (hard) constraint is a restriction on the solution of a search problem. Generic constraint satisfaction problems (CSPs) consist of a set of variables that need to get assigned a value each from their discrete domains, say one of the values *red*, *green*, or *blue*. The constraints impose restrictions on the possible assignments, for example, that variable X cannot be assigned *red* if variable Y is assigned *green*. An example of a CSP is map coloring, where we need to pick a color for every state from among three available colors so that neighboring states receive different colors. We showed how constraints that involve three or more variables can be transformed to constraints that involve only one variable (unary constraints) or two variables (binary constraints). We then discussed different search methods for the resulting CSPs.

The idea behind constraint propagation is to rule out certain assignments to make the subsequent search more efficient. Arc consistency rules out a value x for a variable X if the variable is involved in at least one binary constraint that cannot be satisfied if variable X is assigned value x. (If the values are integers, arc consistency can maintain intervals of values rather than sets of values and is then also referred to as bounds consistency.) Path consistency is more powerful than arc consistency by checking paths of constraints at the same time instead of only individual constraints; for example, a binary constraint between variables X and Y and a binary constraint between variables Y and Z. It is sufficient to check paths of length two. There are also specialized consistency methods, such as the constraint that all variables need to be assigned pairwise different values.

Constraint propagation methods rarely result in only one possible value for each variable. Thus, they do not eliminate the need for search. The simplest possible systematic search method is backtracking; that is, depth-first search. (We will discuss randomized search in Chapter 14.) Backtracking assigns values to the variables one after the other in a fixed order and backtracks immediately if a partial assignment violates some constraint. There are several ways of making backtracking more efficient. Backjumping improves on backtracking by backtracking to the variable that is responsible for the constraint violation instead of the previous variable. Dynamic backtracking improves on backjumping by not forgetting the assignments to the variables between the current one and the one to which it backtracks. Backmarking improves on dynamic backtracking by removing additional constraint checks.

Various heuristics have been studied to decide in which order the various backtracking methods should consider the variables and in which order they should consider the values of the variables (i.e., variable and value ordering). However, it can be inefficient to consider the values of the variables in a fixed order since, after some backtracks, the assignments of values to variables can differ substantially from the ones recommended by the heuristic. It is called a discrepancy to not assign a variable the value recommended by the heuristic. Limited discrepancy search uses the backtracking methods to generate complete assignments of values to variables to increase the number of discrepancies. The simplest version of limited discrepancy search generates in its ith iteration all complete assignments of values to variables with at most $i - 1$ discrepancies and thus replicates the effort of its $(i - 1)$th iteration. Improved limited discrepancy search improves on limited discrepancy search by using a user-provided depth limit to generate in its ith iteration all complete assignments of values to variables with exactly $i - 1$ discrepancies. Often, the heuristic is less reliable toward the top of the search tree, when only a few variables have been assigned values. Depth-bounded discrepancy search improves on limited discrepancy search by using an iteratively increasing depth bound to generate in its ith iteration all complete assignments of values to variables with discrepancies among the first $i - 1$ variables only.

We then discussed important classes of CSPs, some of which deviate from the generic CSPs discussed earlier, but all of which are NP-hard, as well as problem-specific heuristics (e.g., variable or value ordering), pruning rules (often in the form of lower bounds on the cost of completing a solution), and systematic solution techniques that utilize the structure of specific CSPs to find solutions faster. Many of these CSPs exhibit so-called phase transitions. Underconstrained CSPs (i.e., ones with few constraints) are easy to solve because many complete assignments of values to variables are solutions. Similarly, overconstrained CSPs are easy to solve or prove unsolvable because many partial assignments of values to variables already violate the constraints and can thus be dismissed early during the search. However, CSPs between these extremes can be difficult to solve. For some classes of CSPs, it is known when they are are easy or difficult to solve.

A SATISFIABILITY (SAT) problem consists of a propositional formula with Boolean variables that need to get assigned truth values to make the propositional formula true. Propositional formulas can be given in conjunctive normal form, as a conjunction of clauses. Clauses are disjunctions that consist of literals; that is, variables and their negations. A k-SAT problem consists of a propositional formula in conjunctive normal form of which the clauses contain at most k literals. k-SAT problems are NP-hard for $k \geq 3$ but can be solved in polynomial time for $k < 3$. k-SAT problems for $k \geq 3$ are often solved with variants of the Davis-Putnam Logmann-Loveland algorithm, a specialized version of the backtracking methods, but can also make use of structure in the form of backbones and backdoors.

A NUMBER PARTITION problem consists of a set of integers that need to be split into two sets so that the integers in each set sum up to the same value. NUMBER PARTITION problems are NP-hard. They are often solved with specialized versions of the backtracking methods in conjunction with problem-specific heuristics, such as the greedy or KK heuristics.

A BIN PACKING problem consists of a bin capacity and a set of integers that need to be partitioned into as few sets as possible so that the sum of the integers in each set are no larger than the bin capacity. BIN PACKING problems are NP-hard. They are often solved with specialized polynomial-time approximation algorithms or specialized versions of depth-first branch-and-bound methods.

A RECTANGLE PACKING problem consists of a set of rectangles and an enclosing rectangle into which the other rectangles have to be placed without overlap, depending on the problem either in any orientation or with given orientations. RECTANGLE PACKING problems are NP-hard. They are often solved with specialized versions of the backtracking methods in conjunction with rectangle placements that dominate other rectangle placements and problem-specific lower bounds that estimate the amount of unusable space in the enclosing rectangle given a partial placement of rectangles.

A VERTEX COVER problem consists of an undirected graph for which we need to find the smallest set of vertices so that at least one end vertex of every edge is in the set. A CLIQUE problem consists of an undirected graph for which we need to find the largest set of vertices so that all vertices in the set are pairwise connected via single edges. An INDEPENDENT SET problem consists of an undirected graph for which we need to find the largest set of vertices so that no two vertices in the set are connected via a single edge. These problems are closely related and all NP-hard. They are often solved with specialized versions of the backtracking methods in conjunction with problem-specific heuristics.

A GRAPH PARTITION problem consists of an undirected graph of which the vertices have to be divided into two sets with equal cardinality so that the number of edges of which the two end vertices are in different sets is minimal. GRAPH PARTITION problems are NP-hard. They are often solved with specialized versions of the backtracking methods in conjunction with problem-specific heuristics.

Table 13.2 displays the NP problems and the heuristic estimates that have been mentioned in the text. We give rough complexities, where n, m are the input parameters (n: number of items to be packed/number of nodes in the graph; m: number of clauses).

A temporal constraint network problem consists of a number of variables that need to get assigned a real value (interpreted as a time point) each. The constraints impose restrictions on the possible assignments. They consist of a set of intervals each. Unary constraints specify that the value of a given variable is in one of the intervals. Binary constraints specify that the difference of the values of two given variables is in one of the intervals. Temporal constraint network problems are NP-hard. However, they can be solved in polynomial time with a version of the Floyd and Warshall algorithm if the constraints consist of single intervals each, resulting in simple temporal constraint networks. They can also be solved in polynomial time with a version of Dijkstra's algorithm if they are acyclic and the constraints consist of single intervals of which the upper bounds are infinity, resulting in PERT networks.

So far, the constraints imposed restrictions on the possible solutions, the nodes of a search tree. However, the constraints can also impose restrictions on the paths from the root to leaves of a search tree (i.e., path constraints). In this case, backtracking methods can backtrack immediately when the path from the root to the current node violates a constraint because all of its completions then violate the constraint as well. Path constraints are often expressed in linear temporal logic (a common formalism for the specification of desired properties of software systems) and can then be checked incrementally in two ways. First, they can be checked by splitting the logic formula into a part that applies to the current node and is checked immediately, and a part that applies to the remainder of the path and is propagated to the children of the current node. Second, they can be checked by compiling the logic

Table 13.1 NP-hard problems and their heuristics.

Problem	Heuristics	Runtime
k-SAT	# UnSat Clauses	$O(km)$
NUMBER PARTITION	Greedy, KK	$O(n \lg n)$
BIN PACKING	FF, FFD	$O(n \lg n)$
	Bin Completion	Exponential
RECTANGLE PACKING	Wasted Space	Exponential
VERTEX COVER	Maximum Matching	$O(n^3)$
GRAPH PARTITION	e.g., h_1	$O(n^2)$

formula into a Büchi automaton and then using it in parallel to the traversal of the original search space.

We also discussed very briefly a relaxation of CSPs to the case where not all constraints need to be satisfied (soft constraints). For example, each constraint can have an associated cost and we want to minimize the cost of the violated constraints (or, more generally, some objective function that takes into account which constraints are satisfied and which ones are violated), resulting in constraint optimization problems.

Overall, constraint satisfaction and optimization techniques are widely used and available as libraries for many programming languages for several reasons. First, CSPs are important for applications, such as time tabling, logistics, and scheduling. Second, CSPs can be stated easily, namely in a purely declarative form. Third, CSPs can be solved with general solution techniques or specialized solution techniques that utilize the structure of specific CSPs to find solutions faster. The solution techniques are often modular, with several choices for constraint propagation methods and several choices for the subsequent search.

Table 13.2 classifies the different constraint search approaches in this chapter.

Table 13.2 Constraint search algorithms for CSPs, temporal constraint networks (CNs), and path constraints. TEG denotes temporally extended goals, STN denotes simple temporal networks.

Algorithm	Scenario	Propagation	Constraints	Domains
AC-3 (13.2)	CSP	—	Binary	Finite
AC-8 (13.3)	CSP	—	Binary	Finite
Bounds Consistency	CSP	✓	k	Finite
Path Consistency	CSP	✓	k	Finite
Backtracking (13.5)	CSP	AC-x	k	Finite
Pure Backtracking (13.6)	CSP	Consistency	k	Finite
Backjumping (13.7)	CSP	Consistency	k	Finite
Backmarking (13.9)	CSP	Consistency	k	Finite
Dynamic Backtracking	CSP	Consistency	k	Finite
LDS (13.10)	Bin. Trees	—	General	Finite
Improved LDS (13.11)	Bin. Trees	—	General	Finite
Depth-bound LDS (13.12)	Bin. Trees	—	General	Finite
DPLL (13.13)	k-SAT	—	k	Boolean
STN (13.16)	Temp. CN	—	Binary	Infinite
PERT (13.17)	Temp. CN	—	Binary	Infinite
Progression (13.18,13.19)	TEG	✓	LTL	Boolean
Automata	TEG	—	LTL	Boolean

13.10 **EXERCISES**

13.1 Consider the following four CRYPTARITHMS.

```
BLAU * ROT        VITA * MAX            YIN      WEG * STADT
----------        ----------          + YANG    -----------
ANLR              WXXX                 ------     DDAET
 OINL              MWTX                 TEILT       TTGNZ
  ALNE              WIWG                           -------
 ------             WCIG                           DISTANZ
ANTENNE           ---------
                  WICHTIG
```

1. Model the problems as CSPs.
2. Solve the CSPs with a constraint system using bounds consistency.
3. Solve the CSPs with a constraint solver using the all-different constraint.

13.2 Show that path consistency is sufficient to explore paths of length two only.

13.3 We have to assemble a meal containing all vitamins A, B1, B2, B3, B6, B12, C, D, and E with a selection of three fruits. The set of fruits can be assembled from fruit 1 containing B3, B12, C, and E; fruit 2 containing A, B1, B2, and E; fruit 3 containing A, B12, and D; fruit 4 containing A, B1, B3, and B6; fruit 5 containing B1, B2, C, and D; fruit 6 containing B1, B3, and D; and fruit 7 containing B2, B6, and E. Is this possible?
1. Use constraint satisfaction to solve the problem.
2. Model the problem as an SAT instance.
3. Model the problem as a binary CSP.

13.4 Find a path through the following street network with no crossing used more than once and that satisfies the constraints on the number of adjacent road fragments to a block. Start in the top-left corner and exit in the bottom-right corner

2	2			2		3	
2	1	1	3	0	1		
	2	2	3		1	0	2
1		1	1		2	2	2
1	0		1			1	
	1						

1. Model the problem as a satisfiability problem.
2. Solve the problem using an SAT solver.

13.5   **1.** Solve the problems in Figure 13.2 by using a CSP solver.
   2. Generate SUDOKUS automatically. One frequently used method is to first start with a filled SUDOKU, then transpose some rows and columns, and then remove numbers without affecting the uniqueness of the solution.
   3. Illustrate how to use CSP technology to provide hints for a human to solve SUDOKUS.

13.6   **1.** Formalize the BIPARTITE MATCHING problem between a set of n males and f females as a CSP.
   2. Suppose we have m male and f females (of $m + f = n$ persons) to be grouped together and set up a basket experiment, with names on the balls. Now we draw two balls, one after the other, without putting one back. Determine m and f dependent on n so that the probability that the sexes for the first and second ball are different is $1/2$. For example $n = 4$, we have $m = 1$ and $f = 3$, since the probability $1/4 \cdot 3/3 = 1/4$ of drawing first a male then a female and equal to the probability $3/4 \cdot 1/3 = 1/4$ of drawing first a female then a male. You may assume n to be a square number and $f > m$.

13.7   The k-GRAPH COLORING asks for a mapping from the set of nodes to the set of k colors, so that no two adjacent nodes share the same color.
   1. Show that deciding 2-GRAPH COLORING can be decided in polynomial time.
   2. Show that 3-GRAPH COLORING is NP-hard.
   3. Formalize the 3-coloring problem as a CSP.
   4. Show that the graph with edges (1,2), (1,3), (2,3), (2,4), (3,4), (4,5), (5,6), (3,5), (3,6) can be 3-colored by providing mapping to the color set {1,2,3}.

13.8   The n-QUEENS problem aims at placing n nonconflicting queens on a chess board of size $n \times n$. Write a recursive backtracking search program to generate a feasible solution. To ease the search, use an array representing the queen positions in each row. How big can you raise n until CPU time exceeds one hour?

13.9   Show that for the n-QUEENS problem, there is no need to search at all. Take the board to be enumerated from 1 to n along both coordinate axes. We define a knight pattern S at (i, j) to be the set of squares a knight can reach using an up-right jump: $S(i, j) = \{(i, j), (i-1, j+2), (i-2, j+4), (i-3, j+6), \ldots\}$.
   1. Show that for all even n in $\{n \mid (n-2) \bmod 6 \neq 0\} = \{4, 6, 10, 12, 16, \ldots\}$ the pattern $S(n/2, 1) \cup S(n, 2)$ is a solution to n-QUEENS. For $n = 6$ we have:

	1	2	3	4	5	6
1					O	
2			O			
3	O					
4						O
5				O		
6		O				

   2. Show that for an uneven n in $\{n \mid (n-3) \bmod 6 \neq 0\} = \{5, 7, 11, 13, 17, \ldots\}$ we can derive an almost identical solution. An example for $n = 7$ is as follows:

	1	2	3	4	5	6	7
1							○
2					○		
3			○				
4	○						
5						○	
6				○			
7		○					

3. Show that by rearranging the location of the last three queens in $S(n/2, 1) \cup S(n - 1, 2)$ we can find a solution to an even n in $\{n \mid (n - 2) \bmod 6 = 0\} = \{8, 14, 20 \ldots\}$. An example for $n = 8$ is as follows:

	1	2	3	4	5	6	7	8
1							○	
2					○			
3			○					
4	○							
5						○		
6								○
7		○						
8				○				

4. Prove that the pattern for odd n in $\{n \mid (n - 3) \bmod 6 = 0\} = \{9, 15, 21, \ldots\}$ can be found by an extension of $S(\lceil n/6 \rceil, 1) \cup S(n, n/3 + 1)$ followed by an enlargement of $S(2n/3, 2)$ at column $n/3 + 1$. An example for $n = 15$ is as follows:

	1	2	3	4	5	6	7	8	9	10	11	12	13	14	15
1				○											
2			○												
3	○														
4															○
5													○		
6											○				
7									○						
8							○								
9					○										
10		○													
11														○	
12												○			
13										○					
14								○							
15						○									

13.10 Consider an arithmetic constraint for $X = 3Y + 5Z$ where $D_X = [2..7]$, $D_Y = [0..2]$, and $D_Z = [-1..2]$.
1. Show that the constraint is not bounds consistent with D.
2. Find domains for X, Y, and Z that are bounds consistent.

13.11 Determine the propagation rules for the constraint $4X + 3Y + 2Z \leq 9$.
1. Rewrite the expression into three forms, one for each variable.
2. Obtain inequalities based on $\min_D$ and $\max_D$.
3. Test the rules with the initial domain $D_X = D_Y = D_Z = [0..9]$.

13.12 A KNAPSACK has limited weight capacity of 9 units. Product 1 has weight 4, product 2 has weight 3, and product 3 has weight 2. The profits for products are 15 units, 10 units, and 7 units, respectively. Determine the selection of products for the KNAPSACK to obtain a profit of 20 units or more.
1. Specify the CSP corresponding to the problem.
2. Apply bounds consistency to the initial domains $[0..9]$.
3. For the labeling choose branch $X = 0$ first and apply bounds consistency once more.
4. Now choose branch $Y = 1$ and apply bounds consistency to obtain a solution to the problem. What is the value of Z?
5. Determine all alternative solutions to the problem.

13.13 Display the selection of the first three paths in a complete binary tree of height 5 with
1. Linear discrepancy search.
2. Improved LDS.
3. Depth-bounded LDS.

13.14 Show that original LDS generates a total of 19 different paths for a depth-three binary tree, only eight of which are unique.

13.15 To compute the time efficiency of LDS we have to count all internal nodes that are generated. We assume a complete b-ary search tree to a uniform depth d.
1. Show that the total number of nodes generated by improved LDS is the same as the number of nodes generated by depth-first iterative-deepening search.
2. Use your result to prove that the total number of nodes generated by improved LDS is approximated by $b\frac{b}{b-1} + b^2\frac{b}{b-1} + \cdots + b^d\frac{b}{b-1}$.

13.16 Consider the following sequential schedule:

```
  0: (zoom plane city-a city-c) [100]
100: (board dan plane city-c)    [30]
130: (board ernie plane city-c)  [30]
160: (refuel plane city-c)       [40]
200: (zoom plane city-c city-a) [100]
300: (debark dan plane city-a)   [20]
320: (board scott plane city-a)  [30]
350: (refuel plane city-a)       [40]
390: (zoom plane city-a city-c) [100]
490: (refuel plane city-c)       [40]
```

```
530: (zoom plane city-c city-d) [100]
630: (debark ernie plane city-d) [20]
650: (debark scott plane city-d) [20]
```

The action is prefixed by its starting time while the duration of the action is shown in brackets. The precedence relation includes conflicts between flying (zooming) and boarding (debarking, refueling). Refueling, boarding, and debarking actions can be carried out concurrently, while flying and zooming can obviously not.

1. Use PERT scheduling to compute an optimal parallel plan. When do the actions start and end in the schedule?
2. Model and solve the problem using simple temporal networks.

13.17 Partition the numbers 2, 4, 5, 9, 10, 12, 13, and 16 into two sets.
1. Compute the greedy heuristic for it.
2. Compute the KK heuristic for it.
3. Apply CKKA to find a solution to the problem; that is, draw the search tree.

13.18 Show that the running time for NUMBER PARTITION with the DAC strategy of Horowitz and Sahni can be improved to time $O(2^{n/2})$ by a refined sorting strategy.

13.19 For a problem L and a polynomial p let L_p be the subproblem in which only inputs with $w_{max} \leq p(|w|)$ are allowed, where w_{max} is the largest value in the input w. A problem L is *NP-complete in the strong sense*, if L_p is NP-complete. Show
1. NUMBER PARTITION is not complete in the strong sense.
2. TSP is NP-complete in the strong sense.

13.20 With the refined methods for RECTANGLE PACKING it is possible to pack the $1 \times 1, \ldots, 24 \times 24$ squares into a 70×70 square. Verify that the minimum area that must be left is 49 units.

13.21 A related problem attributed to Golumb is the task to find the SMALLEST ENCLOSING SQUARE: For each set of squares from 1×1 to $n \times n$, what is the smallest square that can contain them all? By the search based on wasted space validate the following table. How far can you scale?

2	3	4	5	6	7	8	9	10	11	12	13	14	15
3	5	7	9	11	13	15	18	21	24	27	30	33	36

13.22 Show that SIMPLE MAX CUT can be reduced from 3-SAT.
1. Show that MAX-2-SAT can be reduced from 3-SAT.
2. Show that SIMPLE MAX CUT can be reduced from MAX-2-SAT.

13.23 Improve heuristic h_1 in GRAPH PARTITION by drawing inferences on the free graph that connects free vertices in A' and in B'.
1. Provide a number $N(x)$ of *allowed* edges for x i.e., Type 3 edges that will be added to h_1 if we move x from one component to another.
2. Take as many edges as possible from the free graph and form a subgraph such that no node x will be connected to more than $N(x)$ neighbors. Solve the induced generalized matching problem using network flow efficiently.
3. The computed flow F finally yields the heuristic $h_1(u) + F$. Show that the heuristic is admissible.

13.24   The research in SATISFIABILITY has influenced the interest in more flexible formula specifications. The problem QUANTIFIED BOOLEAN FORMULA (QBF-SAT) asks if formulas of the form
$f' = Q_1 x_1 \cdots Q_n x_n f(x)$ with $Q_i \in \{\exists, \forall\}$ are satisfiable.
  1. Show that 2-QBF-SAT is in P by extending the algorithm for 2-SAT.
  2. Show that QBF-SAT is PSPACE-complete.
     1. For showing QBF-SAT in DTAPE(n), use that $A_{n-1}(f'|_{x=0})$ and $A_{n-1}(f'|_{x=1})$ can be
        merged to the overall evaluation $A_n(f')$ on constant space.
     2. Show that for all L in PSPACE, QBF can be polynomially reduced to L. If M_L is a deter-
        ministic Turing machine, bounded to $p(n)$ space and $2^{p(n)}$ time, for input x, construct a
        QBF formula Q_x of size $O(p(n)^2)$, which is satisfied if and only if M_L accepts x. Avoid
        recursion in both subformulas.

13.25   1. Show that if *LTL-Solve* terminates at a node u with $f_u = false$, no successor of u will ever
        fulfill the imposed path constraint.
     2. Extend the pseudo code to add formula progression to A*.

13.26   Generalize the result of bounded arithmetic constraints $\sum_{i=1}^{n} a_i x_i < a_0$ to b-bit variables $x_i \in$
$\{0, \ldots, 2^b\}$.
  1. Explain the working of Algorithm 13.20 by constructing the BDD for $2x - 3y \le 1$ for 4-bit
     values. The algorithm is initially invoked by calling $Node(1, 0, -a_0)$.
  2. Consider the conjunction/disjunction of several linear arithmetic formulas of the form
     $\sum_{i=1}^{n} a_{i,j} \cdot x_i \le a_{0,j}, 1 \le j \le m$. Show that the satisfiability of a conjunction of m linear
     constraints can be solved in time $O(nb \prod_{j=1}^{m} \sum_{i=1}^{n} a_{i,j})$.

Procedure Node
Input: Inequality constraint C: $\sum_{i=1}^{n} a_i x_i < a_0$
Output: Unreduced BDD G that represents C on the domains of the x_i's

$index \leftarrow j \cdot n + i$	;; Set variable index
if $(i = n)$ **and** $(j = b - 1)$	;; Last level, accept if carry negative
if $(c < 0)$ $l \leftarrow \top$	;; Carry negative
else $l \leftarrow \bot$	;; Carry positive
if $(c + a_v < 0)$ $r \leftarrow \top$	;; Carry plus coefficient negative
else $r \leftarrow \bot$	;; Carry plus coefficient positive
return $new(l, r, index)$	;; Decrease depth
if $(i = n)$	;; Last level, compute carry
if $(even(c))$ $l \leftarrow Node(1, j + 1, c/2)$	;; Carry even
else $l \leftarrow Node(1, j + 1, (c - 1)/2)$	;; Carry odd
if $(even(c + a_v))$ $r \leftarrow Node(1, j + 1, (c - a_v)/2)$	;; Carry plus coefficient even
else $r \leftarrow Node(1, j + 1, (c - a_v - 1)/2)$	;; Carry plus coefficient odd
return $new(l, r, index)$	;; Decrease depth
return $new\ (Node(i + 1, j, c), Node(i + 1, j, c), index)$	;; Recursive call

Algorithm 13.20

BDD construction algorithm for linear and bound arithmetic constraint.

13.11 **BIBLIOGRAPHIC NOTES**

There are many introductory books to CSP solving and programming, like the ones by Mariott and Stuckey (1998), Hentenryck (1989), Tsang (1993), or Rossi, Beek, and Walsh (2006). Most of the problems are very well related to other discussions in the book (e.g., automated planning) and include search heuristics. A surveying online guide to constraint programming is maintained by Roman Barták.

The complexity of *cryptarithms* has been discussed by Eppstein (1987). *Sudoku* (*Su* translates to *number*, *doku* translates to single(ton)) most likely was introduced in the 1970s. Under the name *Kaji Maki* it appeared in the journal *Monthly Nikolist* in 1984.

AC-3 is due to Mackworth (1977). There have been several improvements that have been proposed to enhance the traversal in AC-3/AC-8. For example, AC-4 by Mohr and Henderson (1986) computes the sets of supporting values in optimal worst-case time, and AC-5 by Hentenryck, Deville, and Teng (1992) covers both AC-4 and AC-3. The algorithm AC-6 by Bessiere (1994) further improves AC-4 by remembering just one supporting value for a variable, and AC-7 by Bessiere, Freuder, and Regin (1999) improves AC-6 by exploiting symmetries that are constraints. AC-2000 by Bessiere and Regin (2001) is an adaptive version of AC-3 that either looks for support or propagates deletions; AC-2001 by Bessiere and Regin (2001) and AC-3.1 by Zhang and Yap (2001) are recent improvements of AC-3 to achieve optimality.

The path consistency algorithm presented in the text is also due to Mackworth (1977). He revised it to PC-2 to revise only a subset of relevant paths. Mohr and Henderson (1986) have extended PC-2 to PC-3 based on AC-4, but the extension was unsound, and could delete a consistent value. A correct version of PC-3, denoted as PC-4, has been proposed by Han and Lee (1988). The version PC-5 by Singh (1995) is based on principles of AC-6. The all-different constraint based on matching theory has been presented by Regin (1994).

As search refinements to *chronological backtracking* that upon failure backtrack to the penultimate variable, *backjumping* by Gaschnig (1979c) jumps back to a conflicting one. *Dynamic backtracking* by Ginsberg (1993) upon failure unassigns only the conflicting variable and *backmarking* by Haralick and Elliot (1980) remembers *no-goods* and uses them in subsequent searches.

Not all algorithms that have been tested are complete; for example, bounded backtrack search by Harvey (1995) restricts the number of backtracks and *depth-bounded backtrack search* by Cheadle et al. (2003) restricts the depth where alternatives are explored. In *iterative broadening* by Ginsberg and Harvey (1992) we have a restricted number of successors (breadth) in each node. *Credit search* by Cheadle et al. (2003) is a more recent technique that computes limited credit for exploring alternatives and splits among the alternatives.

The linear discrepancy search scheme has been invented by Harvey and Ginsberg (1995) and later was improved by Korf (1996). Depth-bounded discrepancy search is due to Walsh (1997). A related strategy, called interleaved depth-first search, has been contributed by Meseguer (1997). It searches depth-first several so-called active subtrees in parallel, and assumes a single processor on which it interleaves DFS on active subtrees.

The book by Dechter (2004) includes an introduction to temporal networks and their application. The theorem on the minimal temporal networks is due to Shostak (1981) and to Leiserson and Saxe (1983). The application of PERT to scheduling of partial or completed temporal plans for a heuristic search solver has been proposed by Edelkamp (2003c). A related approach based on simple temporal networks is due to Coles, Fox, Halsey, Long, and Smith (2009).

The theory of NP-completeness was initiated by the theorem of Cook (1971), who has shown that the satisfiability problem SAT is NP-complete by devising a polynomial encoding of the computations of a nondeterministic Turing machine with SAT clauses. Garey and Johnson (1979) have enlarged the theory of NP-completeness to a wide range of problems. Some results refer to joint work by Garey, Johnson, and Stockmeyer (1974).

The problem of phase transition goes back to early work of Erdös and Renyi of analyzing thresholds in random graphs. The research of phase transition in AI was initiated by Cheeseman, Kanefsky, and Taylor (2001). For the phase transition parameter (for the ratio between the number of clauses and the number of variables) in 3-SAT, lower bounds of $2/3, \ldots, 3.42$, and upper bounds of $5.19, \ldots, 4.5$ have been shown. Backbones are studied by Slaney and Walsh (2001). In Zhang (2004b) the connection of backbones and phase transition in 3-SAT problems is discussed. Their effect on local search algorithms has been considered by Zhang (2004a). The hardness of backbones have been addressed (Beacham, 2000). Backdoors have been reported in Ruan, Kautz, and Horvitz (2004). The algorithms to compute strong and weak backdoors have been provided by Kilby, Slaney, Thiebaux, and Walsh (2005).

Aspvall, Plass, and Tarjan (1979) showed that 2-SAT and 2-QBF-SAT are in P. Many good SAT solvers in practice refer to Chaff by Moskewicz, Madigan, Zhao, Zhang, and Malik (2001). Some of the refinements discussed for the DPLL algorithm refer to this implementation. Branch-and-bound has been applied to MAX-SAT by Hsu and McIlraith (2010) and hill-climbing search with gradients to MAX-k-SAT by Sutton, Howe, and Whitley (2010).

Karmarkar and Karp (1982) have devised the polynomial-time approximation algorithm for Number Partition. Later, the conjecture that the value of the final difference in the KK heuristic is of order $O(n^{c \lg n})$ for some constant c was confirmed. Horowitz and Sahni (1974) have shown how to reduce the trivial 2^n algorithm. Schroeppel and Shamir (1981) have improved the algorithm by reducing the space complexity from $O(2^{n/2})$ to $O(2^{n/4})$, without increasing the runtime complexity. In the Shroepel and Shamir algorithm, the subsets are generated on demand maintaining subset sums on four equal-sized subsets. Korf (1998) has extended this approximation to the complete (anytime) algorithm. The extension of the 2- to k-Number Partitioning problem (Multiway Number Partition) has been studied by Korf (2009), with an approach that has been corrected in Korf (2010). The importance of this problem for scheduling where numbers are the time it takes for k-equal processors to process a job and the goal is to minimize the makespan, is obvious.

Optimal Bin Packing has been considered by Korf (2002) in the *bin completion algorithm* with lower bounds for the bin packing problem that has been proposed by Martello and Toth (1990). An improved algorithm based on a faster algorithm to generate all undominated completions of a bin and a better pruning has been presented by Korf (2003b).

Most work on Rectangle Packing deals with approximate rather than optimal solutions. However, in resource constraint scheduling problems and in the design of VLSI chips, where rectangle packing is applied, deriving optimal solutions is of practical interest. Initial results on optimal Rectangle Packing have been given by Korf (2003c), with new results provided in the work by Korf (2004b). The work refers to an article of Gardner (1966). Comparable good results have been achieved by Moffitt and Pollack (2006) who avoid discretization of the rectangles. According to Gardner (1966) smallest enclosing square problem has been solved by Golumb, Conway, and Reid for n up to 17.

Solving Clique problems with state space search methods has been considered by Stern, Kalech, and Felner (2010a). Surprisingly good approximate results to vertex cover have been presented by Richter, Helmert, and Gretton (2007). There is increasing interest in the Canadian Traveler's

Problem with promising results, for example, the ones given by Eyerich, Keller, and Helmert (2010) and by Bnaya, Felner, and Shimony (2009).

Another challenge for heuristic search in constraint processing is the computation of the tree width for the bucket elimination algorithm of Dechter (1999). It is determined by the maximum degree in any elimination order of variables. States are too large in main memory, and reconstruction schemes apply (Dow and Korf, 2007). Zhou and Hansen (2008) have proposed a combination of depth-first and breadth-first search.

Applying temporal logics to constrain the search is a widespread field. There are two concurrent approaches: *formula progression* as applied, for example, by Bacchus and Kabanza (2000); and *automata* as applied in model checking, for example, by Wolper (1983). Which one turns out to be the more efficient overall approach is yet unresolved, but there is some initial data by Kerjean, Kabanza, St-Denis, and Thiebaux (2005) on comparing the two approaches in the context of analyzing plan synthesis problems.

Path constraints provide an important step toward the description of temporal control knowledge by Bacchus and Kabanza (2000) and temporally extended goals by DeGiacomo and Vardi (1999). To take care of both extended goals and control knowledge, Kabanza and Thiebaux (2005) have applied a hybrid algorithm, formula progression for the control knowledge, and *Büchi automata* for analyzing the temporally extended goal. The methods are applied concurrently for an extended state vector that includes currently progressed formula and the current state in the Büchi automaton.

Many planners support search control knowledge like TALPlan (Kvarnström, Doherty, and Haslum, 2000) or TLPlan by Bacchus and Kabanza (2000), while planners for temporally extended goals like MBP (see Lago, Pistore, and Traverso, 2002; Pistore and Traverso, 2001) often do not incorporate heuristic search. Progress on heuristic search model checking for temporally extended goals has been documented by Baier and McIlraith (2006) and Edelkamp (2006). The first one uses derived predicates to compile the properties into, and the second approach applies automata theory to compile the temporally extended goals away, as illustrated here. Rintanen (2000) has compared formula progression as in TLPlan with a direct translation into plan operators. His translation applies all changes to the operators so that produced plans remain unchanged. Instead of PDDL input, he has considered a set of clauses with *next-time* and *until*. Fox, Long, and Halsey (2004) have considered the transformation of *maintenance* and *deadline goals* in the context of PDDL2 planning. The setting is slightly different as they consider formulas of the type $\mathbf{U}\,p\,c$ (and $\mathbf{F}\,p\,c$), where p is the condition until which (or from which) condition c must hold.

Although soft constraints have been extensively studied in the CSP literature, only recently has the search community started to investigate them; see, for example, Brafman and Chernyavsky (2005), Smith (2004), and Briel, Sanchez, Do, and Kambhampati (2004). More recently, plan and preference constraints have been integrated into PDDL, the description language for problems in action planning (Gerevini and Long, 2005). Baier (2009) has tackled planning with soft constraints on temporally extended goals. A set of new heuristics and another search algorithm have been proposed to guide the planner toward preferred plans.

The work of Bartzis and Bultan (2006) has been studied to the efficiency of BDD for bounded arithmetic constraints. The authors have also illustrated how to handle multiplication, overflows, and multiple bounds. The experimental results were impressive, since the approach could solve appropriate model checking problems orders of magnitudes faster than previous state-of-the-art approaches.

Selective Search

The heuristic search strategies considered so far were mainly concerned about a *systematic* enumeration of the underlying state space. Search heuristics accelerated the exploration to arrive at goals fast. In many cases we could show the *completeness* of the search process, meaning that it returns a solution if it exists. Exceptions are partial and beam search methods, which sacrificed completeness for a better time and space performance in successful runs.

Moreover, most approaches that we encountered so far were *deterministic* (meaning that they return the same search result on each trial) even if the underlying search space was not. In rare cases, we already came across the concepts of *randomization*, like when accessing transposition tables with stochastic node caching in Chapter 6. In randomized search we distinguished between *Las Vegas* algorithms, which are always correct but may vary in runtime, and *Monte Carlo* methods, which are only mostly correct. In a randomized algorithm, we can no longer study the worst-case time complexity, but have to consider the average time complexity, averaged over the set of all possible inputs (mostly assuming a uniform distribution among them). This is in contrast to the average time complexity for deterministic algorithms, which we study because of the worst-case analysis being too pessimistic in practice. For both incomplete and randomized searches, *restarting* the algorithms with different parameters counterbalances some of their deficiencies.

In this chapter we study *selective search* algorithms, a generic term to cover aspects of *local search* and *randomized search*. Selective search strategies are *satisficing*, in the sense that they do not necessarily return the optimal solution (though by chance they can), but with very good results in practice.

Local search has a wide range of applicability in combinatorial optimization. Given the (local) *neighborhood* of states, the aim is to optimize an objective function to find a state with optimal global cost. As the algorithms are inherently incomplete, in local search we at least aim for those that are superior to all states in their neighborhood. As seen with general branching rules in CSP problem solving, a neighborhood slightly differs from the set of successors of an implicit search algorithm. Successors do not necessarily have to be valid (i.e., *reachable*) states. Through modifications to the state vector, selective search algorithms often allow "larger" jumps in the search space compared to enumerative methods. One problem that has to be resolved is to guarantee feasibility of the result of the neighbor selection operator.

For state space search problems paths rather than singular nodes have to be evaluated. The aim is to optimize a cost function on the set of possible paths. Similar to the chapter of game playing, in this chapter goal estimates are generalized to *evaluation functions* that govern the desirability of a generated path. In this perspective, lower-bound heuristics are special cases, where the end nodes of the paths are evaluated. As in real-time search (see Ch. 11), move commitment is essential for selective search strategies. Predecessor states once left can no longer be put back on.

The chapter is structured as follows. As the first representatives of local search algorithms with randomization we look at the *Metropolis algorithm, simulated annealing,* and *randomized tabu search.* Next we turn to exploration strategies that are based on mimicking processes in nature. The first attempt is based on simulating the evolution, and the second attempt is based on simulating processes in ant colonies. Both adapt quite nicely to heuristic state space search. We provide algorithms for the *simple* and the *parameter-free genetic algorithm* (GA). Some theoretical insights to GA search are given. Then an introduction to *ant algorithms* and their application to combinatorial optimization problems is given. Besides the *simple ant system,* a variant of *simulated annealing* for computer ants called *algorithm flood* is discussed.

Next we consider *Monte Carlo randomized search* using the MAX-SAT problem as the running example. Randomized strategies are often simpler to implement but their analysis can be involved. We study some complexities to show how derivations may be simplified. Before diving into the algorithms, we reflect the theory of approximation algorithms and the limits of approximation.

Last but not least, we consider optimization with *Lagrange multipliers* for solving nonlinear and constrained optimization problems. Once again, the application to state space search problems is based on the extended neighborhood of paths.

14.1 FROM STATE SPACE SEARCH TO MINIMIZATION

To some extent, selective search algorithms take place in the state space of solutions. We prefer taking the opposite view of *lifted states* instead.

The paradigm of enumerating generation path sequences can be lifted to state space minimization that searches for the best state for a given evaluation function. The idea is simple: In a lifted state space, states are paths. The heuristic estimate of the last state on the path serves as the evaluation got the lifted state.

An extended successor relation, also called *neighborhood,* modifies paths not only at their ending state, but also at intermediate ones; or it merges two different paths into one. For this cases, we have to be careful that paths to be evaluated are feasible.

One option is to think of a path as an integer vector $x \in \mathbf{N}^k$. Let (S, A, s, T) be a state space problem and h be a heuristic. We further assume that the optimal solution length is k. This assumption will be relaxed later on.

The associated state space path $\pi(x)$ generated by x is a path $(u_0, \ldots, u_k)$ of states with $u_0 = s$ and u_{i+1} being the $(x_i \bmod |Succ(u_i)|)$ successor of u_i, $1 \leq i < k$. If $|Succ(u_i)| = 0$ for one $1 \leq i < k$, then $\pi(x)$ is not defined. The *evaluation* of vector x is $h(u_k)$; that is, the heuristic evaluation of the last state on the path $\pi(x)$. If $\pi(x)$ is not defined (e.g., due to a dead-end with $|Succ(u_i)| = 0$) for one i, the evaluation is ∞.

Therefore, the use of the heuristic for path evaluation is immediate. The optimization problem in the lifted state space corresponds to minimize the heuristic estimate. For a goal state we have estimate zero, the optimum. For each individual x of length k we have at most one state with a generating path $\pi(x)$.

This allows us to define various optimization algorithms for each state space problem with known solution length. For modifying paths in the extended successor relation, we do not have to go back to a binary encoding, but modify the integer vectors in $I\!N^k$ directly. For example, a simple change in a selected vector position can generate very different states.

So far we can solve problems with a solution path of fixed length only. There are mainly two different options to devise a general state space search algorithm. First, we can increase the depth in an iterative-deepening manner and wait for the search algorithm to settle. The other option is to allow vectors of different lengths to be part of the modification. In difference to the set of enumerative algorithms considered so far, with state space minimization we allow different changes to the set of paths, not only extensions and deletions at one end.

14.2 HILL-CLIMBING SEARCH

As mentioned in Chapter 6, *hill-climbing* selects the best successor node under some evaluation function, which we denote by f, and commits the search to it. Then the successor serves as the actual node, and the search continues. In other words, hill-climbing (for maximization problems) or gradient descent (for minimization problems) commits to changes that improve the current state until no more improvement is possible. Algorithm 14.1 assumes a state space minimization problem with objective function f to be minimized.

Before dropping into more general selective search strategies, we briefly reflect the main problems. The first problem is the *feasibility problem*. Some of the instances generated may not be valid with respect to the problem constraints: the search space divides into feasible and infeasible regions (see Fig. 14.1, left). The second problem is the *optimization problem*. Some greedily established local optimal solutions may not be globally optimal. In the minimization problem illustrated in Figure 14.1 (right) we have two local optima that have to be exited to eventually find the global optimum.

Procedure Hill-Climbing
Input: State space min. problem with initial state s and neighbor relation *Succ*
Output: State with low evaluation

$u \leftarrow v \leftarrow s; h \leftarrow f(s)$;; Initialize search
do   ;; Loop until local optimum found
   $Succ(u) \leftarrow Expand(u)$;; Generate successors
   for each $v \in Succ(u)$;; Consider successors
      if $(f(v){<}f(u))\ u \leftarrow v$;; Evaluation improved
   while $(u \neq v)$;; Generate successors
   return u ;; Output solution

Algorithm 14.1

Hill-climbing.

One option to overcome local optima is book-keeping previous optima. It may be casted as a statistical machine learning method for large-scale optimization. The approach remembers the optima of all hill-climbing applications to the given function and estimates a function of the optima. Then in stage 1 of the algorithm it uses the ending point as a starting point for hill-climbing on the estimated function of the optima. In a second stage the algorithm uses the ending point as a starting point for hill-climbing on the given function. The idea is illustrated in Figure 14.2. The oscillating function has to be minimized; known optima and the predicted optimal curve are shown. Using this function, the assumed next optima would be used as a starting state for the search.

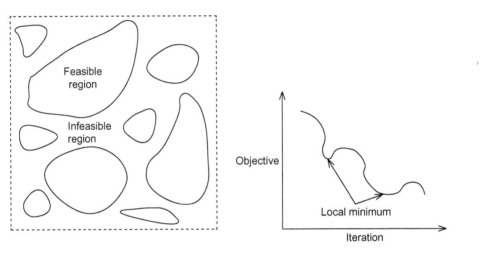

FIGURE 14.1

Problems of feasibility (left) and local optimality (right).

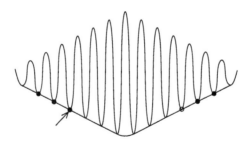

FIGURE 14.2

Improvement of hill-climbing based on bookkeeping. The arrow shows the end of the last hill-climbing iteration; the additional curve is the estimated function to predict the next starting point of hill-climbing after reestimation.

14.3 SIMULATED ANNEALING

Simulated annealing is a local search approach based on the analogy of the *Metropolis algorithm*, which itself is a variant of randomized local search. The Metropolis algorithm generates a successor state v from u by perturbation, transferring u into v with a small random distortion (e.g., random replacement at state vector positions). If the evaluation function f, also called energy in this setting, at state v is lower than at state u then u is replaced by v, otherwise v is accepted with probability $e^{\frac{f(u)-f(v)}{kT}}$, where k is the *Boltzmann constant*. The motivation is adopted from physics. According to the laws of thermodynamics the probability of an increase in energy of magnitude ΔE at temperature T is equal to $e^{-\frac{\Delta E}{kT}}$. In fact, the Boltzmann distribution is crucial to prove that the Metropolis algorithm converges. In practice, the Boltzman constant can be safely removed or easily substituted by any other at the convenience of the designer of the algorithm.

For describing simulated annealing, we expect that we are given a state space minimization problem with evaluation function f. The algorithm itself is described in Algorithm 14.2. The *cooling-scheme* reduces the temperature. It is quite obvious that a slow cooling implies a large increase in the time complexity of the algorithm.

The initial temperature has to be chosen large enough that all operators are allowed, as the maximal difference in cost of any two adjacent states. Cooling is often done by multiplying a constant c to T, so that the value T in iteration t equals $c^k T$. An alternative is $T/\lg(k+2)$.

Procedure Simulated Annealing
Input: State space min. problem, initial temperature T
Output: State with low evaluation

$t \leftarrow 0$	;; Iteration counter
$u \leftarrow s$	;; Start search from initial state
while $(T > \epsilon)$	;; T not too close to 0
$\quad Succ(u) \leftarrow Expand(u)$	;; Generate successors
$\quad v \leftarrow Select(Succ(u))$	;; Choose (random) successor
$\quad$ **if** $(f(v) < f(u))$ $u \leftarrow v$	;; Evaluation improved, select v
$\quad$ **else**	;; Evaluation worse
$\quad\quad r \leftarrow Select(0,1)$	;; Choose random probability
$\quad\quad$ **if** $\left(r < e^{\frac{f(u)-f(v)}{T}} \right)$	;; Check Boltzmann condition
$\quad\quad\quad v \leftarrow u$	;; Continue search at v
$\quad t \leftarrow t+1$	;; Evaluation improved, select v
$\quad T \leftarrow Cooling(T,t)$	;; Decrease T according to iteration count
return u	;; Output solution

Algorithm 14.2

Simulated annealing.

In the limit, we can expect convergence. It has been shown that in an undirected search space with an initial temperature T that is at least as large as the size of the minimal deterioration that is sufficient for leaving the deepest local minimum, simulated annealing converges asymptotically. The problem is that even to achieve an approximate solution we need a worst-case number of iterative steps that is quadratic in the search space, meaning that breadth-first search can perform better.

14.4 TABU SEARCH

Tabu search is a local search algorithm that restricts the feasible neighborhood by neighbors that are excluded. The word *tabu* (or *taboo*) was used by the aborigines of Tonga Island to indicate things that cannot be touched because they are sacred. In tabu search, such states are maintained in a data structure called a *tabu list*. They help avoid being trapped in a local optimum. If all neighbors are *tabu*, a move is accepted that worsen the value of the objective function to which an ordinary deepest decent method would be trapped. A refinement is the *aspiration criterion*: If there is a move in the tabu list that improves all previous solutions the *tabu* constraint is ignored. According to a provided selection criteria tabu search stores only *some* of the previously visited states. The pseudo code is shown in Algorithm 14.3.

One simple strategy for updating the tabu list is to forbid any state that has been visited in the last k steps. Another option is to require that local transformation does not always change the same parts of the state vector or modify the cost function during the search.

Randomized tabu search as shown in Algorithm 14.4 can be seen as a generalization to simulated annealing. It combines the reduction of the successor set by a tabu list with the selection mechanism applied in simulated annealing. Instead of the Boltzmann condition, we can accept successors

---

Procedure Tabu Search
Input: State space min. problem
Output: State with low evaluation

$Tabu \leftarrow \{s\}$;; Initialize tabu list
$best \leftarrow s$;; Initialize currently best state
$Terminate \leftarrow false$;; Initialize termination flag
$u \leftarrow s$;; Start search from initial state
while ($\neg Terminate$) ;; Loop
    ;; Generate successors
    $v \leftarrow Select(Succ(u) \setminus Tabu)$;; Choose (random) successor
    if ($f(v) < f(u)$) $best \leftarrow u$;; Evaluation improved, select v
    $Tabu \leftarrow Refine(Tabu)$;; Update tabu list
    $Terminate \leftarrow Update(Terminate)$;; Modify flag
    $v \leftarrow u$;; Continue with v
return $best$;; Output solution

Algorithm 14.3

Tabu search.

Procedure Randomized Tabu Search
Input: State space min. problem
Output: State with low evaluation

$Tabu \leftarrow \{s\}$	;; Initialize tabu list
$best \leftarrow s$	;; Initialize currently best state
$Terminate \leftarrow false$	;; Initialize termination flag
$u \leftarrow s$	;; Start search from initial state
while ($\neg Terminate$)	;; Loop
	;; Generate successors
$\quad v \leftarrow Select(Succ(u) \setminus Tabu)$	;; Choose (random) successor
$\quad$ **if** ($f(v) < f(u)$) $v \leftarrow best \leftarrow u$	;; Evaluation improved, select v
$\quad$ **else**	;; Evaluation worse
$\quad\quad r \leftarrow Select(0,1)$	;; Choose random probability
$\quad\quad$ **if** $\left(r < e^{\frac{f(u)-f(v)}{T}} \right)$	;; Check Boltzmann condition
$\quad\quad\quad v \leftarrow u$	;; Continue with v
$\quad Tabu \leftarrow Refine(Tabu)$	;; Update tabu list
$\quad Terminate \leftarrow Update(Terminate)$	;; Modify flag
return $best$	;; Output solution

Algorithm 14.4

Randomized tabu search.

---

according to a probability decreasing, for example, with $f(u) - f(v)$. As with standard simulated annealing in both cases, we can prove asymptotic convergence.

14.5 EVOLUTIONARY ALGORITHMS

Evolutionary algorithms have seen a rapid increase in their application scope due to a continuous report of solving hard combinatorial optimization problems. The implemented concepts of *recombination*, *selection*, *mutation*, and *fitness* are motivated by their similarities to natural evolution. In short, the fittest surviving individual will encode the best solution to the posed problem. The simulation of the evolutionary process refers to the genetics in living organisms on a fairly high abstraction level.

Unfortunately, most evolutionary algorithms are of domain-dependent design, while using an explicit encoding of a selection of individuals of the state space, where many exploration problems, especially in Artificial Intelligence applications like puzzle solving and action planning, are described implicitly. As we have seen, however, it is possible to encode paths for general state space problems as individuals in a genetic algorithm.

14.5.1 Randomized Local Search and $(1+1)$ EA

Probably the simplest question for optimization is the following: Given $f : \{0,1\}^n \to \mathbb{R}$, determine the assignment to f with lowest f-value.

Randomized local search (RLS) is a variant that can be casted as an evolutionary algorithm with a population of size 1. In RLS the first state is chosen uniformly at random. Then the offspring v is obtained from u by mutation. A process called *selection* commits the search to successor v if its fitness $f(v)$ is larger than or equal to $f(u)$ (greater than or equal in the case of a minimization problem). The *mutation* operator of RLS as is implemented in Algorithm 14.5 chooses a position $i \in \{1,\ldots,n\}$ in the state vector at random and replaces it with a different randomly chosen value. In the case of bitvectors (which is considered here), the bit is flipped. In the case of vectors from $\Sigma = \{1,\ldots,k\}$, one of the $k - 1$ different values is chosen according to the uniform distribution. RLS is a hill-climber with a small neighborhood and can get stuck in local optima. Therefore, larger neighborhoods of more local changes have been proposed.

The $(1+1)$ EA also works with populations of size 1. The mutation operator changes each position independently from the others with probability $1/n$. The $(1+1)$ EA is implemented in Algorithm 14.6 and always finds the optimum in expected finite time, since each individual in $\{0,1\}^n$ has a positive probability to be produced as offspring of a selected state. Although no worsening is accepted, $(1+1)$ EA is not a pure hill-climber; it allows almost arbitrary big jumps.

Such search algorithms do not know if the best point ever seen is optimal. In the analysis, therefore, we consider the search as an infinite stochastic process. We are interested in the random variable at the first point of time when an optimal input is sampled. The expected value of that variable is referred to as the *expected runtime*.

The expected runtime and success probabilities for RLS and for the $(1+1)$ EA have been studied for various functions. For example, we have the following result.

Theorem 14.1. *(Expected Runtime $(1+1)$ EA) For the function $f(u) = u_1 + \cdots + u_n$ the expected runtime of the $(1+1)$ EA is bounded by $O(n \lg n)$.*

Proof. Let $A_i = \{u \in \{0,1\}^n \mid i - 1 \le f(u) < i\}$. For $x \in A_i$ let $s(u)$ be the probability that mutation changes u into some $v \in A_j$ where $j > i$ and let $s(i) = \min\{s(u) \mid u \in A_i\}$. The expected time to leave A_i is $1/s(i)$, so that for a bound on the total expected runtime we have to compute $\sum_{i=1}^n 1/s(i)$. For our

---

Procedure Randomized Local Search
Input: Boolean function $f : \{0,1\}^n$
Output: State in $\{0,1\}^n$ with low evaluation

$u \leftarrow Select(\{0,1\}^n)$	;; Select initial state vector
while $(\neg Terminate)$	;; Until termination criterion reached
$\quad v \leftarrow u$	;; Local copy of current state
$\quad i \leftarrow Select(\{0,1,\ldots,n\})$	;; Select bit position
$\quad v_i \leftarrow \neg u_i$	;; Mutate bit
$\quad$ **if** $(f(v)<f(u))\ u \leftarrow v$	;; Select successor
$\quad\quad Terminate \leftarrow Update(Terminate)$	;; Modify flag
return u	;; Output solution

Algorithm 14.5

Randomized local search.

Procedure (1 + 1) EA
Input: Boolean function $f : \{0,1\}^n$
Output: State in $\{0,1\}^n$ with low evaluation

$p_m \leftarrow 1/n$	;; Set mutation rate
$u \leftarrow Select(\{0,1\}^n)$	;; Select initial state vector
while $(\neg Terminate)$	;; Until termination criterion reached
for each $i \in \{1,\dots,n\}$	;; Consider all bit positions
if $(Select(0,1) > p_m)$ $v_i \leftarrow u_i$ **else** $v_i \leftarrow \neg u_i$	;; Mutate bits
if $(f(v) < f(u))$ $u \leftarrow v$	;; Select successor
$Terminate \leftarrow Update(Terminate)$	;; Modify flag
return u	;; Output solution

Algorithm 14.6

Randomized $(1 + 1)$ EA.

---

case, inputs from A_i have $n + 1 - i$ neighbors with a larger function value. Therefore,

$$s(i) \geq (n+1-i)\left(\frac{1}{n}\left(1 - \frac{1}{n}\right)^{n-1}\right) \geq (n+1-i)/en.$$

Hence, the total expected runtime is bounded by

$$\sum_{i=1}^{n} 1/s(i) \leq en \sum_{i=1}^{n} 1/(n+1-i) \leq en \sum_{i=1}^{n} 1/i \leq en \cdot (\ln n + 1) = O(n \lg n). \qquad \blacksquare$$

There are also families of functions for which mutation as the only genetic algorithm is provably worse than evolutionary algorithms for which a recombination operator has been defined.

14.5.2 Simple GA

Many genetic algorithms maintain a sample population of states (or their respective path generation vectors) instead of enumerating the state space state by state.

Definition 14.1. *(Simple GA) A simple genetic algorithm, simple GA for short, consists of*

1. *The (initial) population C: A list of n individuals, n even (for proper mating).*
2. *The set of individuals or chromosomes $p \in C$: These can be feasible and infeasible problem solutions, to be coded as a string over some alphabet Σ.*
3. *The evaluation function $e(p)$: A problem depending on an object function to be minimized.*
4. *The fitness function $f(p)$: A nonnegative function, derived from $e(p)$. It correlates positively with reproduction choices $\varphi(p)$ of p.*
5. *The selection function φ with $\sum_{p \in C} \varphi(p) = n$: A general option for the selection function is to take $\varphi(p) = f(p)/\bar{f}$ with $\bar{f} = (1/n)\sum_{p \in C} f(p)$.*

In many cases individuals are bitvectors.

Definition 14.2. *(Genetic Operators) The crossover and mutation operators are defined as follows:*

1. *Crossover: Divide*

$$p = (p_1, \ldots, p_n) \quad \text{and} \quad q = (q_1, \ldots, q_n)$$

   in partial sequences and recombine p' and q' as
   - *1-point crossover:*
     choose random $\ell \in \{1, \ldots, n-1\}$, and set

$$p' = (p_1, \ldots, p_\ell, q_{\ell+1}, \ldots, q_n)$$
$$q' = (q_1, \ldots, q_\ell, p_{\ell+1}, \ldots, p_n)$$

   - *2-point crossover:*
     choose random $\ell, r \in \{1, \ldots, n\}, \ell < r$, and set

$$p' = (p_1, \ldots, p_\ell, q_{\ell+1}, \ldots, q_r, p_{r+1}, \ldots, p_n)$$
$$q' = (q_1, \ldots, q_\ell, p_{\ell+1}, \ldots, p_r, q_{r+1}, \ldots, q_n)$$

   - *uniform crossover:*
     generate random bit mask $b = (b_1, \ldots, b_n)$ and set (bitwise Boolean operations)

$$p' = (b \wedge p) \vee (\neg b \wedge q)$$
$$q' = (b \wedge q) \vee (\neg b \wedge p)$$

2. *Mutation: Each component b of a chromosome is modified with probability p_m; for example, $p_m = 0.1\%$ or $p_m = 1/n$.*

Algorithm 14.7 depicts a general strategy for solving GAs. It is based on the four basic routines *Selection, Recombination/Crossover, Mutation,* and *Terminate.* Subsequently, to solve a problem with a genetic algorithm, we have to choose an encoding for potential solutions, choose an evaluation and a fitness function, and choose parameters n, p_c, p_m, and a termination criteria. The algorithm itself is then implemented, with the help of existing software libraries.

Infeasible solutions shall be sentenced by a surplus term, so that the live expectancy is small. This can be dealt with as follows. The surplus term is a function on the distance of the feasible region and the best infeasible vector is always worse than the best feasible one.

Let us consider an example. The SUBSET SUM problem is given by $w = (w_1, \ldots, w_n) \in \mathbf{N}^n, B \in \mathbf{N}$. The feasible solutions are $x = (x_1, \ldots, x_n) \in \{0, 1\}^n$ with $\sum_{i=1}^n w_i x_i \leq B$. The objective function to be maximized is $P(x) = \sum_{i=1}^n w_i x_i$. This problem can be reformulated as a minimization problem for the simple GA as follows:

$$e(x) = \lambda(x)\,(B - P(x)) + (1 - \lambda(x))\,P(x) \quad \text{with}$$

$$\lambda(x) = \begin{cases} 1 & \text{if } x \text{ is feasible} \\ 0 & \text{otherwise} \end{cases}$$

with fitness $f(x) = \sum_{i=1}^n w_i - e(x)$.

Procedure Simple-Genetic-Algorithm
Input: Initial population of states, evaluation and fitness function e and f,
      recombination and mutation rate p_m and p_r
Output: Individual with high fitness

$t \leftarrow 1$	;; Initialize population counter
$C_t \leftarrow$ initial population with $\|C_t\| = n$ even	;; Draw initial population
loop	;; Until termination
for each $p \in C_t$ calculate $e(p)$	;; Compute individual evaluation
for each $p \in C_t$ compute $f(p)$ from $e(p)$	;; Calculate individual fitness
if (*Terminate*(C_t)) **break**	;; Termination criteria met
$C_{t+1/2} \leftarrow$ *Selection*(C_t)	;; Intermediate generation
$t \leftarrow t + 1$	;; Update population count
$C_t \leftarrow \emptyset$	;; Initialize next generation
while $(\|C_{t-1/2}\| \neq 0)$	;; While individuals left
remove random p, q in $C_{t-1/2}$	;; Take two pair at random
$(p', q') \leftarrow$ *Crossover*(p, q, p_c)	;; p_c = recombination rate
$C_t \cup \{p', q'\}$	;; Append children
for each $p \in C_t, b \in p$	;; p_m = for all bit positions in all individuals
$b \leftarrow$ *Mutation*(b, p_m)	;; p_m = mutation rate
return $p \in C_t$ with max $f(p)$	;; Return solution

Algorithm 14.7

Simple GA on solution strings.

The MAXIMUM CUT problem has a weighted graph $G = (V, E, w)$ as input with $w(u, v) = w(v, u)$ and $w(u, u) = 0$ for all $u \in V$. The set of feasible solutions is $V_0, V_1 \subseteq V$ with $V_0 \cap V_1 = \emptyset, V_0 \cup V_1 = V$. Let $C \leftarrow \{(v, v') \in E \mid v \in V_0, v' \in V_1\}$. The objective function is $W(C) = \sum_{(u,v) \in C} w(u, v)$ and an optimal solution C is a solution with maximal value of $W(C)$. The encoding of V_0, V_1 is given by vectors $x = (x_1, \ldots, x_n)$, with $x_i = 1$ if and only if $i \in V_1$. The formulation of MAXIMUM CUT as maximizing a GA problem reads as follows:

$$e(x) = \sum_{i=1}^{n-1} \sum_{j=i+1}^{n} w(i, j) \left[x_i \left(1 - x_j\right) + x_j \left(1 - x_i\right) \right].$$

Figure 14.3 shows an example of a cut with $n = 10$.

Tests with $n = 100$ show that after 1,000 iterations and 50,000 evaluations, obtained solutions differ from the optimum by at most 5 % (on the average) with only $(5 \cdot 10^4)/2^{100} \approx 4 \cdot 10^{-24}$ % of the entire state space that has been looked at.

14.5.3 Insights to Genetic Algorithm Search

We now come to some insights of GAs, stating that selection and recombination is equal to innovation. Let us consider the iterated analysis of the hyperplane partition in the n-cube, the graph with nodes $\mathbb{B}^n$, where two nodes are connected if the bit-flip (or Hamming) distance is one.

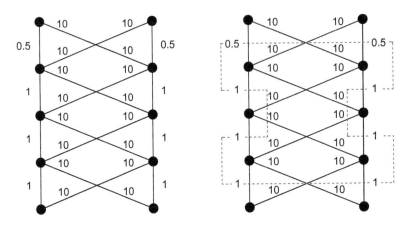

FIGURE 14.3

Cut obtained by GA with 10 generations.

Definition 14.3. *(Schema, Order, Value) A* schema *is a string over the alphabet* $\{0,1,*\}$, *with at least one non-* $*$ *character. The* order $o(s)$ *of a schema s is the number of non-* $*$ *characters in s. The* value $\Delta(s)$ *of a schema s is the length between the maximal and minimal index of a non-* $*$ *character.*

The order of $1**1*****0**$ is 3 and $\Delta(***1**0**10**) = 12 - 5 = 7$. The probability that a 1-point crossover has an intersection in schema s is $\Delta(s)/(n-1)$.

The bit-string x *fits* to schema s, $x \in s$, if s can be changed into x by modifying at most one $*$. Therefore, all x that fit into s are located on a hyperplane. Every $x \in B^n$ belongs to $\sum_{k=0}^{n-1} \binom{n}{k} = 2^n - 1$ hyperplanes. There are $3^n - 1$ different hyperplanes. A random population of size n has many chromosomes that fit to schema s of small order $o(s)$. On the average we have $n/2^{o(s)}$ individuals. The evaluation of x exhibits an implicit parallelism. Since x contains information of over $2^n - 1$ schemas, a GA *senses* schema, so that the representation of good schemas in the upcoming generation is increased.

Due to information loss, convergence to the optimum cannot be expected by recombination alone. We need mutation, which performs small changes to individuals and generates new information. Selection and mutation together are sufficient for performing *randomized local search*.

In Figure 14.4 individuals x with $x_1 = 0$ are better than those of $x_1 = 1$ and survive better. Therefore, the population rate in regions with $f(x) > \bar{f}$ is increased.

We next try to formally quantify the changes when progressing from C_t to C_{t+1}. The result, the *schema theorem*, is fundamental to the theory of GA. Actually, the statement is not a formal theorem but the result of some mathematical observations, important enough to be unrolled here. The *schema theorem* estimates a lower bound of the expected sensing rate of a schema s in going from C_t to C_{t+1}.

Let the cardinality M of a schema s in iteration t be defined as $M(s,t) = |\{x \in C_t \mid x \in s\}|$ and $M(s, t+1/2) = M(s,t)f(s,t)/\bar{f}$, where

$$f(s,t) = \frac{1}{M(s,t)} \sum_{x \in C_t, x \in s} f(x).$$

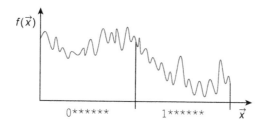

FIGURE 14.4

Representation of good schemas.

The argumentation takes two conservative assumptions: each crossover is destructive, and gains are small. Then, we have

$$M(s,t+1) \geq (1-p_c)M(s,t)\frac{f(s,t)}{\bar{f}} + p_c\left[M(s,t)\frac{f(s,t)}{\bar{f}}(1-d(s,t))\right]$$

$$= M(s,t)\frac{f(s,t)}{\bar{f}}[1-p_c d(s,t)], \qquad (*)$$

where $d(s,t)$ is the probability that a schema s is destroyed in iteration t by a crossover operation. If $x,y \in s$ are recombined there is no loss. Let $P(s,t) = M(s,t)/n$ be the probability that of a random $x \in C_t$ we have $x \in s$, and $d(s,t) = \frac{\Delta(s)}{n-1}(1-P(s,t))$. Then, insertion into $(*)$ and division by n yields a *first version of the schema theorem*

$$P(s,t+1) \geq P(s,t)\frac{f(s,t)}{\bar{f}}\left[1-p_c\frac{\Delta(s)}{n-1}(1-P(s,t))\right].$$

By assuming that the partner of $x \in s$ originates in $C_{t+1/2}$, we have $\tilde{d}(s,t) = \frac{\Delta(s)}{n-1}\left(1-P(s,t)\frac{f(s,t)}{\bar{f}}\right)$. Hence, the *second version of the schema theorem* is

$$P(s,t+1) \geq P(s,t)\frac{f(s,t)}{\bar{f}}\left[1-p_c\frac{\Delta(s)}{n-1}\left(1-P(s,t)\frac{f(s,t)}{\bar{f}}\right)\right].$$

Considering the destructive effect of mutation we have

$$P(s,t+1) \geq P(s,t)\frac{f(s,t)}{\bar{f}}\left[1-p_c\frac{\Delta(s)}{n-1}\left(1-P(s,t)\frac{f(s,t)}{\bar{f}}\right)\right](1-p_m)^{o(s)}.$$

14.6 APPROXIMATE SEARCH

To analyze the quality of a suboptimal algorithm, we take a brief excursion to the theory of *approximation algorithms*.

We say that algorithm A computes a *c-approximation*, if for all inputs I we have

$$m_A(I)/m_{OPT}(I) \geq c \text{ (deterministic) or } E[m_A(I)]/m_{OPT}(I) \geq c \text{ (probabilistic),}$$

where m_A is the value computed by the approximation and m_{OPT} is the value computed by the optimal algorithm to solve the (maximization) problem. By this definition, the value of c is contained in $[0, 1]$.

14.6.1 Approximating TSP

The *algorithm of Christofides* computes a near-optimal tour T with $d(T) \leq 3 \cdot d(T_{opt})/2$, where $d(T_{opt})$ is the cost of the best solution T_{opt}. The algorithm first constructs a MST T'. Let V' be defined as the set of vertices in T' with odd degree. Next it finds a minimum weight matching M on V' (with an $O(|V'|^3)$ algorithm) and constructs a *Euler tour* T'' on the edges of $T' \cup M$. Lastly, it prunes shortcuts in T'' and returns the remaining tour T. The sum of degrees D of all the vertices is $2e$. Therefore, D is even. If D_e is the sum of degrees of the vertices that have even degree, then D_e is also even. Therefore, $D - D_e = 2k$ for some integer value k. This means that the sum of degrees of the vertices that have odd degree each is also an even number. Thus, there are even numbers of vertices having odd degree. Therefore, the minimum weighted matching on the vertices in V' is well defined. The Euler tour based on the MST and the matching M starts and ends at the same vertex and visits all the edges exactly once. It is a complete cyclic tour, which then is truncated by using shortcuts according to the triangular property. We have $d(T) \leq d(T'') = d(T') + d(M) = d(MST) + d(M) \leq d(T_{opt}) + d(M)$. It remains to show that $d(M) \leq d(T_{opt})/2$. Suppose that we have an optimal TSP tour T_o visiting only the vertices that have odd degrees. Then $d(T_o) \leq d(T_{opt})$. We choose alternate edges among the edges on this path. Let M' and M'' be two sets of edges with $d(M') \leq d(M'')$. Consequently, we have $d(T_o) = d(M') + d(M'') \geq 2 \cdot d(M')$. Because we find the minimum matching edges M, we have $d(M) \leq d(M') \leq d(T'')/2 \leq d(T_{opt})/2$. Combining the results, we have $d(T) \leq d(T_{opt}) + d(T_{opt})/2 = 3 \cdot d(T_{opt})/2$.

14.6.2 Approximating MAX-k-SAT

In contrast to the decision problem k-SAT with k literals in each clause, in the optimizing variant MAX-k-SAT we search for the maximal degree of satisfiability. More formally, for a formula with m clauses and n variables the task is to determine

$$\max\{1 \leq j \leq m \mid a \in \{0,1\}^n, a \text{ satisfies } j \text{ clauses}\}.$$

A deterministic 0.5-approximation of MAX-k-SAT is implemented in Algorithm 14.8; $c|_{a_i}$ denotes the simplification of a clause c with regard to assignment a_i to variable x_i. It is not difficult to see that the simple approximation algorithm yields an assignment that is off by at most a factor of 2. We see that for each iteration there are at least as many clauses that are satisfied as there are unsatisfied.

Procedure Approximate-MAX-SAT
Input: Clause set C of a MAX-k-SAT formula
Output: Assignment for variables in C

for each $i \in \{1,\ldots,n\}$;; Loop on set variables
  if $(|\{c \in C \mid x_i \in c\}| > |\{c \in C \mid \overline{x_i} \in c\}|)$
    $a_i \leftarrow$ *true*   ;; x_i appears in more clauses than $\overline{x_i}$
  if $(|\{c \in C \mid \overline{x_i} \in c\}| > |\{c \in C \mid x_i \in c\}|)$
    $a_i \leftarrow$ *false*   ;; $\overline{x_i}$ appears in more clauses than x_i
  $C \leftarrow C \setminus \{c \mid c|_{a_i} = true\}$;; Remove all satisfied clauses
  $C \leftarrow C \setminus \{c \mid c|_{a_i} = false\}$;; Remove all unsatisfied clauses
return a ;; Return found assignment

Algorithm 14.8

Deterministic approximation algorithm for MAX-k-SAT.

14.7 RANDOMIZED SEARCH

The concept of randomization accelerates many algorithms. For example, *randomized quicksort* randomizes the choice of the pivot element to fool the adversary and in choosing an uneven split into two parts. Such algorithms that are always correct and that have better time performance on the average (over several runs) are called *Las Vegas* algorithms. For the concept of randomized search in the *Monte Carlo* setting, we expect the algorithm only to be *mostly* correct (the leading characters MC used in both terms may help to memorize the classification).

In the following we will exemplify the essentials of randomized algorithms in the context of maximizing k-SAT with instances consisting of clauses of the form $u_1 \vee u_2 \vee \cdots \vee u_l$, with $u_i \in \{x_1,\ldots,x_n\} \cup \{\overline{x_1},\ldots,\overline{x_n}\}$. Searching for satisfying assignments for random SAT instances is close to finding a needle in a haystack. Fortunately, there is often more structure in the problem that lets heuristic value selection and assignment strategies be very effective.

The *brute-force* algorithm for SAT takes all 2^n assignments and checks whether they satisfy the formula. The runtime is $O(n \cdot 2^n)$ when testing sequentially, or $O(2^n)$ when testing in the form of a binary search tree.

A simple strategy shows that there is space for improvement. Assigning the first k variables to one of the values yields a tree with 2^k branches. If the k variables are chosen such that the truth value of one clause is determined, then at least one of the 2^k variable assignments evaluates it to false (otherwise the clause would be trivially true for all assignments and could be omitted). Hence, at least one branch induces a backtrack and does not have to be considered further on. This implies that if the variable order is chosen along the clauses, then a backtrack approach runs in time $O((2^k - 1)^{n/k})$. Depending on the structure of the clause, in some cases, more than one branch can be pruned.

The *Monien-Speckenmeyer algorithm* is a deterministic k-SAT solver that includes a recursive procedure shown in Algorithm 14.9, which works on the structure of f. For $k = 3$ the algorithm processes the following assignments: first $u_1 \leftarrow 1$, then $u_1 \leftarrow 0 \wedge u_2 \leftarrow 1$, and finally $u_1 \leftarrow 0 \wedge u_2 \leftarrow 0 \wedge x_3 = 1$.

The recurrence relation for the algorithm is of the form $T(n) \leq T(n-1) + \cdots + T(n-l)$. Assuming $T(n) = \alpha^n$ yields $\alpha^k \leq \alpha^{k-1} + \cdots + \alpha^1 + 1$ for general k and $\alpha^3 \leq \alpha^2 + \alpha + 1$ for $k = 3$ so that $\alpha \approx 1.839$. Therefore, Monien-Speckenmeyer corresponds to an $O(1.839^n)$ algorithm. With some tricks the runtime can be reduced to $O(1.6181^n)$.

Let the probability of finding a satisfying assignment be p. The probability of not finding a satisfying assignment in t trials is $(1-p)^t$. We have $(1-p)^t \leq e^{-tp}$, since $1 - x \leq e^{-x}$. Therefore, the number of iterations t has to be chosen so that $e^{-tp} \leq \epsilon$, by means $t \geq \ln(1/\epsilon)/p$.

Another simple randomized algorithm for k-SAT has been suggested by Paturi, Pudlák and Zane. The iterative algorithm is shown in Algorithm 14.10. It applies one assignment at a time by selecting and setting appropriate variables, continously modifying a random seed.

The state space to be searched is $\{false, true\}^n$. It is illustrated in Figure 14.5. Unsuccessful assignments are represented as hollow nodes, while a satisfying assignment is represented in the form of a black spot. The algorithm of Paturi, Pudlák, and Zane generates candidates for a MAX-k-SAT in the space.

Procedure Monien-Speckenmeyer
Input: MAX-k-SAT Instance f
Output: Assignment for f

if (f trivial) **return** result	;; Termination criterion
$\{u_1, \ldots, u_l\} \leftarrow$ SelectShortest	;; Choose shortest clause
for each $i \in \{1, \ldots, l\}$	;; For all literals
if (MonienSpeckenmeyer($f\|_{u_1 \leftarrow false, \ldots, u_{i-1} \leftarrow false, u_i \leftarrow true}$))	;; Recursive call
return true	;; Propagate success
return false	;; Propagate failure

Algorithm 14.9

Monien-Speckenmeyer algorithm.

Procedure PPZ
Input: MAX-k-SAT instance f
Output: Assignment for f

$\pi \leftarrow$ SelectPermutation$(1, \ldots, n)$	;; Choose random permutation
for each $i \in \{1, \ldots, n\}$	;; For all variables
if ($\{x_{\pi(i)}\} \in f$) $a_{\pi(i)} \leftarrow$ true	;; Set variable
else if ($\{\overline{x_{\pi(i)}}\} \in f$) $a_{\pi(i)} \leftarrow$ false	;; Clear variable
else $a_{\pi(i)} \leftarrow$ Select$(\{false, true\})$	;; Throw coin
$f \leftarrow f\|_{x_{\pi(i)} \leftarrow a_{\pi(i)}}$	;; Simplify with respect to assignment
return $(a_1, \ldots, a_n)$	;; Feedback assignment

Algorithm 14.10

Algorithm of Paturi, Pudlák, and Zane.

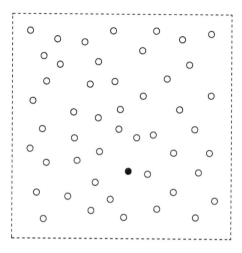

FIGURE 14.5

Solving k-SAT problems with the PPZ algorithm.

Procedure Hamming-Sphere
Input: MAX-k-SAT instance f, current assignment a, depth d
Output: Improved assignment for f

if $(f(a) = true)$ **return** *true*	;; Satisfying assignment found
if $(d = 0)$ **return** *false*	;; Radius of sphere exceeded
$\{l_1,\dots,l_k\} \leftarrow SelectUnsatClause$	;; Choose unsatisfied clause randomly
for each $i \in \{1,\dots,k\}$	;; For all literals in clause
if $(Hamming\text{-}Sphere(flip(a,i),d-1))$	;; Flip and call recursively
return *true*	;; Propagate success
return *false*	;; Indicate failure

Algorithm 14.11

Hamming sphere algorithm.

The success probability p for one trial can be shown to be $p \geq 2^{-n(1-1/k)}$. Subsequently, with $O(2^{n(1-1/k)})$ iterations, we have a success probability of $\geq 1 - o(1)$. For 3-SAT this yields an algorithm with an expected runtime of $O(1.587^n)$.

The *Hamming sphere* algorithm invokes a recursive procedure with parameters (a,d), where a is the current assignment and d is a depth limit. It is implemented in Algorithm 14.11 and illustrated in Figure 14.6. The initial depth value is the radius of the Hamming sphere. The spheres are illustrated as arrows in the circles denoting the spheres. Because the algorithm is called many times we have shown several such spheres, one containing a satisfying assignment.

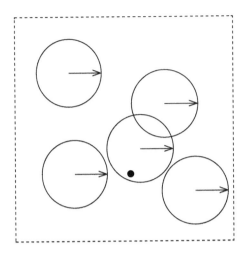

FIGURE 14.6

Solving k-SAT problems with the Hamming sphere algorithm.

The analysis of the algorithm is as follows. The test procedure is called t times with random $a \in \{0, 1\}^n$ and $d = \beta n$. The running time to traverse one sphere is $O(q(n)k^d) \doteq O(k^d)$. The size of the Hamming sphere of radius $\beta n \leq n/2$ is equal to

$$\sum_{i=0}^{\beta n} \binom{n}{i} \doteq \binom{n}{\beta n} \doteq 2^{h(\beta)n} = \left[\left(\frac{1}{\beta} \right)^{\beta} \left(\frac{1}{1-\beta} \right)^{1-\beta} \right]^n.$$

The success probability is $p = 2^{(h(\beta)n)}/2^n = 2^{(h(\beta)-1)n}$. Therefore, $t \in O(2^{(1-h(\beta))n})$ iterations are needed. The running time $O((2^{(1-h(\beta))}k^{\beta})^n)$ is minimal for $\beta = 1/(k+1)$, such that $O((\frac{2k}{k+1})^n)$.

Solving k-SAT with *random walk* works as shown in the iterative procedure of Algorithm 14.12. The algorithm starts with a random assignment and improves that by flipping the assignments to random variables in unsatisfied clauses. This procedure is closely related to the GSAT algorithm introduced in Chapter 13.

The procedure is called t times and is terminated in case of a satisfying assignment. An illustration is provided in Figure 14.7, where the walks are shown as directed curves, one ending at a satisfying assignment.

The analysis of the algorithm bases on a model of the walk in the form of a stochastic automata. It mimics the analysis of the GAMBLER'S RUIN problem. First, we generate a binomial distribution according to the Hamming distances from the goal in a fixed assignment. Second, the transition probabilities of $\geq 1/3$ (improvement toward the goal) and $\leq 2/3$ (distancing from the goal) are set. The probability to encounter the Hamming distance 0 is

$$p = \sum_{j=0}^{n} \binom{n}{j} 2^{-n} q_j \text{ with } q_j \doteq \left(\frac{1}{k-1} \right)^j.$$

Procedure Random-Walk
Input: MAX-k-SAT instance f
Output: Assignment for f

$a \leftarrow Select(\{false,true\}^n)$　　　　　　　　　　　　　;; Any random assignment
for each $i \in \{1,\ldots,3n\}$　　　　　　　;; Random walk to certain number of steps
　　if $(f(a))$ **return** a　　　　　　　　　　　;; Satisfying assignment found
　　$\{l_1,\ldots,l_k\} \leftarrow SelectUnsatClause$　　;; Choose unsatisfied clause randomly
　　$flip(a, Select(\{1,\ldots,k\}))$　　　　　　;; Flip assignment to random variable

Algorithm 14.12

Algorithm random walk.

FIGURE 14.7

Solving k-SAT problems with the random walk algorithm.

For 3-SAT we have

$$q_j \doteq \binom{3j}{2j}\left(\frac{1}{3}\right)^{2j}\left(\frac{2}{3}\right)^{j} \doteq \left[2^{3h(2/3)}\left(\frac{1}{3}\right)\left(\frac{2}{3}\right)^{2}\right]^{j} = \left[\left(\frac{3}{2}\right)^2\left(\frac{3}{1}\right)\left(\frac{4}{3^3}\right)\right]^{j} = \left(\frac{1}{2}\right)^{j}.$$

If we include this result in this equation, we have $p = 2^{-n}\left(1 + \frac{1}{k-1}\right)^{n}$. The average time complexity of the random walk strategy, therefore, is bounded by $\doteq O(1/p) = O\left(\left(2 \cdot \left(1 - \frac{1}{k}\right)\right)^{n}\right)$.

14.8 ANT ALGORITHMS

Genetic algorithms mimic biological evolution. By their success, the research in *bionic algorithms* that model optimization processes in nature has been intensified. Many new algorithms mimic ant search; for example, consider some natural ants while searching for food as shown in Figure 14.8. Ant communication is performed via pheromones. They trade random decision for adapted decision. In contrast to natural ants, *computer ants*

- solve optimizing problems via sequences of decisions;
- choose random decision, while being guided by pheromone and other criteria;
- have a limited memory;
- can detect feasible options; and
- distribute pheromones proportional to the quality of the established solution.

14.8.1 Simple Ant System

Algorithm 14.13 shows a simple ant system to find an optimized solution for the TSP problem. The parameters of the simple ant system algorithm for TSP are

1. the number of ants n. Usually we have $n = c$; that is, each ant starts in another city;
2. values $\alpha, \beta \in [0, \infty)$ include the relative impact of the pheromones in relation to their visibility. If α is too big we have early stagnation or exploitation; if α is too small we have an iterative heuristic or exploration. Suggested setting: $\alpha = 1, \beta = 5$;
3. variable $\rho \in [0, 1]$ influences the memory of the algorithm. If ρ is too big we have an early convergence; if ρ is too small we do not exhibit knowledge. Suggested setting: $\rho = 1/2$; and
4. additional value Q that determines influence of new information in relation to initialization, $\tau_{ij}(0)$, turns out to be not crucial. Suggested setting: $Q = 100$.

In the algorithm we have two subroutines to be implemented.

1. *Choice of city j* for ant k in city i: If i is not defined, j is initialized, otherwise determined by
   - j does not need to be part of an existing tour
   - probability P_{ij} for choosing j is proportional to $1/d_{ij}$ and τ_{ij}

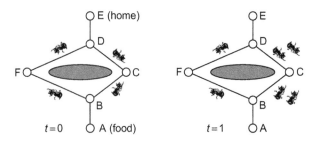

FIGURE 14.8

Ants searching for food.

Procedure Ant-Search
Input: TSP problem instance (for further parameters see below)
Output: Optimized solution

$t \leftarrow 0$;	;; Time
for each $i, j \in \{1,\ldots,c\}$	;; For all cities
$\quad \tau_{ij} \leftarrow Pheromone(i, j, t)$	;; Compute pheromone size
while not (*Terminate*)	;; Termination criterion not met
$\quad t \leftarrow t + 1$	;; Increase iteration count
$\quad$ **for each** $k \in \{1,\ldots,n\}$	;; For all ants
$\quad\quad$ **while not** (*CompleteTour(k)*)	;; Unless Hamiltonian cycle
$\quad\quad\quad j \leftarrow ChooseCity(k)$	;; Selection
$\quad\quad L_k \leftarrow TourLength(k)$	;; Evaluation criteria
$\quad$ **for each** $i, j \in \{1,\ldots,n\}$	;; For all ant pairs
$\quad\quad \tau_{ij} \leftarrow Pheromone(i, j, t)$	;; Compute pheromone level
return *ShortestTour*	

Algorithm 14.13

The ant system algorithm for solving TSP.

with

$$P_{ij} \leftarrow \begin{cases} \dfrac{[\tau_{ij}]^{\alpha} [\eta_{ij}]^{\beta}}{\sum_{h \in \Omega(k)} [\tau_{ih}]^{\alpha} [\eta_{ih}]^{\beta}} & \text{for } j \in \Omega(k) \\ 0 & \text{otherwise} \end{cases}$$

τ_{ij} : pheromone level on (i, j)

α : weight of τ_{ij}

η_{ij} : $1/d_{ij}$ visibility

β : weight of η_{ij}

$\Omega(k)$: set of k unvisited cities

2. *Computation of pheromone size* $\tau_{ij}(t)$ *for* (i, j):
If $t = 0$ then $\tau_{ij}(t)$ is newly initialized, otherwise a fraction $(1 - \rho)$ disappears and ant k distributes Q/L_k:

$$\tau_{ij}(t + 1) \leftarrow \rho \tau_{ij}(t) + \Delta \tau_{ij}$$
$$\Delta \tau_{ij} = \sum_{k=1}^{\mu} \Delta \tau_{ij}^k$$

$$\Delta \tau_{ij}^k = \begin{cases} Q/L_k & \text{for } (i,j) \in \text{Tour}(k) \\ 0 & \text{otherwise} \end{cases}$$

Tests show that the algorithm is successful with parameters ($\alpha = 1$, $\beta = 1$, $\rho = 0.9$, $Q = 1$, $n \leq 33$).

14.8.2 **Algorithm Flood**

Another important option for optimization is *simulated annealing*. Since we are only interested in the main characteristic of this technique we prefer the interpretation as a form of ant search. Suppose ants are walking on a landscape that is slowly flooded by water as shown in Figure 14.9. The hope is that at the end an ant will be positioned on the highest mountain corresponding to the best evaluation possible.

In the pseudo-code presentation in Algorithm 14.14 each ant has a position (initialized with *SelectPosition*) and its position corresponds to a solution of the problem. There are neighbors' positions in *Succ* that can be reached by applying operators. The quality of the solution is measured by the evaluation function *height*. The water level *level* is a slowly rising parameter and the call to *Dry* indicates that only dry ants remain active. Tests show the effectiveness of the algorithm for problems with many neighbors.

As in the case of GAs, *algorithm flood* can be easily adapted to general heuristic search state space problems by using ants' encodings for paths, a suitable neighborhood relation, and the heuristic estimate as the evaluation function.

14.8.3 **Vertex Ant Walk**

A real-time search variant, often mentioned together with ant algorithms, is *vertex ant walk*. It is defined by the rules in Algorithm 14.15 and has no explicit termination criterion.

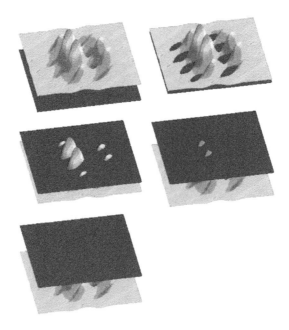

FIGURE 14.9

The flood is rising.

Procedure Flood
Input: State space problem, initial (water) *level*
Output: Evaluation of optimized solution

$t \leftarrow 1$	;; Initialize time
for each $i \in \{1,\dots,n\}$	;; For all ants
$position(i) \leftarrow SelectPosition$	;; Choose start locations
$active(i) \leftarrow true$	;; All ants are active
while not (*Terminate*)	;; Look for termination criterion
for each $i \in \{1,\dots,n\}$	;; For all ants
if (*active*(*i*))	;; As far as alive
$position(i) \leftarrow Succ(i, level)$	;; Successor states
$active(i) \leftarrow Dry(i, l)$	;; Survivors
$level \leftarrow level + Rain$	;; Update water level
$t \leftarrow t + 1$	;; Update iteration count
return $\max\{height(i) \mid i \in \{1,\dots,n\}\}$	;; Return best solution

Algorithm 14.14

Flood algorithm.

Procedure Vertex-Ant-Walk
Input: State space problem with initial state s
Output: Hamiltonian path in state space problem

for each $u \in S$: $(h(u), \tau(u)) \leftarrow (0,0)$	
$u \leftarrow s$	;; Start in initial state
loop	;; Endless loop
$v \in \text{argmin}_{a \in A(v)}\{x \in Succ(u,a) \mid (h(x), \tau(x))\}$	;; Action selection
$\tau(u) \leftarrow t$; $h(u) \leftarrow h(v) + 1$; $t \leftarrow t + 1$	;; Value update
$u \leftarrow a(v)$	;; Action commitment

Algorithm 14.15

Vertex ant walk.

A tie can only occur between yet unvisited states. Once a state is visited, it always has a unique time stamp that avoids further ties.

Theorem 14.2. *(Properties VAW) Algorithm 14.15 fulfills the following properties:*

1. *For (u,v) as an edge in the state space problem graph $G = (V,E)$, it always holds that $|h(u) - h(v)| \leq 1$.*

2. *Let t be the t-th iteration and $h^t = \sum_{v \in V} h^t(u)$ be the h-value in iteration t. At all times t, we have $h^t(G) \geq t$.*

3. *A single ant covers any connected graph within $O(nd)$ steps, where n is the number of vertices and d is the diameter of the graph.*

4. *A Hamiltonian cycle, upon being traversed n consecutive times, becomes a limit cycle of VAW.*

Proof.

1. The result is clearly true for $t = 0$. Inductively, we assume that it is also true at time t. Since $h(v)$ is the minimum among u's neighbors, the maximum difference $|h(x) - h(y)|$ after the update is between u and v, and this difference is equal to 1.

2. Denote the sequence of nodes visited up to time t by $u_1, \ldots, u_t$, and the h-value of a vertex u upon completion of time step t by $h_t(u)$. The only change to h may occur at the vertex currently visited, hence $h_t(G) = h_{t-1}(G) + \Delta_t$, where Δ_i is the offset to $h(G)$ at time i, $\Delta_i = h_i(u_i) - h_{i-1}(u_i)$. According to the VAW rule, upon moving from u_i to u_{i+1} the value of $h_i(u_i)$ is set to $h_i(u_{i+1}) + 1$ and $\Delta_i = h_i(u_{i+1}) - h_{i-1}(u_i) + 1$. Together with $\Delta_i = h_i(u_i) - h_{i-1}(u_i)$ by substituting $i = t - 1$ we have $h_{t-1}(u_t) = h_{t-2}(u_{t-1}) + \Delta_{t-1} - 1$. Recursively applying the analysis, we have

$$h_t(u_t) = h_{t-1}(u_t) + \Delta_t$$
$$= h_{t-2}(u_{t-1}) + \Delta_{t-1} + \Delta_t - 1$$
$$= h_{t-3}(u_{t-2}) + \Delta_t + \Delta_{t-1} + \Delta_t - 3$$
$$\vdots$$
$$= h_0(u_1) - (t - 1) + \sum_{i=1}^{t} \Delta_t.$$

Since $h_t(G) = \sum_{i=1}^{t} \Delta_t$ we finally get $h_t(G) = h_t(u_t) - h_0(u_1) + (t - 1)$. The result follows by the rules $h_0(u_1) = 0$ and $h_t(u_t) \geq 1$.

3. We shall prove a slightly stronger claim: After at most $d(2n - d - 1)/2$ steps the graph is covered. Assume the contrary. Then there is at least one node, say u, for which $h(u) = 0$. According to the first lemma none of u's neighbors can have $h > 1$ and none of u's neighbors' neighbors can have $h > 2$, and so on. Therefore, we have at least one node with $h = 0$, at least one node with $h = 1$, and so on up to $d - 1$. For the rest of the at most $n - d$ nodes we have $h \leq d$. This yields $h(G) \leq \binom{d}{2} + d(n - d) = d(2n - d - 1)/2$. According to the second lemma, the total value of h at time t is at least t, so that after at most $d(2n - d - 1)/2$ steps the graph is covered.

4. If the graph has a Hamiltonian cycle, following this cycle is clearly the shortest way to cover the graph. Recall that a closed path in a graph is a Hamiltonian cycle if it visits each node exactly once. We shall see that a Hamiltonian cycle is a possible limit of VAW. Moreover, if the ant happens to follow the cycle for n consecutive times, it will follow this cycle forever.

   Recall that upon leaving a node u, we have $h_t(u_t) = h_t(u_{t+1}) + 1$. Let us now assume that at time t the ant has completed a sequence of n Hamiltonian cycles. Then u_{t+1} has not been visited since time $t - n + 1$ and $h_t(u_{t+1}) = h_{t-n+1}(u_{t+1}) = h_{t-n+1}(u_{t-n+1})$. Substituting the first equation into the second yields

$$h_t(u_t) = h_{t-n+1}(u_{t-n+1}) + 1$$
$$= h_{t-2(n+1)}(u_{t-2(n+1)}) + 2$$
$$\vdots$$
$$= h_{t-n(n+1)}(u_{t-n(n+1)}) + n$$
$$= h_{t-n(n+1)}(u_t) + n.$$

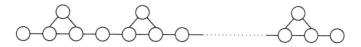

FIGURE 14.10

A hard test-bet for VAW.

During the $(n+1)$st cycle, the ant is confronted with the same relative h pattern with which it was confronted in the first cycle. The value n that is added to each h value does not change the ordering relation between the nodes. Therefore, the same decisions are taken. ∎

The bound of $O(nd)$ is tight. There are examples of graphs, where the cover time is indeed $O(nd)$. Consider a graph that consists of triangles that are connected in a single chain, with one additional node between the triangles (see Fig. 14.10). It is easy to validate that the triangles are in fact *traps* for VAW that cause the ant to go back to its starting point. There are n vertices, and the diameter is about $0.8n$. The time needed to traverse the graph is $\Omega(nd) = \Omega(n^2)$.

The last results hold for a single ant. They are not in general true for *multiple ants*, but it seems reasonable to say that if the graph is large and the ants are fairly distributed in the beginning, the load will be more or less balanced. In *edge ant walk* (EAW) edges rather than nodes are marked. For this process it can be shown that k small-oriented ants can cover a graph in at most $O(\delta \cdot n^2/k)$ steps, where δ is the maximum vertex-degree and n is the number of nodes. In practice, VAW often performs better than *edge ant walk*, since in general, $nd < \delta \cdot n^2$.

14.9 *LAGRANGE MULTIPLIERS

In *continuous nonlinear programming* (CNLP), we have continuous and differential functions f, $h = (h_1, \ldots, h_m)^T$, and $g = (g_1, \ldots, g_r)^T$. The nonlinear program P_c given as

$$\min_x f(x), \text{ where } x = (x_1, \ldots, x_v) \in \mathbb{R}^v$$

subject to

$$h(x) = 0 \text{ and } g(x) \leq 0$$

is to be solved by finding a constrained local minimum x with respect to the continuous neighborhood $N_c(x) = \{x' \mid ||x' - x|| \leq \epsilon\}$ of x for some $\epsilon > 0$.

A point x^* is a *constraint local minimum* (CLM) if x^* is feasible and $f(x^*) \leq f(x)$ for all feasible $x \in N_c(x^*)$.

Based on Lagrange-multiplier vectors $\lambda = (\lambda_1, \ldots, \lambda_m)^T$ and $\mu = (\mu_1, \ldots, \mu_r)^T$, the Lagrangian function of P_c is defined as

$$L(x, \lambda, \mu) = f(x) + \lambda^T h(x) + \mu^T g(x).$$

14.9.1 Saddle-Point Conditions

A *sufficient saddle-point condition* for x^* in P_c is established if there exist λ^* and μ^* such that

$$L(x^*, \lambda, \mu) \leq L(x^*, \lambda^*, \mu^*) \leq L(x, \lambda^*, \mu^*)$$

for all x satisfying $||x - x^*|| < \epsilon$ and all $\lambda \in R^m$ and $\mu \in R^r$. To illustrate that the condition is only sufficient, consider the following CLNP:

$$\min_x f(x) = -x^2 \text{ subject to } h(x) = x - 5 = 0.$$

It is obvious that $x^* = 5$ is a CLM. Differentiating the Lagrangian $L(x, \lambda) = x^2 + \lambda(x - 5)$ with respect to x and evaluating it at $x^* = 5$ yields $-10 + \lambda = 0$, which implies $\lambda^* = 10$. However, since the second derivative is $-2 < 0$, we know that $L(x, \lambda)$ is at a local maximum at x^* instead of a local minimum. Hence, there exists no λ^* that satisfies the sufficient saddle-point condition.

To devise a sufficient and necessary saddle-point condition we take the *transformed Lagrangian* for P_c defined as

$$L_c(x, \alpha, \beta) = f(x) + \alpha^T |h(x)| + \beta^T \max\{0, g(x)\},$$

where $|h(x)|$ is defined as $(|h_1(x)|, \ldots, |h_m(x)|)^T$ and $\max\{0, g(x)\}$ is given by $(\max\{0, g_1(x)\}, \ldots, \max\{0, g_r(x)\})^T$.

A point $x \in R^v$ is *regular* with respect to the constraints, if the gradient vectors of the constraints are linearly independent.

Theorem 14.3. *(Extended Saddle-Point Condition) Suppose $x^* \in R^v$ is regular. Then x^* is a CLM of P_c if and only if there exist finite $\alpha^* \geq 0$ and $\beta^* \geq 0$ such that, for any $\alpha^{**} > \alpha^*$ and $\beta^{**} > \beta^*$, the following condition is satisfied:*

$$L_c(x^*, \alpha, \beta) \leq L_c(x^*, \alpha^{**}, \beta^{**}) \leq L_c(x, \alpha^{**}, \beta^{**}).$$

Proof. The proof consists of two parts. First, given x^*, we need to prove that there exist finite $\alpha^{**} > \alpha^* \geq 0$ and $\beta^{**} > \beta^* \geq 0$ that satisfy the preceding condition. The inequality on the left side is true for all α and β because x^* is a CLM, which implies that $|h(x^*)| = 0$ and $\max\{0, g(x^*)\} \leq 0$.

To prove the inequality on the right side, we know that the gradient vectors of the equality and the active inequality constraints at x^* are linear-independent, because x^* is a regular point. According to the necessary condition on the existence of a CLM by Karush, Kuhn, and Tucker (see Bibliographic Notes) there exist unique λ^* and μ^* that satisfy $\nabla_x L(x^*, \lambda^*, \mu^*) = 0$, where $\mu \geq 0$ and $\mu_j = 0$ if $g_j(x^*) < 0$. When we divide the index sets for h and g into negative and nonnegative sets, we get

- $P_e(x) = \{i \in \{1, \ldots, m\} | h_i(x) \geq 0\}$
- $N_e(x) = \{i \in \{1, \ldots, m\} | h_i(x) < 0\}$
- $A(x) = \{j \in \{1, \ldots, r\} | g_j(x) = 0\}$
- $A_p(x) = \{j \in \{1, \ldots, r\} | g_j(x) \geq 0\}$

Differentiating the Lagrangian function $L(x, \lambda, \mu) = f(x) + \lambda^T h(x) + \mu^T g(x)$ with respect to x yields

$$\nabla_x f(x^*) + \sum_{i=1}^{m} \lambda_i^* \nabla_x h_i(x^*) + \sum_{j=1}^{r} \mu_j^* \nabla_x g_j(x^*) = 0.$$

Assuming $x \in N_c(x^*)$ and $\alpha^* = |\lambda^*|$ and $\beta^* = \mu^*$ we evaluate $L(x, \alpha^{**}, \beta^{**})$ for all $\alpha^{**} > \alpha^*$ and $\beta^{**} > \beta^*$ as follows:

$$L(x, \alpha^{**}, \beta^{**}) = f(x) + \sum_{i=1}^{m} \alpha_i^{**} |h_i(x)| + \sum_{j=1}^{r} \beta_j^{**} \max\{0, g_j(x^*)\}$$

$$= f(x) + \sum_{i \in P_e(x)} \alpha_i^{**} h_i(x) - \sum_{i \in N_e(x)} \alpha_i^{**} h_i(x) + \sum_{j \in A_p(x)} \beta_j^{**} g_j(x^*).$$

Assuming $x = x + \epsilon x$ and using a *Taylor series expansion* of the functions around x^* we have

$$L(x, \alpha^{**}, \beta^{**}) = f(x^*) + \nabla_x f(x^*)^T \epsilon x + + \sum_{i \in P_e(x)} \alpha_i^{**} \nabla_x h_i(x^*)^T \epsilon x$$

$$- \sum_{i \in N_e(x)} \alpha_i^{**} \nabla_x h_i(x^*)^T \epsilon x + \sum_{j \in A_p(x)} \beta_j^{**} \nabla_x g_j(x^*)^T \epsilon x + o(\epsilon x^2).$$

Since

- for all $i \in P_e(x) : \alpha_i^{**} \nabla_x h_i(x^*)^T \epsilon x$
- for all $i \in N_e(x) : \alpha_i^{**} \nabla_x h_i(x^*)^T \epsilon x < 0$
- for all $j \in A_p(x) : \beta_j^{**} \nabla_x g_j(x) \epsilon x > 0$
- for all $j \in A_p(x) \setminus A(x) : \beta_j^{**} \nabla_x g_j(x) \epsilon x > 0$

with $\alpha^{**} > |\lambda^*|$ and $\beta^{**} > \mu^* \geq 0$ we have

$$L(x, \alpha^{**}, \beta^{**}) > f(x^*) + \nabla_x f(x^*)^T \epsilon x + + \sum_{i \in P_e(x)} \lambda_i^{**} \nabla_x h_i(x^*)^T \epsilon x$$

$$- \sum_{i \in N_e(x)} \lambda_i^{**} \nabla_x h_i(x^*)^T \epsilon x + \sum_{j \in A_p(x)} \mu_j^{**} \nabla_x g_j(x^*)^T \epsilon x + o(\epsilon x^2)$$

$$\geq f(x^*) + \nabla_x f(x^*)^T \epsilon x + + \sum_{i=1}^{m} \lambda_i^{**} \nabla_x h_i(x^*)^T \epsilon x$$

$$+ \sum_{j \in A(x)} \mu_j^{**} \nabla_x g_j(x^*)^T \epsilon x + o(\epsilon x^2)$$

$$= f(x^*) + \left(\nabla_x f(x^*) + \sum_{i=1}^{m} \lambda_i^{**} \nabla_x h_i(x^*) + \sum_{j \in A(x)} \mu_j^{**} \nabla_x g_j(x^*) \right)^T \epsilon x + o(\epsilon x^2)$$

$$= f(x^*) + o(\epsilon x^2) \geq f(x^*) = L(x^*, \alpha^{**}, \beta^{**}),$$

which proves the right side of the inequality.

The second part of the proof assumes that the condition is satisfied, and we need to show that x^* is a CLM. Point x^* is feasible because the inequality on the left side can only be satisfied when $h(x^*) = 0$ and $g(x^*) \leq 0$. Since $|h(x^*)| = 0$ and $\max\{0, g(x^*)\} \leq 0$, the inequality of the right side ensures that x^* is a local minimum when compared to all feasible points in $N_c(x^*)$. Therefore, x^* is a CLM. ∎

The theorem requires $\alpha^{**} > \alpha^*$ and $\beta^{**} > \beta^*$ instead of $\alpha^{**} \geq \alpha^*$ and $\beta^{**} \geq \beta^*$ because L_c may not be a strict local minimum when $\alpha^{**} = \alpha^*$ and $\beta^{**} = \beta^*$. Consider the example CNLP with $L_C(x, \alpha) = -x^2 + \alpha|x - 5|$. At the only CLM $x^* = 5$, $L_c(x, \alpha)$ is not a strict local minimum when $\alpha = \alpha^* = 10$, but when $\alpha = 20 > \alpha^*$.

The algorithmic solution according to the theorem is iterative in nature with the pseudo code given in Algorithm 14.16.

Theorem 14.3 transfers to discrete and mixed (continuous and discrete) state spaces. The difference in discrete (mixed) space is the definition discrete (mixed) neighborhood N_d (N_m). Intuitively, N_d represents points that can be reached from y in one step, regardless whether there is a valid action to effect the transition. We require $y' \in N_d(y)$ if and only if $y \in N_d(y')$). A mixed neighborhood $N_m(x, y)$ of a point x in continuous space and a point y in discrete space can be defined as

$$N_m(x, y) = \left\{ (x', y) \mid x' \in N_c(x) \right\} \bigcup \left\{ (x, y') \mid y' \in N_d(y) \right\}.$$

Procedure Extended-Saddle-Point
Input: CNLP for P_c
Output: CLM x^*

$\alpha \leftarrow 0; \beta \leftarrow 0$	;; Initialize Lagrange multipliers
while CLM of P_c not found	;; Until completion
if $(h_i(x) \neq 0$ resp. $g_i(x) \nleq 0)$	;; Determine slack
incr. α_i resp. β_i by δ	;; Update multipliers
while (local minimum not found)	;; Local improvement
perform decent on L_c with respect to x	;; Local search algorithm
return CLM	;; Feedback solution

Algorithm 14.16

Saddle-point iteration method for finding a CLM.

14.9.2 **Partitioned Problems**

The goal of solving state space problems can be reduced to the previous setting. Our formulation assumes that the (possibly continuous) time horizon is partitioned in $k+1$ stages, with u_l local variables, m_l local equality constraints, and r_l local inequality constraints in stage l, $l \in \{0,\dots,k\}$.

Such partitioning decomposes the state variable vector S of the problem into $k+1$ subvectors $S_0,\dots,S_k$, where $S_l = (S_1(l),\dots,S_{u_t}(l))^T$ is a u_l-element state vector in (mixed) state space at stage l, and $S_i(l)$ is the ith dynamic state variable in stage l. Usually u_t is fixed. A solution to such a problem is a path that consists of the assignments of all variables in S. A state space search problem can be written as $\min_S J(S)$ subject to $h_l(S_l) = 0$, $g_l(S_l) \leq 0$, $t = 0,\dots,k$ (the *local constraints*), and $H(S) = 0$, $G(S) \geq 0$ (the *global constraints*). Here, h_l and g_l are vectors of local-constraint functions that involve S_l and time in stage t; and H and G are vectors of global-constraint functions that involve state variables and time in two or more stages.

We define the neighborhood of a solution path $p = (S_0,\dots,S_k)$ as follows. The *partitionable (mixed) neighborhood* of a path p is defined as

$$N(p) = \bigcup_{l=0}^{k} N^{(l)}(p) = \bigcup_{l=0}^{k} \{p' \mid S'_l \in N(S_l) \text{ and } \forall\, i \neq l : S_i = S'_i,\},$$

where $N(p_l)$ is the state space neighborhood of state vector S_l in stage l. Intuitively, $N(p)$ is partitioned into $k+1$ disjoint sets of neighborhoods, each perturbing one of the stages.

Here $N(p)$ includes all paths that are identical to S in all stages except l, where $S(l)$ is perturbed to a neighboring state in $N(S_l)$. For example, let $N(2) = \{1,3\}$ for each stage in a three-stage problem and $p = (2,2,2)$. Then $N(p)$ is given by $\{(1,2,2),(3,2,2)\}$, $\{(2,1,2),(2,3,2)\}$, and $\{(2,2,1),(2,2,3)\}$; that is, the union of the perturbation of p in stages 1, 2, and 3.

Algorithm 14.17 gives the iterative algorithm for computing an optimal solution. For a fixed γ and ν the program finds S_l that solves the following mixed-integer linear program in stage l: $\min_{S_l} J(S) + \gamma^T H(S) + \eta^T G(S)$ subject to $h_l(S_l) = 0$ and $g_l(S_l) \leq 0$. As a result, the solution of the original problem is now reduced to solving multiple smaller subproblems of which the solutions are collectively necessary for the final solution. Therefore, the approach reduces significantly the efforts in finding a solution, since the size of each partition will lead to a reduction of the base of the exponential complexity when a problem is partitioned.

The entire Lagrangian function that is minimized is

$$L(S,\alpha,\beta,\gamma,\eta) = J(S) + \sum_{l=0}^{k} \left\{ \alpha(l)^T |h_l(S_l)| + \beta(l)^T \max\{0, g_l(S_l)\} \right\} + \gamma^T |H(S)| + \eta^T \max\{0, G(S)\}.$$

As in Theorem 14.3, necessary and sufficient conditions for L can be established, showing that algorithm *Lagrangian Search* will terminate with an optimal solution.

Procedure Lagrangian-Search
Input: State space problem
Output: Solution path that minimizes objective function

$\gamma \leftarrow 0; \eta \leftarrow 0$	;; Initialize global Lagrange multipliers
while CLM is not found	;; Global constraints satisfied
incr. γ_i (resp. η_i) by δ if $H_i(S) \neq 0$ (resp. $G_j(S) \not\leq 0$)	;; Update global multipliers
$\alpha(t) \leftarrow 0; \beta(t) \leftarrow 0$	;; Initialize local Lagrange multipliers
while $h(S_l) \neq 0$ or $g(S_l) > 0$	;; Local constraints satisfied
if $(h_i(S_l) \neq 0$ resp. $g_i(S_l) \not\leq 0)$	;; Determine slack
increase $\alpha_i(l)$ resp. $\beta_i(l)$ by δ	;; Update local multipliers
while local minimum of L not found	;; Local improvement
perform decent on L with respect to $S \in N^l(S)$	;; Local search algorithm
return CLM	;; Feedback solution

Algorithm 14.17

Lagrangian method for finding a CLM.

14.10 *NO-FREE-LUNCH

Despite all successes in problem solving, it is clear that a general problem solver which solves all optimization problems is not to be expected. With their *no-free-lunch theorems*, Wolpert and Macready have shown that any search strategy performs exactly the same when averaged over all possible cost functions. If some algorithm outperforms another on some cost function, then the latter one must outperform the former one on others. A universally best algorithm does not exist. Even random searchers will perform the same on average on all possible search spaces. Other no-free-lunch theorems show that even learning does not help. Consequently, there is no universal search heuristic. However, there is some hope. By considering specific domain classes of practical interest, the knowledge of these domains can certainly increase performance. Loosely speaking, we trade the efficiency gain in the selected problem classes with the loss in other classes. The knowledge we encode in search heuristics reflects state space properties that can be exploited.

A good advice for a programmer is to learn different state space search techniques and understand the problem to be solved. The ability to devise effective and efficient search algorithms and heuristics in new situations is a skill that separates the master programmer from the moderate one. The best way to develop that skill is to solve problems.

14.11 SUMMARY

In this chapter, we studied search methods that are not necessarily complete but often find solutions of high quality fast. We did this in the context of solving optimization problems in general and used, for example, traveling salesperson problems as examples. Many of these search methods then also apply to path planning problems, for example, by ordering the actions available in states and then encoding paths as sequences of action indices.

The no-free-lunch theorems show that a universally best-search algorithm does not exist since they all perform the same when averaged over all possible cost functions. Thus, search algorithms need to be specific to individual classes of search problems.

Complete search methods are able to find solutions with maximal quality. Approximate search methods utilize the structure of search problems to find solutions of which the quality is only a certain factor away from maximal. Approximate search methods are only known for a small number of search problems. More general search methods typically cannot make such guarantees. They typically use hill-climbing (local search) to improve an initial random solution repeatedly until it can no longer be improved, a process that is often used in nature, such as in evolution or for path finding by ants. They often find solutions of high quality fast but do not know how good their solutions are.

To use search methods based on hill-climbing, we need to carefully define which solutions are neighbors of a given solution, since search methods based on hill-climbing always move from the current solution to a neighboring solution. The main problem of search methods based on hill-climbing are local maxima since they cannot improve the current solution any longer once they are at a local maximum. Thus, they use a variety of techniques to soften the problem of local maxima. For example, random restarts allow search methods based on hill-climbing to find several solutions and return the one with the highest quality. Randomization allows search methods based on hill-climbing to be less greedy yet simple, for example, by moving to any neighboring solution of the current solution that increases the quality of the current solution rather than only the neighboring solution that increases the quality of the current solution the most. Simulated annealing allows search methods based on hill-climbing to move to a neighboring solution of the current solution that decreases the quality. The probability of making such a move is larger the less the quality decreases and the sooner the move is made. Tabu search allows search methods based on hill-climbing to avoid previous solutions. Genetic algorithms allow search methods based on hill-climbing to combine parts of two solutions (recombinations) and to perturb them (mutations).

Although most of the chapter was dedicated to discrete search problems, we also showed how hill-climbing applies to continuous search problems in the context of hill-climbing for continuous nonlinear programming.

In Table 14.1 we have summarized the selective search strategies as proposed in this chapter. All algorithms find local optimum solutions, but in some cases arguments are given for why the local optimum should not be far off from the global optimum. In this case we wrote *Global* together with a star denoting that this will be achieved only in the theoretical limit, not in practice. We give some hints on the nature of theoretical analyses behind it, and the main principle that is simulated to overcome the state explosion problem.

Table 14.2 summarizes the results of randomized search in k-SAT problems, showing the base α in the runtime complexity of $O(\alpha^n)$. We see that for larger values of k the values converge to 2. In fact, compared to the naive $O(2^k)$ algorithm with base $\alpha = 2$, there is no effective strategy with better α in general SAT problems.

Table 14.1 Overview of selective search algorithms.

Algorithm	Optimum	Neighbors	Principle
Simulated annealing (14.2)	Global*	General	Temperature
Tabu (14.3)	Local	General	Forced cuts
Randomized tabu (14.4)	Local	General	Forced/random cuts
Randomized local search (14.5)	Local	Boolean	Selective/mutation
$(1+1)$ GA (14.6)	Global*	Boolean	Selective/mutation
Simple GA (14.7)	Global*	General	Selective/mutation/recombination
Vertex Ant search (14.15)	Cover	Specific	Pheromones
Ant search (14.13)	Global*	Specific	Pheromones
Flood (14.14)	Local	General	Water level
Lagrangian (14.16,14.17)	CLM	MIXED	Multipliers

Table 14.2 Runtime results for k-SAT.

k-SAT, $k =$	3	4	5	6	7	8
Brute-force	2	2	2	2	2	2
Backtrack	1.91	1.97	1.99	1.99	1.99	1.99
Monien-Speckenmeyer (14.9)	1.61	1.83	1.92	1.96	1.98	1.99
Paturi-Pudlák-Zane (14.10)	1.58	1.68	1.74	1.78	1.81	1.83
Hamming-sphere (14.11)	1.5	1.6	1.66	1.71	1.75	1.77
Random-walk (14.12)	1.33	1.5	1.6	1.66	1.71	1.75

14.12 EXERCISES

14.1 Validate empirically that the phase transition for 3-SAT is located at $m \approx 4.25n$ by randomly generating 3-SAT formulas and running an SAT solver.

14.2 In this exercise we develop a randomized $(3/4)$-approximation of MAX-2-SAT.

1. Give a randomized $(1 - 2^{-k})$-approximation (RA) that simply selects a random assignment. Given clauses C of length k show that the probability that clause C is satisfied is $1 - 2^{-k}$.

2. Illustrate the working of *randomized rounding* (RR) where an SAT formula is substituted by a linear program (LP), for example, clause $C_j = (x_1 \vee \overline{x_2})$ is converted to

$$\max \sum_{j=1}^{m} z_j \quad \text{subject to} \quad y_1 + (1 - y_2) \geq z_j \text{ for } 0 \leq y_i, z_j \leq 1.$$

Then the solutions are computed with an efficient LP solver. The solutions are taken as probabilities to draw Boolean values for the assignment variables.

3. Show that the combined run of RA and RR yields a $(3/4)$-approximation for MAX-2-SAT. Instead of proving the theorem formally, you may work out a small example.

14.3 As another example for a randomized algorithm we chose the probabilistic reduction of three-dimensional matching (3-DM) on 2-SAT. The idea is as follows. With probability of $1/3$ one of the colors in $f : V \to \{1,2,3\}$ is omitted. The resulting problem is converted into a 2-SAT instance with variables $x_{v,j}$ (v for the node and j for the color). The clauses are of the form $(x_{v,i} \lor x_{v,j})$ and $(\overline{x_{u,1}} \lor \overline{x_{v,1}}) \land (\overline{x_{u,2}} \lor \overline{x_{v,2}}) \land (\overline{x_{u,3}} \lor \overline{x_{v,3}})$.

1. Show that the probability of the correct choice of colors is $(2/3)^n$.

2. Show that we need $t \in O(1.5^n \cdot \ln(1/\epsilon)) = O(1.5^n)$ iterations for a running time of $O(poly(n) \cdot 1.5^n) \doteq O(1.5^n)$.

3. Using this reduction principle to show that a CSP with binary constraints (the domain of each variable is D) is solvable in time $O(p(n) \cdot (|D|/2)^n)$.

14.4 Most k-SAT solvers can be extended to constraint satisfaction problems (CSP), where k is the order of the constraints and assignments. For the sake of simplicity assume that the domains of all variables are the same (D).

1. For *Hamming sphere* infer a runtime of $O\left(\left(|D| \cdot \frac{k}{k+1}\right)^n\right)$.

2. For *random walk* establish a runtime of $O((|D| \cdot (1 - 1/k))^n)$. Show that for $k = 2$, this bound for *random walk* matches the one obtained for reduction in the previous exercise.

14.5 The algorithm of Monien-Speckenmeyer has been improved by using *autarkic* assignments. An assignment b is called *autarkic* for f, if all clauses, with at least one b variable, are already satisfied. For example, the assignment $b = (0,0)$ is autarkic for $f = (\neg x_1 \lor x_2 \lor x_4) \land (x_1 \lor \neg x_2 \lor x_3) \land (x_3 \lor \neg x_4) \land (x_3 \lor x_4 \lor x_5)$, since only the first two clauses contain x_1 and x_2, and these clauses are set to 1 by b.

1. Give another autarkic assignment for f.

2. Describe the changes to the algorithm of Monien and Speckenmeyer to include autarkic assignments.

14.6 Change the order of Ws and Bs in _WWWBBB to WWWBBB_. You are allowed to jump over at most two places provided that the target location is free. It is not required that the empty place is in the front.

1. Determine an optimal solution by hand.

2. Use an evaluation function that counts the number of Bs to the left of each W, summed over all three Ws. Apply genetic heuristic search to find a solution.

14.7 Consider Simple-GA on the fitness function $f(x) = 3 - (x - 2)^2$, with $x \in \{1, \ldots, 10\}$ by using a binary string encoding of the two individuals $p = 1$ and $q = 10$.

1. Determine the maximum of the function analytically.

2. Does the algorithm arrive at the optimum using bit mutation and 1-point crossover, both with regard to random bit positions?

14.8 Implement and run genetic heuristic search to the same instance. Use 100 randomly generated paths of length 65 to start with and apply 1,000 iterations of the algorithm.

14.9 Consider the two parents $p = (01001101)$ and $q = (11100011)$ for a crossover application. Obtain the children of p and q obtained by
   1. 1-point crossover (at index $l = 5$).
   2. 1-point crossover ($l = 3$, $r = 6$).
   3. Uniform crossover ($b = (00110011)$).

14.10 Perform VAW on the graph of Figure 14.11.
   1. Denote the tuples $(u_t, h(u_t), \tau(u_t))$, $t \in \{1, \ldots, 18\}$ starting at node 1.
   2. When is the graph completely covered?
   3. How long is the limit cycle?
   4. Denote the node sequence in the final tour as a regular expression.
   5. Is the limit cycle Hamiltonian?

14.11 Perform VAW on the graph of Figure 14.12.
   1. Denote the tuples $(u_t, h(u_t), \tau(u_t))$, $t \in \{1, \ldots, 36\}$ starting at node 1.
   2. When is the graph completely covered?
   3. How long is the limit cycle?
   4. Denote the node sequence in the final tour as a regular expression.
   5. Is the limit cycle Hamiltonian?

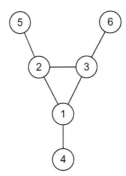

FIGURE 14.11

An example graph for the vertex ant walk.

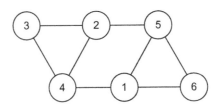

FIGURE 14.12

Another example graph for the vertex ant walk.

14.12 Devise an undirected graph that omits a Hamiltonian path that is not recognized by the VAW process. (There is one with nine nodes.)

14.13 For algorithm *Flood* take function $height(x,y) = -(x-4)^2 + -(y-6)^4$ to be optimized, with respect to a 10×10 grid. Start with $n = 20$ active ants at random position. Initialize W to 0 and increase it by 0.1 for each iteration.

14.14 Express the previous exercises now with real values on $[0,10] \times [0,10]$ as a continuous nonlinear programming task.
  1. What is the constraint local minimum (CLM) for this function?
  2. Express the optimization problem with Lagrangian multipliers.
  3. Is it the global optimum?

14.15 Heuristics for discrete domains are often found by relaxation of the problem formulation from an integer program to a linear program.
  1. Formulate KNAPSACK as a (0/1) integer program.
  2. Relax the integrality constraints to derive an upper bound on KNAPSACK.

14.16 In the LADDER problem a ladder leans across a five-foot fence, just touching a high wall three feet behind the fence.
  1. What is the minimum possible length l of the ladder? Use standard calculus. Hint: The formula $(a+3)^2 + (b+5)^2 = l^2$ describes a circle with center $(-3,-5)$ and radius L. The proportionality of base and height for the two smaller right triangles yields $ab = 15$. Substitute this in the first equation to obtain the single-variable function.
  2. Provide the objective function $F(a,b)$ with constraint function $G(a,b) = 0$ and solve the problem using Lagrange multipliers to find a set of three equations in three unknowns.

14.17 Consider now the TWO LADDER problem with two ladders of lengths l and l' leaning across two walls of given heights $h = 10$ and $h' = 15$ bordering a gap of given width $W = 50$ (see Fig. 14.13). The lower ends of the ladders are placed at distances d' and d' from the walls, so that their upper ends meet at a point above the water. The two ladders are supported in place by each other as well as by the two walls. The problem is to find this minimal sum of l and l'.
  1. Model and solve the problem by ordinary calculus.
  2. Model and solve the problem as a Lagrange optimization problem.

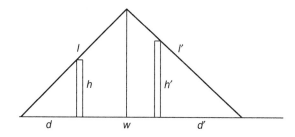

FIGURE 14.13

The TWO LADDER problem.

14.13 BIBLIOGRAPHIC NOTES

Hill-climbing and gradient decent algorithms belong to the folklore of computer science. Algorithm *flood* is a version of *simulated annealing*, which has been introduced by Kirkpatrick, Jr., and Vecchi (1983). Randomized tabu search appeared in Faigle and Kern (1992). Annealing applies to optimization problems where direct methods are trapped; while *simulated tempering*, for example, by Marinari and Parisi (1992) and *swapping* by Zheng (1999) are applied when direct methods perform poorly. The standard approach for sampling via Markov chain Monte Carlo from nonuniform distributions is the Metropolis algorithm (Metropolis, Rosenbluth, Rosenbluth, Teller, and Teller, 1953). There is a nice discussion about lifting space and solution state spaces in the beginning by Hoos and Stützle (2004).

Ant walk generalized the use of *diminishing pebbles* by a model of odor markings. Vertex ant walk has been introduced by Wagner, Lindenbaum, and Bruckstein (1998). It is a reasonable trade-off between sensitive DFS and self-avoiding walk by Madras and Slade (1993). Edge ant walk has been proposed by Wagner, Lindenbaum, and Bruckstein (1996). Thrun (1992) has described *counterbased exploration* methods, which is similar to VAW, but the upper bound shown there on the cover time is $O(n^2 d)$, where d is the diameter and n is the number of vertices.

Satisfiability problems have been referenced in the previous chapter. Known approximation ratios for MAX-SAT are 0.7846; MAX-3-SAT, 7/8, upper bound 7/8; MAX-2-SAT, 0.941, upper bound 21/22=0.954; MAX-2-SAT with additional cardinality constraints, 0.75; see Hofmeister (2003). Many inapproximability results are based on the *PCP theory*, denoting that the class of NP is equal to a certain class of probabilistically checkable proofs (PCP). For example, this theory implies that there is an $\epsilon > 0$, so that it is NP-hard to find an $(1 - \epsilon)$ approximation for MAX-3-SAT. PCP theory has been introduced by Arora (1995). The technical report based on the author's PhD thesis contains the complete proof of the PCP theorem, and basic relations to approximation algorithms.

The algorithms of Monien and Speckenmeyer (1985) and of Paturi, Pudlák, and Zane (1977) have been improved by the analysis of Schöning (2002), who has also studied *random walk* and *Hamming sphere* as presented in the text. Hofmeister, Schöning, Schuler, and Watanabe (2002) have improved the runtime of a randomized solution to 3-SAT to $O(1.3302^n)$, and Baumer and Schuler (2003) have further reduced it to $O(1.329^n)$. A deterministic algorithm with a performance bound of $O((2 - \frac{2}{k+1})^n)$ has been suggested by Dantsin, Goerdt, Hirsch, and Schöning (2000). The $(2^{n-\Theta(n/\lg n)})$ lower-bound result of Miltersen, Radhakrishnan, and Wegener (2005) shows that a conversion of conjunctive normal for (CNF) to disjunctive normal form (DNF) is almost exponential. This suggest that $O(\alpha^n)$ algorithms for general SAT with $\alpha < 2$ are not immediate.

Genetic algorithms are of widespread use with their own community and conferences. Initial work on genetic programming including the *Schema Theorem* has been presented by Holland (1975). A broad survey has been established in the triology by Koza (1992, 1994) and Koza, Bennett, Andre, and Keane (1999). Schwefel (1995) has applied evolutionary algorithms to optimize airplane turbines. Genetic path search has been introduced in the context of model checking by Godefroid and Khurshid (2004).

Ant algorithms also span a broad community with their own conferences. A good starting point is the special issue on *Ant Algorithms and Swarm Intelligence* by Dorigo, Gambardella, Middendorf, and Stützle (2002), and a book by Dorigo and Stützle (2004). The ant algorithm for TSP is due to Gambardella and Dorigo (1996). It has been generalized by Dorigo, Maniezzo, and Colorni (1996).

There is a rising interest in *(particle) swarm optimization algorithms (PSO)*, a population-based stochastic optimization technique that originally has been developed by Kennedy and Eberhart. It closely relates to genetic algorithms with different recombination and mutation operators (Kennedy, Eberhart, and Shi, 2001). Applications include time-tabling as considered by Chu, Chen, and Ho (2006), or stuff scheduling as studied by Günther and Nissen (2010).

Mathematical programming has a long tradition with a broad spectrum of existing techniques especially for continuous and mixed-integer optimization. The book *Nonlinear Programming* by Avriel (1976) provides a good starting point. For CNLP, Karush, Kuhn, and Tucker (see Bertsekas, 1999) have given another necessary condition. If only equality constraints are present in P_c, we have $n + m$ equations with $n + m$ unknowns (x, λ) to be solved by iterative approaches like *Newton's method*. A *static penalty approach* transforms P_c into the unconstraint problem $L_\rho(x, \alpha, \beta) = f(x) + \alpha^T |h(x)|^\rho + \beta^T \max\{0, g(x)\}^\rho$ very similar to the one considered in the text (set $\rho = 1$). However, the algorithm may be hard to carry out in practice because the global optimum of L_ρ needs to hold for all points in the search space, making α and β very large.

Mixed-integer NLP methods generally decompose MINLP into subproblems in such a way that after fixing a subset of the variables, each resulting subproblem is convex and easily solvable, or can be relaxed and approximated. There are four main types: *generalized Benders decomposition* by Geoffrion (1972), *outer approximation* by Duran and Grossmann (1986), *generalized cross-decomposition* by Holmberg (1990), and *branch and reduce methods* by Ryoo and Sahinidis (1996).

There is some notion of completeness for selective algorithms called *probabilistic approximate completeness* (PAC) (Hoos and Stützle, 1999). Randomized algorithms, which are not PAC, are essentially incomplete. The intuition is that if the algorithm is left to run infinitely, a PAC algorithm will almost certainly find a solution, if it exists. In other words, algorithms that are PAC can never get trapped in nonsolution regions of the search space. However, they may still require a very long time to escape from such regions; see, for example, Hoos and Stützle (2004). Whether this theoretical property has practical impact is uncertain. This may change, if combined with results on the failure probability's rate of convergence.

The first *no-free-lunch theorems* have been given by Wolpert and Macready (1996). Culberson (1998b) has given an algorithmic view of *no-free-lunch*. More recent results on the NFL theory have been established by Droste, Jansen, and Wegener (1999, 2002).

Heuristic Search Applications

Action Planning

15

In domain-independent action planning, a running system must be able to find plans and exploit search knowledge fully automatically. In this chapter we concentrate on *deterministic planning* (each action application produces exactly one successor) with no uncertainty in the environment and no observation to infer otherwise inaccessible state variables. The input of a planning problem consists of a set of state variables, an initial state in the form of value assignments to the variables, a goal (condition), and a set of actions. A plan is a sequence (or schedule) of actions that eventually maps the initial state into one that satisfies the goal.

The *problem domain description language* (PDDL) allows flexible specifications of domain models and problem instances. Starting from problems described in STRIPS notation (as introduced in Ch. 1), PDDL has grown to an enormous expressive power, including large fragments of first-order logic to combine propositional expressions, numerical state variables to feature the handling of real-valued quantities, and constraints to impose additional restrictions for the set of valid plans. *Metric planning* introduces planning with costs, and *temporal planning* covers action duration. The agreed standard for PDDL encompasses the following hierarchy of expressiveness.

Level 1: Propositional Planning. This level includes all sorts of propositional description languages. It unifies STRIPS-type planning with the *abstract description language* (ADL). ADL allows typed domain objects and any bounded quantification over these. ADL also includes negated and disjunctive preconditions, and conditional effects. While the former two language extensions can be easily compiled away (by introducing negated predicates and by splitting the actions), the latter ones are *essential* in the sense that their compilation may induce an exponential increase in the problem specification. Propositional planning is decidable, but PSPACE-hard.

Level 2: Metric Planning. This level introduces numerical state variables, so-called *fluents*, and an objective function to be optimized (the *domain metric*) that judges plan quality. Instead of Boolean values to be associated with each grounded atom, the language extension enables the processing of continuous quantities, an important requirement for modeling many real-world domains. This growing expressiveness comes at a high price. Metric planning is *undecidable* even for very restricted problem classes (a decision problem is undecidable if is impossible to construct one computable function that always terminates and leads to a correct answer). This, however, does not mean that metric planners cannot succeed in finding plans for concrete problem instances.

Level 3: Temporal Planning. This level introduces *duration*, which denotes action execution time. The duration can be a constant quantity or a numerical expression dependent on the current assignment to state variables. Two different semantics have been proposed. In the *PDDL* *semantics* each temporal action is divided into an initial, an invariant, and a final happening. Many temporal planners, however, assume the simpler *black-box semantics*. The common task is to find a *temporal plan*, i.e., a set of actions together with their starting times. This plan is either *sequential* (simulating additive action costs) or *parallel* (allowing the concurrent execution of actions). The minimal execution time of such a temporal plan is its *makespan*, and can be included as one objective in the domain metric.

More and more features have been attached to this hierarchy. Domain axioms in the form of *derived predicates* introduce inference rules, and *timed initial facts* allow action execution windows and deadlines to be specified. Newer developments of PDDL focus on temporal and preference constraints for plans. Higher levels support continuous processes and triggered events.

The results of the biennial *international planning competitions* (started in 1998) show that planners keep aligned with the language extensions, while preserving good performances in finding and optimizing plans. Besides algorithmic contributions, the achievements also refer to the fact that computers have increased in their processing power and memory resources.

As a consequence, modern action planning is apparently suited to provide prototypical solutions to specific problems. In fact, action planning becomes more and more application oriented. To indicate the range and flavor of applicability of modern action planning, we list some examples that have been proposed as benchmarks in the context of international planning competitions.

AIRPORT The task is to control the ground traffic on an airport, assigning travel routes and times to the airplanes, so that the outbound traffic has taken off and the inbound traffic is parked. The main problem constraint is to ensure the safety of the airplanes. The aim is to minimize the total travel time of all airplanes.

PIPESWORLD The task is to control the flow of different and possibly conflicting oil derivatives through a pipeline network, so that certain product amounts are transported to their destinations. Pipeline networks are modeled as graphs consisting of areas (nodes) and pipes (edges), where the pipes can differ in length.

PROMELA The task is to validate state properties in systems of communicating processes. In particular, deadlock states shall be detected, i.e., states where none of the processes can apply a transition. For example, a process may be blocked when trying to read data from an empty communication channel.

POWER SUPPLY RESTORATION The task is to reconfigure a faulty electricity network, so that a maximum of nonfaulty lines is supplied. There is uncertainty about the status of the network, and various numerical parameters must be optimized.

SATELLITE The domain is inspired from a NASA application, where satellites have to take images of spatial phenomena and send them back to Earth. In an extended setting, timeframes for sending messages to the ground stations are imposed.

ROVERS The domain (also inspired from a NASA application) models the problem of planning for a group of planetary rovers to explore the planet they are on, for example, by taking pictures and samples from interesting objects.

STORAGE The domain involves spatial reasoning and is about moving a certain number of crates from some containers to some depots by hoists. Inside a depot, each hoist can move according to a specified spatial map connecting different areas of the depot.

TRAVELING PURCHASE PROBLEM A generalization of the TSP. We have a set of products and a set of markets. Each market is provided with a limited amount of each product at a known price. The task is to find a subset of the markets such that a given demand of each product can be purchased, minimizing the routing and the purchasing costs.

OPENSTACK A manufacturer has a number of orders, each for a combination of different products, and can make one product at a time only. The total required quantity of each product is made at the same time. From the time that the first product (included in an order) is made to the time that all products (included in the order) have been made, the order is said to be open. During this time it requires a stack. The problem is to order the production of the different products, so that the maximum number of stacks that are in use simultaneously is minimized.

TRUCKS Essentially, this is a logistics domain about moving packages between locations by trucks under certain constraints. The loading space of each truck is organized by areas: a package can be loaded onto an area of a truck only if the areas between the area under consideration and the truck door are free. Moreover, some packages must be delivered within given deadlines.

SETTLERS The task is to build up an infrastructure in an unsettled area, involving the building of housing, railway tracks, sawmills, etc. The distinguishing feature of the domain is that most of the domain semantics are encoded with numeric variables.

UMTS The task is the optimization of the call setup for mobile applications. A refined schedule for the setup is needed to order and accelerate the execution of the application modules that are invoked during the call setup.

Probably the most important contribution to cope with the intrinsic difficulty of domain-independent planning was the development of search guidance in the form of generic heuristics. In the following, we introduce designs for planning heuristics and show how to tackle more expressive planning formalisms, like metric and temporal planning, as well as planning with constraints.

15.1 OPTIMAL PLANNING

Optimal planners compute the best possible plan. They minimize the number of (sequential or parallel) plan steps or optimize the plan with respect to the plan metric. There are many different proposals for optimal planning, ranging from plan graph encoding, satisfiability solving, integer programming to constraint satisfaction, just to name a few. Many modern approaches consider heuristic search planning based on admissible estimates.

We first introduce optimal planning via layered planning graphs and via satisfiability planning. Next, admissible heuristics are devised that are based on dynamic programming or on pattern databases.

15.1.1 *Graphplan*

Graphplan is a parallel-optimal planner for propositional planning problems. The rough working of the *Graphplan* algorithm is the following. First, the parametric input is grounded. Starting with a planning graph, which only consists of the initial state in the first layer, the graph is incrementally constructed. In one stage of the algorithm, the planning graph is extended with one action and one propositional layer followed by a graph extraction phase. If this search terminates with no solution, the plan horizon is extended with one additional layer. As an example, consider the ROCKET domain for transporting cargo in space (see Fig. 15.1). The layered planning graph is shown in Table 15.1.

In the forward phase the next action layer is determined as follows. For each action and each instantiation of it, a node is inserted, provided that no two preconditions are marked as mutually exclusive (*mutex*). Two propositions *a* and *b* are marked mutex, if all options to generate *a* are exclusive to all options to generate *b*. Additionally, so-called *noop* actions are included that merely propagate existing propositions to the next layer. Next, the actions are tested for exclusiveness and for each action a list of all other actions is recorded, for which they are exclusive. To generate the next propositional layer, the add-effects are inserted and taken as the input for the next stage.

```
(:action move
:parameters (?r - rocket ?from ?to - place)
:precondition (and (at ?r ?from) (has-fuel ?r))
:effect (and (at ?r ?to) (not (at ?r ?from)) (not (has-fuel ?r))))
(:action load
:parameters (?r - rocket ?p - place ?c - cargo)
:precondition (and (at ?r ?p) (at ?c ?p))
:effect (and (in ?c ?r) (not (at ?c ?p))))
(:action unload
:parameters (?r - rocket ?p - place ?c - cargo)
:precondition (and (at ?r ?p) (in ?c ?r))
:effect (and (at ?c ?p) (not (in ?c ?r))))
```

FIGURE 15.1

Some actions in the ROCKET domain.

Table 15.1 Layered planning graph for the ROCKET domain. Propositional and action levels alternate. First propositional level includes the initial state. The action layer i contains all actions with preconditions satisfied in propositional layer $i - 1$. A proposition is added to layer i if it is already contained in layer $i - 1$ or there is an applicable action that has the proposition as an add-effect.

Prop. Level 1	Action Level 1	Prop. Level 2	Action Level 2	Prop. Level 3
	(load b l)	(in b r)	(noop)	(in b r)
	(load a l)	(in a r)	(noop)	(in a r)
	(move l p)	(at r p)	(noop)	(at r p)
			(unload a p)	(at a p)
			(unload b p)	(at b p)
(at a l)	(noop)	(at a l)	(noop)	(at a l)
(at b l)	(noop)	(at b l)	(noop)	(at b l)
(at r l)	(noop)	(at r l)	(noop)	(at r l)
(fuel r)	(noop)	(fuel r)	(noop)	(fuel r)

A fixpoint is reached when the set of propositions no longer changes. As one subtle problem, this test for termination is not sufficient. Consider a goal in BLOCKSWORLD given by (on a b), (on b c), and (on c a). Every two conditions are satisfiable but not all three all together. Thus, the forward phase terminates if the set of propositions *and* the goal set in the previous stage have not changed.

It is not difficult to see that the size of the planning graph is polynomial in the number n of objects, the number m of action schemas, the number p of propositions in the initial state, the length l of the longest add-list, and the number of layers in the planning graph. Let k be the largest number of action parameters. The number of instantiated effects is bounded by $O(ln^k)$. Therefore, the maximal number of nodes in every propositional layer is bounded by $O(p + mln^k)$. Since every action schema can be instantiated in at most $O(n^k)$ different ways, the maximal number of nodes in each action layer is bounded by $O(mn^k)$.

In the generated planning graph, *Graphplan* constructs a valid plan, chaining backward from the set of goals. In contrast to most other planners, this processing works layer by layer to take care of preserving the mutex relations. For a given time step t, *Graphplan* tries to extract all possible actions (including noops) from time step $t - 1$, which has the current subgoal as add-effects. The preconditions for these actions build the subgoals to be satisfied in time step $t - 1$ to satisfy the chosen subgoal at time step t. If the set of subgoals is not solvable, *Graphplan* chooses a different set of actions, and recurs until all subgoals are satisfied or all possible combinations have been exhausted. In the latter case, no plan (with respect to the imposed depth threshold) exists, as it can be shown that *Graphplan* terminates with failure if and only if there is no solution to the current planning problem. The complexity of the backward phase is exponential (and has to be unless PSPACE = P). By its layered construction, *Graphplan* constructs a plan that has the smallest number of parallel plan steps.

15.1.2 *Satplan*

To cast a fully instantiated action planning task as a satisfiability problem we assign to each proposition a time stamp denoting when it is valid. As an example, for the initial state and goal condition of a sample BLOCKSWORLD instance, we may have generated the formula

$$(\text{on } a\,b\,1) \wedge (\text{on } b\,t\,1) \wedge (\text{clear } a\,1) \wedge (\text{on } b\,a\,3).$$

Further formulas express action execution. They include action effects, such as

$$\forall\, x, y, z, i : (\text{on } x\,y\,i) \wedge (\text{clear } x\,i) \wedge (\text{clear } z\,i) \wedge (\text{move } x\,y\,z\,i) \Rightarrow$$
$$(\text{on } x\,z\,i+1) \wedge (\text{clear } y\,i+1)$$

and *noop* clauses for propositions to persist. To express that no action with unsatisfied precondition is executed, we may introduce rules, in which additional action literals imply their preconditions, such as

$$\forall\, x, y, z, i : (\text{move } x\,y\,z\,i) \Rightarrow (\text{clear } x\,i) \wedge (\text{clear } z\,i) \wedge (\text{on } x\,y\,i).$$

Effects are dealt with analogously. Moreover, (for sequential plans) we have to express that at one point in time only one action can be executed. We have

$$\forall x, x', y, y', z, z', i : x \neq x' \vee y \neq y' \vee z \neq z' \Rightarrow \neg(\text{move } x\,y\,z\,i) \vee \neg(\text{move } x'\,y'\,z'\,i).$$

Finally, for a given step threshold N we require that at every step $i < N$ at least one action has to be executed; for all $i < N$ we require

$$\exists x, y, z : (\text{move } x \ y \ z \ i).$$

The only model of this planning problem is (move a b t 1), (move b t a 2). *Satplan* is a combination of a planning problem encoding and an SAT solver. The planner's performance participates in the development of more and more efficient SAT solvers.

Extensions of *Satplan* to parallel planning encode the planning graph and the mutexes of *Graphplan*. For this approach, *Satplan* does not find the plan with the minimal total number of steps, but the one with the minimal number of parallel steps.

15.1.3 Dynamic Programming

One of the first estimates for heuristic search planning is the *max-atom* heuristic. It is an approximation of the optimal cost for solving a relaxed problem in which the delete lists are ignored. An illustration is provided in Figure 15.2 (left).

The heuristic is based on dynamic programming. Consider a propositional and grounded propositional planning problem $P = (S, A, s, T)$ (see Ch. 1) with planning states u and v, and propositions p and q. Value $h(u) = \sum_{p \in T} g(u, p)$ is the sum of the approximations $g(u, p)$, to reach p from u, where

$$g(u, p) = \min\{g(u, p), 1 + \max_{q \in pre(a)} g(u, q) \mid p \in add(a), a \in A\}$$

is a fixpoint equation. The recursion starts with $g(u, p) = 0$, for $p \in u$, and $g(u, p) = \infty$, otherwise. The values of g are computed iteratively, until the values no longer change. The costs $g(u, C)$ for the set C is computed as $g(u, C) = \sum_{p \in C} g(u, p)$. In fact, the cost of achieving all the propositions in a set can be computed as either a sum (if sequentiality is assumed) or as a max (if parallelism is assumed instead). The *max-atom heuristic* chooses the maximum of the cost values with $g(u, C) = \max_{p \in C} g(u, p)$. The pseudo code is shown in Algorithm 15.1. This heuristic is consistent, since by taking the maximum cost values, the heuristic on an edge can decrease by at most 1.

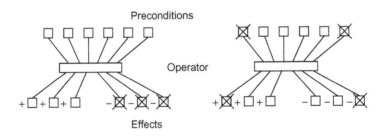

FIGURE 15.2

Schematic view on action abstractions for max-atom (left) and pattern database heuristic (right). The preconditions of the abstract actions are shown in the form of boxes on top of it, while the effects (separated in add (+) and delete (−) effects) are shown in the form of boxes below it. Marked boxes refer to facts that have been eliminated in the relaxation of the problem.

Procedure Max-Atom
Input: State space planning problem P
Output: Max atom heuristic for T

for each $p \in AP$: $g(p) \leftarrow \infty$	;; Initialize distance array to default
for each $p \in u$: $g(p) \leftarrow 0$	;; Initialize distance array to current state
$v \leftarrow u$; $u \leftarrow \emptyset$	;; Initialize relaxed traversal
while $(u \neq v)$	;; Termination criterion: no change
for each $a \in \{a' \in A \mid pre(a') \subseteq v\}$	;; For all enabled actions
$p_{\max} \leftarrow$ **arg max**$_{p \in pre(a)}\{g(p)\}$	;; Most costly precondition
for each $r \in add(a)$	;; Consider all add-effects
if $(1 + p_{\max} \leq g(r))$ $g(r) \leftarrow 1 + p_{\max}$	;; Improve value
$u \leftarrow v$	;; Mark previous state
$v \leftarrow u \cup add(a)$	;; Apply op (without delete list)
return $\max_{p \in T} g(p)$	

Algorithm 15.1

Max-atom heuristic.

As the heuristic determines the backward distance of atoms with respect to the initial state, the previous definition of the heuristic is of use only for *backward* or *regression search*. However, it is not difficult to implement a variant that is applicable to *forward* or *progression search*, too.

The *max-atom* heuristic has been extended to *max-atom-pair* to include larger atom sets, which enlarges the extracted information (without losing admissibility) by approximating the costs of atom pairs:

$$g_2(u, \{p, q\}) = \min\{ \min_{a \in A(p \& q)} [1 + g_2(u, pre(a))],$$

$$\min_{a \in A(p|q)} [1 + g_2(u, pre(a) \cup \{p\}), \min_{a \in A(q|p)} [1 + g_2(u, pre(a) \cup \{q\})],$$

where $p \& q$ denotes that p and q are both contained in the add list of the action, and where $p|q$ denotes that p is contained in the add list and q is neither contained in the add list nor in the delete list. If all goal distances are precomputed, then these distances can be retrieved from a table, yielding a fast heuristic.

The extension to h^m with atom sets of $m \geq 2$ elements has to be expressed with the following recursion:

$$h^m(C) = \begin{cases} 0 & \text{if } C \subseteq u \text{ and } |C| \leq m \\ \min_{(D,O) \in R(C)} \{1 + h^m(D)\} & \text{if } C \not\subseteq u \text{ and } |C| \leq m, \\ \max_{D \subseteq C, |D| = m} h^m(D) & \text{if } |C| > m \end{cases}$$

where $R(C)$ denotes all pairs (D, O) that contain $C \cap add(a) \neq \emptyset$, $C \cap del(a) \neq \emptyset$, and $D = (C \setminus add(a)) \cup pre(a)$. It is rarely used in practice.

It has been argued that the layered arrangement of propositions in *Graphplan* can be interpreted as a special case of a search with h^2.

15.1.4 **Planning Pattern Databases**

In the following, we study how to apply *pattern databases* (see Ch. 4) to action planning. For a fixed state vector (in the form of a set of instantiated predicates) we provide a general abstraction function. The ultimate goal is to create admissible heuristics for planning problems fully automatically.

Planning patterns omit propositions from the planning space. Therefore, in an abstract planning problem with regard to a set $R \subseteq AP$, a domain abstraction is induced by $\phi(u) = u|_R = u \cap R$. (Later on we will discuss how R can be selected automatically.) The interpretation of ϕ is that all Boolean variables for propositions not in R are mapped to *don't care*. An *abstract planning problem* $P|_R = (S|_R, A|_R, s|_R, T|_R)$ of a propositional planning problem (S, A, s, T) with respect to a set of propositional atoms R is defined by $s|_R = s \cap R$, $S|_R = \{u|_R \mid u \in S\}$, $T|_R = \{t|_R \mid t \in T\}$, $A|_R = \{a|_R \mid a \in A\}$, where $a|_R$ for $a = (pre(a), add(a), del(a)) \in A$ is given as $a|_R = (pre(a)|_R, add(a)|_R, del(a)|_R)$. An illustration is provided in Figure 15.2 (right).

This means that abstract actions are derived from concrete ones by intersecting their precondition, add, and delete lists with the subset of predicates in the abstraction. Restriction of actions in the concrete space may yield *noop actions* $\phi_R(a) = (\emptyset, \emptyset, \emptyset)$ in the abstract planning problem, which are discarded from the action set $A|_R$.

A *planning pattern database* with respect to a set of propositions R and a propositional planning problem $P = (S, A, s, T)$ is a collection of pairs (d, v) with $v \in S|_R$ and d being the shortest distance to the abstract goal. Restriction $|_R$ is *solution preserving*; that is, for any sequential plan π for the propositional planning problem P there exists a plan π_R for the abstraction $P|_R = (S|_R, A|_R, s|_R, T|_R)$. Moreover, an optimal abstract plan for $P|_R$ is shorter than or equal to an optimal plan for P. Strict inequality holds if some abstract actions are noops, or if there are even shorter paths in the abstract space. We can also prove consistency of pattern database heuristics as follows. For each action a that maps u to v in the concrete space, we have $\phi(a)(\phi(u)) = \phi(v)$. By the triangular inequality of shortest paths, the abstract goal distance for $\phi(v)$ plus one is larger than or equal to the abstract goal distance $\phi(u)$.

Figure 15.3 illustrates a standard (left) and multiple pattern database (right) showing that different abstractions may refer to different parts of the state vector.

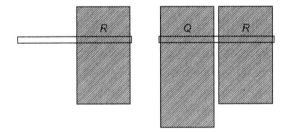

FIGURE 15.3

Standard (left) and multiple pattern (right) databases on sets of propositions R and Q. The horizontal ruler indicates the state vector. The rectangles illustrate the generated pattern databases on top of the selected support atoms (the rectangle widths correspond to the selected sets of propositions and rectangle heights correspond to the sizes of the databases).

Encoding

Propositional encodings are not necessarily the best state space representations for solving propositional planning problems. A multivalued variable encoding is often better. It transforms a propositional planning task into an SAS^+ *planning problem*, which is defined as a quintuple $P = (S, X, A, s, T)$, with $X = \{v_1, \ldots, v_n\}$ being a set of state variables of states in S (each $v \in X$ has finite-domain D_v), A being a set of actions given by a pair (P, E) for preconditions and effects, and s and T being the initial and goal state s, respectively, in the form of a partial assignment. A *partial assignment* for X is a function s over X, such that $s(v) \in D_v$, if $s(v)$ is defined.

The process of finding a suitable multivalued variable encoding is illustrated with a simple planning problem, where a truck is supposed to deliver a package from Los Angeles to San Francisco. The initial state is defined by the atoms (ispackage package), (istruck truck), (location los-angeles), (location san-francisco), (at package los-angeles), and (at truck los-angeles). Goal states have to satisfy the condition (at package san-francisco). The domain provides three action schemas named load to load a truck with a certain package at a certain location, the inverse operation unload, and drive to move a truck from one location to another.

The first preprocessing step will detect that only the at (denoting the presence of a given truck or package at a certain location) and in predicates (denoting that a package is loaded in a certain truck) change over time and need to be encoded. The labeling predicates ispackage, istruck, location are not affected by any action and thus do not need to be specified in a state encoding.

In a next step, some mutual exclusion constraints are discovered. In our case, we will detect that a given object will always be at or in at most one other object, so propositions such as (at package los-angeles) and (in package truck) are mutually exclusive. This result is complemented by *fact space exploration*: Ignoring negative (delete) effects of actions, we exhaustively enumerate all propositions that can be satisfied by any legal sequence of actions applied to the initial state, thus ruling out illegal propositions, such as (in los-angeles package), (at package package), or (in truck san-francisco). Now all the information that is needed to devise an efficient state encoding schema for this particular problem is at the planner's hands. We discover that three multivalued variables are needed. The first one is required for encoding the current city of the truck and the other two variables are required to encode the status of the package.

Using the multivalued variable encoding the number of *possible planning states* shrinks drastically, whereas the number of *reachable planning states* remains unchanged. As another consequence, the multivalued variable encoding provides better predictions to the expected sizes of the abstract planning spaces.

Multiple Pattern Databases

As abstract planning problems are defined by a selection R of atoms there are several different candidates for a pattern database. This remains true when projecting multivalued variables.

We exemplify our considerations in BLOCKSWORLD. The domain is specified with the four action schemas pick-up, put-down, stack, and unstack, and the propositions on, ontable, handempty, and clear. The example problem contains four blocks a, b, c, and d used for grounding. For example, (pick–up a) is defined as the precondition list {(clear a), (ontable a), (handempty)}, the add list {(holding a)}, and the delete list {(ontable a), (clear a), (handempty)}. The goal of the instance is {(on d c), (on c a), (on a b)} and the initial state is given by {(clear b), (ontable d), (on b c), (on c a), (on a d)}.

One possible multivalued variable encoding for the domain, consisting of groups of mutually exclusive propositions, which has been automatically inferred by a static analyzer (as explained earlier) has nine variable domains: D_{v_1} = {(on c a), (on d a), (on b a), (clear a), (holding a)} (for the blocks on top of a); D_{v_2} = {(on a c), (on d c), (on b c), (clear c), (holding c)} (for the blocks on top of c); D_{v_3} = {(on a d), (on c d), (on b d), (clear d), (holding d)} (for the blocks on top of d); D_{v_4} = {(on a b), (on c b), (on d b), (clear b), (holding b)} (for the blocks on top of b); D_{v_5} = {(ontable a), none} (is block a bottom-most in tower); D_{v_6} = {(ontable c), none} (is block c bottom-most in tower); D_{v_7} = {(ontable d), none} (is block d bottom-most in tower); D_{v_8} = {(ontable b), none} (is block b bottom-most in tower); and D_{v_9} = {(handempty), none} (for the gripper). Each state can be expressed by selecting one proposition for each variable and none refers to the absence of all other propositions in the group.

We may select variables with even index to define the abstraction ϕ_{even} and variables with odd index to define the abstraction ϕ_{odd}. The resulting planning databases are depicted in Table 15.2. Note that there are only three atoms present in the goal state so that one of the pattern databases only contains patterns of length one. Abstraction ϕ_{even} corresponds to v_1 and ϕ_{odd} corresponds to the union of v_2 and v_4.

Table 15.2 Two pattern databases for the example problem. Pairs of pattern and goal distances are shown. The upper one refers to the projection onto group of v_1 with its set of possible assignments (on c a), (on d a), (on b a), (clear a), and (holding a). It is generated starting from (on c a). The second database projects to the cross-product of v_2 covering (on a c), (on d c), (on b c), (clear c), (holding c), and v_4 covering (on a b), (on c b), (on d b), (clear b), and (holding b); starting from the partial goal state (on d c), (on a b).

((on c a),0)	
((clear a),1)	
((holding a),2)	
((on b a),2)	
((on d a),2)	

((on d c), (on a b),0)	
((on d c)(clear b),1)	((on a b)(clear c),1)
((on d c)(holding b),2)	((clear c)(clear b),2)
((on d c)(on d b),2)	((on a b)(holding c),2)
((on a c)(on a b) ,2)	
((clear c)(holding b),3)	((clear b)(holding c),3)
((on a c)(clear b),3)	((on d b)(clear c),3)
((holding c)(holding b),4)	((on b c)(clear b),4)
((on a c)(holding b),4)	((on c b)(clear c),4)
((on d b)(holding c),4)	((on a c)(on d b),4)
((on b c)(holding b),5)	((on a b)(on b c),5)
((on d b)(on b c),5)	((on c b)(holding c),5)
((on a c)(on c b),5)	((on c b)(on d c),5)

To construct an explicit-state pattern database, one can use a hash table for storing the goal distance for each abstract state. In contrast, *symbolic planning pattern databases* are planning pattern databases that have been constructed with BDD exploration for latter use either in symbolic or explicit heuristic search. Each search layer is represented by a BDD. In planning practice, a better scaling seems to favor symbolic pattern database construction.

Pattern Addressing

To store the pattern databases, large hash tables are required. The estimate of a state is then a mere hash lookup (one for each pattern database). To improve efficiency of the lookup, it is not difficult to devise an incremental hashing scheme.

First, we assume a propositional encoding. For $u \subseteq AP = \{p_1, p_2, \ldots, p_{|AP|}\}$ we select $h(u) = \left(\sum_{p_i \in u} 2^i \right) \mod q$ as the hash function with prime q denoting the size of the hash table. The hash value of $v = (u \setminus del(a)) \cup add(a)$ can be incrementally calculated as

$$
h(v) = \left(\sum_{a_i \in (u \setminus del(a)) \cup add(a)} 2^i \right) \mod q = \left(\sum_{p_i \in u} 2^i - \sum_{p_i \in del(a)} 2^i + \sum_{p_i \in add(a)} 2^i \right) \mod q
$$

$$
= \left(\left(\sum_{p_i \in u} 2^i \right) \mod q - \left(\sum_{p_i \in del(a)} 2^i \right) \mod q + \left(\sum_{p_i \in add(a)} 2^i \right) \mod q \right) \mod q
$$

$$
= \left(h(u) - \left(\sum_{p_i \in del(a)} 2^i \right) \mod q + \left(\sum_{p_i \in add(a)} 2^i \right) \mod q \right) \mod q.
$$

Of course, hashing induces a (clearly bounded) number of collisions that have to be resolved by using one of the techniques presented in Chapter 3.

Since $2^i \mod q$ can be precomputed for all $p_i \in AP$, we have an incremental running time to compute the hash address that is of order $O(|add(a)| + |del(a)|)$, which is almost constant for most propositional planning problems (see Ch. 1). For constant time complexity we store $\left(\sum_{p_i \in add(a)} 2^i \right) \mod q - \left(\sum_{p_i \in del(a)} 2^i \right) \mod q$ together with each action a. Either complexity is small, when compared with the size of the planning state.

It is not difficult to extend incremental hash addressing to multivalued variables. According to the partition into variables, a hash function is defined as follows. Let $v_{i_1}, v_{i_2}, \ldots, v_{i_k}$ be the selected variables in the current abstraction and $offset(k) = \prod_{l=1}^{k} |D_{v_{i_{l-1}}}|$. Furthermore, let $variable(p)$ and $value(p)$ be, respectively, the variable index and the position of proposition p in its variable group. Then, the hash value of state u is

$$
h(u) = \sum_{p \in u} value(p) \cdot offset(variable(p)) \mod q.
$$

The incremental computation of $h(v)$ for $v = (u \setminus del(a)) \cup add(a)$ is immediate.

Automated Pattern Selection

Even in our simple example planning problem, the number of variables and the sizes of the generated pattern databases for ϕ_{even} and ϕ_{odd} differ considerably. Since we perform a complete exploration for pattern database construction, time and space resources may become exhausted. Therefore, an automatic way to find a balanced partition with regard to a given memory limit is required. Instead of imposing a bound on the total size for all pattern databases altogether, we impose a threshold for the sizes of the individual pattern databases, which has to be adapted to a given infrastructure.

As shown in Chapter 4, one option for pattern selection is PATTERN PACKING: According to the domain sizes of the variables, it finds a selection of pattern databases so that their combined sizes do not exceed the given threshold.

In the following, we consider genetic algorithms for improved pattern selection, where *pattern genes* denote which variable appears in which pattern. Pattern genes have a two-dimensional layout (see Fig. 15.4). It is recommended to initialize the genes with PATTERN PACKING. To avoid that all genes of the initial population are identical, the variable ordering for PATTERN PACKING can be randomized.

A *pattern mutation* flips bits with respect to a small probability. This allows us to add or delete variables in patterns. We extended the mutation operator to enable insertion and removal of entire patterns. Using selection, an enlarged population produced by recombination is truncated to its original size, based on their fitness. The (normalized) fitness for the population is interpreted as a distribution function for selecting the next population. Consequently, genes with higher fitness are chosen with higher probability.

The higher the distance-to-goal values in abstract space, the better the quality of the corresponding database in accelerating the search in the concrete search space. As a consequence, we compute the mean heuristic value for each of the databases and superimpose it over a pattern partitioning. If PDB_i,

	v_1	v_2	v_3	v_4	v_5	v_6	v_7	v_8	$\cdots$	n
1	1	0	0	0	1	1	0	1	$\cdots$	1
2	0	0	1	0	1	0	1	0	$\cdots$	0
3	0	1	1	0	1	1	0	1	$\cdots$	1
4	1	0	0	1	0	0	1	1	$\cdots$	0
5	0	1	0	0	1	0	1	0	$\cdots$	0
6	1	0	1	0	0	1	0	0	$\cdots$	0
7	0	0	0	1	1	0	1	0	$\cdots$	1
8	0	1	1	0	0	1	0	0	$\cdots$	0
$\vdots$	$\vdots$	$\vdots$	$\vdots$	$\vdots$	$\vdots$	$\vdots$	$\vdots$	$\vdots$	$\ddots$	$\vdots$
p	1	1	0	0	0	0	0	1	$\cdots$	0

FIGURE 15.4

Gene representation of a planning pattern selection. In the columns variables are listed; in the rows the patterns are enumerated. In the first pattern, the v_1, v_5, v_6, v_8, and v_n are present, whereas in the second pattern v_3, v_5, and v_7 are chosen.

$1 \le i \le p$ is the ith pattern database and $h^i_{\max}$ its maximal h-value, then the fitness for gene g is

$$\overline{h}(g) = \max_{i=1}^{p} \sum_{x=1}^{h^i_{\max}} \frac{i \cdot |\{u \in PDB_i \mid h(u) = x\}|}{|PDB_i|},$$

or

$$\overline{h}(g) = \sum_{i=1}^{p} \sum_{x=1}^{h^i_{\max}} \frac{i \cdot |\{u \in PDB_i \mid h(u) = x\}|}{|PDB_i|},$$

where the operator depends on the disjointness of the multiple pattern databases.

15.2 SUBOPTIMAL PLANNING

For suboptimal planning we first introduce the causal graph heuristic based on the multivalued variable encoding. Then we consider extensions of the relaxed planning heuristic (as introduced in Ch. 1) to metric and temporal planning domains.

15.2.1 Causal Graphs

There are two main problems of the relaxed planning heuristic (see Ch. 1). First, unsolvable problems can become solvable, and, second, the distance approximations may become weak. Take, for example, the two LOGISTICS problems in Figure 15.5. In both cases, we have to deliver a package to its destination (indicated with a shaded arrow) using some trucks (initially located at the shaded nodes). In the first case (illustrated on the left) a relaxed plan exists, but the concrete planning problem (assuming traveling constraints induced by the edges) is actually unsolvable.

In the second case (illustrated on the top right) a concrete plan exists. It requires moving the truck to pick up the package and return it to its home. The relaxed planning heuristic returns a plan that is about half as good. If we scale the problem as indicated to the lower part of the figure, heuristic search planners based on the relaxed planning heuristic quickly fail.

The *causal graph analysis* is based on the following *multivalued variable encoding* $X = \{v_1, v_2, v_c\}$, $D_{v_1} = D_{v_2} = \{A, B, C, D, E, F\}$, $D_{v_c} = \{A, B, C, D, E, t_1, t_2\}$, $A = \{(\{v_1 \leftarrow A\}, \{v_1 \leftarrow B\}), (\{v_1 \leftarrow A\}, \{v_1 \leftarrow C\}), (\{v_1 \leftarrow A\}, \{v_1 \leftarrow D\}), (\{v_2 \leftarrow A\}, \{v_2 \leftarrow B\}), \ldots, (\{v_c \leftarrow F, v_1 \leftarrow F\}, \{v_c \leftarrow t_1\}), \ldots\}$, $s = \{v_1 \leftarrow C, v_2 \leftarrow F, v_c \leftarrow E\}$, and $T = \{v_c \leftarrow B\}$.

The *causal graph* of an SAS$^+$ planning problem P with variable set X is a directed graph (X, A'), where $(u, v) \in A'$ if and only if $u \ne v$ and there is an action $(pre, eff) \in A$, such that $eff(v)$ is defined and either $pre(u)$ or $eff(u)$ is defined. This implies that an edge is drawn from one variable to another if the change of the second variable is dependent on the current assignment of the first variable. The causal graph of the first example (Fig. 15.5, left) is shown in Figure 15.6. These (in practice acyclic) graphs are divided into high-level (v_c) and low-level variables (v_1 and v_2).

Given an SAS$^+$ planning problem with $v \in X$, the *domain transition graph* G_v is a directed labeled graph with node set D_v. Being a projection of the original state space it contains an edge (d, d') if

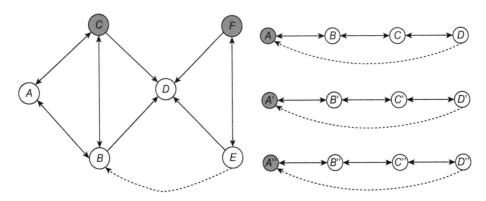

FIGURE 15.5

Problems with the relaxed planning heuristic. The relaxed plan for the first problem (left) is to move the right truck to pick up the package, move to D, and drop it. Then move the left truck to D, pick up the package, move it to B, and drop it. For the second problem (right) in the relaxed plan the package is teleported from D to A as (at truck A) is already true in the initial state.

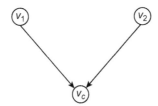

FIGURE 15.6

The causal graph for the example problem with one variable for the truck and two variables for the packages. Edges are drawn if the variables labeling the nodes are dependent. More precisely, an edge connects v_i and v_j if the change of v_j depends on the current assignment of v_i.

there is an action (pre, eff) with $pre(v) = d$ (or $pre(v)$ undefined) and $eff(v) = d'$. The edge is labeled by $pre(X \backslash \{v\})$. The domain transition graph for the example problem is shown in Figure 15.7.

Plan existence in SAS$^+$ planning problems is provably hard. Hence, depending on the structure of the domain transition graph(s), a heuristic search planning algorithm approximates the original problem. The approximation, measured in the number of executed plan steps, is used as a (nonadmissible) heuristic to guide the search in the concrete planning space.

Distances are measured between different value assignments to variables. The (minimal) cost $\delta_v(d, d')$ to change the assignment of v from d to d' is computed as follows. If v has no causal predecessor, $\delta_v(d, d')$ is the shortest path distance from d to d' in the domain transition graph, or ∞, if no such path exists. Let X_v be the set of variables that have v and all immediate predecessors of v in the causal graph of P. Let P_v be the subproblem induced by X_v with the initial value of v being d and the goal value of v being d'. Furthermore, let $\delta_v(d, d') = |\pi|$, where π is the shortest plan computed by the approximation algorithm (see later). The costs of the low-level variables are the shortest path

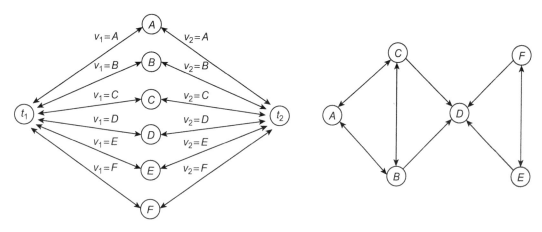

FIGURE 15.7

The domain transition graph for the cargo variable v_c, which is at the location A, B, C, D, E, or F, or in the truck t_1 or t_2 (left), and for the truck variables v_1 and v_2 that are moving between locations on a map (right).

costs in the domain transition graph, and 1 for the high-level variables. Finally, we define the heuristic estimate $h(u)$ of the multivalued planning state u as

$$h(u) = \sum_{v \in X} \delta_v(d_s(v), d_T(v)).$$

The approximation algorithm uses a queue for each high-level variable. It has polynomial running time but there are solvable instances for which no solution is obtained. Based on a queue Q it roughly works as shown in Algorithm 15.2.

Applied to an example (see Fig. 15.5, right), Q initially contains the elements $\{A, B, C, D, t\}$. The stages of the algorithms are as follows. First, we remove D from the queue, such that $u = (v_H \leftarrow D, v_L \leftarrow A)$. Choosing (pickup D) yields $\pi(t) = ((\text{move A B}), (\text{move B C}), (\text{move C D}), (\text{pickup D}))$. Next, we remove t from the queue, such that $u = (v_H \leftarrow t, v_L \leftarrow D)$. Choosing (drop A) yields $\pi(A) = ((\text{move A B}), (\text{move B C}), (\text{move C D}), (\text{pickup D}), (\text{move D C}), (\text{move C B}), (\text{move B A}), (\text{drop A}))$. Choosing (drop B), (drop C), (drop D) produces similar but shorter plans. Afterward, we remove C from the queue, such that $u = (v_H \leftarrow C, v_L \leftarrow C)$ yields no improvement. Subsequently, B is removed from the queue, such that $u = (v_H \leftarrow B, v_L \leftarrow B)$ yields no improvement. Lastly, A is removed from the queue and the algorithm terminates and returns $\pi(A)$.

15.2.2 Metric Planning

Metric planning involves reasoning about continuous state variables and arithmetic expressions. An example for an according PDDL action is shown in Figure 15.8.

Many existing planners terminate with the first solution they find. Optimization in metric planning, however, calls for improved exploration algorithms.

The state space of a metric planning instance is the set of assignments to the state variables with valid values. The logical state space is the result of projecting the state space to the components that

Procedure Causal Graph
Input: State space planning problem P
Output: Causal graph heuristic for T

if $(d_H = d_s(v_H))$ $\pi(d_H) \leftarrow \emptyset$	;; Initialize plan
else $\pi(d_H) \leftarrow \perp$	;; High-level plan undefined
$Q \leftarrow D_H$	;; Initialize queue with high-level variables
while $Q \neq \emptyset$	;; No solution found
Delete d_H from Q that minimizes $|\pi(d_H)|$	;; Given that $\pi(d_H)$ is defined
$\pi \leftarrow \pi(d_H)$	;; Initialize partial plan
for each t from d_H to d'_H with precondition *pre*	;; High-level transition
if (*pre* satisfied) ;; Search in domain transition graph of low-level variables	
$\pi_L \leftarrow$ min-plan satisfying pre	;; Minimal step plan
$\pi' \leftarrow (\pi, \pi_L, t)$	;; Concatenate plans
if $(|\pi(d'_H)| > |\pi'|)$	;; Improvement found
$\pi(d'_H) \leftarrow \pi'$	;; Update partial plan

Algorithm 15.2

Approximation of a plan with causal graph.

```
(:action fly
 :parameters (?a - aircraft ?c1 ?c2 - city)
 :precondition (and (at ?a ?c1)
                    (>= (fuel ?a)
                        (* (distance ?c1 ?c2) (slow-burn ?a))))
 :effect (and (not (at ?a ?c1)) (at ?a ?c2)
              (increase total-fuel-used
                        (* (distance ?c1 ?c2) (slow-burn ?a)))
              (decrease (fuel ?a)
                        (* (distance ?c1 ?c2) (slow-burn ?a)))))
```

FIGURE 15.8

An action in PDDL, Level 2. The parameters in the action *fly* are typed, *fuel* and *slow-burn* are unary predicates, and *distance* is a binary predicate. Moreover, *total-fuel-used* is a global variable that is increased by the amount *fuel* is decreased.

are responsible for representing predicates. Analogously, the numerical state space is the result of projecting the state space to the components that represent functions. Figure 15.10 shows an instantiated problem, which refers to the domain BOXES shown in Figure 15.9.

In metric planning problems, preconditions and goals are of the form $exp \otimes exp'$, where exp and exp' are arithmetic expressions over the sets of variables and operators $\{+, -, *, /\}$ and where $\otimes$ is selected from $\{\geq, \leq, >, <, =\}$. Assignments are of the form $v \leftarrow exp$ with head v and exp being an arithmetic expression (possibly including v). Additionally, a domain metric can be specified which has to be

```
(define (domain Boxes)
(:predicates (in-A-Box1) (in-A-Box2) (in-B-Box1)
             (in-B-Box2) (in-C-Box1) (in-C-Box2))
(:functions (weight-Box1) (weight-Box2))
(:action move-A-Box1-Box2
 :precondition (in-A-Box1)
 :effect (and (not (in-A-Box1)) (in-A-Box2)
              (decrease weight-Box1 5) (increase weight-Box2 5)))
(:action move-A-Box2-Box1
 :precondition (in-A-Box2)
 :effect (and (not (in-A-Box2)) (in-A-Box1)
              (decrease weight-Box2 5) (increase weight-Box1 5)))
(:action move-B-Box1-Box2
 :precondition (in-B-Box1)
 :effect (and (not (in-B-Box1)) (in-B-Box2)
              (decrease weight-Box1 3) (increase weight-Box2 3)))
(:action move-B-Box2-Box1
 :precondition (in-B-Box2)
 :effect (and (not (in-B-Box2)) (in-B-Box1)
              (decrease weight-Box2 3) (increase weight-Box1 3)))
(:action move-C-Box1-Box2
 :precondition (in-C-Box1)
 :effect (and (not (in-C-Box1)) (in-C-Box2)
              (decrease weight-Box1 8) (increase weight-Box2 8)))
(:action move-C-Box2-Box1
 :precondition (in-C-Box2)
 :effect (and (not (in-C-Box2)) (in-C-Box1)
              (decrease weight-Box2 8) (increase weight-Box1 8))))
```

FIGURE 15.9

The domain Boxes. We have two boxes and three objects. Each object has an individual weight and is located in exactly one of the boxes. Box containment is described using two predicates. The sum of all weights in one box is described using two functions. Using six actions every object can change its location.

```
(define (problem Equality)
(domain Boxes)
(:init (in-A-Box1) (in-B-Box1) (in-C-Box1)
       (= weight-Box1 16))
(:goal (= weight-Box1 weight-Box2)))
```

FIGURE 15.10

The problem Equality. Initially all boxes are contained in the first box. The goal is to move the boxes such that both boxes have the same weight.

minimized or maximized over the end states of all valid plans. Costs in the domain metric refer to assignments to the numerical state variables.

Metric planning is an essential language extension. Since we can encode the working of random access machines in real numbers, even the decision problem, whether or not a plan exists, is *undecidable*. The undecidability result show that in general we cannot prove that a problem obeys no solution. However, if there is one, we may be able to find it. Moreover, as metric planning problems may span infinite state spaces, heuristics to guide the search process are even more important than for finite-domain planning problems. For example, we know that A* is complete even on infinite graphs, given that the cumulated costs of every infinite path is unbounded.

Heuristic Estimate

The metric version of the propositional relaxed planning heuristic analyzes an extended layered planning graph, where each fact layer includes the encountered propositional atoms and numerical variables. The forward construction of the planning graph iteratively applies actions until all goals are satisfied. In the backward greedy plan extraction phase the atoms and variables in the preconditions are included in a pending queue as still to be processed. In contrast to the propositional relaxed planning heuristic, multiple applications of actions have to be granted, otherwise the inference of a numeric goal, say 100, by a single increment operator does not approximate the hundred steps needed. For this case, numeric conditions in the pending queue need to be propagated backward through a selected action.

As a consequence, we have to determine the *weakest precondition* using the *Hoare calculus*, a well-known concept to determine the partial correctness of computer programs. Its assignment rule states that $\{p[x \setminus t]\}\, x \leftarrow t;\, \{p\}$, where x is a variable, p is a postcondition, and $[x \setminus t]$ is the substitution of t in x. As an example consider the assignment $u \leftarrow 3x + 17$ with postcondition p given as $u < 5x$. To find the weakest precondition we take $t = 3x + 17$, such that $p[u \setminus t]$ evaluates to $3x + 17 < 5x$ and $x > 8.5$. For the application in relaxed metric planning, assume that an assignment of the form $h \leftarrow exp$ is subject to a postcondition exp'. The weakest precondition of it is established by substituting the occurrence of h in exp' with exp. In a tree representation this corresponds to insert exp at all leaves that correspond to h as subtrees in exp'. Usually, a simplification algorithm refines the resulting representation of $exp[h \setminus exp']$.

In Algorithm 15.3 we illustrate the plan construction process in pseudo code. For each layer t in the relaxed planning graph a set of active propositional and numerical constraints is determined. We use $p(\cdot)$ to select valid propositions and $v(\cdot)$ to select the variables. To determine the set of applicable actions A_t, we assume to have implemented a recursive procedure *Test*. The input of this procedure is a numerical expression and a set of intervals $[min_t^i, max_t^i]$, $1 \le i \le |X|$ that describe lower and upper assignment bounds for each variable v_i. The output is a Boolean value that indicates whether the current assignment fits into the corresponding bounds. We also assume a recursive implementation for *Update* to adjust the bounds min_t and max_t to min_{t+1} and max_{t+1} according to a given expression exp.

For the extraction process as shown in Algorithm 15.4 we first search for the minimal layer in which the chosen condition is satisfied. The propositional and numerical *pending queues* in layer i are denoted by $p(G_i)$ and $v(G_i)$. These pending queues represent the conditions for the particular layer that have to be achieved while constructing the relaxed plan. Although the initialization for the propositional part given the compound goal condition is rather simple (see with the relaxed planning heuristic in Ch. 1), for the initialization of the numerical condition queue the variable intervals $[min_i, max_i]$ for an increasing layer i are utilized to test the earliest satisfaction of the goal condition.

Procedure Relax
Input: Current planning state u, planning goal T
Output: Relaxed planning graph

$P_0 \leftarrow p(u)$	;; Initialize propositions
for each $i \in \{1,\ldots,\lvert X\rvert\}$	;; For each variable index
$\quad \min_0^i \leftarrow \max_0^i \leftarrow v^i(u)$	;; Initialize propositions and intervals
$t \leftarrow 0$	;; Initialize iteration counter
while $(p(T) \nsubseteq P_t$ **or** $\exists exp \in v(T) : Test(exp, \min_t, \max_t))$	;; Information to process
$\quad A_t \leftarrow \{a \in A \mid p \in pre(a) \subseteq P_t,$	;; Update action set
$\qquad \forall exp \in v(pre(a)) : Test(exp, \min_t, \max_t)\}$	
$\quad P_{t+1} \leftarrow P_t \cup \bigcup_{pre(a)\subseteq P_t} add(a)$	;; Update propositional information
$\quad [\min_{t+1}, \max_{t+1}] \leftarrow [\min_t, \max_t]$	;; Initialize interval information
$\quad$ **for** $a \in A_t, exp \in v(eff(a))$	;; Traverse action set
$\qquad Update(exp, \min_t, \max_t, \min_{t+1}, \max_{t+1})$	;; Update interval information
$\quad$ **if** (*relaxed problem unsolvable*) **return** ∞	;; Termination criterion, failure
$\quad t \leftarrow t+1$	;; Increase iteration counter

Algorithm 15.3

Plan graph construction for numerical relaxed planning heuristic.

Now the constructed planning graph is traversed backward, layer by layer. To find the set of active actions, we reuse the set A_i and recompute the vectors $\min_{i+1}$ and $\max_{i+1}$ as determined in the forward phase. We continue until either an add-effect of an action in A_i is detected or the numerical conditions of an effect become satisfied. In both cases we add the corresponding action to the relaxed plan and propagate the propositional preconditions of the chosen action to the layer in the relaxed planning graph, where they are satisfied for the first time as still to be processed.

The remaining code fragment (starting with *for each* $exp' \in v(eff(a))$ considers how numeric postconditions are propagates by themselves. For the ease of presentation we restrict to ordinary assignments. After an assignment is chosen, we determine the weakest precondition for the expression as described earlier. It is also added to the pending queue of the shallowed level, in which it is satisfied. This layer can easily be determined by iteratively calling *Test* for the layers $j \in \{1,\ldots,i\}$.

For example, if we have a postcondition of $v \geq 100$ and an assignment $v \leftarrow v+1$ in one of the action effects, the weakest precondition to be progressed (according to Hoare's assignment rule) is $v+1 \geq 100$, which is equivalent to $v \geq 99$. The latest layer in which this condition is satisfied might be the one where we started. So if we have the interval $[0, 100]$ for v in the current layer i, and $[0, 75]$ in the previous layer $i-1$, we include the action in the relaxed plan 25 times until $v \leq 75$, at which time the condition is included in the pending queue of layer $i-1$.

15.2.3 Temporal Planning

Temporal planning domains include temporal modifiers *at start*, *over all*, and *at end*, where label *at start* denotes the preconditions and effects at invocation time of the action, *over all* refers to an

Procedure Extract
Input: Relaxed planning graph, planning goal T
Output: Approximation for relaxed plan length

$A \leftarrow \emptyset$;; Initialize relaxed plan
for $i \in \{1, \dots, t\}$;; Process layers forward
     $p(G_i) \leftarrow \{g \in p(T) \mid layer(g) = i\}$;; Initialize propositional information in Layer i
     for each $exp \in v(T)$;; Initialize numerical information in Layer i
         if ($Test(exp, min_i \, max_i)$) $v(G_i) \leftarrow v(G_i) \cup \{exp\}$; $v(T) \leftarrow v(T) \setminus \{exp\}$
for $i \in \{t, \dots, 1\}$;; Process layers backward
     $[min_{i+1}, max_{i+1}] \leftarrow [min_i, max_i]$;; Reinitialize interval information
     for each $a \in A_i$;; Retraverse action set in Layer i
         for each $exp \in v(eff(a))$;; For each numerical effect
             $Update$ $(exp, min_i, max_i, min_{i+1}, max_{i+1})$;; Recompute interval information
         for $e \in add(a)$ $e \in p(G_i)$;; Add-effect condition matches list
             $A \leftarrow A \cup \{a\}$; $p(G_i) \leftarrow p(G_i) \setminus add(a)$;; Update propositional list
             for each $p \in p(pre(a))$:   ;; Update propositional information
                 $p(G_{layer(p)}) \leftarrow p(G_{layer(p)}) \cup \{p\}$
             for each $exp \in v(pre(a))$;; Update numerical information
                 $v(G_{layer(exp)}) \leftarrow v(G_{layer(exp)}) \cup \{exp\}$
         for each $exp \in v(G_i)$;; Traverse numerical list
             if $Test(exp, min_{i+1}, max_{i+1})$;; Interval condition match
             $A \leftarrow A \cup \{a\}$; $v(G_i) \leftarrow v(G_i) \setminus \{exp\}$;; Update numerical list
             $p(G_i) \leftarrow p(G_i) \setminus add(a)$;; Update propositional list
             for each $p \in p(pre(a))$;; Update propositional information
                 $p(G_{layer(p)}) \leftarrow p(G_{layer(p)}) \cup \{p\}$
             for each $exp \in v(pre(a))$;; Update numerical information
                 $v(G_{layer(exp)}) \leftarrow p(G_{layer(exp)}) \cup \{exp\}$
             for each $exp' \in v(eff(a))$;; Matching effect found
                 $exp \leftarrow exp[head(exp') \setminus exp']$;; Compute weakest precondition
             for each $j \in \{1, \dots, i\}$;; Determine earliest matching layer
                 if ($Test(exp, min_j, max_j)$) $l \leftarrow j$
             $v(G_l) \leftarrow v(G_l) \cup \{exp\}$;; Update numerical information
return $|A|$;; Estimate is size of action set

Algorithm 15.4

Extraction of a numerical relaxed plan.

invariance condition that must hold, and *at end* refers to the finalization conditions and consequences of the action. An example for a PDDL action with numbers and durations is shown in Figure 15.11.

Temporal Model

There are mainly two different options to translate the temporal information back to metric planning problems with preconditions and effects. In the first case, the compound action is split into three smaller parts: one for action invocation, one for invariance maintenance, and one for action termination. This is the suggested semantic of PDDL2.1 (see Fig. 15.12, top right). As expected, there are no effects

```
(:durative-action fly
 :parameters (?a - aircraft ?c1 ?c2 - city)
 :duration (= ?duration (/ (distance ?c1 ?c2) (slow-speed ?a)))
 :condition (and (at start (at ?a ?c1))
                 (at start (>= (fuel ?a)
                              (* (distance ?c1 ?c2) (slow-burn ?a)))))
 :effect (and (at start (not (at ?a ?c1)))
              (at end (at ?a ?c2))
              (at end (increase total-fuel-used
                             (* (distance ?c1 ?c2) (slow-burn ?a))))
              (at end (decrease (fuel ?a)
                             (* (distance ?c1 ?c2) (slow-burn ?a))))))
```

FIGURE 15.11

An action in PDDL, Level 3.

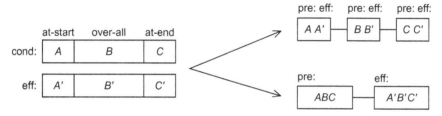

FIGURE 15.12

Compiling temporal modifiers into actions. The original action (left) with preconditions and effects partitioned in at-start, at-end, and over-all events, respectively, is transformed into either the intended semantics (top right) or into the black-box semantic (bottom right).

in the invariance pattern, so that $B' = \emptyset$. Moreover, for benchmarks it is uncommon that new effects in at-start are preconditioned for termination control or invariance maintenance, such that $A' \cap (B \cup C) = \emptyset$. In these problems, a simpler model can be applied, using only one untimed variant for each temporal action (see Fig. 15.12, bottom right). For most planning benchmarks there are no deficiencies by assuming this temporal model, in which each action starts immediately after a previous one has terminated.

These black-box semantics allow the modifiers to be dropped since conditions are checked at the beginning and effects are checked at the end. The instantiation of a timed version of the BOXES domain is provided in Figure 15.13.

Action Dependency

The purposes of defining action dependency are twofold. First, at least one execution order of two independent actions can be pruned from the search tree and, more importantly, it is possible to compute optimal schedules of sequential plans with respect to the generated action sequence and its causal

```
(define (domain Boxes)
(:predicates (in-A-Box1) (in-A-Box2) (in-B-Box1)
             (in-B-Box2) (in-C-Box1) (in-C-Box2))
(:functions (weight-Box1) (weight-Box2) )
(:durative-action move-A-Box1-Box2
 :duration (= ?duration 2.5) :condition (in-A-Box1)
 :effect (and (not (in-A-Box1)) (in-A-Box2)
              (decrease weight-Box1 5) (increase weight-Box2 5)))
(:durative-action move-A-Box2-Box1
 :duration (= ?duration 2.5) :condition (in-A-Box2)
 :effect (and (not (in-A-Box2)) (in-A-Box1)
              (decrease weight-Box2 5) (increase weight-Box1 5)))
(:durative-action move-B-Box1-Box2
 :duration (= ?duration 0.9) :condition (in-B-Box1)
 :effect (and (not (in-B-Box1)) (in-B-Box2)
              (decrease weight-Box1 3) (increase weight-Box2 3)))
(:durative-action move-B-Box2-Box1
 :duration (= ?duration 0.9) :condition (in-B-Box2)
 :effect (and (not (in-B-Box2)) (in-B-Box1)
              (decrease weight-Box2 3) (increase weight-Box1 3)))
(:durative-action move-C-Box1-Box2
 :duration (= ?duration 6.45) :condition (in-C-Box1)
 :effect (and (not (in-C-Box1)) (in-C-Box2)
              (decrease weight-Box1 8) (increase weight-Box2 8)))
(:durative-action move-C-Box2-Box1
 :duration (= ?duration 6.45) :condition (in-C-Box2)
 :effect (and (not (in-C-Box2)) (in-C-Box1)
              (decrease weight-Box2 8) (increase weight-Box1 8))))
```

FIGURE 15.13

The domain Boxes stated for black-box semantics.

structure. If all actions are dependent (or void with respect to the optimizer function), the problem is inherently sequential and no schedule leads to any improvement.

Two grounded actions are *dependent* if one of the following conditions holds:

1. The propositional precondition set of one action has a nonempty intersection with the add or the delete lists of the other one (*propositional conflict*).
2. The head of a numerical modifier of one action is contained in some condition of the other one. Intuitively, an action modifies variables that appear in the condition of the other (*direct numerical conflict*).
3. The head of the numerical modifier of one action is contained in the formula body of the modifier of the other one (*indirect numerical conflict*).

In an implementation (at least for temporal and numerical planning) the dependence relation is computed beforehand and tabulated for constant time access. To improve the efficiency of precomputation, the set of leaf variables is maintained in an array, once the grounded action is constructed. To detect domains for which any parallelization leads to no improvement, a planning domain is said to be *inherently sequential* if all actions in any sequential plan are dependent or instantaneous (i.e., with zero duration). The static analyzer may check an approximation by comparing each action pair prior to the search.

Parallelizing Sequential Plans

A *parallel plan* $\pi_c = ((a_1, t_1), \ldots, (a_k, t_k))$ is a *schedule* of actions $a_i \in A$, $i \in \{1, \ldots, k\}$ that transforms the initial state s into one of the goal states $t \in T$, where a_i is executed at time t_i. A precedence ordering $\preceq_d$ induced by the set of actions $\{a_1, \ldots, a_k\}$ and a dependency relation is given by $a_i \preceq_d a_j$, if a_i and a_j are dependent and $1 \leq i < j \leq k$.

Precedence is not a partial ordering, since it is neither reflexive nor transitive. By computing the transitive closure of the relation, however, precedence could be extended to a partial ordering. A sequential plan $a_1, \ldots, a_k$ produces an acyclic set of precedence constraints $a_i \preceq_d a_j$, $1 \leq i < j \leq k$ on the set of actions. It is also important to observe that the constraints are already topologically sorted according to $\preceq_d$ by taking the node ordering $\{1, \ldots, k\}$.

Let $d(a)$ for $a \in A$ be the *duration* of action a in a sequential plan. For a *parallel plan* $\pi_c = ((a_1, t_1), \ldots, (a_k, t_k))$ that respect $\preceq_d$, we have $t_i + d(a_i) \leq t_j$ for $a_i \preceq_d a_j$, $1 \leq i < j \leq k$. An *optimal parallel plan* with regard to a sequence of actions $a_1, \ldots, a_k$ and precedence ordering $\preceq_d$ is a parallel plan $\pi^* = ((a_1, t_1), \ldots, (a_k, t_k))$ with minimal execution time among all alternative parallel plans $\pi_c = ((a_1, t_1'), \ldots, (a_k, t_k'))$ that respect $\preceq_d$.

Possible implementation of such schedulers can be based on the *project evaluation and review technique* or on *simple temporal networks* (see Ch. 13).

15.2.4 Derived Predicates

Derived predicates are predicates that are not affected by any of the actions available to the planner. Instead, the predicate's truth values are derived by a set of *rules* of the form **if** $\phi(x)$ **then** $P(x)$. An example of a derived predicate is the *above* predicate in BLOCKSWORLD, which is true between blocks x and y, whenever x is transitively (possibly with some blocks in between) on y. This predicate can be defined recursively as follows:

```
(:derived (above ?x ?y - block)
   (or (on ?x ?y) (exists (?z - block) (and (on ?x ?z) (above ?z ?y))))).
```

The semantics, roughly, are that an instance of a derived predicate is satisfied if and only if it can be derived using the available rules. More formally, let R be the set of rules for the derived predicates, where the elements of R have the form $(P(x), \phi(x)) -$ *if* $\phi(x)$ *then* $P(x)$. Then $D(u)$, for a set of basic facts u, is defined as follows:

$$D(u) = \bigcap \{v \supseteq u \mid \forall (P(x), \phi(x)) \in R : \forall c, |c| = |x| : (v \models \phi(c) \Rightarrow P(c) \in v)\}.$$

This definition uses the standard notations of the modeling relation $\models$ between states (represented as sets of facts in our case) and formulas, and of the substitution $\phi(c)$ of the free variables in formula $\phi(x)$ with a constant vector c. In words, $D(u)$ is the intersection of all supersets of u that are closed under application of the rules R. $D(u)$ can be computed by the simple process shown in Algorithm 15.5.

Procedure *Derive*
Input: State u, rule set R
Output: Extension for state u

$v \leftarrow u$;; Make a copy of input state
while $(\exists c : |c| = |x|, v \models \phi(c), P(c) \notin v, (P(x), \phi(x)) \in R)$;; Choose instantiation
$\quad v \leftarrow v \cup \{P(c)\}$;; Update copy
$D(u) \leftarrow v$;; Update derived set

Algorithm 15.5

Fixpoint for applying a set of rules to a planning state.

Hence, derivation rules can be included in a forward chaining heuristic search planner by inferring the truth of the derived rule for each step.

Suppose that we have grounded all derived predicates to the rules (p, ϕ). In ϕ there can be further derived predicates, which by the acyclic definition of derived predicates cannot be directly or indirectly dependent from p. For the rule (p, ϕ) the values p and ϕ are equivalent. This implies that p is nothing more than a macro for the expression ϕ. All derived predicates can be eliminated from the planning instance by the substitution with more complex descriptions. The advantage with regard to alternative methods for handling derived predicates is that the state vector does not have to be extended.

15.2.5 Timed Initial Literals

Timed initial literals are an extension for temporal planning. Syntactically they are a very simple way of expressing a certain restricted form of exogenous events: facts that will become true or false at time points that are known to the planner in advance, independent of the actions that the planner chooses to execute. Timed initial literals are thus deterministic unconditional exogenous events.

An illustrative example considers a planning task for shopping. There is a single action that achieves the goal, which requires a shop to be open as its precondition. The shop opens at time step 9 relative to the initial state, and closes at time step 20. We can express the shop opening times by two timed initial literals:

```
(:init (at 9 (shop-open)) (at 20 (not (shop-open)))).
```

Timed initial literals can be inserted into a heuristic search planner as follows. We associate with each (grounded) action so-called *action execution time windows* that specify the interval of a save execution. This is done by eliminating the preconditions that are related to the time initial literal. For ordinary literals and STRIPS actions, the conjunction of precondition leads to the intersection of action execution time windows. For repeated literals or disjunctive precondition lists, time windows have to be kept, while simple execution time windows can be integrated into the PERT scheduling process.

15.2.6 State Trajectory Constraints

State trajectory or *plan constraints* provide an important step of PDDL toward *temporal control knowledge* and *temporally extended goals*. They assert conditions that must be satisfied during the execution of a plan. Through the decomposition of temporal plans into plan happenings, state trajectory constraints feature all levels of the PDDL hierarchy. For example, the constraint *a fragile block can never have something above it* can be expressed as

```
(always (forall (?b - block) (implies (fragile ?b) (clear ?b)))).
```

As illustrated in Chapter 13 plan constraints can be compiled away. The approach translates the constraints in linear temporal logic and compiles them into finite-state automata. The automata are simulated in parallel to the search. The initial state of the automaton is added to the initial state of the problem and the automation transitions are compiled to actions. A synchronization mechanism controls that the original actions and the automata actions alternate. Planning goals are extended with the accepting states of the automata.

15.2.7 Preference Constraints

Annotating individual goal conditions or state trajectory constraints with *preferences* model soft constraints and allow the degree of satisfaction to be scaled with respect to hard constraints that have to be fulfilled in a valid plan. The plan objective function includes special variables referring to the violation of the preference constraints and allows planners to optimize plans.

Quantified preference rules like

```
(forall (?b - block) (preference p (clear ?b)))
```

are grounded (one for each block), while the inverse expression

```
(preference p (forall (?b - block) (clear ?b)))
```

leads to only one constraint.

Preferences can be treated as variables using conditional effects, so that the heuristics derived earlier remain appropriate for effective plan-finding.

15.3 BIBLIOGRAPHIC NOTES

Drew McDermott and a committee have created the specification language (PDDL) in 1998 in the form of a Lisp-like input language description format that includes planning formalisms like STRIPS by Fikes and Nilsson (1971). Later, ADL as proposed by Pednault (1991) was used. Planning in temporal and metric domains started in 2002. For this purpose, Fox and Long (2003) developed the PDDL hierarchy, of which the first three levels were shown in the text. This hierarchy was attached later. Domain axioms in the form of derived predicates introduce inference rules, and timed initial facts allow deadlines to be specified (Hoffmann and Edelkamp, 2005). Newer developments of PDDL focus on temporal and preference constraints (Gerevini and Long, 2005) and object fluents (Geffner, 2000). Complexity analyses for standard benchmarks have been provided by Helmert (2003, 2006a). Approximation properties of such benchmarks have been studied by Helmert, Mattmüller, and Röger (2006). The complexity of planning with multivalued variables (SAS^+ planning) has been analyzed by Bäckström and Nebel (1995).

Graphplan has been developed by Blum and Furst (1995), and *Satplan* is due to Kautz and Selman (1996). The set of admissible heuristics based on dynamic programming have been proposed by Haslum and Geffner (2000). Planning with pattern databases has been invented by Edelkamp (2001a), and the extension to symbolic pattern databases has been addressed by Edelkamp (2002). Various packing algorithms have been suggested by Haslum, Bonet, and Geffner (2005). Incremental hashing for planning pattern databases has been proposed by Mehler and Edelkamp (2005). The automated pattern selection for domain-independent explicit-state and symbolic heuristic search planning with genetic algorithms has been proposed by Edelkamp (2007). Zhou and Hansen (2006b) have used general abstractions for planning domains together with structured duplicate detection (see Ch. 8).

The relaxed planning heuristic as proposed by Hoffmann and Nebel (2001) has been analyzed by Hoffmann (2001), providing a heuristic search topology for its effectiveness in known benchmark domains. Bonet and Geffner (2008) have derived a functional representation of the relaxed planning heuristic in symbolic form as a DNNF. Alcázar, Borrajo, and Linares López (2010) have proposed using information extracted from the last actions in the relaxed plan to generate intermediate goals backward.

Hoffmann (2003) has shown how to extend the heuristic by omitting the delete list to numerical state variables. An extension of the approach to nonlinear tasks has been given by Edelkamp (2004). A unified heuristic for deterministic planning has been investigated by Rintanen (2006). Coles, Fox, Long, and Smith (2008) have refined the heuristic by solving linear programs to improve the relaxation. Fuentetaja, Borrajo, and Linares López (2008) have introduced an approach for dealing with cost-based planning that involves the use of look-ahead states to boost the search, based on a relaxed plan graph heuristic. How to add search diversity to the planning process has been studied by Linares López and Borrajo (2010).

Borowsky and Edelkamp (2008) have proposed an optimal approach to metric planning. State sets and actions are encoded as Presburger formulas and represented using minimized finite-state machines. The exploration that contributes to the planning via a model checking paradigm applies symbolic images to compute the finite-state machine for the sets of successors.

The causal graph heuristic has been discussed extensively by Helmert (2006b) and been implemented in the *Fast-Downward* planner. Helmert and Geffner (2008) have shown that the causal graph heuristic can be viewed as a variant of the max-atom heuristic with *additional context*. They have provided a recursive functional description of the causal graph heuristic that, without restriction to the dependency graph structure, extends the existing one.

Automated planning pattern database design has been studied by Haslum, Botea, Helmert, Bonet, and Koenig (2007). A more flexible design that goes back to work by Dräger, Finkbeiner, and Podelski (2009) has been pursued by Helmert, Haslum, and Hoffmann (2007), and pattern database heuristics for nondeterministic planning have been studied by Mattmüller, Ortlieb, Helmert, and Bercher (2010). In Katz and Domshlak (2009) structural pattern database heuristics have been proposed that lead to polynomial-time calculations based on substructures of the causal graph. Moreover, a general method for combining different heuristics has been given. Good heuristics have also been established by the extraction of landmarks in Richter, Helmert, and Westphal (2008), a work that refers to Hoffmann, Porteous, and Sebastia (2004). A theoretical analysis of the advances in the design of heuristics has lead to the heuristic LM-cut with very good results (Helmert and Domshlak, 2009). Bonet and Helmert (2010) have improved this heuristic by computing hitting sets.

Alternative characterizations that have been derived of h^m have been given by Haslum (2009). Limits of heuristic search in planning domains have been documented by Helmert and Röger (2008).

Pruning techniques for the use of actions have been studied by Wehrle, Kupferschmid, and Podelski (2008). A reduced set of actions has been looked at in Haslum and Jonsson (2000). It is known that achieving approximate solutions in BLOCKSWORLD is easy (Slaney and Thiébaux, 2001) and that domain-dependent cuts drastically reduce the search space. For compiling temporal logic control into PDDL, Rintanen (2000) has compared formula progression as in TLPlan by Bacchus and Kabanza (2000) with a direct translation into planning actions.

For efficient optimization in complex domains, planner LPG by Gerevini, Saetti, and Serina (2006) and SGPlan by Chen and Wah (2004) apply Lagrangian optimization techniques to gradually improve a (probably invalid) first plan. Both planners extend the relaxed planning heuristics; the first one optimizes an *action graph* data structure, and the latter applies *constraint partitioning* (into less restricted subproblems). As shown in Gerevini, Saetti, and Serina (2006), the planner LPG-TD can efficiently deal with multiple action time windows. The outstanding performance of constraint partitioning, however, is likely due to manual help.

Further planers like Crikey by Coles, Fox, Halsey, Long, and Smith (2009) link planning and scheduling algorithms into a planner that is capable of solving many problems with *required* concurrency, as defined by Cushing, Kambhampati, Mausam, and Weld (2007). Alternatively, we can build domain-independent (heuristic) forward chaining planners that can handle durative actions and numeric variables. Planners like Sapa by Do and Kambhampati (2003) follow this approach. Sapa utilizes a temporal version of planning graphs first introduced in TGP by Smith and Weld (1999) to compute heuristic values of time-stamped states. A more recent approach has been contributed by Eyerich, Mattmüller, and Röger (2009).

Automated System Verification

The presence of a vast number of computing devices in our environment imposes a challenge for designers to produce reliable software. In medicine, aviation, finance, transportation, space technology, and communication, we are more and more aware of the *critical role* correct hardware and software plays. Failure leads to financial and commercial disaster, human suffering, and fatalities. However, systems are harder to verify than in earlier days. Testing if a system works as intended becomes increasingly difficult. Nowadays, design groups spend 50% to 70% of the design time on verification. The cost of the late discovery of bugs is enormous, justifying the fact that, for a typical microprocessor design project, up to half of the overall resources spent are devoted to its verification. In this chapter we give evidence of the important role of heuristic search in this context.

The process of fully automated property verification is referred to as *model checking* and will cover most of the presentation here. Given a formal model of a system and a property specification in some form of temporal logic, the task is to validate whether or not the specification is satisfied in the model. If not, a model checker returns a counterexample for the system's flawed behavior helping the system designer to debug the system. The major disadvantage of model checking is that it scales poorly; for a complete verification each state has to be looked at. With the integration of heuristics into the search process (known as *directed model checking*) we look at various options for improved search. The applications range from checking models of communication protocols, Petri nets, real-time as well as graph transition systems, to the verification of real software. We emphasize the tight connection between model checking and action planning.

Another aspect of automated system verification that is especially important for AI applications is to check whether or not a *knowledge-based system* is *consistent* or contains *anomalies*. We address how symbolic search techniques can be of help here. We give examples of symbolic search in solving (multiple-fault) diagnosis problems.

Most of the work in heuristic search for automated system verification concentrates on accelerated falsification. With *directed automated theorem proving*, algorithms like A* and greedy best-first search are integrated in a deductive system. As theorem provers draw inferences on top of axioms of an underlying logic, the state space is the set of proof trees. More precisely, sets of clauses for a proof state are represented in the form of a finite tree and rules describe how a clause is obtained by manipulating a finite set of other input clauses. Inference steps are performed mainly via resolution. Since such systems are provided in functional programming languages, we look at functional implementations of search algorithms.

16.1 MODEL CHECKING

Model checking has evolved into one of the most successful verification techniques. Examples range from mainstream applications such as protocol validation, software checking, and embedded system verification, to exotic areas such as business work-flow analysis and scheduler synthesis. The success of model checking is largely based on its ability to efficiently locate errors. If an error is found, a model checker produces a counterexample that shows how the errors occur, which greatly facilitates debugging. In general, counterexamples are executions of the system, which can be paths (if linear logics are used) or trees (if branching logics are used).

However, while current model checkers find error states efficiently, the counterexamples are often unnecessarily complex, which hampers error explanation. This is due to the use of *naive* search algorithms.

There are two primary approaches to model checking. First, *symbolic model checking* applies a symbolic representation for the state set, usually based on binary decision diagrams. Property validation in symbolic model checking amounts to some form of symbolic fixpoint computation. *Explicit-state model checking* uses an explicit representation of the system's global state graph, usually given by a state transition function. An explicit-state model checker evaluates the validity of the temporal properties over the model, and property validation amounts to a partial or full exploration of a certain state space. The success of model checking lies in its potential for *push-button* automation and in its error reporting capabilities. A model checker performs an automated complete exploration of the state space of a software model, usually using a depth-first search strategy. When a property violating a state is encountered the search stack contains an error trail that leads from an initial system state into the encountered state. This error trail greatly helps software engineers in interpreting validation results.

The sheer size of the reachable state space of realistic software models imposes tremendous challenges on model checking technology. Full exploration of the state space is often impossible, and approximations are needed. Also, the error trails reported by depth-first search model checkers are often exceedingly lengthy—in many cases they consist of multiple thousands of computation steps, which greatly hampers error interpretation.

In the design process of systems two phases are distinguished. In a first *explanatory phase*, we want to locate errors fast; in a second *fault-finding* phase, we look for short error trails. Since the requirements of the two phases are not the same, different strategies apply. In safety property checking the idea is to use state evaluation functions to guide the state space exploration into a property violating state. Greedy best-first search is one of the most promising candidate for the first phase, but yield no optimal solution counterexamples. For the second phase, the A* algorithm has been applied with success. It delivers optimally short error trails if the heuristic estimate for the path length to the error trail is admissible. Even in cases where this cannot be guaranteed, A* delivers very good results.

The use of heuristic search renders erstwhile unanalyzable problems to ones that are analyzable for many instances. The quality of the results obtained with A* depends on the quality of the heuristic estimate, and heuristic estimates were devised that are specific for the validation of concurrent software, such as specific estimates for reaching deadlock states and invariant violations.

16.1.1 Temporal Logics

Models with propositionally labeled states can be described in terms of *Kripke structures*. More formally, a Kripke structure is a quadruple $M = (S, R, I, L)$, where S is a set of states, R is the transition relation between states using one of the enabled operators, I is the set of initial states, and $L : S \to 2^{AP}$ is a state labeling function. This formulation is close to the definition of a state space problem in Chapter 1 up to the absence of terminal states. That I may contain more than one start state helps to model some uncertainty in the system. In fact, by considering the set of possible states as one *belief state* set, this form of uncertainty can be compiled away.

For model checking, the desired property of the system is to be specified in some form of temporal logic. We already introduced *linear temporal logic* (LTL) in Chapter 13. Given a Kripke structure and a temporal formula f, the *model checking problem* is to find the set of states in M that satisfy f, and check whether the set of initial states belongs to this state set. We shortly write $M \models f$ in this case.

The model checking problem is solved by searching the state space of the system. Ideally, the verification is completely automatic. The main challenge is the *state explosion problem*. The problem occurs in systems with many components that can interact with each other, so that the number of global states can be enormous. We observe that any propositional planning problem can be modeled as an LTL model checking problem as any propositional goal g can be expressed in the form of a counterexample to the temporal formula $f = \mathbf{A}(\mathbf{G} \neg g)$ in LTL. If the problem is solvable, the LTL model checker will return a counterexample, which manifests a solution for the planning problem.

The inverse is also often true. Several model checking problems can be modeled as state space problems. In fact, the class of model checking problems that fit into the representation of a state space problem with a simple predicate should be evaluated at each individual state. Such problems are called *safety properties*. The intuition behind such a property is to say that something bad should not happen. In contrast, *liveness properties* refer to infinite runs with (*lasso*-shaped) counterexamples. The intuition is to say that something good will eventually occur.

In *automata-based model checking* the model and the specification are both transformed into automata for accepting infinite words. Such automata look like ordinary automata but accept if during the simulation of an infinite word one accepting state is visited infinitely often. This assumes that a system can be modeled by an automaton, which is possible when casting all states in the underlying Kripke structure for the model as being accepting. Any LTL formula can be transformed into an automata over infinite words even if this construction may be exponential in the size of the formula. Checking correctness is reduced to checking language emptiness. More formally, the model checking procedure validates that a model represented by an automaton M satisfies its specification represented by an automaton M'. The task is to verify if the *language induced by the model* is included in the *language induced by the specification*, $L(M) \subseteq L(M')$ for short. We have $L(M) \subseteq L(M')$ if and only if $L(M) \cap \overline{L(M')} = \emptyset$. In practice, checking language emptiness is more efficient than checking language inclusion. Moreover, we often construct the property automaton N for negation of the LTL formula, avoiding the posterior complementation of the automaton over infinite words. The property automaton is nondeterministic, such that both the model and the formula introduce branching to the search process.

16.1.2 The Role of Heuristics

Heuristics are evaluation functions that order the set of states to be explored, such that the states that are closer to the goal are considered first. Most search heuristics are state-to-goal distance estimates that are based on solving simplifications or *abstractions* of the overall search problems. Such heuristics are computed either *offline*, prior to the search in the concrete state space, or *online* for each encountered state (set). In a more general setting, heuristics are evaluation functions on generating paths rather than on states only.

The design of *bug hunting estimates* heavily depends on the type of error that is searched for. Example error classes for safety properties are system deadlocks, assertion or invariance violations. To guide the search, the error description is analyzed and evaluated for each state. In *trail-directed* search we search for a short counterexample for a particular error state that has been generated, for example, by simulating the system.

Abstractions often refer to *relaxations* of the model. If the abstraction is an *overapproximation* (each behavior in the abstract space has a corresponding one in the concrete space, which we will assume here), then a correctness proof for the specification in the abstract space implies the correctness in the concrete space.

Abstraction and heuristics are two sides of the same medal. Heuristics correspond to exact distances in some abstract search space. This leads to the general approach of *abstraction-directed model checking* (see Fig. 16.1). The model under verification is abstracted into some abstract model checking problem. If the property holds, then the model checker returns true. If not, in a *directed model checking* attempt the *same* abstraction can be used to guide the search in the concrete state space to falsify the property. If the property does not hold, a counterexample can be returned, and if it does hold, the property has been verified.

This framework does not include recursion as in *counterexample-guided error refinement*, a process illustrated in Figure 16.2. If the abstraction (heuristic) turns out to be too coarse, it is possible to iterate the process with a better one.

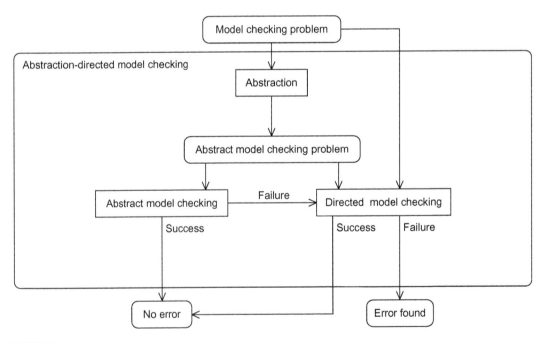

FIGURE 16.1

Abstraction-directed model checking. First, an abstraction is computed. If the abstract system is not correct, the abstraction serves as a heuristic for guiding the search toward the error.

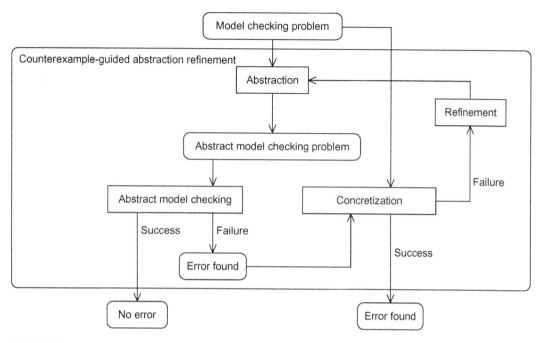

FIGURE 16.2

Counterexample-guided error refinement. First, an abstraction is computed. If the abstract system is not correct, based on the validity of the counterexample, either it is returned or the abstraction is refined and the system iterates.

16.2 COMMUNICATION PROTOCOLS

Communication protocols are examples for finite reactive concurrent asynchronous systems that are applied to organize the communication in computer networks. One important representative of this class is TCP/IP, which organizes the information exchange in the Internet. Control and data flows are essential for communication protocols and are organized either by access to global/shared variables or via communication queues, which are basically FIFO channels. Guards are Boolean predicates associated with each transition and determine whether or not it can be executed. Boolean predicates over variables are conditions on arithmetic expressions, while predicates over queues are either static (e.g., *capacity*, *length*) or dynamic (e.g., *full*, *empty*). Boolean predicates can be combined via ordinary Boolean operations to organize the flow of control.

In the following we introduce search heuristics used in the analysis of (safety properties for) communication protocols, mainly to detect *deadlocks* and violations of *system invariants* or *assertions*.

16.2.1 Formula-Based Heuristic

System invariants are Boolean predicates that hold in every global system state u. When searching for invariant violations it is helpful to estimate the number of system transitions until a state is reached where the invariant is violated. For a given formula f, let $h_f(u)$ be an estimate of the number of transitions required until a state v is reached where f holds, starting from state u. Similarly, let $\bar{h}_f(u)$ denote the heuristic for the number of transitions necessary until f is violated.

In Figure 16.3, we illustrate a recursive definition of h_f as a function of f. In the definition of h_f for $f = f_1 \wedge f_2$ the use of addition suggests that f_1 and f_2 are independent, which may not be true. Consequently, the estimate is not a lower bound, affecting the optimality of algorithms like A*. If the aim is to obtain short but not necessarily optimal paths, we may tolerate inadmissibilities; otherwise, we may replace addition by maximization.

Formulas describing system invariants may contain other terms, such as relational operators and Boolean functions over queues. We extend the definition of h_f and $\bar{h}_f$ as shown in Figure 16.4.

Note that the estimate is coarse but nevertheless very effective in practice. It is possible to refine these definitions for specific cases. For instance, $h_{a=b}$ can be defined as $a - b$ in case $a \geq b$ and a is only ever decremented and b is only ever incremented.

The control state predicate definition is given in Figure 16.5. The distance matrix δ_i can be computed with the ALL PAIRS SHORTEST PATHS algorithm of Floyd and Warshall in cubic time (see Ch. 2).

The statement `assert` extends the model with logical assertions. Given that an assertion a labels a transition $t = (u, v)$, with $t \in T_i$, then we say a is violated if the formula $f = u_i \wedge \neg a$ is satisfied.

f	$h_f(u)$	$\bar{h}_f(u)$
$true$	0	∞
$false$	∞	0
a	**if** a **then** 0 **else** 1	**if** a **then** 1 **else** 0
$\neg f_1$	$\bar{h}_{f_1}(u)$	$h_{f_1}(u)$
$f_1 \vee f_2$	$\min\{h_{f_1}(u), h_{f_2}(u)\}$	$\bar{h}_{f_1}(u) + \bar{h}_{f_2}(u)$
$f_1 \wedge f_2$	$h_{f_1}(u) + h_{f_2}(u)$	$\min\{\bar{h}_{f_1}(u), \bar{h}_{f_2}(u)\}$

FIGURE 16.3

Definition of h_f for Boolean expressions f. Value a is a basic proposition; f_1 and f_2 are logical subformulas.

f	$h_f(u)$	$\bar{h}_f(u)$
$full(q)$	$capacity(q) - length(q)$	if $full(q)$ then 1, else 0
$empty(q)$	$length(q)$	if $empty(q)$ then 1, else 0
$q?[t]$	length of minimal prefix of q without t ($+1$ if q lacks message tagged with t)	if $head(q) \neq t$ then 0, else maximal prefix of t's
$a \otimes b$	if $a \otimes b$ then 0, else 1	if $a \otimes b$ then 1, else 0

FIGURE 16.4

Definition of h_f for queue expressions and relational operators in f. Function $q?[t]$ refers to the expression that is true when the message at the head of queue q is tagged with a message of type t. All other predicates are self-explaining. Symbol $\otimes$ is a wild card for the relational operators $=, \neq, \leq, <, >$, or $\geq$.

f	$h_f(u)$	$\overline{h}_f(u)$
s_i	$\delta_i(u_i, s_i)$	if $u_i = s_i$ 1, else 0

FIGURE 16.5

Definition of h_f for control state predicates in f. The value $\delta_i(u_i, v_i)$ is the minimal number of transitions necessary for the process i to reach state u_i starting from state v_i.

$label(t)$	$executable(t, u)$
q?x, q asynchronous channel	$\neg empty(q)$
q?t, q asynchronous channel	$q?[t]$
q!m, q asynchronous channel	$\neg full(q)$
condition c	c

FIGURE 16.6

Function *executable* for asynchronous communication operations and Boolean conditions, where x is a variable, and t is a tag.

16.2.2 Activeness Heuristic

In concurrent systems, a *deadlock* occurs if at least a subset of processes and resources is in a cyclic wait situation. State u is a *deadlock* if there is no outgoing transition from u to a successor state v and at least one end state of a process of the system is not *valid*. A local control state can be labeled as end to indicate that it is valid; that is, that the system may terminate if the process is in that state.

Some statements are always executable; among others, assignments, else statements, and run statements used to start processes. Other statements, such as send or receive operations or statements that involve the evaluation of a guard, depend on the current state of the system. For example, a send operation q!m is only executable if the queue q is not full, indicated by the predicate $\neg full(q)$. Asynchronous untagged receive operations (q?x, with x variable) are not executable if the queue is empty; the corresponding formula is $\neg empty(q)$. Asynchronous tagged receive operations (q?t, with t tag) are not executable if the head of the queue is a message tagged with a tag different from t; yielding the formula $q?[t]$. Moreover, conditions are not executable if the value of the condition corresponding to the term c is false.

The Boolean function *executable*, ranging over tuples of statements and global system states, is summarized for asynchronous operations and Boolean conditions in Figure 16.6.

To estimate the smallest number of transitions from the current state to a deadlock state, we observe that in a deadlock state all processes are necessarily blocked. Hence, the *active process heuristics* use the number of active or nonblocked processes in a given state:

$$h_a(u) = \sum_{P_i \in P \wedge active(i,u)} 1,$$

where $active(i, u)$ is defined as

$$active(i, u) \equiv \bigvee_{t = (u_i, v_i) \in T_i} executable(t).$$

Assuming that the range of h_a is contained in $\{0,\ldots,|P|\}$, the active processes heuristic is not very informative for protocols involving a small number of processes.

Deadlocks are global system states in which no progress is possible. Obviously, in a deadlock state each process is blocked in a local state that does not possess an enabled transition. It is not trivial to define a logical predicate that characterizes a state as a deadlock state that could at the same time be used as an input to the estimation function h_f. We first explain what it means for a process P_i to be blocked in its local state u_i. This can be expressed by the predicate $blocked_i$, which states that the program counter of process P_i must be equal to u_i and that no outgoing transition t from state u_i is executable:

$$blocked_i(u_i) \equiv \bigwedge_{t=(u_i,v_i)\in T_i} \neg executable(t,u_i).$$

Suppose we are able to identify those local states in which a process i can block; that is, in which it can perform a potentially blocking operation. Let C_i be the set of potentially blocking states within process i. A process is blocked if its control resides in some of the local states contained in C_i. Hence, we define a predicate for determining whether a process P_i is blocked in a global state u as the disjunction of $blocked_i(c)$ for every local state c contained in C_i:

$$blocked_i(u) \equiv \bigvee_{c\in C_i} blocked_i(c).$$

Deadlocks, however, are global states in which *every* process is blocked. Hence, the disjunction of $blocked_i(u)$ for every process P_i yields a formula that establishes whether a global state u is a deadlock state or not:

$$deadlock(u) = \bigwedge_{i=1}^{n} blocked_i(u).$$

Now we address the problem of identifying those local states in which a process can block. We call these states *dangerous*. A local state is dangerous if every outgoing local transition can block. Note that some transitions are always executable, for example, those corresponding to assignments. To the contrary, conditional statements and communication operations are not always executable. Consequently, a local state that has only potentially nonexecutable transitions should be classified as dangerous. Additionally, we may allow the protocol designer to identify states as dangerous. Chaining backward from these states, local distances to critical program counterlocations can be computed in linear time.

The deadlock characterization formula *deadlock* is constructed before the verification starts and is used during the search by applying the estimate h_f, with f being a *deadlock*. Due to the first conjunction of the formula, estimating the distance to a deadlock state is done by summing the estimated distances for blocking each process separately. This assumes that the behavior of processes is entirely independent and obviously leads to a nonoptimistic estimate. We estimate the number of transitions required for blocking a process by taking the minimum estimated distance for a process to reach a local dangerous state and negate the enabledness of each outgoing transition in that state. This could lead again to a nonadmissible estimate, since we are assuming that the transitions performed to reach the dangerous state have no effect on disabling the outgoing transitions of that state.

It should be noted that *deadlock* characterizes many deadlock states that are never reached by the system. Consider two processes P_i, P_j having local dangerous states u, v, respectively. Assume that u has an outgoing transition for which the enabledness condition is the negation of the enabledness condition for the outgoing transition from v. In this particular case it is impossible to have a deadlock in which P_i is blocked in local state u and P_j is blocked in local state v, since either one of the two transitions must be executable. As a consequence the estimate could prefer states unlikely to lead to deadlocks. Another concern is the size of the resulting formula.

16.2.3 **Trail-Directed Heuristics**

We describe now two heuristics that exploit the information of an already established error state. The first heuristic is designed to focus at exactly the state that was found in the error trail, while the second heuristic focuses on equivalent error states.

Hamming Distance

Let u be a global state given in a suitable binary vector encoding, as a vector $(u_1, \ldots, u_k)$. Further on, let v be the error state we are searching for. One estimate for the number of transitions necessary to get from u to v is called the *Hamming distance* $h_d(u, v)$ that is defined as:

$$h_d(u, v) = \sum_{i=1}^{k} |u_i - v_i|.$$

Obviously, in a binary encoding, $|u_i - v_i| \in \{0, 1\}$ for all $i \in \{1, \ldots, k\}$. Obviously, computing $h_d(u, v)$ is available in time linear in the size of the (binary) encoding of a state. The heuristic is not admissible, since one transition might change more than one position in the state vector at a time. Nevertheless, the Hamming distance reveals a valuable ordering of the states according to their goal distances.

FSM Distance

Another distance metric centers around the local states of component processes. The *FSM heuristic* is the sum of the goal distances for each local process P_i, $i \in \{1, \ldots, n\}$. Let u_i be the program counter of state u in process i. Moreover, let $\delta_i(u_i, v_i)$ be the shortest path distance between the program counters u_i and v_i in P_i. Then

$$h_m(u) = \sum_{i=1}^{n} \delta_i(u_i, v_i).$$

Another way for defining the FSM heuristic is by constructing the Boolean predicate f as $\bigwedge_{i \in \{1, \ldots, n\}} u_i = v_i$. Applying the formula-based heuristic yields $h_f(u) = h_m(u)$.

Since the distances between local states can be precomputed, each one can be gathered in constant time resulting in an overall time complexity that is linear to the number of processes of the system.

In contrast to the Hamming distance, the FSM distance abstracts from the current queue load and from values of the local and global variables. We expect that the search will then be directed into equivalent error states that could potentially be reachable through shortest paths. The reason is that some kind of errors depend on the local state of each component process, while variables play no role.

16.2.4 **Liveness Model Checking**

The *liveness as safety model checking* approach proposes to convert a liveness model checking problem into a safety model checking problem by roughly doubling the state vector size. The most important observation is that the exploration algorithms do not have to be rewritten.

In the *lifted search space* we search for shortest lasso-shaped counterexamples, without knowing the start of the cycle beforehand. We use the consistent heuristic

$$h_a(u) = \min\{\delta_N(u_N, v_N) \mid v \text{ is accepting in } N\}$$

of distances in N for finding accepting states in the original search space.

States in the *lifted search space* are abbreviated by tuples (u, v), with u recording the start state of the cycle, and v being the current search state. If we reach an accepting state, we immediately switch to a secondary search. Therefore, we observe two distinct cases: *primary search*, for which the accepting state has not yet reached; and *cycle detection search*, for which an accepting state has to be revisited. The state $u = v$ reached in secondary search is the goal. Because it is a successor of a secondary state, we can distinguish the situation from reaching such a state for the first time.

For all extended states $x = (u, v)$ in the lifted search space, let $h_a(x) = h_a(u)$ and $h_m(x) = h_m(u, v)$. Now we are ready to merge the heuristics to one estimate:

$$h(x) = \begin{cases} h_a(u) & \text{if } u = v \\ h'_m(u, v) & \text{if } u \neq v. \end{cases} \qquad (16.1)$$

As each counterexample has to contain at least one accepting state in N, for primary states x we have that $h = h_a(x)$ is a lower bound. For secondary states x, we have

$$h(x) = h_m(u, v) = \max\{h_m(u, v), \delta_N(u_N, v_N)\},$$

a lower bound to close the cycle and the lasso in total. Therefore, h is admissible. Moreover, we can strengthen the result.

It is not difficult to see that h is consistent; that is, $h(x) - h(x') \leq 1$ for all successor states x' of x. As both h_a and h'_m are monotone, only one of them is true at a time. Hence, we have to show that h is monotone in case of reaching an accepting state. Here we have that a predecessor x with an evaluation of $h(x) = h_a(x) = 0$ spawns successors x' with evaluation values of $h_m(x') > 0$. However, this incurs no problem as $h(x) - h(x') \leq 1$ preserves monotonicity.

The model checking algorithm for directed external LTL search is an extension of external A* (see Ch. 8), which traverses the bucket file list along growing $f = g + h$ diagonals. On disk we store (packed) state pairs. Figure 16.7 illustrates a prototypical execution.

16.2.5 **Planning Heuristics**

To encode communication protocols in PDDL, each process is represented by a finite-state automaton. Since is not difficult to come up with a specialized description, we are interested in a generic translation routine; the propositional encoding should reflect the graph structures of the processes and the communication queues.

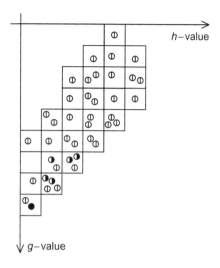

FIGURE 16.7

Directed model checking LTL. For primary nodes (illustrated using two white half circles) heuristic h_a applies, whereas for secondary nodes (illustrated using circles half white/half black) estimate h_m applies. Once a terminal state with matching half circles (illustrated using two black half circles) is reached, an accepting cycle is established.

In the example problem for converting the DINING PHILOSOPHERS problem (see Ch. 10) the initial state is shown in Figure 16.8.

The encoding of the communication structure is based on representing updates in the channel as changes in an associated graph. The *message-passing* communication model realizes the ring-based implementation of the queue data structure. A queue is either empty (or full) if both pointers refer to the same queue state. A queue may consist of only one queue state, so the successor bucket of queue state 0 is the queue state 0 itself. In this case the grounded propositional encoding includes actions where the add and the delete lists share an atom. Here we make the standard assumption that deletion is done first. In Figure 16.8 (bottom) the propositions for one queue and the connection of two queues to one process are shown.

Globally shared and local variables are modeled using numerical variables. The only difference of local variables compared to shared ones is their restricted visibility scope, so that local variables are simply prefixed with the process in which they appear. If the protocol relies on pure message passing, no numerical state variable is needed, yielding a pure propositional model for the DINING PHILOSOPHERS problem.

The PDDL domain encoding uses seven actions, named *activate-trans*, *queue-read*, *queue-write*, *advance-queue-head*, *advance-empty-queue-tail*, *advance-nonempty-queue-tail*, and *process-trans*. We show the activation of a process in Figure 16.9.

Briefly, the actions encode the protocol semantics as follows. Action *activate-trans* activates a transition in a process of a given type from local state s_1 to s_2. Moreover, the action sets the predicate *activate*. This Boolean flag is a precondition of the *queue-read* and *queue-write* actions, which set propositions that initialize the reading/writing of a message. For queue Q in an activated transition

```
(is-a-process philosopher-0 philosopher)
(at-process philosopher-0 state-1)
(trans philosopher trans-3 state-1 state-6)
(trans philosopher trans-4 state-6 state-3)
(trans philosopher trans-5 state-3 state-4)
(trans philosopher trans-3 state-4 state-5)
(trans philosopher trans-6 state-5 state-6)
[...]
(is-a-queue forks-0 queue-1)
(queue-head forks-0 qs-0)
(queue-tail forks-0 qs-0)
(queue-next queue-1 qs-0 qs-0)
(queue-head-msg forks-0 empty)
(queue-size forks-0 zero)
(settled forks-0)
[...]
(writes philosopher-0 forks-0 trans-3) (trans-msg trans-3 fork)
(reads philosopher-0 forks-0 trans-4)  (trans-msg trans-4 fork)
(reads philosopher-0 forks-1 trans-5)  (trans-msg trans-5 fork)
(writes philosopher-0 forks-1 trans-6) (trans-msg trans-6 fork)
```

FIGURE 16.8

PDDL encoding for one philosopher's process, for a (single-cell) communication channel, and for connecting communication to local state transitions.

```
(:action activate-trans
 :parameters (?p - process ?pt - proctype
              ?t - transition ?s1 ?s2 - state)
 :precondition (and
    (forall (?q - queue) (settled ?q))
    (trans ?pt ?t ?s1 ?s2)
    (is-a-process ?p ?pt) (at-process ?p ?s1)
 :effect (and (activate ?p ?t)))
```

FIGURE 16.9

Testing if a transition is enabled and activating it. A pending process is activated if all queues have finalized their updates and if there is a transition that matches the current process state.

querying message m, this corresponds to the expression $Q?m$, respectively $Q!m$. After the read/write operation has been initialized, the queue update actions: *advance-queue-head*, *advance-empty-queue-tail*, or *advance-nonempty-queue-tail* have to be applied. The actions respectively update the head and the tail positions, as needed to implement the requested read/write operation. The actions also set a *settled* flag, which is a precondition of every queue access action. Action *process-trans* can then be invoked. It executes the transition from local state s_1 to s_2; that is, sets the new local process state and resets the flags.

```
(:derived (blocked-trans ?p - process ?t - transition)
   (exists (?q - queue ?m - message ?n - number)
     (and (activate ?p ?t) (reads ?p ?q ?t) (settled ?q)
           (trans-msg ?t ?m) (queue-size ?q ?n) (is-zero ?n))))))

(:derived (blocked ?p - process)
   (exists (?s - state ?pt - proctype)
     (and (at-process ?p ?s) (is-a-process ?p ?pt)
       (forall (?t - transition)
         (or (blocked-trans ?p ?t)
             (forall (?s2 - state) (not (trans ?pt ?t ?s ?s2)))))))))
```

FIGURE 16.10

Derivation of a deadlock in a concurrent system in PDDL. A process is blocked if all its enabled transitions are blocked and a system is in a deadlock if all processes are blocked.

If the read message does not match the requested message, or the queue capacity is either too small or too large, then the active local state transition will block. If all active transitions in a process block, the process itself will block. If all processes are blocked, we have a deadlock in the system. Detection of such deadlocks can be implemented, either as a collection of specifically engineered actions or, more elegantly, as a set of derived predicates. In both cases we can infer, along the lines of argumentation outlined earlier, that a process/the entire system is blocked. The goal condition that makes the planners detect the deadlocks in the protocols is simply a conjunction of atoms requiring that all processes are blocked. The PDDL description for the derivation of a deadlock based on blocked read accesses is shown in Figure 16.10.

Extensions to feature LTL properties with PDDL are available via state trajectory constraints or temporally extended goals.

16.3 PROGRAM MODEL CHECKING

An important application of automated verification lies in the inspection of real software, because they can help to detect subtle bugs in safety-critical programs. Earlier approaches to *program model checking* rely on abstract models that were either constructed manually or generated from the source code of the investigated program. As a drawback, the program model may abstract from existing errors, or report errors that are not present in the actual program. The new generation of program model checkers builds on architectures capable of interpreting compiled code to avoid the construction of abstract models. The used architectures include *virtual machines* and *debuggers*.

We exemplify our considerations in program model checking on the object code level. Based on a virtual processor, it performs a search on machine code, compiled, for example, from a c/c++ source. The compiled code is stored in ELF, a common object file format for binaries. Moreover, the virtual machine was extended with multithreading, which makes it also possible to model-check concurrent programs. Such an approach provides new possibilities for *model checking software*. In the design phase we can check whether the specification satisfies the required properties or not. Rather than using

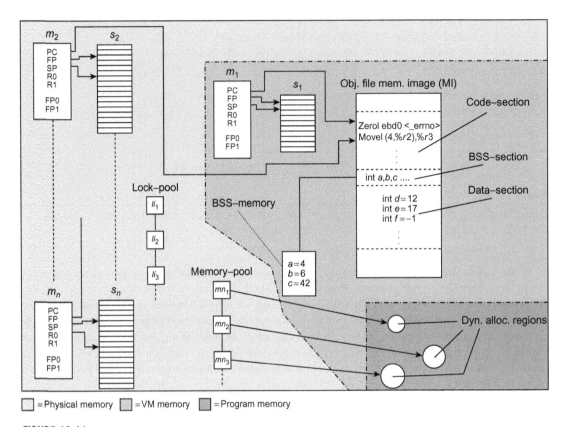

FIGURE 16.11

A state in an assembly language level model checker. Accessed and nonreleased shared variables are maintained in the lock pool, dynamic memory blocks are maintained in the memory pool, the current execution structure (of the active thread) is kept in stacks, and global data such as the program itself and some global variables are already reserved in the object code file that is loaded before the model checker is started.

a model written in the input language of a model checker, the developers provide a test implementation written in the same programming language as the end product.

In *assembly language level program model checking* there are no syntactic or semantic restrictions to the programs that can be checked as long as they can be compiled. Figure 16.11 displays the components of a state, which is essentially composed of the stack contents and machine registers of the running threads, as well as the lock- and memory-pools. The pools store the set of locked resources and the set of dynamically allocated memory regions. The other sections contain the program's global variables.

The state vector in Figure 16.11 can be large and we may conclude that model checking machine code is infeasible due to the memory required to store the visited states. In practice, however, most states of a program differ only slightly from their immediate predecessors. If memory is only allocated

```
#include "IVMThread.h"
#include "MyThread.h"
extern int glob;

class IVMThread;
MyThread::MyThread()
 :IVMThread::IVMThread(){
}
void MyThread::start() {
  run();
  die();
}
void MyThread::run() {
  glob=(glob+1)*ID;
}
void MyThread::die() {
}
int MyThread::id_counter;
```

```
#include <assert.h>
#include "MyThread.h"
#define N 2

class MyThread;
MyThread * t[N];
int i,glob=0;

void initThreads () {
  BEGINATOMIC
    for(i=0;i<N;i++) {
      t[i]=new MyThread();
      t[i]->start();
    }
  ENDATOMIC
}
void main() {
  initThreads();
  VASSERT(glob!=8);
}
```

FIGURE 16.12

The source of the program glob. The main program applies an atomic block of code to create the threads. Such a block is defined by a pair of BEGINATOMIC and ENDATOMIC statements. Upon creation, each thread is assigned a unique identifier ID by the constructor of the super class. An instance of MyThread uses ID to apply the statement glob=(glob+1)*ID. The VASSERT statement evaluates the Boolean expression glob!=8.

for changed components, by using pointers to unchanged components in the predecessor state, it is possible to explore large parts of the program's state space before running out of memory.

Figure 16.12 shows an example program, which generates two threads from an abstract thread class that accesses the shared variable glob. If the model checker finds an *error trail* of program instructions that leads to the line of the VASSERT statement, and the corresponding system state violates the Boolean expression, the model checker prints the trail and terminates. Figure 16.13 shows the error trail. The assertion is only violated if Thread 3 is executed before Thread 2. Otherwise, glob would take the values 0, 2, and 9.

Heuristics have been successfully used to improve error detection in concurrent programs. States are evaluated by an estimator function, measuring the distance to an error state, so that states closer to the faulty behavior have a higher priority and are considered earlier in the exploration process. If the system contains no error, there is no gain.

Deadlock Heuristics

The model checker automatically detects deadlocks during the program exploration. A thread can gain and release exclusive access to a resource using the statements VLOCK and VUNLOCK, which take as their parameter a pointer to a base type or structure. When a thread attempts to lock an already locked

```
Step 1: Thread 1 - Line 10 src-file: glob.c -   initThreads
Step 2: Thread 1 - Line 16 src-file: glob.c -   main
Step 3: Thread 3 - Line 15 src-file: MyThread.cc -   MyThread::run
Step 4: Thread 3 - Line 16 src-file: MyThread.cc -   MyThread::run
Step 5: Thread 2 - Line 15 src-file: MyThread.cc -   MyThread::run
Step 6: Thread 2 - Line 16 src-file: MyThread.cc -   MyThread::run
Step 7: Thread 1 - Line 20 src-file: glob.c -   main
Step 8: Thread 1 - Line <unknown> src-file: glob.c -   main
```

FIGURE 16.13

The error trail for the glob program. First, the instances of MyThread are generated and started in one atomic step. Then the run-method of Thread 3 is executed, followed by the run-method of Thread 2. After step 3, we have glob=(0+1)*3=3 and after step 5 we have glob=(3+1)*2=8. Finally, the line containing the VASSERT statement is reached.

resource, it must wait until the lock is released by the thread that holds it. A deadlock describes a state, where all running threads wait for a lock to be released. An appropriate example for the detection of deadlocks is the *most-block heuristic*. It favors states, for which more threads are blocked.

Structural Heuristics

Another established estimate used for error detection in concurrent programs is the *interleaving heuristic*. It relies on a quantity for maximizing the interleaving of thread executions. The heuristic does not assign values to states but to paths. The objective is that by prioritizing interleavings concurrency bugs are found earlier in the exploration process.

The *lock heuristic* additionally prefers states with more variable locks and more threads alive. Locks are the obvious precondition for threads to become blocked and only threads that are still alive can get in a blocked mode in the future.

If threads have the same program code and the threads differ only in their (thread) *ID*, their internal behavior is only slightly different. In the *thread-ID* heuristic the threads are ordered linear according to their ID. This means that we avoid all those executions in the state exploration, where for each pair of threads, a thread with a higher ID has executed less instruction than threads with a lower ID. States that do not satisfy this condition will be explored later in a way not to disable complete exploration.

Finally, we may consider the access to shared variables. In the *shared variable heuristic* we prefer a change of the active thread after a global read or write access.

Trail-directed heuristics target *trail-directed* search; that is, given an error trail for the instance, find a possibly shorter one. This turns out to be an apparent need of the application programmer, for whom long error trails are an additional burden to simulate the system and to understand the nature of the faulty behavior.

Examples for the trail-directed heuristic are the aforementioned Hamming distance and FSM heuristics. In assembly language level program model checking the FSM heuristic is based on the finite-state automaton representation of the object code that is statically available for each compiled class.

The export of parsed programs into planner input for applying a tool-specific heuristic extends to include real numbers, threading, range statements, subroutine calls, atomic regions, deadlocks, as well as assertion violation detection. Such an approach, however, is limited by the static structure of PDDL, which hardly covers dynamic needs as present in memory pools, for example.

16.4 ANALYZING PETRI NETS

Petri nets are fundamental to the analysis of distributed systems, especially infinite-state systems. Finding a particular marking corresponding to a property violation in Petri nets can be reduced to exploring a state space induced by the set of reachable markings. Typical exploration approaches are undirected and do not take into account any knowledge about the structure of the Petri net.

More formally, a standard Petri net is a 4-tuple (P, T, I^-, I^+), where $P = \{p_1, \ldots, p_n\}$ is the set of *places*, $T = \{t_1, \ldots, t_m\}$ is the set of *transitions* with $1 \leq n, m < \infty$, and $P \cap T = \emptyset$. The backward and forward incidence mappings I^- and I^+, respectively, map elements of $P \times T$ and $T \times P$ to the set of natural numbers and fix the Petri net structure and the transition labels.

A *marking* maps each place to a number; with $M(p)$ we denote the number of *tokens* at place p. It is natural to represent M as a vector of integers.

Markings correspond to states in a state space. Petri nets are often supplied with an initial marking M_0, the initial state. A transition t is *enabled* if all its input places contain at least one token, $M(p) \geq I^-(p, t)$ for all $p \in P$. If a transition is fired, it deletes one token from each of its input places and generates one on each of its output places. A transition t enabled at marking m may *fire* and generate a new marking $M'(p) = M(p) - I^-(p, t) + I^+(p, t)$ for all $p \in P$, written as $M \rightarrow M'$.

A marking M' is *reachable* from M, if $M \xrightarrow{*} M'$, where $\xrightarrow{*}$ is the reflexive and transitive closure of $\rightarrow$. The *reachability set* $R(N)$ of a Petri net N is the set of all markings M reachable from M_0.

A Petri net N is *bounded* if for all places p there exists a natural number k, such that for all M in $R(N)$ we have $M(p) \leq k$. A transition t is *live*, if for all M in $R(N)$, there is a M' in $R(N)$ with $M \xrightarrow{*} M'$ and t is enabled in M'. A Petri net N is *live* if all transitions t are *live*. A *firing sequence* $\sigma = t_1, \ldots, t_n$ starting at M_0 is a finite sequence of transitions such that t_i is enabled in M_{i-1} and M_i is the result of firing t_i in M_{i-1}.

In the analysis of complex systems, *places* model conditions or objects such as program variables, *transitions* model activities that change the values of conditions and objects, and *markings* represent the specific values of the condition or object, such as the value of a program variable.

An example of an ordinary Petri net for the DINING PHILOSOPHERS example with 2 and 4 philosophers is provided in Figure 16.14. Different philosophers correspond to different columns, and the places in the rows denote their states: *thinking*, *waiting*, and *eating*. The markings for the 2-philosophers case correspond to the initial state of the system; for the 4-philosophers case, we show the markings that resulted in a deadlock.

There are two different analysis techniques for Petri nets: the *analysis of the reachability set* and the *invariant analysis*. The latter approach concentrates on the Petri net structure. Unfortunately, invariant analysis is applicable only if studying $|P| \times |T|$ is tractable. Hence, we concentrate on the analysis of the reachability set. Recall that the number of tokens for a node in a Petri net is not bounded a priori, so that the number of possible states is infinite.

Heuristics estimate the number of transitions necessary to achieve a condition on the goal marking. Evaluation functions in the context of Petri nets associate a numerical value to each marking to

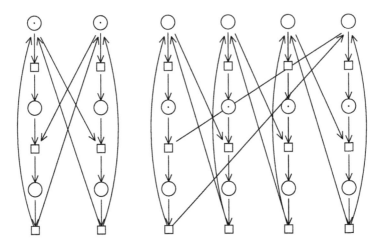

FIGURE 16.14

Place-transition Petri nets for 2- and 4-DINING PHILOSOPHERS. The graphical representation consists of circles for places, dots for tokens, rectangles for transitions, and arrows for arcs between places and transitions. The left net is in its initial states; the net to the right is in a deadlock state. Moreover, the left net can be viewed as an abstraction of the right net.

prioritize the exploration of some successors with respect to some others. The *shortest firing distance* $\delta_N(M,M')$ in a net N is defined as the length of the shortest firing sequence between M and M'. The distance is infinite if there exists no firing sequence between M and M'. Moreover, $\delta_N(M,\psi)$ is the shortest path to a marking that satisfies condition ψ starting at M, $\delta_N(M,\psi) = \min\{\delta_N(M,M') \mid M' \models \psi\}$. Subsequently, heuristic $h(M)$ estimates $\delta_N(M,\psi)$. It is *admissible*, if $h(M) \leq \delta_N(M,\psi)$ and *monotone* if $h(M) - h(M') \leq 1$ for a successor marking M' of M. Monotone heuristics with $h(M') = 0$ for all $M' \models \psi$ are admissible.

We distinguish two search stages. In the explanatory mode, we explore the set of reachable markings having just the knowledge on what kind of error ϕ we aim at. In this phase we are just interested in finding such errors fast, without aiming at concise counterexample firing sequences. For the fault-finding mode we assume that we know the marking where the error occurs. This knowledge is to be inferred by simulation, test, or a previous run in the explanatory mode. To reduce the firing sequence a heuristic estimate between two markings is needed.

Hamming Distance Heuristic

A very intuitive heuristic estimate is the *Hamming distance heuristic*

$$h_H(M,M') = \sum_{p \in P} [M(p) \neq M'(p)].$$

Here, the truth of $[M(p) \neq M'(p)]$ is interpreted as an integer in $\{0,1\}$. Since a transition may add or delete more than one token at a time, the heuristic is neither admissible nor consistent. However, if we divide $h_H(M,M')$ by the maximum number of infected places of a transition, we arrive at an admissible value. In the 4-DINING PHILOSOPHERS problem, an initial estimate of 4 matches the shortest firing distance to a deadlock.

Subnet Distance Heuristic

A more elaborate heuristic that approximates the distance between M and M' works as follows. Via abstraction function ϕ it projects the place transition network N to $\phi(N)$ by omitting some places, transitions, and corresponding arcs. In addition, the initial set of marking M and M' is reduced to $\phi(M)$ and $\phi(M')$. As an example, the 2-DINING PHILOSOPHERS Petri net in Figure 16.14 (left) is in fact an abstraction of the 4-DINING PHILOSOPHERS Petri net to its right.

The *subnet distance heuristic* is the shortest path distance required to reach $\phi(M')$ from $\phi(M)$, formally

$$h_\phi(M,M') = \delta_{\phi(N)}(\phi(M),\phi(M')).$$

In the example of 4-DINING PHILOSOPHERS we obtain an initial estimate of 2. The heuristic estimate is admissible, i.e., $\delta_N(M,M') \geq \delta_{\phi(N)}(\phi(M),\phi(M'))$. Let M be the current marking and M'' be its immediate successor. To prove that the heuristic h_ϕ is consistent, we show that $h_\phi(M) - h_\phi(M'') \leq 1$. Using the definition of h_ϕ, we have that

$$\delta_{\phi(N)}(\phi(M),\phi(M')) \leq 1 + \delta_{\phi(N)}(\phi(M''),\phi(M')).$$

This inequality is always true since the shortest path cost from $\phi(M)$ to $\phi(M')$ cannot be greater than the shortest path cost that traverses $\phi(M'')$ (triangular property).

To avoid recomputations, it is appropriate to precompute the distance prior to the search and to use table lookups to guide the exploration. The subnet distance heuristic completely explores the coverage of $\phi(N)$ and runs an ALL PAIRS SHORTEST PATHS algorithm on top of it.

If we apply two different abstractions ϕ_1 and ϕ_2, to preserve admissibility, we can only take their maximum,

$$h^{\max}_{\phi_1,\phi_2}(M,M') = \max\{h_{\phi_1}(M,M'), h_{\phi_2}(M,M')\}.$$

However, if the supports of ϕ_1 and ϕ_2 are disjoint—that is, the corresponding set of places and the set of transitions are disjoint $\phi_1(P) \cap \phi_2(P) = \emptyset$ and $\phi_1(T) \cap \phi_2(T) = \emptyset$—the sum of the two individual heuristics

$$h^{\text{add}}_{\phi_1,\phi_2}(M,M') = h_{\phi_1}(M,M') + h_{\phi_2}(M,M')$$

is still admissible. If we use an abstraction for the first two and the second two philosophers we obtain the perfect estimate of four firing transitions.

Activeness Heuristic

While the preceding two heuristics measure the distance from one marking to another, it is not difficult to extend them for a goal by taking the minimum of the distance of the current state to all possible markings that satisfy the desired goal. However, as we concentrate on deadlocks, specialized heuristics can be established that bypass the enumeration of the goal set.

A deadlock in a Petri net occurs if no transition can fire. Therefore, a simple distance estimate to the deadlock is simply to count the number of *active transitions*. In other words, we have

$$h_a(M) = \sum_{t \in T} enabled(t).$$

As with the Hamming distance the heuristic is not consistent nor admissible, since one firing transition can change the enableness of more than one transition. For our running example we find four active transitions in the initial states.

Planning Heuristics

In the following we derive a PDDL encoding for Petri nets, so that we can use in-built planning heuristic to accelerate the search. We declare two object types `place` and `transition`. To describe the topology of the net we work with the predicates (`incoming ?s - place ?t - transition`) and (`outgoing ?s - place ?t - transition`), representing the two sets I^- and I^+. For the sake of simplicity all transitions have weight 1. The only numerical information that is needed is the number of tokens at a place. This marking mapping is realized via the fluent predicate (`number-of-tokens ?p - place`). The transition firing action is shown in Figure 16.15.

The initial state encodes the net topology and the initial markings. It specifies instances to the predicates `incoming` and `outgoing` and a numerical predicate (`number-of-tokens`) to specify M_0. The condition that a transition is blocked can be modeled with a derived predicate as follows:

```
(:derived blocked (?t - transition)
    (exists (?p - place)
       (and (incoming ?p ?t) (= (number-of-tokens ?p) 0))))
```

Consequently, a deadlock to be specified as the goal condition is derived as

```
(:derived deadlock (forall (?t - transition) (blocked ?t)))
```

It is obvious that the PDDL encoding inherits a one-to-one correspondence to the original Petri net.

```
(:action fire-transition
 :parameters (?t - transition)
 :preconditions
    (forall (?p - place)
       (or (not (incoming ?p ?t))
          (> (number-of-tokens ?p) 0)))
 :effects
    (forall (?p - place)
       (when (incoming ?p ?t) (decrease (number-of-tokens ?p))))
    (forall (?p - place)
       (when (outgoing ?t ?p) (increase (number-of-tokens ?p)))))
```

FIGURE 16.15

Numerical planning action of a Petri net transition.

16.5 EXPLORING REAL-TIME SYSTEMS

Real-time model checking with timed automata is an important verification scenario, and cost-optimal reachability analysis as considered here has a number of industrial applications including resource-optimal scheduling.

16.5.1 Timed Automata

Timed automata can be viewed as an extension of classic finite automata with clocks and constraints defined on these clocks. These constraints, when corresponding to states, are called *invariants*, and restrict the time allowed to stay at the state. When connected to transitions these constraints are called *guards*. They restrict the use of the transitions. The clocks C are real-valued variables and measure durations. The values of all the clocks in the system are denoted as a vector, also called *clock valuation function*, $v : C \rightarrow R^+$. The constraints are defined over clocks and can be generated by the following grammar: For $x, y \in C$, a constraint α is defined as

$$\alpha ::= x \prec d \mid x - y \prec d \mid \neg \alpha \mid (\alpha \wedge \alpha),$$

where $d \in Z$ and $\prec \in \{<, \leq\}$. These constraints yield two different kinds of transitions. The first one (*delay* transition) is to wait for some duration in the current state s, provided the *invariant*(s) holds. This lets only the clock variables increase. The other operation (*edge* transition) resets some clock variables while taking the transition t. The operation is possible given that the *guard*(t) holds. We allow an edge transition to be taken without an increase in time.

Trajectories are alternating sequences of states and transitions and define a path within the automata. The reachability task is to determine if the goal in the form of partial assignment to the ordinary and clock variables can be reached or not. The optimal reachability problem is to find a trajectory that minimizes the overall path length.

For a reachability analysis on timed automata, we face the problem of an infinite-state space. This infiniteness is due to the fact that the clocks are real-valued and, hence, an exhaustive state space exploration suffers from infinite branching. This problem was solved with the introduction of a partitioning scheme based on regions. A region automata creates finitely many partitions of the infinite-state space based on the equivalent classes of the clock valuations. In model checking tools, though, a coarser representation called a *zone* is used. Formally, a *zone* Z over a set of clocks C is a finite conjunction of difference constraints of the form $x - y \leq d$ or $x - y < d$, with $x, y \in C$ and integer d.[1]

The semantics for *delay* and *edge transitions* in a timed automata are based on some basic operations. We restrict to changes in clock variables. For a clock vector u and a zone Z we write $u \in Z$ if u satisfies the constraints in Z. The two main operations on (clock) zones are: clock *reset* $\{x\}Z = \{u[0/x] \mid u \in Z\}$ that resets all the clocks x, and *delay* (d time units) $Z^\uparrow = \{u + d \mid u \in Z\}$. The reachability problem in timed automata can then be reduced to the reachability analysis in *zone automata*. In a zone automata, each state is basically a *symbolic state* corresponding to one or many states in the original timed automata. The new state is represented as a tuple (l, Z), with l being the

---

[1] Unary constraints $x \leq d$ or $x < d$ are rewritten as $x - x_0 \leq d$ and $x - x_0 < d$ for some start time clock variable x_0, $x - y \geq d$ as $y - x \leq -d$ and $x = y$ as $x - y \leq 0$ and $y - x \leq 0$.

discrete part containing the local state of the automata, and Z is the convex $|C|$-dimensional hypersurface in Euclidean space. Semantically, (l,Z) now represents the set of all states (l,u) with $u \in Z$. Let $B(C)$ denote the set of constraints defined on clocks C and let 2^C denote the power set of C. Formally, a timed automata is a tuple (S, l_0, A, Inv, T), where S is the set of states, (l_0, Z_0) is the initial state with an empty zone, $A \subseteq S \times B(C) \times 2^C \times S$ is the transition relation making states to their successors, given the constraints on the edge are satisfied, $Inv : S \to B(C)$ assigns invariants to the states, and T is the set of final states.

16.5.2 Linearly Priced Timed Automata

Linearly priced timed automata are timed automata with (linear) cost variables. For the sake of brevity, we restrict their introduction to one cost variable c. Cost increases at states with respect to a predefined rate and in transitions with respect to an update operation. The cost-optimal reachability problem is to find a trajectory that minimizes the overall path costs. Figure 16.16 shows a timed automata. The minimum cost of reaching location s_3 with cost 13 corresponds to the trajectory $(d(0), t_1, d(4), t_2)$ of waiting 0 steps in s_1 and then taking the transition to s_2, where four time steps are spent until the transition to the goal in s_3.

Similar to timed automata, for priced timed automata we use the notion of *priced zones* to represent the symbolic states. Let Δ_Z be the unique clock valuation of Z such that for all $u \in Z$ and $\forall x \in C$, we have $\Delta_Z \leq u(x)$; that is, it represents the lowest corner of the $|C|$-dimensional hyper-surface representing a zone. In the following, Δ_Z is referred to as the zone offset. For the internal state representation, we exploit the fact that prices are linear cost hyperplanes of zones. A *priced zone PZ* is a triple (Z, c, r), where Z is a zone, integer c describes the cost of Δ_Z, and $r : C \to \mathbf{Z}$ gives the rate for a given clock. In other words, prices of zones are defined by the respective slopes that the cost function hyperplane has in the direction of the clock variable axes. Furthermore, with $f : PZ \to \mathbf{Z}$, we denote the cost evaluation function based on priced zones PZ. The cost value f for a given clock $x \in C$ in the priced zone $PZ = (Z, c, r)$ can then be computed as $c + \sum_{x \in C} r(x)(v(x) - \Delta_z(x))$. Formally, a linearly priced timed automata over clocks C is a tuple $(S, l_0, A, Inv, Price, T)$, where S is a finite set of locations; (l_0, PZ_0) is the initial state with empty priced zone PZ_0; $A \subseteq S \times B(C) \times 2^C \times S$ is the set of transitions, each consisting of a parent state, the guard on the transition, the clocks to reset, and the successor state; Inv assigns invariants to locations; and $Prize : (S \cup A) \to \mathbf{N}$ assigns prices to the states and transitions.

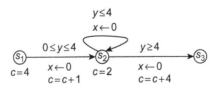

FIGURE 16.16

Example of a priced timed automaton with three states s_1 (*init*), s_2 (*intermediate*), s_3 (*goal*) with two clock variables x and y and the clock constraints defined on the transitions. The rate of cost variable c is 4 at s_1 and 2 at s_2.

16.5.3 **Traversal Politics**

In priced real-time systems, the costs f denote a monotonic increasing function implying that for all $(u,v) \in A$ we have $f(u) \leq f(v)$. It is clear that breadth-first search does not guarantee a cost-optimal solution. A natural extension is to continue the search when a goal is encountered and keep on searching until a *better* goal is found or the state space is exhausted. Such a branch-and-bound algorithm is an extension to uninformed search and *prunes* all the states that do not improve on the last solution cost. Given that the cost function is monotone, the algorithm always terminates with an optimal solution. The underlying traversal policy for branch-and-bound can be borrowed from either breadth-first search, depth-first search, or best-first search.

Heuristics are either provided by the user, or inferred automatically by generalizing the FSM distance heuristic to include clock variables. The automated construction of the heuristic shares similarities with the ones for metric planning and is involved.

One of the involved differences between real-time reachability and ordinary reachability analysis is the *zone inclusion check*. In (delayed) duplicate elimination we omit all identical states from further consideration, whereas in real-time model checking we have to check inclusions of the form $Z \subseteq Z'$ to detect duplicate states. Once Z is *closed under entailment*, in the sense that no constraint of Z can be strengthened without reducing the solution set, the time complexity for inclusion checking is linear to the number of constraints in Z.

Subsequently, while porting real-time model checking algorithms to an external device, we have to provide an option for the elimination of zones. Since we cannot define a *total order* on zones, trivial external sorting schemes are useless in our case. In external breadth-first search we exploit the fact that two states (l, Z) and (l', Z') are comparable only when $l = l'$. This motivates the definition of *zone union* U, where all zones correspond to the states sharing a common discrete part l, and for all $Z, Z' \in U$, we have $Z \nsubseteq Z'$. Duplicate states can now be removed by first sorting with respect to the discrete part l, which will cluster all states, sharing the same l-value, and then performing a one-to-one comparison among all such states. The result of this phase is a file where states are sorted according to the discrete parts l forming duplicate free zone unions. This one-to-one comparison of all the zones for a particular l can only be performed I/O-efficiently when all the states sharing the same l can be read into the main memory. The same approach of internalizing zone unions is available during set refinement with respect to predecessor files. We load both the zone union from the predecessor file and the one in the unrefined file and check for the entailment condition.

16.6 **ANALYZING GRAPH TRANSITION SYSTEMS**

Graphs are a suitable formalism for software and hardware systems involving issues such as communication, object orientation, concurrency, distribution, and mobility. The properties of such systems mainly regard aspects such as temporal behavior and structural properties. They can be expressed, for instance, by logics used as a basis for a formal verification method, the main success of which is due to the ability to find and report errors.

Graph transition systems extend traditional transition systems by relating states with graphs and transitions with *partial graph morphisms*. Intuitively, a partial graph morphism associated to a transition represents the relation between the graphs associated to the source and the target state of the transition; that is, it models the merging, insertion, addition, and renaming of graph items (nodes or edges), where the cost of merged edges is the least one among the edges involved in the merging.

As an example, consider the ARROW DISTRIBUTED DIRECTORY PROTOCOL, a solution to ensure exclusive access to mobile objects in a distributed system. The distributed system is given as an undirected graph G, where vertices and edges, respectively, represent nodes and communication links. Costs are associated with the links in the usual way, and a mechanism for optimal routing is assumed.

The protocol works with a minimal spanning tree of G. Each node has an arrow that, roughly speaking, indicates the *direction* in which the object lies. If a node owns the object or is requesting it, the arrow points to itself; we say that the node is *terminal*. The directed graph induced by the arrows is called L. Roughly speaking, the protocol works by propagating requests and updating arrows such that at any moment the paths induced by arrows, called *arrow paths*, either lead to a terminal owning the object or waiting for it.

More precisely, the protocol works as follows: Initially, L is set such that every path leads to the node owning the object. When a node u wants to acquire the object, it sends a request message $find(u)$ to $a(u)$, the target of the arrow starting at u, and sets $a(u)$ to u; that is, it becomes a terminal node. When a node u of which the arrow does not point to itself receives a $find(w)$ message from a node v, it forwards the message to node $a(u)$ and sets $a(u)$ to v. On the other hand, if $a(u) = u$ (the object is not necessarily at u but will be received if not) the arrows are updated as in the previous case, but this time the request is not forwarded but enqueued. If a node owns the object and its queue of requests is not empty, it sends the object to the (unique) node u of its queue sending a $move(u)$ message to v. This message goes *optimally* through G. Figure 16.17 illustrates two states of a protocol instance with six nodes $v_0, \ldots, v_5$.

We might be interested in properties like *Can node v_i be a terminal? Can node v_i be terminal and all arrow paths end at v_i? Can a node v be terminal? Can a node v be terminal and all arrow paths end at v?*

The properties of a graph transition system can be expressed using different formalisms. We can use, for instance, a temporal graph logic, which combines temporal and graph logics. A similar alternative is *spatial logics*, which combines temporal and structural aspects. In graph transformation systems, we can use rules to find certain graphs: The goal might be to find a match for a certain transformation

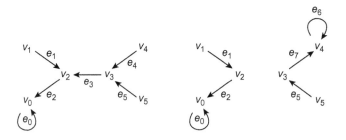

FIGURE 16.17

Three states of the directory. The state on the left is the initial one: node v_0 has the object and all paths induced by the arrows lead to it. The state on the right of the figure is the result of two steps: node v_4 sends a request for the object through its arrow and v_3 processes it by updating the arrows properly; that is, the arrow points now to v_4 instead of v_2.

rule. For the sake of simplicity and generality, however, we consider that the problem of satisfying or falsifying a property is reduced to the problem of finding a set of *goal states* characterized by a goal graph and the existence of an injective morphism.

It is of practical interest to identify particular cases of goal functions as the following goal types: (1) ψ is an identity—the exact graph G is looked for; (2) ψ is a restricted identity—an exact subgraph of G is looked for; (3) ψ is an isomorphism—a graph isomorphic to G is looked for; (4) ψ is any injective graph morphism—the most general case.

Note that there is a type hierarchy, since goal type 1 is a subtype of goal types 2 and 3, which are of course subtypes of the most general goal type 4. The computational complexity of the goal function varies according to the previous cases. For goals of types 1 and 2, the computational efforts needed are just $O(|G|)$ and $O(|\psi(G)|)$, respectively. Unfortunately, for goal types 3 and 4, due to the search for isomorphisms, the complexities increase to a term exponential in $|G|$ for GRAPH ISOMORPHISM and to a term exponential in $|\psi(G)|$ for SUBGRAPH ISOMORPHISM.

We consider two analysis problems. The first one consists of finding a goal state, and the second problem aims at finding an optimal path to a goal state. The two problems can be solved with traditional graph exploration algorithms. For the reachability problem, for instance, we can use depth-first search, hill-climbing, best-first search, Dijkstra's algorithm (and its simplest version, breadth-first search), or A*. For the optimality problem, only the last two are suitable.

Removable Items Heuristic

For graph transformation systems, graph morphisms are induced by graph transformation rules while in communication protocols by the operations of the processes. In most cases, such transitions are usually local and involve a few insertions/deletions/mergings of items. As a heuristic we can thus determine, prior to the analysis, the number of items deleted and erased by graph morphisms so that it is not difficult to derive consistent heuristics.

Isomorphism Heuristics

The main drawback of the preceding for goals of type 4 is evident. If state graphs have more edges and nodes than the goal graph the resulting heuristic is completely blind. Thus, we propose functions inspired by heuristics to decide GRAPH ISOMORPHISM or SUBGRAPH ISOMORPHISM. For instance, if we have to decide whether two graphs are isomorphic, we would check first whether the two graphs have the same number of items. If so, we could continue trying to match nodes with the same in- and out-degrees.

Obviously, none of the two heuristics presented in this section is consistent or admissible in general, and we could define other versions of the heuristics by changing some of the parameters used: the order criteria, the distance between vectors, and so on. The idea of these heuristics is, indeed, to illustrate the wide variety of nonadmissible heuristics we could define.

Hamming Distance Heuristic

The Hamming distance of two bit vectors is the number of vector indices on which the bits differ. As there are many different encodings of a graph, we choose a simple one based on the image of the state representation in the memory. As more than one bit can change within one transition (e.g., the last one before reaching the goal), the heuristic is neither admissible nor consistent.

Planning Heuristics

Finally, we can profit from specific heuristics available in the concrete tool that performs the analysis. To apply a planner to graph transition systems, we first need a propositional description of graph transition systems in PDDL. Due to the parametric description facility provided by planning formalism, it is easy to define morphisms and partial morphisms as actions. For example, a morphism that inverses an edge can be specified as follows:

```
(:action morphism-inverse
:parameters(?u ?v - node)
:precondition (and (link ?u ?v))
:effect
  (and (not (link ?u ?v)) (link ?v ?u)))
```

A graph transition problem can be described with the help of predicates defining the graph in the initial state. The whole graph can be described by the use of link predicates defining the edges between different nodes of the graph.

Fortunately, PDDL provides a very neat and elegant mechanism to formulate our goals' criteria. In the following we address methods to describe the following goals.

Property 1 goal (subgraph): Perhaps the most simple to describe are the type 1 goals, as we only search for a specific subgraph. As is evident from the PDDL specification of the domain, the subgraph can easily be declared by using the (link u v) predicates.

Property 2 goal (exact graph): For a *Property 2* goal, we look for an exact matching of the goal graph in the state space. Just like for the previous type, we can describe the whole graph with (link u v) predicates.

Property 3 goal (subgraph isomorphism): Given a goal graph G, the state space is searched for a state that contains a subgraph isomorphic to G. In such cases, goals are strictly more expressive and need an existential quantification over all the nodes to be described succinctly. A goal of type 3 can then be included as

```
(:goal (exists (?n0 ?n1 - node) (link ?n0 ?n1))
```

Property 4 goal (isomorphism): Given a goal graph G, the state space is searched for a node that contains a graph isomorphic to G. Having the existential quantifier in our hands, we can describe G using (link u v) predicates, for example,

```
(:goal (exists ?n0 ?n1 ?n2 ?n3 ?n4 ?n5 - node)
 (and (link ?n0 ?n0) (link ?n1 ?n0) (link ?n2 ?n0) (link ?n3 ?n1)
      (link ?n4 ?n0) (link ?n5 ?n4))
```

In practice, heuristic search planners can outperform general tools for verifying graph transition systems. But, similar to program model checking applications, the static structure of a plan that models the approach is not able to cover dynamic behaviors in graph transition systems.

16.7 ANOMALIES IN KNOWLEDGE BASES

Knowledge-based systems (KBSs) are used in several applications. Especially when applied to business settings, errors in a KBS can cause considerable damage. Most KBSs are rule based. Checking for anomalies in a given knowledge-based system is a very important task. A popular classification of such anomalies are

1. *Redundancy*: A rule can be omitted without affecting the system's inferences.
2. *Conflict*: Incompatible inferences can be made from valid initial data.
3. *Circularity*: An inference depends on itself.
4. *Deficiency*: No useful conclusions are produced for some valid input set.

Consider the following example for determining the academic status of a person with a knowledge base consisting of five rules:

- (R1): *member-of-university*$(X) \wedge$ *unrolled*$(X) \rightarrow$ *student*(X)
- (R2): *student*$(X) \wedge \neg$*has-degree*$(X,D) \rightarrow$ *undergraduate*(X)
- (R3): *student*$(X) \wedge$ *has-degree*$(X,D) \rightarrow$ *graduate*(X)
- (R4): *enrolled*$(X) \wedge \neg$*has-degree*$(X,D) \rightarrow$ *undergraduate*(X)
- (R5): $\neg$*student*$(X) \rightarrow$ *staff*(X)

Moreover, let *member-of-university*(a), *enrolled*(a), and *has-degree*$(a, bachelor)$ be the possible inputs and *undergraduate*(a), *graduate*(a), and *staff*(a) be mutually incompatible outputs. To check this rule base, goals are *labeled*. As the first goal is reachable via two paths (via rule R4 or via rules R1 and R2), we get two possible *environments*: $\{$*enrolled*$(a), \neg$*has-degree*$(a, bachelor)\}$ and $\{$*member-of-university*(a), *enrolled*$(a), \neg$*has-degree*$(a, bachelor)\}$, so that we obtain a redundancy. The rule base also contains a *conflict*, namely the conjunction of *staff*(a), and *undergraduate*(a) contains the valid combination $\{\neg$*member-of-university*(a), *enrolled*$(a), \neg$*has-degree*$(a, bachelor)\}$.

The efficiency of a labeling approach clearly depends on the compactness of the generated labels. It is not difficult to see that these may require exponential size, with the exponent being in the depth of the rule sets. Henceforth, more efficient representations like BDDs are needed.

The symbolic approach encodes the system's input in binary form, traverses the rule base, thereby constructing the BDDs instead of labels that describe the input and output dependencies of the system, checking these BDD labels against each other, and reporting any anomaly.

In the example we can choose a three-bit unary encoding (x_1, x_2, x_3), respectively denoting the truth or absence of the inputs *member-of-university*(a), *enrolled*(a), and *has-degree*$(a, bachelor)$. Traversing the rule base either by forward or backward chaining gives the BDD representation for the labels. For every rule instance in the inference space, a BDD is constructed using the labels of the literals in its antecedent. The label of the corresponding hypothesis is obtained by computing the disjunct of the rule labels of all rule instances having that hypothesis as a consequent. In the example we obtain the BDD representations for *undergraduate*$(a) = x_2 \wedge \neg x_3$, for *graduate*$(a) = x_1 \wedge x_2 \wedge x_3$, and for *staff*$(a) = \neg x_1 \wedge \neg x_2$. The redundancy anomaly is found during exploration by performing a containment operation on the set of BDD labels. The incompatible output anomaly is established by conjoining the output BDDs for *undergraduate*(a) and for *staff*(a).

16.8 DIAGNOSIS

In diagnosis, we are not only concerned with detecting errors, but additionally with explaining them. Application areas for such (model-based) diagnosis are *intelligent tutoring*, *intelligent authoring*, and *intelligent debugging systems*, in which the mistakes of a novice student, author, or programmer have to be uncovered based on a model of an experienced one. The scenario differs from detecting errors in formal verification as introduced for directed model checking as one practical application of heuristic search technology.

Finding a good diagnosis with respect to some existing flaws in a system is a guided search in itself. Once we have found a misconception, we have to search for the flaw in the argumentation according to the *subject model* of the problem. This is done by propagating the error in the model and *probing* on more and more specific issues. The subject model or *qualitative dependency network* is an augmented undirected graph that is generated in a process called *qualitative simulation*. The edges represent discrete variables with values of a certain range. In the easiest case a variable is Boolean stating that a condition is true or false (*the velocity of a car is positive*). In other cases a variable represents a set of quantities (*the acceleration of a car is large*). The nodes in the network manipulate and propagate the information found at incident edges. They represent the qualitative knowledge and the influence the variables have on each other (*if the velocity of a car is positive and the brakes are pushed, the velocity will decrease*).

Dependency networks are constructed by an expert, explored in an empirical study, or inferred with an inductive learning algorithm. In the diagnosis task we match the knowledge of the learner to the network. The main objective is to efficiently store and propagate the input information within the network. If a misconception arises, we aim to pose only a few questions to pinpoint a wrong inference. In our scenario we allow the learner to make multiple faults according to the model and simulate all possible worlds he or she might be in. Since a diagnosis task is a search in a space of different hypothesis on the values of variables, we deal with uncertainties in background knowledge.

16.8.1 General Diagnostic Engine

The *general diagnostic engine* (GDE) is a framework for performing model-based diagnostics. It is traditionally exemplified by arithmetic dependency networks, in which we have devices such as adders (A_i) and multipliers (M_i). Edges connect the devices as illustrated in Figure 16.18 to an overall graph structure. Variables labeling the edges can be assigned to specific values and the information according to the setting is broadcast within the network. Devices can malfunction and therefore lead to contradictions. The set of possible assignments to the variables is restricted to a small integer range. This implies that all different values can be encoded using only a few bits. A *probe* of an edge is an assignment to a

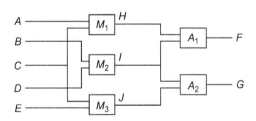

FIGURE 16.18

An arithmetic dependency network with multiplier and adder devices.

variable that reflects the supervised background knowledge received in an interaction with the learner. The access to this knowledge is often computationally expensive.

We distinguish two main stages in one iteration of a GDE. On one hand, we have to update the model according to a given probe, and on the other hand, we have to discriminate the candidates for the next probe. In the following we focus on the first issue. GDE is based on an architecture called *assumption-based truth maintenance system* (ATMS). Besides the dependency network structure, an ATMS maintains database *entries* (v, j_v), with v being an assignment to a variable and j_v being its *justification*. A justification is a set of devices that have been used to derive that variable V is assigned to v. Different justifications for a single variable value might exist. Starting with an empty database the learner instantiates variables one after the other. These variables are *final*, since we have full knowledge of their values. The consequences are drawn with respect to the functionality of the used devices and lead to an assumption on the valuation of the other variables in the network. If the assumption is not confirmed by the learner, we call a value a *no-good*.

In the example the assignments A to 1, B to 1, C to 1, and D to 1 forces F to equal 2 with justification $\{M_1, M_2, A_1\}$. The assignment F to 1 is a *no-good*. Unfortunately, the approach to propagate the values in the network with a simple depth-first search is not sufficient. We need some form of iteration. The new information has to be propagated in the network until no further changes can be achieved, and it has to be offered at every edge of each device node. The database at device node k with degree n for the operation $\otimes$ is updated as follows: Take *every* combination of entries $(v_1, j_{v_1}), \ldots, (v_{n-1}, j_{v_{n-1}})$ for the variables $V_1, \ldots, V_{n-1}$, calculate $v_n = \otimes(v_1, \ldots, v_{n-1})$ with justification $j_{v_n} = \bigcup_{i=1}^{n-1} j_{v_i} \cup \{k\}$, and insert the pair (v_n, j_{v_n}) into the database. Especially in large models these efforts are tremendous, such that merging the inputs reveals the bottleneck of the overall propagation.

16.8.2 Symbolic Propagation

The set of possible propagations of variables in a discrete domain at a given device consists of instantiations to the incident variables $(v_1, \ldots, v_n)$. As seen earlier, BDDs can be utilized to efficiently describe sets of states. In the case of a diagnosis problem a state is a pair consisting of a variable assignment and set of devices that causes the variable to have this particular value.

We have already seen that if we restrict the values to a finite domain, we can represent the Boolean operations *Add* and *Mult* with parameters a, b, and c in the form of a BDD. The key idea in using BDDs is that they do not only apply to a single element but to the whole set that is described at the inputs. For example, combining the BDD characterization of the set $\{1, 3, 7\}$ with the BDD representation of $\{2, 4\}$ and with the BDD for *Mult* directly leads to the description of the BDD representation for the set $\{1, 2, 3, 4, 6, 12, 14, 21, 28\}$. Moreover, the relational description allows us to apply the BDDs in the reverse direction. For example, the *Subtract* and *Div* operators can be obtained by swapping the variable sets a and c in *Add* and *Mult*.

Let $A(a)$ and $B(b)$ be the BDD representations of the different value assignments of the input variables for a device that realizes a Boolean function $F(a, b, c)$. The relational product $C(c) = \exists a, b \ (A(a) \land B(b) \land F(a, b, c))$ computes the desired output BDD. The other two propagation rules are obtained similarly. The justification of the result can be derived by merging the justifications of the inputs. We extend the result with the influence of the currently operating unit and we only allow to execute the operation if both inputs do not already rely on the unit. Therefore, we build the BDD

Result based on the disjunct on all triples of justifications satisfying these additional constraints. As the number of units n and thus the number of bits to encode a justification are big and the power set is exponential in n, we might doubt that this BDD can be constructed, but we explicitly build the BDD for $c_i = a_i \vee b_i$ on every index i and build the conjunct for all $i \in \{1, \ldots, n\}$.

Let $A(a, j_a)$ be the description of the first input and $B(b, j_b)$ be the description of the second input. Then we have

$$C(c, j_c) = \exists a, j_a, b, j_b \; (A(a, j_a) \wedge B(b, j_b) \wedge F(a, b, c) \wedge Result \; (j_a, j_b, j_c)).$$

The implementation of the proposed *diagnosis system* based on BDDs is simple. Any *diagnostic variable* consists of a marker *final*, a BDD *bdd* representing all possible value/justification pairs, and the variable sets for addressing *value* and *just*. Diagnostic variables are linked to at least two devices to inform the devices if a change to a BDD has been obtained. There are four cases to terminate the propagation:

- *The output is final:* We have full knowledge of the output values.
- *One input BDD is the zero function:* We prevent propagation.
- *The output BDD is the zero function:* Either the computation on the restricted domain is not possible or one boundary condition to the relation *Result* is met.
- *The result implies the output BDD:* The output value has already been calculated or no new information is available.

16.9 AUTOMATED THEOREM PROVING

Standard theorem proving procedures draw inferences on sets of clauses. For theorem proving in *predicate logic* SAT solver technology is frequently applied.

To illustrate how *automated theorem proving* can be casted a variant to state space search we recall the resolution rule for predicate logic. From sentences $P_1 \vee P_2 \vee \ldots \vee P_n$ and $\neg P_1 \vee Q_2 \vee \ldots \vee Q_m$ we derive resolvents $P_2 \vee \ldots \vee P_n \vee Q_2 \vee \ldots \vee Q_m$, for example, from P and $\neg P \vee Q$, we derive Q.

In *first-order logic* we are given sentences $P_1 \vee \ldots \vee P_n$ and $Q_1 \vee \ldots \vee Q_m$, where each P_j and Q_k is a literal. If P_j and $\neg Q_k$ *unify* with substitution list Θ, we can derive the resolvent sentence $subst(\Theta, P_1 \vee \ldots \vee P_{j-1} \vee P_{j+1} \vee \ldots \vee P_n \vee Q_1 \vee \ldots \vee Q_{k-1} \vee Q_{k+1} \vee \ldots \vee Q_m)$. For example, from clauses $P(x, f(a)) \vee P(x, f(y)) \vee Q(y)$ and $\neg P(z, f(a)) \vee \neg Q(z)$, we can derive the resolvent clause $P(z, f(y)) \vee Q(y) \vee \neg Q(z)$ using $\Theta = x/z$.

Unification itself is a *pattern matching* procedure, which takes two atomic sentences, called literals, as input, returns *failure* if no match is obtained, and a substitution list, Θ, if a match is found. The equation $unify(p, q) = \Theta$ means $subst(\Theta, p) = subst(\Theta, q)$ for two atomic sentences p and q, where Θ is called the *most general unifier (mgu)*, variables are implicitly universally quantified, and to make literals match, we replace variables by terms. Examples are $parents(x, father(x), mother(Justus))$, $parents(Justus, father(y), z)$ with mgu $\{x/Justus, y/Justus, z/mother(Justus)\}$, and $parents(x, father(x), mother(Justus))$, $parents(Max, father(y), mother(y))$ with unification *failure*.

The pseudo-code linear-time algorithm that returns the mgu is provided in Algorithm 16.1. Note that the mgu not unique, the variable can never be replaced by a term containing that variable, and it is important to check occurrences before making a recursive call.

Procedure Unify
Input: Terms p,q, partial substitution list θ
Output: Complete unification list θ

$(r,s) \leftarrow Scan(p,q)$	;; First terms, where p and q *disagree*
if $((r,s) = (\emptyset,\emptyset))$ **return** $(\theta,success)$	;; Match found
if *variable*(r)	;; Process p
$\quad \theta \leftarrow \theta \cup \{r/s\}$	;; Extend substitution list
$\quad Unify(subst(\theta,p),subst(\theta,q),\theta)$	;; Recursive call
else if variable(s)	;; Process q
$\quad \theta \leftarrow \theta \cup \{s/r\}$	;; Extend substitution list
$\quad Unify(subst(\theta,p),subst(\theta,q),\theta)$	;; Recursive call
else return *failure*	;; No unification available

Algorithm 16.1

The unification algorithm for first-order logic.

Procedure Resolution-Refutation
Input: *KB* set of consistent, *true* sentences in first-order logic
$\quad\quad Q$ goal sentence that we want to derive
Output: *success* if $KB \models Q$, and *failure* otherwise

$KB \leftarrow KB \cup \{\neg Q\}$	;; Proof by contradiction
while $(false \notin KB)$	;; Potentially endless loop
$\quad (S_1,S_2) \leftarrow SelectUnify(KB)$	;; Sentences containing literals that unify
$\quad$ **if** $((S_1,S_2) = (\emptyset,\emptyset))$ **return** *failure*	;; No contradiction possible
$\quad resolvent \leftarrow ResolutionRule(S_1,S_2)$	;; Compute resolvent
$\quad KB \leftarrow KB \cup \{resolvent\}$	;; Extend knowledge base
return *success*	;; Contradiction found

Algorithm 16.2

Resolution refutation procedure.

The *resolution refutation procedure* realizes proof-by-contradiction with an implementation displayed in Algorithm 16.2. Given a consistent set of axioms *KB* and a goal sentence Q, we have to show that $KB \models Q$; that is, every interpretation I that satisfies *KB* satisfies Q. Since interpretation I either satisfies Q or $\neg Q$, we have $(KB \models Q)$ if and only if $(KB \wedge \neg Q \models false)$.

Since the resolution rule is only applicable with sentences that are in the form $P_1 \vee P_2 \vee \ldots \vee P_n$, the question remains, how to convert every sentence in first-order logic into this form. Fortunately, every sentence in first-order logic can be converted to a logically equivalent sentence that is in a *normal form* called *clause form*.

The nine steps to obtain a clause form are as follows. First, we eliminate all equivalences by replacing each instance of the form $(P \Leftrightarrow Q)$ with the equivalent expression $((P \Rightarrow Q) \wedge (Q \Rightarrow P))$. Then we eliminate all implications by replacing each instance of the form $(P \Rightarrow Q)$ with $(\neg P \vee Q)$. Next, we reduce the scope of each negation symbol to a single predicate by applying equivalences such as converting $\neg\neg P$ to P; $\neg(P \vee Q)$ to $\neg P \wedge \neg Q$; $\neg(P \wedge Q)$ to $\neg P \vee \neg Q$; $\neg(\forall x)P$ to $(\exists x)\neg P$; and $\neg(\exists x)P$ to $(\forall x)\neg P$. Afterward, we standardize the variables and rename all variables so that each quantifier has its own unique variable name; convert $(\forall x)P(x)$ to $(\forall y)P(y)$ if there is another place where variable x is already used. Next, we eliminate existential quantification by introducing *Skolem functions*; that is, convert $(\exists x)P(x)$ to $P(c)$, where c is a brand new constant symbol that is not used in any other sentence. Value c is called a *Skolem constant*. More generally, if the existential quantifier is within the scope of a universal quantified variable, then introduce a Skolem function that depends on the universally quantified variable. Function f is called a *Skolem function*, and must be a new name that does not occur in any other sentence in the entire KB. Subsequently, we remove universal quantification symbols by first moving them all to the left end and making the scope of each the entire sentence, and then just dropping the first part. Afterward, we distribute *and* over *or* to obtain a conjunction of disjunctions. Next, we split each conjunct into a separate clause. Finally, we standardize variables so that each clause contains unique variable names.

The resolution procedure can be thought of as the bottom-up construction of a search tree, where the leaves are the clauses produced by KB and the negation of the goal. When a pair of clauses generates a new resolvent clause, we add a new node to the tree with arcs directed from the resolvent to the two parent clauses. It succeeds when a node containing the *false* clause is produced, becoming the root node of the tree. This suggests a breadth-first exploration. Level 0 clauses are those from the original axioms and the negation of the goal. Level k clauses are the resolvents computed from two clauses, one of which must be from Level $k - 1$ and the other from any earlier level. Breadth-first exploration is complete, but very inefficient.

To control the resolution's search, different suggestions have been made. The *set-of-support approach* requires that at least one parent clause must be from the negation of the goal or one of the *descendants* of such a goal clause. The strategy is complete, when we assume that all possible set-of-support clauses are derived. In *unit resolution*, at least one parent clause must be a *unit clause*, one containing a single literal. This strategy is not complete in general, but complete for *Horn clauses*. For *input resolution*, at least one parent from the set of original clauses (from the axioms and the negation of the goal) strategy is not complete in general, but complete for Horn clauses.

16.9.1 Heuristics

A *top-down proof* creates a proof tree, where the node label of each interior node corresponds to the conclusion, and the node labels of its children correspond to the premises of an inference step. Leaves of the proof tree are either axioms or instances of settled theorems. A proof state represents the *outer fragment of a proof tree*: the top node represents the goal and all leaves representing the subgoals of the proof state. All proven leaves can be discharged, because they are not needed for further considerations. If all subgoals have been solved, the proof is successful.

One estimate for the remaining distance to the goal is the number of internal nodes of the current proof state. An illustrative competitor is the string length of a proof state representation. The number of trees with k internal nodes and the number of strings with length k are both finite, such that for this *internal node heuristic* and the *string length heuristic* the number of proof states with fixed heuristic value k are finite.

This is the basis for the design of guided search algorithms with guaranteed progress. At first glance, heuristic search according to the representation size of a theorem seems not to be a good choice, since it exploits very poor knowledge. But even these vague parts of information can speed up computation by magnitudes.

The third heuristic we suggest is the number of open subgoals in the current proof state. This heuristic is the only one that is admissible when we assume that one inference step can close at most one open subgoal at a time. This also proves that the *open subgoal heuristic* is consistent.

In contrast to the *internal node heuristic* and the *string length heuristic* by the limited range of information, the *open subgoal heuristic* can have infinite plateaus of states with the same estimate value. In this case, greedy best-first search frequently fails to terminate. On the other hand, in regular state spaces, even weaker heuristics may yield fast solutions in greedy search.

16.9.2 Functional A* Search

In a *forward proof*, axioms and already proven theorems are combined to generate new theorems. In a *backward proof*, we start with the theorem to prove, which is step-by-step reduced to new subgoals. With a tactic, basic inference steps are combined to larger case-sensitive and proof-searching rules using axioms, memorized theorems, or assumptions. For increasing performance in some basic object logics, tableau theorem provers have been integrated, but their inference is not generic for all object logics. The inference process is hidden in the *auto* tactic.

Greedy best-first search expands the states with minimal evaluation function value first. It is attracted by local optima not complete even for finite graphs. In contrast, DFS and BFS are complete since DFS uses global memory to store already proven subgoals, and BFS could omit the pruning of duplicate states.

In a functional implementation of A* (see Alg. 16.3), one input parameter is the heuristic function h (we have not expelled the input and output parameters since the input are all mappings and the function declaration itself is assigned to the output). Furthermore, the successor generation function Γ, goal predicate *Goal*, and the initial state s are passed to the algorithms as parameters, where the goal function helps filtering the successor states. The priority queue *Open* is represented by a list of triples (g, f, u), sorted by ascending f-values. For the sake of brevity we have omitted reopening of already expanded nodes on shorter generating paths. If the heuristic function h is consistent, $h(v) - h(u) + 1 \geq 0$ for all $(u, v) \in E$, this is no restriction. In this case, on every path the priority f is monotone. All reweighted edges are positive, and the correctness argument of Dijkstra's algorithm applies. All extracted nodes will have correct f-values. The implementation of A* in Algorithm 16.3 uses simultaneous recursion. Keywords and function declarations are set in bold and variables and function calls are set in italics.

In contrast to the imperative setting, in functional A*, *insert* implements dictionary updates within the set of horizon nodes. If the state is already contained in the priority queue, no insertion takes place, thus avoiding duplicates within the queue. However, since the *Closed* list of already expanded states is not modeled, even on finite graphs the functional pure heuristic search derivate $f(v) = (g, h(v), v)$ is no longer complete.

Global expanded node maintenance in *Closed* is integrated in the pseudo codes of Algorithm 16.3 as follows: Set *Closed* is supplied as an additional parameter—in A* to the *relax* function, and in IDA* to the *depth* function. In A*, *Closed* is initialized to the empty list at the very beginning, while in IDA*, *Closed* is reinitialized in each iteration. Instead of (*map f succs*) visited states are first eliminated

```
Functional A* (s, Goal, h, Γ) =                          ;; Interface
  let func relax(succs, t, g) =                           ;; Definition subroutine
    let func f(v) = (g, g + h(v), v)                      ;; Local merit computation
        l ← (filter Goal succs)                           ;; Search for terminal state
    in if (l ≠ []) then l else                            ;; Termination in case goal is found
        Open(foldr (insert, (map f succs), t))            ;; Insert successors calling . . .
                                                          ;; . . . priority queue update
    end                                                   ;; End first subroutine
  and                                                     ;; Recursive definition
    func Open [] = [] |                                   ;; Main case
    Open ((g, f, u) :: t) =                               ;; Call subroutine
      relax (Γ(u), t, g + 1)                              ;; End second subroutine
  in                                                      ;; Initial call
    relax (Γ(s), [], 0)
  end
```

Algorithm 16.3

Functional implementation of the A* algorithm.

by (*map f eliminate(Closed, succs)*). The dictionary for *Closed* can be implemented through lists, balanced trees, or low-level hash tables.

16.10 BIBLIOGRAPHIC NOTES

Approver by Hajek (1978) is probably the first tool for the automated verification of communication protocols. It has already applied guidances to search the state space. The tool was capable of dealing with a broader class of concurrent systems than the classic communication protocols, for instance, like mutual exclusion algorithms. The *SpotLight* system by Yang and Dill (1998) has applied A* to combat the state explosion problem. A general search strategy, called the *target enlargement analysis*, computed nodes around the goal by applying some preimages starting from the target description before starting the forward search. With this respect, this technique shares similarities with *perimeter search* (see Ch. 9). A first study of symbolic-guided model checking algorithm simulating the A* exploration has been provided by Reffel and Edelkamp (1999).

Heuristic search model checking for the analysis of communication protocols has been suggested by Edelkamp, Leue, and Lluch-Lafuente (2004b). The authors coined the term *directed model checking* and implemented a guided variant of the explicit-state model checker SPIN (Holzmann, 2004). For liveness properties the authors contribute an improved nested-DFS algorithm based on the classification of the automata representation of the property in strongly connected components. Later, trail-improvement and partial-order reduction has been included to the system (Edelkamp, Leue, and Lluch-Lafuente, 2004c). Jabbar and Edelkamp (2005) have provided the first external directed model checker to analyze models beyond main memory capacity. Jabbar and Edelkamp (2006) have parallelized the approach with almost linear speedup. Edelkamp and Jabbar (2006c) have extended the scenario to LTL properties based on the *liveness as safety model checking* approach as proposed by Schuppan and Biere (2004).

Counterexample-guided error refinement has been suggested by Clarke, Grumberg, Jha, Lu, and Veith (2001). Pattern/abstraction database heuristics have been introduced independently by Edelkamp and Lluch-Lafuente (2004) (for explicit-state model checking) and by Qian and Nymeyer (2004) (for symbolic model checking). An automated translation of communication protocol specifications from Promela to PDDL has been suggested by Edelkamp (2003b). With two scalable protocol designs, namely the deadlock solution to the DINING PHILOSOPHERS problem and the OPTICAL TELEGRAPH protocol, the domain has served as a benchmark for the international planning competition (Hoffmann et al., 2006).

Directed model checking the machine code has been proposed by Mehler (2005) based on work of Leven, Mehler, and Edelkamp (2004). The architecture refers to model checking Java programs through extending its virtual machines by Visser, Havelund, Brat, and Park. (2000), and by model checking via steered debuggers as proposed by Mercer and Jones (2005). A related approach has been proposed by Robby, Dwyer, and Hatcliff (2003). Externalization and parallelization have been discussed by Edelkamp, Jabbar, and Sulewski (2008a).

Petri nets have been invented by Petri (1962) as a means of describing concurrency and synchronization in distributed systems. They have been used for action planning by Fabiani and Meiller (2000) and by Hickmott, Rintanen, Thiebaux, and White (2006). Heuristics for Petri nets are due to Bonet, Haslum, Hickmott, and Thiébaux (2008) as well as to Edelkamp and Jabbar (2006a). The transcriptions are automated, each predicate is represented by a place, and each action is realized as a transition.

Model checking with timed automata as invented by Alur and Dill (1994) is a decidable subfield of the analysis of hybrid automata (see Henzinger, Kopke, Puri, and Varaiya, 1995) with a number of industrial applications. UPPAAL, as proposed by Larsen, Larsson, Petterson, and Yi (1997), is one very successful verification tool based on timed automata. It can be used for modeling, simulation, and validation of real-time systems. It deals with nondeterministic processes with finite control structure, channel or shared variable communication, and real-valued clocks. UPPAAL CORA developed by Larsen et al. (2001) is the extension of UPPAAL designed for efficient cost-optimal reachability analysis in priced timed automata. UPPAAL CORA is also competitive in resource-optimal scheduling as shown by Rasmussen, Larsen, and Subramani (2004). Heuristics for UPPAAL have been proposed by Kupferschmid, Hoffmann, Dierks, and Behrmann (2006). External branch-and-bound for real-time domains has been proposed by Edelkamp and Jabbar (2006b). A connection from mu-calculus parity games and symbolic planning has been drawn by Bakera, Edelkamp, Kissmann, and Renner (2008).

The graphical nature of designs appears explicitly in approaches like *graph transformation systems* (Rozenberg, 1997), and implicitly in other modeling formalisms like algebras for *concurrent communicating processes* (Milner, 1989). A formal definition of the ARROW DISTRIBUTED DIRECTORY PROTOCOL has been given by Demmer and Herlihy (1998). Edelkamp, Jabbar, and Lluch-Lafuente (2006) have integrated graph transition systems into an ordinary model checker (SPIN) and suggest many of the heuristics discussed in the text. Converting graph transition systems into inputs for planners has been suggested by Edelkamp and Jabbar (2005). The scenario tries to solve the optimization problems with respect to some cost algebra (Edelkamp, Jabbar, and Lluch-Lafuente, 2005).

The classification for different knowledge-based anomalies has been proposed by Preece and Shinghal (1994). Ginsberg (1988) and Rousset (1988) were the first to propose a rule-chain checking technique. BDD implementation for validating knowledge bases have been proposed by Torasso and Torta (2003) and Mues and Vanthienen (2004).

Single-fault analysis is equivalent to satisfiability of Boolean formulas, and thus NP-complete (Meriott and Stuckey, 1998). In the text we consider multiple faults and tackle a harder problem (Kleer and Williams, 1987). One LISP implementation can be found in the textbook by Forbus and de Kleer (1993).

Automated theorem proving for the verification of systems is of rising interest. As a trivial example, all bounded model checkers based on SMV by McMillan (1993) that perform SAT-based exploration apply theorem proving techniques. On the other hand, many theorem provers, like PVS by Owre, Rajan, Rushby, Shankar, and Srivas (1996), include model checking units. Directed automated theorem proving and the functional application of A* has been invented by Edelkamp and Leven (2002). A self-contained introduction to an interactive theorem prover developed at Cambridge University and TU Munich, has been provided by Nipkow, Paulson, and Wenzel (2002). Standard functional heap priority queue representation is described by Okasaki (1998). He used a priority queue representation based on linear lists and also omits the *Closed* list. There are different state-of-the art generic higher-order logic (HOL) theorem proving systems to which directed search appears applicable, like the HOL (Gordon, 1987) and COQ (Barras et al., 1997).

Vehicle Navigation

Navigation is a ubiquitous need to satisfy today's mobility requirements. Current navigation systems assist almost any kind of motion in the physical world including sailing, flying, hiking, driving, and cycling. This success in the mass market has been largely fueled by the advent of the GLOBAL POSITIONING SYSTEM (GPS), which provides a fast, accurate, and cost-efficient way to determine one's geographical position anywhere on the Earth. GPS is most useful in combination with a digital map; *map matching* can provide the user with the information of where he or she is located with regard to it. However, for use in a vehicle, it is not only desirable to know the current position, but also to obtain directions of how to get from the current position to a (possibly unknown) target. To solve this problem, *route finding* has become a major application area for heuristic search algorithms.

In this chapter, we briefly review the interplay of search algorithms and other components of navigation systems, and we discuss particular algorithmic challenges arising in this field.

17.1 COMPONENTS OF ROUTE GUIDANCE SYSTEMS

Let us first give a brief overview of the different components of a navigation system. Apart from the routing algorithm, relevant aspects include the generation and processing of suitable *digital maps*, *positioning*, *map matching*, *geocoding*, and *user interaction*. The next sections discuss these topics in turn.

17.1.1 Generation and Preprocessing of Digital Maps

Digital maps are usually represented as graphs, where the nodes represent intersections and the edges are unbroken road segments that connect the intersections. Nodes are associated with a geographical location. Between intersections intermediate nodes of degree 2 (so-called *shape points*) approximate a road's geometry.

Each segment has a unique identifier and additional associated attributes, such as the name, the road type (e.g., highway, on-/off-ramp, city street), speed information, address ranges, and the like. Generally, no information about the number of lanes is provided. The straightforward representation for a two-way road is by means of a single undirected segment. However, for navigation purposes a representation that breaks them up into two unidirectional links of opposite direction is often more convenient.

Today's commercially available digital maps have achieved an accuracy in the range of a few to a few tens of meters, as well as a coverage for all the major highway road network and urban regions in the industrialized world. They are produced based on a variety of sources: digitization of legacy (paper) maps, aerial photographs, and data collection by specialized field personnel with proprietary equipment, such as optical surveying instruments and high-precision GPS receivers. Maps can be digitized by hand, tracing each map's lines with a cursor, or automatically with scanners. Since maps are bound to change continually over time, updates have to be supplied on a regular basis, typically once or twice a year.

Besides navigation, the combination of enhanced digital roadmaps and precise positioning systems enables a much wider range of novel in-car applications that improve safety and convenience, such as curve speed warning, lane departure detection, predictive cruise control for fuel savings, and more. However, for such applications current commercial maps still lack some necessary features and accuracy, such as accurate altitude, lane structure, and intersection geometry. A number of national and international research efforts are currently under way to investigate the potential of these technologies, like the U.S. Department of Transportation project *EDMap* and its European Union counterpart *NextMap*, which are similar in scope. The objective of EDMap was to develop and evaluate a range of digital map database enhancements that might enable or improve the performance of driver assistance systems under development or consideration by automakers. The project partners included several automotive manufacturers and map suppliers.

Alternative approaches to the traditional labor- and equipment-intensive process of map generation have been researched, and prototypical systems have been developed. One such proposition is statistical in spirit: It is based on a large quantity of possibly noisy data from GPS traces for a fleet of vehicles, as opposed to a small number of highly accurate points obtained from surveying methods. It is assumed that the input probe data are obtained from vehicles that go about their usual business unrelated to the task of map construction, possibly piggybacking on other applications based on positioning systems. The data are *(semi-)automatically* processed in different stages. After data cleanup and outlier removal, traces from different cars are split into sections that belong to the same segment and pooled together, based on an initial inaccurate map, or unsupervised road clustering. Then, each segment geometry is refined using spine fitting. The histogram of distances of GPS points to the road centerline is used to determine the number and position of lanes; finally, observed lane transitions at intersections help to connect the lanes to intersection models.

In a separate project, techniques for offline and online generation of sparse maps has been developed, tailored to use in small, portable devices. The map is based on a collection of entire routes. Intersection points are identified, and segments comprise not individual roads, but subsections of traces not intersecting other traces. Heuristic search methods are needed to estimate if traces represent the same road.

Regardless of the way a digital map has been generated, for navigation purposes it has to be brought in efficiently manageable data structures. The requirements of a routing component are often different from the map display and map matching component, and need a separate representation. For routing, we do not need to explicitly store shape points, only the combined distance and travel times of the line segments between two intersections is relevant for routing. Still, many intersection nodes of degree 2 remain. These nodes can be eliminated by merging the adjacent edges through adding their distance and travel time values.

To find roads that are close to a given location, we cannot afford to sift extensively through large networks. Appropriate *spatial data structures* access methods (e.g., R-tree, CCAM) have been developed that allow fast location-based retrieval, such as *range queries*. Recently, some general-purpose databases have begun incorporating spatial access methods.

17.1.2 **Positioning Systems**

Positioning system is a general term to identify and record the location of an object on the Earth's surface. There are three types of positioning systems commonly in use: standalone, satellite-based, and terrestrial radio-based.

Stand-alone Positioning Systems

Dead reckoning (DR) is the typical standalone technique that sailors commonly used in earlier times before the development of satellite navigation. To determine the current position, DR incrementally integrates the distance traveled and the direction of travel relative to a known start location. A ship's direction used to be determined by magnetic compass, and the distance traveled was computed by the time of travel and the speed of the vehicle (posing the technical challenge of building mechanical clocks that work with high accuracy in an environment of rough motions and changing climates). In modern land-based navigation, however, various sensor devices can be used, such as wheel rotation counters, gyroscopes, and inertial measurement units (IMUs). A common drawback of dead reckoning is that the estimation errors increase with the distance to the known initial position, so that frequent updates with a fixed position are necessary.

Satellite-Based Positioning Systems

With a GPS receiver, users anywhere on the surface of the Earth (or in space around the Earth) can determine their geographic position in latitude (north–south, ascending from the equator), longitude (east–west), and elevation. Latitude and longitude are usually given in units of degrees (sometimes delineated to degrees, minutes, and seconds); elevation is usually given in distance units above a reference such as mean sea level or the *geoid*, which is a model of the shape of the Earth.

The GLOBAL POSITIONING SYSTEM was originally designed by the United States Department of Defense for military use. It comprises 24 satellites orbiting at about 12,500 miles above the Earth's surface. The satellites circle the Earth about twice in a 24-hour period. Each GPS satellite transmits radio signals that can be used to compute a position. These signals are currently transmitted on two different radio frequencies, called *L1* and *L2*. The civilian access code is transmitted on *L1* and is freely available to any user, but the precise code is transmitted on both frequencies, and can be used only by the U.S. military.

To calculate a position, a GPS receiver uses a principle called *triangulation* (to be precise: *trilateration*), a method for determining a position based on the distance from other points or objects that have known locations.

The satellite's radio signals carry two key pieces of information—its position and velocity—and a digital timing signal based on an accurate atomic clock on board the satellite. GPS receivers compare this timing information to timing information generated by a clock within the receiver itself to determine the time it took the radio signal to travel from the satellite to the receiver (and hence its distance, taking into account the speed of light).

Since each satellite measurement constrains the location to lie on a sphere around it, the information of *three* satellites leaves only two possible positions, one of which can generally be ruled out for not lying on the Earth's surface. So, although in principle three satellites are sufficient for localization, in practice another one is needed to compensate for inaccuracies in the receiver's quartz clock.

Obviously with such a sophisticated system, many things can cause errors in the positional computation and limit the accuracy of measurement. Apart from clock errors, major noise sources are:

- Atmospheric interference: The signal is deflected by the ionosphere, and has to travel a longer distance, particularly for satellites that stand low over the horizon.
- Multipath: The signal is reflected at nearby buildings, trees, and such, so that the receiver has to distinguish between the original signal and its echo.
- Due to the various external gravitational influences, the satellite's orbit can deviate from the theoretical prediction.

To achieve higher position accuracy, most GPS receivers utilize what is called *differential GPS (DGPS)*. A DGPS receiver utilizes information from one or more stationary base-station GPS receivers. The base-station GPS receiver calculates a position from the satellite signals, and its difference from the accurately known real position. Under the valid assumption that nearby locations experience a similar error (e.g., due to atmospheric noise), the difference is broadcast to the mobile receivers, who add it to their computed position. Publicly available differential correction sources can be classified as either local area or wide area broadcasts. Local area differential corrections are usually broadcast from land-based radio towers and are calculated from information collected by a single base station. The most common local area differential correction source is a free service maintained by the U.S. Coast Guard. Wide area differential corrections are broadcast from geostationary satellites and are based on a network of GPS base stations spread throughout the intended coverage area. A common source for different corrections used by many low-cost GPS receivers is the *Wide Area Augmentation System (WAAS)*. It is broadcast on the same radio frequency as the GPS signals; therefore, the receivers can conveniently obtain it using the same antenna.

The European *Galileo* program will build a civilian global navigation satellite system that is interoperable with GPS and the Russian GLONASS. By offering dual frequencies as standard, however, Galileo will deliver real-time positioning accuracy down to the meter range, which is unprecedented for a publicly available system. It is planned to reach full operational capability with a total of 30 satellites.

Terrestrial Radio-Based Positioning Systems

Apart from satellite-based navigation, terrestrial radio-based positioning systems have been designed for specific applications (e.g., offshore navigation). They commonly employ direction or angle of arrival (AOA), absolute timing or time of arrival (TOA), and differential time of arrival (TDOA) techniques to determine the position of a vehicle. For example, *LORAN-C* consists of a number of base stations at known locations that keep sending a synchronized signal. By noting the time difference between the signals received from two different stations, the position can be constrained to a hyperbola; exact location requires a second pair of base stations.

Indoor navigation systems generally use infrared and short-range radios, or *radio frequency identification (RFID)*. The mobile networking community uses a technique known as *cell identification (Cell-ID)*.

Hybrid Positioning Systems

We have seen that dead reckoning can maintain the position independently of the availability of external sources, however, it needs regular fixes with known positions or the error will increase steeply with the distance traveled. On the other hand, satellite-based or terrestrial positioning systems can provide an accurate position, but are not available everywhere or all the time (e.g., GPS needs a clear view of the sky, rendering it unreliable in tunnels or urban canyons). Therefore, many practically deployed positioning systems employ a combination of fixed positioning and dead reckoning. Most factory-installed navigation systems use a combination of (D)GPS with wheel rotation counters, gyroscopes, and steering wheel sensors. A universal, principled way of integrating several noisy sensors into a consistent estimate is the *Kalman filter*. To use the Kalman filter to estimate the internal state of a process given only a sequence of noisy observations, we must supply a time-dependent model of the process. In our case, it must be specified how variables like speed and acceleration at a discrete time instant t evolve from a given state at time $t - 1$. In addition, we have to define how the observed outputs depend on the system's state, and how the controls affect it. Then, the process can be essentially modeled as a Markov chain built on linear operators perturbed by Gaussian noise.

Factory-installed vehicle navigation systems can offer a higher positional accuracy than handheld devices due to the integration of built-in sensors. Due to the big gap in cost, however, the latter ones are becoming more and more popular, especially in Europe.

17.1.3 Map Matching

Map matching means associating a position given as a longitude/latitude pair with the most probable location with regard to a map. With perfect knowledge of the location and flawless maps, this would be a trivial step. However, GPS positions might sometimes deviate from the true position by tens to hundreds of meters; and in addition, digital maps contain inaccuracies in the geometry of roads, spurious or missing segments. Moreover, roads are usually represented as lines, and intersections simplified as points where segments meet. Real roads, however, particularly multilane highways, have a nonnegligible width; real intersections also have a considerable extent, and can comprise turn lanes.

Geometric techniques utilize only the estimated location(s) and the road segments. We can distinguish between point-to-point matching, point-to-curve matching, and curve-to-curve matching. In *point-to-point matching* (see Fig. 17.1), the objective is to find the closest node n_i to the measured position p (e.g., the location predicted by GPS). Generally, the Euclidean distance is used to find the

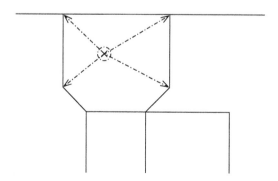

FIGURE 17.1

Point-to-point map matching: The current GPS position is associated with the closest intersection.

distance between p and n_i. The number of nodes n_i is quite large in a road network; however, this number can be reduced using a range query with a suitable window size and the appropriate spatial access method (e.g., R-tree, CCAM). Point-to-point matching gives inaccurate results when we are in the middle of a segment, far away from intersections.

In *point-to-curve matching* (see Fig. 17.2), the objective is to find the closest curve from the measured point. Since most common map segments are represented as a sequence of line segments (a so-called *polyline*), we find the minimum distance between p and any point on some line segments l_i. The procedure consists of *projecting* a point on a line segment (see Fig. 17.3). Generally, we can first retrieve a set of candidate segments with a range query centered on p. Then, each line segment of each road is tested in turn.

To improve efficiency, a *bounding box* can be associated with each segment. Formally, the *axis-parallel bounding box* for a set of coordinates P is defined as the smallest enclosing rectangle

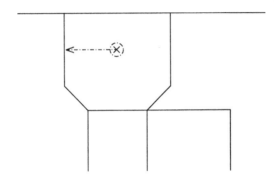

FIGURE 17.2

Point-to-curve map matching: The current GPS position is associated with the closest (interpolated) point on a line segment.

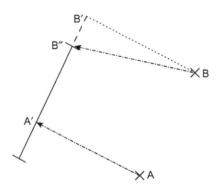

FIGURE 17.3

Projection of a point onto a line segment. An intermediate point A' on the line segment is found that has minimal distance from the current GPS position A. As in the case of point B, the closest point B' on the line can lie outside the segment; in this case, the distance is defined with regard to the closest end point B''.

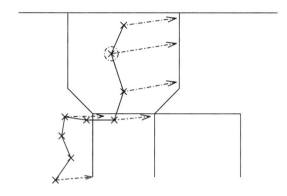

FIGURE 17.4

Curve-to-curve map matching: The history of the trace is used for disambiguation of possible routes. Knowing the (most likely) previous segments restricts the feasible matches of the current position that are consistent with the road network.

$[x_1, x_2] \times [y_1, y_2]$ for P; that is, $x_1 = \min\{x \mid (x, y) \in P\}$, $y_1 = \min\{y \mid (x, y) \in P\}$, $x_2 = \max\{x \mid (x, y) \in P\}$, $y_2 = \max\{y \mid (x, y) \in P\}$. Then, irrelevant segments can be excluded with little effort by computing the distance of p to the bounding box first; we continue with the actual sequence of projections only if it is sufficiently small (i.e, smaller than the best line segment found so far). Apart from the location of a vehicle, it is also often worthwhile to take into account the *heading* (direction of travel) of the vehicle for disambiguation between two close segments running in different directions, for example, in the vicinity of intersections.

Still, point-to-curve matching has limitations. For example, a frequently observed problem in current navigation systems is that a vehicle on a freeway is mapped to an exit ramp, which runs almost parallel (or vice versa). Due to map inaccuracy and the width of lanes, the *closest* line segment is indeed on the wrong street. In this case, taking into account only proximity and heading of the current position is not enough.

A more accurate geometric method, *curve-to-curve matching* (see Fig. 17.4), uses not only the current point p_n, but an entire (segment of the) polyline of historical positions $p_0, p_1, \ldots, p_n$, the so-called *trace* of the vehicle, simultaneously to find the most probable line segment. The knowledge of a vehicle's previous segment constrains the subsequent segment to one of the outgoing edges of its head node. Since alternative candidate routes have to be maintained in parallel and simultaneously extended, it turns out that heuristic search algorithms, most notably A*, provide the best map matching results. Each state in the search consists of a match between a position p_i and a line segment, and its successors are all matches of p_{i+1} that are *consistent* with the map; that is, they are matched either to the same segment, or to any segment that is connected to it in the direction of travel. As a cost measure, we can apply projected point distance, heading difference, or a weighted combination of the two.

Often, digital maps have a higher *relative accuracy* than *absolute accuracy*; that means that the distance error between adjacent shape points is much smaller than the distance between the latitude/longitude position of a shape point and its ground truth. In other words, the map can be locally shifted. An effective way of compensating for these types of inaccuracies is to use a cost function in the A* algorithm that penalizes discrepancies between the driven distance, as estimated from the vehicle trace, and the distance between the matching start and end points according to the digital map.

In summary, a search algorithm (heuristic or not) performing curve-to-curve matching can correct for GPS and map inaccuracies much more effectively than simple point-to-curve matching. In exchange, considerably more computation effort is involved. Therefore, it is used where accuracy is of primary concern, such as in automatic lane keeping or *map generation* (see the previous section); if rapid response is more important than occasional errors, such as in most navigation systems, point-to-curve matching is employed.

17.1.4 Geocoding and Reverse Geocoding

Geocoding is the term used for determining a location along a measured network; typically this means transforming a textual description, such as a street address, into a location. Conversely, reverse geocoding maps a given position into a normalized description of a feature location. Reverse geocoding, therefore, includes *map matching*, to be discussed in the next section.

Often, maps do not contain information about individual buildings, but address ranges for street segments. Geocoding then applies interpolation: If the address range of a street segment spans the address being geocoded, a point location will be created where that address should be. For instance, 197 will be located 97% of the way from the 100 end of the 100–199 block of Main Street (to be precise: $97 / 99 \cdot 100 = 97.97\%$). Another limitation is the network data used—if there are inaccuracies in the street network, the geocoding process will produce unexpected results.

17.1.5 User Interface

The market acceptance of commercial routing systems depends largely not only on the quality of the map data and the speed and accuracy of the search algorithm, but also on the interaction with the user. This starts with the convenience of entering start and target destinations, which involves geocoding (see Sec. 17.1.4), but also search capabilities and tolerance against variations of address format, slight spelling errors, and so on. Speech recognition plays an important role for in-vehicle systems.

After a route has been found, the system provides the driver with spoken and/or visual advice to guide him to his destination. If available, a graphical map display must look appealing, and find the right scale and detail of presentation. For offline navigation, a textual route description is generated; in on-board systems, the position of the car is used in combination with the current route to determine the necessary advice and the timing of giving advice. Usually, the driver first receives a warning that he should prepare to make a certain turn ahead of time so that he can actually make the necessary preparations, such as changing lanes and slowing down. Then the actual advice is given. While the driver is progressing toward his destination, the car navigation system monitors the progress of the car by comparing the current position and the presented route. Of course, not all drivers (correctly) follow all instructions. If the car is not positioned on the current route for a certain amount of time, then the system concludes the driver has deviated from his route, and a new route needs to be planned from the position of the car to the destination.

17.2 ROUTING ALGORITHMS

The route planning algorithm implemented in most car navigation systems is an approximation algorithm based on A*. The problem can become challenging due to the large size of maps that have to be stored (it is an example of a graph that has to be stored *explicitly*). Moreover, constraints on the available computation time of the algorithm are often very tight due to real-time operation. As we will see, to speed up computation, some shortcut heuristics are applied that sometimes result in nonoptimal solutions. Often, at the start an initial route is presented to the driver. As the driver progresses along the proposed route, the system can recalculate the route to find successive improvements.

Car navigation systems usually provide the option to choose among several different optimization criteria. In general, the driver can choose between planning a fastest route, a shortest route, and a route giving preference or penalties to freeways. Also, options to avoid toll roads or ferries may be available. In the future, we expect to see an increase in the *personalization* of planned routes, by an increasing adaptation of the used cost functions to the preferences of the individual driver.

Another aspect of the quality of routes in real-life situations concerns traffic conditions. Information can be static (e.g., average rush-hour and off-peak speeds) or be received online wirelessly (e.g., by radio (RDS) or cell phone). Taking traffic information into account for route planning is a major challenge of a navigation system.

Another real-life requirement that is often overlooked when applying heuristic search to a road network is the existence of *traffic rules*. At a particular intersection, the driver, for example, may not be allowed to make a right turn. Traffic rules can be modeled by a cost function on pairs of adjacent edges. If a traffic rule exists that forbids the driver to go from one road segment to another, then an infinite cost is associated with that pair of adjacent edges. In extension, this formalism also allows us to flexibly encode travel time estimates for intersections (on average, left turns take more time than right turns or straight continuations). The cost of a path P with edges $e_0, \ldots, e_n$ is defined as

$$w(P) = \sum_{i=0}^{n} w_e(e_i) + \sum_{i=0}^{n-1} w_r(e_i, e_{i+1}),$$

where w_e is the edge cost and w_r is the cost associated with turning from e_i to e_{i+1}.

In the straightforward formalization of the state space, intersections are identified with nodes, and road segments between them as edges. However, this is no longer feasible in the presence of turn restrictions. Because an optimum route may contain a node more than once, the standard A* algorithm cannot be used to determine the optimum route. However, an optimum route does not contain an edge more than once. To plan optimum routes in a graph with rules, a modified A* algorithm can be used that evaluates edges instead of nodes. The g-value of an edge e reflects the path cost from the start node up to the head node of e. Additionally, a value g_n associated with each node n is maintained, which keeps track of the minimum of all g-values of edges ending in n.

17.2.1 Heuristics for Route Planning

When trying to find a *shortest* route, the edge costs are equal to the length of the edge. The (modified) A* algorithm can use an h-value based on the *Euclidean distance*, or bee line, from the geographical location $L(u)$ associated with the node u to the location of the destination t. The Euclidean distance between Cartesian coordinates $p_1 = (x_1, y_1)$ and $p_2 = (x_2, y_2)$ is defined as

$$d(p_1, p_2) = \|p_1 - p_2\|_2 = \sqrt{(x_1 - x_2)^2 + (y_1 - y_2)^2},$$

where $\| \cdot \|_2$ denotes the so-called L_2-norm. The heuristic $h(u) = d(L(u), L(t))$ is a lower bound, since the shortest way to the goal must be at least as long as the air distance. It is also consistent, since for adjacent nodes u and v, $h(u) = \|L(t) - L(u)\|_2 \le \|L(t) - L(v)\|_2 + \|L(v) - L(u)\|_2 = \|L(t) - L(v)\|_2 + \|L(u) - L(v)\|_2 \le h(v) + w(u, v)$ by the triangle inequality of the Euclidean plane. Therefore, no reopening is needed in the algorithm.

As for the *fastest* route, it is common to estimate travel time based on *road classes*. Every segment of the road network has been assigned a certain road class. This road class can be used to indicate the importance of a road: the higher the road class number the less important the road. For example, edges with road class 0 are mainly freeways, and edges with road class 1 are mainly highways. An average speed is associated with each road class, and the cost of an edge is determined as its length, divided by this speed. The Euclidean distance divided by the overall maximum speed v_{max} can be used as a h-value to plan fastest routes.

Many route planning systems allow the user to prefer a combination between the fastest route and the shortest route. We can express this using a preference parameter τ that determines the relative weights of a linear combination of the two. We define h_τ as the heuristic estimate for a node u in this extended model as

$$h_\tau(u) = \tau \cdot \frac{1}{v_{max}} \cdot \|L(u) - L(t)\|_2 + (1 - \tau) \cdot \|L(u) - L(t)\|_2$$

$$= \|L(u) - L(t)\|_2 \cdot \left(\frac{\tau}{v_{max}} + (1 - \tau) \right).$$

Since τ and v_{max} are constant for the entire graph and $\|L(u) - L(t)\|_2$ never overestimates the actual edge cost, h_τ never overestimates the actual path cost; that is, it is admissible.

17.2.2 Time-Dependent Routing

Certain properties of a road network change over time. Roads may be closed during specific time periods. For example, a road can be closed for construction work during several hours or days. Particularly during rush hours, the driving time of a route is typically longer. To take this into account, the basic model has been extended to handle *time-dependent costs*. The weight functions w_e and w_r accept an additional argument, representing time. We also define analogous functions $t_e(e, t)$ and $t_r(e_1, e_2, t)$ that denote the time needed to pass an edge and for turning between edges at time t, respectively (for the case of the shortest route, $t_e = w_e$ and $t_r = w_r$). This formalism also allows, for example, for modeling phases of stoplights. The cost of a path $P = (e_0, \ldots, e_n)$ at departure time t_0 is calculated as

$$w(P, t_0) = w_e(e_0, t_0) + \sum_{i=1}^{n} w_e(e_i, t_i + t_r(e_{i-1}, e_i, t_i)) + \sum_{i=1}^{n} w_r(e_{i-1}, e_i, t_i),$$

where $t_{i+1} = t_i + t_r(e_{i-1}, e_i, t_i) + t_e(e_i, t_i + t_r(e_{i-1}, e_i, t_i))$ denotes the arrival time at the head node of edge e_{i+1}.

In this formalism, however, some assignments of time-dependent costs lead to complications. As an extreme case, suppose that for a ferry that operates only during certain times, we assign a weight of infinity outside that interval. Then a vehicle starting at a certain time might not find a possible route with finite weight at all, whereas it can be possible for a later departure. It can be optimal to *delay* the arrival at a node u if the cost of the time-route from node u to the destination decreases more than the cost of the time-route from the starting point to node u increases by delaying the arrival. This means that cycles or large detours can be actually beneficial. It has been shown that finding an optimal route for the general case of time-dependent weights is NP-hard.

To apply (a variant of) Dijkstra's algorithm or the A* algorithm, we have to ensure the precondition of *Bellman's principle of optimality*; that is, that every partial time-route of an optimum time-route is itself an optimum time-route (see Sec. 2.1.3). Let $h^*(e,t_0)$ denote the minimum travel time to get to the goal, starting at time t_0 from the tail node of edge e. Then the road graph is called *time-consistent* if for all times $t_1 \leq t_2$, and every pair of adjacent edges e_1 and e_2, we have

$$t_1 + t_r(e_1,e_2,t_1) + h^*(e_2,t_1 + t_r(e_1,e_2,t_1)) \leq t_2 + t_r(e_1,e_2,t_2) + h^*(e_2,t_2 + t_r(e_1,e_2,t_2)).$$

Roughly speaking, this condition states that leaving a node later can perhaps reduce the duration of traversing an edge, but it cannot decrease the arrival time at the goal. Time consistency of a road graph implies that the Bellman condition holds.

To show time consistency, it turns out that we do not have to explicitly inspect the routes between all pairs of start and destination nodes; instead, it is sufficient to check every pair of adjacent edges. More precisely, we have to verify the condition that for all times $t_1 \leq t_2$ and every pair of adjacent edges e_1 and e_2, we have

$$t_1 + t_r(e_1,e_2,t_1) + t_e(e_2,t_1 + t_r(e_1,e_2,t_1)) \leq t_2 + t_r(e_1,e_2,t_2) + t_e(e_2,t_2 + t_r(e_1,e_2,t_2)).$$

Then time consistency of the road graph follows from a straightforward induction on the number of edges in the solution path.

The model can be generalized to the case that we are trying to minimize a cost measure different from travel time, for example, distance. Then, besides time consistency, the feasibility of the search algorithm requires *cost consistency*. A road graph is called *cost consistent* if for every minimum-cost time-route $(e_1,\ldots,e_n)$ departing at time t_0 from node s to node d, the partial route $(e_1,\ldots,e_i)$ departing at t_0 is also an optimal route from s to e_i. In addition, if there are two minimum-cost time-routes from node s to edge e_i with identical cost, then the time-route $(e_1,\ldots,e_i)$ is the one with the earliest arrival time at the head node of e_i. Unlike for time consistency, unfortunately, there is no easy way of verifying cost consistency without planning the routes between all pairs of nodes.

Under the aforementioned properties of time and cost consistency, the Bellman equation holds, and we can apply the A* algorithm for route finding. The only modification we have to make is to keep track of the arrival time at the end node of each edge, and to use this arrival time to determine the (time-dependent) cost of its adjacent edges.

17.2.3 Stochastic Time-Dependent Routing

The time-dependent costs from the last section can be used to model a variety of delays in travel time, for example, congestion during rush hours, traffic lights timing, timed speed or turn restrictions, and many more conditions. However, it goes without saying that the *exact* progress a particular driver will make at a certain time is unknown. In this section, we are concerned with attempts to model the *uncertainty* of the prediction.

In the most general setting, the cost and driving time of an edge e is a random variable described by a *probability density function* $f(e,t)$. However, in such a formalism the complexity of calculating the stochastic cost of a route can be tremendous; it involves a detailed computation of all possible combinations of realized travel times for the edges in the route. To see this, consider a trip consisting of only two edges, e_1 and e_2. The probability that the trip takes k seconds is equal to a very lengthy sum, namely, of the probability that e_1 takes 1 second and e_2 takes $k - 1$ seconds, plus the probability that e_1 takes 2 seconds and e_2 $k - 2$ seconds, and so on. In the continuous case, we have to form an integral, or more precisely, what is known as a *convolution*. These operations would be computationally infeasible for practical route planning algorithms.

One way out is to consider only probability density functions of certain parametric forms with nice properties. Thus, it has been proposed that if the travel times are exponentially or Erlang distributed and the travel time profiles have a simple form, then the expected travel time and variance of the travel time of a stochastic time-route can be computed exactly. However, in the following we discuss a different approach.

First, costs and travel times of adjacent edges are assumed to be independent. Turn restrictions are assumed to be certain, and not included in the stochastic modeling. Each edge carries two pieces of information: the mean μ and the standard deviation σ of the cost. The model also includes two factors β and γ to reflect the driver's preferences. The *estimated cost* of a stochastic path P is defined as $w(P,t_0) = \mu(w(P,t_0)) + \beta \cdot \sigma(w(P,t_0))$; in turn, the mean and standard deviation of the weight of the path is computed as

$$\mu(w(P,t_0)) = \mu(w_e(e_0,t_0)) + \sum_{i=1}^{n} \mu(w_e(e_i,t_i + t_r(e_{i-1},e_i,t_i))) + \sum_{i=1}^{n} w_r(e_{i-1},e_i,t_i)$$

$$\sigma(w(P,t)) = \sigma(w_e(e_0,t_0)) + \sum_{i=1}^{n} \sigma(w_e(e_i,t_i + t_r(e_{i-1},e_i,t_i))),$$

with $t_{i+1} = t_i + t_r(e_{i-1},e_i,t_i) + \mu(t_e(e_i,t_i + t_r(e_{i-1},e_i,t_i))) + \sigma(t_e(e_i,t_i + t_r(e_{i-1},e_i,t_i)))$.

Minimizing the estimated cost gives the driver the option to indicate his willingness of taking uncertainty into account when planning a route. For example, for $\beta = 1$ a decrease of 10 minutes in the expected travel time and a decrease of 10 minutes in the standard deviation of the travel time are considered equally desirable. For higher values of β, reducing uncertainty becomes more important than reducing the expected travel time. For lower values of β, the situation is exactly the other way around. The factor γ is used to increase the travel time per edge. For $\gamma = 0$, the driving time is assumed to be equal to the expected driving time. Setting $\gamma > 0$ means the driver is pessimistic about the actual driving time. The larger it is, the more likely the driver will arrive at his destination before the estimated arrival time. This is especially useful for individuals that have an important appointment.

Exactly as in the previous section, we have to ensure the time consistency of the graph to guarantee the Bellman precondition. Taking into account the preference parameters, we have to show for all allowed values for β (or γ), for all times $t_1 \leq t_2$, and all pairs of adjacent edges e_1 and e_2, that

$$t_1 + t_r(e_1,e_2,t_1) + \mu(t_e(e_2,t_1 + t_r(e_1,e_2,t_1))) + \beta \cdot \sigma(t_e(e_2,t_1 + t_r(e_1,e_2,t_1))) \leq$$
$$t_2 + t_r(e_1,e_2,t_2) + \mu(t_e(e_2,t_2 + t_r(e_1,e_2,t_2))) + \beta \cdot \sigma(t_e(e_2,t_2 + t_r(e_1,e_2,t_2))).$$

Consequently, the test needs to be performed with the minimum and the maximum allowed value for β.

17.3 CUTTING CORNERS

As mentioned earlier, the requirement of real-time operation, combined with a road graph that can consist of millions of nodes, poses hard time and memory constraints on the search algorithm. Therefore, various pruning schemes have been proposed. Some of the techniques described in Chapter 10 can be applied; in the following, we introduce some methods that are specific to geometric domains.

Nonadmissible pruning reduces computation time or memory requirements by compromising the guarantee of finding an optimal solution. For example, most commercial navigation systems of today incorporate the rationale that when far away from start and goal, the optimal route most likely uses only freeways, highways, and major connections. The system maintains maps on different levels of detail (based on the road class), where the highest one might only contain the highway network, and the lowest level is identical to the entire map. Given a start and destination point, it selects a section of the lowest-level map only within a limited range of both; within larger ranges, it might use an intermediate level, and for the highest distance only the top-level map. This behavior reduces computation time considerably, while still being a good solution in most cases.

Similarly, we know that the Euclidean distance is overly optimistic most of the time. Multiplying it by a small factor, say, 1.1, yields more realistic estimates and can reduce the computation time dramatically, while the solution is often almost identical. This is an instance of nonoptimal A* described in Chapter 6.

The next two sections present two *admissible* schemes for the reduction of search time.

17.3.1 Geometric Container Pruning

In a domain like route planning, where a multitude of shortest path queries have to be answered on the same problem graph, it is possible to accelerate search by means of pieces of information computed prior to the arrival of the queries. As an extreme case, we could compute and memorize all distances and starting edges for the paths between all pairs of nodes using the Floyd-Warshall (Ch. 2) or Johnson's algorithm; this can reduce the query processing to a mere linear backtracking from target to source. However, the space required for saving this information is $O(n^2)$, which is often not feasible because of n being very large. In the next section, we present an approach that reduces the search time in return for more reasonable memory requirements.

Research on annotating a graph by *geometric containers* to guide a search algorithm has shown significant gains in terms of the number of expanded nodes. The basic idea is to reduce the size of the search space of Dijkstra's algorithm or the A* algorithm by pruning edges that can be safely ignored because they are already known not to lie on a shortest path to the target. The two stages for geometric speedups are as follows:

1. In a preprocessing step, for each edge $e = (u, v)$, store the set of nodes t such that a shortest path from u to t starts with this particular edge e (as opposed to other edges emanating from u).
2. While running Dijkstra's algorithm or A*, do not insert edges into the priority queue of which the stored set does not contain the target.

Procedure Create-Containers
Input: Explicit-state space problem graph $G = (V, E, w)$
Output: Rectangular containers $Box : e \to V' \subseteq V$

for each $s \in V$	;; All nodes serve as initial node
$Insert(Open, (s, 0))$	;; Insert init node with zero priority
for each $v \in V \setminus \{s\}$	;; For all other nodes
$Insert(Open, (v, \infty))$	;; Insert into list with infinite cost
while $(Open \neq \emptyset)$	;; As long as there are horizon nodes
$u \longleftarrow DeleteMin(Open)$	;; Extract best one
$Succ(u) \leftarrow Expand(u)$	;; Generate successors by node expansion
for each $v \in Succ(u)$	;; For all successor nodes
if $(f(v) > f(u) + w(u, v))$	;; If better path established
$f(v) \leftarrow f(u) + w(u, v)$	;; Update costs
$DecreaseKey(Open, (v, f(v)))$	;; Update priority queue
if $(u = s)$	;; Special case, initial node reached
$ancestor(v) \leftarrow (s, v)$	;; No contraction at s
else	;; Usual case
$ancestor(v) \leftarrow ancestor(u)$	;; Contraction of shortest path tree
for each $y \in V \setminus \{s\}$	;; For all nodes
$Enlarge(Box(ancestor(y)), y)$	;; Update bounding-box container

Algorithm 17.1

Creating shortest path containers.

The problem that arises is that for n nodes in the graph we would need $O(n^2)$ space to store this information, which is not practically feasible. Hence, we do not remember the set of possible target nodes explicitly, but approximations of it, so-called *geometric containers*. For containers with constant space requirement, the overall storage will be in $O(n)$.

A simple example for a container would be an axis-parallel rectangular bounding box around all possible targets. However, this is not the only container class we can think of. Other options are enclosing circles or the convex hull of a set of points P, which is defined as the smallest convex set that contains P. Recall that a set $M \subseteq S$ is called *convex* if for every two elements $a, b \in M$ the line segment between a and b is also completely contained in M.

A container will generally contain nodes that do not belong to the target node set. However, this does not hurt an exploration algorithm in the sense that it still returns the correct result, but increases only the search space. Incorporating this geometric pruning scheme into an exploration algorithm like Dijkstra or A* will retain its completeness and optimality, since all shortest paths from the start to the goal node are preserved.

The containers can be computed by Algorithm 17.1 in time $O(n^2 \lg n)$. It essentially solves a sequence of single-source-all-targets problems, for all nodes; a variable $ancestor(u)$ remembers the respective outgoing edge from s used on the shortest path to u. Figure 17.5 shows the result of computing a container for the starting point C and the resulting container for edge (C, D).

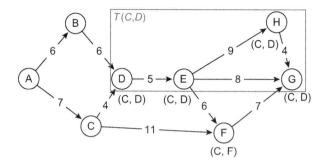

FIGURE 17.5

Example for creating the target container for C.

Procedure Bounding-Box-Graph-Search
Input: Graph G, start node s, target node t
Output: Shortest path from s to t

$[\ldots]$
while $(Open \neq \emptyset)$;; Search space not explored completely
  $u \longleftarrow DeleteMin(Open)$;; Take most promising state
  if $(Goal(u))$ **return** $Path(u)$;; Terminate with shortest path
  $Succ(u) \leftarrow Expand(u)$;; Generate successors
  for each $v \in Succ(u)$;; Consider all successors
    if $(t \notin Box(u,v))$ **continue**   ;; Enforce pruning
    $Improve(u,v)$;; Otherwise, continue search

Algorithm 17.2

Bounding-box graph search algorithm.

The application of containers in explicit graph search is shown in Algorithm 17.2. While running any optimal exploration algorithm on query (s,t), we do not insert edges into the horizon list that are definitely not part of a shortest path to the target. The time required for the computation of these containers pays off well during the main search. Empirical results show a reduction of 90% to 95% in the number of explored nodes in rail networks of different European countries. Figure 17.6 illustrates the effect of bounding-box pruning in the reduction of traversed edges.

It is instructive to compare shortest path pruning to the related approach of pattern database heuristics (see Ch. 15). In the latter case, state-to-goal instead of state-to-state information is stored. Pattern databases are used to refine the search for a fixed goal and varying initial state. In contrast, shortest path pruning uses precomputed shortest path information for a varying initial state and goal state.

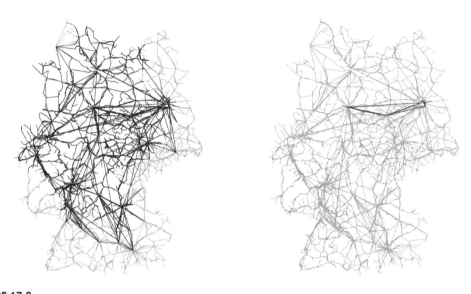

FIGURE 17.6

Shortest path search without (left) and with (right) container pruning (bold edges are searched).

17.3.2 Localizing A*

Consider the execution of the A* algorithm on a search space that is slightly larger than the internal memory capacity of the computer, yet not as large to require external search algorithms. We often cannot simply rely on the operating system's virtual memory mechanism for moving pages to and from the disk; the reason is that A* does not respect locality at all; it explores nodes strictly according to the order of f-values, regardless of their neighborhood, and hence jumps back and forth in a spatially unrelated way only for marginal differences in the estimation value.

In the following, we present a heuristic search algorithm to overcome this lack of locality. *Local A** is a practical algorithm that takes advantage of the geometric embedding of the search graph. In connection with *software paging*, it can lead to a significant speedup. The basic idea is to organize the graph structure such that node locality is preserved as much as possible, and to prefer to some degree local expansions over those with globally minimum f-value. As a consequence, the algorithm cannot stop with the first solution found; we adopt the Node-Ordering-A* framework of Chapter 2. However, the overhead in the increased number of expansions can be significantly outweighed by the reduction in the number of page faults.

In the application of the algorithm to *route planning* we can partition the map according to the two-dimensional physical layout, and store it in a tile-wise fashion. Ideally, the tiles should roughly have a size such that a few of them fit into main memory.

The *Open* list is represented by a new data structure, called HEAP OF HEAPS (see Fig. 17.7). It consists of a collection of k priority queues $H_1, \ldots, H_k$, one for each page. At any instant, only one of the heaps, H_{active}, is designated as being *active*. One additional priority queue $\mathcal{H}$ keeps track of the root nodes of all H_i with $i \neq active$. It is used to quickly find the overall minimum across all of these heaps.

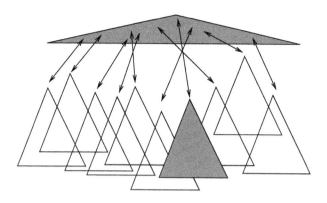

FIGURE 17.7

Example for the HEAP OF HEAPS data structure.

Procedure IsEmpty
Output: Boolean value, indicating if number of elements is zero

    return $\bigwedge_{i=1}^{k} IsEmpty(H_i)$;; All *Open* lists empty

Procedure Insert
Input: Node u with key $f(u)$
Side effect: Updated structure

    if $(\phi(u) \neq active \wedge f(u) < f(Min(H_{\phi(u)})))$;; If improvement to overall heap
        $DecreaseKey(\mathcal{H},(H_{\phi(u)},f(u)))$;; Update overall heap
    $Insert(H_{\phi(u)},(u,f(u)))$;; Inserting in relevant heap

Procedure DecreaseKey
Input: Node u with key $f(u)$
Side effect: Updated structure

    if $(\phi(u) \neq active \wedge f(u) < f(Min(H_{\phi(u)})))$;; If improvement to overall heap
        $DecreaseKey(\mathcal{H},(H_{\phi(u)},f(u)))$;; Update overall heap
    $DecreaseKey(H_{\phi(u)},(u,f(u)))$;; Forward operation to relevant heap

Algorithm 17.3

Access operations on HEAP OF HEAPS.

Let node u be mapped to tile $\phi(u)$. The following priority queue operations are delegated to the member priority queues H_i in the straightforward way. Whenever necessary, $\mathcal{H}$ is updated accordingly.

The *Insert* and *DecreaseKey* operations (see Alg. 17.3) can affect all heaps. However, the hope is that the number of adjacent pages of the active page is small and that they are already in memory or

---

Procedure DeleteSome
Output: Node u with minimal key
Side effect: Updated structure

  CheckActive   ;; Evaluate page changing condition
  return *DeleteMin*(H_{active})   ;; Perform extraction

Procedure CheckActive
Side effect: Updated structure

  if (*IsEmpty*(H_{active}) $\vee$;; Forced change if active page is empty
    ($f(Min(H_{active})) - f(Min(Min(\mathcal{H}))) > \Delta$;; First condition satisfied
     $\wedge f(Min(H_{active})) > \Lambda$))   ;; Second condition satisfied
    Insert($\mathcal{H}, H_{active}, f(Min(H_{active}))$)   ;; Flush current active page
    $H_{active} \leftarrow DeleteMin(H)$;; Find next active page

Algorithm 17.4

Maintenance of active heap.

---

have to be loaded only once; for example, in route planning, with a rectangular tiling each heap can have at most four neighbor heaps. All other pages and priority queues remain unchanged and thus do not have to reside in main memory. The working set of the algorithm will consist of the active heap and its neighbors for some time, until it shifts attention to another active heap.

To improve locality of the search, *DeleteMin* is substituted by a specialized *DeleteSome* operation that prefers node expansions with respect to the current page. Operation *DeleteSome* performs *DeleteMin* on the active heap (see Alg. 17.4).

As the aim is to minimize the number of switches between pages, the algorithm favors the *active* page by continuing to expand its nodes, although the minimum f-value might already exceed the minimum of all remaining priority queues. There are two control parameters: an *activeness bonus* Δ and an estimate Λ for the cost of an optimum solution. If the minimum f-value of the active heap is larger than that of the remaining heaps plus the *activeness bonus* Δ, the algorithm may switch to the priority queue satisfying the minimum root f-value. Thus, Δ discourages page switches by determining the proportion of a page to be explored. As it increases to large values, in the limit each activated page is searched to completion. However, the active page still remains valid, unless Λ is exceeded. The rationale behind this second heuristic is that we can often provide a heuristic for the total least-cost path that is, on the average, more accurate than that obtained from h, but that might be overestimating in some cases.

With this implementation of the priority queue, the algorithm Node-Ordering-A* remains essentially unaltered; the data structure and page handling is transparent to the algorithm. Traditional A* arises as a special case for $\Delta = 0$ and $\Lambda < h^*(s)$, where $h^*(s)$ denotes the actual minimum cost of a path between the source and a goal node. Optimality is guaranteed, since we leave the heuristic estimates unaffected by the heap prioritizing scheme, and since each node inserted into the HEAP OF HEAPS must eventually be returned by a DeleteMin operation.

The algorithm has been incorporated into a commercially available route planning system. The system covers an area of approximately 800 × 400 km at a high level of detail, and comprises approximately 910,000 nodes (road junctions) linked by 2,500,000 edges (road elements).

For long-distance routes, conventional A* expands the nodes in a spatially uncorrelated way, jumping to a node as far away as some 100 km, but possibly returning to the successor of the previous one in the next step. Therefore, the working set gets extremely large, and the virtual memory management of the operating system leads to excessive paging and is the main burden on the computation time.

As a remedy, we achieve memory locality of the search algorithm by exploiting the underlying spatial relation of connected nodes. Nodes are geographically sorted according to their coordinates in such a way that neighboring nodes tend to appear close to each other. A page consists of a constant number of successive nodes (together with the outgoing edges) according to this order. Thus, pages in densely populated regions tend to cover a smaller area than those representing rural regions. For not too small sizes, the connectivity within a page will be high, and only a comparably low fraction of road elements cross the boundaries to adjacent pages. Figure 17.8 shows some bounding rectangles of nodes belonging to the same page.

There are three parameters controlling the behavior of the algorithm with respect to secondary memory: the algorithm parameters Δ and Λ and the (software) page size. The latter one should be adjusted so that the active page and its adjacent pages together roughly fit into available main memory. The optimum solution estimate Λ is obtained by calculating the Euclidean distance between the start and the goal and adding a fixed percentage. Figure 17.9 juxtaposes the number of page faults to the number of node expansions for varying page size and Δ. We observe that the rapid decrease of page faults compensates the increase of expansions (note the logarithmic scale). Using an activeness bonus

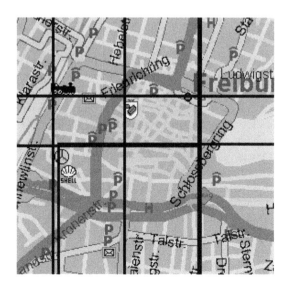

FIGURE 17.8

Granularity of the partition (lines indicate page boundaries).

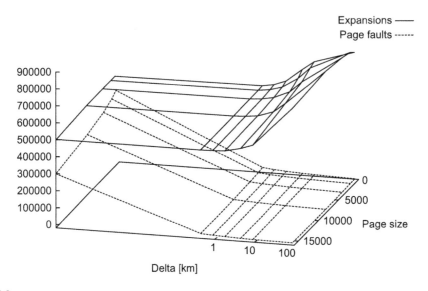

FIGURE 17.9

Number of page faults and node expansions for varying page size and activeness bonus Δ.

of about 2 km suffices to decrease the value by more than one magnitude for all page sizes. At the same time the number of expanded nodes increases by less than 10%.

17.4 BIBLIOGRAPHIC NOTES

Astronomical positioning and dead reckoning are nautical techniques thousands of years old. However, though determining latitude had been mastered early on, measuring longitude proved to be extremely harder. Thus, English ships were being wrecked, thousands of lives were lost, and precious cargo wasn't making its scheduled delivery. Competing with the most renowned astronomers of his time, in the early 1700s a simple clockmaker named John Harrison thought that a well-built clock with a dual face would solve the problem. Sobel (1996) has given a fascinating account of Harrison's struggle against enormous obstacles put in his way by an ingrained scientific establishment.

Comprehensive overviews of the components of modern navigation systems and their interaction can be found in Schlott (1997) and Zhao (1997). Advanced vehicle safety applications and the requirements they impose on future digital maps are discussed in the final reports of the EDMap (CAMP Consortium, 2004) and NextMAP (Ertico, 2002) projects. An approach to generate high-precision digital maps from unsupervised GPS traces has been described in Schrödl, Wagstaff, Rogers, Langley, and Wilson (2004). An incremental learning approach for constructing maps based on GPS traces has been proposed by Brüntrup, Edelkamp, Jabbar, and Scholz (2005). GPS route planning on the superposition of traces is proposed by Edelkamp, Jabbar, and Willhalm (2003). It determines intersections of GPS traces efficiently using the *sweepline* segment intersection algorithm of Bentley and Ottmann (1979), which is one of the first output-sensitive algorithms in computational geometry. The geometric travel planning approach included Voronoi diagrams for query point location search and A* heuristic graph traversal for finding the optimal route. Winter (2002) has discussed modifications to the search algorithm to accommodate turn restrictions in road networks. Our account of time-dependent and stochastic routing is based on the excellent work of Flinsenberg (2004), which should also be consulted for further references on different aspects of routing algorithms. An overview of research concerning real-time vehicle routing problems has been presented by Ghiani, Guerriero, Laporte, and Musmanno (2003).

Shortest path containers have been introduced by Wagner and Willhalm (2003) and been adapted to dynamic edge changes in Wagner, Willhalm, and Zaroliagis (2004). Contraction hierarchies by Geisberger and Schieferdecker (2010) and transit-route routing by Bast, Funke, Sanders, and Schultes (2007) further speed up search. This approach links to initial work by Schulz, Wagner, and Weihe (2000) on shortest path angular sectors. A GPS route planner implementation using shortest path containers in A* has been provided by Edelkamp et al. (2003). Further algorithmic details on dynamic changes to the inferred structures have been discussed in Jabbar (2003). Local A* based on the Heap of Heaps data structure has been proposed by Edelkamp and Schrödl (2000) in the context of a commercial route planning system.

Computational Biology

18

Computational biology or *bioinformatics* is a large research field on its own. It is dedicated to the discovery and implementation of algorithms that facilitate the understanding of biological processes. The field encompasses different areas, such as building evolutionary trees and operating on molecular sequence data. Many approaches in computational biology refer to statistical and machine learning techniques. We concentrate on aspects for which the paradigm of state space search applies.

First of all, we observe a tight analogy between biological and computational processes. For example, generating test sequences for a computational system relates to generating experiments for a biological system. On the other hand, many biochemical phenomena reduce to the interaction between defined sequences.

We selected two problems as representatives for the field and in which heuristics have been applied for increasing the efficiency of the exploration. On one hand, we analyze BIOLOGICAL PATHWAY problems, which have been intensively studied in the field of molecular biology for a long time. We show how these problems can be casted as state space search problems and we illustrate how one problem can be implemented as a planning domain to participate from the general planning heuristics.

On the other hand, we consider what has been denoted as the *holy grail* in DNA and protein analyses. Throughout the book, we have already made several references to MULTIPLE SEQUENCE ALIGNMENT. The core of this chapter aims at providing a coherent perspective and points out recent trends in research of this ubiquitous problem in computational biology.

18.1 BIOLOGICAL PATHWAY

The understanding of biological networks, such as (metabolic and signal transduction) pathways, is crucial for understanding molecular and cellular processes in the organism or system under study. One natural way to study biological networks is to compare known with newly discovered networks and look for similarities between them.

A BIOLOGICAL PATHWAY is a sequence of chemical reactions in a biological organism. Such pathways specify mechanisms that explain how cells carry out their major functions by means of molecules and reactions that produce regular changes. Many diseases can be explained by defects in pathways, and new treatments often involve finding drugs that correct those defects. An example of signaling pathways in a cell is illustrated in Figure 18.1.

We can model parts of the functioning of a pathway as a search problem by simply representing chemical reactions as actions. One example of the BIOLOGICAL PATHWAY domain is the pathway of the

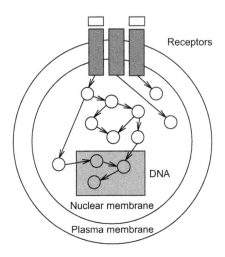

FIGURE 18.1

Signaling pathways in a cell.

mammalian cell cycle control. There are different kinds of basic actions corresponding to the different kinds of reactions that appear in the pathway.

A simple qualitative encoding of the reactions of the pathway has five different actions: an action for choosing the initial substrates, an action for increasing the quantity of a chosen substrate (in the propositional version, quantity coincides with presence, and it is modeled through a predicate indicating if a substrate is available or not), an action modeling biochemical association reactions, an action modeling biochemical association reactions requiring catalysts, and an action modeling biochemical synthesis reactions. An encoding as a planning domain is provided in Figure 18.2.

The goals refer to substances that must be synthesized by the pathway, and are disjunctive with two disjuncts each. Furthermore, there is a limit on the number of input substrates that can be used in the pathway.

In extended versions both the products that must be synthesized by the pathway and the number of the input substrates that are used by the network are turned into preferences. The challenge here is finding paths that achieve a good trade-off between the different kinds of preferences.

Reactions have different durations and can happen if their input substrates reach some concentration level. Moreover, reactions generate their products in specific quantities. The refined goals are summations of substance concentrations that must be generated by the pathway.

18.2 MULTIPLE SEQUENCE ALIGNMENT

Despite their limitation to the moderate number of sequences, the research on *exact* algorithms for the MULTIPLE SEQUENCE ALIGNMENT problem is still going on, trying to push the practical boundaries further. They still form the building block of heuristic techniques, and incorporating them into existing

```
(define (domain pathways)
(:requirements :typing :adl)
(:types simple complex - molecule)
(:predicates
  (association-reaction ?x1 ?x2 - molecule ?x3 - complex)
  (catalyzed-association-reaction ?x1 ?x2 - molecule ?x3 - complex)
  (synthesis-reaction ?x1 ?x2 - molecule)
  (possible ?x - molecule) (available ?x - molecule)
  (chosen ?s - simple) (next ?l1 ?l2 - level) (num-subs ?l - level))

(:action choose
 :parameters (?x - simple ?l1 ?l2 - level)
 :precondition (and (possible ?x) (not (chosen ?x))
                    (num-subs ?l2) (next ?l1 ?l2))
 :effect (and (chosen ?x) (not (num-subs ?l2)) (num-subs ?l1)))

(:action initialize
  :parameters (?x - simple)
  :precondition (and (chosen ?x))
  :effect (and (available ?x)))

(:action associate
 :parameters (?x1 ?x2 - molecule ?x3 - complex)
 :precondition (and (association-reaction ?x1  ?x2  ?x3)
                    (available ?x1) (available ?x2))
 :effect (and  (not (available ?x1)) (not (available ?x2)) (available ?x3)))

(:action associate-with-catalyze
 :parameters (?x1 ?x2 - molecule ?x3 - complex)
 :precondition (and (catalyzed-association-reaction ?x1 ?x2 ?x3)
                    (available ?x1) (available ?x2))
 :effect (and (not (available ?x1)) (available ?x3)))

(:action synthesize
 :parameters (?x1 ?x2 - molecule)
 :precondition (and (synthesis-reaction ?x1 ?x2) (available ?x1))
 :effect (and (available ?x2)))
```

FIGURE 18.2

PDDL encoding of Biological Pathway.

tools could improve them. For example, an algorithm iteratively aligning two groups of sequences at a time could do this with three or more, to better avoid local minima. Moreover, it is theoretically important to have the "gold standard" available for evaluation and comparison, even if not for all problems.

Since MSA can be cast as a minimum-cost path finding problem, it is amenable to heuristic search algorithms developed in the AI community; these are actually among the currently best approaches. Therefore, though many researchers in this area have often used puzzles and games in the past to study heuristic search algorithms, recently there has been a rising interest in MSA as a test bed with practical relevance.

A number of exact algorithms have been developed that compute alignments for a moderate number of sequences. Some of them are constrained by available memory, some by the required computation time, and some by both. It is helpful to roughly group the approaches into two categories: those based on the dynamic programming paradigm, which proceed primarily in breadth-first fashion; and best-first search, utilizing lower and/or upper bounds to prune the search space. Some recent research, including the one introduced in Section 18.2.2, attempts to beneficially combine these two approaches.

The earliest MULTIPLE SEQUENCE ALIGNMENT algorithms were based on dynamic programming (see Sec. 2.1.7). We have seen how Hirschberg's algorithm (see Sec. 6.3.2) is able to reduce the space complexity by one dimension from $O(N^k)$ to $O(kN^{k-1})$, for k sequences of length at most N, by deleting each row as soon as the next one is completed; only a few relay nodes are maintained. To finally recover the solution path, a *divide-and-conquer* strategy recomputes the (much easier) partial problems between the relays.

Section 6.3.1 described how dynamic programming can be cast in terms of Dijkstra's algorithm, to do essentially the same, but relieving us from the necessity of explicitly allocating a matrix of size N^3; this renders dynamic programming quickly infeasible when more than two sequences are involved. Reference counting has been introduced for *Closed* list reduction, already having a big practical impact on the feasibility of instances.

For integer edge costs, the priority queue (also referred to as the heap) can be implemented as a bucket array pointing to doubly linked lists, so that all operations can be performed in constant time. To expand a vertex, at most $2^k - 1$ successor vertices have to be generated, since we have the choice of introducing a gap in each sequence. Thus, like dynamic programming, Dijkstra's algorithm can solve the MULTIPLE SEQUENCE ALIGNMENT problem in $O(2^k N^k)$ time and $O(N^k)$ space for k sequences of length $\leq N$.

On the other hand, although dynamic programming and Dijkstra's algorithm can be viewed as variants of breadth-first search, we achieve best-first search if we expand nodes v in the order of an estimate (lower bound) of the total cost of a path from s to the t passing through v. Rather than the g-value as in Dijkstra's algorithm, we use $f(v) := g(v) + h(v)$ as the heap key, where $h(v)$ is a lower bound on the cost of an optimal path from v to t; most of the time, the sum of optimal pairwise alignments is used.

Unfortunately, the standard linear-memory alternative to A*, IDA*, is not applicable in this case: Although it works best in tree-structured spaces, lattice-structured graphs like in the MULTIPLE SEQUENCE ALIGNMENT problem induce a huge overhead in duplicate expansions due to the huge number of paths between any two given nodes.

It should be mentioned that the definition of the MULTIPLE SEQUENCE ALIGNMENT problem as given earlier is not the only one; it competes with other attempts at formalizing biological meaning, which is often imprecise or depends on the type of question the biologist investigator is pursuing. In the following, we are only concerned with *global alignment* methods, which find an alignment of entire sequences. *Local* methods, in contrast, are geared toward finding maximally similar partial sequences, possibly ignoring the remainder.

18.2.1 **Bounds**

Let us now have a closer look on how lower and upper bounds are derived.

Obtaining an inaccurate *upper bound* on $\delta(s,t)$ is fairly easy, since we can use the cost of *any* valid path through the lattice. Better estimates are available from heuristic linear-time alignment programs.

In Section 1.7.6, we have already seen how lower bounds on the k-alignment are often based on optimal pairwise alignments; usually, prior to the main search, these subproblems are solved in a backward direction, by ordinary dynamic programming, and the resulting distance matrix is stored for later access.

Let U^* be an upper bound on the cost of an optimal multiple sequence alignment G. The sum of all optimal alignment costs $L_{i,j} = d(s_{i,j}, t_{i,j})$ for pairwise subproblems $i, j \in \{1, \ldots, k\}, i < j$, call it L, is a lower bound on G. Carrillo and Lipman pointed out that by the additivity of the sum-of-pairs cost function, any pairwise alignment induced by the optimal multiple sequence alignment can at most be $\delta = U - L$ larger than the respective optimal pairwise alignment. This bound can be used to restrict the number of values that have to be computed in the preprocessing stage and have to be stored for the calculation of the heuristic: For the pair of sequences i, j, only those nodes v are feasible such that a path from the start node $s_{i,j}$ to the goal node $t_{i,j}$ exists with total cost no more than $L_{i,j} + \delta$. To optimize the storage requirements, we can combine the results of two searches. First, a forward pass determines for each relevant node v the minimum distance $d(s_{i,j}, v)$ from the start node. The subsequent backward pass uses this distance like an exact heuristic and stores the distance $d(v, t_{i,j})$ from the target node only for those nodes with $d(s_{i,j}, v) + d(v, t_{i,j}) \leq d(s,t) + \delta$.

Still, for larger alignment problems the required storage size can be extensive. In some solvers, the user is allowed to adjust δ individually for each pair of sequences. This makes it possible to generate at least heuristic alignments if time or memory doesn't allow for the complete solution; moreover, it can be recorded during the search if the δ-bound was actually reached. In the negative case, optimality of the found solution is still guaranteed; otherwise, the user can try to run the program again with slightly increased bounds.

The general idea of precomputing simplified problems and storing the solutions for use as a heuristic is the same as in searching with pattern databases. However, these approaches usually assume that the computational cost can be amortized over many search instances to the same target. In contrast, many heuristics are instance-specific, such that we have to strike a balance.

18.2.2 **Iterative-Deepening Dynamic Programming**

As we have seen, a fixed search order as in dynamic programming can have several advantages over pure best-first selection.

- Since *Closed* nodes can never be reached more than once during the search, it is safe to delete useless ones (those that are not part of any shortest path to the current *Open* nodes) and to apply path compression schemes, such as the Hirschberg algorithm. No sophisticated schemes for avoiding *back leaks* are required, such as core set maintenance and dummy node insertion into *Open*.
- Besides the size of the *Closed* list, the memory requirement of the *Open* list is determined by the *maximum* number of nodes that are open *simultaneously at any time* while the algorithm is running. When the f-value is used as the key for the priority queue, the *Open* list usually contains all nodes with f-values in some range $(f_{min}, f_{min} + \delta)$; this set of nodes is generally spread across

the search space, since g (and accordingly $h = (f - g)$) can vary arbitrarily between 0 and $f_{min} + \delta$. As opposed to that, if dynamic programming proceeds along levels of antidiagonals or rows, at any iteration at most k levels have to be maintained at the same time, and hence the size of the *Open* list can be controlled more effectively.

- For practical purposes, the running time should not only be measured in terms of iterations, but we should also take into account the execution time needed for an expansion. By arranging the exploration order such that edges with the same head node (or more generally, those sharing a common coordinate prefix) are dealt with one after the other, much of the computation can be cached, and edge generation can be sped up significantly. We will come back to this point in Section 18.2.5.

The remaining issue of a static exploration scheme consists of adequately bounding the search space using the h-values. A* is known to be minimal in terms of the number of node expansions. If we knew the cost $\delta(s,t)$ of a cheapest solution path beforehand, we could simply proceed level by level of the grid, however, only immediately prune generated edges e whenever $f(e) > \delta(s,t)$. This would ensure that we only generate those edges that would have been generated by algorithm A* as well. An upper threshold would additionally help reduce the size of the *Closed* list, since a node can be pruned if all of its children lie beyond the threshold; additionally, if this node is the only child of its parent, this can give rise to a propagating chain of ancestor deletions.

We propose to apply a search scheme that carries out a series of searches with successively larger thresholds until a solution is found (or we run out of memory or patience). The use of such an upper bound parallels that in the IDA* algorithm.

18.2.3 Main Loop

The resulting algorithm, which we will refer to as *iterative-deepening dynamic programming* (IDDP), is sketched in Algorithm 18.1. The outer loop initializes the threshold with a lower bound (e.g., $h(s)$), and, unless a solution is found, increases it up to an upper bound. In the same manner as in the IDA* algorithm, to make sure that at least one additional edge is explored in each iteration, the threshold has to be increased correspondingly at least to the minimum cost of a fringe edge that exceeded the previous threshold. This fringe increment is maintained in the variable *minNextThresh*, initially estimated as the upper bound, and repeatedly decreased in the course of the following expansions.

In each step of the inner loop, we select and remove a node from the priority queue of which the level is minimal. As explained later in Section 18.2.5, it is favorable to break ties according to the lexicographic order of target nodes. Since the total number of possible levels is comparatively small and known in advance, the priority queue can be implemented using an array of linked lists; this provides constant time operations for insertion and deletion.

Edge Expansion

The expansion of an edge e is partial (see Alg. 18.2). A child edge might already exist from an earlier expansion of an edge with the same head vertex; we have to test if we can decrease the g-value. Otherwise, we generate a new edge if its f-value exceeds the search threshold of the current iteration and its memory is immediately reclaimed. In a practical implementation, we can prune unnecessary accesses to partial alignments *inside* the calculation of the heuristic as soon as the search threshold has already been reached.

Procedure IDDP
Input: Edges e_s, e_t, LOWER BOUND L, UPPER BOUND U^*
Output: Optimal alignment

$U \leftarrow L$	;; Initialize threshold
while $(U \leq U^*)$	;; Outer loop, iterative-deepening phases
$Open \leftarrow \{s_e\}$	;; Initialize frontier list
$U' \leftarrow U$	;; Inner loop
while $(Open \neq \emptyset)$	;; Bounded dynamic programming
Remove e from $Open$ with min. $level(e)$	;; Select edge for expansion
if $(e = e_t)$	;; Optimal alignment found
return $Path(e_s, e_t)$	;; Find actual alignment
$Expand(e, U, U')$	;; Generate and process successors, Alg. 18.2
$\Delta \leftarrow ComputeIncr$	;; Compute search threshold for next iteration
$U \leftarrow \max\{U + \Delta, U'\}$	;; Update search threshold

Algorithm 18.1

Iterative-deepening dynamic programming.

Procedure Expand
Input: Edge e, threshold U, next threshold U'
Side effects: Initialize/update g-values of successors of e

for each c in $Succ(e)$	;; Retrieve child or tentatively generate it if not ...
	;; ... yet existing, set Boolean variable $created$ accordingly
$g' \leftarrow g(e) + GapCost(e,c) + GetCost(c)$	;; Determine new g-value
$f = g' + h(c)$	;; Determine new f-value
if $((f \leq U)$ **and** $(g' < g(c)))$	;; Shorter path than current best found ...
$g(c) \leftarrow g'$	;; ... estimate within threshold
$UpdateEdge(e,c,h)$	;; Edge relaxation (Alg. 18.3)
else if $(f > U)$	;; Larger path than currently best
$U' \leftarrow \min\{U', f\}$	;; Record minimum of pruned edges
if($created$)	;; Child new
$Delete(c)$	;; Make sure only promising edges are stored
if $(ref(e) = 0)$	;; Reference count zero
$DeleteRec(e)$	;; No promising children could be inserted into the heap

Algorithm 18.2

Edge expansion in IDDP.

The relaxation of a successor edge within the threshold is performed by the subprocedure *UpdateEdge* (see Alg. 18.3). This is similar to the corresponding relaxation step in A*, updating the child's g- and f-values, its parent pointers, and inserting it into *Open*, if it is not already contained. However, in contrast to best-first search, it is inserted into the heap according to the antidiagonal level

---

Procedure UpdateEdge
Input: Edges p (parent), c (child), HEAP $Open$
Side effects: Update $Open$, delete unused ancestors of c

$ref(p) \leftarrow ref(p) + 1$;; Increment reference count of new parent
$ref(ancestor(c)) \leftarrow ref(ancestor(c)) - 1$;; Decrement reference count of old one
if $(ref(ancestor(c)) = 0)$;; The former parent has lost its last child ...
   $DeleteRec(ancestor(c))$;; ... and becomes useless

$ancestor(c) \leftarrow p$;; Update ancestor
if (c **not in** $Open$)   ;; Not yet generated
   Insert c into $Open$ with $level(c)$

Algorithm 18.3

Edge relaxation step for IDDP.

Procedure DeleteRec
Input: Edge e

if $(ancestor(e) \neq \emptyset)$
   $ref(ancestor(e)) \leftarrow ref(ancestor(e)) - 1$;; Decrease reference counter
if $(ref(ancestor(e)) = 0)$;; No remaining reference
   $DeleteRec(ancestor(e))$;; Recursive call
$Delete(e)$;; Remove edge from memory

Algorithm 18.4

Recursive deletion of edges that are no longer part of any solution path.

---

of its head vertex. Note that in the event that the former parent loses its last child, propagation of deletions (see Alg. 18.4) can ensure that only those *Closed* nodes continue to be stored that belong to some solution path. Edge deletions can also ensure deletion of dependent vertex and coordinate data structures (not shown in the pseudo code). The other situation that gives rise to deletions is if immediately after the expansion of a node no children are pointing back to it (the children might either be reachable more cheaply from different nodes, or their f-value might exceed the threshold).

The correctness of the algorithm can be shown analogously to the soundness proof of A*. If the threshold is smaller than $\delta(s,t)$, dynamic programming will terminate without encountering a solution; otherwise, only nodes are pruned that cannot be part of an optimal path. The invariant holds that there is always a node in each level that lies on an optimal path and is in the *Open* list. Therefore, if the algorithm terminates only when the heap runs empty, the best found solution stored will indeed be optimal.

The iterative-deepening strategy results in an overhead computation time due to reexpansions, and we are trying to restrict this overhead as much as possible. More precisely, we want to minimize the ratio $v = n_{IDDP}/n_{A^*}$, where n_{IDDP} and n_{A^*} denote the number of expansions in *IDDP* and A*, respectively. We choose a threshold sequence $U_1, U_2, \dots$ such that the number of expansions n_i in stage i satisfies $n_i = 2n_{i-1}$; if we can at least double n_i in each iteration, we will expand at most four times as many nodes as A*.

Procedure *ComputeIncr* stores the sequence of expansion numbers and thresholds from the previous search stages, and then uses curve fitting for extrapolation (in the first few iterations without sufficient data available, a very small default threshold is applied). We found that the distribution of nodes $n(U)$ with an f-value smaller or equal to threshold U can be modeled very accurately according to the exponential approach $n(U) = A \cdot B^U$. Consequently, to attempt to double the number of expansions, we choose the next threshold according to $U_{i+1} = U_i + \frac{1}{\lg_2 B}$.

18.2.4 Sparse Representation of Solution Paths

When the search progresses along antidiagonals, we do not have to fear back leaks, and are free to prune *Closed* nodes. We only want to delete them lazily and incrementally when being forced to by the algorithm approaching the computer's memory limit, however.

When deleting an edge e, the backtrack pointers of its child edges that refer to it are redirected to the respective predecessor of e, the reference count of which is increased accordingly. In the resulting *sparse solution path* representation, backtrack pointers can point to any optimal ancestors.

After termination of the main search, we trace back the pointers starting with the goal edge; this is outlined Alg. 18.5, which prints out the solution path in reverse order. Whenever an edge e points back to an ancestor e' that is not its direct parent, we apply an auxiliary search from start edge e' to goal edge e to reconstruct the missing links of the optimal solution path. The search threshold can now be fixed at the known solution cost; moreover, the auxiliary search can prune those edges that cannot be ancestors of e because they have some coordinate greater than the corresponding coordinate in e. Since also the shortest distance between e and e' is known, we can stop at the first path that is found at this cost. To improve the efficiency of the auxiliary search even further, the heuristic could be recomputed to suit the new target. Therefore, the cost of restoring the solution path is usually marginal compared to that of the main search.

Which edges are we going to prune, in which order? For simplicity, assume for the moment that the *Closed* list consists of a single solution path. According to the Hirschberg approach, we would keep only one edge, preferably lying near the center of the search space (e.g., on the longest antidiagonal), to minimize the complexity of the two auxiliary searches. With additional available space allowing us

---

Procedure Path
Input: Edges e_s, e
Side effects: Output MSA solution

if $(e = e_s)$ **return**	;; End of recursion
if $(target(ancestor(e)) \neq source(e))$	;; Relay node
$IDDP(ancestor(e), e, f(e), f(e))$	;; Recursive path reconstruction
$OutputEdge(e)$	;; Print information
$Path(e_s, ancestor(e))$	;; Continue path construction

Algorithm 18.5

Divide-and-conquer solution reconstruction in reverse order.

to store three relay edges, we would divide the search space into four subspaces of about equal size (e.g., additionally storing the antidiagonals halfway between the middle antidiagonal and the start node respectively the target node). By extension, to incrementally save space under diminishing resources we would first keep only every other level, then every fourth, and so on, until only the start edge, the target edge, and one edge halfway on the path would be left.

Since in general the *Closed* list contains multiple solution paths (more precisely, a tree of solution paths), we would like to have about the same density of relay edges on each of them. For the case of k sequences, an edge reaching level l with its head node can originate with its tail node from level $l-1,\ldots,l-k$. Thus, not every solution path passes through each level, and deleting every other level could result in leaving one path completely intact, while extinguishing another totally. Thus, it is better to consider contiguous *bands* of k levels each, instead of individual levels. Bands of this size cannot be skipped by any path. The total number of antidiagonals in an alignment problem of k sequences of length N is $k \cdot N - 1$; thus, we can decrease the density in $\lfloor \lg N \rfloor$ steps.

A technical implementation issue concerns the ability to enumerate all edges that reference some given prunable edge, without explicitly storing them in a list. However, the reference counting method described earlier ensures that any *Closed* edge can be reached by following a path bottom-up from some edge in *Open*. The procedure is sketched in Algorithm 18.6. The variable *sparse* denotes the interval between level bands that are to be maintained in memory. In the inner loop, all paths to *Open* nodes are traversed in a backward direction; for each edge e' that falls into a prunable band, the pointer of the successor e on the path is redirected to its respective backtrack pointer. If e was the last edge referencing e', the latter one is deleted, and the path traversal continues up to the start edge. When all *Open* nodes have been visited and the memory bound is still exceeded, the outer loop tries to double the number of prunable bands by increasing *sparse*.

Procedure SparsifyClosed
Input: Size n

```
for each sparse in {1,…,⌊lg n⌋}              ;; Increase interval between stored level bands
    while (usedMem > maxMem and ∃e ∈ Open GetLastSparse(e) < sparse)
        pred ← ancestor(e)                          ;; Trace back solution path
        while (pred ≠ ∅ and GetLastSparse(e) < sparse)
            SetLastSparse(sparse)                    ;; Mark to avoid repeated traceback
            if (⌊level(GetHead(pred))/k⌋ mod 2^sparse ≠ 0)        ;; In prunable band
                ancestor(e) ← ancestor(pred)                     ;; Adjust pointer and …
                ref(ancestor(e)) ← ref(ancestor(e)) + 1                ;; … reference
                ref(pred) ← ref(pred) − 1                ;; Decrease reference count
                if (ref(pred) = 0)          ;; Last remaining edge referring to predecessor
                    DeleteRec(pred)                ;; Predecessor not in prunable band
            else                                            ;; Continue traversal
                e ← ancestor(e)                             ;; Choose continuation
            pred ← ancestor(e)                          ;; Set according predecessor
```

Algorithm 18.6

Sparsification of *Closed* list under restricted memory.

The procedure *SparsifyClosed* is called regularly during the search, for example, after each expansion. However, a naive version as described earlier would incur a huge overhead in computation time, particularly when the algorithm's memory consumption is close to the limit. Therefore, some optimizations are necessary. First, we avoid tracing back the same solution path at the same (or lower) *sparse* interval by recording for each edge the interval when it was traversed the last time (initially zero); only for an increased variable *sparse* can there be anything left for further pruning. In the worst case, each edge will be inspected $\lfloor \lg N \rfloor$ times. Second, it would be very inefficient to actually inspect each *Open* node in the inner loop, just to find that its solution path has been traversed previously, at the same or higher *sparse* value; however, with an appropriate bookkeeping strategy it is possible to reduce the time for this search overhead to $O(k)$.

18.2.5 Use of Improved Heuristics

As we have seen, the estimator h_{pair}, the sum of optimal pairwise goal distances, gives a lower bound on the actual path length. The tighter the estimator is, the smaller the search space the algorithm has to explore.

Beyond Pairwise Alignments

Kobayashi and Imai suggested applying more powerful heuristics by considering optimal solutions for subproblems of size $m > 2$. They proved that the following heuristics are admissible and more informed than the pairwise estimate.

- $h_{all,m}$ is the sum of all m-dimensional optimal costs, divided by $\binom{k-2}{m-2}$.
- $h_{one,m}$ splits the sequences into two sets of sizes m and $k - m$; the heuristic is the sum of the optimal cost of the first subset, plus that of the second one, plus the sum of all two-dimensional optimal costs of all pairs of sequences in different subsets. Usually, m is chosen close to $k/2$.

These improved heuristics can reduce the main search effort by orders of magnitudes. However, in contrast to pairwise subalignments, time and space resources devoted to compute and store higher-dimensional heuristics are in general no longer negligible compared to the main search. Kobayashi and Imai noticed that even for the case $m = 3$ of triples of sequences, it can be impractical to compute the entire subheuristic $h_{all,m}$. As one reduction, they show that it suffices to restrict the search to nodes where the path cost does not exceed the optimal path cost of the subproblem by more than

$$\delta = \binom{k-2}{m-2} U - \sum_{i_1,\dots,i_m} d(s_{i_1,\dots,i_m}, t_{i_1,\dots,i_m}).$$

This threshold can be seen as a generalization of the Carrillo-Lipman bound. However, it can still incur excessive overhead in space and computation time for the computation of the $\binom{k}{m}$ lower-dimensional subproblems. A drawback is that it requires an upper bound, on which the accuracy of the algorithm's efficiency also hinges. We could improve this bound by applying more sophisticated heuristic methods, but it seems counterintuitive to spend more time doing so that we would rather use to calculate the exact solution. In spite of its advantages for the main search, the expensiveness of the heuristic calculation appears as a major obstacle.

An alternative is to partition the heuristic into (hyper-) cubes using a hierarchical *oct-tree* data structure; in contrast to "full" cells, "empty" cells only retain the values at their surface. When the main search tries to use one of them, its interior values are recomputed on demand. Still, this work assumes that each node in the entire heuristic is calculated at least once using dynamic programming.

One cause of the dilemma lies in the implicit assumption that a *complete* computation is necessary. The previous bound δ refers to the worst-case scenario, and can generally include many more nodes than actually required in the main search. However, since we are only dealing with the heuristic, we can actually afford to miss some values occasionally; although this might slow down the main search, it cannot compromise the optimality of the final solution. Therefore, we propose to generate the heuristics with a much smaller bound δ. Whenever the attempt to retrieve a value of the m-dimensional subheuristic fails during the main search, we simply revert to replacing it by the sum of the $\binom{m}{2}$-optimal pairwise goal distances it covers.

The IDDP algorithm lends itself well to make productive use of higher-dimensional heuristics. First and most important, the strategy of searching to adaptively increasing thresholds can be transferred to the δ-bound as well.

Second, as far as a practical implementation is concerned, it is important to take into account not only how a higher-dimensional heuristic affects the number of node expansions, but also their time complexity. This time is dominated by the number of accesses to subalignments. With k sequences, in the worst case an edge has $2^k - 1$ successors, leading to a total of $(2^k - 1)\binom{k}{m}$ evaluations for $h_{all,m}$. One possible improvement is to enumerate all edges emerging from a given vertex in lexicographic order, and to store partial sums of heuristics of prefix subsets of sequences for later reuse. In this way, if we allow for a cache of linear size, the number of accesses is reduced to $\sum_{i=m}^{i=k} 2^i \binom{i-1}{m-1}$; correspondingly, for a quadratic cache we only need $\sum_{i=m}^{i=k} 2^i \binom{i-2}{m-2}$ evaluations. For instance, in aligning 12 sequences using $h_{all,3}$, a linear cache reduces the evaluations to about 37% within one expansion.

As mentioned earlier, in contrast to A*, IDDP gives us the freedom to choose any particular expansion order of the edges within a given level. Therefore, when we sort edges lexicographically according to the target nodes, much of the cached prefix information can be shared additionally across consecutively expanded edges. The higher the dimension of the subalignments, the larger the savings.

Trade-Off between Computation of Heuristic and Main Search

As we have seen, we can control the size of the precomputed subalignments by choosing the bound δ up to which f-values of edges are generated beyond the respective optimal solution cost. There is obviously a trade-off between the auxiliary and main searches. It is instructive to consider the *heuristic miss ratio r*, the fraction of calculations of the heuristic h during the main search when a requested entry in a partial MULTIPLE SEQUENCE ALIGNMENT has not been precomputed. The optimum for the main search is achieved if the heuristic has been computed for every requested edge ($r = 0$). Going beyond that point will generate an unnecessarily large heuristic containing many entries that will never be actually used. On the other hand, we are free to allocate less effort to the heuristic, resulting in $r > 0$ and consequently decreasing performance of the main search. Generally, the dependence has an S-shaped form.

Unfortunately, in general we do not know in advance the right amount of auxiliary search. As mentioned earlier, choosing δ according to the Carrillo-Lipman bound will ensure that every requested subalignment cost will have been precomputed; however, in general we will considerably overestimate the necessary size of the heuristic.

As a remedy, algorithm IDDP gives us the opportunity to recompute the heuristic in each threshold iteration in the main search. In this way, we can adaptively strike a balance between the two.

When the currently experienced fault rate r rises above some threshold, we can suspend the current search, recompute the pairwise alignments with an increased threshold δ, and resume the main search with the improved heuristics.

Like for the main search, we can accurately predict the auxiliary computation time and space at threshold δ using an exponential fitting. Due to the lower dimensionality, it will generally increase less steeply; however, the constant factor might be higher for the heuristic, due to the combinatorial number of $\binom{k}{m}$ alignment problems to be solved.

A doubling scheme as explained previously can bound the overhead to within a constant factor of the effort in the last iteration. In this way, when also limiting the heuristic computation time by a fixed fraction of the main search, we can ensure as an expected upper bound that the overall execution time stays within a constant factor of the search time that would be required when using only the pairwise heuristic.

If we knew the exact relation between δ, r, and the speedup of the main search, an ideal strategy would double the heuristic whenever the expected computation time is smaller than the time saved in the main search. However, this dependence is more complex than simple exponential growth; it varies with the search depth and specifics of the problem. Either we would need a more elaborate model of the search space, or the algorithm would have to conduct explorative searches to estimate the relation.

18.3 BIBLIOGRAPHIC NOTES

Gusfield (1997) and Waterman (1995) have given comprehensive introductions to computational molecular biology. The definition of a pathway has been given by Thagard (2003). The *mammalian cell cycle control* has been described by Kohn (1999). It appeared as an application domain in the fifth international planning competition in 2006, where it was modeled by Dimopoulos, Gerevini, and Saetti. A recent search tool for the alignment of metabolic pathways has been presented by Pinter, Rokhlenko, Yeger-Lotem, and Ziv-Ukelson (2005). Given a query pathway and a collection of pathways, it finds and reports all approximate occurrences of the query in the collection.

Bosnacki (2004) has indicated a natural analogy between biochemical networks and (concurrent) systems with an unknown structure. Both are considered as a black box with unknown internal workings about which we want to check some property; that is, verify some hypothesis about their behavior. Test sequences can be casted as counterexamples obtained by search as observed by Engels, Feijs, and Mauw (1997). A suitable algorithm for inducing a model of a system has been developed by Angluin (1987). The algorithm requires an oracle that in this case is substituted by a conformance testing. Unlike model checking that is applied to the model of the system, (conformance) testing is performed on the system implementation. Also, conformance testing does not try to cover all execution sequences of the implementation. Rather than understanding the networks, the goal of Rao and Arkin (2001) is to design biological networks for a certain task.

FASTA and BLAST (see Altschul, Gish, Miller, Myers, and Lipman, 1990), are standard methods for database searches. Davidson (2001) has employed a local beam search scheme. Gusfield (1993) has proposed an approximation called the *star-alignment*. Out of all the sequences to be aligned, one *consensus sequence* is chosen such that the sum of its pairwise alignment costs to the rest of the sequences is minimal. Using this "best" sequence as the center, the other ones are aligned using the "once a gap, always a gap" rule. Gusfield has shown that the cost of the optimal alignment is greater than or equal to the cost of this star alignment, divided by $(2 - 2/k)$. The program MSA due to Gupta, Kececioglu, and Schaffer (1996) allows the user to adjust δ to values below the *Carrillo-Lipman bound* individually for each pair of sequences (Carrillo and Lipman, 1988).

For MULTIPLE SEQUENCE ALIGNMENT problems in higher dimensions, A* is clearly superior to dynamic programming. However, in contrast to the Hirschberg algorithm, it still has to store all the explored nodes in the *Closed* list to avoid "back leaks." As a remedy, Korf (1999) and Korf and Zhang (2000) have proposed to store a list of forbidden operators with each node, or to place the parents of a deleted node on *Open* with an f-value ∞. The approach by Zhou and Hansen (2004a) only requires the boundary to be stored.

The main algorithm IDDP as described in this chapter has been published by Schrödl (2005). The work by Korf, Zhang, Thayer, and Hohwald (2005) refers to a related incremental dynamic programming algorithm called *iterative-deepening bounded dynamic programming*.

McNaughton, Lu, Schaeffer, and Szafron (2002) have suggested an oct-tree data structure for storing the heuristic function. A different line of research tries to restrict the search space of the breadth-first approaches by incorporating bounds. Ukkonen (1985) has presented an algorithm for the pairwise alignment problem, which is particularly efficient for similar sequences; its computation time scales as $O(dm)$, where d is the optimal solution cost.

Another approach for MULTIPLE SEQUENCE ALIGNMENT is to make use of the lower bounds h from A*. The key idea is the following: Since all nodes with an f-value lower than $\delta(s,t)$ have to be expanded anyway to guarantee optimality, we might as well explore them in any reasonable order, like that of Dijkstra's algorithm or dynamic programming, if we only knew the optimal cost. Even slightly higher upper bounds will still help pruning. Spouge (1989) has proposed to bound dynamic programming to nodes v where $g(v) + h(v)$ is smaller than an upper bound for $\delta(s,t)$.

Linear bounded diagonal alignment (LBD-Align) by Davidson (2001) uses an upper bound to reduce the computation time and memory in solving a pairwise alignment problem by dynamic programming. The algorithm calculates the dynamic programming matrix one antidiagonal at a time, starting in the top-left corner, and working down toward the bottom-right corner. While A* would have to check the bound in every expansion, *LBD-Align* only checks the top and bottom cell of each diagonal. If, for example, the top cell of a diagonal has been pruned, all the remaining cells in that row can be pruned as well, since they are only reachable through it; this means that the pruning frontier on the next row can be shifted one down. Thus, the pruning overhead can be reduced from a quadratic to a linear amount in terms of the sequence length.

Progresses have been made to improve the scaling of the MULTIPLE SEQUENCE ALIGHNMENT algorithms. Niewiadomski, Amaral, and Holte (2006) have applied large-scale parallel frontier search with delayed duplicate detection to solve challenging (Balibase) instances, and Zhou and Hansen (2006a) have successfully improved the sparse-memory graph search with a breadth-first heuristic search.

Robotics

19

Sven Koenig and Craig Tovey

A difference between search in robotics and typical search testbeds in artificial intelligence, like the EIGHT-PUZZLE or the RUBIK'S CUBE, is that state spaces in robotics are continuous and need to be discretized. Another difference is that robots typically have a priori incomplete knowledge of the state spaces. In these cases, they cannot predict with certainty which observations they will make after they have moved nor the feasibility or outcomes of their future moves. Thus, they have to search in nondeterministic state spaces, which can be time consuming due to the large number of resulting contingencies. Complete AND-OR searches (i.e., minimax searches) minimize the worst-case trajectory length but are often intractable since the robots have to find large conditional plans. Yet, search has to be fast for robots to move smoothly. Thus, we need to speed up search by developing robot-navigation methods that sacrifice the minimality of their trajectories.

19.1 SEARCH SPACES

Consider the motion-planning problem of changing an unblocked start configuration of a robot to a goal configuration. This is a search problem in the *configuration space*, where the configuration of a robot is typically specified as a vector of real numbers. For example, the configuration of a mobile robot that is omnidirectional and not subject to acceleration constraints is given by its coordinates in the workspace. Configurations are either unblocked (i.e., possible or, alternatively, in *freespace*) or blocked (i.e., impossible or, alternatively, part of obstacles). Configurations are blocked, for example, because the robot would intersect an obstacle in the workspace. The configuration space is formed by all configurations.

An example motion-planning problem in a two-dimensional workspace with a robot arm that has two joints and is bolted to the ground at the first joint is shown in Figure 19.1(a). An obstacle blocks one quadrant of the plane. The robot arm has to move from its start configuration to the goal configuration. There are different choices of defining the configuration space. If we only want to find an unblocked trajectory from the start configuration to the goal configuration then the choice is usually unimportant. However, if the planning objective includes the optimization of some cost, such as minimizing time or energy, then it is preferable to define the configuration space so that this cost is represented as a norm-induced or other natural metric on the configuration space. One configuration space is shown in Figure 19.1(b), where the configurations are given by the two joint angles θ_1 and θ_2. The region in the

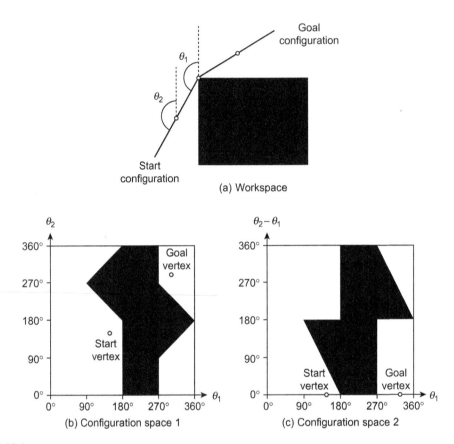

FIGURE 19.1

Robot arm example.

figure wraps around because angles are measured modulo $360°$, so that the four corners in the figure represent the same configuration. Some configurations are blocked because the robot arm would inter-sect an obstacle in the workspace (but they could also be blocked because a joint angle is out of range). Horizontal movement in the figure requires the robot arm to actuate both joints. Movement along the diagonal with slope one results if only the first joint actuates. Thus, horizontal movement requires more energy than diagonal movement, contrary to what the figure suggests visually. It may then be preferable to define the vertical axis of the configuration space as $\theta_2 - \theta_1$, as shown in Figure 19.1(c).

Robot moves in the workspace are continuous out of physical necessity. The configuration space is therefore continuous and thus needs to get discretized to allow us to use search methods to find trajectories from the start configuration to the goal configuration. We model the configuration space as a (vertex-blocked) graph $G = (\hat{V}, V, E)$, where $\hat{V}$ is the set of (blocked and unblocked) vertices, $V \subseteq \hat{V}$ is the set of unblocked vertices, and $E \subseteq \hat{V} \times \hat{V}$ is the set of edges. The configuration of the robot is represented by exactly one unblocked vertex at any instant. We say, for simplicity, that the robot visits that vertex. Edges connect vertices that correspond to configurations that the robot can potentially move between. The vertices are blocked or unblocked depending on whether the corresponding configurations are blocked or unblocked. The robot needs to move on a trajectory in the resulting graph from the vertex that corresponds to the start configuration to the vertex that corresponds to the goal configuration. We assume that paths and trajectories do not contain blocked vertices (unless stated otherwise) and measure their lengths as well as all other distances in number of moves (i.e., edge traversals).

We can obtain the graph in different ways.

- We can obtain the graph by partitioning the configuration space into cells (or some other regular or irregular tessellation of the space), where a cell is considered unblocked if and only if it does not contain obstacles. The vertices are the cells and are unblocked if and only if the corresponding cells are unblocked. Edges connect adjacent cells (i.e., cells that share a border) and are thus (about) equally long.

    One problem is the granularity of the discretization. If the cells are large, then an existing trajectory might not be found, as shown in Figure 19.2. Blocked configurations are black, and unblocked configurations are white. The circle and cross show the start and goal configuration, respectively. On the other hand, the smaller we make the cells, the more numerous they become, which results in a quadratic explosion. It can therefore make sense to have cells of different sizes: small cells close to obstacles in configuration space to be able to find gaps between them and large cells otherwise. One particular method for obtaining a nonuniform discretization is the *parti-game algorithm*. It starts with large cells and splits them as needed while trying to move the robot from the start configuration to the cell that contains the goal configuration (goal cell). A simplified version of the parti-game algorithm is illustrated in Figure 19.3. It starts with a uniform coarse-grained discretization of the configuration space. The vertices of the graph represent the cells, and edges connect vertices that correspond to adjacent cells. Thus, it initially ignores obstacles and makes the optimistic assumption that it can move from each cell to any adjacent cell (*freespace assumption*). It uses the graph to find a shortest path from its current cell to the goal cell. It then follows the path

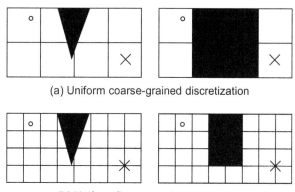

(a) Uniform coarse-grained discretization

(b) Uniform fine-grained discretization

FIGURE 19.2

Cell-based discretization.

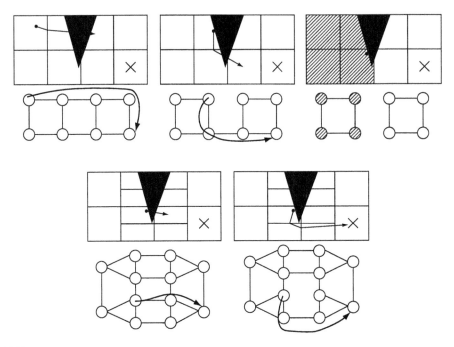

FIGURE 19.3

Parti-game algorithm.

by always moving toward the center of the successor cell of its current cell. If it gets blocked by an obstacle (which can be determined in the workspace and thus without modeling the shape of obstacles in the configuration space), then it is not always able to move from its current cell to the successor cell and therefore removes the corresponding edge from the graph. It then replans and finds another shortest path from its current cell to the goal cell. If it finds such a path, then it repeats the process. If it does not find such a path, then it uses the graph to determine from which cells it can reach the goal cell (*solvable cells*) and from which cells it cannot reach the goal cell (*unsolvable cells*, shaded gray in the figure). It then splits all unsolvable cells that border solvable cells (and have not yet reached the resolution limit) along their shorter axes. (It also splits all solvable cells that border unsolvable cells along their shorter axes to prevent adjacent cells from having very different sizes, which is not necessary but makes it efficient to determine the neighbors of a cell with kd-trees.) It deletes the vertices of the split cells from the graph and adds one vertex for each new cell, again assuming that it can move from each new cell to any adjacent cell and vice versa. (It could remember where it got blocked by obstacles to delete some edges from the graph right away but does not. Rather, it deletes the edges automatically when it gets blocked again by the obstacles in the future.) It then replans and finds another shortest path from its current cell to the goal cell and repeats the process until the goal cell is reached or no cell can be split any further because the resolution limit is reached. The final discretization is then used as initial discretization for the next motion-planning problem in the same configuration space.

- We can also obtain the graph by picking a number of unblocked configurations (including the start and goal configurations). The vertices are these configurations and are unblocked. Edges connect vertices of which the connecting straight line (or path of some simple controller) does not pass through obstacles (which can perhaps be determined in the workspace and thus without modeling the shapes of obstacles in the configuration space). We can leave out long edges (e.g., edges longer than a threshold) to keep the graph sparse and the edges about equally long. In case all obstacles are polygons, we can pick the corners of the polygons as configurations (in addition to the start and goal configurations). The resulting graph is called the *visibility graph*. A shortest trajectory in the visibility graph is also a shortest trajectory in a two-dimensional configuration space (but not necessarily in a three- or higher-dimensional configuration space). However, the obstacles are often not polygons and can only be approximated with complex polygons, resulting in a large number of configurations and thus large search times. *Probabilistic roadmaps* therefore pick a number of unblocked configurations randomly (in addition to the start and goal configurations). The larger the number of picked configurations, the larger the search time tends to be. On the other hand, the larger the number of picked configurations, the more likely it is that a trajectory is found if one exists and the shorter the trajectory tends to be. So far, we assumed that the configuration space is first discretized and then searched. However, it is often faster to pick random configurations during the search. *Rapidly exploring random trees*, for example, grow search trees by picking configurations randomly and then try to connect them to the search tree.

There are also other models of the configuration space, for example, *Voronoi graphs*, which have the advantage that trajectories remain as far away from obstacles as possible and the safety distance to obstacles is thus maximal.

By definition, the robot cannot leave the connected component of unblocked vertices in which it starts. We therefore assume that the graph has only one component of unblocked vertices (i.e., that there is a path between any two unblocked vertices). We draw our examples principally from robot-navigation problems in (two-dimensional four-neighbor) grid graphs, where the configuration space is the workspace itself, and thus use the terms "terrain" and "position" in the following instead of "configuration space" and "configuration." In general, grid graphs model (two-dimensional four-neighbor) GRIDWORLDS of square cells. GRIDWORLDS (including evidence and occupancy grids) are widely used to model the terrain of mobile robots by partitioning it into square cells, lend themselves readily to illustration, and form challenging testbeds for search under a priori incomplete knowledge.

19.2 SEARCH UNDER INCOMPLETE KNOWLEDGE

We assume that the graph is undirected and make the following minimal assumptions about the robot capabilities throughout this chapter, called the base model: The robot is able to move from its current vertex to any desired adjacent unblocked vertex. The robot is capable of error-free moves and observations. For example, it can identify its absolute position with GPS or its relative position with respect to its start position with dead-reckoning (which keeps track of how the robot has moved in the terrain). The robot is able to identify vertices uniquely, which is equivalent to each vertex having a unique identifier that the robot might a priori not know. The robot is able to observe at least the identifier and blockage status of its current vertex and all vertices adjacent to its current vertex. The robot always

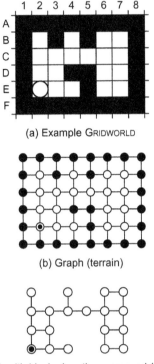

(a) Example GRIDWORLD

(b) Graph (terrain)

(c) Graph with blocked vertices removed (freespace)

FIGURE 19.4

Different kinds of graphs.

makes the same observation when it visits the same vertex. The robot is able to remember the sequence of moves that it has executed and the sequence of observations it has made in return.

The base model guarantees that the robot can maintain the subgraph of the graph, including the vertices (with their identifiers and their blockage status) and the edges (i.e., vertex neighborships) that the robot either a priori knew about or has observed already. In a *minimal base model*, the robot is able to observe exactly the identifier of its current vertex and the identifier and blockage status of all vertices adjacent to its current vertex. We will give an example of a robot that has the capabilities required by the minimal base model shortly in the context of Figure 19.4.

19.3 FUNDAMENTAL ROBOT-NAVIGATION PROBLEMS

Robots typically have a priori only incomplete knowledge of their terrain or their current position. We therefore study three fundamental robot-navigation problems under a priori incomplete knowledge that underlie many other robot-navigation problems.

Mapping means to obtain knowledge of the terrain, often the blockage status of all positions, called a map. There are two common approaches of handling a priori incomplete knowledge of the terrain. The first approach of handling incomplete knowledge of the terrain is characterized by the robot a priori knowing the topology of the graph. The second approach of handling a priori incomplete knowledge of the terrain is characterized by the robot a priori not knowing anything about the graph, not even its topology.

The objective of the robot is to know everything about the graph that it possibly can, including its topology and the blockage status of every vertex. The robot either a priori knows the topology of the graph and the identifier of each vertex but not which vertices are blocked (Assumption 1) or neither the graph nor the identifier or blockage status of each vertex (Assumption 2). Assumption 1 is a possible assumption for grid graphs, and Assumption 2 is a possible assumption for grid graphs, visibility graphs, probabilistic roadmaps, and Voronoi graphs. The graph can contain blocked and unblocked vertices under Assumption 1 but contains only unblocked vertices under Assumption 2.

An example GRIDWORLD is shown in Figure 19.4(a). Blocked cells (and vertices) are black, and unblocked cells are white. The circle shows the current cell of the robot. We assume that the robot has only the capabilities required by the minimal base model. It always observes the identifier and blockage status of the adjacent cells in the four compass directions and then moves to an unblocked adjacent cell in one of the four compass directions, resulting in a grid graph. This grid graph is shown in Figure 19.4(b) for Assumption 1 and in Figure 19.4(c) for Assumption 2. Initially, the robot knows that it visits cell E2 and observes that cells E1 and F2 are blocked and cells E3 and D2 are unblocked. We denote this observation using a "+" for an unblocked adjacent cell and a "−" for a blocked adjacent cell in the compass directions north, west, south, and east (in this order). Thus, the initial observation of the robot is denoted as "D2 +, E1 −, F2 −, E3 +" or "+ − − +" in short.

The example in Figure 19.5 shows that it can make a difference whether we make Assumption 1 or 2. The robot moves along the arrow. Figures 19.5(c) and (d) show the knowledge of the robot. Cells (and vertices) that the robot knows to be blocked are black, cells (and vertices) that the robot knows to be unblocked are white, and cells (and vertices) of which the blockage status is unknown to the robot are gray. The circle shows the current cell of the robot. The robot needs to enter the center cell to rule out the possibility that it operates in the graph shown in Figure 19.6 under Assumption 2. On the other hand, it does not need to enter the center cell to know the graph under Assumption 1.

Localization means to identify the current position of a robot, usually a mobile robot rather than a robot arm. We assume that the robot has a map of the terrain available and a priori knows its orientation relative to the map (e.g., because it is equipped with a compass) but not its start position. The robot a priori knows the graph, including which vertices are blocked. Its objective is to localize, which means to identify its current vertex or the fact that its current vertex cannot be identified uniquely because the a priori known map has at least two isomorphic connected components of unblocked vertices and it is located in one of them. The robot a priori does not know the identifier of each vertex. Thus, the robot is not trivially localized after it observes the identifier of a vertex. This assumption is, for example, realistic if the robot uses dead-reckoning to identify the vertices.

Goal-directed navigation in a priori unknown terrain means to move a robot to a goal position in a priori unknown terrain. The robot a priori knows the topology of the graph and the identifier of each vertex but not which vertices are blocked. It knows the goal vertex but may not know the geometric embedding of the graph. Its objective is to move to the goal vertex.

(a) Example GRIDWORLD

(b) Graph

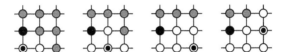

(c) Knowledge of the robot: Assumption 1

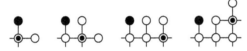

(d) Knowledge of the robot: Assumption 2

FIGURE 19.5

A priori knowledge of the graph.

FIGURE 19.6

Alternative graph.

19.4 SEARCH OBJECTIVE

We perform a worst-case analysis of the trajectory length because robot-navigation methods with small worst-case trajectory lengths always perform well, which matches the concerns of empirical robotics researchers for guaranteed performance. We describe upper and lower bounds on the worst-case trajectory length in graphs with the same number of unblocked vertices. The lower bounds are usually proved by example and thus need to be derived scenario by scenario since the trajectories depend on both the graph and the knowledge of the graph. The upper bounds, however, hold for all scenarios of topologies of graphs and observation capabilities of the robot that are consistent with the base model.

Researchers sometimes use online rather than worst-case criteria to analyze robot-navigation methods. For example, they are interested in robot-navigation methods with a small *competitive ratio*. The competitive ratio compares the trajectory length of a robot to the trajectory length needed by an omniscient robot with complete a priori knowledge to verify that knowledge. For localization, for example, the robot a priori knows its current vertex and only needs to verify it. Minimizing the ratio of these quantities minimizes regret in the sense that it minimizes the value of k such that the robot could have localized k times faster if it had a priori known its current vertex. The competitive ratio has little relation to the worst-case trajectory length if robots do not have complete a priori knowledge. Furthermore, the difference in trajectory length between robot-navigation methods that do and do not have a priori complete knowledge is often large. For goal-directed navigation, for example, the robot can follow a shortest path from the start vertex to the goal vertex if it a priori knows the graph, but usually has to try out many promising paths on average to get from the start vertex to the goal vertex if it a priori does not know the graph. This trajectory length can increase with the number of unblocked vertices while the shortest path can remain of constant length, making the competitive ratio arbitrarily large.

19.5 SEARCH APPROACHES

A robot is typically able to observe the identifier and blockage status of only those vertices that are close to its current vertex. The robot thus has to move in the graph to observe the identifier and blockage status of new vertices, either to discover more about the graph or its current vertex. Therefore, it has to find a reconnaissance plan that determines how it should move to make new observations, which is called *sensor-based search*. The reconnaissance plan is a conditional plan that can take into account the a priori knowledge of the robot and the entire knowledge that it has already gathered (namely, the sequence of moves that it has executed and the sequence of observations it has made in return) when determining the next move of the robot. A deterministic plan specifies the move directly while a randomized plan specifies a probability distribution over the moves. No randomized plan that solves one of the robot-navigation problems has a smaller average worst-case trajectory length (where the average is taken with respect to the randomized choice of moves by the randomized plan) than a deterministic plan with minimal worst-case trajectory length. We therefore consider only deterministic plans.

The robot can either first determine and then execute a complete conditional plan (offline search) or interleave partial searches and moves (online search). We now discuss these two options in greater detail, using localization as an example. Localization consists of two phases, namely hypothesis generation and hypothesis elimination. Hypothesis generation determines all vertices that could be the current vertex of the robot since they are consistent with the current observation made by it. This phase simply involves going through all unblocked vertices and eliminating those that are inconsistent with the observation. If the set contains more than one vertex, hypothesis elimination then tries to determine which vertex in this set is the current vertex by moving the robot in the graph. We discuss in the following how hypothesis elimination can use search to determine how to move the robot.

19.5.1 Optimal Offline Search

Offline search finds a complete and thus potentially large conditional plan before the robot starts to move. A *valid localization plan* eventually correctly identifies either the current vertex of the robot or the fact that the current vertex cannot be identified uniquely, no matter which unblocked vertex the robot starts in.

Consider, for example, the localization problem from Figure 19.7. Figure 19.8 shows part of the state space that the robot can move to from the start state. The states are sets of cells, namely the cells that the robot could be in. Initially, the robot observes "+ − − −". The question marks indicate the cells that are consistent with this observation, namely cells E2, E4, and E6. The start state thus contains these three cells. (The robot can rule out cell B7 since it knows its orientation relative to the map.) Every state that contains only one cell is a goal state. In every nongoal state, the robot can choose a move (OR nodes of the state space), described as a compass direction. It then makes a new observation (AND nodes of the state space). The state space is nondeterministic since the robot cannot always predict the observation and thus the successor state resulting from a move.

Deterministic localization plans assign a move to each OR node in the state space. Valid deterministic localization plans with minimal worst-case trajectory length can be found with a complete AND-OR search (i.e., minimax search), resulting in *decision trees* (i.e., trees where the root is the start state, all leaf nodes are goal states, every AND node has all of its successor nodes included, and every OR node has at most one of its successor nodes included) since states cannot repeat in valid localization plans with minimal worst-case trajectory length. Such a decision tree is shown in Figure 19.9. However, it is intractable to perform a complete AND-OR search. This is not surprising since the states are sets of unblocked vertices and their number is thus large (although not all sets of

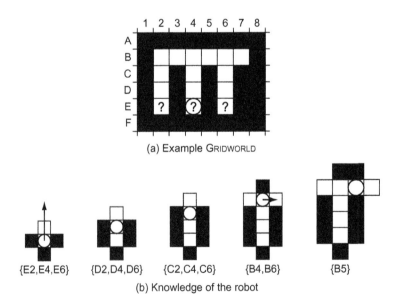

(a) Example GRIDWORLD

{E2,E4,E6}   {D2,D4,D6}   {C2,C4,C6}   {B4,B6}   {B5}

(b) Knowledge of the robot

FIGURE 19.7

Greedy localization.

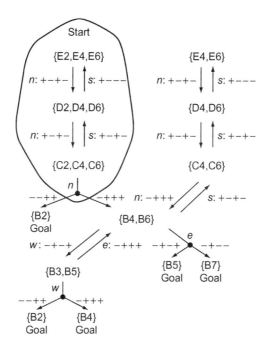

FIGURE 19.8

Partial state space for localization.

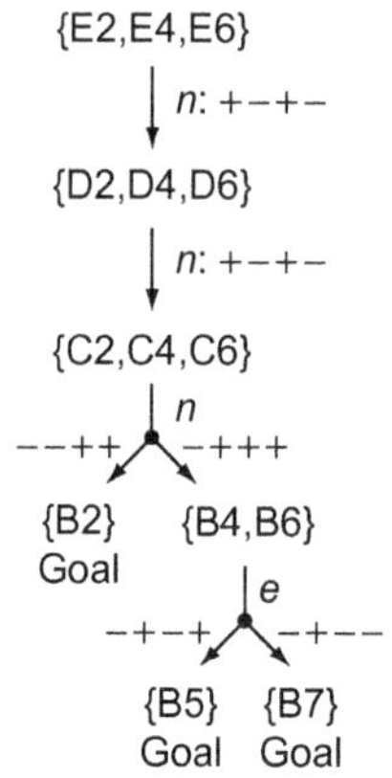

FIGURE 19.9

Localization plan with minimal worst-case trajectory length.

unblocked vertices can appear in practice). In fact, it is NP-hard to localize with minimal worst-case trajectory length and thus very likely needs exponential search time, which is consistent with results that show the complexity of offline search under a priori incomplete knowledge to be high in general.

19.5.2 **Greedy Online Search**

To search fast, we need to speed up search by developing robot-navigation methods that sacrifice the minimality of their trajectories. If done correctly, the suboptimality of the trajectory and thus the increase in the execution time are outweighed by the decrease of the search time so that the sum of search and execution times (i.e., the problem-completion time) decreases substantially, which is the idea behind *limited rationality*. For robot-navigation problems under a priori incomplete knowledge, this can be done by interleaving searches and moves to obtain knowledge about the graph or the current vertex in the graph early and then using this knowledge for the new searches right away. This knowledge makes subsequent searches faster since it reduces the uncertainty of the robot about the graph or its current vertex, which reduces the size of the state space that the robot can move to from its current state and thus also the amount of search performed for unencountered situations.

Search in deterministic state spaces is fast. *Greedy online search* makes use of this property to solve search problems in nondeterministic state spaces by interleaving myopic searches in deterministic state spaces and moves. The result is a trade-off between search and execution time. We now introduce two greedy online search approaches, namely agent-centered search and assumption-based search. They differ in how they make search deterministic.

Agent-centered search methods (in nondeterministic state spaces) search with limited lookahead by performing partial AND-OR searches, forward from the current state, instead of a complete one. They restrict the search to the part of the state space around the current state (resulting in local search), which is the part of the state space that is immediately relevant for the robot in its current situation because it contains the states that the robot will soon be in. Thus, agent-centered search methods decide on the part of the state space to search and then how to move within it. Then, they execute these moves (or only the first move) and repeat the overall process from the resulting state. Consequently, agent-centered search methods avoid a combinatorial explosion by finding only prefixes of complete plans.

Since agent-centered search methods do not search all the way from the current state of the robot to a goal state, they need to avoid moving in a way that cycles forever. The agent-centered search methods that we describe in this chapter do this by making the lookahead large enough so that the subsequent execution obtains new knowledge, although real-time heuristic search methods can be used to get away with smaller lookaheads. Furthermore, the agent-centered search methods that we describe in this chapter use a simple approach to make search fast, namely by searching exactly in all of the deterministic part of the non-deterministic state space around the current state, with the objective to execute a move with more than one possible successor state and thus obtain new knowledge quickly. This is the part of the state space in Figure 19.8 that has a border around it. The robot then traverses the path, the last move of which has more than one possible successor state. It then observes the resulting state and repeats the process from the state that actually resulted from the move instead of all states that could have resulted from it.

Figure 19.10(b) illustrates agent-centered search. The shaded areas represent the search spaces of agent-centered search, one for each search episode between consecutive moves. The shaded areas together are much smaller than the shaded area of the large triangle in Figure 19.10(a) that represents the search space of an optimal offline search method but the resulting trajectory is not shortest.

Assumption-based search methods, on the other hand, search all the way from the current state to a goal state but make assumptions about the successor states of moves by ignoring some of them.

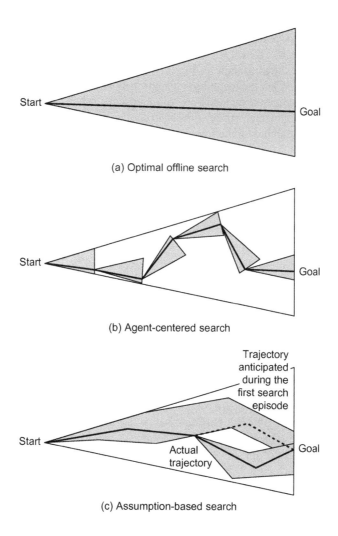

(a) Optimal offline search

(b) Agent-centered search

(c) Assumption-based search

FIGURE 19.10

Greedy online search.

Therefore, assumption-based search methods find a complete plan (under the assumptions made) from the current state to the goal state and execute the plan. If a move results in a successor state that was ignored during the search, then they repeat the overall process from the state that resulted from the move. Consequently, assumption-based search methods avoid a combinatorial explosion because they ignore some successor states of moves and thus do not consider all contingencies. The agent-centered search methods that we describe in this chapter use a simple approach to make search fast, namely by ignoring all successor states of each move but one, which makes the state space effectively deterministic.

Figure 19.10(c) illustrates assumption-based search. The shaded areas represent the search spaces of assumption-based search, one for each search episode. The shaded areas together are much smaller than the shaded area of the large triangle in Figure 19.10(a) that represents the search space of an optimal offline search method but the resulting trajectory is not shortest.

Greedy online robot-navigation methods are commonsense robot-navigation methods that have often been discovered and implemented by empirical robotics researchers. We study greedy localization, greedy mapping, and search with the freespace assumption. They are related and can be analyzed in a common framework.

19.6 GREEDY LOCALIZATION

Greedy localization uses agent-centered search to localize a robot. Greedy localization maintains a set of hypotheses, namely the unblocked vertices that the robot could be in because they are consistent with all previous observations. It always reduces the size of this set with as few moves as possible, until this is no longer possible. This corresponds to moving on a shortest path from its current vertex to a closest informative vertex until it can no longer move to an informative vertex. We define an informative vertex to be an unblocked vertex with the property that the robot can obtain knowledge about its current vertex that allows it to reduce the size of its set of hypotheses. Note that a vertex becomes and remains uninformative once the robot has visited it.

Figure 19.7 illustrates the trajectory of greedy localization. Initially, it can be in cells E2, E4, and E6. The fastest way to reduce the size of the set of hypotheses in this situation is to move north twice. It could then observe "− − + +", in which case it must be in cell B2. It could also observe "− + + +", in which case it can be in cells B4 and B6. Either way, it has reduced the size of its set of hypotheses. After the robot executes the moves, it observes "− + + +" and thus can be in cells B4 and B6. The fastest way to reduce the size of its set of hypotheses in this situation is to move east. It could then observe "− + − +", in which case it must be in cell B5. It could also observe "− + − −", in which case it must be in cell B7. Either way, it has reduced the size of its set of hypotheses. After the robot executes the move, it observes "− + − +" and thus knows that it is cell B5 and has localized, in this particular case with minimal worst-case trajectory length.

Greedy localization can use deterministic search methods and has low-order polynomial search times in the number of unblocked vertices because it performs an agent-centered search in exactly all of the deterministic part of the nondeterministic state space around the current state, namely exactly up to the instant when it executes a move that has more than one possible successor state and then reduces the size of its set of hypotheses, as shown with a border in Figure 19.8.

It is NP-hard to localize better than logarithmically close to minimal worst-case trajectory length, including in grid graphs. Moreover, robots are unlikely to be able to localize in polynomial time with a trajectory length that is within a factor $o(\log^2|V|)$ of minimal. We analyze the worst-case trajectory length of greedy localization as a function of the number of unblocked vertices, where the worst case is taken over all graphs of the same number of unblocked vertices (perhaps with the restriction that localization is possible), and all start vertices of the robot and all tie-breaking strategies are used to decide which one of several equally close informative vertices to visit next. The worst-case trajectory length of greedy localization is $\Omega\left(\frac{|V|\log|V|}{\log\log|V|}\right)$ moves in graphs $G = (\hat{V}, V, E)$ under the minimal base model and thus is not minimal. This statement continues to hold in grid graphs where localization is possible. It is $O(|V|\log|V|)$ moves in graphs $G = (\hat{V}, V, E)$ and thus is rather small. These results assume that the graph has only one connected component of unblocked vertices but that the a priori known map of the graph can be larger than the graph and contain more than one connected component of unblocked vertices.

19.7 GREEDY MAPPING

Greedy mapping uses agent-centered search to learn a graph. The robot a priori knows either the topology of the graph and the identifier of each vertex but not which vertices are blocked or neither the graph nor the identifier or blockage status of each vertex. The robot maintains the currently known subgraph of the graph, regardless of what other knowledge it obtains. It always moves on a shortest path from its current vertex to a closest informative vertex in the currently known subgraph until it cannot move to an informative vertex any longer. We define an informative vertex to be an unblocked vertex with the property that the robot can obtain new knowledge for its map in it. Note that a vertex becomes and remains uninformative once the robot has visited it. (An alternative version of greedy mapping always moves to a closest unvisited vertex.)

Figure 19.11 illustrates the trajectory of greedy mapping if the robot a priori knows the topology of the graph and the identifier of each vertex but not which vertices are blocked. Arrows show the paths determined by greedy mapping whenever greedy mapping determines them. The robot then traverses these paths without search, and an arrow is thus only shown for the first move on each path. Greedy mapping can use deterministic search methods and has a low-order polynomial search time in the number of unblocked vertices because it performs an agent-centered search in exactly all of the deterministic parts of the nondeterministic state space around the current state, namely exactly up to the instant when it executes a move that has more than one possible successor state and thus obtains new knowledge for its map. Greedy mapping has to search frequently. It can calculate the shortest paths from the current vertex to a closest informative vertex efficiently with *incremental heuristic search methods*, which combine two principles for searching efficiently, namely heuristic search (i.e., using estimates of the goal distances to focus the search) and incremental search (i.e., reusing knowledge obtained during previous search episodes to speed up the current one).

We analyze the worst-case trajectory length of greedy mapping as a function of the number of unblocked vertices, where the worst case is taken over all graphs of the same number of unblocked vertices, and all possible start vertices of the robot and all possible tie-breaking strategies are used to decide which one of several equally close informative vertices to visit next. The worst-case trajectory length of greedy mapping is $\Omega\left(\frac{|V|\log|V|}{\log\log|V|}\right)$ moves in graphs $G = (\hat{V}, V, E)$ under the minimal base model in case the robot a priori knows neither the graph nor the identifier or blockage status of each vertex. This statement continues to hold in grid graphs in case the robot a priori knows the topology of the graph and the identifier of each vertex but not which vertices are blocked. This lower bound shows that the worst-case trajectory length of greedy mapping is slightly superlinear in the number of unblocked vertices and thus not minimal (since the worst-case trajectory length of depth-first search is linear

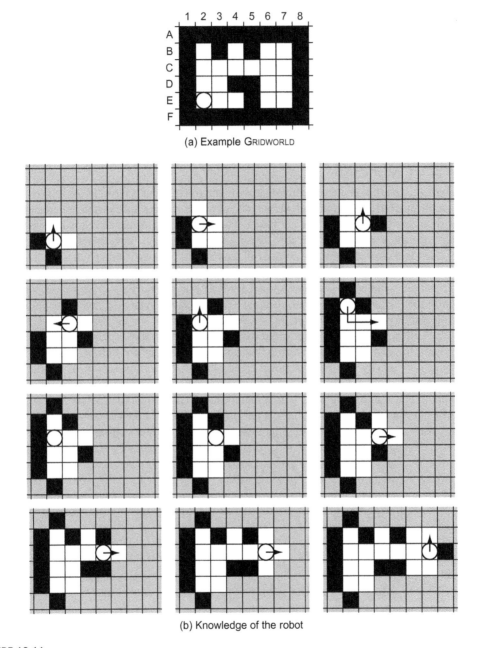

(a) Example GRIDWORLD

(b) Knowledge of the robot

FIGURE 19.11

Greedy mapping.

in the number of unblocked vertices). The worst-case trajectory length of greedy mapping is also $O(|V|\log|V|)$ moves in graphs $G = (\hat{V}, V, E)$, whether the robot a priori knows the topology of the graph or not. The small upper bound is close to the lower bound and shows that there is only a small penalty to pay for the following qualitative advantages of greedy mapping over depth-first search. First, greedy mapping is reactive to changes of the current vertex of the robot, which makes it easy to integrate greedy mapping into complete robot architectures because it does not need to have control of the robot at all times. Second, it is also reactive to changes in the knowledge that the robot has of the graph since each search makes use of all of the knowledge that the robot has of the graph. It takes new knowledge into account immediately when it becomes available and changes the moves of the robot right away to reflect its new knowledge.

Uninformed real-time heuristic search methods can also be used for mapping graphs but their worst-case trajectory lengths are typically $\Theta(|V|^2)$ moves or worse in graphs $G = (\hat{V}, V, E)$, whether the robot a priori knows the topology of the graph or not, and thus is larger than the ones of greedy mapping.

19.8 SEARCH WITH THE FREESPACE ASSUMPTION

Search with the freespace assumption uses assumption-based search for goal-directed navigation in a priori unknown terrain. Search with the freespace assumption maintains the blockage status of the vertices that the robot knows so far. It always moves on a shortest presumed unblocked path from its current vertex to the goal vertex until it visits the goal vertex or can no longer find a presumed unblocked path from its current vertex to the goal vertex. A *presumed unblocked path* is a sequence of adjacent vertices that does not contain vertices that the robot knows to be blocked. The robot moves on the presumed unblocked path toward the goal vertex but immediately repeats the process if it observes a blocked vertex on the planned path. Thus, it repeatedly makes the first move on a shortest presumed unblocked path from the current vertex to the goal vertex. This allows it to either follow the path successfully or obtain knowledge about the graph. If the robot visits the goal vertex, it stops and reports success. If it fails to find a presumed unblocked path from its current vertex to the goal vertex, it stops and reports that it cannot move to the goal vertex from its current vertex and, since the graph is undirected, neither from its start vertex.

Figure 19.12 illustrates the trajectory of search with the freespace assumption. The cross shows the goal cell. Search with the freespace assumption can use deterministic search methods and has a low-order polynomial search time in the number of vertices (but not necessarily unblocked vertices). It can calculate the shortest presumed unblocked paths efficiently with incremental heuristic search methods. The computational advantage of incremental heuristic search methods, such as D* (Lite), over search from scratch is much larger for search with the freespace assumption than for greedy mapping.

We analyze the worst-case trajectory length of search with the freespace assumption as a function of the number of unblocked vertices, where the worst case is taken over all graphs of the same number of unblocked vertices, and all start and goal vertices of the robot and all tie-breaking strategies are used to decide which one of several equally short presumed unblocked paths to move along. The worst-case trajectory length of search with the freespace assumption is $\Omega\left(\frac{|V|\log|V|}{\log\log|V|}\right)$ moves in graphs $G = (\hat{V}, V, E)$ under the minimal base model and thus is not minimal since the worst-case trajectory length of depth-first search is linear in the number of unblocked vertices. This statement continues to hold in grid graphs. It is $O(|V|\log^2|V|)$ moves in graphs $G = (\hat{V}, V, E)$ and $O(|V|\log|V|)$ moves in

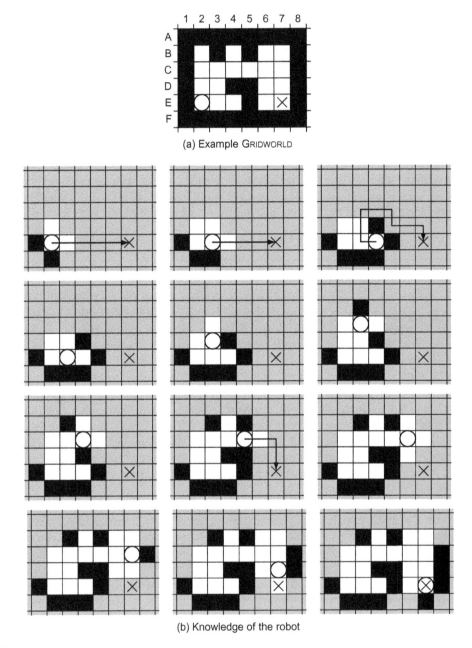

(a) Example GRIDWORLD

(b) Knowledge of the robot

FIGURE 19.12

Search with the freespace assumption.

planar graphs $G = (\hat{V}, V, E)$, including grid graphs. The small upper bound is close to the lower bound and shows that there is only a small penalty to pay for the following qualitative advantages of search with the freespace assumption over depth-first search. First, search with the freespace assumptions attempts to move in the direction of the goal vertex. Second, it reduces its trajectory length over time (although not necessarily monotonically) when it solves several goal-directed navigation problems in the same terrain and remembers the blockage status of the vertices that the robot knows so far from one goal-directed navigation problem to the next one. Eventually, it moves along a shortest trajectory to the goal vertex because the freespace assumption makes it explore vertices with unknown blockage status and thus might result in the discovery of shortcuts.

19.9 BIBLIOGRAPHIC NOTES

Overviews on motion planning and search in robotics have been given by Choset et al. (2005), LaValle (2006), and, for robot navigation in unknown terrain, Rao, Hareti, Shi, and Iyengar (1993). The parti-game algorithm has been described by Moore and Atkeson (1995). Greedy online search is related to sensor-based search, which has been described by Choset and Burdick (1994). It can be implemented efficiently with incremental heuristic search methods, including D* by Stentz (1995) and D* Lite by Koenig and Likhachev (2005); see also the overview by Koenig, Likhachev, Liu, and Furcy (2004).

Greedy localization has been described and analyzed by Mudgal, Tovey, and Koenig (2004); Tovey and Koenig (2000); and Tovey and Koenig (2010). It is implemented by the Delayed Planning Architecture (with the viable plan heuristic) by Genesereth and Nourbakhsh (1993) and Nourbakhsh (1997). Variants of greedy localization have been used by Fox, Burgard, and Thrun (1998) and Nourbakhsh (1996). Minimax LRTA* by Koenig (2001a) is a real-time heuristic search method that generalizes the Delayed Planning Architecture to perform agent-centered searches in only a part of the deterministic part of the nondeterministic state space. It deals with the problem that it might then not be able to reduce the size of its set of hypotheses and thus needs to avoid infinite cycles with a different method, namely real-time heuristic search. The NP-hardness of localization has been analyzed by Dudek, Romanik, and Whitesides (1998) and Koenig, Mitchell, Mudgal, and Tovey (2009). Guibas, Motwani, and Raghavan (1992) gave a geometric polynomial time method for robots with long-distance sensors in continuous polygonal terrain to determine the set of possible positions that are consistent with their initial observation. Localization has been studied principally with respect to the competitive ratio criterion of Sleator and Tarjan (1985), starting with Papadimitriou and Yannakakis (1991). Examples include Baeza-Yates, Culberson, and Rawlins (1993); Dudek, Romanik, and Whitesides (1998); Fleischer, Romanik, Schuierer, and Trippen (2001); and Kleinberg (1994).

Greedy mapping has been described and analyzed by Koenig, Smirnov, and Tovey (2003) and Tovey and Koenig (2003). Variants of greedy mapping have been used by Thrun et al. (1998); Koenig, Tovey, and Halliburton (2001b); and Romero, Morales, and Sucar (2001). Mapping with depth-first search has been described by Wagner, Lindenbaum, and Bruckstein (1999). Mapping has been studied principally with respect to the competitive ratio criterion. Examples include Deng, Kameda, and Papadimitriou (1998); Hoffman, Icking, Klein, and Kriegel (1997); Albers and Henzinger (2000); and Deng and Papadimitriou (1990).

Search with the freespace assumption has been described by Stentz (1995b) and described and analyzed by Koenig, Smirnov, and Tovey (2003); Mudgal, Tovey, Greenberg, and Koenig (2005);

and Mudgal, Tovey, and Koenig (2004). Variants of search with the freespace assumption have been used by Stentz and Hebert (1995) and, due to their work and follow-up efforts, afterwards widely in DARPA's unmanned ground vehicle programs and elsewhere. Goal-directed navigation in a priori unknown terrain has been studied principally with respect to the competitive ratio criterion. Examples include Blum, Raghavan, and Schieber (1997) and Icking, Klein, and Langetepe (1999). The most closely related results to the ones described in this chapter are the bug algorithms by Lumelsky and Stepanov (1987).

Bibliography

Adelson-Velskiy, G., Arlazarov, V., & Donskoy, M. (2003). Some methods of controlling the search tree in chess programs. *Artificial Intelligence, 6*(4), 361–371.

Aggarwal, S., Alonso, R., & Courcoubetis, C. (1988). Distributed reachability analysis for protocol verification environments. In *Discrete Event Systems: Models and Application*, Vol. 103 of *Lecture Notes in Control and Information Sciences* (pp. 40–56).

Aggarwal, A., & Vitter, J. S. (1987). Complexity of sorting and related problems. In *ICALP* no. (pp. 467–478).

Aggarwal, A., & Vitter, J. S. (1988). The input/output complexity of sorting and related problems. *Journal of the ACM, 31*(9), 1116–1127.

Agre, P., & Chapman, D. (1987). Pengi: An implementation of a theory of activity. In *AAAI*, (pp. 268–272).

Aho, A. V., & Corasick, M. J. (1975). Efficient string matching: An aid to bibliographic search. *Communications of the ACM, 18*(6), 333–340.

Ahuja, R. K., Magnanti, T. L., & Orlin, J. B. (1989). Networks flows. In *Handbooks in Operation Research and Management Science*. North-Holland.

Ajwani, D., Malinger, I., Meyer, U., & Toledo, S. (2008). Graph search on flash memory. MPI-TR.

Akers, S. B. (1978). Binary decision diagrams. *IEEE Transactions on Computers, 27*(6), 509–516.

Albers, S., & Henzinger, M. (2000). Exploring unknown environments. *SIAM Journal on Computing, 29*(4), 1164–1188.

Alcázar, V., Borrajo, D., & Linares López, C. (2010). Using backwards generated goals for heuristic planning. In *ICAPS* (pp. 2–9).

Allen, J. D. (2010). *The Complete Book of Connect 4: History, Strategy, Puzzles*. Sterling Publishing.

Allis, L. V. (1998). *A knowledge-based approach to connect-four. The game is solved: White wins*. Master's thesis, Vrije Univeriteit, The Netherlands.

Allis, L. V., van der Meulen, M., & van den Herik, H. J. (1994). Proof-number search. *Artificial Intelligence, 66*, 91–124.

Altschul, S., Gish, W., Miller, W., Myers, E., & Lipman, D. (1990). Basic local alignment search tool. *Journal of Molecular Biology, 215*, 403–410.

Alur, R., & Dill, D. L. (1994). A theory of timed automata. *Theoretical Computer Science, 126*(2), 183–235.

Ambite, J., & Knoblock, C. (1997). Planning by rewriting: Efficiently generating high-quality plans. In *AAAI* (pp. 706–713).

Amir, A., Farach, M., Galil, Z., Giancarlo, R., & Park, K. (1994). Dynamic dictionary matching. *Journal of Computer and System Sciences, 49*(2), 208–222.

Amir, A., Farach, M., Idury, R. M., La Poutré, J. A., & Schäffer, A. (1995). Improved dynamic dictionary matching. *Information and Computation, 119*(2), 258–282.

Anantharaman, T. S., Campbell, M. S., & Hsu, F. H. (1990). Singular extensions: Adding selectivity to brute force search. *Artificial Intelligence, 43*(1), 99–110.

Anderson, K., Schaeffer, J., & Holte, R. C. (2007). Partial pattern databases. In *SARA* (pp. 20–34).

Angluin, D. (1987). Learning regular sets from queries and counterexamples. *Information and Computation, 75*, 87–106.

Aragon, C. R., & Seidel, R. G. (1989). Randomized search trees. In *FOCS* (pp. 540–545).

Arge, L. (1996). *Efficient external-memory data structures and applications*. PhD thesis, University of Aarhus.

Arge, L., Knudsen, M., & Larsen, K. (1993). Sorting multisets and vectors in-place. In *WADS* (pp. 83–94).

Arora, S. (1995). Probabilistic checking of proofs and hardness of approximation problems. Technical Report CS-TR-476-94, Princeton University.

Aspvall, B., Plass, M. B., & Tarjan, R. E. (1979). A linear-time algorithm for testing the truth of certain quantified Boolean formulas. *Information Processing Letters, 8*(3), 121–123.

Atkinson, M. D., Sack, J. R., Santoro, N., & Strothotte, T. (1986). Min-max heaps and generalized priority queues. *Communications of the ACM, 29*, 996–1000.

Auer, P., Cesa-Bianchi, N., & Fischer, P. (2002). Finite-time analysis of the multiarmed bandit problem. *Machine Learning, 47*(2/3), 235–256.

Ausiello, G., Italiano, G., Marchetti-Spaccamela, A., & Nanni, U. (1991). Incremental algorithms for minimal length paths. *Journal of Algorithms, 12*(4), 615–638.

Avriel, M. (1976). *Nonlinear Programming: Analysis and Methods*. Prentice-Hall.

Bacchus, F., & Kabanza, F. (2000). Using temporal logics to express search control knowledge for planning. *Artificial Intelligence, 116*, 123–191.

Bäckström, C., & Nebel, B. (1995). Complexity results for SAS$^+$ planning. *Computational Intelligence, 11*(4), 625–655.

Baeza-Yates, R., Culberson, J., & Rawlins, G. (1993). Searching in the plane. *Information and Computation, 2*, 234–252.

Baeza-Yates, R., & Gonnet, G. H. (1992). A new approach to text searching. *Communications of the ACM, 35*(10), 74–82.

Bagchi, A., & Mahanti, A. (1983). Search algorithms under different kinds of heuristics—A comparative study. *Journal of the ACM, 30*(1), 1–21.

Bagchi, A., & Mahanti, A. (1985). Three approaches to heuristic search in networks. *Journal of the ACM, 32*(1), 1–27.

Baier, J. (2009). *Effective search techniques for non-classical planning via reformulation*. PhD thesis, University of Toronto.

Baier, J., & McIlraith, S. A. (2006). Planning with first-order temporally extended goals using heuristic search. In *AAAI* (pp. 788–795).

Bakera, M., Edelkamp, S., Kissmann, P., & Renner, C. D. (2008). Solving mu-calculus parity games by symbolic planning. In *MOCHART* (pp. 15–33).

Balch, T., & Arkin, R. (1993). Avoiding the past: A simple, but effective strategy for reactive navigation. In *International Conference on Robotics and Automation* (pp. 678–685).

Baldan, P., Corradini, A., König, B., & König, B. (2004). Verifying a behavioural logic for graph transformation systems. *ENTCS, 104*, 5–24.

Ball, M., & Holte, R. C. (2008). The compression power of BDDs. In *ICAPS* (pp. 2–11).

Ball, T., Majumdar, R., Millstein, T. D., & Rajamani, S. K. (2001). Automatic predicate abstraction of C programs. In *PLDI* (pp. 203–213).

Barnat, J., Brim, L., Cerná, I., Moravec, P., Rockai, P., & Simecek, P. (2006). DiVinE—A tool for distributed verification. In *CAV* (pp. 278–281).

Barnat, J., Brim, L., & Chaloupka, J. (2003). Parallel breadth-first search LTL model-checking. In *IEEE International Conference on Automated Software Engineering* (pp. 106–115). IEEE Computer Society.

Barnat, J., Brim, L., & Simecek, P. (2007). I/O-efficient accepting cycle detection. In *CAV* (pp. 316–330).

Barras, B., Boutin, S., Cornes, C., Courant, J., Filliatre, J. C., Giménez, E., et al. (1997). The Coq Proof Assistant Reference Manual—Version V6.1. Technical Report 0203, INRIA.

Barto, A., Bradtke, S., & Singh, S. (1995). Learning to act using real-time dynamic programming. *Artificial Intelligence, 72*(1), 81–138.

Bartzis, C., & Bultan, T. (2006). Efficient BDDs for bounded arithmetic constraints. *International Journal on Software Tools for Technology Transfer, 8*(1), 26–36.

Bast, H., Funke, S., Sanders, P., & Schultes, D. (2007). Fast routing in road networks with transit nodes. *Science, 316*(5824), 566.

Batalin, M., & Sukhatme, G. (2004). Coverage, exploration and deployment by a mobile robot and communication network. *Telecommunication Systems Journal: Special Issue on Wireless Sensor Networks, 26*(2), 181–196.

Baumer, S., & Schuler, R. (2003). Improving a probabilistic 3-SAT algorithm by dynamic search and independent clause pairs. In *SAT* (pp. 150–161).

Beacham, A. (2000). *The complexity of problems without backbones.* Master's thesis, Department of Computing Science, University of Alberta.

Behrmann, G., Hune, T. S., & Vaandrager, F. W. (2000). Distributed timed model checking—How the search order matters. In *CAV* (pp. 216–231).

Bellman, R. (1958). On a routing problem. *Quarterly of Applied Mathematics, 16*(1), 87–90.

Bentley, J. L., & Ottmann, T. A. (2008). Algorithms for reporting and counting geometric intersections. *Transactions on Computing, 28*, 643–647.

Bercher, P., & Mattmüller, R. (2008). A planning graph heuristic for forward-chaining adversarial planning. In *ECAI* (pp. 921–922).

Berger, A., Grimmer, M., & Müller-Hannemann, M. (2010). Fully dynamic speed-up techniques for multi-criteria shortest path searches in time-dependent networks. In *SEA* (pp. 35–46).

Berlekamp, E. R., Conway, J. H., & Guy, R. K. (1982). *Winning Ways.* Academic Press.

Bertsekas, D. P. (1999). *Nonlinear Programming.* Athena Scientific.

Bessiere, C. (1994). Arc-consistency and arc-consistency again. *Artificial Intelligence, 65*, 179–190.

Bessiere, C., & Regin, J.-C. (2001). Refining the basic constraint propagation algorithm. In *IJCAI* (pp. 309–315).

Bessiere, C., Freuder, E. C., & Regin, J.-C. (1999). Using constraint metaknowledge to reduce arc consistency computation. *Artificial Intelligence, 107*, 125–148.

Biere, A. (1997). μcke-efficient μ-calculus model checking. In *CAV* (pp. 468–471).

Biere, A., Cimatti, A., Clarke, E., & Zhu, Y. (1999). Symbolic model checking without BDDs. In *TACAS* (pp. 193–207) .

Bisani, R. (1987). Beam search. In *Encyclopedia of Artificial Intelligence* (pp. 56–58).

Bistarelli, S., Montanari, U., & Rossi, F. (1997). Semiring-based constraint satisfaction and optimization. *Journal of the ACM, 44*(2), 201–236.

Bjørnsson, Y., Bulitko, V., & Sturtevant, N. (2009) "TBA*: Time-Bounded A*," Proceedings of the International Joint Conference on Artificial Intelligence, 431–436.

Bloem, R., Ravi, K., & Somenzi, F. (2000). Symbolic guided search for CTL model checking. In *DAC* (pp. 29–34).

Bloom, B. (1970). Space/time trade-offs in hashing coding with allowable errors. *Communication of the ACM, 13*(7), 422–426.

Blum, A., & Furst, M. L. (1995). Fast planning through planning graph analysis. In *IJCAI* (pp. 1636–1642).

Blum, A., Raghavan, P., & Schieber, B. (1991). Navigation in unfamiliar terrain. In *STOC* (pp. 494–504).

Blum, A., Raghavan, P., & Schieber, B. (1997). Navigating in unfamiliar geometric terrain. *SIAM Journal on Computing, 26*(1), 110–137.

Bnaya, Z., Felner, A., & Shimony, S. E. (2009). Canadian traveler problem with remote sensing. In *IJCAI* (pp. 437–442).

Bollig, B., Leucker, M., & Weber, M. (2001). Parallel model checking for the alternation free μ-calculus. In *TACAS*, (pp. 543–558).

Bonasso, R., Kortenkamp, D., & Murphy, R. (1998). *Xavier: A Robot Navigation Architecture Based on Partially Observable Markov Decision Process Models.* MIT Press.

Bonet, B. (2008). Efficient algorithms to rank and unrank permutations in lexicographic order. In *AAAI-Workshop on Search in AI and Robotics.*

Bonet, B., & Geffner, H. (2000). Planning with incomplete information as heurstic search in belief space. In *AIPS* (pp. 52–61).

Bonet, B., & Geffner, H. (2001). Planning as heuristic search. *Artificial Intelligence, 129*(1–2), 5–33.

Bonet, B., & Geffner, H. (2005). An algorithm better than AO*? In *AAAI* (pp. 1343–1348).

Bonet, B., & Geffner, H. (2006). Learning depth-first: A unified approach to heuristic search in deterministic and non-deterministic settings, and its application to MDPs. In *ICAPS* (pp. 142–151).

Bonet, B., & Geffner, H. (2008). Heuristics for planning with penalties and rewards formulated in logic and computed through circuits. *Artificial Intelligence, 172*, 1579–1604.

Bonet, B., & Helmert, M. (2010). Strengthening landmark heuristics via hitting sets. In *ECAI* (pp. 329–334).

Bonet, B., Haslum, P., Hickmott, S. L., & Thiébaux, S. (2008). Directed unfolding of petri nets. *T. Petri Nets and Other Models of Concurrency, 1*, 172–198.

Bonet, B., Loerincs, G., & Geffner, H. (2008). A robust and fast action selection mechanism for planning. In *AAAI* (pp. 714–719).

Bornot, S., Morin, R., Niebert, P., & Zennou, S. (2002). Black box unfolding with local first search. In *TACAS* (pp. 241–257).

Borowsky, B., & Edelkamp, S. (2008). Optimal metric planning with state sets in automata representation. In *AAAI* (pp. 874–879).

Bosnacki, D. (2004). Black box checking for biochemical networks. In *CMSB* (pp. 225–230).

Bosnacki, D., Edelkamp, S., & Sulewski, D. (2009). Efficient probabilistic model checking on general purpose graphics processors. In *SPIN* (pp. 32–49).

Botea, A., Müller, M., & Schaeffer, J. (2005). Learning partial-order macros from solutions. In *ICAPS* (pp. 231–240).

Botelho, F. C., Pagh, R., & Ziviani, N. (2007). Simple and space-efficient minimal perfect hash functions. In *WADS* (pp. 139–150).

Botelho, F. C., & Ziviani, N. (2007). External perfect hashing for very large key sets. In *CIKM* (pp. 653–662).

Brafman, R., & Chernyavsky, Y. (2005). Planning with goal preferences and constraints. In *ICAPS* (pp. 182–191).

Barto, A. G., Bradtke, S. J., & Singh, S. P. (1995). Learning to act using real-time dynamic programming. *Artificial Intelligence, 72*(1), 81–138.

Breiman, L., Friedman, J. H., Olshen, R. A., & Stone, C. J. (1984). *Classification and Regression Trees*. Wadsworth.

Breitbart, Y., Hunt, H., & Rosenkrantz, D. (1992). Switching circuits by binary decision diagrams. *Bell System Technical Journal, 38*, 985–999.

Breitbart, Y., Hunt, H., & Rosenkrantz, D. (1995). On the size of binary decision diagrams representing Boolean functions. *Theoretical Computer Science, 145*, 45–69.

Brengel, K., Crauser, A., Meyer, U., & Ferragina, P. (1999). An experimental study of priority queues in external memory. In *WAE* (pp. 345–359).

Breyer, T. M., & Korf, R. E. (2008). Recent results in analyzing the performance of heuristic search. In *AAAI, Workshop on Search Techniques in Artificial Intelligence and Robotics*.

Breyer, T. M., & Korf, R. E. (2010a). Independent additive heuristics reduce search multiplicatively. In *AAAI* (pp. 33–38).

Breyer, T. M., & Korf, R. E. (2010b). 1.6-bit pattern databases. In *AAAI* (pp. 39–44).

Briel, M., Sanchez, R., Do, M., & Kambhampati, S. (2004). Effective approaches for partial satisfaction (oversubscription) planning. In *AAAI* (pp. 562–569).

Brodal, G. S. (1996). Worst-case efficient priority queues. In *SODA* (pp. 52–58).

Brodnik, A., & Munro, J. M. (1999). Membership in constant time and almost-minimum space. *SIAM Journal of Computing, 28*(3), 1627–1640.

Brooks, R. (1986). A robust layered control system for a mobile robot. *IEEE Journal of Robotics and Automation, RA-2*, 14–23.

Bruegmann, B. (1993). *Monte-Carlo Go*. Unpublished manuscript.

Bruengger, A., Marzetta, A., Fukuda, K., & Nievergelt, J. (1999). The parallel search bench ZRAM and its applications. *Annals of Operation Research, 90*, 25–63.

Brumitt, B., & Stentz, A. (1998). GRAMMPS: A generalized mission planner for multiple mobile robots. In *ICRA*.

Brüntrup, R., Edelkamp, S., Jabbar, S., & Scholz, B. (2005). Incremental map generation with GPS traces. In *ITSC*, 2005.

Bruun, A., Edelkamp, S., Katajainen, J., & Rasmussen, J. (2010). Policy-based benchmarking of weak heaps and their relatives. In *SEA* (pp. 424–435).

Bryant, R. E. (1992). Symbolic Boolean manipulation with ordered binary-decision diagrams. *ACM Computing Surveys, 24*(3), 142–170.

Buchsbaum, A., Goldwasser, M., Venkatasubramanian, S., & Westbrook, J. (2000). On external memory graph traversal. In *Symposium on Discrete Algorithms (SODA)* (pp. 859–860).

Bulitko, V., & Lee, G. (2006). Learning in real-time search: A unifying framework. *Journal of Artificial Intelligence Research, 25*, 119–157.

Bulitko, V., Sturtevant, N., & Kazakevich, M. (2005). Speeding up learning in real-time search via automatic state abstraction. In *AAAI* (pp. 1349–1354).

Burgard, W., Fox, D., Moors, M., Simmons, R., & Thrun, S. (2000). Collaborative multi-robot exploration. In *ICRA* (pp. 476–481).

Burns, E., Lemons, S., Ruml, W., & Zhou, R. (2009a). Suboptimal and anytime heuristic search on multi-core machines. In *ICAPS* (2009a).

Burns, E., Lemons, S., Zhou, R., & Ruml, W. (2009b). Best-first heuristic search for multi-core machines. In *IJCAI* (pp. 449–455).

Bylander, T. (1994). The computational complexity of propositional STRIPS planning. *Artificial Intelligence*, 165–204.

Caires, L., & Cardelli, L. (2003). A spatial logic for concurrency (part I). *Information and Computation, 186*(2), 194–235.

CAMP Consortium. (2004). Enhanced digital mapping project final report. Submitted to the U.S. department of transportation, federal highway administration, and national highway traffic and safety administration, 11, 2004.

Campbell Jr., M., Hoane, A. J., & Hsu, F. (2002). Deep blue. *Artificial Intelligence, 134*(1–2), 57–83.

Cantone, D., & Cinotti, G. (2002). QuickHeapsort, an efficient mix of classical sorting algorithms. *Theoretical Computer Science, 285*(1), 25–42.

Carlsson, S. (1987). The deap—A double-ended heap to implement double-ended priority queues. *Information Processing Letters, 26*, 33–36.

Carrillo, H., & Lipman, D. (1988). The multiple sequence alignment problem in biology. *SIAM Journal of Applied Mathematics, 5*(48), 1073–1082.

Cederman, D., & Tsigas, P. (2008). *A practical quicksort algorithm for graphics processors*. Technical Report 2008-01, Chalmers University of Technology.

Chakrabarti, P. P., Ghose, S., Acharya, A., & DeSarkar, S. C. (1989). Heuristic search in restricted memory. *Artificial Intelligence, 41*(2), 197–221.

Chakrabarti, S., van den Berg, M., & Dom, B. (1999). Focused crawling: A new approach to topic-specific web resource discovery. *Computer Networks, 31*, 1123–1640.

Charikar, M., Indyk, P., & Panigrahy, R. (2002). New algorithms for subset query, partial match, orthogonal range searching, and related problems. In *ICALP* (pp. 451–462).

Cheadle, A. M., Harvey, W., Sadler, A. J., Schimpf, J., Shen, K., & Wallace, M. G. (2003). ECLiPSe: An introduction. Technical Report.

Cheeseman, P., Kanefsky, B., & Taylor, W. (2001). Where the really hard problems are. In *IJCAI* (pp. 331–340).

Chen, Y., & Wah, B. W. (2004). Subgoal partitioning and resolution in planning. In *Proceedings of the International Planning Competition*.

Cherkassy, B. V., Goldberg, A. V., & Ratzig, T. (1997a). Shortest path algorithms: Theory and experimental evaluation. *Mathematical Programming, 73*, 129–174.

Cherkassy, B. V., Goldberg, A. V., & Silverstein, C. (1997b). Buckets, heaps, list and monotone priority queues. In *SODA* (pp. 82–92).

Choset, H., & Burdick, J. (1994). Sensor based planning and nonsmooth analysis. In *ICRA* (pp. 3034–3041).

Choset, H., Lynch, K., Hutchinson, S., Kantor, G., Burgard, W., Kavraki, L., et al. (2005). *Principles of Robot Motion*. MIT Press.

Choueka, Y., Fraenkel, A. S., Klein, S. T., & Segal, E. (1986). Improved hierarchical bit-vector compression in document retrieval systems. *ACM SIGIR* (pp. 88–96).

Christofides, N. (1976). Worst-case analysis of a new heuristic for the travelling salesman problem. Technical Report 388, Graduate School of Industrial Administration, Carnegie-Mellon University.

Chu, S. C., Chen, Y. T., & Ho, J. H. (2006). Timetable scheduling using particle swarm optimization. In *ICICIC* (Vol. 3, pp. 324–327).

Cimatti, A., Giunchiglia, E., Giunchiglia, F., & Traverso, P. (1997). Planning via model checking: A decision procedure for AR. In *ECP* (pp. 130–142).

Clarke, E. M., Grumberg, O., Jha, S., Lu, Y., & Veith, H. (2001). Counterexample-guided abstraction refinement. In *CAV* (pp. 154–169).

Clarke, E. M., Grumberg, O., & Long, D. E. (1994). Model checking and abstraction. *ACM Transactions on Programming Languages and Systems, 16*(5), 1512–1542.

Cleaveland, R., Iyer, P., & Yankelevich, D. (1995). Optimality in abstractions of model checking. In *Static Analysis Symposium* (pp. 51–53).

Clune, J. (2007). Heuristic evaluation functions for general game playing. In *AAAI* (pp. 1134–1139).

Coego, J., Mandow, L., & Pérez de-la Cruz, J.-L. (2009). A new approach to iterative deepening multiobjective A*. In *AI*IA* (pp. 264–273).

Cohen, J. D. (1997). Recursive hashing functions for n-grams. *ACM Transactions on Information Systems, 15*(3), 291–320.

Coles, A., Fox, M., Halsey, K., Long, D., & Smith, A. (2009). Managing concurrency in temporal planning using planner-scheduler interaction. *173*(1), 1–44.

Coles, A., Fox, M., Long, D., & Smith, A. (2008). A hybrid relaxed planning GraphLP heuristic for numeric planning domains. In *ICAPS* (pp. 52–59).

Cook, S. A. (1971). The complexity of theorem-proving procedures. In *STOC* (pp. 151–158).

Cook, D. J., & Varnell, R. C. (1998). Adaptive parallel iterative deepening A*. *Journal of Artificial Intelligence Research, 9*, 136–166.

Cooperman, G., & Finkelstein, L. (1992). New methods for using Cayley graphs in interconnection networks. *Discrete Applied Mathematics, 37/38*, 95–118.

Cormen, T. H., Leiserson, C. E., & Rivest, R. L. (1990). *Introduction to Algorithms*. MIT Press.

Corradini, A., Montanari, U., Rossi, F., Ehrig, H., Heckel, R., & Löwe, M. (1997). Algebraic approaches to graph transformation I: Basic concepts and double pushout approach. In G. Rozenberg (Ed.), *Handbook of Graph Grammars and Computing by Graph Transformation* (Vol. 1, chap. 3). Foundations. World Scientific.

Coulom, R. (2006). Efficient selectivity and backup operators in Monte-Carlo tree search. In *CG* (pp. 72–83).

Cox, I. (1997). Blanche—An experiment in guidance and navigation of an autonomous robot vehicle. *SIAM Journal on Computing, 26*(1), 110–137.

Crauser, A. (2001). *External memory algorithms and data structures in theory and practice*. PhD thesis, MPI-Informatik, Universität des Saarlandes.

Culberson, J. C. (1998a). Sokoban is PSPACE-complete. In *FUN* (pp. 65–76).

Culberson, J. C. (1998b). On the futility of blind search: An algorithmic view of no free lunch. *Evolutionary Computing, 6*(2), 109–127.

Culberson, J. C., & Schaeffer, J. (1998). Pattern databases. *Computational Intelligence, 14*(4), 318–334.

Cung, V.-D., & LeCun, B. (1994). A suitable data structure for parallel A*. Technical Report 2165, INRIA, France.

Cushing, W., Kambhampati, S., Mausam, & Weld, D. S. (2007). When is temporal planning really temporal? In *IJCAI* (pp. 1852–1859).

Dakin, R. J. (1965). A tree-search algorithm for mixed integer programming problems. *The Computer Journal, 8*, 250–255.

Dantsin, E., Goerdt, A., Hirsch, E. A., & Schöning, U. (2000). Deterministic k-SAT algorithms based on covering codes and local search. In *ICALP* (pp. 236–247).

Davidson, A. (2001). A fast pruning algorithm for optimal sequence alignment. In *Symposium on Bioinformatics and Bioengineering* (pp. 49–56).

Davis, H. W. (1990). Cost-error relationship in A*. *Journal of the ACM, 37*(2), 195–199.

Dayhoff, M. O., Schwartz, R. M., & Orcutt, B. C. (1978). A model of evolutionary change in proteins. *Atlas of Protein Sequences and Structures, 5*.

Dean, T. L., & Boddy, M. (1988). An analysis of time-dependent planning. In *AAAI*.

Dean, T. L., Kaelbling, L., Kirman, J., & Nicholson, A. (1995). Planning under time constraints in stochastic domains. *Artificial Intelligence, 76*(1–2), 35–74.

Dearden, R. (2001). Structured prioritised sweeping. In *ICML* (pp. 82–89).

DeChampeaux, D., & Sint, H. J. (1977). An improved bi-directional heuristic search algorithm. *Journal of the ACM, 24*(2), 177–191.

Dechter, R. (1999). Bucket elimination: A unifying framework for reasoning. *Artificial Intelligence*, 41–85.

Dechter, R. (2004). *Constraint Processing*. Morgan Kaufmann.

Dechter, R., & Pearl, J. (1983). The optimality of A* revisited. In *AAAI* (pp. 59–99).

DeGiacomo, G., & Vardi, M. Y. (1999). Automata-theoretic approach to planning for temporally extended goals. In *ECP* (pp. 226–238).

Delort, C., & Spanjaard, O. (2010). Using bound sets in multiobjective optimization: Application to the biobjective binary knapsack problem. In *SEA* (pp. 253–265).

Demaine, E. D., Demaine, M. L., & O'Rourke, J. (2000). PushPush and Push-1 are NP-hard in 2D. In *Canadian Conference on Computational Geometry* (pp. 211–219).

Dementiev, R., Kettner, L., Mehnert, J., & Sanders, P. (2004). Engineering a sorted list data structure for 32-bit key. In *ALENEX/ANALC* (pp. 142–151).

Dementiev, R., Kettner, L., & Sanders, P. (2005). STXXL: Standard template library for XXL data sets. In *ESA* (pp. 640–651).

Demmer, M. J., & Herlihy, M. (1998). The arrow distributed directory protocol. In *DISC* (pp. 119–133).

Deng, X., Kameda, T., & Papadimitriou, C. (1998). How to learn an unknown environment I: The rectilinear case. *Journal of the ACM, 45*(2), 215–245.

Deng, X., & Papadimitriou, C. (1990). Exploring an unknown graph. In *FOCS* (pp. 355–361).

Deo, N., & Pang, C. (1984). Shortest path algorithms: Taxonomy and annotations. *IEEE Transactions on Systems Science and Cybernetics, 14*, 257–323.

Dial, R. B. (1969). Shortest-path forest with topological ordering. *Communications of the ACM, 12*(11), 632–633.

Dietterich, T. G. (2000). Hierarchical reinforcement learning with the maxq value function decomposition. *Journal of Artificial Intelligence Research, 13*, 227–303.

Dietzfelbinger, M., Karlin, A., Mehlhorn, K., Meyer auf der Heide, F., Rohnert, H., & Tarjan, R. E. (1994). Dynamic perfect hashing: Upper and lower bounds. *SIAM Journal of Computing, 23*, 738–761.

Dijkstra, E. W. (1959). A note on two problems in connexion with graphs. *Numerische Mathematik, 1*, 269–271.

Dijkstra, E. W., & Scholten, C. S. (1979). Termination detection for diffusing computations. *Information Processing Letters, 11*(1), 1–4.

Diligenty, M., Coetzee, F., Lawrence, S., Giles, C. M., & Gori, M. (2000). Focused crawling using context graphs. In *International Conference on Very Large Databases* (pp. 527–534).

Dillenburg, J. F. (1993). *Techniques for improving the efficiency of heuristic search.* PhD thesis, University of Illinois at Chicago.

Dillenburg, J. F., & Nelson, P. C. (1994). Perimeter search. *Artificial Intelligence, 65*(1), 165–178.

Dinh, H. T., Russell, A., & Su, Y. (2007). On the value of good advice: The complexity of A* search with accurate heuristics. In *AAAI* (pp. 1140–1145).

Do, M. B., & Kambhampati, S. (2003). Sapa: A multi-objective metric temporal planner. 20, 155–194.

Doran, J., & Michie, D. (1966). Experiments with the graph traverser program. In *Proceedings of the Royal Society of London* (Vol. 294, pp. 235–259).

Dorigo, M., Gambardella, L. M., Middendorf, M., & Stützle, T. (Eds.). (2002). *IEEE Transactions on Evolutionary Computation: Special Issue on Ant Algorithms and Swarm Intelligence.*

Dorigo, M., Maniezzo, V., & Colorni, A. (1996). The ant system: Optimization by a colony of cooperating agents. *IEEE Transactions on Systems, Man and Cybernetics, 26*(1), 29–41.

Dorigo, M., & Stützle, T. (Eds.). (2004). *Ant Colony Optimization.* MIT Press.

Dow, P. A., & Korf, R. E. (2007). Best-first search for treewidth. In *AAAI* (pp. 1146–1151).

Dräger, K., Finkbeiner, B., & Podelski, A. (2009). Directed model checking with distance-preserving abstractions. *International Journal on Software Tools for Technology Transfer, 11*(1), 27–37.

Driscoll, J. R., Gabow, H. N., Shrairman, R., & Tarjan, R. E. (1988). Relaxed heaps: An alternative to fibonacci heaps with applications to parallel computation. *Communications of the ACM, 31*(11).

Droste, S., Jansen, T., & Wegener, I. (1999). Possibly not a free lunch but at least a free appetizer. In *GECCO* (pp. 833–839).

Droste, S., Jansen, T., & Wegener, I. (2002). Optimization with randomized search heuristics—The (A)NFL theorem, realistic scenarios, and difficult functions. *Theoretical Computer Science, 287*, 131–144.

Dudek, G., Romanik, K., & Whitesides, S. (1995). Localizing a robot with minimum travel. In *SODA* (pp. 437–446).

Dudek, G., Romanik, K., & Whitesides, S. (1998). Localizing a robot with minimum travel. *Journal on Computing, 27*(2), 583–604.

Duran, M. A., & Grossmann, I. E. (1986). An outer approximation algorithm for a class of mixed-integer nonlinear programs. *Mathematical Programming, 36*, 306–307.

Dutt, S., & Mahapatra, N. R. (1994). Scalable load balancing strategies for parallel A* algorithms. *Journal of Parallel and Distributed Computing, 22*(3), 488–505.

Dutt, S., & Mahapatra, N. R. (1997). Scalable global and local hashing strategies for duplicate pruning in parallel A* graph search. *IEEE Transactions on Parallel and Distributed Systems, 8*(7), 738–756.

Dutton, R. D. (1993). Weak-heap sort. *BIT, 33*, 372–381.

Eckerle, J. (1998). *Heuristische Suche unter Speicherbeschränkungen.* PhD thesis, University of Freiburg.

Eckerle, J., & Lais, T. (1998). Limits and possibilities of sequential hashing with supertrace. In *FORTE/PSTV.* Kluwer.

Eckerle, J., & Ottmann, T. A. (1994). An efficient data structure for the bidirectional search. In *ECAI* (pp. 600–604).

Eckerle, J., & Schuierer, S. (1995). Efficient memory-limited graph search. In *KI* (pp. 101–112).

Edelkamp, S. (1997). Suffix tree automata in state space search. In *KI* (pp. 381–385).

Edelkamp, S. (1998a). Updating shortest paths. In *ECAI* (pp. 655–659).

Edelkamp, S. (1998b). *Datenstrukturen and lernverfahren in der zustandsraumsuche.* PhD thesis, University of Freiburg.

Edelkamp, S. (2001a). Planning with pattern databases. In *ECP* (pp. 13–24).

Edelkamp, S. (2001b). Prediction of regular search tree growth by spectral analysis. In *KI* (pp. 154–168).

Edelkamp, S. (2002). Symbolic pattern databases in heuristic search planning. In *AIPS* (pp. 274–293).

Edelkamp, S. (2003a). Memory limitation in artificial intelligence. In P. Sanders, U. Meyer, & J. F. Sibeyn (Eds.), *Memory Hierarchies* (pp. 233–250).

Edelkamp, S. (2003b). Promela planning. In *SPIN* (pp. 197–212).

Edelkamp, S. (2003c). Taming numbers and durations in the model checking integrated planning system. *Journal of Artificial Research, 20*, 195–238.

Edelkamp, S. (2004). Generalizing the relaxed planning heuristic to non-linear tasks. In *KI* (pp. 198–212).

Edelkamp, S. (2005). External symbolic heuristic search with pattern databases. In *ICAPS* (pp. 51–60).

Edelkamp, S. (2006). On the compilation of plan constraints and preferences. In *ICAPS* (pp. 374–377).

Edelkamp, S. (2007). Automated creation of pattern database search heuristics. In *MOCHART* (pp. 35–50).

Edelkamp, S., & Eckerle, J. (1997). New strategies in real-time heuristic search. In S. Koenig, A. Blum, T. Ishida, & R. E. Korf (Eds.), *AAAI Workshop on Online Search* (pp. 30–35).

Edelkamp, S., & Helmert, M. (2001). The model checking integrated planning system MIPS. *AI-Magazine* (pp. 67–71).

Edelkamp, S., & Jabbar, S. (2005). Action planning for graph transition systems. In *ICAPS, Workshop on Verification and Validation of Model-Based Planning and Scheduling Systems* (pp. 58–66).

Edelkamp, S., & Jabbar, S. (2006a). Action planning for directed model checking of Petri nets. *ENTCS, 149*(2), 3–18.

Edelkamp, S., & Jabbar, S. (2006b). Externalizing real-time model checking. In *MOCHART* (pp. 67–83).

Edelkamp, S., & Jabbar, S. (2006c). Large-scale directed model checking LTL. In *SPIN* (pp. 1–18).

Edelkamp, S., Jabbar, S., & Bonet, B. (2007). External memory value iteration. In *ICAPS* (pp. 414–429).

Edelkamp, S., Jabbar, S., & Lluch-Lafuente, A. (2005). Cost-algebraic heuristic search. In *AAAI* (pp. 1362–1367).

Edelkamp, S., Jabbar, S., & Lluch-Lafuente, A. (2006). Heuristic search for the analysis of graph transition systems. In *ICGT* (pp. 414–429).

Edelkamp, S., Jabbar, S., & Schrödl, S. (2004a). External A*. In *KI* (pp. 233–250).

Edelkamp, S., Jabbar, S., & Sulewski, D. (2008a). Distributed verification of multi-threaded C++ programs. *ENTCS, 198*(1), 33–46.

Edelkamp, S., Jabbar, S., & Willhalm, T. (2003). Geometric travel planning. In *ITSC* (Vol. 2, pp. 964–969).

Edelkamp, S., & Kissmann, P. (2007). Externalizing the multiple sequence alignment problem with affine gap costs. In *KI* (pp. 444–447).

Edelkamp, S., & Kissmann, P. (2008a). Symbolic classification of general multi-player games. In *ECAI* (pp. 905–906).

Edelkamp, S., & Kissmann, P. (2008b). Symbolic classification of general two-player games. In *KI* (pp. 185–192).

Edelkamp, S., & Kissmann, P. (2008c). Limits and possibilities of BDDs in state space search. In *AAAI* (pp. 1452–1453).

Edelkamp, S., Kissmann, P., & Jabbar, S. (2008b). Scaling search with symbolic pattern databases. In *MOCHART* (pp. 49–64).

Edelkamp, S., & Korf, R. E. (1998). The branching factor of regular search spaces. In *AAAI* (pp. 299–304).

Edelkamp, S., Leue, S., & Lluch-Lafuente, A. (2004b). Directed explicit-state model checking in the validation of communication protocols. *International Journal on Software Tools for Technology Transfer, 5*(2–3), 247–267.

Edelkamp, S., Leue, S., & Lluch-Lafuente, A. (2004c). Partial order reduction and trail improvement in directed model checking. *International Journal on Software Tools for Technology Transfer, 6*(4), 277–301.

Edelkamp, S., & Leven, P. (2002). Directed automated theorem proving. In *LPAR* (pp. 145–159).

Edelkamp, S., & Lluch-Lafuente, A. (2004). Abstraction in directed model checking. In *ICAPS, Workshop on Connecting Planning Theory with Practice*.

Edelkamp, S., & Meyer, U. (2001). Theory and practice of time-space trade-offs in memory limited search. In *KI* (pp. 169–184).

Edelkamp, S., & Reffel, F. (1998). OBDDs in heuristic search. In *KI* (pp. 81–92).

Edelkamp, S., Sanders, P., & Simecek, P. (2008c). Semi-external LTL model checking. In *CAV* (pp. 530–542).

Edelkamp, S., & Schrödl, S. (2000). Localizing A*. In *AAAI* (pp. 885–890).

Edelkamp, S., & Stiegeler, P. (2002). Implementing HEAPSORT with $n \lg n - 0.9n$ and QUICKSORT with $n \lg n + 0.2n$ comparisons. *ACM Journal of Experimental Algorithmics, 7*(5).

Edelkamp, S., & Sulewski, D. (2008). Flash-efficient LTL model checking with minimal counterexamples. In *SEFM* (pp. 73–82).

Edelkamp, S., & Sulewski, D. (2010). Efficient probabilistic model checking on general purpose graphics processors. In *SPIN* (pp. 106–123).

Edelkamp, S., Sulewski, D., & Yücel, C. (2010a). GPU exploration of two-player games with perfect hash functions. In *SOCS* (pp. 23–30).

Edelkamp, S., Sulewski, D., & Yücel, C. (2010b). Perfect hashing for state space exploration on the GPU. In *ICAPS* (pp. 57–64).

Edelkamp, S., Sulewski, D., Barnat, J., Brim, L., & Simecek, P. (2011). Flash memory efficient LTL model checking. *Science of Computer Programming, 76*(2), 136–157.

Edelkamp, S., & Wegener, I. (2000). On the performance of WEAK-HEAPSORT. In *STACS* (pp. 254–266).

Elmasry, A. (2010). The violation heap: A relaxed fibonacci-like heap. In *COCOON* (pp. 479–488).

Elmasry, A., Jensen, C., & Katajainen, J. (2005). *Relaxed weak queues: An alternative to run-relaxed heaps.* Technical Report CPH STL 2005-2, Department of Computing, University of Copenhagen.

Elmasry, A., Jensen, C., & Katajainen, J. (2008a). Two new methods for constructing double-ended priority queues from priority queues. *Computing, 83*(4), 193–204.

Elmasry, J., Jensen, C., & Katajainen, J. (2008b). Multipartite priority queues. *ACM Transactions on Algorithms, 5*(1), 1–19.

Elmasry, A., Jensen, C., & Katajainen, J. (2008c). Two-tier relaxed heaps. *Acta Informatica, 45*(3), 193–210.

Engels, A., Feijs, L. M. G., & Mauw, S. (1997). Test generation for intelligent networks using model checking. In *TACAS* (pp. 384–398).

Eppstein, D. (1987). On the NP-completeness of cryptarithms. *SIGACT News, 18*(3), 38–40.

Eppstein, D., & Galil, Z. (1988). Parallel algorithmic techniques for compinatorial computation. *Annual Review of Computer Science, 3*, 233–283.

Ertico. (2002). Nextmap for transport telematics systems. Final Report, 06-2002.

Even, S., & Gazit, H. (1985). Updating distances in dynamic graphs. *Methods of Operations Research, 49*, 371–387.

Even, S., & Shiloach, Y. (1981). An on-line edge deletion problem. *Journal of the ACM, 28*(1), 1–4.

Evett, M., Hendler, J., Mahanti, A., & Nau, D. S. (1990). PRA*: A memory-limited heuristic search procedure for the connection machine. In *Frontiers in Massive Parallel Computation* (pp. 145–149).

Eyerich, P., Keller, T., & Helmert, M. (2010). High-quality policies for the Canadian traveler's problem. In *AAAI* (pp. 51–58).

Eyerich, P., Mattmüller, R., & Röger, G. (2009). Using the context-enhanced additive heuristic for temporal and numeric planning. In *ICAPS* (pp. 130–137).

Fabiani, P., & Meiller, Y. (2000). Planning with tokens: An approach between satisfaction and optimisation. In *PUK*.

Fadel, R., Jakobsen, K. V., Katajainen, J., & Teuhola, J. (1997). External heaps combined with effective buffering. In *Australasian Theory Symposium* (pp. 72–78).

Faigle, U., & Kern, W. (1992). Some convergence results for probabilistic tabu search. *Journal of Computing, 4*, 32–37.

Feige, U. (1996). A fast randomized LOGSPACE algorithm for graph connectivity. *Theoretical Computer Science, 169*(2), 147–160.

Feige, U. (1997). A spectrum of time-space tradeoffs for undirected $s - t$ connectivity. *Journal of Computer and System Sciences, 54*(2), 305–316.

Felner, A. (2001). *Improving search techniques and using them in different environments*. PhD thesis, Bar-Ilan University.

Felner, A., & Alder, A. (2005). Solving the 24 puzzle with instance dependent pattern databases. In *SARA* (pp. 248–260).

Felner, N. R., Korf, R. E., & Hanan, S. (2004a). Additive pattern database heuristics. *Journal of Artificial Intelligence Research, 22*, 279–318.

Felner, A., Meshulam, R., Holte, R. C., & Korf, R. E. (2004b). Compressing pattern databases. In *AAAI* (pp. 638–643).

Felner, A., Moldenhauer, C., Sturtevant, N. R., & Schaeffer, J. (2010). Single-frontier bidirectional search. In *AAAI*.

Felner, A., & Ofek, N. (2007). Combining perimeter search and pattern database abstractions. In *SARA* (pp. 414–429).

Felner, A., & Sturtevant, N. R. (2009). Abstraction-based heuristics with true distance computations. In *SARA*.

Felner, A., Shoshani, Y., Altshuler, Y., & Bruckstein, A. (2006). Multi-agent physical A* with large pheromones. *Autonomous Agents and Multi-Agent Systems, 12*(1), 3–34.

Felner, A., Zahavi, U., Schaeffer, J., & Holte, R. C. (2005). Dual lookups in pattern databases. In *IJCAI* (pp. 103–108).

Feng, Z., & Hansen, E. A. (2002). Symbolic heuristic search for factored Markov decision processes. In *AAAI* (pp. 714–719).

Feuerstein, E., & Marchetti-Spaccamela, A. (1993). Dynamic algorithms for shortest paths in planar graphs. *Theoretical Computer Science, 116*(2), 359–371.

Fikes, R. E., & Nilsson, N. J. (1971). Strips: A new approach to the application of theorem proving to problem solving. *Artificial Intelligence, 2*, 189–208.

Finnsson, H., & Björnsson, Y. (2008). Simulation-based approach to general game playing. In *AAAI* (pp. 1134–1139).

Fleischer, R., Romanik, K., Schuierer, S., & Trippen, G. (2001). Optimal robot localization in trees. *Information and Computation, 171*, 224–247.

Flinsenberg, I. C. M. (2004). *Route planning algorithms for car navigation*. PhD thesis, Technische Universiteit Eindhoven, Eindhoven, The Netherlands.

Forbus, K. D., & de Kleer, J. (1993). *Building Problem Solvers*. MIT Press.

Ford, L. R., & Fulkerson, D. R. (1962). *Flows in Networks*. Princeton University Press.

Forgy, C. L. (1982). Rete: A fast algorithm for the many pattern/many object pattern match problem. *Artificial Intelligence, 19*, 17–37.

Fotakis, D., Pagh, R., & Sanders, P. (2003). Space efficient hash tables with worst case constant access time. In *STACS* (pp. 271–282).

Foux, G., Heymann, M., & Bruckstein, A. (1993). Two-dimensional robot navigation among unknown stationary polygonal obstacles. *IEEE Transactions on Robotics and Automation, 9*(1), 96–102.

Fox, D., Burgard, W., & Thrun, S. (1998). Active Markov localization for mobile robots. *Robotics and Autonomous Systems, 25*, 195–207.

Fox, M., & Long, D. (1999). The detection and exploration of symmetry in planning problems. In *IJCAI* (pp. 956–961).

Fox, M., & Long, D. (2003). PDDL2.1: An extension to PDDL for expressing temporal planning domains. *Journal of Artificial Intelligence Research, 20*, 61–124.

Fox, M., Long, D., & Halsey, K. (2004). An investigation on the expressive power of PDDL2.1. In *ECAI* (pp. 586–590).

Franceschini, G., & Geffert, V. (2003). An in-place sorting with $o(n\lg n)$ comparisons and $o(n)$ moves. In *FOCS* (pp. 242–250).

Franciosa, P., Frigioni, D., & Giaccio, R. (2001). Semi-dynamic breadth-first search in digraphs. *Theoretical Computer Science, 250*(1–2), 201–217.

Frank, I., & Basin, D. (1998). Search in games with incomplete information: A case study using bridge card play. *Artificial Intelligence, 100*, 87–123.

Fredman, M. L., & Tarjan, R. E. (1987). Fibonacci heaps and their uses in improved network optimization algorithm. *Journal of the ACM, 34*(3), 596–615.

Fredman, M. L., Komlós, J., & Szemerédi, E. (1984). Storing a sparse table with $o(1)$ worst case access time. *Journal of the ACM, 3*, 538–544.

Fredman, M. L., Sedgewick, R., Sleator, D. D., & Tarjan, R. E. (1986). The pairing heap: A new form of self-adjusting heap. *Algorithmica, 1*(1), 111–129.

Fredriksson, K., Navarro, G., & Ukkonen, E. (2005). Sequential and indexed two-dimensional combinatorial template matching allowing rotations. *Theoretical Computer Science, 347*(1–2), 239–275.

Frigioni, D., Marchetti-Spaccamela, A., & Nanni, U. (1996). Fully dynamic output bounded single source shortest path problem. In *SODA* (pp. 212–221).

Frigioni, D., Marchetti-Spaccamela, A., & Nanni, U. (1998). Semidynamic algorithms for maintaining single source shortest path trees. *Algorithmica, 22*(3), 250–274.

Frigioni, D., Marchetti-Spaccamela, A., & Nanni, U. (2000). Fully dynamic algorithms for maintaining shortest paths trees. *Journal of Algorithms, 34*(2), 251–281.

Fuentetaja, R., Borrajo, D., & Linares López, C. (2008). A new approach to heuristic estimations for cost-based planning. In *FLAIRS* (pp. 543–548).

Furcy, D. (2004). *Speeding up the convergence of online heuristic search and scaling up offline heuristic search.* PhD thesis, Georgia Institute of Technology.

Furcy, D., Felner, A., Holte, R. C., Meshulam, R., & Newton, J. (2004). Multiple pattern databases. In *ICAPS* (pp. 122–131).

Furcy, D., & Koenig, S. (2000). Speeding up the convergence of real-time search. In *AAAI* (pp. 891–897).

Furtak, T., Kiyomi, M., Uno, T., & Buro, M. (2005). Generalized Amazons is PSPACE-complete. In *IJCAI* (pp. 132–137).

Gabow, H. N., & Tarjan, R. E. (1989). Faster scaling algorithms for network problems. *SIAM Society for Industrial and Applied Mathematics, 18*(5), 1013–1036.

Galand, L., Perny, P., & Spanjaard, O. (2010). Choquet-based optimisation in multiobjective shortest path and spanning tree problems. *European Journal of Operational Research, 204*(2), 303–315.

Gambardella, L. M., & Dorigo, M. (1996). Solving symmetric and asymmetric tsps by ant colonies. In *Conference on Evolutionary Computation (IEEE-EC)* (pp. 20–22).

Garavel, H., Mateescu, R., & Smarandache, I. (2001). Parallel state space construction for model-checking. In *SPIN* (pp. 216–234).

Gardner, M. (1966). The problems of Mrs. Perkin's quilt and other square packing problems. *Scientific American, 215*(3), 59–70.

Garey, M. R., & Johnson, D. S. (1979). *Computers and Intractibility: A Guide to the Theory of NP-Completeness.* Freeman & Company.

Garey, M. R., Johnson, D. S., & Stockmeyer, L. (1974). Some simplified NP-complete problems. In *STOC* (pp. 47–63).

Gaschnig, J. (1979a). *Performance measurement and analysis of certain search Algorithms.* PhD thesis, Carnegie-Mellon University.

Gaschnig, J. (1979b). A problem similarity approach to devising heuristics: First results. In *IJCAI* (pp. 434–441).

Gaschnig, J. (1979c). *Performance Measurement and Analysis of Certain Search Algorithms*. PhD thesis, Department of Computer Science, Carnegie-Mellon University.

Gasser, R. (1995). *Harnessing computational resources for efficient exhaustive search*. PhD thesis, ETH Zürich.

Gates, W. H., & Papadimitriou, C. H. (1976). Bounds for sorting by prefix reversal. *Discrete Math.*, 27, 47–57.

Geffner, H. (2000). *Functional Strips: A More Flexible Language for Planning and Problem Solving* (pp. 188–209). Kluver.

Geisberger, R., & Schieferdecker, D. (2010). Heuristic contraction hierarchies with approximation guarantee. In *SOCS* (pp. 31–38).

Geldenhuys, J., & Valmari, A. (2003). A nearly memory optimal data structure for sets and mappings. In *SPIN* (pp. 236–150).

Gelly, S., & Silver, D. (2007). Combining online and offline knowledge in UCT. In *ICML* (Vol. 227, pp. 273–280).

Genesereth, M., & Nourbakhsh, I. (1993). Time-saving tips for problem solving with incomplete information. In *AAAI* (pp. 724–730).

Geoffrion, A. M. (1972). Generalized Benders decomposition. *Journal of Optimization Theory and Applications, 10*(4), 237–241.

Gerevini, A., & Long, D. (2005). *Plan constraints and preferences in PDDL3*. Technical Report, Department of Electronics for Automation, University of Brescia.

Gerevini, A., Saetti, A., & Serina, I. (2006). An approach to temporal planning and scheduling in domains with predictable exogenous events. *Journal of Artificial Intelligence Research, 25*, 187–231.

Ghiani, G., Guerriero, F., Laporte, G., & Musmanno, R. (2003). Real-time vehicle routing: Solution concepts, algorithms and parallel computing strategies. *European Journal of Operational Research, 151*, 1–11.

Ghosh, S., Mahanti, A., & Nau, D. S. (1994). ITS: An efficient limited-memory heuristic tree search algorithm. In *AAAI* (pp. 1353–1358).

Ginsberg, M. L. (1988). Knowledge-base reduction: A new approach to checking knowledge bases for inconsistency and redundancy. In *AAAI* (pp. 585–589).

Ginsberg, M. L. (1993). Dynamic backtracking. *Journal of Artificial Intelligence Research, 1*, 25–46.

Ginsberg, M. L. (1996). Partition search. In *AAAI* (pp. 228–233).

Ginsberg, M. L. (1999). Step toward an expert-level bridge-playing program. In *IJCAI* (pp. 584–589).

Ginsberg, M. L., & Harvey, W. (1992). Iterative broadening. *Artificial Intelligence, 55*, 367–383.

Godefroid, P. (1991). Using partial orders to improve automatic verification methods. In *CAV* (pp. 176–185).

Godefroid, P., & Khurshid, S. (2004). Exploring very large state spaces using genetic algorithms. *International Journal on Software Tools for Technology Transfer, 6*(2), 117–127.

Goetsch, G., & Campbell, M. S. (1990). Experiments with the null-move heuristic. In *Computers, Chess, and Cognition* (pp. 159–181).

Gooley, M. M., & Wah, B. W. (1990). Speculative search: An efficient search algorithm for limited memory. In *IEEE International Workshop on Tools with Artificial Intelligence* (pp. 194–200).

Gordon, M. (1987). HOL: A proof generating system for higher-order logic. In G. Birtwistle & P. A. Subrahmanyam (Eds.), *VLSI Specification, Verification, and Synthesis*. Kluwer.

Goto, S., & Sangiovanni-Vincentelli, A. (1978). A new shortest path updating algorithm. *Networks, 8*(4), 341–372.

Govindaraju, N. K., Gray, J., Kumar, R., & Manocha, D. (2006). GPUTeraSort: High performance graphics coprocessor sorting for large database management. In *SIGMOD* (pp. 325–336).

Graf, S., & Saidi, H. (1997). Construction of abstract state graphs with PVS. In *CAV* (pp. 72–83).

Groce, A., & Visser, W. (2002). Model checking Java programs using structural heuristics. In *ISSTA* (pp. 12–21).

Grumberg, O., Heyman, T., & Schuster, A. (2006). A work-efficient distributed algorithm for reachability analysis. *Formal Methods in System Design, 29*(2), 157–175.

Guibas, L., Motwani, R., & Raghavan, P. (1992). The robot localization problem in two dimensions. In *SODA* (pp. 259–268).

Guida, G., & Somalvico, M. (1979). A method for computing heuristics in problem solving. *Information and Computation, 19*, 251–259.

Günther, M., & Nissen, V. (2010). Particle swarm optimization and an agent-based algorithm for a problem of staff scheduling. In *EvoApplications (2)* (pp. 451–461).

Gupta, S., Kececioglu, J., & Schaffer, A. (1996). Improving the practical space and time efficiency of the shortest-paths approach to sum-of-pairs multiple sequence alignment. *Journal of Computational Biology*.

Gusfield, D. (1993). Efficient methods for multiple sequence alignment with guaranteed error bounds. *Bulletin of Mathematical Biology, 55*(1), 141–154.

Gusfield, D. (1997). *Algorithms on Strings, Trees, and Sequences: Computer Science and Computational Biology*. Cambridge University Press.

Gutmann, J., Fukuchi, M., & Fujita, M. (2005). Real-time path planning for humanoid robot navigation. In *IJCAI* (pp. 1232–1237).

Hachtel, G. D., & Somenzi, F. (1992). A symbolic algorithm for maximum network flow. *Methods in System Design, 10*, 207–219.

Hajek, J. (1978). Automatically verified data transfer protocols. In *International Computer Communications Conference* (pp. 749–756).

Han, C., & Lee, C. (1988). Comments on Mohr and Henderson's path consistency algorithm. *Artificial Intelligence, 36*, 125–130.

Hansen, E. A., Zhou, R., & Feng, Z. (2002). Symbolic heuristic search using decision diagrams. In *SARA* (pp. 83–98).

Hansen, E. A., & Zilberstein, S. (1998). Heuristic search in cyclic AND/OR graphs. In *AAAI* (pp. 412–418).

Hansen, E. A., & Zilberstein, S. (2001). LAO*: A heuristic search algorithm that finds solutions with loops. *Artificial Intelligence, 129*, 35–62.

Hansson, O., Mayer, A., & Valtorta, M. (1992). A new result on the complexity of heuristic estimates for the A* algorithm (research note). *Artificial Intelligence, 55*, 129–143.

Haralick, R. M., & Elliot, G. L. (1980). Increasing tree search efficiency for constraint satisfaction problems. *Artificial Intelligence, 14*, 263–314.

Harris, M., Sengupta, S., & Owens, J. D. (2007). Parallel prefix sum (scan) with CUDA. In H. Nguyen (Ed.), *GPU Gems 3* (pp. 851–876). Addison-Wesley.

Hart, P. E., Nilsson, N. J., & Raphael, B. (1968). A formal basis for heuristic determination of minimum path cost. *IEEE Transactions on on Systems Science and Cybernetics, 4*, 100–107.

Harvey, W. D. (1995). *Nonsystematic backtracking search*. PhD thesis, Stanford University.

Harvey, W. D., & Ginsberg, M. L. (1995). Limited discrepancy search. In *IJCAI* (pp. 607–613).

Haslum, P. (2006). Improving heuristics through relaxed search—An analysis of TP4 and HSP* a in the 2004 planning competition. *Journal of Artificial Intelligence Research, 25*, 233–267.

Haslum, P. (2009). hm(p)=h1(pm): Alternative characterisations of the generalisation from hmax to hm. In *ICAPS*.

Haslum, P., Bonet, B., & Geffner, H. (2005). New admissible heuristics for domain-independent planning. In *AAAI* (pp. 1163–1168).

Haslum, P., Botea, A., Helmert, M., Bonet, B., & Koenig, S. (2007). Domain-independent construction of pattern database heuristics for cost-optimal planning. In *AAAI* (pp. 1007–1012).

Haslum, P., & Geffner, H. (2000). Admissible heuristics for optimal planning. In *AIPS* (pp. 140–149).

Haslum, P., & Jonsson, P. (2000). Planning with reduced operator sets. In *AIPS* (pp. 150–158).

Haverkort, B. R., Bell, A., & Bohnenkamp, H. C. (1999). On the efficient sequential and distributed generation of very large Markov chains from stochastic Petri nets. In *Workshop on Petri Net and Performance Models* (pp. 12–21). IEEE Computer Society Press.

Hawes, N. (2002). An anytime planning agent for computer game worlds. In *CG, Workshop on Agents in Computer Games*.

Hebert, M., McLachlan, R., & Chang, P. (1999). Experiments with driving modes for urban robots. In *Proceedings of the SPIE Mobile Robots*.

Heinz, E. A. (2000). *Scalable Search in Computer Chess*. Vierweg.

Heinz, A., & Hense, C. (1993). Bootstrap learning of alpha-beta-evaluation functions. In *ICCI* (pp. 365–369).

Helmert, M. (2002). Decidability and undecidability results for planning with numerical state variables. In *AIPS* (pp. 303–312).

Helmert, M. (2003). Complexity results for standard benchmark domains in planning. *Artificial Intelligence, 143*(2), 219–262.

Helmert, M. (2006a). New complexity results for classical planning benchmarks. In *ICAPS* (pp. 52–62).

Helmert, M. (2006b). The Fast Downward planning system. *Journal of Artificial Intelligence Research, 26*, 191–246.

Helmert, M., & Domshlak, C. (2009). Landmarks, critical paths and abstractions: What's the difference anyway? In *ICAPS* (pp. 162–169).

Helmert, M., & Geffner, H. (2008). Unifying the causal graph and additive heuristics. In *ICAPS* (pp. 140–147).

Helmert, M., Haslum, P., & Hoffmann, J. (2007). Flexible abstraction heuristics for optimal sequential planning. In *ICAPS* (pp. 176–183).

Helmert, M., Mattmüller, R., & Röger, G. (2006). Approximation properties of planning benchmarks. In *ECAI* (pp. 585–589).

Helmert, M., & Röger, G. (2008). How good is almost perfect? In *AAAI* (pp. 944–949).

Helmert, M., & Röger, G. (2010). Relative-order abstractions for the pancake problem. In *ECAI* (pp. 745–750).

Henrich, D., Wurll, Ch., & Wörn, H. (1998). Multi-directional search with goal switching for robot path planning. In *IEA/AIE* (pp. 75–84).

Henzinger, T. A., Kopke, P. W., Puri, A., & Varaiya, P. (1995). What's decidable about hybrid automata? In *STOC* (pp. 373–381).

Hernádvölgyi, I. T. (2000). Using pattern databases to find macro operators. In *AAAI* (p. 1075).

Hernádvölgyi, I. T. (2003). *Automatically generated lower bounds for search*. PhD thesis, University of Ottawa.

Hernádvögyi, I. T., & Holte, R. C. (1999). *PSVN*: A vector representation for production systems. Technical Report 99-04, University of Ottawa.

Hernández, C., & Meseguer, P. (2005). LRTA*(k). In *IJCAI* (pp. 1238–1243).

Hernández, C., & Meseguer, P. (2007a). Improving HLRTA*(k). In *CAEPIA* (pp. 110–119).

Hernández, C., & Meseguer, P. (2007b). Improving LRTA*(k). In *IJCAI* (pp. 2312–2317).

Hickmott, S., Rintanen, J., Thiebaux, S., & White, L. (2006). Planning via Petri net unfolding. In *IJCAI* (pp. 1904–1911).

Hirschberg, D. S. (1975). A linear space algorithm for computing common subsequences. *Communications of the ACM, 18*(6), 341–343.

Hoey, J., St-Aubin, R., Hu, A., & Boutilier, C. (1999). SPUDD: Stochastic planning using decision diagrams. In *UAI* (pp. 279–288).

Hoffman, F., Icking, C., Klein, R., & Kriegel, K. (1997). A competitive strategy for learning a polygon. In *SODA* (pp. 166–174).

Hoffmann, J. (2001). Local search topology in planning benchmarks: An empirical analysis. In *IJCAI* (pp. 453–458).

Hoffmann, J. (2003). The Metric FF planning system: Translating "ignoring the delete list" to numerical state variables. *Journal of Artificial Intelligence Research, 20*, 291–341.

Hoffmann, J., & Edelkamp, S. (2005). The deterministic part of IPC-4: An overview. *Journal of Artificial Intelligence Research, 24*, 519–579.

Hoffmann, J., Edelkamp, S., Thiebaux, S., Englert, R., Liporace, F., & Trüg, S. (2006). Engineering realistic bench-marks for planning: The domains used in the deterministic part of IPC-4. *Journal of Artificial Intelligence Research*, Submitted.

Hoffmann, J., & Koehler, J. (1999). A new method to query and index sets. In *IJCAI* (pp. 462–467).

Hoffmann, J., & Nebel, B. (2001). Fast plan generation through heuristic search. *Journal of Artificial Intelligence Research, 14*, 253–302.

Hoffmann, J., Porteous, J., & Sebastia, L. (2004). Ordered landmarks in planning. *Journal of Artificial Intelligence Research, 22*, 215–278.

Hofmeister, T. (2003). An approximation algorithm MAX2SAT with cardinality constraints. In *ESA* (pp. 301–312).

Hofmeister, T., Schöning, U., Schuler, R., & Watanabe, O. (2002). A probabilistic 3-SAT algorithm further improved. In *STACS* (pp. 192–202).

Holland, J. (1975). *Adaption in natural and artificial systems*. PhD thesis, University of Michigan.

Holmberg, K. (1990). On the convergence of the cross decomposition. *Mathematical Programming, 47*, 269–316.

Holte, R. C. (2009). Common misconceptions concerning heuristic search. In *SOCS* (pp. 46–51).

Holte, R. C., & Hernádvölgyi, I. T. (1999). A space-time tradeoff for memory-based heuristics. In *AAAI* (pp. 704–709).

Holte, R. C., Grajkowski, J., & Tanner, B. (2005). Hierarchical heuristic search revisited. In *SARA* (pp. 121–133).

Holte, R. C., Perez, M. B., Zimmer, R. M., & Donald, A. J. (1996). Hierarchical A*: Searching abstraction hierarchies. In *AAAI* (pp. 530–535).

Holzer, M., & Schwoon, S. (2001). *Assembling molecules in Atomix is hard*. Technical Report 0101, Institut für Informatik, Technische Universität München.

Holzmann, G. J. (1997). State compression in SPIN. In *3rd Workshop on Software Model Checking*.

Holzmann, G. J. (1998). An analysis of bitstate hashing. *Formal Methods in System Design, 13*(3), 287–305.

Holzmann, G. J. (2004). *The Spin Model Checker: Primer and Reference Manual*. Addison-Wesley.

Holzmann, G. J., & Bosnacki, D. (2007). The design of a multicore extension of the SPIN model checker. *IEEE Transactions on Software Engineering, 33*(10), 659–674.

Holzmann, G. J., & Puri, A. (1999). A minimized automaton representation of reachable states. *International Journal on Software Tools for Technology Transfer, 2*(3), 270–278.

Hoos, H., & Stützle, T. (1999). Towards a characterisation of the behaviour of stochastic local search algorithms for SAT. *Artificial Intelligence, 112*, 213–232.

Hoos, H. H., & Stützle, T. (2004). *Stochastic Local Search: Foundations & Applications*. Morgan Kaufmann.

Hopcroft, J. E., & Ullman, J. D. (1979). *Introduction to Automata Theory, Languages and Computation*. Addison-Wesley.

Horowitz, E., & Sahni, S. (1974). Computing partitions with applications to the knapsack problem. *Journal of the ACM, 21*(2), 277–292.

Hsu, E., & McIlraith, S. (2010). Computing equivalent transformations for applying branch-and-bound search to MAX-SAT. In *SOCS* (pp. 111–118).

Hüffner, F., Edelkamp, S., Fernau, H., & Niedermeier, R. (2001). Finding optimal solutions to Atomix. In *KI* (pp. 229–243).

Huyn, N., Dechter, R., & Pearl, J. (1980). Probabilistic analysis of the complexity of A*. *Artificial Intelligence, 15*, 241–254.

Ibaraki, T. (1978). m-depth serach in branch-and-bound algorithms. *Computer and Information Sciences, 7*(4), 315–373.

Ibaraki, T. (1986). Generalization of alpha-beta and SSS* search procedures. *Artificial Intelligence, 29*, 73–117.

Icking, C., Klein, R., & Langetepe, E. (1999). An optimal competitive strategy for walking in streets. In *STACS* (pp. 110–120).

Ikeda, T., & Imai, T. (1994). A fast A* algorithm for multiple sequence alignment. *Genome Informatics Workshop* (pp. 90–99).

Inggs, C., & Barringer, H. (2006). CTL* model checking on a shared memory architecture. *Formal Methods in System Design, 29*(2), 135–155.

Ishida, T. (1992). Moving target search with intelligence. In *AAAI* (pp. 525–532).

Ishida, T. (1997). *Real-Time Search for Learning Autonomous Agents.* Kluwer Academic Publishers.

Italiano, G. (1988). Finding paths and deleting edges in directed acyclic graphs. *Information Processing Letters, 28*(1), 5–11.

Jabbar, S. (2003). *GPS-based navigation in static and dynamic environments.* Master's thesis, University of Freiburg.

Jabbar, S. (2008). *External memory algorithms for state space exploration in model checking and action planning.* PhD thesis, Technical University of Dortmund.

Jabbar, S., & Edelkamp, S. (2005). I/O efficient directed model checking. In *VMCAI.* (pp. 313–329).

Jabbar, S., & Edelkamp, S. (2006). Parallel external directed model checking with linear I/O. In *VMCAI* (pp. 237–251).

Jabbari, S., Zilles, S., & Holte, R. C. (2010). Bootstrap learning of heuristic functions. In *SOCS* (pp. 52–60).

Jájá, J. (1992). *An Introduction to Parallel Algorithms.* Addision Wesley.

Jaychandran, G., Vishal, V., & Pande, V. S. (2006). Using massively parallel simulations and Markovian models to study protein folding: Examining the Villin head-piece. *Journal of Chemical Physics, 124*(6), 164903–14.

Jensen, R. M. (2003). *Efficient BDD-based planning for non-deterministic, fault-tolerant, and adversarial domains.* PhD thesis, Carnegie-Mellon University.

Jensen, R. M., Bryant, R. E., & Veloso, M. M. (2002). Set A*: An efficient BDD-based heuristic search algorithm. In *AAAI* (pp. 668–673).

Jensen, R. M., Hansen, E. A., Richards, S., & Zhou, R. (2006). Memory-efficient symbolic heuristic search. In *ICAPS* (pp. 304–313).

Johnson, D. S. (1977). Efficient algorithms for shortest paths in sparse networks. *Journal of the ACM, 24*(1), 1–13.

Jones, D. T., Taylor, W. R., & Thornton, J. M. (1992). The rapid generation of mutation data matrices from protein sequences. *CABIOS, 3,* 275–282.

Junghanns, A. (1999). *Pushing the limits: New developments in single-agent search.* PhD thesis, University of Alberta.

Junghanns, A., & Schaeffer, J. (1998). Single agent search in the presence of deadlocks. In *AAAI* (pp. 419–424).

Junghanns, A., & Schaeffer, J. (2001). Sokoban: Improving the search with relevance cuts. *Theoretical Computing Science, 252*(1–2), 151–175.

Kabanza, F., & Thiebaux, S. (2005). Search control in planing for termporally extended goals. In *ICAPS* (pp. 130–139).

Kaindl, H., & Kainz, G. (1997). Bidirectional heuristic search reconsidered. *Journal of Artificial Intelligence Research, 7,* 283–317.

Kaindl, H., & Khorsand, A. (1994). Memory-bounded bidirectional search. In *AAAI* (pp. 1359–1364).

Kale, L., & Saletore, V. A. (1990). Parallel state-space search for a first solution with consistent linear speedups. *International Journal of Parallel Programming, 19*(4), 251–293.

Kaplan, H., Shafrir, N., & Tarjan, R. E. (2002). Meldable heaps and boolean union-find. In *STOC* (pp. 573–582).

Karmarkar, N., & Karp, R. M. (1982). *The differencing method of set partitioning.* Technical Report UCB/CSD 82/113, Computer Science Division, University of California, Berkeley.

Karp, R. M., & Rabin, M. O. (1987). Efficient randomized pattern-matching algorithms. *IBM Journal of Research and Development, 31*(2), 249–260.

Kask, K., & Dechter, R. (1999). Branch and bound with mini-bucket heuristics. In *IJCAI* (pp. 426–435).

Katajainen, J., & Vitale, F. (2003). Navigation piles with applications to sorting, priority queues, and priority deques. *Nordic Journal of Computing, 10*(3), 238–262.

Katz, M., & Domshlak, C. (2009). Structural-pattern databases. In *ICAPS* (pp. 186–193).

Kautz, H., & Selman, B. (1996). Pushing the envelope: Planning propositional logic, and stochastic search. In *ECAI* (pp. 1194–1201).

Kavraki, L., Svestka, P., Latombe, J.-C., & Overmars, M. (1996). Probabilistic roadmaps for path planning in high-dimensional configuration spaces. *IEEE Transactions on Robotics and Automation, 12*(4), 566–580.

Keller, T., & Kupferschmid, S. (2008). Automatic bidding for the game of Skat. In *KI* (pp. 95–102).

Kennedy, J., & Eberhart, R. C. Particle swarm optimization. In *IEEE International Conference on Neural Networks* (Vol. IV, pp. 1942–1948).

Kennedy, J., Eberhart, R. C., & Shi, Y. (2001). *Swarm Intelligence*. Morgan Kaufmann.

Kerjean, S., Kabanza, F., St-Denis, R., & Thiebaux, S. (2005). Analyzing LTL model checking techniques for plan synthesis and controller synthesis. In *MOCHART*.

Kilby, P., Slaney, J., Thiebaux, S., & Walsh, T. (2005). Backbones and backdoors in satisfiability. In *AAAI* (pp. 1368–1373).

Kirkpatrick, S., Gelatt Jr., C. D., & Vecchi, M. P. (1983). Optimization by simulated annealing. *Science, 220*, 671–680.

Kishimoto, A. (1999). *Transposition table driven scheduling for two-player games*. Master's thesis, University of Alberta.

Kishimoto, A., Fukunaga, A., & Botea, A. On the scaling behavior of HDA*. In *SOCS* (pp. 61–62).

Kishimoto, A., Fukunaga, A. S., & Botea, A. (2009). Scalable, parallel best-first search for optimal sequential planning. In *ICAPS* (pp. 201–208).

Kissmann, P., & Edelkamp, S. (2010a). Instantiating general games using Prolog or dependency graphs. In *KI* (pp. 255–262).

Kissmann, P., & Edelkamp, S. (2010b). Layer-abstraction for symbolically solving general two-player games. In *SOCS*.

Kleer, J., & Williams, B. C. (1987). Diagnosing multiple faults. *Artificial Intelligence* (pp. 1340–1330).

Klein, D., & Manning, C. (2003). A* parsing: Fast exact Viterbi parse selection. In *North American chapter of the association for computational linguistics* (pp. 40–47).

Klein, P., & Subramanian, S. (1993). Fully dynamic approximation schemes for shortest path problems in planar graphs. In *WADS* (pp. 443–451).

Kleinberg, J. (1994). The localization problem for mobile robots. In *Proceedings of the Symposium on Foundations of Computer Science* (pp. 521–533).

Knight, K. (1993). Are many reactive agents better than a few deliberative ones? In *IJCAI* (pp. 432–437).

Knoblock, C. A. (1994). Automatically generating abstractions for planning. *Artificial Intelligence, 68*(2), 243–302.

Knuth, D. E., Morris, J. H., & Prat, V. R. (1977). Fast pattern matching in strings. *Journal of Computing, 6*(1), 323–350.

Knuth, D. E., & Plass, M. F. (1981). Breaking paragraphs into lines. *Software—Practice and Experience, 11*, 1119–1184.

Kobayashi, H., & Imai, H. (1998). Improvement of the A* algorithm for multiple sequence alignment. *Genome Informatics* (pp. 120–130).

Kocsis, L., & Szepesvári, C. (2006). Bandit based Monte-Carlo planning. In *ICML* (pp. 282–293).

Koenig, S. (2001a). Minimax real-time heuristic search. *Artificial Intelligence, 129*(1–2), 165–197.

Koenig, S. (2001b). Agent-centered search. *AI Magazine, 22*(4), 109–131.

Koenig, S. (2004). A comparison of fast search methods for real-time situated agents. In *AAMAS* (pp. 864–871).

Koenig, S., & Likhachev, M. (2003). D* lite. In *AAAI* (pp. 476–483).

Koenig, S., & Likhachev, M. (2005). Fast replanning for navigation in unknown terrain. *Transactions on Robotics*.

Koenig, S., & Likhachev, M. (2006). Real-time adaptive A*. In *AAMAS* (pp. 281–288).

Koenig, S., Likhachev, M., Liu, Y., & Furcy, D. (2004). Incremental heuristic search in artificial intelligence. *AI Magazine, 24*(2), 99–112.

Koenig, S., Mitchell, J., Mudgal, A., & Tovey, C. (2009). A near-tight approximation algorithm for the robot localization problem. *Journal on Computing, 39*(2), 461–490.

Koenig, S., & Simmons, R.G. (1993). Complexity analysis of real-time reinforcement learning. In *AAAI* (pp. 99–105).

Koenig, S., & Simmons, R. G. (1995). Real-time search in non-deterministic domains. In *IJCAI* (pp. 1660–1667).

Koenig, S., & Simmons, R. G. (1996a). The effect of representation and knowledge on goal-directed exploration with reinforcement-learning algorithms. *Machine Learning, 22*(1/3), 227–250.

Koenig, S., & Simmons, R. G. (1996b). Easy and hard testbeds for real-time search algorithms. In *AAAI* (pp. 279–285).

Koenig, S., & Simmons, R. (1998a). Xavier: A robot navigation architecture based on partially observable Markov decision process models. In R. Bonasso, D. Kortenkamp, & R. Murphy (Eds.), *Artificial Intelligence Based Mobile Robotics: Case Studies of Successful Robot Systems* (pp. 91–122). MIT Press.

Koenig, S., & Simmons, R. G. (1998b). Solving robot navigation problems with initial pose uncertainty using real-time heuristic search. In *AIPS* (pp. 145–153).

Koenig, S., Smirnov, Y., & Tovey, C. (2003). Performance bounds for planning in unknown terrain. *Artificial Intelligence, 147*(1–2), 253–279.

Koenig, S., & Szymanski, B. (1999). Value-update rules for real-time search. In *AAAI* (pp. 718–724).

Koenig, S., Szymanski, B., & Liu, Y. (2001). Efficient and inefficient ant coverage methods. *Annals of Mathematics and Artificial Intelligence, 31*, 41–76.

Koenig, S., Tovey, C., & Halliburton, W. (2001). Greedy mapping of terrain. In *ICRA* (pp. 3594–3599).

Kohavi, Z. (1978). *Switching and Finite Automata Theory* (2nd ed.). McGraw-Hill.

Kohn, K. (1999). Molecular interaction map of the mammalian cell cycle control and DNA repair systems. *Molecular Biology of the Cell, 10*(8), 2703–2734.

Korf, R. E. (1985a). Depth-first iterative-deepening: An optimal admissible tree search. *Artificial Intelligence, 27*(1), 97–109.

Korf, R. E. (1985b). Macro-operators: A weak method for learning. *Artificial Intelligence, 26*, 35–77.

Korf, R. E. (1990). Real-time heuristic search. *Artificial Intelligence, 42*(2–3), 189–211.

Korf, R. E. (1991). Multiplayer alpha-beta pruning. *Artificial Intelligence, 48*(1), 99–111.

Korf, R. E. (1993). Linear-space best-first search. *Artificial Intelligence, 62*, 41–78.

Korf, R. E. (1996). Improved limited discrepancy search. In *IJCAI* (pp. 286–291).

Korf, R. E. (1997). Finding optimal solutions to Rubik's Cube using pattern databases. In *AAAI* (pp. 700–705).

Korf, R. E. (1998). A complete anytime algorithm for number partitioning. *Artificial Intelligence, 106*, 181–203.

Korf, R. E. (1999). Divide-and-conquer bidirectional search: First results. In *IJCAI* (pp. 1184–1191).

Korf, R. E. (2002). A new algorithm for optimal bin packing. In *AAAI* (pp. 731–736).

Korf, R. E. (2003a). Breadth-first frontier search with delayed duplicate detection. In *MOCHART* (pp. 87–92).

Korf, R. E. (2003b). An improved algorithm for optimal bin packing. In *IJCAI* (pp. 1252–1258).

Korf, R. E. (2003c). Optimal rectangle packing: Initial results. In *ICAPS* (pp. 287–295).

Korf, R. E. (2004a). Best-first frontier search with delayed duplicate detection. In *AAAI* (pp. 650–657).

Korf, R. E. (2004b). Optimal rectangle packing: New results. In *ICAPS* (pp. 142–149).

Korf, R. E. (2008). Minimizing disk I/O in two-bit breadth-first search. In *AAAI* (pp. 317–324).

Korf, R. E. (2009). Multi-way number partitioning. In *IJCAI* (pp. 538–543).

Korf, R. E. (2010). Objective functions multi-way number partitioning. In *SOCS* (pp. 71–72).

Korf, R. E., & Chickering, D. M. (1994). Best-first minimax search: Othello results. In *AAAI* (Vol. 2, pp. 1365–1370).

Korf, R. E., & Felner, A. (2002). Disjoint pattern database heuristics. In *Chips Challenging Champions: Games, Computers and Artificial Intelligence* (pp. 13–26). Elsevier Sience.

Korf, R. E., & Felner, A. (2007). Recent progress in heuristic search: A case study of the four-peg towers of hanoi problem. In *IJCAI* (pp. 2324–2329).

Korf, R. E., & Reid, M. (1998). Complexity analysis of admissible heuristic search. In *AAAI* (pp. 305–310).

Korf, R. E., Reid, M., & Edelkamp, S. (2001). Time complexity of Iterative-Deepening-A*. *Artificial Intelligence, 129*(1–2), 199–218.

Korf, R. E., & Schultze, T. (2005). Large-scale parallel breadth-first search. In *AAAI* (pp. 1380–1385).

Korf, R. E., & Taylor, L. A. (1996). Finding optimal solutions to the twenty-four puzzle. In *AAAI* (pp. 1202–1207).

Korf, R. E., & Zhang, W. (2000). Divide-and-conquer frontier search applied to optimal sequence alignment. In *AAAI* (pp. 910–916).

Korf, R. E., Zhang, W., Thayer, I., & Hohwald, H. (2005). Frontier search. *Journal of the ACM, 52*(5), 715–748.

Koza, J. R. (1992). *Genetic Programming: On the Programming of Computers by Means of Natural Selection.* MIT Press.

Koza, J. R. (1994). *Genetic Programming II: Automatic Discovery of Reusable Programs.* MIT Press.

Koza, J. R., Bennett, H. B., Andre, D., & Keane, M. A. (1999). *Genetic Programming III: Darvinian Invention and Problem Solving.* Morgan Kaufmann.

Kristensen, L., & Mailund, T. (2003). Path finding with the sweep-line method using external storage. In *ICFEM* (pp. 319–337).

Krueger, J., & Westermann, R. (2003). Linear algebra operators for GPU implementation of numerical algorithms. *ACM Transactions on Graphics, 22*(3), 908–916.

Kumar, V. (1992). Branch-and-bound search. In S. C. Shapiro (Ed.), *Encyclopedia of Artificial Intelligence* (pp. 1468–1472). New York: Wiley-Interscience.

Kumar, V., Ramesh, V., & Rao, V. N. (1987). Parallel best-first search of state-space graphs: A summary of results. In *AAAI* (pp. 122–127).

Kumar, V., & Schwabe, E. J. (1996). Improved algorithms and data structures for solving graph problems in external memory. In *IEEE-Symposium on Parallel and Distributed Processing* (pp. 169–177).

Kunkle, D., & Cooperman, D. (2008). Solving Rubik's Cube: Disk is the new RAM. *Communications of the ACM, 51*(4), 31–33.

Kupferschmid, S., Dräger, K., Hoffmann, J., Finkbeiner, B., Dierks, H., Podelski, A., et al. (2007). Uppaal/DMC—Abstraction-based heuristics for directed model checking. In *TACAS*, (pp. 679–682).

Kupferschmid, S., & Helmert, M. (2006). A Skat player based on Monte-Carlo simulation. In *CG* (pp. 135–147).

Kupferschmid, S., Hoffmann, J., Dierks, H., & Behrmann, G. (2006). Adapting an AI planning heuristic for directed model checking. In *SPIN*, (pp. 35–52).

Kvarnström, J., Doherty, P., & Haslum, P. (2000). Extending TALplanner with concurrency and resources. In *ECAI* (pp. 501–505).

Kwa, J. (1994). BS*: An admissible bidirectional staged heuristic search algorithm. *Artificial Intelligence, 38*(2), 95–109.

Laarman, A., van de Pol, J., & Weber, M. (2010). Boosting multi-core reachability performance with shared hash tables. In *FMCAD*.

Lago, U. D., Pistore, M., & Traverso, P. (2002). Planning with a language for extended goals. In *AAAI* (pp. 447–454).

Land, A. H., & Doig, A. G. (1960). A tree-search algorithm for mixed integer programming problems. *Econometria, 28*, 497–520.

Langley, P. (1996). *Elements of Machine Learning.* Morgan Kaufmann.

Larsen, B. J., Burns, E., Ruml, W., & Holte, R. C. (2010). Searching without a heuristic: Efficient use of abstraction. In *AAAI*.

Larsen, K. G., Larsson, F., Petterson, P., & Yi, W. (1997). Efficient verification of real-time systems: Compact data structures and state-space reduction. In *IEEE Real Time Systems Symposium* (pp. 14–24).

Larsen, K. G., Behrmann, G., Brinksma, E., Fehnker, A., Hune, T. S., Petterson, P., et al. (2001). As cheap as possible: Efficient cost-optimal reachability for priced timed automata. In *CAV* (pp. 493–505).

Latombe, J.-C. (1991). *Robot Motion Planning*. Kluwer Academic Publishers.

LaValle, S. (2006). *Planning Algorithms*. Cambridge University Press.

LaValle, S., & Kuffner, J. (2000). Rapidly-exploring random trees: Progress and prospects. In *Workshop on the Algorithmic Foundations of Robotics*.

Lawler, E. L. (1976). *Combinatorial Optimization: Networks and Matroids*. Holt, Rinehart, and Winston.

Lee, C. Y. (1959). Representation of switching circuits by binary-decision programs. *Bell Systems Technical Journal, 38*, 985–999.

Lehmer, H. D. (1949). Mathematical methods in large-scale computing units. In *Symposium on Large-Scale Digital Calculating Machinery* (pp. 141–146). Harvard University Press.

Leiserson, C. E., & Saxe, J. B. (1983). A mixed integer linear programming problem which is efficiently solvable. In *CCCC* (pp. 204–213).

Lerda, F., & Sisto, R. (1999). Distributed-memory model checking with SPIN. In *SPIN* (pp. 22–39).

Lerda, F., & Visser, W. (2001). Addressing dynamic issues of program model checking. In *SPIN* (pp. 80–102).

Leven, P., Mehler, T., & Edelkamp, S. (2004). Directed error detection in C++ with the assembly-level model checker StEAM. In *SPIN* (pp. 39–56).

Li, Y., Harms, J., & Holte, R. C. (2005). IDA* MCSP: A fast exact MCSP algorithm. In *International conference on communications* (pp. 93–99).

Li, Y., Harms, J. J., & Holte, R. C. (2007). Fast exact multiconstraint shortest path algorithms. In *International Conference on Communications*.

Likhachevm, M. (2005). *Search-based planning for large dynamic environments*. PhD thesis, Carnegie Mellon University.

Likhachev, M., & Koenig, S. (2002). Incremental replanning for mapping. In *IROS* (pp. 667–672).

Likhachev, M., & Koenig, S. (2005). A generalized framework for Lifelong Planning A*. In *ICAPS* (pp. 99–108).

Lin, C., & Chang, R. (1990). On the dynamic shortest path problem. *Journal of Information Processing, 13*(4), 470–476.

Littman, M. (1994). Memoryless policies: Theoretical limitations and practical results. In *From Animals to Animats 3: International Conference on Simulation of Adaptive Behavior*.

Linares López, C. (2008). Multi-valued pattern databases. In *ECAI* (pp. 540–544).

Linares López, C. (2010). Vectorial pattern databases. In *ECAI* (pp. 1059–1060).

Linares López, C., & Borrajo, D. (2010). Adding diversity to classical heuristic planning. In *SOCS* (pp. 73–80).

Linares López, C., & Junghanns, A. (2003). Perimeter search performance. In *CG* (pp. 345–359).

Lluch-Lafuente, A. (2003a). *Directed search for the verification of communication protocols*. PhD thesis, University of Freiburg.

Lluch-Lafuente, A. (2003b). Symmetry reduction and heuristic search for error detection in model checking. In *MOCHART* (pp. 77–86).

Love, N. C., Hinrichs, T. L., & Genesereth, M. R. (2006). *General game playing: Game description language specification*. Technical Report LG-2006-01, Stanford Logic Group.

Luckhardt, C. A., & Irani, K. B. (1986). An algorithmic solution of n-person games. In *AAAI* (pp. 158–162).

Lumelsky, V. (1987). Algorithmic and complexity issues of robot motion in an uncertain environment. *Journal of Complexity, 3*, 146–182.

Lumelsky, V., & Stepanov, A. (1987). Path-planning strategies for a point mobile automaton moving amidst unknown obstacles of arbitrary shape. *Algorithmica, 2*, 403–430.

Mackworth, A. K. (1977). Consistency in networks of relations. *Artificial Intelligence, 8*(1), 99–118.

Madani, O., Hanks, S., & Condon, A. (1999). On the undecidability of probabilistic planning and infinite-horizon partially observable Markov decision problems. In *AAAI* (pp. 541–548).

Madras, N., & Slade, G. (1993). *The Self-Avoiding Walk*. Birkenhauser.

Mahapatra, N. R., & Dutt, S. (1999). Sequential and parallel branch-and-bound search under limited memory constraints. *The IMA Volumes in Mathematics and Its Applications—Parallel Processing of Discrete Problems, 106*, 139–158.

Mandow, L., & Pérez de-la Cruz, J.-L. (2010a). A note on the complexity of some multiobjective A* search algorithms. In *ECAI* (pp. 727–731).

Mandow, L., & Pérez de-la Cruz, J.-L. (2010b). Multiobjective A* search with consistent heuristics. *Journal of the ACM, 57*(5).

Manzini, G. (1995). BIDA*. *Artificial Intelligence, 75*(2), 347–360.

Marais, H., & Bharat, K. (1997). Supporting cooperative and personal surfing with a desktop assistant. In *ACM Symposium on User Interface, Software and Technology* (pp. 129–138).

Mares, M., & Straka, M. (2007). Linear-time ranking of permutations. In *ESA* (pp. 187–193).

Marinari, E., & Parisi, G. (1992). Simulated tempering: A new Monte Carlo scheme. *Europhysics Letters, 21*, 451–458.

Mariott, K., & Stuckey, P. (1998). *Programming with Constraints*. MIT Press.

Marsland, T. A., & Reinefeld, A. (1993). *Heuristic search in one and two player games*. Technical Report TR 93-02, University of Alberta, Edmonton, Canada.

Martelli, A. (1977). On the complexity of admissible search algorithms. *Artificial Intelligence, 8*, 1–13.

Martello, S., & Toth, P. (1990). Lower bounds and reduction procedures for the bin packing problem. *Discrete Applied Mathematics, 28*, 59–70.

Matthies, L., Xiong, Y., Hogg, R., Zhu, D., Rankin, A., Kennedy, B., et al. (2002). A portable, autonomous, urban reconnaissance robot. *Robotics and Autonomous Systems, 40*, 163–172.

Mattmüller, R., Ortlieb, M., Helmert, M., & Bercher, P. (2010). Pattern database heuristics for fully observable nondeterministic planning. In *ICAPS* (pp. 105–112).

McAllester, D. A. (1988). Conspiricy-number-search for min-max searching. *Artificial Intelligence, 35*, 287–310.

McAllester, D., & Yuret, D. (2002). Alpha-beta-conspiracy search. *ICGA Journal, 25*(2), 16–35.

McCreight, E. M. (1976). A space-economical suffix tree construction algorithm. *Journal of the ACM, 23*(2), 262–272.

McCreight, E. M. (1985). Priority search trees. *SIAM Journal of Computing, 14*(2), 257–276.

McMillan, K. L. (1993). *Symbolic Model Checking*. Kluwer Academic Press.

McNaughton, M., Lu, P., Schaeffer, J., & Szafron, D. (2002). Memory-efficient A* heuristics for multiple sequence alignment. In *AAAI* (pp. 737–743).

Mehler, T. (2005). *Challenges and applications of assembly-level software model checking*. PhD thesis, Technical University of Dortmund.

Mehler, T., & Edelkamp, S. (2005). Incremental hashing with pattern databases. In *ICAPS Poster Proceedings*.

Mehler, T., & Edelkamp, S. (2006). Dynamic incremental hashing in program model checking. *ENTCS, 149*(2).

Mehlhorn, K. (1984). *Data Structures and Algorithms (2): NP Completeness and Graph Algorithms*. Springer.

Mehlhorn, K., & Meyer, U. (2002). External-memory breadth-first search with sublinear I/O. In *ESA* (pp. 723–735).

Mehlhorn, K., & Näher, S. (1999). *The LEDA Platform of Combinatorial and Geometric Computing*. Cambridge University Press.

Mercer, E., & Jones, M. (2005). Model checking machine code with the GNU debugger. In *SPIN* (pp. 251–265).

Merino, P., del Mar Gallardo, M., Martinez, J., & Pimentel, E. (2004). aSPIN: A tool for abstract model checking. *International Journal on Software Tools for Technology Transfer, 5*(2–3), 165–184.

Meriott, K., & Stuckey, P. (1998). *Programming with Constraints*. MIT Press.

Mero, L. (1984). A heuristic search algorithm with modifiable estimate. *Artificial Intelligence, 23*, 13–27.

Meseguer, P. (1997). Interleaved depth-first search. In *IJCAI* (pp. 1382–1387).

Metropolis, N., Rosenbluth, A. W., Rosenbluth, M. N., Teller, A. H., & Teller, E. (1953). Equation of state calculations by fast computing machines. *Journal of Chemical Physics, 21*, 1087–1092.

Milner, R. (1989). *Communication and Concurrency*. Prentice-Hall.

Milner, R. (1995). An algebraic definition of simulation between programs. In *IJCAI* (pp. 481–489).

Miltersen, P. B., Radhakrishnan, J., & Wegener, I. (2005). On converting CNF to DNF. *Theoretical Computer Science, 347*(1–2), 325–335.

Minato, S., Ishiura, N., & Yajima, S. (1990). Shared binary decision diagram with attributed edges for efficient boolean function manipuation. In *DAC* (pp. 52–57).

Miura, T., & Ishida, T. (1998). Statistical node caching for memory bounded search. In *AAAI* (pp. 450–456).

Moffitt, M. D., & Pollack, M. E. (2006). Optimal rectangle packing: A Meta-CSP approach. In *ICAPS* (pp. 93–102).

Mohr, R., & Henderson, T. C. (1986). Arc and path consistency revisited. *Artificial Intelligence, 28*(1), 225–233.

Monien, B., & Speckenmeyer, E. (1985). Solving satisfiability in less than 2^n steps. *Discrete Applied Mathematics, 10*, 287–294.

Moore, A., & Atkeson, C. (1993). Prioritized sweeping: Reinforcement learning with less data and less time. *Machine Learning, 13*(1), 103–130.

Moore, A., & Atkeson, C. (1995). The parti-game algorithm for variable resolution reinforcement learning in multi-dimensional state spaces. *Machine Learning, 21*(3), 199–233.

Moskewicz, M., Madigan, C., Zhao, Y., Zhang, L., & Malik, S. (2001). Chaff: Engineering an efficient SAT solver. In *DAC* (pp. 236–247).

Mostow, J., & Prieditis, A. E. (1989). Discovering admissible heuristics by abstracting and optimizing. In *IJCAI* (pp. 701–707).

Mudgal, A., Tovey, C., Greenberg, S., & Koenig, S. (2005). Bounds on the travel cost of a Mars rover prototype search heuristic. *SIAM Journal on Discrete Mathematics* 19(2): 431-447.

Mudgal, A., Tovey, C., & Koenig, S. (2004). Analysis of greedy robot-navigation methods. In *Proceedings of the International Symposium on Artificial Intelligence and Mathematics*.

Mues, C., & Vanthienen, J. (2004). Improving the scalability of rule base verification. In *KI* (pp. 381–395).

Müller, M. (1995). *Computer go as a sum of local games*. PhD thesis, ETH Zürich.

Müller, M. (2001). Partial order bounding: A new approach to evaluation in game tree search. *Artificial Intelligence, 129*(1–2), 279–311.

Müller, M. (2002). Proof set search. *CG* (pp. 88–107).

Munagala, K., & Ranade, A. (1999). I/O-complexity of graph algorithms. In *SODA* (pp. 687–694).

Munro, J. I., & Raman, V. (1996). Selection from read-only memory and sorting with minimum data movement. *Theoretical Computer Science, 165*, 311–323.

Myrvold, W., & Ruskey, F. (2001). Ranking and unranking permutations in linear time. *Information Processing Letters, 79*(6), 281–284.

Nau, D. S. (1983). Pathology on game trees revisited, and an alternative to minimaxing. *Artificial Intelligence, 21*, 221–244.

Nau, D. S., Kumar, V., & Kanal, L. (1984). General branch and bound, and its relation to A* and AO*. *Artificial Intelligence, 23*, 29–58.

Needleman, S., & Wunsch, C. (1981). A general method applicable to the search for similarities in the amino acid sequences of two proteins. *Journal of Molecular Biology, 48*, 443–453.

Nguyen, V. Y., & Ruys, T. C. Incremental hashing for SPIN. In *SPIN* (pp. 232–249).

Niewiadomski, R., Amaral, J. N., & Holte, R. C. (2006). Sequential and parallel algorithms for frontier A* with delayed duplicate detection. In *AAAI*.

Nilsson, N. J. (1980). *Principles of Artificial Intelligence*. Tioga Publishing Company.

Nipkow, T., Paulson, L. C., & Wenzel, M. (2002). *Isabelle/HOL—A Proof Assistant for Higher-Order Logic*, Vol. 2283 of *LNCS*. Springer.

Nourbakhsh, I. (1996). *Robot Information Packet*. AAAI Spring Symposium on Planning with Incomplete Information for Robot Problems.

Nourbakhsh, I. (1997). *Interleaving Planning and Execution for Autonomous Robots*. Kluwer Academic Publishers.

Nourbakhsh, I., & Genesereth, M. (1996). Assumptive planning and execution: A simple, working robot architecture. *Autonomous Robots Journal, 3*(1), 49–67.

Okasaki, C. (1998). *Purely Functional Data Structures* (chap. 3). Cambridge University Press.

Osborne, M. J., & Rubinstein, A. (1994). *A Course in Game Theory*. MIT Press.

Ostlin, A., & Pagh, R. (2003). Uniform hashing in constant time and linear space. In *ACM Symposium on Theory of Computing* (pp. 622–628).

Owen, G. (1982). *Game Theory*. Academic Press.

Owens, J. D., Houston, M., Luebke, D., Green, S., Stone, J. E., & Phillips, J. C. (2008). GPU computing. *Proceedings of the IEEE, 96*(5), 879–899.

Owre, S., Rajan, S., Rushby, J. M., Shankar, N., & Srivas, M. K. (1996). PVS: Combining specification, proof checking, and model checking. In *CAV* (pp. 411–414).

Pagh, R., & Rodler, F. F. (2001). Cuckoo hashing. In *ESA* (pp. 121–133).

Pai, D. K., & Reissell, L.-M. (1998). Multiresolution rough terrain motion planning. *IEEE Transactions on Robotics and Automation, 14* (1), 19–33.

Papadimitriou, C., & Tsitsiklis, J. (1987). The complexity of Markov decision processes. *Mathematics of Operations Research, 12*(3), 441–450.

Papadimitriou, C., & Yannakakis, M. (1991). Shortest paths without a map. *Theoretical Computer Science, 84*(1), 127–150.

Parberry, I. (1995). A real-time algorithm for the $(n^2 - 1)$-puzzle. *Information Processing Letters, 56*, 23–28.

Park, S. K., & Miller, K. W. (1988). Random number generators: Good ones are hard to find. *Communications of the ACM, 31*, 1192–1201.

Paturi, R., Pudlák, P., & Zane, F. (1977). Satisfiability coding lemma. In *FOCS* (pp. 566–574).

Pearl, J. (1985). *Heuristics*. Addison-Wesley.

Pednault, E. P. D. (1991). Generalizing nonlinear planning to handle complex goals and actions with context-dependent effects. In *IJCAI* (pp. 240–245).

Peled, D. A. (1996). Combining partial order reductions with on-the-fly model-checking. *Formal Methods in Systems Design, 8*, 39–64.

Peled, D. A. (1998). Ten years of partial order reduction. In *CAV* (pp. 17–28).

Pemberton, J., & Korf, R. E. (1992). Incremental path planning on graphs with cycles. In *ICAPS* (pp. 179–188).

Pemberton, J., & Korf, R. E. (1994). Incremental search algorithms for real-time decision making. In *ICAPS* (pp. 140–145).

Petri, C. A. (1962). *Kommunikation mit automaten*. PhD thesis, Universität Bonn.

Phillips, J. C., Braun, R., Wang, W., Gumbart, J., Tajkhorshid, E., Villa, E., Chipot C., Skeel, R. D., Kalé, L, & Schulten K. (2005). Scalable molecular dynamics with NAMD. *Journal of Computational Chemistry, 26*(16), 1781–1802.

Pijls, W., & Kolen, A. (1992). *A general framework for shortest path algorithms*. Technical Report 92-08, Erasmus Universiteit Rotterdam.

Pinter, R. Y., Rokhlenko, O., Yeger-Lotem, E., & Ziv-Ukelson, M. (2005). Alignment of metabolic pathways. *BioInformatics, 21*(16), 3401–3408.

Pirzadeh, A., & Snyder, W. (1990). A unified solution to coverage and search in explored and unexplored terrains using indirect control. In *ICRA* (pp. 2113–2119).

Pistore, M., & Traverso, P. (2001). Planning as model checking for extended goals in non-deterministic domains. In *IJCAI* (pp. 479–486).

Plaat, A., Schaeffer, J., Pijls, W., & de Bruin, A. (1996). Best-first fixed-depth minimax algorithms. *Artificial Intelligence, 87*(1–2), 255–293.

Pohl, I. (1969). *Bi-directional and heursitic search in path problems*. Technical Report, Stanford Linear Accelerator Center.

Pohl, I. (1971). Bi-directional search. *Machine Intelligence, 6*, 127–140.

Pohl, I. (1977a). Heuristic search viewed as a path problem. *Artificial Intelligence, 1*, 193–204.

Pohl, I. (1977b). Practical and theoretical considerations in heuristic search algorithms. *Machine Intelligence, 8*, 55–72.

Politowski, G., & Pohl, I. (1984). D-node retargeting in bidirectional heuristic search. In *AAAI* (pp. 274–277).

Powley, C., & Korf, R. E. (1991). Single-agent parallel window search. *IEEE Transaction on Pattern Analysis and Machine Intelligence, 4*(5), 466–477.

Preditis, A. (1993). Machine discovery of admissible heurisitics. *Machine Learning, 12*, 117–142.

Preece, A., & Shinghal, R. (1994). Foundations and application of knowledge base verification. *International Journal on Intelligent Systems Intelligence, 9*(8), 683–701.

Prendinger, H., & Ishizuka, M. (1998). APS, a prolog-based anytime planning system. In *Proceedings 11th International Conference on Applications of Prolog (INAP)*.

Provost, F. (1993). Iterative weakening: Optimal and near-optimal policies for the selection of search bias. In *AAAI* (pp. 769–775).

Qian, K. (2006). *Formal verification using heursitic search and abstraction techniques*. PhD thesis, University of New South Wales.

Qian, K., & Nymeyer, A. (2003). Heuristic search algorithms based on symbolic data structures. In *ACAI* (pp. 966–979).

Qian, K., & Nymeyer, A. (2004). Guided invariant model checking based on abstraction and symbolic pattern databases. In *TACAS* (pp. 497–511).

Ramalingam, G., & Reps, T. (1996). An incremental algorithm for a generalization of the shortest-path problem. *Journal of Algorithms, 21*, 267–305.

Rao, C., & Arkin, A. (2001). Control motifs for intracellular regulatory networks. *Annual Review of Biomedical Engineering, 3*, 391–419.

Rao, N., Hareti, S., Shi, W., & Iyengar, S. (1993). *Robot navigation in unknown terrains: Introductory survey of non-heuristic algorithms*. Technical Report ORNL/TM–12410, Oak Ridge National Laboratory, TN.

Rao, V. N., Kumar, V., & Korf, R. E. (1991). Depth-first vs. best-first search. In *AAAI* (pp. 434–440).

Rapoport, A. (1966). *Two-Person Game Theory*. Dover.

Rasmussen, J. I., Larsen, K. G., & Subramani, K. (2004). Resource-optimal scheduling using priced timed automata. In *TACAS* (pp. 220–235).

Ratner, D., & Warmuth, M. K. (1990). The $(n^2 - 1)$-puzzle and related relocation problems. *Journal of Symbolic Computation, 10*(2), 111–137.

Reffel, F., & Edelkamp, S. (1999). Error detection with directed symbolic model checking. In *FM* (pp. 195–211).

Regin, J.-C. (1994). A filtering algorithm for constraints of difference in CSPS. In *AAAI* (pp. 362–367).

Reinefeld, A., & Marsland, T. A. (1994). Enhanced iterative-deepening search. *IEEE Transactions on Pattern Analysis and Machine Intelligence, 16*(7), 701–710.

Reingold, O. (2005). Undirected st-connectivity in log-space. In *STOC* (pp. 376–385).

Reisch, S. (1981). Hex ist PSPACE-vollständig. *Acta Informatica, 15*, 167–191.

Rensink, A. (2003). Towards model checking graph grammars. In *Workshop on Automated Verification of Critical Systems*, Technical Report DSSE-TR-2003 (pp. 150–160).

Rich, E., & Knight, K. (1991). *Artificial Intelligence*. McGraw-Hill.

Richter, S., Helmert, M., & Gretton, C. (2007). A stochastic local search approach to vertex cover. In *KI* (pp. 412–426).

Richter, S., Helmert, M., & Westphal, M. (2008). Landmarks revisited. In *AAAI* (pp. 975–982).

Rintanen, J. (2000). Incorporation of temporal logic control into plan operators. In *ECAI* (pp. 526–530).

Rintanen, J. (2003). Symmetry reduction for SAT representations of transition systems. In *ICAPS* (pp. 32–41).

Rintanen, J. (2006). Unified definition of heuristics for classical planning. In *ECAI* (pp. 600–604).

Rivest, R. L. (1976). Partial-match retrieval algorithms. *SIAM Journal of Computing, 5*(1), 19–50.

Robby, Dwyer, M. B., & Hatcliff, J. (2003). Bogor: An extensible and highly-modular software model checking framework. In *ESEC* (pp. 267–276).

Rohnert, H. (1985). A dynamization of the all pairs least cost path problem. In *STACS* (pp. 279–286).

Romein, J. W., & Bal, H. E. (2003). Solving Awari with parallel retrograde analysis. *Computer, 36*(10), 26–33.

Romein, J. W., Plaat, A., Bal, H. E., & Schaeffer, J. (1999). Transposition table driven work scheduling in distributed search. In *AAAI* (pp. 725–731).

Romero, L., Morales, E., & Sucar, E. (2001). An exploration and navigation approach for indoor mobile robots considering sensor's perceptual limitations. In *ICRA* (pp. 3092–3097).

Rossi, F., van Beek, P., & Walsh, T. (2006). *Handbook of Constraint Programming (Foundations of Artificial Intelligence)*. New York: Elsevier Science.

Rousset, P. (1988). On the consistency of knowledge bases, the COVADIS system. *Computational Intelligence, 4*, 166–170.

Rozenberg, G. (Ed.). (1997). *Handbook of Graph Grammars and Computing by Graph Transformations*. World Scientific.

Ruan, Y., Kautz, H., & Horvitz, E. (2004). The backdoor key: A path to understanding problem hardness. In *AAAI*.

Russell, S. (1992). Efficient memory-bounded search methods. In *ECAI* (pp. 1–5). Wiley.

Russell, S., & Norvig, P. (2003). *Artificial Intelligence: A Modern Approach*. Prentice-Hall.

Russell, S., & Wefald, E. (1991). *Do the Right Thing–Studies in Limited Rationality*. MIT Press.

Ryoo, H. S., & Sahinidis, N. V. (1996). A branch-and-reduce approach to global optimization. *Journal of Global Optimization, 8*(2), 107–139.

Sacerdoti, E. (1997). Planning in a hierarchy of abstraction spaces. *Artificial Intelligence, 5*, 115–135.

Samadi, M., Felner, A., & Schaeffer, J. (2008a). Learning from multiple heuristics. In *AAAI* (pp. 357–362).

Samadi, M., Siabani, M., Holte, R. C., & Felner, A. (2008b). Compressing pattern databases with learning. In *ECAI* (pp. 495–499).

Samuel, A. L. (1959). Some studies in machine learning using the game of checkers. *IBM Journal on Research and Development, 3*, 210–229.

Sanders, P., Meyer, U., & Sibeyn, J. F. (2002). *Algorithms for Memory Hierarchies*. Springer.

Savitch, W. J. (1970). Relationships between nondeterministic and deterministic tape complexities. *Journal of Computer and System Sciences, 4*(2), 177–192.

Sawatzki, D. (2004a). A symbolic approach to the all-pairs shortest-paths problem. In *WG* (pp. 154–167).

Sawatzki, D. (2004b). Implicit flow maximization by iterative squaring. In *SOFSEM* (pp. 301–313).

Schaeffer, J. (1986). *Experiments in search and knowledge*. PhD thesis, University of Waterloo.

Schaeffer, J. (1989). The history heuristic and alpha-beta search enhancements in practice. *IEEE Transactions on Pattern Analysis and Machine Intelligence, 11*, 1203–1212.

Schaeffer, J. (1997). *One Jump Ahead: Challenging Human Supremacy in Checkers*. Springer.

Schaeffer, J., Björnsson, Y., Burch, N., Kishimoto, A., & Müller, M. (2005). Solving checkers. In *IJCAI* (pp. 292–297).

Schaeffer, J., Burch, N., Björnsson, Y., Kishimoto, A., Müller, M., Lake, R., et al. (2007). Checkers is solved. *Science, 317*(5844), 1518–1522.

Schapire, R. (1992). *The Design and Analysis of Efficient Learning Algorithms*. MIT Press.

Schiffel, S., & Thielscher, M. (2007). Fluxplayer: A successful general game player. In *AAAI* (pp. 1191–1196).

Schlott, S. (1997). *Vehicle Navigation: Route Planning, Positioning and Route Guidance*. Landsberg/Lech, Germany: Verlag Moderne Industrie.

Schofield, P. D. A. (1967). Complete solution of the eight puzzle. In *Machine Intelligence 2* (pp. 125–133). Elsevier.

Schöning, U. (2002). A probabilistic algorithm for k-SAT based on limited local search and restart. *Algorithmica, 32*(4), 615–623.

Schrage, L. (1979). A more portable Fortran random number generator. *ACM Transactions on Mathematical Software, 5*(2), 132–138.

Schrödl, S. (1998). Explanation-based generalization in game playing: Quantitative results. In *ECML* (pp. 256–267).

Schrödl, S. (2005). An improved search algorithm for optimal multiple sequence alignment. *Journal of Artificial Intelligence Research, 23*, 587–623.

Schrödl, S., Wagstaff, K., Rogers, S., Langley, P., & Wilson, C. (2004). Mining GPS traces for map refinement. *Data Mining Knowledge Discovery, 9*(1), 59–87.

Schroeppel, R., & Shamir, A. (1981). A $t = o(2^{n/2})$, $s = o(2^{n/4})$ algorithm for certain NP-complete problems. *SIAM Journal of Computing, 10*(3), 456–464.

Schulz, F., Wagner, D., & Weihe, K. (2000). Dijkstra's algorithm on-line: An empirical case study from public railroad transport. *Journal of Experimental Algorithmics, 5*(12), 110–114.

Schuppan, V., & Biere, A. (2004). Efficient reduction of finite state model checking to reachability analysis. *International Journal on Software Tools for Technology Transfer, 5*(2–3), 185–204.

Schwefel, H.-P. (1995). *Evolution and Optimum Seeking*. Wiley.

Sen, A. K., & Bagchi, A. (1988). Average-case analysis of heuristic search in tree-like networks. In *Search in Artificial Intelligence* (pp. 131–165).

Sen, A. K., & Bagchi, A. (1989). Fast recursive formulations for best-first search that allow controlled use of memory. In *IJCAI* (pp. 297–302).

Shannon, C. E. (1950). Programming a computer to play chess. *Philosophical Magazine, 41*(7), 256–275.

Shostak, R. (1981). Deciding linear inequalities by computing loop residues. *Journal of the ACM, 28*, 769–779.

Shue, L., Li, S., & Zamani, R. (2001). An intelligent heuristic algorithm for project scheduling problems. In *Annual Meeting of the Decision Sciences Institute*.

Shue, L., & Zamani, R. (1993). An admissible heuristic search algorithm. In *International Symposium on Methodologies for Intelligent Systems* (pp. 69–75).

Sieling, D. (1994). *Algorithmen und untere Schranken für verallgemeinerte OBDDs*. PhD thesis, Technical University of Dortmund.

Silver, D. (20050. Cooperative pathfinding. In *Conference on Artificial Intelligence and Interactive Digital Entertainment* (pp. 117–122).

Simmons, R., Apfelbaum, D., Burgard, W., Fox, D., Moors, M., Thrun, S., & Younes, H (1997). Coordination for multi-robot exploration and mapping. In *AAAI* (pp. 852–858).

Simmons, R., Goodwin, R., Koenig, S., O'Sullivan, J., & Armstrong, G. (2001). Xavier: An autonomous mobile robot on the web. In R. Goldberg & R. Siegwart (Eds.), *Beyond Webcams: An Introduction to Online Robots*. MIT Press.

Singh, M. (1995). Path consistency revised. In *IEEE International Conference on Tools with Artificial Intelligence* (pp. 318–325).

Singh, K., & Fujimura, K. (1993). Map making by cooperating mobile robots. In *ICRA* (pp. 254–259).

Slaney, J., & Thiébaux, S. (2001). Blocks world revisited. *Artificial Intelligence* (pp. 119–153).

Slaney, J., & Walsh, T. (2001). Backbones in optimization and approximation. In *IJCAI* (pp. 254–259).

Sleator, D., & Tarjan, R. (1985). Amortized efficiency of list update and paging rules. *Communications of the ACM, 28*(2), 202–208.

Smith, D. E. (2004). Choosing objectives in over-subscription planning. In *ICAPS* (pp. 393–401).

Smith, S. J. J., Nau, D. S., & Throop, T. A. (1998). Computer bridge—A big win for AI planning. *AI Magazine, 19*(2), 93–106.

Smith, D. E., & Weld, D. S. (1999). Temporal planning with mutual exclusion reasoning. In *IJCAI* (pp. 326–337).

Sobel, D. (1996). *Longitude: The True Story of a Lone Genius Who Solved the Greatest Scientific Problem of His Time*. Penguin Books.

Sobrinho, J. L. (2002). Algebra and algorithms for QoS path computation and hop-by-hop routing in the internet. *IEEE/ACM Transactions on Networking, 10*(4), 541–550.

Spira, P., & Pan, A. (1975). On finding and updating spanning trees and shortest paths. *SIAM Journal on Computing, 4*, 375–380.

Spouge, J. L. (1989). Speeding up dynamic programming algorithms for finding optimal lattice paths. *SIAM Journal of Applied Mathematics, 49*(5), 1552–1566.

Stasko, J. T., & Vitter, J. S. (1987). Pairing heaps: Experiments and analysis. *Communications of the ACM, 30*(3), 234–249.

Stentz, A. (1995a). Optimal and efficient path planning for unknown and dynamic environments. *International Journal of Robotics and Automation, 10*(3), 89–100.

Stentz, A. (1995b). The focussed D* algorithm for real-time replanning. In *Proceedings of the International Joint Conference on Artficial Intelligence* (pp. 1652–1659).

Stentz, A. (1997). Best information planning for unknown, uncertain, and changing domains. In *AAAI Workshop on Online Search* (pp. 110–113).

Stentz, A., & Hebert, M. (1995). A complete navigation system for goal acquisition in unknown environments. *Autonomous Robots, 2*(2), 127–145.

Stephen, G. A. (1994). *String Searching Algorithms*. World Scientific Publishing.

Stern, U., & Dill, D. L. (1996). Combining state space caching and hash compaction. In *Methoden des Entwurfs und der verifikation digitaler systeme, 4. GI/ITG/GME Workshop* (pp. 81–90). Shaker Verlag.

Stern, U., & Dill, D. L. (1997). Parallelizing the Murϕ Verifier. In *CAV* (pp. 256–267).

Stern, R., Kalech, M., & Felner, A. (2010a). Searching for a *k*-clique in unknown graphs. In *SOCS* (pp. 83–89).

Stern, R., Puzis, R., & Felner, A. (2010b). Potential search: A greedy anytime heuristic search. In *SOCS* (pp. 119–120).

Stockman, G. C. (1997). A minimax algorithm better than alpha-beta. *Artificial Intelligence, 12*(2), 179–196.

Sturtevant, N. (2008). An analysis of UCT in multi-player games. In *CG* (pp. 37–49).

Sturtevant, N., & Bowling, M. (2006). Robust game play against unknown opponents. In *AAAI* (pp. 96–109).

Sturtevant, N., & Korf, R. E. (2000). On pruning techniques for multi-player games. In *AAAI* (pp. 201–207).

Sturtevant, N., Zhang, Z., Holte, R. C., & Schaeffer, J. (2008). Using inconsistent heuristics on A* search. In *AAAI, Workshop on Search Techniques in Artificial Intelligence and Robotics*.

Sulewski, D., Edelkamp, S., & Kissmann, P. (2011). Exploiting the computational power of the graphics cards: Optimal state space planning on the GPU. In *ICAPS* (pp. 242–249). Submitted.

Sutherland, I. (1969). A method for solving arbitrary-wall mazes by computer. *IEEE Transactions on Computers, C–18*(12), 1092–1097.

Sutton, R. (1991). DYNA, an integrated architecture for learning, planning, and reacting. *SIGART Bulletin, 2*(4), 160–163.

Sutton, R. S. (1988). Learning to predict by the methods of temporal differences. *Machine Learning, 3*, 9–44.

Sutton, A. M., Howe, A. E., & Whitley, L. D. (2010). Directed plateau search for MAX-k-SAT. In *SOCS* (pp. 90–97).

Svennebring, J., & Koenig, S. (2004). Building terrain-covering ant robots. *Autonomous Robots, 16*(3), 313–332.

Tarjan, R. E. (1983). *Data Structures and Network Algorithms*. SIAM.

Taylor, L. A. (1997). *Pruning duplicate nodes in depth-first search*. PhD thesis, Computer Science Department, University of California, Los Angeles.

Tesauro, G. (1995). Temporal difference learning and TD-Gammon. *Communication of the ACM, 38*(3), 58–68.

Thagard, P. (2003). Pathways to biomedical discovery. *Philosophy of Science, 70*, 2003.

Thayer, S., Digney, B., Diaz, M., Stentz, A., Nabbe, B., & Hebert, M. (2000). Distributed robotic mapping of extreme environments. In *SPIE: Mobile Robots XV and Telemanipulator and Telepresence Technologies VII* (Vol. 4195).

Thayer, J., & Ruml, W. Finding acceptable solutions faster using inadmissible information. In *SOCS* (pp. 98–99).

Thayer, J., & Ruml, W. (2010). Anytime heuristic search: Frameworks and algorithms. In *SOCS*.

Thorpe, P. (1994). *A hybrid learning real-time search algorithm*. Master's thesis, Computer Science Department, University of California, Los Angeles.

Thorup, M. (1999). Undirected single-source shortest paths with positive integer weights in linear time. *Journal of the ACM, 46*, 362–394.

Thorup, M. (2000). On RAM priority queues. *SIAM Journal of Computing, 30*, 86–109.

Thrun, S. (1992). The role of exploration in learning control. In *Handbook for Intelligent Control: Neural, Fuzzy and Adaptive Approaches*. Van Nostrand Reinhold.

Thrun, S. (2000). Probabilistic algorithms in robotics. *AI Magazine, 21*(4), 93–109.

Thrun, S., Bücken, A., Burgard, W., Fox, D., Fröhlinghaus, T., Hennig, D., et al. (1998). Map learning and high-speed navigation in RHINO. In D. Kortenkamp, R. Bonasso, & R. Murphy (Eds.), *Artificial Intelligence Based Mobile Robotics: Case Studies of Successful Robot Systems* (pp. 21–52). MIT Press.

Thrun, S., Burgard, W., & Fox, D. (2005). *Probabilistic Robotics*. MIT Press.

Torasso, P., & Torta, G. (2003). Computing minimal-cardinality diagnoses using BDDs. In *KI* (pp. 224–238).

Tovey, C., & Koenig, S. (2000). Gridworlds as testbeds for planning with incomplete information. In *AAAI* (pp. 819–824).

Tovey, C., & Koenig, S. (2003). Improved analysis of greedy mapping. In *Proceedings of the International Conference on Intelligent Robots and Systems* (pp. 3251–3257).

Tovey, C., & Koenig, S. (2010). Localization: Approximation and performance bounds for minimizing travel distance. *IEEE Transactions on Robotics, 26*(2), 320–330.

Tromp, J. (2008). Solving connect-4 on medium board sizes. *ICGA Journal, 31*(2), 110–112.

Tsang, T. (1993). *Foundations of Constraint Satisfaction*. Academic Press.

Turing, A. M., Strachey, C., Bates, M. A., & Bowden, B. V. (1953). Digital computers applied to games. In B. V. Bowden (Ed.), *Faster Than Thought* (pp. 286–310). Putnam.

Ukkonen, E. (1985). Algorithms for approximate string matching. *Information and Control, 64*, 110–118.

Valmari, A. (1991). A stubborn attack on state explosion. In *CAV* (pp. 156–165).

Valtorta, M. (1984). A result on the computational complexity of heuristic estimates for the A* algorithm. *Information Sciences, 34*, 48–59.

van den Herik, H. J., & Herschberg, I. S. (1986). A data base on data bases. *ICCA Journal* (pp. 29–34).

van Emde Boas, P., Kaas, R., & Zijlstra, E. (1977). Design and implementation of an efficient priority queue. *Mathematical Systems Theory, 10*, 99–127.

Van Hentenryck, P. (1989). *Constraint Satisfaction in Logic Programming*. MIT Press.

Van Hentenryck, P., Deville, Y., & Teng, C.-M. (1992). A generic arc-consistency algorithm and its specializations. *Artificial Intelligence, 57*, 291–321.

van Leeuwen, J., & Wood, D. (1993). Interval heaps. *The Computer Journal, 36*, 209–216.

Visser, W., Havelund, K., Brat, G., & Park, S. (2000). Model Checking Programs. In *ICSE* (pp. 3–12).

Wagner, I. A., Lindenbaum, M., & Bruckstein, A. M. (1996). Smell as a computational resource—A lesson we can learn from the ant. In *Israeli Symposium on Theory of Computing and Systems (ISTCS)*, (Vol. 24, pp. 219–230).

Wagner, I. A., Lindenbaum, M., & Bruckstein, A. M. (1998). Efficiently searching a graph by a smell-oriented vertex process. *Annals of Mathematics and Artificial Intelligence, 24*, 211–223.

Wagner, I., Lindenbaum, M., & Bruckstein, A. (1999). Distributed covering by ant robots using evaporating traces. *IEEE Transactions on Robotics and Automation, 15*(5), 918–933.

Wagner, D., & Willhalm, T. (2003). Geometric speed-up techniques for finding shortest paths in large sparse graphs. In *ESA* (pp. 776–787).

Wagner, D., Willhalm, T., & Zaroliagis, C. (2004). Dynamic shortest path containers. *ENTCS, 92*, 65–84.

Wah, B. (1991). *MIDA*: An IDA* search with dynamic control*. Technical Report 91-09, Center for Reliable and High Performance Computing, Coordinated Science Laboratory, University of Illinois.

Wah, B., & Shang, Y. (1994). Comparative study of IDA*-style searches. In *IJCAI* (pp. 290–296).

Walsh, T. (1997). Depth-bounded discrepancy search. In *IJCAI* (pp. 1388–1393).

Wang, C. (1991). Location estimation and uncertainty analysis for mobile robots. In I. Cox & G. Wilfong (Eds.), *Autonomous Robot Vehicles*. Springer.

Waterman, M. S. (1995). *Introduction to Computational Biology: Maps, Sequences, and Genomes*. Chapman and Hall.

Wegener, I. (2000). *Branching Programs and Binary Decision Diagrams—Theory and Applications*. SIAM.

Wehrle, M., Kupferschmid, S., & Podelski, A. (2008). Useless actions are useful. In *ICAPS* (pp. 388–395).

Wickelgren, W. A. (1995). *How to Solve Mathematical Problems*. Dover.

Wijs, A. (1999). *What to do next? Analysing and optimising system behaviour in time*. PhD thesis, Vrije Universiteit Amsterdam.

Winter, S. (2002). Modeling costs of turns in route planning. *GeoInformatica* (pp. 345–361).

Woelfel, P. (2006). Symbolic topological sorting with OBDDs. *Journal of Discrete Algorithms, 4*(1), 51–71.

Wolper, P. (1983). Temporal logic can be more expressive. *Information and Control, 56*, 72–99.

Wolpert, D. H., & Macready, W. G. (1996). *No free lunch theorems for search*. Technical Report, The Santa Fe Institute, NM.

Yang, B., Bryant, R. E., O'Hallaron, D. R., Biere, A., Coudert, O., Janssen, G., et al. (1998). A performance study of BDD based model checking. In *FMCAD* (pp. 255–289).

Yang, F., Culberson, J. C., Holte, R. C., Zahavi, U., & Felner, A. (2008). A general theory of additive state space abstractions. *Journal of Artificial Intelligence Research, 32*, 631–662.

Yang, C. H., & Dill, D. L. (1998). Validation with guided search of the state space. In *DAC* (pp. 599–604).

Yanovski, V., Wagner, I., & Bruckstein, A. (2003). A distributed ant algorithm for efficiently patrolling a network. *Algorithmica, 37*, 165–186.

Yoshizumi, T., Miura, T., & Ishida, T. (2000). A* with partial expansion for large branching factor problems. In *AAAI* (pp. 923–929).

Younger, D. H. (1967). Recognition and parsing of context-free languages in time n^3. *Information and Control, 10*(2), 189–208.

Zahavi, U., Felner, A., Burch, N., & Holte, R. C. (2008a). Predicting the performance of IDA* with conditional distributions. In *AAAI* (pp. 381–386).

Zahavi, U., Felner, A., Holte, R. C., & Schaeffer, J. (2008b). Duality in permutation state spaces and the dual search algorithm. *Artificial Intelligence, 172*(4–5), 514–540.

Zahavi, U., Felner, A., Schaeffer, J., & Sturtevant, N. R. (2007). Inconsistent heuristics. In *AAAI* (pp. 1211–1216).

Zelinsky, A. (1992). A mobile robot exploration algorithm. *IEEE Transactions on Robotics and Automation, 8*(6), 707–717.

Zhang, W. (1998). Complete anytime beam search. In *AAAI* (pp. 425–430).

Zhang, W. (2004a). Configuration landscape analysis and backbone guided local search for satisfiability and maximum satisfiability. *Artificial Intelligence, 158*(1), 1–26.

Zhang, W. (2004b). Phase transition and backbones of 3-SAT and Maximum 3-SAT. In *Principles and Practice of Constraint Programming (CP)*.

Zhang, W., Sen, A. K., & Bagchi, A. (1999). An average-case analysis of graph search. In *AAAI* (pp. 757–762).

Zhang, Z., Sturtevant, N. R., Holte, R. C., Schaeffer, J., & Felner, A. (2009). A* search with inconsistent heuristics. In *IJCAI* (pp. 634–639).

Zhang, Y., & Yap, R. H. C. (2001). Making AC-3 an optimal algorithm. In *IJCAI* (pp. 316–321).

Zhao, Y. (1997). *Vehicle Location and Navigation Systems*. Artech House Inc.

Zheng, Z. (1999). *Analysis of swapping and tempering monte carlo Algorithms*. PhD thesis, York University.

Zhou, R., & Hansen, E. A. (2002a). Memory-bounded A* graph search. In *Conference of the Florida Artificial Intelligence Research Society (FLAIRS)*.

Zhou, R., & Hansen, E. A. (2002b). Multiple sequence alignment using A*. In *AAAI*. Student abstract.

Zhou, R., & Hansen, E. A. (2003a). Sparse-memory graph search. In *IJCAI* (pp. 1259–1268).

Zhou, R., & Hansen, E. A. (2003b). Sweep A*: Space-efficient heuristic search in partially-ordered graphs. In *ICTAI* (pp. 688–695).

Zhou, R., & Hansen, E. A. (2004a). Breadth-first heuristic search. In *ICAPS* (pp. 92–100).

Zhou, R., & Hansen, E. A. (2004b). Space-efficient memory-based heuristics. In *AAAI* (pp. 677–682).

Zhou, R., & Hansen, E. A. (2004c). Structured duplicate detection in external-memory graph search. In *AAAI* (pp. 683–689).

Zhou, R., & Hansen, E. A. (2005a). External-memory pattern databases using structured duplicate detection. In *AAAI*.

Zhou, R., & Hansenm, E. A. (2005b). Beam-stack search: Integrating backtracking with beam search. In *ICAPS* (pp. 90–98).

Zhou, R., & Hansen, E. A. (2006a). A breadth-first approach to memory-efficient graph search. In *AAAI* (pp. 1695–1698).

Zhou, R., & Hansen, E. A. (2006b). Domain-independent structured duplicate detection. In *AAAI* (pp. 1082–1087).

Zhou, R., & Hansen, E. A. (2007a). Edge partitioning in external-memory graph search. In *IJCAI* (pp. 2410–2417).

Zhou, R., & Hansen, E. A. (2007b). Parallel structured duplicate detection. In *AAAI* (pp. 1217–1222).

Zhou, R., & Hansen, E. A. (2008). Combining breadth-first and depth-first strategies in searching for treewidth. In *AAAI, Workshop on Search Techniques in Artificial Intelligence and Robotics*.

Zhou, R., Schmidt, T., Hansen, E. A., Do, M., & Uckun, S. (2010). Edge partitioning in parallel structured duplicate detection. In *SOCS* (pp. 137–138).

Zilberstein, S., & Russell, S. (1993). Anytime sensing, planning and action: A practical model for robot control. In *IJCAI* (pp. 1402–1407).

Zilles, S., & Holte, R. C. (2010). The computational complexity of avoiding spurious states in state space abstraction. *Artificial Intelligence, 174*(14), 1072–1092.

Zobrist, A. (1970). *A new hashing method with application for game playing*. Technical Report, School of Electronic Engineering Science, University of Wisconsin, Madison. Reprinted in *ICCA Journal* 13(2), 69–73.

Zomaya, A. (1996). *The Parallel and Distributed Computing Handbook*. McGraw-Hill.

Index

(1+1) EA, 639–641
$\alpha\beta$-algorithm, 527
$\alpha\beta$-branch-and-bound, 550
$\alpha\beta$-pruning, 525–529
f-LRTA*, 488
f-optimality, 243
λ-reduction, 108
c-approximation, 646
h-value surface, 468, 481, 482, 499
k-beam search, 251
k-best first search, 250–251, 274
k-SAT, 593, 620, 646–651
k-satisfiability, 593
(pseudo) Boolean function, 640
Closed list, 48, 81, 89, 110, 111, 151–153, 167, 227, 251, 254–265, 280, 385, 768
DecreaseKey operation, 53, 90, 104, 108, 753
DeleteMin operation, 90, 92, 157, 324
Graphplan, 675–677, 679, 697
Insert operation, 51, 96, 128, 325, 356, 358
Open list, 48, 49, 50, 59, 60, 81, 89, 90, 110, 151–152, 167, 227, 236, 247, 254, 257, 262, 752, 766
Satplan, 317, 677–678, 697
$(n^2 - 1)$-PUZZLE, 3, 10, 11, 19, 20, 29, 89, 116, 170, 177, 179, 211, 228, 283, 335, 407, 420
n-QUEENS, 624

1-LEVEL BUCKET, 90, 157, 265, 299, 306
2-LEVEL BUCKET, 92
2-SAT, 593, 596, 630, 665
2-SAT backdoor, 596
AIRPORT, 674
ALGEBRAIC DECISION DIAGRAM, 312
ALL PAIRS SHORTEST PATHS, 47, 62, 86, 450, 579, 706, 719
AMAZONS, 523, 568
AND INVERTER GRAPH, 312
ARROW DISTRIBUTED DIRECTORY PROTOCOL, 724, 735
ARROW PUZZLE, 187, 447
ATOMIC HEAP, 157
ATOMIX, 42–43, 46
AWARI, 568
BACKGAMMON, 11, 45, 562

BIN PACKING, 178, 572, 598, 599, 602, 620, 630
BINARY DECISION DIAGRAM, 283, 286
BINARY SEARCH TREE, 97, 98
BINOMIAL TREE, 104, 105
BIOLOGICAL PATHWAY, 759
BIPARTITE MATCHING, 624
BITONIC SORT, 404, 405
BLOCKSWORLD, 11, 29, 30, 296, 615, 616, 677, 681, 695, 699
BLOOM FILTER, 134, 158
BRIDGE, 10, 45, 536, 538, 568
BUCKET SORT, 342, 343
BUFFERED REPOSITORY TREE, 324, 325
BURNED PANCAKE, 363, 364
CANADIAN TRAVELER'S PROBLEM, 630
CENTURY PUZZLE, 21
CHEAP NECKLACE, 41
CHECKERS, 10, 423, 522, 534, 560, 568
CHESS, 10, 465, 520, 522, 530, 535, 537, 543, 560
CIRCUIT VALUE problem, 374
CLIQUE, 604, 620, 630
COMPONENT TREE, 157
CONNECT, 4, 10, 45, 521, 568
CRYPTARITHM, 574, 579
DAD'S PUZZLE, 20, 21
DECISION TREE, 286
DECOMPOSABLE NEGATIONAL NORMAL FORM, 312
DICTIONARY, 111
DINING PHILOSOPHERS, 158, 460, 711, 717, 735
DONKEY PUZZLE, 20
EIGHT QUEENS, 573, 586
EIGHT-PUZZLE, 19, 20, 45, 118, 163, 172, 208, 432, 450, 458, 477, 773
EXTERNAL MERGESORT, 323, 343
EXTERNAL QUICKSORT, 323, 324
FIBONACCI HEAP, 104–106, 157
FIFTEEN-PUZZLE, 10, 19, 45, 115, 168, 191, 205, 208, 284, 309, 340, 343, 370, 389, 412, 414, 425, 440, 446
FROGS AND TOADS, 42
GAMBLER'S RUIN, 650
GENERAL SLIDING TILE PUZZLE, 20, 45

GENERALIZED SUFFIX TREE, 89, 146, 151
GO, 521, 562, 567–568
GRAPH COLORING, 577, 624
GRIDWORLD, 50, 52, 165, 255, 257, 435, 440, 512
GRIPPER, 300, 301
HEAP, 98, 152, 752
HEX, 523, 568
HOBBITS AND ORCS, 82
INDEPENDENT SET, 604, 620
INVERTED TRIE, 147, 148, 150
KNAPSACK, 84, 87, 598, 626
KNIGHT'S TOUR, 83, 84
LADDER, 667
LOGISTICS, 11, 30, 685
LONELY EIGHT, 574, 575
METRIC TSP, 25, 45
MINIMUM SPANNING TREE, 26, 200
MISSIONARY AND CANNIBALS, 82
MORPION SOLITAIRE, 538, 565, 568
MULTIPLE SEQUENCE ALIGNMENT, 3, 26–29, 62, 84, 255, 270, 325, 329, 365, 760, 770, 772
NIM, 521, 564
NINE-MEN-MORRIS, 521, 522, 568
NUMBER PARTITION, 572, 588, 596, 597, 620, 630
OPENSTACK, 675
PAIRING HEAP, 100
PANCAKE, 363, 364
PATRICIA TRIE, 143
PATTERN PACKING, 178, 684
PEG, 551
PERFECT WEAK HEAP, 107
PIPESWORLD, 674
POWER SUPPLY RESTORATION, 674
PROMELA, 674
QUANTIFIED BOOLEAN FORMULA, 628
QUICK-HEAPSORT, 157
QUICKSORT, 157, 321, 404
RACETRACK, 44
RADIX HEAP, 93–96, 157
RADIX SORT, 343
RAILROAD SWITCHING, 12–14, 23
RANK-RELAXED WEAK QUEUE, 158
RECTANGLE PACKING, 572, 601–604, 620, 630

RELAXED WEAK QUEUE, 106–108, 110, 157–158
RIVER CROSSING, 83
ROUTE PLANNING, 24–25
ROVERS, 674
RUBIK'S CUBE, 10, 22
RUN-RELAXED WEAK QUEUE, 157
SAME GAME, 565
SATELLITE, 674
SEQUENTIAL ORDERING, 189, 192
SET COVERING, 577
SETTLERS, 675
SINGLE SOURCE SHORTEST PATHS, 47, 62, 196, 298, 311, 319, 324, 325
SKAT, 566, 568
SMALLEST ENCLOSING SQUARE, 627
SOKOBAN, 3, 9, 10, 22, 23, 45, 89, 116, 138, 284, 301, 305, 317, 441, 442, 445, 450, 453, 459, 463
STAR abstraction, 163
STOCHASTIC SHORTEST PATH, 553
STORAGE, 674
STRIPS, 29, 30, 38, 42, 163, 186, 365, 453, 463, 673, 696
STRIPS ABSTRACTION, 163
STRIPS PLANNING, 29, 453
STRONGLY CONNECTED COMPONENT, 311
SUBSET SUM, 642
SUDOKU, 574, 579
SUFFIX LIST, 131, 133, 134, 137, 152, 158
SUFFIX TREE, 142, 143, 147, 150, 153, 159
SUFFIX TRIE, 143
TSP, 25–26, 646
THIRTY-FIVE-PUZZLE, 45, 187, 295, 335, 348, 398
THREE-PUZZLE, 35
TIC-TAC-TOE, 521, 544, 545, 563, 566
TOPOLOGICAL SORTING, 311, 318
TOURNAMENT TREE, 324
TOWERS-OF-HANOI, 10, 179, 370, 418, 424, 427
TRAVELING PURCHASE PROBLEM, 675
TRIE, 139, 141, 143, 147
TRUCKS, 675
TWENTY-FOUR-PUZZLE, 19, 45, 172, 174, 191, 208, 223
TWO LADDER, 667
UMTS, 675
VERTEX COVER, 572, 604, 620

WEAK QUEUE, 107, 152
WEAK-HEAPSORT, 157
WUSEL, 43, 46
64-bit compression, 406

A
A*, 69–75
ABC procedure, 537
abstract description language, 673
abstract planning problem, 680
abstract problem graph, 343, 392
abstraction, 161, 185, 191, 703
abstraction database heuristic, 735
abstraction refinement, 161
abstraction transformation, 161, 162, 165
abstraction-directed model checking, 704
AC load balancing strategy, 387
AC-3, 576–577, 581, 629
AC-8, 576–577, 581, 629
acceptor processor, 388
Ackermann function, 41
action, 3, 12, 30, 35, 285, 694
action cost partitioning, 312
action execution time window, 696
action graph, 699
action planning, 3, 11, 29–32, 192, 280, 296, 673–699
action-execution step, 469–470
action-selection step, 469
action-value function, 540
active process heuristic, 707
activeness heuristic, 707–709, 719–720
adaptive sort, 356
ADD, 312, 569
adding finite-domain variables (with BDDs), 289
additional context, 698
additive penalty, 446
adjacency list, 15, 326, 328
adjacency matrix, 14, 47, 62, 210
ADL, 673, 697
admissible compression, 184
admissible heuristic, 18, 162, 171, 174, 697
admissible macro, 450
admissible pruning, 429, 430, 458–459
admissible weight function, 198, 204, 205
affine gap cost, 28, 65, 66
agent-centered search, 465–466, 514
Aho-Corasick algorithm, 435–438

algebraic decision diagram, 569
algorithm A, 58
algorithm flood, 634, 654
alive procedure, 444
all-different constraint, 571, 575, 579, 580
alphametic, 574
amino acid, 26, 27, 46
amortized complexity, 7, 92
ample set, 453–455, 464
ample set construction, 454
ancestor (of a node), 15
AND/OR graph, 552–559
anomaly (in a knowledge-based system), 701
ant algorithm, 652–657
antidiagonal, 63, 255, 767, 768
anytime A*, 277
anytime repairing A*, 246–250
API, 401
approximation, 26, 28, 34
approximation algorithm, 45, 599, 630, 645, 647, 687, 744
ARA*, 247–249
arc consistency, 571, 575–579
arc consistent (CSP), 575
arc consistent (variable pair), 575
arithmetic CSP, 578
arity, 8
array compaction, 406–407
arrow path, 724
articulation, 24
aspiration criterion, 638
aspiration search, 530–531
assembly language level program model checking, 714, 716
assertion, 706
assertion violation, 717
assignment costs, 686
assignment graph, 580
assumption based truth maintenance system, 729
asymptotic branching factor, 206–211
asynchronous distribution, 379
asynchronous IDA*, 382–385
asynchronous parallel search, 420
asynchronous search, 375, 380, 384
asynchronous setting, 369, 379, 420
ATMS, 729
atom, 8, 42–43
auto tactic, 733
automata-based model checking, 703

automated theorem proving, 730–734
automatically inferred pruning
    knowledge, 429
average macro solution length, 450

B

back leak, 259, 260, 763, 767, 772
back-propagation, 443
backbone, 595–596
backdoor, 595–596
backjumping, 583–584
backmarking, 585–587
backtracking, 581–582
backup induction, 554
backward edge, 455
backward proof, 733
backward search, 679
ball, 22
base model, 777
BDD, 283, 286–290
beam search, 251
beam width, 251, 266
beam-stack, 267
beam-stack search, 266–270
belief state, 504–506, 703
Bellman equation, 36, 37, 67, 747
Bellman-Ford algorithm, 47, 81, 86, 311
best-first minimax search, 567
best-first search (for two-player games),
    533–534
best-fit, 599
BFS, 51–53
BFS level, 177, 272–273, 292, 294, 298,
    326, 348, 402
BFS number, 362
BFS tree, 331
BHFFA, 410, 411, 427
bibliographic search problem, 433
bidirectional heuristic front-to-front
    algorithm, 410, 411, 427
bidirectional heuristic search, 370
bidirectional search, 408–419
big-oh notation, 7
bin completion, 599–600
binary constraint, 573
binary constraint network, 609
binary CSP, 573
binary search tree, 98, 385
bioinformatics, 759
bionic algorithm, 652
bipartite graph, 24, 579
birthday problem, 406

bit-state hashing, 134–136
black-box semantic, 674, 693, 694
blank, 19
BLAST, 771
blast tactic, 733
blind search, 16, 291–299
block, 4, 401
block (in a rank sequence), 107
block size, 321
BnB, 198–201
Boltzman constant, 636
Boolean constraint, 571
bootstrap method, 540
bootstrapping, 442, 458, 524
bound variable, 8
bounded model checking, 317, 736
bounding, 198
bounding box, 742
bounds consistency, 577–578
box, 22
branch-and-bound, 198–201
branch-and-bound search tree, 199, 201
branching, 198, 571
branching factor, 15, 206–211
branching partitioning, 310, 312
branching rule, 379, 581
breadth-first duplicate detection search,
    431
breadth-first heuristic search, 261–264
breadth-first search, 47, 51–53
brute-force algorithm, 647
brute-force branching factor, 216, 217
brute-force search tree, 206, 211, 215,
    216
Büchi automaton, 615–617, 631
bug hunting estimate, 704
business work-flow analysis, 702

C

cache anomalies, 321
cache-oblivious algorithm, 361
canonicalize, 447
Carrillo-Lipman bound, 769, 770, 772
CAS, 378
cascading cut, 105, 107
causal graph, 685–687
causal graph analysis, 685
central processing unit (CPU), 370
chairman, 108
character, 113
characteristic equation, 209
characteristic function, 283–285

children layer, 389
Christofides' algorithm, 646
chronological backtracking, 629
Church-Turing thesis, 5
circularity anomaly, 727
CKKA, 598
clause, 592
clause form, 731
cleaning transformation, 108, 109
client, 378, 398, 399
clique pattern database compression, 184
CLM, 657
clock valuation function, 721
clock variable, 721
closed under entailment, 723
closed world assumption, 29
clustering, 388
CNLP, 657, 669
coalescing, 401
collapse compression, 137
combinatorial game theory, 521, 568
communication protocol, 705–713
commutative action, 453
compare-and-swap, 378, 425
complete binary tree, 98
complete deductive system, 9
complete greedy algorithm, 598
complete Karmakar-Karp algorithm, 598
complete search process, 633
completeness (of a search algorithm),
    456
complexity theory, 5–6
compound statement, 4
computability theory, 4–5
computable function, 5
computational biology, 9, 27, 757
computer ant, 634, 652
concise hash function, 403
configuration, 12
configuration space, 773–777
conflict analysis, 288
conflict anomaly, 727
congruence relation, 447
conjunctive normal form, 8, 620
consistency, 575–580
consistency (in a knowledge-based
    system), 701
consistent formula, 8
consistent heuristic, 3, 18
consolidate, 105
consolidation, 104–106
conspiracy number search, 567

conspiracy search, 537
constant, 8
constrain operator, 309
constraint, 572
constraint function, 618
constraint graph, 583, 609
constraint local minimum, 657
constraint modeling, 571
constraint optimization, 618–619
constraint optimization problem, 572, 618
constraint partitioning, 699
constraint propagation, 571
constraint satisfaction problem, 572, 581
constraint search, 571
continuous nonlinear programming, 657
contracted locus, 143
control knowledge, 612, 631
control knowledge in LRTA*, 479
convex hull, 43
convex set, 750
Cook's theorem, 286
cooling scheme, 637
correct deductive system, 9
cost, 14
cost (of an action), 35
cost consistency, 747
cost function, 53, 618
cost structure, 77, 78
cost-to-go function, 66
counterexample, 703
counterexample guided error refinement, 704, 705, 735
credit search, 629
critical node, 528
critical path, 611
critical role (of correct software), 701
critical tree, 528, 529, 534
cross-over operator, 642
crypto-arithmetic puzzle, 574
CSP, 572
cubie, 22
cuckoo hashing, 128–130
cuckoo process, 128, 129
cut, 105
cycle argument, 474, 483
cycle detection search, 426, 710

D

DAG, 325
dangerous state, 708

data abstraction, 161
data partitioning, 384
data stream, 344
Datalog, 550
Davis-Putnam Logmann-Loveland algorithm, 594
dead reckoning, 739
dead-end detection, 430
dead-end pruning, 458–459
deadlock, 705, 707, 708
deadlock formula, 708
debugger, 713
decidable logic, 9
decidable problem, 5
decision problem, 5
decision tree, 529
decomposed state, 444
deductive system, 9
Deep Blue, 10
deep cut-off, 526
Deep Fritz, 10, 520
deep pruning, 547
Deep Thought, 521
deficiency anomaly, 727
delay transition, 721
delayed duplicate detection, 319, 359
delayed expansion strategy, 309
dependency network, 728
dependent actions, 693
depth-bounded discrepancy search, 591
depth-first branch-and-bound, 195, 199
depth-first iterative-deepening, 195, 201
depth-first search, 47, 50–51
depth-slicing, 375
derived predicate, 674, 695–696
descendant (of a node), 15
deterministic planning, 673
deterministic search model, 36
deterministic Turing machine, 591
DFBnB, 195, 199
DFID, 195, 201
DFS, 50
diagnosis, 727–730
diagnosis system, 730
diagnostic variable, 730
diagonizable matrix, 209
diamond property, 454
difference bound matrix, 312
difference constraint, 721
digital (binary) sum, 564
digital map, 737
Dijkstra's algorithm, 47

diminishing pebble, 668
direct conflict, 694
direct numerical conflict, 694
directed acyclic graph, 325
directed automated theorem proving, 701
directed model checking, 701
directed state space problem, 23
discount, 65
disjoint hash function, 403
disjoint pattern database, 173–177
disjoint state abstraction, 175
disjunctive normal form, 8
disjunctive partitioning, 312
disk striping, 321
distance, 13
distance move, 452
distant move pair, 452
distributed algorithm, 369
distributed memory model, 397
distributed response strategy, 376
distributed search, 369–427
divide-and-conquer, 62
divide-and-conquer algorithm, 196–197
divide-and-conquer beam search, 266
divide-and-conquer beam stack search, 267
divide-and-conquer bidirectional search, 257
divide-and-conquer decomposition search, 568
divide-and-conquer forward frontier search, 257–259
divide-and-conquer solution reconstruction, 262
DNA, 26
domain abstraction, 163
domain expert pruning knowledge, 429
domain metric, 673
domain range, 577
domain splitting, 581
domain transition graph, 685
domain-independent planning, 673
dominance condition, 604
dominance condition on feasible bin completions, 599
don't care (proposition), 680
donor processor, 388
double bit-state hashing, 251
double hashing, 124
DPLL, 594
dual encoding, 573

dual pattern database, 179–180
duality, 180
duplicate (node), 49
duplicate (string), 432
duplicate detection scope, 265
duration, 695
dynamic backtracking, 584–585
dynamic incremental hashing, 155
dynamic load balancing, 384
dynamic perfect hashing, 127
dynamic programming, 62–68, 255, 543, 678–679
dynamic pruning, 458
dynamic substring pruning, 438
dynamic variable reordering, 288

E

early duplicate detection, 328, 391
early merging, 359, 390
edge, 12
edge ant walk, 493, 501, 657
edge counting, 493
edge partitioning, 364
edge transition, 721
edit distance, 28
effective branching factor, 23
efficiency, 372
eigenvalue problem, 209
ELF, 713
eligibility trace, 567
embarrassing parallel, 398
embedded system verification, 702
embedding, 162
enabledness preserving action, 453
encapsulated variable, 573
endgame database, 522
enforced hill climbing, 240–242
equilibrium distribution, 212
equilibrium fraction (of nodes), 206, 207
equivalence class, 447
error, 539
error trail, 715
essential language extension, 673
Euclidean distance, 25, 745
Euler tour, 328, 374
evaluation, 634
evaluation function, 633, 641
evaluation function parameter, 542
eventually (operator), 613
evolutionary algorithm, 639–645
evolutionary distance, 28
executed action, 35

existential elimination, 9
existential introduction, 9
exit distance, 276
expand queue, 394
expansion (of a node), 15, 49
expected cost, 520
expected return, 36
expected reward, 520
explanation-based learning, 543
explanatory phase, 702
explicit graph, 14
explicit state space graph, 15
explicit-state model checking, 702
explicit-state pattern database, 683
explicit-state search, 283
exploitation (of the search space), 274
exploration (of a node), 15
exploration (of the search space), 274
exploration-exploitation dilemma, 542
Extended IDA*, 276
extended locus, 143
extended successor relation, 634
extended weight function, 198
external A*, 320
external A* search, 334
external B-tree, 362
external BFS, 326, 328, 360
external binary search tree, 362
external breadth-first branch-and-bound, 320, 330–332
external breadth-first heuristic search, 331, 332, 347
external breadth-first search, 319
external depth-first search, 319, 325
external Dijkstra search, 324
external Dijkstra's algorithm, 47, 53–57
external enforced hill climbing, 320, 332–334
external explicit-graph DFS, 325–326
external explicit graph search algorithm, 324–328
external explicit-graph BFS, 326–328
external linked list, 361
external memory data structure, 323
external pattern database, 346–347
external queue, 361
external scanning, 323
external sorting, 323, 341
external stack, 361
external symbolic pattern database, 348
external value iteration, 349–353

F

fact, 29
fact space exploration, 681
factorial base, 118
factorial base (of a permutation), 118
fail-safe variant, 526
failure function, 435
FALCONS, 489
fast learning and converging search, 489
FASTA, 763, 771
fault-finding phase, 702
feasibility problem, 635
feasible object set, 599
features, 542
fellow, 108
Fibonacci number, 40
FIFO, 51
finite state controller, 559
finite state machine pruning, 435–438
firing sequence, 717
first fail, 581
first order logic, 730
first-fit, 621
first-fit decreasing, 599
first-in first-out, 51
first-in-first-out (paging strategy), 320
first-order predicate logic, 8
fitness, 639
fitness function, 641
fixpoint, 31
fixpoint (computation), 289
FKS hashing, 128
FKS hashing scheme, 126–127
Floyd-Warshall algorithm, 47, 62
fluent, 673
folding, 388
forbidden word, 431
formula progression, 614–615
formula-based heuristic, 705–707
forward checking, 581
forward expansion, 554
forward proof, 733
forward pruning, 537
forward search, 679
forward set simplification, 293, 309
forward-chaining search, 449
free ball, 441
free variable, 8
freespace, 773
frequency (of pattern searches), 445
fringe search, 231–233
front-to-front, 410

frontier search, 257–259, 319, 346, 389
frontier set simplification, 293
FSM distance heuristic, 709
full state hashing, 375
fully expanded, 453
function, 8
functional A*, 733–735

G

GA, 634, 641–643
Galileo, 740
game description language, 550
game theory, 550, 567, 568
game tree, 524–525
gap, 28, 63, 273
gap opening, 27
GDE, 728–729
GDL, 550
general cost structure, 76, 78
general diagnostic engine, 728–729
general game playing, 11, 45, 550–552
general purpose GPU programming, 400
generalization of dead-end pattern, 441
generalized suffix tree, 89, 146–151, 438
generation (of a node), 61, 173, 224
generic search model, 29, 36–37
genetic operator, 642
geocoding, 744
global hashing, 388
global positioning system, 737, 739
global sequence alignment, 762
global variable, 199, 201, 709, 714
globally (operator), 613
goal constraint, 571, 613
goal preference, 617
goal state, 26, 37, 291, 298, 457, 474,
        491, 561, 634, 725
golden ratio, 113
GPGPU, 400
GPS, 11, 739
GPU, 370, 400–408
GPU-based search, 370, 405
gradient decent, 668
gradient descent, 539, 542, 635
graph leveling, 388
graph morphism, 723, 725
graph transition system, 723–726
graphics processing unit (GPU), 370,
        400
greedy best-first search, 73, 87, 243,
        307–308, 497, 733
greedy heuristic, 597

greedy plan extraction, 31, 690
greedy policy, 37
grounded planning domain, 30
GSAT algorithm, 595

H

Hamming distance heuristic, 718–719,
        725
Hamming sphere algorithm, 649, 650
hand-off, 377
hard constraint, 571, 619, 697
hard problem, 591–609
hardware verification, 9, 318
harmless dead-end, 276
harmonic number, 136
harmonic sum, 136
hash compaction, 136–137, 158
hash table folding, 183
hash-based distribution, 375
hash-based duplicate detection, 342–343,
        359, 388
hash-based partitioning, 404–406
head (of a string), 143
heap, 97–110
heap property, 98
heap store, 107
heap-ordered multiway tree, 100
heuristic, 15–19, 26, 47, 75, 161,
        302–309, 465, 477–479,
        597–598, 607–608, 690–691,
        703–704, 707–713, 715–720
heuristic function, 69, 75, 212, 304, 608
heuristic knowledge in LRTA*, 479–480
heuristic search, 47, 68, 121, 261–264,
        302–309, 418–419, 572
heuristic search algorithm, 16, 68, 263,
        347, 752, 762
hierachical A*, 165–167
high-level variable, 687
hill-climbing, 240–242, 280, 332–334,
        635–636, 668
Hirschberg's algorithm, 256, 257, 762
history heuristic, 530, 567
Hoare calculus, 690
holy grail, 759
homomorphism, 162
horizon effect, 537, 562
Horn backdoor, 596
Horn clause, 732
Horner's rule (for evaluating
        polynimials), 114

Huffman compression, 185
hyper-arc consistency, 577
hyperarcs, 553
hypercube, 27
hypergraph, 552, 553

I

I/O efficiency, 319, 324, 354, 364, 388,
        723
IDA*, 195, 203–218, 233, 236, 251–254,
        276, 346, 382–385
IDDP, 764, 770, 772
IDLA*, 439
IE, 219
ILP, 618
image, 283, 290, 310
immediate duplicate detection, 353, 361,
        365
immediate reward, 540
implicit graph, 15, 47, 48, 328–342
implicit state space graph, 15
improved limit discrepancy search, 589,
        591
in-order traversal, 385
in-place locking, 378
inadmissible macro, 450
inadmissible pruning, 266
inclusion check, 722
inconsistent node, 244
incremental duplicate learning A*,
        438–440
incremental hashing, 111, 113, 116, 158,
        375
incremental pruning, 459
incremental state space generation, 15
indel, 27, 28
independence ratio, 375, 377
independent action, 453
inductive logic programming, 542
inference rule, 9, 32, 674, 697
infinite path, 56, 65, 613, 615, 690
influence, 452–453
informed search, 68, 81
inherently sequential, 694, 695
initial population, 641
initial state, 12, 31, 33, 41, 166, 183,
        284, 304, 346, 429, 449, 697, 720
initial state set, 286
input resolution, 732
instruction-level paralellism, 369
integer linear program, 618, 661

intelligent authoring, 727
intelligent debugging, 728
intelligent tutoring, 727
interleaved variable ordering, 288
interleaving heuristic, 716
internal node heuristic, 732, 733
international planning competition, 45, 674, 735, 771
interpretation, 8
invariant analysis, 717
invariant constraint, 721
inverse, 119, 161, 167, 431, 703
inverse macro, 452
inversible action, 170, 180, 433
inversion, 20, 120
inverted index, 118
invisible action, 454
Isabelle, 736
isolated field procedure, 441
isomorphism heuristic, 725
iterative broadening, 251, 252, 280, 629
iterative deepening (in two-player search), 525
iterative deepening A*, 195, 204–218, 233, 236, 251, 254, 276, 345, 382, 385
iterative expansion, 219
iterative threshold search, 233–235, 279
iterative-deepening dynamic programming, 763–764
ITS, 233–235, 279

K

Kalman filter, 741
Karmakar-Karp heuristic, 597–598
kernel, 259, 401
knowledge-based system, 701, 726–727
Kripke structure, 702, 703

L

labeling, 524, 571, 581, 681, 727
Lagrange multiplier, 634, 657–660
language (induced by the model), 703
language (induced by the specification), 703
Las Vegas algorithm, 633, 647
lasso, 703, 710
last-in first-out, 50, 320
last-in-first-out (paging strategy), 320
lattice, 27, 255
layered plan graph construction, 677
lazy state space generation, 15

lcp, 440
LDFS, 569
LDS, 588–591, 619–620
leader (of a run), 108
learning DFS, 569
learning real-time A*, 466–473
least-recently-used (paging strategy), 320
leftmost tip node, 234
Lehmer generator, 116
Lempel-Ziv compression, 185
lexicographic rank, 118, 159
LIFO, 50, 320
lifted search space, 710
lifted state space, 634
limit discrepancy search, 588–591, 619–620
linear conflict heuristic, 21
linear probing, 123, 354, 358
linear program, 618, 661
linear speedup, 372
linear temporal logic, 613, 621, 697, 703
linearly priced timed automaton, 722
list ranking, 374
literal, 8, 592
little-oh notation, 7
live transition, 717
liveness as safety model checking, 710, 735
liveness property, 703
LM load balancing strategy, 387
load balancing, 375, 378, 385, 387
local hashing, 388, 425
local pattern, 23
local search, 465, 633, 638, 663
local search space, 468, 472, 479, 482, 487, 498, 499, 561
local sequence alignment, 762
local variable, 661, 711
locality, 116, 264–265, 343, 347
locality (for delayed duplicate detection), 343
locality (for structured duplicate detection), 343
locality (of abstract state space graph), 347
locality (of state vector), 116
locally consistent, 581
lock heuristic, 716
lock-free hash table, 378, 426
lock-free hashing, 378–379
locking, 387

logistics, 571, 622, 675
lollipop state space, 511
long run minimization (of solution costs), 480
longest common prefix, 146, 440
loosely called action, 471
loss backup, 543
low-level variable, 685, 686
lower bound, 7, 10, 18, 28, 45, 86, 130, 199, 299, 302, 340–342, 397, 477, 479, 606
LP, 618
LRTA*, 466–496
LRTA* improvement (for fast-acting agents), 480
LRTA* improvement (for slowly-acting agents), 480
LRTA* with lookahead, 473–474
LTL, 613, 621, 697, 703

M

machine learning, 191–192, 463, 539, 561, 636, 759
macro, 450
macro action, 22, 191, 430, 450
macro learning, 450, 459
macro operator, 450
macro problem solving, 449–452, 459
macro table, 450–452
makespan, 630, 674
mammalian cell cycle control, 760, 771
Manhattan distance heuristic, 21, 115, 334, 374, 414, 446
map matching, 737, 741–744
marked node, 107–108
marking (in a Petri net), 717
Markov chain, 35, 741
Markov decision process, 35–36, 495, 519
Markov decision process problem, 35, 65–68, 495
master, 378, 380, 391, 394, 395, 398, 400
matching, 579
matrix multiplication, 374, 579
MAX-k-SAT, 630, 646–647, 648
max-atom heuristic, 678–679
max-atom-pair heuristic, 679
maximal pattern size, 445
maximum flow, 24, 580
maximum matching, 580, 606, 607
maximum weighted bipartite matching, 174

maxMem, 187, 235, 266
MDP, 35–36, 65–68, 495
member (of a run), 107
membership problem, 111
memorizing, 441
memory aware recursive best-first search, 219
memory hierarchy, 319, 322
memory leak, 237
memory locality, 320, 755
memory-enhanced test framework, 532–533, 562
merge (weak-heap), 102
merging strategy, 356
merit function, 69
message-passing, 711
metric planning, 673, 687–691
Metropolis algorithm, 634, 637
Min-LRTA*, 482–483, 493
min-max LRTA*, 494–495, 504–506
min-max-learning real-time A*, 494–495, 504–506
minimal constraint network, 609
minimal matching (heuristic), 24
minimal temporal constraint network, 610
minimax, 519, 525
misplaced-tile heuristic, 21
mistake-bounded error model, 480, 495
modal operator, 613
model automaton, 615, 703
model checking, 701, 702, 704, 710, 713–717, 721
model checking object code, 713
model checking problem, 703–704, 710
model checking software, 713
model counting, 287
model relaxation, 704
model-based diagnosis, 727
molecule, 42
Monien-Speckenmeyer algorithm, 647–648
monotone heuristic, 18, 718
Monte Carlo algorithm, 633, 647
Monte Carlo policy evaluation, 68
Monte Carlo randomized search, 634
Monte Carlo sampling, 538, 552
Monte Carlo search, 537, 562
Moore's Law, 319
most general unifier, 730
most-blocked heuristic, 716
motion-planning problem, 773, 776

move, 12
move ordering, 529–530
move-alternation property, 272
MRBFS, 219
MST, 26, 646
MTD(f), 532, 534
multiobjective search, 48, 79–80
multiplayer game, 10, 538, 547–549
multiple pattern database, 172–173, 681–683
multiple-goal heuristic search, 370, 418–419
multiplicative hashing, 113
multiplying finite-domain variables (with BDDs), 289
multivalued pattern database, 191
multivalued variable encoding, 681, 682, 685
multiway tree, 100
mutation operator, 640, 642, 684
mutex action, 676
mutex proposition, 676
mutually exclusive lock, 385
mutually substring free, 439

N

NAND-flash, 353
navigation, 737
navigationpile, 155–156
negmax, 519, 524, 525, 530
neighborhood, 633, 634
next time (operator), 613
no-free-lunch theorem, 662, 663
no-good, 600, 729
node, 12
node counting, 491–492, 500–501, 502, 512
node expansion efficiency, 116
node ordering, 234, 255, 382, 695
node store, 107, 108
nondeterministic environment, 519
nondeterministic search model, 29, 36
nondeterministic Turing machine, 5, 6, 591, 593
noop, 31
noop action, 676, 680
normal form, 731
NP, 6
NP-complete, 25, 175, 178, 593
NP-complete problem, 6, 591
NP-containment, 591
NP-hardness, 591

nucleotide base, 26
null move, 537
null-window search, 531, 532

O

objective function, 25, 79, 572, 617, 618, 633, 635, 638, 642, 643
observed action, 35
obstacle, 42
oct-tree data structure, 769
off-chip global memory, 401
off-chip local memory, 401
off-line heuristic, 703
on-chip register, 401
on-chip shared memory, 401
on-demand pattern database, 183
on-line heuristic, 703
on-the-fly state space generation, 15
open addressing, 121, 123, 131, 133, 134, 136, 153
open subgoal heuristic, 733
operations research, 198
operator, 12
optical storage media, 195
optimal alignment, 11, 27, 28, 255
optimal parallel plan, 695
optimal plan, 37, 300, 301, 675
optimal policy, 36, 65, 349, 539, 540, 560
optimal solution, 14, 25, 28
optimal value function, 36, 37, 68, 540, 541
optimality (of a search algorithm), 53, 78, 81, 198, 251, 440, 450
optimization problem, 79, 199, 331, 598, 634, 635, 662
oracle, 6
order preserving (hash function), 347
ordered hashing, 124, 125, 136, 406
ordered search tree algorithm, 198
original maze, 445
orthogonal hash function, 342
othello, 567
out-degree (of a node), 15
outer fragment (of a proof tree), 732
overall distribution, 212–213
overapproximation, 704
overconsistent A*, 244–246
overconsistent node, 245
overconstraint SAT problem, 595
oversubscribed problem, 571

P

PAC, 669
page, 320
page fault, 320, 752, 755, 756
page frame, 320
paging strategy, 320
pair transformation, 108, 109
pairing, 100
parallel A*, 388
parallel algorithm, 6, 369, 371–374
parallel branch-and-bound, 379–380
parallel depth-first branch-and-bound, 379
parallel depth-first search, 369, 379
parallel external A*, 388, 392–398
parallel external breadth-first search, 370, 388–391
parallel external search, 370, 388
parallel global A*, 385–387
parallel IDA*, 379, 382
parallel local A*, 385, 387–388
parallel memory model, 388
parallel merging, 374
parallel plan, 31, 675, 677, 695
parallel random access machine, 370–372, 374, 388
parallel search, 369, 370, 385, 397, 418, 420, 421, 522
parallel sorting, 374, 406
parallel state space search, 369, 374
parallel structured duplicate detection, 391–392, 393
parameter-free genetic algorithm, 634
parametric planning domain, 30, 448
paranoid assumption, 547
parent (of a node), 15
parent layer, 262, 389
parent transformation, 108, 109
parity, 20, 119
parity (of permutation), 119, 294
partial A*, 251–254
partial assignment, 573, 594, 605, 619, 620, 681, 721
partial expansion A*, 270–271
partial IDA*, 251–254
partial order reduction, 430, 453–458
partial path, 26, 143, 153
partial position, 442, 444, 446
partial solution, 26, 554, 558, 602, 604
partial state hashing, 375
partial state storage, 251, 253
partial sum, 373

partially expanded, 453
partially expanded node, 236
partially observable Markov decision process, 35, 507
particle swarm optimization, 669
partition function, 375
partition search, 535–536
partitionable (mixed) neighborhood, 661
partitioned transition relation, 315
path consistency, 571, 578, 580, 581
path consistent CSP, 579
path constraint, 571, 612–617, 621
path-max heuristic, 237
pattern database, 161, 167–168, 172–177, 177–185, 294–296, 346–348, 398–400, 680
pattern database partitioning, 312
pattern gene, 684
pattern mutation, 684
pattern search, 445–446
pattern selection problem, 178
pattern store, 445
pattern trie compaction, 185
Paturi-Pudlák-Zane algorithm, 648
PDDL, 30, 32, 33, 674, 688, 692–693, 696–697, 710–712, 720, 726, 761
PDDL semantic, 673–674
PDISK, 388
penalty, 446
penalty table, 445–446
pending queue, 690, 691
perfect hash function, 118–121, 126, 271, 284
perfect hash table, 139, 168, 295
perfect hashing, 111, 118, 126, 152, 153, 169
perfect heuristic, 16, 17
perfect information game, 524
persistent set, 464
PERT, 611–612, 621, 696
Petri net, 701, 717–720
phase transition, 595, 620
pipelined instruction fetching, 369
pipelining, 344–345
place (in a Petri net), 717
plan constraint, 616, 617, 696–697
planar graph, 325
planning heuristic, 710–713, 720, 726
planning pattern, 680
planning pattern database, 680–685
planning process, 674, 698
ply, 524, 525, 538

policy, 36, 519
policy iteration, 65–67, 558
polynomial reduction, 6, 593, 599, 606
polynomial-time transformation, 591
POMDP, 35, 507
portal heuristic, 192
positioning, 737
possible planning state, 681
postorder, 287
potential violating node, 107
PRAM, 370–372, 374, 388
PRAM architecture, 370
precedence ordering, 695
predecessor link, 50
predecessor pruning, 433
predicate logic, 8, 9, 730
preference constraint, 617, 697
prefix sum, 373
prefix-optimal, 78
preimage, 283, 295
Presburger automaton, 312
priced zone, 722
primary search, 710
primary state, 710
principal-variation, 524
principal-variation search, 532
principle of optimality, 53, 62, 66, 78
principle variation tree, 529
priority queue, 53, 89
priority search tree, 385
probabilistic environment, 519, 520, 560
probabilistic LRTA*, 495–496
probabilistic search model, 36
probabilitstic approximate completeness, 669
probing, 728
problem domain description language, 30, 673
problem graph, 13
process, 369
processor, 369
processor core, 369
production system, 3, 32
program model checking, 713–717
progression search, 679
project evaluation and review technique, 611–612, 695
proof number search, 567, 568
proof set search, 567
property automaton, 703
propositional conflict, 694
propositional formula, 8, 620

propositional logic, 8
propositional planning, 673
protein, 26
protocol validation, 702
pruning, 429
pruning pair, 432
pruning set, 449
pseudo code, 3
pseudo random number, 117, 158
PSO, 669
PSPACE, 6
PSPACE complete, 23, 30, 46
PSVN, 35
pure backtracking, 581, 586
push-button automation, 702

Q

Q-learning, 540, 542, 543, 560
Q-value, 37
quantifier, 8
quantitative dependency network, 728
queue, 51
quotient space, 112
quotient state space, 447

R

Rabin and Karp hashing, 113–115
RAID, 321
RAM, 358
random access memory, 358
random communication, 387
random walk algorithm, 651
randomization, 633, 634, 647, 663
randomized hashing, 126
randomized local search, 639–641
randomized quicksort, 647
randomized search, 633, 634
randomized tabu search, 638–639, 663
rank hashing (of a permutation), 272
rank sequence, 107
rapid restart, 595
RBFS, 219–220
reopening (of nodes), 73
reweighted problem graph, 47
reweighting transformation, 69
reachability analysis, 545–546
reachability set, 717
reachable marking, 717
reachable planning state, 681
reachable state, 228, 568, 702
reached (node), 48
read-only media, 195

real-time A*, 491
real-time adaptive A*, 484
real-time dynamic programming, 569
real-time heuristic search, 465, 514
real-time model checking, 721, 723
real-time search, 465, 654
reasonable state space, 475, 483, 492, 493
recognized dead-end, 276, 334
recombination, 639
recovering solution quality, 255
recursive best-first search, 195, 219–220
recursively enumerable set, 5
reduced and ordered BDD, 286
reducibility of a heuristic, 446
redundancy anomaly, 727
redundant array of independent disks, 321
redundant array of inexpensive disks, 321
refine queue, 395
refined threshold determination, 195
refuted node, 526
region automaton, 721
regression search, 679
regular rank sequence, 107
regular search space, 195
reinforcement learning, 483, 540
relational product, 288, 290
relaxation, 54
relaxation (of a planning problem), 30
relaxation (of an action), 30
relaxed planning heuristic, 30, 34, 685, 686, 690, 691, 698
relaxed problem, 31, 162
relay search, 348–349
relay solution, 348
relevance analysis, 461, 462
relevance cut, 452–453
relevant flag, 443
remaining area, 604
removable item heuristic, 725
reset search space, 492
residual, 67
resolution refutation procedure, 731
resource-optimal scheduling, 721
restart, 594, 633
restrict operator, 309–310
Rete algorithm, 142, 159
retrograde analysis, 167, 519, 543–544
reversible state space problem, 23
revise procedure, 576

revolving search method, 465
reward (for an action), 35
RIDA*, 219, 280
right-most tip node, 234
robotics, 9, 11
roll-out, 11
rote learning, 539
round-and-robin, 387
RTA*, 491
RTAA*, 484
rule, 695
run transformation, 108
run-length compression, 185

S

safely explorable state space, 475, 477, 491–493, 495
safety property, 702
SAS$^+$ planning problem, 681, 685, 686
SAT, 593
satisfiability, 593
satisfiability problem, 620
satisfiable formula, 8
satisficing search strategy, 633
scanning (a file), 319
schema theorem, 644
scope, 8
search, 9
search algorithm, 3, 10, 11, 47, 197, 243, 256, 269, 274, 313, 385–388, 562, 582, 584, 587, 622, 664, 751
search constraint, 571
search discrepancy, 588
search frontier, 48
search heuristic, 16
search skeleton, 219
search tree, 48, 195
search tree problem space, 198
secondary state, 710
selection, 639, 640
selection function, 641
selective search, 633
semi-decidable set, 5
semi-external search, 365
semi-virtual connection, 523
semiring, 579
sentence, 8
sequential plan, 674
serialization (of a problem), 462
set (of individuals), 641
set-of-support approach, 732
shallow cut-off, 526, 548

shallow pruning, 547–549
shared variable, 705, 711, 714
shared variable heuristic, 716
shortcut (string), 432
shortest firing sequence, 718
sibling transformation, 108
sifting algorithm, 288
signaling pathway, 759, 760
signature (of permutation), 119
simple ant system, 634, 652–653
simple GA, 641–643
simple genetic algorithm, 641–643
simple temporal constraint network, 610
simple temporal network, 609–611
simplemaxcut, 606
simulated annealing, 634, 663, 664
single instruction multiply data, 401
single-agent puzzle, 3
singleton, 108
singleton transformation, 108
singular extension, 537
Skolem constant, 732
Skolem function, 732
SLA*, 488
SLA*T, 488
SMGS, 259–261
soft constraint, 617
software checking, 713
software paging, 320, 752
software verification, 9
solid state disk, 353
solution, 13
solution (of a CSP), 572
solution certificate, 6
solution depth, 206
solution path, 14
solution preserving abstraction, 163
solution preserving pruning, 429
solution preserving restriction, 680
solution reconstruction, 227
solved node, 554
sorting (a file), 319
space explosion problem, 283
sparse graph, 14–15
sparse memory-graph search, 259–261
spatial logic, 724
specialized consistency, 571, 575,
    579–580
speedup, 369, 372
splay operation (for treaps), 386
split value, 346
splittability of a heuristic, 446

splitter, 324
spurious solution path, 161
spurious state, 188
SRAM, 401
SSD, 353
stack, 50
stack splitting, 380–382
stage algorithm, 636
standard variable ordering, 288
state, 12
state (of a node), 108
state caching algorithm, 274
state explosion problem, 283, 663
state reconstruction, 253–254
state space, 3
state space of solutions, 634
state space partitioning function, 375
state space problem, 12–14
state space problem graph, 13
state trajectory constraint, 696–697
state-action pair, 471
state-caching algorithm, 227
static evaluation function, 524
static load balancing, 375
static penalty approach, 669
static pruning, 429
step counter, 550
sterile node, 215
stochastic node caching, 231
stone, 22
strategy (in two-player games), 529
streaming data, 344
streaming multiprocessor, 401
streaming processor, 401
string length heuristic, 732
string matching, 115, 374
strong backdoor, 596
strong preimage, 546
strong solution, 568
structured duplicate detection, 343–344,
    359
stubborn set, 464
stuck procedure, 441
substring query, 142
subgraph pattern database compression,
    184
subject model, 728
subnet distance heuristic, 719
subset dictionary, 443
substitution matrix, 27
substring acceptor, 433
substring matching, 438

substring pruning, 430–433, 458
substring pruning automaton, 437
subtree rotation (for treaps), 386
succeed-first principle, 581
successor (of a node), 15
sufficient saddle point condition, 658
suffix link, 143
sum-of-pairs alignment cost function, 27
super-goal, 370
super-linear speedup, 372
super-string query, 142
supervised learning, 540
surjective transformation, 164
swapping, 320
symbolic A*, 302–305
symbolic Bellman-Ford algorithm, 47,
    57, 60, 62, 311
symbolic breadth-first search, 284
symbolic breadth-first tree search,
    291–292
symbolic model checking, 317, 702
symbolic pattern database, 294–296
symbolic planning pattern database, 683
symbolic reachability analysis, 545
symbolic retrograde analysis, 544–547
symbolic search, 283
symbolic shortest path algorithm, 311
symbolic shortest-path search, 298–299
symmetric action, 459
symmetry, 179–180, 447
symmetry pattern database lookup, 179,
    180
symmetry reduction, 430, 447–449, 459
synchronous distribution, 379
synchronous parallel search, 420
synchronous pruning automaton, 433
synchronous search, 380
synchronous setting, 369, 379
system invariant violation, 705
systematic state space enumeration, 633
systematic tie breaking, 489

T

taboo, 638
tabu list, 638
tabu neighbor, 638
tabu search, 638–639
tail (of a string), 143
Taylor series expansion, 659
temporal constraint, 572
temporal constraint network, 609–612,
    621

temporal control knowledge, 696
temporal credit assignment problem, 540
temporal difference learning, 540, 541
temporal graph logic, 724
temporal logic, 571, 702–703
temporal plan, 674
temporal planning, 673–674, 691–695
temporally extended goal, 612, 622, 696
terminal node, 143, 524, 528, 554, 724
termination-checking step, 471, 489
test maze, 445
theorem proving, 9, 730–732
thickness of search frontier, 265
thread, 401
time consistency, 747, 748
time tabling, 571, 622
timed automaton, 722
timed initial fact, 674
timed initial literal, 696
tip edge, 234
tip node, 234
token (in a Petri net), 717
tool-specific heuristic, 716
top-down proof, 732
topological order, 63, 75, 255
total duplicate identification, 49
trail-directed heuristic, 709, 716
trail-directed search, 704, 716
trajectory, 721
transformed Lagrangian, 658
transition, 12
transition (in a Petri net), 717
transition guard, 721
transition relation, 285, 288–290, 310
transposed matrix, 209
transposition table, 228–231, 530
transposition-driven scheduling, 375,
      376
transputer, 385
treap, 385–387
tree partial locking protocol, 387
tree width, 631
trial-based real-time dynamic
      programming, 512, 514
triangle inequality, 26, 746
triangle inequality (of Euclidean plane),
      25, 746
trie, 139, 185, 435
trivial heuristic, 73, 235

true distance heuristic, 192
truth table, 8
TSP, 25–26, 200, 201, 646, 652
Turing machine, 4–6, 32–33, 591, 593
Turing machine configuration, 33, 592
Turing test, 567
two-bit breadth-first search, 271–273
two-person game theory, 567

U
UCT, 11, 538
unblocked state, 775
undecidability, 32
undecidability (of metric planning), 690
undecidable, 3, 30, 32, 690
underconstraint SAT problem, 595
underconsistent node, 245
unification, 443, 730, 731
uninformed search, 16, 47, 81, 165, 169,
      284, 723
uninteruptable power supply, 321
union-find data structure, 154
unique table, 313
unit, 369
unit clause, 732
unit cost problem graph, 14, 306–308
unit propagation, 594, 596
unit resolution, 732
universal hashing, 111, 116
unrecognized dead-end, 276, 334
unsupervised learning, 540
until (operator), 613
unweighted problem graph, 14, 242, 338,
      347, 450
UPS, 321
used operator, 262
user interaction, 737
user view serialization, 387

V
valid end state, 441
valleys in h-value surface, 482
value function, 36, 37, 67, 68, 349, 519
value iteration, 65–68, 349
value selection, 581
value-update step, 469–473
variable ordering (in a BDD), 287, 288
variable ordering (of a CSP), 581
variable permutation, 448

variable transposition, 448, 449
vector notation (of productions system),
      35
vectorial pattern database, 191
verification of a solution, 6
vertex ant walk, 654–657, 666
video RAM, 401–407
virtual connection, 523
virtual machine, 713
virtual memory, 319, 320, 752
virtual search tree, 274
VLOCK, 715
von Neumann architecture, 321
VRAM, 401–407
VUNLOCK, 715

W
wait-free hash table, 425
wasted space, 602–604
wave-shaping, 409, 410
weak backdoor, 596
weak preimage, 546
weakest precondition, 690, 691
weight, 13–14
weight function, 53
weighted A*, 243–244
weighted problem graph, 14, 69, 73
weighted search space, 14, 432
weighted state space problem, 14, 16, 18
weighted transition relation, 286, 299
well-formed formula, 8
win backup, 543, 544
work queue, 375, 390, 394
workspace, 773, 774
worst macro solution length, 450
worst-fit, 599
worst-fit decreasing, 599

Z
zero-initialized edge counting, 493
zero-initialized LRTA*, 477, 479, 492,
      514
zero-initialized node counting, 492
zero-sum game, 524, 547, 560–561
Zobrist hashing, 564
zone, 721
zone union, 723
zugzwang, 537

Printed and bound by CPI Group (UK) Ltd, Croydon, CR0 4YY

03/10/2024

01040320-0003